WHERE TO FIND IT

Chapter

	1	2	3	4	5	6	7	8	9	10	11	12	13	14	15
Operations Management															
Inventory management			√											√	
Economic order quantity			√								√				
Production lot size			√												
Single period decisions											√		√		
Production/inventory planning			√	√		√	√	√						√	
Equipment replacement									√			√		√	
Preventive maintenance											√				
Distribution/logistics				√					√						
Location analysis	√	√						√							
Supplier management												√			
Environmental management												√			
Service systems														√	√
Project management/scheduling									√	√	√		√		
Job shop scheduling										√					
Assembly line balancing										√					
Vehicle routing										√					
Marketing															
Marketing allocation	√									√		√			
Media selection	√														
Direct mail advertising											√				
Advertising strategies			√			√		√			√				
Finance															
Financial analysis	√	√	√	√			√				√		√		
Investment planning									√	√		√			√
Capital budgeting								√							
Asset allocation							√								

MANAGEMENT SCIENCE

MODELING, ANALYSIS AND INTERPRETATION

JEFFREY D. CAMM
University of Cincinnati

JAMES R. EVANS
University of Cincinnati

SOUTH-WESTERN College Publishing

An International Thomson Publishing Company

Acquisitions Editor: Jack C. Calhoun
Publisher/Team Director: Valerie Ashton
Development Editor: Dennis Hanseman
Production Editor: Rebecca Roby
Marketing Manager: Scott D. Person
Production House: Publication Services
Cover Design: Craig LaGesse Ramsdell
Internal Design: Joe Devine

MI61AA
Copyright© 1996
by South-Western College Publishing
Cincinnati, Ohio

1 2 3 4 5 6 7 8 MT 1 0 9 8 7 6 5
Printed in the United States of America

Library of Congress Cataloging-in-Publication Data

Camm, Jeffrey D.
    Management science : modeling, analysis, and interpretation /
Jeffrey D. Camm, James R. Evans.
      p. cm.
    Includes index.
    ISBN 0-538-82738-6
    1. Management science.   2. Industrial management–Mathematical models.   3. Problem solving–Mathematical models.   I. Evans. James R., 1950– . II. Title.
HD30.25.C36   1995   94-33273
658–dc20   CIP

ITP
I(T)P   International Thomson Publishing
South-Western College Publishing is an ITP Company. The ITP trademark is used under license.

 This book is printed on acid-free paper that meets Environmental Protection Agency standards for recycled paper.

PREFACE

Management science—the use of mathematical models and quantitative approaches to improve decision making—originated some 50 years ago in military applications. The discipline flourished in business and industry during the 1950s and early 1960s as computing power developed and researchers refined the mathematics underlying the various approaches. During the 1970s and 1980s, however, quantitative modeling was often viewed as irrelevant to contemporary business problems. Today, the use of management science is stronger than ever, and it is being used extensively by many of the world's leading companies.

Many factors have contributed to the renaissance of management science. These include increases in computing power, data availability, and software availability; a better-educated work force; and a renewed drive for quality and company performance. Powerful workstations coupled with effective optimization and simulation software can now solve extremely large planning problems. More than at any time in history, strategic data are available through corporate information systems. Scanner data, geodemographic data, and electronic data interchange provide companies with abundant information that can be exploited to increase competitive advantage. Management science provides the means to extract valuable insights from these data. Furthermore, the tools of management science—optimization, statistics, and simulation modeling—are now available to millions of potential users as basic components of spreadsheet packages. Upper management, schooled in the 1960s in management science, are more accepting of solutions based on these tools. The emphasis on Total Quality Management and Business Process Reengineering as approaches to improving business practice in a globally competitive economy has forced companies to reexamine their operations. Indeed, these are exciting times for the discipline of management science.

About the Book

Management Science: Modeling, Analysis, and Interpretation offers a new and fresh approach to the study of management science. More than any other current management science text, this book emphasizes, as the title suggests, *modeling* business problems, *analyzing* the models, and *interpreting* the results obtained from these models.

The book's content is logically organized into three major parts. Chapters 1 through 3 of the book provide an introduction to management science, spreadsheets, and model development. Chapters 4 through 10 focus on deterministic management science models, and Chapters 11 through 15 are devoted to probabilistic models.

We have designed many unique features into this book:

1. A distinct modeling, not algorithmic, focus. A great deal of attention is paid to the process by which we build mathematical models. Influence diagrams are used as a way to structure problems. The analysis of models and their sensitivity to assumptions and input data are stressed throughout the book. It has been the authors' experience in consulting that one rarely, if ever, "runs a model to get a solution." Rather, by varying input data and assumptions, a model is used to provide a variety of possible alternatives from which to choose. This point is emphasized in many of the examples, problems, and cases presented. Finally, we stress the importance of properly interpreting the results obtained from the various models presented, and when possible, we explain why these solutions make sense on an intuitive basis. Intuitive solutions, or a recognition of why a nonintuitive solution is optimal is important in the acceptance of any management science study. Many key concepts or "tips" to the student are highlighted throughout the book.

2. Unique coverage of important contemporary topics. The content of the book was designed to be current and relevant, and many chapters and sections are unique among competing management science books. For example, Chapter 3, "Developing and Using Management Science Models," presents a practical approach to the modeling and problem solving process, reminiscent of the roots of management science as developed by Churchman, Ackoff, and Arnoff. Chapter 8, "Integer Programming Modeling and Analysis" discusses the role of problem formulation in efficiently solving integer programs. Chapter 10, "Heuristics and Approximation," focuses on the practical solution of difficult problems along the lines that management science professionals actually practice. Chapter 11 presents unique perspectives on the use of statistical analysis and the development of probabilistic models. Chapter 13, "Computer Simulation and Risk Analysis," provides a contemporary coverage of simulation and its applications to assess risk. This is one of the growing applications of management science in business. Similarly, Chapter 14, "Simulating Dynamic Systems," provides a more realistic and practical coverage of dynamic simulation than any competing book. In Chapter 15, "Modeling and Analysis of Queueing Systems," we discuss behavioral issues in managing waiting lines. Many more examples appear throughout the book.

3. Heavy reliance on spreadsheets and widely available software. Most students today rely on spreadsheets as much as many of us relied on calculators just a few years ago. Thus, we emphasize spreadsheets—both LOTUS 1-2-3 and EXCEL—for the analysis of problems. These packages were chosen because they are the tools most likely to be available to professionals in the workplace. Our goal is *not* to *teach* spreadsheets, but how to *use* them in the analysis and solution of management science problems. This is reflected in Chapter 2, "Spreadsheets and Management Science," which addresses spreadsheets from the perspective of management science, the use of the 1-2-3 and Excel linear programming solvers in Chapter 5, and in many other places in the book. The optimization package LINDO and the simulation package *Crystal Ball* are also used where appropriate.

   Each book comes with a disk that contains most of the spreadsheets presented in the text examples. We encourage the student to use these spreadsheets to further explore the ideas presented in each chapter.

4. Use of real applications and examples throughout. We rely heavily on real applications taken from applied journals such as *Interfaces,* from the Edelman Award competition for best application of management science, and from the extensive consulting experience of the authors. Each chapter also summarizes a real application of chapter material in the

"Management Science Practice" section. Discussion questions allow this feature to be used for case analysis and class discussions.

5. Extensive worked-out examples and solved problems. Each chapter is replete with examples to illustrate practical applications, and contains a section of additional examples and solved problems.

6. Comprehensive end-of-chapter exercises. To help the student and instructor, chapter review exercises are broken into four parts:

a. *Terms to Understand.* These are key terms and major concepts that students ought to be able to define or explain *in their own words* for "level 1" mastery of the chapter material.
b. *Questions.* These call for non-numerical answers to issues associated with the chapter material. Some focus on basic review of important concepts, and others are designed to stretch the students' minds or apply ideas creatively to familiar situations. These questions can be used effectively for class discussions, particularly with students who have business experience.
c. *Problems.* Each chapter has a variety of problems designed to test the student's mastery of quantitative material. Some are similar to examples in the chapter; others are model challenging. Most can be analyzed or solved using spreadsheet software, and students should be encouraged to do so.
d. *Cases.* Cases include more challenging problems, especially those that require judgment, creativity, and sensitivity analysis to address. Many are based on actual experiences of our students or on our own work.

Ancillaries

To support instructors and students, two ancillaries are available:

1. An *Instructor's Manual* contains answers to all problems and cases in the book.

2. A *Student Study Guide,* prepared by Scott Shafer of Auburn University, contains review questions, problems, and tips designed to aid students in mastering the material in the book.

Acknowledgments

A project of this magnitude required the help and cooperation of many people. We would particularly like to thank our reviewers.

Warren Boe
University of Iowa

Burton Dean
San Jose State University

Geoffrey Churchill
Georgia State University

Van Enns
University of Calgary

Russell Fenske
University of Wisconsin, Milwaukee

Raj Jagannathan
University of Iowa

Samuel Graves
Boston College

Edward P.C. Kao
University of Houston

Randolph Hall
University of California, Berkeley

Jerrold May
University of Pittsburgh

Terry Harrison
Pennsylvania State University

Richard McClure
Miami University

Rick Hesse
Mercer University

Stephen Powell
Dartmouth College

Their many helpful suggestions have made this a better book.

Finally, we wish to thank sincerely our editor, Dennis Hanseman, whose support and practical knowledge of management science helped bring this project to fruition.

Jeffrey D. Camm
James R. Evans

14 SIMULATING DYNAMIC SYSTEMS   750

15 MODELING AND ANALYSIS OF QUEUEING SYSTEMS   787

PART 1

MANAGEMENT

SCIENCE

MODELING

CHAPTER 1

INTRODUCTION TO MANAGEMENT SCIENCE AND PROBLEM SOLVING

INTRODUCTION

- Making the right decisions about overbooking airline flights, determining the number of discount fares to offer on a flight, and controlling reservations to account for connecting flights over its entire system has saved American Airlines over $500 million per year [Smith et al., 1992].
- GTE, the largest local telephone company in the United States, invests $300 million annually in customer access facilities. By designing the customer access network, GTE network planners improved productivity by over 500 percent and saved an estimated $30 million annually in network construction costs [Jack et al., 1992].
- Weyerhaeuser is one of the largest forest products companies in the world. The proper utilization of its raw material product (trees) has a drastic impact on revenue. Frontline decision makers known as "woods buckers" must decide how to cut trees into logs of various sizes, considering factors such as length, curvature, diameter, and knots. By developing a new set of cutting guidelines, Weyerhaeuser realized over $100 million in increased profits [Lembersky and Chi, 1986].

Each of these companies has achieved remarkable bottom-line results. They did it through the use of management science.

> *Management science* is the scientific discipline devoted to the analysis and solution of complex decision problems.

Management science is concerned with deciding scientifically how best to design and operate systems, usually under conditions requiring the allocation of scarce resources. It uses the language of mathematics and the power of computers to help decision makers make choices by quantitatively estimating and forecasting the implications of these choices. Management science is a multidisciplinary field, using any branch of science—such as mathematics, statistics, economics, sociology, and psychology—that may have knowledge or methods useful in understanding or analyzing a particular decision.

Management science does not apply solely to multimillion dollar corporate projects. All businesses, whether large or small, can use management science effectively. Managers encounter numerous problems on a daily basis. These include forecasting demand for products and services, determining the best product mix, locating facilities, controlling inventory, allocating resources, improving customer service and quality, and scheduling employees, transportation vehicles, and production. Management science techniques can be used to solve problems and improve managerial decisions in all of these areas. Management science is a growing and dynamic profession; *Money* magazine noted that management science will be one of the fastest-growing careers of the 1990s.

The purpose of this book is to introduce you to this discipline by focusing on its applications and value in the world of business. This book is not intended to make you an expert in the mathematics and technical procedures used to solve management science problems or in the development of sophisticated computer systems; these are the domain of skilled management scientists. Rather, the goal of this book is to help you learn to develop and understand a variety of management science approaches used to analyze and solve business problems. As a student of marketing, operations management, finance, accounting, or a related area of business, *you*, not the management scientist, must recognize when problems can be solved using management science. It is therefore important that you learn the language of management science, understand how problems are solved using management science approaches, and be able to communicate with management scientists. Personal computer technology, spreadsheets, and special software packages now provide every manager with the ability to apply management science, and you may find many opportunities to apply these techniques in your future careers.

In this chapter we introduce you to the basic concepts of management science that provide the foundation for the rest of the book. We begin with a brief history to help you understand the nature of the profession.

A BRIEF HISTORY

Management science is a relatively young field, with its roots reaching back to Frederick W. Taylor's work around the turn of the twentieth century. Taylor, who studied production at a very detailed level by focusing on work methods, proposed a "science of management" based on observation, measurement and analysis of work, improvement in work methods, and economic incentives. Other pioneers saw the potential uses of mathematics in emerging fields such as telephone communications and control of manufacturing inventories.

As a formal discipline, management science was born from efforts to improve military operations prior to and during World War II. Radar was developed to provide an early means of detecting air attacks in Great Britain; however, in 1937 a major air-defense exercise showed that although radar was very successful at early detection, it had poor tracking capabilities. A subsequent exercise involving five radar stations along the coast revealed major problems with combining and coordinating the sometimes-conflicting data from the stations. The superintendent of the Radar Research Station described this problem as an "operational achievement falling short of requirements" and proposed that "research into the operational aspects of the system should begin." This led to the term *operational research* to describe a formal, scientific approach to improving military operations. The United States, however, adopted the term *operations research*.

To study radar and other wartime problems, the British formed teams of researchers from disciplines such as statistics, physics, mathematics, and astronomy. One of the problems these teams investigated was the size of convoys—groups of merchant ships escorted by naval vessels—used to cross the Atlantic Ocean. Convoys were crucial in bringing supplies and munitions from the United States and so were prime targets for German U-boat attacks. The British Admiralty had long believed that small convoys were less susceptible to detection by U-boats and consequent shipping losses. The operational research group analyzed convoys during 1941 and 1942 and discovered that large convoys lost not only a smaller proportion of ships, but also fewer ships in total. Statistical evidence showed that the number of ships sunk was not related to the size of the convoy. Rather than simply report the statistical correlations, the group went one step further. They proved that, under reasonable assumptions, their observed data could be explained *mathematically*. Convinced of their conclusions, the scientists pressed the Admiralty to change its policy, which it did in 1943. The decision to use large convoys has since been acclaimed as one of the great command decisions that contributed to the Allied victory.

In the United States as well, scientists became involved in national defense efforts during the early war years. The Anti-Submarine Warfare Operations Research Group was established in 1942 to improve methods of searching for submarines and to protect U.S. ships. As applications expanded, the name was shortened in 1943 to the Operations Research Group. All branches of the armed forces subsequently developed operations research efforts.

After the war, scientists recognized that the mathematical tools and techniques developed for military applications could be applied successfully to problems in business and industry. A significant amount of research was carried on in public and private "think tanks" during the late 1940s and through the 1950s. As the focus on business applications expanded, the term *management science* became more prevalent. Today, many people use the terms *operations research* and *management science* interchangeably.

In the academic sector, operations research and management science grew within industrial engineering departments, with a principal focus on manufacturing applications. By the late 1960s many business schools were developing similar programs and expanding the applications to the traditional areas of business such as marketing, finance, and accounting.

Today, management science is an established profession. In 1952, the Operations Research Society of America (ORSA) was founded, and in 1957 the International Federation of Operational Research Societies (IFORS) was established in Europe. Shortly after ORSA was formed, The Institute of Management Sciences (TIMS) was established. TIMS' goal was to bring together all of the management sciences internationally, including many of the behavioral and social sciences in addition to operations research (which was viewed as having a distinct mathematical bias). These societies recently merged as INFORMS—the Institute for Operations Research and Management Science. Because the term *management science* is generally viewed as broader in scope than *operations research*, we will use it in this book.

APPLICATIONS OF MANAGEMENT SCIENCE

Management science is applied in every industry in both the private and public sectors, and in this section we present a sampling of the huge scope of management science applications. Complete descriptions of these applications can be found in the references at the end of this chapter, and we encourage you to read them. Many more examples will be described throughout the book.

Scheduling Airline Crews

The monthly scheduling of airline crews to flights is enormously complex, due to union and FAA work rules and the sheer overall size of the problem. American Airlines, for instance, has over 16,000 flight attendants, over 2,300 flight segments per day, and over 500 aircraft. Crews reside in 12 different cities, called crew bases; a crew must therefore be assigned to a sequence of flights (typically lasting three days) that starts and ends at the same crew base. Total crew costs exceed $1.3 billion annually; a 1 percent improvement in crew utilization therefore translates into a $13 million savings each year. American Airlines has developed and refined a scheduling system called TRIP—Trip Reevaluation and Improvement Program—using a variety of management science techniques. [Anbil et al., 1991]

Telecommunications Planning

L. L. Bean, the widely known retailer of high-quality outdoor goods and apparel, handles much of its sales volume through catalog sales and telemarketing operations. During one peak selling season, the service level provided to incoming calls was unacceptable; during certain periods 80 percent of the calls received a busy signal, and those that did not often had to wait up to 10 minutes before speaking with a sales agent. A management science project was conducted to determine how best to allocate their telecommunications resources. The project determined the best number of phone lines and agents to have on duty for each half hour of the selling season. During the next year, customer service and profits improved significantly [Quinn et al., 1991].

Transportation Planning

Reynolds Metals Company spends over $250 million annually to deliver its products and receive raw materials. Shipments are made by truck, rail, ship, and air across a network of over 120 shipping locations, including plants, warehouses, and suppliers. Truck shipments account for over half of the company's annual freight costs. The company had had a decentralized operating philosophy, in which divisions and plants had been responsible for managing their own freight operations, selecting their own carriers, negotiating freight rates, and dispatching shipments. With this system, service standards were not uniform, quality varied, and shipment status was not monitored. The company recognized that a sizable cost advantage could be obtained by centralizing the transportation operations and improving the system for dispatching trucks. The management science group played a major role in implementing the program and making it successful [Moore et al., 1991].

Search for Sunken Treasure

Management science techniques were used to devise a search plan to find a ship, the *Central America*, which sank in 1857 off the coast of South Carolina with three tons of gold on board. The search plan incorporated historical accounts of the storm and the shipwreck, mathematical analysis of drift due to ocean currents and winds, and estimates of the navigational instruments of the period. The plan was used to convince investors that their investment had a reasonable chance of success and led to the discovery of the ship in 1989 [Stone, 1992].

Financial Strategies

The secondary mortgage market is a market created for issuing and trading securities built from portfolios of mortgages, primarily single-family mortgages. The market has grown to a size comparable to the corporate bond market. Prudential Securities, one of the top three firms in this market, uses a full range of management science methods to predict the prepayment of mortgages, to estimate the value of mortgage-backed securities and adjustable-rate mortgages under various interest-rate scenarios, and to structure the best portfolios of mortgage-backed securities [Ben-Dov et al., 1992].

Telephone Network Planning

All telephone company customers are connected directly by physical facilities to central offices and indirectly to all other customers by connections between central offices. The parts of the telephone network that connect customers' homes and businesses to a central office are called customer access facilities. When the marketing forecast for future demand indicates that the present customer access facilities will be inadequate, the company must add new facilities. The planning task is to find an expansion plan—that is, locations, sizes, and timing for facilities to the network—to meet forecasted customer demand at the minimum discounted price. With the advent of new switching and transmission technologies such as fiber-optic cables, the multiyear planning for telephone facilities investments has become exceedingly complex. GTE has used sophisticated management science technology to develop a planning system that addresses this problem, resulting in millions of dollars of savings [Jack et al., 1992].

Automated Postal Technology

The United States Postal Service processes over 500 million pieces of mail each day, delivering them to 100 million locations. Part of their success is the use of the most advanced technology and systems for sorting, processing, and moving the mail. A critical aspect of their planning is the evaluation of alternative technology investments. Management science tools help to project the ramifications of automated equipment not only on other types of equipment, but also on the work force, facilities, and other costs of operation. The system quantifies the effects of candidate automation strategies and provides a common basis that all corporate departments can use to examine the operating improvements attributed to alternative programs and the resulting financial impacts [Cebry et al., 1992].

A list of additional applications of management science is given in Table 1.1.

TABLE 1.1
Applications of
management science

Finance

Pension fund management and
  investment
Cash management
Portfolio management
Financial planning and control

Human Resources Management

Work shift scheduling
Labor–management negotiation
Personnel evaluation and selection
Recruitment and promotion

International Business

Global financing and capital
  structure
International marketing channels
Global manufacturing and plant
  location

Marketing and Transportation

Advertising budget allocation
New product sales analysis
Market mix analysis
Media planning
Retail promotion strategy
Distribution planning
Fleet configuration
Airline operations planning

Production

Inventory planning and
  control
Facility layout
Product mix analysis

Education

Library management
Teaching assignment
  scheduling
Classroom assignment
Selection of MBA students

Health Care

Nurse scheduling
Financial planning
Diagnosis and therapy
Blood distribution

Natural Resources

Hydroelectric system
  management
Mining project evaluation
Water pollution control

Miscellaneous

Police beat design
Ski-area design
Crisis management
Energy planning

(Source: H.B. Eom and S.M. Lee, "A Survey of Decision Support System Applications (1971–April 1988),"
Interfaces, Vol. 20, no. 3, May-June 1990, 65–79.)

PROBLEM SOLVING

As the examples in the previous section show, management science is devoted to solving
important problems.

> A *problem* is a confusing or troublesome situation, or an opportunity for improve-
> ment, whose solution is not obvious.

Problem solving is the activity associated with selecting an appropriate solution that resolves the situation or leads to an improvement. Problem solving consists of several phases:

1. Recognizing the problem
2. Defining the problem
3. Structuring the problem
4. Analyzing the problem
5. Interpreting results and selecting a solution
6. Implementing the solution

Managers at different organizational levels face different types of problems. In a manufacturing firm, for instance, top managers face decisions of allocating financial resources, building or expanding facilities, determining product mix, and strategically sourcing production. Middle managers in operations develop distribution plans, production and inventory schedules, and staffing plans. Finance managers analyze risks, determine investment strategies, and make pricing decisions. Marketing managers develop advertising plans and make sales force allocation decisions. At the shop floor, or supervisory level, problems involve the size of daily production runs, individual machine schedules, and worker assignments. Whatever the problem, the first step is to realize that it exists.

In a highly competitive business environment it is usually not difficult to identify problems; it is more difficult to identify opportunities. A renewed focus on continuous improvement has been driven by the quest for improved quality. Quality improvement takes many forms: improving the design of products and services, improving manufacturing and service processes, and improving the quality of business decisions. Managers must be very sensitive to opportunities for improving quality. Today, management science plays an important role in quality improvement.

The second step in the problem solving process is to define the problem. This involves stating goals and objectives, characterizing the alternative courses of action (or decisions) from which a manager can choose, and identifying any constraints on the solution. *Goals* are stated as specific targets to be achieved, such as "obtain a 10 percent reduction in cost" or "answer the telephone within 3 rings." *Objectives*, on the other hand, are usually stated as an ideal level of accomplishment, such as "minimizing cost" or "maximizing profit." *Decisions* represent the actions that a manager can take to achieve objectives and goals. *Constraints* are limitations or requirements that are imposed on any solution, such as "do not exceed the allowable budget" or "ensure that all demand is met."

Decision making is the process of selecting a course of action among several alternatives. The individuals responsible for this selection are called *decision makers*. Clearly, if only one course of action exists or can be viably selected, or if there is no discernible difference in outcomes associated with any of the potential courses of action, a problem does not exist.

Managers must be able to measure how well a decision achieves their goals and objectives. To do this, they must understand relationships among various elements of a problem. This is easier to do if the problem can be structured in a form that is more convenient to work with, and this is where management science begins to play an important role. For most management science problems, a *model* of the problem can provide structure to the information about the problem in order to facilitate analysis. A model can be a simple picture, a spreadsheet, or a set of mathematical equations.

Models require data, and an important part of modeling is obtaining good data. Managers must collect, "clean," and organize data in a useful form. For many models, managers must estimate or forecast important inputs, a process that requires good support from the information systems function in an organization.

A completed model helps managers to gain insight into the nature of the relationships among components of a problem, aids intuition, and provides a vehicle for communication. Analysis involves some sort of experimentation or solution process. Problem analysis may involve evaluating various scenarios, finding a solution that meets certain goals, determining the best solutions, or analyzing risks associated with various decision alternatives. Management scientists have spent decades developing and refining a variety of approaches to address different types of problems. Much of this book is devoted to helping you understand these techniques and gain a basic facility in using them.

Interpreting the results from the analysis phase is crucial in making good decisions. Models cannot capture every detail of the real problem, and managers must understand the limitations of models and their underlying assumptions.

Implementing a solution simply means putting it to work. This means translating the management science model back to the decision-maker's problem—the real world. Managers must not forget the importance of political and behavioral issues in implementation.

We will now discuss each of these phases in more detail and provide some examples.

RECOGNIZING PROBLEMS

How are problems recognized? Problems exist when there is a gap between the present and some desired state of affairs. For example, a grocery store manager might believe that customer waiting lines are too long, or a consumer products manager might feel that distribution costs are too high. This recognition might result from comparing performance with some other reference group (our store versus our competitor), a universal standard (4.0 GPA or a .300 batting average), prior performance (what the company did last year), or an arbitrary target (desired market share or industry average). Benchmarking—comparing your performance to the world leader—is common practice today in identifying problems and opportunities.

Russell Ackoff, a pioneer of management science, notes that managers are often only aware of *symptoms* of problems. He calls this a *mess*—"a system of external conditions that produces dissatisfaction"—or alternatively, a set of intertwined problems. You must be able to extract the real problems from the mess.

The term *Type III error* is often used to describe solving the wrong problem.[1] Managers and management scientists often ignore this type of error, and consequently waste effort and expense on irrelevant problem solving. It is easy to focus on the most obvious problems rather than on the most important problems.

---

[1]You probably recall the terms "Type I error" and "Type II error" from statistics. A Type I error is concluding that something is not true when it actually is; a Type II error is concluding that something is true when it actually is false.

> Finding the "true" problem is an important step of any management science activity.

A good example of identifying the real problem involved a major airport in Texas. Airport passengers frequently complained about delays in getting baggage delivered to the baggage claim area. The "obvious" problem might be defined as, "How can we design a more efficient baggage-handling system?" This problem definition begs for a (costly) engineering solution. (Does Denver International come to mind?) A good problem solver might ask the question, "Why do we want to do this?" A response might be, "To reduce the time to deliver the baggage." Further questioning of "Why do we want to reduce the delivery time?" might lead to the response, "To eliminate the complaints." This creates a new problem definition: "How can I eliminate complaints?" This, in fact, was the *real* problem. How was it resolved? By moving the baggage claim area farther from the arrival gates! While the actual delivery time did not change, the *perception* did, because passengers did not have to wait as long. The complaints disappeared!

DEFINING PROBLEMS

Defining a problem involves stating goals and objectives to be achieved and decisions that would achieve them. In many situations, there are multiple goals and objectives. For example, the grocery store manager who believes that waiting lines are too long might have the objectives of maximizing customer service and minimizing costs. Possible decisions might include hiring additional employees (how many?), building larger facilities (what size?), or acquiring new scanner technology (what kind?). Customer service might be measured by the length of waiting lines or the average time that customers wait. Costs might be measured as discounted present value. Notice that the objectives conflict: the decisions that will improve customer service will increase cost. Thus, the manager must make a trade-off between these objectives.

In a similar fashion, the consumer products company manager who feels that distribution costs are too high might investigate redesigning the distribution system. This might involve deciding on new locations for manufacturing plants and warehouses (where?), new assignments of products to plants (which ones?), and the amount of each product to ship from different warehouses to customers (how much?). The goal of cost reduction might be measured by the total delivered cost of the product. While there is only one objective in this case, the manager would probably want to ensure that a specified level of customer service is achieved with the redesign. This is an example of a constraint.

Defining problems is not a trivial task. The complexity of a problem increases when

- The number of potential courses of action is large.
- The problem belongs to a group rather than to an individual.
- The problem solver has several competing objectives.
- External groups or individuals are affected by the problem.

- The problem solver and the true owner of the problem—the person who experiences the problem and is responsible for getting it solved—are not the same.
- Time limitations are important.

These factors make it difficult to develop meaningful objectives and characterize the range of potential decisions. In defining problems, it is important to involve all people who make the decisions or who may be affected by them.

STRUCTURING PROBLEMS

Structuring a problem involves developing some type of model.

> A *model* is a representation or abstraction of a real object, idea, or system.

Models capture the most important features of a problem and present them in a form that is easy to interpret. Models are used extensively in business and society for description, explanation, prediction, and control. Models complement decision makers' intuition and often provide insights that intuition cannot. One early application of management science in marketing involved a study of sales operations [Brown et al., 1956]. Sales representatives had to divide their time between large and small customers and between acquiring new customers and keeping old ones. The problem was to determine how the representatives should best allocate their time. Intuition suggested that they should concentrate on large customers and that it was much harder to acquire a new customer than to keep an old one. However, intuition could not tell whether they should concentrate on the 500 largest or the 5,000 largest customers or how much effort to spend on acquiring customers. Models of sales force effectiveness and customer response patterns provided the insight to make these decisions.

Types of Models

Models can be qualitative or quantitative and can range from simple "mental models" to sophisticated computer models. *Qualitative* models usually involve a picture or diagram that depicts the relationships among the elements of a problem. *Quantitative* models usually involve mathematical relationships.

We may classify models into three categories, according to their intended use:

1. Descriptive models
2. Predictive models
3. Prescriptive models

Descriptive models simply tell "what is." They describe relationships and provide information for evaluation. Descriptive models are useful for several reasons. First, they provide one approach to the construction of other models that will be used to find best decisions. Second, they provide managers with a framework for comparing different modes of operation and yield insight into the behavior of business systems. Finally, they provide a theory that can be tested through observation and experimentation.

Predictive models are aimed at forecasting or predicting future events. For example, we may wish to predict the pattern of sales of a new product over time in order to plan production and inventory levels or sales efforts. Predictive models often involve statistical analysis of historical data. We will study statistical models in Chapter 11.

The goal of *prescriptive models* is to recommend the best decisions to satisfy an objective. In a highly competitive world where one percentage point can mean a difference of hundreds of thousands of dollars or more, managers would like to find the best possible solutions.

Descriptive Models

One simple descriptive model is called an *influence diagram* since it describes how various factors of a problem influence others. An influence diagram shows the relationships between various quantities and is a useful approach for conceptualizing the elements of any model and their relationships to one another. The elements of the model are represented by circles called *nodes*. *Branches* connect the nodes and show which elements influence another. Influence diagrams are excellent brainstorming tools, particularly in group meetings. The following example shows how to construct simple influence diagrams.

EXAMPLE 1. A PROFIT MODEL

The general equation that describes profit is

$$\text{Profit} = \text{Revenue} - \text{Cost}$$

Since revenue and cost influence profit, a simple influence diagram that shows these relationships is given in Figure 1.1.

We can develop a more detailed model by noting that revenue depends on (is influenced by) the unit price and quantity sold; and total cost is a function of unit cost, quantity produced, and relevant fixed costs. The enhanced model is shown in Figure 1.2.

FIGURE 1.1   *A simple influence diagram for profit*

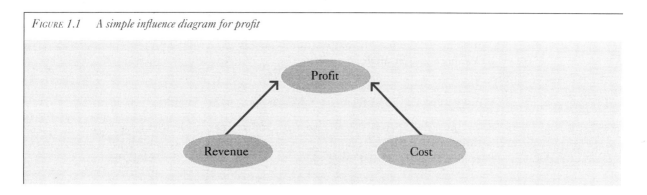

FIGURE 1.2   *An enhanced influence diagram for profit*

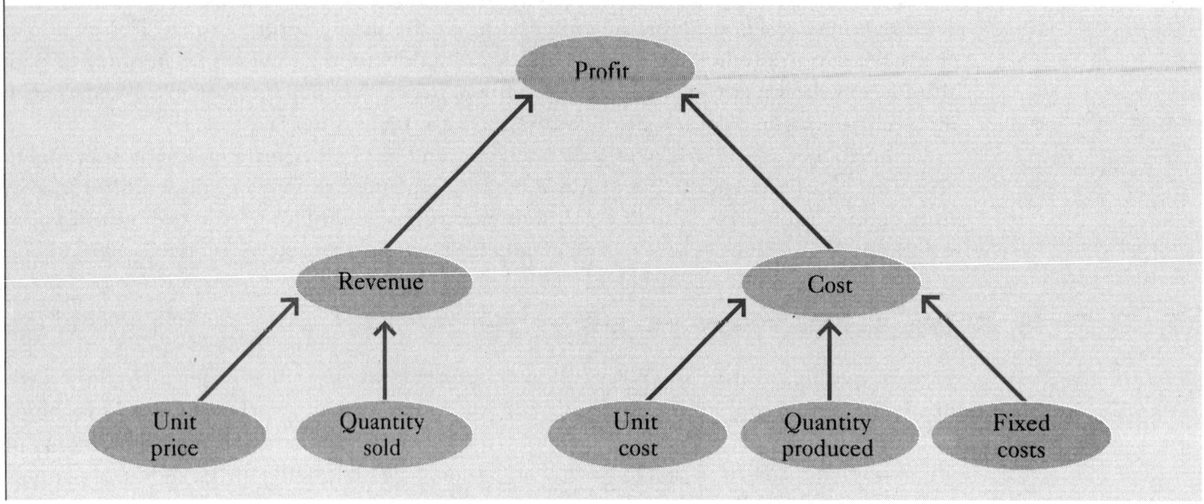

An important principle of modeling is to start simple and embellish the model as necessary.

Descriptive models often form the basis for detailed mathematical models and can help a decision-maker conceptualize and provide insights into the nature of a problem. Thus, it is good practice to first attempt to structure a problem using a simple influence diagram.

Descriptive models are also used to represent other decision processes. For example, we might study how managers make certain types of decisions, such as the choice of research and development projects or stock selection. By documenting the sequence of steps performed in making such decisions we arrive at a descriptive model, usually a logical flowchart. This model might be used to better understand the process with the goal of improving it.

Descriptive models may also be mathematical. We may use influence diagrams to guide the development of mathematical models. The following example shows how to do this for the profit model (Example l).

EXAMPLE 2. DEVELOPING A MATHEMATICAL MODEL FOR PROFIT

We must first specify the precise nature of the relationships among the various quantities in Figure 1.1. Revenue is computed by multiplying the unit price of the item by the quantity sold. Thus,

$$\text{Profit} = (\text{Unit price})(\text{Quantity sold}) - \text{Cost}$$

Cost is often expressed as fixed cost plus variable cost. Therefore, we have

$$\text{Profit} = (\text{Unit price})(\text{Quantity sold})$$
$$- [\text{ Fixed cost} + (\text{Unit cost})(\text{Quantity produced})]$$

By defining

$$P = \text{profit}$$
$$p = \text{unit price}$$
$$c = \text{unit cost}$$
$$F = \text{fixed cost}$$
$$S = \text{quantity sold}$$
$$Q = \text{quantity produced}$$

we have

$$P = pS - [F + cQ]$$

This model does not tell a manager how much to produce nor what price to charge; it simply describes the relationships among these quantities in mathematical terms.

Models contain two types of quantities:
1. Constants, called *parameters,* and
2. Quantities that can change, called *variables.*

Variables may be *controllable,* in the sense that the decision-maker can manipulate them freely, or *uncontrollable.* Uncontrollable variables may assume different values, but they cannot be directly controlled by the decision-maker. In Example 2, for instance, the quantities p, c, and F would generally be constants; they are the parameters in the model. The quantity sold, S, may vary, but the decision-maker cannot directly manipulate this value; thus, S is an uncontrollable variable. However, Q, the quantity produced, is a controllable variable, since the decision-maker can decide on its value. Controllable variables are also called *decision variables.*

Predictive Models

Predictive models aim to predict the effect of alternative decisions or forecast future events. For instance, a basic principle in economic theory is that the demand rate (an uncontrollable variable) for a product is negatively related to its price (a controllable variable). Many different mathematical models can describe this phenomenon. In small ranges around the current price, we often assume a linear relationship:

$$D = a - bp$$

where D is the demand rate, p is the unit price, and a and b are constants that relate the demand rate to price. An alternative model assumes that price elasticity—the ratio of the percentage change in demand to the percentage change in price—is constant. In this case, the model is

$$D = ap^{-b}$$

Each of these is a predictive model of the demand. If the model is appropriate, setting a value for price will provide a prediction of demand. The task of the modeler is to select or build an appropriate model that represents the behavior of the real situation. This involves critical examination of assumptions and often requires testing with real data.

Prescriptive Models

A prescriptive mathematical model has four components:

- Controllable (decision) variables
- Uncontrollable variables and parameters
- Constraints
- An objective function

We defined variables and parameters previously. Constraints are limitations or require-ments imposed on acceptable values of the decision variables. The outcome of a decision is the joint result of the decision-maker's choice and the true values of the uncontrollable variables. The *objective function* is a specified relationship between the controllable and un-controllable variables. Typically, the decision-maker seeks to maximize or minimize the objective function. The following example illustrates the development of a prescriptive model.

EXAMPLE 3. A PRODUCT MIX MODEL

A manufacturer of high-tech radar detectors assembles two models: LaserStop and SpeedBuster. Both models use many of the same electronic components. Two of these components, which have very high quality and reliability requirements, can only be obtained from a single overseas manufacturer. For the next month, the supply of these components is limited to 6,000 of component A and 3,500 of component B. Table 1.2 shows the number of each component required for each product and the profit per unit of product sold. How many of each product should be assembled during the next month to maximize the manufacturer's profit, assuming that the firm can sell all it produces?

Since we have an objective of profit maximization, this will be a prescriptive model. Profit can be computed as the quantity sold times the profit/unit, added for

TABLE 1.2
Data for radar detector assemblies

	Component Requirements/ unit		Profit/ unit
	A	B	
LaserStop	12	6	$24
SpeedBuster	12	10	$40

both products. To simplify the presentation, let us define LS to represent the number of units of LaserStops to assemble, and SB the number of units of SpeedBusters to make. Then an expression for profit is

$$\text{Profit} = 24\,\text{LS} + 40\,\text{SB}$$

We also observe that we have limited quantities of the two components. Since only 6,000 of component A will be available, the number of component A used in assembling both products cannot exceed 6,000. Since each product requires 12 of component A, the number of component A that will be used is

$$\text{Quantity used} = 12\,\text{LS} + 12\,\text{SB}$$

This number must be *less than or equal* to the number available (6,000), or

$$12\,\text{LS} + 12\,\text{SB} \le 6,000$$

Similarly, for component B, we have a constraint

$$6\,\text{LS} + 10\,\text{SB} \le 3,500$$

Mathematically, there is no reason why the values of LS and SB cannot be less than zero. However, in terms of the real world situation, this is illogical. Thus, we must also add constraints restricting these quantities to be at least zero, or

$$\text{LS} \ge 0$$

$$\text{SB} \ge 0$$

Therefore, the complete model is

$$\text{Maximize Profit} = 24\,LS + 40\,SB$$

subject to the constraints

$$12\,\text{LS} + 12\,\text{SB} \le 6,000$$

$$6\,\text{LS} + 10\,\text{SB} \le 3,500$$

$$\text{LS} \ge 0$$

$$\text{SB} \ge 0$$

Using the model, we wish to find the best combination of products that satisfy all constraints and maximize profit. This is an example of an *optimization problem*.

Problems in which we seek to minimize or maximize some objective function are called *optimization problems*. Any solution that satisfies all constraints is called a *feasible solution*. A feasible solution that minimizes or maximizes the objective is called an *optimal solution*.

Probabilistic Models

The models we discussed thus far are *deterministic*. Models that include randomness are called *probabilistic* (or sometimes *stochastic*).

> A *deterministic model* is one in which all model input information is assumed to be known with certainty or represented as such. A *probabilistic model* is one in which some of the model input information is not known with certainty and is usually described using probabilities.

For instance, suppose that customer demand is an important element of some model. We can make the assumption that the demand is known with certainty; say 5,000 units per month. In this case we would be dealing with a deterministic model. On the other hand, suppose we have evidence to indicate that demand is normally distributed, with a mean of 5,000 units per month and a standard deviation of 600 units per month. If this assumption is used in a model, we would be dealing with a probabilistic model. In general, whenever a model includes a probabilistic element it can be classified as a probabilistic model. We will discuss probabilistic models further in Chapter 11.

Data Preparation

As we noted, models need data. For many models, such as the product mix model in Example 3, data are easy to obtain from company records or the accounting department. Other models require data that must be estimated using statistical analysis. Care must be taken when working with data, and every effort should be made to ensure that data are sufficiently accurate. Sample data do not always reflect reality. People do not always behave the same when observed, nor do they always act as they say they act. Poor data can result in poor solutions. In one application the authors have seen, a distribution system design model relied on data obtained from the corporate finance department. Transportation costs were determined using a formula based on the latitude and longitude of the locations of plants and customers. But when the solution was represented on a geographic information system (GIS) mapping program, one of the customers was in the Atlantic Ocean! (This also shows the value of graphical representations of models and solutions).

ANALYZING PROBLEMS

Models are used in management science to analyze problems in several ways.

Models Are Used to Understand the Behavior of Systems in Order to Evaluate Alternative Decisions. Descriptive models, in particular, provide this capability. For example, suppose that we combine the demand–price and profit models discussed in Examples 1 and 2:

$$D = ap^{-b}$$

$$P = (p - c)Q - F$$

If we assume that all demand can be sold, or that $D = Q$, then we have

$$P = (p - c)ap^{-b} - F$$

Suppose that an economist determines that the constants in the demand–price model are a = 600,000 and b = 2.1. The unit cost of the product is $18 and fixed costs amount to $3,500. Table 1.3 shows the demand and profit as price varies between $20 and $40. This information is displayed on the graph in Figure 1.3. We see that as price increases, demand falls and profit increases, although at a decreasing rate. Eventually, at a price of about $34, profit reaches a maximum and begins to decline. If an important managerial goal is to establish a strong market share, then it may not be appropriate to set the price too high, even though profit can be maximized. This model provides managers with the information to make trade-offs between profit and market share.

Models Are Used to Find Acceptable or Optimal Solutions to Optimization Problems. In Example 3 we developed a product mix model with the objective of maximizing profit:

TABLE 1.3
Demand and
profit calculations

Price	Demand	Profit
20	1,112	($1,276.60)
21	1,003	($489.68)
22	910	$140.19
23	829	$644.70
24	758	$1,048.40
25	696	$1,370.52
26	641	$1,626.22
27	592	$1,827.58
28	548	$1,984.28
29	509	$2,104.13
30	474	$2,193.48
31	443	$2,257.51
32	414	$2,300.49
33	388	$2,325.90
34	365	$2,336.67
35	343	$2,335.22
36	324	$2,323.56
37	305	$2,303.38
38	289	$2,276.11
39	273	$2,242.95
40	259	$2,204.90

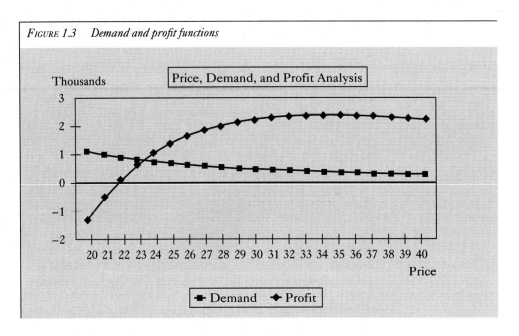

FIGURE 1.3   *Demand and profit functions*

$$\text{Maximize Profit} = 24\,\text{LS} + 40\,\text{SB}$$

subject to the constraints

$$12\,\text{LS} + 12\,\text{SB} \le 6{,}000$$
$$6\,\text{LS} + 10\,\text{SB} \le 3{,}500$$
$$\text{LS} \ge 0$$
$$\text{SB} \ge 0$$

We would like to have a method to find an optimal solution.

An *algorithm* is a systematic procedure that finds a feasible or an optimal solution to a problem.

Researchers in management science have developed algorithms to solve many types of optimization problems, and we will discuss some of these in this book. However, we will not be concerned with the detailed mechanics of these algorithms, since they are widely available on personal computers; our focus will be on the use of the algorithms to solve the models we develop.

If possible, we would like an algorithm that finds an optimal solution. However, some models are so complex that it is impossible to solve them optimally in a reasonable amount of computer time, because of the extremely large number of computations that may be required. (Some problems may not be possible to solve in your lifetime, even on the fastest available computer!) For many optimization problems, therefore, a manager might be satisfied with a solution that is good but not optimal. Other reasons why managers may not be concerned with finding an optimal solution to a model include the following:

- Inexact or limited data used to estimate uncontrollable quantities in models may contain more error than that of a nonoptimal solution.
- The assumptions used in a model make it an inaccurate representation of the real problem, making the "best" solution moot.
- Managers may not need the very best solution; anything better than the present one will often suffice, so long as it can be obtained at a reasonable cost and in a reasonable amount of time.

If an algorithm is guaranteed to find an optimal solution to a problem, we say it is an *exact algorithm*. Algorithms without such guarantees are called *heuristic algorithms* or simply *heuristics* from a Greek word meaning "to discover."

A *heuristic* is a rule that is typically guided by common sense and will generally provide good, but not necessarily optimal, solutions.

For example, a heuristic approach to finding a solution to the product mix problem might be to produce as many units of the product as possible with the largest unit profit. In this case, we would attempt to produce as many SpeedBusters as possible while producing no LaserStops. We must ensure that the solution is feasible. Thus, if LS = 0, the first constraint must satisfy

$$12 \text{ SB} \leq 6{,}000$$

or

$$\text{SB} \leq 6{,}000/12 = 500$$

From the second constraint we have

$$10 \text{ SB} \leq 3{,}500$$

or

$$\text{SB} \leq 3{,}500/10 = 350$$

We can therefore produce at most 350 SpeedBusters without violating a constraint. The total profit would be 40(350) = \$14,000. Surprisingly, this is an optimal solution! Simple approaches based on common sense often yield very good solutions; however, they generally do not guarantee optimal solutions to all problems. (If the unit profit on LaserStops is increased by just \$1, producing LS = 0 and SB = 350 would not be an optimal solution. Can you find a better one in this case?) We will see how to solve this problem in Chapter 5.

Models Are Used to Examine the Sensitivity of Solutions to Changes in the Data.
Because data are often inexact estimates or subject to uncontrollable variation, it is important to understand how solutions may change as the data changes.

> *Sensitivity analysis* involves seeing what happens to model results when changes are made in the model data.

For example, using our heuristic solution to the product mix problem, suppose that an additional 10 units of component B are available. If the constraint on component B is changed to

$$10 \, \text{SB} < 3{,}510$$

then we see that SB $\leq$ 351. We can produce an additional SpeedBuster and increase profits by \$40. This type of information can enable a manager to determine the value of trying to obtain additional resources. Other questions that might be asked are: How will total profit change as the unit profits are changed? How will profits be affected if a contract requires production of 50 LaserStops? Because a model is only a representation of the real problem, sensitivity analysis is an important element of problem analysis.

Dramatic increases in the performance and accessibility of computers have facilitated the analysis of management science problems in practice. Today we are able to use desktop personal computers to solve problems with thousands of decision variables that would have required large and expensive mainframe computers twenty-five years ago. The ability to use personal computers allows managers to build and experiment with models in their offices. This ability has been enhanced through the development of decision support systems.

> A *decision support system (DSS)* is a set of computer-based tools used by a manager in connection with his or her problem-solving and decision-making duties.[2]

DSSs include three components:

1. Data management. The data management component includes information databases and allows the user to input, retrieve, update, and manipulate data.
2. Model management. The model management component consists of various statistical tools and management science models and allows the user to easily build, manipulate, and solve models.
3. Communication system. The communication system component provides the interface necessary for the user to interact with the data and model management components.

---

[2]William E. Leigh and Michael E. Doherty, *Decision Support and Expert Systems*, Cincinnati, OH: South-Western Publishing Co., 1986.

Decision support systems provide the technology for managers without a high level of technical expertise to use management science models productively.

INTERPRETING RESULTS AND SELECTING A SOLUTION

The information provided by management science models is only one component in decision making. Managers should never implement model solutions blindly, because many important considerations usually cannot be included in formal models. Quantitative information must therefore be integrated with qualitative analysis drawn from managers' experience and judgment. The more well-structured a problem is, the more the manager can rely on management science model results. As problems become more fuzzy and strategic in nature, more weight is usually placed on qualitative issues. Nevertheless, management science models can provide information that better supports a manager's intuition, or that the manager may never have realized.

IMPLEMENTING SOLUTIONS

Any solution must be accepted by the problem owners, and solutions must be checked against the problem definition. An elegant solution simply will not make sense relative to the actual problem if careless errors have been made. In the worst case, the wrong solution is implemented. Also, the cost of solving the problem should never exceed the benefits that will accrue. This may seem obvious, but it is seldom considered at the early stages of problem solving.

Management scientists often believe that problems only involve technical issues. In reality, many political and social problems must be addressed to get a solution to be used. Managers must accept the solution and believe that it will benefit them. Workers on the factory floor who must use the solution must be able to do so with minimal training and effort. Ensuring that a solution to a management science problem is implemented successfully requires providing adequate resources, motivating managers and workers, eliminating resistance to change, modifying organizational policies, and developing trust. Problems (and their solutions!) affect people: customers, suppliers, and employees. Thus, people must be an important part of the problem solving process. Sensitivity to political and organizational issues is an important skill that management scientists must possess when looking beyond the technical solutions.

A case in point is a study conducted for the New York City Department of Sanitation that focused on allocating 450 new street cleaners throughout the city. A mathematical model was developed to allocate the cleaners in an optimal fashion based on the marginal improvement that could be achieved with additional cleaners. The model suggested that many of the new cleaners be assigned to districts that were already quite clean. In the final allocation, however, most of the new street cleaners went to the dirtiest districts, but each district was assigned some as a political compromise. The value of the model was not in providing an optimal solution, but in predicting the effects of alternative decisions.

SUMMARY OF THE PROBLEM SOLVING PROCESS

Figure 1.4 summarizes the process of solving problems using management science. We must emphasize that this process is *not* necessarily sequential and "clean." Often it is necessary to go back to earlier steps as new information arises. Management science focuses on three major themes: modeling, analysis, and interpretation. These themes define the focus of this book. The other aspects of this process are vitally important, but they relate more to managerial issues.

MANAGEMENT SCIENCE PRACTICE

In each chapter we provide a detailed discussion of one application described in the chapter introduction. These are designed to show how concepts developed in the chapter have been put into practice by companies using management science. Here we discuss how American Airlines uses management science for overbooking problems.

FIGURE 1.4   *Problem solving with management science*

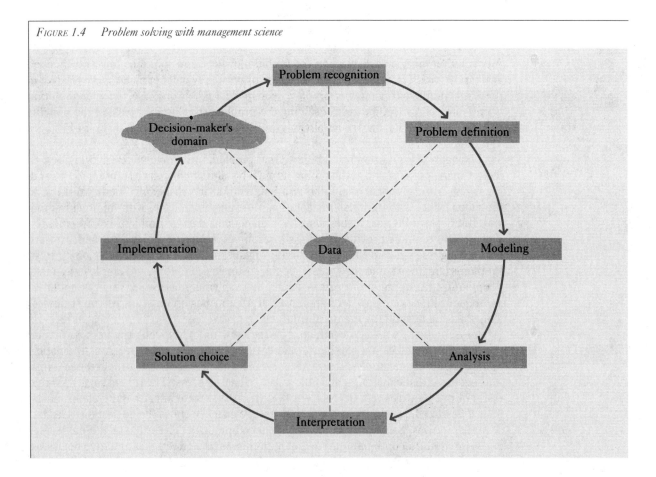

The Airline Overbooking Problem[3]

Airlines allow customers to cancel unpaid reservations with no penalty. Even after purchasing a ticket, many passengers may cancel or miss their flights and receive at least partial refunds. Those who do not formally cancel a reservation and do not show up are considered no-shows. On average, about half of all reservations made for a flight are cancelled or become no-shows. American Airlines estimates that about 15 percent of seats on sold-out flights would be unused if reservation sales were limited to aircraft capacity.

By properly setting reservation levels higher than seating capacity, American is able to compensate for passenger cancellations and no-shows. However, poor overbooking decisions can be costly. If reservation levels are set too low (more passengers than expected cancel or do not show up), then flights depart with empty seats that could have been filled. With overbooking, the airline takes the risk that more passengers may show up for a flight than there are seats on the aircraft. The airline must compensate such passengers for their inconvenience and must accommodate them on other flights.

The cost of oversales consists of compensation for the inconvenience (in the form of vouchers that can be redeemed on a future flight), hotel and meal accommodations if necessary, and a seat on a later flight, either on American or some other airline. If the passenger is put on another airline, American must pay the other airline for transportation. The oversale cost is not constant. The more oversales that occur on a flight, the higher the voucher offer will be and the more likely that unaccommodated passengers will have to be transported on another airline. Therefore, the total oversale cost grows at an increasing rate.

American Airlines Decision Technologies (AADT), the management science consulting branch of the company, developed an optimization model that maximizes net revenue associated with overbooking decisions. In choosing the best overbooking level for a flight, the model balances the additional revenue that can be gained by selling a reservation against the cost of the additional oversale risk. This is shown in Figure 1.5. When there is little or no overbooking, total revenue equals net revenue. The optimal overbooking level occurs at the maximum of the net revenue curve, where net revenue is the difference between total passenger revenue and oversale cost.

The number of oversales allowed by using this model, however, may sometimes degrade passenger service to an unacceptable level. To prevent this problem, AADT added a constraint to limit the expected number of oversales on each flight. The complete model accounts for

- The additional revenue generated by adding more reservations
- The probability distribution of passenger cancellations and no-shows
- The expected number of oversales
- The maximum number of oversales allowed
- The likelihood that a passenger who cannot secure a reservation on one flight will choose another American Airlines flight (called the recapture probability)

Because these factors vary with the amount of time before departure, overbooking levels are recalculated several times before departure. Four forecasts are needed for the model:

---

[3]Adaptation and figure from Smith *et al.*, "Field Management at American Airlines," *Interfaces*, Vol. 22, No. 1, Jan–Feb 1992, pp. 8–31.

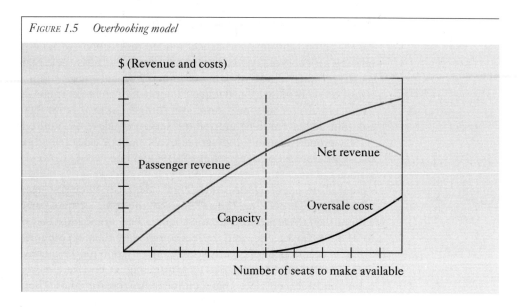

FIGURE 1.5   *Overbooking model*

1. The probability that a passenger will cancel
2. The probability that a passenger with an active reservation will not show up
3. The recapture probability
4. The oversale cost

AADT uses forecasting models to estimate the probabilities.

Discussion Questions

1. Economic theory states that the optimum net revenue occurs at a point where marginal revenue equals marginal cost. Does this apply to the overbooking situation? Discuss this question in terms of Figure 1.5.
2. What relationship do you think would exist between the optimum overbooking level and the recapture probability? If the recapture probability increases, would the overbooking level be higher or lower?
3. What data are needed to generate the four forecasts needed by the model?

MORE EXAMPLES AND SOLVED PROBLEMS

We conclude each chapter of this book with a set of additional examples and solved problems. These are designed to reinforce the ideas developed in the chapter, to provide "tips" that will help you become a better modeler and problem solver, and to provide practice for completing the problems and exercises at the end of the chapters. To obtain the full benefit from these examples, you should try to work them on your own before continuing. In this chapter, we focus on some elementary modeling principles. The next chapter will expand on these principles in developing more comprehensive models in management science.

Example 4. From Models to Influence Diagrams

In Example 3, we developed the following model:

$$\text{Maximize Profit} = 24\,\text{LS} + 40\,\text{SB}$$
$$12\,\text{LS} + 12\,\text{SB} \le 6{,}00 \text{ (component A use)}$$
$$6\,\text{LS} + 10\,\text{SB} \le 3{,}500 \text{ (component B use)}$$
$$\text{LS} \ge 0$$
$$\text{SB} \ge 0$$

Let us break this model down into its basic components. The decision variables are LS and SB, the number of units of each product to produce. If numerical values are assigned to these variables, then we know the number of units of component A (12 LS + 12 SB) and the number of units of component B (6 LS + 10 SB) that are used. We also know the profit (24 LS + 40 SB). We also have limited availabilities of each component A and B (6,000 and 3,600) that restrict the usage of each component. Finally, we have nonnegativity requirements (LS $\ge$ 0 and SB $\ge$ 0) for the decision variables.

By decomposing a model in this fashion it is easy to draw an influence diagram as shown in Figure 1.6. In this diagram, we have included the data in the problem, which clearly show the relationships among the elements of the problem.

Figure 1.6   An influence diagram for the radar detector model

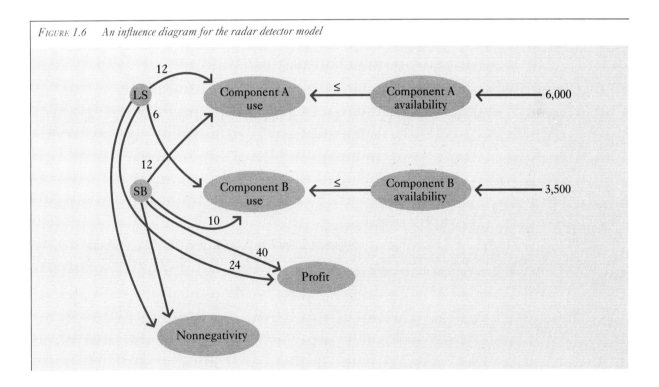

It is easy to construct an influence diagram from a mathematical model. The art of modeling is to develop the influence diagram *first*, and then to define the appropriate mathematical relationships.

EXAMPLE 5. A MARKETING MEDIA SELECTION MODEL

Marketing managers have various media alternatives, such as radio, TV, magazines, etc., in which to advertise. They must determine which to use, the number of insertions in each, and the timing of insertions to maximize advertising effectiveness within a limited budget. Suppose that three media options are available: radio, TV, and newspaper. Let R, T, and N be the number of ads placed in each of these media, respectively. Table 1.4 provides some basic data. The exposure value is a measure of the number of people exposed to the advertisement and is derived from market research studies. The minimum and maximum number of units are those desired by the client firm. A total budget of $40,000 is available. The objective is to maximize the total exposure value.

The structure of this model is similar to the radar detector example. If R radio ads are placed, the resulting exposure is $2,000R$. Similarly, T and N television and newspaper ads yield total exposure values of $3,500T$ and $2,700N$. Therefore, any media mix results in a total exposure

$$\text{Total exposure} = 2,000R + 3,500T + 2,700N$$

The amount spent on this mix cannot exceed the budget:

$$\text{Expenses} = 500R + 2,000T + 200N \leq 40,000$$

Finally, we must meet the minimum and maximum requirements for each medium:

$$0 \leq R \leq 15$$

$$12 \leq T$$

$$6 \leq N \leq 30$$

The complete model is

$$\text{maximize } 2,000R + 3,500T + 2,700N$$

subject to the constraints

$$500R + 2,000T + 200N \leq 40,000$$

$$0 \leq R \leq 15$$

$$12 \leq T$$

$$6 \leq N \leq 30$$

*TABLE 1.4
Media
selection data*

Medium	Cost/ad	Exposure value	Minimum units	Maximum units
Radio	$500	2,000	0	15
TV	$2,000	3,500	12	—
Newspaper	$200	2,700	6	30

This model has several limitations. First, it assumes that each exposure has a constant effect, but in reality repeated exposures have diminishing returns. The model also assumes constant media costs, but discounts often apply for multiple ads in a particular medium. The model assumes that exposure is additive; that is, it does not consider audience duplication and replication. Finally, the model fails to consider when the advertisements should be scheduled.

> All models have limitations. It is important to understand the assumptions of any model to use them effectively in problem solving.

EXAMPLE 6. LOCATING A DISTRIBUTION FACILITY

Distribution centers are used as buffers between manufacturing plants and markets to take advantage of bulk transportation and improve customer service. The location of distribution centers should take into account the locations of plants and markets, the volume of goods moved, and transportation costs. A reasonable approach is to find a "central" location that includes these factors.

A simple approach is to find the "center of gravity," the location that minimizes the weighted distance between the distribution center and the supply and demand locations. The weighted distance is the distance multiplied by the volume shipped. Suppose that location i has map coordinates (x_i, y_i) and an annual volume of W_i. Let (c_x, c_y) be the map coordinate of the center of gravity. The center of gravity is found from the following equations:

$$c_x = \frac{\sum_i x_i W_i}{\sum_i W_i}$$

$$c_y = \frac{\sum_i y_i W_i}{\sum_i W_i}$$

Why do these coordinates define the center of gravity? The answer lies in the name itself and derives from a simple physical analogy. Suppose we have a board in which holes are drilled at the locations of existing facilities. Pass a string through each hole and tie them together. Place a weight at the other end of each string corresponding to the shipping volume at that location. Now shake the board gently until the knot tying the strings together comes to a rest. In a frictionless world, that will be the location that minimizes the total weighted distance to all locations! The equations above are simply a mathematical representation of this point.

To illustrate this model, suppose that an electronics firm in Fort Worth, Texas, manufactures for three main markets in Minneapolis, San Diego, and Columbus, Ohio. The monthly demands at the markets are 12,000, 16,000, and 5,000 units respectively. The total shipments from Fort Worth are therefore 33,000 units. Using approximate latitudes and longitudes, map coordinates of these cities are

Ft. Worth: (33, 98)

Minneapolis: (45, 93)

San Diego: (32.5, 117.5)

Columbus: (40, 84)

The center of gravity is

$$c_x = \frac{33(33,000) + 45(12,000) + 32.5(16,000) + 40(5,000)}{33,000 + 12,000 + 16,000 + 5,000} = 35.6$$

$$c_y = \frac{98(33,000) + 93(12,000) + 117.5(16,000) + 84(5,000)}{33,000 + 12,000 + 16,000 + 5,000} = 100.8$$

This location is near the Texas-Oklahoma border. Of course, many other considerations must be included in the decision, such as highway access, labor supply, and facility cost.

Simple models can provide insights into the nature of complex systems and provide starting points for more detailed analyses.

EXAMPLE 7. A SPEAKER SCHEDULING PROBLEM

The Management Development Center at a local university is sponsoring a half-day (four-hour) seminar on applications of management science. There are six speakers, each planning to speak one hour. If they were scheduled in six different time slots, the seminar would extend beyond the planned four-hour period. Because of the participants' divergent interests, certain speakers can be scheduled simultaneously. The following matrix shows which speakers *should not* be scheduled at the same time:

		Speaker					
		1	2	3	4	5	6
	1				x	x	
	2						
Speaker	3				x	x	x
	4	x		x		x	x
	5	x		x	x		x
	6			x	x	x	

Any assignment of speakers that avoids conflicts is a feasible solution. We would like to design an algorithm that finds one. We can develop a simple model of this problem by drawing a picture. Each speaker corresponds to a point (circle), and a line is drawn between two points if the speakers should not be scheduled at the same time. This is shown in Figure 1.7. How might you find a feasible solution?

Notice that a solution exists if you can label the six points in Figure 1.7 (speakers) with four letters A, B, C, and D (corresponding to the four time slots) so that no two points with a connecting line have the same label. An algorithm to do this might start with any speaker, say speaker 1, and assign that speaker to time slot A. Next, select any speaker without a label, say 5. Assign this speaker to any time slot that avoids conflicts with speakers already assigned. Therefore, you would assign to speaker 5 any time slot except A. Now repeat this procedure. If we choose speaker 4 next, we cannot assign time slot A or B, so we might choose C. We repeat this until all speakers are assigned a time slot. A solution is shown in Figure 1.8.

FIGURE 1.7   *Model for the speaker scheduling problem*

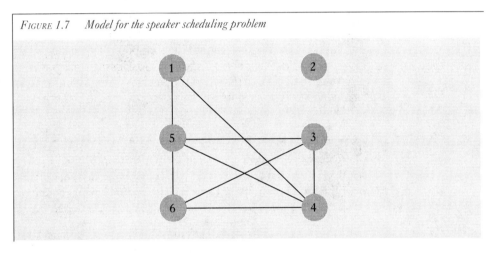

FIGURE 1.8   *A solution for the speaker scheduling problem*

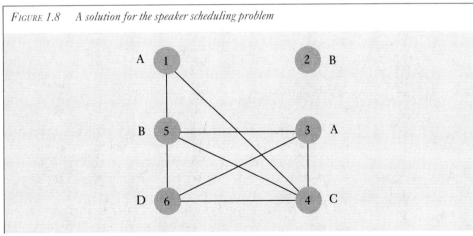

However, there is no guarantee that this approach will ensure that a feasible solution is found. To illustrate this, suppose that we started with speaker 5, and assign time slot A. Next choose speaker 1, assigning time slot B; then speaker 6, assigning time slot C; and next speaker 3, assigning time slot D. If we choose speaker 4 next, none of the time slots can be assigned without a conflict. This situation is shown in Figure 1.9.

> It might seem easy to design a simple algorithm for a problem; it is far more difficult to guarantee that it will work. Developing good management science algorithms that are proven to work is the job of management sciences researchers.

The methods that you will learn in this book have been studied extensively by many researchers. In practice, however, you might find yourself having to develop an ad hoc method to solve some problem. By having a better understanding of techniques that have been developed by management science researchers, you will be better equipped to attack unconventional problem situations.

SUMMARY

In this chapter we introduced management science, a scientific discipline devoted to the analysis of complex decision problems. The field has grown rapidly since the Second World War and has been used successfully in all areas of business and industry, services, government, and nonprofit organizations to improve the effectiveness and efficiency of systems and processes.

The problem solving process is central to management science application. This process consists of

- Problem recognition
- Problem definition
- Problem structuring
- Problem analysis
- Results interpretation and solution selection
- Solution implementation

In most cases, management science problems have the objective of optimizing some quantity such as profit or cost. Models are used to provide structure to a problem and simplify the process of finding solutions.

Models have several advantages to problem solvers:

- Models enable decision-makers to anticipate what will happen in the future.
- Models enable decision-makers to evaluate alternative actions without carrying out experiments on the real system.
- Models allow decision-makers to study systems and the interactions within them, therefore helping to explain how systems operate.
- Models improve on decision making based exclusively on intuitive judgment and provide guidance as to the best courses of action to take.

Algorithms and heuristics are developed to solve management science problems. It is important to realize, however, that any practical decision problem has organizational and political consequences. Users of management science must look beyond technical issues when developing models and implementing the solutions.

Finally, we wish to point out that even if a model is never solved, the *process* of model building can be of immense benefit in helping the decision-maker to understand the structure of the problem better. Models help you to organize your thoughts and provide structure to a "mess" of facts, decisions, and data.

CHAPTER REVIEW EXERCISES

I. Terms to Understand

You should be able to define the following terms:

a. Management science (p. 2)
b. Problem (p. 7)
c. Problem solving (p. 8)
d. Goals (p. 8)
e. Objectives (p. 8)
f. Decisions (p. 8)
g. Constraints (p. 8)
h. Decision making (p. 8)
i. Model (p. 8, 11)
j. Type III error (p. 9)
k. Descriptive model (p. 11)
l. Predictive model (p. 12)
m. Prescriptive model (p. 12)

n. Influence diagram (p. 12)
o. Controllable variable (p. 14)
p. Uncontrollable variable (p. 14)
q. Objective function (p. 15)
r. Optimization problem (p. 16)
s. Feasible solution (p. 16)
t. Optimal solution (p. 16)
u. Deterministic model (p. 17)
v. Stochastic model (p. 17)
w. Algorithm (p. 19)
x. Heuristic (p. 20)
y. Sensitivity analysis (p. 21)
z. Decision support system (p. 21)

II. Discussion Questions

1. Why is management science a multidisciplinary field? How can different disciplines contribute to solving a management science problem?
2. How has the widespread growth of computers contributed to the effective application of management science? What do you foresee in the future?
3. List five problems from your own experience (personal, professional, or school) that you think might benefit from a management science analysis and explain your reasoning.
4. What role can management science play in quality and continuous improvement?
5. Explain the difference between problems and their symptoms. Why is it important to get to the true problem rather than attack only the symptoms?
6. Describe the major phases of problem solving.
7. Why are models used in most management science problems? Summarize the major uses of models in management science.
8. How would you recognize when a prescriptive model, rather than a descriptive or predictive model, is appropriate for a decision problem?
9. Explain the four components of prescriptive models.
10. Why do we have to develop heuristics for some problems?
11. How does an exact algorithm differ from a heuristic algorithm?
12. Why must social and political concerns be addressed when solving management science problems?
13. In this chapter we have seen the importance of defining and analyzing a problem prior to attempting to find a solution. A story exists concerning one of the earliest operations research groups in World War II, which was conducting a study of the optimum utilization of Spitfire and Hurricane aircraft during the Battle of Britain. Whenever one of the planes returned from battle, the bullet holes were carefully plotted. By repeatedly recording this over time, and studying the clusters of data, the group was able to estimate the regions of the aircraft most likely to be hit by enemy gunfire, with the objective of reinforcing these regions with special armor. What difficulties do you see here?
14. Discuss some of the problems associated with the following quantitative "solutions":[4]
    a. A manufacturing firm wanting to estimate the sales of one of its products asked a sample of retailers to pick two days per month at random and record the number sold on those days. The two-day totals were then multiplied by 15 to yield monthly sales estimates.
    b. A researcher noted that commercial establishments in certain high-crime areas spent far more money on protective devices than those in safer districts. This was quite unnecessary, he stated, for the heavily protected stores sustained no greater burglary rates than their counterparts in other areas.
    c. According to Barnett (see footnote 4), *The New York Times* reported that "If you live in Detroit, you have a better than 2000 to 1 chance of *not* being killed by one of your fellow citizens. Optimists searching for perspective in the statistics of murder insist those odds are pretty good." This figure was obtained by converting Detroit's annual murder rate to a simple fraction.
15. As the population of major cities expands, municipal governments must make decisions about expanding existing airports or building new regional airports.
    a. List and discuss the key issues that are relevant to these decisions.
    b. How might management science techniques be used?
    c. Who are the major constituencies? What objectives do they have?
    d. Discuss the difficulty in making trade-offs among these objectives.

---

[4]Adapted from Arnold Barnett, "Misapplications Reviews: An Introduction," *Interfaces*, Vol. 12, No. 5, October 1982, pp. 47–49.

16. How might management science be used in the following situations?
    a. Making and marketing a new product
    b. Deciding where to locate a new plant
    c. Determining a personal investment plan
17. Trucks that enter a state must file a route plan with the state government. They are not allowed to travel on roads with prohibitive weight restrictions. On the other hand, the trucker wants to reach his or her destination in the shortest possible time. How might management science help to solve this problem?
18. You wish to determine the schedule of your courses next term.
    a. What is your objective? How would you measure it?
    b. What are your alternative courses of action?
    c. What data do you need to find a solution?
    d. How would you construct an optimal schedule?
19. In driving to your campus (or any other location) describe how management science can help you find an optimal route. Do you always drive the optimal route? If not, why not?

III. Problems

1. A (greatly) simplified model of the national economy can be described as follows.[5] The national income is the sum of three components: consumption, investment, and government spending. Consumption is related to the total income of all individuals and to the taxes they pay on income. Taxes are related to income by the tax rate. Investment is also related to the size of the total income. Use this information to draw an influence diagram by recognizing that the phrase "*A* is related to *B*" implies that *A* influences *B* in the model.
2. In Problem 1, if we assume that the phrase "*A* is related to *B*" can be translated into mathematical terms as "$A = kB$" where k is some constant, construct a mathematical model for the information provided.
3. Four key marketing decision variables are price (P), advertising (A), logistics (L), and product quality (Q). Consumer demand is influenced by these variables. The simplest model for describing demand in terms of these variables is

$$D = k - pP + aA + lL + qQ$$

where k, p, a, l, and q are constants. Discuss the assumptions of this model. Specifically, how does each variable affect demand? How do the variables influence each other? What limitations might this model have? How can it be improved?
4. Return on investment (ROI) is computed in the following manner: ROI is equal to turnover multiplied by earnings as a percent of sales. Turnover is sales divided by total investment. Total investment is current assets (inventories, accounts receivable, and cash) plus fixed assets. Earnings equals sales minus the cost of sales. The cost of sales consists of mill cost of sales, selling expenses, freight and delivery, and administrative costs. Construct an influence diagram that relates these variables. Define symbols and use the influence diagram to develop a mathematical model. What kind of a model is it?
5. Total marketing effort is a term used to describe the critical decision factors that affect demand: price, advertising, distribution, and product quality. Define the variable x to represent total marketing effort. A typical model that is used to predict demand as a function of total marketing effort is

$$D = ax^b$$

---

[5]T. G. Lewis and B. J. Smith, *Computer Principles of Modeling and Simulation*, Boston: Houghton Mifflin, 1979.

Suppose that a is a positive number. Different model forms result from varying the constant b. Sketch the graphs of this model for $b = 0$, $b = 1$, $0 < b < 1$, $b < 0$, and $b > 1$. What does each model tell you about the relationship between demand and marketing effort? What assumptions are implied? Are they reasonable? How would you go about selecting the appropriate model?

6. A consumer products company has collected the following data relating monthly demand to the price of one of its products:

Price	Demand
$12	2,080
$14	2,006
$16	1,950
$18	1,870

What type of model is appropriate? Can you determine a good model for this data?

7. A common problem in marketing is finding a set of price levels and marketing efforts for several products in a product line that would maximize profit subject to budget and production capacity constraints. Data available include the demand for each product, the unit cost of producing each product, fixed costs, available budget, total production capacity, and amount of production capacity used by each unit of output of product i.

a. Construct an influence diagram showing the relationships among these factors.

b. Suppose that the demand depends on price and marketing effort. How would your influence diagram change?

c. Discuss the general form of a mathematical model that might be developed for this problem.

8. A manufacturer of mini-CD players is preparing to set the price on a new model. Demand is thought to depend on the price and is represented by the model

$$D = 2000 - 3p$$

The accounting department estimates that the total costs can be represented by

$$C = 5,000 + 40D$$

Develop a model for the total profit. Can you find the price for which profit is maximized?

9. A firm produces two products. The following data are available:

Inputs	Cost/unit of input	Production requirements per unit of output Product 1	Product 2
Material (lbs.)	$ 3	3.0	2.0
Machine hours	$70	.1	.2
Labor hours	$ 9	.2	.3
Selling hours	$30	.5	.2
Advertising $	$ 2	2.5	1.5

Develop an influence diagram and a mathematical model for the cost per unit of output for a product. Using the data above, determine the unit cost for each product.

10. A model for sales is

$$S = nks$$

where n = the number of consumers in the market, k = percentage of consumers who purchase from the company, and s = average purchase size per month. Suppose that n = 4000, k = .18, and s = $125. Determine the sensitivity of sales to a 5 percent change in each of these factors. On which factor(s) should a manager focus initiatives in an effort to improve sales?

11. A group of students is asked to rate five different brands of beer according to two characteristics: flavor and body (lightness or heaviness). Each brand is rated on a scale from 1 to 7 for each characteristic. Each student is also asked to rate the "ideal" beer. The results of the survey are

Brand	Flavor	Body
A	3	5
B	6	3
C	5	2
D	2	3
E	3	1
Ideal	6	5

Develop a model for predicting the degree of similarity among brands. Can you develop a model to predict consumer preferences (in rank order)?

12. Cashiers in stores typically provide change by giving as many coins of the highest denomination first, followed by as many of the next highest denomination, etc., until the total amount is reached.
    a. What "problem" is the cashier actually solving?
    b. Is this procedure an exact algorithm for solving this problem?
    c. What would happen if our currency system had 20-cent pieces?

13. An investor is considering investing in two stocks: The Quincunx Corporation (QC) and Red Bead Development (RBD). Project returns are $5 per share for QC, and $3 per share of RBD. The cost per share for QC is $20 while the cost per share of RBD is $15. The investor has $2,000 to invest. How should the money be allocated?
    a. Draw an influence diagram of this problem.
    b. Define symbols and develop a mathematical model for this decision problem.
    c. Using trial and error, attempt to find the optimal solution.

14. A regional airline trains flight attendants in groups. Due to turnover, employees leave at a constant rate over time. The decision problem involves determining the number of employees to train in each group and the timing of the training sessions. If the group is too large, the employees will be underutilized and excess costs will be incurred. On the other hand, if the group is too small, then the training courses must be repeated very often and additional training costs will be realized.
    a. Define the decision and uncontrollable variables in this problem.
    b. Assuming that the airline wishes to minimize training costs, define some symbols and construct an appropriate model.

15. A business traveler is to make six round-trips between Boston and Washington, DC, during the next month. Three primary airlines serving this route are BosAir (BA), Air National (AN), and East Coast Airlines (ECA). The traveler is a member of the frequent flier clubs, and flights on ECA generate credits on BA. The mileage award structure is

BA: 1,000 miles per flight plus 5,000 extra miles if the number of flights in one month is at least two, and another 5,000 miles if the number of flights in one month is at least six.

AN: 1,500 miles per flight plus 10,000 bonus miles if the number of flights in one month is at least six.

ECA: 2,000 miles (on BA) per flight, plus 10,000 bonus miles if the number of flights during the month is at least five.

Because of the rules governing the exchange of bonus miles for free travel, the traveler values each AN mile as roughly 5/4 of one BA mile. The traveler's objective is to maximize the equivalent number of BA miles.

a.   Develop a procedure for solving this problem.

b.   What are some of the practical considerations that might affect the solution but are difficult to model?

16.   The old East Prussian city of Königsberg was built at the junction of two rivers and the two islands formed by them. Seven bridges connected the islands to each other and to the rest of the city, as shown in Figure 1.10. A Swiss mathematician, Leonhard Euler, was asked if one could start from any point, cross each bridge exactly once, and return to the starting point. Can you find a solution to this problem? If not, what might be a more practical objective? Can you think of some practical problems that are similar to this one? (Hint: Consider city government and other municipal services.)

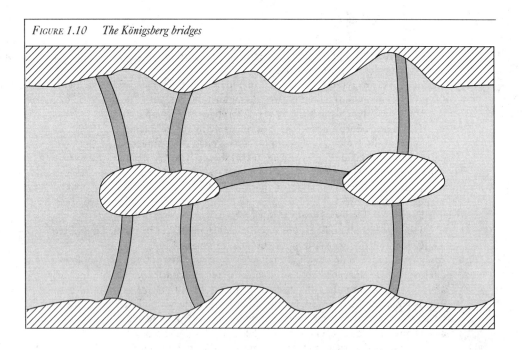

FIGURE 1.10   *The Königsberg bridges*

17.   A puzzle consists of four cubes, painted in four colors. The problem is to arrange the cubes in a straight line so that each color shows on each of the four sides. The color configuration of the four blocks is shown in Figure 1.11. Using arguments from your prior probability and statistics classes, compute the number of possible solutions. Can you construct a pictorial model of this problem that easily leads to the solution?

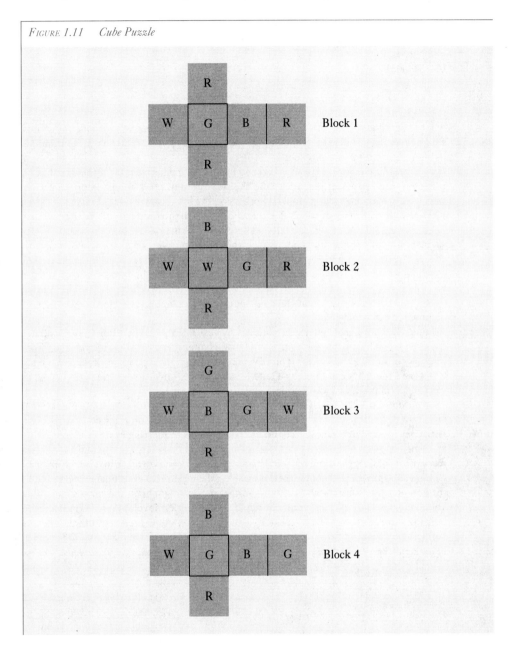

FIGURE 1.11   Cube Puzzle

IV. Projects and Cases

1. For each of the applications described in the "Applications of Management Science" section, discuss some of the issues that a management science project group would most likely have addressed. What types of individuals might have composed the groups? What types of models might they have applied? What data would they have had to gather?

2. Using knowledge developed from previous courses or interviews with faculty, develop a list of management science applications in each of the following functional disciplines of business:
    a. Accounting
    b. Marketing
    c. Finance
    d. Operations management
    e. Information systems
3. Select a decision problem that you currently face (for example, finding a job, improving your grades, buying a car) and discuss how you would apply the problem solving approach (definition, analysis, solution, and implementation) to your problem.
4. A supermarket has been experiencing long lines during peak periods of the day. The problem is noticeably worse on certain days of the week, and the peak periods are sometimes different according to the day of the week. There are usually enough workers on the job to open all cash registers. The problem is knowing when to call some of the workers stocking shelves up to the front to work the checkout counters. How might management science models help the supermarket? What data would be needed to develop these models?
5. Almost all colleges and universities face the following type of exam scheduling problem. There are *M* classes, whose exams need to be scheduled over *D* days. There are typically several periods per day in which to schedule the exams. If a student has more than one exam scheduled in a particular time slot, that student should be given a deferral for the conflict. A good schedule will minimize the number of conflicts. What data would be necessary to construct a model to solve this problem? How might the university's information technology play a key role?
6. A major metropolitan hospital's Outpatient Physical Therapy Department[6] is expanding to supply services to the Center for Occupational Health (COH). COH offers disability management services aimed at preventing injuries on the job and easing injured workers' transition back to work. Companies make contracts with COH, and the Physical Therapy Department designs on-site work transition programs to return injured workers to their original jobs within a certain time frame.

    Currently, the Physical Therapy Department supplies 1.5 full-time equivalent (FTE) therapists to COH (a total of 60 hours per week). The physical therapist treats an injured worker three times each week for two hours per treatment. Because of rapid growth, DOH is requesting more available FTEs to meet demand.

    The company sites are located throughout the state, so physical therapists must travel to and from the work sites (possibly combining several patients and work sites in one trip) and return home the same day. How would you approach the problem of determining the minimum additional number of FTEs necessary to treat the new demand? Discuss what further information you might need and suggest possible solution approaches.
7. Your company has eight new product opportunities under development. Top management has allocated a new investment budget of $1.5 million. Data for each product are given in the following table. How would you go about making a decision on which products to choose? Develop any models that you believe would help you make this decision. What assumptions, either implicit or explicit, have you made?

Product	Price	Annual Sales	Annual Cost	Initial Investment
1	10	10,000	80,000	160,000
2	1	500,000	475,000	400,000
3	1,000	200	180,000	250,000
4	50	100,000	4,000,000	750,000
5	3	1,000	2,500	2,000
6	20	80,000	1,500,000	500,000
7	500	50	20,000	30,000
8	20	200,000	3,800,000	500,000

---

[6] Thanks to Emmy Ziller for providing the information for this case.

REFERENCES

Ackoff, Russell L., "Beyond Problem Solving," *Decision Sciences*, Vol. 5, No. 2, 1974, pp. x–xv.

Anbil, Ranga, Eric Gelman, Bruce Patty, and Rajan Tanga. "Recent Advances in Crew-Pairing Optimization at American Airlines." *Interfaces*, Vol. 21, No. 1, January–February 1991, pp. 62–74.

Barnett, Arnold. "Misapplications Reviews: High Road to Glory." *Interfaces*, Vol. 17, No. 5, September–October 1987, pp. 51–54.

Ben-Dov, Yosi, Lakhbir Hayre, and Vincent Pica. "Mortgage Valuation Models at Prudential Securities." *Interfaces*, Vol. 22, No. 1, January–February 1992, pp. 55–71.

Brightman, Harvey J. *Group Problem Solving: An Improved Managerial Approach*, Atlanta, GA: Business Publishing Division, Georgia State University, 1988.

Brown, A. A., F. L. Hulswit, and J. D. Detelle. "A Study of Sales Operations." *Operations Research*, pp. 296–308, 1956.

Cebry, Michael E., Anura H. deSilva, and Fred J. DiLisio. "Management Science in Automating Postal Operations: Facility and Equipment Planning in the United States Postal Service." *Interfaces*, Vol. 22, No. 1, January–February 1992, pp. 110–130.

Collins, Dwight E. and Thomas E. Baker. "Using OR to Add Value in Manufacturing." *OR/MS Today*, December 1989, 22–26.

De Witt, Calvin W., Leon S. Lason, Allan D. Waren, Donald A. Brenner, and Simon A. Melhem. "OMEGA: An Improved Gasoline Blending System for Texaco." *Interfaces*, Vol. 19, No. 1, January–February 1989, 85–101.

Falconer, N. "On the Size of Convoys: An Example of the Methodology of Leading Wartime OR Scientists." *Operational Research Quarterly*, Vol. 27, No. 2, 1976, pp. 315–327.

Hall, John R. Jr. "An Issue Oriented History of TIMS." *Interfaces*, Vol. 13, No. 4, 1983, pp. 9–19.

Jack, Carolyn, Sheng-Roan Kai, and Alexander Shulman. "NETCAP – An Interactive Optimization System for GTE Telephone Network Planning." *Interfaces*, Vol. 22, No. 1, January–February 1992, pp. 72–89.

Kotler, Philip. *Marketing Decision Making: A Model Building Approach*, New York: Holt, Rinehart and Winston, 1968.

Lardner, Harold. "The Origins of Operational Research." *Operations Research*, Vol. 32, No. 2, 1984, pp. 465–475.

Lembersky, Mark R. and Uli H. Chi. "Weyerhaeuser Decision Simulator Improves Timber Profits." *Interfaces*, Vol. 16, No. 1, January–February 1986, 6–15.

Makuch, William M., Jeffrey L. Dodge, Joseph G. Ecker, Donna C. Granfors, and Gerald J. Hahn. "Managing Consumer Credit Delinquency in the US Economy: A Multi-Billion Dollar Management Science Application." *Interfaces*, Vol. 22, No. 1, January–February 1992, pp. 90–109.

Mehra, Satish. "Applying MS/OR Techniques to Small Businesses." *Interfaces*, Vol. 20, No. 2, March–April 1990, pp. 38–41.

Moore, E. William Jr., Janice M. Warke, and Lonny R. Gorban. "The Indispensable Role of Management Science in Centralizing Freight Operations at Reynolds Metals Company." *Interfaces*, Vol. 21, No. 1, January–February 1991, pp. 107–129.

Morris, Michele, "15 Fast-Track Careers," *Money*, June 1990, pp. 108–129.

Quinn, Phil, Bruce Andrews, and Henry Parsons. "Allocating Telecommunications Resources at L. L. Bean, Inc." *Interfaces*, Vol. 21, No. 1, January–February 1991, pp. 75–91.

Riccio, Lucius J., Joseph Miller, and Ann Litke. "Polishing the Big Apple: How Management Science Has Helped Make New York Streets Cleaner." *Interfaces*, Vol. 16, No. 1, January–February 1986, 83–88.

Smith, Barry C., John F. Leimkuhler, and Ross M. Darrow. "Yield Management at American Airlines." *Interfaces*, Vol. 22, No. 1, January–February 1992, pp. 8–31.

Stone, Lawrence D. "Search for the SS *Central America*: Mathematical Treasure Hunting." *Interfaces*, Vol. 22, No. 1, January–February 1992, pp. 32–54.

Watson, C. E. "The Problems of Problem Solving." *Business Horizons*, Vol. 19, August 1976, pp. 88–94.

CHAPTER 2

SPREADSHEETS

AND

MANAGEMENT

SCIENCE

INTRODUCTION

- One of the difficult decisions facing managers responsible for maintaining motor vehicle and construction equipment fleets is whether or not to implement oil analysis programs. A model developed for maintenance managers for the Southern Company was used to determine optimum policies for equipment and to assess the sensitivity of the results to various changes in the model parameters. The model, developed in LOTUS 1-2-3, provided the insight and financial analysis that justified improved maintenance policies, especially those using oil sampling strategies [Mellichamp et al., 1993].

- Bethlehem Steel Corporation uses a LOTUS 1-2-3 spreadsheet model for production planning and cost analysis. Based on an optimization of product flows through a steelmaking plant, the model is used to assess the impact of changes in product demands, facility capacities, and costs. Questions that are addressed include How many shifts per week would the plate mill run if this year's demand for steel plate products were 500,000 tons? and How would the final costs of products be affected if the price of natural gas increased by 20 percent? [Baker et al., 1987].

- A spreadsheet model developed by an internal consulting group at Du Pont helped the company to evaluate new strategies for one of its principal businesses. A key element of this model was the assessment of uncertainties such as competitors' strategies, market size, market share, and prices. The strategy that was ultimately chosen was expected to increase the value of the business by $175 million [Krumm and Rolle, 1992].

Personal computers have brought modeling to the fingertips of every manager, and one of the most exciting developments in microcomputing is the *electronic spreadsheet*. Spreadsheet software such as LOTUS 1-2-3, Microsoft®Excel, and Quattro Pro automate the way most individuals work with numerical data. They provide the means to manage data, formulas, and graphics simultaneously, using intuitive representations instead of abstract mathematical notation. Although the early applications of spreadsheets were primarily in accounting and finance, spreadsheets have developed into the most friendly and powerful general-purpose managerial tools available for doing basic numerical computation. Spreadsheets are also excellent tools for working with mathematical models in management science.

The purpose of this chapter is to review some of the key concepts, skills, and applications of spreadsheets in management science. We will use spreadsheets throughout this book whenever appropriate and we assume that you have a basic familiarity with spreadsheets, perhaps having used them in accounting or finance courses. Most of the spreadsheet examples in this book were implemented on LOTUS 1-2-3 4.01 for Windows or Excel 5.0. If you use other spreadsheet software, you may find some differences and should consult your software manual for the appropriate syntax or procedures.

GOOD SPREADSHEET DESIGN FOR MODEL BUILDING[1]

One of the particularly useful aspects of spreadsheet software is its ability to provide a creative, flexible tool for users of various skill levels to create anything from a simple worksheet to a complex decision model with relative ease. The worksheet structure and simple menu interface provide a framework useful for solving a wide variety of problems in business and management science. Useful spreadsheets should have several properties.

- First, the spreadsheet must provide accurate results. Because the formulas and functions are more susceptible to undetected errors than standard computer programs, the user must be careful. Good design and documentation can make an application more understandable and less vulnerable to incorrect use. Cross-checking, batch totals, and breaking down lengthy formulas into smaller steps can help to reduce errors. Careful and complete testing should help to detect errors and verify results.
- Second, spreadsheets need to be understood by both their creators and their users. Clear and complete descriptions and a consistent approach to the layout greatly contribute toward comprehensibility.
- Third, spreadsheets often need to be adapted to changes in a problem or application. In designing a spreadsheet (or any mathematical model for that matter) you should consider possible future uses or variations of the proposed model.
- Fourth, spreadsheets need to be efficient; the user should be able to readily locate and observe the critical portions of the worksheet.

Although elaborate and complex spreadsheet models can be designed to handle everything from detailed investment analysis to complex management science applications, spreadsheet models can also be developed to solve simple problems. We provide some general recommendations on building spreadsheet models, focusing on constructing and documenting them. Each time you begin to build a model, you may want to review these suggestions.

- *Planning saves time and trouble.* Although there are many ways to correct design problems with spreadsheet models (e.g., Insert, Delete, Move), much time will be saved if you lay out a tentative structure for the model on paper before turning the computer on. Pay particular attention to global formats and alignment. These should be entered on the worksheet before any entries are made. You can always override the global commands later (with Range commands) if specific cells require special formatting or alignment.
- *Use all available resources.* When you have a question, don't hesitate to examine the manual that accompanies the software. Many good books exist that provide a quick reference or tutorial (see, for instance, [Smith, 1990]). Newer versions of spreadsheet software have on-line help capabilities. Windows-based software provides spreadsheet command and on-line help capabilities at the click of a mouse and is extremely easy to use.

---

[1]Adapted from Thommes, 1992, and Smith, 1990.

- *Document your worksheet.* You should design your model so that six months from now you can remember the purpose of the template and how it works. First, choose a file name for your model that is both descriptive and simple. This will help eliminate the frustration of typing incorrect file names when loading your model. You may wish to put a short written description of what the model does on the worksheet. Where appropriate, include important instructions and explanatory notes on the face of the worksheet.

- *Use an effective layout.* A common strategy for laying out a spreadsheet is to separate areas of different use. In general, a good layout should be vertical rather than horizontal. Every spreadsheet should begin with an identification that is easily viewed. The identification should include a descriptive title, and usually the author's name and date of creation. For many applications, data will be entered by the user; a *data section* area, which will hold these data, should be separate from the work area. Another area of the worksheet will normally contain assumptions, definitions, and formulas. At a minimum, this section should contain a listing and definition of all constants and input variables used in the spreadsheet. To enhance the flexibility of the spreadsheet, all possible constants and variables that may change in the future should be identified. The work area might include lookup tables, intermediate calculations, or other data. When the spreadsheet is modified, this area will frequently require enlargements or additions, and this should be anticipated when allocating space. Finally, an output area will contain calculated results and descriptive labels. Some input data may need to be repeated to enhance understanding and readability. Such input data should be referenced only with cell references or range names.

  Without a data section, specific numerical values would have to be entered directly into the worksheet at the cells in which they are used. If the data change, the new values must be reentered directly into all appropriate formulas in the model. As we will illustrate in Example 1, this "direct-entry" model can be inefficient and cumbersome if the change in data involves revising many formulas.

  With a data section, all of the input data will be placed in one spot on the template, and all formulas in the answer will reference the appropriate cells in the data section. If new information is provided, changes are made to the data section only; no formulas need to be revised.

- *Pay attention to alignment and format.* Put labels over all columns. Use the currency and comma formats where appropriate. Use an integer format (no decimal places) where decimal accuracy is not needed. Use uppercase and lowercase letters just as you would in a handwritten or typed report. Arrange all worksheet data in either columns or rows, not a combination of both. A visually consistent worksheet is easier to read and reduces the possibility of mistakes. Your model may perform a sophisticated analysis, but if it is cluttered and difficult to read, no one will appreciate your brilliance.

- *Use the printer wisely.* When printing your model, you do not have to print all the cells used to calculate your answer. It is a common practice to place "scratch pads" and tables out of sight if they clutter up your printout or do not provide useful information to the template user.

- *Write clear formulas.* Clear formulas speed up calculations by eliminating unnecessary computation, reducing errors, and making it easier to maintain your spreadsheet.

Complex calculations should be divided into several cells. Explanatory comments should be placed next to formula cells if appropriate.

- *Always keep flexibility in mind.* One of the most powerful features of a spreadsheet program is its ability to perform instant recalculation when new data are entered. You can capitalize on this ability by designing your models to accept new input without having to alter previously entered formulas. This is another important reason to use a data section at the top of the worksheet.

- *Learn to use the Copy command.* It can be used frequently when setting up many spreadsheet models and it will save you both time and trouble once you get used to it. If you make a mistake when copying, simply do it over.

- *Use "advanced" spreadsheet capabilities.* Don't be afraid to use the functions. Functions such as @IF can add a great deal of power and flexibility to your models and the same is true of the @HLOOKUP and @VLOOKUP commands. You can begin to develop very sophisticated spreadsheet models when you learn to use these commands.

- *Use sample data during development.* In general, if you develop a model with a data section, you should enter some sample data before programming your answer. Developing a "blank" spreadsheet model with correct formulas and format is quite difficult.

- *Protect your worksheet from hardware and software failures.* As important as this is, many people still fail to do this (until they learn the hard way at least once). Also, protect your worksheet from accidental changes. Always keep a printout of the model on file. Should you ever lose or destroy a model saved on a disk, you can reconstruct it much faster if you have a printout of the original. Keep a printout of the "cell contents" on file. Keep a backup copy of your model on a disk separate from the one containing the original model. As you are developing a model, save it on disk at frequent intervals. Use the Worksheet and Range Protect options to prevent mistaken entry into or erasure of important cells.

These are some of the basic concepts, but the reader interested in learning more should refer to the books cited in footnote 1.

EXAMPLE 1. A PROFIT CALCULATION SPREADSHEET

Figure 2.1 shows a spreadsheet for the profit model developed in Chapter 1 (Example 2). The range A3..B8 contains the parameters and uncontrollable variables. The only decision variable, quantity produced, is entered in cell B10. The outputs of the model are given in the range A14..B18. Formulas and assumptions are provided on the right side of the spreadsheet. In this particular model, we assume that all production can be sold. Thus, even though the value of Sales will always be the same as the quantity produced, the spreadsheet allows you to easily change this assumption and input a different value for Sales. Figure 2.2 shows the output when a value of 40,000 is entered for quantity produced.

Note that the formulas for revenue and cost refer to the cells in the input section. As noted earlier, it is easier to change the input data than to modify the formulas.

FIGURE 2.1   Spreadsheet for profit analysis

	A	B	C	D	E	F	G
1	**Profit Calculation Spreadsheet**						
2							
3	Parameters and uncontrollable variables			Formulas and assumptions			
4							
5	Unit Price	$40					
6	Unit Cost	$24					
7	Fixed Cost	$400,000					
8	Sales	0		Assume sales = quantity produced			
9							
10	Decision variable						
11							
12	Quantity produced						
13							
14	Model outputs						
15							
16	Revenue	$0		Revenue = unit price * sales			
17	Cost	$400,000		Cost = fixed cost + unit cost * quantity produced			
18	Profit	($400,000)					

Selected cell formulas

	A	B
5	Unit Price	40
6	Unit Cost	24
7	Fixed Cost	400000
8	Sales	+B12
9		
10	Decision variable	
11		
12	Quantity produced	
13		
14	Model outputs	
15		
16	Revenue	+B5*B8
17	Cost	+B7+B6*B12
18	Profit	+B16-B17

FIGURE 2.2   Profit calculation for $Q = 40,000$

	A	B	C	D	E	F	G
1	**Profit Calculation Spreadsheet**						
2							
3	Parameters and uncontrollable variables			Formulas and assumptions			
4							
5	Unit Price	$40					
6	Unit Cost	$24					
7	Fixed Cost	$400,000					
8	Sales	40000		Assume sales = quantity produced			
9							
10	Decision variable						
11							
12	Quantity produced	40000					
13							
14	Model outputs						
15							
16	Revenue	$1,600,000		Revenue = unit price * sales			
17	Cost	$1,360,000		Cost = fixed cost + unit cost * quantity produced			
18	Profit	$240,000					

SPREADSHEET SKILLS FOR MODELERS

Spreadsheet software continually evolves to provide users with increasingly sophisticated ways to organize, analyze, and present information. We assume that you are familiar with the fundamentals of a popular spreadsheet program and have used it for accounting, financial, or other types of business applications. You should be comfortable with basic user skills, including the following:

- Moving around a spreadsheet
- Entering and editing data and formulas
- Copying cell contents
- Performing basic arithmetic calculations
- Relative and absolute addressing
- Creating and using range names
- Formatting data and text
- Retrieving, saving, and printing files
- Creating simple graphs

In addition to these basic skills, you should be familiar with @functions and what-if tables. These spreadsheet capabilities are extremely useful in management science applications, and we will use them throughout the book.

@Functions/ = Functions

@Functions in LOTUS 1-2-3 (= Functions in EXCEL 5.0) are used to perform special calculations in cells. You should consult the manual corresponding to your particular version of software to determine what functions are available. For management science applications, the most useful functions in LOTUS 1-2-3 are:

@MIN—finds the smallest value in a list

@MAX—finds the largest value in a list

@SUM—finds the sum of values in a list

@AVG—averages a list of values

@STD—finds the population standard deviation (using n in the denominator)

@STDS—finds the sample standard deviation (using $n-1$ in the denominator)

@NORMAL—returns information about the normal distribution

@POISSON—returns information about the Poisson distribution

@SQRT—finds the positive square root of a number

@RAND—generates a uniform random number between O and 1

@Functions may be linked with other standard arithmetic operations and can also be combined with one another. For instance, we may wish to compute a standard normal value using the formula (where μ = mean, and σ = standard deviation).

$$z = \frac{x - \mu}{\sigma}$$

Suppose that 50 values that define the distribution are stored in the range A3..A53 and that the value of x is in cell B5. If we wish to place the value of z in cell D8, we would write this formula in cell D8:

$$(+\text{B5 - @AVG(A3..A53))/@STD(A3..A53)}$$

Three other @Functions that deserve special explanation are @IF, @VLOOKUP, and @HLOOKUP.

@IF(CONDITION,A,B). This function allows you to choose one of two values to enter into a cell. If the specified condition is true, value A will be put in the cell. If the condition is false, value B will be entered. For example,

$$\text{C2:@IF(A8} = 2, 7, 8)$$

states that if the value in cell A8 is 2, the number 7 will be assigned to cell C2; if the value in cell A8 is not 2, the number 8 will be assigned to cell C2. "Conditions" may include

$=$ equal to

$>$ greater than

$<$ less than

$>=$ greater than or equal to

$<=$ less than or equal to

$<>$ not equal to

@VLOOKUP(A,X..Y,C) and @HLOOKUP(A,X..Y,C). These functions allow you to look up a value in a table. They are similar in concept to the @IF function, but they allow the program to pick an answer from an entire table of values. VLOOKUP stands for a vertical lookup table; HLOOKUP stands for a horizontal lookup table.

The function @VLOOKUP uses three arguments:

1. The value to look up
2. The table range
3. The number of the column whose value we want (the left-hand column is zero)

To illustrate this, suppose we want to place in cell G14 a number 1, 2, or 3, depending on the contents of cell B9. If the value in cell B9 is .55 or less, then G14 should be 1; if it is greater than .55 but .85 or less, then G14 should be 2; and if it is greater than .85, then cell G14 should be 3. We must first put the data in a table in cells B4 through C6:

A	B	C
4	0	1
5	0.55	2
6	0.85	3

Now consider the formula

$$G14:@VLOOKUP(B9,B4..C6,1)$$

The @VLOOKUP function takes the value in cell B9 and searches for a corresponding value in the first column of the range B4..C6. The search ends when the first value greater than the value in cell B9 is found. The program returns to the next lower value in column B, picks the number found in the cell one column to its immediate right, and enters it in cell G14. Suppose the number in cell B9 is .624. The function would search column B until it finds the first number larger than .624. This is .85 in cell B6. Then it returns to the next lower row (row 5) and picks the number in column C as the value of the function. Thus, the value placed in cell G14 is 2. @HLOOKUP works in a similar fashion, except that the search is along rows instead of columns.

What-If Tables

What-if tables, called *data tables* in early versions of LOTUS 1-2-3, allow you to perform repeated "what-if" analyses and present the results in a table. A what-if table shows the results of substituting different values in formulas. To create a what-if table, you fill a range with values for the variables that you wish to evaluate. Then the program calculates the formulas with every combination of values for the variables and enters the results in the worksheet. What-if tables are particularly useful for generating data for graphs. The following example shows an application of what-if tables.

EXAMPLE 2. A WHAT-IF TABLE FOR PROFIT ANALYSIS

We will extend the profit calculation spreadsheet in Example 1 to find the break-even point using a what-if table. This is shown in Figure 2.3. The *input cell* is where LOTUS 1-2-3 temporarily stores the different values for the variable while calculating the formula. Since the decision variable is quantity produced, the input cell is B12. The table range, B22..E38, contains the input values, the formulas, and the cells below the formulas where the results are displayed. The input cell must be outside the table range. Formulas begin in the second column of the first row of the table range. We therefore enter the formulas for revenue, cost, and profit in cells C22, D22, and E22. Each formula should refer to the input cell. In the first column of the table range, beginning in the second row, we enter the input values we want to evaluate. In this example, we filled the range B23..B38 starting with 15,000 in increments of 1,000. Pressing the function key F8 calculates the table. Figure 2.4 shows graphs of revenue, cost, and profit prepared from this table. We see that the break-even point occurs at a quantity of 25,000.

One of the advantages of what-if tables is that you can easily change the input values and, by pressing F8, recalculate the table. This allows you to perform sensitivity analyses very easily.

FIGURE 2.3   What-if table calculations

	A	B	C	D	E	F	G
1	**Profit Calculation Spreadsheet**						
2							
3	Parameters and uncontrollable variables			Formulas and assumptions			
4							
5	Unit Price	$40					
6	Unit Cost	$24					
7	Fixed Cost	$400,000					
8	Sales	0		Assume sales = quantity produced			
9							
10	Decision variable						
11							
12	Quantity produced						
13							
14	Model outputs						
15							
16	Revenue	$0		Revenue = unit price * sales			
17	Cost	$400,000		Cost = fixed cost + unit cost * quantity produced			
18	Profit	($400,000)					
19							
20	What-if Table						
21		Quantity	Revenue	Cost	Profit		
22			$0	$400,000	($400,000)		
23		15000	$600,000	$760,000	($160,000)		
24		16000	$640,000	$784,000	($144,000)		
25		17000	$680,000	$808,000	($128,000)		
26		18000	$720,000	$832,000	($112,000)		
27		19000	$760,000	$856,000	($96,000)		
28		20000	$800,000	$880,000	($80,000)		
29		21000	$840,000	$904,000	($64,000)		
30		22000	$880,000	$928,000	($48,000)		
31		23000	$920,000	$952,000	($32,000)		
32		24000	$960,000	$976,000	($16,000)		
33		25000	$1,000,000	$1,000,000	$0		
34		26000	$1,040,000	$1,024,000	$16,000		
35		27000	$1,080,000	$1,048,000	$32,000		
36		28000	$1,120,000	$1,072,000	$48,000		
37		29000	$1,160,000	$1,096,000	$64,000		
38		30000	$1,200,000	$1,120,000	$80,000		

MANAGEMENT SCIENCE APPLICATIONS OF SPREADSHEETS

Spreadsheets facilitate the process of analyzing problems in management science. We may categorize the major applications of spreadsheets in management science into four categories:

1. Data analysis
2. What-if analysis
3. Goal seeking and optimization
4. Risk analysis

FIGURE 2.4   *Revenue, cost, and profit curves*

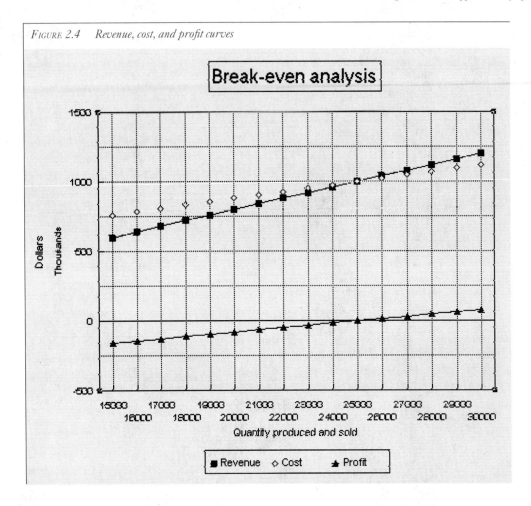

Data Analysis

Spreadsheets provide a basic capability for organizing, summarizing, and displaying data used in the development of management science models. Preparing inputs to models may involve summarizing empirical data, estimating parameters such as averages, standard deviations, and coefficients for profit and cost functions, or selecting probability distributions to model observed phenomena. The graphing capabilities of spreadsheets provide a powerful way of displaying relationships among variables, showing trends, and other useful visual communication.

EXAMPLE 3. ESTIMATING AVERAGE SERVICE TIME

A division of a retail sales corporation is evaluating its order entry customer service area. Management has received some complaints from customers about the length of time they are waiting to talk to a sales representative. An important problem is determining the number of sales representatives they need to reduce customer waiting time.

One of the steps in addressing this problem is to determine the average time that a sales representative spends on an order. In reviewing the company's records, the management science team was able to gather data over a five-month period reporting the average time (in seconds) spent on a call with a customer during each month and the monthly average time spent after the call completing the paperwork.

Figure 2.5 shows a spreadsheet designed to compute the weighted average call time. The upper portion of the worksheet contains the input data; the lower portion summarizes the calculations. Adding the average time on call and average time after

FIGURE 2.5   A spreadsheet for data analysis

	A	B	C	D	E
1	Average Service Time Calculation				
2					
3	Input Data				
4		Average	Average		
5	Month	Time on call	Time after call	Total calls	Percent
6	October	127	23	12,567	22.34%
7	November	124	18	11,325	20.13%
8	December	114	17	10,898	19.37%
9	January	100	23	11,153	19.82%
10	February	103	24	10,319	18.34%
11			Total	56,262	
12					
13	Work Area				
14		Average			
15	Month	Total time	Fraction of calls	Time*fraction	
16	October	150	0.223	33.50	
17	November	142	0.201	28.58	
18	December	131	0.194	25.37	
19	January	123	0.198	24.38	
20	February	127	0.183	23.29	
21			Weighted avg.	135.14	

Cell formulas

	A	B	C	D	E
1	Average Service Time Calculation				
2					
3	Input Data				
4		Average	Average		
5	Month	Time on call	Time after call	Total calls	Percent
6	October	127	23	12567	+D6/$D$11
7	November	124	18	11325	+D7/$D$11
8	December	114	17	10898	+D8/$D$11
9	January	100	23	11153	+D9/$D$11
10	February	103	24	10319	+D10/$D$11
11			Total	@SUM(D6..D10)	
12					
13	Work Area				
14		Average			
15	Month	Total time	Fraction of calls	Time*fraction	
16	October	+B6+C6	+E6	+B16*C16	
17	November	+B7+C7	+E7	+B17*C17	
18	December	+B8+C8	+E8	+B18*C18	
19	January	+B9+C9	+E9	+B19*C19	
20	February	+B10+C10	+E10	+B20*C20	
21			Weighted avg.	@SUM(D16..D20)	

call for each month produces the total time. By multiplying the total time each month by the fraction of calls that month and summing, we can obtain the overall average service time.

Although this is a simple example, spreadsheets are invaluable in processing large amounts of raw data to determine inputs to management science models.

What-If Analysis

What-if analysis is perhaps the most important use of spreadsheets in management science. What-if analysis is the study of various decision strategies or environments, using many different inputs, generating many different outputs, and conducting sensitivity analyses to answer a variety of what-if questions. In Chapter 1 we discussed the use of models to study system behavior and evaluate alternative decisions; the data in Table 1.3 and the graph in Figure 1.3 were developed using a spreadsheet. The Management Science Practice case study later in this chapter is an excellent example of what-if analysis. We will use spreadsheets throughout this book to evaluate alternatives and perform sensitivity analyses.

Goal-Seeking and Optimization

Many management science problems involve seeking solutions to satisfy a decision maker's goals or to optimize some objective. Although spreadsheet models are only descriptive, they can facilitate the process of seeking good solutions to problems by allowing a manager to quickly see the effects of changes in the decision variables of a model.

Figure 2.6 illustrates the relationship between the decision maker and the spreadsheet. The decision maker enters values for the variables and parameters of a model; the spreadsheet evaluates the consequences of these decisions. The decision maker must intelligently search among potential solutions to find one that is acceptable. This is a big limitation of spreadsheets and is one of the reasons why it is appropriate to learn about management science algorithms that find optimal solutions to models. We will see, however, that for certain types of problems we may optimize the spreadsheet model using special software.

FIGURE 2.6   *Decision making using spreadsheets*

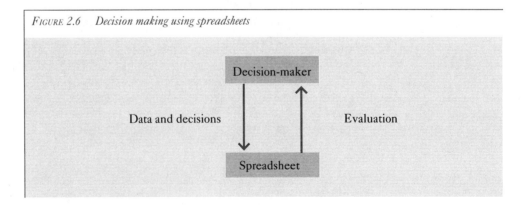

The automatic recalculation feature of spreadsheets allows a decision maker to evaluate many different scenarios very easily. This provides a means of interactively seeking the best solutions for a given problem. The decision maker can evaluate a set of decisions, modify one or more values, and reevaluate the modified scenario until an acceptable set of decision values have been reached. This process requires that the decision maker knows the problem area well and that he or she has good set of rules to guide the decision process.

Decision makers generally use two types of search processes to seek good or optimal solutions: enumerative and heuristic searches. An *enumerative search* consists of evaluating a set of potential solutions, one of which is hoped to be the best. A *heuristic search* depends on intelligently modifying solutions to work toward the best. The following examples illustrate each method.

EXAMPLE 4. ENUMERATIVE ANALYSIS OF ADVERTISING STRATEGIES

A firm needs to decide on the best level of advertising budget to maximize net profit. Based on data analysis, a management science team estimated that profit is governed by the following equations (all values are expressed in millions of dollars):

$$\text{Sales} = 2.1 + 4.3(1 - e^{-1.4(\text{budget})})$$

$$\text{Cost} = .38 + .55\text{Sales}$$

$$\text{Gross profit} = \text{Sales} - \text{Cost}$$

$$\text{Net profit} = \text{Gross profit} - \text{Budget}$$

In the first formula, e is the number 2.71828....

Figure 2.7 shows a spreadsheet using a what-if table to enumerate net profit for a range of budget values. A graph of net profit generated from this table is shown in Figure 2.8. We see that the maximum profit occurs for a budget of about $700,000. We might wish to change the input values and search within a finer grid around this value. This is easy to do using the what-if table.

EXAMPLE 5. SEEKING AN OPTIMAL SOLUTION WITH HEURISTIC SEARCH

In Chapter 1 we developed a model to determine the mix of two models of radar detectors that maximizes profit. Figure 2.9 shows a spreadsheet designed to evaluate any product mix. The top portion of the worksheet lists the input data and the values of the decision variables are entered in cells B14 and B15. The lower portion of the worksheet evaluates the proposed solution and cell B23 computes the total profit. We must also ensure that the solution is feasible. Cells B20 and B21 compute the number of components A and B that are used for a particular solution. In cells C20 and C21 we subtract the usage from the availability to compute the excess number of components available. For the solution to be feasible, these values must not be negative.

A trial solution, LS = 100 and SB = 300, is shown in Figure 2.10. The profit is $14,400; however, since the excess for component B is negative, this solution is not feasible. If we reduce SB to 250, we obtain the solution shown in Figure 2.11. The solution is feasible and has a profit of $12,400. We may continue to experiment with different values for the decision variables until we find an acceptable solution.

FIGURE 2.7   *What-if analysis of budget alternatives*

	A	B	C	D	E	F	G
1	**Advertising Budget Allocation**						
2							
3	Decision variable			Formulas and Assumptions			
4							
5	Budget	$0.00		All data in millions of dollars			
6							
7							
8							
9							
10	Model outputs						
11							
12	Sales	$2.100		Sales = 2.1 + 4.3*(1 - exp(-1.4*budget))			
13	Cost	$1.535		Cost = .38 + .55*sales			
14	Gross profit	$0.565		Gross profit = sales - cost			
15	Net profit	$0.565		Net profit = gross profit - budget			
16							
17	What if Table						
18			Budget	Sales	Cost	Gross Profit	Net Profit
19				$2.100	$1.535	$0.565	$0.565
20			$0.00	$2.100	$1.535	$0.565	$0.565
21			$0.05	$2.391	$1.695	$0.696	$0.646
22			$0.10	$2.662	$1.844	$0.818	$0.718
23			$0.15	$2.914	$1.983	$0.932	$0.782
24			$0.20	$3.150	$2.113	$1.038	$0.838
25			$0.25	$3.370	$2.233	$1.136	$0.886
26			$0.30	$3.575	$2.346	$1.229	$0.929
27			$0.35	$3.766	$2.451	$1.315	$0.965
28			$0.40	$3.944	$2.549	$1.395	$0.995
29			$0.45	$4.110	$2.640	$1.469	$1.019
30			$0.50	$4.265	$2.726	$1.539	$1.039
31			$0.55	$4.409	$2.805	$1.604	$1.054
32			$0.60	$4.544	$2.879	$1.665	$1.065
33			$0.65	$4.669	$2.948	$1.721	$1.071
34			$0.70	$4.786	$3.012	$1.774	$1.074
35			$0.75	$4.895	$3.072	$1.823	$1.073
36			$0.80	$4.997	$3.128	$1.869	$1.069
37			$0.85	$5.092	$3.181	$1.911	$1.061
38			$0.90	$5.180	$3.229	$1.951	$1.051
39			$0.95	$5.263	$3.275	$1.988	$1.038
40			$1.00	$5.340	$3.317	$2.023	$1.023

Searching for an optimal solution, either enumeratively or heuristically, will not generally guarantee that an optimal solution will be found. For prescriptive models, it is best to use an algorithm that will find an optimal solution.

Risk Analysis

Risk analysis studies the effects of uncertainty in making decisions. It is much easier to analyze or solve models in which all data are known with certainty. In practice, however, decision makers often develop models in which the value of one or more variables is uncertain. A good example is the airline overbooking problem discussed in Chapter 1. As another example, in developing and marketing new products, a firm cannot predict

FIGURE 2.8   *Net profit curve*

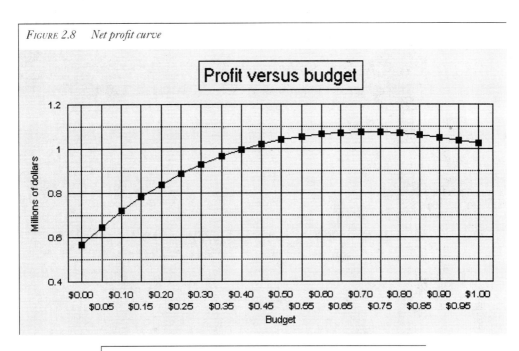

FIGURE 2.9   *Spreadsheet for radar detector example*

	A	B	C	D	E
1	**Product Mix Model**				
2					
3	*Input data*				
4					
5		Component	Requirements		
6		A	B		Unit Profit
7	LS	12	6		$24
8	SB	12	10		$40
9	Availability	6000	3500		
10					
11					
12	*Decision variables*				
13					
14	Number LS				
15	Number SB				
16					
17	*Model outputs*				
18					
19		Usage	Excess		
20	Component A	0	6000		
21	Component B	0	3500		
22					
23	Profit	$0.00			

Selected cell formulas

	A	B	C
17	*Model outputs*		
18			
19		Usage	Excess
20	Component A	+B7*B14+B8*B15	+B9-B20
21	Component B	+C7*B14+C8*B15	+C9-B21
22			
23	Profit	+E7*B14+E8*B15	

57

FIGURE 2.10   Infeasible solution

	A	B	C	D	E
1	**Product Mix Model**				
2					
3	*Input data*				
4					
5		Component	Requirements		
6		A	B		Unit Profit
7	LS	12	6		$24
8	SB	12	10		$40
9	Availability	6000	3500		
10					
11					
12	*Decision variables*				
13					
14	Number LS	100			
15	Number SB	300			
16					
17	*Model outputs*				
18					
19		Usage	Excess		
20	Component A	4800	1200		
21	Component B	3600	-100		
22					
23	Profit	$14,400.00			

FIGURE 2.11   Feasible solution

	A	B	C	D	E
1	**Product Mix Model**				
2					
3	*Input data*				
4					
5		Component	Requirements		
6		A	B		Unit Profit
7	LS	12	6		$24
8	SB	12	10		$40
9	Availability	6000	3500		
10					
11					
12	*Decision variables*				
13					
14	Number LS	100			
15	Number SB	250			
16					
17	*Model outputs*				
18					
19		Usage	Excess		
20	Component A	4200	1800		
21	Component B	3100	400		
22					
23	Profit	$12,400.00			

exactly what competitors will do, what effects advertising strategies will have on sales, or whether production costs are forecast accurately. To complicate matters, objective data to characterize the uncertainty often do not exist or are very difficult to obtain. Thus, in many case, we can quantify risk only subjectively.

Quantifying risk means determining all the possible values a risky variable could take and determining the relative likelihood of each value. This information usually is summarized in the form of a probability distribution. We may repeatedly sample from this distribution and evaluate the spreadsheet to develop a risk profile of the distribution of possible outcomes from the model. This information can help a decision maker develop the insight needed to make a good decision.

We present a simple example of risk analysis next to illustrate the basic ideas. In Part III of this book we deal exclusively with modeling uncertainty in decision problems.

EXAMPLE 6. RISK ANALYSIS

For the profit model illustrated in Example 1, suppose that uncertainty exists about both the unit cost and the sales. In this case we cannot assume that we can sell all that we produce, and that therefore sales is truly uncontrollable. Let us assume that the unit cost is $24 with probability .7 or $26 with probability .3. We can also approximate the range of sales by three estimates:

Low estimate: Sales = 20,000 with probability .25

Moderate estimate: Sales = 50,000 with probability .5

High estimate: Sales = 80,000 with probability .25

Risk analysis involves repeated sampling from these probability distributions to generate distributions for the variables of interest. In this example, the key variable is net profit.

To sample from these distributions in a LOTUS 1-2-3 spreadsheet, we use the functions @RAND and @IF. The function @RAND generates a *random number*, that is, a number which is uniformly distributed between 0 and 1. To sample a value for the unit cost, we first generate a random number. If the value of the random number is less than .7, then the unit cost is 24, otherwise, the unit cost is 26. Since random numbers are uniformly distributed between 0 and 1, we would expect that approximately 70 percent of the time our sample would have a unit cost of 24, and 30 percent of the time a unit cost of 26. To put the correct number in a spreadsheet cell, we use the formula

@IF(@RAND<.7, 24, 26)

To sample from the sales distribution, we may nest the IF functions as follows:

@IF(@RAND<.5, 50000, @IF(@RAND<.5, 20000, 80000))

This function first determines if the value of a random number is less than .5. If so, then the sales is assigned a value of 50,000. If not, we know that sales must be either 20,000 or 80,000 with equal probability. The nested @IF formula makes this determination. In Chapter 13 we will see how to sample from any probability distribution more easily using the @VLOOKUP function.

Figure 2.12 shows a spreadsheet in which we sample the unit cost and sales from their respective distributions and compute the net profit fifty times for a

FIGURE 2.12   Risk analysis spreadsheet

	A	B	C	D	E	F	G
1	**Risk Analysis**						
2							
3	Parameters and uncontrollable variables			Formulas and assumptions			
4							
5	Unit Price	$40		Revenue = unit price * sales			
6	Unit Cost	$24		Cost = fixed cost + unit cost * quantity produced			
7	Fixed Cost	$400,000		Unit cost is 24 with probability .7			
8	Sales	40000		and 26 with probability .3			
9							
10	Decision variable			Sales have the following probability distribution:			
11							
12	Quantity produced	40000		Sales	Probability		
13				20,000	0.25		
14	Model outputs			50,000	0.50		
15				80,000	0.25		
16	Revenue	$1,600,000					
17	Cost	$1,360,000					
18	Profit	$240,000					
19							
20							
21	Risk analysis table						
22							
23	Sample	Unit cost	Sales	Profit			
24	1	26	80000	$1,760,000			
25	2	24	20000	($560,000)			
26	3	26	50000	$560,000			
27	4	24	20000	($560,000)			
28	5	24	20000	($560,000)			
29	6	24	80000	$1,840,000			
30	7	24	50000	$640,000			
31	8	24	20000	($560,000)			
32	9	24	80000	$1,840,000			
33	10	26	20000	($640,000)			
34	11	24	50000	$640,000			
35	12	24	20000	($560,000)			
36	13	26	50000	$560,000			
37	14	24	80000	$1,840,000			
38	15	24	50000	$640,000			
39	16	24	80000	$1,840,000			
40	17	24	50000	$640,000			
41	18	24	50000	$640,000			
42	19	26	20000	($640,000)			
43	20	24	50000	$640,000			
44	21	24	50000	$640,000			
45	22	24	50000	$640,000			
46	23	24	50000	$640,000			
47	24	24	50000	$640,000			
48	25	24	50000	$640,000			
49	26	24	20000	($560,000)			
50	27	24	20000	($560,000)			
51	28	26	20000	($640,000)			
52	29	24	80000	$1,840,000			
53	30	24	50000	$640,000			
54	31	24	50000	$640,000			
55	32	24	50000	$640,000			
56	33	24	20000	($560,000)			
57	34	24	20000	($560,000)			
58	35	24	50000	$640,000			
59	36	26	50000	$560,000			
60	37	24	20000	($560,000)			
61	38	24	50000	$640,000			
62	39	24	20000	($560,000)			
63	40	24	50000	$640,000			
64	41	26	80000	$1,760,000			
65	42	26	50000	$560,000			
66	43	24	50000	$640,000			
67	44	24	20000	($560,000)			
68	45	24	50000	$640,000			
69	46	26	80000	$1,760,000			
70	47	24	20000	($560,000)			
71	48	24	80000	$1,840,000			
72	49	24	80000	$1,840,000			
73	50	26	50000	$560,000			
74							
75			min	($640,000)			
76			max	$1,840,000			
77			average	$478,400			
78			std. dev.	$850,937			

production quantity of 40,000. We see that the net profit may be as low as − $640,000 or as high as $1,840,000. The average is $478,400, and the standard deviation is $850,937. Although the expected value is positive, there is considerable risk of operating at a loss. This is better illustrated by the chart in Figure 2.13, which shows the net profit for each sample. In 16 of the 50 samples, the firm would incur a loss. This may be a risk that the decision-maker does not want to take.

MANAGEMENT SCIENCE PRACTICE

In this section we describe the spreadsheet model developed by the Southern Company to analyze oil sampling decisions for vehicle maintenance.

The Oil Sampling Decision Model[2]

One of the many maintenance options available to motor vehicle and construction equipment managers of the Southern Company is oil analysis. The practice of periodically taking samples of the lubricating oil from engines, transmissions, and other components

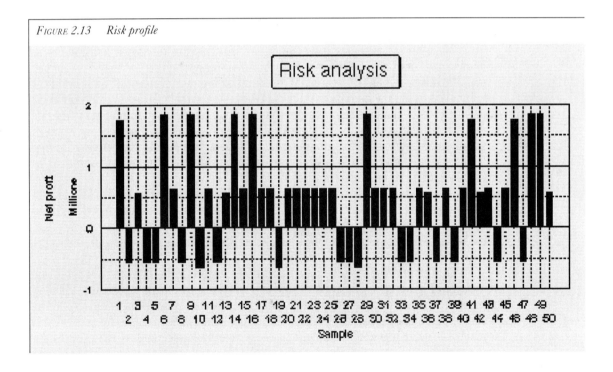

FIGURE 2.13   *Risk profile*

_____

[2]Adapted from [Mellichamp et al., 1993].

and subjecting the samples to physical and chemical tests has become an accepted practice in maintaining equipment. Traces of various kinds of metals or contaminants in the sample indicate potential failures, which can often be avoided by preventive maintenance. Failure to detect such problems usually leads to emergency maintenance and equipment downtime.

In most cases the diagnostic interpretation of laboratory tests of oil samples is imprecise and subject to uncertainty. False signals can be associated with a sample; for instance, a sample containing high levels of iron may be thought to indicate excessive wear of a critical component when in fact no problem exists. If the manager acts on the indication of excessive iron, the expensive equipment teardown may turn out to be unnecessary. A critical question, then, is whether an oil sampling program is warranted.

A task force of fleet managers and maintenance experts identified four strategies to consider:

1. No preventive maintenance: repair components only when failures occur.
2. Sample only: take oil samples at regular intervals and perform whatever preventive maintenance is indicated by the oil analysis.
3. Change oil only: change oil at regular intervals, take no samples, and perform repairs whenever failures occur.
4. Change oil and sample: change oil on a regular basis, take samples at regular intervals, and repair as indicated by the oil analysis.

To analyze these strategies it was necessary to describe the particular outcomes that might occur under each scenario. For example, under the first strategy—no preventive maintenance—if a failure occurs, then emergency maintenance will be required. If no failure occurs, no maintenance is necessary. If an oil sample is taken, different decisions may be chosen, depending on the results of the sample. If the sample identifies a defective component as defective, then preventive maintenance will be accomplished. If the sample indicates a defective component as nondefective (a false result), then emergency maintenance will be required later. The diagram shown in Figure 2.14 summarizes the decisions that can be selected.

To model these strategies the team had to determine cost parameters, the probability of failure and the risk that the sampling will provide incorrect indications of the true state of the components. Figure 2.15 shows an example of the spreadsheet model that was developed for automobiles and light trucks, although values have been altered slightly to avoid disclosing proprietary information.

The formulas used in this model are simple applications of expected value and are shown in Figure 2.16. For instance, the expected cost of emergency maintenance under strategy 1, pC_eN is found by multiplying the expected number of failures (pN) by the cost of emergency repair (C_e). The emergency maintenance cost under strategy 2 is the same, except that the emergency repair cost must be multiplied by the probability that the sample will indicate that a defective component is not defective (Type I error, α).

Because a spreadsheet was used, sensitivity analysis on the model parameters was easy to perform. Some key studies include the following:

FIGURE 2.14   *Maintenance strategies and potential outcomes*

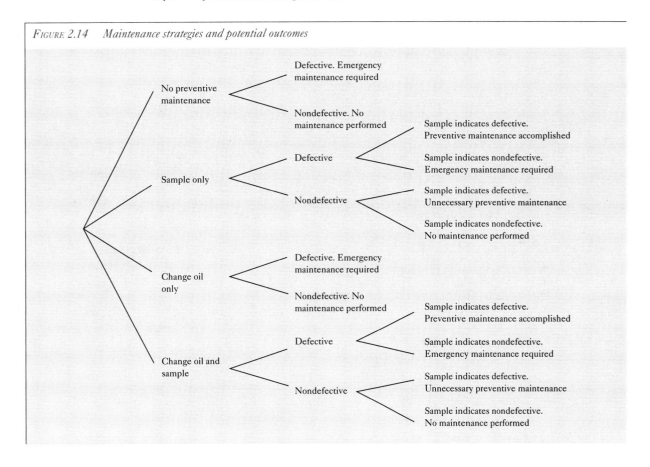

Oil Analysis Effectiveness. Managers wanted to know how much better their oil analysis capabilities would have to be for them to prefer strategy 4 to strategy 3. Experimenting with the probability estimates showed that oil analysis would have to be at least 97 percent effective in distinguishing defective from nondefective components.

Repair Cost Variation. A second question was "How much would repair costs have to change to cause strategy 3 to be preferred to strategy 4 for construction equipment engines?" The model showed that decreasing emergency repair cost from $12,000 to $6,000 would cause indifference.

Probability of Failure. The probability of failure with no regular maintenance was the only parameter for which the task force was unable to find historical data. This was an important parameter to study, and it was found that changes in the most likely estimates had to be fairly substantial before a different strategy would be preferred.

FIGURE 2.15   *LOTUS 1-2-3- spreadsheet model for automobiles and light trucks*

Probability Definitions

Probability of a component failure with no regular maintenance	0.1
Probability of a component with regular oil changes	0.04
Probability that oil analysis will identify a defective component as defective	0.7
Probability that oil analysis will identify a defective component as nondefective	0.3
Probability that oil analysis will identify a nondefective component as defective	0.2
Probability that oil analysis will identify a nondefective component as nondefective	0.8

Cost Definitions

Emergency repair	$1,200.00
Preventive maintenance to restore a defective component	500.00
Preventive maintenance on a nondefective component	250.00
Oil change	14.80
Oil analysis	20.00

Other Data

Number of vehicles	100

Cost Analysis	Strategy 1 Do Nothing	Strategy 2 Sample Only	Strategy 3 Oil Change	Strategy 4 Both
Oil changes	0.00	$370.00	$1,480.00	$1,480.00
Oil analysis	0.00	2,000.00	0.00	2,000.00
Preventive maintenance	0.00	8,000.00	0.00	6,200.00
Emergency maintenance	$12,000.00	3,600.00	4,800.00	1,440.00
Total cost	$12,000.00	$13,970.00	$6,280.00	$11,120.00

Discussion Questions

1. Explain the rationale for each expected cost formula in Figure 2.16 by constructing influence diagrams to show how each formula was developed.
2. Discuss other what-if questions that the spreadsheet model might be used to address.
3. What conclusions does the model suggest and why was it useful?

MORE EXAMPLES AND SOLVED PROBLEMS

EXAMPLE 7. ENUMERATIVE SEARCH FOR SOLVING THE PRODUCT MIX MODEL

In Example 5, we showed how a spreadsheet can be used to seek an optimal solution to the radar detector product mix model using heuristic search. We can use what-

FIGURE 2.16   *Spreadsheet formulas*

Cost Element	Strategy 1 (Do Nothing)	Strategy 2 (Sample Only)	Strategy 3 (Oil Change Only)	Strategy 4 (Both)
Oil change	0	$p*(1-\alpha)*C_c*N$ $+(1-p)*\beta*C_c*N$	C_c*N	C_c*N
Oil analysis	0	C_a*N	0	C_a*N
Preventive maintenance	0	$p*(1-\alpha)*C_d*N$ $+(1-p)*\beta*C_f*N$	0	$p'*(1-\alpha)*C_d*N$ $+(1-p')*\beta*C_f*N$
Emergency maintenance	$p*C_e*N$	$p*\alpha*C_e*N$	$p'*C_e*N$	$p'*\alpha*C_e*N$

Parameter definitions:

p = failure probability associated with strategies 1 and 2
p' = failure probability associated with strategies 3 and 4
α = type I error probability resulting from oil analysis
β = type II error probability resulting from oil analysis
C_c = cost to perform a routine oil change
C_a = cost to analyze an oil sample per unit under strategies 2 and 4
C_e = cost of repairing a component that fails
C_d = cost to repair a component identified through oil analysis as potentially defective
C_f = cost to discover that a component identified as potentially defective through oil analysis is actually
    = not defective (teardown and out-of-service-costs)
N = number of vehicles in fleet

if tables to enumerate various values for the decision variables. Figure 2.17 shows two-variable what-if tables for profit and excess availability of components A and B when LS varies from 95 to 105 and SB varies from 290 to 320. The tables for excess availability are necessary to ensure that the solution we choose is feasible. Within these ranges, we see that the best feasible solution occurs when LS = 100 and SB = 290. We might wish to search around a finer grid of unit values of SB close to 290 to find a better solution. What-if tables allow you to do this easily simply by changing the values in the range. We emphasize that there is no guarantee that the optimal solution will be found, but it should be possible to find a very good solution.

EXAMPLE 8. A SPREADSHEET FOR THE CENTER-OF-GRAVITY MODEL

Example 6 in Chapter 1 describes the center-of-gravity model. A spreadsheet for finding the center-of-gravity location and conducting sensitivity analysis, such as the

FIGURE 2.17   *What-if analysis for the product mix problem*

	A	B	C	D	E	F	G
25	What if Table - Profit		Number SB				
26		0	290	295	300	310	320
27	Number LS	95	$13,880	$14,080	$14,280	$14,680	$15,080
28		96	$13,904	$14,104	$14,304	$14,704	$15,104
29		97	$13,928	$14,128	$14,328	$14,728	$15,128
30		98	$13,952	$14,152	$14,352	$14,752	$15,152
31		99	$13,976	$14,176	$14,376	$14,776	$15,176
32		100	$14,000	$14,200	$14,400	$14,800	$15,200
33		101	$14,024	$14,224	$14,424	$14,824	$15,224
34		102	$14,048	$14,248	$14,448	$14,848	$15,248
35		103	$14,072	$14,272	$14,472	$14,872	$15,272
36		104	$14,096	$14,296	$14,496	$14,896	$15,296
37		105	$14,120	$14,320	$14,520	$14,920	$15,320
38							
39	What if Table - Excess A		Number SB				
40		6000	290	295	300	310	320
41	Number LS	95	1380	1320	1260	1140	1020
42		96	1368	1308	1248	1128	1008
43		97	1356	1296	1236	1116	996
44		98	1344	1284	1224	1104	984
45		99	1332	1272	1212	1092	972
46		100	1320	1260	1200	1080	960
47		101	1308	1248	1188	1068	948
48		102	1296	1236	1176	1056	936
49		103	1284	1224	1164	1044	924
50		104	1272	1212	1152	1032	912
51		105	1260	1200	1140	1020	900
52							
53	What if Table - Excess B		Number SB				
54		3500	290	295	300	310	320
55	Number LS	95	30	-20	-70	-170	-270
56		96	24	-26	-76	-176	-276
57		97	18	-32	-82	-182	-282
58		98	12	-38	-88	-188	-288
59		99	6	-44	-94	-194	-294
60		100	0	-50	-100	-200	-300
61		101	-6	-56	-106	-206	-306
62		102	-12	-62	-112	-212	-312
63		103	-18	-68	-118	-218	-318
64		104	-24	-74	-124	-224	-324
65		105	-30	-80	-130	-230	-330

example in Figure 2.18, is easy to construct. To find the center of gravity, we use the @function

$$@SUMPRODUCT(RANGE1, RANGE2)$$

FIGURE 2.18   *Spreadsheet for center-of-gravity model*

	A	B	C	D
1	Center of Gravity Model			
2				
3	*Parameters and uncontrollable variables*			
4				
5	*Location*	*x-coordinate*	*y-coordinate*	*Demand*
6	Ft. Worth	22	9	33,000
7	Minneapolis	24	21	12,000
8	San Diego	5	11	16,000
9	Columbus	33	17	5,000
10				
11	*Model outputs*			
12				
13	Center of gravity			
14	x-coordinate	19.08		
15	y-coordinate	12.27		

Selected cell formulas

	A	B	C	D
1	Center of Gravity Model			
2				
3	*Parameters and uncontrollable variables*			
4				
5	*Location*	*x-coordinate*	*y-coordinate*	*Demand*
6	Ft. Worth	22	9	@SUM(D7..D9)
7	Minneapolis	24	21	12000
8	San Diego	5	11	16000
9	Columbus	33	17	5000
10				
11	*Model outputs*			
12				
13	Center of gravity			
14	x-coordinate	@SUMPRODUCT(B6..B9,D6..D9)/@SUM(D6..D9)		
15	y-coordinate	@SUMPRODUCT(C6..C9,D6..D9)/@SUM(D6..D9)		

This function computes the sum of the product of data in two named ranges. That is, it multiplies each value in RANGE1 by the corresponding value in RANGE2 and sums these products.

EXAMPLE 9. AIRLINE DISCOUNTING POLICY RISK ANALYSIS

We discussed issues of airline overbooking and yield management in the Management Science Practice section in Chapter 1. This example illustrates how risk analysis may be used to analyze discount policies. Most airlines offer discount fares for advanced purchase. Assume that only two fares are available, full and discount. The airline must make the decision of whether or not to accept the next request for a discount seat. If it accepts the discount request, the revenue it earns is the discount fare. If it rejects the discount request, two outcomes are possible. First, rejecting the discount request may result in an additional empty seat and no additional revenue. Alternatively, the remaining seat may be filled by a full-fare passenger, either because full-fare passenger demand is sufficient to fill the seats or because discount-fare passengers choose to pay full-fare when told the discount fare is not available.

This decision situation is illustrated by the diagram in Figure 2.19. The decision depends on the probability, p, of getting a full-fare request when a discount request is rejected. The optimal decision can be easily found through a simple expected-value calculation. The expected value of rejecting the request is computed by multiplying the probability of selling the full-fare ticket by the revenue earned and adding that product to the product of one minus the probability of not selling the full-fare ticket times the revenue earned ($0), or,

$$\text{Expected value} = p\ (\$\text{full fare}) + (1 - p)(\$0)$$

$$= p\ (\$\text{full fare})$$

If this value is larger than the discount fare, then the discount seat request *should* be rejected.

The value of p is uncertain, making the decision risky. To illustrate this with an example, suppose that the full fare is $560 and the discount fare is $400. The airline estimates that the value of p lies somewhere in the range from 0.65 to 0.80. Figure 2.20 shows a spreadsheet for conducting the risk analysis.

If we assume that the values within the range .65 to .80 are equally likely, then we may sample probabilities from this range in a spreadsheet using the formula (where μ = mean, and σ = standard deviation).

.65 + @RAND*15

Recall that @RAND provides a number randomly between 0 and 1. If @RAND is zero, the sample outcome is therefore .65. If @RAND is one, the sample outcome

FIGURE 2.19   *Airline discount fare request decision*

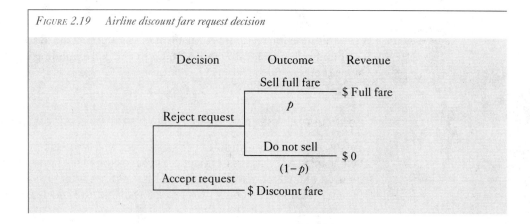

FIGURE 2.20   Airline discounting risk analysis spreadsheet

	A	B	C	D	E	F	G
1	Airline Discounting Policy Risk Analysis						
2							
3	Parameters and uncontrollable variables				Assumptions		
4							
5	Full fare	$560.00			Probability of selling full fare varies		
6	Discount fare	$400.00			between .65 and .80		
7							
8	Risk analysis table						
9							
10	Sample	p	Revenue		Sample	p	Revenue
11	1	0.692	$560		51	0.653	$0
12	2	0.713	$560		52	0.734	$560
13	3	0.664	$0		53	0.665	$0
14	4	0.671	$560		54	0.721	$560
15	5	0.686	$560		55	0.738	$560
16	6	0.694	$560		56	0.752	$560
17	7	0.748	$560		57	0.665	$560
18	8	0.699	$560		58	0.692	$560
19	9	0.734	$0		59	0.701	$560
20	10	0.717	$0		60	0.748	$0
21	11	0.668	$0		61	0.740	$560
22	12	0.701	$560		62	0.793	$560
23	13	0.720	$560		63	0.740	$0
24	14	0.716	$560		64	0.726	$560
25	15	0.732	$560		65	0.650	$0
28	18	0.693	$560		68	0.798	$560
29	19	0.731	$0		69	0.704	$560
30	20	0.656	$0		70	0.793	$560
31	21	0.757	$560		71	0.665	$560
32	22	0.798	$560		72	0.728	$560
33	23	0.789	$560		73	0.799	$560
34	24	0.701	$560		74	0.682	$0
35	25	0.797	$560		75	0.687	$560
36	26	0.699	$0		76	0.698	$560
37	27	0.782	$560		77	0.784	$560
38	28	0.677	$560		78	0.688	$560
39	29	0.772	$560		79	0.756	$560
40	30	0.766	$560		80	0.799	$560
41	31	0.738	$560		81	0.684	$560
42	32	0.716	$560		82	0.675	$560
43	33	0.716	$560		83	0.674	$560
44	34	0.773	$560		84	0.719	$0
45	35	0.781	$560		85	0.654	$560
46	36	0.757	$560		86	0.789	$560
47	37	0.759	$560		87	0.786	$0
48	38	0.739	$560		88	0.676	$560
49	39	0.730	$0		89	0.712	$0
50	40	0.790	$560		90	0.705	$560
51	41	0.664	$0		91	0.663	$560
52	42	0.752	$560		92	0.664	$560
53	43	0.765	$560		93	0.734	$0
54	44	0.768	$560		94	0.695	$0
55	45	0.669	$0		95	0.718	$0
56	46	0.793	$0		96	0.664	$0
57	47	0.676	$560		97	0.678	$560
58	48	0.709	$560		98	0.695	$560
59	49	0.664	$560		99	0.759	$0
60	50	0.752	$560		100	0.758	$560
61			sum $21,840.00				sum $20,160.00
62						Average	$420.00

	A	B	C
10	Sample	p	Revenue
11	1	0.65+@RAND*0.15	@IF(@RAND<B11,560,0)
12	2	0.65+@RAND*0.15	@IF(@RAND<B12,560,0)
13	3	0.65+@RAND*0.15	@IF(@RAND<B13,560,0)
14	4	0.65+@RAND*0.15	@IF(@RAND<B14,560,0)
15	5	0.65+@RAND*0.15	@IF(@RAND<B15,560,0)

FIGURE 2.20   (continued)

is .80. As @RAND varies from 0 to l, we obtain probabilities between .65 and .80. Once a value of p is generated, the revenue is computed using the @IF function. If a random number is less than p, the airline receives the full fare; otherwise it receives nothing.

Figure 2.20 shows the results of l00 samples. The average revenue is $420, suggesting that the airline should accept the discount fare request. In practice, airlines regularly estimate the value of p based on the remaining available seats and the distribution of demand several times before the departure of each flight and adjust seat allocations accordingly.

EXAMPLE 10. A LOCAL AREA NETWORK PRINTER DECISION PROBLEM [3]

In this example we present a more complete case study of problem solving, drawing upon the concepts presented in Chapter 1 as well as applications of spreadsheets introduced in this chapter.

Local Area Networks, or LANs, link several computers together to share common software and hardware, allowing companies to reduce costs by pooling computer resources. One problem that faces many companies is determining the best use of printers on a LAN. The company must decide if it should invest in several less expensive, slow printers; in fewer, more-expensive, high-speed printers; or in some combination. The first step is to define the problem clearly.

Problem Definition.   A variety of factors affect service, including

- Printer demand
- Job size
- Printer capacity
- Number of printers
- Types of printers
- User behavior
- Number of users

---

[3]We are indebted to our students, Rob Maretsky, Jim Borngesser, Laura Meeks, Pam Rakolta, Scott Simmonds, and Calixte Gbe, for developing this example

To better understand the logical relationships among these factors we might draw a simple pictorial model, such as the diagram in Figure 2.21, that describes the factors affecting printer service time. Figure 2.21 shows that printer service time is determined by printer demand, job size, and printer capacity. The number of users affects printer demand; user behavior affects both the demand and job size; and the number and types of printers determine printer capacity.

For instance, from Figure 2.21, we see that the only decisions the manager faces are the number and types of printers to choose. The number of users and user behavior are important inputs in determining printer service time, but they cannot be controlled by the manager.

We might also think about the costs involved in making this decision. As printer capacity is increased, the direct costs of purchasing the equipment and maintaining it will also increase. On the other hand, the costs of user dissatisfaction from waiting for print jobs and lost work productivity will decrease with higher printer capacity. In sketching these relationships, the manager might arrive at another graphical model, shown in Figure 2.22. This model shows the trade-off between printer costs and user costs. In reality, the problem therefore involves multiple and conflicting objectives. However, because it is virtually impossible to quantify the user costs, the manager might, for example, define the problem as finding the minimum-cost printer configuration that will achieve an average of a 30-second wait for a print job.

FIGURE 2.21   *An influence diagram for print job turnaround*

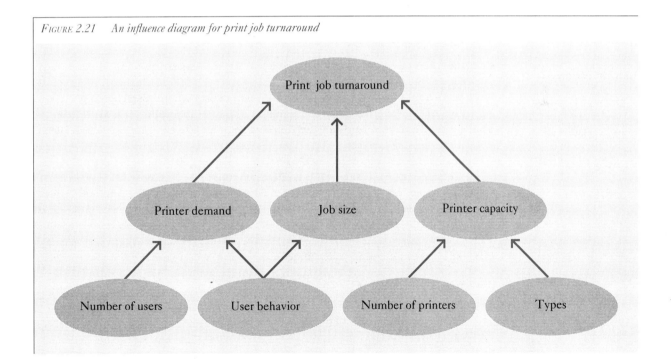

FIGURE 2.22   *Cost model for printer capacity*

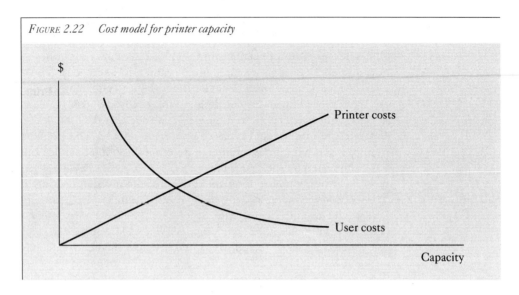

Structuring the Problem. To better understand the environment in which printers are used, data was collected from a LAN consisting of 15 users and two printers, each of which prints 6 pages per minute. The data collected showed print job sizes, time between print jobs, bytes per second throughput, the user requesting the job, and printer location. These data were collected by a BASIC program that queried the network for print traffic information every 5 seconds. Once the raw data file was created, the information was transferred to a spreadsheet for analysis. An illustration is shown in Figure 2.23.

The size of a print job affects the throughput of the printer. A large print job typically indicates graphical output, whereas a smaller job indicates textual output. The average throughput times were therefore broken into two ranges, 0–100K bytes and greater than 100K bytes.

The objective is to design a LAN system for a new department of 60 employees. Since the data were collected for a LAN environment of 15 users, the demand data on printer usage was aggregated by user to develop a user profile that could be extrapolated to the larger department. What-if experiments were performed to determine the aggregate printer capacity that would be necessary to achieve the service goal of a 30-second average wait time. The experiments indicated that an aggregate capacity of 6,500 bytes per second was required.

The manager considered two types of printers: a slow model that prints 6 pages per minute (or 1,974.81 bytes per second) and costs $1,400, and a fast model that prints 16 pages per minute (or 5,266.15 bytes per second) but costs $3,250. The manager's decision problem is "How many printers of each type should be purchased to meet the goal of providing at least 4,500 bytes per second of print capacity at minimum total cost?"

FIGURE 2.23   *Example spreadsheet file*

Sample: 10-11 am 2/24/93
PP-2 Printers/6ppm   **Start Time 39693**

User	Printer	Submit	TB Jobs (secs)	Print Size	Finish	Start Print Time (secs)	
RM	W	40455	761	11,247	40476	21	
RM	W	40496	41	35,294	40512	16	
SB	W	40496	0	407,319	40596	100	
RM	W	40682	186	6,886	40703	21	
KJ	E	41137	455	21,161	41159	22	
KJ	E	41457	320	21,161	41479	22	
KJ	E	41661	204	21,161	41671	N/A	Job Killed
KJ	E	41757	96	21,161	41779	22	
KD	E	42377	620	10,392	42399	22	
BN	E	42497	120	705,514	42578	81	
RM	W	42813	316	48,929	42856	43	

A simple spreadsheet model, such as the example shown in Figure 2.24, can be constructed to assist in making this decision. In cells B11 and B12 we input the number of each type of printer; these are the decision variables. The total cost is computed as

Total cost = $1,400 * number of slow printers + $3, 250 * number of fast printers

This is found in cell B16.

The aggregate capacity of the printers is computed as

$$\text{Aggregate capacity} = 1,974.81 * NS + 5,266.15 * NF$$

This is found in cell B17.

Finally, we can compute the difference between the aggregate capacity and the required capacity and show this in cell Bl9. If this difference is negative, it means that the particular decision made does not meet the requirement.

We may develop a mathematical model and represent the decision variables for the LAN problem by defining SP as the number of slow printers to purchase and FP as the number of fast printers to purchase. The uncontrollable variables are the cost and speed of each type and the required print capacity. If SP slow printers and FP fast printers are purchased, their combined print capacity will be

$$1,974.81 \text{ SP} + 5,266.15 \text{ FP}   \text{bytes per second}$$

This is simply a mathematical representation of the formula in cell B17 of the spreadsheet.

In order to meet the goal of at least 6,500 bytes per second of print capacity, we must ensure that the aggregate capacity is at least equal to the required capacity. Thus, we have the constraint

$$1,974.81 \text{ SP} + 5,266.15 \text{ FP} \geq 6,500$$

FIGURE 2.24   *Spreadsheet model for LAN decision problem*

A	A	B	C
1	Local Area Network Analysis		
2			
3	*Input Data*		
4			
5		Speed	Unit Cost
6	Slow printers	1974.81	$1,400
7	Fast printers	5266.15	$3,250
8			
9	*Decision Variables*		
10			
11	Number of slow printers		
12	Number of fast printers		
13			
14	*Model Outputs*		
15			
16	Total cost	$0	
17	Aggregate capacity	0	
18	Required capactity	6500	
19	Difference	-6500	

The purchase cost of the printers would be

$$\text{Total cost} = 1,400 \text{ SP} + 3,250 \text{ FP}$$

This formula is in cell B16 of the spreadsheet.

Finally, by recognizing that the variables cannot be negative and that we cannot buy a fractional number of printers, we can ensure that the values of both decision variables are nonnegative, or greater than or equal to zero, and are integer-valued. By *integer-valued* we mean that the decision variables must be whole numbers. The complete mathematical model is

$$\text{Minimize } 1,400 \text{ SP} + 3,250 \text{ FP}$$

subject to

$$1,974.81 \text{SP} + 5,266.15 \text{FP} \geq 6,500$$

$$\text{SP} \geq 0, \ \text{FP} \geq 0 \text{ and integer}$$

Solving this model would provide the best values for the decision variables.

Analyzing the Problem.   Figures 2.25 through 2.28 show several alternative solutions. The first solution does not meet the capacity requirement. Increasing the number of slow printers to 4 meets the requirement at a total cost of $5,600. If we choose two fast printers, the requirement can be met at a cost of $6,500. Finally, selecting one printer of each type meets the requirement at a cost of $4,650. This appears to be the best solution.

FIGURE 2.25   *First alternative solution*

	A	B	C
1	Local Area Network Analysis		
2			
3	*Input Data*		
4			
5		Speed	Unit Cost
6	Slow printers	1974.81	$1,400
7	Fast printers	5266.15	$3,250
8			
9	*Decision Variables*		
10			
11	Number of slow printers	3	
12	Number of fast printers	0	
13			
14	*Model Outputs*		
15			
16	Total cost	$4,200	
17	Aggregate capacity	5924.43	
18	Required capactity	6500	
19	Difference	-575.57	

FIGURE 2.26   *Second alternative solution*

	A	B	C
1	Local Area Network Analysis		
2			
3	*Input Data*		
4			
5		Speed	Unit Cost
6	Slow printers	1974.81	$1,400
7	Fast printers	5266.15	$3,250
8			
9	*Decision Variables*		
10			
11	Number of slow printers	4	
12	Number of fast printers	0	
13			
14	*Model Outputs*		
15			
16	Total cost	$5,600	
17	Aggregate capacity	7899.24	
18	Required capactity	6500	
19	Difference	1399.24	

FIGURE 2.27   *Third alternative solution*

	A	B	C
1	Local Area Network Analysis		
2			
3	*Input Data*		
4			
5		Speed	Unit Cost
6	Slow printers	1974.81	$1,400
7	Fast printers	5266.15	$3,250
8			
9	*Decision Variables*		
10			
11	Number of slow printers	0	
12	Number of fast printers	2	
13			
14	*Model Outputs*		
15			
16	Total cost	$6,500	
17	Aggregate capacity	10532.3	
18	Required capactity	6500	
19	Difference	4032.3	

FIGURE 2.28   *Fourth alternative solution*

	A	B	C
1	Local Area Network Analysis		
2			
3	*Input Data*		
4			
5		Speed	Unit Cost
6	Slow printers	1974.81	$1,400
7	Fast printers	5266.15	$3,250
8			
9	*Decision Variables*		
10			
11	Number of slow printers	1	
12	Number of fast printers	1	
13			
14	*Model Outputs*		
15			
16	Total cost	$4,650	
17	Aggregate capacity	7240.96	
18	Required capactity	6500	
19	Difference	740.96	

SUMMARY

Spreadsheets are indispensable tools for performing numerical computations and solving quantitative problems in management science. Good spreadsheets should provide accurate results, be easily understood by their creators and users, be adaptable to changes in a problem or application, and use computing resources efficiently. Well-designed spreadsheets should separate areas for different uses, such as input data, work areas, and output. Spreadsheet users in management science should have basic user skills and be familiar with some advanced capabilities such as @functions and what-if tables.

We identified four major applications of spreadsheets in management science: data analysis, what-if analysis, goal seeking and optimization, and risk analysis. When solving practical problems in management science we often use several of these approaches.

CHAPTER REVIEW EXERCISES

I. Terms to Understand

a.	Electronic spreadsheet (p. 43)	e.	What-if analysis (p. 51)
b.	Data section (p. 45)	f.	Enumerative search (p. 55)
c.	@Functions (p. 48)	g.	Heuristic search (p. 55)
d.	What-if table (p. 50)	h.	Risk analysis (p. 56)

II. Discussion Questions

1. Explain the key properties that well-designed spreadsheets should have.
2. Discuss approaches to good spreadsheet design. What is the value of a data section?
3. Using the manual that accompanies your spreadsheet package, prepare a list of the spreadsheet skills that you are comfortable with. What skills not on the list would help you the most?
4. Explain the purpose of a what-if table. Describe how to construct one using your spreadsheet package.
5. Discuss applications of spreadsheets for data analysis. What specific features of spreadsheets facilitate basic statistical analysis?
6. Describe two ways spreadsheets may be used to find solutions to satisfy a decision maker's goals or that optimize some objective.
7. Explain what we mean by "quantifying risk." What are some of the issues and difficulties involved with this practice?
8. In Figure 2.22, discuss the appropriate form of the printer cost function. Should it be linear or increase at an increasing or decreasing rate?

III. Problems

1. Modify the profit calculation spreadsheet (Figure 2.1) to include economies of scale as follows. If production is 20,000 or less, the unit cost is $24. The unit cost for the next 5,000 units is $22.50, and the unit cost for all remaining units is $21.00.
2. Using the spreadsheet developed in Problem 1, find the break-even point.
3. Develop a generic spreadsheet for computing the return on investment as described in Problem 4 in Chapter 1. How helpful was the influence diagram in developing this spreadsheet?
4. Develop a spreadsheet to answer the questions posed in Problem 5 in Chapter 1. Use the graphing capabilities of the software to generate graphs as requested.
5. Develop a spreadsheet for Problem 9 in Chapter 1. Use the spreadsheet to calculate the unit cost for each product.

6. A major consumer products company is faced with a decision of choosing between two manufacturing processes for a new product. Process 1 is highly capital-intensive. The annual production cost is estimated to be $40,000 in fixed expenses and $1.10 per unit in variable expenses. Process 2 is more labor-intensive; the corresponding production costs will be $24,000 in fixed expenses and $2.25 per unit invariable expenses. Develop a spreadsheet with a what-if table to determine the range of sales for which process 1 is preferable. Find the break-even point to the nearest 100 units.

7. A company manufactures four products on three machines. The production schedule for the next 6 months is

Product	Month 1	Month 2	Month 3	Month 4	Month 5	Month 6
1	150	150	150	150	150	150
2	250	0	250	0	250	0
3	75	75	75	75	75	75
4	0	100	0	100	0	100

The number of hours each product requires on each machine is

Machine	1	2	3	4
1	.25	.15	.15	.25
2	.30	.20	.35	.50
3	.20	.25	.15	.10

Set-up times are 20 percent of the machine processing times. The number of machine hours available during the next six months is

Machine	Month 1	Month 2	Month 3	Month 4	Month 5	Month 6
1	120	60	60	60	60	60
2	180	60	180	60	180	60
3	120	60	120	60	120	60

Design a spreadsheet to determine if there is enough machine capacity to meet all demand. If not, determine how much and where additional capacity is needed.

8. Design a spreadsheet to perform sensitivity analysis for the sales model for Problem 10 in Chapter 1.

9. Develop a spreadsheet and what-if table to estimate the optimal price for Problem 8 in Chapter 1.

10. Develop a spreadsheet for Problem 13 in Chapter 1. Use the spreadsheet to seek an optimal solution by
    a. heuristic search
    b. enumerative search

11. A manufacturer of small electrical components estimates the following for a new design:
    Fixed costs = $10,000 per year
    Unit revenue = $.45
    Direct material cost per unit = $.15
    Direct labor cost per unit = $.10
    Overhead cost per unit = $.05
    Construct a spreadsheet model to find the break-even point and examine the sensitivity of the break-even point to the estimates of fixed costs and direct labor costs. What effect does a 10 percent error in either of these figures have?

12. The Radio Shop sells two popular models of portable sport radios, model A and model B. The sales of these products are not independent of each other (in economics, we call these *substitutable products*, because if the price of one increases, sales of the other will increase). The store wishes to establish a pricing policy to maximize revenue from these products. A study of price and sales data shows the following relationships between the quantity sold (N) and prices (P) of each model:

$$N_A = 19.5 - 0.6P_A + 0.25P_B$$

$$N_B = 30.1 + 0.08P_A - 0.5P_B$$

   a. Construct a model for the total revenue.
   b. Develop a spreadsheet with a two-variable what-if table to determine the optimal prices for each product in order to maximize total revenue.

13. Consider the situation in Problem 11. Suppose that direct material costs are uncertain and estimated to be $.12 with probability 0.2, $.15 with probability 0.4, and $.20 with probability 0.4. Use a spreadsheet-based risk analysis to determine the level of annual sales required to achieve a 10 percent return on investment. Explain the reasoning for your recommendation.

14. A company's research and development group has identified a potential new product. The firm will continue to develop this product only if it expects to make a profit in the first year. Variable costs are estimated to be $60 per unit and fixed costs are $450,000. Marketing personnel think that the product can sell for $160. At this price, they believe that sales will range from a low estimate of 3,000 with probability 0.3, a medium estimate of 5,000 with probability 0.4, and a high estimate of 8,000 with probability 0.3. Using a spreadsheet analysis, how risky is continued development of this product?

15. Show how to use the @VLOOKUP function instead of the @IF function to sample outcomes from the probability distributions used in Example 6. Discuss how you may generalize this approach to any discrete probability distribution. Apply your answer to the following:

Sales	Probability
10,000	.40
15,000	.25
20,000	.20
25,000	.10
30,000	.05

16. Refer to the situation in Problem 6 and the results from Problem 15. Suppose that the distribution in Problem 15 represents the best estimate of sales. Perform a risk analysis and make a recommendation for choosing one of the two production processes.

IV. Projects and Cases

1. This project refers to the Southern Company spreadsheet model in the Management Science Practice section of this chapter. First, construct an influence diagram from the spreadsheet model. Second, implement the spreadsheet model and answer the following questions.
   a. How does the total cost of each strategy change as the probability changes that oil analysis will identify a defective component as nondefective?
   b. How does the total cost of each strategy change as the probability changes that oil analysis will identify a nondefective component as defective?
   c. How sensitive are the strategies to the probability of a component failure with no regular maintenance?

d. How sensitive are the strategies to the cost of preventive maintenance?

e. How sensitive are the strategies to the cost of emergency repair?

Use what-if tables and graphs as necessary and write a report to the manager of the maintenance function.

2. Kurbe Marketing Research[4]

Each year, Kurbe Marketing Research (KMR) conducts hundreds of research studies for a variety of clients. Throughout the year, the demand for telephone research varies. KMR conducts most of its research projects in-house and if it cannot handle all of the work, it must subcontract some of the telephone interviewing at a lower profit margin.

KMR faces conflicting objectives. It needs to have telephone services available when clients need data collected, yet it needs to keep its costs down in order to remain competitive and earn a profit. Costs include the fixed costs of facilities and supervision, general overhead ($125,000 per month), the costs of operating computer-assisted telephone interviewing stations, or CATIs, ($3,000 per month per CATI) and the cost of operators ($1,500 per month per operator). The key decision variable is the number of CATIs to have. If the number of CATIs is high, costs would increase, but the amount of subcontracted work would decrease. If the number is low, subcontracting would increase while costs would decrease. Each CATI can handle $9,000 of research demand per month.

KMR has determined that it receives 15% of the revenue for all work subcontracted to an outside vendor. Table 2.1 provides the average monthly demands for the past several years.

Month	Demand
Jan	940
Feb	820
Mar	575
Apr	860
May	695
Jun	320
Jul	840
Aug	700
Sep	245
Oct	770
Nov	150
Dec	170

a. Construct an influence diagram for monthly profit.

b. Develop a spreadsheet for computing the total annual profit from both in-house and subcontracting work for a variable number of CATIs.

c. Make a recommendation for the optimal number of CATIs to have.

d. Examine the sensitivity of your solution if demand estimates vary by 6 percent in either direction. Does this change your recommendation?

---

[4]We gratefully acknowledge our students Anita Anderson, Ken Brown, Jerry Tepe, and Jeanne Vennemeyer for developing this case.

REFERENCES

Baker, G. L., William A. Clark, Jr., J. J. Frund, and R. E. Wendell, "Production Planning and Cost Analysis on a Microcomputer," *Interfaces*, vol. 17, No. 4, July–August 1987, pp. 53–60.

Krumm, F. V. and C. F. Rolle, "Management and Application of Decision and Risk Analysis in Du Pont," *Interfaces*, vol. 23, No. 3, May–June 1993, pp. 84–93.

Mellichamp, J. M., D. M. Miller, and O-J. Kwon, "The Southern Company Uses a Probability Model for Cost Justification for Oil Sample Analysis," *Interfaces*, vol. 23, No. 3, May–June 1993, pp. 118–124.

Smith, G. N., *LOTUS 1-2-3 Quick, Second Edition*, Boston: boyd & fraser Publishing Co., 1990.

Thommes, M. C., *Proper Spreadsheet Design*, Boston: boyd & fraser Publishing Co., 1992.

Vazsonyi, A., "Where We Ought to Be Going: The Potential of Spreadsheets," *Interfaces*, Vol. 23, No. 5, September–October 1993, pp. 26–39

CHAPTER 3

DEVELOPING

AND USING

MANAGEMENT

SCIENCE MODELS

INTRODUCTION

- The epidemics of acquired immunodeficiency syndrome (AIDS) and the human immunodeficiency virus (HIV) are extremely serious. Because intravenous drug users are known to be a high-risk group due to the common practice of needle sharing, policy makers need to understand the basic behavior of the spread of the disease and to evaluate the effects of interventions such as needle cleaning programs [Homer and St. Clair, 1991].

- The rules of ice hockey specify that only six players can be on the ice at any one time. The rules do not require that one of these players be the goalie, so whenever a team is behind near the end of the game, it may elect to "pull its goalie" and use the extra player in an offensive capability. If you pull your goalie your chances of scoring go up a little, but your opponent's chances go up a lot. Nevertheless, this strategy is often used. A logical question to consider is "What is the optimal time to pull the goalie?" [Morrison and Wheat, 1986].

- The phenomenon of "windshear" was recognized in 1970 by the National Transportation Safety Board as a cause or contributing factor in several airline accidents, many of which were fatal. Since the aviation community has become aware of this phenomenon, a great many actions have been taken, such as the development of Doppler radar and other alert systems. An important issue is whether or not airport operations should be suspended whenever a thunderstorm cell exists within some prescribed distance from the control tower. What should this distance be, and what delays can be expected in the air traffic system? [Machol and Barnett, 1988].

These problems are quite different from the typical business applications that we encountered in the first two chapters and show the wide applicability of management science. However, such unique and ill-structured problems require a significant amount of creativity to model.

The process by which an experienced management scientist arrives at a model is highly intuitive [Morris, 1967]. We cannot provide a "recipe" for constructing models. Effective modeling is more of an art than a science. This raises the question of how you can develop this intuition. One approach is to gain experience through studying the modeling efforts of others and to develop models largely by imitation and practice. Establishing an analogy or association between your particular problem and previously developed models can play an important role in determining where to start. Research shows that people tend to classify problems in a familiar context. This can make the modeling task easier. It is therefore important to study common types of models in order to make this classification process easier. In subsequent chapters we will see many examples of different types of models.

Modeling by imitation, however, has its drawbacks. It tends to inhibit creativity and to limit one's ability to develop useful models for unique situations. An alternative approach is to provide a set of guiding principles and process tips for developing good models. Developing a mathematical model has little to do with mathematical skills; rather, it requires good logical thinking and a mastery of some basic concepts. In this chapter we focus on these ideas.

PRINCIPLES OF MODEL BUILDING

A model is a way of structuring a poorly defined situation. We might think of modeling as similar to drawing a picture of a person or a landscape. Each artist views the object differently, and even though many features may be the same, the details may differ as the artist includes his or her own perspectives and experience. As this analogy suggests, the possible ways of modeling a particular problem are endless.

> There is more than one correct way to model a given problem!

Good models, like good art, should have some basic characteristics. Models should be

- *Simple.* They should be easy to understand and be good communication vehicles that translate easily into decision-makers' language.
- *Complete.* Models should reflect reality and include the important elements of the problem you are modeling.
- *Robust.* It should be difficult to obtain bad answers from models.
- *Consistent.* Results should follow logically from the assumptions underlying the model.
- *Flexible.* You should be able to enhance and update your model as new information becomes available.

Various factors influence the model development process (Figure 3.1). These include the system and the environment in which the model arises, the purpose of the model, the assumptions underlying the model, the data that are available, the solution methods and software that might be used, and the quality of the solution that is required. Model builders must address each of these issues.

Understand the System and its Environment

The first step in good model development is to understand the system and the environment in which the model will be used. This can often be facilitated by drawing some type of picture of the problem. There are many ways to do this: You may create a picture of the physical system itself, an influence diagram, or a flowchart that describes how the system operates. A *flowchart* is a picture of the sequence of steps in a process, and flowcharts help us to visualize the interconnections within a system. Flowcharts may help to pinpoint sources of data and reveal obstacles to implementing the results of models.

Determine the Purpose of Modeling

The purpose of modeling is to gain insight from reality, for example, by quantifying the trade-offs that a decision-maker might face. Different models have different purposes. The first step in developing a model is to fully understand the objective of the problem solving effort. What do we want the model to do—predict? evaluate? optimize? If we wish

FIGURE 3.1   *Factors influencing the model development process*

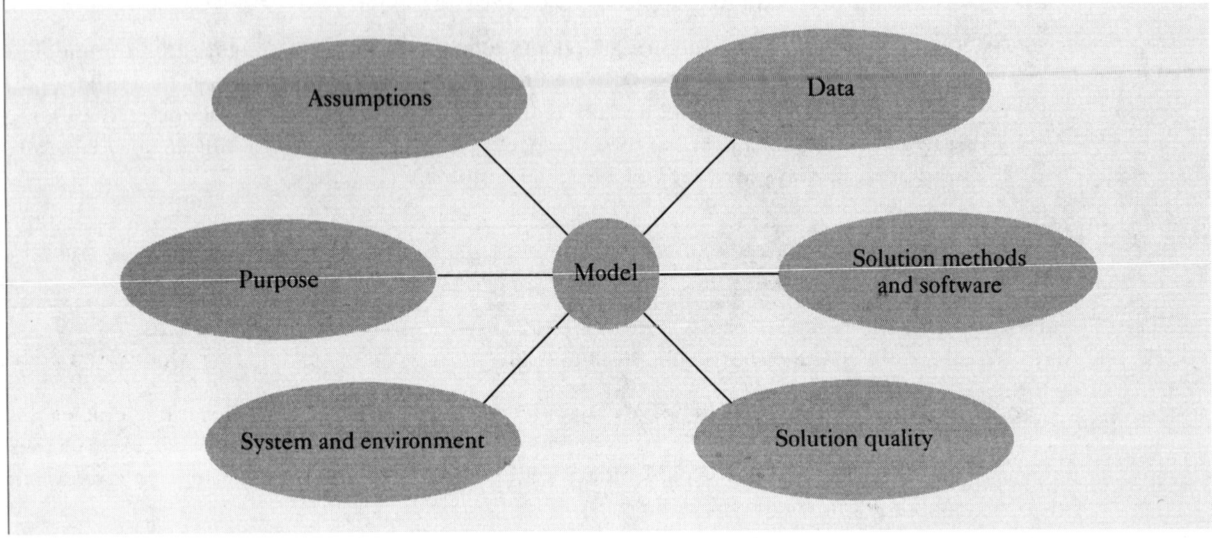

to use the model to predict future outcomes or to evaluate the result of proposed changes in the system, then a descriptive model is appropriate. If, on the other hand, we wish to determine the best course of action to follow, then a prescriptive model is necessary. Descriptive models can be constructed by drawing flowcharts and influence diagrams, or by developing systems of mathematical relationships that describe the connections between elements of the system. If the model is prescriptive, then we must define one or more objectives to be optimized, as well as constraints which restrict the optimization. We often start with descriptive models to develop better understanding of the system, and then evolve toward prescriptive models for better decision making.

Understand Problem Assumptions

Models depend on a variety of assumptions. Assumptions are often necessary to account for information that is not available or to simplify the model so that it may be manipulated or solved easily. If assumptions are unrealistic, then the output obtained from the model probably will also be unrealistic. It is important to make assumptions explicit so that users of the model are aware of its limitations.

Know What Data Are Available

The more information that we have about a problem, the better we can consider different perspectives and develop a useful model. As a general rule, we should use the minimum amount of data that is necessary. However, data must be viewed carefully, because data do not always reflect reality: people will not always behave according to the rules (such as when work standards are developed by time and motion studies); people will not always do what they say for the reasons they say; and data can be affected by organizational politics.

A systems flowchart often provides clues as to *where* relevant data can be obtained. Another useful technique is to work in the system to learn how it really operates. For example, if you are working on a model for police dispatching, ride the squad cars; if you are working on an inventory problem, work in the warehouse. While such activities may not always be feasible, there are many aspects of a system that can be learned only by doing.[1]

Explore Available Solution Methods and Software

A model is of limited value if it cannot be solved. We must consider the capabilities and availability of software packages and computers. There are basically two types of software available for solving management science problems. The first type consists of special purpose "canned" computer packages for specific types of models. For example, special computer packages exist for specific management science techniques such as linear programming problems, simulation problems, and network analysis problems that we will study in later chapters. The advantage of such packages is their efficiency and ease of use. The second type of software consists of general purpose programming languages such as QuickBasic, FORTRAN, or PASCAL, and other general purpose modeling packages such as spreadsheets. General purpose languages and packages are often used for problems that do not fall into a "neat" model category that can be solved by a special purpose package. It often takes much longer to develop a computer program that works correctly using general purpose software. Often, consultants might be called in to design specific software systems for a particular problem.

Assess the Solution Quality

The quality of the solution obtained from a model is influenced by its complexity and the computer software and hardware that are available. In general, the more detailed a model is, the better it will reflect reality. However, it is silly to develop a large, complex mathematical model that would require hours to solve on a supercomputer when only a personal computer is available. You might have to resort to a simple model that will provide only approximate results. Similarly, your boss might need an answer in two days, and you only have a spreadsheet package available. The model and solution approach that you develop might have to be creatively adapted to your particular environment.

It is also important to determine how accurate the solution needs to be. If upper management is only interested in a "ballpark" estimate that falls within a few million dollars, for instance, a relatively simple model might suffice. If, on the other hand, more accuracy is required, then a more complex model is warranted.

We will illustrate these principles with the following example.

---

[1] This theme is eloquently and entertainingly expressed by R. E. D. "Gene" Woolsey in many columns in the management science practitioner journal *Interfaces*. We encourage you to read these.

EXAMPLE 1. AN INVENTORY MANAGEMENT PROBLEM

In managing the inventory of retail goods, managers must make a fundamental decision about how much and when to order. These decisions have economic impacts, due to the nature of the costs involved. Inventory costs fall into four major categories:

1. Purchase costs
2. Order preparation costs
3. Inventory holding costs
4. Shortage costs

The costs of purchasing the items may be constant for any quantity ordered, or discounts might be given as an incentive to order larger quantities. Order preparation costs involve the time spent preparing and placing orders, such as clerical, telephone, receiving, and inspection time. Inventory holding costs include all expenses associated with carrying inventory, such as rent on storage space, utilities, insurance, taxes, and the cost of capital. Shortages can be either a back order in which the customer will wait for an item that is out of stock, or a lost sale in which the customer purchases the item elsewhere. Back orders incur additional costs for shipping, invoicing, and labor; lost sales result in lost profit opportunities and possible future loss of revenues.

These costs are influenced by the amount ordered and the timing of the ordering decision. For example, if many small orders are placed, then the ordering cost will be high, but little inventory will be carried, reducing holding costs. On the other hand, if few large orders are placed, then ordering costs will be low, but inventory holding costs will be high. Similarly, if orders are placed too early, excessive holding will result. If orders are placed too late, the firm risks running out of stock and incurring shortages. Thus, decision-makers seek a minimum cost balance among these costs. Establishing such trade-offs is typical of many management science problems. Let us first describe the typical inventory system and its environment.

System and Environment. Most inventory systems operate on a *continuous review* policy. In a continuous review system, the *inventory position*—the amount on hand plus any amount on order but not yet received minus back orders—is monitored continuously. Whenever the inventory position falls to or below a level r, called the *reorder point*, an order for a fixed amount, say Q, units is placed. Figure 3.2 illustrates the operation of a continuous review system from the viewpoint of both stock level and the inventory position. The dark curve is the stock level and the light curve is the inventory position. As we move to the right, the stock level is initially the same as the inventory position. When it reaches the reorder point, an order for Q units is placed, and the inventory position is increased by Q. The amount of time it takes for an order to arrive is called the *lead time*. During the lead time, the stock level continues to decrease as new demands are met. When the order arrives, the stock level increases by Q, and the stock level and inventory position are again equal. If the stock level hits zero and demands continue to arrive, back orders accumulate until an order arrives. When an order arrives, the accumulated back order demand is filled and the remainder becomes the stock level. Notice that the inventory position does not change when an order arrives because the inventory position was updated when the order was placed. Figure 3.3 is a flowchart that describes the logical operation of such a continuous review system with back orders.

Purpose. For this situation, we might be interested in developing a total cost model to evaluate various inventory policies and strategies; for instance, the impact of smaller, more frequent deliveries (just-in-time purchasing) on the cost. Or, our goal might be to determine the order quantity that minimizes total cost. We will do both for this example.

Assumptions. We need to make several important assumptions:

1. Only a single inventory item is considered.
2. The entire quantity arrives at one time.
3. The demand for the item is constant over time.
4. No shortages are allowed.

For many inventory situations, assumptions 1 and 2 are usually valid. However, assumptions 3 and 4 are critical. If the demand varies considerably or exhibits randomness, then the model would not provide useful results to the decision-maker. On the other hand, if demand is not *exactly* constant, but generally smooth, then assuming

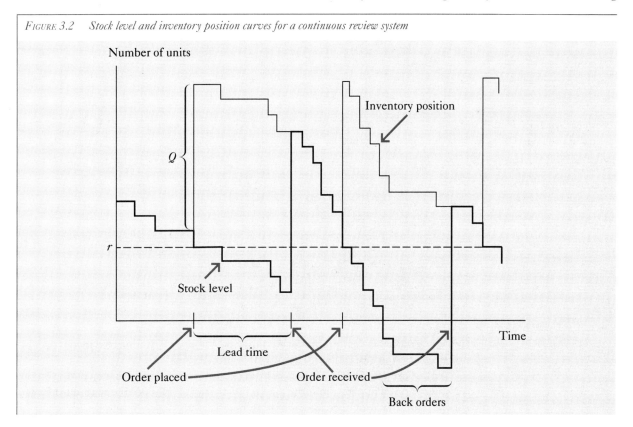

FIGURE 3.2   *Stock level and inventory position curves for a continuous review system*

FIGURE 3.3   *Flowchart for a continuous review inventory system*

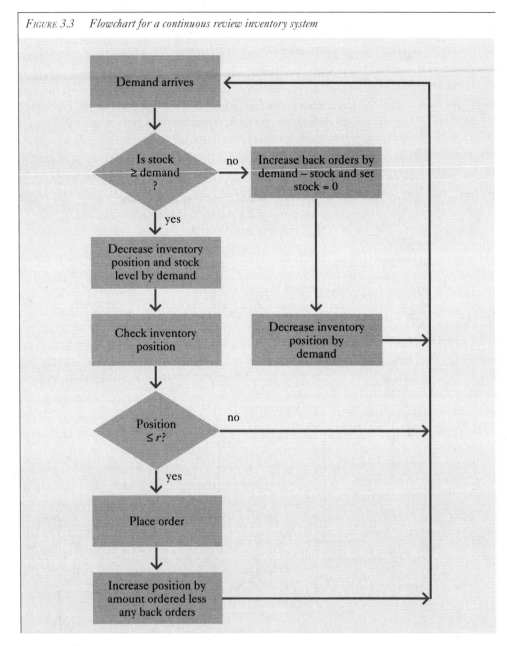

constancy probably is appropriate. Assumption 4 may be questionable in practice, but it is made to simplify the model that will be developed.

With these assumptions, the stock level and inventory position curves in Figure 3.2 smooth out and take the form shown in Figure 3.4. Notice that with no shortages allowed, the stock level curve cannot fall below zero.

FIGURE 3.3   *(continued)*

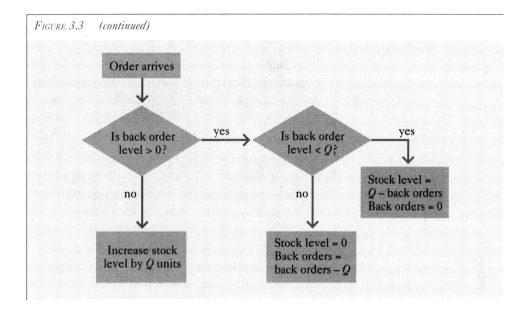

FIGURE 3.4   *Stock level and inventory position curves under simplifying assumptions*

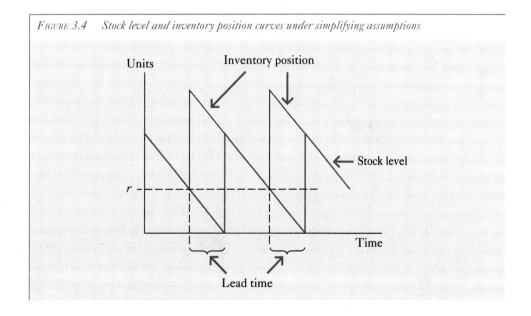

Data. The key data requirements for this model are the annual demand, holding cost per unit, and ordering cost. The annual demand is never known with certainty; it must be based on a forecast. We must be cautious, because forecasts are often wrong and subject to error. The holding cost is normally computed as a percentage of the item's unit price. The percentage used—called the *carrying charge rate*—is one of the more difficult pieces of data to estimate. Clearly, the holding cost rate should be at least as great as the cost of capital (at which the firm can invest elsewhere), but beyond that, it is virtually impossible to account for all of the costs (none of which will remain constant) associated with holding inventory, particularly on a unit-by-unit basis. The ordering cost likewise is difficult to estimate. Thus, it should be clear that any model that is developed will have inaccurate data at best. For this example, suppose that annual demand is 15,000 units, ordering cost is $200 per order, unit cost is $22, and the carrying charge rate is 20 percent.

Solution Methods. Because of the inaccuracy of the data, it would be useful for the manager to be able to investigate the effects of variability in the data on the cost and decisions that may be recommended. A useful means of doing this is with a spreadsheet.

Solution Quality. The solution quality depends on the assumptions that we made. We saw that these assumptions greatly simplify the situation, but the question remains as to how serious this departure from reality is. By relaxing some assumptions, we might be able to develop a more realistic model, but it might be too difficult to analyze mathematically. Since our purpose is to evaluate economic issues, considerable insight can be gained from a simple model, so we will decide to keep it as simple as possible.

GUIDELINES FOR DEVELOPING MANAGEMENT SCIENCE MODELS

In this section we present a variety of tips and techniques that can assist in the model-building process. These ideas are designed to help you approach modeling in a more structured fashion and to improve the quality of the models you develop. Later, we will use the inventory example to illustrate these concepts.

Organize Information and Define Variables

The fundamental purpose of a model is simple: to transform a set of inputs into outputs. This is illustrated in Figure 3.5. The first information that we need is therefore a list of inputs and outputs. The inputs consist of

- decision variables.
- parameters and uncontrollable variables.

In Chapter 2 we saw this guideline in practice while developing spreadsheet models. By listing all variables and parameters along with their dimensions, we are in a better position to combine them into a reasonable model.

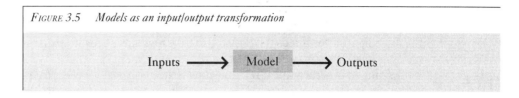

FIGURE 3.5   *Models as an input/output transformation*

Inputs ⟶ Model ⟶ Outputs

Draw a Picture

A useful method of organizing input and output information is to draw a picture depicting the relationships among these quantities. A graphical representation allows the modeler to see more clearly the relationships between various parts of the system being studied, and provides clues for defining the mathematical relationships. Influence diagrams, introduced in Chapter 1, are a useful graphical device because they help you to see the pieces of a model and to build it up in a logical fashion.

If an influence diagram is constructed correctly, the inputs will have no arrows pointing into them, since they must be set externally by the decision-maker. This makes a useful check of the validity of the model.

> An easy way of determining if a model is complete is to determine if all quantities that are not influenced by others are either decision variables or known values.

Establish Symbols

Once the variables and constraints have been defined, we may establish symbols for the variables and translate the constraints and objectives into mathematical relations. We typically denote decision variables by letters toward the end of the alphabet, while we denote uncontrollable variables and parameters with letters from the beginning of the alphabet. This is certainly not a rule! Often it is better to use descriptive names or acronyms to make the model easier to read, and we will do this in the spreadsheet examples throughout this book. With mathematical equations and formulas, we will tend to use letters or acronyms to conserve space.

Construct the Model

Constructing the model involves writing down any relationships between variables in mathematical terms. The relationships identify the model constraints and objectives. Constraints tie the decision variables together with the uncontrollable variables and parameters. In many problems, relationships may be stated explicitly in the problem statement; in others we may have to rely on experience and general knowledge to discover them. For example, a problem may state that "the quantity produced in department A cannot exceed department A's capacity." This relationship is clear. In other problems, you might have to recognize that "profit = revenue − cost" or that money received in July must "go somewhere;" that is, be saved or spent in August. We must be careful to look for any mathematical relationships that are logically necessary but may not be directly stated in the problem. Most prescriptive models (see Chapter 1) usually have a variety of constraints as well as an objective function.

> In developing any model, it is usually good practice to break the problem down into smaller, more manageable pieces, and to develop detailed models for each one. Then combine the pieces into the overall model.

Solve or Analyze the Model

We would like to have some method that can find an optimal solution to a model, or can provide us with useful information in order to make a decision. As we discussed in Chapter 1, various techniques for solving or analyzing models are available. We may use a spreadsheet or an algorithm to find an optimal solution. In addition, we may want to perform sensitivity analyses on the model and solution.

EXAMPLE 2. DEVELOPING AND SOLVING A MODEL FOR INVENTORY MANAGEMENT

We will illustrate these modeling guidelines using the inventory management situation introduced in Example 1.

Organize Information and Define Variables. Let us first define the inputs and outputs in this problem. The output of the model is the total annual inventory cost. The inputs to the model are

1. Annual demand.
2. Unit cost.
3. Ordering cost.
4. Carrying charge rate.

These inputs are assumed to be uncontrollable; the only controllable input (decision variable) is the amount to order.

Draw a Picture. An influence diagram for the total inventory cost is shown in Figure 3.6. We break down the total cost into the holding cost term and ordering cost term. Holding cost is a function of the holding cost per unit and the number of units in inventory. As described earlier, the unit holding cost is based on the cost of the item and the carrying charge rate. Ordering cost is a function of the number of orders placed

FIGURE 3.6   *Influence diagram for total inventory cost*

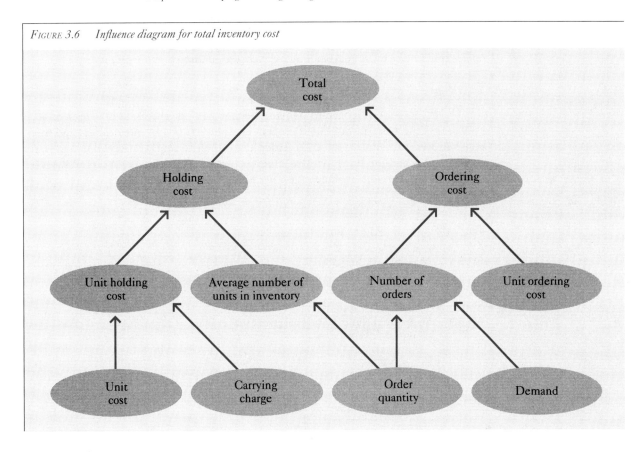

and the cost of each order. Both the number of units in inventory and the number of orders placed depend on the order quantity.

Establish Symbols. For the inventory cost model, let

$$Q = \text{order quantity}$$
$$D = \text{annual demand}$$
$$C = \text{unit cost of the item}$$
$$C_0 = \text{cost per order placed}$$
$$i = \text{inventory carrying charge per unit}$$

Construct the Model. To develop a total cost model, we can use the influence diagram in Figure 3.6 for guidance. Let us first deal with the ordering cost. With an annual demand D and order quantity Q, the number of orders that must be placed each year is D/Q. Therefore the total annual ordering cost is

Annual ordering cost = (number of orders per year)(cost per order) = $(D/Q)C_0$

Inventory holding cost per unit is computed as a fixed percentage of the unit cost of the item. Thus, if C is the unit cost of the item and i is the annual carrying charge rate (expressed as a decimal fraction), the cost of holding one unit for one year is

$$\text{Holding cost per unit} = iC$$

The assumption of constant demand becomes important in determining an expression for the average number of units in inventory. If Q units are ordered and then received when the inventory level is depleted, then the inventory will decrease to zero at a constant rate until the next order arrives. Since the inventory level starts at Q and ends at zero, the average inventory is

$$\text{Average inventory} = (Q + 0)/2 = Q/2$$

Thus, the annual inventory holding cost is

$$\text{Annual inventory holding cost} = (\text{average inventory})(\text{annual holding cost per unit})$$
$$= (Q/2)iC = iCQ/2$$

We may now express the total annual inventory cost as

$$\text{Total annual cost} = DC_0/Q + iCQ/2$$

Using the data we have for this specific example, we have

$$\text{Total annual cost} = (15,000)(200)/Q + (.2)(22)Q/2$$
$$= 3,000,000/Q + 2.2Q$$

We would like to find the value of Q that minimizes the total annual cost.

Solve or Analyze the Model. We may set up a simple spreadsheet for the inventory cost model as shown in Figure 3.7. In the top half of the spreadsheet we input the data. In the bottom half, we set up a what-if table to examine the effects of different order quantities on the costs. Figure 3.8 provides more insight into the nature of the solution through a graph generated from the spreadsheet data. It shows that the order cost decreases, while the holding cost increases as the order quantity increases. The total cost curve appears to reach a minimum somewhere around 1,200. This may not be the true optimal solution, because we only studied order quantities in increments of 100. However, it appears that the optimal order quantity lies somewhere between 1,100 and 1,300. With the spreadsheet, we could easily construct a what-if table for order quantities within this range and get closer to the optimal solution. From the graph (as well as from the table in the spreadsheet), we clearly see that this model finds a minimum cost trade-off between the order cost and the holding cost.

FIGURE 3.7 *Spreadsheet for the economic order quantity model*

	A	B	C	D
1	**Inventory Cost Model**			
2				
3	*Parameters and uncontrollable variables*			
4				
5	Annual Demand Rate	15000		
6	Ordering Cost	$200.00		
7	Unit Cost	$22.00		
8	Carrying Charge Rate	0.2		
9				
10	*Decision variable*			
11				
12	Order Quantity	500		
13				
14	*Model Outputs*			
15				
16	Order cost	$6,000.00		
17	Inventory cost	$1,100.00		
18	Total cost	$7,100.00		
19				
20				
21	*What-if Table*			
22				
23	Order Quantity	Order cost	Inventory cost	Total cost
24		$6,000.00	$1,100.00	$7,100.00
25	500	$6,000.00	$1,100.00	$7,100.00
26	600	$5,000.00	$1,320.00	$6,320.00
27	700	$4,285.71	$1,540.00	$5,825.71
28	800	$3,750.00	$1,760.00	$5,510.00
29	900	$3,333.33	$1,980.00	$5,313.33
30	1000	$3,000.00	$2,200.00	$5,200.00
31	1100	$2,727.27	$2,420.00	$5,147.27
32	1200	$2,500.00	$2,640.00	$5,140.00
33	1300	$2,307.69	$2,860.00	$5,167.69
34	1400	$2,142.86	$3,080.00	$5,222.86
35	1500	$2,000.00	$3,300.00	$5,300.00

Selected cell formulas

	A	B
14	*Model Outputs*	
15		
16	Order cost	+$B$5*$B$6/$B$12
17	Inventory cost	+$B$8*$B$7*$B$12/2
18	Total cost	+B16+B17

The spreadsheet approach does not guarantee that the best solution will be found. Using calculus, we can develop a mathematical solution showing that the value of Q that minimizes the total cost is[2]

$$Q^* = \sqrt{2D\,C_0/i\,C}$$

ECONOMIC ORDER QUANTITY

---

[2]The mathematical derivation can be found in the chapter appendix. Remember, it is the role of management science researchers to develop these formulas; it is the role of the manager to *use* them!

FIGURE 3.8   *Inventory cost curves*

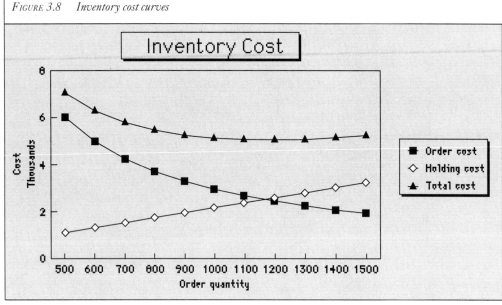

(This value is called the *economic order quantity (EOQ)* and the model is sometimes called the *economic order quantity model*.) Substituting the values of the uncontrollable variables, we have

$$Q^* = \sqrt{2(15,000)(200)/(0.20)(22)} = 1,167.75 \text{ or } 1,168$$

This results in a total cost of

$$\text{TC} = (15,000)(200)/1,168 + .2(22)(1,168)/2 = \$5,138$$

We probably could have found this solution by repeatedly constructing what-if tables over successively smaller ranges. The advantages of a mathematical solution procedure are that it is easier to apply and that it guarantees an optimal solution. Whenever possible, you should use an exact solution method rather than relying on a heuristic procedure.

One issue that the model does not address directly is the decision of when to order; that is, the reorder point. If we order too early, we will have more stock than we need and incur unnecessary holding costs. If we order too late, we run the risk of running out of stock before the order is received. Ideally, we would like the order to be received at the same time we run out of stock. Therefore, the reorder decision depends on the lead time. We should set the reorder point to be the inventory level that provides enough stock to satisfy all demand during the lead time. If the demand rate, D, is constant as assumed, and the lead time is t, then the reorder point should be equal to Dt.

To illustrate this for the numerical example, we have $D = 15,000$ units per year. Suppose that the lead time is one week, or .0192 years. The demand during the lead time is $(15,000)(.0192) = 288$ units. If we place an order when the inventory position reaches 288, then the order will arrive when the stock level falls to zero. This is illustrated in Figure 3.9.

> Decisions often must be made with logic, rather than just the output of mathematical models.

EVALUATING MODELS

We should critically evaluate models for their appropriateness and validity. Some important questions that we should address include the following.

- How obvious is the interpretation of the model? Are the results intuitive to the decision-maker?

FIGURE 3.9   *Computing the reorder point*

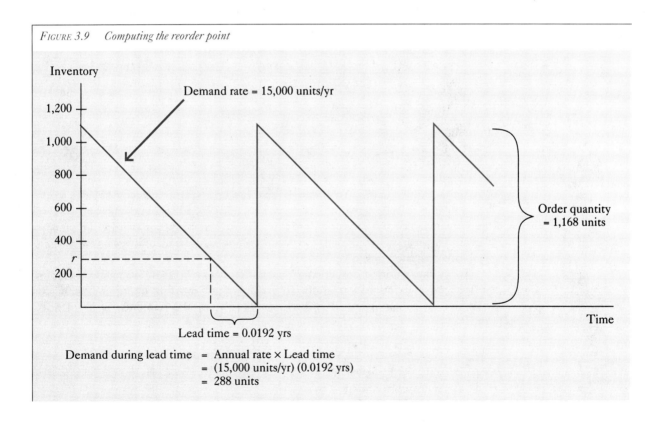

- Do the outputs of the model change as one would expect in response to changes in the inputs?
- How does any recommended course of action from the model compare with the decision-maker's intuition?

The better the ability of a decision-maker to understand a model and believe in its results, the more likely it is that he or she will accept it and use it. Models that are appealing to a management scientist are not necessarily as appealing to a manager! Many practitioners suggest that models should be simple functions of only a few key decision variables with clear physical interpretations.

Validity refers to how well a model represents reality. A "perfect" model corresponds to the real world in every respect; unfortunately, no such model has ever existed, and never will exist in the future, because it is impossible to include every detail of real life in one model. One technique for judging the validity of a model is to identify and examine the assumptions made in a model to see how they agree with the manager's perception of the real world. The closer the agreement, the higher the validity.

The model must be able to predict performance that would be observed in the actual system, and modelers should ask such questions as, What are the consequences of a deviation of the model from reality? What are the chances that the real system will respond as the model indicates? Does the model provide practical value to management? Let us examine the inventory model from this perspective.

EXAMPLE 3. VALIDITY OF THE ECONOMIC ORDER QUANTITY MODEL

To obtain a quick sense of the validity of the EOQ model, let us examine the two terms that constitute the total cost:

1. Ordering cost, DC_0/Q
2. Holding cost, $iCQ/2$

As the order quantity Q increases, we can see that the ordering cost decreases, because Q is in the denominator. This makes sense because fewer orders of larger size are being placed. At the same time, however, the holding cost increases (because Q is in the numerator) because larger orders will increase the average inventory. The model therefore appears to reflect what we would observe in practice. These observations were demonstrated in Figure 3.8.

Today, many firms are practicing "just-in-time" purchasing, in which frequent orders for small quantities are made. To make the just-in-time concept economically attractive, the ordering cost must be low. By analyzing the economic order quantity formula:

$$Q^* = \sqrt{2DC_0/iC}$$

we see that as C_0 decreases, so does Q^*, as does the total cost. Here again, the model reflects what we would expect to happen.

Management scientists often state that the purpose of modeling is to obtain insight, not numbers. A useful means of achieving this insight is through sensitivity analysis. Sensitivity analysis is important to managers because most data are at best estimates of the real values. Mathematical models provide a convenient basis for performing sensitivity analysis.

EXAMPLE 4. SENSITIVITY ANALYSIS FOR THE ECONOMIC ORDER QUANTITY MODEL

To illustrate this, let us consider the numerical instance of the economic order quantity model that we discussed. Recall that $D = 15,000$, $C_0 = 200$, $C = 22$, and $i = .20$. The optimal order quantity is given by

$$Q^* = \sqrt{2DC_0/iC}$$

and the total annual cost is

$$\text{TC} = DC_0/Q + iCQ/2$$

Now suppose that we err by 10 percent in our estimate of the annual demand, meaning that D can be as low as 13,500 or as high as 16,500. How would this affect the total cost? Note that since we do not realize that our estimate is wrong, we would still use $Q^* = 1,168$, but that the actual cost would be computed using the true value of D. (If demand is lower, we would order less frequently; if it is higher, we would order more frequently.)

Thus, if $D = 13,500$, the total cost actually incurred is

$$\text{TC} = (13,500)(200)/1,168 + .2(22)(1,168)/2 = \$4,881$$

The optimal order quantity corresponding to $D = 13,500$ would be

$$Q^* = \sqrt{2DC_0/iC} = \sqrt{2(13,500)(200)/.2(22)} = 1,108 \text{ with an annual cost}$$

$$\text{TC} = (13,500)(200)/1,108 + .2(22)(1,108)/2 = \$4,874, \text{ a difference of only \$7.}$$

If $D = 16,500$, the total cost is

$$\text{TC} = (16,500)(200)/1,168 + .2(22)(1,168)/2 = \$5,395$$

The optimal order quantity would have been

$$Q^* = \sqrt{2DC_0/iC} = \sqrt{2(16,500)(200)/.2(22)} = 1,225$$

with a total cost of

$$\text{TC} = (16,500)(200)/1,225 + .2(22)(1,225)/2 = \$5,389, \text{ a difference of only \$6.}$$

A more detailed summary is provided on the spreadsheet in Figure 3.10 (differences with the calculations above are due to rounding to whole numbers). We see that relatively large errors in demand forecasting have little effect on the minimum cost. This can also be seen in Figure 3.8 by observing that the total cost curve is quite

FIGURE 3.10   *Sensitivity analysis spreadsheet for demand*

	A	B	C	D	E
1	**Inventory Cost Model Sensitivity Analysis**				
2					
3	*Parameters and uncontrollable variables*				
4					
5	Annual Demand Rate	15000			
6	Ordering Cost	$200.00			
7	Unit Cost	$22.00			
8	Carrying Charge Rate	0.2			
9					
10	*Model outputs*				
11					
12	Optimal order quantity	1167.75			
13	Order cost	$2,569.05			
14	Inventory cost	$2,569.05			
15	Total cost	$5,138.09			
16					
17					
18	*Sensitivity Analysis Table*				
19					
20		Demand	Actual cost	EOQ	Minimum Cost	Difference
21		13000	$4,795.55	1087.11	$4,783.30	$12.25
22		13500	$4,881.19	1107.82	$4,874.42	$6.77
23		14000	$4,966.82	1128.15	$4,963.87	$2.95
24		14500	$5,052.46	1148.12	$5,051.73	$0.73
25		15000	$5,138.09	1167.75	$5,138.09	$0.00
26		15500	$5,223.73	1187.05	$5,223.03	$0.70
27		16000	$5,309.36	1206.05	$5,306.60	$2.76
28		16500	$5,395.00	1224.74	$5,388.88	$6.12
29		17000	$5,480.63	1243.16	$5,469.92	$10.71
30		17500	$5,566.27	1261.31	$5,549.77	$16.49

Selected cell formulas

	A	B
10	*Model outputs*	
11		
12	Optimal order quantity	@SQRT(2*$B$5*$B$6/($B$8*$B$7))
13	Order cost	+$B$5*$B$6/$B$12
14	Inventory cost	+$B$8*$B$7*$B$12/2
15	Total cost	+B13+B14
16		
17		
18	*Sensitivity Analysis Table*	
19		
20	Demand	Actual cost
21	13000	+A21*$B$6/$B$12+$B$8*$B$7*$B$12/2
22	13500	+A22*$B$6/$B$12+$B$8*$B$7*$B$12/2
23	14000	+A23*$B$6/$B$12+$B$8*$B$7*$B$12/2
24	14500	+A24*$B$6/$B$12+$B$8*$B$7*$B$12/2
25	15000	+A25*$B$6/$B$12+$B$8*$B$7*$B$12/2
26	15500	+A26*$B$6/$B$12+$B$8*$B$7*$B$12/2
27	16000	+A27*$B$6/$B$12+$B$8*$B$7*$B$12/2
28	16500	+A28*$B$6/$B$12+$B$8*$B$7*$B$12/2
29	17000	+A29*$B$6/$B$12+$B$8*$B$7*$B$12/2
30	17500	+A30*$B$6/$B$12+$B$8*$B$7*$B$12/2

FIGURE 3.10   (continued)

	C	D	E
20	EOQ	Minimum Cost	Difference
21	@SQRT(2*A21*$B$6/($B$8*$B$7))	+A21*$B$6/C21+$B$8*$B$7*C21/2	+B21-D21
22	@SQRT(2*A22*$B$6/($B$8*$B$7))	+A22*$B$6/C22+$B$8*$B$7*C22/2	+B22-D22
23	@SQRT(2*A23*$B$6/($B$8*$B$7))	+A23*$B$6/C23+$B$8*$B$7*C23/2	+B23-D23
24	@SQRT(2*A24*$B$6/($B$8*$B$7))	+A24*$B$6/C24+$B$8*$B$7*C24/2	+B24-D24
25	@SQRT(2*A25*$B$6/($B$8*$B$7))	+A25*$B$6/C25+$B$8*$B$7*C25/2	+B25-D25
26	@SQRT(2*A26*$B$6/($B$8*$B$7))	+A26*$B$6/C26+$B$8*$B$7*C26/2	+B26-D26
27	@SQRT(2*A27*$B$6/($B$8*$B$7))	+A27*$B$6/C27+$B$8*$B$7*C27/2	+B27-D27
28	@SQRT(2*A28*$B$6/($B$8*$B$7))	+A28*$B$6/C28+$B$8*$B$7*C28/2	+B28-D28
29	@SQRT(2*A29*$B$6/($B$8*$B$7))	+A29*$B$6/C29+$B$8*$B$7*C29/2	+B29-D29
30	@SQRT(2*A30*$B$6/($B$8*$B$7))	+A30*$B$6/C30+$B$8*$B$7*C30/2	+B30-D30

flat around the optimal solution. In Figure 3.10, we illustrate the effects of errors in the annual demand as it is varied from 13,000 to 17,500. In the ACTUAL COST column, we compute the total cost using the actual order quantity (1,167.75). In the next column, EOQ, we compute the economic order quantity for the given level of demand, followed by the minimum cost using *this* order quantity. The last column shows the difference.

This analysis shows that errors in estimating the demand and using the wrong order quantity have little impact on the total cost. We would therefore say that this model is *robust* with respect to changes in demand. In an end-of-chapter exercise, we will ask you to investigate the sensitivity of the other values in the model.

MODEL ENRICHMENT

Modeling may be viewed as a process of enrichment or elaboration [Morris, 1967]. That is, we begin with simple models, often quite different from reality, and move toward more elaborate models that capture the complexity of the real situation. However, the more complex a model is, the less likely it is that it will be accepted by the user. Model builders should therefore take care not to make models more complex than necessary.

There are several ways to enrich models. You could change constants into variables, add new variables, relax some assumptions, or add randomness to the model. For example, in the EOQ model, you might assume that demand is random rather than fixed, or add some constraints. Limitations on warehouse space might require that inventory not exceed a specified amount of warehouse space. To illustrate this, suppose that each item requires two square feet of space. If only 2,000 square feet of warehouse space is available, we see that the solution of ordering 1,168 units would not be feasible. In our model, we would add the constraint:

$$2Q \leq 2,000$$

The enhanced model becomes

$$\text{Minimize } DC_0/Q + iCQ/2$$

$$\text{subject to}$$

$$2Q \leq 2,000$$

Solving this model would tell us the quantity of items to order in order to minimize total inventory cost and meet the warehouse space constraint. Can you tell what the optimal solution is? (Hint: How will the total cost graph in Figure 3.8 be affected by the constraint?)

Another way to enrich this inventory model is to consider multiple items. We will use a subscript to denote the item number. We could enhance the model that includes the warehouse constraint by having two items as follows:

$$\text{Minimize } D_1 C_{01}/Q_1 + i\,C_1 Q_1/2 + D_2 C_{02}/Q_2 + i\,C_2 Q_2/2$$

subject to

$$f_1 Q_1 + f_2 Q_2 \leq L$$

where f_1 and f_2 are the per-unit space requirements for items 1 and 2, and L is the available warehouse capacity. It is not easy to see how to approach this problem. Often when we enrich a model, we must develop new solution approaches.

MANAGEMENT SCIENCE PRACTICE

In this section we discuss efforts at structuring and modeling a highly-unstructured problem situation—the spread of HIV among intravenous (IV) drug users. The management science community has addressed this vital health issue, particularly the task of evaluating policy alternatives in the face of limited hard data.

Modeling HIV Transmission Through Needle Sharing[3]

By 1986, 17 percent of newly reported AIDS cases in the U.S. were attributable to IV drug use. By 1987 this figure had risen to 20 percent. Intravenous drug users therefore represent a key target group for behavioral change efforts. Researchers in Los Angeles developed a model focusing on the dynamic consequences of HIV transmission through needle sharing. To develop a useful model, several assumptions were made:

1. Only drug users who inject frequently enough to be considered addicts can become infected.
2. The total addicted population in a given area may be considered a collection of small cliques—groups of individuals who mutually share needles. Needles from one clique may be shared with other cliques.
3. The nonsharing population is fixed in size and the sharing population is initially constant.
4. Needle sharing is the only route of HIV transmission (i.e., sexual transmission is not considered).

---

[3] Adapted from Homer and St. Clair, 1991.

5. All members of a particular clique share the same HIV infection status. One implication of this assumption is that all sharers may be at risk for infection while nonsharers face no such risk.
6. An uninfected sharer risks infection with a fixed probability whenever an infectious needle is used or not effectively cleaned.
7. A stock of used needles is maintained in proportion to the sharer population. These are disposable and discarded after an average number of uses.

The model is a rather complex set of mathematical equations whose simultaneous solution provides predictions of the behavior of key variables in the system over time. The model starts at time zero with an initial IV drug user population and an initial sharer fraction of that population. As time progresses, the total user population changes only when the population of sharers changes, while the nonsharer population remains fixed. The population of sharers is subdivided into two stocks: uninfected sharers and infected sharers, initialized so that the stock of infected sharers is only a tiny fraction (0.01 percent) of all sharers at time zero.

The model consists of two basic parts: a population model and a shared-needle model. The model's basic stock-and-flow structure for population is shown in Figure 3-11. New entries to the uninfected sharer population eventually leave this stock either by (1) quitting addictive IV drug use, (2) through "standard loss," that is, migration or non-HIV death, or (3) by becoming infected. Those who become infected eventually leave the

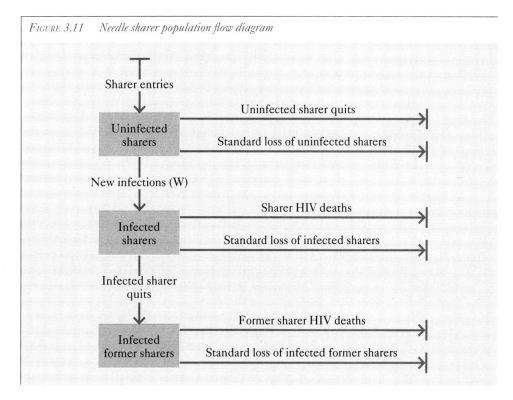

FIGURE 3.11   *Needle sharer population flow diagram*

infected sharer stock either by (1) quitting addictive IV drug use, (2) through standard loss, or (3) through HIV death. Finally, those infected sharers who have quit addictive IV drug use eventually leave the infected former sharer stock either (1) through standard loss or (2) through HIV death.

Some typical equations in this model are

$$P_s = P_{su} + P_{si}$$

$$P = P_s + P_0[1 - F_{sp0}]$$

$$F_{is} = P_{si}/P_s$$

$$F_{ip} = P_{si}/P$$

where

P_s = sharer population
P_{su} = uninfected sharers
P_{si} = infected sharers
P = IV drug user population
P_0 = initial IV drug user population
F_{sp0} = initial sharer fraction of IV drug user population
F_{is} = infected fraction of sharers
F_{ip} = infected fraction of IV drug users

These equations are quite straight-forward and easy to model. Other equations model the rates of change of these variables over time and other aspects of the model in Figure 3.11. A more complicated equation represents infection risk per use:

$$\beta = \alpha[1 - c][1 - (1/\mu)]\phi$$

where

β = infection risk per use
α = infection risk per infectious needle use
c = effective cleaning fraction of shared uses
μ = uses per needle before discard
ϕ = infectious fraction of uninfected sharers' used needles

This says that an uninfected sharer may, with a given probability, become infected with HIV by using an infectious needle contaminated with HIV. The probability of an uninfected sharer using a needle which is infectious is expressed as the product of two factors. The first factor represents the probability that the needle has been used previously; this reuse fraction is determined by the average number of uses per needle prior to being discarded. The second factor represents the probability that a previously used needle currently in the possession of an uninfected sharer is infectious. You can see that quite a bit of modeling effort went into developing this equation alone. Figure 3.12 shows the conceptual model from which the shared needle equations are developed.

The model was used to predict behavior patterns and to analyze intervention strategies. Figures 3.13 to 3.15 show the model predictions of key population categories and the annual incidence of new infections, population fractions and the infectious fraction

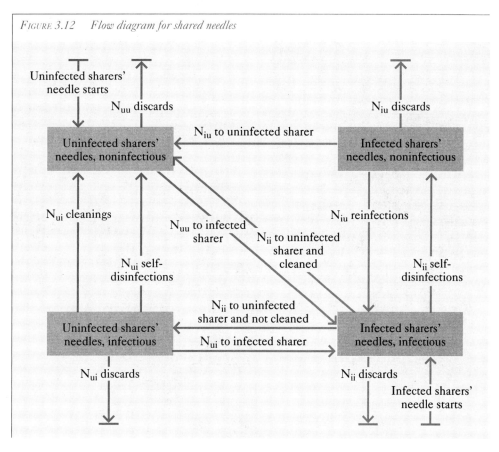

FIGURE 3.12   Flow diagram for shared needles

Uninfected sharers' needle starts

N_{uu} discards

N_{iu} discards

N_{iu} to uninfected sharer

Uninfected sharers' needles, noninfectious

Infected sharers' needles, noninfectious

N_{ui} cleanings

N_{uu} to infected sharer

N_{ii} to uninfected sharer and cleaned

N_{iu} reinfections

N_{ui} self-disinfections

N_{ii} self-disinfections

N_{ii} to uninfected sharer and not cleaned

Uninfected sharers' needles, infectious

N_{ui} to infected sharer

Infected sharers' needles, infectious

N_{ui} discards

N_{ii} discards

Infected sharers' needle starts

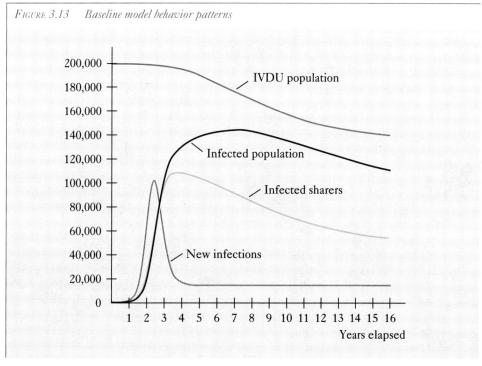

FIGURE 3.13   Baseline model behavior patterns

IVDU population

Infected population

Infected sharers

New infections

200,000
180,000
160,000
140,000
120,000
100,000
80,000
60,000
40,000
20,000
0

1 2 3 4 5 6 7 8 9 10 11 12 13 14 15 16

Years elapsed

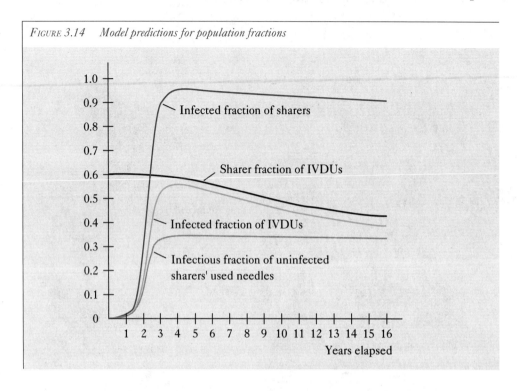

FIGURE 3.14   *Model predictions for population fractions*

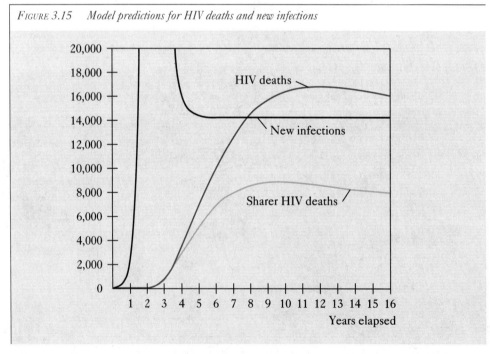

FIGURE 3.15   *Model predictions for HIV deaths and new infections*

of uninfected sharers' used needles, and HIV deaths over a 16-year time horizon. These graphs show how the key variables reach an equilibrium.

The model can assist policy makers in studying the potential benefits of campaigns to increase the effective cleaning of shared needles. The following questions were addressed:

- How important is the magnitude of such a campaign?
- How important is the timeliness of the campaign?
- How might the openness of needle sharing affect the impacts of the campaign's magnitude and timeliness?
- If the campaign results in a greater attraction to needle sharing, to what extent might its benefits be undermined?

Figure 3.16 shows a summary of several policy scenarios in which the effective cleaning fraction is changed at different rates and compared to the baseline (scenario # 1). Scenarios 2 through 5 address the first two questions raised above. In scenario # 2, the parameter c is increased to 30 percent (from an initial value of 10 percent) for all 16 years; in scenario # 3, c is increased to 50 percent; in scenario # 4, c is increased to 50 percent, but not until the second year; and in scenario # 5, c is increased to 50 percent, but not until the fourth year. The results show the critical importance of both the magnitude and timeliness of the cleaning campaign.

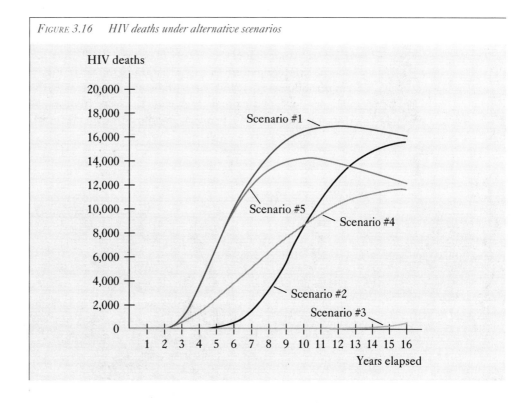

FIGURE 3.16   *HIV deaths under alternative scenarios*

Discussion Questions

1. Why were so many assumptions made in developing this model?
2. Discuss the results of scenarios 2 through 5 in Figure 3.16. How do they compare with one another? What implications do they have for the size and timing of a needle cleaning campaign?
3. How might this model be used to examine policy interventions other than a needle-cleaning campaign? For example, what other parameters might be varied and what would these mean?

MORE EXAMPLES AND SOLVED PROBLEMS

In this section we present further examples that illustrate the process of developing management science models. While some of these may appear to be quite complicated, applying the guidelines developed in this chapter will help you to focus your thinking.

EXAMPLE 5. A MODEL OF AN INSPECTION PROCESS

Assembled cellular telephones move through a series of inspection stations to test their transmission performance and range sensitivity. If the unit is found to be functioning improperly, then it is routed to an adjustment station where a technician either adjusts or replaces some of the electronic components. After adjustment, the unit is sent back to an inspection station for retest. Units that pass the test are sent to a packing area. Historical data shows that 98 percent of all units pass the inspection.

A descriptive picture of this situation is shown in Figure 3.17. This is different from the influence diagrams we introduced in Chapter 1 in that it illustrates the movement, or "flow" of the products through the inspection and adjustment system. Models such as this are useful to managers who deal with manufacturing or service systems.

FIGURE 3.17   A model of an inspection process

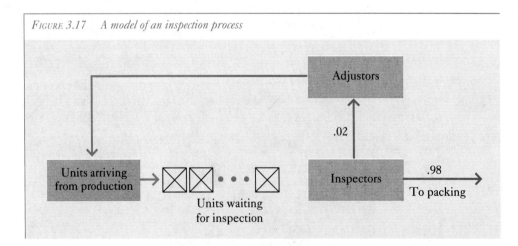

A picture of a system often helps to begin the modeling process. It also provides a means of communicating aspects of the model with the managers who own the problem.

EXAMPLE 6. PRODUCTION LOT SIZE MODEL

The *production lot size* model is similar to the economic order quantity model. However, instead of the ordered quantity of the item being delivered all at once, it is produced at a steady rate for some period of time, say 100 units per day, 500 units per week, and so on. Thus, if D represents the annual demand rate and P represents the annual production rate, during periods of production, inventory increases at the net rate of $P - D$ units. When production is not occurring, however, inventory decreases at the rate of D units per year. This is illustrated in Figure 3.18. Similar to the EOQ model, C_0 represents the ordering cost (sometimes called the *setup cost*), and iC represents the holding cost per unit. We develop a model for the total annual cost in terms of Q, the amount to produce.

From Figure 3.18, we can see that the only difference between the two figures is that the "delivery" (production) occurs over a period of time rather than instantaneously. A model for this situation should therefore be quite similar to the economic

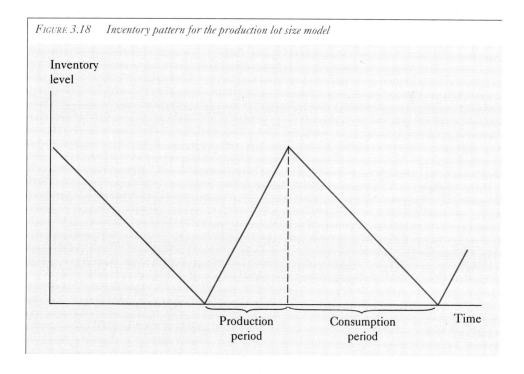

FIGURE 3.18   *Inventory pattern for the production lot size model*

order quantity model. Since Q is the production quantity, we will produce a total of Q units each time production commences. Since production occurs at a fixed rate of P units per year, it will take Q/P years to produce the entire quantity Q (Q units divided by P units per year equals Q/P years). During this time, inventory builds up from zero at a rate of $P - D$ units per year. Therefore, at the end of the production cycle, a total of $(P - D)Q/P = (1 - D/P)Q$ units will be in stock. Since production and demand occur at constant rates, the average inventory will be one-half of this maximum inventory, or $0.5(1 - D/P)Q$ units. Thus the annual holding cost is

$$0.5(1 - D/P)QiC$$

The number of production runs, or setups, per year will be the same as in the EOQ case, or D/Q. Thus, the annual setup cost is

$$(D/Q)C_0$$

The total cost is therefore

$$0.5(1 - D/P)QiC + (D/Q)C_0$$

Notice that the only difference between this model and that for the economic order quantity is the term $(1 - D/P)$. Also, if P were infinite (that is, if all items are delivered instantaneously), the term D/P would drop out and the model would be the same as the EOQ model. What about the optimal order quantity? Recall that the EOQ formula is

$$Q^* = \sqrt{2DC_0/iC}$$

If you compare both models closely, you might guess that the optimal lot size would be

$$Q^* = \sqrt{2DC_0/iC(1 - D/P)}$$

This, in fact, is exactly the formula for the optimal order quantity. Again, as P becomes infinite, the solution becomes the same as the EOQ.

Many models are minor variations or extensions of others. Recognizing this often helps in the modeling process.

EXAMPLE 7. MULTIPERIOD PRODUCTION PLANNING

Suzie's Sweatshirts is a home-based company that makes upscale, hand-painted sweatshirts for children. Forecasts of sales for the next year are

$$
\begin{array}{ll}
\text{Autumn}: & 125 \\
\text{Winter}: & 350 \\
\text{Spring}: & 75
\end{array}
$$

Shirts are purchased for $15. The cost of capital is 24 percent per year (or 6 percent per quarter); thus, the holding cost per shirt is .06(15) = $.90 per quarter. The shirts are painted by part-time workers who earn $4.50 per hour during the autumn. Because of the high demand for part-time help during the winter holiday season, labor rates are higher in the winter, and Suzie must pay the workers $6.00 per hour. In the spring, labor is more difficult to keep, and Suzie finds that she must pay $5.50 per hour to get qualified help. Each shirt takes 1.5 hours to complete. How should Suzie plan production over the three quarters to minimize the combined production and inventory holding costs?

The decision variables in this problem are the number of shirts to produce during each of the three quarters. Thus, we may define the variables as

$$x_A = \text{number produced in autumn}$$
$$x_W = \text{number produced in winter}$$
$$x_S = \text{number produced in spring}$$

We note that Suzie has the option of producing more than the demand in a particular quarter. Thus, inventory may be held to the next period. We define I_A, I_W, and I_S to be the number of shirts held in inventory at the end of the autumn, winter, and spring quarters, respectively. We illustrate this in Figure 3.19.

The production cost per shirt is computed by multiplying the labor rate by the number of hours required to produce a shirt. Thus, the unit cost in the autumn is ($4.50)(1.5) = $6.75; in the winter, ($6.00)(1.5) = $9.00; and in the spring, ($5.50)(1.5) = $8.25.

The objective function is to minimize the total cost of production and inventory. (Since the cost of the shirts themselves is constant, it is not relevant to the problem we are addressing.) The total cost function is therefore

$$6.75x_A + 9.00x_W + 8.25x_S + .90(I_A + I_W + I_S)$$

The constraints of the problem are implied from Figure 3.19. For each quarter, we note that we must maintain a "material balance" of shirts:

Inventory from last quarter + production this quarter − inventory held to next quarter
= demand

FIGURE 3.19

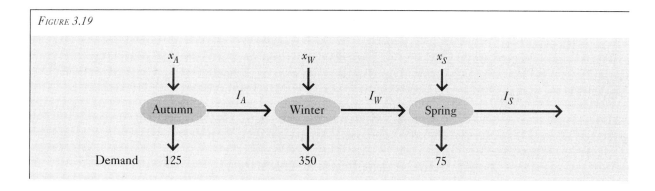

Thus, for the autumn we have

$$0 + x_A - I_A = 125$$

For the winter we have

$$I_A + x_W - I_W = 350$$

and for the spring:

$$I_W + x_S - I_S = 75$$

We also note that all variables must be greater than or equal to zero. The complete model is

$$\text{Minimize } 6.75x_A + 9.00x_W + 8.25x_S + .90(I_A + I_W + I_S)$$

subject to

$$x_A - I_A = 125$$

$$I_A + x_W - I_W = 350$$

$$I_W + x_S - I_S = 75$$

$$x_A, x_W, x_S, I_A, I_W, I_S \geq 0$$

Constraints in problems with multiple time periods often result from material balance equations that link successive time periods.

Example 8. Automobile Fuel Consumption

Automobiles have different fuel economies (mpg), and commuters drive different distances to work or school. Suppose that a state Department of Transportation (DOT) is interested in measuring the average monthly fuel consumption of commuters in a certain city. The DOT might sample a group of commuters and collect information on the number of miles driven per day, number of driving days per month, and the fuel economy of their cars.

We may develop a model for the amount of gasoline consumed, but we must first define some symbols for the data. Let

G = gallons of fuel consumed per month
m = miles per day driven to and from work or school
d = number of driving days per month
f = fuel economy in miles per gallon

We seek an expression for G in terms of m, d, and f.

By examining the dimensions, it is often easy to help identify the correct model, and *always* easy to verify if a model is correct by checking to see how the dimensions "cancel out:"

$$G = (m \text{ miles/day})(d \text{ days/month})/(f \text{ miles/gallon})$$

$$= md/f \text{ (miles/day)(days/month)(gallons/mile)}$$

$$= md/f \text{ (miles/month)(gallon/mile)}$$

$$= md/f \text{ (gallons/month)}$$

When developing *any* model, always pay attention to the *dimensions* of each number and variable.

EXAMPLE 9. ALLOCATION OF ADVERTISING

A brand manager for a major consumer products company must determine how much time to allocate between radio and television advertising during the next month. Market research has provided estimates of the audience exposure for each minute of advertising in each medium. Costs per minute of advertising are also known, and the manager has a limited budget. The manager has decided that because television ads have been found to be much more effective than radio ads, at least 70 percent of the time should be allocated to television.

A model for this problem has two decision variables: the amount of time spent on radio ads and the amount of time spent on TV ads. The actual values of these variables influence

1. the audience exposure
2. the total cost of advertising
3. the total time spent advertising

Moreover, advertising expenditures are related to the available budget, and the total time spent advertising is related to the minimum requirement for TV ads. These relationships are summarized in Figure 3.20.

Suppose that we have the following data for this problem:

	Exposure/minute	Cost/minute
Radio	150	$400
TV	800	$2000

A total budget of $25,000 is available for advertising. A mathematical model for the optimal advertising strategy can be developed as follows.

First define symbols for the decision variables. Let R = time spent on radio ads and T = time spent on TV ads. Since our objective is to maximize the total audience exposure, we note that for every minute of radio advertising, we receive 150 units of

FIGURE 3.20   *Influence diagram for advertising allocation problem*

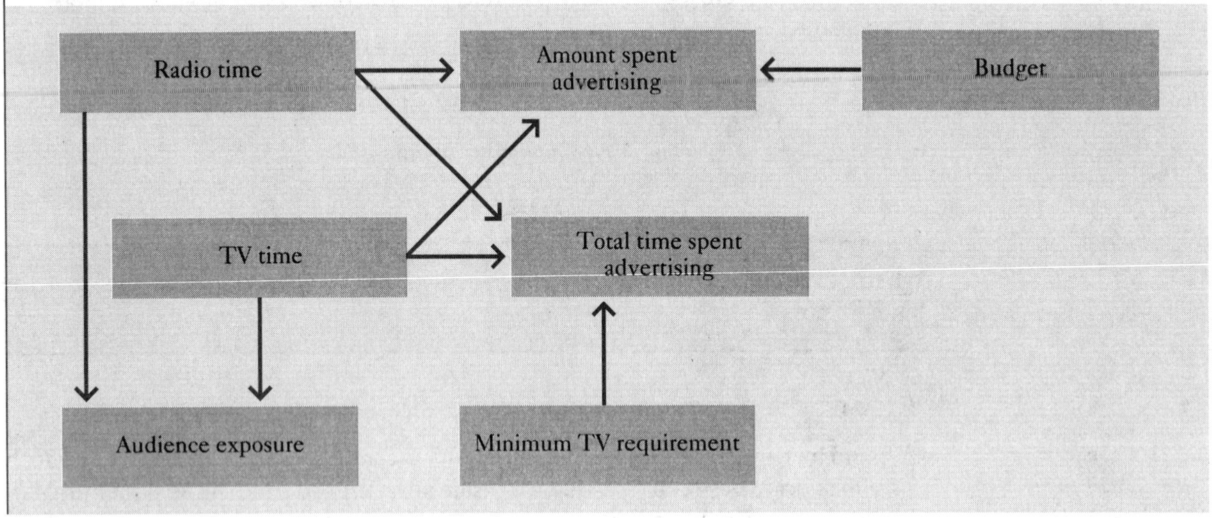

exposure, and for every minute of TV advertising, we receive 800 units of exposure. Thus, we seek to maximize

$$\text{Total Exposure} = 150R + 800T$$

We have a limited budget, therefore the total amount of money spent on the ads cannot exceed the $25,000 allotted:

$$400R + 2000T \leq 25,000$$

Another constraint is that television ads must be at least 70 percent of the total. Since the total minutes spent on both types of media is $T + R$, we have

$$T \geq .7(T + R)$$

Note that this can be rewritten using algebra as

$$.3T - .7R \geq 0$$

The complete model (with the restrictions that no time allocations can be negative) is

$$\text{Maximize Total Exposure} = 150R + 800T$$

subject to the constraints

$$400R + 2000T \leq 25,000$$

$$.3T - .7R \geq 0$$

$$T \geq 0, \quad R \geq 0$$

Influence diagrams help you see relationships among elements of a model before you try to develop the mathematical relationships.

EXAMPLE 10. MAXIMIZING AIRLINE REVENUE

The demand for airline travel is quite sensitive to price. Typically there is an inverse relationship between demand and price; when price decreases, demand increases and vice-versa. One major airline has found that when the price (p) for a round trip between Chicago and Los Angeles is $600, the demand ($D$) is 500 passengers per day. When the price is reduced to $300, demand is 1,200 passengers per day. The airline needs to develop an appropriate mathematical model that will determine what price to charge in order to maximize the total revenue.

We recognize that revenue is (price)(demand). We also know that price is related to demand; therefore, we need to express demand as a function of price. We are not given this function, but only two data points (p,D) as (600,500) and (300, 1,200) as shown in Figure 3.21. Without any other information, we have to assume a linear relationship between p and D; that is, $D = ap + b$, where a and b are the slope and intercept, respectively. Since both points must satisfy this equation, we have:

$$500 = a(600) + b$$

$$1,200 = a(300) + b$$

Using algebra to solve these equations simultaneously, we obtain

$$D = (-7/3)p + 1,900$$

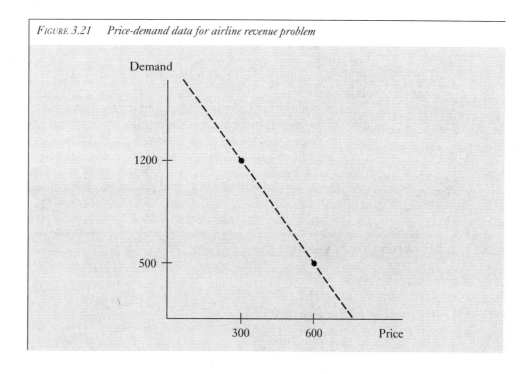

FIGURE 3.21   *Price-demand data for airline revenue problem*

Now we can develop the following expression for revenue (R)

$$R = (\text{price})(\text{demand})$$
$$= pD = p[(-7/3)p + 1,900]$$
$$= (-7/3)p^2 + 1,900p$$

The airline's optimization problem is to maximize R.

> Developing models often involves *making assumptions* and performing some "pre-processing" using basic techniques of mathematics and statistics.

SUMMARY

In this chapter we examined the modeling process more closely and suggested a variety of principles and guidelines to facilitate the process of model building. As with any project, modeling requires good planning. You must understand the system you wish to model, the purpose of the model, assumptions which will guide the model formulation, the data that will be available as input to the model, the solution methods and software that are available, and the quality of the solution that will be required. Without addressing these questions, it is difficult to develop models that will serve the purpose of the managers who use them.

We suggested several guidelines for approaching the modeling process. First, organize your information and define variables. Next, draw a picture if possible and write down some symbols for the unknown quantities in the model. Use this information to develop specific functions and mathematical relationships. To solve a model, use a spreadsheet or special algorithms.

A major purpose of models is to provide insight into a problem. All modeling should therefore be accompanied by sensitivity analysis. Spreadsheets are wonderful mechanisms for doing this because of their built-in capability to address "what-if" questions. In solving problems throughout this book, we encourage you to try to develop spreadsheet models, even if they are not asked for. You will find that they will improve your understanding of the models and your ability to develop more complex models for many decision situations.

CHAPTER REVIEW EXERCISES

I. Terms to Understand

You should be able to define the following terms:

a. Flowchart (p. 83)
b. Continuous review (p. 86)
c. Inventory position (p. 86)
d. Reorder point (p. 86)

e. Lead time (p. 86)
f. Back order (p. 86)
g. Carrying charge rate (p. 90)
h. Economic order quantity (EOQ) (p. 96)
i. Economic order quantity model (p. 98)

j. Robust model (p. 101)
k. Production lot size (p. 109)
l. Setup cost (p. 109)
m. Dimensions (p. 113)

II. Discussion Questions

1. Why is modeling considered more of an art than a science?
2. Explain the two basic ways of learning to model. What are the relative advantages or disadvantages of each?
3. Describe the characteristics of good models.
4. Describe the factors that influence the development of models in management science. What role should the user (not the developer) of the model play with respect to these factors?
5. Why is it necessary to make simplifying assumptions when building models?
6. How do you determine what level of solution quality to have in a particular model?
7. Explain how a continuous review inventory system works.
8. What key assumptions are made in the economic order quantity model?
9. Describe the practical guidelines suggested for developing management science models.
10. Explain how pictures and other graphic aids can help in the modeling process.
11. Explain the value of sensitivity analysis to managerial decision-making.
12. Why should one begin with a simple model and gradually elaborate it?
13. Explain various ways of enriching models.
14. Why are symbols used in constructing models?
15. Evaluate the advisability and practicality of working in a system in order to learn how it operates.
16. For the inspection process problem (Example 5), discuss what additional data are needed and how to acquire these data.

III. Problems

1. A periodic review inventory system operates as follows. The inventory position is checked only at fixed intervals of time. If the inventory position is at or below the reorder point when checked, then an order is placed for enough stock to bring the inventory position up to a fixed amount called the reorder level.
    a. Draw stock level and inventory position curves similar to Figure 3.2 that illustrates the operation of such a system.
    b. Explain how you might determine the optimal time between reviews. What are the important trade-offs in this problem?
2. Given the following list of characteristics associated with inventory systems (a more comprehensive list than is applicable to the EOQ model), construct an influence diagram that describes the structure of the system.
    a. Stock on hand
    b. Cost of holding inventory
    c. Obsolescence rate
    d. Interest rate
    e. Demand
    f. Probability of stockout
    g. Lead time
    h. Cost of a stockout
    i. Total stockout costs
    j. Reorder quantity
    k. Reorder costs
    l. Total costs
3. A firm would like to order its key component by using the EOQ formula. The demand for the component is 6,000 units per year, ordering cost is $75.00 per order, cost per unit is $3.50, and the holding cost rate is 8 percent. Write out the total cost model and give the EOQ for this component. What assumptions does this model make? Explore the sensitivity of this model to changes in the annual demand by looking at this scenario with annual demands of 4,000, 5,000, 7,000, and 8,000.

4. Consider the scenario of Problem 3. Explore the sensitivity of the model with respect to the holding cost rate by calculating the EOQ and total cost as the holding cost rate varies from .04 to .12 in increments of .02. Is the model more or less sensitive to changes in the holding cost rate than it is to changes in the annual demand? Explain your answer in terms of the graph of the total cost function and its components.

5. Refer back to Problem 14 in Chapter 1. Explain why this problem is analogous to the economic order quantity model. Suppose that the airline requires five new flight attendants per month. The fixed cost of each training session is $25,000. New flight attendants are paid $1,750 per month. Flight attendants who are certified may not be used immediately; however, the airline continues to pay them and considers this a "holding cost" necessary to maintain a necessary work force. Construct the total cost model and determine the optimal size of the training program.

6. Sunshine Tanning Products of Honolulu experiences roughly a constant demand of 10,000 bottles of tanning oil per year. The maximum annual rate of production is 50,000 bottles per year, with a setup cost of $400 per run. The inventory holding rate (annual) is 20 percent and the per-unit cost of production is $1.35 per bottle. Write out the total cost model for this scenario. Using trial and error, try to find the production run size that will minimize cost.

7. A textbook produced by South-Eastern Publishing has an annual demand of 6,000 copies. The production cost for each book is $15.00. Holding cost is based on a 15 percent annual rate, and production setup costs are $130 per setup. The equipment used can produce books at an annual rate of 20,000 copies. Assuming 250 working days per year, setup the total cost model for the optimal production lot size and find the optimal production quantity.

8. A *stockout* is a demand that cannot be supplied from inventory. While stockouts may be undesirable from a customer service point-of-view, they are often economical, especially for high-value items where the holding cost is extremely high. The following figure shows the inventory pattern for a back order situation under the assumption that demand is constant. Note that B represents the amount of back orders that accumulate when an order of size Q is received. The inventory cycle is divided into two parts: T_1 days when inventory is available, and T_2 days when back orders accumulate. Using the same notation as the economic order quantity model, and letting C_B = annual cost to maintain one unit on back order, develop a model for the total annual cost (ordering + holding + back order). Hint: assume that the back order cost is C_B times the average back order level.

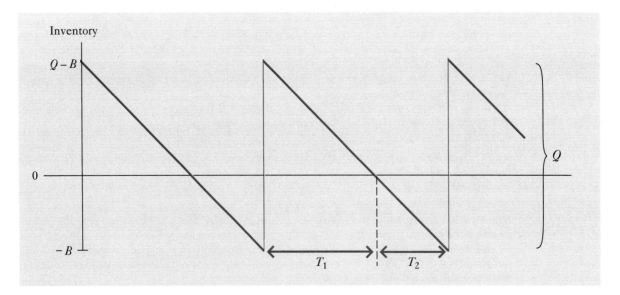

9. For the back order model in Problem 8, we can show that the optimal order quantity Q^* and the optimal back order level B^* are:

$$Q^* = \sqrt{\frac{2D\,C_0(C_h + C_B)}{C_h C_B}}$$

$$B^* = Q^* \frac{C_h}{C_h + C_B}$$

where $C_h = iC$. Let $D = 3,000$, $i = .20$, $C = \$70$, $C_0 = \$50$, and $C_B = \$25$. Develop a spreadsheet and show, using sensitivity analysis approaches, that these formulas provide the minimum total cost.

10. Consider the product mix model for radar detectors formulated in Chapter 1:

$$\text{maximize} \quad 24\,\text{LS} + 40\,\text{SB}$$

$$12\,\text{LS} + 12\,\text{SB} \leq 6,000$$

$$6\,\text{LS} + 10\,\text{SB} \leq 3,500$$

$$\text{LS, SB} \geq 0$$

Show how to work through the formulation of this model step-by-step using the guidelines developed in this chapter.

11. Barry Green, owner of Barry's Landscape and Lawn Service, is currently planning for the fertilizing of the lawn at his largest account, Greenwood Community College. He has a fixed fee agreement, so it is to his advantage to minimize the cost he incurs in fertilizing the lawn. The contract between Barry's and Greenwood specifies that at least 10 pounds of nitrogen, seven pounds of phosphorus and five pounds of potash will be placed on the lawn. Barry can purchase three different fertilizers from his supplier. The amount of nitrogen, phosphorus, and potash in 100 pounds of each of the three fertilizers, as well as the cost per 100 pounds, is shown in the table below. Barry can buy as much of these fertilizers as he wants and can mix the different fertilizers together himself if he so desires, before applying the fertilizer to the lawn.

The data represent the number of lbs. of each nutrient present in 100 lbs. of each fertilizer type.

Fertilizer Type	Nitrogen	Phosphorus	Potash	Cost
1.	3	2	5	$4.50
2.	1	4	4	$6.00
3.	2	5	5	$8.00

Using the guidelines suggested in this chapter, formulate a model which will allow fertilization of the lawn at least cost.

12. Set up a spreadsheet for Barry Green's problem (see Problem 11). Using trial and error, attempt to find the optimal solution. Your spreadsheet should allow you to easily determine the feasibility of any solution.

13. A company specializing in fuel additives has decided to produce two new products, A and B. There is currently excess capacity at two of the company's processing plants in Lexington, KY and San Jose, CA. The available capacity per month (in hours) is 15 in Lexington and 50 in San Jose. Projections of demand for the two new products for the next month are 500 gallons of A and 650 gallons of B. Each gallon of A takes 1 minute to process and each gallon of B takes 2 minutes. Because of differences in the cost of labor and natural resources in the two locations, the cost per gallon for each of the products differs by location. Each gallon of product A costs $1.20 to produce in Lexington and $1.90 in San Jose. Each gallon of B costs

$1.00 in Lexington and $1.90 in San Jose. Use the guidelines in this chapter to develop a model that will minimize the cost of production while meeting demand projections.

14. An oil change costs $15 and must be performed every 3,000 miles. Develop a mathematical model showing the monthly cost of oil changes for x miles driven per day. (What assumptions must you make?)

15. A rock concert promoter knows that if ticket prices are $20, a capacity crowd of 12,000 can be expected for a certain concert. However, at higher prices, fewer people will be expected to attend. The promoter feels that for each $1 increase in price, 300 fewer tickets will be sold.

    a. Construct a model for revenue as a function of the *additional* premium charged over the base price of $20.

    b. Construct a model for revenue as a function of the ticket price itself, and show that this model is equivalent to the one developed in part a.

16. An investor has $100,000 to invest. She has 25 different stocks under consideration. The expected return over the next year for each stock has been estimated. For diversification, she wishes to restrict the amount invested in any one stock to no more than $5000. Obviously, she wants to maximize her return.

    a. Develop an influence diagram for this problem.

    b. Define the controllable and uncontrollable variables.

    c. How is this problem similar to the advertising strategy model discussed in this chapter? How is it different?

17. A forest fire is burning down a narrow valley 3 miles wide at a speed of 40 feet per minute. The fire can be contained by cutting a fire break through the forest across the valley. It takes 30 seconds for one person to clear one foot of the firebreak. The value of lost timber is $4000 per square mile. Each person hired is paid $12 per hour, and it costs $30 to transport and supply each person with the appropriate equipment.

    Construct a mathematical model for determining how many people should be sent to contain the fire, and for determining the best location for the firebreak. Develop a spreadsheet to help you in finding the optimal solution.[4]

18. A company produces a single product whose demand varies significantly by quarter; demand projections for the upcoming four quarters are 2,500, 1,000, 3,200, and 2,700 units. Seasonal variations in the availability of a raw material used in producing the product cause its per unit production cost to vary over time. The cost per unit for production in the next four quarters is expected to be $120, $100, $125, and $120. The holding cost per unit is expected to be $15 per unit for the next quarter and is expected to remain at that level for all four quarters. Develop a model that will satisfy demand and yield the cost minimizing production plan.

19. A model that represents the cost of electricity in an office workroom is shown below.

$$\text{Cost} = [n/m + (1 - n/m)(1 - p)]WNC/1{,}000$$

where

$$W = \text{wattage/bulb}$$
$$N = \text{number of bulbs in the system}$$
$$C = \text{cost of electricity (\$/kwh)}$$
$$n = \text{usage (people/hour)}$$
$$1/m = \text{average time used per person}$$
$$p = \text{proportion of people who turn the lights off}$$

---

[4]This is a simplified version of a real application studied by G. M. Parks, "Development and Application of a Model for Suppression of Forest Fires," *Management Science*, Vol. 10, pp. 760–766 (1964).

Suppose that $n = 3$, $m = 10$, $W = 75$, $N = 10$, $C = \$.0142$, and $p = 0.6$. Show the sensitivity of the cost with respect to changes in n, C and p (individually). Draw a graph of the cost as a function of changes in these parameters.

20. A natural gas pipeline is to be run from a supply terminal across a river that is 1,000 yards wide to a factory that is 2,500 yards downstream. The construction cost is \$28 per yard underground and \$24 per yard under water. Construct a mathematical model to determine the best configuration of the pipeline (i.e., how much should be under water and how much underground) to minimize the total cost. Use a spreadsheet to find the optimal solution.

IV. Projects and Cases

1. Select a real system and a decision problem with which you are familiar. Write a report analyzing the issues in developing a model for this decision problem using the issues discussed in this chapter.

2. An effective transportation system is essential in today's society. However, the cost of transportation is continually increasing, and transportation issues have therefore become areas of controversy in urban areas. One important facet of the transportation planning process is the availability and quality of parking. Parking locations, particularly in the central business district, must be convenient and reasonably priced. Moreover, parking availability affects the environment and the modes of transportation chosen by a community's citizens. Lack of adequate parking facilities increases the demand for alternative transportation such as mass transit.

Some of the more critical questions that must be answered are
   a. Where should parking facilities be located?
   b. Should new facilities be constructed, or should old ones be expanded?
   c. How many vehicles should each facility be equipped to serve?
   d. Should the facilities be open lots or enclosed garages? Self-service or attendant-operated?
   e. What price structure should be established?
   f. When should facilities be constructed to anticipate future demands and integrate effectively with other aspects of transportation planning?

Construct an influence diagram that describes the salient features and relationships of this problem. How might management science models address these problems? What types of models might be used? Discuss the factors discussed under "Recognizing Problems" in Chapter 1 that will influence the modeling process.

3. A music club offers new members four free compact discs upon signing up. The member need only buy *one* CD within the next year at half price and then receives three more CDs free. The member may cancel at anytime thereafter. Clearly, the music club must make a profit or it would not stay in business. How might you develop a model to determine the club's expected profits (at net present value) over, say, a five-year period? What factors influence the decision to offer such an incentive to join (draw an influence diagram)? Use the guidelines given under "Good Spreadsheet Design for Model Building" in Chapter 2 to propose a useful model.

4. The American Baseball League consists of 14 teams organized into two divisions: the Western Division—with Seattle, Oakland, California, Texas, Kansas City, Minnesota, and Chicago—and the Eastern Division—with Milwaukee, Detroit, Cleveland, Toronto, Baltimore, New York and Boston. One of the issues facing the League each year is the assignment of umpire crews to the series during the course of the season. A series consists of two, three, or four consecutive games with the same opponent in the same city.

Several considerations must be taken into account. Of primary concern is achieving a balance among assignments. A particular umpire crew should be assigned approximately an equal number of times with each team during the season, and these assignments should be spread rather evenly throughout the schedule. A second concern is to reduce excessive travel.

A number of other requirements must be satisfied.

1. A crew cannot travel from city A to city B if the last game in city A is a night game and the first game in city B is a day game on the next day.
2. A crew cannot travel from any West coast city to Chicago or any Eastern Division city without a day off.
3. Any crew traveling from a night game on the West coast to Kansas City or Texas must have a day off.
4. No crew should be assigned to the same team for two or more consecutive series.

Questions:

a. How would you define the decision variables in this problem?
b. What uncontrollable variables would be important in this problem?
c. Can you identify any constraints?
d. What is the appropriate objective function? Could there be more than one?
e. Would computers be important in solving this problem?
f. What social or political issues might affect any solution?
g. Develop an influence diagram that relates the major variables in the problem.
h. Why might you believe that management science techniques could be appropriate?

5. A county engineer contacted a consultant for some assistance. He had received an MBA, taken a course in management science, and was convinced that there was a better way to route the salt trucks and snow plows in his county. He was on the verge of purchasing new trucks because the current fleet was unable to meet demand adequately. At a cost of at least $75,000 per truck, this was an important problem.

    During an interview, the engineer revealed that the county had 12 trucks that were dispatched from a central location and assigned to 12 routes. These routes were formed after geographically partitioning the county into 12 regions. Some trucks, however, could not salt their entire route in one load but had to return to the salt depot to refill. Data on the road network, truck capacities, salting rates, average vehicle speeds, and so forth were readily available.

    Several problems were raised, including, How can we keep critical road segments clear by rush hour? How can we revise routing plans for contingencies (equipment breakdowns, for example)? How many trucks should be purchased (do they come in different sizes)? The county was interested in making the amount of deadheading (not to be confused with fans of the Grateful Dead—rather, time on the route that is not spent on productive work) as small as possible, as well as minimizing the time to service all roads in the county. The routes had to be chosen so that no vehicle salt capacity is exceeded.

    Questions:

    a. How would you define the decision variables in this problem?
    b. What uncontrollable variables would be important in this problem?
    c. Can you identify any constraints?
    d. What is the appropriate objective function? Could there be more than one?
    e. How important would information technology be in solving the engineer's problem?
    f. What social or political issues might affect any solution?
    g. Develop an influence diagram that relates the major variables in the problem.
    h. Why might you believe that management science techniques could be appropriate?

REFERENCES

Evans, James R. "Spreadsheets and Optimization: Complementary Tools for Decision Making," *Production and Inventory Management*, First Quarter, 1986, pp. 36–45.

Homer, Jack B. and Christian L. St. Clair. "A Model of HIV Transmission through Needle Sharing," *Interfaces*, Vol. 21, No. 3, May–June 1991, pp. 26–49.

Machol, R. E. and A. Barnett. "Thunderstorms and Aviation Safety—A Dialogue," *Interfaces*, Vol. 18, No. 2, March–April 1988, pp. 20–27.

Morris, W. T. "On the Art of Modeling," *Management Science*, Vol. 13, No. 12, August 1967, pp. B-707–717.

Morrison, D. G. and R. D. Wheat. "Misapplications Reviews: Pulling the Goalie Revisited," *Interfaces*, Vol. 16, No. 6, November–December 1986, pp . 28–34.

Tersine, R. J. and E. T. Grasso, "Models: A Structure for Managerial Decision Making," *Industrial Management*, Vol. 21, March–April, 1979, pp. 6–11.

Woolsey, G., "A Requiem for the EOQ: An Editorial," *Production and Inventory Management*, Vol. 29, No. 3, Third Quarter 1988, pp. 68–72.

APPENDIX: DERIVATION OF THE EOQ FORMULA

The total annual cost is

$$\text{TC} = DC_0/Q + iCQ/2$$

To find the order quantity that minimizes cost, we set the derivative $d\,\text{TC}/dQ$ equal to zero and solve for Q:

$$d\,\text{TC}/dQ = -DC_0/Q^2 + iC/2 = 0$$
$$iCQ^2 = 2DC_0$$
$$Q^2 = 2DC_0/iC$$
$$Q = \sqrt{2DC_0/iC}$$

To verify that this is indeed the minimum cost solution, we check the second derivative:

$$d^2\text{TC}/dQ^2 = 2DC_0/Q^3$$

Since the value of the second derivative is positive for all positive values of Q, this proves that we have found the minimum cost solution.

PART 2

DETERMINISTIC MODELS IN MANAGEMENT SCIENCE

CHAPTER 4

LINEAR

PROGRAMMING

(LP)

MODELING

INTRODUCTION

- The U.S. Forest Service is responsible for the management of 191 million acres of national forest land that produces 12 billion board feet of timber, 200 million visitor recreation days, and 10 million animal unit months of grazing annually. The lands are contained in 154 designated national forests managed by supervisors in 121 forest offices. Nearly all of the 121 offices use large and complex linear programming models to perform forest-level planning. Linear programming models are used to allocate forest land to different management strategies in order to maximize the discounted net value of land and to schedule maintenance and product flows [Field, 1984].

- GE Capital provides credit card services for a consumer credit business that exceeds $12 billion in total outstanding dollars. Managing delinquent accounts is a problem of paramount importance to the profitability of the company. Different collection strategies may be used for delinquent accounts, including mailed letters, interactive taped telephone messages, live telephone calls, and legal procedures. Accounts are categorized by outstanding balance and expected payment performance, which is based on factors like customer demographics and payment history. GE uses a multiple time period linear programming model to determine the most effective collection strategy to apply to its various categories of delinquent accounts. This approach has reduced annual losses due to delinquency by $37 million [Makuch et al., 1992].

- Citgo Petroleum Corporation used a variety of management science and statistical techniques to improve profits by roughly $70 million per year. A major component of the systems approach is the use of linear programming. Multiple period linear programming models are used at the refineries to determine optimal run levels for various products based on resource usage and product yields, to determine optimal crude and feedstock acquisition, and to control the cost of inventory. Citgo management estimates that the manufacturing LP model and the resulting improvements in refinery management saved approximately $50 million (in 1985) through improvements in refinery yield and reduced labor costs [Klingman et al., 1987].

Each of these examples involves planning in order to optimize some objective. For example, the objective of GE capital is to maximize net collections, Citgo seeks to minimize costs, and the U.S. Forest Service seeks to maximize land value. In addition, these planning problems involve limited resources such as personnel, equipment, and wood harvesting capacity. All organizations have similar objectives and all are faced with limited resources that make attaining these objectives challenging. When we formulate these problems mathematically, we call them *mathematical programming problems*.

A *mathematical programming problem* is a problem in which we seek to maximize or minimize some objective function in the presence of restrictions, which can be represented mathematically using inequalities and equalities.

Clearly, we cannot express all managerial decision problems as mathematical programming problems. However, we can model and solve a wide variety of practical planning and operational problems with mathematical programming. The term "programming" was coined because these models find the best "program," or course of action, to follow.

The U.S. Forest Service, GE Capital, and Citgo Petroleum all use a particular type of mathematical programming model known as a *linear program (LP)*. Linear programming is the subject of this chapter; other types of mathematical programming models will be discussed in Chapters 7, 8, and 9.

THE STRUCTURE OF LINEAR PROGRAMMING MODELS

We have already seen examples of linear programming models in Chapters 1 and 2. The product mix model (Example 3) and the media selection model (Example 5) in Chapter 1 are linear programming models.

Recall that the product mix example concerned the question of how many LaserStop and SpeedBuster radar detectors to make in order to maximize profit. We defined the controllable variables of the model as LS = the number of units of LaserStop to produce and SB = the number of units of SpeedBuster to produce. The objective is to maximize profit. Each LaserStop yields a profit of $24, and each SpeedBuster gives a profit of $40. However, profit maximization is restricted by the fact that there are limited quantities of the two components that both products require. Only 6,000 units of component A and 3,500 units of component B are available. Each LaserStop requires 12 units of component A and six units of component B. Each SpeedBuster requires 12 units of component A and 10 units of B. The model developed in Chapter 1 is as follows:

$$\text{Maximize } 24\,\text{LS} + 40\,\text{SB} \quad \text{Objective Function}$$

$$\text{subject to}$$

$$12\,\text{LS} + 12\,\text{SB} \leq 6,000$$

$$6\,\text{LS} + 10\,\text{SB} \leq 3,500 \quad \text{Constraints}$$

$$\text{LS, SB} \geq 0$$

This product mix model is a linear programming model with two nonnegative controllable (decision) variables, two constraints (not counting nonnegativity restrictions), and a maximization objective. The uncontrollable parameters (or model inputs) are the profit per unit for each product, the per-unit requirements for the limited components for each product, and the number of units of each component available. In terms of general linear programming terminology, we refer to the profit per unit as *objective function coefficients*, the per-unit requirements for the limited components for each product as *constraint coefficients*, and the quantities of component A and B (as well as the 0 in the nonnegativity restrictions) as the *right-hand side values*.

What characteristics of this mathematical model make it a *linear* program? We answer this question next.

Characteristics of Linear Programs

Recall from Chapter 1 that models can be categorized as logical or mathematical, prescriptive, predictive or descriptive, and deterministic or probabilistic. How would we classify an LP model such as the product mix example? LP models are certainly mathematical since they involve mathematical functions and relationships. Furthermore, since we are maximizing or minimizing the objective function, that is, finding the **best** course of action, LPs are prescriptive. Finally, since the inputs to these models are assumed to be known and fixed, LPs are deterministic. For example, in the product mix problem, the profit per unit, per-unit component requirements, and the availability are known constants.

We have previously mentioned that the term "program" in linear programming refers to the fact that in solving these models, we are seeking the best "program" or course of action to follow, according to our objective. What is the significance of the adjective "linear"?

> To be a *linear* program, the following three conditions must be met.
> 1. The objective and constraints must be represented using *linear functions* of the decision variables.
> 2. Constraints must be of a $\leq$, $\geq$, or = type.
> 3. Variables can assume any fractional numerical value.

The first condition means that all decision variables can be raised *only* to the first power and can be multiplied *only* by a constant term. Therefore, nonlinear terms such as x^2, xy, and 2^x are prohibited. The linearity assumption implies that with respect to the decision variables, the rate of change of the objective function and constraints is always a constant. For example, in the product mix example, the unit profit of a product is the same for every unit, regardless of volume.

The second condition states that constraints in a linear program must be represented with inequalities ($\leq$, $\geq$) or equalities (=). A constraint using a strict inequality ($<$ or $>$) is therefore not permitted. To see why, suppose we have the problem

$$\text{Maximize } x$$

$$\text{subject to}$$

$$x + 4y < 5$$

You can see that $x = 5$ is not feasible. Can you find any value of x that maximizes the objective and is feasible? For any value of x strictly less than 5, we can always find a number closer to 5 that gives a larger value for the objective function. Therefore, such a constraint does not define a limit that allows us to effectively search for an optimal solution.

The third condition is that decision variables are allowed to assume any fractional values. Many problems deal with commodities for which fractional quantities are valid, such as problems involving fluids or the allocation of time or funds. Also, models whose decision variables are rates—for example, the number of units to produce per day—can have fractional values. The fraction is simply work in process at the end of the day.

On the other hand, suppose that we are trying to decide the number of different models of high-cost machine tools to purchase. In this case, fractional values do not make sense. If the LP solution is 8.6, dropping the .6 or rounding to 9 could have serious resource and cost implications. Since we cannot purchase or effectively use .6 of a machine, we would require a model and solution method that *forces* the variables to assume integer values. Such models are known as *integer linear programming* models. In general, integer linear programs are simply linear programs with integer restrictions placed on the decision variables. We will discuss integer linear programs in Chapter 8.

For now, we will also assume that all decision variables must be nonnegative; that is, greater than or equal to zero. This is not a limiting restriction in most applications, and as we shall see in Chapter 7, can be overcome through a clever modeling technique. These assumptions ensure that the model has all of the characteristics required to use solution techniques developed especially for linear programs. In Chapter 5 we will provide intuitive explanations of the techniques and discussions as to why these assumptions are needed.

In the next section, we discuss the process of building LP models.

BUILDING LP MODELS

No matter what your future job may be, and regardless of whether you work in a service or manufacturing operation, you will be more effective if you can recognize problems that can be solved using management science. How can you determine if a decision problem can be modeled and solved using a linear programming model? The following questions provide some guidance.

1. Can the objective be stated clearly as a linear function that should be maximized or minimized?
2. Can all of the important restrictions be defined and expressed as linear inequalities or equalities?
3. Are all of the assumptions of a linear program satisfied?
4. Are the required input data available, and can the data be trusted?

If you can answer "yes" to these questions, then you can benefit from using an LP model. Of course, the estimated cost associated with model development—debugging, data collection and verification, and solution—must be weighed against the potential benefits associated with the solution. The issues discussed in Chapters 1 and 3 should be reviewed.

Three helpful questions can assist you in developing an LP model:

1. *What am I trying to decide?* Define the appropriate variables that represent decisions you can control.
2. *What is the objective to be maximized or minimized?* Write the objective function as a linear function of the decision variables.
3. *How is the problem restricted?* Write the constraints as linear functions of the decision variables with ≤, ≥, or = relationships.

We elaborate on each of these three pieces of LP modeling in the following sections.

Defining Decision Variables

What am I trying to decide? By answering this question, you will be forced to define what outputs or solution you expect from the analysis. By defining what you mean by a solution to the problem, you have defined the *decision variables* for the LP model. For example, in the product mix example, we needed to know how many LaserStops and SpeedBusters to produce. This led us to the decision variables LS = number of LaserStops to produce and SB = number of SpeedBusters to produce.

Building the Objective Function

What is the objective to be maximized or minimized? The answer to this question will often be straightforward once the decision variables have been defined. For example, for the product mix scenario, we obviously wanted to know how many LaserStops and SpeedBusters to produce *to maximize profit*. Because we were given the per-unit profit for each product, we were able to describe profit as a linear function of the decision variables. However, it is important that you understand exactly what is meant by profit in linear programming models. This requires that you thoroughly understand the difference between fixed and variable costs.

When building a linear programming model it is important to understand which costs are relevant to the decision under consideration and which costs have no bearing on that decision. *Fixed costs*, sometimes referred to as *sunk costs*, do not affect the optimal strategy because these costs have already been incurred or have to be incurred regardless of the decision made. *Variable costs* are those *incremental costs* incurred based on the decision. Only variable costs relative to the decision being made should be included in the model.

> Sunk costs should not be included in linear programming models.

As an example, consider the radar detector product mix model. We have 6,000 units of component A and 3,500 units of component B on hand. If the company owns these components, then the cost of these components is a sunk cost. Since the cost has already been incurred, that cost is no longer relevant to the decision we need to make. Our objective is to now utilize these materials (units of component A and B) in an optimal fashion, but there is nothing we can do about the cost of these goods!

To see this mathematically, suppose that each component A costs us \$.01 and each unit of component B costs \$.02. Then we can write our objective in terms of *net profit* as

$$\text{Max } 24\,\text{LS} + 40\,\text{SB} - .01(6{,}000) - .02(3{,}500)$$

or

$$\text{Max } 24\,\text{LS} + 40\,\text{SB} - 130$$

There is clearly nothing we can do in terms of our decision variables in order to change the deduction of \$130 we must take for the cost of the components; all we can do is to maximize the sum of the first two terms of the objective function. Maximizing net profit is the same as maximizing our original objective function, in the sense that the same optimal values of LS and SB will be given (the way to maximize net profit is to maximize our original objective function).

In accounting terms, the coefficients of $24 and $40 are really *per-unit contribution margins*. They are the per-unit contribution toward the payoff of fixed costs and profit. In linear programming models, we will often refer to a profit maximizing objective function. It is important that you realize that *profit* here means contribution to fixed costs and profit, and that fixed costs are not explicitly included in the model because they are not relevant to the decision being made.

Of course, not all LP models have profit maximization as their objective. Examples of other objectives include variable cost minimization, maximization of machine utilization, minimization of inventory, and so forth.

Building the Constraint Set

When constructing the constraints of the problem, we must be able to describe the restrictions of the problem as linear functions of the decision variables with $\leq$, $\geq$, or $=$ relationships. Often, it is helpful to think of the constraint as *forcing a relationship between two entities*. For example, in the product mix problem we know that the number of units of component A used cannot exceed the number of units of A available. The number of units of A used is $12\,LS + 12\,SB$. This must be less-than-or-equal-to the number available: 6,000, or $12\,LS + 12\,SB \leq 6,000$. This is a typical resource usage constraint where the entity *usage of the resource* cannot exceed the entity *resource availability*. As described in Chapter 3, influence diagrams can be helpful in visualizing and organizing these relationships.

Most restrictions in a problem can be gleaned from a careful reading of the scenario. This was the case for the product mix model with regard to the usage and availability of the two components A and B. We refer to restrictions that are explicitly stated in the scenario as *explicit constraints*. *Implicit constraints* are those which are not explicitly stated in the problem, but are required for the LP model to accurately model the scenario. A simple example of implicit constraints in the product mix model are the *nonnegativity restrictions* on the decision variables LS and SB. While not explicitly stated, it is clear that we cannot produce a negative number of LaserStops or SpeedBusters. To be mathematically precise, however, these constraints must be added to the model. Other types of implicit constraints are often required to relate decision variables to one another when one set of decision variables defines another. We will see these types of implicit constraints in some of the examples later in this chapter.

Dimensionality Checking

A quick verification of the correctness of any linear programming model is to check the dimensionality of the model. The dimension of a term in the model can be defined as the unit of measure of that term. Inconsistencies in dimensions within the objective function or within a particular constraint indicate that an error has been made in constructing the model.

> When building a linear programming model, you should always check the *dimensionality* of each term in the model. All terms in the objective function should have the same dimension. Likewise, all terms of each constraint should have the same dimensions.

We will illustrate a dimensionality check with the product mix LP.

$$\text{Maximize } 24\,\text{LS} + 40\,\text{SB} \quad \text{Objective Function}$$

subject to

$$12\,\text{LS} + 12\,\text{SB} \le 6{,}000$$

$$6\,\text{LS} + 10\,\text{SB} \le 3{,}500 \quad \text{Constraints}$$

$$\text{LS}, \text{SB} \ge 0$$

Consider the objective function term $24\,\text{LS}$. This term's dimensionality is (dollars/LaserStop)(quantity of LaserStops) = dollars. The term $40\,\text{SB}$ is likewise in dollars, so that the dimension of the objective function is dollars plus dollars = dollars.

What is the dimension of each of the constraints? Let's consider the first constraint. The right-hand side of the inequality is the number of units of component A available. Therefore, the mathematical expression on the left-hand side of the inequality, which represents the number of units of component A we use, should be in terms of the number of units of component A: (number of component A / LaserStop) (quantity of LaserStops) + (number of component A / SpeedBuster) (quantity of SpeedBusters) = (component A for LaserStops) + (component A for SpeedBusters). The component B constraint is similarly in units of component B.

While passing the dimensionality check does not necessarily imply that your model is correct, if your model fails the dimensionality check, you can be sure that your model is incorrect.

Next, we will use the modeling process described in this section to illustrate the development of several LP models.

Some Examples of LP Modeling

EXAMPLE 1. THE KNAPSACK PROBLEM

A simple example of a linear program is known as the knapsack problem. The name comes from the following scenario. A knapsack can be filled with some commodity up to a point where the weight becomes too much of a burden to carry. The problem is to maximize the value of the commodities carried while taking into account the weight restriction.

For example, consider the case of an independent trucker who can haul different liquid commodities in gallon containers. She has the option of four different commodities whose weights and profits per gallon are shown in Table 4.1. The volume of fluids will not be a problem until the weight restriction on the vehicle comes into play. The

Commodity:	1	2	3	4
Profit/gal.	$1.90	$1.02	$ .92	$2.40
lbs./gal.	3.4	2.0	1.6	4.3

maximum haul by weight is 1 ton (2,000 lbs.). What amounts of which commodities should be hauled in order to maximize profit?

As discussed in Chapter 1, influence diagrams are sometimes a useful first step in model development because they clarify how the pieces of the problem are related. An influence diagram of the trucking problem is shown in Figure 4.1. Let us use the three basic questions previously discussed to guide the formulation process.

What does the trucker need to decide? The amount of each commodity to haul. We can define decision variables to reflect this as follows:

$$COM1 = \text{number of gallons of commodity 1 hauled}$$
$$COM2 = \text{number of gallons of commodity 2 hauled}$$
$$COM3 = \text{number of gallons of commodity 3 hauled}$$
$$COM4 = \text{number of gallons of commodity 4 hauled}$$

What is the objective to be maximized or minimized? The trucker would like to maximize the profit realized from the haul. Since the profits per gallon are given in Table 4.1, we can calculate total profit from the haul as a linear function of the decision variables by simply multiplying the number of gallons hauled by the profit per gallon [(gallons)($/gallon) = $]. Summing over all four commodities gives total profit.

$$1.90\,COM1 + 1.02\,COM2 + .92\,COM3 + 2.40\,COM4$$

How is the problem restricted? The truck can haul a maximum of 1 ton (2,000 lbs.). This restriction must be represented by a constraint that relates the weight of the

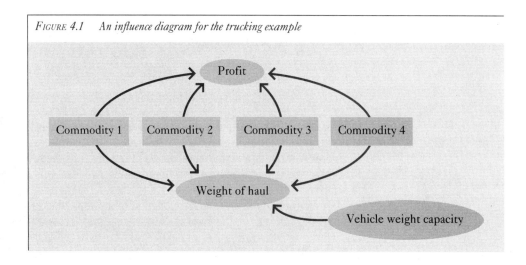

FIGURE 4.1   An influence diagram for the trucking example

haul to the truck's weight capacity. The weight of the haul can be represented as a function of the decision variables in a manner similar to total profit. The total weight of a particular commodity is the number of gallons hauled multiplied by the weight per gallon of that commodity [(lbs./gal.)(gals.) = lbs.]. The total weight of the haul is the sum of the weights over all four commodities and must not exceed 2,000 pounds. This restriction can be written as

$$3.4\,COM1 + 2.0\,COM2 + 1.6\,COM3 + 4.3\,COM4 \leq 2,000$$

Since it is impossible to carry a negative load, the decision variables must be restricted to be nonnegative. The entire LP model can now be stated as:

$$\text{Maximize } 1.90\,COM1 + 1.02\,COM2 + .92\,COM3 + 2.40\,COM4$$

$$\text{subject to}$$

$$3.4\,COM1 + 2.0\,COM2 + 1.6\,COM3 + 4.3\,COM4 \leq 2,000$$

$$COM1, COM2, COM3, COM4 \geq 0$$

Let us perform a dimensionality check of this model. The objective function terms are each of the form (profit/gallon) (gallons) = profit (in dollars). The left-hand side of the constraint is the sum of terms of the form (pounds/gallon) (gallons) = pounds, and the right-hand side is 2,000 pounds. Hence the model we have developed is consistent in its dimensionality.

Any linear program with only a single constraint (not counting the nonnegativity restrictions on the decision variables) is known as a knapsack problem. Such problems often arise in applications like the transport of goods, where commodities need to be packed into a transport vehicle, the design of cutting patterns in the clothing and paper industries, and the allocation of a fixed budget to various investment alternatives.

EXAMPLE 2. THE COLORADO CATTLE COMPANY

The Colorado Cattle Company (CCC) can purchase three types of raw feed ingredients from a wholesale distributor. The company's cattle have certain nutritional requirements with respect to fat, protein, calcium, and iron. Each cow requires at least 10 units of calcium, no more than 7.5 units of fat, at least 12 units of iron, and at least 15 units of protein per day. Table 4.2 shows the amount of fat, protein, calcium, and iron in each pound of the three feed ingredients. Grade 1 feed costs $.25, grade 2, $.10, and grade 3, $.08 per pound. The cattle can be fed a mixture of the three types

*TABLE 4.2
Colorado Cattle
Company data*

Feed Ingredients (Units Per Pound)		
	Grade 1	Grade 2	Grade 3
Calcium	.7	.8	0
Fat	.5	.6	.4
Iron	.9	.8	.8
Protein	.8	1.5	.9

of raw feed. CCC would like to feed its herd as cheaply as possible. This scenario is illustrated with an influence diagram in Figure 4.2.

What is the Colorado Cattle Company trying to decide? The objective is to minimize the cost of feeding the cattle. We can determine how to feed each cow at minimum cost while taking into account the nutritional requirements. Once we know how to feed a single cow at minimum cost , we can simply order the amounts required per cow times the number of cattle in the herd. What we really need to decide is how much of each feed ingredient to buy per cow per day.

We begin by defining decision variables to designate those quantities which we control that are as yet unknown. CCC has control over how much of each grade to feed a cow. We can therefore define the following:

GRADE1 = amount (in lbs.) of grade 1 to use per day in feeding a cow
GRADE2 = amount (in lbs.) of grade 2 to use per day in feeding a cow
GRADE3 = amount (in lbs.) of grade 3 to use per day in feeding a cow.

What is the objective to be maximized or minimized? The stated objective is to minimize the daily cost of feeding a cow. One of the three grades of feed, or a combination of the grades, can be used. The cost of feeding is simply the amount of each feed multiplied by its cost [(lbs.)($/lb.) = $] for each grade added together. The cost per day of feeding a cow can then be represented as

$$.25 \, \text{GRADE1} + .10 \, \text{GRADE2} + .08 \, \text{GRADE3}$$

How is the problem restricted? The daily nutritional requirements must be met. Consider the calcium requirement. The amount of calcium in the daily feed must be at least 10 units. As shown in the influence diagram in Figure 4.2, calcium enters the feed through grades 1 and 2 only. Each pound of grade 1 gives the cow .7 units of calcium and each pound of grade 2 gives .8. We can mathematically state the amount of calcium

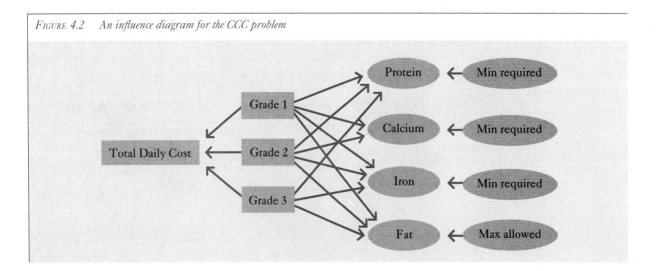

FIGURE 4.2   *An influence diagram for the CCC problem*

in the daily feed by multiplying the amount of each grade used by its contribution of calcium [(lbs.)(units/lb.) = units]. The requirement that the cow must have at least 10 units of calcium is expressed as

$$.7 \, GRADE1 + .8 \, GRADE2 + 0 \, GRADE3 \geq 10$$

The left-hand side of this inequality is simply the amount of calcium in the mix. That amount, in turn, must be at least 10 units, as shown on the right-hand side. Similarly for iron, the number of units in the daily feed must be at least the minimum requirement:

$$.9 \, GRADE1 + .8 \, GRADE2 + .8 \, GRADE3 \geq 12$$

and for protein:

$$.8 \, GRADE1 + 1.5 \, GRADE2 + .9 \, GRADE3 \geq 15$$

The fat restriction places an upper limit on how much fat can be included. The amount of fat in the feed is represented mathematically in the same fashion as the other nutrients, but it is related with a less-than-or-equal-to sign because we are given an upper bound on the amount that can be in the feed. Therefore, that requirement is expressed as

$$.5 \, GRADE1 + .6 \, GRADE2 + .4 \, GRADE3 \leq 7.5$$

Finally, while fairly obvious, it is also true that we cannot buy negative amounts of feed, so that each decision variable must be nonnegative. The complete linear program can now be stated as

Minimize $.25 \, GRADE1 + .1 \, GRADE2 + .08 \, GRADE3$ *Cost*

subject to

$$.7 \, GRADE1 + .8 \, GRADE2 + 0 \, GRADE3 \geq 10 \quad Calcium$$
$$.9 \, GRADE1 + .8 \, GRADE2 + .8 \, GRADE3 \geq 12 \quad Iron$$
$$.8 \, GRADE1 + 1.5 \, GRADE2 + .9 \, GRADE3 \geq 15 \quad Protein$$
$$.5 \, GRADE1 + .6 \, GRADE2 + .4 \, GRADE3 \leq 7.5 \quad Fat$$
$$GRADE1, GRADE2, GRADE3 \geq 0$$

Some classes of linear programming models have such wide applicability that they have been given special names. The LaserStop and SpeedBuster LP, as we have seen, falls into the general class of LPs known as *product mix problems*, because it deals with optimizing some objective (profit) by determining the mix of products to produce, while also satisfying resource availability requirements. Likewise, as discussed in Example 1, many problems can be classified as *knapsack problems*. The Colorado Cattle Company problem is an example of a general LP known as the *diet problem*. The diet problem concerns the minimization of the cost of a diet which meets certain minimum nutritional requirements.

While you will often encounter completely unique decision-making scenarios, you will enhance your modeling ability by understanding these generic categories of problems. Often your scenario will fall into one of these categories with some special twist. For example, you might solve a diet LP which minimizes the amount of red meat in your diet while meeting the recommended daily nutritional requirements and remaining within a budget constraint. Though slightly different from the CCC scenario, the structure of the constraint set for the nutritional requirements will be very similar. We will be discussing a variety of other classes of LP problems later in this chapter. Before doing so, however, we wish to discuss the importance of using linear programming from an intuitive point of view.

TRADE-OFFS, THE POWER OF LINEAR PROGRAMMING SOLUTIONS

In this section we discuss trial-and-error solutions of spreadsheet models in order to gain insight into the interactions between variables and the trade-offs between the objective function and constraints in LP models. Obviously, the drawback to trial-and-error approaches is that there is no guarantee that you will find the optimal solution. In fact, as we shall see, with trial-and-error approaches, it can be difficult to find a *feasible* solution, much less an optimal solution. Fortunately, we have software packages that can find optimal solutions to LP models very easily. These packages, which are even available in the spreadsheet environment, have rendered the trial-and-error approach to solving LP models obsolete. In the next chapter we will discuss the LINDO solver, as well as the LP solvers now available in LOTUS 1-2-3 and EXCEL.

EXAMPLE 3. TRIAL-AND-ERROR APPROACH TO THE KNAPSACK PROBLEM

For convenience, the knapsack problem in Example 1 is repeated below.

$$\text{Maximize } 1.90\,COM1 + 1.02\,COM2 + .92\,COM3 + 2.40\,COM4$$

subject to

$$3.4\,COM1 + 2.0\,COM2 + 1.6\,COM3 + 4.3\,COM4 \leq 2,000$$
$$COM1, COM2, COM3, COM4 \geq 0$$

Figure 4.3 shows a LOTUS 1-2-3 spreadsheet model of this scenario. With the exception of cells B22, C22, B24, and B15 through B18, all cells are simply data or label cells. Cells B15 through B18 hold the quantities of commodities 1 through 4 to haul. These cells correspond to the decision variables of our model. B24 contains of the formula "+C6*B15 + C7*B16 + C8*B17 + C9*B18" which computes the objective function value (profit), given the values placed in cells B15 through B18. Note that we could also use the @SUMPRODUCT function to describe this, namely @SUMPRODUCT (C6..C9, B15..B18).Cell B22 contains the formula "+B6*B15 + B7*B16 + B8*B17 + B9*B18;" that is, the weight of the haul, given the values in cells B15 through B18. Finally, cell C22 gives the amount of unused weight capacity (+B10−B22). Note that if cell C22 has a negative value, the load is too heavy for the truck (the capacity constraint of our model is violated).

As we saw in Chapter 2, spreadsheets like the one in Figure 4.3 provide a way to evaluate various alternatives in terms of feasibility and objective function value. By intelligently selecting values to haul, we can attempt to find a feasible solution with high profit. Figure 4.3 shows the resulting weight required and profit generated

FIGURE 4.3   *Spreadsheet model for Example 1, Trucking Problem*

A	A	B	C	D
1	Trucking Problem Model			
2				
3	*Parameters and uncontrollable variables:*			
4				
5	Commodity	Pounds/gal.	Profit/gal.	
6	1	3.4	$1.90	
7	2	2	$1.02	
8	3	1.6	$0.92	
9	4	4.3	$2.40	
10	Availability	2000		
11				
12	*Decision Variables:*			
13				
14	Commodity	Gallons		
15	1	500		
16	2	0		
17	3	0		
18	4	0		
19				
20	*Model Outputs:*			
21		Used	Unused	
22	Weight	1700	300	
23				
24	Profit	$950.00		

Selected cell formulas

A	A	B	C
20	*Model Outputs:*		
21		Used	Unused
22	Weight	+B6*B15+B7*B16+B8*B17+B9*B18	+B10-B22
23			
24	Profit	+C6*B15+C7*B16+C8*B17+C9*B18	

by hauling 500 gallons of commodity 1. Notice that we have 300 pounds of weight capacity remaining. The weight restriction being the only real operational constraint, there is no reason not to use all of the capacity (to maximize profit, the trucker should always carry as much as the truck can handle). A trial-and-error approach might begin by selecting the commodity with the highest profit per gallon. This would lead to the selection of commodity 4. The truck can haul 465.11627 gallons of commodity $4(2000/4.3 = 465.11627)$, which will give a profit of $1,116.28. This solution is shown in Figure 4.4a. We can proceed with a trial-and-error approach by checking the resulting profit for solution by hauling only commodity 1, only commodity 2, and only commodity 3, in order to see if any of these yield a profit higher than the $1,116.28 we have found. These solutions are shown in Figures 4.4b, 4.4c, and 4.4d. Of the four solutions we generated, the highest profit is achieved by hauling 1,250 gallons of commodity 3. We could continue to investigate solutions involving more than one type of commodity. However, by using an LP solver we can find that the optimal solution is to haul 1,250 gallons of commodity 3 (and none of commodities 1, 2, and 4) for a

FIGURE 4.4a   Solution to Example 1, only commodity 4

	A	B	C	D
1	Trucking Problem Model			
2				
3	Parameters and uncontrollable variables:			
4				
5	Commodity	Pounds/gal	Profit/gal.	
6	1	3.4	$1.90	
7	2	2	$1.02	
8	3	1.6	$0.92	
9	4	4.3	$2.40	
10	Availability	2000		
11				
12	Decision Variables:			
13				
14	Commodity	Gallons		
15	1	0		
16	2	0		
17	3	0		
18	4	465.1163		
19				
20	Model Outputs:			
21		Used	Unused	
22	Weight	2000	0	
23				
24	Profit	$1,116.28		

FIGURE 4.4b   Solution to Example 1, only commodity 1

	A	B	C	D
1	Trucking Problem Model			
2				
3	Parameters and uncontrollable variables:			
4				
5	Commodity	Pounds/gal	Profit/gal.	
6	1	3.4	$1.90	
7	2	2	$1.02	
8	3	1.6	$0.92	
9	4	4.3	$2.40	
10	Availability	2000		
11				
12	Decision Variables:			
13				
14	Commodity	Gallons		
15	1	588.2353		
16	2	0		
17	3	0		
18	4	0		
19				
20	Model Outputs:			
21		Used	Unused	
22	Weight	2000	0	
23				
24	Profit	$1,117.65		

FIGURE 4.4c   Solution to Example 1, only commodity 2

	A	B	C	D
1	Trucking Problem Model			
2				
3	Parameters and uncontrollable variables:			
4				
5	Commodity	Pounds/gal	Profit/gal.	
6	1	3.4	$1.90	
7	2	2	$1.02	
8	3	1.6	$0.92	
9	4	4.3	$2.40	
10	Availability	2000		
11				
12	Decision Variables:			
13				
14	Commodity	Gallons		
15	1	0		
16	2	1000		
17	3	0		
18	4	0		
19				
20	Model Outputs:			
21		Used	Unused	
22	Weight	2000	0	
23				
24	Profit	$1,020.00		

FIGURE 4.4d   Solution to Example 1, only commodity 3

	A	B	C	D
1	Trucking Problem Model			
2				
3	Parameters and uncontrollable variables:			
4				
5	Commodity	Pounds/gal	Profit/gal.	
6	1	3.4	$1.90	
7	2	2	$1.02	
8	3	1.6	$0.92	
9	4	4.3	$2.40	
10	Availability	2000		
11				
12	Decision Variables:			
13				
14	Commodity	Gallons		
15	1	0		
16	2	0		
17	3	1250		
18	4	0		
19				
20	Model Outputs:			
21		Used	Unused	
22	Weight	2000	0	
23				
24	Profit	$1,150.00		

total profit of $1,150. That is, this solution gives the highest profit of the solutions we generated and is in fact the best the trucker can achieve. Let us see why this solution makes sense. The key to understanding the solution is to realize that we must consider the *profit per pound* of capacity used for each commodity. For each liquid, profit per pound is profit per gallon divided by pounds per gallon [(profit/gal)/(lbs/gal) = profit/lb]. The profits generated per pound are $.5588, $.51, $.575, and $.5581 for commodities 1 through 4 respectively. Commodity 3 has the highest profit per pound and consequently is the commodity that maximizes *total* profit. The LP solution considers simultaneously the profit contribution and the contribution to the weight restriction.

We were lucky enough to find the optimal solution to the knapsack problem using trial and error. However, imagine trying to use this approach on a problem with many more variables and constraints. As the number of constraints and variables becomes larger, it becomes increasingly more difficult to assimilate all of the trade-offs involved. As the following Colorado Cattle Company example illustrates, just finding a feasible solution can sometimes be difficult, even for small models.

EXAMPLE 4. TRIAL-AND-ERROR APPROACH TO THE DIET PROBLEM

Consider the CCC example. Recall that the decision variables are how much of each grade to include in the feed per day:

$$\text{Minimize } .25\text{GRADE1} + .1\text{GRADE2} + .08\text{GRADE3}$$

subject to

$$.7\text{GRADE1} + .8\text{GRADE2} + 0\text{GRADE3} \geq 10 \quad \text{(Calcium)}$$

$$.9\text{GRADE1} + .8\text{GRADE2} + .8\text{GRADE3} \geq 12 \quad \text{(Iron)}$$

$$.8\text{GRADE1} + 1.5\text{GRADE2} + .9\text{GRADE3} \geq 15 \quad \text{(Protein)}$$

$$.5\text{GRADE1} + .6\text{GRADE2} + .4\text{GRADE3} \leq 7.5 \quad \text{(Fat)}$$

$$\text{GRADE1, GRADE2, GRADE3} \geq 0$$

Is the solution to this LP as obvious as the solution to the knapsack problem? The presence of multiple constraints makes this problem much more difficult. A naive approach might be to try to buy all grade 3 feed, since it is the cheapest, but this is impossible because there is no way that the calcium requirement can be met by using only grade 3. A solution containing only grade 3 will be infeasible; that is, it will not satisfy the constraint set.

Figure 4.5a shows a spreadsheet model for the CCC scenario. The decision variables are cells B15, C15, and D15. Cells C20, C21, C22, and C24 correspond to the left-hand side of the constraints in our LP model (C20 is B7*B15+C7*C15+D7*D15, C21 is B8*B15+C8*C15+D8*D15, and C22 is B9*B15+C9*C15+D9*D15). Cells C20, C21, and C22 indicate the amount by which the current solution is in excess of the minimum requirements (formulae B20−E7, B21−E8 and B22−E9). C24 indicates the amount by which the current solution falls short of the maximum amount of 7.5 units of fat (F10−B24). The cost function is given in cell B26

FIGURE 4.5   *Spreadsheet model for the Colorado Cattle Company*

	A	B	C	D	E	F
1	Colorado Cattle Company Model					
2						
3	Parameters and uncontrollable variables:					
4						
5	Grade	1	2	3		
6	Cost / lb.	$0.25	$0.10	$0.08	Minimum	Maximum
7	Calc. / lb.	0.7	0.8	0	10	
8	Iron / lb.	0.9	0.8	0.8	12	
9	Prot. / lb.	0.8	1.5	0.9	15	
10	Fat / lb.	0.5	0.6	0.4		7.5
11						
12	Decision Variables:					
13						
14	Grade	1	2	3		
15	Quantity	0	12.5	0		
16						
17						
18	Model Outputs:					
19		Amount	Excess			
20	Calcium	10	0			
21	Iron	10	-2			
22	Protein	18.75	3.75			
23		Amount	Available			
24	Fat	7.5	0			
25						
26	Total Cost	$1.25				

Selected cell formulas

	A	B	C
18	Model Outputs:		
19		Amount	Excess
20	Calcium	+B15*B7+C15*C7+D15*D7	+B20-E7
21	Iron	+B15*B8+C15*C8+D15*D8	+B21-E8
22	Protein	+B15*B9+C15*C9+D15*D9	+B22-E9
23		Amount	Available
24	Fat	+B15*B10+C15*C10+D15*D10	+F10-B24
25			
26	Total Cost	+B6*B15+C6*C15+D6*D15	

(B6*B15+C6*C15+D6*D15). Because grades 2 and 3 are the cheapest, perhaps we can find a feasible solution made up of these two grades. We need at least 12.5 pounds of grade 2 to meet the calcium requirement ((10 units)/(.8 units/lb) = 12.5 lbs), but that takes us exactly to the limit of fat (.6(12.5) = 7.5). Adding *any* grade 3 (to satisfy the iron restriction) will add fat and consequently violate the fat constraint. This leads to another infeasible solution, as demonstrated in the spreadsheet in Figure 4.5. (The −2 in cell C21 indicates that the solution of 12.5 pounds of grade 2 falls short of the iron requirement by two units).

Determining a feasible solution to an LP can be difficult. The beauty of the linear programming solution technique we will discuss in the next chapter (the approach used by LP solvers) is that it not only allows us to determine if feasible solutions exist, but to find the *best* solution (in terms of the objective function) by taking into account the trade-offs between contributions of decision variables in the constraints and the objective function.

The optimal solution for the Colorado Cattle Company generated by the LINDO LP solver is far less obvious than that of the knapsack problem: 8 pounds of grade 1, 5.5 pounds of grade 2, and .5 pounds of grade 3, for a total cost of $2.59 per cow per day. The solution is shown on our spreadsheet model in Figure 4.5b. Do you think you could have generated this solution by trial and error as we did for the trucking problem?

Somewhat counterintuitively, we are using only .5 lbs. of the cheapest grade. A look at the constraint set shows that grade 3 is relatively comparable to grade 2 in its contribution of fat and iron, but considerably lower in calcium and protein. Also, notice that the iron and calcium minimum requirements are met exactly and that this solution contains the maximum amount of fat allowed. As previously discussed, LPs consider the contributional trade-offs in arriving at the optimal solution. Another view is that LP solution techniques are able to determine which of the inequality constraints should hold exactly as equalities; that is, which resources or limitations cause the bottleneck in the process (keep us from doing even better). In the CCC solution in Figure 4.5b, if we could somehow lower the minimum requirements on calcium or iron, or raise the amount of fat allowed, we might be able to feed the cow for less than $2.59 per day.

Together, these two examples illustrate the fundamental power of linear programming. LP models provide a means of finding solutions that satisfy all of the restrictions

FIGURE 4.5b   Optimal Solution to the CCC model

	A	B	C	D	E	F
1	Colorado Cattle Company Model					
2						
3	Parameters and uncontrollable variables:					
4						
5	Grade	1	2	3		
6	Cost / lb.	$0.25	$0.10	$0.08	Minimum	Maximum
7	Calc. / lb.	0.7	0.8	0	10	
8	Iron / lb.	0.9	0.8	0.8	12	
9	Prot. / lb.	0.8	1.5	0.9	15	
10	Fat / lb.	0.5	0.6	0.4		7.5
11						
12	Decision Variables:					
13						
14	Grade	1	2	3		
15	Quantity	8	5.5	0.5		
16						
17						
18	Model Outputs:					
19		Amount	Excess			
20	Calcium	10	0			
21	Iron	12	0			
22	Protein	15.1	0.1			
23		Amount	Available			
24	Fat	7.5	0			
25						
26	Total Cost	$2.59				

of the problem *and* of determining the most efficient use of resources by *simultaneously* taking into account the restrictions and the objective function. The power of linear programming stems from the fact that the trade-offs among the constraints and between the constraints and the objective are considered systematically by the algorithm used to solve the LP. The algorithm the computer uses to solve LP models eliminates the need to use trial-and-error. In Chapter 5 we will provide an intuitive understanding of *how* computerized algorithms are able to solve LP models. Even very small problems can sometimes have less-than-obvious solutions (as in the CCC example). In practice, planning problems that are modeled as LPs having thousands of variables and thousands of constraints are routinely solved on microcomputers. Indeed, large LP models can have over a million variables.

MATHEMATICAL NOTATION FOR LP MODELS

When building larger and more complicated LP models, it is convenient to use something called a *subscripted decision variable*. By using subscripted variables rather than a larger variable name which is perhaps more immediately descriptive, we will be able to write larger LPs in a more compact from. Subscripted variables coupled with summation notation provide a convenient way to write many LP models in shorthand. We will often use subscripted variables and summation notation to simplify the presentation, so it is important that you have a complete understanding of them.

As an example, suppose that we are trying to decide how much of $100,000 to invest in each of four options: Certificates of Deposit, a Growth Mutual Fund, a Growth and Income Mutual Fund, and a Bond Mutual Fund. We could define the decision variables CD, GROWTH, G&I, and BOND as the amount in dollars to invest in each of these options. A constraint indicates that we can invest no more money than we have available can then be written as

$$CD + GROWTH + G\&I + BOND \leq 100,000$$

Instead of using these variable definitions, we could define the following subscripted variables:

$$x_i = \text{the amount in dollars to invest in option } i$$

with $i = 1,2,3,4$ corresponding to the four options in the order that they were listed ($i = 1$ is Certificates of Deposit, $i = 2$ is Growth Mutual Fund, etc.). In general, the subscript is used to denote various alternatives. Our constraint can now be written as

$$x_1 + x_2 + x_3 + x_4 \leq 100,000$$

We can also use summation notation to write the investment constraint in a more compact form. The symbol $\sum$ (the Greek letter sigma) is used to signify the addition of elements. The investment amount limitation can be expressed in summation notation as

$$\sum_{i=1}^{4} x_i \leq 100,000$$

Now suppose that the problem really has forty options rather than just four. Trying to write the above constraint with forty different descriptive variable names like we originally defined will be quite cumbersome. Using summation notation, it is just as easy to write a sum similar to the one above.

$$\sum_{i=1}^{40} x_i \leq 100{,}000$$

When convenient, particularly when discussing larger, more realistic models, we will use subscripted variables and summation notation.

APPLICATIONS OF LP MODELS

LP models have been used in virtually every area of business. In this section we continue to demonstrate the LP modeling process by illustrating the construction of LP model examples in operations management, finance, and marketing.

EXAMPLE 5. PRODUCTION PLANNING OVER TIME

Both GE Capital and Citgo applied multiple time period linear programming models in the scenarios described at the beginning of this chapter. We illustrate here the development of this type of model.

The planning department of a small company must determine aggregate production levels for a product over each of the next four quarters. Table 4.3 shows the relevant cost and demand data. The inventory holding cost is per unit and is based on the end-of-quarter inventory. The cost of production varies over time. There are currently 10 units in inventory. The company would like to know how many units to produce and how many units to hold in inventory each quarter, so as to satisfy demand at minimum cost.

What is the company trying to decide? Production levels for each of the next four quarters need to be determined. We can define the following decision variables:

$$q_i = \text{quantity to produce in quarter } i \quad i = 1, 2, 3, 4$$

What is the objective to be maximized or minimized? The company wishes to minimize total variable cost, which is made up of variable production costs and holding costs. In order to develop the appropriate objective function, we need to be able to represent each of these costs as a function of the decision variables. It is often easier to model—and to explain the meaning of the model—if explicit variables are defined for any entity that contributes to the objective. Certainly the production cost can be handled easily by taking the per-unit cost times the q_i for each quarter i ((Cost/unit)× (units)=cost). The other cost component, holding cost, must also be represented. We can define the following extra decision variables as

$$I_i = \text{inventory at the end of quarter } i \quad i = 1, 2, 3, 4$$

TABLE 4.3
Multi-period
production planning
problem data

Quarter	Demand	Production Cost/Unit	Inventory Holding Cost/Unit
1	100	$200	$10
2	150	$195	$10
3	120	$210	$10
4	180	$200	$10

The objective function can now be written as

$$\text{Min } 200q_1 + 195q_2 + 210q_3 + 200q_4 + 10I_1 + 10I_2 + 10I_3 + 10I_4$$

How is the problem restricted? The only explicit restriction in this problem is that demand must be satisfied. However, there is an implicit constraint set that is required. We must link the inventory variables to the production variables. The values of the inventory variables in a particular quarter are determined by the amounts of production and demand in that quarter, so they can be expressed as functions of the decision variables associated with production levels. Inventory levels, I_i, are defined by *inventory balance equations* which state that

ending inventory = beginning inventory + production − demand

These can be written in terms of our decision variables as

$$I_1 = 10 + q_1 - 100$$
$$I_2 = I_1 + q_2 - 150$$
$$I_3 = I_2 + q_3 - 120$$
$$I_4 = I_3 + q_4 - 180$$

Each of these equations is really an example of an implicit constraint which we mentioned in our discussion of the LP model building process. However, because the inventory variables are required to be nonnegative, these equations also ensure that the explicit restrictions that demand be met are enforced. A dimensionality check of these equations shows that the left and right-hand sides are each measured in units of product.

Consequently, the model in its entirety is

$$\text{Min } 200q_1 + 195q_2 + 210q_3 + 200q_4 + 10I_1 + 10I_2 + 10I_3 + 10I_4$$

subject to

$$I_1 = 10 + q_1 - 100$$
$$I_2 = I_1 + q_2 - 150$$
$$I_3 = I_2 + q_3 - 120$$
$$I_4 = I_3 + q_4 - 180$$
$$q_i, I_i \geq 0 \quad i = 1, 2, 3, 4$$

The solution to this model is to produce 90 units in quarter 1, 270 units in quarter 2 with 120 units held in inventory for quarter 3, produce no units in quarter 3, and 180 units in quarter 4. The total cost is $107,850 (production cost of $106,650 plus holding cost of $1,200).

EXAMPLE 6. VOHIO OIL BLENDING PROBLEM

Three input ingredients go into the production of two types of fuel at Vohio Oil. The major distinguishing feature of the two end products (regular and super) is the octane level required. Regular fuel must have a minimum octane level of 90, and super's level must be at least 100. The octane levels of the three inputs as well as their availability for the coming two-week period are known. Likewise, the maximum demand for the end products along with the revenue generated per barrel are known. These data are summarized in Table 4.4. Develop an LP model to determine how much of each end product to produce in order to maximize contribution to profit.

What is it that Vohio needs to decide? Vohio needs to decide how much of each input to use in the production of regular and super in order to maximize profit. Implicit in this decision is the decision of how much regular and super to produce. Let's define the following decision variables:

$$RB = \text{number of barrels of regular to produce for the two-week period}$$
$$SB = \text{number of barrels of super to produce for the two-week period}$$
$$R_i = \text{number of barrels of input } i \text{ used to make regular}$$
$$S_i = \text{number of barrels of input } i \text{ used to make super}$$

What is the objective to be maximized or minimized? Vohio would like to maximize profit (that is, contribution towards fixed costs and profit). The objective function can thus be stated mathematically as

$$\text{Max } 18.5\,RB + 20\,SB - 16.5R_1 - 16.5S_1 - 14R_2 - 14S_2 - 17.5R_3 - 17.5S_3$$

How is the problem restricted? First, we know that we have limited amounts of inputs 1, 2, and 3. We can use these inputs in the production of regular or super fuel. We can express the availability of the inputs using inequalities:

TABLE 4.4
Data for the Vohio Oil Company blending problem

Input	Cost/bbl.	Octane	Available (barrels)
1	16.50	100	110,000
2	14.00	87	350,000
3	17.50	110	300,000

	Revenue/barrel	Max Demand (barrels)
Regular	18.50	350,000
Super	20.00	500,000

$$R_1 + S_1 \le 110,000$$
$$R_2 + S_2 \le 350,000$$ *availability*
$$R_3 + S_3 \le 300,000$$

We assume that inputs 1, 2, and 3 are the only inputs into regular and super. Therefore, the amount of regular produced is simply the sum of the amounts of inputs 1, 2, and 3 we decide to use in the production of regular (and similarly for super).

$$\text{RB} = R_1 + R_2 + R_3$$
$$\text{SB} = S_1 + S_2 + S_3$$ *3 suppliers*

We have upper bounds on the amounts of regular and super we should produce:

$$\text{RB} \le 350,000$$

$$\text{SB} \le 500,000$$

The octane requirements define the two products. We need to enforce the octane requirement of 90 for regular and 100 for super. Regular, for example, will have an octane level dependent on which percentage of the total comes from input 1, 2, or 3. Hence, we can think of the octane level as a weighted average of the octane levels of the inputs, where the weights are the fraction of the total made up of that input. For regular produced, the octane level will be

$$(100)\frac{R_1}{\text{RB}} + (87)\frac{R_2}{\text{RB}} + (110)\frac{R_3}{\text{RB}}$$ *Octane*

Furthermore, this octane level for regular must be at least 90.

$$(100)\frac{R_1}{\text{RB}} + (87)\frac{R_2}{\text{RB}} + (110)\frac{R_3}{\text{RB}} \ge 90$$

Note that this equation is nonlinear, because we have decision variables divided by other decision variables. We can however, linearize the constraint by multiplying both sides of the inequality by *RB*, which yields

$$100R_1 + 87R_2 + 110R_3 \ge 90\,\text{RB}$$

In a similar manner, we can ensure an octane level of at least 100 on super.

$$100S_1 + 87S_2 + 110S_3 \ge 100\,\text{SB}$$

The entire model for Vohio, including nonnegativity of the decision variables, can be written as

$$\text{Max } 18.5\,\text{RB} + 20\,\text{SB} - 16.5R_1 - 16.5S_1 - 14R_2 - 14S_2 - 17.5R_3 - 17.5S_3$$

subject to

$$R_1 + S_1 \le 110,000$$
$$R_2 + S_2 \le 350,000$$
$$R_3 + S_3 \le 300,000$$
$$\text{RB} = R_1 + R_2 + R_3$$
$$\text{SB} = S_1 + S_2 + S_3$$

$$RB \leq 350,000$$
$$SB \leq 500,000$$
$$100R_1 + 87R_2 + 110R_3 \geq 90\,RB$$
$$100S_1 + 87S_2 + 110S_3 \geq 100\,SB$$
$$RB, SB, R_i, S_i \geq 0 \quad i = 1, 2, 3$$

The solution to this model is to produce 260,000 gallons of regular (from 0 gallons of input 1, 180,434.8 gallons of input 2, and 79,565.2 gallons of input 3) and 500,000 gallons of super (from 110,000 gallons of input 1, 169,565.2 of input 2, and 220,434.8 gallons of input 3). The plan yields a profit of $2,845,000.

EXAMPLE 7. MABOPS INC.: THE TRANSPORTATION PROBLEM

MaBops Inc. must plan the shipment of its product, MSX, a high performance personal computer. The company must determine how to ship the MSX from its factories to its distribution centers on a weekly basis. MaBops' plants are located in Los Angeles, Denver, Pensacola, and Cincinnati. Warehouses (distribution centers) are located in Houston, Las Vegas, New Orleans, Chicago, and Boise (see Figure 4.6). Table 4.5

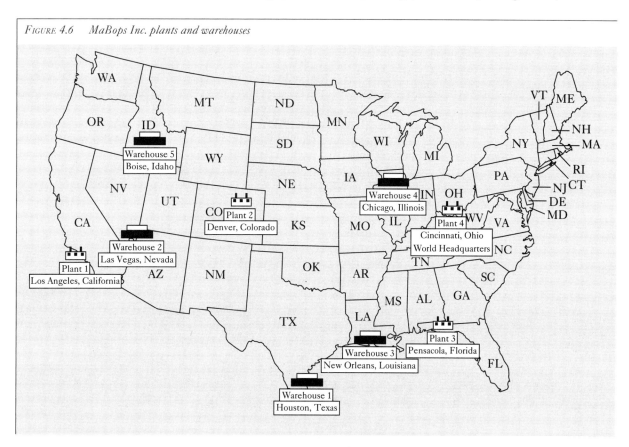

FIGURE 4.6   MaBops Inc. plants and warehouses

shows the weekly availability of the MSX at each plant and the next week's projected demand required at each warehouse. The per-unit cost (in dollars) of shipping from each plant to each warehouse is given in Table 4.5. We would like to develop a model to prescribe the least costly method of shipping the product.

What is it that MaBops needs to decide? The volume to ship from each plant to each warehouse must be determined. Define the following decision variables:

$$x_{ij} = \text{amount to ship from plant } i \text{ to warehouse } j$$

$$i = 1, 2, 3, 4$$

$$j = 1, 2, 3, 4, 5$$

These types of variables are called *double subscripted variables*. They are useful in defining decision variables when the natural way to think about the process being modeled is through some sort of pairing of entities. Here, for example, MaBops is deciding how much to ship between pairs of plants and warehouses. In the definition above, the first subscript in the variable refers to the plant number and the second to the warehouse number.

What is the objective to be maximized or minimized? MaBops wants to minimize the total cost of shipping its goods next week. This objective can be expressed in terms of the decision variables as

$$\text{Min } 5x_{11} + 1x_{12} + 5x_{13} + 7x_{14} + 4x_{15} + 9x_{21} + 7x_{22} + 8x_{23} + 3x_{24}$$
$$+ 5x_{25} + 3x_{31} + 4x_{32} + 3x_{33} + 8x_{34} + 6x_{35} + 4x_{41} + 5x_{42} + 6x_{43} + 2x_{44} + 7x_{45}$$

min cost₁,₁
ie plant1 plant2

How is the problem restricted? The problem is restricted in two ways. First, the capacity (availability of the product) at each plant cannot be exceeded. Second, the demand at

TABLE 4.5
*MaBops Inc. capacity
and demand data*

Plant	Capacity	Warehouse	Demand
1. Los Angeles	15,000	1. Houston	8,000
2. Denver	20,000	2. Las Vegas	11,000
3. Pensacola	17,500	3. New Orleans	15,000
4. Cincinnati	10,000	4. Chicago	10,000
		5. Boise	15,000

*MaBops Inc. per unit
shipping cost*

TO: FROM:	Houston (1)	Las Vegas (2)	New Orleans (3)	Chicago (4)	Boise (5)
LA (1)	$5	1	5	7	4
Denv.(2)	9	7	8	3	5
Pens. (3)	3	4	3	8	6
Cinc. (4)	4	5	6	2	7

each warehouse must be satisfied. Note that in order for this type of shipping problem to be feasible; that is, for all demand to be satisfied, the total capacity over all plants must be at least as much as the total demand over all warehouses. This is the case here because the total capacity is 62,500 and total demand is 59,000. MaBops has the capacity to meet demand.

Every plant needs a capacity constraint that ensures that the amount shipped from a plant does not exceed its capacity. Consider, for example, plant 1 (Los Angeles). The total amount shipped from plant 1 to the warehouses 1, 2, 3, 4, and 5 cannot exceed 15,000. The amount shipped from plant 1 can be represented mathematically as

$$x_{11} + x_{12} + x_{13} + x_{14} + x_{15}$$

The amounts shipped from each of the other three plants can likewise be mathematically represented. The capacity constraints can therefore be written as functions of the decision variables as follows:

$$x_{11} + x_{12} + x_{13} + x_{14} + x_{15} \leq 15,000 \quad \text{Capacity}$$
$$x_{21} + x_{22} + x_{23} + x_{24} + x_{25} \leq 20,000 \quad \text{''}$$
$$x_{31} + x_{32} + x_{33} + x_{34} + x_{35} \leq 17,500 \quad \text{''}$$
$$x_{41} + x_{42} + x_{43} + x_{44} + x_{45} \leq 10,000 \quad \text{''}$$

The demand constraints, one for each warehouse, are similar. At warehouse 1 (Houston), for example, the total amount shipped into the warehouse from plants 1, 2, 3, and 4, must be *greater-than-or-equal-to* the demand. The amount shipped into Houston can be represented mathematically as:

$$x_{11} + x_{21} + x_{31} + x_{41}$$

The demand constraints can therefore be written as:

$$x_{11} + x_{21} + x_{31} + x_{41} \geq 8,000 \quad \text{demand}$$
$$x_{12} + x_{22} + x_{32} + x_{42} \geq 11,000 \quad \text{''}$$
$$x_{13} + x_{23} + x_{33} + x_{43} \geq 15,000 \quad \text{''}$$
$$x_{14} + x_{24} + x_{34} + x_{44} \geq 10,000 \quad \text{''}$$
$$x_{15} + x_{25} + x_{35} + x_{45} \geq 15,000 \quad \text{''}$$

The entire model for MaBops' shipping appears as:

$$\text{Min } 5x_{11} + 1x_{12} + 5x_{13} + 7x_{14} + 4x_{15} + 9x_{21} + 7x_{22} + 8x_{23} + 3x_{24}$$
$$+ 5x_{25} + 3x_{31} + 4x_{32} + 3x_{33} + 8x_{34} + 6x_{35} + 4x_{41} + 5x_{42} + 6x_{43} + 2x_{44} + 7x_{45}$$

subject to

$$
\begin{array}{ll}
x_{11} + x_{12} + x_{13} + x_{14} + x_{15} \leq 15,000 & x_{12} + x_{22} + x_{32} + x_{42} \geq 11,000 \\
x_{21} + x_{22} + x_{23} + x_{24} + x_{25} \leq 20,000 & x_{13} + x_{23} + x_{33} + x_{43} \geq 15,000 \\
x_{31} + x_{32} + x_{33} + x_{34} + x_{35} \leq 17,500 & x_{14} + x_{24} + x_{34} + x_{44} \geq 10,000 \\
x_{41} + x_{42} + x_{43} + x_{44} + x_{45} \leq 10,000 & x_{15} + x_{25} + x_{35} + x_{45} \geq 15,000 \\
x_{11} + x_{21} + x_{31} + x_{41} \geq 8,000 &
\end{array}
$$

$$x_{ij} \geq 0 \quad i = 1, 2, 3, 4 \quad j = 1, 2, 3, 4, 5$$

The solution to the MaBops model is shown in Figure 4.7. The total cost of shipping is $183,000. From the figure, the solution is somewhat intuitive, especially when the capacities of the plants are considered. For example, most warehouses are served by the point nearest to them.

Notice that the solution is integral. That is, none of the optimal values of the decision variables are fractional. Some LP models have special characteristics that guarantee that the solution will not be fractional. MaBops is an example of a such a special LP called the *transportation problem*. The LP transportation problem has a special structure that ensures that as long as the capacities and demands are integer, the shipping amounts prescribed by the model will also be integer. The special structure is that every decision variable appears in exactly two constraints, with a coefficient of one in each. For example, x_{23} appears in the second plant constraint and the third warehouse constraint. Likewise, x_{34} appears in the third plant constraint and the fourth warehouse constraint. In general, x_{ij} appears in exactly two constraints with coefficients of one: the ith plant constraint and the jth warehouse constraint. This structure defines what we mean by a Transportation LP model.

FIGURE 4.7   *MaBops Inc. optimal shipping plan*

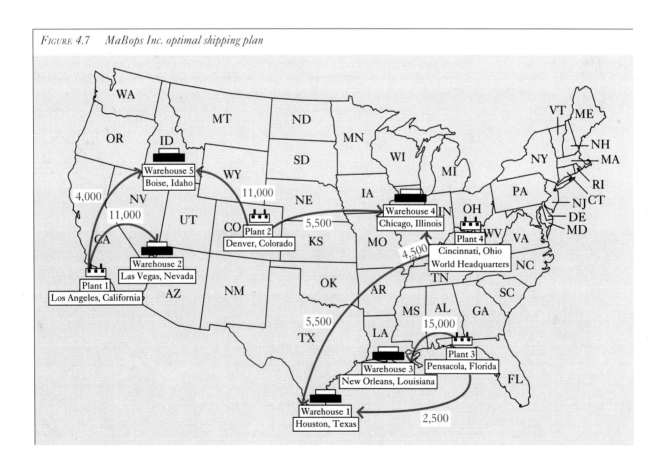

A Transportation Problem LP with integer supplies and demands will have an integer optimal solution.

Using summation notation, we can write our MaBops model as

$$\text{Min } 5x_{11} + 1x_{12} + 5x_{13} + 7x_{14} + 4x_{15} + 9x_{21} + 7x_{22} + 8x_{23} + 3x_{24} + 5x_{25}$$
$$+3x_{31} + 4x_{32} + 3x_{33} + 8x_{34} + 6x_{35} + 4x_{41} + 5x_{42} + 6x_{43} + 2x_{44} + 7x_{45}$$

subject to

$$\sum_{j=1}^{5} x_{1j} \leq 15{,}000$$

$$\sum_{j=1}^{5} x_{2j} \leq 20{,}000$$

$$\sum_{j=1}^{5} x_{3j} \leq 17{,}500 \qquad \text{Capacity}$$

$$\sum_{j=1}^{5} x_{4j} \leq 10{,}000$$

$$\sum_{i=1}^{4} x_{i1} \geq 8{,}000$$

$$\sum_{i=1}^{4} x_{i2} \geq 11{,}000$$

$$\sum_{i=1}^{4} x_{i3} \geq 15{,}000 \qquad \text{demand}$$

$$\sum_{i=1}^{4} x_{i4} \geq 10{,}000$$

$$\sum_{i=1}^{4} x_{i5} \geq 15{,}000$$

$$x_{ij} \geq 0 \quad i = 1, 2, 3, 4 \quad j = 1, 2, 3, 4, 5$$

In its general form, the *transportation problem* with *m* origins and *n* destinations can be written as

$$\text{Min} \sum_{i=1}^{m} \sum_{j=1}^{n} c_{ij} x_{ij}$$

subject to

$$\sum_{j=1}^{n} x_{ij} \le s_i \qquad i = 1, 2, \ldots m$$

$$\sum_{i=1}^{m} x_{ij} \ge d_j \qquad j = 1, 2, \ldots n$$

$$x_{ij} \ge 0 \text{ for all } i \text{ and } j$$

where the c_{ij} are the per unit cost of shipping from origin i to destination, the s_i are the supplies available at origin i, and the d_j, are the demands at destination j. The notation to the right of the constraints signifies that there are m supply constraints (written by fixing i =1, then i =2, etc.) and likewise n demand constraints.

Example 8. Grad & Sons Insurance: Portfolio Selection

Grad & Sons Insurance carries an investment portfolio of bonds, stocks, and other investment alternatives such as real estate. At the beginning of next year, $500,000 will be available for investment in the four options OP1, OP2, OP3, and OP4. The expected annual rates of return on these four options are .06, .09, .07, and .11. The risk factor per dollar invested is a measure of the inherent uncertainty of the expected return, so a low risk factor is desirable. The risk factors per dollar invested for the four investment alternatives are subjective estimates of the possible loss the investor could incur in the worst case analysis (0 is no risk, 1 means the investor could lose everything), which have been provided by a Grad & Sons analyst. They are .02, .05, .04, and .075, respectively. For diversification, no single alternative can be more than $200,000. Management needs a return of at least .08, but would like to minimize the risk taken to achieve that return.

What is it that Grad & Sons management needs to decide? Management needs to plan how to invest the $500,000 which will become available next year. Four alternatives are given, so we can define the following decision variables:

$$A_j = \text{amount (in dollars) to invest in alternative } i$$
$$i = 1, 2, 3, 4$$

What is the objective to be maximized or minimized? Management wishes to minimize the risk of the portfolio. Since the risk factors are on a per-dollar basis, one way to describe total risk mathematically is by multiplying the risk factor for each alternative by the number of dollars invested in that alternative ($(risk/$) = risk), and then summing. We caution that some risk factors, such as standard deviations of previous returns, are not additive. If risk were measured by standard deviations, the interrelationships between the various alternatives would have to be considered. Here, the risk factors are subjective. The objective function can thus be written as

$$\text{Min} \quad .02A_1 + .05A_2 + .04A_3 + .075A_4$$

How is the problem restricted? The problem is restricted in terms of a minimum return needed, diversification, and the total amount available for investment. The first restriction states that the expected return must be at least .08($500,000), or $40,000. The return from the portfolio can be expressed as the sum of the individual investment returns.

$$.06A_1 + .09A_2 + .07A_3 + .11A_4 \geq 40,000$$

Note that the left-hand side of the constraint is in dollars—(dollars returned / dollar invested) (dollars invested) = dollars—as is the right-hand side.

The diversification restriction requires that each individual investment not be more than $200,000:

$$A_1 \leq 200,000$$

$$A_2 \leq 200,000$$

$$A_3 \leq 200,000$$

$$A_4 \leq 200,000$$

Finally, the total investment will be $500,000.

$$A_1 + A_2 + A_3 + A_4 = 500,000$$

Along with nonnegativity, the entire model can therefore be written as:

$$\text{Min } .02A_1 + .05A_2 + .04A_3 + .075A_4$$

subject to

$$.06A_1 + .09A_2 + .07A_3 + .11A_4 \geq 40,000$$

$$A_1 \leq 200,000$$

$$A_2 \leq 200,000$$

$$A_3 \leq 200,000$$

$$A_4 \leq 200,000$$

$$A_1 + A_2 + A_3 + A_4 = 500,000$$

$$A_1, A_2, A_3, A_4 \geq 0$$

The solution from an LP solver is to invest $200,000 in each of OP1 and OP2, $25,000 in OP3 and $75,000 in OP4. This plan yields an expected return of eight percent with a risk of 20,625 (or on a per-dollar basis, 20,625/500,000 = .04125).

EXAMPLE 9. OPTIMAL ALLOCATION OF MARKETING EFFORT AMONG NONINTERACTING PRODUCTS[1]

Phillips Inc. sells two products—1 and 2—and uses two marketing instruments—advertising and selling—to stimulate demand for these products. There is no interaction between the two products in the sense that the price, cost, or demand of one

---

[1]This problem is adapted from Kotler, Philip. *Marketing Decision Making: A Model Building Approach*. Holt Reinhart and Winston, 1971: pp. 171–173.

product will not affect the demand of the other product. The company must determine the amount of selling and advertising resources to devote to each of the products in the coming quarter. Phillips has budgeted $25,000 for advertising and has allotted a total of 5,000 hours of labor to selling for the quarter. Based on past data and managerial judgment, Phillips has estimated that a dollar of advertising will yield $8 profit when spent on product 1 and $15 when spent on product 2. These estimates hold over the entire range of the advertising budget. Management has likewise estimated the productivity of personal selling. An hour of personal selling devoted to product 1 will generate a profit of $25 and an hour devoted to product 2 will generate a profit of $45. These estimates are assumed to hold over the ranges of personal selling hours allowable by the company. Company policy stipulates that at least 2,000, but no more than 3,500 hours of labor can be used on each product. Company policy also dictates that at least $6,000 but no more than $18,000 be spent on advertising for each product.

What does Phillips need to decide? Phillips needs to decide how many labor hours for selling and how much money for advertising to allocate to each of its two products. We therefore need to define a set of decision variables that accurately represent these decisions:

$$A_i = \text{amount of advertising dollars to spend on product } i$$
$$S_i = \text{number of hours of selling to allocate to product } i$$
$$i = 1, 2$$

What is the objective to be maximized or minimized? Phillips would like to maximize the next quarter's profit contribution realized from the allocation of its advertising budget and its selling hours allotment. This can be expressed mathematically as

$$\text{Max } 8A_1 + 15A_2 + 25S_1 + 45S_2$$

How is the problem restricted? First, both advertising and personal selling have limited budgets. For advertising the budget is in dollars, and for selling it is in labor hours. We must ensure that the total dollars expended on advertising does not exceed the budget. This can be expressed in terms of our decision variables as

$$A_1 + A_2 \le 25,000$$

Likewise, the total number of hours allocated to selling for the two products cannot exceed 5,000 hours:

$$S_1 + S_2 \le 5,000$$

Furthermore, we have upper and lower bounds on the amount of advertising dollars and selling hours that can be allocated to each product. The advertising allocations must be no less than $6,000 and no more than $18,000.

$$A_1 \ge 6,000$$
$$A_1 \le 18,000$$
$$A_2 \ge 6,000$$
$$A_2 \le 18,000$$

The number of hours allocated to selling of each of the products must be at least 2,000 hours, but no more than 3,500 hours.

$$S_1 \geq 2,000$$
$$S_1 \leq 3,500$$
$$S_2 \geq 2,000$$
$$S_2 \leq 3,500$$

Policy on sales

The entire model can be stated as

$$\text{Max } 8A_1 + 15A_2 + 25S_1 + 45S_2$$

subject to

$$A_1 + A_2 \leq 25,000$$
$$S_1 + S_2 \leq 5,000$$
$$A_1 \geq 6,000$$
$$A_1 \leq 18,000$$
$$A_2 \geq 6,000$$
$$A_2 \leq 18,000$$
$$S_1 \geq 2,000$$
$$S_1 \leq 3,500$$
$$S_2 \geq 2,000$$
$$S_2 \leq 3,500$$
$$A_i, S_i \geq 0 \quad i = 1, 2$$

advertising policy

Sales policy

Check the dimensionality of the objective function and constraints in order to convince yourself that there are no dimensionality problems in the model we developed. The solution to the model is to invest $7,000 in advertising for product 1 and $18,000 in advertising for product 2, and to allocate 2,000 hours to selling product 1 and 3,000 hours to selling product 2. This plan will yield a profit of $511,000.

MANAGEMENT SCIENCE PRACTICE[2]

To comply with the National Forest Management Act of 1976, operations research analysts were placed in almost all of the national forest headquarters to perform forest-level planning using large and complex linear programming models. In this section we describe in more detail the use of linear programming to manage the United States' national forests.

---

[2]Adapted from Field, Richard C. "National Forest Planning is Promoting US Forest Service Acceptance of Operations Research." *Interfaces*, Vol. 14, No.5, Sept.–Oct., 1984, pp.67–76.

Land Management at the National Forest Service

The National Forest Service is responsible for the management of over 191 million acres of national forest in 154 designated national forests. The National Forest Management Act of 1976 mandated the development of a comprehensive plan to guide the management of each national forest. Linear programming models are among the tools used to assist managers in this monumental and complex problem.

Decisions need to be made regarding the use of land in each of the national forests. The overall management objective is "to provide multiple use and the sustained yield of goods and services from the National Forest System in a way that maximizes long-term net public benefits in an environmentally sound manner." Linear programming models are used to decide the number of acres of various types in each forest to be used for the many possible usage strategies. For example, the decision variables of the model are variables such as the number of acres in a particular forest to be used for timber, the number of acres to be used for recreational purposes of various types, and the number of acres to be left undisturbed.

The general linear programming model has as its objective the maximization of the net discounted value of the forest over the planning time horizon. Constraints include the availability of land of different types, bounds on the amount of land dedicated to certain uses, and resources available to manage land under different strategies (for example, recreational areas must be staffed; harvesting the land requires a budget for labor, the transport of goods, and replanting). These LP planning models are quite large. Some have over 6,000 constraints and over 120,000 decision variables! The data requirements for these models are quite intense, requiring the work of literally hundreds of agricultural resource specialists to estimate reasonable values for the inputs to the model. These same specialists are also utilized to ensure that the solutions from the large LP models make sense operationally. That is, specialists are actively involved in the construction of these models and interpretation of the results, a necessity for the success of any management science application.

Discussion Questions

1. What would be involved in estimating the value of different land use strategies to be used as objective function coefficients in the LP model? For example, how would you estimate the value of land assigned to harvest timber next year? To be used for camping next year?

2. In general, would you say that the linear programming model just described is a knapsack problem, a blending problem, a diet problem, a product mix problem, or none of these? Why?

3. Models similar to the one described in this section are used by private land developers to maximize the profit they realize from their land holdings. What do you think the decision variables would be in this scenario? What kinds of constraints would be needed?

MORE EXAMPLES AND SOLVED PROBLEMS

EXAMPLE 10. M-KART INC: CAPACITY UTILIZATION

M-Kart Inc. produces two types of golf carts, T1 and T2. The T1 is a gasoline-powered model; the T2 is electric. Management is currently trying to plan the best utilization of the company's machinery and labor for the next month. There are four departments: fabrication and finishing (shared by both products), the T1 engine installation department, and the T2 engine installation department. Every unit of T1 must pass through the fabrication and T1 engine installation departments, and then the finishing department. Likewise, each T2 requires capacity in the fabrication, T2 engine installation, and finishing departments. Table 4.6 shows the capacity of each department in terms of the maximum number of T1 and T2 that the department could produce. (In the case of the fabrication and finishing departments, these numbers reflect the amounts as if each product were the only one produced). The marginal contribution for each unit of T1 is $250 and each unit of T2 is $375. Because of the extensive growth in the number of public golf courses throughout the U.S., the company has recently been able to sell everything it can produce. Management wants to know the most profitable use of its departmental capacities.

What is it that M-Kart needs to decide? Management would like to know how to use their existing capacity to generate the most profit. Note that this problem is very similar to the LaserStop and SpeedBuster problem—the question of how to most effectively utilize capacity is similar to how to most effectively utilize the available components required by each radar detector. Furthermore, the question of how to most effectively utilize the capacity boils down to how many of each cart to produce, because the capacity only generates profit through the production of the carts. Consequently, this problem, like the radar detector example, is really a *product mix problem*. We can define the following decision variables:

$$NT_1 = \text{number of T1 carts to produce next month}$$
$$NT_2 = \text{number of T2 carts to produce next month}$$

What is the objective to be maximized or minimized? M-Kart wishes to maximize the profit realized next month. The marginal contribution per cart of each T1 and T2 is known, so this objective can be written as

$$\text{Max } 250\,NT_1 + 375\,NT_2$$

TABLE 4.6
M-Kart departmental capacities

	T1	T2
Fabrication	3,500	2,500
Finishing	1,500	3,500
T1 Eng. Install.	2,000	0
T2 Eng. Install.	0	1,500

How is the problem restricted? The production of the carts is limited by the available capacity in each of the four departments. We need to ensure that the amount of capacity used in production does not exceed the available capacity in each department.

Beginning with the fabrication department, we know that no more than 3,500 T1 carts and no more than 2,500 T2 carts can be processed. Furthermore, these upper limits are what could be produced if each of these products was the sole product. We can think of T1 and T2 as competing for this shared capacity in the fabrication department. If we decide to make NT_1 units of T1, how much of the fabrication capacity has been used? Well, if only T1 carts were fabricated, then the 100% utilization in that department would be 3,500 units. If we make NT_1 units, then we have therefore used (NT_1/3,500) of the available capacity. Suppose for example, that we produce 1,400 T1 carts next month; we will use (1,400/3,500)=4/10=.4 of the available fabrication capacity. Likewise, the fraction of available fabrication capacity used by the production of T2 carts will be NT_2/2,500. Because the two products must share the fabrication department, we must ensure that these two fractions added together do not exceed one (total capacity). Hence the restriction for the fabrication department can be written as

$$\frac{NT_1}{3,500} + \frac{NT_2}{2,500} \leq 1$$

Similarly, the two carts compete for finishing capacity. This restriction can be written as

$$\frac{NT_1}{1,500} + \frac{NT_2}{3,500} \leq 1$$

Since the products do not compete for capacity in the engine installation departments, these restrictions are somewhat simpler. They can be expressed as $NT_1 \leq 2,000$ and $NT_2 \leq 1,500$. Finally, nonnegativity must be enforced: $NT_1, NT_2 \geq 0$.

The entire M-Kart profit maximizing model can thus be written as

$$\text{Max } 250\,NT_1 + 375\,NT_2$$

subject to

$$\frac{NT_1}{3,500} + \frac{NT_2}{2,500} \leq 1$$

$$\frac{NT_1}{1,500} + \frac{NT_2}{3,500} \leq 1$$

$$NT_1 \leq 2,000$$

$$NT_2 \leq 1,500$$

$$NT_1, NT_2 \geq 0$$

We note in passing that the multiplication of a constraint by a positive number does not alter the optimal solution (We note that it can affect the interpretation of the solution, which we will discuss in Chapter 6). We can thus multiply both sides of the first constraint by 35,000 (since both 3,500 and 2,500 divide evenly into it) and the second constraint by 10,500 (since both 1,500 and 3,500 divide evenly into it), to give an equivalent model:

$$\text{Max } 250\,\text{NT}_1 + 375\,\text{NT}_2$$

$$\text{subject to}$$

$$10\,\text{NT}_1 + 14\,\text{NT}_2 \leq 35,000 \quad \text{\small Production}$$

$$7\,\text{NT}_1 + 3\,\text{NT}_2 \leq 10,500 \quad \text{\small Finishing}$$

$$\text{NT}_1 \leq 2,000$$

$$\text{NT}_2 \leq 1,500$$

$$\text{NT}_1, \text{NT}_2 \geq 0$$

The computer solution to the M-Kart model yields a profit of $776,785. However, this solution calls for a fractional number of T1 carts. We can think of a fractional amount of T1 as work in process at the end of the period. Note however, that we cannot really generate the marginal contribution associated with the fractional amounts so that the operational solution cannot be fractional. The optimal profit with integer numbers of T1 and T2 carts is $776,750.

A spreadsheet model of the M-Kart scenario is shown in Figure 4.8. The solution shown in the spreadsheet is a nonoptimal solution of 1,000 of each type of cart. Notice that there is unused capacity in every department. Problem 5 at the end of this chapter asks you to use trial-and-error with this spreadsheet to find a solution whose objective function value is as close as possible to the optimal value of $776,750.

EXAMPLE 11. TIME-BASED FINANCIAL PLANNING

An investor is considering four investment options over the next five years. Because he anticipates taking a leave from his job at the end of the fifth year, he would like to maximize the amount of cash on hand at that time. Investment *A* is a one-year investment alternative. It pays back $1.15 per dollar invested at the end of the year. A dollar invested in alternative *B* returns $1.55 three years later. Alternative *C* is a long term project in which a dollar invested today yields $2.20 at the end of the fifth year. Alternative *D* is an annual option, but will not become available until the start of year three. It will return $1.20 per dollar invested per year. The investor currently has $30,000 on hand to invest.

Since the time horizons on these alternatives vary, we must be careful to keep track of the funds that will become available in a given year. A flow diagram will be helpful in keeping things straight. A flow diagram for this problem appears in Figure 4.9. Each node represents the beginning of a year (node 6 is the start of the sixth year). Note that because the one-year alternative *A* is available every year, all cash will be invested at all times (there is no reason to hold cash, because it can be earning

Figure 4.8 M-Kart spreadsheet model

	A	B	C	D	E	F
1	M-KART INC.					
2						
3	*Parameters and uncontrollable variables:*					
4				Capacity		
5	Model	Profit/Unit	Fabrication	Finishing	T1 Engine	T2 Engine
6	T1	$250.00	3500	1500	2000	0
7	T2	$375.00	2500	3500	0	1500
8						
9						
10	*Decision Variables:*					
11		Number				
12	T1	1000				
13	T2	1000				
14						
15						
16	*Model Outputs:*					
17		% Capacity Used				
18	Department	T1	T2	Total		
19	Fabrication	28.6%	40.0%	68.6%		
20	Finishing	66.7%	28.6%	95.2%		
21	T1 Engine	50.0%		50.0%		
22	T2 Engine		66.7%	66.7%		
23						
24	Total Profit	$625,000				

Selected cell formulas

	A	B	C	D
16	*Model Outputs:*			
17		% Capacity Used		
18	Department	T1	T2	Total
19	Fabrication	+B12/C6	+B13/C7	+B19+C19
20	Finishing	+B12/D6	+B13/D7	+B20+C20
21	T1 Engine	+B12/E6		+B21
22	T2 Engine		+B13/F7	+C22
23				
24	Total Profit	+B6*B12+B7*B13		

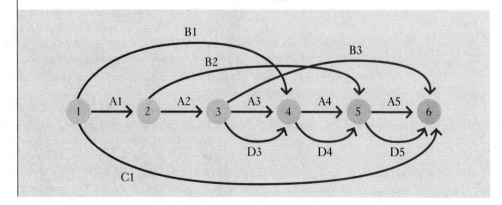

Figure 4.9 A flow diagram for the investment planning problem

interest in alternative A and will be available for reinvesting at the start of the next year). In terms of our flow diagram, any cash that becomes available at the start of a year will be invested.

What is it that the investor is trying to decide? How much to invest in each alternative in each year needs to be decided.

$$A_i = \text{amount(\$) to invest in alternative } A \text{ at the start of year } i$$
$$B_i = \text{amount(\$) to invest in alternative } B \text{ at the start of year } i$$
$$C_i = \text{amount(\$) to invest in alternative } C \text{ at the start of year } i$$
$$D_i = \text{amount(\$) to invest in alternative } D \text{ at the start of year } i$$

What is the objective to be maximized or minimized? The investor wishes to maximize the cash on hand at the beginning of the sixth year. From Figure 4.9, we see that investments in options A and D in year five, investment in option B at the start of year three, and investment in option C at the start of the first year, will all mature at the start of year six. The amount of cash on hand will be the sum of the amount invested multiplied by the return. Hence the objective function can be written as

Max Payback

$$\text{Max } 1.15A_5 + 1.55B_3 + 2.20C_1 + 1.20D_5$$

How is the problem restricted? The problem is restricted in several ways. First, not every investment option will be available in every year. The flow diagram in Figure 4.9 shows which alternatives are available in each year, taking into account that the investor wants all money to be available at the start of the sixth year. Second, we must keep track of the amount of money available at the start of each year and relate it to the investment alternatives available that year. Because option A is available in every year and returns money the following year, we can assume that all of the funds will be invested at any point in time. Consequently, we can set the amount available equal to the amount invested at the start of each year.

Consider the start of the first year. The amount available for investment is the $30,000 on hand. Where can this $30,000 be invested? From Figure 4.9, alternatives A, B, and C are available, so that setting the amount invested equal to the amount available can be written as

$$A_1 + B_1 + C_1 = 30,000$$

For the start of the second year, only those funds invested in alternative A will be available for reinvestment (see Figure 4.9), and the amount available will be 1.15 times the amount invested in A at the start of year one. Alternatives A and B are the options available for reinvesting. Again, setting the amount invested equal to the amount available can be written as

$$A_2 + B_2 = 1.15A_1$$

Similarly for the start of year three; the funds available are 1.15 of the amount invested in alternative A in year two.

$$A_3 + B_3 + D_3 = 1.15A_2$$

In year four, funds are available from investments in A and D during year three, and B from year one. Reinvestment alternatives include options A and D.

$$A_4 + D_4 = 1.15A_3 + 1.55B_1 + 1.20D_3 \qquad 4^{th} \text{ year}$$

At the start of year five, funds become available from investments in A and D in year four, and investments in B from year two.

$$A_5 + D_5 = 1.15A_4 + 1.20D_4 + 1.55B_2 \qquad 5^{th} \text{ year}$$

The entire LP model for this investment problem is then written as

$$\text{Max } 1.15A_5 + 1.55B_3 + 2.20C_1 + 1.20D_5$$

subject to

$$A_1 + B_1 + C_1 = 30{,}000$$

$$A_2 + B_2 = 1.15A_1$$

$$A_3 + B_3 + D_3 = 1.15A_2$$

$$A_4 + D_4 = 1.15A_3 + 1.55B_1 + 1.20D_3$$

$$A_5 + D_5 = 1.15A_4 + 1.55B_2 + 1.20D_4$$

$$A_i, B_i, C_i, D_i \geq 0 \text{ for all } i$$

The solution to this LP is to invest all available money in investment A in the first two years and in investment D the last three years. This strategy will result in $68,558.40 at the start of year six.

EXAMPLE 12. SALES REP TERRITORY ASSIGNMENT: THE ASSIGNMENT PROBLEM

Special case of transportation model

Running Spot (RS) Shoes of Philadelphia, PA produces high quality hand-made track shoes. The success of this fast growing company in the Northeast, combined with a positive market analysis conducted by a Philadelphia marketing research firm, has convinced the company to attempt to expand nationwide.

The success of this expansion will be highly dependent on the efforts of its six sales representatives who will make calls to sporting goods stores, running shops, universities, and some of the larger high schools in their assigned regions. RS has promoted six people to the position of sales representative with the understanding that five of them will have to relocate to other parts of the country (one will remain in Philadelphia to cover the Northeast region). RS management has no indication of the potential success of any particular rep in a given region, so it would like to use the regional preferences of the six people as it decides which rep will be assigned to each region.

Management has asked each rep to assign a weighting between 0 and 1 to each region, where a 1 indicates a strong preference for being assigned to that region, and a 0 a strong desire not to be assigned there. The results of the preference survey are shown in Table 4.7. RS management seeks an assignment of reps to regions so that total preference score (the sum of the individual's preferences) is maximized.

On the surface it may not appear that this problem will lend itself to linear programming modeling as we have seen it. However, this problem is solvable by linear programming if viewed in the right manner. In particular, it is a special case of the transportation problem we have seen in the MaBops Inc. shipping example.

We can think of each of the sales reps as a plant with capacity of one, and each of the regions as a warehouse with demand of one. The preferences can be thought of as a profit associated with "shipping" one unit from a particular sales rep to a particular region. Because the structure of this problem is the same as that of the transportation problem (it has only capacity and demand constraints, as in Example 7), and the capacities and the supplies are integer, the solution will also be integer. Furthermore, because the capacities and demands are all ones, the amount "shipped" from a rep to a region will be either 0 or 1 in the optimal solution! We can then interpret the solution by understanding 1 as a match between a rep and a region, and 0 as not being a match. Having outlined an LP approach to this assignment problem, we return to our process of LP model building.

What is it that RS Shoes is trying to decide? RS management seeks an assignment of sales reps to sales regions. We can define the following decision variables:

$$x_{ij} = 1 \text{ if rep } i \text{ is assigned to region } j, \; 0 \text{ if not}$$

where $i = 1, 2, 3, 4, 5, 6$ are the sales reps in order from top to bottom and $j = 1, 2, 3, 4, 5, 6$ are the sales regions from left to right in Table 4.7.

What is the objective to be maximized or minimized? Management wishes to maximize the preference score measured as the sum of the preferences of the individual reps. Using the decision variables we have defined, we can express this as a linear function.

$$\text{Max } 1x_{11} + .8x_{12} + .7x_{13} + .6x_{14} + .1x_{15} + .1x_{16} + .4x_{21} + .4x_{22} + \ldots\ldots + .1x_{66}$$

When one of the x_{ij}s takes on a value of 1, that is, when sales rep i is assigned to region j, then that preference score is added to the total.

How is the problem restricted? The constraint set is similar in structure to the model constraints in the MaBops problem. Because we have six reps and six regions, we are

TABLE 4.7
Regional preference scores of the RS sales reps

	NW (1)	NM (2)	NE (3)	SW (4)	SM (5)	SE (6)
1. Bob	1.0	.8	.7	.6	.1	.1
2. Nancy	.4	.4	.4	.8	.7	.9
3. Karen	1.0	1.0	.2	1.0	1.0	1.0
4. Bart	.8	.1	.1	.8	.3	.7
5. Jill	.8	.2	.2	.9	.9	.9
6. Tom	.6	1.0	.8	.1	.1	.1

looking for a direct match: every rep must be assigned to exactly one region (capacity of one) and every region must be assigned exactly one rep (demand of one).

For example, the restriction on Bob (sales rep 1) is

$$x_{11} + x_{12} + x_{13} + x_{14} + x_{15} + x_{16} = 1$$ total demand

Likewise for the other five reps.

The demand restriction for region 1 can be written as

$$x_{11} + x_{21} + x_{31} + x_{41} + x_{51} + x_{61} = 1$$ total supply

Likewise for the other five regions.

The entire assignment model for RS Shoes can thus be written as

$$\text{Max } 1x_{11} + .8x_{12} + .7x_{13} + .6x_{14} + .1x_{15} + .1x_{16} + .4x_{21} + .4x_{22} + \ldots\ldots + .1x_{66}$$

subject to

$$x_{11} + x_{12} + x_{13} + x_{14} + x_{15} + x_{16} = 1$$
$$x_{21} + x_{22} + x_{23} + x_{24} + x_{25} + x_{26} = 1$$
$$x_{31} + x_{32} + x_{33} + x_{34} + x_{35} + x_{36} = 1$$
$$x_{41} + x_{42} + x_{43} + x_{44} + x_{45} + x_{46} = 1$$
$$x_{51} + x_{52} + x_{53} + x_{54} + x_{55} + x_{56} = 1$$
$$x_{61} + x_{62} + x_{63} + x_{64} + x_{65} + x_{66} = 1$$
demand

$$x_{11} + x_{21} + x_{31} + x_{41} + x_{51} + x_{61} = 1$$
$$x_{12} + x_{22} + x_{32} + x_{42} + x_{52} + x_{62} = 1$$
$$x_{13} + x_{23} + x_{33} + x_{43} + x_{53} + x_{63} = 1$$
$$x_{14} + x_{24} + x_{34} + x_{44} + x_{54} + x_{64} = 1$$
$$x_{15} + x_{25} + x_{35} + x_{45} + x_{55} + x_{65} = 1$$
$$x_{16} + x_{26} + x_{36} + x_{46} + x_{56} + x_{66} = 1$$
supply

$$x_{ij} \geq 0 \text{ for all } i \text{ and } j$$

The solution to the RS Shoes assignment model is Bob—NE, Nancy—SE, Karen—SW, Bart—NW, Jill—SM, and Tom—NM, with a total preference score of 5.3.

The *assignment problem* with m items in the first set to be assigned to n items in the second set is

Assignment problem general form

$$\text{Max (or Min) } \sum_{i=1}^{m} \sum_{j=1}^{n} c_{ij}x_{ij}$$

subject to

$$\sum_{j=1}^{n} x_{ij} \leq 1 \quad i = 1, 2, \ldots m$$

$$\sum_{i=1}^{m} x_{ij} = 1 \quad j = 1, 2, \ldots n$$

$$x_{ij} \geq 0 \text{ for all } i \text{ and } j$$

In its general form, it is easy to see that the assignment problem is simply a special case of the transportation problem with all supplies and demands equal to one. To be feasible, it must be that $m \geq n$. Also note that when $m = n$, that is, when there has to be an exact match, the first set of constraints can be written as equality constraints. This is in fact the case in the RS Shoes example.

The assignment problem is a special case of the transportation problem. The LP assignment model will yield an integer solution of zeros and ones.

SUMMARY

In this chapter we have discussed the terminology, notation, and assumptions of linear programming models. In situations where the assumptions hold, linear programming models provide a powerful technique for optimizing an objective under constrained conditions.

We have seen a variety of applications of linear programming models in the functional areas of business. There are also many applications of these types of models in the military and in government. The text by Gass, 1985, lists citations for over 1,000 applications of linear programming-based models. Building LP models is an art that requires practice, and to this end, we provide ample opportunity to enhance your skills with the problem set that follows.

In this chapter we briefly discussed the potential benefit of linear programming-based solutions. The next chapter provides more detail about how to solve LP models using a computer, and Chapter 6 focuses on how to effectively interpret the output from these computer solutions.

Finally, in this chapter we have seen two examples of very special LP models: the transportation and assignment problem models. The special characteristic of these models is that if their constraints have integer right-hand sides, then their solution values will also be integer. In Chapter 8 we will focus on integer programming models, that is, linear programming models where some or all of the decision variables are restricted to be integer. What differentiates integer programming models from linear programming models is that, more often than not, the integer restriction will not be as easily satisfied as in the transportation and assignment problems.

CHAPTER REVIEW EXERCISES

I. Terms to Understand

a. Mathematical programming (p. 127)

b. Linear programming (p. 128)

c. Nonnegativity constraint (p. 132)

d. Objective function coefficient (p. 128)

e. Constraint coefficient (p. 128)

f. Right-hand side values (p. 128)

g. Decision variable (p. 131)

II. Discussion Questions

1. What assumptions must be satisfied before a problem can be modeled using linear programming? Describe four scenarios: two where the assumptions would be satisfied, and two where at least one of the assumptions would be violated.

2. To what does the term *program* in linear program refer? Explain.

3. Linear programs often yield solutions with fractional values for the decision variables. In what kinds of applications would this pose a problem? When would this not be of much concern?

4. Consider Example 5, *Production Planning Over Time*. In the solution given why do you think inventory is carried from the first to the second quarter?

5. What special property does the transportation problem have? Why might it be important in some scenarios?

III. Problems

1. Tommy's Tables produces two types of tables, regular and deluxe. These two models use the same legs (each table requires four), but the deluxe is larger because it has more surface area. It takes .5 hours to finish a regular table and 1 hour to finish a deluxe table. This week Tommy has 45 hours of labor available for finishing and 240 usable table legs on hand in the shop. Each regular table produces a profit of $200, and each deluxe produces a profit of $425. Develop an LP model which will yield the number of regulars and deluxes to produce in order to maximize profit. Also construct a spreadsheet model of this scenario. Find the best solution you can using trial-and-error.

2. Kilgore's Deli is a small delicatessen located near a major university. Kilgore's does a large walk-in carry-out lunch business. The deli offers two luncheon chili specials, Wimpy and Dial 911. At the beginning of the day Kilgore needs to decide how much of each special to make (he always sells out of whatever he makes). The profit on one serving of Wimpy is $.45 and a serving of Dial 911 yields a profit of $.58. Each serving of Wimpy requires .25 pounds of beef, .25 cups of onions, and 5 ounces of Kilgore's special sauce. Each serving of Dial 911 requires .25 pounds of beef, .4 cups of onions, 2 ounces of Kilgore's special sauce, and 5 ounces of hot sauce. Today, Kilgore has 20 pounds of beef, 15 cups of onions, 88 ounces of Kilgore's special sauce, and 60 ounces of hot sauce on hand. Develop an LP model that will tell Kilgore how many servings of Wimpy and Dial 911 to make in order to maximize his profit today.

3. A company has $400,000 to invest for the coming year. The company intends to invest in one or more of the following four options (expected returns are for the year): option 1 will pay 5 percent; option 2, 4.7 percent; option 3, 4 percent; and option 4, 5.75 percent. The company has decided that no more than $200,000 should be invested in any one option. Formulate an LP model which will yield the investment strategy that will maximize the expected return. Can you solve your model by simple inspection as we did with the knapsack problem? How is this problem similar to the knapsack problem? Construct a spreadsheet model based on your LP model and find the best solution you can using trial-and-error.

4. The Valdaz Coffee Company produces two premium blends of coffee, Tastee and Tastier. These coffees are blended from a mixture of four types of coffee beans, ($b1,b2,b3$, and $b4$). The profit per pound for Tastee is $1.34. Tastier has a per-pound profit of $1.48. The per-pound blend requirements of $b1$, $b2$, $b3$ and $b4$ to make a pound of Tastee and Tastier, as well as the current availability of the beans are shown in the following figure. Assuming that Valdaz can sell everything it produces, formulate a linear programming model that will yield the amount of each blend to produce in order to maximize profit.

	Tastee Requirements per pound	Tastier Requirements per pound	Available
b1	.2 pounds	.5 pounds	2500 pounds
b2	.6 pounds	.1 pounds	1500 pounds
b3	.2 pounds	0 pounds	700 pounds
b4	0 pounds	.4 pounds	600 pounds

5. Reread Example 10, the M-Kart problem on capacity utilization. Use the spreadsheet model in Figure 4.8 to find the best solution you can using trial-and-error.

6. Very Good (VG) Juice Company produces five different juices: cherry, apple, orange, pineapple, and lemon. VG statisticians report to management with monthly projections of the minimum (based on previous retail orders) and maximum sales for each. In the past, these projections have been accurate, even though the demand is very seasonal. Each month, management is faced with the decision of how much of each product to produce for the next month. Virtually no finished product inventory is carried, but ample supplies of the raw materials are on hand. What makes the production decision difficult is that the products yield different profits and require different amounts of machine time in the three processes (blending, straining, and bottling) each employs. The relevant data (per 1,000 gal) as well as the minutes available per process, appear in the following table. Formulate a linear program that will prescribe how much of each product to produce given next month's projections.

	Apple	Cherry	Lemon	Orange	Pineapp	Avail.
Blend	23	22	18	19	19	5,000
Strain	22	40	20	34	22	3,000
Bottle	10	10	10	10	10	5,000

	Apple	Cherry	Lemon	Orange	Pineapp
Profit ($/1000 gal.)	$800	$320	$1,120	$1,440	$800
Max Sales (000)	20	30	50	50	20
Min Sales (000)	10	15	20	40	10

7. The Decatur Nut Company packages and sells three different half-pound canned peanut mixes: Party Nuts, Mixed, and Delightful Mix. These generate a per-can revenue of $2.25, $3.37, and $6.49 respectively. Party Nuts are simply 100 percent peanuts. Mixed consists of 55 percent peanuts, 25 percent cashews, 10 percent Brazil nuts, and 10 percent hazelnuts. Delightful Mix is made up of 40 percent cashews, 20 percent Brazil nuts, and 40 percent hazelnuts. The company has on hand 500 pounds of peanuts, 175 pounds of cashews, 100 pounds of Brazil nuts, and 80 pounds of hazelnuts. The company would like to mix these nuts in a way that will yield maximum revenue. Formulate this problem as a linear program.

8. A company produces four products with current variable costs of $9, $6.50, $5, and $7.50 per pound, respectively. Because the company works on a contractual basis with retailers, it knows the demands for each product for the next three months. These are specified in the following table. Due to a new labor contract, the variable cost of each of the products will increase by 5 percent at the beginning of month three. There are currently 50 pounds of each product on hand, and company policy dictates that at the end of the coming three-month period, there must also be an inventory of 50 pounds of each product.

   These four products share a common bottleneck machine which is available for 320 hours per month (two shifts of eight hours each per day, five days per week, four weeks per month). Product 1 needs .05 hours of the bottleneck per pound, product 2 requires .05 hours/pound, product 3 requires .2 hrs/pound, and product 4 requires .1 hours/pound. The cost of holding inventory per pound per month is 10 percent of the cost of the product. Develop an LP model to meet demand and minimize the cost of production and inventory.

Demands for Each Product by Month

Product	Month 1	Month 2	Month 3
1	1,000	800	1,000
2	1,000	900	500
3	600	600	500
4	0	200	500

9. Consider the scenario where a company produces a single product. Demands for the next four quarters are known to be 700, 1,200, 550, and 1,000 units, respectively. The production cost of the product is $125 per unit. The per-unit cost to hold one unit in inventory is 25 percent of the cost of the product per quarter. An inventory buffer level of 25 units must be maintained in every quarter. Due to capacity limitations, no more than 1,000 units can be produced in any given quarter. Develop an LP model that will yield a production plan that minimizes total cost (defined as the sum of the cost of production and holding).

10. The Coger Company is a midwestern producer of canned soups. The company's food processing plants are located in Columbus, OH and Indianapolis, IN. Distribution centers are located in Toledo, OH, Dayton, OH, Bowling Green, KY, and St. Louis, MO. The new director of logistical planning, who was brought in to improve the efficiency of operations, has decided to use mathematical modeling to optimize the cost of shipping the goods from the processing plants to the distribution centers. The cost of shipping a case of soup from each processing center to each distribution center is given in the following table. The weekly capacity at the two processing centers as well as the weekly requirements at the distribution centers are provided in another table. Develop an LP model the logistical director could use to minimize the cost of shipping while meeting capacity and demand requirements.

Per Case Cost of Shipping

	Toledo	Dayton	Bowl. Gr.	St. Louis
Columbus	$1.75	$1.25	$3.25	$5.60
Indy	$1.90	$1.25	$2.50	$3.00

Weekly Capacity	(cases)	Weekly Demand	
Columbus	3,000	Toledo	1,200
Indianapolis	4,000	Dayton	1,800
		Bowling Gr.	900
		St. Louis	2,500

11. Newberg Brewery has received an order for 100 gallons of 3 percent beer (that is, 3 percent alcoholic content). However, 3 percent beer is not one of this small brewery's regular products. The four types of beer in stock are two nonalcoholic beers (NA1, .25 percent alcohol and NA2, .5 percent alcohol), a light beer (L1, 5.8 percent alcohol), and a stout beer (S1, 6.3 percent alcohol). There are 1,000 gallons of each of these products on hand. Rather than attempting to brew a 3 percent beer from scratch, the brewmaster, who has had a particularly bad day, has decided to mix amounts of existing stock, perhaps with some water (0 percent alcoholic content), to satisfy this small order (which he considers a real nuisance!). He hopes that whatever mixture he uses does not taste too bad. In case the taste is bad and he has to start over, he would like to minimize the cost of this mixture. A gallon of NA1 costs $.45, NA2 costs $.50/gallon, L1 costs $.65/gallon and S1 costs $.90/gallon. Water is free. Develop a model that will find the least cost blend of the existing stock and water which will result in a 3% "beer."

12. The scheduler for a softball league is in the process of scheduling the umpires for each game in the coming week. There are five games that week and he has six umpires available. Every game needs exactly one umpire and an umpire should not be assigned to more than one game in a week. Because a new cycle (rotation of umpires) is beginning, it does not matter which umpire takes a break this coming week. The following table shows the number of times (in the past) that each umpire has been scheduled for a game involving either team in each of next week's games. The scheduler wishes to start out this cycle with a matching of umpires to games that avoids placing umpires with teams they have seen many times. Develop a model that will match umpires to games next week, in a manner that will minimize the sum of the number of times the umpires have previously been paired with the teams.

Number of times each umpire has been paired with the teams playing in next week's games

Umpire	Game 1	Game 2	Game 3	Game 4	Game 5
1	2	1	2	2	2
2	3	0	1	4	1
3	2	2	2	2	0
4	3	2	0	2	3
5	3	3	4	1	0
6	0	1	1	5	1

13. A financial planner is developing an investment portfolio for a client who has $75,000 to invest. The client is new to investing and therefore wishes to refrain from investing directly in stocks. The planner has therefore identified six funds: three growth and income (G&I), two index funds (I), and a money market fund (MM). The five year annual rate of return, while far from a guarantee, is used by the planner as an estimate of the expected future annual return. These rates are shown in the following table. The client wishes to put no more than 50 percent of her investment in any one fund and would like at least twice as much in growth and income as in the money market fund. Develop an LP model to give the investment strategy that will maximize her expected return subject to the conditions above.

Five-Year Annual Rate of Return

	G&I 1	G&I 2	G&I 3	I1	I2	MM
Rate:	15%	10%	16%	10%	13%	8%

14. A company produces two products. Production time for both products involves processing time in two different departments, A and B. Each unit of product 1 requires .5 minutes of time in department A and one minute in department B. Each unit of product 2 requires two minutes in department A and 3 minutes in department B. Because of the complicated nature of the work in Department A, there is a 2 percent scrap rate on the work in process for product 1 and a 1 percent scrap rate on product 2 work in process. That is, only 98 percent of the product 1 work in process is usable after it is processed in department A, and likewise for 99 percent of product 2. This coming week there are 20 hours of time available in department A and 15 available in department B. The per-unit profits of products 1 and 2 are \$4.50 and \$8.75 respectively. Develop an LP model to prescribe a production plan that will maximize profit.

15. Corry is an undergraduate management major at the University of Cincinnati. He has just finished the requirements for the mandatory management science course. The grading for the course is composed of a midterm exam, a final exam, individual assignments, and class participation. The final exam was on Monday, and Corry picked up his final exam grade on Tuesday, so he now knows all of the scores which will factor into his overall grade. He has earned an 86 percent on the midterm, a 94 percent on the final, 93 percent on the individual assignments and an 85 percent in participation. The benevolent management science instructor is allowing each student in the class to determine their own weights for each of the four components that will determine their final grade. Of course, there are some restrictions on the weightings used to arrive at an overall course grade:

    1. The participation grade can be no more than 15 percent (.15).
    2. The midterm exam score must count at least twice as much as the individual assignment score.
    3. The final exam score must count at least three times as much as the individual assignment score.
    4. Each of the four components must count for at least 10 percent (.10) of the course grade.
    5. The weights used must sum to one and be nonnegative.

    Develop a model that will yield the set of valid weights which will maximize his score for the course.

16. Drew's Sporting Goods, a sporting goods chain, will be sponsoring a Gun and Knife show in January of next year, and is currently developing a morning radio advertisement plan. Five of the largest radio stations have been flagged as good choices for the campaign. Their cost per half minute for advertising on each station is shown in the following table.

Station	Cost/.5 Minute
Rock 102.7	\$200
Country 100	\$150
Country 103.1	\$250
All Talk 700	\$500
All Sports 55	\$100

The company has allocated \$15,000 for morning radio advertisements. To ensure a broad reach, at least five minutes of advertisement should be purchased on each of these five stations and no more than 15 minutes should be bought on any one station. The company has decided that at least as many minutes of advertisements should be purchased on the two country stations (combined) as on the other three stations (combined). Develop a model that will maximize the number of .5 minute advertisements purchased, subject to the stated restrictions.

17. Epsilon Airlines is a national airline that services predominantly the eastern and southeastern United States. Over 60 percent of Epsilon's passengers book directly through the company's own reservation system. Because the airline industry is so competitive, it is especially important that customers not have to wait to make reservations. Epsilon analysts have estimated the minimum number of reservationists needed by day of the week, for the months of June and July and the first two weeks of August (the typical family summer vacation period). These estimates are shown in the following table.

Day	Minimum Number of Reservationists Needed
Monday	75
Tuesday	50
Wednesday	45
Thursday	60
Friday	90
Saturday	75
Sunday	45

A union contract stipulates that each reservationist must work five consecutive days and then have two days off. Each reservationist receives the same weekly salary. Assume that this schedule cycles, and ignore the start-up and stopping of this schedule. Develop a model that will minimize the labor cost of reservations while meeting the minimum requirements stated above and abiding by the union contract. You may ignore the practical requirement that the number of reservationists must be integer.

18. A large midwestern consumer goods corporation has asked SALS Marketing Inc. to develop an advertising campaign for one of its new products. SALS has promised a plan that will yield the highest possible exposure rating, a measurement of the ability to reach the appropriate demographic group, which is correlated with demand produced per dollar spent on advertising. The options for advertisements with their respective costs (per unit of advertising) and per-unit exposure ratings are given in the following table.

Of course, certain restrictions exist for the advertising campaign. The corporation has budgeted $800,000 for the campaign, but to restrict overexposure to any particular audience, wants **no more** than $300,000 put into any one medium. Also, to ensure a broad range of exposure, **at least** $100,000 must be spent in each medium. Develop an LP model of this situation.

Media		Cost per Unit	Exposure per Unit
Magazines:	Literary	$7,500	15,000
	News	$10,000	22,500
	Topical	$15,000	24,000
Newspapers:	Major Evening	$3,000	75,000
	Major Morning	$2,000	37,500
Television:	Morning	$20,000	275,000
	Mid-day	$10,000	180,000
	Evening	$60,000	810,000
Radio:	Morning	$15,000	180,000
	Mid-day	$15,000	17,000
	Evening	$10,000	16,000

19. A couple wishes to maximize the amount of cash they have on hand when they retire in five years. They are considering two investments (*A* and *B*) which will be renewable annually, one (*C*) that will be available at the start of year three and be annually renewable thereafter, and finally, one (*D*) that is available at the start of the third year and pays back at the end of the fifth year. The couple has a lump sum note of $11,000 due at the end of year two. They currently have $200,000 available for investment. The return per dollar invested is given in the following table.

Investment	Term	Net Return per Dollar Invested
A	Annual	6.5%
B	Annual	6.0%
C	Annual (after year 2)	7.0%
D	3 Years (years 3,4,5)	19.0%

   Investments *A* and *B* are not independent. Each year, at least as much must be invested in *B* as is invested in *A*. Develop a model to provide the plan that will maximize the cash available at the start of the sixth year.

20. Old Towne Brewery is a new, small, locally run brewery in Boston, MA. Old Towne produces five different beers, all sold in six-packs of twelve-ounce bottles. The five products with their variable cost (per six-pack) and contribution (defined as the selling price − variable cost per six pack) are shown in the following table. The total production cost for this month will be the variable costs plus the fixed costs for the plant and overhead, which amount to $5,000. Old Towne has orders that it has already committed to fill this month (in six-packs): 100 Stout, 100 Paul R, 100 Kings, 400 Light, and 80 Kings NA. The projections for this coming month indicate that the brewery can sell no more than 1,000 six-packs of Stout and 1,500 each of the other four types of beer. The brewery's accountant, who also has the misfortune of being the production scheduler, would like to schedule production so that profit is maximized this month.

Old Towne Brewery Product Data

Product	Variable Cost	Contribution
Stout	$4.75	$1.25
Paul R	2.90	1.10
Kings	3.20	.60
Light	2.80	.70
Kings NA	3.00	.90

IV. Projects and Cases

1. The first stage in ice cream making is the blending of ingredients so as to obtain a mix that meets prespecified requirements as to the percentage of certain constituents.[3] The desired composition is

---

[3] This problem is based on the Hendrie's Ice Cream scenario discussed in Chapter 3 of the text by Dano.

1. Fat	16.00%
2. Serum solids	8.00%
3. Sugar solids	16.00%
4. Egg solids	.35%
5. Stabilizer	.25%
6. Emulsifier	.15%
7. Water	59.25%

The mix is composed of ingredients from the following list.

Ingredient	Cost ($/lb.)
1. 40% cream	$1.19
2. 23% cream	.70
3. Butter	2.32
4. Plastic cream	2.30
5. Butter oil	2.87
6. 4% milk	.25
7. Skim condensed milk	.35
8. Skim milk powder	.65
9. Liquid sugar	.25
10. Sugared frozen fresh egg yolk	1.75
11. Powdered egg yolk	4.45
12. Stabilizer	2.45
13. Emulsifier	1.68
14. Water	.00

The number of pounds of a constituent found in a pound of an ingredient is shown in the following table. Note that a pound of stabilizer contributes only to the stabilizer requirement (one pound), one pound of emulsifier contributes only to the emulsifier requirement (one pound), and that water contributes to none of the requirements (it simply adds to the composition's volume and weight).

	Ingredient													
Constituent	1	2	3	4	5	6	7	8	9	10	11	12	13	14
1	.4	.2	.8	.8	.9	.1				.5	.6			
2	.1			.1		.1	.3	1						
3									.7	.1				
4										.4	.4			
5												1		
6													1	
7	.5	.8	.2	.1	.1	.8	.7		.3					1

The ice cream is produced in batches of 100 pounds. Develop an LP model that will prescribe how much of each ingredient to use in order to produce the ice cream at minimum cost. Develop a spreadsheet model based on your LP model and find the best solution you can using trial-and-error.

2.   The Calhoun Textile Mill[4]

The Calhoun Textile Mill is in the process of deciding on a production schedule. It wishes to know how to weave the various fabrics it will produce during the coming quarter. The sales department has confirmed orders for each of the 15 fabrics that are produced by Calhoun. These demands are given in the following table. Also given in this table is the variable cost for each fabric. The mill operates continuously during the quarter: 13 weeks, 7 days a week, and 24 hours a day.

There are two types of looms: dobbie and regular. Dobbie looms can be used to make all fabrics, and are the only looms that can weave certain fabrics, such as plaids. The rate of production for each fabric on each type of loom is also given in the table. Note that if the production rate is zero, the fabric cannot be woven on that type of loom. Also, if a fabric can be woven on each type of loom, then the production rates are equal. Calhoun has 90 regular looms and 15 dobbie looms. For this exercise, assume the time requirement to change over a loom from one fabric to another is negligible.

Fabrics woven at Calhoun proceed to the finishing department in the mill and then are sold. Any fabrics that are not woven in the mill because of limited capacity will be bought on the outside market, finished at the Calhoun Mill, and sold at the selling price. Management would like to know how to allocate the looms to the fabrics and which fabrics to buy on the market. Develop an LP model of Calhoun's problem. Construct a spreadsheet model based on your LP model and find the best solution you can using trial-and-error.

Calhoun Textile Mill Data

Fabric	Demand (Yds.)	Dobbie (Yd./Hr.)	Regular (Yd./Hr.)	Mill Cost ($/Yd.)	Sub. Cost ($/Yd.)
1	16,500	4.653	0.00	.6573	.80
2	52,000	4.653	0.00	.555	.70
3	45,000	4.653	0.00	.655	.85
4	22,000	4.653	0.00	.5542	.70
5	76,500	5.194	5.194	.6097	.75
6	110,000	3.809	3.809	.6153	.75
7	122,000	4.185	4.185	.6477	.80
8	62,000	5.232	5.232	.488	.60
9	7,500	5.232	5.232	.5029	.70
10	69,000	5.232	5.232	.4351	.60
11	70,000	3.733	3.733	.6417	.80
12	82,000	4.185	4.185	.5675	.75
13	10,000	4.439	4.439	.4952	.65
14	380,000	5.232	5.232	.3128	.45
15	62,000	4.185	4.185	.5029	.70

---

[4]Based on Camm et al., 1987.

REFERENCES

Bradley, Stephen P., Arnoldo C. Hax, and Thomas L. Magnanti. *Applied Mathematical Programming.* Reading, Massachusetts: Addison-Wesley Publishing Company, 1977.

Camm, Jeffrey D., P.M. Dearing, and Suresh K. Tadisina. "The Calhoun Textile Mill Case: An Exercise on the Significance of Linear Programming Modeling." *IIE Transactions*, Vol.19, No. 1, March 1987, pp. 23–28.

Dano, Sven. *Linear Programming In Industry.* Wien: Springer-Verlag, 1974.

Dantzig, George B. "Reminiscences About the Origins of Linear Programming." *Operations Research Letters*, Vol. 1, No. 2, April 1982, pp. 43–48.

Dantzig, George B. "The Diet Problem." *Interfaces*, Vol. 20, No. 4, July–August 1990, pp. 43–47.

Evans, James R. and Jeffrey D. Camm. "Using Pictorial Representations in Teaching Linear Programming Modeling." *IIE Transactions*, Vol. 22, No. 2, June 1990, pp. 191–195.

Field, Richard C. "National Forest Planning is Promoting US Forest Service Acceptance of Operations Research," *Interfaces*, Vol. 14, No. 5, September–October 1984, pp. 67–76.

Gass, Saul I. *Linear Programming.* 5th edition. New York: McGraw Hill Book Company, 1985.

Klingman, Darwin, Nancy Phillips, David Steiger, and Warren Young. "The Successful Deployment of Management Science throughout Citgo Petroleum Corporation," *Interfaces*, Vol. 17, No. 1, January–February, 1987, pp. 4–25.

Kotler, Philip. *Marketing Decision Making: A Model Building Approach.* Holt Reinhart and Winston: 1971: pp. 171–173.

Makuch, William M., Jeffrey L. Dodge, Joseph E. Ecker, Donna C. Granfors, and Gerald J. Hahn. "Managing Consumer Credit Delinquency in the U.S. Economy: A Multi-Billion Dollar Management Science Application." *Interfaces*, Vol. 22, No. 1, January–February 1992, pp. 90–109.

CHAPTER 5

SOLVING

LINEAR

PROGRAMMING

MODELS

In Chapter 4 we discussed modeling issues and applications of linear programming. In this chapter, we turn our attention to solving linear programs. The solution procedure is complex enough that it is almost always performed by a computer. Standard computer output provides a variety of information for managerial analysis in addition to the optimal solution. You will find it easier to interpret this computer output if you have an intuitive understanding of how computer software solves linear programs.

In this chapter we discuss some important geometric concepts underlying linear programming models and how these concepts are related to solution techniques. It is not our goal to teach you the mathematics required to solve LPs. Rather, we want to develop your intuition so that you will be a more intelligent user of LP models.

THE GEOMETRY OF LINEAR PROGRAMS

To gain intuition and better understand the geometry of linear programs, we will study examples with only two decision variables. Pictures of two-dimensional problems are easy to illustrate and have the basic characteristics of practical problems that have more decision variables. Recall that a feasible solution to a linear program is a set of values for the decision variables that satisfies *all* the constraints. Linear programs generally have an infinite number of feasible solutions.

> The set of feasible solutions to a linear program is called the *feasible region*.

How can we characterize the feasible region of a linear program geometrically? The constraints of any LP are one of the following three types.

1. Less than or equal to ($\leq$).
2. Greater than or equal to ($\geq$).
3. Equal to ($=$).

Types 1 and 2 are called *inequality* constraints; type 3 is called an *equality* constraint. Because we assume that all constraints are linear functions of the decision variables, we can easily characterize the feasible region.

Graphing Inequality Constraints

In a problem with only two decision variables (x_1, x_2), we can draw the feasible region on a two-dimensional coordinate system. Let us begin by considering the simplest constraints in an LP model, namely that the decision variables must be nonnegative. These constraints are $x_1 \geq 0$ and $x_2 \geq 0$. The constraint $x_1 \geq 0$ corresponds to all points on or to the right of the x_2 axis; the constraint $x_2 \geq 0$ corresponds to all points on or above the x_1 axis (see Figure 5.1). Taken together, these nonnegativity restrictions imply that any feasible solution must be restricted to the first (upper-right) quadrant.

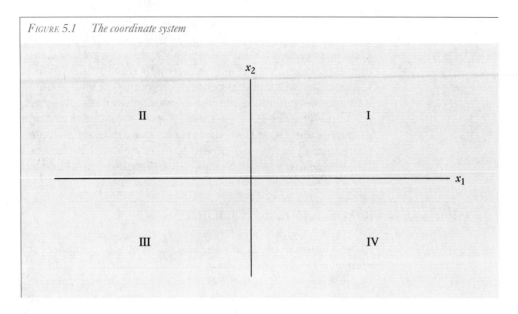

FIGURE 5.1   *The coordinate system*

In two dimensions, an equality constraint is simply a line. As an example, consider the constraint $5x_1 + 2x_2 = 20$. To graph a line in two dimensions, we need to find two points that lie on the line. As long as the right-hand side term is not zero, the two points that are easiest to find are the x_1 and x_2 intercepts (the points where the line crosses the x_1 and x_2 axes). To find the x_2 intercept we set $x_1 = 0$ and solve for x_2. We find that $x_2 = 20/2 = 10$. Likewise, to find the x_1 intercept we set $x_2 = 0$, obtaining $x_1 = 20/5 = 4$. Thus, two points that lie on the line $5x_1 + 2x_2 = 20$ are (0,10) and (4,0); the line extending through these points is shown in Figure 5.2. In three dimensions an equality constraint forms a *plane*; in higher dimensions, we call it a *hyperplane*.

Now consider the inequality constraint $5x_1 + 2x_2 \leq 20$. Notice that all points on the line $5x_1 + 2x_2 = 20$ satisfy this inequality. In addition, all points (x_1, x_2) for which $5x_1 + 2x_2$ is *strictly less than* 20 also satisfy the constraint. Where can these points be found? In Figure 5.2 we can see that a straight line divides the plane into two parts, which we call *halfspaces*. One halfspace consists of all points for which $5x_1 + 2x_2 \geq 20$; the *other* halfspace consists of all points for which $5x_1 + 2x_2 \leq 20$. We need only to determine which halfspace corresponds to our constraint by testing any point on either side of the line. For example, the point (0,0) is easy to test to see whether it satisfies the inequality constraint $5x_1 + 2x_2 \leq 20$. If we substitute (0,0) into the left-hand side of the inequality, we have $5(0) + 2(0) = 0 < 20$. Therefore, the side of the line containing (0,0) is the halfspace that satisfies the constraint, and all points in this halfspace will also satisfy the constraint. If we had found that (0,0) did *not* satisfy the constraint, then it would be true that any point in the *other* halfspace would satisfy it. Figure 5.3 (on page 182) shows the halfspace for $5x_1 + 2x_2 \leq 20$.

We may determine the set of feasible points for each constraint of a linear program in a similar fashion. For any inequality constraint, we first find the line corresponding to

FIGURE 5.2   *The line* $5x_1 + 2x_2 = 20$

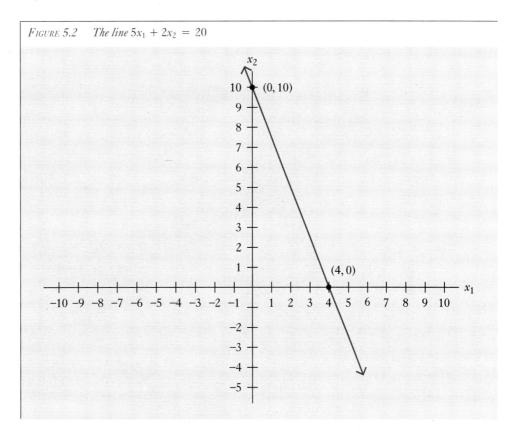

the constraint as an equality. We refer to this line as the *constraint line*. Then we determine which halfspace satisfies the inequality.

As another example, let us consider a greater-than-or-equal-to constraint, $2x_1 + 3x_2 \geq 6$. We can graph this constraint using the same approach we used with the less-than-or-equal-to constraint. We first find two points on the constraint line $2x_1 + 3x_2 = 6$. When we set $x_1 = 0$, we obtain $x_2 = 2$. When we set $x_2 = 0$, we obtain $x_1 = 3$. We therefore have two points that lie on the line: (0,2) and (3,0). We pick a point that is not on the constraint line in order to determine which halfspace the inequality defines. For example, let us use (0,0). Since $2(0) + 3(0) = 0 < 6$, the halfspace corresponding to $2x_1 + 3x_2 \geq 6$ is the side of the line that does not contain the point (0,0). This halfspace is shown in Figure 5.4 (on page 182).

In graphing the constraints in the previous two examples, we were able to find two points on the line defined by the constraint by finding the intercepts (we set one variable to 0 and solved for the second, and vice versa). If the line passes through the origin (0,0), both intercepts will be the same, and we will need to find another point on the line. We can do this by picking any non-zero value for one of the variables and solving for the second variable.

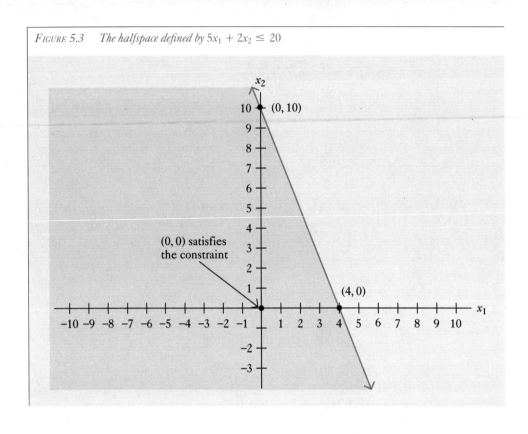

FIGURE 5.3   *The halfspace defined by* $5x_1 + 2x_2 \leq 20$

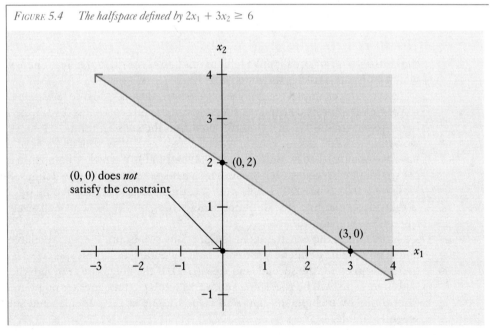

FIGURE 5.4   *The halfspace defined by* $2x_1 + 3x_2 \geq 6$

For example, consider the constraint $x_1 - x_2 \leq 0$. We first graph the line $x_1 - x_2 = 0$. If we set $x_1 = 0$, then $x_2 = 0$. Obviously, setting $x_2 = 0$ will result in the same point, so let us simply choose a value for x_1 that is not 0. Suppose we set $x_1 = 10$. Then $10 - x_2 = 0$ or $x_2 = 10$. We now have two points on the constraint line: $(0,0)$ and $(10,10)$, as shown in Figure 5.5. The halfspace is determined in the same manner as before, by picking a point *not on the line* and testing to see if that point satisfies the constraint. Pick a point and test it to ensure that we have shaded in the correct halfspace in Figure 5.5.

In the previous examples, the intercepts of the constraint lines were in the first quadrant. This is not always the case. Consider for example, the constraint $-3x_1 + 2x_2 \leq 12$. We first graph the line $-3x_1 + 2x_2 = 12$. If we set $x_1 = 0$, then $x_2 = 12/2 = 6$. If we set $x_2 = 0$, then $x_1 = 12/(-3) = -4$. Thus, we have two points on the constraint line: $(0,6)$ and $(-4,0)$, as shown in Figure 5.6. Testing a point not on the line indicates that the halfspace shown in Figure 5.6 (for example, the point $(0,0)$) does satisfy the inequality.

FIGURE 5.5   *The halfspace defined by* $x_1 - x_2 \leq 0$

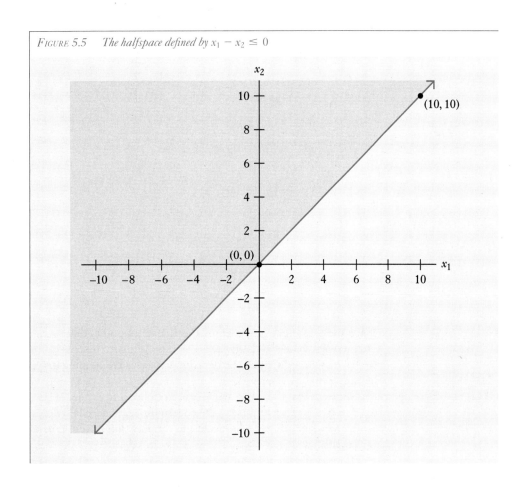

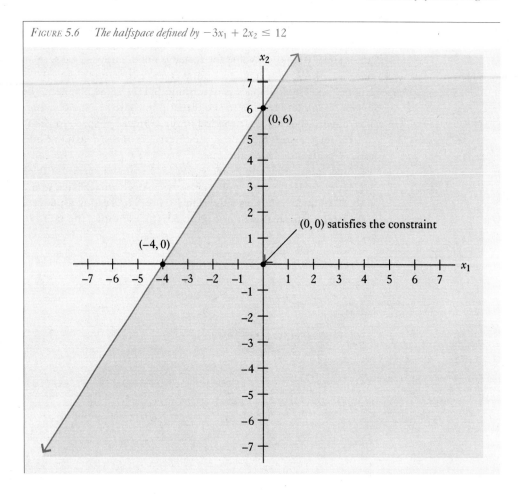

FIGURE 5.6   *The halfspace defined by* $-3x_1 + 2x_2 \leq 12$

Finding the Feasible Region

Since the feasible region for an LP is the set of points that satisfies all constraints, it must be the *intersection* of all halfspaces corresponding to the constraints. Furthermore, because we have assumed that all the decision variables are nonnegative, the feasible region must lie in the first quadrant.

Suppose that the nonnegativity restrictions and the set of constraints shown in Figures 5.3, 5.4, 5.5, and 5.6 represent the constraint set of an LP. By plotting all of the constraints on the same graph, we can locate the intersection of the halfspaces. The intersection of the constraints $5x_1 + 2x_2 \leq 20$, $2x_1 + 3x_2 \geq 6$, $x_1 - x_2 \leq 0$, $-3x_1 + 2x_2 \leq 12$, and the first quadrant is shown in Figure 5.7.

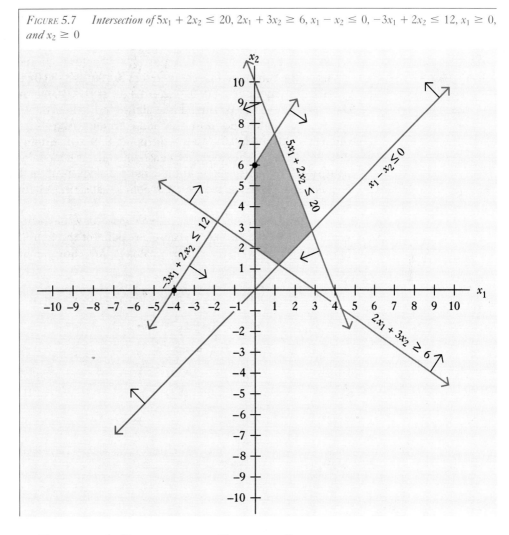

FIGURE 5.7   *Intersection of* $5x_1 + 2x_2 \leq 20$, $2x_1 + 3x_2 \geq 6$, $x_1 - x_2 \leq 0$, $-3x_1 + 2x_2 \leq 12$, $x_1 \geq 0$, *and* $x_2 \geq 0$

EXAMPLE 1. GRAPHING THE FEASIBLE REGION

Consider the linear program

$$\text{Max } 2x_1 + 3x_2$$
$$\text{subject to}$$
$$1.25x_1 + x_2 \leq 100$$
$$x_1 + x_2 \geq 30$$
$$x_1 \leq 50$$
$$x_2 \leq 75$$
$$x_1, x_2 \geq 0$$

To draw the feasible region, we must find the halfspace corresponding to each constraint and its intersection in the first quadrant. We begin by graphing the first constraint. To plot the constraint line, we need two points on the line $1.25x_1 + x_2 = 100$. If we set $x_1 = 0$, then $x_2 = 100$. Setting $x_2 = 0$ yields $x_1 = 100/(1.25) = 80$. The two points on the constraint line are therefore (0,100) and (80,0); this line is shown in Figure 5.8. Testing the point (0,0) $[1.25(0) + (0) = 0 < 100]$ indicates that the halfspace corresponding to this constraint is as shown in Figure 5.8.

The constraint line for the second constraint is $x_1 + x_2 = 30$. This line passes through (0,30) and (30,0). We test the point (0,0) to determine the halfspace: $0 + 0 = 0 < 30$. Therefore the side of the constraint line not containing (0,0) is the appropriate halfspace. This halfspace is shown with the halfspace of the first constraint in Figure 5.9. The shaded area is the region of points that satisfies both $1.25x_1 + x_2 \leq 100$ and $x_1 + x_2 \geq 30$.

The third constraint is called a *simple upper bound* on the variable x_1. What does the graph of $x_1 \leq 50$ look like? Because any point of the form $(50, x_2)$ satisfies $x_1 = 50$ (any value of x_2 will work), the constraint line corresponding to this constraint is

---

FIGURE 5.8   *The graph of* $1.25x_1 + x_2 \leq 100$ *in the first quadrant*

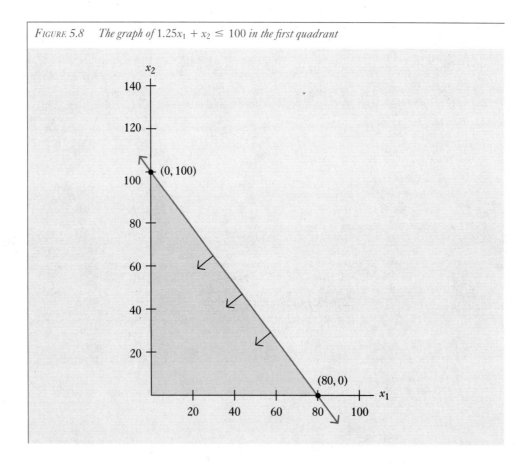

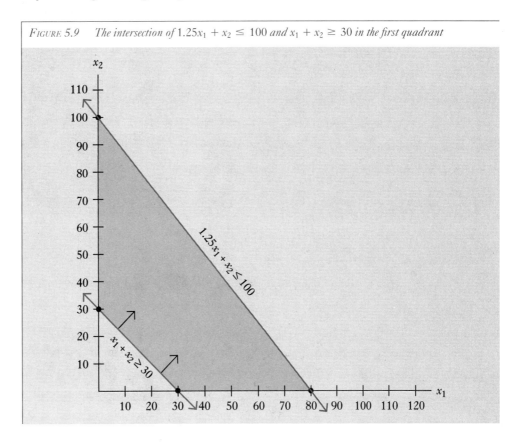

FIGURE 5.9   The intersection of $1.25x_1 + x_2 \leq 100$ and $x_1 + x_2 \geq 30$ in the first quadrant

a vertical line crossing the x_1 axis at 50. This is shown graphically in Figure 5.10. To determine which side of the line satisfies the inequality, we test point $(0,0)$. This point does satisfy the inequality because $0 < 50$, so the side of the line containing $(0,0)$ satisfies the constraint. The halfspace and its intersection with the halfspaces of the first two constraints in the first quadrant are shown in Figure 5.10.

The fifth constraint, $x_2 \leq 75$, is a simple upper bound on the variable x_2. Any point of the form $(x_1, 75)$ satisfies the constraint line $x_2 = 75$. Therefore, the constraint line is a horizontal line that crosses the x_2 axis at 75. All points in the halfspace below the line satisfy the inequality, as shown in Figure 5.11. (Again, check a point to assure yourself that this is correct.) Figure 5.11 shows the intersection of this constraint with the other three constraints in the first quadrant; the shaded area in Figure 5.11 is the feasible region.

Equality Constraints

Some LP models have equality constraints. In graphing inequality constraints with two variables, we saw that an equality constraint is simply a straight line. Suppose, for

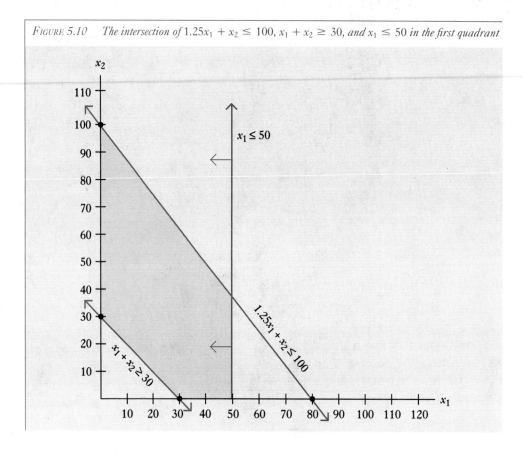

FIGURE 5.10   *The intersection of* $1.25x_1 + x_2 \leq 100$, $x_1 + x_2 \geq 30$, *and* $x_1 \leq 50$ *in the first quadrant*

example, that the constraint $-5x_1 + 7x_2 = 150$ is added to the problem in Example 1. This line passes through the points $(0, 21.43)$ and $(-30, 0)$ as shown in Figure 5.12. The feasible region for this new problem consists of all points in the feasible region shown in Figure 5.11 *that are also on the line* $-5x_1 + 7x_2 = 150$. Geometrically, the new feasible region is the *line segment* that intersects the region defined by the inequality constraints (see Figure 5.12). Notice how an equality constraint strongly restricts the size of the feasible region (compare Figure 5.11 to Figure 5.12).

Corner Points, Binding Constraints, and Optimal Solutions

The points labeled *a* through *f* in Figure 5.11 are known as the *corner points* of the feasible region. Note that corner points correspond to the intersection of two constraint lines. For example, consider point *c*. This point is formed by the intersection of the constraint lines

FIGURE 5.11   The feasible region for Example 1

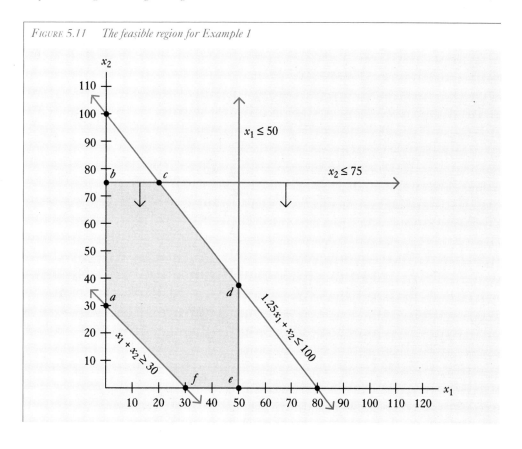

$1.25x_1 + x_2 = 100$ and $x_2 = 75$. The point c therefore satisfies both of the following equations.

$$1.25x_1 + x_2 = 100$$
$$x_2 = 75$$

Substituting $x_2 = 75$ from the second equation into the first yields

$$1.25x_1 + 75 = 100$$

or

$$1.25x_1 = 25$$

or

$$x_1 = 25/1.25 = 20$$

Point c is therefore (20,75).

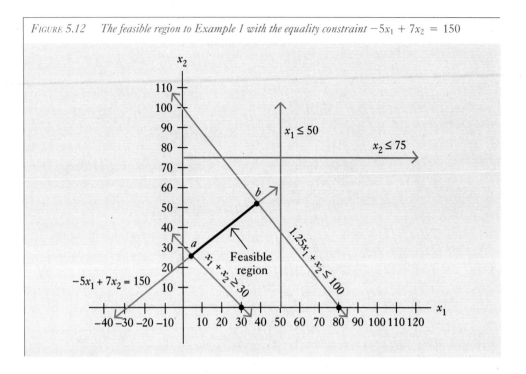

The constraints whose lines intersect at a corner point are called *binding constraints* at that corner point. Binding constraints at a corner point are those constraints that hold as equalities at that point.

The values of x_1 and x_2 at the other corner points in Figure 5.11 can be found in a similar manner by solving simultaneously the constraint lines of the binding constraints at the point. We can find the coordinates of point d for example, by solving the equations $1.25x_1 + x_2 = 100$ and $x_1 = 50$.

$$1.25(50) + x_2 = 100$$

or

$$x_2 = 100 - 1.25(50) = 37.5$$

Point d is therefore (50, 37.5). Corner point a in Figure 5.11 can be found by solving the equations $x_1 = 0$ and $x_1 + x_2 = 30$, which clearly yield the coordinates (0,30). The other corner point values can be easily calculated in a similar manner; their coordinates are point b, (0,75); point e, (50,0); and point f, (30,0).

The corner points of the feasible region in Figure 5.12 are the points labeled a and b. We can obtain the coordinates of point a by solving the equations $x_1 + x_2 = 30$ and $-5x_1 + 7x_2 = 150$ simultaneously. We solve the first equation for x_1: $x_1 = 30 - x_2$ and substitute into the second:

$$-5(30 - x_2) + 7x_2 = 150 \qquad \text{or} \qquad -150 + 12x_2 = 150$$

which yields

$$12x_2 = 300 \qquad \text{or} \qquad x_2 = 300/12 = 25$$

Substituting the value of x_2 back into the first equation yields the value of x_1.

$$x_1 + (25) = 30 \qquad \text{or} \qquad x_1 = 5$$

Hence the coordinates of point a are (5,25). In a similar manner we can solve the equations $-5x_1 + 7x_2 = 150$ and $1.25x_1 + x_2 = 100$ to get the coordinates of (40,50) for point b.

Corner points are important concepts in linear programs, because

> If an optimal solution to a linear program exists, it will occur at a corner point of the feasible region.

As we will discuss in the next section, this powerful result comes from the fact that the constraints and objective of a linear program are linear functions of the decision variables.

The fact that the solution to an LP can be found at a corner point suggests that one approach to solving a linear program would be to search *intelligently* among the corner points of the feasible region and to find the point that optimizes the objective function. This corresponds to trying to find which set of constraints to make binding. This is, in fact, the approach used by the most popular technique for solving linear programs, the simplex method. An intuitive explanation of the simplex algorithm is given in the Appendix of this chapter.

The Significance of Linearity

The assumption of a linear objective function and linear constraints is extremely important. Linearity ensures that the objective and the feasible region are what mathematicians call "well-behaved." This means that the feasible region has no disjointed pieces or jagged sides that could hamper our search for an optimal solution. It is the linearity assumption that implies that the solution to an LP will be a corner point.

Figure 5.13 shows a table of objective function values $Z = 2x_1 + 3x_2$ for selected feasible values of x_1 and x_2 for Example 1. The selected values for x_1 range from 0 to 60 in increments of 5, and those for x_2 range from 0 to 100 in increments of 5. A "." in the cell indicates that the (x_1, x_2) is infeasible (does not satisfy the constraint set). Notice that the shape of the set of feasible cells resembles that of the feasible region in Figure 5.11. There are some slight differences due to the fact that we have only snapshots of the discrete increments of 5 in each cell; nonetheless, this spreadsheet can give us a feel for how the objective function behaves. Notice that as we move from the cells in the lower part of the table toward those in the upper part, the objective function values increase.

FIGURE 5.13   *A spreadsheet table for Example 1*

A	A	B	C	D	E	F	G	H	I	J	K	L	M	N	O
1															
2															
3								x1							
4		.	0	5	10	15	20	25	30	35	40	45	50	55	60
5		100	.	.	.	.	.	.	.	.	.	.	.	.	.
6		95	.	.	.	.	.	.	.	.	.	.	.	.	.
7		90	.	.	.	.	.	.	.	.	.	.	.	.	.
8		85	.	.	.	.	.	.	.	.	.	.	.	.	.
9		80	.	.	.	.	.	.	.	.	.	.	.	.	.
10		75	225	235	245	255	265	.	.	.	.	.	.	.	.
11		70	210	220	230	240	250	.	.	.	.	.	.	.	.
12		65	195	205	215	225	235	245	.	.	.	.	.	.	.
13		60	180	190	200	210	220	230	240	.	.	.	.	.	.
14		55	165	175	185	195	205	215	225	235	.	.	.	.	.
15	x2	50	150	160	170	180	190	200	210	220	230	.	.	.	.
16		45	135	145	155	165	175	185	195	205	215	.	.	.	.
17		40	120	130	140	150	160	170	180	190	200	210	.	.	.
18		35	105	115	125	135	145	155	165	175	185	195	205	.	.
19		30	90	100	110	120	130	140	150	160	170	180	190	.	.
20		25	.	85	95	105	115	125	135	145	155	165	175	.	.
21		20	.	.	80	90	100	110	120	130	140	150	160	.	.
22		15	.	.	.	75	85	95	105	115	125	135	145	.	.
23		10	.	.	.	.	70	80	90	100	110	120	130	.	.
24		5	.	.	.	.	65	75	85	95	105	115	.	.	.
25		0	.	.	.	.	.	60	70	80	90	100	.	.	.

The same can be said as we move from left to right. This merely confirms what we already knew; that higher values for x_1 and x_2 give us a higher objective function value.

Figure 5.14 shows lines connecting constant values of the objective function. These constant objective function value lines are known as *objective function contours*. Notice that the contours are parallel to one another and that the value of the objective function increases in one direction (here, up and to the right) and decreases in the other direction. The optimal solution to the LP is the feasible point (or set of points) that are on the highest-valued contour line. Therefore, we can easily solve a two-variable problem by first graphing the feasible region and then plotting objective function contour lines in the direction of increase (for a maximization problem) or decrease (for a minimization problem) until we find the best feasible point.

EXAMPLE 2. FINDING AN OPTIMAL SOLUTION GRAPHICALLY

Let us continue our analysis of the model in Example 1. We have found the feasible region (see Figure 5.11), but still seek the optimal solution. We may use objective function contours to identify the optimal solution graphically.

Using this contour approach, we first plot $Z = 2x_1 + 3x_2$, for two values, say $Z = 100$ and $Z = 200$. (Note that this is the same as plotting an equality constraint.) These are shown in Figure 5.15. We move parallel contours in the direction of increased objective function value (because we are maximizing) until we find the last feasible point(s) that intersects with a contour. As shown in Figure 5.15, corner point *c* must

FIGURE 5.14   Contours for Example 1

	A	B	C	D	E	F	G	H	I	J	K	L	M	N	O
1															
2															
3								x1							
4		.	0	5	10	15	20	25	30	35	40	45	50	55	60
5		100	.	.	.	.	.	.	.	.	.	.	.	.	.
6		95	.	.	.	.	.	.	.	.	.	.	.	.	.
7		90	.	.	.	.	.	.	.	.	.	.	.	.	.
8		85	.	.	.	.	.	.	.	.	.	.	.	.	.
9		80	.	.	.	.	.	.	.	.	.	.	.	.	.
10		75	225	235	245	255	265	.	.	.	.	.	.	.	.
11		70	210	220	230	240	250	.	.	.	.	.	.	.	.
12		65	195	205	215	225	235	245	.	.	.	.	.	.	.
13		60	180	190	200	210	220	230	240	.	.	.	.	.	.
14		55	165	175	185	195	205	215	225	235	.	.	.	.	.
15	x2	50	150	160	170	180	190	200	210	220	230	.	.	.	.
16		45	135	145	155	165	175	185	195	205	215	.	.	.	.
17		40	120	130	140	150	160	170	180	190	200	210	.	.	.
18		35	105	115	125	135	145	155	165	175	185	195	205	.	.
19		30	90	100	110	120	130	140	150	160	170	180	190	.	.
20		25	.	85	95	105	115	125	135	145	155	165	175	.	.
21		20	.	.	80	90	100	110	120	130	140	150	160	.	.
22		15	.	.	.	75	85	95	105	115	125	135	145	.	.
23		10	.	.	.		70	80	90	100	110	120	130	.	.
24		5	.	.	.	.		65	75	85	95	105	115	.	.
25		0	.	.	.	.	.		60	70	80	90	100	.	.

Contour labels at right: 240, 210, 165

FIGURE 5.15   Feasible region and contours for Example 1

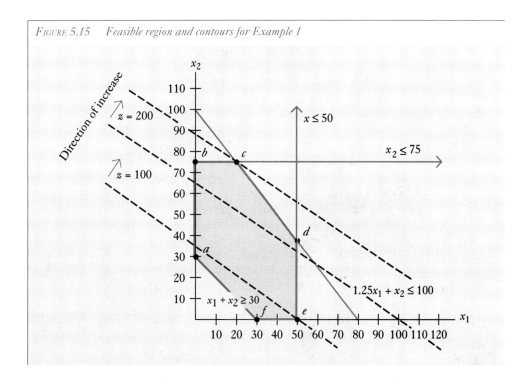

be the optimal solution. We can find the optimal objective function value, x_1, and x_2 values by solving the system of constraint lines for the constraints that are binding at point c. Point c is formed by the intersection of $1.25x_1 + x_2 = 100$ and $x_2 = 75$. We have already seen that the solution to this set of equations yields the point (20,75). Substituting $x_1 = 20$ and $x_2 = 75$ into the objective function yields $2(20) + 3(75) = 265$. We will use a * superscript to denote optimal values. We say therefore that $x_1^* = 20$, $x_2^* = 75$, and $z^* = 265$.

The geometry here provides insight into the reason why corner points are optimal solutions. Because the objective function is linear, the contours are parallel lines. Consequently, the best objective function will be found on a border of the feasible region. Because the constraints are linear, the feasible region is a set of points whose borders are straight lines. An optimal solution will therefore always occur at the intersection of the lines representing the borders and the best contour.

These concepts described for two-variable problems generalize to larger problems. Although we cannot visualize their feasible regions and objective function contours, the optimal solutions to LP problems with many variables and constraints can be found at the intersection of constraints.

CATEGORIZING LINEAR PROGRAMMING OUTPUTS

There are four possible outcomes to a linear programming model:

1. Unique optimal solution
2. Alternate optimal solutions
3. Unboundedness
4. Infeasibilty

When an LP has a *unique optimal solution*, it means that there is exactly one solution that will result in the maximum (or minimum) objective. If an LP has *alternate optimal solutions*, the objective is maximized (or minimized) by more than a single plan. This is good news because this type of solution gives management more flexibility in achieving the objective. A problem is *unbounded* if the objective can be maximized to infinity (or minimized to negative infinity). Ordinarily, this means that the real system has not been correctly modeled. Finally, if an LP is *infeasible*, it means that there is no plan that satisfies all of the restrictions of the problem. If this occurs, some of the restrictions originally imposed will have to be relaxed in order to obtain a feasible solution.

As we have seen, Example 2 is an example of a unique optimal solution. The point (20,75) gives an objective function value of 265. Every other feasible point lies on a lower valued contour, therefore every other feasible solution has an objective function value strictly less than 265. Examples 3 through 5 illustrate geometrically the other three possible outcomes for two dimensional problems.

EXAMPLE 3. ALTERNATE OPTIMAL SOLUTIONS

A linear program may have alternate optimal solutions. We illustrate this with the following example.

$$\text{Min } 4x_1 + 4x_2$$

subject to

$$x_1 + 2x_2 \leq 10$$

$$x_1 + x_2 \geq 1.5$$

$$x_2 \leq 4$$

$$x_1, x_2 \geq 0$$

As shown in Figure 5.16, the constraint line corresponding to the first inequality passes through the points (10,0) and (0,5). The second constraint line passes through the points (1.5,0) and (0,1.5). The third is a horizontal line through the point (0,4). The complete feasible region is the intersection of the three halfspaces in the first quadrant shown in Figure 5.16. Select a point on either side of each line to convince yourself that we have chosen the correct halfspaces.

This feasible region has five corner points, labeled *a-e*. We plot objective function contours for any two values of $Z = 4x_1 + 4x_2$, say $Z = 40$ and $Z = 20$ as shown in Figure 5.17. We continue to move in the direction of decreased objective function value until we find the lowest-valued contour that intersects the feasible region. As shown in Figure 5.17, the lowest valued contour lies directly over the second constraint line, $x_1 + x_2 = 1.5$.

Points *a* and *b both* achieve the smallest objective function value (remember that this is a minimization problem). Point *a* has coordinates (1.5,0) with objective function value $4(1.5) + 4(0) = 6$. Point *b* has coordinates (0,1.5) with objective function value $4(0) + 4(1.5) = 6$. This LP therefore has *two* optimal corner point solutions. In fact, there are an infinite number of solutions. Any point on the line segment connecting points *a* and *b* will have an objective function value of 6. For example, the point (1,0.5) lies on the line segment; it has an objective function value $Z = 4(1) + 4(.5) = 6$. Choose some other points on the line segment and check the objective function value to convince yourself that this is true.

An *alternate optimal solution* occurs when more than one corner point has the best objective function value. In this situation, an infinite number of optimal solutions exist.

Although any alternate optimal solution is as good as any other, there may be qualitative factors that make one solution more attractive than the others. The decision-maker will therefore have a variety of plans from which to choose. Unfortunately, computer programs designed to solve LP models typically only report one of the many possible alternate optimal solutions.

FIGURE 5.16   Feasible region for Example 3

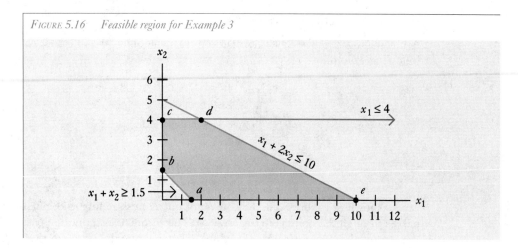

FIGURE 5.17   Feasible region and contours for Example 3

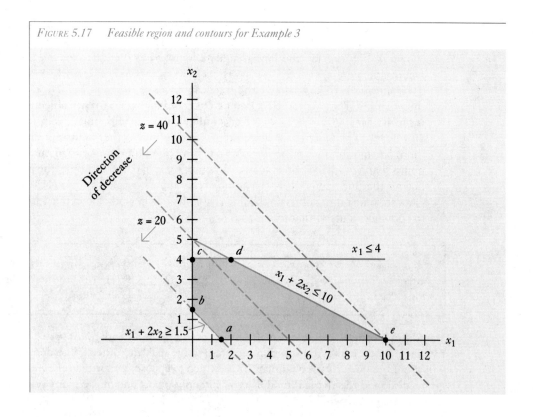

EXAMPLE 4. UNBOUNDED PROBLEM

Next, consider the LP shown below:

$$\text{Max } 2x_1 + 5x_2$$

$$\text{subject to}$$

$$x_1 + x_2 \geq 6$$

$$x_1 - x_2 \leq 4$$

$$x_1, x_2 \geq 0$$

The feasible region for this example is shown in Figure 5.18. Note that unlike the feasible regions for the first two examples, this region does not have a border on all sides. The feasible region extends to infinity along the two lines labeled e_1 and e_2. Two constraints intersect at the point (5,1), so we have two corner points: a (0,6)

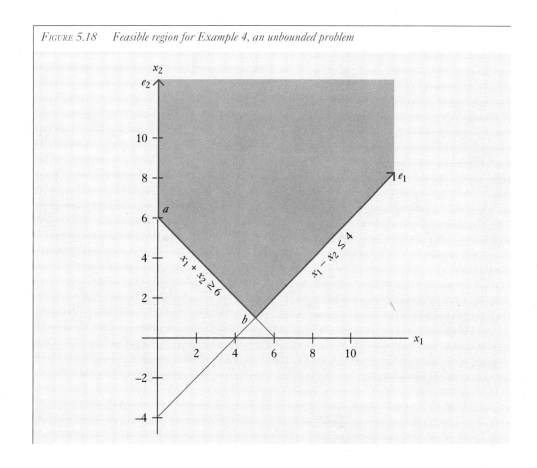

FIGURE 5.18   *Feasible region for Example 4, an unbounded problem*

and b (5,1). The objective function contours for values of $Z = 25$ and $Z = 40$ are shown in Figure 5.19. Note that the direction of increase in the contours is toward the open side of the feasible region. We can continue to plot contours corresponding to higher objective function values and still intersect the feasible region. Because there is no constraint to stop us, we can continue to pick points yielding increasingly larger objective function values. We can push the value of the objective function to infinity and still remain feasible.

> A linear program is *unbounded* if it has an open feasible region, and the direction of improved objective function values is in the direction of the open side of the feasible region. In this case no optimal solution exists.

An unbounded problem must have an open feasible region. (Any problem that has a feasible region bordered on all sides cannot be an unbounded.) *However, a problem with*

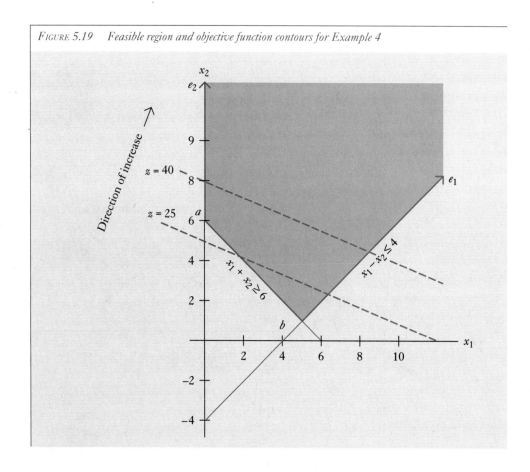

FIGURE 5.19   *Feasible region and objective function contours for Example 4*

an open feasible region is not necessarily unbounded. To see this, consider the problem in Example 4, but with a minimization objective. The minimization problem has the same feasible region and contours shown in Figure 5.19, but we now seek the feasible point or points on the lowest-valued contour. As we move the contours to lower and lower values, we see that point b will be the feasible point on the lowest-valued contour. Corner point b has coordinates (5,1) with $Z = 15$. The optimal solution therefore occurs at corner point b, and because the objective function value of all other feasible points is strictly greater than that at b, it is a unique optimal solution.

It is also possible, of course, for an LP with an open feasible region to have alternate optimal solutions, either along a side of the feasible region defined by corner points or along a constraint line of the open area.

Since we live in a world of limited resources, an unbounded problem typically means that some constraint or set of constraints has been left out of the model. It is impossible, for example, to maximize profit to infinity or to minimize cost to negative infinity. If you have an unbounded problem, you should check to make sure that all of the restrictions of the problem are in the model and that the model inputs have the appropriate sign.

Example 5. Infeasible Problem

The fourth possible outcome of an LP is infeasibility. Consider the following LP:

$$\text{Max } 1.1x_1 - 2x_2$$
$$\text{subject to}$$
$$x_1 + x_2 \leq 3$$
$$x_2 \geq 4$$
$$x_1 - x_2 = 1$$
$$x_1, x_2 \geq 0$$

Graphs of the three constraints are shown in Figure 5.20. (Remember that only points on the line satisfy the constraint in the equality case.) We see that there is no point that satisfies all constraints simultaneously. Consequently, the feasible region is empty.

An LP whose feasible region is empty is called *infeasible*.

Infeasible problems can occur in practice. For example, a company could be in the enviable position of having increasing demand for its product, but find that it no longer has the capacity to satisfy this demand. As we shall see later in this chapter, output from computer LP solvers can often provide valuable information about how to change the model to ensure that a feasible solution exists. In the situation just described, for example, the company might be able to learn how much capacity needs to be added to its facility to ensure that demand is satisfied.

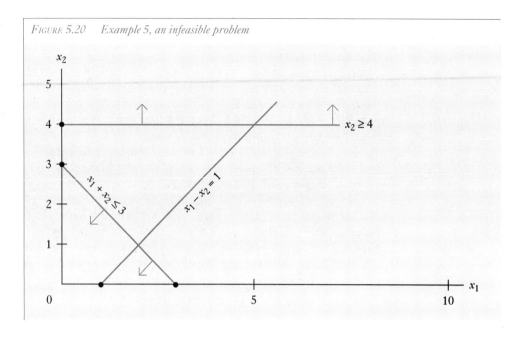

FIGURE 5.20   *Example 5, an infeasible problem*

Summary of Graphical LP Solution

The following steps summarize the simple graphic approach we have been using to solve two-dimensional linear programs.

1. Draw the feasible region. (If the region is empty, then stop; the problem is infeasible. Otherwise go to step 2.)
2. Select two values for the objective function and plot their associated contours. Continue plotting contours parallel to the first two in the direction of increase (for a max) or decrease (for a min) as determined by them. Continue plotting contours until there is no longer any intersection with the feasible region. If it is impossible to leave the feasible region as you move in that direction, then the problem is unbounded. Otherwise go to step 3.
3. If the best contour that intersects the feasible region contains only a single feasible point, then that point is the unique optimal solution. If the best contour lies on a border, any point on that border is an optimal solution. In either case, solve for the optimal solution by solving the set of binding constraints at that corner point (or set of corner points).

To the best of the authors' knowledge, no one is making any money solving linear programming problems graphically (with the possible exception of management science textbook authors!), because this approach can only be used for two-variable problems. There are not many two-dimensional problems in practice. However, the geometry of LP models provides important insight into the solution of larger LP models.

STANDARD FORM

Linear programs can have any mix of less-than-or-equal-to, greater-than-or-equal-to, or equality constraints. Computer programs that solve linear programs preprocess a model and convert it into what is called *standard form*.

> A linear program is said to be in standard form if (1) all constraints (excluding the nonnegativity constraints) are expressed as equalities, (2) all variables are restricted to be nonnegative, (3) all variables appear on the left-hand side of the constraints, and (4) all constant quantities appear on the right-hand side of the constraints.

To express a problem in standard form, we must have a way to convert inequality constraints to equalities. Consider for example the inequality $5x_1 + x_2 \leq 10$. We may define a new decision variable for this constraint, known as a *slack variable*. The slack variable represents the amount by which the left-hand side of the less-than-or-equal-to constraint is less than the right-hand side. Alternatively, a slack variable can be thought of as the amount that must be added to the left-hand side in order to make it equal to the right-hand side. For the inequality $5x_1 + x_2 \leq 10$, we add a slack variable s_1 to the left-hand side to give $5x_1 + x_2 + s_1 = 10$. Because we assume nonnegativity ($s_1 \geq 0$), the original inequality is enforced (a negative value for s_1 would mean that the left-hand side of the original constraint is greater than the right-hand side).

Suppose, for example, that $x_1 = 0$ and $x_2 = 8$. The constraint in standard form would be $5(0) + 8 + s_1 = 10$. In this case $s_1 = 2$, indicating that the left-hand side of the original inequality is two less than ten.

In standard form, we write all variables on the left-hand side of the constraints. However, as we have seen in Chapter 4, in formulating a model, we might have some variables on the right-hand side in order to make the constraints more understandable. Should this occur, simply move those variables to the left-hand side, taking care to change the sign and collect like terms as you learned in algebra.

For example, consider the constraint $3x_1 \leq x_1 + x_2 + x_3$. We first move any variables on the right-hand side to the left: $3x_1 - x_1 - x_2 - x_3 \leq 0$ or $2x_1 - x_2 - x_3 \leq 0$. Then we add a nonnegative slack variable, say s_2, to the left-hand side: $2x_1 - x_2 - x_3 + s_2 = 0$.

> To convert a less-than-or-equal-to constraint to standard form, move all variables to the left-hand side (changing signs appropriately), add a nonnegative slack variable to the left-hand side, and replace the $\leq$ with $=$.

We can likewise convert a greater-than-or-equal-to inequality to standard form. For a greater-than-or-equal-to constraint, we define a nonnegative variable called a *surplus variable*. The value of a surplus variable indicates the amount by which the left-hand side is greater than the right-hand side. That is, the value of the surplus variable is the amount we must subtract from the left-hand side in order to make it equal to the right-hand side.

For example, consider the inequality $2x_1 - x_2 \geq 6$. Define a nonnegative surplus variable for this constraint, say s_3. We subtract s_3 from the left-hand side: $2x_1 - x_2 - s_3 = 6$. If $x_1 = 5$ and $x_2 = 1$, then $2(5) - 1 - s_3 = 6$, so $s_3 = 3$.

Any greater-than-or-equal-to constraint can be converted to an equality using this logic.

> To convert a greater-than-or-equal-to constraint to standard form, move all variables to the left-hand side (changing signs appropriately), subtract a nonnegative surplus variable from the left-hand side, and replace the $\geq$ with $=$.

EXAMPLE 6. PUTTING A PROBLEM IN STANDARD FORM

Recall the LP model in Example 2:

$$\text{Max } 2x_1 + 3x_2$$
$$\text{subject to}$$
$$1.25x_1 + x_2 \leq 100$$
$$x_1 + x_2 \geq 30$$
$$x_1 \leq 50$$
$$x_2 \leq 75$$
$$x_1, x_2 \geq 0$$

We may put this model in standard form by adding a nonnegative slack variable to each less-than-or-equal-to constraint and subtracting a nonnegative surplus variable from each greater-than-or-equal-to constraint. Hence, the model in standard form is

$$\text{Max } 2x_1 + 3x_2$$
$$\text{subject to}$$
$$1.25x_1 + x_2 + s_1 = 100$$
$$x_1 + x_2 - s_2 = 30$$
$$x_1 + s_3 = 50$$
$$x_2 + s_4 = 75$$
$$x_1, x_2, s_1, s_2, s_3, s_4 \geq 0$$

As we have seen, the solution to this model is $x_1^* = 20$ and $x_2^* = 75$ (point c in Figure 5.15). Substituting these values into the constraints gives us

$$1.25(20) + (75) + s_1 = 100$$
$$20 + 75 - s_2 = 30$$
$$20 + s_3 = 50$$
$$75 + s_4 = 75$$

Solving for the slack and surplus variables, we have $s_1^* = 0$, $s_2^* = 65$, $s_3^* = 30$, and $s_4^* = 0$. Recall from Figure 5.15 that the first and fourth constraints are binding (their constraint lines intersect to form the optimal corner point c). Because point c is on the constraint lines for the first and fourth constraints, they hold as equalities and s_1^* and s_4^* are zero. The solution to a problem in standard form immediately tells us which constraints are binding—those with zero slack or surplus.

Slack variables (for $\leq$ constraints) and surplus variables (for $\geq$ constraints) have a value of zero for binding constraints.

Example 7. The Colorado Cattle Company Model in Standard Form

Recall that the management of the Colorado Cattle Company wishes to minimize the daily cost of feeding a cow using three different grades of feed, subject to limitations on calcium, iron, protein and fat. The LP model is

$$\text{Min } .25x_1 + .1x_2 + .08x_3$$

$$\text{subject to}$$

$$.7x_1 + .8x_2 + 0x_3 \geq 10 \quad \text{(Calcium)}$$
$$.9x_1 + .8x_2 + .8x_3 \geq 12 \quad \text{(Iron)}$$
$$.8x_1 + 1.5x_2 + .9x_3 \geq 15 \quad \text{(Protein)}$$
$$.5x_1 + .6x_2 + .4x_3 \leq 7.5 \quad \text{(Fat)}$$
$$x_1, \ x_2, \ x_3 \geq 0$$

Constraints

where x_i (i =1,2,3), is the amount of grade i (in pounds) to put into the mix per cow per day. Let us put this model in standard from. First consider the calcium constraint. Because it is a greater-than-or-equal-to constraint, the left-hand side, which represents the number of units of calcium in the mix—given we use amounts x_1, x_2, and x_3 of each of the three grades respectively—can add up to any amount *equal to or greater than* 10. If the left-hand side is strictly greater than 10, then we have included more calcium than required.

To convert this constraint to an equality, we introduce the slack variable s_1, which we define as the amount by which the number of units of calcium exceeds the minimum requirement of 10. An equivalent way to write the calcium constraint is

$$.7x_1 + .8x_2 + 0x_3 - s_1 = 10$$

Using similar logic, we define s_2 and s_3 as the amounts exceeding the minimum requirement for iron and protein, respectively.

$$.9x_1 + .8x_2 + .8x_3 - s_2 = 12$$
$$.8x_1 + 1.5x_2 + .9x_3 - s_3 = 15$$

The fat constraint states that the units of fat must be equal to or less than 7.5. We could have less fat than the maximum limit. Define a slack variable s_4 as the amount by which the left-hand side is less than 7.5. The amount of fat used, plus s_4, must then add to 7.5.

$$.5x_1 + .6x_2 + .4x_3 + s_4 = 7.5$$

The complete model for the Colorado Cattle Company in standard form is

$$\text{Min} \quad .25x_1 + .1x_2 + .08x_3$$

subject to

$$.7x_1 + .8x_2 + 0x_3 - s_1 = 10$$
$$.9x_1 + .8x_2 + .8x_3 - s_2 = 12$$
$$.8x_1 + 1.5x_2 + .9x_3 - s_3 = 15$$
$$.5x_1 + .6x_2 + .4x_3 + s_4 = 7.5$$
$$x_1, \ x_2, \ x_3, \ s_1, \ s_2, \ s_3, \ s_4 \geq 0$$

In Chapter 4, we learned that the solution to this model is 8 lbs. of grade 1, 5.5 lbs of grade 2 and .5 lbs. of grade 3 for a total cost of \$2.59 per cow per day ($x_1^* = 8$, $x_2^* = 5.5$, $x_3^* = .5$, and $Z^* = 2.59$). Substituting these values into the constraints yields

$$.7(8) + .8(5.5) + 0(.5) - s_1 = 10$$
$$.9(8) + .8(5.5) + .8(.5) - s_2 = 12$$
$$.8(8) + 1.5(5.5) + .9(.5) - s_3 = 15$$
$$.5(8) + .6(5.5) + .4(.5) + s_4 = 7.5$$

Solving for the slack and surplus variables, we find $s_1^* = 0, s_2^* = 0, s_3^* = .1$, and $s_4^* = 0$. Hence, the minimum requirements on calcium and iron are exactly met. There are .1 units of excess protein and the diet is exactly at its limit with respect to fat.

In the next section we discuss the use of computer packages to solve LP models. Because we typically will not have a graph of the feasible region, the only way we will be able to tell if a constraint is binding is to see if its slack or surplus variable is zero.

COMPUTER IMPLEMENTATION OF LP MODELS

A wide variety of linear programming solvers are currently available[1]. Because of its popularity in academic circles, we will be using the microcomputer LP solver LINDO (Linear Interactive Discrete Optimizer) to demonstrate computer model building and solution

---

[1] For an interesting account of the history of LP solvers, see 'History of the Development of LP Solvers,' William Orchard-Hays, *Interfaces*, Vol.20, No. 4, July–August, 1990, pp.61–73.

interpretation. The more popular spreadsheet packages such as LOTUS 1-2-3, the LOTUS add-on *What's Best!*,®and EXCEL now allow us to solve LP models in a spreadsheet environment. We will also discuss the use of spreadsheet solvers in this chapter.

The LINDO LP Solver

LINDO (Linear Interactive Discrete Optimizer) is a software package created to solve mathematical programming models. In Figure 5.21 we illustrate the use of LINDO to solve the Colorado Cattle Company model. As you can see, the model input is similar to the way that you would write out the model by hand, a characteristic that has made the LINDO package popular as an educational tool. When LINDO is started, the computer responds with a colon; this prompt means that the system is ready for a command. We start by typing the objective function using "min" or "max." Next the computer responds with a question mark. This means that the computer is accepting model input (we can continue with the objective function or enter constraints). The *!* allows us to put comments behind input. After entering the objective function, we type *st* after the question mark prompt to indicate that the lines that follow are constraints. Notice that $<$ and $>$ symbols are used to represent $\leq$ and $\geq$. The *End* command signals that we are finished entering the model.

LINDO assumes that all variables are nonnegative, so that we are not required to explicitly list the nonnegativity constraints. Because the simplex algorithm requires that

FIGURE 5.21   *LINDO model input for the Colorado Cattle Co. LP*

```
 : min .25X1 + .1X2 + .08X3
 ? st
 ?   .7X1 + 8X2 > 10                    !calcium
 ?   .9X1 + 8X2 + .8X3 > 12             !iron
 ?   .8X1 + 1.5X2 + .9X3 > 15           !protein
 ?   .5X1 + 6X2 + .4X3 < 7.5            !fat
 ?end

 :look all

 MIN      0.25X1 + 0.1X2 + 0.08X3
 SUBJECT TO
    2) 0.7X1 + 0.8X2 >=  10
    3) 0.9X1 + 0.8X2 + 0.8X3 >= 12
    4) 0.8X1 + 1.5X2 + 0.9X3 >= 15
    5) 0.5X1 + 0.6X2 + 0.4X3 <= 7.5
 END
```

the model be in standard form, LINDO internally puts in slack and surplus variables. However, LINDO requires that we input the model so that the right-hand side of every constraint is a constant.

The *Look all* command tells LINDO to list the model as it has been interpreted. This allows us to check for any errors we may have inadvertently entered. If the model does contain errors, the "edit" command may be used to correct mistakes. Notice that > and < have been converted to >= and <= and that the objective function is labeled row 1, the first constraint row 2, etc. To solve the problem, we simply type GO at the colon prompt. After the solution is displayed, LINDO will ask you if you would like sensitivity analysis information. We suggest that you always respond yes. Sensitivity analysis will be further described in the next chapter. The following example illustrates the solution output from LINDO for the Colorado Cattle Company model.

EXAMPLE 8. LINDO SOLUTION TO THE CCC MODEL

The LINDO model solution output for the CCC problem is shown in Figure 5.22. The LP optimum was found in four iterations. This means that the computer had to evaluate four corner points to reach the optimal solution. The optimal objective function value is $2.59; that is, the minimum-cost diet that satisfies the four restrictions will cost $2.59 per cow per day. The optimal values for the decision variables can be found in the section labeled *variable* and *value* (the values of the slacks or surpluses can be found directly below in the row section). Here, $x_1^* = 8$, $x_2^* = 5.5$, $x_3^* = .5$.

The optimal plan calls for a mixture of 8 pounds of feed one, 5.5 pounds of feed two, and .5 pounds of feed 3. The first, second, and fourth constraints corresponding to calcium, iron, and fat, are binding because their slack or surplus values are zero. This means that the recommended plan exactly meets the minimum requirements of 10 units of calcium and 12 units of iron and is at the limit of 7.5 units of fat. The surplus of .1 in the third constraint means that the minimum requirement of 15 units of protein is exceeded by .1 units (that is, this mixture will give the cow 15.1 units of protein).

Notice that at this point we have completely defined the solution. We know how much of each feed type to use, the total cost, and how much of each of the four nutrients the plan will provide. The remaining pieces of the output in Figure 5.22, "Reduced Cost," "Dual Prices," and the section "Ranges In Which The Basis Is Unchanged," will be discussed in the next chapter.

Solving LP Models in a Spreadsheet

As previously mentioned, linear programming solvers are becoming a standard part of spreadsheet packages. LOTUS 1-2-3 and Microsoft EXCEL both contain "Solvers" that

---

FIGURE 5.22 *LINDO solution output for the CCC LP model*

LP OPTIMUM FOUND AT STEP   4

OBJECTIVE FUNCTION VALUE

1)   2.5900000

VARIABLE	VALUE	REDUCED COST
X1	8.000000	0.000000
X2	5.500000	0.000000
X3	0.500000	0.000000

ROW	SLACK OR SURPLUS	DUAL PRICES
2)	0.000000	-0.310000
3)	0.000000	-0.670000
4)	0.100000	0.000000
5)	0.000000	1.140000

NO. ITERATIONS =   4

RANGES IN WHICH THE BASIS IS UNCHANGED:

OBJ COEFFICIENT RANGES

VARIABLE	CURRENT COEF	ALLOWABLE INCREASE	ALLOWABLE DECREASE
X1	0.250000	INFINITY	0.142500
X2	0.100000	0.162857	INFINITY
X3	0.080000	0.177143	2.680000

RIGHTHAND SIDE RANGES

ROW	CURRENT RHS	ALLOWABLE INCREASE	ALLOWABLE DECREASE
2	10.000000	0.137930	4.000000
3	12.000000	0.054794	1.999999
4	15.000000	0.099999	INFINITY
5	7.500000	1.000000	0.016949

can solve linear programs. Spreadsheet add-ons such as *What's Best!* and *What-If Solver* are also popular. All of these packages bring the power of linear programming to the desktops of millions of people who are already comfortable with spreadsheets. We will again use the

Colorado Cattle Company LP model to illustrate how to use the Solver option in LOTUS 1-2-3 and Microsoft EXCEL.

The LOTUS 1-2-3 Solver. In this section we describe how to use the Solver in LOTUS 1-2-3 Version 4 for Windows. Let us assume that we have constructed a spreadsheet model for the Colorado Cattle Company Problem. The Lotus 1-2-3 *Solver* option can be found by selecting *Range, Analyze* and then *Solver* from the 1-2-3 control panel. After selecting the *Solver* option, the *Solver Definition* dialog box will appear. Within this dialog box we must specify the *adjustable cells* (the cells that correspond to the decision variables of the LP model), the *constraint cells* (cells that have the constraints of the LP model as formulas), the *optimal cell* (the cell containing the objective function formula), and whether the objective function is to be maximized or minimized. The constraint cells are cells that contain formulas that correspond to the constraint set of the LP model. *Unlike LINDO, the LOTUS Solver does not assume that the adjustable cells must be nonnegative.* Nonnegativity constraints must therefore be explicitly stated.

Additionally, Solver allows us to specify the number of "answers" we would like to find. Obviously the term *answers* should not be interpreted as optimal solutions (because we might have a unique optimal solution), but this option gives us the potential to see a variety of feasible solutions.

EXAMPLE 9. LOTUS 1-2-3 SOLVER SOLUTION TO THE CCC MODEL

Figure 5.23 shows the spreadsheet model for the Colorado Cattle Company that we discussed in Chapter 4, as well as some selected cell formulas. In order to use the *Solver* option, we must literally build the constraint formulas and place them in separate cells that we will be able to identify in the *Solver Definition* dialog box. Figure 5.24 shows the formulas for the constraint cells, which have been placed in the range E20 through E28. Notice that the nonnegativity restrictions have been stated in cells E26 through E28. Figure 5.25 shows how the model is defined in the *Solver Definition* dialog box. Once this definition is complete, the model is solved by clicking the *Solve* button in the upper right-hand corner. The optimal values of the decision variables will appear in the adjustable cells.

Figure 5.26 shows the solution for the CCC model. Note that a 1 in a constraint cell indicates that the constraint is satisfied and a zero means that the constraint is violated. Due to roundoff error, the calcium and iron constraints appear to be violated (there are zeros in their constraint cells). This is not the case, because the excess for these constraints is really zero (see cells C20 and C21). We see that the LOTUS Solver found the same solution as LINDO: 8 pounds of Grade 1, 5.5 pounds of Grade 2, and .5 pounds of Grade 3 for a cost of $2.59. From the model output section we see that the minimum number of units of calcium and iron are exactly met and that we have .1 extra units of protein. This solution contains exactly the limit of 7.5 units of fat.

FIGURE 5.23   Colorado Cattle Company LOTUS spreadsheet model

A	A	B	C	D	E	F
1	Colorado Cattle Company Model					
2						
3	Parameters and uncontrollable variables:					
4						
5	Grade	1	2	3		
6	Cost / lb.	$0.25	$0.10	$0.08	Minimum	Maximum
7	Calc. / lb.	0.7	0.8	0	10	
8	Iron / lb.	0.9	0.8	0.8	12	
9	Prot. / lb.	0.8	1.5	0.9	15	
10	Fat / lb.	0.5	0.6	0.4		7.5
11						
12	Decision Variables:					
13						
14	Grade	1	2	3		
15	Quantity	0	8	0		
16						
17						
18	Model Outputs:					
19		Amount	Excess			
20	Calcium	6.4	-3.6			
21	Iron	6.4	-5.6			
22	Protein	12	-3			
23		Amount	Available			
24	Fat	4.8	2.7			
25						
26	Total Cost	$0.80				

Selected cell formulas

A	A	B	C
18	Model Outputs:		
19		Amount	Excess
20	Calcium	+B15*B7+C15*C7+D15*D7	+B20-E7
21	Iron	+B15*B8+C15*C8+D15*D8	+B21-E8
22	Protein	+B15*B9+C15*C9+D15*D9	+B22-E9
23		Amount	Available
24	Fat	+B15*B10+C15*C10+D15*D10	+F10-B24
25			
26	Total Cost	+B6*B15+C6*C15+D6*D15	

A variety of reports can be generated once the model has been solved by the LOTUS Solver. We defer the discussion of these reports until the next chapter.

The Microsoft EXCEL Solver. The Solver in EXCEL is somewhat different than the Solver in LOTUS 1-2-3 because the constraint set of the LP model is constructed within

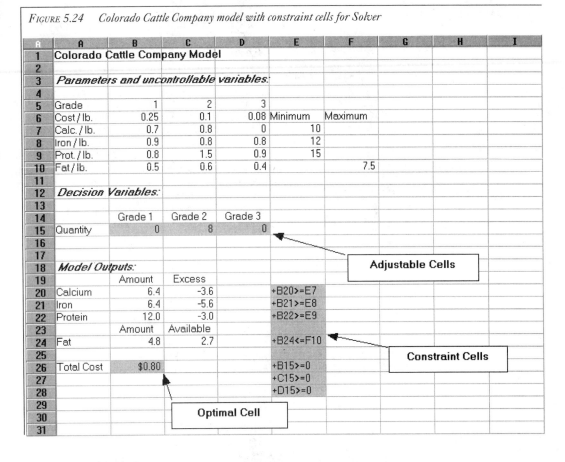

FIGURE 5.24   *Colorado Cattle Company model with constraint cells for Solver*

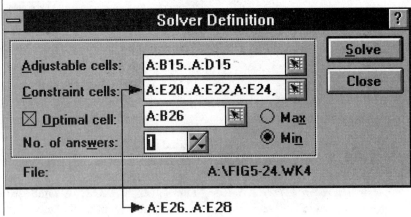

FIGURE 5.25   *Solver definition box for the Colorado Cattle Company LP model*

FIGURE 5.26   *Solution to the Colorado Cattle Company model using the LOTUS Solver*

	A	B	C	D	E	F	G	H	I
1	Colorado Cattle Company Model								
2									
3	*Parameters and uncontrollable variables:*								
4									
5	Grade	1	2	3					
6	Cost / lb.	0.25	0.1	0.08	Minimum	Maximum			
7	Calc. / lb.	0.7	0.8	0	10				
8	Iron / lb.	0.9	0.8	0.8	12				
9	Prot. / lb.	0.8	1.5	0.9	15				
10	Fat / lb.	0.5	0.6	0.4		7.5			
11									
12	*Decision Variables:*								
13									
14		Grade 1	Grade 2	Grade 3					
15	Quantity	8	5.5	0.5					
16									
17									
18	*Model Outputs:*								
19		Amount	Excess						
20	Calcium	10.0	-0.0		0.00				
21	Iron	12.0	-0.0		0.00				
22	Protein	15.1	0.1		1.00				
23		Amount	Available						
24	Fat	7.5	0.0		1.00				
25									
26	Total Cost	$2.59			1.00				
27					1.00				
28					1.00				
29									
30									
31									

Adjustable Cells

Constraint Cells

Optimal Cell

the dialog box. EXCEL's dialog box is referred to as the *Solver Parameters* dialog box. Again, let us assume we have constructed an EXCEL spreadsheet model of the LP. From the control panel, we select *Tools*, and, then *Solver*. The *Solver Parameters* dialog box will appear. *Set Cell* is the term used to specify the objective function cell, and the decision variable cells are referred to as *Changing Cells*. We specify these cells in the appropriate box of the dialog box. The objective function is also flagged as a max or min. The constraints are constructed in the constraint box and can be edited by using the *Add*, *Change* or *Delete* buttons. *As in LOTUS, the EXCEL Solver does not assume nonnegativity of the changing cells, so that nonnegativity constraints must be stated explicitly in the constraint box. For an LP model, the Options button should be selected and then the option "Assume Linear Model" should be chosen.* The *Solve* button from the *Solver Parameters* dialog box invokes the Solver. The optimal values of the changing cells will appear in the original spreadsheet, and a variety of reports are available. As with LOTUS 1-2-3, we defer a discussion of these reports until the next chapter. We illustrate the use of the EXCEL Solver next.

EXAMPLE 10. EXCEL SOLVER SOLUTION TO THE CCC MODEL

Figure 5.27 shows an EXCEL spreadsheet for the Colorado Cattle Company model (all cell formulas are the same as those discussed for the LOTUS Spreadsheet). The *Solver Parameters* dialog box used to define the LP is shown in Figure 5.28. With this problem definition, we select *Options*, and *Assume Linear Model*, then return to the *Solver Parameters* dialog box and select *Solve*. The solution appears in Figure 5.29. This solution obviously matches that found by LINDO and LOTUS Solver.

MORE EXAMPLES AND SOLVED PROBLEMS

In this section we provide additional examples of using LINDO and the LOTUS and EXCEL solvers to solve LP problems and interpretation of the output.

FIGURE 5.27   EXCEL spreadsheet for the Colorado Cattle Company model

	A	B	C	D	E	F	G	H
1	Colorado Cattle Company Model							
2								
3	*Parameters and uncontrollable variables*							
4								
5	Grade	1	2	3				
6	Cost/lb.	$0.25	$0.10	$0.08	Minimum	Maximum		
7	Calc./lb.	0.7	0.8	0	10			
8	Iron/lb.	0.9	0.8	0.8	12			
9	Prot./lb.	0.8	1.5	0.9	15			
10	Fat/lb.	0.5	0.6	0.4		7.5		
11								
12	*Decision Variables*							
13								
14	Grade	1	2	3				
15	Quantity	0	8	0				
16								
17						Changing Cells		
18	*Model Outputs:*							
19		Amount	Excess					
20	Calcium	6.4	-3.6					
21	Iron	6.4	-5.6					
22	Protein	12	-3					
23		Amount	Available					
24	Fat	4.8	2.7					
25								
26	Total Cost	$0.80						
27								
28				Set Cell				
29								

FIGURE 5.28   The Solver Parameters dialog box for the CCC model

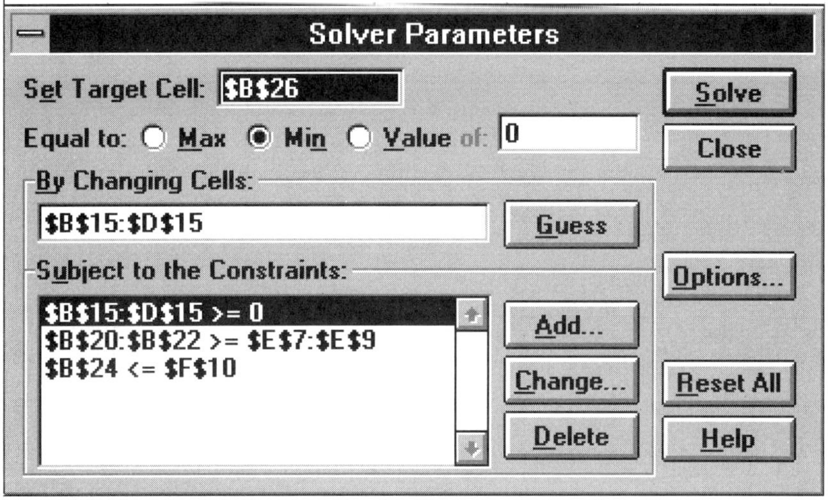

FIGURE 5.29   The solution obtained for the Colorado Cattle Company model using the EXCEL Solver

	A	B	C	D	E	F
1	Colorado Cattle Company Model					
2						
3	*Parameters and uncontrollable variables*					
4						
5	Grade	1	2	3		
6	Cost/lb.	$0.25	$0.10	$0.08	Minimum	Maximum
7	Calc./lb.	0.7	0.8	0	10	
8	Iron/lb.	0.9	0.8	0.8	12	
9	Prot./lb.	0.8	1.5	0.9	15	
10	Fat/lb.	0.5	0.6	0.4		7.5
11						
12	*Decision Variables*					
13						
14	Grade	1	2	3		
15	Quantity	8	5.5	0.5		
16						
17						
18	*Model Outputs:*					
19		Amount	Excess			
20	Calcium	10.00	0.00			
21	Iron	12.00	0.00			
22	Protein	15.10	0.10			
23		Amount	Available			
24	Fat	7.50	0.00			
25						
26	Total Cost	$2.59				

$= \$B\$20 - \$E\$7$

$= \$B\$21 - \$C\$8$

$= \$B\$22 - \$E\$9$

EXAMPLE 11. UNBOUNDED SOLUTIONS

Figure 5.30 shows the LINDO model and solution for Example 4, which is an example of an unbounded problem. LINDO informs us that the problem is unbounded and that the variables that make the problem unbounded are x_2 and the slack variable in the last constraint (notice that these two variables have extremely large values of 99 million). To see why the output makes sense, consider the graph for this problem shown in Figure 5.31. The problem is unbounded because we can continue to move along the edge e_2 (increasing the value of x_2 and the slack in row 3) and increase the objective function without limit.

EXAMPLE 12. AN INFEASIBLE PROBLEM

Figure 5.32 shows the LINDO model and solution for Example 5, an example of an infeasible model. LINDO finds that there are no feasible solutions and indicates which constraints are violated. The current (infeasible) solution is $x_1 = 2$ and $x_2 = 1$. As indicated by its negatively valued surplus variable, however, the row 3 constraint

---

FIGURE 5.30   *LINDO model and output for an unbounded problem*

```
MAX     2 X1 + 5 X2
SUBJECT TO
        2)   X1 + X2 >= 6
        3)   X1 − X2 <= 4
    END

UNBOUNDED SOLUTION AT STEP 3 REDUCED COST= − 5.00000
    UNBOUNDED VARIABLES ARE:


    SLK   2
          X2
    SLK   3


              OBJECTIVE FUNCTION VALUE

        1)        30.000000

VARIABLE          VALUE          REDUCED COST
        X1              .000000          3.000000
        X2        99999900.000000          .000000

ROW        SLACK OR SURPLUS       DUAL PRICES
        2)              .000000          5.000000
        3)        99999900.000000          .000000

NO. ITERATIONS = 3
```

FIGURE 5.31   *The feasible region for Example 11*

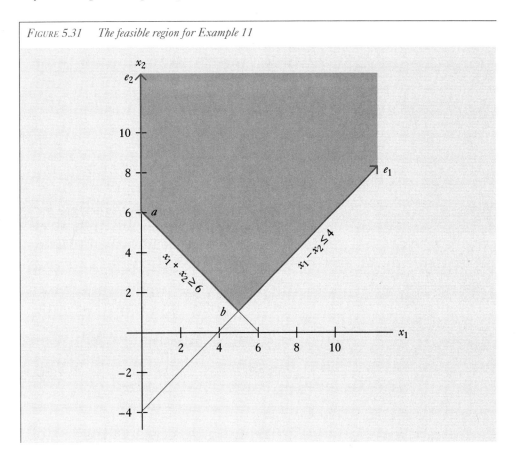

is violated. Note that the value for the surplus is -3 and that if we decrease the right-hand side of row 3 by three, the constraint would be feasible. Rows with negative slack can therefore give us clues as to where changes need to be made in order to make the model feasible.

EXAMPLE 13. ALTERNATE OPTIMAL SOLUTIONS

Recall the model of Example 3, which we used to illustrate the existence of alternate optimal solutions:

$$\text{Min } 4x_1 + 4x_2$$
$$\text{subject to}$$
$$x_1 + 2x_2 \leq 10$$
$$x_1 + x_2 \geq 1.5$$
$$x_2 \leq 4$$
$$x_1, x_2 \geq 0$$

Figure 5.32   LINDO model and output for an infeasible LP

```
MAX      1.1 X1  − 2 X2
SUBJECT TO
        2)    X1 + X2 <= 3
        3)    X2 >= 4
        4)    X1 − X2 = 1
   END
```

NO FEASIBLE SOLUTION AT STEP   1
SUM OF INFEASIBILITIES = 3.00000

VIOLATED ROWS HAVE NEGATIVE SLACK,
OR (EQUALITY ROWS) NONZERO SLACKS.
ROWS CONTRIBUTING TO INFEASIBILITY
HAVE NONZERO DUAL PRICE.

           OBJECTIVE FUNCTION VALUE

        1)   0.20000005

VARIABLE	VALUE	REDUCED COST
X1	2.000000	0.000000
X2	1.000000	0.000000

ROW	SLACK OR SURPLUS	DUAL PRICES
2)	0.000000	0.500000
3)	− 3.000000	− 1.000000
4)	0.000000	0.500000

NO. ITERATIONS = 1

The computer solution does not explicitly tell us that a problem has alternate optimal solutions. However, it is possible to tell when alternate optimal solutions exist by using pieces of the output we have not yet discussed (e.g. reduced costs and dual prices in LINDO). For the most part, this requires a technical understanding of how the simplex algorithm solves LPs. In fact, many texts spend a fair amount of time discussing the intricacies of determining when alternate optimal solutions exist, and then do not elaborate on how to get to the other alternate optimal solutions that have not been reported! Indeed, for many LP solvers, it is often difficult to get to other alternate optimal solutions because the user does not have direct control over the moves the solver makes. The Solver in LOTUS 1-2-3, however, allows us to specify the number of solutions we would like to report. This option gives us a chance to find and report alternate optimal solutions. A LOTUS 1-2-3 spreadsheet model of the above LP model appears in Figure 5.33 with selected cell formulas shown (including the constraint cells). The *Solver Definition* dialog box for this problem is shown in Figure 5.34. Note that we have requested three solutions.

After selecting *Solve*, three solutions are reported, as shown in Figures 5.35, 5.36, and 5.37. The Solver has found two alternate optimal solutions with objective function

FIGURE 5.33   *LOTUS 1-2-3 model for Example 13*

	A	B	C	D	E	F	G	H	I
1	Example 13								
2									
3	Parameters and uncontrollable variables:								
4									
5	Objective	4	4						
6				Right-Hand Side					
7	Constraint 1	1	2	10					
8	Constraint 2	1	1	1.5					
9	Constraint 3	0	1	4					
10									
11	Decision Variables:								
12									
13	Quantity	2	2	←	Adjustable Cells				
14									
15	Model Outputs:								
16			Left-Hand Side						
17	Constraint 1		6.00			1.00			
18	Constraint 2		4.00			1.00	Constraint Cells		
19	Constraint 3		2.00			1.00			
20						1.00			
21	Objective		16.00			1.00			
22									
23									
24				Optimal Cell					
25									
26									

Selected cell formulas

	A	B	C	D	E	F	G	H	I
15	Model Outputs:								
16			Left-Hand Side						
17	Constraint 1		+B7*B13+C7*C13			+C17<=D7	Constraint Cells		
18	Constraint 2		+B8*B13+C8*C13			+C18>=D8			
19	Constraint 3		+B9*B13+C9*C13			+C19<=D9			
20						+B13>=0			
21	Objective		+B5*B13+C5*C13			+C13>=0			
22									
23									
24				Optimal Cell					
25									
26									

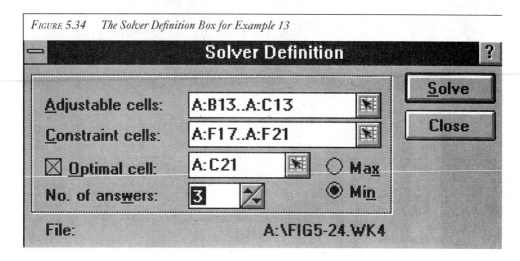

FIGURE 5.34   *The Solver Definition Box for Example 13*

FIGURE 5.35   *First solution reported by Solver*

A	A	B	C	D	E	F
1	Example 13					
2						
3	*Parameters and uncontrollable variables:*					
4						
5	Objective	4	4			
6				Right-Hand Side		
7	Constraint 1	1	2	10		
8	Constraint 2	1	1	1.5		
9	Constraint 3	0	1	4		
10						
11	*Decision Variables:*					
12						
13	Quantity	1.5	0			
14						
15	*Model Outputs:*					
16			Left-Hand Side			
17	Constraint 1		1.50			1.00
18	Constraint 2		1.50			1.00
19	Constraint 3		0.00			1.00
20						1.00
21	Objective		6.00			1.00

value 6, and the third solution was one that was in our original spreadsheet (Figure 5.33 on page 218).

Whether or not LOTUS Solver accurately reports alternate optimal solutions depends on the starting solution we use (we began in this example with the solution

FIGURE 5.36   *Second solution reported by Solver*

	A	B	C	D	E	F
1	Example 13					
2						
3	*Parameters and uncontrollable variables:*					
4						
5	Objective	4	4			
6				Right-Hand Side		
7	Constraint 1	1	2	10		
8	Constraint 2	1	1	1.5		
9	Constraint 3	0	1	4		
10						
11	*Decision Variables:*					
12						
13	Quantity	0	1.5			
14						
15	*Model Outputs:*					
16			Left-Hand Side			
17	Constraint 1		3.00			1.00
18	Constraint 2		1.50			1.00
19	Constraint 3		1.50			1.00
20						1.00
21	Objective		6.00			1.00

FIGURE 5.37   *Third solution reported by Solver*

	A	B	C	D	E	F
1	Example 13					
2						
3	*Parameters and uncontrollable variables:*					
4						
5	Objective	4	4			
6				Right-Hand Side		
7	Constraint 1	1	2	10		
8	Constraint 2	1	1	1.5		
9	Constraint 3	0	1	4		
10						
11	*Decision Variables:*					
12						
13	Quantity	2	2			
14						
15	*Model Outputs:*					
16			Left-Hand Side			
17	Constraint 1		6.00	∘		1.00
18	Constraint 2		4.00			1.00
19	Constraint 3		2.00			1.00
20						1.00
21	Objective		16.00			1.00

$x_1 = 2$ and $x_2 = 2$), because LOTUS uses an algorithm that is considerably different than the simplex algorithm. The details of this algorithm are beyond the scope of this book.

EXAMPLE 14. MaBops Transportation Model

In the MaBops transportation model from Chapter 4, we defined x_{ij} as the amount to ship from plant i to distribution center j, where there are four plants and five distribution centers. Supplies at the plants and demands at the distribution centers are known, and we wish to minimize shipping costs. The LINDO model and solution are shown in Figure 5.38.

   We see from the LINDO output that the cheapest shipping cost is $182,000. The optimal shipping quantities are 11,000 units from Los Angeles to Las Vegas, 4,000 units from Los Angeles to Boise, 5,500 units from Denver to Chicago, 11,000 units from Denver to Boise, 2,500 units from Pensacola to Houston, 15,000 units from Pensacola to New Orleans, 5,500 units from Cincinnati to Houston, and 4,500 units from Cincinnati to Chicago. Note that rows 2,4, and 5 are binding because they have zero slack. Row 3 is nonbinding and has a slack value of 3,500. Hence all plants except for the Pensacola plant will utilize 100 percent of available capacity under this plan. Pensacola has a remaining capacity of 3,500 units and therefore will be operating at only 82.5 percent capacity. We will discuss the remaining portions of the MaBops LINDO output in the next chapter.

EXAMPLE 15. Radar Detector Product Mix Model

An EXCEL spreadsheet model of the LaserStop and SpeedBuster LP model from Chapter 2 is shown in Figure 5.39, along with selected cell formulas. Recall that we have 6,000 units of component A and 3,500 units of component B available. Each LaserStop requires 12 units of A and 6 units of B and yields a profit of $24. Each SpeedBuster requires 6 units of A and 10 units of B and yields a profit of $40. We would like to know how many LaserStops and SpeedBusters to produce in order to maximize profit. We select *Tools* and *Solver* from the EXCEL menu. The *Solver Parameters* dialog box appears in Figure 5.40. We have centered cell B3 in the *Set Cell* entry box, entered cells B14 through B15 in the *Changing Cells* entry box, and defined the constraints on components A and B (B20 ≤ B9 and B21 ≤ C9) as well as nonnegativity (B14 through B15 ≥ 0). The Max button has been chosen.

   After selecting *Options* and *Assume Linear Model*, we return to the *Solver Parameters* dialog box and select *Solve*. The solution appears in Figure 5.41. Maximum profit of $14,000 can be obtained by producing all SpeedBusters (350 units) and no LaserStops. All 3,500 units of component B are used, but we have 1,800 units of component A left over.

FIGURE 5.38   *MaBops LINDO model and solution output*

MIN   5 X11 + X12 + 5 X13 + 7 X14 + 4 X15 + 9 X21 + 7 X22 + 8 X23
       + 3 X24 + 5 X25 + 3 X31 + 4 X32 + 3 X33 + 8 X34 + 6 X35 + 4 X41
       + 5 X42 + 6 X43 + 2 X44 + 7 X45

SUBJECT TO
        2)   X11 + X12 + X13 + X14 + X15 <= 15000 ! LA
        3)   X21 + X22 + X23 + X24 + X25 <= 20000 ! Denver
        4)   X31 + X32 + X33 + X34 + X35 <= 17500 ! Pensacola
        5)   X41 + X42 + X43 + X44 + X45 <= 10000 ! Cincinnati
        6)   X11 + X21 + X31 + X41 =   8000   ! Houston
        7)   X12 + X22 + X32 + X42 = 11000   ! Las Vegas
        8)   X13 + X23 + X33 + X43 = 15000   ! New Orleans
        9)   X14 + X24 + X34 + X44 = 10000   ! Chicago
       10)   X15 + X25 + X35 + X45 = 15000   ! Boise
END

OBJECTIVE FUNCTION VALUE

        1)   182000.00

VARIABLE	VALUE	REDUCED COST
X11	0.000000	1.000000
X12	11000.000000	0.000000
X13	0.000000	1.000000
X14	0.000000	5.000000
X15	4000.000000	0.000000
X21	0.000000	4.000000
X22	0.000000	5.000000
X23	0.000000	3.000000
X24	5500.000000	0.000000
X25	11000.000000	0.000000
X31	2500.000000	0.000000
X32	0.000000	4.000000
X33	15000.000000	0.000000
X34	0.000000	7.000000
X35	0.000000	3.000000
X41	5500.000000	0.000000
X42	0.000000	4.000000
X43	0.000000	2.000000
X44	4500.000000	0.000000
X45	0.000000	3.000000

ROW	SLACK OR SURPLUS	DUAL PRICES
2)	0.000000	1.000000
3)	3500.000000	0.000000
4)	0.000000	2.000000
5)	0.000000	1.000000
6)	0.000000	−5.000000
7)	0.000000	−2.000000
8)	0.000000	−5.000000
9)	0.000000	−3.000000
10)	0.000000	−5.000000

NO. ITERATIONS = 8
RANGES IN WHICH THE BASIS IS UNCHANGED

OBJ COEFFICIENT RANGES

VARIABLE	CURRENT COEF	ALLOWABLE INCREASE	ALLOWABLE DECREASE
X11	5.000000	INFINITY	1.000000
X12	1.000000	4.000000	INFINITY
X13	5.000000	INFINITY	1.000000
X14	7.000000	INFINITY	5.000000
X15	4.000000	1.000000	4.000000
X21	9.000000	INFINITY	4.000000
X22	7.000000	INFINITY	5.000000
X23	8.000000	INFINITY	3.000000
X24	3.000000	1.000000	1.000000
X25	5.000000	3.000000	1.000000
X31	3.000000	2.000000	1.000000
X32	4.000000	INFINITY	4.000000
X33	3.000000	1.000000	INFINITY
X34	8.000000	INFINITY	7.000000
X35	6.000000	INFINITY	3.000000
X41	4.000000	1.000000	2.000000
X42	5.000000	INFINITY	4.000000
X43	6.000000	INFINITY	2.000000
X44	2.000000	1.000000	1.000000
X45	7.000000	INFINITY	3.000000

RIGHTHAND SIDE RANGES

ROW	CURRENT RHS	ALLOWABLE INCREASE	ALLOWABLE DECREASE
2	15000.000000	11000.000000	3500.000000
3	20000.000000	INFINITY	3500.000000
4	17500.000000	5500.000000	2500.000000
5	10000.000000	5500.000000	3500.000000
6	8000.000000	3500.000000	5500.000000
7	11000.000000	3500.000000	11000.000000
8	15000.000000	3500.000000	5500.000000
9	10000.000000	3500.000000	5500.000000
10	15000.000000	3500.000000	11000.000000

FIGURE 5.39   EXCEL spreadsheet model for the radar detector problem

	A	B	C	D	E	F
1	Product Mix Model					
2						
3	Parameters and uncontrollable variables:					
4						
5		Component Requirements				
6		A	B		Unit Profit	
7	LS	12	6		$24	
8	SB	12	10		$40	
9	Availability	6000	3500			
10						
11						
12	Decision Variables:					
13						
14	Number LS	0				
15	Number SB	0				
16						
17	Model Outputs:					
18						
19		Usage	Excess			
20	Component A	0	6000			
21	Component B	0	3500			
22						
23	Profit	$0				
24						
25						

Changing Cells → (points to B14:B15)

Set Cell → (points to B23)

Selected cell formulas

	A	B	C
17	Model Outputs:		
18			
19		Usage	Excess
20	Component A	=+B7*B14+B8*B15	=+B9-B20
21	Component B	=+C7*B14+C8*B15	=+C9-B21
22			
23	Profit	=+E7*B14+E8*B15	

223

FIGURE 5.40   The EXCEL Solver Parameters dialog box settings for the radar detector problem

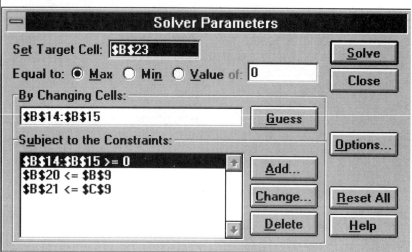

FIGURE 5.41   The solution to the radar detector problem

	A	B	C	D	E
1	Product Mix Model				
2					
3	*Parameters and uncontrollable variables:*				
4					
5		Component Requirements			
6		A	B		Unit Profit
7	LS	12	6		$24
8	SB	12	10		$40
9	Availability	6000	3500		
10					
11					
12	*Decision Variables:*				
13					
14	Number LS	0			
15	Number SB	350			
16					
17	*Model Outputs:*				
18					
19		Usage	Excess		
20	Component A	4200	1800		
21	Component B	3500	0		
22					
23	Profit	$14,000			

SUMMARY

In this chapter we have discussed the geometry of linear programming, the possible outcomes of a linear program, and how to solve LP models on the computer and interpret the solution output.

The feasible region is the set of all points that satisfies the constraints. Corner points of the feasible region are formed by the intersection of two or more constraint lines. If a solution to an LP exists, we know that a solution can be found at a corner point of the feasible region. The constraints whose constraint lines form a corner point, are binding at that corner point.

There are four possible outcomes to a linear program:

1. Unique optimal solution
2. Alternate optimal solutions
3. Unboundedness
4. Infeasibility

We have a unique optimal solution when there is a single corner point whose objective function value is strictly better than the objective function value of every other feasible point. If two or more points of the feasible region have the best objective function value, the LP has alternate optimal solutions. If the objective function can be maximized to infinity or minimized to negative infinity, the LP is unbounded. Finally, if the feasible region is empty, the problem is infeasible.

We have seen how to put any LP model into standard form. All variables must be on the left-hand side of the constraint. Any inequality constraints must be converted to equality constraints either by adding a slack variable to the left-hand side ($\leq$ constraints), or by subtracting a surplus variable from the left-hand side ($\geq$ constraints). Binding constraints always have slack values of zero.

The LINDO LP solver is a package designed to solve LP models. The Solver option in LOTUS 1-2-3 and EXCEL may be used to solve LP models in spreadsheets. In this chapter we illustrated how to solve LP models with these packages and how to interpret the basic solution output, such as the optimal objective function value, the optimal value of the decision variables, and the characteristics of binding constraints. LINDO and the EXCEL Solver also provide important extra information known as sensitivity analysis. In Chapter 6 we focus on solution interpretation and sensitivity analysis.

CHAPTER REVIEW EXERCISES

I. Terms to Understand

a. Feasible region (p. 179)
b. Binding constraint (p. 190)
c. Unique optimal solution (p. 194)
d. Alternate optimal solutions (p. 195)

e. Unbounded problem (p. 198)
f. Infeasible problem (p. 199)
g. Slack variable (p. 201)
h. Surplus variable (p. 201)

II. Discussion Questions

1. Is it possible for a real-world LP model to be infeasible? Explain.
2. Describe a scenario in which one alternate optimal solution to an LP model might be preferred over another.
3. Describe the relationship between binding constraints and corner points.
4. Explain why the following statement is *false*: "An LP problem with an unbounded feasible region must be unbounded."
5. Think of a company you deal with that probably uses linear programming computer models. What application(s) do you think they analyze using LP models? Describe those applications.

III. Problems

1. Consider the following LP problem:

$$\text{Min } 6x_1 + 2x_2$$
$$\text{subject to}$$
$$3x_1 + 2x_2 \geq 60$$
$$x_2 \leq 70$$
$$-10x_1 + 10x_2 \geq 100$$
$$x_1, x_2 \geq 0$$

   a. Graph the feasible region for this LP.
   b. Give the coordinates of the corner points.
   c. Put the problem in standard form and identify the values of the variables and their values at each corner point.
   d. What is the optimal solution?
2. Consider the LP in problem 1. Replace the minimization with maximization and solve.
3. Recall the radar detector example. LS = the number of LaserStops to produce and SB = the number of SpeedBusters to produce.

$$\text{Max } 24LS + 40SB$$
$$\text{subject to}$$
$$12LS + 12SB \leq 6,000 \quad (\text{component } A)$$
$$6LS + 10SB \leq 3,500 \quad (\text{component } B)$$
$$LS, SB \geq 0$$

   a. Graph the feasible region for this problem.
   b. Put the problem in standard form.
   c. Identify the coordinates of each corner point.
   d. Verify geometrically that an optimal solution is the solution shown in Figure 5.41.
4. Recall the Tommy's Table production problem from Chapter 4 (Problem 1). Solve this problem graphically.
   a. How many regular and how many deluxe tables should be produced to maximize profit?
   b. What is the maximum profit achievable?
   c. Which resources are used completely (which constraints are binding) at the optimal solution?

5.   Solve the following problem graphically:

$$\text{Max } 1.2x_1 + 0.5x_2$$

$$\text{subject to}$$

$$x_1 - x_2 \leq 5$$

$$x_1 \leq 10$$

$$2x_1 + 3x_2 \geq 20$$

$$x_1, x_2 \geq 0$$

6.   Consider the LINDO model and solution output shown below.
   a.   What is the optimal objective function value?
   b.   What are the optimal values of the decision variables?
   c.   Which constraints are binding at the optimal solution?

```
MAX      10 X1 + 6 X2
SUBJECT TO
        2)   2 X1 + 3 X2 <= 90
        3)   4 X1 + 2 X2 <= 80
        4)   X2 >= 15
        5)   5 X1 + X2 = 25
END

        OBJECTIVE FUNCTION VALUE

        1)   150.00000
```

VARIABLE	VALUE	REDUCED COST
X1	.000000	20.000000
X2	25.000000	.000000

ROW	SLACK OR SURPLUS	DUAL PRICES
2)	15.000000	.000000
3)	30.000000	.000000
4)	10.000000	.000000
5)	.000000	6.000000

NO. ITERATIONS = 2

RANGES IN WHICH THE BASIS IS UNCHANGED:

VARIABLE	OBJ COEFFICIENT RANGES CURRENT COEF	ALLOWABLE INCREASE	ALLOWABLE DECREASE
X1	10.000000	20.000000	INFINITY
X2	6.000000	INFINITY	4.000000

RIGHTHAND SIDE RANGES

ROW	CURRENT RHS	ALLOWABLE INCREASE	ALLOWABLE DECREASE
2	90.000000	INFINITY	15.000000
3	80.000000	INFINITY	30.000000
4	15.000000	10.000000	INFINITY
5	25.000000	5.000000	10.000000

7. Consider the LINDO model and solution output for the infeasible LP problem shown below.
   a. Which constraints are currently violated?
   b. Graph the constraint set for this problem.
   c. Show the solution reported by LINDO, and illustrate geometrically which constraints are violated.

```
MIN    3 X1  +  4  X2
SUBJECT TO
    2)     X1 + X2 >= 20
    3)     3 X1 + 2 X2 <= 90
    4)     X1 >= 80
END

NO FEASIBLE SOLUTION AT STEP      1
SUM OF INFEASIBILITIES = 50.0000


VIOLATED ROWS HAVE NEGATIVE SLACK,
OR (EQUALITY ROWS) NONZERO SLACKS.
ROWS CONTRIBUTING TO INFEASIBILITY
HAVE NONZERO DUAL PRICE.


              OBJECTIVE FUNCTION VALUE

        1)        90.000000

VARIABLE         VALUE              REDUCED COST
      X1        30.000000              .000000
      X2         .000000               .666667

ROW       SLACK OR SURPLUS          DUAL PRICES
      2)       10.000000              .000000
      3)        .000000               .333333
      4)      - 50.000000           - 1.000000
NO. ITERATIONS = 1
WARNING, SOLUTION MAY BE NONOPTIMAL/NONFEASIBLE
```

RANGES IN WHICH THE BASIS IS UNCHANGED:

OBJ COEFFICIENT RANGES

VARIABLE	CURRENT COEF	ALLOWABLE INCREASE	ALLOWABLE DECREASE
X1	3.000000	−3.000000	INFINITY
X2	4.000000	INFINITY	2.000000

RIGHTHAND SIDE RANGES

ROW	CURRENT RHS	ALLOWABLE INCREASE	ALLOWABLE DECREASE
2	20.000000	10.000000	INFINITY
3	90.000000	INFINITY	−150.000000
4	80.000000	−50.000000	INFINITY

8. Recall the Vohio Oil Blending example from Chapter 4. Three input ingredients go into the production of two types of fuel at Vohio. The major distinguishing feature of the two end products (regular and super) is the octane level required. Regular fuel must have a minimum octane level of 90 and super's level must be at least 100. The octane levels of the three inputs as well as their availability for the coming two-week period are known. Likewise, the maximum demand for the end products along with the revenue generated per barrel are known. These data are summarized in the table below. In Chapter 4, we developed an LP model to determine how much of each end product to produce in order to maximize contribution to profit.

Input	Cost/bbl.	Octane	Available (barrels)
1	16.50	100	110,000
2	14.00	87	350,000
3	17.50	110	300,000

	Revenue/barrel	Max Demand (barrels)
Regular	18.50	350,000
Super	20.00	500,000

We defined the following decision variables:

RB = number of barrels of regular to produce for the two week period
SB = number of barrels of super to produce for the two week period
R_i = number of barrels of input i used to make regular
S_i = number of barrels of input i used to make super

The LP model is then

$$\text{Max } 18.5\,RB + 20\,SB - 16.5\,R_1 - 16.5\,S_1 - 14\,R_2 - 14\,S_2 - 17.5\,R_3 - 17.5\,S_3$$

subject to

$$
\begin{array}{lll}
R_1 + S_1 \le 110,000 & \quad & \text{Input 1} \\
R_2 + S_2 \le 350,000 & & \text{Input 2} \\
R_3 + S_3 \le 300,000 & & \text{Input 3} \\
RB = R_1 + R_2 + R_3 & & \\
SB = S_1 + S_2 + S_3 & & \\
RB \le 350,000 & & \text{Regular Demand} \\
SB \le 500,000 & & \text{Super Demand} \\
100\,R_1 + 87\,R_2 + 110R_3 \ge 90\,RB & & \text{Regular Octane} \\
100\,S_1 + 87\,S_2 + 110S_3 \ge 100\,SB & & \text{Super Octane} \\
RB,\, SB,\, R_i,\, S_i,\, \ge 0 & & i = 1,2,3
\end{array}
$$

The LINDO model and solution output appear below. Notice that the octane constraints had to be modified so that all decision variables are on the left-hand side.

a. What is the optimal objective function value?
b. How much of each input should be used in the production of regular? Super?
c. Which restrictions form the bottleneck for Vohio?
d. What are the octane levels for regular and super?

```
MAX     18.5 RB + 20 SB − 16.5 R1 − 16.5 S1 − 14 R2 − 14 S2 −
        17.5 R3 − 17.5 S3

   SUBJECT TO
        2)    R1 + S1 <= 110000              ! Input 1
        3)    R2 + S2 <= 350000              ! Input 2
        4)    R3 + S3 <= 300000              ! Input 3
        5)    RB − R1 − R2 − R3 = 0
        6)    SB − S1 − S2 − S3 = 0
        7)    RB <= 350000                   ! Regular Demand
        8)    SB <= 500000                   ! Super Demand
        9)    − 90 RB + 100 R1 + 87 R2 + 110 R3 >= 0    ! Reg. Octane
       10)    − 100 SB + 100 S1 + 87 S2 + 110 S3 >= 0  ! Sup. Octane
   END
                  OBJECTIVE FUNCTION VALUE

            1)          2845000.0
   VARIABLE         VALUE            REDUCED COST
         RB      260000.000000           .000000
         SB      500000.000000           .000000
         R1           .000000            .000000
         S1      110000.000000           .000000
```

R2	180434.800000	.000000
S2	169565.200000	.000000
R3	79565.220000	.000000
S3	220434.800000	.000000

ROW	SLACK OR SURPLUS	DUAL PRICES
2)	.000000	2.000000
3)	.000000	4.500000
4)	.000000	1.000000
5)	.000000	18.500000
6)	.000000	18.500000
7)	90000.000000	.000000
8)	.000000	1.500000
9)	1050000.000000	.000000
10)	.000000	.000000

NO. ITERATIONS = 5
RANGES IN WHICH THE BASIS IS UNCHANGED:

		OBJ COEFFICIENT RANGES	
VARIABLE	CURRENT COEF	ALLOWABLE INCREASE	ALLOWABLE DECREASE
RB	18.500000	1.500000	1.000000
SB	20.000000	INFINITY	1.500000
R1	−16.500000	.000000	INFINITY
S1	−16.500000	INFINITY	.000000
R2	−14.000000	.000000	.000000
S2	−14.000000	.000000	.000000
R3	−17.500000	2.653846	.000000
S3	−17.500000	.000000	2.653846

		RIGHTHAND SIDE RANGES	
ROW	CURRENT RHS	ALLOWABLE INCREASE	ALLOWABLE DECREASE
2	110000.000000	90000.000000	105000.000000
3	350000.000000	90000.000000	180434.800000
4	300000.000000	90000.000000	52500.000000
5	.000000	11666.670000	260000.000000
6	.000000	11666.670000	37727.270000
7	350000.000000	INFINITY	90000.000000
8	500000.000000	105000.000000	90000.000000
9	.000000	1050000.000000	INFINITY
10	.000000	1050000.000000	4150000.000000

9. Recall the Phillips Inc. problem (Example 9 in Chapter 4). Phillips sells two products and is trying to determine the optimal amount of advertising dollars and direct selling hours to allocate to each of the products in the next quarter. The total advertising budget for the quarter is $25,000 and there are a total of 5,000 labor hours for direct selling. A dollar of advertising will generate $8 in profit if applied to product 1 and $15 if applied to product 2. An hour of selling will generate $25 in profit if spent on product 1 and $45 if spent on product 2. Company policy stipulates that between $6,000 and $18,000 be allocated to each product and between 2,000 and 3,500 hours of labor be allocated to each product. A LOTUS spreadsheet model with the optimal solution from the LOTUS Solver is shown in the following figure. Suppose that the company is willing to use another 1,000 hours of labor for selling (a new total of 6,000 hours available). Solve a modified model using either the LOTUS or EXCEL solver to determine the value of these extra 1,000 hours. How should these extra 1,000 hours be allocated?

	A	B	C	D
1	Phillips Inc.			
2				
3	Parameters and uncontrollable variables:			
4				
5			Profit	
6		Advertising ($/$)		Selling ($/hr.)
7	Product 1	$8		$25
8	Product 2	$15		$45
9				
10		Advertising $		Selling Hours
11	Min	$6,000		2000
12	Max	$18,000		3500
13				
14	Total	$25,000		5000
15				
16				
17	Decision variables:			
18				
19				
20		Advertising	Selling Hrs.	
21	Product 1	$7,000	2000	
22	Product 2	$18,000	3000	
23				
24	Model outputs:			
25		Used	Remaining	
26	Advertising	$25,000	$0	
27	Selling Hours	5000	0	
28				
29	Profit	$511,000		
30				
31				
32				
33				

10. Recall the Grad & Sons portfolio selection example (Example 8 in Chapter 4). Options OP1 through OP4 have the expected rates of return of .06, .09, .07, and .11 for the coming year. We have $500,000 to invest. No more than $200,000 should be invested in any one alternative. The risk factors per dollar invested for the four options are .02, .05, .04, and .075 respectively. We wish to minimize risk while achieving a

A	A	B	C
1	Grad & Sons Portfolio Model		
2			
3	Parameters and uncontrollable variables:		
4			
5		Expected Return	Risk Factor
6	OP1	0.06	0.02
7	OP2	0.09	0.05
8	OP3	0.07	0.04
9	OP4	0.11	0.075
10			
11	Investment Amount	$500,000	
12	Diversification Bound	$200,000	
13	Minimum Return	0.08	
14			
15	Decision variables:		
16		Investment	
17	OP1	$200,000	
18	OP2	$200,000	
19	OP3	$25,000	
20	OP4	$75,000	
21			
22	Model outputs:		
23		Dollars	
24	Return	$40,000	0.08
25	Risk	$20,625	0.04125
26			
27			

return of at least 8 percent. A LOTUS spreadsheet model for this problem appears in the figure above. The solution from the LOTUS solver is the one shown in the spreadsheet. We are interested in the trade-off between risk and return. Solve a series of modified LP models by varying the required return from 5 percent to 10 percent. Plot the risk versus required return. Which risk/return pair would you recommend?

11. The Intensive Care Unit at General Hospital has the following day shift staffing requirements:

Day	Minimum Number of Nurses Required
Sunday	16
Monday	15
Tuesday	12
Wednesday	14
Thursday	15
Friday	18
Saturday	19

Nurses work five consecutive days and then take two days off. Each nurse earns $700 per 5 day work week.

a. Develop an LP model that minimizes the staffing cost while meeting the minimum requirements for each day.

b. Find the optimal solution to your model using an LP solver.

c. Which days form the bottleneck in this problem (which constraints are binding)?

Problems 12 through 20 refer to problems first stated at the end of Chapter 4.

12. Solve the Valdaz Coffee Company problem (problem 4 in Chapter 4) using an LP solver.
     a.   What is the maximum profit?
     b.   How much of each blend (Tastee and Tastier) should be produced?
     c.   Which bean availability keeps Valdaz from achieving even higher profits?

13. Solve the Very Good Juice Company problem (problem 6 in Chapter 4) using an LP solver.
     a.   What is the maximum profit?
     b.   How much of each juice should be produced?
     c.   Which products are at their maximum sales level? Minimum sales level?
     d.   Which department(s) are candidates for capacity expansion?

14. Solve the Decatur canned peanut problem (problem 7 in Chapter 4) using an LP solver.
     a.   What is the maximum revenue?
     b.   How many cans of Party Nuts, Mixed, and Delightful Mix should be produced?
     c.   Which types of nuts are completely used and which are in excess?

15. Solve the four-product production planning model (problem 8 in Chapter 4) using an LP solver. Give the optimal amounts of production of the four products in each month, the amounts to hold in inventory, and the total cost.

16. Solve the Coger Company problem (problem 10 in Chapter 4) using an LP solver.
     a.   What is the optimal shipping cost?
     b.   How much should be shipped from each plant to each distribution center?
     c.   Which plant(s) are utilizing 100 percent of capacity?
     d.   Coger is considering putting a plant of capacity 4,000 in St. Louis and closing either the Columbus or Indianapolis plants. Make a recommendation based on shipping costs by solving modified versions of your original Coger model.

17. Solve the financial planning problem (problem 13 in Chapter 4) using an LP solver.
     a.   What is the optimal investment strategy? What is the expected return for this strategy?
     b.   Update the model you solved in part *a* in order to incorporate the following new restriction. At least as much must be invested in Income funds as is invested in Growth & Income. Solve the model and discuss any differences in the new solution.

18. Solve Corry's grade problem (problem 15 in Chapter 4) using an LP solver. What is Corry's maximal overall score?

19. Solve the Drew's Sporting Goods advertising problem (problem 16 in Chapter 4) using an LP solver.

20. Solve the advertising problem (problem 18 in Chapter 4) using an LP solver.
     a.   What is the optimal objective function value?
     b.   How much should be invested in each advertising option?
     c.   Which of the media are at their upper limit? Lower limit?

IV. Projects and Cases

1. Schneider's Sweet Shop

    Schneider's Sweet Shop specializes in homemade candies and ice cream. Schneider produces its ice cream in-house, in batches of 50 pounds. The first stage in ice cream making is the blending of ingredients so as to obtain a mix that meets prespecified requirements as to the percentage of certain constituents. The desired composition is

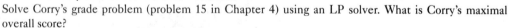

1. Fat	16.00 %		5. Stabilizer	.25 %
2. Serum Solids	8.00 %		6. Emulsifier	.15 %
3. Sugar Solids	16.00 %		7. Water	59.25 %
4. Egg Solids	.35 %			

The mix can be composed of ingredients from the following list

Ingredient	Cost ($/lb.)
1. 40% Cream	$1.19
2. 23% Cream	.70
3. Butter	2.32
4. Plastic Cream	2.30
5. Butter Oil	2.87
6. 4% Milk	.25
7. Skim Condensed Milk	.35
8. Skim Milk Powder	.65
9. Liquid Sugar	.25
10. Sugared Frozen Fresh Egg Yolk	1.75
11. Powdered Egg Yolk	4.45
12. Stabilizer	2.45
13. Emulsifier	1.68
14. Water	.00

The number of pounds of a constituent found in a pound of an ingredient is shown in the following table. Note that a pound of stabilizer contributes only to the stabilizer requirement (one pound), one pound of emulsifier contributes only to the emulsifier requirement (one pound), and that water contributes only to the water requirement (one pound).

Young Jack Schneider has recently acquired the shop from his father. Jack's father has in the past used the following mixture: 9.73 pounds of plastic cream, 3.03 pounds of skim milk powder, 11.37 pounds of liquid sugar, .44 pounds of sugared frozen fresh egg yolk, .12 pounds of stabilizer, .07 pounds of emulsifier, and 25.24 pounds of water (the scale at Schneider's is only accurate to 100ths of a pound). Jack feels that perhaps it is possible to produce the ice cream in a more cost-effective manner. He would like for you to find the cheapest mix for producing a batch of ice cream that meets the requirements specified above. (That is, solve the model developed in Case 1 of Chapter 4 for a 50-pound batch).

Constituent										Ingredient				
	1	2	3	4	5	6	7	8	9	10	11	12	13	14
1	.4	.2	.8	.8	.9	.1				.5	.6			
2	.1			.1		.1	.3	1						
3									.7	.1				
4										.4	.4			
5												1		
6													1	
7	.5	.8	.2	.1	.1	.8	.7		.3					1

As an aside, Jack is also curious about the cost effect of being a little more flexible in the requirements listed above. He wants to know the cheapest mix if the composition meets the following tolerances:

1. Fat   15.00–17.00 %
2. Serum Solids   7.00– 9.00 %
3. Sugar Solids   15.50–16.50 %
4. Egg Solids   .30– .40 %
5. Stabilizer   .20– .30 %
6. Emulsifier   .10– .20 %
7. Water   58.00– .50 %

Write a report which compares the cost of Jack's father's approach, the cost of following the strict requirements, and the cost if the more flexible requirements are followed.

2.   The Calhoun Textile Mill Revisited

Refer to the Calhoun Textile Mill case (Case 2) in Chapter 4. Management would like to know how to allocate looms to fabrics and which fabrics (and how much) should be bought on the market. Develop and solve an LP model to answer these questions. Develop a report for management that tells how much of each fabric to produce on dobbie and regular looms, and how much to purchase on the outside market. For any fabrics purchased on the outside market, give a rationale as to why this fabric(s) was chosen for outside purchase. Rerun your model with one extra dobbie loom. How much cheaper would the production cost be if this extra loom was available (ignore the cost of the loom)?

REFERENCES

Bazaraa, M., J. Jarvis and H. Sherali, *Linear Programming and Network Flows*. 2nd ed. New York: John Wiley and Sons.

Dantzig, George B. 'Reminisces About the Origins of Linear Programming,' *OR Letters*, Vol. 1, No. 2, 1982, pp. 43–48.

Hooker, J.N., 'Karmarkar's Linear Programming Algorithm,' *Interfaces*, Vol. 14, No. 4, July–August 1986, pp. 75–90.

Orchard-Hays, William, 'History of the Development of LP Solvers,' *Interfaces*, Vol. 20, No. 4, July–August 1990, pp.61–73.

Schrage, Linus, *LINDO User's Manual Release 5.0*. San Francisco, CA: The Scientific Press, 1991.

Wild, William Jr., and Otis Porter, 'The Startling Discovery Bell Labs Kept in the Shadows,' *Business Week*, September 21, 1987, pp.69–76.

APPENDIX

An Intuitive Explanation of the Simplex Algorithm

In 1947, George Dantzig[2] developed a technique called the simplex algorithm, which has since been widely used in business and industry to solve many practical problems. The simplex method solves linear programs by characterizing corner points algebraically and by moving systematically from one corner point of the feasible region to another, using algebraic manipulations to improve the objective function. We shall not describe the algebraic details of the simplex method; rather, we will describe it intuitively and use two-dimensional examples to explain the concepts.

[2]For a delightful account of the history of the development of Linear Programming, refer to George B. Dantzig. 'Reminiscences About the Origins of Linear Programming,' *Operations Research Letters*, Vol. 1, No. 2, 1982, pp. 43–48.

Corner Points and Basic Feasible Solutions

The simplex algorithm requires that an LP model be in standard form before the search for the optimal solution can begin. The method always starts at a corner point. For two-dimensional problems, we saw that corner points are characterized by their binding constraints; the slack and surplus variables with value zero indicate which constraints are binding. How can we generalize this notion to higher dimensions?

Fortunately, this can be done rather easily. For a linear programming problem in standard form, assume that we have n variables (including slack and surplus variables) and m equations. If we set $n - m$ of the variables to zero and can solve the remaining system of equations uniquely, then we have found what is known as a *basic solution*. Basic solutions correspond to points where constraints (including the variable axes) intersect. When the constraints intersect to form a corner point of the feasible region, the solution is referred to as a *basic feasible solution*. A basic feasible solution is obtained when $n - m$ variables are set to zero and the solution to the remaining $m \times m$ system of equations yields a nonnegative solution. We call the variables set to zero *nonbasic variables*, and those that remain in the system of equations *basic variables*. When we set $n - m$ variables to zero, we are left with m equations in the m unknown basic variables. This system can be solved using standard techniques of algebra (note that it is possible that one or more of these basic variables can also be zero, a condition known as *degeneracy*).

EXAMPLE A. THE SIMPLEX ALGORITHM

We will use the following example to show how the corner points can be characterized and how the simplex algorithm operates. Consider the following problem:

$$\text{Max } 2x_1 + 3x_2$$
$$\text{subject to}$$
$$1.25x_1 + x_2 \leq 100$$
$$x_1 \leq 50$$
$$x_2 \leq 75$$
$$x_1 + x_2 \geq 30$$
$$x_1, \ x_2 \geq 0$$

The feasible region is shown in Figure 5A.1.

This example can be put into standard form by adding slack variables to the left-hand side of the first three constraints and subtracting a surplus variable from the left-hand side of the last constraint.

$$\text{Max } 2x_1 + 3x_2$$
$$\text{subject to}$$
$$1.25x_1 + x_2 + s_1 = 100$$
$$x_1 + s_2 = 50$$
$$x_2 + s_3 = 75$$
$$x_1 + x_2 - s_4 = 30$$
$$x_1, \ x_2, \ s_1, \ s_2, \ s_3, \ s_4 \geq 0$$

FIGURE 5A.1   *The feasible region for Example A*

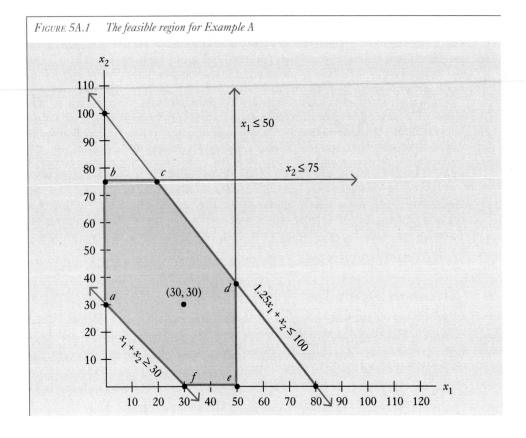

Now, consider point c in Figure 5A.1. Because point c is formed by the intersection of the first and third constraints, we know that s_1 and s_3 must be zero there. This reduces the system of equations to

$$1.25x_1 + x_2 = 100$$
$$x_1 + s_2 = 50$$
$$x_2 = 75$$
$$x_1 + x_2 - s_4 = 30$$

The nonbasic variables at this point are s_1 and s_3, and the remaining variables are basic variables. Notice that this system has *four* equations and *four* unknowns. If this *square system of equations* (a system having the same number of unknowns as equations) has a solution, it can be solved quite efficiently on a computer.

The third equation can be used to substitute 75 for x_2 wherever it appears in the other equations.

$$1.25x_1 + 75 = 100$$
$$x_1 + s_2 = 50$$
$$x_1 + 75 - s_4 = 30$$

which simplifies to

$$1.25x_1 = 25$$

$$x_1 + s_2 = 50$$

$$x_1 - s_4 = -45$$

Solving the first equation gives $x_1 = 25/1.25 = 20$, and this can be substituted to give two equations in two unknowns.

$$20 + s_2 = 50$$

$$20 - s_4 = -45$$

or $s_2 = 30$ and $s_4 = 65$.

Thus, the solution is $x_1 = 20, x_2 = 75, s_2 = 30$, and $s_4 = 65$ (recall that we set nonbasics $s_1 = 0$ and $s_3 = 0$ because the point is formed by the first and third constraints). This is a basic feasible solution because we have set $6 - 4 = 2$ variables to zero and obtained a nonnegative solution to the remaining system of four variables and four constraints.

How does a basic feasible solution differ from any other feasible solution? The point (30,30) in Figure 5A.1 is a feasible solution, but is not a basic feasible solution. If we substitute $x_1 = 30$ and $x_2 = 30$ into the constraints in standard form, we find that $s_1 = 32.5, s_2 = 20, s_3 = 45$, and $s_4 = 30$. It is not basic because we have not set $n - m = 6 - 4 = 2$ of the variables equal to zero.

Finding an Optimal Solution

As the previous discussion suggests, basic feasible solutions correspond to corner points of the feasible region. We know that if an optimal solution to an LP exists, we can find it at a corner point. By only considering basic feasible solutions, we will only consider the corner points and *not* points like (30,30). This is precisely what the simplex algorithm does; it moves from one basic feasible solution to another (one corner point to another) by swapping a variable that was basic with one that was nonbasic. When a nonbasic variable is swapped with a basic variable, we are geometrically moving to a *neighboring* corner point (a corner point connected to the current point by a border of the feasible region). The simplex algorithm chooses which neighboring corner point to move to by considering how the objective function changes as we move along the border of the feasible region.

Figure 5A.2 shows contour lines for $Z = 2x_1 + 3x_2$ with Z=0, Z=30, and Z=60 for Example A. Point f is the first corner point (basic feasible solution) touched as we increase the value of the objective function. The simplex algorithm begins its search of the feasible region at point f. Although we will not go into the details here, this geometric approach using objective function contours can be characterized algebraically.

At point f, $x_2 = 0$ and the last constraint is binding, so the surplus variable $s_4 = 0$. These two variables are nonbasic. x_1 is positive clearly, and because point f does not lie on the first three constraints, s_1, s_2, and s_3 are also positive. These four variables are basic. We find the values of the basic variables by solving the constraint set with x_2 and $s_4 = 0$.

The simplex algorithm proceeds by moving to the next neighboring corner point along the border with the greatest rate of change for the objective function. Geometrically, this is the border that is closest to the direction of improvement for the objective function. By direction of improvement, we mean the direction of the movement of the objective function contours as we move to better objective function values. We have labeled this direction ∇Z in Figure 5A.3 (this direction is always perpendicular to the contours). As shown in Figure 5A.3,

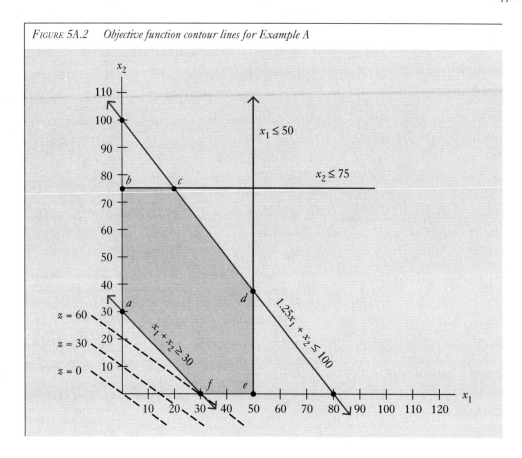

FIGURE 5A.2   Objective function contour lines for Example A

the angle between ∇Z and the f—e border is smaller than that between ∇Z and the f—a border. Therefore, as shown in Figure 5A.3, the simplex algorithm will leave point f and go to point e. Note that at point e, $x_2 = 0$ and the second constraint is binding ($s_2 = 0$). These two variables are nonbasic and the remaining four variables are basic. From the previous point f, we have simply swapped s_4 and s_2 as nonbasic elements. We can now find the values of the new basic variables by solving the constraint set with $s_2 = 0$ and $x_2 = 0$.

As shown in Figure 5A.4, the simplex algorithm proceeds from point e to point d and then to point c, based on the objective function contours. At point c, no neighboring corner point lies on a contour with a better objective function value, so point c must be the optimal solution. Table 5A-1 summarizes the progression of the simplex algorithm on the model of Example A. Note that as we move from one corner point to the next, there is a change of one variable in the basic and nonbasic sets. We can summarize the simplex algorithm in the following manner:

1. Find an initial basic feasible solution (a solution with $n - m$ variables set to zero such that the remaining variables yield a nonnegative solution to the $m \times m$ system). If none exists, stop; the problem is infeasible. Otherwise go to step 2.

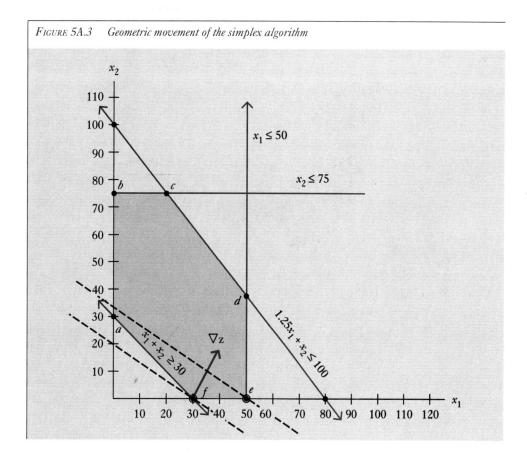

FIGURE 5A.3   *Geometric movement of the simplex algorithm*

2. Check to see if moving along the border of the feasible region from the current point will improve the objective function value. If not, stop; the current basic feasible solution is optimal. If improvement is possible go to step 3.

3. Move to the neighboring corner point by moving along the border closest to the direction of improvement (∇Z). If there is no next corner point as you move along the border, then the problem is unbounded. Otherwise, swap one of the basic variables with a nonbasic variable, so that the set of nonbasic variables are the variables which must equal zero at the new point. The basic variable values of the new point can be obtained by solving the $m \times m$ system. Go to step 2.

Step 1 of the simplex, finding a starting basic feasible solution, is referred to as *phase 1* of the simplex algorithm. We have avoided the details of how this is done on the computer. Let it suffice to say that a different phase 1 LP is solved to determine feasibility. The output from phase 1 is a starting corner point (basic feasible solution) if one exists. Otherwise we know that the problem is infeasible.

The simplex algorithm has performed well on a wide variety of practical problems, but it has been shown to be "inefficient in the worst case," to use the terminology of mathematicians. This means that for some problems the simplex algorithm could run for a very long time. Motivated by this fact and the extremely large LP models used in the telecommunications industry, AT&T Bell Labs' Narendra Karmarkar developed a different approach

FIGURE 5A.4   *Movement of the simplex algorithm*

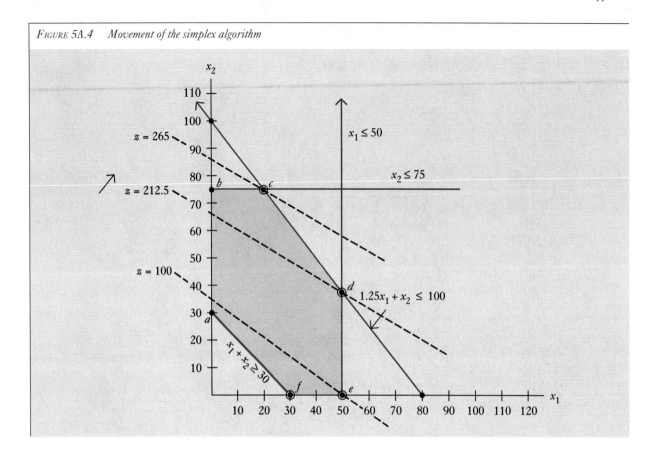

to solving linear programs in 1984. Karmarkar was able to show that his algorithm is efficient, even in the worst case, and he was able to solve some very large telecommunications LP models in impressively small amounts of computer time. Although the mathematics involved is beyond the scope of this book, the underlying concept of Karmarkar's algorithm is very appealing. Instead of trying to find the optimal solution by moving around the edges of the feasible region, Karmarkar's algorithm cuts across the interior of the feasible region.

AT&T's program based on Karmarkar's algorithm (called KORBX) has been used to solve very large problems, and a considerable amount of research has investigated these types of algorithms (generally referred to as interior point methods). To date however, the simplex algorithm remains by far the most popular LP solution technique.

TABLE 5A.1
*The simplex algorithm
steps for Example A*

Point	Nonbasic	Basics	Objective Value
f	s_4, x_2	s_1, s_2, s_3, x_1	60
e	s_2, x_2	s_1, s_3, s_4, x_1	100
d	s_1, s_2	s_3, s_4, x_1, x_2	212.5
c	s_1, s_3	s_2, s_4, x_1, x_2	265

CHAPTER 6

INTERPRETING

LP SOLUTIONS

AND MODEL

SENSITIVITY

INTRODUCTION

The parameters of an LP model are the *objective function coefficients, constraint coefficients,* and the *right-hand side* constants (we will assume that all variables have been moved to the left-hand side of the constraints in the formulation). Because LP models are deterministic, all of the parameters are assumed to be known and constant. In reality, some of the parameters might only be estimates and may be subject to error or variation. Therefore, what is "optimal" to the model may not be "optimal" to the real problem.

In addition to these uncertainties, a manager using an LP model for planning will likely be interested in analyzing a variety of scenarios. Typically, these scenarios are variations of some "base case," and are generated by changes in the base case model parameters. For example, a production planning model may have the forecasted demand per period as input. A production planner might be interested in how costs change as the demand in a particular period is increased or decreased from the forecasted value. Likewise, indications of how the model outputs would change as the selling price or the cost of raw material might change would also be of interest. If extra resources become available, a planner might want to know which of the resources that are completely used in the base case model solution should be increased.

Sensitivity analysis provides information about the sensitivity of a solution in an LP model to changes in the input parameters. Sensitivity analysis addresses questions such as, What effect would a 5 percent error in estimating a cost coefficient mean? How much would an additional unit of a scarce resource be worth? If the sales V.P. orders a price increase, should we change our production plan? These are important questions that can help managers to evaluate an LP solution and make a decision.

One way of addressing these questions is to solve the base case LP model with new parameter values in order to determine the effects of parameter changes. However, if information on only a single parameter change is desired, solvers such as LINDO and EXCEL may provide the desired sensitivity analysis information without resolving the model. At virtually no extra computational cost, LINDO and EXCEL provide information on

- How much an objective function coefficient may vary before the current solution no longer remains optimal.
- How much the objective function value can change when the right-hand side constant in a constraint changes.

In this chapter we discuss how to obtain and interpret sensitivity analysis information for linear programs. As in Chapter 5, we first build your intuition by discussing some geometric issues.

THE GEOMETRY OF LP MODEL CHANGES

As we mentioned, a manager might be interested in how changes in the unit cost or profit affects the solution to an LP model. He or she might also be interested in changes in constraint coefficients and constraint right-hand side values. For example, a manager might want to know how the model solution and its objective function value are affected by changes in the hours required per unit of production or changes to the machine time available.

As we shall see, some changes to LP models change *only* the objective function value. Other changes may affect *only* the optimal values of the decision variables. Still other changes affect *both* the objective function value *and* the optimal values of the decision variables. We will refer to a change in the optimal objective function value as a change in the LP's *value*. A change in the optimal values of the decision variables will be referred to as a change in the *solution* of the LP.

Changes in Objective Function Coefficients

Suppose that we find that one of the objective function coefficients in an LP model that we have already solved is incorrect. This could happen if, for example, a profit or cost coefficient has been miscalculated or perhaps has been entered incorrectly into the computer model. Will this change the LP's value or solution? As we shall see, it may or may not, depending on the magnitude of the error.

When we change an objective function coefficient in an LP model, the slope of the objective function changes. The feasible region is not affected by any change in the objective function. Consequently, whether or not an objective function coefficient change results in a new solution depends on whether or not the new slope of the objective function contours leads to a different optimal corner point.

E XAMPLE 1. CHANGING OBJECTIVE FUNCTION COEFFICIENTS

Recall Example 1 from Chapter 5:

$$\text{Max } 2x_1 + 3x_2$$
$$\text{subject to}$$
$$1.25x_1 + x_2 \leq 100$$
$$x_1 + x_2 \geq 30$$
$$x_1 \leq 50$$
$$x_2 \leq 75$$
$$x_1, x_2 \geq 0$$

The feasible region is shown with objective function contours in Figure 6.1. Recall that point c is the optimal solution. Let us consider changes for the objective function coefficient of x_1, which is currently equal to 2. Suppose that the coefficient should be 1. As shown in Figure 6.2, corner point c would still remain optimal. In fact, as you can see from Figure 6.2, point c will remain the optimal solution as long as the slope of the objective function contours remains between the slopes of the constraint lines at corner point c ($1.25x_1 + x_2 = 100$ and $x_2 = 75$). The slope of the constraint line is the coefficient of x_1 when the equation has been solved for x_2. For example, for $1.25x_1 + x_2 = 100, x_2 = -1.25x_1 + 100$, so the slope is -1.25 (or $-5/4$). The slope of $x_2 = 75$ is zero. Therefore, point c remains the solution so long as the slope of the objective function is between -1.25 and zero. If the coefficient of x_1 is

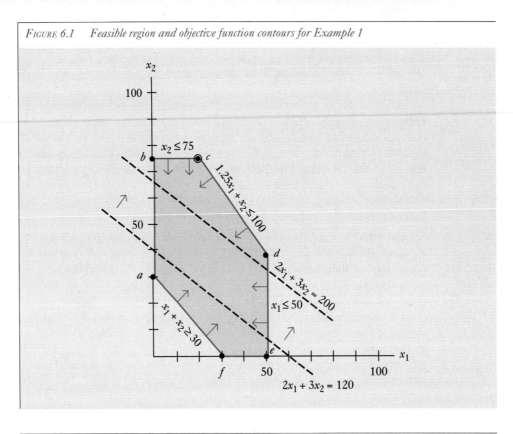

FIGURE 6.1   *Feasible region and objective function contours for Example 1*

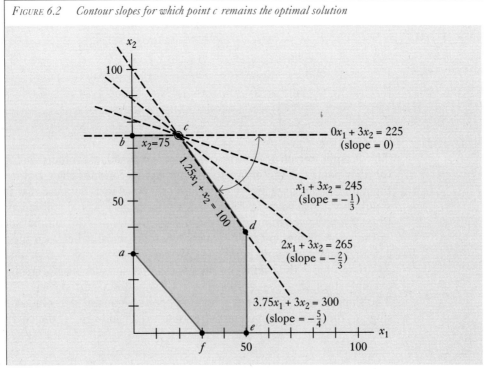

FIGURE 6.2   *Contour slopes for which point c remains the optimal solution*

1, the slope of the objective function is $-1/3$ ($x_2 = (-1/3)x_1 + Z$). Since $-1/3$ is between -1.25 and zero, the current solution remains optimal.

Note that while the solution point c remains optimal for the objective function $x_1 + 3x_2$, the *value* changes. The original value was $2(20) + 3(75) = 265$. The new value, as shown in Figure 6.2, is $(20) + 3(75) = 245$.

Although we will not go into the details here, it is possible to calculate those values for the coefficient of x_1 that keep the slope of the objective function between -1.25 and 0 when the coefficient of x_2 remains equal to 3. As shown in Figure 6.2, the slope of the objective function is equal to -1.25 when x_1's coefficient is 3.75, and the slope is 0 when x_1's coefficient is 0. Consequently, the current solution remains optimal for values from 0 to 3.75 for the coefficient of x_1.

If the change in the objective function coefficient is such that the slope of the objective function is not between the slopes of the constraint lines of the current solution, then that point is no longer optimal. For example, consider a value of 10 for the coefficient of x_1. The contour for $10x_1 + 3x_2$ is shown in Figure 6.3. As shown, we can move beyond the old optimal point, c, to higher-valued contours until we reach point d, the new optimal solution. Here the solution has changed to $x_1 = 50$, $x_2 = 37.5$ and the value has changed to $10(50) + 3(37.5) = 612.5$.

FIGURE 6.3   *Optimal solution for objective function* $10x_1 + 3x_2$

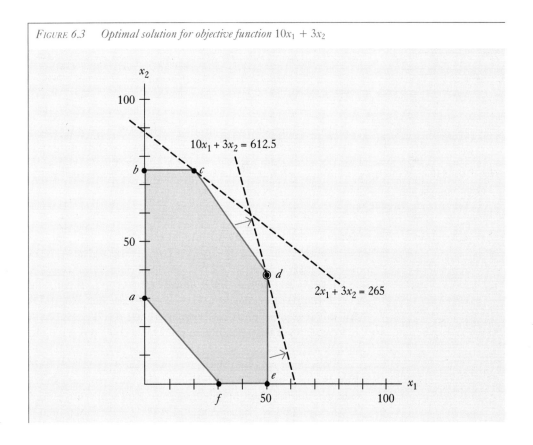

Changes in Right-hand Sides of Constraints

Suppose the value of the right-hand side of some constraint is changed. For example, a manager might find that she has a budget cut, necessitating a decrease in the right-hand side value of the budget constraint in her LP planning model. Will this affect the solution and optimal value of the LP?

Changes in the right-hand side values of an inequality constraint may or may not have an impact on the optimal LP solution and value. When we change the right-hand side of an inequality constraint, the constraint shifts parallel to itself (similar to what we saw when we plotted objective function contours for different values of the objective function). With such a change, the feasible region may become larger or smaller, depending on the direction of the shift. In fact, if the constraint is redundant, it is possible that the feasible region will remain unchanged. In the remainder of this section, we assume that the constraint in question is *not* a redundant constraint.

We say that a constraint has been *tightened* if the new value of the right-hand side makes the constraint more difficult to satisfy; that is, fewer points satisfy the modified constraint than satisfied the original constraint. We say that a constraint has been *relaxed* if more points satisfy the constraint with the modified right-hand side than with the original constraint. We can therefore make the observations shown in the following table.

TABLE 6.1
Tightening and relaxing constraints

	Constraint Type	
	$\leq$	$\geq$
Right-Hand Side Increase	Relaxation	Tightening
Right-Hand Side Decrease	Tightening	Relaxation

For example, a budget constraint that dictates that we may not invest more cash than we have available is relaxed if the budget is increased, and tightened if it is decreased. On the other hand, a constraint specifying a minimum daily requirement of a nutrient is relaxed if that minimum is lowered and tightened if the minimum is increased.

EXAMPLE 2. CHANGING THE RIGHT-HAND SIDE OF A CONSTRAINT

Suppose we modify the LP model in Example 1 by increasing the right-hand side value of the constraint $x_1 + x_2 \geq 30$ to 35. This tightens the constraint, because fewer points satisfy $x_1 + x_2 \geq 35$. This change eliminates a portion of the feasible region, as shown in Figure 6.4. Note, however, that the optimal solution does not change.

If we relax the constraint $x_1 + x_2 \geq 30$ by changing the right-hand side to 25, the feasible region expands, as shown in Figure 6.4. The optimal point still remains point c, so we can see that relaxing or tightening a constraint will not necessarily change the optimal solution.

Consider changing the constraint $1.25x_1 + x_2 \leq 100$. Suppose that the right-hand side is increased to 110; this relaxes the constraint, as shown in Figure 6.5. We see that we can increase the objective function by moving to higher-valued contours, out to point g. The x_1 and x_2 values at point g can be obtained by solving the constraint

FIGURE 6.4   Tightening and relaxing the constraint $x_1 + x_2 \geq 30$

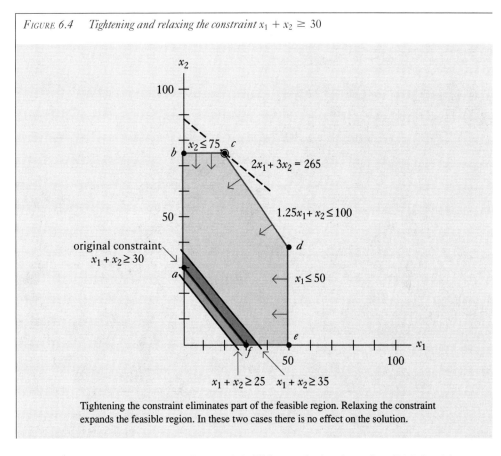

Tightening the constraint eliminates part of the feasible region. Relaxing the constraint expands the feasible region. In these two cases there is no effect on the solution.

lines $1.25x_1 + x_2 = 110$ and $x_2 = 75$. This results in the point $(28,75)$ with a new objective function value of $2(28) + 3(75) = 281$. This is an increase of 16 over the old objective function value of 265 at point c.

As shown in Figure 6.6, we may continue to increase the objective function value by increasing the right-hand side of the constraint $1.25x_1 + x_2 \leq 100$ until it is no longer a binding constraint. The optimal point defined by the intersection of the constraint lines $1.25x_1 + x_2 = 100$ and $x_2 = 75$ moves to the left as the right-hand side of 100 is increased. This allows us to reach higher-valued contours. The effect is only valid for an increase of 37.5, because as shown in Figure 6.6, for an increase larger than 37.5, the first constraint is no longer binding. Instead, the optimal corner point is defined by the constraint lines $x_1 = 50$ and $x_2 = 75$.

Changes in Constraint Coefficients

Suppose that we change a coefficient in a constraint. This alters the slope of that constraint and may or may not affect the optimal solution. Whether or not a new optimal solution and value results from a coefficient depends on which constraint is changed,

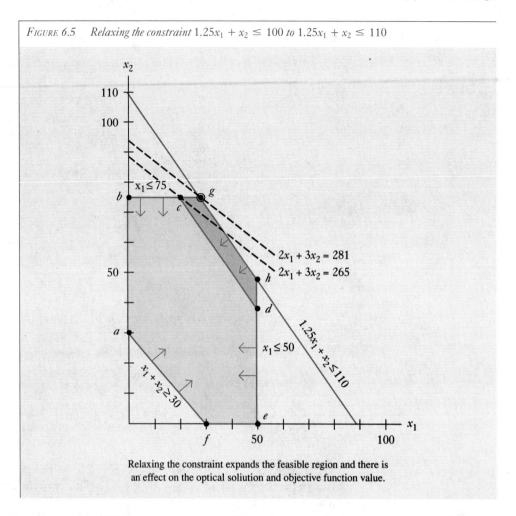

FIGURE 6.5   *Relaxing the constraint* $1.25x_1 + x_2 \leq 100$ *to* $1.25x_1 + x_2 \leq 110$

Relaxing the constraint expands the feasible region and there is
an effect on the optical soliution and objective function value.

which coefficient is changed, and the magnitude of the change. The sensitivity of the
model solution to constraint coefficients is *not* easily determined and consequently is not a
part of routine LP solver computer output. Essentially, determining the effect of a change
in a constraint coefficient requires that we delete the old constraint from the model and
then add the new constraint to the remaining constraint set. We discuss adding new constraints and deleting existing constraints in the next section.

Adding and Deleting Constraints

What effect can the addition of a constraint have on the optimal solution to an LP? The
straightforward answer to this question is,

FIGURE 6.6   *Geometry of an increase in the right-hand side for the constraint* $1.25x_1 + x_2 \leq 100$

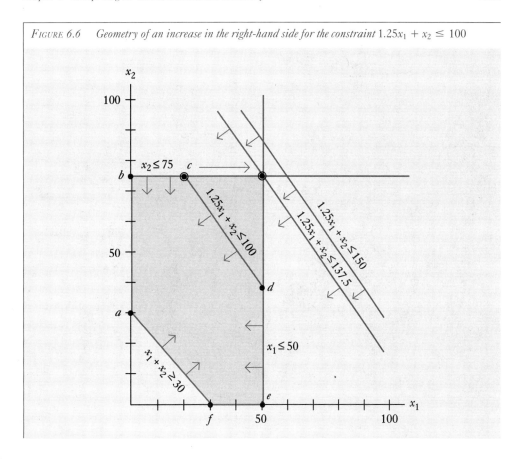

When adding a constraint to an LP, if the current optimal solution satisfies the constraint, that solution will remain optimal. If the current optimal solution does not satisfy the new constraint, the model must be resolved with the new constraint.

EXAMPLE 3. ADDING A CONSTRAINT

Consider adding the constraint $2x_1 + x_2 \geq 60$ to the problem in Example 1. The current solution is $x_1 = 20$ and $x_2 = 75$. We first check to see that the current solution satisfies the constraint $2(20) + 75 = 40 + 75 = 115 > 60$. Therefore, (20,75) remains the optimal solution. Figure 6.7 shows the feasible region for Example 1 with the added constraint $2x_1 + x_2 \geq 60$. Although the feasible region is now smaller, point c (20,75) has not been eliminated and remains optimal.

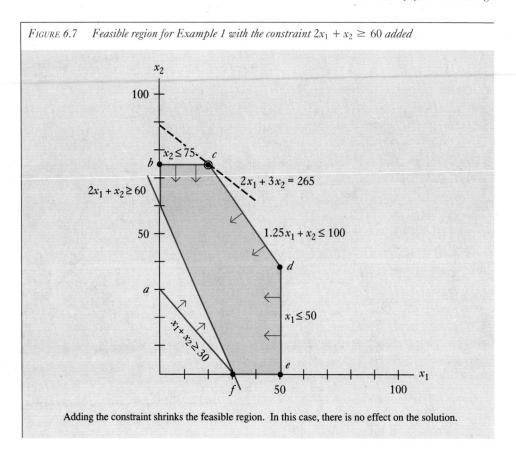

Adding the constraint shrinks the feasible region. In this case, there is no effect on the solution.

Now consider adding the constraint $x_1 \leq 15$. The current solution of $x_1 = 20$ and $x_2 = 75$ does not satisfy the new constraint. We must therefore resolve the model with this new constraint added to the constraint set. As shown in Figure 6.8, we see that the new optimal solution is point h. The values of x_1 and x_2 at point h are $x_1 = 15$ and $x_2 = 75$. The new objective function value is $2(15) + 3(75) = 255$. Note that the objective function value is smaller.

We turn our attention now to deleting a constraint. If the deleted constraint was redundant, there will be no change in the feasible region and the current solution will remain optimal. If the deleted constraint was not redundant, then the feasible region will expand. If the expansion of the feasible region creates a new feasible point that has a better objective function value than the current optimal solution, then the current solution will no longer be optimal. This can occur only when we delete a constraint that is *binding* at the optimal solution.

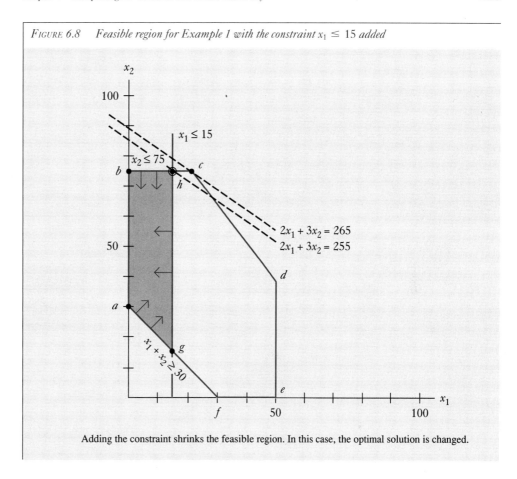

FIGURE 6.8   *Feasible region for Example 1 with the constraint* $x_1 \leq 15$ *added*

Adding the constraint shrinks the feasible region. In this case, the optimal solution is changed.

Deleting a nonbinding constraint at the current optimal solution does not change the optimal solution. Deleting a binding constraint at the current optimal solution may change the optimal solution, so the model must be resolved to find out.

EXAMPLE 4. DELETING A CONSTRAINT

Consider deleting the constraint $x_1 + x_2 \geq 30$ from the constraint set of Example 1. The new expanded feasible region is shown in Figure 6.9. Note that this constraint was not binding at our solution of $x_1 = 20$ and $x_2 = 75$; therefore there is no effect on the optimal solution. This is confirmed in Figure 6.9, as point c is still optimal.

   Suppose on the other hand, that we delete the constraint $x_1 \leq 75$. This is a binding constraint at our optimal solution point c. This expands the feasible region, as shown in Figure 6.10. The new optimal solution is $x_1 = 0$ and $x_2 = 100$, which

FIGURE 6.9 *Feasible region for Example 1 with the constraint* $x_1 + x_2 \geq 30$ *deleted*

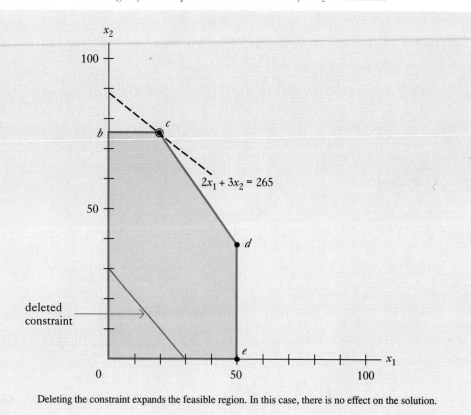

Deleting the constraint expands the feasible region. In this case, there is no effect on the solution.

we have labeled point i in Figure 6.10. The new objective function value is $2(0) + 3(100) = 300$.

Because making the feasible region smaller cannot improve the objective function value and expanding the feasible region cannot worsen the objective function value, we can make the following generalizations about adding or deleting constraints.

> Adding a constraint to an LP model will either leave the optimal objective function value the same or make it worse. Deleting a constraint will either leave the optimal objective function value the same or make it better.

Next we turn our attention to sensitivity analysis using LP solvers on the computer.

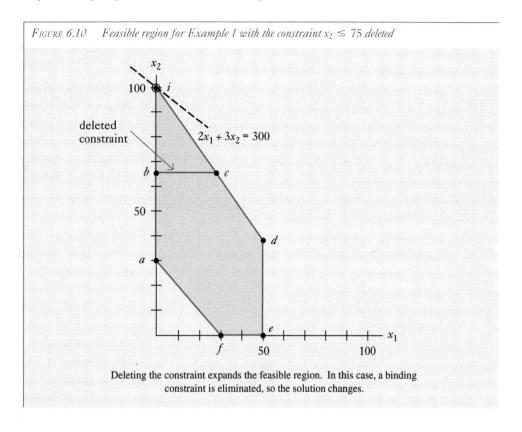

FIGURE 6.10   *Feasible region for Example 1 with the constraint $x_2 \leq 75$ deleted*

Deleting the constraint expands the feasible region. In this case, a binding
constraint is eliminated, so the solution changes.

COMPUTER IMPLEMENTATION OF LP SENSITIVITY ANALYSIS

For practical planning problems, we would like LP solvers to provide sensitivity analysis
information automatically. Fortunately, LP solvers such as LINDO and EXCEL can handle and provide information on larger problems than the two-variable problems we discussed in the previous section. We begin with a more complete discussion of the LINDO
output introduced in Chapter 5.

LINDO

Figure 6.11 shows the model and solution output for Example 1. LINDO provides a
variety of information in addition to the optimal values of the decision variables, slacks
and surpluses, and objective function value. These include

1. reduced costs,
2. dual prices,
3. objective function coefficient ranges, and
4. right-hand side ranges.

The *reduced costs* in the variable section tell how much the objective function coefficient of a variable would have to change for that variable to become positive in the solution. In the model in Figure 6.11, x_1 and x_2 are both in the solution, so their reduced costs are zero.

The *dual prices* are the improvement in the objective function value for an increase of one in the right-hand side of a constraint, while all other parameters in the model are fixed. These values are known as dual prices because they are the variable values in a related LP known as the dual problem. A positive dual price is how much the objective function value is *improved* by an increase of one in the right-hand side. A negative dual price indicates how much the objective function would be *worsened* by an increase in the right-hand side.

The dual price for the first constraint in Figure 6.11 is 1.6. This indicates that the objective function value will be improved by 1.6 for an increase of one in the right-hand side of that constraint. In fact, this is what we found in Example 2, as shown in Figure 6.5. We increased the right-hand side of the constraint by 10 to 110 and the objective function value improved (increased) by $1.6 \times 10 = 16$ to 281.

Dual prices are valid only within a certain range. This means that a dual price will only hold for a per-unit increase of the right-hand side up to a certain total increase. The range is given in the *Right-hand Side Ranges* section of the LINDO output.

For example, consider the first constraint (row 2) in Figure 6.11. We have seen that the dual price of 1.6 indicates that an increase in the right-hand side of this constraint will improve the objective function by 1.60 per unit of increase. Checking the allowable increase in the *Right-hand Side Ranges* section shows that this dual price is valid for an increase up to 37.5 units. Recall that in Example 2, this is precisely the allowable change before the first constraint no longer remains binding at the optimal point (see Figure 6.6).

Dual prices are symmetric; that is, a *decrease* in the right-hand side of a constraint will result in a change in sign opposite to that of the dual price. A decrease in the right-hand side of the first constraint in Figure 6.11 will worsen the objective function by 1.60 per unit. This relationship holds for a decrease of 25 (the allowable decrease shown in the *Right-hand Side Ranges* section of Figure 6.11.). The geometry is shown in Figure 6.12. The optimal point formed by the constraint lines $1.25x_1 + x_2 = 100$ and $x_2 = 75$ moves to the left as the right-hand side of 100 is decreased. The result of this is that only lower-valued contours are reachable. For decreases beyond the allowable 25, the constraint $x_2 \leq 75$ is no longer binding and the optimal point is formed by the constraint lines $1.25x_1 + x_2 = y$ and $x_1 = 0$, where y is the new right-hand side.

In Figure 6.11, observe that nonbinding constraints have zero dual prices. This indicates that there is no change in the objective function value for increases or decreases in these right-hand sides (all other parameters are held fixed) for the ranges given in the *Right-hand Side Ranges* section. Since nonbinding constraints do not form the optimal corner point, there is an amount by which their right-hand sides can change and not have an impact on the solution or value. In Figure 6.11, notice that the dual price of zero for row 3 holds for an increase of 65 and a decrease of infinity. Clearly, given that the constraint is nonbinding, decreasing its right-hand side will never change the solution. Increasing its right-hand side, however, will eventually make the current solution infeasible. (This

---

FIGURE 6.11   LINDO model and solution output for Example 1

```
MAX        2 X1 + 3 X2
SUBJECT TO
        2)   1.25 X1 + X2 <= 100
        3)   X1 + X2 >= 30
        4)   X1 <= 50
        5)   X2 <= 75
END
```

LP OPTIMUM FOUND AT STEP   4

OBJECTIVE FUNCTION VALUE

    1)   265.00000

VARIABLE	VALUE	REDUCED COST
X1	20.000000	.000000
X2	75.000000	.000000

ROW	SLACK OR SURPLUS	DUAL PRICES
2)	.000000	1.600000
3)	65.000000	.000000
4)	30.000000	.000000
5)	.000000	1.400000

NO. ITERATIONS = 4

RANGES IN WHICH THE BASIS IS UNCHANGED:

	OBJ COEFFICIENT RANGES		
VARIABLE	CURRENT COEF	ALLOWABLE INCREASE	ALLOWABLE DECREASE
X1	2.000000	1.750000	2.000000
X2	3.000000	INFINITY	1.400000

	RIGHTHAND SIDE RANGES		
ROW	CURRENT RHS	ALLOWABLE INCREASE	ALLOWABLE DECREASE
2	100.000000	37.500000	25.000000
3	30.000000	65.000000	INFINITY
4	50.000000	INFINITY	30.000000
5	75.000000	25.000000	37.000000

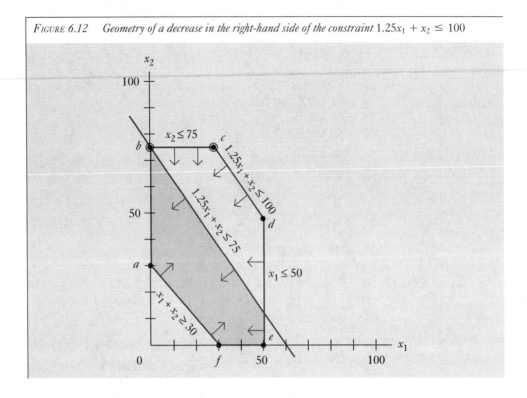

can be seen in Figure 6.3 by plotting the constraint $x_1 + x_2 \geq 30$ for higher values of its right-hand side.) If we increase the constraint $x_1 + x_2 \geq 30$ by 65, point c will be on the constraint line $x_1 + x_2 = 95$. If the right-hand side is increased beyond the value of 95, point c is no longer feasible, and the solution and value will change. A similar geometric observation can be made for row 4. These observations generalize to all LP solutions.

> The dual price for a nonbinding constraint is zero.

The dual price of 1.4 for the last constraint in the model of Figure 6.11 may be interpreted in the same way as the dual price of 1.6 for the first constraint. We ask you to explore the geometry of changing this right-hand side in a problem at the end of this chapter.

The *objective function coefficient ranges* give the allowable change in the objective function coefficient for which the current solution remains optimal, given that all other parameters in the model are held fixed. For example, in Figure 6.11, the objective function coefficient of x_1, currently 2, can increase by up to 1.75 or decrease by as much as 2, and the current solution of $x_1 = 20$ and $x_2 = 75$ will remain optimal. As long as the coefficient remains in the range 0 to 3.75, we do not have to rerun the model. However, if the coefficient is changed within the allowable range, then the objective function value will change (we may calculate this value easily by plugging the current solution into the new objective function).

EXAMPLE 5. INTERPRETING LINDO SOLUTION OUTPUT

The LINDO model and solution output for the Colorado Cattle Company model discussed in Chapters 4 and 5 is shown in Figure 6.13. The solution is to use 8 pounds of grade 1, 5.5 pounds of grade 2, and 0.5 pounds of grade 3, for a total daily cost of $2.59 per cow. Since all three grades are in the solution, all of the reduced costs are zero. The protein constraint is not binding and consequently has a dual price of zero.

We interpret the nonzero dual prices of rows 2, 3, and 5 as follows. The dual price of −0.31 for row 2 indicates that as the right-hand side (amount of required calcium) increases, the objective function value is loosened by $0.31 per unit of increase. This price holds for an increase of only 0.13793 in the calcium requirement. We interpret the dual price for the iron requirement in a similar manner.

The positive dual price associated with the fat constraint indicates that increasing the allowable fat by 1 unit improves, i.e., decreases, the objective function by $1.14. This price holds for an increase of one unit.

The differences in the signs of the dual prices make sense if you consider that these are the rates of change for an *increase* in the right-hand side. Increasing the right-hand side of a greater-than-or-equal-to constraint tightens that constraint. We know from the previous section that this cannot help the objective function value. The dual prices on the greater-than-or-equal-to constraints are therefore negative, indicating that the objective function value will worsen. Increasing the right-hand side of a less-than-or-equal-to constraint relaxes that constraint. A relaxation cannot hurt the objective function value. The positive dual price on the fat constraint indicates this.

The small *Right-hand Side Ranges* indicate that this model is fairly sensitive to changes in the constraint right-hand sides. The fat constraint, whose dual price is large (in absolute value) relative to those of the other constraints, suggests that this constraint in particular is a candidate for relaxation if we wish to lower cost. This means that a relatively easy way to lower cost would be to allow more fat into the mix.

The ranges of the objective function coefficients are large relative to the current coefficients, indicating that this model is not very sensitive to changes in the cost coefficients.

Table 6.2 summarizes the interpretation of LINDO sensitivity analysis.

FIGURE 6.13   *LINDO model and output for the CCC problem*

```
MIN        0.25 X1 + 0.1 X2 + 0.08 X3              ! CCC LP Model
SUBJECT TO
       2)    0.7 X1 + 0.8 X2 >= 10                 ! Calcium
       3)    0.9 X1 + 0.8 X2 + 0.8 X3 >= 15 ! Iron
       4)    0.8 X1 + 1.5 X2 + 0.9 X3 >= 15 ! Protein
       5)    0.5 X1 + 0.6 X2 + 0.4 X3 >= 15 ! Fat
END
```

LP OPTIMUM FOUND AT STEP   4

OBJECTIVE FUNCTION VALUE

1)   2.5900002

VARIABLE	VALUE	REDUCED COST
X1	8.000000	0.000000
X2	5.500000	0.000000
X3	0.500000	0.000000

ROW	SLACK OR SURPLUS	DUAL PRICES
2)	0.000000	−0.310000
3)	0.000000	−0.670000
4)	0.100000	0.000000
5)	0.000000	1.140000

NO. ITERATIONS = 4

RANGES IN WHICH THE BASIS IS UNCHANGED:

OBJ COEFFICIENT RANGES

VARIABLE	CURRENT COEF	ALLOWABLE INCREASE	ALLOWABLE DECREASE
X1	0.250000	INFINITY	0.142500
X2	0.100000	0.162857	INFINITY
X3	0.080000	0.177143	2.680000

RIGHTHAND SIDE RANGES

ROW	CURRENT RHS	ALLOWABLE INCREASE	ALLOWABLE DECREASE
2	10.000000	0.137930	4.000000
3	12.000000	0.054794	1.999999
4	15.000000	0.099999	INFINITY
5	7.000000	1.000000	0.016949

TABLE 6.2
Interpreting LINDO
sensitivity analysis

Reduced cost indicates the minimum amount by which the objective function coefficient of a variable will have to change before that variable will be in the solution at a positive amount. In a max problem, this is the minimum amount that the coefficient will have to increase. For a min problem, it is the minimum amount the coefficient will have to decrease.

Dual price indicates the improvement in the objective function value for an increase of one unit in the right-hand side of a constraint. A negative dual price indicates a detrimental effect on the objective function (negative improvement).

Improvement for a maximization problem means an increase in its objective function value (worsening means a decrease in its value).

Improvement for a minimization problem means a decrease in the objective function value (worsening means an increase in its value). Dual prices are symmetric: the effect of decreasing a right-hand side value can be obtained by changing the sign of the dual price.

Right-hand side range indicates the range over which dual prices are valid.

Objective function coefficient range gives the allowable increase and decrease in the objective function coefficient of a variable. As long as a change falls within that range, the current solution remains optimal.

Caveat: These ranges assume only a *single change* in the input data. If multiple changes occur, we must re-run the model with those changes.

Excel Solver

When solving an LP using EXCEL, the solution returns to the spreadsheet model. In addition to the solution in the spreadsheet, it is possible to generate three reports. EXCEL will generate an Answer Report, a Sensitivity Report, and a Limits Report. In these reports, Solver labels the cells by searching for the first text to the left and above each changing cell. The objective function cell is referred to as the Target Cell in these reports.

The Answer Report shows the basic information we discussed in the previous chapter: optimal changing cell values, the optimal Target Cell value, the optimal values of all cell formulas, which constraints are binding, and the values of the slack or surplus variables. The original values of the changing cells (those that were in the spreadsheet when Solver was invoked) are also given.

The Sensitivity Report provides all of the same sensitivity information that we described for LINDO. For each changing cell (decision variable), EXCEL gives the optimal value and reduced cost. EXCEL also provides the objective function coefficient and its allowable increase and decrease for each changing cell. These changes are the objective function coefficient changes for which the current solution remains optimal if all other parameters remain fixed. For each constraint cell, the report gives the final value, the shadow price (the equivalent of LINDO's dual price), the right-hand side, and the allowable change in the right-hand side for the shadow price. The *shadow price* given by EXCEL is interpreted as the *rate of change* in the objective function value as the right-hand side value of a constraint is *increased*. A positive shadow price indicates an increase in the objective function, and a negative shadow price indicates a decrease. The rate of change of the objective function value for a *decrease* in the right-hand side can be obtained by changing the sign of the shadow price.

This leads to an important distinction that needs to be made between EXCEL and LINDO. The sign interpretation for EXCEL's shadow price is different than LINDO's dual price. In LINDO, a negative dual price "hurts" the objective function value and a positive dual price "helps" the objective function value. In EXCEL, the sign of the shadow price is exactly the change in the objective function (positive means an increase and negative means a decrease), without regard to whether the objective is max or min.

The Limits Report tells how the changing cells can vary with everything else in the model fixed (parameter cells *and* other changing cell values) while maintaining feasibility. The associated Target Cell value for this change is also given. We emphasize that the Limits Report information is *not* sensitivity analysis as we have discussed it; it does not really describe how sensitive the model is to the input parameters. The Limits Report rather indicates the allowable change *in the value of a changing cell* with all other model entities fixed.

EXAMPLE 6. INTERPRETING EXCEL SOLVER OUTPUT

Figure 6.14 shows the EXCEL spreadsheet model for the Colorado Cattle Company problem; the solution shown is the optimal solution found by Solver. The Answer Report generated by EXCEL is shown in Figure 6.15. The original (infeasible) solution in the spreadsheet when Solver was invoked was zero pounds of each grade. The column labeled "Final Value" gives the optimal values of the objective function and adjustable cells. The constraint section indicates which constraints are binding.

The Solver Sensitivity Report for the CCC model is shown in Figure 6.16. Compare these results with the LINDO output in Figure 6.13 (note that $1E + 30$ is essentially infinity). All information is the same as in LINDO, with the exception of the signs on the shadow and dual prices. EXCEL's shadow prices indicate that as the calcium and iron requirements are increased, cost will increase at a rate of $.31 and $.67, respectively. If the amount of fat allowed is increased, cost will decrease at a rate of $1.14. The allowable changes for which these prices are valid are given in the constraints section.

Finally, the Limits Report for the CCC model is shown in Figure 6.17. The report shows the optimal target cell and adjustable cell values, along with the lower limit on each adjustable cell, its resulting target cell value, the upper limit, and its resulting target cell value. In this case, note that the lower and upper limit values are the same as the optimal values for each changing cell. This indicates that the value of each adjustable cell cannot be altered and maintain feasibility while all else in the model remains fixed. This indicates that the CCC problem is very strongly restricted (something you already know if you tried to generate a feasible solution using trial and error as discussed in Chapter 4!).

FIGURE 6.14   EXCEL spreadsheet model for the CCC problem

	A	B	C	D	E	F	G	H
1	Colorado Cattle Company Model							
2								
3	Parameters and uncontrollable variables							
4								
5	Grade	1	2	3				
6	Cost/lb.	$0.25	$0.10	$0.08	Minimum	Maximum		
7	Calc./lb.	0.7	0.8	0	10			
8	Iron/lb.	0.9	0.8	0.8	12			
9	Prot./lb.	0.8	1.5	0.9	15			
10	Fat/lb.	0.5	0.6	0.4		7.5		
11								
12	Decision Variables							
13								
14		Grade 1	Grade 2	Grade 3				
15	Quantity	8	5.5	0.5				
16								
17							Changing Cells	
18	Model Outputs:							
19		Amount	Excess					
20	Calcium	10	0.0					
21	Iron	12	0.0					
22	Protein	15.1	0.1					
23		Amount	Available					
24	Fat	7.5	0.0					
25								
26	Total Cost	$2.59						
27								
28						Set Cell		
29								

FIGURE 6.15   EXCEL Solver Answer Report for the CCC problem

Target Cell (Min)

Cell	Name	Original Value	Final Value
$B$26	Total Cost	$0.00	$2.59

Adjustable Cells *or changing cells*

Cell	Name	Original Value	Final Value
$B$15	Quantity Grade 1	0	8
$C$15	Quantity Grade 2	0	5.5
$D$15	Quantity Grade 3	0	0.5

Constraints

Cell	Name	Cell Value	Formula	Status	Slack
$B$20	Calcium Amount	10	$B$20>=$E$7	Binding	0
$B$21	Iron Amount	12	$B$21>=$E$8	Binding	0
$B$22	Protein Amount	15.1	$B$22>=$E$9	Not Binding	0.1
$B$24	Fat Amount	7.5	$B$24<=$F$10	Binding	0
$B$15	Quantity Grade 1	8	$B$15>=0	Not Binding	8
$C$15	Quantity Grade 2	5.5	$C$15>=0	Not Binding	5.5
$D$15	Quantity Grade 3	0.5	$D$15>=0	Not Binding	0.5

(handwritten annotations:)

minimize cost of feeding
$= .25x_1 + .1x_2 + .08x_3$
$= $B6 + $C6 + $D6$

changing cells

FIGURE 6.16   The EXCEL Sensitivity Report for the CCC model

Changing Cells

Cell	Name	Final Value	Reduced Cost	Objective Coefficient	Allowable Increase	Allowable Decrease
$B$15	Quantity Grade 1	8	0	0.25	1E+30	0.1425
$C$15	Quantity Grade 2	5.5	0	0.1	0.162857143	1E+30
$D$15	Quantity Grade 3	0.5	0	0.08	0.177142857	2.68

Constraints

Cell	Name	Final Value	Shadow Price	Constraint R.H. Side	Allowable Increase	Allowable Decrease
$B$20	Calcium Amount	10	0.31	10	0.137931034	4
$B$21	Iron Amount	12	0.67	12	0.054794521	2
$B$22	Protein Amount	15.1	0	15	0.1	1E+30
$B$24	Fat Amount	7.5	-1.14	7.5	1	0.016949153

FIGURE 6.17   The EXCEL Limits Report for the CCC model

Cell	Target Name	Value
$B$26	Total Cost	$2.59

Cell	Adjustable Name	Value	Lower Limit	Target Result	Upper Limit	Target Result
$B$15	Quantity Grade 1	8	8	2.59	8	2.59
$C$15	Quantity Grade 2	5.5	5.5	2.59	5.5	2.59
$D$15	Quantity Grade 3	0.5	0.5	2.59	0.5	2.59

LOTUS 1-2-3 Solver

The Solver in LOTUS 1-2-3 for Windows (Release 4) provides three solution reports. In addition to the spreadsheet solution, an Answer Table, a How Solved Report, and a What-If Limits Report may also be generated after the Solver has optimized the LP model. Unfortunately, none of these reports provide sensitivity analysis as we have described it. Like the EXCEL Solver, the LOTUS Solver labels cells by using the first text cell above and to the left of each cell.

The Answer Table shows the optimal values for the adjustable cells and supporting cells (cells that are functions of the adjustable cells). If multiple answers are found (recall that this may mean multiple feasible solutions, not necessarily alternate optimal solutions) then these may be reported. In addition, the highest and lowest values of each adjustable and supporting cell are listed for all feasible solutions. The What-If Limits Table reports these limits exclusively (that is, the What-If Table is a subset of the Answer Table).

The How Solved Report is the most descriptive of the three reports. It indicates whether the problem is a max or min problem, the cell location and optimal value of the objective function cell, the optimal values of the adjustable cells, and a listing of the binding and nonbinding constraints.

LOTUS 1-2-3 Release 4 for Windows provides no information with regard to objective function coefficient ranges, dual prices or right-hand side ranges. The only way to evaluate possible changes is to make those changes in the model and to resolve them.

EXAMPLE 7. INTERPRETING LOTUS SOLVER OUTPUT

A LOTUS 1-2-3 spreadsheet model of the optimal solution found by Solver for the Colorado Cattle Company model is shown in Figure 6.18. The Answer Table is shown in Figure 6.19. Notice that a second-best solution costing $2.63 is reported in addition to the optimal solution. This is a nice feature of LOTUS, because a manager can select from a variety of solutions even if they might not all be optimal. Reasons external to the model might make the selection of a nonoptimal solution preferable if it is "not too far from optimal." The lowest and highest values for each of the adjustable and supporting cells over all feasible solutions found are also given.

The How Solved Report for the CCC problem is shown in Figure 6.20. The sets of binding and nonbinding constraints are shown at the bottom of the output, as are the optimal values of the decision variables and the optimal objective function value.

SENSITIVITY-BASED LP MODELING

As we have seen, LP solution output can provide us with much more than just an answer. LINDO and EXCEL provide information concerning the sensitivity of the solution to the model input parameters. Knowing that this information is available after solving the model should affect *how* we model a problem. Models that are mathematically equivalent (models that provide the correct optimal solution) may not be equivalent in the sensitivity information that they provide. We will use a previous example to show how we can better formulate models from the perspective of sensitivity analysis.

EXAMPLE 8. SUZIE'S SWEATSHIRTS REVISITED

In Chapter 3 we presented a multiperiod production planning problem (Example 7). Suzie's Sweatshirts makes upscale, hand-painted sweatshirts for children. Forecasts of sales for next year are 125 for the Autumn season, 350 for Winter, and 75 for Spring. The cost of the shirts is $15 each (a sunk cost). The cost of capital is 24% per year or 6% per quarter (season). Hence the holding cost per sweatshirt is .06($15) = $.90 per quarter. The hourly rates for painting the sweatshirts are $4.50 in the Autumn, $6.00 in the Winter, and $5.50 in the Spring. Each sweatshirt takes 1.5 hours to complete. Therefore, the costs for painting the sweatshirts are as follows: (1.5)($4.50) = $6.75, (1.5)($6.00) = $9.00, and (1.5)($5.5) = $8.25 in each of

FIGURE 6.18   *The LOTUS 1-2-3 model for the CCC problem*

A	A	B	C	D	E	F	G	H	I
1	Colorado Cattle Company Model								
2									
3	*Parameters and uncontrollable variables:*								
4									
5	Grade	1	2	3					
6	Cost / lb.	0.25	0.1	0.08	Minimum	Maximum			
7	Calc. / lb.	0.7	0.8	0	10				
8	Iron / lb.	0.9	0.8	0.8	12				
9	Prot. / lb.	0.8	1.5	0.9	15				
10	Fat / lb.	0.5	0.6	0.4		7.5			
11									
12	*Decision Variables:*								
13									
14		Grade 1	Grade 2	Grade 3					
15	Quantity	8	5.5	0.5					
16									
17									
18	*Model Outputs:*								
19		Amount	Excess						
20	Calcium	10.0	0.0		+B20>=E7				
21	Iron	12.0	0.0		+B21>=E8				
22	Protein	15.1	0.1		+B22>=E9				
23		Amount	Available						
24	Fat	7.5	0.0		+B24<=F10				
25									
26	Total Cost	$2.59			+B15>=0				
27					+C15>=0				
28					+D15>=0				
29									
30									
31									

Adjustable Cells

Constraint Cells

Optimal Cell

FIGURE 6.19   *The LOTUS 1-2-3 answer table for the CCC model*

Solver Table Report - Answer table
Worksheet: D:\BOOK\FIGURES\CCCSOLV.WK4

Optimal cell

Cell	Name	Lowest value	Highest value	Answers Optimal (#1)	2
A:B26	Total Cost	$2.59	$2.63	$2.59	$2.63

Adjustable cells

Cell	Name	Lowest value	Highest value	Answers Optimal (#1)	2
A:B15	Grade 1 Quantity	8.00000000000000001	8.21917808219178082	8.00000000000000001	8.21917808219178082
A:C15	Grade 2 Quantity	5.30821917808219178	5.5	5.5	5.30821917808219178
A:D15	Grade 3 Quantity	0.499999999999999999	0.51369863013698301	0.499999999999999999	0.51369863013698301

Supporting formula cells

Cell	Name	Lowest value	Highest value	Answers Optimal (#1)	2
A:B20	Amount Calcium	10.0	10.0	10.0	10.0
A:B21	Amount Iron	12.0	12.1	12.0	12.1
A:B22	Amount Protein	15.0	15.1	15.1	15.0
A:B24	Amount Fat	7.5	7.5	7.5	7.5

FIGURE 6.20   *The How Solved Report for the CCC model from LOTUS 1-2-3*

Solver Table Report - How solved
Worksheet: D:\BOOK\FIGURES\CCCSOLV.WK4

Optimal answer (#1)

Answer #1 is one of 2 which satisfies all of the constraints.

This answer minimizes the value of cell A:B26 (Total Cost).

For this answer, the optimal cell attained the following value:

Optimal Cell

Cell	Name	Value
A:B26	Total Cost	$2.59

For this answer, Solver changed the values in the following adjustable cells:

Adjustable cells

Cell	Name	Value
A:B15	Grade 1 Quantity	8.00000000000000001
A:C15	Grade 2 Quantity	5.5
A:D15	Grade 3 Quantity	0.499999999999999999

These values make the following constraints binding:

Binding constraints

Cell	Name	Formula
A:E20	Calcium	+B20>=E7
A:E21	Iron	+B21>=E8
A:E24	Fat	+B24<=F10

The following constraints are not binding for this answer:

Nonbinding constraints

Cell	Name	Formula	Becomes binding if written as
A:E22	Protein	+B22>=E9	+B22>=E9+0.0999999999999999952
A:E26		+B15>=0	+B15>=0+8.00000000000000001
A:E27		+C15>=0	+C15>=0+5.5
A:E28		+D15>=0	+D15>=0+0.499999999999999999

the three quarters respectively. How should Suzie plan production over the three quarters in order to minimize the combined production and holding costs?

We defined the following decision variables:

X_A =   number of sweatshirts to produce in Autumn
X_W =   number of sweatshirts to produce in Winter
X_S =   number of sweatshirts to produce in Spring
I_A =   inventory to be held at the end of Autumn
I_W =   inventory to be held at the end of Winter
I_S =   inventory to be held at the end of Spring

We developed a simple LP model with the objective of minimizing the cost of production and inventory subject to inventory balance equations. A listing of the LINDO model and its solution appears in Figure 6.21. The solution is to produce 475 sweatshirts in the Autumn quarter, none in the Winter, and 75 in the Spring. This necessitates holding 350 sweatshirts in inventory at the end of the Autumn quarter. The total cost of production and inventory is $4,140. The dual prices indicate that an increase in demand in the Autumn quarter will increase cost by $6.75 per sweatshirt. An increase in the demand in the winter quarter will increase cost by $7.65 per sweatshirt (we will make the sweatshirt in Autumn and hold it inventory, so the cost is $6.75 + $.90 = $7.65). Finally, an increase in demand in the Spring will increase cost by $8.25. These prices hold for the ranges in the *Right-hand Side Ranges* section.

The reduced costs indicate how much cheaper each cost would have to be in order for the associated variable to become attractive enough to be positive. For example, the objective function coefficient ranges indicate that the coefficient of $6.75 for Autumn production can decrease by $.30 or increase by $1.35 (with all other parameters fixed) and the current solution will remain optimal. Similar ranges are defined for production coefficients in the other quarters and for the inventory holding costs.

The problem with this formulation is that it does not give any sensitivity analysis on the hourly wage rates. Furthermore, it does not indicate the sensitivity to the cost of capital (.06). If the cost of capital is incorrect, the error will affect all three inventory coefficients. Sensitivity analysis, however, only allows for a single change, not simultaneous changes.

Let us reformulate this model by adding some additional variables.

$$H_A = \text{labor hours used in Autumn}$$
$$H_W = \text{labor hours used in Winter}$$
$$H_S = \text{labor hours used in Spring}$$
$$V = \text{dollar value of total inventory}$$

The following model is equivalent to our original model in the sense that the same optimal solution will be given (can you show this?).

$$\text{Min } 4.5H_A + 6H_W + 5.5H_S + .06V$$

subject to

$$X_A - I_A = 125$$
$$X_W + I_A - I_W = 350$$
$$I_W + X_S - I_S = 75$$
$$H_A = 1.5x_A$$
$$H_W = 1.5x_W$$
$$H_S = 1.5x_S$$
$$15I_A + 15I_W + 15I_S = V$$
$$x_j, I_j, H_j, I_j \geq 0 \text{ for all } j$$

FIGURE 6.21   *LINDO model and solution output for Example 1*

```
MIN       6.75 XA + 9 XW + 8.25 XS + 0.9 IA + 0.9 IW + 0.9 IS
SUBJECT TO
        2)   XA − IA = 125                        ! Autumn
        3)   XW + IA − IW = 350                   ! Winter
        4)   XW + IW − IS = 75                    ! Spring
END
```

LP OPTIMUM FOUND AT STEP   2

OBJECTIVE FUNCTION VALUE

1)   4140.00000

VARIABLE	VALUE	REDUCED COST
XA	475.000000	0.000000
XW	0.000000	1.350000
XS	75.000000	0.000000
IA	350.000000	0.000000
IW	0.000000	0.300000
IS	0.000000	9.150000

ROW	SLACK OR SURPLUS	DUAL PRICES
2)	.000000	−6.750000
3)	.000000	−7.650000
4)	.000000	−8.250000

NO. ITERATIONS = 2

RANGES IN WHICH THE BASIS IS UNCHANGED:

	OBJ COEFFICIENT RANGES		
VARIABLE	CURRENT COEF	ALLOWABLE INCREASE	ALLOWABLE DECREASE
XA	6.750000	1.350000	0.300000
XW	9.000000	INFINITY	1.350000
XS	8.250000	0.300000	9.150000
IA	0.900000	1.350000	0.300000
IW	0.900000	INFINITY	0.300000
IS	0.900000	INFINITY	9.150000

	RIGHTHAND SIDE RANGES		
ROW	CURRENT RHS	ALLOWABLE INCREASE	ALLOWABLE DECREASE
2	125.000000	INFINITY	475.000000
3	350.000000	INFINITY	350.000000
4	75.000000	INFINITY	75.000000

The fourth through sixth constraints are needed to define the labor hour variables (1.5 hrs./unit × units = hrs.) and the seventh constraint defines V, the total value of all inventory held. Since the cost of capital is multiplied by the value of total inventory in the objective function, we will get an objective function coefficient range on the cost of capital in this model.

The LINDO model and its solution are shown in Figure 6.22 (on pages 271 and 272). The solution is the same as the original model; however, this new model gives coefficient ranges on relevant data: the hourly wage rates by quarter and the cost of capital. Note that the model solution is relatively insensitive to an increase in the cost of capital (allowable increase is .09), but rather sensitive to a decrease (allowable decrease is only .01). This is not at all clear from the sensitivity analysis provided by the original model.

Two general modeling principles can be gleaned from Example 8. First, we must define a separate variable to associate with any parameter for which we would like sensitivity information. We must logically link these variables with the original variables through constraints by defining these new variables in the constraint set. Second, if a group of variables have a common parameter, we must define a variable that is the sum of these variables and then place the aggregate variable in the objective function with the common coefficient. This second technique, which we used to get sensitivity analysis for the cost of capital, eliminates the problem of multiple changes that would occur in the objective function as the common parameter changes (this problem occurs often in multiperiod models where variables for different time periods share a common coefficient).

PRESENTING LP MODEL OUTPUT FOR MANAGERIAL INTERPRETATION: A CASE STUDY

In this section we describe how to present the information obtained from a linear programming analysis. Managers almost always want sound alternatives from which to choose when making decisions. You should view linear programming as a means of providing alternatives rather than providing "the answer." Always keep in mind that the goal of management science is to *assist* management in making *informed decisions*.

Typically, an LP-based analysis will begin with a *base case scenario*. Sensitivity analysis of the base case scenario can give insight into where further investigation is warranted. Parameters to which the model solution is highly sensitive or constraints with large dual prices should be considered for further study. It is usually prudent to make additional

---

FIGURE 6.22   *LINDO model and solution output for Example 1*

```
MIN       4.5 HA + 6 HW + 5.5 HS + 0.06 V
SUBJECT TO
     2)   XA  −  IA = 125
     3)   IA +  XW  −  IW = 350
     4)   IW +  XS  −  IS = 75
     5)   HA  −  1.5  −  XA = 0
     6)   HA  −  1.5  −  XW = 0
     7)   HS  −  1.5  −  XS = 0
     8)   − V  +  15 IA +  15 IW +  15 IS = 0
END

LP OPTIMUM FOUND AT STEP        2


        OBJECTIVE FUNCTION VALUE


     1)      4140.00000


VARIABLE              VALUE          REDUCED COST
     HA          712.500000              .000000
     HW            0.000000              .900000
     HS          112.500000              .000000
      V          5250.000000             .000000
     XA          475.000000              .000000
     IA          350.000000              .000000
     XW             .000000              .000000
     IW             .000000              .300000
     XS           75.000000              .000000
     IS             .000000             9.150000


     ROW     SLACK OR SURPLUS          DUAL PRICES
     2)              .000000            − 6.750000
     3)              .000000            − 7.650000
     4)              .000000            − 8.250000
     5)              .000000            − 4.500000
     6)              .000000            − 5.100000
     7)              .000000            − 5.500000
     8)              .000000              .060000

NO. ITERATIONS = 2

RANGES IN WHICH THE BASIS IS UNCHANGED:
```

	OBJ COEFFICIENT RANGES		
VARIABLE	CURRENT COEF	ALLOWABLE INCREASE	ALLOWABLE DECREASE
HA	4.500000	.900000	.200000
HW	6.000000	INFINITY	.900000
HS	5.500000	.200000	6.100000
V	.060000	.090000	.010000
XA	.000000	1.350000	.300000
IA	.000000	1.350000	.300000
XW	.000000	INFINITY	1.350000
IW	.000000	INFINITY	.300000
XS	.000000	.300000	9.150000
IS	.000000	INFINITY	9.150000

	RIGHTHAND SIDE RANGES		
ROW	CURRENT RHS	ALLOWABLE INCREASE	ALLOWABLE DECREASE
2	125.000000	INFINITY	475.000000
3	350.000000	INFINITY	350.000000
4	.000000	INFINITY	75.000000
5	.000000	INFINITY	712.000000
6	.000000	.000000	525.000000
7	.000000	INFINITY	112.500000
8	.000000	5250.000000	INFINITY

runs of the base case model with these sensitive parameters altered. In this way a variety of solutions will be generated covering different possible scenarios.

Finally, the old saying that "a picture is worth a thousand words" has endured because it is true! Graphs and charts are powerful tools that provide intuition and allow management to understand alternatives quickly. In this regard, the spreadsheet LP solvers have an advantage over most dedicated LP solvers such as LINDO. The spreadsheet solvers have easily accessible graphing capabilities that allow us to display the solutions or to show the effects of changing parameters on these solutions.

EXAMPLE 9. MANAGERIAL INFORMATION FOR SUZIE'S SWEATSHIRTS

An EXCEL spreadsheet model of the Suzie's Sweatshirt problem is shown in Figure 6.23. Using the model we developed in Example 8 in the previous section, the decision variables are the quantity to produce in each quarter, the amount of inventory to hold at the end of each quarter, the number of labor hours used each quarter, and the total inventory value over all quarters (this cell, F15, corresponds to the decision variable V in the model shown in Figure 6.22). The optimal solution is shown in the spreadsheet in Figure 6.23. Notice that we have included more than just the minimum amount of information in the output section. Total production, inventory, and hours are reported, along with cost breakdowns and the percentage of the total

---

FIGURE 6.23   *EXCEL model for Suzie's Sweatshirts*

	A	B	C	D	E	F	G
1	Suzie's Sweatshirts						
2							
3	*Parameters and uncontrollable inputs:*						
4							
5		Hourly Wage	Demand				
6	Autumn	$4.50	125		Cost of Capital	6%	
7	Winter	$6.00	350		Cost per Shirt	$15.00	
8	Spring	$5.50	75		Holding Cost	$0.90	
9							
10					Hours per Shirt	1.5	
11							
12	*Decision Variables:*						
13							
14		Quantity	Inventory	Hours			
15	Autumn	475.0	350.0	712.5	Inventory Value	5250	
16	Winter	0.0	0.0	0.0			
17	Spring	75.0	0.0	112.5			
18							
19							
20	*Model outputs:*						
21							
22		Production	Inventory	Hours			
23	Total	550.0	350.0	825.0			
24							
25							
26		Balance			Cost		Percent
27	Autumn	125.0		Holding	$315.00		8%
28	Winter	350.0		Production	$3,825.00		92%
29	Spring	75.0		Total	$4,140.00		100%
30							

of each cost. Any information that management might need to consider should be included in the output section.

Figure 6.24 shows two simple graphics that could be used in a presentation or report. The pie chart shows that holding cost is only 8% of the total cost. The three-dimensional bar graph shows that Suzie should produce in Autumn and hold inventory for Winter and then produce in the Spring.

Suppose that Suzie is comfortable with most of the parameters we have used in the model. For example, she is fairly confident of the demands she has estimated, the wage rates are fixed, and the cost of the sweatshirts will be $15. She is less sure about her cost of capital, because it depends on, among other things, the interest rate. We should therefore investigate the model's sensitivity to the assumed cost of capital.

The EXCEL solver sensitivity analysis for this LP model is shown in Figure 6.25. From the first line we see that the objective function coefficient of .06 can increase by as much as .09 or decrease by as much as .01, and the current solution will

FIGURE 6.24   *Graphics for the solution to Suzie's Sweatshirts*

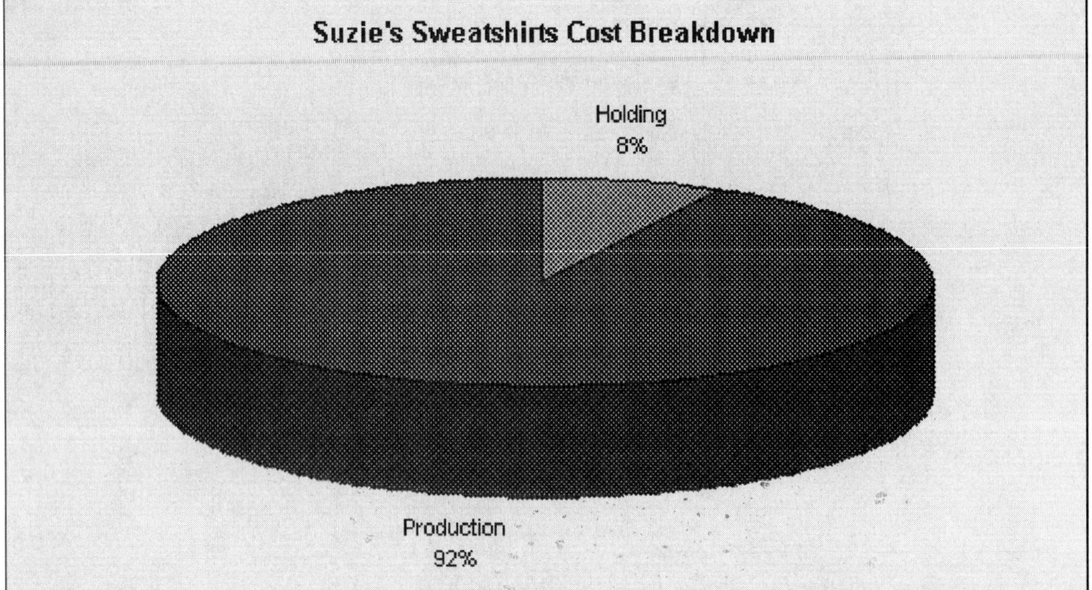

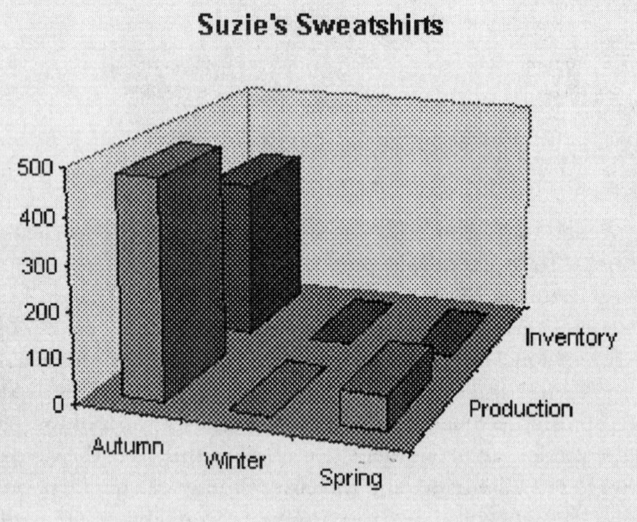

FIGURE 6.25   *Sensitivity analysis for the Suzie's Sweatshirts model*

Changing Cells

Cell	Name	Final Value	Reduced Cost	Objective Coefficient	Allowable Increase	Allowable Decrease
$F$15	Inventory Value	5250	0	0.06	0.090000005	0.010000002
$B$15	Autumn Quantity	475.0	0.0	0	1.350000068	0.300000075
$C$15	Autumn Inventory	350.0	0.0	0	1.350000068	0.300000075
$D$15	Autumn Hours	712.5	0.0	4.5	0.900000045	0.200000005
$B$16	Winter Quantity	0.0	1.4	0	1E+30	1.350000065
$C$16	Winter Inventory	0.0	0.3	0	1E+30	0.300000075
$D$16	Winter Hours	0.0	0.0	6	1E+30	0.900000043
$B$17	Spring Quantity	75.0	0.0	0	0.300000075	9.149999927
$C$17	Spring Inventory	0.0	9.1	0	1E+30	9.149999927
$D$17	Spring Hours	112.5	0.0	5.5	0.200000042	6.099999951

Constraints

Cell	Name	Final Value	Shadow Price	Constraint R.H. Side	Allowable Increase	Allowable Decrease
$B$27	Autumn Balance	125.0	6.7	125	1E+30	475
$B$28	Winter Balance	350.0	7.6	350	1E+30	350
$B$29	Spring Balance	75.0	8.2	75	1E+30	75
$D$16	Winter Hours	0.0	6.0	0	1E+30	0
$D$17	Spring Hours	112.5	5.5	0	1E+30	112.5
$D$15	Autumn Hours	712.5	4.5	0	1E+30	712.5
$F$15	Inventory Value	5250	0.06	0	1E+30	5250

remain optimal. This means that the current solution is optimal as long as the cost of capital is between .05 and .15. This suggests that the solution is relatively insensitive to increases in interest rates, but rather sensitive to decreases. What we can do is to resolve the model for interest rates slightly outside of the range .05 to .15 in order to see the effect on the solution.

Figure 6.26 shows the solution and sensitivity analysis for a capital cost of 4%. Notice that this solution allocates all production in the Autumn quarter. With the lower cost of capital, inventory becomes more cost-effective, and we can take complete advantage of the lower wages in the Autumn. Furthermore, the sensitivity analysis indicates that this solution is optimal for a decrease in the cost of capital of up to .19 (while this is mathematically correct, we know that we cannot have a negative cost of capital) and an increase of .01. This implies that the solution shown in Figure 6.26 is the optimal solution when the cost of capital is between 0% and 5%. Note that at exactly 5% the solutions in Figure 6.23 and 6.26 are alternate optimal solutions (5% is at the high end of the range of 4% and at the low end of the range of 6%).

The solution and sensitivity analysis for the 16% cost of capital is shown in Figure 6.27. In this solution no inventory is held and production is equal to the demand in each quarter because the high cost of capital makes holding inventory too expensive. Note from the sensitivity analysis (first line), that this solution is optimal for an increase in the cost of capital of infinity and a decrease of .01 (at 15% this solution and the solution shown in Figure 6.23 are alternate optimal solutions). Hence, the solution shown in Figure 6.27 is optimal for any cost of capital higher than 15%.

FIGURE 6.26   The solution and sensitivity analysis for a 4% cost of capital

	A	B	C	D	E	F	G
1	Suzie's Sweatshirts						
2							
3	Parameters and uncontrollable inputs:						
4							
5		Hourly Wage	Demand				
6	Autumn	$4.50	125		Cost of Capital	4%	
7	Winter	$6.00	350		Cost per Shirt	$15.00	
8	Spring	$5.50	75		Holding Cost	$0.60	
9							
10					Hours per Shirt	1.5	
11							
12	Decision Variables:						
13							
14		Quantity	Inventory	Hours			
15	Autumn	550.0	425.0	825.0	Inventory Value	7500	
16	Winter	0.0	75.0	0.0			
17	Spring	0.0	0.0	0.0			
18							
19							
20	Model outputs:						
21							
22		Production	Inventory	Hours			
23	Total	550.0	500.0	825.0			
24							
25							
26		Balance			Cost		Percent
27	Autumn	125.0		Holding	$300.00		7%
28	Winter	350.0		Production	$3,712.50		93%
29	Spring	75.0		Total	$4,012.50		100%
30							

Changing Cells

Cell	Name	Final Value	Reduced Cost	Objective Coefficient	Allowable Increase	Allowable Decrease
$F$15	Inventory Value	7500	0	0.04	0.01	0.19
$B$15	Autumn Quantity	550.0	0.0	0	0.299999994	8.549999999
$C$15	Autumn Inventory	425.0	0.0	0	0.299999994	8.549999999
$D$15	Autumn Hours	825.0	0.0	4.5	0.199999996	5.699999999
$B$16	Winter Quantity	0.0	1.7	0	1E+30	1.650000064
$C$16	Winter Inventory	75.0	0.0	0	0.299999994	8.549999999
$D$16	Winter Hours	0.0	0.0	6.00000003	1E+30	1.100000043
$B$17	Spring Quantity	0.0	0.0	0	1E+30	0.299999994
$C$17	Spring Inventory	0.0	8.6	0	1E+30	8.550000002
$D$17	Spring Hours	0.0	0.2	5.499999997	1E+30	0.199999996

Constraints

Cell	Name	Final Value	Shadow Price	Constraint R.H. Side	Allowable Increase	Allowable Decrease
$B$27	Autumn Balance	125.0	6.7	125	1E+30	550
$B$28	Winter Balance	350.0	7.4	350	1E+30	425
$B$29	Spring Balance	75.0	8.0	75	1E+30	75
$D$16	Winter Hours	0.0	6.0	0	1E+30	0
$D$17	Spring Hours	0.0	5.3	0	0	112.5
$D$15	Autumn Hours	825.0	4.5	0	1E+30	825
$F$15	Inventory Value	7500	0.04	0	1E+30	7500

	A	B	C	D	E	F	G
1	**Suzie's Sweatshirts**						
2							
3	*Parameters and uncontrollable inputs:*						
4							
5		Hourly Wage	Demand				
6	Autumn	$4.50	125		Cost of Capital	16%	
7	Winter	$6.00	350		Cost per Shirt	$15.00	
8	Spring	$5.50	75		Holding Cost	$2.40	
9							
10					Hours per Shirt	1.5	
11							
12	*Decision Variables:*						
13							
14		Quantity	Inventory	Hours			
15	Autumn	125.0	0.0	187.5	Inventory Value	0	
16	Winter	350.0	0.0	525.0			
17	Spring	75.0	0.0	112.5			
18							
19							
20	*Model outputs:*						
21							
22		Production	Inventory	Hours			
23	Total	550.0	0.0	825.0			
24							
25							
26		Balance			Cost		Percent
27	Autumn	125.0		Holding	$0.00		0%
28	Winter	350.0		Production	$4,612.50		100%
29	Spring	75.0		Total	$4,612.50		100%

Changing Cells

Cell	Name	Final Value	Reduced Cost	Objective Coefficient	Allowable Increase	Allowable Decrease
$F$15	Inventory Value	0	0.009999995	0.16	1E+30	0.009999995
$B$15	Autumn Quanitity	125	0	0	3.000000075	0.149999932
$C$15	Autumn Inventory	0	0	0	3.000000075	0.149999932
$D$15	Autumn Hours	187.5	0	4.5	2.00000005	0.099999955
$B$16	Winter Quanitity	350	0	0	0.149999931	1.500000034
$C$16	Winter Inventory	0	3.0	0	1E+30	3.000000075
$D$16	Winter Hours	525	0	6.00000003	0.099999954	1.000000022
$B$17	Spring Quanitity	75	0	0	3.000000076	10.50000013
$C$17	Spring Inventory	0	10.5	0	1E+30	10.50000013
$D$17	Spring Hours	112.5	0	5.500000043	2.00000005	7.000000087

Constraints

Cell	Name	Final Value	Shadow Price	Constraint R.H. Side	Allowable Increase	Allowable Decrease
$B$27	Autumn Balance	125.0	6.8	125	1E+30	125
$B$28	Winter Balance	350.0	9.0	350	1E+30	350
$B$29	Spring Balance	75.0	8.3	75	1E+30	75
$D$16	Winter Hours	525.0	6.0	0	1E+30	525.0000013
$D$17	Spring Hours	112.5	5.5	0	1E+30	112.5
$D$15	Autumn Hours	187.5	4.5	0	1E+30	187.5
$F$15	Inventory Value	0	0.150000005	0	0	5250

From the analyses in Figures 6.25, 6.26, and 6.27, we have completely captured the sensitivity of the solution to changes in the cost of capital. The three different solutions and the range over which they are optimal are

Cost of Capital	Production (Inventory)		
	Autumn	Winter	Spring
0%–5%	550 (425)	0 (75)	0 (0)
5%–15%	475 (350)	0 (0)	75 (0)
≥ 15%	125 (0)	350 (0)	75 (0)

This information is depicted graphically in Figure 6.28, where we have graphed the production quantities per quarter for the different solutions. This picture (or alternatively, the same type of graph of inventory) shows very clearly that the model yields solutions that appeal to one's sense of intuition. If the cost of capital is low, holding inventory is cheaper and Suzie should produce everything in the Autumn when the wage rates are low. For a medium cost of capital, inventory is justified from Autumn to Winter, but is not cheap enough to hold until Spring. Finally, for a high cost of capital, holding inventory is very expensive and a zero inventory policy becomes optimal.

As the coming Autumn approaches, Suzie perhaps will have a better estimate of the cost of capital, and based on the more reliable estimate, she now has alternatives from which to choose.

FIGURE 6.28   *Solutions for different costs of capital*

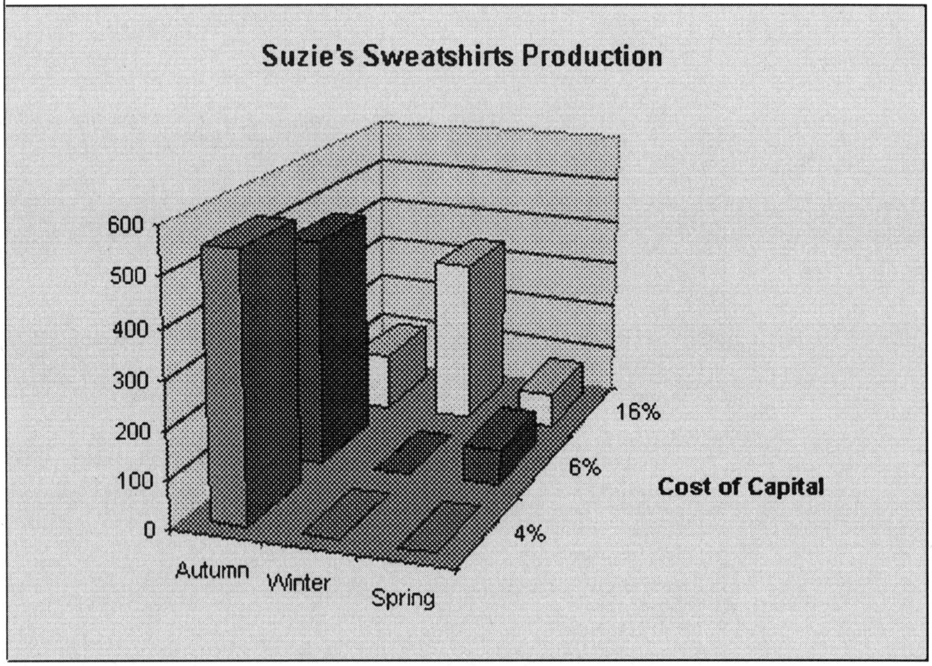

MORE EXAMPLES AND SOLVED PROBLEMS

EXAMPLE 10. MABOPS TRANSPORTATION PROBLEM REVISITED

In the MaBops transportation model from Chapter 4 (Example 6), we defined x_{ij} as the amount to ship from plant i to distribution center j, where there are four plants and five distribution centers. Supplies at the plants and demands at the distribution centers are known, along with the per-unit shipping costs from each plant to each distribution center. We wish to minimize shipping costs. The LINDO model and solution are shown in Figure 6.29.

The reduced cost for each of the variables indicates how much cheaper the per-unit cost of shipping would have to be before that shipping route would be selected. For example, the per-unit cost of shipping from Los Angeles to Houston (the coefficient of x_{11}) would have to be \$4 or lower before that routing would be selected (\$5 less the reduced cost of \$1).

The dual prices for the plant constraints (rows 2–5) indicate the benefit (decrease in shipping cost) of increasing the capacity of a plant by 1 unit. Pensacola (row 4) has a dual price of 2, which is twice as large as the dual price of any other plant. This means that the model is more sensitive to capacity at Pensacola than at the other plants. An expansion decreases cost by \$2 per unit. This makes Pensacola the best choice for possible expansion, assuming that the cost of expansion is the same at all plants. Also note that we have excess capacity at the Denver plant, as indicated by the positive slack in row 3.

The dual prices for rows 6–11 (the demands at the distribution centers) indicate how much the objective function will be worsened (recall that a negative sign indicates that the objective function will be hurt) by an increase of one unit in demand at the distribution centers. For example, if demand at the Houston distribution center is increased by 1, cost will go up by \$5. These dual prices and those previously discussed are valid only for a single change in the model, and only over the right-hand side ranges given in the last section of the output.

Finally, the objective coefficient ranges indicate that the model is particularly sensitive to the cost of $x_{15}, x_{24}, x_{25}, x_{31}, x_{41}$, and x_{44}. These data should be carefully scrutinized for accuracy.

EXAMPLE 11. SUNK VS. VARIABLE COST AND SHADOW PRICE INTERPRETATION

The following example, based on a problem from Winston,[1] illustrates why we need to consider the distinction between sunk and variable costs when interpreting shadow prices.

A company produces two products from a raw material. Up to 90 pounds of the raw material can be purchased at a price of \$10 per pound. One pound of raw material

---

[1]Winston, Wayne L. *Operations Research: Applications and Algorithms.* Duxbury, 3rd Edition, 1994, problem 8, p.324.

FIGURE 6.29   *MaBops LINDO model and solution output*

```
MIN       5 X11 + X12 + 5 X13 + 7 X14 + 4 X15 + 9 X21 + 7 X22
          + 8 X23 + 3 X24 + 5 X25 + 3 X31 + 4 X32 + 3 X33 + 8 X34
          + 6 X35 + 4 X41 + 5 X42 + 6 X43 + 2 X44 + 7 X45
SUBJECT TO
        2)  X11 + X12 + X13 + X14 + X15 <= 15000 ! LA
        3)  X21 + X22 + X23 + X24 + X25 <= 20000 ! Denver
        4)  X31 + X32 + X33 + X34 + X35 <= 17500 ! Pensacola
        5)  X41 + X42 + X43 + X44 + X54 <= 10000 ! Cincinnati
        6)  X11 + X21 + X31 + X41  = 8000       ! Houston
        7)  X12 + X22 + X32 + X43  = 11000      ! Las Vegas
        8)  X13 + X23 + X33 + X43  = 15000      ! New Orleans
        9)  X14 + X24 + X34 + X44  = 10000      ! Chicago
       10)  X15 + X25 + X35 + X45  = 15000      ! Boise
END
```

LP OPTIMUM FOUND AT STEP   8

                OBJECTIVE FUNCTION VALUE

        1)   182000.00

VARIABLE	VALUE	REDUCED COST
X11	.000000	1.000000
X12	11000.000000	.000000
X13	.000000	1.000000
X14	.000000	5.000000
X15	4000.000000	.000000
X21	.000000	4.000000
X22	.000000	5.000000
X23	.000000	3.000000
X24	5500 .000000	.000000
X25	11000.000000	.000000
X31	2500.000000	.000000
X32	.000000	4.000000
X33	15000.000000	.050000
X34	.000000	7.000000
X35	.000000	3.000000
X41	5500.000000	.000000
X42	.000000	4.000000
X43	.000000	2.000000
X44	4500.000000	.000000
X45	.000000	3.000000

ROW	SLACK OR SURPLUS	DUAL PRICES
2)	.000000	1.000000
3)	3500.000000	.000000
4)	.000000	2.000000
5)	.000000	1.000000
6)	.000000	−5.000000
7)	.000000	−2.000000
8)	.000000	−5.000000
9)	.000000	−3.000000
10)	.000000	−5.000000

NO. ITERATIONS = 8

RANGES IN WHICH THE BASIS IS UNCHANGED:

	OBJ COEFFICIENT RANGES		
VARIABLE	CURRENT COEF	ALLOWABLE INCREASE	ALLOWABLE DECREASE
X11	5.000000	INFINITY	1.000000
X12	1.000000	4.000000	INFINITY
X13	5.000000	INFINITY	1.000000
X14	7.000000	INFINITY	5.000000
X15	4.000000	1.000000	4.000000
X21	9.000000	INFINITY	4.000000
X22	7.000000	INFINITY	5.000000
X23	8.000000	INFINITY	3.000000
X24	3.000000	1.000000	1.000000
X25	5.000000	3.000000	1.000000
X31	3.000000	2.000000	1.000000
X32	4.000000	INFINITY	4.000000
X33	3.000000	1.000000	INFINITY
X34	8.000000	INFINITY	7.000000
X35	6.000000	INFINITY	3.000000
X41	4.000000	1.000000	2.000000
X42	5.000000	INFINITY	4.000000
X43	6.000000	INFINITY	2.000000
X44	2.000000	1.000000	1.000000
X45	7.000000	INFINITY	3.000000

RIGHTHAND SIDE RANGES

ROW	CURRENT RHS	ALLOWABLE INCREASE	ALLOWABLE DECREASE
2	15000.000000	11000.000000	3500.000000
3	20000.000000	INFINITY	3500.000000
4	17500.000000	5500.000000	2500.000000
5	10000.000000	5500.000000	3500.000000
6	8000.000000	3500.000000	5500.000000
7	11000.000000	3500.000000	11000.000000
8	15000.000000	2500.000000	5500.000000
9	10000.000000	3500.000000	5500.000000
10	15000.000000	3500.000000	11000.000000

is needed to produce one pound of product 1, but one pound of raw material makes only .3 pounds of product 2. The production of one pound of product 1 requires 2 hours of labor, and one pound of product 2 requires 10 hours of labor. Product 1 sells for $11.50/pound and product 2 for $40/pound. There are 200 hours of labor available, and at most 40 pounds of product 2 can be sold. The company would like to maximize contribution to profit and fixed costs.

We can define these decision variables.

Q_1 = quantity of product 1 to produce
Q_2 = quantity of product 2 to produce
P_1 = amount of raw material to use for product 1
P_2 = amount of raw material to use for product 2
RM = total amount of raw material to purchase

The LINDO model and solution are shown in Figure 6.30. The objective is to maximize revenue, less the cost of raw material. The first constraint (row 2) requires that the amount of raw material purchased be at least as much as the total used. Row 3 limits the amount of raw material purchased to 90 units or less. The third constraint (row 4) requires that labor used be less than or equal to the labor available. The limitation on the production of product 2 is given by constraint four (row 5) and constraints in rows six and seven relate the production raw material requirements to the amounts produced.

The solution shows that 70 units of product 1 and 6 units of product 2 should be produced. All of the 200 hours of labor are used (row 4 is binding), and all 90 pounds of the available raw material are purchased (row 3 is binding). Row 5 is the only nonbinding constraint. We focus our discussion on the sensitivity of the model to raw material parameters.

First, consider the sensitivity of the solution to the cost per pound of raw material. The objective function coefficient range indicates that the *coefficient* of −10 can increase by up to infinity or decrease by as much as .499999 with everything else held fixed, and the current solution will remain optimal. Do *not* interpret this to mean that the cost per pound can increase by infinity or decrease by .49999. An increase in the coefficient is a decrease in the cost, because the cost is subtracted

FIGURE 6.30   Variable cost raw material model

```
MAX        11.5 Q1 + 40 Q2 − 10 RM
SUBJECT TO
        2)    RM − P1 − P2 >= 0
        3)    RM <= 90
        4)    2 Q1 + 10 Q2 <= 200
        5)    Q2 <= 40
        6)  − Q1 + P1 = 0
        7)  − Q2 + 0.3 P2 = 0
END
```

OBJECTIVE FUNCTION VALUE

        1)   145.00000

VARIABLE	VALUE	REDUCED COST
Q1	70.000000	.000000
Q2	6.000000	.000000
RM	90.000000	.000000
P1	70.000000	.000000
P2	20.000000	.000000

ROW	SLACK OR SURPLUS	DUAL PRICES
2)	.000000	−10.500000
3)	.000000	.500000
4)	.000000	.500000
5)	34.000000	.000000
6)	.000000	−10.500000
7)	.000000	−35.000000

        NO. ITERATIONS =   4

RANGES IN WHICH THE BASIS IS UNCHANGED:

OBJ COEFFICIENT RANGES

VARIABLE	CURRENT COEF	ALLOWABLE INCREASE	ALLOWABLE DECREASE
Q1	11.500000	.500000	.166666
Q2	40.000000	.833332	1.666668
RM	−10.000000	INFINITY	.499999
P1	.000000	.500000	.166666
P2	.000000	.250000	.500000

ROW	CURRENT RHS	ALLOWABLE INCREASE	ALLOWABLE DECREASE
	RIGHTHAND SIDE RANGES		
2	.000000	23.333340	10.000000
3	90.000000	10.000000	23.333340
4	200.000000	70.000010	20.000000
5	40.000000	INFINITY	34.000000
6	.000000	23.333340	10.000000
7	.000000	7.000000	2.000000

in the objective function. The correct interpretation is that the cost can range from negative infinity to 10.4999 and the current solution will still remain optimal.

When interpreting the dual price for raw material, we must be careful to recognize costs that are included in the objective function. The dual price for row 3 indicates that the objective function will benefit $.50 for each one-unit increase in the available raw material. This dual price is valid for an increase of up to 10 units of raw material. Because the cost per unit of $10 is included in the objective function, the *dual price here is the maximum premium we should pay above and beyond the normal cost of the raw material* (the $10 cost in the objective function). Hence, the maximum we should ever pay for extra raw material is $10.50 per unit.

Suppose that the cost of the raw material was a sunk cost (we have *already purchased* all 90 units that are now available for production). To alter our model, we need to redefine the variable RM as the amount of raw material used in production and to delete the last term of the objective function because it is now a constant ($-\$10 \times 90 = -\$900$). The new model and its solution are shown in Figure 6.31. Notice that the solution is the same (we purchased all 90 pounds of the raw material in the first model, so the solutions should be the same). However, compare the dual price for row 3 in the two models. In Figure 6.31, the dual price is $10.50. In the model in Figure 6.31, the cost of the raw material is considered a sunk cost and is therefore not included in the objective function. The dual price of $10.50 is the *maximum we should be willing to pay for another pound of raw material*.

FIGURE 6.31   Sunk cost raw material model

```
MAX     11.5 Q1+40 Q2
SUBJECT TO
        2)   RM − P1 − P2 >= 0
        3)   RM <= 90
        4)   2 Q1 + 10 Q2 <= 200
        5)   Q2 <= 40
        6) − Q1 + P1 = 0
        7) − Q2 + 0.3 P2 = 0
END
```

OBJECTIVE FUNCTION VALUE

1)   1045.0000

VARIABLE	VALUE	REDUCED COST
Q1	70.000000	.000000
Q2	6.000000	.000000
RM	90.000000	.000000
P1	70.000000	.000000
P2	20.000000	.000000

ROW	SLACK OR SURPLUS	DUAL PRICES
2)	.000000	− 10.500000
3)	.000000	10.500000
4)	.000000	.500000
5)	34.000000	.000000
6)	.000000	− 10.500000
7)	.000000	− 35.000000

NO. ITERATIONS = 4

RANGES IN WHICH THE BASIS IS UNCHANGED:

OBJ COEFFICIENT RANGES

VARIABLE	CURRENT COEF	ALLOWABLE INCREASE	ALLOWABLE DECREASE
Q1	11.500000	.500000	3.500000
Q2	40.000000	17.500000	1.666668
RM	.000000	INFINITY	10.500000
P1	.000000	.500000	3.500000
P2	.000000	5.250000	.500000

RIGHTHAND SIDE RANGES

ROW	CURRENT RHS	ALLOWABLE INCREASE	ALLOWABLE DECREASE
2	.000000	23.333340	10.000000
3	90.000000	10.000000	22.333340
4	200.000000	70.000010	20.000000
5	40.000000	INFINITY	34.000000
6	.000000	23.333340	10.000000
7	.000000	7.000000	2.000000

What we have seen in this example generalizes to other problems. If the cost of the resource is included in the objective function, the dual price indicates the maximum premium over the cost included in the objective that we should pay for an additional unit of this resource. If the cost of the resource is not included in the objective (that is, if the cost is considered sunk), then the dual price is the maximum price we should pay for an additional unit of the resource.

EXAMPLE 12. PHILLIPS INC. REVISITED

p. 148

Recall the Phillips Inc. marketing problem (Chapter 4, Example 9). Phillips Inc. sells two products, 1 and 2, and uses two marketing instruments, advertising and selling, to stimulate demand for these products. There is no interaction between the two products in the sense that the price, cost, or demand of one product will not affect the demand of the other product. The company must decide on the amount of selling and advertising resources to devote to each of the products in the coming quarter. Phillips has budgeted $25,000 for advertising and has allotted a total of 5,000 hours of labor for selling for the quarter. Based on past data and managerial judgment, Phillips has estimated that a dollar of advertising will yield $8 profit when spent on product 1 and $15 when spent on product 2. These estimates hold over the entire range of the advertising budget. Management has likewise estimated the productivity of personal selling: an hour of personal selling devoted to product 1 will generate a profit of $25 and an hour devoted to product 2 will generate a profit of $45. These estimates are assumed to hold over the ranges of personal selling hours allowable by the company. Company policy stipulates that at least 2,000, but no more than 3,500 hours of labor can be used on each product. Company policy also dictates that at least $6,000 but no more than $18,000 be spent on advertising for each product.

In Chapter 4 we developed this model:

Let A_i = amount of advertising dollars to spend on product i
S_i = number of hours of selling to allocate to product i
$i = 1, 2$

$$\text{Max } 8A_1 + 15A_2 + 25S_1 + 45S_2$$

subject to

$$A_1 + A_2 \leq 25,000$$

$$S_1 + S_2 \leq 5,000$$

$$A_1 \geq 6,000 \qquad S_1 \geq 2,000$$
$$A_1 \leq 18,000 \qquad S_1 \leq 3,500$$

$$A_2 \geq 6,000 \qquad S_2 \geq 2,000$$
$$A_2 \leq 18,000 \qquad S_2 \leq 3,500$$

$$A_i, S_i \geq 0 \qquad i = 1, 2$$

An EXCEL model of this scenario is shown in Figure 6.32. The solution shown is the optimal solution found by the EXCEL Solver.

Figure 6.33 shows the breakdown of profit, use of advertising, and use of selling hours by product (this information was easily graphed from the spreadsheet from cells B31 and B32, B21 and B22, and D21 and D22).

FIGURE 6.32   EXCEL model for Phillips Inc.

	A	B	C	D
1	**Phillips Inc.**			
2				
3	*Parameters and uncontrollable inputs:*			
4				
5			Profit	
6		Advertising ($/$)		Selling ($/hr.)
7	Product 1	$8.00		$25.00
8	Product 2	$15.00		$45.00
9				
10		Adv $ / Prod.		Selling Hrs/ Prod.
11	Min	$6,000.00		2000
12	Max	$18,000.00		3500
13				
14		Advertising $		Selling Hours
15	Total Available	$25,000.00		5000
16				
17				
18	*Decision variables:*			
19				
20		Advertising		Selling Hours
21	Product 1	$7,000.00	Product 1	2000
22	Product 2	$18,000.00	Product 2	3000
23				
24				
25	*Model outputs:*			
26		Used	Remaining	
27	Advertising	$25,000.00	$0.00	
28	Selling Hours	5000	0	
29				
30		Profit		
31	Product 1	$106,000.00		
32	Product 2	$405,000.00		
33	Total	$511,000.00		

Selected cell formulas

	A	B	C
25	*Model outputs:*		
26		Used	Remaining
27	Advertising	=B21+B22	=B15-B27
28	Selling Hours	=D21+D22	=D15-B28
29			
30		Profit	
31	Product 1	=B7*B21+D7*D21	
32	Product 2	=B8*B22+D8*D22	
33	Total	=B31+B32	

FIGURE 6.33   *Graphical display of profit, advertising, and selling hours by product*

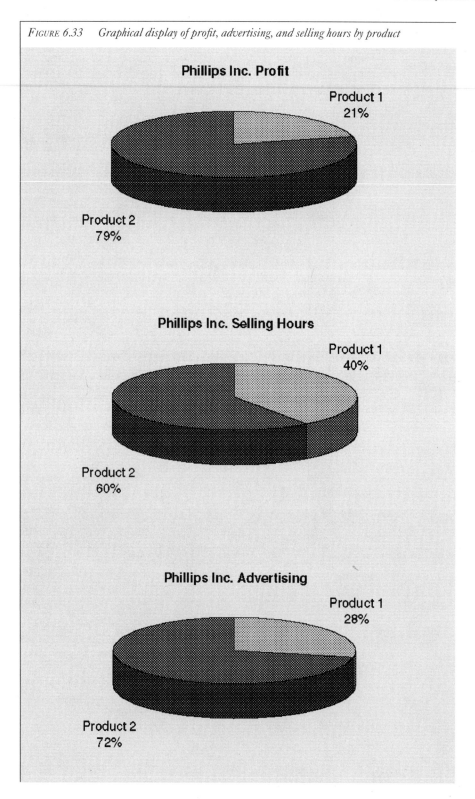

Figure 6.34 shows the sensitivity report from Solver. The objective function co-efficient ranges indicate that the solution is rather insensitive to a change in an objective function coefficient value. The constraints section indicates that the profit will increase at a rate of $8 for an increase in the advertising budget. This price holds for an increase in budget of $11,000. The shadow price on the selling hours constraint indicates that profit will increase by $45 for each one-unit increase in the selling hours. This holds for an increase up to 500 hours. (Note that EXCEL does not include simple upper and lower bound constraints in the constraint section, as we have in this model on advertising and selling.)

Suppose that Phillips is particularly interested in the value of adjusting the advertising budget. We can perform a more detailed analysis of that model parameter, but we will limit our analysis to a budget between $12,000 and $36,000 because this is the range implied by the simple upper and lower bounds on advertising for each product.

Notice from the sensitivity analysis in Figure 6.34 that the $8 shadow price holds for an increase of $11,000 (and −$8 for a decrease of up to $1,000). Therefore, this price of $8 holds for every one dollar increase in advertising budget from $24,000 to $36,000. We therefore know that the optimal profit for a budget of $24,000 is $511,000 − $8 × (1000) = $503,000 and the optimal profit for a budget of $36,000 is $511,000 + $8 × (11,000) = $599,000. We need to rerun the model to find the budget effect for a budget between $12,000 and $24,000.

Figure 6.35 shows the optimal solution and sensitivity analysis for the model with a budget of $12,000. The optimal profit is $323,000. The shadow price for the advertising budget constraint is $15 and this price holds for an increase of $12,000. Therefore,

---

FIGURE 6.34   EXCEL Solver Sensitivity Report for Phillips Inc.

Changing Cells

Cell	Name	Final Value	Reduced Cost	Objective Coefficient	Allowable Increase	Allowable Decrease
$B$21	Product 1 Advertising	$7,000.00	$0.00	8	1E+30	7
$B$22	Product 2 Advertising	$18,000.00	$7.00	15	1E+30	7
$D$21	Product 1 Selling Hours	2000	-20	25	20	1E+30
$D$22	Product 2 Selling Hours	3000	0	45	1E+30	20

Constraints

Cell	Name	Final Value	Shadow Price	Constraint R.H. Side	Allowable Increase	Allowable Decrease
$B$27	Advertising Used	$25,000.00	$8.00	25000	11000	1000
$B$28	Selling Hours Used	5000	45	5000	500	1000

the $15 shadow price holds for a budget from $12,000 to $24,000. We have therefore completely captured the effect of advertising over the range of $12,000 to $36,000. Figure 6.36 shows our findings (a range for which there is a constant shadow price is linear and the "elbows" occur where the shadow price changes).

FIGURE 6.35 *Optimal solution and sensitivity analysis for Phillips Inc. for an advertising budget of $12,000*

	A	B	C	D
1	Phillips Inc.			
2				
3	*Parameters and uncontrollable inputs:*			
4				
5			Profit	
6		Advertising ($/$)		Selling ($/hr.)
7	Product 1	$8.00		$25.00
8	Product 2	$15.00		$45.00
9				
10		Adv $ / Prod.		Selling Hrs/ Prod.
11	Min	$6,000.00		2000
12	Max	$18,000.00		3500
13				
14		Advertising $		Selling Hours
15	Total Available	$12,000.00		5000
16				
17				
18	*Decision variables:*			
19				
20		Advertising		Selling Hours
21	Product 1	$6,000.00	Product 1	2000
22	Product 2	$6,000.00	Product 2	3000
23				
24				
25	*Model outputs:*			
26		Used	Remaining	
27	Advertising	$12,000.00	$0.00	
28	Selling Hours	5000	0	
29				
30		Profit		
31	Product 1	$98,000.00		
32	Product 2	$225,000.00		
33	Total	$323,000.00		

FIGURE 6.35 *(continued)*

Changing Cells

Cell	Name	Final Value	Reduced Cost	Objective Coefficient	Allowable Increase	Allowable Decrease
$B$21	Product 1 Advertising	$6,000.00	($7.00)	8	7	1E+30
$B$22	Product 2 Advertising	$6,000.00	$0.00	15	1E+30	7
$D$21	Product 1 Selling Hours	2000	-20	25	20	1E+30
$D$22	Product 2 Selling Hours	3000	0	45	1E+30	20

Constraints

Cell	Name	Final Value	Shadow Price	Constraint R.H. Side	Allowable Increase	Allowable Decrease
$B$27	Advertising Used	$12,000.00	$15.00	12000	12000	0
$B$28	Selling Hours Used	5000	45	5000	500	1000

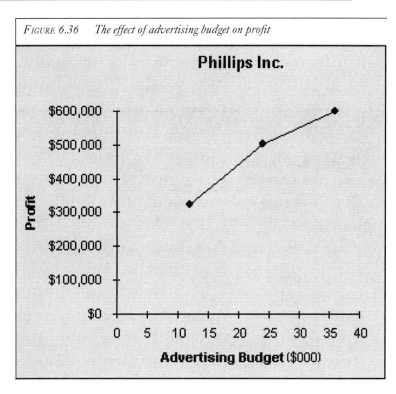

FIGURE 6.36   *The effect of advertising budget on profit*

SUMMARY

In this chapter we discussed how to thoroughly analyze linear programming models. In addition to the optimal solution, packages such as LINDO and EXCEL provide important information known as sensitivity analysis.

Sensitivity analysis indicates how sensitive the optimal solution is to changes in the input parameters such as objective function coefficients and the right-hand side values of the constraints. Dual prices indicate the change in the objective function value for an increase of one unit in the right-hand side of a constraint. However, note that a dual price is guaranteed to hold only for changes within the right-hand side range of its constraint.

Objective function coefficient ranges provided by sensitivity analysis indicate the changes in the objective function coefficients for which the current solution remains optimal. Both right-hand side ranges and objective function coefficient ranges are valid only for a single change in the model.

Through the use of sensitivity analysis, a variety of solutions can be generated, by taking into account the sensitivity of the solution to key input parameters. Through a thorough analysis of the LP model, you can provide management with valuable information that may help them hedge against changes in the model data and that allows them to make a more fully informed decision.

Sensitivity analysis should affect how we build LP models because variable definition and constraint structure may have an impact on the usefulness of the sensitivity analysis information. As we have seen, two models that are equivalent in terms of the optimal solution obtained may not yield equally useful sensitivity analysis.

CHAPTER REVIEW EXERCISES

I. Terms to Understand

a. Sensitivity analysis (p. 244)
b. Constraint tightening (p. 248)
c. Constraint relaxation (p. 248)
d. Reduced cost (p. 256)
e. Dual price (p. 256)

f. Right-hand side range (p. 256)
g. Objective function coefficient range (p. 258)
h. Shadow price (p. 261)

II. Discussion Questions

1. Describe how a $\leq$ constraint is relaxed. How is a $\geq$ constraint relaxed? Give geometric examples of each.
2. Respond to the following statement with regard to sensitivity analysis: "The purpose of mathematical programming is system insight, not output numbers."
3. Describe the geometric effect of changing an objective coefficient in a two-variable LP problem.
4. Consider the following two (equivalent) constraints:

$$0.5x_1 + 0.25x_2 \leq 4$$

(total hours used $\leq$ total hours available)

and

$$30x_1 + 15x_2 \leq 240$$

(total minutes used $\leq$ total minutes available)

How would you interpret the dual price for each of these constraints? How do you think the dual prices would compare numerically?
5. Describe the difference(s) in interpreting sensitivity information from LINDO versus the EXCEL Solver.

III. Problems

1. Consider the following LINDO LP problem and solution output:

```
MIN        2 X1 + X2
SUBJECT TO
        2)        3X1 + X2 >= 60
        3)        X1 + X2 >= 40
        4)        3X1 + 2X2 <= 180
END
              OBJECTIVE FUNCTION VALUE

        1)           50.000000

    VARIABLE          VALUE           REDUCED COST
        X1          10.000000             .000000
        X2          30.000000             .000000

        ROW     SLACK OR SURPLUS      DUAL PRICES
        2)           .000000            - .500000
        3)           .000000            - .500000
        4)          90.000000             .000000

NO. ITERATIONS = 2

RANGES IN WHICH THE BASIS IS UNCHANGED:
                    OBJ COEFFICIENT RANGES
    VARIABLE        CURRENT         ALLOWABLE        ALLOWABLE
                      COEF          INCREASE         DECREASE
        X1          2.000000        1.000000         1.000000
        X2          1.000000        1.000000          .333333

                    RIGHTHAND SIDE RANGES
        ROW         CURRENT         ALLOWABLE        ALLOWABLE
                      RHS           INCREASE         DECREASE
         2          60.000000       60.000000        20.000000
         3          40.000000       20.000000        20.000000
         4         180.000000        INFINITY        90.000000
```

a. Verify the optimal solution shown by drawing the feasible region and objective function contours.

b. Show the validity of the objective function coefficient ranges on the graph.

c. According to the LINDO output, what will be the optimal objective function value if the right-hand side of row 2 is increased by 5 (that is, if row 2 becomes $3x_1 + x_2 \geq 65$)?

d.   Verify your answer to part *c* geometrically.
e.   Geometrically demonstrate the validity of the right-hand range given for row 2.

2.   Consider the LP from Example 1 of this chapter. The LINDO model and solution are shown in the following figure.

```
MAX          2 X1 + 3 X2
SUBJECT TO
         2)        1.25 X1 + X2 <= 100
         3)        X1 + X2 >= 30
         4)        X1 <= 50
         4)        X2 <= 75
END
LP OPTIMUM FOUND AT STEP            4

               OBJECTIVE FUNCTION VALUE

         1)        265.00000

VARIABLE          VALUE              REDUCED COST
     X1          20.000000               .000000
     X2          75.000000               .000000

    ROW     SLACK OR SURPLUS      DUAL PRICES
     2)          .000000            1.600000
     3)         65.000000            .000000
     4)         30.000000            .000000
     5)          .000000            1.400000

NO. ITERATIONS =      4
```

RANGES IN WHICH THE BASIS IS UNCHANGED:

OBJ COEFFICIENT RANGES

VARIABLE	CURRENT COEF	ALLOWABLE INCREASE	ALLOWABLE DECREASE
X1	2.000000	1.750000	2.000000
X2	3.000000	INFINITY	1.400000

RIGHTHAND SIDE RANGES

ROW	CURRENT RHS	ALLOWABLE INCREASE	ALLOWABLE DECREASE
2	100.000000	37.500000	25.000000
3	30.000000	65.000000	INFINITY
4	50.000000	INFINITY	30.000000
5	75.000000	25.000000	37.500000

a. The feasible region for this problem appears in Figure 6.1. Show geometrically, the validity of the objective function coefficient range for x_2.

b. Demonstrate geometrically the validity of the dual price of 1.4 for row 5 and its right-hand side range (allowable increase of 25 and allowable decrease of 37.5).

3. Consider the following LINDO model and solution output.

```
MAX        X1 + 0.75 X2
SUBJECT TO
        2)          − 2 X1 + X2 >= 12
        3)           7 X1 + 3 X2 <= 42
        4)               X2 <=12.5
END
OBJECTIVE FUNCTION VALUE

        1)          9.6250000


VARIABLE          VALUE              REDUCED COST
    X1            .250000                .000000
    X2          12.500000                .000000


    ROW    SLACK OR SURPLUS         DUAL PRICES
     2)          .000000              − .500000
     3)         2.750000                .000000
     4)          .000000              1.250000


NO. ITERATIONS = 2
```

RANGES IN WHICH THE BASIS IS UNCHANGED:

OBJ COEFFICIENT RANGES

VARIABLE	CURRENT COEF	ALLOWABLE INCREASE	ALLOWABLE DECREASE
X1	1.000000	INFINITY	1.000000
X2	.750000	INFINITY	1.250000

RIGHTHAND SIDE RANGES

ROW	CURRENT RHS	ALLOWABLE INCREASE	ALLOWABLE DECREASE
2	12.000000	.500000	.785714
3	42.000000	INFINITY	2.750000
4	12.500000	.423077	.500000

a. What are the optimal values of the decision variables and objective function?

b. Which constraints are binding?

c. Verify your answers to parts *a* and *b* by solving the problem graphically.
d. Why do rows 2 and 4 have dual prices that are opposite in sign? Explain this using the graph you developed in part *c*.
e. Show the validity of the objective function coefficient and right-hand side ranges using your graph from part *c*.

4. In the radar detector example from Chapter 1, LS = the number of LaserStops to produce and SB = the number of SpeedBusters to produce. The per-unit profit, for these two products are $24 and $48 respectively. Each LaserStop requires 12 units of component A and 6 units of component B. Each SpeedBuster requires 12 units of component A and 10 units of component B. The LINDO model and solution output appear in the following figure.

```
MAX      24 LS + 40 SB
SUBJECT TO
        2)      12 LS + 12 SB <= 6000
        3)      6 LS + 10 SB <= 3500
END



            OBJECTIVE FUNCTION VALUE

        1)          14000.000

VARIABLE            VALUE           REDUCED COST
    LS           0.000000              0.000000
    SB         350.000000              0.000000


    ROW    SLACK OR SURPLUS          DUAL PRICES
    2)         1800.000000              0.000000
    3)            0.000000              4.000000

NO. ITERATIONS =       1

RANGES IN WHICH THE BASIS IS UNCHANGED:
                    OBJ COEFFICIENT RANGES
VARIABLE        CURRENT         ALLOWABLE       ALLOWABLE
                COEF            INCREASE        DECREASE
    LS          24.000000       0.000000        INFINITY
    SB          40.000000       INFINITY        0.000000

                    RIGHTHAND SIDE RANGES
    ROW         CURRENT         ALLOWABLE       ALLOWABLE
                RHS             INCREASE        DECREASE
    2           6000.000000     INFINITY        1800.000000
    3           3500.000000     1500.000000     3500.000000
```

a.   If you have not already done so in Problem 3 in Chapter 5, graph the feasible region and objective function contours for this problem in order to verify the LINDO solution.

b.   From your graph in part *a*, you should recognize that the solution is not unique. What are the values of the decision variables at the other optimal corner point? Why might this other corner point be a preferred solution?

c.   In light of the fact that there are alternative optimal solutions, explain the value of the reduced cost for LS.

d.   Verify the objective function coefficient ranges using your graph.

e.   Suppose that you have been offered 500 units of component B at a price of \$3.75 per unit. Is this a deal you would take? Why?

f.   Suppose that we add a constraint that at least twice as many LaserStops must be produced as Speed-Busters. Will the optimal solution given above by LINDO change? Will the optimal objective function value change? Explain your answers using your graph from part a.

5.   Recall the production planning over time LP model discussed in Example 5 of Chapter 4. The cost per unit of production is \$200, \$195, \$210, and \$200 for the next four quarters. The holding cost is \$10 per unit per quarter regardless of the quarter. There are currently 10 units in inventory and the demands for the next four quarters are 100, 150, 120, and 180. We defined the following decision variables:

$$Q_i = \text{number of units to produce in quarter } i, \ i = 1, 2, 3, 4$$

$$I_i = \text{number of units held in inventory at the end of quarter } i, \ i = 1, 2, 3, 4$$

The LINDO model and solution appear below.

```
MIN    200 Q1 + 195 Q2 = 210 Q3 + 200 Q4 + 10 I1 + 10 I12 + 10 I3
       + I0 I4
SUBJECT TO
       2)   Q1 − I1 = 90
       3)   Q2 + I1 − I2 = 150
       4)   Q2 + I2 − I3 = 120
       5)   Q2 + I3 − I4 = 180
END


           OBJECTIVE FUNCTION VALUE

       1)        107850.00

VARIABLE              VALUE          REDUCED COST
     Q1           90.000000              .000000
     Q2          270.000000              .000000
     Q3             .000000             5.000000
     Q4          180.000000              .000000
     I1             .000000            15.000000
     I2          120.000000              .000000
     I3             .000000            15.000000
     I4             .000000           210.000000
```

ROW	SLACK OR SURPLUS	DUAL PRICES
2)	.000000	− 200.500000
3)	.000000	− 195.500000
4)	.000000	− 205.000000
5)	.000000	− 200.000000

NO. ITERATIONS = 4

RANGES IN WHICH THE BASIS IS UNCHANGED:

OBJ COEFFICIENT RANGES

VARIABLE	CURRENT COEF	ALLOWABLE INCREASE	ALLOWABLE DECREASE
Q1	200.000000	INFINITY	15.000000
Q2	195.000000	5.000000	15.000000
Q3	210.000000	INFINITY	5.000000
Q4	200.000000	15.000000	210.000000
I1	10.000000	INFINITY	15.000000
I2	10.000000	5.000000	15.000000
I3	10.000000	INFINITY	15.000000
I4	10.000000	INFINITY	210.000000

RIGHTHAND SIDE RANGES

ROW	CURRENT RHS	ALLOWABLE INCREASE	ALLOWABLE DECREASE
2	90.000000	INFINITY	90.000000
3	150.000000	INFINITY	270.000000
4	120.000000	INFINITY	120.000000
5	180.000000	INFINITY	180.000000

a. Interpret the solution.
b. Determine which constraints are binding.
c. Interpret the dual prices for the binding constraints.
d. Suppose that the cost per unit of production in quarter one is really $210. What can you say about the model solution?

6. Consider the output and model shown in Problem 5. This model's output does not really indicate the sensitivity of the solution to the holding cost of $10 per unit per quarter. The ranges on the coefficients of the inventory variables assume that only one coefficient changes. If the $10 estimate is incorrect and is incorrect for all four quarters, then multiple changes will result in the model we have developed. Change the model given in Problem 5 so that the sensitivity analysis will give an indication of how sensitive the solution is to this $10 input. Solve your new model with an LP solver. (*Hint:* define a variable that is the *total* amount of inventory held.)

7. Recall the Grad & Sons Investment problem from Chapter 4 (Example 8). Grad & Sons Insurance carries an investment portfolio of bonds, stocks, and other investment alternatives such as real estate. At the beginning of next year, $500,000 will be available for investment in four alternatives: OP1, OP2, OP3, and

OP4. The expected annual rate of return on these four options are .06, .09, .07, and .11. The risk factor per dollar invested is a measure of the inherent uncertainty of the expected return, so that a low risk factor is desirable. The risk factors per dollar invested for the four investment alternatives are subjective estimates of the possible loss the investor could incur in the worst case analysis (0 is no risk, 1 if the investor could lose everything) that have been provided by a Grad & Sons analyst. They are .02, .05, .04, and .075, respectively. For diversification, no single alternative can be more than $200,000. Management needs a return of at least .08, but would like to minimize the risk taken to achieve that return. In Chapter 4 we defined the following decision variables:

A_i = amount (in dollars) to invest in alternative i
$i = 1, 2, 3, 4$

The LINDO model and solution appear in the following figure.

```
MIN     0.02 A1 + 0.05 A2 + 0.04 A3 + 0.075 A4
SUBJECT TO
    2)   0.06 A1 + 0.09 A2 + 0.07 A3 + 0.11 A4 >= 40000
    3)   A1 <= 200000
    4)   A2 <= 200000
    5)   A3 <= 200000
    6)   A4 <= 200000
    7)   A1 + A2 + A3 + A4 = 500000
END


LP OPTIMUM FOUND AT STEP          6

        OBJECTIVE FUNCTION VALUE

    1)        20625.000

VARIABLE          VALUE          REDUCED COST
    A1        200000.000000          .000000
    A2        200000.000000          .000000
    A3         25000.009766          .000000
    A4         74999.992188          .000000


    ROW     SLACK OR SURPLUS       DUAL PRICES
    2)           0.000000          -0.875000
    3)           0.000000           0.011250
    4)           0.000000           0.007500
    5)      174999.984375           0.000000
    6)      125000.007813           0.000000
    7)           0.000000           0.021250

NO. ITERATIONS = 6
```

RANGES IN WHICH THE BASIS IS UNCHANGED:

OBJ COEFFICIENT RANGES

VARIABLE	CURRENT COEF	ALLOWABLE INCREASE	ALLOWABLE DECREASE
A1	0.020000	0.011250	INFINITY
A2	0.050000	0.007500	INFINITY
A3	0.040000	0.035000	0.009000
A4	0.075000	0.045000	0.015000

RIGHTHAND SIDE RANGES

VARIABLE	CURRENT COEF	ALLOWABLE INCREASE	ALLOWABLE DECREASE
2	40000.000000	1000.000366	2999.999756
3	200000.000000	20000.007813	139999.984375
4	200000.000000	50000.027344	200000.000000
5	200000.000000	INFINITY	174999.984375
6	200000.000000	INFINITY	125000.007813
7	500000.000000	42857.136719	9090.913086

a. Which constraints are binding?
b. Interpret the dual price for row 2 (the return constraint).
c. Interpret the dual prices for rows 3 and 4.
d. Interpret the dual price for row 7.
e. Suppose that the risk factor on option alternative 3 increases to .06. Will the current solution stay optimal? Why or why not?

8. Ohio Valley Wines makes two types of wines, A and B. The cost of grapes for producing these wines is a sunk cost. Company policy dictates that at least 40%, but no more than 70% of all wine produced must be type A. It is estimated that demand for A is related to promotion in a linear manner: every dollar spent on the promotion of A increases the quantity demanded by five bottles above the forecasted demand without advertising. Likewise, every dollar spent on the promotion of B generates a demand of eight bottles of B over the forecasted demand. The demand for A is estimated to be 15,000 bottles and the demand for B is estimated to be 8,000 bottles. Ohio Valley Wines has a budget of $10,000 for promotion.

Type A wine sells for $13.25 per bottle and B sells for $7.75 per bottle. Ohio Valley Wines would like to maximize contribution to profit and fixed costs by deciding on the optimum levels of promotion and production for each of the wines.

Let Q_A = quantity (in bottles) of Wine A to produce
        Q_B = quantity (in bottles) of Wine B to produce
        P_A = dollars to spend promoting Wine A
        P_B = dollars to spend promoting Wine B

The LINDO model and solution are shown in the following figure.

```
MAX      13.25 QA + 7.75 QB
SUBJECT TO
         2)       0.6 QA − 0.4 QB >= 0
         3)       0.3 QA − 0.7 QB <=0
         4)       QA − 5 PA <= 15000
         5)       QB − 8 PB <= 8000
         6)       PA + PB <= 10000
END
```

OBJECTIVE FUNCTION VALUE

       1)   914929.60

VARIABLE	VALUE	REDUCED COST
QA	55211.270000	.000000
QB	23661.970000	.000000
PA	8042.253000	.000000
PB	1957.747000	.000000

ROW	SLACK OR SURPLUS	DUAL PRICES
2)	23661.970000	.000000
3)	.000000	.598592
4)	.000000	13.070420
5)	.000000	8.169014
6)	.000000	65.352110

NO. ITERATIONS = 4
RANGES IN WHICH THE BASIS IS UNCHANGED:

OBJ COEFFICIENT RANGES

VARIABLE	CURRENT COEF	ALLOWABLE INCREASE	ALLOWABLE DECREASE
QA	13.250000	INFINITY	.850000
QB	7.750000	.531250	38.666660
PA	.000000	309.333300	4.250000
PB	.000000	4.250000	309.333300

RIGHTHAND SIDE RANGES

ROW	CURRENT RHS	ALLOWABLE INCREASE	ALLOWABLE DECREASE
2	.000000	23661.970000	INFINITY
3	.000000	13900.000000	27096.780000
4	15000.000000	190333.300000	46333.330000
5	8000.000000	19857,140000	81571.430000
6	10000.000000	INFINITY	9266.667000

a. How much of each wine should be produced, and what is the optimal allocation of the advertising budget?

b. Interpret the dual prices of rows 3 through 6.

c. In a manner similar to that used in the Phillips Inc. problem (Example 12) in this chapter, analyze the effect of advertising budget on revenue.

9. Recall the Vohio Oil Blending example from Chapter 4. Three input ingredients go into the production of two types of fuel at Vohio. The major distinguishing feature of the two end products (regular and super) is the octane level required. Regular fuel must have a minimum octane level of 90 and super's level must be at least 100. The octane levels of the three inputs as well as their availability for the coming two-week period are known. The maximum demand for the end products, and the revenue generated per barrel are also known. These data are summarized in the following table.

Input	Cost/bbl.	Octane	Available (barrels)
1	16.50	100	110,000
2	14.00	87	350,000
3	17.50	110	300,000

	Revenue/barrel	Max Demand (barrels)
Regular	18.50	350,000
Super	20.00	500,000

In Chapter 4, we developed an LP model to determine how much of each end product to produce in order to maximize contribution to profit.

We defined the following decision variables as

RB = number of barrels of regular to produce for the two-week period
SB = number of barrels of super to produce for the two-week period
R_i = number of barrels of input i used to make regular
S_i = number of barrels of input i used to make super

The LINDO model we developed in Chapter 4 and its solution appear in the following figure.

```
MAX     18.5 RB + 20 SB − 16.5 R1 .5 S1 − 14 R2 −
                14 S2 − 17.5 R3 − 17.5 S3
SUBJECT TO
        2)    R1 + S1 <= 110000    ! Input 1
        3)    R2 + S2 <= 350000    ! Input 2
        4)    R3 + S3 <= 300000    ! Input 3
        5)    RB − R1 − R2 − R3 =     0
        6)    SB − S1 − S2 − S3 =     0
        7)    RB <= 350000    ! Regular Demand
        8)    SB <= 500000    ! Super Demand
        9) − 90 RB + 100 R1 + 87 R2 + 110 R3 >= 0    ! Reg. Octane
       10) − 100 SB + 100 S1 + 87 S2 + 110 S3 >= 0    ! Sup. Octane
END


        OBJECTIVE FUNCTION VALUE

        1)      2845000.0

VARIABLE          VALUE        REDUCED COST
      RB     260000.000000          .000000
      SB     500000.000000          .000000
      R1          .000000          .000000
      S1     110000.000000          .000000
      R2     180434.800000          .000000
      S2     169565.200000          .000000
      R3      79565.220000          .000000
      S3     220434.800000          .000000


    ROW     SLACK OR SURPLUS     DUAL PRICES
      2)          .000000          2.000000
      3)          .000000          4.500000
      4)          .000000          1.000000
      5)          .000000         18.500000
      6)          .000000         18.500000
      7)     90000.000000          .000000
      8)          .000000          1.500000
      9)   1050000.000000          .000000
     10)          .000000          .000000

NO. ITERATIONS = 5
```

RANGES IN WHICH THE BASIS IS UNCHANGED:

OBJ COEFFICIENT RANGES

VARIABLE	CURRENT COEF	ALLOWABLE INCREASE	ALLOWABLE DECREASE
RB	18.500000	1.500000	1.000000
SB	20.500000	INFINITY	1.500000
R1	− 16.500000	.000000	INFINITY
S1	− 16.500000	INFINITY	.000000
R2	− 14.000000	.000000	.000000
S2	− 14.000000	.000000	.000000
R3	− 17.500000	2.653846	.000000
S3	− 17.500000	.000000	2.653846

RIGHTHAND SIDE RANGES

ROW	CURRENT RHS	ALLOWABLE INCREASE	ALLOWABLE DECREASE
2	110000.000000	90000.000000	105000.000000
3	350000.000000	90000.000000	180434.800000
4	300000.000000	90000.000000	52500.000000
5	.000000	11666.670000	260000.000000
6	.000000	11666.670000	37727.270000
7	350000.000000	INFINITY	90000.000000
8	500000.000000	105000.000000	90000.000000
9	.000000	1050000.000000	INFINITY
10	.000000	1050000.000000	4150000.000000

a. Interpret the dual prices for rows 2 through 4.
b. What would be the effect on the objective function value if the maximum demand for super increased by 12,000 barrels?
c. Suppose that the selling price of super drops to $19 per barrel. Does the current solution remain optimal? Why or why not?

10. Consider the following LINDO model and solution for the Vohio Oil blending problem discussed in Problem 9.

```
MAX      18.5 RB + 20 SB − 16.5 INPUT1 − 14 INPUT2 − 5 INPUT3
SUBJECT TO
     2)   −INPUT1+R1+S1 = 0
     3)   −INPUT2+R2+S2 = 0
```

```
 4) − INPUT3 + R3 + S3 = 0
 5)   INPUT1 <= 110000
 6)   INPUT2 <= 350000
 7)   INPUT3 <= 300000
 8)   RB − R1 − R2 − R3 = 0
 9)   SB − S1 − S2 − S3 = 0
10)   RB <= 350000
11)   SB <= 500000
12) − 90 RB + 100 R1 + 87 R2 + 110 R3 >= 0
13) − 100 SB + 100 S1 + 87 S2 + 110 S3 >= 0
```

END

OBJECTIVE FUNCTION VALUE

```
 1)      2845000.0
```

VARIABLE	VALUE	REDUCED COST
RB	260000.000000	.000000
SB	500000.000000	.000000
INPUT1	110000.000000	.000000
INPUT2	350000.000000	.000000
INPUT3	300000.000000	.000000
R1	.000000	.000000
S1	110000.000000	.000000
R2	180434.800000	.000000
S2	169565.200000	.000000
R3	79565.220000	.000000
S3	220434.800000	.000000

ROW	SLACK OR SURPLUS	DUAL PRICES
2)	.000000	18.500000
3)	.000000	18.500000
4)	.000000	18.500000
5)	.000000	2.000000
6)	.000000	4.500000
7)	.000000	1.000000
8)	.000000	18.500000
9)	.000000	18.500000
10)	90000.000000	.000000
11)	.000000	1.500000
12)	105000.000000	.000000
13)	.000000	.000000

NO. ITERATIONS = 5

RANGES IN WHICH THE BASIS IS UNCHANGED:

OBJ COEFFICIENT RANGES

VARIABLE	CURRENT COEF	ALLOWABLE INCREASE	ALLOWABLE DECREASE
RB	18.500000	1.500000	1.000000
SB	20.000000	INFINITY	1.500000
INPUT1	−16.500000	INFINITY	2.000000
INPUT2	−14.000000	INFINITY	4.500000
INPUT3	−17.500000	INFINITY	1.000000
R1	.000000	.000000	INFINITY
S1	.000000	INFINITY	.000000
R2	.000000	.000000	.000000
S2	.000000	.000000	.000000
R3	.000000	2.653846	.000000
S3	.000000	.000000	2.653846

RIGHTHAND SIDE RANGES

ROW	CURRENT RHS	ALLOWABLE INCREASE	ALLOWABLE DECREASE
2	.000000	90000.000000	105000.000000
3	.000000	90000.000000	180434.800000
4	.000000	90000.000000	52500.000000
5	110000.000000	90000.000000	105000.000000
6	350000.000000	90000.000000	180434.800000
7	300000.000000	90000.000000	52500.000000
8	.000000	11666.670000	260000.000000
9	.000000	11666.670000	37727.270000
10	350000.000000	INFINITY	90000.000000
11	500000.000000	105000.000000	90000.000000
12	.000000	1050000.000000	INFINITY
13	.000000	1050000.000000	4150000.000000

Here, INPUT1, INPUT2, and INPUT3 are the total amounts of inputs 1, 2, and 3 to use. This model is equivalent to the original model in Problem 9 in the sense that they both yield the same optimal solution. Why might this new model be preferred over the original model?

11. Assume that the inputs in the Vohio Oil blending problem are a sunk cost. That is, assume that rows 5, 6, and 7 in Problem 10 are amounts Vohio has already purchased and made available for the production of regular and super (the last three terms in the objective function would be deleted). How would this affect the interpretation of the dual prices for these constraints?

12. Using the Vohio Oil model given in Problem 10, analyze the effect of increasing or decreasing maximum demand for super in a manner similar to that used in the Phillips Inc. example in this chapter (Example 12). Plot the optimal objective function value as a function of demand for super.

13. Rick's Barbecue produces two types of barbecue sauce, Southern Tang and Yankee Sweet. These sauces are made from two secret ingredients, known only as *A* and *B*. Southern Tang is made up of between 40% and 70% of *A*, and the remainder is made up of *B*. Yankee Sweet is made up of between 80% and 90% *A*, and the remainder is *B*. Southern Tang sells for $2.45 per quart and Yankee Sweet sells for $2.15 per quart. There are 120 quarts of ingredient *A* at a price of $1.00 per quart available for tomorrow's production. There are 45 quarts of ingredient *B* available at $.85 per quart. Rick would like to plan tomorrow's production in order to maximize contribution to profit and fixed costs (assume that Rick can sell everything he produces). An EXCEL Spreadsheet for Rick's problem is shown in the following figure. The values shown in the spreadsheet are the optimal solution found by Solver. The answer report and sensitivity analysis from Solver are also shown.

	A	B	C	D	E
1	**Rick's Barbeque**				
2					
3	*Parameters and uncontrollable inputs:*				
4				Ingredients	
5		Selling Price/ Quart	Max A	Min A	
6	Southern Tang	$2.45	70%	40%	
7	Yankee Sweet	$2.15	90%	80%	
8					
9		Cost/Quart	Available		
10	A	$1.00	120		
11	B	$0.85	45		
12					
13					
14	*Decision variables:*				
15		A	B	Total	
16	Southern Tang	99.7	42.7	142.5	
17	Yankee Sweet	20.3	2.3	22.5	
18	Total	120.0	45.0		
19					
20	*Model outputs:*				
21		Revenue			
22	Southern Tang	$349.12			
23	Yankee Sweet	$48.38			
24		Cost		Used	Available
25	A	$120.00		120	0
26	B	$38.25		45	0
27					
28	Profit	$239.25			

Target Cell (Max)

Cell	Name	Original Value	Final Value
$B$28	Profit Cost	$239.25	$239.25

Adjustable Cells

Cell	Name	Original Value	Final Value
$B$16	Southern Tang A	99.8	99.7
$C$16	Southern Tang B	42.8	42.8
$B$17	Yankee Sweet A	20.3	20.3
$C$17	Yankee Sweet B	2.3	2.3
$B$18	Total A	120.0	120.0
$C$18	Total B	45.0	45.0
$D$16	Southern Tang Total	142.5	142.5
$D$17	Yankee Sweet Total	22.5	22.5

Constraints

Cell	Name	Cell Value	Formula	Status	Slack
$B$16	Southern Tang A	99.7	$B$16<=$C$6*$D$1	Binding	.0
$B$17	Yankee Sweet A	20.3	$B$17<=$C$7*$D$1	Binding	.0
$B$16	Southern Tang A	99.7	$B$16>=$D$6*$D$1	Not Binding	42.7
$B$17	Yankee Sweet A	20.3	$B$17>=$D$7*$D$1	Not Binding	2.3
$D$16	Southern Tang Total	142.5	$D$16=$B$16+$C$1	Binding	.0
$D$17	Yankee Sweet Total	22.5	$D$17=$B$17+$C$1	Binding	.0
$B$18	Total A	120.0	$B$18=$B$16+$B$17	Binding	.0
$D$25	A Used	120	$D$25<=$C$10	Binding	0
$D$26	B Used	45	$D$26<=$C$11	Binding	0
$C$18	Total B	45.0	$C$18=$C$16+$C$1	Binding	.0
$B$16	Southern Tang A	99.7	$B$16>=0	Not Binding	99.7
$C$16	Southern Tang B	42.8	$C$16>=0	Not Binding	42.8
$B$17	Yankee Sweet A	20.3	$B$17>=0	Not Binding	20.3
$C$17	Yankee Sweet B	2.3	$C$17>=0	Not Binding	2.3
$B$18	Total A	120.0	$B$18>=0	Not Binding	120.0
$C$18	Total B	45.0	$C$18>=0	Not Binding	45.0
$D$16	Southern Tang Total	142.5	$D$16>=0	Not Binding	142.5
$D$17	Yankee Sweet Total	22.5	$D$17>=0	Not Binding	22.5

Changing Cells

Cell	Name	Final Value	Reduced Cost	Objective Coefficient	Allowable Increase	Allowable Decrease
$B$16	Southern Tang A	99.7	.0	0	2.857142857	0.333333333
$C$16	Southern Tang B	42.7	.0	0	6.666666666	1
$B$17	Yankee Sweet A	20.3	.0	0	0.333333333	0.740740741
$C$17	Yankee Sweet B	2.3	.0	0	1	6.666666667
$B$18	Total A	120.0	.0	-1	1E+30	1
$C$18	Total B	45.0	.0	-0.85	1E+30	2.65
$D$16	Southern Tang Total	142.5	.0	2.45	2	0.3
$D$17	Yankee Sweet Total	22.5	.0	2.15	0.3	0.666666667

Constraints

Cell	Name	Final Value	Shadow Price	Constraint R.H. Side	Allowable Increase	Allowable Decrease
$B$16	Southern Tang A	99.7	1.5	0	4.5	17.1
$B$17	Yankee Sweet A	20.3	1.5	0	1.5	4.5
$B$16	Southern Tang A	99.7	.0	0	42.75	1E+30
$B$17	Yankee Sweet A	20.3	.0	0	2.25	1E+30
$D$16	Southern Tang Total	142.5	3.5	0	6.428571428	31.66666667
$D$17	Yankee Sweet Total	22.5	3.5	0	1.666666667	31.66666666
$B$18	Total A	120.0	-2.0	0	15	285
$D$25	A Used	120	1	120	285	15
$D$26	B Used	45	3	45	6.428571429	31.66666667
$C$18	Total B	45.0	-3.5	0	31.66666667	6.428571429

a. What is the maximum contribution to profit and fixed cost found by the EXCEL solver? How many quarts of Southern Tang and Yankee Sweet should Rick make?

b. Interpret the shadow prices on the availability of ingredients A and B (cells $D$25 and $D$26 in the Constraints section of the sensitivity report).

c. Suppose that the cost of ingredient A increases to $1.50 per quart before Rick can purchase what he needs for tomorrow. Will the current solution remain optimal? Why or why not?

d. Suppose that 50 more quarts of ingredient A become available (over and above the 120 already available) at a price of $1.50 per quart. Should Rick purchase the 50 extra quarts of A? Why or why not?

14. Welz's Widgets has four production plants located in Atlanta, Cincinnati, Chicago, and Salt Lake City. It currently has 12 distribution centers located in Portland, San Jose, Las Vegas, Tucson, Colorado Springs, Kansas City, St. Paul, Austin, Jackson, Montgomery, Cleveland, and Pittsburgh. The monthly capacity is known for each plant, and the monthly demand at each of the distribution centers is known. The per-unit shipping cost from each plant to each distribution center is also known. Welz is interested in minimizing the cost of transporting its widgets from its plants to its distribution centers.

An EXCEL spreadsheet model for this scenario is shown in the following figure. The solution shown is the optimal solution found by the EXCEL solver. The decision variables are the quantity to ship from each plant to each location. In addition to the spreadsheet, the sensitivity report is also provided.

a. What is the minimum monthly cost of shipping?

b. Which plants will operate at capacity in this solution?

c. Suppose that 500 units of extra capacity are available (and that the cost of this extra capacity is a sunk cost). To which plant should this extra capacity go? Why?

d. Suppose that the cost of shipping from Atlanta to Jackson increased to $0.45 per unit. Would the current solution remain optimal? Why or why not?

e. Of the routes currently chosen for shipment, which seems the most cost-sensitive?

Velz's Widgets

Parameters and uncontrollable inputs:

Shipping Cost Per Unit

	Portland	San Jose	Las Vegas	Tuscon	Colo. Springs	Kansas City	St. Paul	Austin	Jackson	Montgomery	Cleveland	Pitts.	Supply
Atlanta	$2.17	$2.10	$1.75	$1.50	$1.20	$0.68	$0.92	$0.81	$0.35	$0.14	$0.56	$0.53	15000
Cincinnati	$1.97	$2.02	$1.68	$1.53	$1.10	$0.55	$0.61	$0.97	$0.57	$0.49	$0.22	$0.27	35000
Chicago	$1.71	$1.83	$1.53	$1.41	$0.94	$0.42	$0.37	$0.98	$0.67	$0.67	$0.34	$0.41	15000
Salt Lake City	$0.63	$0.57	$0.35	$0.58	$0.39	$0.93	$0.39	$1.08	$1.34	$1.55	$1.57	$1.69	35000
Demand	5000	15600	4250	3750	4570	7500	3000	8700	3250	12300	9600	16700	

Decision variables:

	Portland	San Jose	Las Vegas	Tuscon	Colo. Springs	Kansas City	St. Paul	Austin	Jackson	Montgomery	Cleveland	Pitts.
Atlanta	0	0	0	0	0	0	0	0	2700	12300	0	0
Cincinnati	0	0	0	0	0	0	0	8150	550	0	9600	16700
Chicago	0	0	0	0	0	7500	3000	550	0	0	0	0
Salt Lake City	5000	15600	4250	3750	4570	0	0	0	0	0	0	0
Total To:	5000	15600	4250	3750	4570	7500	3000	8700	3250	12300	9600	16700

Model outputs:

Total From:

Atlanta	15000
Cincinnati	35000
Chicago	11050
Salt Lake City	33170

Total To:

Portland	San Jose	Las Vegas	Tuscon	Colo. Springs	Kansas City	St. Paul	Austin	Jackson	Montgomery	Cleveland	Pitts.
5000	15600	4250	3750	4570	7500	3000	8700	3250	12300	9600	16700

Total Cost: $39,792.80

Changing Cells

Cell	Name	Final Value	Reduced Cost	Objective Coefficient	Allowable Increase	Allowable Decrease
$B$22	Atlanta Portland	0	1.77	2.17	1E+30	1.77
$C$22	Atlanta San Jose	0	1.76	2.1	1E+30	1.76
$D$22	Atlanta Las Vegas	0	1.63	1.75	1E+30	1.63
$E$22	Atlanta Tuscon	0	1.15	1.5	1E+30	1.15
$F$22	Atlanta Colo. Sprngs	0	1.04	1.2	1E+30	1.04
$G$22	Atlanta Kansas City	0	0.49	0.68	1E+30	0.49
$H$22	Atlanta St. Paul	0	0.78	0.92	1E+30	0.78
$I$22	Atlanta Austin	0	0.06	0.81	1E+30	0.06
$J$22	Atlanta Jackson	2700	0	0.35	0.06	0.13
$K$22	Atlanta Montgomery	12300	0	0.14	0.13	1E+30
$L$22	Atlanta Cleveland	0	0.56	0.56	1E+30	0.56
$M$22	Atlanta Pitts.	0	0.48	0.53	1E+30	0.48
$B$23	Cincinnati Portland	0	1.35	1.97	1E+30	1.35
$C$23	Cincinnati San Jose	0	1.46	2.02	1E+30	1.46
$D$23	Cincinnati Las Vegas	0	1.34	1.68	1E+30	1.34
$E$23	Cincinnati Tuscon	0	0.96	1.53	1E+30	0.96
$F$23	Cincinnati Colo. Sprngs	0	0.72	1.1	1E+30	0.72
$G$23	Cincinnati Kansas City	0	0.14	0.55	1E+30	0.14
$H$23	Cincinnati St. Paul	0	0.25	0.61	1E+30	0.25
$I$23	Cincinnati Austin	8150	0	0.97	0.01	0.09
$J$23	Cincinnati Jackson	550	0	0.57	0.09	0.06
$K$23	Cincinnati Montgomery	0	0.13	0.49	1E+30	0.13
$L$23	Cincinnati Cleveland	9600	0	0.22	0.11	1E+30
$M$23	Cincinnati Pitts.	16700	0	0.27	0.13	1E+30
$B$24	Chicago Portland	0	1.08	1.71	1E+30	1.08
$C$24	Chicago San Jose	0	1.26	1.83	1E+30	1.26
$D$24	Chicago Las Vegas	0	1.18	1.53	1E+30	1.18
$E$24	Chicago Tuscon	0	0.83	1.41	1E+30	0.83
$F$24	Chicago Colo. Sprngs	0	0.55	0.94	1E+30	0.55
$G$24	Chicago Kansas City	7500	0	0.42	0.14	1E+30
$H$24	Chicago St. Paul	3000	0	0.37	0.25	1E+30
$I$24	Chicago Austin	550	0	0.98	0.09	0.01
$J$24	Chicago Jackson	0	0.09	0.67	1E+30	0.09
$K$24	Chicago Montgomery	0	0.3	0.67	1E+30	0.3
$L$24	Chicago Cleveland	0	0.11	0.34	1E+30	0.11
$M$24	Chicago Pitts.	0	0.13	0.41	1E+30	0.13
$B$25	Salt Lake City Portland	5000	0	0.63	1.08	1E+30
$C$25	Salt Lake City San Jose	15600	0	0.57	1.26	1E+30
$D$25	Salt Lake City Las Vegas	4250	0	0.35	1.18	1E+30
$E$25	Salt Lake City Tuscon	3750	0	0.58	0.83	1E+30
$F$25	Salt Lake City Colo. Sprngs	4570	0	0.39	0.55	1E+30
$G$25	Salt Lake City Kansas City	0	0.51	0.93	1E+30	0.51
$H$25	Salt Lake City St. Paul	0	0.62	0.99	1E+30	0.62
$I$25	Salt Lake City Austin	0	0.1	1.08	1E+30	0.1
$J$25	Salt Lake City Jackson	0	0.76	1.34	1E+30	0.76
$K$25	Salt Lake City Montgomery	0	1.18	1.55	1E+30	1.18
$L$25	Salt Lake City Cleveland	0	1.34	1.57	1E+30	1.34
$M$25	Salt Lake City Pitts.	0	1.41	1.69	1E+30	1.41

Constraints

Cell	Name	Final Value	Shadow Price	Constraint R.H. Side	Allowable Increase	Allowable Decrease
$B$33	Atlanta Total From:	15000	-0.23	15000	550	2700
$B$34	Cincinnati Total From:	35000	-0.01	35000	550	3950
$B$35	Chicago Total From:	11050	0	15000	1E+30	3950
$B$36	Salt Lake City Total From:	33170	0	35000	1E+30	1830
$E$34	Total To: Portland	5000	0.63	5000	1830	5000
$F$34	Total To: San Jose	15600	0.57	15600	1830	15600
$G$34	Total To: Las Vegas	4250	0.35	4250	1830	4250
$H$34	Total To: Tuscon	3750	0.58	3750	1830	3750
$I$34	Total To: Colo. Sprngs	4570	0.39	4570	1830	4570
$J$34	Total To: Kansas City	7500	0.42	7500	3950	7500
$K$34	Total To: St. Paul	3000	0.37	3000	3950	3000
$L$34	Total To: Austin	8700	0.98	8700	3950	550
$M$34	Total To: Jackson	3250	0.58	3250	3950	550
$N$34	Total To: Montgomery	12300	0.37	12300	2700	550
$O$34	Total To: Cleveland	9600	0.23	9600	3950	550
$P$34	Total To: Pitts.	16700	0.28	16700	3950	550

15. A farmer needs to decide how many acres of corn, oats, soybean, and wheat to plant this year. An acre of corn planted for sale later yields $52.5 in revenue. Because the farmer has livestock, he must plant 25 acres of corn for feed (these generate no immediate revenue). He likewise must plant 35 acres of oats for feed, but an acre of oats planted for sale later generates $27 in revenue. An acre of soybeans yields $50 in revenue and an acre of wheat yields $48 in revenue. The farmer has already committed to sell 10 acres of oats and 5 acres of wheat. Upper limits on the demand of each commodity are 120 acres of corn, 150 acres of oats, 180 acres of soybeans, and 150 acres of wheat. The farmer has 400 acres of available land to plant. His budget for extra help in harvesting the crops is $5,000. It takes $6 per acre for extra help to harvest corn and oats, $30 per acre to harvest soybeans, and $21 per acre to harvest wheat. The farmer would like to know how many acres of each crop to plant so as to maximize revenue from the harvest.

    An EXCEL spreadsheet, sensitivity report, and answer report for this problem follow.

  a. What is the maximum revenue achieved? How much of each crop should be planted?

  b. Which constraints are binding?

  c. How will revenue change if 20 more acres become available?

  d. In your opinion, is this solution very sensitive to the objective function coefficients (revenue per acre)? Explain your response.

Problems 16 through 20 on page 314 refer to problems at the end of Chapters 4 and 5. Each problem requests that you solve a model on the computer. Use a package that provides sensitivity analysis, such as LINDO or EXCEL Solver.

	A	B	C	D	E	F	G	H
1	Farmer's Problem							
2								
3	*Parameters and uncontrollable inputs:*							
4								
5		Corn	Oats	Soybeans	Wheat			
6	Revenue/Acre	$52.50	$27.00	$50.00	$48.00		Budget	$5,000.00
7	Feed Acres	25	35	0	0		Acres	400
8	Sales Committed	0	10	0	5			
9	Max Sales	120	150	180	150			
10	Harvest Help/Acre	$6.00	$6.00	$30.00	$21.00			
11								
12								
13	*Decision variables:*							
14		For Sale	For Feed					
15	Corn	120	25					
16	Oats	55.41666667	35					
17	Soybeans	14.58333333	0					
18	Wheat	150	0					
19								
20								
21								
22	*Model outputs:*							
23		Planted			Used	Available		
24	Corn	145		Budget	$5,000.00	$0.00		
25	Oats	90.41666667						
26	Soybeans	14.58333333						
27	Wheat	150						
28	Total	400						
29	Unplanted	0						
30								
31								
32	Total Revenue	$15,725.42						

Target Cell (Max)

Cell	Name	Original Value	Final Value
$B$32	Total Revenue	$15,725.42	$15,725.42

Adjustable Cells

Cell	Name	Original Value	Final Value
$B$15	Corn For Sale	120	120
$C$15	Corn For Feed	25	25
$B$16	Oats For Sale	55.41666667	55.41666667
$C$16	Oats For Feed	35	35
$B$17	Soybeans For Sale	14.58333333	14.58333333
$C$17	Soybeans For Feed	0	0
$B$18	Wheat For Sale	150	150
$C$18	Wheat For Feed	0	0

Constraints

Cell	Name	Cell Value	Formula	Status	Slack
$B$28	Total Planted	400	$B$28<=$H$7	Binding	0
$E$24	Budget Used	$5,000.00	$E$24<=$H$6	Binding	$0.00
$C$15	Corn For Feed	25	$C$15=$B$7	Binding	0
$C$16	Oats For Feed	35	$C$16=$C$7	Binding	0
$C$17	Soybeans For Feed	0	$C$17=$D$7	Binding	0
$C$18	Wheat For Feed	0	$C$18=$E$7	Binding	0
$B$15	Corn For Sale	120	$B$15>=$B$8	Not Binding	120
$B$16	Oats For Sale	55.41666667	$B$16>=$C$8	Not Binding	45.41666667
$B$17	Soybeans For Sale	14.58333333	$B$17>=$D$8	Not Binding	14.58333333
$B$18	Wheat For Sale	150	$B$18>=$E$8	Not Binding	145
$B$15	Corn For Sale	120	$B$15<=$B$9	Binding	0
$B$16	Oats For Sale	55.41666667	$B$16<=$C$9	Not Binding	94.58333333
$B$17	Soybeans For Sale	14.58333333	$B$17<=$D$9	Not Binding	165.4166667
$B$18	Wheat For Sale	150	$B$18<=$E$9	Binding	0

Changing Cells

Cell	Name	Final Value	Reduced Cost	Objective Coefficient	Allowable Increase	Allowable Decrease
$B$15	Corn For Sale	120	25.5	52.5	1E+30	25.5
$C$15	Corn For Feed	25	-27	0	27	1E+30
$B$16	Oats For Sale	55.41666667	0	27	23	17
$C$16	Oats For Feed	35	-27	0	27	1E+30
$B$17	Soybeans For Sale	14.58333333	0	50	85	10.6
$C$17	Soybeans For Feed	0	-50	0	50	1E+30
$B$18	Wheat For Sale	150	6.625	48	1E+30	6.625
$C$18	Wheat For Feed	0	-41.375	0	41.375	1E+30

Constraints

Cell	Name	Final Value	Shadow Price	Constraint R.H. Side	Allowable Increase	Allowable Decrease
$B$28	Total Planted	400	21.25	400	58.33333333	36.33333333
$E$24	Budget Used	$5,000.00	$0.96	5000	1090	350

16. Recall the Coger Company transportation problem of Chapter 4 (Problem 10). You were asked to solve this problem in Chapter 5 (Problem 16). If you have not already done so, formulate and solve this problem on the computer.
    a, What is the value of adding capacity at the Columbus plant? At the Indianapolis plant? Over what ranges are these values valid? Give some rationale for these values (and ranges).
    b. How much cheaper would the shipping cost from Columbus to Bowling Green have to be before that route becomes attractive from a cost point of view?
    c. Suppose that the demand at St. Louis increases by 700 cases. How much would the total shipping cost increase?
    d. Suppose that the capacity at the Columbus plant decreases to 2,500 cases due to machinery problems. Will the current plan remain optimal? Why or why not?
17. Review the Very Good Juice Company problem from Chapter 4 (Problem 6). In Chapter 5 you were asked to solve this problem on the computer (Problem 13). If you have not already done so, solve this problem on the computer. What effect would an increase of capacity in the straining department have on profit? Analyze the effect of the straining department capacity on profit in a manner similar to the analysis done in the Phillips Inc. problem for advertising budget (Example 12 of this chapter).
18. Review the Valdaz Coffee Company problem from Chapter 4 (Problem 4). In Chapter 5 you were asked to solve this problem on the computer (Problem 12). If you have not already done so, solve this problem on the computer.
    a. Which of the coffee beans, b1, b2, b3, and b4, are completely used in the solution?
    b. How would you interpret the dual prices if the coffee beans are a sunk cost? How would this interpretation change if the cost of the beans is not sunk, but has been included in the contribution to profit coefficients?
    c. Is this solution very sensitive to the profit coefficient accuracy? Explain your response.
19. Review the Drew's Sporting Goods marketing problem in Chapter 4 (Problem 16). In Chapter 5 you were asked to solve this problem on the computer (Problem 19). If you have not already done so, solve this problem on the computer.
    a. Which constraints are binding?
    b. Interpret the dual price for each of the binding constraints.
    c. According to the dual prices, which station is best for lowering the minimum number of .5-minute spots from the current required level of ten?
20. Review the General Hospital staffing problem from Chapter 5 (Problem 11). If you have not already done so, solve this problem on the computer.
    a. Interpret the dual prices for all binding constraints.
    b. Does the model you solved yield valid sensitivity information on the $700 salary all nurses earn? If not, develop a model that does yield valid sensitivity on this input (*hint:* define a decision variable that is the total number of nurses on staff, and use it in the objective function). Are you surprised by the allowable changes for the $700 coefficient? Give a rationale as to why the allowable changes make sense.

IV. Projects and Cases

1. CinTech Co. Manufacturing

CinTech Co. manufactures seven different products denoted $A, B, C, D, E, F,$ and G. The seven products have three raw materials in common (R1 and R2) and share two processes (P1 and P2). There are 500 pounds of R1, 750 pounds of R2, and 350 pounds of R3 available for next week's production. There are 60 hours available for P1 and 80 hours available for P2 next week. The per-unit requirements, per-unit contribution to profit, and fixed costs for the seven products are shown in the following table.

	A	B	C	D	E	F	G
Contr.	$10	$12	$8	$15	$1	$10	$19
R1	.1	3	.2	.1	.2	.1	.2
R2	.2	.1	.4	.2	.2	.3	.4
R3	.2	.1	.1	.2	.1	.2	.3
P1	.02	.03	.01	.04	.01	.02	.04
P2	.04	.0	.02	.02	.06	.03	.05

Due to prior commitments, a minimum of 300 units of *A* must be produced. Because of limitations in other processes, a maximum of 700 units of *B* can be produced per week. For similar reasons, at most 400 units of *E* can be produced next week.

As the rising new star analyst in the company, you have been asked to develop a production plan that will maximize contribution to profit and overhead while satisfying the restrictions placed on production.

a.   Develop an LP model that will yield the optimal production plan for next week. Solve your model on the computer and prepare a detailed report of your recommendations for management.

b.   You have finished your report and are now in a meeting with the Sales Manager, the Production Manager, and the Chief Buyer. Answer each of the following questions independently. (Some of these might require new runs of the model. If so, indicate that, and describe how you would answer the question later in the day.)

   i.   The Sales Manager feels that it would be possible to increase the selling price of product *F* by $2 per unit. What is your reply?

   ii.   The Chief Buyer thinks it is unlikely that she can obtain any more of R1 from the current source. However, there is another supplier, but his quoted price is $10 higher. Should we consider buying additional R1 from the other supplier?

   iii. The firm to which CinTech has agreed to supply 300 units of *A* has requested that it be increased to 350. How should the Sales Manager respond?

   iv.   The Production Manager thinks he can obtain 20 extra hours of P1 at a total increase in cost of $1,500. Is this a good idea?

   v.   The Sales Manager feels that product *B* is priced too low. He feels that the price for *B* should be raised to $14 per unit. However, he estimates that demand at this price will be a maximum of 600. What will be the optimal contribution to profit and fixed costs if this is implemented?

2.   **Coffee Express**

Coffee Express is a chain of gourmet coffee shops that makes its own flavored blends of gourmet coffee. Three of the most popular blends are Columbian-Chocolate, Columbian-Raspberry, and Chocolate-Raspberry. These are blended from three types of beans: Columbian, Chocolate-flavored, and Raspberry-flavored, which are purchased from a wholesaler. The *percent* composition of the three beans in each blend, the availability of each type of bean, and the selling price per pound are given in the table below. Processing costs are $.63 per pound. Coffee Express is interested in maximizing contribution to profit and fixed costs.

Blend	Price	Columbian	Chocolate	Raspberry
Choc-Rasp	$6.35	50%	25%	25%
Col-Choc	$6.00	50%	50%	0%
Col-Rasp	$6.85	60%	0%	40%
Pounds Available		5,000	3,000	2,000

a.   Let A, B, and C correspond to the three different blends. Define x_A, x_B, and x_C as the number of pounds of blends A, B, and C to produce. Formulate a linear programming model only in terms of these variables.
b.   Let x1A represent the number of pounds of Columbian beans to use in blend A, x2A the number of pounds of Chocolate beans to use in blend A, and x3A the number of pounds of Raspberry beans to use in blend A, and similarly for the other blends. Formulate a linear programming model only in terms of these variables.
c.   Verify that your models are correct by solving them using the computer. You should get the same value for the objective function and consistent results.
d.   Would the model that is used make any difference in terms of managerial information? Explain.

3. **Welz's Widgets Distribution System Redesign**
    In the Welz's Widgets transportation problem from this chapter (Problem 14), Welz currently has four plants and 12 distribution centers. The current monthly capacity at each of the four plants, the monthly demand at each distribution center, and the per-unit cost of shipping from each plant to each distribution center are given in the following table.

Welz's Widgets

Shipping Cost Per Unit

	Portland	San Jose	Las Vegas	Tucson	Colo. Springs	Kansas City	St. Paul	Austin	Jackson	Montgomery	Cleveland	Pitts.	Supply
Atlanta	$2.17	$2.10	$1.75	$1.50	$1.20	$0.68	$0.92	$0.81	$0.35	$0.14	$0.56	$0.53	15000
Cincinnati	$1.97	$2.02	$1.68	$1.53	$1.10	$0.55	$0.61	$0.97	$0.57	$0.49	$0.22	$0.27	35000
Chicago	$1.71	$1.83	$1.53	$1.41	$0.94	$0.42	$0.37	$0.98	$0.67	$0.67	$0.34	$0.41	15000
Salt Lake City	$0.63	$0.57	$0.35	$0.58	$0.39	$0.93	$0.99	$1.08	$1.34	$1.55	$1.57	$1.69	35000
Demand	5000	15600	4250	3750	4570	7500	3000	8700	3250	12300	9600	16700	

Welz is interested in redesigning its distribution system from a production capacity perspective. The current distribution centers are doing a good job of satisfying customers, so they will remain as is. However, Welz would like to consolidate its production facilities into only two plants. Total production capacity is 100,000 units per month, so Welz would like to have two facilities, each with capacity of 50,000 units per month. The candidate locations are the four locations of the current plants.

Assume that production costs, the raw material costs, and the cost of expansion at each location are equal, so that the decision should be based on minimizing transportation costs. Develop a recommendation and a report for management as to which locations should be used for the two production facilities.

REFERENCES

Bazaraa, M., J. Jarvis, and H. Sherali. *Linear Programming and Network Flows*. 2nd ed. New York: John Wiley and Sons, 1990.

Camm, J. D., and T. H. Burwell. "Sensitivity Analysis in Linear Programming Models with Common Inputs," *Decision Sciences* Vol. 22, No. 3, 1991, pp.512–518.

Gal, Tomas. *Postoptimal Analysis, Parametric Programming and Related Topics*. London: McGraw-Hill, 1979.

Perry, C., and K. C. Crellin. "The Precise Management Meaning of a Shadow Price." *Interfaces* Vol. 12, No. 2, April, 1982, pp.61–62.

Shearn, D. C. S. "Postoptimal Analysis in Linear Programming—The Right Examples." *IIE Transactions* Vol. 16, No.1, 1984, pp. 99–101.

Winston, Wayne L. *Operations Research: Applications and Algorithms*. Belmont, CA: Duxbury Press, 3rd ed., 1994.

CHAPTER 7

MULTIPLE-OBJECTIVE

LINEAR

PROGRAMMING

MODELS

INTRODUCTION

3 goals

- Investing in a trucking terminal is one of the most crucial decisions a trucking firm faces. An important part of this decision is site selection because a poor location decision for a terminal can result in a loss of valued customers due to low quality service. If the company uses independent truckers (who own their own equipment), a poor site selection could also lead to a loss of reliable company workers, because the cost of traveling from home to the terminal and back is borne by the truckers. The liquid food division of Truck Transport Corporation used goal programming to evaluate potential sites for the relocation of their East St. Louis terminal (one of five terminals the division operates). The goal programming model was used to evaluate each site with respect to customer and driver satisfaction, transportation cost to the major customers, and the transportation cost to the homes of its independent truckers. The company chose a site based on the results of the goal programming analysis. The recommendation was implemented with minimal driver and customer turnover and no significant increase in transportation cost to the drivers [Schniederjans et al., 1982].

- The allocation of funds to competing research and development (R&D) projects can have a dramatic impact on the future growth of a company. Top management at Lord Corporation used goal programming to analyze the alternatives in allocating funds to 25 proposed R&D projects. Management established a variety of goals, including the following: (1) no program should consume more than 10% of the R&D budget; (2) sales growth should exceed 15%; (3) the discounted cash flow rate of return should exceed 30%; (4) projects should have five-year capital limits; and (5) the company should promote constructive change in the industry and be involved in the development of new technology. The goal programming approach allowed management to assess the conflict between the company's financial goals and the goals relating to corporate purpose, and to reach an allocation of R&D funds in line with the stated objectives of the company [Salvia and Ludwig, 1979].

- Designing a tax structure that generates the revenue required for city services and is equitable is a difficult problem that many cities face. The problem has many conflicting objectives, including maintaining adequate revenue levels for the funding of high-quality municipal services and schools, reducing property taxes to slow the flight of residents to the suburbs, reducing sales and payroll taxes to entice business investment, and minimizing the tax burden on low-income taxpayers. The city of Peoria, Illinois used multiobjective linear programming in order to better understand the alternative plans available and the trade-offs between conflicting objectives. The analysis provided a variety of solutions for consideration. The solution chosen called for an increase in the sales tax on general and durable goods, instituting a gasoline tax, and reducing property taxes and sales taxes on food and drugs. The solution maintains the revenue level required for services while shifting some of the burden to noncity residents [Chrisman et al., 1989].

In each of these examples, managers had several, and often conflicting, goals that they wanted to achieve. For example, the Truck Transport Corporation had objectives relating to customer and driver satisfaction and transportation costs. Solutions that might be good for customers, both in terms of satisfaction and cost, might be poor with respect to driver satisfaction and cost. Thus, the company had to find a solution that balanced these objectives. Similarly, the Lord Corporation and the City of Peoria had multiple goals they wanted to achieve.

In this chapter, we study *multiobjective linear programming*. Multiobjective LPs have the same assumptions as ordinary LPs: their objectives and constraint set must be linear functions of the decision variables, constraints must be of the =, ≤, or ≥ type, and fractional values for the decision variables are allowed. The major difference is that multi-objective LPs are better able to model practical problems that have multiple or conflicting objectives. The techniques we study in this chapter therefore allow us to greatly expand the types of problems that we can address with linear programming.

MULTIPLE OBJECTIVES IN LINEAR PROGRAMMING MODELS

It is sometimes difficult to specify a single objective for a given planning scenario. For example, a firm may wish to maximize profit and minimize the loss of customer goodwill simultaneously. An investor may wish to maximize expected return, but at the same time be sensitive to risk. A manufacturing firm might wish to maximize the amount of produc-tion capacity used, but keep little on-hand inventory. When multiple objectives exist and they are in conflict with one another, we need an approach for modelling and evaluating the trade-offs among the conflicting objectives. To illustrate this, consider the following example.

EXAMPLE 1. MULTIPLE CONFLICTING OBJECTIVES

Mary Trump has $1,000 she would like to invest in two options. Option 1 has an expected return of 6%. The risk associated with that option is measured by a risk factor, which is a measure of possible variation in the return. Option 1's risk factor is 4% (roughly speaking, it is likely that the real return on option 1 will be between 2% and 10%). Option 2 is a risk-free option that has a fixed return of 3%. Mary knows that it is not a good idea to put all of her eggs in one basket, so she has decided to invest at least $200, but no more than $700 in each of the two options. She would like to maximize return, but would also like to keep the risk at a minimum level. Because the bounds on each investment will force some diversification, Mary decided to ignore risk and develop an LP model to maximize expected return. She developed the following model.

x_1 = the amount (in dollars) to invest in option 1
x_2 = the amount (in dollars) to invest in option 2

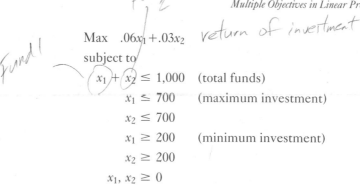

Max $.06x_1 + .03x_2$ *return of investment*
subject to
$$x_1 + x_2 \leq 1{,}000 \quad \text{(total funds)}$$
$$x_1 \leq 700 \quad \text{(maximum investment)}$$
$$x_2 \leq 700$$
$$x_1 \geq 200 \quad \text{(minimum investment)}$$
$$x_2 \geq 200$$
$$x_1, x_2 \geq 0$$

The feasible region and objective function contours for this model are shown in Figure 7.1. Point *d* is the unique optimal solution ($x_1 = 700, x_2 = 300$, with an expected return of $51). Note that this model completely ignores the risk factor information. The linear function that describes risk is $.04x_1 + 0.0x_2$, so that point *d* has a risk of $.04(700) + 0.0(300) = \$28$. (Note that this risk function applies only because option 2 is risk-free. Normally one cannot add measures of variation to obtain the risk of a portfolio.)

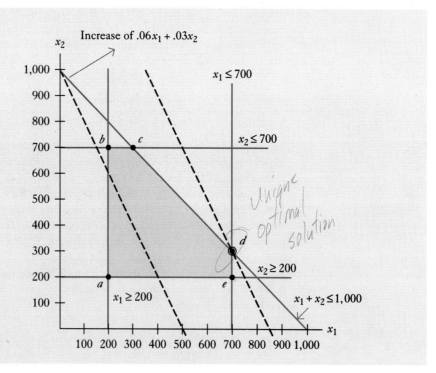

FIGURE 7.1   *The feasible region and objective function contours for the model that maximizes expected return*

Suppose that Mary completely ignores the return objective and makes her objective one of minimizing risk. The feasible region remains the same, but the expected return objective function will be replaced by the risk function $.04x_1 + 0.0x_2$.

$$\text{Min } .04x_1 + 0x_2 \quad ^0$$

subject to

$$x_1 + x_2 \leq 1,000 \quad \text{total funds}$$
$$x_1 \leq 700 \quad \Big\} \text{ max investment}$$
$$x_2 \leq 700$$
$$x_2 \geq 200 \quad \Big\} \text{ min investment cut}$$
$$x_2 \geq 200$$
$$x_1, x_2 \geq 0$$

The feasible region and contours for this model are shown in Figure 7.2. This model has alternate optimal solutions; corner points a ($x_1 = 200, x_2 = 200$, risk $= \$0$) and b ($x_1 = 200, x_2 = 700$, risk $= 0$) are optimal, as are any points on the line segment from a to b.

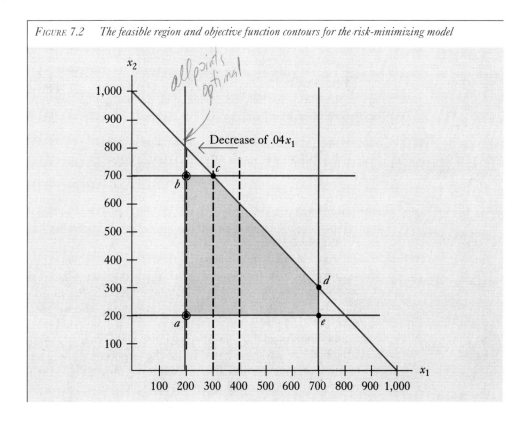

FIGURE 7.2 *The feasible region and objective function contours for the risk-minimizing model*

Mary's second model completely ignores return. The alternate optimal corner point solutions (points *a* and *b*) both give a risk of $28, but point *a* has an expected return of .06(200) + .03(200) = $18, and point *b* has an expected return of .06(200) + .03(700) = $33. If Mary is concerned about both risk and return, she would clearly never choose point *a* over point *b*, because point *b* has the same risk with a higher expected return. With regard to the two objectives of minimizing risk and maximizing return, we say that point *a* *is dominated* by point *b*. A point is dominated if there is another feasible point with strictly better return and the same risk, or a point with a smaller amount of risk for the same return. Mary now is faced with the decision of which of the investment plans to choose.

Plan	Option 1	Option 2	Expected Return	Risk
I	$700	$300	$51	$28
II	$200	$700	$33	$ 8

Plan I has a high return, but also a high risk; plan II has low risk, but a lower return. Neither solution is "better" than the other. Which solution she chooses will be determined by how Mary feels about the trade-off between risk and return (higher expected return comes at the expense of higher risk). How an individual makes such a choice will be addressed in Chapter 12, where we discuss decision analysis.

To assist managers in making decisions with multiple objectives, we need a method of dealing with the trade-offs among them. We will describe two approaches: *weighted objectives* and *absolute priorities*.

Weighted Objective Approach

A simple approach to handling multiple conflicting objectives is to weight the different objectives according to their importance, combine them into a single linear objective, and then solve the linear program with this new combined objective. This approach relies on the subjective judgment of the decision-maker to determine the relative importance of each of the objectives.

We may assume without loss of generality that the weightings of each objective are nonnegative and that they sum to one. Any statement like *objective 1 is 4 times as important as objective 2* can be modeled according to the above rule by simply normalizing the weights. Because 4 + 1 = 5, the first objective would be weighted by 4/5 = .8, and the second objective by 1/5 = .2. If objectives 1 and 2 are roughly the same order of magnitude and we minimize the combined weighted objective = .8 (objective 1) + .2 (objective 2), then objective 1 will have four times the importance of objective 2.

It is important to realize that the multiple objectives must have the same order of magnitude. If the decision variables have objective function coefficients of approximately the same magnitude, then this requirement will be satisfied. If the coefficients vary a great amount over the different objectives, then one or more of the objectives will have to be scaled by dividing through by a constant. Otherwise, an objective that has much larger coefficients than other objectives will have an excessive amount of importance in the combined objectives.

To illustrate this, suppose that we would like to maximize (objective 1) $= 2x_1 + x_2$. Suppose that we would also like to maximize (objective 2) $= 210x_1 + 320x_2$, and that objective 1 is three times as important as objective 2. We would use the following weights to normalize: $3/(3 + 1) = .75$ for objective 1 and $1/(3 + 1) = .25$ for objective 2. The combined objective is $.75(2x_1 + x_2) + .25(210x_1 + 320x_2) = 54x_1 + 80.75x_2$. Notice that the coefficients are relatively large, and that x_2's coefficient is much larger than that of x_1, even though x_1's coefficient is twice that of x_2's in our most important objective. Because objective 2's coefficients are so large relative to objective 1's, our weightings are insignificant. If we scale the second objective by dividing it by 100, its coefficients are the same magnitude as objective 1's, and the combined objective is $.75(2x_1 + x_2) + .25(2.1x_1 + 3.2x_2) = 2.025x_1 + 1.55x_2$. Now objective 1 will have three times the influence of objective 2 in determining the coefficients of the combined objective. Notice that this combined objective more closely matches objective 1 in terms of the differences in the coefficients of x_1 and x_2.

EXAMPLE 2. WEIGHTED OBJECTIVE APPROACH TO MULTIPLE OBJECTIVES

Suppose that Mary, the investor from Example 1, believes that maximizing expected return is four times as important as minimizing risk. We can create a single objective using the following steps:

1. Because we have both max and min objectives, we must convert one of them so that we can combine the objectives into a single objective. We can convert the minimization of the risk function to a maximization objective by changing the signs of the coefficients; that is, {Min $.04x_1$} is the same as {Max $- .04x_1$}.

2. Multiply each objective by its weight and add them together. By weighting the return objective by .8 and the risk objective by .2 in this combined objective, the return objective will have four times the influence of the risk objective. We use weights of .8 and .2 to give: .8 (expected return) + .2 $(-\text{risk}) = .8(.06x_1 + .03x_2) + .2(-.04x_1) = .04x_1 + .024x_2$.

We can now solve Mary's problem with the linear program.

$$\text{Max } .04x_1 + .024x_2$$

subject to

$$x_1 + x_2 \leq 1{,}000$$
$$x_1 \leq 700$$
$$x_2 \leq 700$$
$$x_1 \geq 200$$
$$x_2 \geq 200$$
$$x_1, x_2 \geq 0$$

The optimal solution to this problem is point d, as shown in Figure 7.3. The optimal solution is \$700 in option 1 and \$300 in option 2, with an objective function value of 35.2. The objective function has no direct meaning other than the optimal value of the combined weighted objectives. Of more interest is that the expected profit at point d is $.06(700) + .03(300) = \$51$ and the risk is $.04(700) = \$28$. (Note that $.8(51) + .2(-28) = 35.2$). Thus, we must evaluate each objective at the optimal point.

The weighted objective function approach can be summarized in the following manner.

The Weighted Objective Approach

1. Decide the relative importance of each objective.
2. Convert all objectives to either maximizations or minimizations. An objective can be converted to the other type by changing the signs on its coefficients.
3. Make sure that the objectives are all of the same order of magnitude. This may require scaling one or more of the objectives.
4. Create a weighted objective by multiplying each objective by its weight and adding together all objectives.
5. Solve the linear program with the combined weighted objective.
6. Evaluate each objective at the optimal solution to determine the achievement of each individual objective.

The combined weighting approach provides a means of generating a variety of solutions for different importance weightings. In Example 2, for instance, for general weights w_1 for expected return and w_2 for risk, Mary's objective could be written as $\text{Max } w_1(.06x_1 + .03x_2) + w_2(-.04x_1)$ or $\text{Max } (.06w_1 - .04w_2)x_1 + .03w_1x_2$. Table 7.1 gives the objective function, the solution, and the expected return and risk as we vary the weights by .1.

As we saw in Example 1, the extreme of ignoring return ($w_1 = 0$) as an objective results in alternative optimal solutions (points a and b in Figure 7.2). The other extreme of ignoring risk ($w_2 = 0$) results in a unique optimal solution (point d in Figure 7.1). Objectives that are compromises between these two extremes may lead to solutions different than the solutions obtained by any of the individual objectives. Point c, which is the optimal solution for equal weightings in Figure 7.3, is an example of this.

Figure 7.4 is a plot of risk and return for each of the corner point solutions generated, as well as corner point e in Figure 7.3 (which is $x_1 = 200$, $x_2 = 200$, return = \$48 and risk = \$28). Any points below the dashed border connecting points $b, c,$ and d, are dominated points according to the definition we established in Example 1.

FIGURE 7.3   *The optimal solution of Mary's investment problem with weightings of .8 for return and .2 for risk*

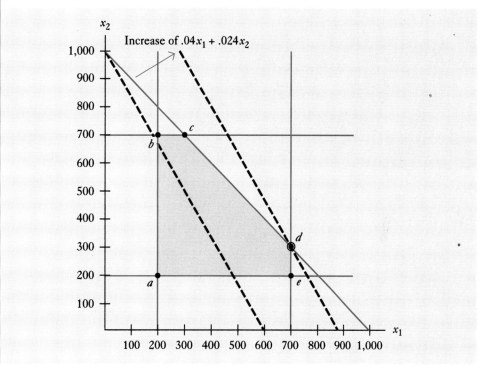

TABLE 7.1
Solutions for various weightings of return and risk

w_1	w_2	Objective Function	x_1	x_2	Return	Risk
.0	1.0	$-.04x_1 + .00x_2$	200	200	$18	$8
			200	700	$33	$8
.1	.9	$-.03x_1 + .003x_2$	200	700	$33	$8
.2	.8	$-.02x_1 + .006x_2$	200	700	$33	$8
.3	.7	$-.01x_1 + .009x_2$	200	700	$33	$8
.4	.6	$.00x_1 + .012x_2$	200	700	$33	$8
.5	.5	$.01x_1 + .015x_2$	300	700	$39	$12
.6	.4	$.02x_1 + .018x_2$	700	300	$51	$28
.7	.3	$.03x_1 + .021x_2$	700	300	$51	$28
.8	.2	$.04x_1 + .024x_2$	700	300	$51	$28
.9	.1	$.05x_1 + .027x_2$	700	300	$51	$28
1.0	.0	$.06x_1 + .03x_2$	700	300	$51	$28

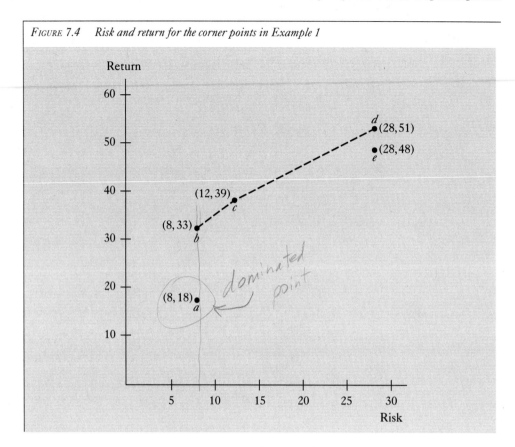

Figure 7.4 *Risk and return for the corner points in Example 1*

Absolute Priorities Approach

*high to low
solve
series
of
LPs*

A second approach to dealing with multiple objectives in linear programs is known as the *absolute priorities approach*. In this approach, we rank objectives from highest to lowest priority and then solve a series of linear programs. We use the objective function in the first LP problem as the highest priority objective . In the second LP, we use the objective function of the highest priority goal as a constraint, fixed at the value achieved in the first LP. We then solve the second LP and record its objective value. The third LP has the third ranking objective as its objective, and constraints that set the first and second objectives equal to the values found in the first two LPs. We continue this process of replacing each objective with the next one in the priority list and locking in all previous objectives at their achieved values until all objectives have been evaluated.

EXAMPLE 3. ABSOLUTE PRIORITIES APPROACH TO MULTIPLE OBJECTIVES

In Mary's investment problem, there are only two objectives. Suppose that Mary determines that maximizing return is a higher-priority objective than minimizing risk.

Priority 1 objective: Max $.06x_1 + .03x_2$ — return of investment

Priority 2 objective: Min $.04x_1$ — risk.

We solve the first problem using the priority 1 objective.

$$\text{Max } .06x_1 + 0.3x_2$$

subject to

$$x_1 + x_2 \leq 1{,}000 \quad \text{total investment}$$
$$x_1 \leq 700 \quad \Big\rbrace \quad \text{max investment in each fund}$$
$$x_2 \leq 700$$
$$x_1 \geq 200 \quad \Big\rbrace \quad \text{min investment in each fund}$$
$$x_2 \geq 200$$
$$x_1, x_2 \geq 0$$

As we have already seen in Example 1, this leads to the unique solution $x_1 = 700, x_2 = 300$ (point d in Figure 7.1). The maximum return is $51. Next, we solve for the priority 2 objective while ensuring that the value of expected return remains $51. from point d

$$\text{Min } .04x_1$$

subject to

$$x_1 + x_2 \leq 1{,}000$$
$$x_1 \leq 700$$
$$x_2 \leq 700$$
$$x_1 \geq 200$$
$$x_2 \geq 200$$
$$.06x_1 + .03x_2 = 51$$
$$x_1, x_2 \geq 0$$

Note that because there is only one point in the feasible region that yields a maximum profit of $51, the feasible region for this problem is a single point, namely point d in Figure 7.1. As we have seen, the risk associated with this point is $28. Anytime a higher-priority objective leads to a unique optimal solution, the feasible region for the lower-priority goals will be a single point, and no change in the solution can occur as lower priority objectives are introduced. However, if there are alternative optimal solutions for an objective, then this approach finds the alternative optimal solution that best satisfies the next objective.

important

To see what would happen if the objective priorities are reversed, suppose that Mary ranks risk minimization as her first priority. Thus, she first solves the LP.

reversing priorities now

$$\text{Min } .04x_1$$

subject to

$$x_1 + x_2 \leq 1{,}000$$
$$x_1 \leq 700$$
$$x_2 \leq 700$$
$$x_1 \geq 200$$
$$x_2 \geq 200$$
$$x_1, x_2 \geq 0$$

From Figure 7.2, we know that points *a* and *b* (and all points on the line segment from *a* to *b*) are alternative optimal solutions to this problem with objective function values of $8. In the second LP, we maximize return and make the risk objective a constraint set equal to 8.

$$\text{Max } .06x_1 + .03x_2$$

subject to

$$x_1 + x_2 \leq 1{,}000$$
$$x_1 \leq 700$$
$$x_2 \leq 700$$
$$x_1 \geq 200$$
$$x_2 \geq 200$$
$$.04x_1 = 8$$
$$x_1, x_2 \geq 0$$

The feasible region for this problem is the line segment from *a* to *b* in Figure 7.2. The unique solution to this problem is point *b*, because of all solutions with a risk of $8, it has the highest return ($33). Therefore, point *b* is the solution for this ranking of priorities.

see p. 325 for figure

The advantage the absolute priorities approach to multiple objectives has over the weighted objective approach is that only a ranking of the priorities (rather than a specification of weights) is required. However, the absolute priorities approach does not really trade off one objective with another, and as we have seen, once a unique solution is encountered, the achievement of the objectives of lower ranking is fixed. In the next section, we discuss an alternative approach, called goal programming, that implicitly creates a more flexible model that increases the existence of alternative optimal solutions.

GOAL PROGRAMMING

Goal programming is an approach to multiple objective scenarios in which each of the objectives has a *target* or goal. For example, rather than specifying that machine utilization should be maximized, a manager might wish to "come as close as possible to 95%

capacity utilization." A company might wish to minimize the amount by which they are under their sales target of $2,000,000, while minimizing overtime. A distribution manager might seek to minimize the amount of inventory held over some buffer target level, while also minimizing the number of back orders over some specified allowance.

Because weighting or absolute priorities approaches may be used, goal programming is similar to the approaches we have already discussed in this chapter. Its distinguishing feature is that the objectives can be stated as minimizing deviations from prespecified goals. We describe goals mathematically, using constraints known as soft constraints or goal constraints.

Hard Versus Soft Constraints *in Goal Programming*

In most LPs, constraints represent limitations or requirements that must be met. If these constraints are not under the control of the decision-maker, we call them *hard constraints*. For example, we may have only a limited supply of raw material available—a manager might not be able to get more, or production might be limited by the available machinery.

In other situations, constraints are somewhat arbitrary. For example, a division manager might have a limited operating budget, but the budget might be negotiable. For planning purposes, the budget is simply a target. Corporate management might allow it to be exceeded if other important objectives can be improved. Thus, the budget constraint would be an example of a *soft constraint* because it can be violated.

The solution to an ordinary LP does not allow a constraint to be violated. Thus, we need a way of modeling soft constraints. To show how to do this, consider Mary's investment problem from Example 1.

EXAMPLE 4. USING DEVIATIONAL VARIABLES

Suppose that Mary wants to maximize return as the objective, subject to the specified constraints on budget and investment amounts in each option, along with some added restriction on the maximum amount of risk. For example, suppose that Mary's desired maximum amount of risk is $12. We would simply add the constraint $.04x_1 \leq 12$.

On the other hand, suppose that Mary sets a risk target of $12, but is flexible enough that risk could be either above or below that target level. This means that the constraint could allow either slack or surplus, and this idea provides the modeling key. We write the constraint as an equality with both slack and surplus variables.

risk target $.04x_1 + s_1 - r_1 = 12.$ *goal restraint*

Here, s_1 is a slack variable that gives the amount of risk under 12, and r_1 is a surplus variable that gives the amount of risk over 12. Both s_1 and r_1 are nonnegative. The actual risk is therefore allowed to be less than or greater than 12. This is called a goal constraint.

In a similar fashion, suppose that Mary sets a goal of $45 for the expected return. We can model this as a goal constraint.

return target $.06x_1 + .03x_2 + s_2 - r_2 = 45.$

Here, s_2 is a slack variable, indicating the shortfall of the target of $45, and r_2 is a surplus variable for the amount of profit over the target of $45.

If we add these constraints to the model in Example 1, we get

$$\text{Min} \ .04x_1$$

subject to

$$x_1 + x_2 \leq 1{,}000$$
$$x_1 \leq 700$$
$$x_2 \leq 700$$
$$x_1 \geq 200$$
$$x_2 \geq 200$$
$$.04x_1 + s_1 - r_1 = 12 \quad \text{risk target}$$
$$.06x_1 + .03x_2 + s_2 - r_2 = 45 \quad \text{return target}$$
$$x_1, x_2, s_1, s_2, r_1, r_2 \geq 0$$

These goal constraints really place no new restrictions on the problem. It is feasible to be above or below the target of $12 for risk and to be above or below the target of $45 return. The feasible region for this model is shown in Figure 7.5. The bold lines indicate the points that meet each goal exactly. Notice that in this example, the two goal lines do not intersect in the original feasible region. This indicates that it will not be possible to satisfy both goals exactly. Also, notice that if we try to use hard constraints $.04x_1 \leq 12$ and $.06x_1 + .03x_2 \geq 45$ to limit risk and ensure return, the problem will be infeasible!

Soft constraints define how far the solution is off target. The slack and surplus variables associated with each goal are sometimes referred to as *deviational variables* because they indicate how far the solution deviates from the target.

We may use these deviational variables to define an objective function to minimize deviations from the goals. For example, because r_1 measures the amount by which the risk exceeds 12, if we replace the objective in Example 4 with the objective of {Min r_1}, the LP would minimize the amount of risk over Mary's target of 12. Thus, any solution with risk less than or equal to 12 will yield an objective function value of zero. An objective of {Min $s_1 + r_1$} would minimize the amount of risk above or below the target of 12. Hence, this objective seeks to meet the target of 12 exactly. Only those solutions with a risk of 12 will give an objective function value of zero.

For multiple objectives involving deviational variables, we can either use weighted combinations of the deviational variables as the objective function, or a sequential absolute priorities approach.

Weighted Objective Approach

The weighted objective approach in goal programming uses linear weighted combinations of deviational variables as the objective of the linear program. To make sure that

FIGURE 7.5   *The feasible region of Example 1 with soft constraints for expected return and risk*

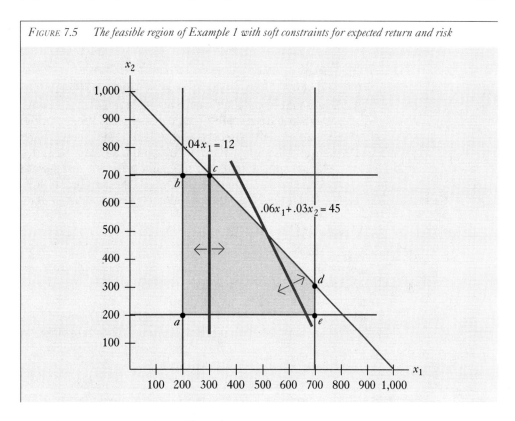

the weights have the desired effect of enforcing relative importance, we must ensure that each constraint is roughly the same order of magnitude.

EXAMPLE 5. GOAL PROGRAMMING USING A WEIGHTED OBJECTIVE

We continue Mary Trump's investment problem. Suppose that Mary sets goals for the expected return at \$45 and risk at \$12. She wishes to achieve an expected return of at least \$45 and a risk no greater than \$12. Thus, she wants to drive s_2 and r_1 to zero if possible. She considers the return goal three times as important as the risk goal, so we may use weights of .75 for s_2 and .25 for r_1. We note that the soft constraints are both in dollars, and that their right-hand side values are comparable in size. The weighting will therefore have the desired effect. We can use the following model:

$$\text{Min } .25r_1 + .75s_2$$
subject to
$$
\begin{aligned}
x_1 + x_2 &\le 1{,}000 \\
x_1 &\le 700 \\
x_2 &\le 700 \\
x_1 &\ge 200 \\
x_2 &\ge 200
\end{aligned}
\left.\rule{0pt}{5.5em}\right\} \text{hard constraints}
$$

$$.04x_1 + s_1 - r_1 = 12$$
$$.06x_1 + .03x_2 + s_2 - r_2 = 45$$
$$\left.\right\} \text{ soft constraints}$$
$$x_1, x_2, s_1, r_1, s_2, r_2 \geq 0$$

The LINDO model and solution are shown in Figure 7.6. With these weightings, Mary should invest $500 in each of the options, which results in an expected return of exactly $45 and a risk of $20 (note that $r_1 = 8$ in the solution). Because the weight for expected return is three times that of risk, the amount of return under $45 is driven to zero and the risk goal cannot be completely achieved.

As shown in Figure 7.7, the point $x_1 = 500$ and $x_2 = 500$ is formed by the intersection of the budget constraint and the goal line for return. On the goal line for expected return, the solution found is the point closest to the goal line for risk.

Absolute Priority Goals *in Goal Programming*

We can also use the absolute priorities approach to solve goal programs. When we can specify targets or goal levels and can rank them in order of importance, we can solve the problem using the absolute priorities approach discussed previously. The highest priority goal is used as the objective function in the first LP and then it is locked into its level of achievement by a constraint in the second LP. The second LP's objective is the second highest priority goal. This process is continued until all of the goals have been optimized.

EXAMPLE 6. GOAL PROGRAMMING USING ABSOLUTE PRIORITIES

Consider Example 5, where Mary has expected return and risk goals of $45 and $12, respectively. Rather than specify the relative importance weights, she may wish to simply rank her goals in order of importance. For example, suppose that minimizing the amount under an expected return of $45 is ranked first, and minimizing the amount of risk over $12 is ranked second.

Priority 1 Goal: Min s_2 *expected return of $45*
Priority 2 Goal: Min r_1 *amount of risk*

Mary would first solve the LP

$$\text{Min } s_2$$
$$\text{subject to}$$
$$x_1 + x_2 \leq 1,000$$
$$x_1 \leq 700$$
$$x_2 \leq 700$$
$$x_1 \geq 200$$
$$x_2 \geq 200$$
$$.04x_1 + s_1 - r_1 = 12 \quad \text{risk}$$
$$.06x_1 + .03x_2 + s_2 - r_2 = 45 \quad \text{return}$$
$$x_1, x_2, s_1, r_1, s_2, r_2 \geq 0$$

```
MIN        0.25 R1 + 0.75 S2
SUBJECT TO
        2)   X1 + X2 <= 1000
        3)   X1 <= 700
        4)   X2 <= 700
        5)   X1 >= 200
        6)   X2 >= 200
        7)  -R1 + 0.04X1 + S1  = 12
        8)   S2 + 0.06X1 + 0.03X2 - R2 = 45
END

        OBJECTIVE FUNCTION VALUE

        1)      2.0000000
```

VARIABLE	VALUE	REDUCED COST
R1	8.000001	.000000
S2	.000000	.416667
X1	500.000000	.000000
X2	500.000000	.000000
S1	.000000	.250000
R2	.000000	.333333

ROW	SLACK OR SURPLUS	DUAL PRICES
2)	.000000	.010000
3)	200.000000	.000000
4)	200.000000	.000000
5)	300.000000	.000000
6)	300.000000	.000000
7)	.000000	.250000
8)	.000000	-.333333

NO. ITERATIONS = 5

RANGES IN WHICH THE BASIS IS UNCHANGED:

OBJ COEFFICIENT RANGES

VARIABLE	CURRENT COEF	ALLOWABLE INCREASE	ALLOWABLE DECREASE
R1	.250000	.312500	.250000
S2	.750000	INFINITY	.416667
X1	.000000	.012500	.010000
X2	.000000	.012500	.012500
S1	.000000	INFINITY	.250000
R2	.000000	INFINITY	.333333

333

ROW	RIGHTHAND SIDE RANGES		
	CURRENT RHS	ALLOWABLE INCREASE	ALLOWABLE DECREASE
2	1000.000000	100.000000	150.000000
3	700.000000	INFINITY	200.000000
4	700.000000	INFINITY	200.000000
5	200.000000	300.000000	INFINITY
6	200.000000	300.000000	INFINITY
7	12.000000	8.000001	INFINITY
8	45.000000	5.999999	6.000000

The LINDO model and solution are shown in Figure 7.8. The first goal is totally satisfied because $s_2 = 0$. The solution is to invest \$500 in each option. The geometry of this LP is shown in Figure 7.9. The shaded region is the set of alternative optimal solutions to this LP. Any point in the shaded region is feasible to the hard constraints and gives $s_2 = 0$ (the amount by which the expected return is under \$45 is zero for

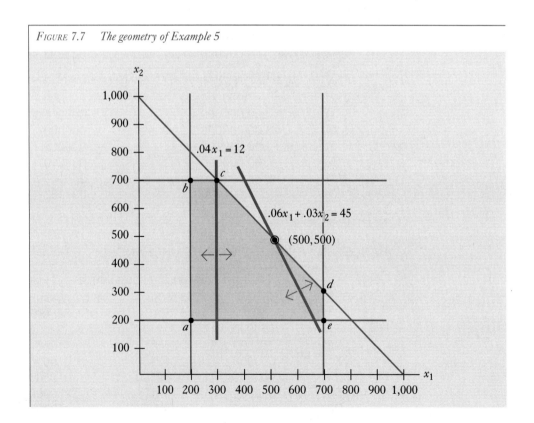

FIGURE 7.7   *The geometry of Example 5*

FIGURE 7.8   *The LINDO model and solution for the first LP of the absolute priority goal programming approach with deviational variables*

```
MIN        S2
SUBJECT TO
        2) X1 + X2 <= 1000
        3) X1 <= 700
        4) X2 <= 700
        5) X1 >= 200
        6) X2 >= 200
        7) 0.04X1 - R1 + S1 = 12
        8) S2 + 0.06X1 + 0.03X2 - R2 = 45
END



                OBJECTIVE FUNCTION VALUE


        1)      .00000000


        VARIABLE            VALUE        REDUCED COST
            S2            .000000            1.000000
            X1         500.000000             .000000
            X2         500.000000             .000000
            R1           8.000001             .000000
            S1            .000000             .000000
            R2            .000000             .000000


        ROW     SLACK OR SURPLUS        DUAL PRICES
            2)            .000000             .000000
            3)         200.000000             .000000
            4)         200.000000             .000000
            5)         300.000000             .000000
            6)         300.000000             .000000
            7)            .000000             .000000
            8)            .000000             .000000


    NO. ITERATIONS = 5



    RANGES IN WHICH THE BASIS IS UNCHANGED:
```

OBJ COEFFICIENT RANGES

VARIABLE	CURRENT COEF	ALLOWABLE INCREASE	ALLOWABLE DECREASE
S2	1.000000	INFINITY	1.000000
X1	.000000	.030000	.000000
X2	.000000	.000000	.030000
R1	.000000	.750000	.000000
S1	.000000	INFINITY	.000000
R2	.000000	INFINITY	.000000

RIGHTHAND SIDE RANGES

ROW	CURRENT RHS	ALLOWABLE INCREASE	ALLOWABLE DECREASE
2	1000.000000	100.000000	150.000000
3	700.000000	INFINITY	200.000000
4	700.000000	INFINITY	200.000000
5	200.000000	300.000000	INFINITY
6	200.000000	300.000000	INFINITY
7	12.000000	8.000001	INFINITY
8	45.000000	5.999999	6.000000

FIGURE 7.9   *The geometry of the first LP model in the absolute priorities approach, Example 6*

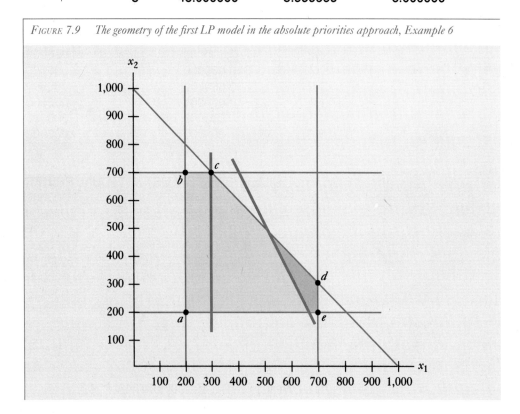

these points; that is, they all give an expected return of $45 or higher). The second LP Mary must solve is to minimize r_1 with the added restriction that $s_2 = 0$. With this added restriction, the feasible region for the second LP is the set of points shaded in Figure 7.9. The LINDO model and solution output are shown in Figure 7.10. Note that the solution did not change. This is because the solution to the first LP is the point in the shaded region that is closest to the goal line for risk and it gives the smallest value of r_1. Because $r_1 = 8$, the second goal is not completely satisfied.

FIGURE 7.10   *The LINDO model and solution to the second LP in the absolute-priorities approach to Example 2.*

```
MIN        R1
SUBJECT TO
          2) X1 + X2 <= 1000
          3) X1 <= 700
          4) X2 <= 700
          5) X1 >= 200
          6) X2 >= 200
          7) 0.04X1 − R1 + S1 = 12
          8) S2 + 0.06X1 + 0.03X2 − R2 = 45
          9) S2 = 0
END

          OBJECTIVE FUNCTION VALUE

       1)      8.0000010
```

VARIABLE	VALUE	REDUCED COST
R1	8.000001	.000000
X1	500.000000	.000000
X2	500.000000	.000000
S1	.000000	1.000000
S2	.000000	.000000
R2	.000000	1.333333

ROW	SLACK OR SURPLUS	DUAL PRICES
2)	.000000	.040000
3)	200.000000	.000000
4)	200.000000	.000000
5)	300.000000	.000000
6)	300.000000	.000000

7)	.000000	1.000000
8)	.000000	−1.333333
9)	.000000	1.333333

NO. ITERATIONS = 5

RANGES IN WHICH THE BASIS IS UNCHANGED:

OBJ COEFFICIENT RANGES

VARIABLE	CURRENT COEF	ALLOWABLE INCREASE	ALLOWABLE DECREASE
R1	1.000000	INFINITY	1.000000
X1	.000000	INFINITY	.040000
X2	.000000	.020000	INFINITY
S1	.000000	INFINITY	1.000000
S2	.000000	INFINITY	INFINITY
R2	.000000	INFINITY	1.333333

RIGHTHAND SIDE RANGES

ROW	CURRENT RHS	ALLOWABLE INCREASE	ALLOWABLE DECREASE
2	1000.000000	100.000000	150.000000
3	700.000000	INFINITY	200.000000
4	700.000000	INFINITY	200.000000
5	200.000000	300.000000	INFINITY
6	200.000000	300.000000	INFINITY
7	12.000000	8.000001	INFINITY
8	45.000000	5.999999	6.000000
9	.000000	6.000000	.000000

SUMMARY OF THE MULTIOBJECTIVE APPROACHES

Table 7.2 provides a summary of when to use each of the four approaches to multiobjective scenarios. The weighted objective approach requires subjective weighting factors, but the absolute priorities approach requires only a ranking of the objectives. Goal programming requires that the objectives have goals or targets, whereas no targets are required for the multiobjective LP approach.

TABLE 7.2
Summary of the multi-objective approaches

	Weighted Objective	Absolute Priorities
Multiobjective LP	No Targets	No Targets
	Importance Weights	Ranking of Objectives
Goal Programming	Targets	Targets
	Importance Weights	Ranking of Goals

MANAGEMENT SCIENCE PRACTICE[1]

In the opening scenario, we discussed the issues faced by Truck Transport Corporation in selecting a site for a trucking terminal. Deciding whether or not a new facility is needed and where it should be located is not a trivial matter. Typically, a facility location analysis will consist of three stages. First, a market study is conducted to ascertain whether or not changes in demand warrant a closer look at the relocation of an existing facility or perhaps the creation of a new facility. Second, if stage one indicates that a new location is prudent, a broad region is identified for possible location of the facility. Finally, the third stage involves the actual site selection within the region defined by stage two. In this Management Science Practice case, we discuss the third stage of a site selection project at Truck Transport Corporation.

Goal Programming for Site Selection: Truck Transport Corporation

The liquid foods division of Truck Transport Corporation uses five terminals to service its customers. Each terminal must recruit and maintain a force of independent truckers. The independent truckers own their own vehicles, but work for the company delivering goods to its customers. Truck Transport Company, after proceeding through stages one and two of the location analysis, has decided on five potential sites for the relocation of its East St. Louis terminal. The need for a systematic approach to evaluating each of the five candidates was met with the application of a goal programming model.

Because the problem had multiple conflicting objectives, a goal programming model was used to evaluate the candidate sites. The traditional objective of minimizing the cost of the transportation of goods to the customers had to be considered, but because Truck Transport used independent truckers, their satisfaction with a new facility also had to be taken into account. The cost of driving a truck from the trucker's home to the terminal is a cost borne by the trucker, and if the new facility put an excessive cost on the drivers, they might jump ship and go to another trucking company. The willingness (or lack of willingness) of each trucker currently on the work force to work with certain managers assigned to the existing or the new facility also needed to be considered. Previous studies

[1] Adapted from Schniederjans *et al.* "An Application of Goal Programming to Resolve a Site Location Problem," *Interfaces* Vol. 12, No. 3, June 1982, pp. 65–72.

had shown that dissatisfaction with managers at different terminals was a major reason for drivers leaving the firm. Likewise, certain customers did not work well with some of the managers. Truck Transport therefore needed to develop a model that considered both customer and employee satisfaction, as well as the cost of drivers getting to and from work and the cost of the transport of goods to its customers. The company used data for 12 major customers and 22 drivers in the goal programming model. The following five goals (in order of priority) were used.

1. Minimize the deviation from the average number of trips required by each of the customers. Minimize the deviation from the requested number of trips for each driver.
2. Minimize the number of undesirable assignments of drivers to terminal managers.
3. Minimize the number of undesirable assignments of customers to terminal managers.
4. Minimize the transportation cost between the drivers' homes and the terminals.
5. Minimize the transportation cost from the terminals to the customers.

The goal programming model had 170 decision variables, 128 deviational variables, and 65 goal constraints. The model was run five times, each with the four fixed sites and one of the five candidate sites as the fifth location. The results appear in Table 7.3.

Each of the five candidate sites satisfies the first three goals. The required number of trips per driver and customer were satisfied and no drivers or customers were assigned to unacceptable terminals. The numbers given in Table 7.3 for the fourth and fifth goals are the estimated increase in cost for the trips from the drivers' homes to the terminals and from the terminals to the customers. Positive deviations for each candidate facility indicate that increases in these costs will occur regardless of the site that is selected. Because site B causes the least amount of increase for both the drivers and the customers, it was chosen as the site to replace the current East St. Louis terminal.

Six months after the move to location B, the operations manager reported that driver turnover was normal for the period, no significant change in customers occurred, and no complaints concerning excessive transportation costs from home to terminal were registered by the drivers.

Discussion Questions

1. Truck Transport chose site B as the solution because it dominated the other solutions. Which of the four remaining sites do you believe is the next best solution? Why?

TABLE 7.3
The results of the five goal programming runs for the truck transport site location problem

		Goal Deviations By Candidate Site				
Priority		A	B	C	D	E
1 (Required Trips)		0	0	0	0	0
2 (Driver Preference)		0	0	0	0	0
3 (Customer Satisfaction)		0	0	0	0	0
4 (Driver Transportation Cost)		17.3	3.2	10.2	25.1	8.0($000)
5 (Customer Transportation Cost)		13.7	1.4	1.6	23.0	2.5($000)

2. What costs that are not explicitly mentioned here might be relevant to the site location decision? Give a rationale as to why these costs were not considered.
3. Why do you think Truck Transport chose the priority of goals 1 through 5 as they did? Generally speaking, how might the solution differ if the order of priority was reversed?

MORE EXAMPLES AND SOLVED PROBLEMS

EXAMPLE 7. PRODUCTION PLANNING AND ZERO INVENTORY

A company is planning production of one of its products for the next four weeks. The demand for these weeks will be 90, 100, 150, and 180 units. The cost to hold a unit in inventory is $10 per unit per week. The cost to produce a unit is $200 in weeks 1, 2, and 4, and $210 in week 3. The production planner's responsibility is to develop a cost-minimizing production schedule.

The production planner has lately been reading about the "just-in-time" philosophy of production. If possible, he would like to develop a schedule that has a minimum amount of inventory. However, he recognizes that cost minimization should be the number one priority (if holding inventory is cost-effective, then it should be carried). He has decided on the following ranking of objectives:

Priority 1: Minimize total cost
Priority 2: Minimize the amount of inventory held

We can solve this problem using multiobjective linear programming with absolute priorities. Let

$$X_i = \text{the number of units to produce in week } i$$

$$I_i = \text{the number of units to hold in inventory at the end of week } i.$$

The only constraints for this model are inventory balance equations and nonnegativity. To first minimize total cost (production cost + inventory cost), we use an LP model with that objective and inventory balance equations (for each week: starting inventory + production − ending inventory = demand). This model is shown in Figure 7.11. The cost-minimizing solution (also shown in Figure 7.11) is to produce 90 in week 1, 270 in week 2, 180 in week 4, and to carry 120 units in inventory from period 2 to 3. The minimum total cost is $109,200.

FIGURE 7.11   *LINDO model and solution to Example 7 with cost minimization objective.*

```
MIN       200 X1 + 200 X2 + 210 X3 + 200 X4 +
             10 I1 + 10 I2 + 10 I3 + 10 I4
SUBJECT TO
          2)   X1 − I1 = 90
          3)   X2 + I1 − I2 = 150
          4)   X3 + I2 − I3 = 120
          5)   X4 + I3 − I4 = 180
END
```

OBJECTIVE FUNCTION VALUE

1)   109200.00

VARIABLE	VALUE	REDUCED COST
X1	90.000000	.000000
X2	270.000000	.000000
X3	.000000	.000000
X4	180.000000	.000000
I1	.000000	10.000000
I2	120.000000	.000000
I3	.000000	20.000000
I4	.000000	210.000000

ROW	SLACK OR SURPLUS	DUAL PRICES
2)	.000000	−200.000000
3)	.000000	−200.000000
4)	.000000	−210.000000
5)	.000000	−200.000000

NO. ITERATIONS = 4

RANGES IN WHICH THE BASIS IS UNCHANGED:

OBJ COEFFICIENT RANGES

VARIABLE	CURRENT COEF	ALLOWABLE INCREASE	ALLOWABLE DECREASE
X1	200.000000	INFINITY	10.000000
X2	200.000000	.000000	20.000000
X3	210.000000	INFINITY	.000000
X4	200.000000	20.000000	210.000000
I1	10.000000	INFINITY	10.000000
I2	10.000000	.000000	20.000000
I3	10.000000	INFINITY	20.000000
I4	10.000000	INFINITY	210.000000

RIGHTHAND SIDE RANGES

ROW	CURRENT RHS	ALLOWABLE INCREASE	ALLOWABLE DECREASE
2	90.000000	INFINITY	90.000000
3	150.000000	INFINITY	270.000000
4	120.000000	INFINITY	120.000000
5	180.000000	INFINITY	180.000000

The second LP has the minimization of total inventory as its objective, with total cost fixed at $109,200. The LINDO model and solution output are shown in Figure 7.12. The new model has an additional constraint that sets the cost function equal to $109,200.

As shown in Figure 7.12 (to the delight of the production planner), there is a solution with a total cost of $109,200 and no inventory. The production plan satisfies both of his objectives.

FIGURE 7.12   *LINDO model and solution of Example 7 with inventory minimization objective.*

```
MIN        I1+I2+I3+I4
SUBJECT TO
       2) − I1 + X1 = 90
       3)   I1 − I2 + X2 = 150
       4)   I2 − I3 + X3 = 120
       5)   I3 − I4 + X4 = 180
       6)   10 I1 + 10 I2 + 10 I3 + 10 I4 + 200 X1 + 200 X2 +
                   210 X3 + 200 X4 = 109200
END

LP OPTIMUM FOUND AT STEP        3

            OBJECTIVE FUNCTION VALUE

        1)        .00000000

VARIABLE            VALUE          REDUCED COST
   I1            .000000             1.000000
   I2            .000000             1.000000
   I3            .000000             1.000000
   I4            .000000             1.000000
   X1          90.000000              .000000
   X2         150.000000              .000000
   X3         120.000000              .000000
   X4         180.000000              .000000


   ROW      SLACK OR SURPLUS        DUAL PRICES
    2)            .000000              .000000
    3)            .000000              .000000
    4)            .000000              .000000
    5)            .000000              .000000
    6)            .000000              .000000
```

NO. ITERATIONS = 3

RANGES IN WHICH THE BASIS IS UNCHANGED:

OBJ COEFFICIENT RANGES

VARIABLE	CURRENT COEF	ALLOWABLE INCREASE	ALLOWABLE DECREASE
I1	1.000000	INFINITY	1.000000
I2	1.000000	INFINITY	1.000000
I3	1.000000	INFINITY	1.000000
I4	1.000000	INFINITY	1.000000
X1	.000000	INFINITY	1.000000
X2	.000000	.952381	1.000000
X3	.000000	1.000000	1.000000
X4	.000000	1.000000	1.000000

RIGHTHAND SIDE RANGES

ROW	CURRENT RHS	ALLOWABLE INCREASE	ALLOWABLE DECREASE
2	90.000000	.000000	.000000
3	150.000000	.000000	.000000
4	120.000000	.000000	.000000
5	180.000000	.000000	.000000
6	109200.000000	.000000	.000000

EXAMPLE 8. CUSTOMER SATISFACTION

Heil Inc. is a company that produces custom-made stained glass windows. The company employs 35 craftsmen who each work a 40 hour week. Heil has orders in hand for next week, and its two major customers, Halmart and Window Warehouse, have ordered 150 and 120 windows respectively. Each window requires 10 hours of craftsman time. The owner of the company, Tom Heil, realizes that too much overtime would be required to meet these orders, and he would like to keep overtime under 200 hours. He has decided on the following goals:

1. Meet half of each customer's demand.
2. Keep overtime to 200 hours.
3. Meet each customer's demand.

Tom has decided that goal 1 is three times as important as goal 3 and that goal 2 is twice as important as goal 3. We define x_1 as the number of windows to produce for customer 1 and x_2 as the number of windows to produce for customer 2. A goal programming formulation of this scenario is

$$\text{Min } .1s_2 + .1s_3 + .3s_4 + .3s_5 + .2r_6$$

$$\text{subject to}$$

$$10x_1 + 10x_2 + s_1 - r_1 = 1{,}400$$
$$x_1 + s_2 - r_2 = 150$$
$$x_2 + s_3 - r_3 = 120$$
$$x_1 + s_4 - r_4 = 75$$
$$x_2 + s_5 - r_5 = 60$$
$$r_1 + s_6 - r_6 = 200$$
$$x_1, x_2, s_i, r_i \geq 0 \quad i = 1, 2, 3, 4, 5, 6$$

The first constraint specifies the deviations from the number of available worker hours (s_1 is unused hours and r_1 is overtime). Constraints two and three define the deviations from the customer demands (s_2 and s_3 are unmet demand, r_2 and r_3 are production in excess of demand). Constraints four and five define the deviations from the goal of meeting half of each customer's demand (s_4 and s_5 are amounts short of half of the demand, and r_4 and r_5 are the amounts over). Finally, the last constraint specifies the overtime target of 200 hours (recall that r_1 = the amount of overtime; s_6 is the amount that overtime is under 200, and r_6 is overtime in excess of 200 hours).

The objective function minimizes the amount of unmet demand (s_2 and s_3), the amount by which production is under half of each customer's demand (s_4 and s_5), and the amount of overtime in excess of 200 hours (r_6). The weightings are set in accordance with the importance of each goal.

The LINDO model and solution are shown in Figure 7.13. The solution is to produce 100 windows for Halmart and 60 for Window Warehouse. Note that the first two goals are completely met ($s_4 = 0, s_5 = 0$, and $r_6 = 0$) so that half of each customer's demand is met and no more than 200 hours of overtime are used. The third goal is not met. We are 50 short of meeting Halmart's demand ($s_2 = 50$) and 60 short of Window Warehouse's demand ($s_3 = 60$).

EXAMPLE 9. ALLOCATION OF ASSETS[2]

Goal programming has been used for financial portfolio development for over twenty years. The conflict between return and risk as well as the existence of various investor objectives make goal programming an ideal tool for portfolio construction. As we have previously mentioned, however, we need to be careful about how risk is measured. Not all measures of risk lend themselves to linear analysis. Arbitrate pricing theory (APT) provides a means of measuring risk in a form that can be incorporated into a linear model.

APT provides estimates of the sensitivity of a particular asset (investment) to a specific risk factor. The investor specifies a target level for the weighted risk factor. A linear constraint which requires that the weighted risk be equal to the desired level can then be constructed.

---

[2]Based on Schniederjans, M., Zorn, T., and R. Johnson. "Allocating Total Wealth: A Goal Programming Approach." *Computers and Operations Research* Vol. 20, No. 7, 1993, pp. 679–685.

FIGURE 7.13   *The LINDO model and solution to Example 8.*

```
MIN        0.3 S4+0.3 S5+0.1 S2+0.1 S3+0.2 R6
SUBJECT TO
       2)  − R1 + 10 X1 + 10 X2 + S1 = 1400
       3)    S2 + X1 − R2 = 150
       4)    S3 + X2 − R3 = 120
       5)    S4 + X1 − R4 = 75
       6)    S5 + X2 − R5 = 60
       7)  − R6 + R1 + S6 = 200
END
```

OBJECTIVE FUNCTION VALUE

       1)   11.000000

VARIABLE	VALUE	REDUCED COST
S4	.000000	.300000
S5	.000000	.300000
S2	50.000000	.000000
S3	60.000000	.000000
R6	.000000	.190000
R1	200.000000	.000000
X1	100.000000	.000000
X2	60.000000	.000000
S1	.000000	.010000
R2	.000000	.100000
R3	.000000	.100000
R4	25.000000	.000000
R5	.000000	.000000
S6	.000000	.010000

ROW	SLACK OR SURPLUS	DUAL PRICES
2)	.000000	.010000
3)	.000000	−.100000
4)	.000000	−.100000
5)	.000000	.000000
6)	.000000	.000000
7)	.000000	.010000

NO. ITERATIONS = 5

For example, John has $200,000 he would like to allocate to life insurance, bond mutual funds, stock mutual funds, and savings. The expected (1 year) returns are 6%, 6.5%, 11%, and 4% respectively. He has established the following lower and upper bounds on the allocations to the alternatives:

Asset	Lower Bound	Upper Bound
1. Life Insurance	$5,000	$10,000
2. Bond Mutual Funds	$60,000	None
3. Stock Mutual Funds	$30,000	None
4. Savings	None	None

s_i = shortfall of target

R_i = surplus

He considers two risk factors important: unexpected inflation and the spread between long and short-term interest rates. The risk factors per dollar allocated to each of the assets and the weighted target for these risk factors are given below.

	Asset				
Factor	1	2	3	4	Target
Inflation	−.5	1.8	2.1	−.3	1.0
Interest Spread	.4	−.5	0.0	−1.1	0.0

John's priorities are (in order of importance) to meet the bound restrictions, to achieve his desired risk levels, and to maximize return on investments.

We define x_i as the dollar amount to allocate to asset i; $i = 1, 2, 3, 4$. The following constraint set can be used with the various objectives for John's allocation problem.

$$
\begin{aligned}
x_1 + s_1 - r_1 &= 5,000 && \text{lower bound} \\
x_1 + s_2 - r_2 &= 10,000 && \text{upper bound} \\
x_2 + s_3 - r_3 &= 60,000 && \text{lower bound} \\
x_3 + s_4 - r_4 &= 30,000 && \text{lower bound} \\
-.5x_1 + 1.8x_2 + 2.1x_3 - .3x_4 + s_5 - r_5 &= 200,000 && \text{total investment} \\
.4x_1 - .5x_2 + 0x_3 - 1.1x_4 + s_6 - r_6 &= 0 && \text{interest spread} \\
.06x_1 + .065x_2 + .11x_3 + .04x_4 + s_7 - r_7 &= 22,000 && \text{expected return} \\
x_1 + x_2 + x_3 + x_4 &= 200,000 && \text{budget restraint} \\
x_i, s_j, r_j &\ge 0 \quad i = 1,2,3,4 \quad j = 1,2,\ldots 7
\end{aligned}
$$

Fund 1

The first four constraints are goal constraints on the bounds of allocation. The fifth and sixth constraints are the risk constraints (the right-hand side values are the desired risk factor ×200, 000). The seventh constraint is the expected return on investment constraint (we know that the expected return can be no more than the highest return of 11%, so the right-hand side has been set to 11% ×200, 000). Finally we have the budget constraint and nonnegativity restrictions.

The objectives to be used in an absolute priorities manner are

Priority 1: Min $(s_1 + r_2 + s_3 + s_4)$ *minimize bound restrictions*
Priority 2: Min $(r_5 + r_6)$ *achieve desired risk levels*
Priority 3: Min s_7 *maximize return on investments*

An EXCEL model and solution (from Solver) to the first LP are shown in Figure 7.14. The optimal objective function value is equal to zero, indicating that the objective of meeting the bound constraints is completely satisfied. The solution is to allocate $10,000 to life insurance, $60,000 to bond mutual funds, $56,667 to stock mutual funds, and $73,333 to savings. The return is $13,667. Note also that $r_5 = r_6 = 0$ (cells F25 and F26), so that this solution also satisfies the second priority goal. Therefore, there is no need to solve the LP with the second priority objective. Instead, we simply

FIGURE 7.14   The EXCEL model and solution to the first priority objective in Example 9

	A	B	C	D	E	F	G	H	I	J
1	Allocation of Assets									
2										
3	Parameters and uncontrollable inputs:									
4					Factors					
5		Lower Bound	Upper Bound	Inflation	Interest Spread	Return				
6	Life Insurance	$5,000	$10,000	-0.5	0.4	6%				
7	Bond Mutual Funds	$60,000		1.8	-0.5	7%				
8	Stock Mutual Funds	$30,000		2.1	0	11%				
9	Savings			-0.3	-1.1	4%				
10										
11			Target	1	0					
12										
13	Budget	$200,000								
14	Max Return	11%								
15										
16										
17	Decision variables:									
18										
19		Investment			Deviations					
20	Life Insurance	$10,000			s	r				
21	Bond Mutual Funds	$60,000		1	0.00	5000.00		Insurance Lower Bound		
22	Stock Mutual Funds	$56,667		2	0.00	0.00		Insurance Upper Bound		
23	Savings	$73,333		3	0.00	0.00		Bonds Lower Bound		
24				4	0.00	26666.67		Stocks Lower Bound		
25				5	0.00	0.00		Inflation Target		
26				6	106666.67	0.00		Interest Rate Spread Target		
27				7	8333.33	0.00		Return Target		
28										
29	Model Outputs:									
30		Value	Deviation	Total	Target					
31	Insurance Lower Bound	$10,000	($5,000)	$5,000	$5,000					
32	Insurance Upper Bound	$10,000	$0	$10,000	$10,000					
33	Bonds Lower Bound	$60,000	$0	$60,000	$60,000					
34	Stocks Lower Bound	$56,667	($26,667)	$30,000	$30,000					
35	Inflation Target	200000.00	0.00	200000.00	200000					
36	Interest Rate Spread Target	-106666.67	106666.67	0.00	0					
37	Return Target	$13,667	$8,333	$22,000	$22,000					
38										
39	Total Investment	$200,000								
40										
41	Priority 1	0								
42	Priority 2	0								
43	Priority 3	$8,333								

Selected Cell Formulas

	A	B	C	D	E
29	**Model Outputs:**				
30		Value	Deviation	Total	Target
31	Insurance Lower Bound	=+B20	=+E21-F21	=B31+C31	=+B6
32	Insurance Upper Bound	=+B20	=+E22-F22	=B32+C32	=+C6
33	Bonds Lower Bound	=+B21	=+E23-F23	=B33+C33	=+B7
34	Stocks Lower Bound	=+B22	=+E24-F24	=B34+C34	=+B8
35	Inflation Target	=+D6*B20+D7*B21+D8*B22+D9*B23	=+E25-F25	=B35+C35	=+D11*B13
36	Interest Rate Spread Target	=+E6*B20+E7*B21+E8*B22+E9*B23	=+E26-F26	=B36+C36	=+E11*B13
37	Return Target	=+F6*B20+F7*B21+F8*B22+F9*B23	=+E27-F27	=B37+C37	=+B13*B14
38					
39	Total Investment	=B20+B21+B22+B23			
40					
41	Priority 1	=+E21+F22+E23+E24			
42	Priority 2	=+F25+F26			
43	Priority 3	=+E27			

lock in the first two objectives as achieved and solve the LP with the third priority objective. We therefore add the constraints B41 = 0 and B42 = 0 to the constraint set in Solver, and solve the model with B43 as the objective function. The solution remains the same as that shown in Figure 7.14, indicating that the third goal cannot be completely satisfied (the solution that satisfies the first two goals yields a return $8,333 less than the maximum expected return).

SUMMARY

In this chapter we discussed several approaches to linear programming problems with multiple objectives. First, we may combine the multiple objectives into a single objective by taking a weighted combination of the objectives. The weights represent the relative importance of each objective.

The second approach, the absolute priorities approach, is sequential. The highest priority objective is used as the objective in the first LP model. The optimal objective function value of the first LP model is then fixed via a constraint in a second LP. The objective of the second LP is the objective that ranked second in priority. This procedure is continued until all of the objectives have been optimized with higher priority objectives that have been set equal to their previously achieved values via constraints.

Goal programming provides a means of modeling conflicting objectives with target values. Soft constraints are used to define deviations above or below the target value for the objectives. The objectives can then be defined in terms of minimizing the deviations from the target for each objective. Either the combined weighting approach or absolute priorities approach can be applied to the deviational variables.

The major advantage of the goal programming approach is the flexibility of the soft constraints. Soft constraints provide a greater number of feasible alternatives between conflicting objectives. The weighted objective approach requires the solution of only a single LP model, but requires subjective importance weightings from the user. The absolute priorities approach requires only a ranking of the multiple objectives, but requires multiple LP runs in order to obtain a solution.

CHAPTER REVIEW EXERCISES

I. Terms to Understand

a. Weighted objective approach (p. 322)
b. Absolute priorities approach (p. 326)
c. Goal programming (p. 328)
d. Target (p. 328)

e. Hard constraint (p. 329)
f. Soft constraint (p. 329)
g. Deviational variable (p. 330)

II. Discussion Questions

1. Discuss the following statement: "A goal constraint with deviational variables for the amounts above or below the target value is really no constraint at all."
2. Describe the advantages and disadvantages of the weighted objective function approach versus the absolute priorities approach to solving linear programs with multiple objectives.
3. Explain why, given target values for multiple conflicting objectives, we typically cannot simply choose one of them as our objective and force the target values for the other objectives with hard constraints.
4. Give two examples where soft constraints for goals might be more appropriate than hard constraints.
5. How might the weighted objective approach be used to implement the absolute priorities approach to multiple objectives? That is, is there an approach based on weighting factors that would allow the absolute priorities approach to be solved in one LP?

III. Problems

1. Anderson Manufacturing produces two products. A unit of product 1 yields a profit of $35. A unit of product 2 gives a profit of $45. Anderson has committed to providing its customers with 100 units of product 1 and 200 units of product 2 next week. However, demand is so heavy that as many as 500 units of each can be sold. Each unit of product 1 requires 3 minutes of machine time and each unit of product 2 requires 4 minutes of machine time. Unfortunately, there are only 40 hours (2,400 minutes) of machine time available next week. Anderson's objectives are

   Priority 1: Use 100% of available machine capacity.
   Priority 2: Make as much product 2 as possible (up to the demand of 500 units).

   a. Formulate the constraint set for this scenario.
   b. Graph the feasible region and find the optimal solution with Priority 1 as the objective function.
   c. Set the first priority equal to the value achieved in part *b* and replace the objective with priority 2. What is the feasible region for this second problem? Find the optimal solution.

2. Stephanie is considering four investment alternatives. The four alternatives are shown in the following table.

Alternative	Return
1. Casino Bonds	10%
2. Municipal Bonds	7%
3. Certificates of Deposit	4%
4. Savings Bonds	5%

Stephanie needs a return of at least 8%. She would like to achieve this return while satisfying, in order, the following objectives. She has $10,000 to invest.

Priority 1: Invest as much as possible in both certificates of deposit and savings bonds.

Priority 2: Invest as much as possible in savings bonds. Formulate the linear programming constraint set for this scenario and solve the problem using the absolute priorities approach.

3.   Reconsider Stephanie's investment problem (problem 2). Rather than using the priorities specified in problem 2, Stephanie has decided to use a weighted objective function approach to her problem. She would like to use the following weights.

Alternative	Objective weighting
1. Casino Bonds	.4
2. Municipal Bonds	.3
3. Certificates of Deposit	.1
4. Savings Bonds	.2

Stephanie has assigned these weightings according to her assessment of the perceived risk (based on the possibility of default and the length of time of each investment). The rationale for these weightings is that a minimizing objective will avoid higher-valued weightings. Solve the linear program for Stephanie with the objective of minimizing the dollars invested in each alternative multiplied by their weighting factors.

4.   RJ Company produces two types of fuel additives. The first type, $F1$, is used in large trucks. The second type, $F2$, is used in school buses. The projected demand for next quarter is 6,000 gallons of $F1$ and 4,000 gallons of $F2$. There is a limited amount of the three inputs used to produce these products. The following table shows the amount of input required for a gallon of each product as well as the amount of each input available.

Gallons of input required per gallon of product			
	Input A	Input B	Input C
$F1$	.3	.3	.4
$F2$	.35	.1	.55
Available	2,400	1,500	4,000	(gallons)

Given available resources, it will be impossible to satisfy the demand for both products. RJ would like to analyze different possibilities with regard to the amounts of production of $F1$ and $F2$ in a manner similar to the analysis conducted for the investment problem in this chapter (see Table 7.1). Let w_1 be the importance weighting placed on $F1$ production and w_2 the importance weighting on $F2$. Define $F1$ as the number of gallons of $F1$ to produce and $F2$ as the number of gallons of $F2$ to produce. The objective function to be used in the analysis is a linear combination of these decision variables with the coefficients w_1 and w_2. That is, the objective function is Max $w_1 F1 + w_2 F2$.

  a.   Formulate the constraint set of the linear programming model for this scenario.
  b.   Graph the feasible region.
  c.   Distribute the weights so that $w_1 + w_2 = 1$. Use a computer LP solver such as LINDO or the EXCEL or LOTUS Solvers to solve the linear programs as w_1 is varied from 0 to 1 in increments of .1. Keep track of the different solutions found. How many different solutions were generated? Relate your findings to the graph you developed in part b.

5. Consider the following production planning problem. A company that produces a single product has a production capacity of 2,500 units per week. Projected demand for the next six weeks is 2,000, 2,900, 1,500, 1,700, 3,000, and 2,300 units. The company places equal importance on minimizing the amount of inventory and lost sales.

  a.   Formulate and solve this problem as a linear program.
  b.   Suppose the company becomes more service oriented, so that minimizing lost sales is twice as important as minimizing the amount of inventory carried. Solve for the optimal production plan.

6. Refer to the Anderson Manufacturing scenario presented in Problem 1. Suppose that 10 hours of overtime are available for production and that Anderson has the following goals (in order of importance) instead of the priorities presented in Problem 1.

Goal 1: Minimize the amount of overtime used.

Goal 2: Maximize profit.

  a.   Formulate this problem as a goal program.
  b.   Graph the feasible region, including the goal constraints.
  c.   Solve the problem using the absolute priorities approach, and illustrate the solution of each of the LPs on your graph.

7. Refer to problem 6. Resolve part c, reversing the order of the goals.

8. Reconsider the asset allocation model described in Example 9 of this chapter. Resolve this problem using the following priorities.

Priority 1: Min s_7

Priority 2: Min $(r_5 + r_6)$

Priority 3: Min $(s_1 + r_2 + s_3 + s_4)$

How does this solution compare with the solution presented in Example 9?

9. Milicro Manufacturing[3] has five vendors from which it may purchase its key component part. Historical records provide information with regard to the quality of each vendor's product and their on-time delivery record. This information, along with the price quote from each vendor, is summarized in the following table.

	Vendor				
	1	2	3	4	5
Quality (% Accepted)	90%	89%	95%	88%	90%
On-Time Deliveries (%)	80%	70%	90%	85%	87%
Price Quote (per unit)	$14.50	$12.00	$15.00	$14.00	$14.50

---

[3] Based on Buffa, F. and W. Jackson. "A Goal Programming Model for Purchase Planning." *Journal of Purchasing and Materials Management,* Fall 1983, pp. 27–34.

Milicro needs 5,000 units of this key component next month and is currently trying to decide on a purchase plan. Company policy dictates that no single vendor should receive more than 50% of the total purchase. In order of importance, the company has the following goals.

> Goal 1: An average acceptance rate of 90%.
> Goal 2: An on-time delivery average of 85%.
> Goal 3: Average unit cost of $14.25 or lower.

   a. Formulate this scenario as a linear goal program.
   b. Solve the linear goal program using the absolute priorities approach.
   c. Solve the linear goal program using the absolute priorities approach with the following priorities:

> Goal 1: An on-time delivery average of 85%.
> Goal 2: An average acceptance rate of 90%.
> Goal 3: Average unit cost of $14.25 or lower.

   d. Compare and contrast the solutions to parts *b* and *c*.

10. Consider the Milicro Manufacturing scenario presented in the last problem using the priorities presented in part *c*. Investigate the effect of the on-time delivery target on the achievement of the other goals by solving the problem using absolute priorities for average on-time delivery targets of 75%, 80%, 85%, and 90%. Graph the average acceptance rate achieved as a function of the on-time delivery target. Also graph the average cost per unit as a function of the on-time delivery target. Which of the four target values for on-time delivery would you recommend?

11. Cincy Sausage[4] produces a variety of meat products, including their specialty, Big Red Sausage. In addition to a secret blend of spices, the Big Red is comprised of beef head, pork jowls, mutton, and water. For each of these ingredients, the cost per pound, amount of fat per pound, and the amount of protein per pound is shown in the following table.

	Beef head	Pork jowls	Mutton	Water
Cost / pound	$.15	$.10	$.08	$.00
Fat / pound	.05	.25	.10	.00
Protein / pound	.20	.25	.08	.00

Cincy uses the following goals, in order of importance, when producing Big Red.

Priority 1: Big Red should consist of at least 18% protein.
Priority 2: Big Red should consist of at most 10% fat.
Priority 3: Roughly equal amounts of beef and pork should be used.
Priority 4: Cost per pound should not exceed $0.10.

Cincy is about to produce a 75-pound batch of Big Red.
   a. Formulate this production scenario as a linear goal program.
   b. Find the solution using the absolute priorities approach.

12. Refer to Problem 9, the Milicro Manufacturing problem.
   a. Resolve the problem using the weighted objective function approach with the following weights:

---

[4]Based on Steuer, Ralph. "Sausage Blending Using Multiple Objective Programming." *Management Science* Vol. 30, No. 11, November 1984, pp. 1376–1384.

Goal	Weights
An average acceptance rate of 90%	.4
An on-time delivery average of 85%	.3
Average unit cost of $14.25 or lower.	.3

Report the achievement of each goal.

b.   Resolve the linear program using equal weights for all three goals. Report how each goal is achieved.

13. Refer to Problem 11, the Cincy Sausage production problem. Resolve the problem using a weighted objective function approach with the following weights:

Priority	Weight
1	.4
2	.4
3	.0
4	.2

Report the achievement of each goal.

14. Recall the production planning over time scenario discussed in Chapter 4. The planning department of a small company is faced with determining aggregate production levels for a product over each of the next four quarters. The following table shows the relevant cost and demand data. The inventory holding cost is per-unit and is based on the end-of-quarter inventory; there are currently 10 units in inventory. The cost of production varies over time.

Quarter	Demand	Production Cost/Unit	Inventory Holding Cost/Unit
1	100	$200	$10
2	150	$195	$10
3	120	$210	$10
4	180	$200	$10

Suppose that there is also a production rate change cost (for example, costs associated with overtime or layoffs). An increase in the amount of production from one quarter to the next costs $6 per unit of increase. A decrease in the amount of production from one quarter to the next costs $4 per unit of decrease. This quarter's production was 110 units.

The company would like to know how many units to produce and how many units to hold in inventory each quarter, in order to satisfy demand at minimum cost. Formulate an LP model for this problem and solve for the optimal production schedule using the computer. (*Hint:* before the model is solved, it is unknown whether or not there will be an increase or a decrease in production level from one quarter to the next; that is, we do not know if the difference between a quarter's production and the previous quarter's production is positive or negative. Model this as a soft constraint with a target of zero for this difference.)

15. Refer to Problem 14. Suppose that management has set the following goals.

Goal 1: Keep total cost to no more than $110,000.
Goal 2: Minimize production rate fluctuations in quarters 3 and 4 (targets = 0).
Goal 3: Minimize inventory held (targets = 0).

Formulate the problem as a goal program and solve using the absolute priorities approach. To what extent is each goal satisfied?

16. A company has three manufacturing cells on its shop floor, and wants to find the best location for a tool crib used by each of the cells. The shop floor has been marked to show the location of the cells as shown in the following figure. Cell 1 is located at point (1,2), cell 2 is at (3,5), and cell 3 is located at point (5,3). The objective is to find the location that minimizes the sum of the distances from the cells to the crib. Assume that distances are measured in a rectangular fashion. For example, the distance from the cell (1,2) to location (3,1) is $|1 - 3| + |2 - 1| = 2 + 1 = 3$, as shown in the figure. Formulate this problem as a goal program. Solve for the optimal location using a computer LP solver.

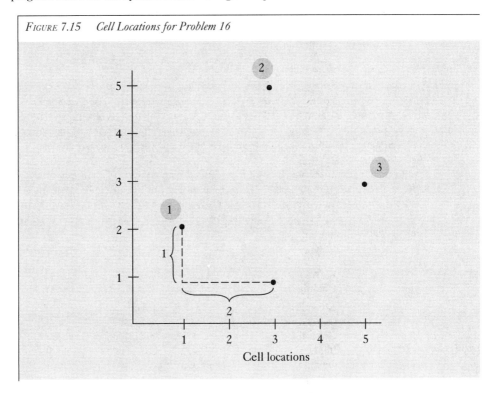

FIGURE 7.15   Cell Locations for Problem 16

17. Refer to Problem 16. Suppose that the average numbers of special tools required per day from the crib are 10 for cell 1, 12 for cell 2, and 38 for cell 3. Solve the location problem with the distances from each of the cells weighted by the demands (use the demands as weights in a goal programming model). Compare the solution to that obtained in Problem 16.

18. Refer to Problem 16. Change the objective to minimize the maximum distance to any of the cells. That is, find the location of the crib that minimizes the furthest walk from any of the three cells.

19. A company is planning a five year investment strategy for its $1 million capital on hand. The company is considering the following options: stocks, bonds, certificates of deposit, and a savings account. A stock investment is expected to yield 12% two years after investment. Bond investments yield a 20% profit three years after investment. Certificates of deposit are annual and are expected to yield a profit of 5%. Any money not invested in stocks or bonds will be invested in the savings account that yields 3.5%. An additional $250,000 will be received at the end of year 2, and an $85,000 obligation must be paid at the end of year 4. The company has the following goals:

Priority 1: The allocation of funds should be sensitive to risk. Therefore, no more than $400,000 should be invested in any one option, with the exception of the savings account.
Priority 2: At least $100,000 should be kept in the savings account for operational expenses.
Priority 3: Maximize the amount of capital on hand at the end of the fifth year.

    a.   Formulate this problem as a goal programming problem.
    b.   Solve the goal program using absolute priorities with an LP solver. Describe how well each goal is achieved.

20.   Resolve the goal programming problem given in Problem 19, with the priorities reversed.
    a.   Describe how well each goal is achieved.
    b.   Compare part *a*'s solution with the solution from Problem 19.

IV. Projects and Cases

1.   A. Riggs and Company provides a variety of business software for managing accounts, inventory, work orders, and so on. For the past several years, license fees were based on the size of the computers on which the software would be used. As a result, larger companies typically paid more for the software than smaller companies. This generated many complaints, particularly because many larger companies felt that they were being penalized inappropriately for small software packages that were a minor function of their business.

    A pricing committee was formed to address this issue. One of their key objectives is to maintain the same total revenue as from the old pricing system. Specifically, software revenues for the next year should be as close to $90 million as possible. Secondly, the price for each application package should be as close to the industry average as possible, while not falling below a certain price. These prices are shown in the following table.

Software Package	Industry Average	Minimum Price	Current Demand
General Accounting	$2,200	$1,200	2,000
General Ledger	$3,000	$2,000	6,000
Budgeting	$1,100	$ 200	6,000
Payroll	$4,000	$3,000	2,500
Inventory	$2,200	$1,200	3,000
Order Entry	$2,500	$1,500	3,000
Billing	$5,000	$4,000	1,000
Scheduling	$4,000	$3,000	1,500
Materials Planning	$3,000	$2,000	1,700

    a.   What prices should be charged for each package if
        I.   the total revenue goal is twice as important as the industry average target goals?
        II.   the total revenue goal is defined as the priority 1 goal in the absolute priority approach?
    b.   Investigate the sensitivity of the solution to increases in the revenue target. In particular, repeat part *a* for increases in the revenue target of 2% and 5%.
2.   Keith Frey is a recruiter for the U.S. Navy. His recruiting responsibilities include physicians, medics, pilots, nuclear power technicians, and general officers. Each year, he has a goal of recruiting a certain number

in each field. Keith is evaluated on the number of "points" earned in this effort. More difficult specialty fields earn higher points, but take more time to recruit. The following table shows the relevant data.

Field	Minimum Number	Points Earned per Recruit	Days Required per Recruit	Cost per Recruit
Physician	2	4,700	45	$2,000
Pilot	6	3,400	20	$800
Medics	3	3,200	15	$700
Nucl. Tech.	6	2,400	12	$600
Gen. Officer	3	1,950	14	$50
ROTC	85	500	5	$75

Keith's office staff has a total of 920 days to devote to recruiting efforts; this cannot be exceeded. He would like his total cost not to exceed $29,000 if possible. In addition, Keith would like to earn at least 150,000 points.

Keith would like to know how many recruits of each type he should try to recruit. His first priority is to not exceed the budget and the second priority is his point goal. He is also interested in the achievement of total points as a function of the budget.

3. DuckTail Casual Clothes[5] specializes in preppie clothes sold nationwide in college book stores. The sales force consists of six full-time sales people and five part-time sales people. The sales manager is paid a fixed salary plus 5% of total sales above the sales quota set by upper management. The sales manager sets the sales quotas for the sales force. She specifies group targets for the full and part-time groups. The full-time sales people are paid a fixed salary plus 10% of the total sales above their group sales quota. Full-time sales people are scheduled for 168 hours of regular time per month per person. On average, a full-time person sells $74 worth of goods per hour. The part-time people are paid an hourly wage plus 12% of the sales above their quotas set by the sales manager. Part timers may work up to 50 hours per month per person, and on average sell $60 worth of goods per hour.

The sales quota has been set at $100,000 for next month. The sales manager has set a goal of $72,000 for the full-time group and $28,000 for the part-timers.

The sales manager has set the following goals, in order of importance.

1. Achieve the sales quota of $100,000.
2. The group of full-time people should meet their sales quota of $72,000.
3. The part-time group should meet their sales quota of $28,000.
4. Overtime hours required of full-timers should be limited to 32 hours per person.
5. Each part-time salesperson should work 50 hours this month.
6. The manager would like a bonus of $600 next month. It would also be great if each full-time and part-time salesperson received a bonus of $200.

Formulate and solve this problem using absolute priority goal programming. The solution should indicate the number of hours each salesperson should work next month. (Assume that each full-time person will work the same number of hours. Likewise, assume that each part-time person should work the same number of hours.) Describe how well each of the six goals is achieved.

---

[5] Based on Tabucanon, Mario T. *Multiple Criteria Decision Making in Industry.* New York: Elsevier Science Publishers, 1988, pp. 254–259.

REFERENCES

Buffa, F., and W. Jackson. "A Goal Programming Model for Purchase Planning." *Journal of Purchasing and Materials Management*, Fall 1983, pp. 27–34.

Chrisman, J., T. Fry, G. Reeves, H. Lewis, and R. Weinstein. "A Multiobjective Linear Programming Methodology for Public Sector Tax Planning." *Interfaces*, Vol. 15, No. 5, September–October 1989, pp. 13–22.

Goicoechea, A., D. Hansen, and L. Duckstein. *Multiobjective Decision Analysis with Engineering and Business Applications*. New York: John Wiley and Sons, 1982.

Rosenthal, R., "Principles of Multiobjective Optimization." *Decision Sciences*, Vol. 16, No.2, Spring 1985, pp. 133–152.

Salvia, A. and W. Ludwig. "An Application of Goal Programming at Lord Corporation." *Interfaces*, Vol. 9, No. 4, August 1979, pp. 129–133.

Schniederjans, M., N. Kwak, and M. Helmer. "An Application of Goal Programming to Resolve a Site Location Problem." *Interfaces*, Vol. 12, No. 3, June 1982, pp. 65–72.

Schniederjans, M., T. Zorn, and R. Johnson. "Allocating Total Wealth: A Goal Programming Approach." *Computers and Operations Research*, Vol. 20, No. 7, 1993, pp. 679–685.

Steuer, Ralph. "Sausage Blending Using Multiple Objective Programming." *Management Science*, Vol. 30, No. 11, November 1984, pp. 1376–1384.

Tabucanon, Mario T. *Multiple Criteria Decision Making in Industry*. New York: Elsevier Science Publishers, 1988.

White, D. "A Bibliography on the Applications of Mathematical Programming Multi-Objective Methods." *Journal of the Operational Research Society*, Vol. 41, No. 8, August 1990, pp. 669–691.

CHAPTER 8

INTEGER

PROGRAMMING

MODELING AND

ANALYSIS

INTRODUCTION

- Labor-intensive service sector operations such as airlines must deal constantly with staffing problems in the face of fluctuating demand. If the staff is too small, the firm cannot serve its customers well, resulting in lost sales and the loss of customer good will. A staff that is too large can meet customer demand, but incurs unnecessary labor cost. Qantas Airways uses an integer programming model to determine a staff size for its telephone reservation system that will incur the least cost while meeting projected demand. The integer programming model uses demand forecasts by month, day, and half-hour intervals to optimize the staff size over time. The staff size must be an integer, because it is impossible to have a fractional number of people on hand to serve the customers. During the first two years of use, the model saved over $235,000 in labor costs [Gaballa and Pearce, 1979].

- Manufacturers of steel, paper, and textiles must plan cutting patterns carefully in order to convert the bulk product to the smaller units sold to customers. Over the course of a year, the use of cutting patterns that minimize trim waste while satisfying the demand for various sized products can save considerable cost. Eastman Kodak Co. uses integer programming models to determine how to cut the large bulk rolls of photographic color paper they manufacture into the sized products customers need. The optimal number of times to use a certain cutting pattern must be an integer value. Likewise, the number of times a product appears in a cutting pattern must be integer, because fractional amounts of the products are of no use to the customers. Using the integer programming models to prescribe cutting patterns that minimize waste, Kodak saved over $2 million dollars in the first year of implementation [Farley, 1991].

- American Airlines employs over 8,000 pilots and over 16,000 flight attendants. Total crew cost, including salaries, fringe benefits, and expenses, is the second largest cost incurred by the airline (fuel cost is the largest). Airlines can save quite a bit of money by efficiently scheduling flight crews (pilots and attendants) to flights. Using integer programming models that can model assignment decisions, American can schedule its crews to flights in a way that minimizes the cost of lodging and meals, while also satisfying Federal Aviation Administration rules and pay guarantees. The integer programming-based scheduling system called TRIP (Trip Evaluation and Improvement Program) took over 15 labor-years to develop and refine, but saves an estimated $20 million annually in crew costs. American Airlines Decision Technologies, the management science group at American, is now a separate subsidiary of American's parent corporation and has sold TRIP to ten major airlines and one railroad [Anbil, Gelman, Patty, and Tanga, 1991].

These examples of applications at Qantas, Kodak, and American Airlines illustrate the power of integer programming models, which can be applied to a wide variety of situations. In fact, in terms of the range of applications, integer programming models are among the most practical and flexible mathematical programming models. Unfortunately, this range and flexibility does not come without a cost. Integer programming models are much more difficult to solve than corresponding linear programs, and require increased computational effort. In this chapter, we introduce you to a variety of applications for integer programming, and describe methods for solving integer programs.

LINEAR INTEGER PROGRAMS

A mathematical programming model in which the decision variables are restricted to integer values is called an *integer program*. Using the terminology from Chapter 4, we can have a nonlinear integer programming model or a linear integer programming model. Due to its complexity, we will not discuss nonlinear optimization in this book. When we refer to an integer programming (IP) model, we will be assuming that the model is linear in the decision variables. Consequently, the model-building approaches we used in the construction of linear programming models in Chapter 4 are applicable to the building of integer programming models.

> A *linear integer program* (IP) is a linear program in which the decision variables are restricted to integer values.

As we discussed in Chapter 4, fractional-valued decision variables are unacceptable in many mathematical programming applications. Some examples are those in which the decision variables represent quantities of high-cost items such as ships, the number of people hired or fired, or logical choices like whether not a facility should be placed at a certain location. In the examples of applications at Qantas and Kodak, the nature of the decision variables required that they be integer valued (you cannot have a fraction of a person on hand to staff your reservation desk, and it is not possible to utilize a fraction of some cutting pattern). American Airlines needed to decide whether or not a certain crew should be assigned to a flight leg, which necessitates the use of an integer variable that is either a 0 (crew not assigned to this flight leg) or a 1 (crew is assigned to this flight leg). Variables of the type described for Qantas and Kodak are called *general integer variables*, while the 0-1 variable described for American is called a *binary variable*. We elaborate on these two types of decision variables in the remainder of this section.

General Integer Variables

General integer variables are decision variables which can take on any feasible *integer* value.

EXAMPLE 1. QUEEN CITY INC.

Queen City Inc. manufactures machine tools. The production planner who oversees the production of two of Queen City's more profitable machines needs to determine how many of each to produce this month. The two machines, TopLathe and Big-Press, each require a certain component. Each TopLathe requires 10 of these components and each BigPress requires 7. Only 49 components are available this month. Production and marketing are not very well coordinated at Queen City, but the planner knows that the sales people are usually happy if production provides them with 5 machines per month. The profit for a TopLathe is $50,000 and $34,000 on a BigPress. Assuming that labor and other components are available, how many of each product should Queen City produce in order to maximize profit? We take the same approach in formulating this problem as we did for linear programs in Chapter 4.

First, what is it that Queen City needs to decide? The planner needs to decide how many TopLathes and how many BigPresses to manufacture this month. We define the following decision variables:

$$x_1 = \text{the number of TopLathes to produce this month}$$
$$x_2 = \text{the number of BigPresses to produce this month}$$

These decision variables must be nonnegative and cannot be fractional, so we must ensure that $x_1, x_2 \geq 0$ *and integer.*

What is the objective to be maximized or minimized? The objective is to maximize profit. Each TopLathe generates a profit of $50,000, and each BigPress generates $34,000. The objective can therefore be represented as a function of the decision variables:

$$\text{Max} \quad 50,000x_1 + 34,000x_2$$

How is the problem restricted? Queen City has only a limited supply of the component. We must develop a constraint that relates the number of units of the component used in production to the number available. Because each TopLathe requires 10 components and each BigPress requires 7, the total number of components used in production can be represented as $10x_1 + 7x_2$. This must not exceed the number available, so

$$10x_1 + 7x_2 \leq 49$$

The second constraint requires that at least five machines must be produced to keep the sales people happy. The total production is $x_1 + x_2$, so we can represent this constraint as

$$x_1 + x_2 \geq 5$$

The complete model for Queen City's production planning problem is

$$\text{Max} \quad 50,000x_1 + 34,000x_2$$
$$\text{subject to}$$
$$10x_1 + 7x_2 \leq 49$$
$$x_1 + x_2 \geq 5$$
$$x_1, x_2 \geq 0 \text{ and integer}$$

The solution to this model is to produce no TopLathes and seven BigPresses for a profit of \$238,000 ($x_1^* = 0, x_2^* = 7$, z^* (the objective function value) $= 238,000$). We will discuss how the computer solves integer programming models later in this chapter.

Binary Integer Variables

Variables that can only assume a value of either 0 or 1 are known as *binary variables* or *zero-one variables*. Mathematically, we can express a binary variable x_i as a general integer variable by writing it as

$$0 \leq x_i \leq 1 \text{ and integer}$$

Binary variables are extremely useful because they enable us to model logical yes-or-no decisions in optimization models. For example, binary variables can be used to model decisions such as whether or not to open a new facility, whether or not to produce product this month, and whether or not to undertake a project.

EXAMPLE 2. BURKE CONSTRUCTION

Tom Burke, owner of Burke Construction, is trying to determine which projects to undertake during the winter quarter (January, February, and March). Because he has a limited work force, Tom knows that he will not be able to complete all of his construction projects without subcontracting some of them. He has committed to complete five projects this winter and has estimated the profit to his company for each. He has also estimated the amount of labor each project will require (in total hours) and what the profit to his company will be if he subcontracts the project to one of the smaller companies in town. These estimates are shown in Table 8.1.

Tom has 4800 labor hours available per quarter (10 workers $\times$ 40 hours/week $\times$ 12 weeks $= 4,800$ hours). In order to maximize profit, which jobs should Tom schedule for his company, and which should be subcontracted? Assume that projects will not be partially subcontracted; a project will either be done completely by Burke Construction or it will be completely subcontracted. Again, let us follow the guidelines presented in Chapter 4.

What is it that Burke needs to decide? Tom needs to determine which projects to undertake with his company directly and which to subcontract. We can define the following decision variables:

TABLE 8.1
Data for Burke
Construction

Project:	1	2	3	4	5
Profit	\$30,000	\$10,000	\$26,000	\$18,000	\$20,000
Subcontr Profit	\$ 6,000	\$ 2,000	\$ 8,000	\$ 9,000	\$ 4,500
Labor Hours	1,300	950	1,000	1,400	1,600

$$x_i = 1 \text{ if project } i \text{ is undertaken directly, 0 if not, } i = 1, 2, 3, 4, 5.$$

$$y_i = 1 \text{ if project } i \text{ is subcontracted, 0 if not, } i = 1, 2, 3, 4, 5.$$

What is the objective to be maximized or minimized? The objective is to maximize profit, and can be stated mathematically as

$$\text{Max} \quad 30x_1 + 10x_2 + 26x_3 + 18x_4 + 20x_5 + 6y_1 + 2y_2 + 8y_3 + 9y_4 + 4.5y_5$$

(Note that the objective function is expressed in thousands of dollars.)

How is the problem restricted? Burke has a limited number of labor hours available, and the number of labor hours used depends on which projects Burke selects to complete. The total number of hours used must not exceed the number available.

$$1,300x_1 + 950x_2 + 1,000x_3 + 1,400x_4 + 1,600x_5 \leq 4,800$$

Finally, each project is either completed directly by Burke or subcontracted. In terms of our decision variables, this means that exactly one of x_i and y_i must be equal to 1. We can express this as

$$x_i + y_i = 1 \quad i = 1, 2, 3, 4, 5$$

The complete model for Burke Construction can be written as

$$\text{Max} \quad 30x_1 + 10x_2 + 26x_3 + 18x_4 + 20x_5 + 6y_1 + 2y_2 + 8y_3 + 9y_4 + 4.5y_5$$

subject to

$$1,300x_1 + 950x_2 + 1,000x_3 + 1,400x_4 + 1,600x_5 \leq 4,800$$

$$x_i + y_i = 1 \quad i = 1, 2, 3, 4, 5$$

$$0 \leq x_i \leq 1 \text{ and integer} \quad i = 1, 2, 3, 4, 5$$

$$0 \leq y_i \leq 1 \text{ and integer} \quad i = 1, 2, 3, 4, 5$$

The solution to the Burke Construction model is to undertake projects 1, 2, 3, and 4, and to subcontract project 5 ($x_i^* = 1$, $i = 1, 2, 3, 4$, $x_5^* = 0$, $y_i^* = 0$, $i = 1, 2, 3, 4$, and $y_5^* = 1$). This plan results in a profit of \$88,500.

The decision variables in Example 2 are *all* binary variables. This type of model is known as a *binary integer program*.

A *binary integer program* (BIP) is an integer program in which all of the decision variables are restricted to either zero or one.

Many planning models have a combination of both integer and continuous variables. Any model in which at least one decision variable is restricted to be integer (general or binary) and at least one variable is allowed to be fractional is known as a *mixed integer program*.

A *mixed integer program* (MIP) is a linear program in which some, but not all of the variables are restricted to be integer (either general or binary).

EXAMPLE 3. CHEMCO INC.

Chemco Inc. produces a wide variety of chemical products. One of their most important products is liquid chlorine. To meet contractual agreements, Chemco must supply 800, 500, 450, and 900 gallons of liquid chlorine respectively in the next four weeks. There are currently 100 gallons of liquid chlorine in storage, and storage is limited to 1,500 gallons. The weekly production capacity is 1,000 gallons. The production manager needs to find the most cost-effective way to meet these demands. She knows that there is a trade-off between the cost of holding the product in inventory and the cost of setting up and cleaning the processing machines. That is, longer production runs mean fewer setups but higher inventory levels, whereas shorter production runs result in lower inventory levels but more setups. The setup and cleaning of the machines costs $500, and it costs $1 per gallon per week to hold inventory. The plant is closed on weekends so that the $500 setup and cleaning is incurred for every week there is production.

What is it that Chemco needs to decide? The production manager would like to know how much and when to produce the liquid chlorine in order to satisfy demand and minimize the cost of setups and inventory. Specifically, we need to decide when (during which weeks) to produce, how many gallons to produce in those weeks, and consequently when and how much to hold in inventory. We can define the following decision variables:

$$x_i = \text{number of gallons of chlorine to produce in week } i$$
$$I_i = \text{number of gallons to hold in inventory at the end of week } i$$
$$y_i = 1 \text{ if we produce in week } i, 0 \text{ if we do not}$$
$$i = 1, 2, 3, 4$$

What is the objective to be maximized or minimized? The objective is to maximize the cost of setups and inventory. This may be described mathematically as

$$\text{Min } 500y_1 + 500y_2 + 500y_3 + 500y_4 + 1I_1 + 1I_2 + 1I_3 + 1I_4$$

How is the problem restricted? We would like to find how the inventory is related to demand and the amount produced. As we have seen in Chapter 4, this can be accomplished through the use of inventory balance equations. Recall that these balance equations state that for every period,

Ending inventory = starting inventory + amount produced − demand

We currently have 100 gallons in inventory, and the projected demand is 800, 500, 450, and 900 gallons. The balance equations are therefore

$$100 + x_1 - 800 = I_1$$
$$I_1 + x_2 - 500 = I_2$$
$$I_2 + x_3 - 450 = I_3$$
$$I_3 + x_4 - 900 = I_4$$

We must ensure that the model forces $y_i = 1$ whenever production occurs in period i; that is, when x_i is positive. This is done by using the constraint

$$x_i \leq 1{,}000 y_i, \quad i = 1, 2, 3, 4. \quad \text{production capability}$$

If $y_i = 0$ (no setup occurs), then $x_i \leq 0$ and because of nonnegativity restrictions, x_i must equal zero. On the other hand, if $y_i = 1$, then x_i is allowed to be less than or equal to 1,000 (the production capacity). This type of constraint is known as a *fixed charge constraint*. It does not allow production unless the fixed (setup) charge is incurred. We note that while it is feasible for $y_i = 1$ and $x_i = 0$, this will *never* be optimal if y_i has a positive cost. Hence, in any optimal solution, $y_i = 1$ only when $x_i > 0$.

Finally, inventory must not exceed 1,500 gallons in each period.

$$I_i \leq 1{,}500, \quad i = 1, 2, 3, 4.$$

The complete model for Chemco can be written as

$$\text{Min } 500 y_1 + 500 y_2 + 500 y_3 + 500 y_4 + 1 I_1 + 1 I_2 + 1 I_3 + 1 I_4$$

subject to

$$100 + x_1 - 800 = I_1$$
$$I_1 + x_2 - 500 = I_2$$
$$I_2 + x_3 - 450 = I_3$$
$$I_3 + x_4 - 900 = I_4$$
$$x_i \leq 1{,}000 y_i \quad i = 1, 2, 3, 4$$
$$I_i \leq 1{,}500 \quad i = 1, 2, 3, 4$$
$$x_i \geq 0 \quad i = 1, 2, 3, 4$$
$$0 \leq y_i \leq 1 \quad \text{and integer} \quad i = 1, 2, 3, 4$$

The solution to the Chemco problem is to produce 700 gallons in period 1, 950 gallons in period 2, and 900 gallons in period 4, for a total cost of $1,950. No production occurs in period 3 because it is cheaper to produce period 3's demand in period 2 (the holding cost is 450 gallons × ($1/gallon) = $450) and avoid a setup ($500).

THE GEOMETRY OF INTEGER PROGRAMS

As with linear programs, we can learn a lot about integer programs by examining the geometry of two-dimensional problems. From simple geometrical examples, we can gain insight into how the computer solves integer programming models, and see how integer programs are related to linear programs.

Let us reconsider the Queen City Inc. example from the previous section (Example 1). The model is

$$\text{Max} \quad 50,000x_1 + 34,000x_2$$

subject to

$$10x_1 + 7x_2 \le 49$$
$$x_1 + x_2 \ge 5$$
$$x_1, x_2 \ge 0 \text{ and integer}$$

This is an example of a general integer program (all of the decision variables are restricted to be integer). Suppose that we ignore the integer restrictions and solve this example as a linear program. To determine the feasible region, we graph each constraint. The first constraint passes through the points (4.9,0) and (0,7). The second constraint passes through the points (5,0) and (0,5). The feasible region is shown in Figure 8.1. By examining the corner points, we find the solution to the LP is $x_1^* = 4.66667$, $x_2^* = .33333$, and $z^* = 244666.67$.

The problem we get when we ignore, or *relax*, the integer restrictions of an IP is called the *linear programming relaxation* of the integer program. The linear programming

50,000 (4.6667)
+
34000 (.33333)

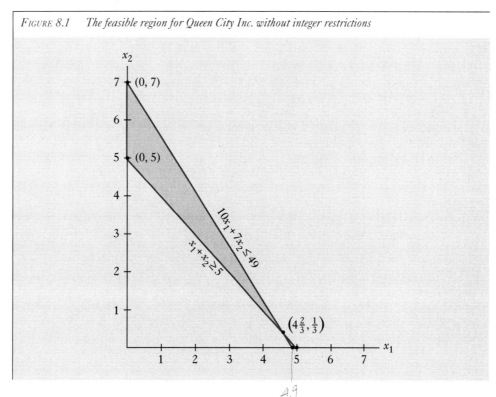

FIGURE 8.1   *The feasible region for Queen City Inc. without integer restrictions*

relaxation is often used as the starting point in the solution of integer programs. If the optimal decision variable values to the LP relaxation turn out to be integer, then that solution must also be optimal to the integer program. However, if the solution to the LP relaxation has fractional values, then the solution to the LP relaxation is not feasible for the integer program. This is the case in the Queen City example. More work must be done to find the optimal solution to the integer program.

The feasible region to the integer program in Example 1 is the set of *integer* points within the feasible region of the LP relaxation. These are shown in Figure 8.2 as dark dots in the feasible region of the LP relaxation. Note that rounding the solution to the LP relaxation in this example (to point (5,0)) is not feasible. In fact, even truncating (that is, dropping the decimal fraction) the solution to the LP relaxation (to point (4,0)) is also infeasible. Even if rounding or truncating the solution to the LP relaxation results in a feasible integer solution, it may be far from the optimal solution to the original integer problem.

Figure 8.3 shows the objective function values for all feasible integer solutions using the table option in EXCEL. The "." indicates an infeasible cell. By examining all feasible integer points, we see that the optimal solution is (0,7) with an objective function value of $238,000. In Figure 8.2, notice how far away the IP solution is from the solution to the LP relaxation. Thus, feasible integer points "close" to the LP relaxation may not be optimal. The fact that the solution to the IP turned out to be a corner point of the

---

FIGURE 8.2   *The set of feasible integer points to the Queen City example*

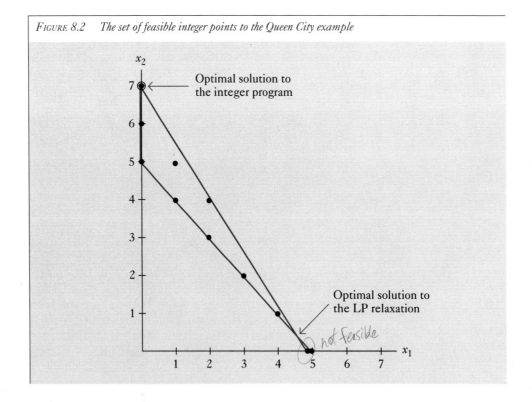

FIGURE 8.3   *Objective function values table for Example 1*

	A	B	C	D	E	F	G	H	I	J	K	L	M
1													
2													
3													
4													
5		10	.	.	.	.	.	.	.	.	.	.	.
6		9	.	.	.	.	.	.	.	.	.	.	.
7		8	.	.	.	.	.	.	.	.	.	.	.
8		7	238	.	.	.	.	.	.	.	.	.	.
9		6	204	.	.	.	.	.	.	.	.	.	.
10	x2	5	170	220	.	.	.	.	.	.	.	.	.
11		4	.	186	236	.	.	.	.	.	.	.	.
12		3	.	.	202	.	.	.	.	.	.	.	.
13		2	.	.	.	218	.	.	.	.	.	.	.
14		1	.	.	.	.	234	.	.	.	.	.	.
15		0	.	.	.	.	.	.	.	.	.	.	.
16			0	1	2	3	4	5	6	7	8	9	10
17													
18							x1						

feasible region is purely coincidence. It is possible to have feasible regions such that none of the corner points are integer valued.

In Chapter 5 we noted that the simplex algorithm for linear programs always finds corner point solutions. If the solution to an IP does not occur at a corner point, how can we use the simplex algorithm to solve integer programs? The geometry in the two-dimensional example gives us some clues as to how the simplex algorithm can be used to solve integer programs. Suppose that the feasible region of the LP relaxation can be "trimmed" or broken up in some way so that fractional corner points are eliminated and that the remaining corner points are integer. Then the simplex algorithm would find the optimal integer solution. Two commonly used approaches to solving IP problems do just that. These approaches, *cutting planes* and *branch and bound*, are briefly discussed in the next section (a more detailed description of branch and bound is given in the Appendix). p.421

COMPUTER IMPLEMENTATION OF IP MODELS

Most computer packages designed to solve integer programming models begin by solving the LP relaxation. This is the case for LINDO and the EXCEL Solver, the packages we discussed in Chapter 4 (LOTUS 1-2-3 Release 4.0 for Windows does not have integer programming capability). When you solve an integer program on the computer, you will notice immediately that the solution takes more time than the solution of a linear program. This is because a series of linear programs must be solved in order to find the optimal integer solution. This is true of both of the branch and bound approach and the cutting plane approach to solving integer programs.

The Branch and Bound Approach

The *branch and bound* approach to integer programming is a "divide and conquer" strategy. The feasible region of the LP relaxation is broken into subregions (branching) in such a way that only non-integer solutions are discarded. Subregions then become the feasible regions for the series of LP's solved. Eventually, integer solutions will be found as corner points to subregions.

Important bounding information allows us to discard entire subregions from consideration. The LP relaxation objective function value of a subregion gives the best value we can possibly find for an integer solution in the subregion (bounding). This is called that subregion's *potential*. If we have already found an integer solution better than a subregion's potential, we may discard that subregion from consideration (this is known as *fathoming* the branch associated with that subregion). Hence, the importance of finding a good integer solution early in the search process is evident because it allows many subregions to be discarded and consequently speeds up the solution process. The Appendix at the end of the chapter provides a more detailed description of branch and bound, along with an example.

The Cutting Plane Approach

The *cutting plane* approach to solving integer programs is quite different from branch and bound. It attempts to add constraints to the LP relaxation to force the optimal corner point to become integer-valued. Care must be taken to avoid "cutting off" any feasible integer solutions. An inequality constraint that does not eliminate any feasible integer solutions is known as a *valid inequality*. A valid inequality that eliminates some fractional solutions is known as a *cutting plane*.

The cutting plane approach begins with the solution to LP relaxation and develops a valid inequality that eliminates the non-integer solution. This valid inequality is appended to the original problem as a constraint and the problem is resolved. If the solution to the revised problem is integer, we have found the optimal integer solution; if not, the process is repeated. Thus, a series of linear programs must be solved, one for each time a new cutting plane must be added to the problem.

Recent work has combined the branch and bound and cutting plane approaches. Valid inequalities that can be generated easily are added to the LP relaxation constraint set *prior* to branch and bound. The branch and bound procedure is then applied to this "tighter" LP relaxation. The LP relaxation is tighter in the sense that many of the fractional solutions that would have to be eliminated by branching have already been eliminated by preprocessing the problem with cuts. Also, a tighter model generally provides better bounds so that branches can be fathomed more quickly. Later in this chapter we will discuss preprocessing prior to branch and bound and developing tight models in more detail.

Interpreting IP Model Solution Output

LINDO uses branch and bound to solve integer, binary, and mixed integer programs. The commands *Gin* and *Int* are used to designate variables as general integer or binary integer variables. The general format used from the ":" mode in LINDO is *Gin variable* to make *variable* a general integer variable and *Int variable* to make *variable* a binary variable.

The regular *Go* command is used to solve the model. After entering the *Go* command, LINDO begins branch and bound. Branch and bound information will come to the screen, including the value of the LP relaxation. Also, any improvement found in the integer solution will be listed on the screen. (Note that the command *Page 0* will eliminate the need to hit the space bar in order to continue the scroll of the screen. We recommend entering *Page 0* before entering *Go*. The general command is *Page #*, where # is the number of lines before the page break occurs.) When the branch and bound algorithm is finished, the message LAST INTEGER SOLUTION IS THE BEST FOUND RE-INSTALLING BEST SOLUTION will come to the screen, followed by the colon prompt. To see the solution, use the *Sol* command. *Sol* causes the solution to be listed on the screen.

EXAMPLE 4. GENERAL INTEGER VARIABLES IN LINDO

The LINDO model input for Example 1 is shown in Figure 8.4. The GIN command is used to make the variables x_1 and x_2 general integer variables. The LINDO branch and bound output for Example 1 appears in Figure 8.5. Notice that LINDO found and listed three integer solutions. Optimality was proven after nine branches (subregions) and over all LP's solved, 21 iterations of the simplex algorithm were needed. The other information is information concerning the branching process and is not very relevant for our purposes. The solution output (obtained by using the SOL command) is shown in Figure 8.6. The optimal solution is $x_1^* = 0$, $x_2^* = 7$, with $z^* = \$238,000$.

FIGURE 8.4   LINDO model input for Example 1

```
:Max 50000x1 + 34000x2
?        st
?        10x1 + 7x2 < 49
?        x1 + x2 > 5
?        END
: GIN x1
: GIN x2
```

FIGURE 8.5   The LINDO branch and bound output for Example 1

```
LP OPTIMUM FOUND AT STEP        2
OBJECTIVE VALUE =     244666.700
SET        X1 TO <=      4 AT      1, BND =    .2437E+06 TWIN =
-.1000E+31          4
SET        X2 TO <=      1 AT      2, BND =    .2340E+06 TWIN =
.2430E+06          7


NEW INTEGER SOLUTION OF        234000.000  AT BRANCH  2 PIVOT
    7
```

OBJECTIVE FUNCTION VALUE
1)   234000.00

VARIABLE   VALUE   REDUCED COST
   X1   4.000000   −50000.000000
   X2   1.000000   −34000.000000

ROW   SLACK OR SURPLUS   DUAL PRICES
 2)   2.000000   .000000
 3)   .000000   .000000

NO. ITERATIONS =   7
BRANCHES =   2 DETERM. = 1.000E   0
BOUND ON OPTIMUM: 243000.0
FLIP   X2 TO >=   2 AT   2 WITH BND =   243000.00
SET   X1 TO <=   3 AT   3, BND = .2423E+06 TWIN =
−.1000E+31   9
SET   X2 TO <=   2 AT   4, BND = .2180E+06 TWIN =
.2420E+06   11
FLIP   X2 TO >=   3 AT   4 WITH BND =   242000.00
SET   X1 TO <=   2 AT   5, BND = .2409E+06 TWIN =
−.1000E+31
SET   X2 TO <=   4 AT   6, BND = .2360E+06 TWIN =
.2400E+06

NEW INTEGER SOLUTION OF   236000.000   AT BRANCH   6 PIVOT
     16

OBJECTIVE FUNCTION VALUE

1)   236000.00

VARIABLE   VALUE   REDUCED COST
   X1   2.000000   −50000.000000
   X2   4.000000   −34000.000000

ROW   SLACK OR SURPLUS   DUAL PRICES
 2)   1.000000   .000000
 3)   1.000000   .000000

NO. ITERATIONS =   16 BRANCHES =   6 DETERM. = 1.000E   0
BOUND ON OPTIMUM: 240000.0
FLIP   X2 TO >=   5 AT   6 WITH BND =   240000.00

SET   X1 TO <=   1 AT   7, BND =   .2394E+06 TWIN =
−.1000E+31   18
SET   X2 TO <=   5 AT   8, BND =   .2200E+06 TWIN =
.2390E+06   20
FLIP   X2 TO >=   6 AT   8 WITH BND =   239000.00
SET   X1 TO <=   0 AT   9, BND =   .2380E+06 TWIN =
−.1000E+31   21

NEW INTEGER SOLUTION OF   238000.000   AT BRANCH   9 PIVOT
21

       OBJECTIVE FUNCTION VALUE

   1)   238000.00

VARIABLE   VALUE   REDUCED COST
   X1   .000000   −1428.570000
   X2   7.000000   .000000

   ROWSLACK OR SURPLUS   DUAL PRICES
   2)   .000000   4857.143000
   3)   2.000000   .000000

NO. ITERATIONS = 21
BRANCHES = 9 DETERM.= 1.000E   0
BOUND ON OPTIMUM: 238000.0
DELETE   X1 AT LEVEL   9
DELETE   X2 AT LEVEL   8
DELETE   X1 AT LEVEL   7
DELETE   X2 AT LEVEL   6
DELETE   X1 AT LEVEL   5
DELETE   X2 AT LEVEL   4
DELETE   X1 AT LEVEL   3
DELETE   X2 AT LEVEL   2
DELETE   X1 AT LEVEL   1
ENUMERATION COMPLETE. BRANCHES = 9 PIVOTS = 21

LAST INTEGER SOLUTION IS THE BEST FOUND
RE-INSTALLING BEST SOLUTION...

EXAMPLE 5. BINARY INTEGER VARIABLES IN LINDO

To illustrate the *Int* command for binary variables, consider the model presented in Example 2. The LINDO model input for this example is shown in Figure 8.7. The solution is shown in Figure 8.8. The solution took four branches and 13 iterations.

FIGURE 8.6   *The LINDO solution output for Example 1*

OBJECTIVE FUNCTION VALUE

1)   238000.00

VARIABLE	VALUE	REDUCED COST
X1	.000000	−50000.000000
X2	7.000000	−34000.000000

ROW	SLACK OR SURPLUS	DUAL PRICES
2)	.000000	.000000
3)	2.000000	.000000

NO. ITERATIONS = 21
BRANCHES = 9 DETERM.= 1.000E   0

FIGURE 8.7   *LINDO model input for Example 2*

```
: Max 30x1 + 10x2 + 26x3 + 18x4 + 20x5 + 6y1 +
? 2y2 + 8y3 + 9y4 + 4.5y5
? st
? 1300x1 + 950x2 + 1000x3 + 1400x4 + 1600x5 < 4800
? x1 + y1 = 1
? x2 + y2 = 1
? x3 + y3 = 1
? x4 + y4 = 1
? x5 + y5 = 1
? end
: int x1
: int x2
: int x3
: int x4
: int x5
: int y1
: int y2
: int y3
: int y4
: int y5
```

FIGURE 8.8   LINDO solution for a BIP (Example 2)

OBJECTIVE FUNCTION VALUE

1)   88.500000

VARIABLE	VALUE	REDUCED COST
X1	1.000000	− 30.000000
X2	1.000000	− 10.000000
X3	1.000000	− 26.000000
X4	1.000000	− 18.000000
X5	0.000000	− 20.000000
Y1	0.000000	− 6.000000
Y2	0.000000	− 2.000000
Y3	0.000000	− 8.000000
Y4	0.000000	− 9.000000
Y5	1.000000	− 4.500000

ROW	SLACK OR SURPLUS	DUAL PRICES
2)	150.000000	0.000000
3)	0.000000	0.000000
4)	0.000000	0.000000
5)	0.000000	0.000000
6)	0.000000	0.000000
7)	0.000000	0.000000

NO. ITERATIONS = 13
BRANCHES = 4 DETERM.= 1.000E   0

Finally, we conclude this section with an important note regarding sensitivity analysis of integer programs. The sensitivity analysis provided by solving the LP relaxation and any of the LP's corresponding to the subproblems are not relevant to the IP. This is because they refer to the sensitivity of the LP relaxation's solution or only to the LP associated with a particular subregion, and *not* to the sensitivity of the original IP. The components of the sensitivity analysis discussed in Chapter 6, such as objective function coefficient ranges, right-hand side ranges, and dual prices, assume that the decision variables' values can be fractional. Therefore, this information is not meaningful for the integer program.

Standard sensitivity analysis is not meaningful for integer programs because it assumes that fractional variable values are possible. To determine the sensitivity of an integer program to its parameters, the model must be resolved with different parameter settings.

Solving IP Models on a Spreadsheet

The EXCEL Solver also has integer programming capability. Model input for integer programming is exactly the same as described for linear programming in Chapter 5. Once a basic spreadsheet has been constructed, select the *Solver* option from the *Tools* menu. This invokes the *Solver Parameters* dialog box which allows you to specify the *Target Cell* (objective function), the *Changing Cells* (decision variables) and constraints. Recall that nonnegativity of the decision variables is not assumed, so these restrictions must be entered as constraints along with the other explicit constraints in the problem. Constraints are entered into the model by selecting the *Add* option in the constraint section.

Through the *Add* option, a decision variable or set of decision variables can be restricted to integer values by selecting the *int* option as the relation in the *Add Constraint* dialog box. To specify a binary variable, restrict the variable to be less-than-or-equal to 1 and integer.

Before attempting to solve a linear integer program, select the *Options* button from the *Solver Parameters* dialog box. Select *Assume Linear Model* to ensure that EXCEL uses the simplex algorithm. Also, check the setting of the *Tolerance* option. For example, with a Tolerance setting of 10%, Solver guarantees that the solution it reports will be within 10% of the true optimal solution. By requesting a solution within some tolerance (for example, 5% or 10%) of optimality rather than requiring the true optimal solution, the solution time may be drastically cut. *However, if the true optimal solution is desired, Tolerance must be set to 0%.* As with linear programming models, the solution process is started by selecting the *Solve* button in the *Solver Parameters* dialog box.

EXAMPLE 6. SOLVING AN INTEGER PROGRAMMING MODEL USING EXCEL SOLVER

Recall the Queen City Inc. production planning problem (Example 1). The integer programming model we developed is

$$\text{Max} \quad 50{,}000x_1 + 34{,}000x_2$$
$$\text{subject to}$$
$$10x_1 + 7x_2 \leq 49$$
$$x_1 + x_2 \geq 5$$
$$x_1, \ x_2 \geq 0 \text{ and integer}$$

where x_1 = the number of TopLathes to produce this month and x_2 = the number of BigPresses to produce this month.

The first constraint restricts to 49 the number of components used (each TopLathe requires 10 and each BigPress requires 7). The second constraint ensures marketing's request that we produce at least five machines.

An EXCEL spreadsheet model, along with cell formulas for this scenario, is shown in Figure 8.9. Figure 8.10*a* shows how the changing cells are restricted to integer using the *Add Constraint* dialog box and Figure 8.10*b* shows the complete model in the *Solver Parameters* dialog box. Before solving the model, the *Solver Options* box was invoked.

FIGURE 8.9   *EXCEL spreadsheet model and formulas for Queen City Inc.*

	A	B	C	D	E	F
1	Queen City Inc.					
2						
3	*Parameters and uncontrollable inputs:*					
4						
5		Components	Profit/unit			
6	TopLathe	10	$50,000		Total Required	5
7	BigPress	7	$34,000			
8						
9	Available	49				
10						
11						
12	*Decision variables:*					
13						
14		Quantity				
15	TopLathe	0				
16	BigPress	0				
17						
18						
19	*Model outputs:*					
20						
21		TopLathe	BigPress	Total		
22	Quantity	0	0	0		
23	Components Used	0	0	0		
24	Profit	$0	$0	$0		

Selected cell formulas

	A	B	C	D
19	*Model outputs:*			
20				
21		TopLathe	BigPress	Total
22	Quantity	=B15	=B16	=B22+C22
23	Components Used	=B6*B15	=B7*B16	=B23+C23
24	Profit	=C6*B15	=C7*B16	=B24+C24

FIGURE 8.10a   The Add Constraint *dialog box to enforce integer restrictions for Queen City Inc.*

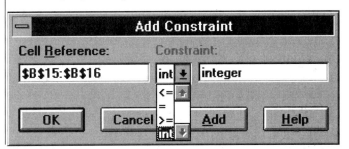

FIGURE 8.10b   *The* Solver Parameters *box for Queen City Inc.*

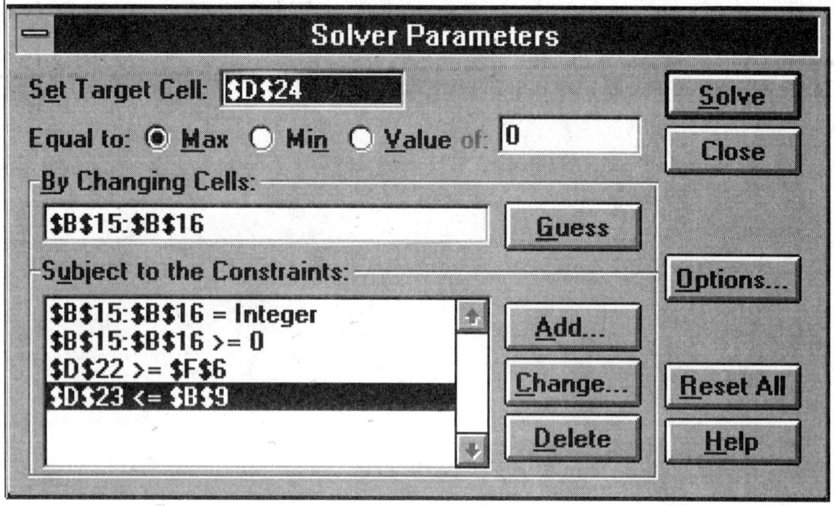

As shown in Figure 8.11, the *Tolerance* is set to zero to ensure that we find the optimal solution, and the *Assume Linear Model* option has been selected. The solution is shown in the spreadsheet in Figure 8.12. The optimal solution is to produce no TopLathes and 7 BigPresses, for a profit of $238,000.

FIGURE 8.11   *The* Solver Options *settings for Queen City Inc.*

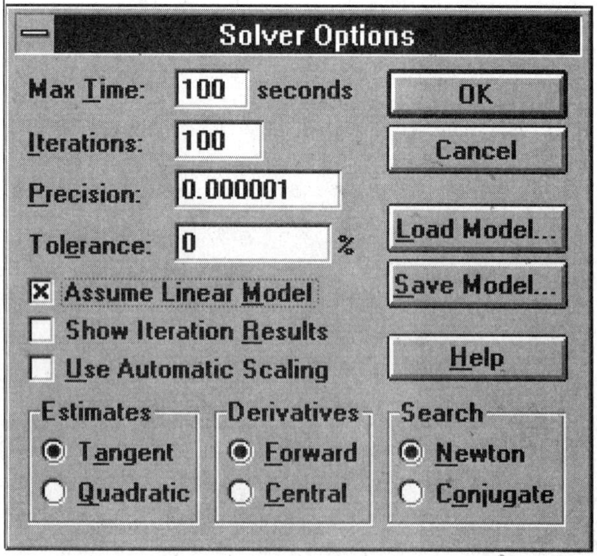

FIGURE 8.12   *The EXCEL solver solution to the Queen City Inc. problem*

	A	B	C	D	E	F
1	Queen City Inc.					
2						
3	Parameters and uncontrollable inputs:					
4						
5		Components	Profit/unit			
6	TopLathe	10	$50,000		Total Required	5
7	BigPress	7	$34,000			
8						
9	Available	49				
10						
11						
12	Decision variables:					
13						
14		Quantity				
15	TopLathe	0				
16	BigPress	7				
17						
18						
19	Model outputs:					
20						
21		TopLathe	BigPress	Total		
22	Quantity	0	7	7		
23	Components Used	0	49	49		
24	Profit	$0	$238,000	$238,000		

DEVELOPING TIGHT MODELS

As we previously discussed, the branch and bound approach used by most computer packages begins by solving the LP relaxation. If the variables that are restricted to be integer turn out to be integer-valued, then the optimal solution has been found, and no branching is necessary. However, in those cases where the solution to the LP relaxation has fractional values for variables which are restricted to be integer, the amount of branching that needs to be done in order to find the optimal IP solution is related to the difference between the objective function value of the LP relaxation and the objective function value of the (unknown) optimal integer solution. That is, the tightness of the bound provided by the LP relaxation relative to the unknown IP optimal objective function value determines how much extra work will be required to find the optimal integer solution. Loosely speaking, a tight IP model is one whose LP relaxation provides an objective function value close to the IP's optimal objective function value.

Large amounts of computer time can be saved by developing tight IP models. One thing you will quickly find out is that solving IP models is not as fast as solving LP models. You may find yourself waiting a very long time for a solution from even relatively small IP models. Consequently, as a model builder, you should be aware of some of the simple techniques that can be used to improve the IP solution process. Most of these techniques are very logical, and although many of them seem trivial, they can save you many minutes and even hours of computer time. The next example illustrates two simple constraint adjustments which can lead to tighter models.

EXAMPLE 7. DEVELOPING A TIGHTER INTEGER PROGRAMMING MODEL

Consider the integer program

$$\text{Max} \quad 8x_1 + 7x_2$$
$$\text{subject to}$$
$$12x_1 + 10x_2 \leq 45$$
$$x_2 \leq 2.5$$
$$x_1, x_2 \geq 0 \text{ and integer}$$

The optimal solution to the LP relaxation of this model is $x_1 = 1.66667$, $x_2 = 2.5$, with an objective function value $= 30.83333$. Two branches and a total of six iterations of the simplex algorithm are required to find the optimal integer solution, which is $x_1 = 2$, $x_2 = 2$, with an objective function value of 30.

Suppose, however, that we inspect the model more closely before attempting to solve it. Notice that x_2 is required to be integer and that the second constraint is $x_2 \leq 2.5$. Clearly, this constraint will never be binding in any optimal integer solution. Because x_2 has to be integer, the second constraint can be replaced by $x_2 \leq 2$. Note that this constraint is valid because no integer solutions are lost.

Next, notice that both coefficients in the first constraint are even numbers (12 and 10). Because both x_1 and x_2 have to be integer, it is not possible for the left-hand side of the constraint to take on an odd value. However, the right-hand side is an odd number (45). Consequently, this constraint can never be binding in the optimal integer solution. Therefore, the right-hand side of the first constraint can be tightened to 44.

The new, tighter model is

$$\text{Max} \quad 8x_1 + 7x_2$$
$$\text{subject to}$$
$$12x_1 + 10x_2 \leq 44$$
$$x_2 \leq 2$$
$$x_1, x_2 \geq 0 \text{ and integer}$$

The solution to the LP relaxation of this model appears in Figure 8.13, and the solution is integer! By using simple logic, we developed a tighter, equivalent model which found an optimal integer solution without having to resort to branch and bound. We will not always be this lucky, but tightening IP models in this fashion can cut down considerably on the amount of branching required to find the optimal IP solution. Of course, extreme caution must be used to make sure you have tightened the IP in a valid manner; that is, that you have not eliminated any feasible integer solutions.

FIGURE 8.13   *LINDO solution to the tightened IP in Example 7*

```
MAX        8 X1 + 7 X2
SUBJECT TO
        2)      12 X1 + 10 X2 <= 44
        3)      X2 <= 2
END

LP OPTIMUM FOUND AT STEP         2

            OBJECTIVE FUNCTION VALUE

        1)              30.000000

    VARIABLE              VALUE        REDUCED COST
        X1             2.000000            .000000
        X2             2.000000            .000000

        ROW    SLACK OR SURPLUS        DUAL PRICES
        2)             .000000            .666667
        3)             .000000            .333333
```

NO. ITERATIONS = 2

In addition to tightening constraints, it is often possible to logically determine the optimal values of certain integer variables prior to solving the IP model. These variables can then be locked in or "pegged" to their optimal value before solving the problem. This is known as *variable pegging*. We will illustrate this using the Chemco MIP model of Example 3.

EXAMPLE 8. PEGGING VARIABLES IN INTEGER PROGRAMS

In the Chemco model (Example 3), x_i = the amount of chlorine (in gallons) to produce in week i, I_i = the amount of chlorine (in gallons) in inventory at the end of week i, and y_i = 1 if we produce in week i, 0 if we do not. The model is

$$\text{Min}\quad 500y_1 + 500y_2 + 500y_3 + 500y_4 + 1I_1 + 1I_2 + 1I_3 + 1I_4$$

$$\text{subject to}$$

$$100 + x_1 - 800 = I_1$$

$$I_1 + x_2 - 500 = I_2$$

$$I_2 + x_3 - 450 = I_3$$

$$I_3 + x_4 - 900 = I_4$$

$$x_i \le 1{,}000\, y_i \quad i = 1, 2, 3, 4$$

$$I_i \leq 1,500 \quad i = 1, 2, 3, 4$$
$$x_i \geq 0 \quad i = 1, 2, 3, 4$$
$$0 \leq y_i \leq 1 \text{ and integer} \quad i = 1, 2, 3, 4$$

Notice from the first constraint that we have 100 gallons currently in inventory and a demand of 800 gallons in week 1. Therefore, we *must* produce at least 700 gallons in week 1 in order to satisfy demand. Consequently, we know that $y_1^* = 1$. Furthermore, notice that we require a total of $1,300 - 100 = 1,200$ gallons of production by the end of the second week. Because we can produce a maximum of 1,000 gallons in any one week, it is clear that we know we *must* produce in week 2 as well as week 1. Therefore, we can peg y_2 to 1; that is, $y_2^* = 1$.

Furthermore, we can tighten the model in the constraint $x_4 \leq 1,000y_4$. The demand in period 4 is only 900. Because we have no required ending inventory, the optimal solution must have $I_4^* = 0$, because holding inventory costs money. Because $I_4^* = 0$, we know that no more than 900 gallons will be produced in period 4. We can therefore tighten the fifth constraint to $x_4 \leq 900y_4$. This causes the y_4 value to be closer to its required value of 1 when x_4 is positive in the LP relaxation. For example, using the original constraint in the LP relaxation, if $x_4 = 500$, then $y_4 = .5$. With the new constraint, when $x_4 = 500$, $y_4 = .55$, resulting in a higher cost, and consequently a better bound. The .55 is closer to the actual value y_4 must assume in the IP solution if x_4 is positive (namely 1). For fixed charge constraints of this type, the coefficient of the binary fixed charge variable should usually be set to the lowest valid bound on the production variable for that time period. This is usually the production capacity or the sum of the demand from that period to the end of the planning horizon.[1]

The original Chemco model had an LP relaxation objective function value of \$1,275 and took 5 branches with 20 iterations to solve the IP. The tightened model with pegged variables, whose solution is shown in Figure 8.14, took only 1 branch and 9 iterations to find the optimal IP solution. Tightening the LP and pegging variables caused the LP relaxation of the tightened model to yield an objective closer to the true optimal value of \$1,950, (the objective function value of its LP relaxation was \$1,725 vs. \$1,275 for the original model) and thus eliminated some of the branching required with the original model. While a drop from five branches to one might not seem so great, imagine how much improvement might be experienced in a larger, real life model. The computer cost savings can be tremendous.

Although many of the techniques for tightening LP relaxations and pegging variables are problem-specific, LINDO has a feature that will perform some general tightening procedures similar to those we have seen. *It is highly recommended that you use this capability if you are solving a model with integer variables on LINDO.* The command is *Titan* and must be used from the command (colon) mode in LINDO prior to using the *Go* command.

We conclude this section with an example of the use of the *Titan* command in LINDO.

---

[1] For further discussion of this point see the reference by Camm, Raturi, and Tsubakitani.

FIGURE 8.14   *The LINDO output to the tightened Chemco MIP model*

```
MIN       500Y1 + 500Y2 + 500 Y3 + 500Y4 + I1 + I2 + I3 + I4
SUBJECT TO
        2)  −I1 + 1X = 700
        3)   I1 − I2 + X2 = 500
        4)   I2 − I3 + X3 = 450
        5)   I3 − I4 + X4 = 900
        6)  −1000Y1 + X1 <= 0
        7)  −1000Y2 + X2 <= 0
        8)  −1000Y3 + X3 <= 0
        9)  −900Y4 + X4 <= 0
       10)   I1 <= 1500
       11)   I2 <= 1500
       12)   I3 <= 1500
       13)   I4 <= 1500
       14)   Y1 = 1
       15)   Y2 = 1
END
INTE      4
```

OBJECTIVE FUNCTION VALUE

        1)   1950.0000

VARIABLE	VALUE	REDUCED COST
Y1	1.000000	500.000000
Y2	1.000000	500.000000
Y3	0.000000	−500.000000
Y4	1.000000	500.000000
I1	0.000000	1.000000
I2	450.000000	0.000000
I3	0.000000	2.000000
I4	0.000000	1.000000
X1	700.000000	0.000000
X2	950.000000	0.000000
X3	0.000000	0.000000
X4	900.000000	0.000000

ROW	SLACK OR SURPLUS	DUAL PRICES
2)	0.000000	0.000000
3)	0.000000	0.000000
4)	0.000000	− 1.000000
5)	0.000000	0.000000
6)	300.000000	0.000000
7)	50.000000	0.000000
8)	0.000000	1.000000
9)	0.000000	0.000000
10)	1500.000000	0.000000
11)	1050.000000	0.000000
12)	1500.000000	0.000000
13)	1500.000000	0.000000
14)	0.000000	0.000000
15)	0.000000	0.000000

NO. ITERATIONS = 10
BRANCHES = 1 DETERM. = 1.000E   0

EXAMPLE 9. USING THE TITAN COMMAND IN LINDO

Recall the Queen City Inc. problem (Example 1). Figure 8.15 (on page 385) shows the model and solution after the use of the *Titan* command. *SUB* and *SLB* stand for simple upper bound and simple lower bound respectively. The *Titan* command has added the constraints $x_1 \leq 4$, $x_2 \geq 1$, and $x_2 \leq 7$. Can you deduce why each of these constraints is valid? The original model took 9 branches and 21 iterations. The tightened model took 8 branches and 18 iterations.

MANAGEMENT SCIENCE PRACTICE[2]

Service sector operations such as airlines, hotels, and restaurants must deal constantly with staffing problems in the face of fluctuating demand. If the staff is too small, the firm cannot serve its customers well. This can result in lost sales and the loss of customer good will. A staff that is too large can meet customer demand, but labor costs might be excessive. Below we discuss how Qantas Airways uses an integer programming model to determine the least cost staff size in its telephone reservation system to meet projected demand.

---

[2] Adaptation from Gaballa and Pearce,"Telephone Sales Manpower Planning at Qantas," *Interfaces*, Vol. 9, No. 3, May 1979, pp. 1–9.

An Airline Staffing Problem

The airline industry has been and continues to be an extremely competitive industry. Survival depends on maximizing efficiency in operations and capturing a sufficient share of the customer market. Qantas Airways decided to analyze the size of its reservation staff, because an oversized staff is inefficient, but an undersized staff will result in lost market share. The fluctuation of demand over time makes the search for an optimal staff size a formidable task.

FIGURE 8.15   *Model and solution for Queen City Inc. using* Titan

```
MAX        50000 X1+34000 X2        ⎫
SUBJECT TO                          ⎪
        2)   10 X1 + 7 X2 <=    49  ⎬  Original model
        3)   X1 + X2 >=    5        ⎪
END                                 ⎭
        GIN  2


REDUCTIONS:
     BNDS: 6 IN       4PASSES.
COEFFICIENTS:    0
MAX        50000 X1+34000 X2        ⎫
SUBJECT TO                          ⎪
        2)   10 X1 + 7 X2 <=    49  ⎪
        3)   X1 + X2 >=    5        ⎪
END                                 ⎬  model after Titan
SUB        X1        4.00000        ⎪
GIN        X1                       ⎪
SLB        X2        1.00000        ⎪
SUB        X2        7.00000        ⎪
GIN        X2                       ⎭
            OBJECTIVE FUNCTION VALUE

        1)            238000.00


VARIABLE           VALUE           REDUCED COST
     X1           .000000          - 50000.000000
     X2          7.000000          - 34000.000000


     ROW     SLACK OR SURPLUS      DUAL PRICES
     2)            .000000             .000000
     3)           2.000000             .000000


NO. ITERATIONS = 18
BRANCHES = 8 DETERM. = 1.000E     0
```

Qantas began its analysis by collecting demand data (number of calls) by month over a two-year period. Then, for a three-month period, data were collected on a half-hour basis. The data showed that demand varied by time of day and day of the week, but that for a given month, variation over weeks was insignificant. Therefore, a typical or average week could be used for a given month's planning purposes.

The integer programming model uses demand forecasts to optimize staff size over time. The model assumes that

1. Shifts start only on the hour or half hour.
2. Shifts start during the hours of 7:00 a.m. to 9:30 a.m., plus one shift which starts at 3:00 p.m. (7 possible shifts).
3. The length of shifts starting between 8:30–9:30 is 8.5 hours with a one-hour lunch; all other shifts are eight hours with a half-hour lunch.
4. Lunch breaks are scheduled over a two-hour interval for the eight-hour shifts and over a two-and-a-half-hour interval for the eight-and-a-half-hour shift, commencing on the hour and half-hour. A day runs from 7:00 a.m. to 11:00 p.m. (32 half-hour intervals).

The model is shown below:

$$\text{Min} \sum_{j=1}^{7} S_j$$

subject to

$$
\begin{aligned}
S_1 &\geq R_1 \\
S_1 + S_2 &\geq R_2 \\
S_1 + S_2 + S_3 &\geq R_3 \\
S_1 + S_2 + S_3 + S_4 &\geq R_4 \\
S_1 + S_2 + S_3 + S_4 + S_5 &\geq R_5 \\
S_1 + S_2 + S_3 + S_4 + S_5 + S_6 &\geq R_6 \\
S_1 + S_2 + S_3 + S_4 + S_5 + S_6 - L_{11} &\geq R_7 \\
S_1 + S_2 + S_3 + S_4 + S_5 + S_6 - L_{21} - L_{12} &\geq R_8 \\
S_1 + S_2 + S_3 + S_4 + S_5 + S_6 - L_{31} - L_{22} - L_{13} &\geq R_9 \\
S_1 + S_2 + S_3 + S_4 + S_5 + S_6 - L_{41} - L_{32} - L_{23} - L_{14} &\geq R_{10} \\
S_1 + S_2 + S_3 + S_4 + S_5 + S_6 - L_{42} - L_{33} - L_{14} - L_{24} - L_{15} &\geq R_{11} \\
S_1 + S_2 + S_3 + S_4 + S_5 + S_6 - L_{43} - L_{24} - L_{34} - L_{15} - L_{25} - L_{16} &\geq R_{12} \\
S_1 + S_2 + S_3 + S_4 + S_5 + S_6 - L_{34} - L_{44} - L_{25} - L_{35} - L_{16} - L_{26} &\geq R_{13} \\
S_1 + S_2 + S_3 + S_4 + S_5 + S_6 - L_{44} - L_{35} - L_{45} - L_{26} - L_{36} &\geq R_{14} \\
S_1 + S_2 + S_3 + S_4 + S_5 + S_6 + S_7 - L_{45} - L_{36} - L_{46} &\geq R_{15} \\
S_1 + S_2 + S_3 + S_4 + S_5 + S_6 + S_7 - L_{46} &\geq R_{16} \\
S_2 + S_3 + S_4 + S_5 + S_6 + S_7 &\geq R_{17} \\
S_3 + S_4 + S_5 + S_6 + S_7 &\geq R_{18} \\
S_4 + S_5 + S_6 + S_7 &\geq R_{19} \\
S_4 + S_5 + S_6 + S_7 &\geq R_{20} \\
S_5 + S_6 + S_7 - L_{17} &\geq R_{21} \\
S_6 + S_7 - L_{27} &\geq R_{22} \\
S_7 - L_{37} &\geq R_{23} \\
S_7 - L_{47} &\geq R_{24} \\
S_7 &\geq R_{25}^*,
\end{aligned}
$$

where R_{25}^* is the *minimum* staff requirement in the time intervals 25 to 32; i.e., from 1,900 to 2,200 hours.

$$\sum_{i=1}^{4} L_{ij} - S_j = 0 \qquad j = 1, 2, \ldots, 7.$$

$$S_j, L_{ij} \geq 0 \text{ and integer}$$

In this model,

$$R_k = \text{staff requirements for time interval } k = 1, 2, \ldots 32$$
$$s_j = \text{number of staff on shift } j, \ j = 1, 2, \ldots 7$$
$$L_{ij} = \text{number of staff from shift } j \text{ taking their lunch break in period } i; i = 1, 2, 3, 4, \ j = 1, 2, \ldots 7$$

Outputs from the model include

1. Number of staff per shift.
2. Start and finish time of each shift.
3. Lunch schedule for each shift.
4. Total staff needed for the day.

Using the output of the daily IP model, a manual approach was developed for devising a minimum workforce schedule permitting each employee two consecutive days off. This approach is used for each month's typical week.

The use of this IP model and the manual workforce schedule saved over $200,000 over two years in the Sydney office alone. Because of the success of this approach in the reservations sales office, similar approaches were later used in other offices and in other customer contact areas such as passenger sales and check-in facilities.

Discussion Questions

1. Give a verbal description of the objective function and each of the constraints shown in the IP model.
2. Discuss in detail two other service sector operations that could benefit from this type of workforce planning model. Describe in detail any differences between your scenarios and that of Qantas and the corresponding changes that would be needed in the model.
3. Rather than changing the workforce levels, some retail and service corporations deal with fluctuating demand by attempting to change the demand patterns. Rather than deal with wide swings in demand through work force adjustments, they attempt to change the distribution of demand over time to meet the service level they can provide. Give some examples of this approach.

PRESENTING IP MODEL OUTPUT FOR MANAGERIAL INTERPRETATION: A CASE STUDY

EXAMPLE 10. TINDALL BOOKSTORES[3]

Tindall Bookstores is a major national retail chain with stores principally located in shopping malls. For many years, the company has published a Christmas catalog that was sent to current customers on file. This strategy generated additional mail order business while also attracting customers to the stores. The cost effectiveness of this strategy, however, was never determined. In 1991 John Harris, Vice-President of Marketing, conducted a major study on the effectiveness of direct-mail delivery of Tindall's Christmas catalog. The results were favorable: patrons who were catalog recipients spent more, on average, than did comparable non-recipients. These revenue gains more than compensated for the costs of production, handling, and mailing, which had been substantially reduced by cooperative allowances from suppliers.

With the continuing interest in direct-mail as a vehicle for delivering holiday catalogs, Harris continued to investigate how new customers could most effectively be reached. One of these ideas involved purchasing mailing lists of magazine subscribers through a list broker. In order to determine which magazines might be more appropriate, a mail questionnaire was administered to a sample of 6,625 current customers to ascertain which magazines they regularly read. Seventy-four magazines were selected for the survey. The assumption behind this strategy is that subscribers of magazines which a high proportion of current customers read would be viable targets for future purchases at Tindall stores. Tindall therefore needed to determine which magazine lists to purchase in order to maximize its ability to reach potential customers.

Data from the customer survey have begun to trickle in. Harris has asked us to develop a prototype model for this problem that can be used later to decide which lists to purchase. The returned questionnaire indicates which of the 74 magazines a customer subscribes to; so far only 53 surveys have been returned. To keep the prototype model manageable, Harris has instructed us to go ahead with the model development using the data from the 53 returned surveys and using only the first ten magazines in the questionnaire. The costs of the first ten lists are given in Table 8.2, and the budget is $3,000.

What is it that needs to be decided? We need to decide which magazine lists to purchase in order to maximize the number of customers reached using the budget of $3,000. Let $x_j = 1$ if magazine list j is purchased, 0 if not, $j = 1, 2 \ldots 10$. We must also know which customers can be reached by a particular list, so let $y_i = 1$ if customer i is reached by the purchased lists, 0 if not; $i = 1, 2, \ldots 53$.

---

[3]This problem is based on the case by the same name developed by James R. Evans of the University of Cincinnati, and was sponsored by the Direct Marketing Policy Center, University of Cincinnati.

TABLE 8.2
Data for Tindall
Bookstores
survey

List	1	2	3	4	5	6	7	8	9	10
Cost(000)	$1	$1	$1	$1.5	$1.5	$1.5	$1	$1.2	$.5	$1.1

Current Survey Results:

Customer	Magazines	Customer	Magazines
1	10	28	4,7
2	1,4	29	6
3	1	30	3,4,5,10
4	5,6	31	4
5	5	32	8
6	10	33	1,3,10
7	2,9	34	4,5
8	5,8	35	1,5,6
9	1,5,10	36	1,3
10	4,6,8,10	37	3,5,8
11	6	38	3
12	3	39	2,7
13	5	40	2,7
14	2,6	41	7
15	8	42	4,5,6
16	6	43	NONE
17	4,5	44	5,10
18	7	45	1,2
19	5,6	46	7
20	2,8	47	1,5,10
21	7,9	48	3
22	6	49	1,3,4
23	3,6,10	50	NONE
24	NONE	51	2,6
25	5,8	52	NONE
26	3,10	53	2,5,8,9,10
27	2,8		

What is the objective to be maximized or minimized? We wish to maximize the number of current customers reached. The objective function is simply the sum of the $y_i s$:

$$\text{Max} \sum_{i=1}^{53} y_i$$

How is the problem restricted? First, no more than $3,000 can be spent on the purchase of lists. Using the cost data from Table 8.2, the cost to purchase the lists cannot exceed $3,000:

$$1{,}000x_1 + 1{,}000x_2 + 1{,}000x_3 + 1{,}500x_4 + 1{,}500x_5 + 1{,}500x_6$$
$$+ 1{,}000x_7 + 1{,}200x_8 + 500x_9 + 1{,}100x_{10} \leq 3{,}000$$

Second, we need a constraint that ensures that a customer is counted as reached only if we purchase a list from one of his or her magazines. This ties together the y_i and x_j variables. We can construct such a constraint using the information from Table 8.2 and the fact that we are using binary variables. Consider customer number two, who subscribes to magazines 1 and 4. This means that y_1 should be set to one only if x_1 or x_4 (or both) equal 1. Note also that if x_1 and x_4 are one, then we still only want to count customer one once (that is, $y_2 = 1$ means that customer one has been reached and is *not* the number of times customer one has been reached). The following constraint will accomplish this for customer two:

$$y_2 \leq x_1 + x_4$$

If x_1 and x_4 are both 0, then we have $y_2 \leq 0$, so that $y_2 = 0$ because the variables are nonnegative. If either x_1 or x_4 is a 1, then y_2 is allowed to be a 1. We need one of these constraints for each customer. Let a_{ij} be binary data based on the survey results in Table 8.2, where $a_{ij} = 1$ if customer i subscribes to magazine j, and $a_{ij} = 0$ if customer i does not subscribe to magazine j. The generic constraint can be written as

$$y_i \leq \sum_{j=1}^{10} a_{ij} x_j \qquad i = 1, 2, \ldots 53$$

Let c_j be the cost of list j. The complete prototype model is then

$$\text{Max} \sum_{i=1}^{53} y_i$$

subject to

$$\sum_{j=1}^{10} c_j x_j \leq 3{,}000 \quad \text{no more than \$3000}$$

$$y_i - \sum_{j=1}^{10} a_{ij} x_j \leq 0 \qquad i = 1, 2 \ldots 53$$

$$y_i = 0, 1 \qquad i = 1, 2, \ldots 53$$

$$x_j = 0, 1 \qquad j = 1, 2, \ldots 10$$

The LINDO model is shown in Figure 8.16, and its solution appears in Figure 8.17. The optimal solution is to purchase lists for magazines 3, 5, and 9. This solution means that the budget of \$3,000 is completely used (row 55 is binding) and that 26 of the 53 respondents (49%) will be reached.

FIGURE 8.16   The LINDO model for the Tindall Bookstore problem

MAX $Y1 + Y2 + Y3 + Y4 + Y5 + Y6 + Y7 + Y8 + Y9 + Y10 + Y11$
               $+ \ Y12 + Y13 + Y14 + Y15 + Y16 + Y17 + Y18 + Y19 + Y20 +$
               $Y21 + Y22 + Y23 + Y24 + Y25 + Y26 + Y27 + Y28 + Y29 +$
               $Y30 + Y31 + Y32 + Y33 + Y34 + Y35 + Y36 + Y37 + Y38 +$
               $Y39 + Y40 + Y41 + Y42 + Y43 + Y44 + Y45 + Y46 + Y47 +$
               $Y48 + Y49 + Y50 + Y51 + Y52 + Y53$

SUBJECT TO

2) $Y1 - X10 <= 0$
3) $Y2 - X1 - X4 <= 0$
4) $Y3 - X1 <= 0$
5) $Y4 - X5 - X6 <= 0$
6) $Y5 - X5 <= 0$
7) $Y6 - X10 <= 0$
8) $Y7 - X2 - X9 <= 0$
9) $Y8 - X5 - X8 <= 0$
10) $Y9 - X10 - X1 - X5 <= 0$
11) $Y10 - X10 - X4 - X6 - X8 <= 0$
12) $Y11 - X6 <= 0$
13) $Y12 - X3 <= 0$
14) $Y13 - X5 <= 0$
15) $Y14 - X6 - X2 <= 0$
16) $Y15 - X8 <= 0$
17) $Y16 - X6 <= 0$
18) $Y17 - X4 - X5 <= 0$
19) $Y18 - X7 <= 0$
20) $Y19 - X5 - X6 <= 0$
21) $Y20 - X2 - X8 <= 0$
22) $Y21 - X9 - X7 <= 0$
23) $Y22 - X6 <= 0$
24) $Y23 - X10 - X6 - X3 <= 0$
25) $Y24 <= 0$
26) $Y25 - X5 - X8 <= 0$
27) $Y26 - X10 - X3 <= 0$
28) $Y27 - X2 - X8 <= 0$
29) $Y28 - X4 - X7 <= 0$
30) $Y29 - X6 <= 0$
31) $Y30 - X10 - X4 - X5 - X3 <= 0$
32) $Y31 - X4 <= 0$
33) $Y32 - X8 <= 0$
34) $Y33 - X10 - X1 - X3 <= 0$
35) $Y34 - X4 - X5 <= 0$
36) $Y35 - X1 - X5 - X6 <= 0$

37) Y36 − X1 − X3 <= 0
38) Y37 − X5 − X8 − X3 <= 0
39) Y38 − X3 <= 0
40) Y39 − X2 − X7 <= 0
41) Y40 − X2 − X7 <= 0
42) Y41 − X7 <= 0
43) Y42 − X4 − X5 − X6 <= 0
44) Y43 <= 0
45) Y44 − X10 − X5 <= 0
46) Y45 − X1 − X2 <= 0
47) Y46 − X7 <= 0
48) Y47 − X10 − X1 − X5 <= 0
49) Y48 − X3 <= 0
50) Y49 − X1 − X4 − X3 <= 0
51) Y50 <= 0
52) Y51 − X6 − X2 <= 0
53) Y52 <= 0
54) Y53 − X10 − X5 − X2 − X9 − X8 <= 0
55) 1100 X10 + 1000 X1 + 1500 X4 + 1500 X5 + 1500 X6 +
     1000 X2 + 500 X9 + 1200 X8 + 1000 X3 + 1000 X7 <= 3000

END
INTE   63

FIGURE 8.17   *The LINDO solution to the Tindall Bookstore IP model*

OBJECTIVE FUNCTION VALUE

1)   26.000000

VARIABLE	VALUE	REDUCED COST
Y1	.000000	− 1.000000
Y2	.000000	− 1.000000
Y3	.000000	− 1.000000
Y4	1.000000	− 1.000000
Y5	1.000000	− 1.000000
Y6	.000000	− 1.000000
Y7	1.000000	− 1.000000
Y8	1.000000	− 1.000000
Y9	1.000000	− 1.000000
Y10	.000000	− 1.000000
Y11	.000000	− 1.000000
Y12	1.000000	− 1.000000
Y13	1.000000	− 1.000000

Y14	.000000	− 1.000000
Y15	.000000	− 1.000000
Y16	.000000	− 1.000000
Y17	1.000000	− 1.000000
Y18	.000000	− 1.000000
Y19	1.000000	− 1.000000
Y20	.000000	− 1.000000
Y21	1.000000	− 1.000000
Y22	.000000	− 1.000000
Y23	1.000000	− 1.000000
Y24	.000000	− 1.000000
Y25	1.000000	− 1.000000
Y26	1.000000	− 1.000000
Y27	.000000	− 1.000000
Y28	.000000	− 1.000000
Y29	.000000	− 1.000000
Y30	1.000000	− 1.000000
Y31	.000000	− 1.000000
Y32	.000000	− 1.000000
Y33	1.000000	− 1.000000
Y34	1.000000	− 1.000000
Y35	1.000000	− 1.000000
Y36	1.000000	− 1.000000
Y37	1.000000	− 1.000000
Y38	1.000000	− 1.000000
Y39	.000000	− 1.000000
Y40	.000000	− 1.000000
Y41	.000000	− 1.000000
Y42	1.000000	− 1.000000
Y43	.000000	− 1.000000
Y44	1.000000	− 1.000000
Y45	.000000	− 1.000000
Y46	.000000	− 1.000000
Y47	1.000000	− 1.000000
Y48	1.000000	− 1.000000
Y49	1.000000	− 1.000000
Y50	.000000	− 1.000000
Y51	.000000	− 1.000000
Y52	.000000	− 1.000000
Y53	1.000000	− 1.000000
X10	.000000	.000000
X1	.000000	.000000
X4	.000000	.000000
X5	1.000000	.000000
X6	.000000	.000000

X2	.000000	.000000
X9	1.000000	.000000
X8	.000000	.000000
X3	1.000000	.000000
X7	.000000	.000000

ROW	SLACK OR SURPLUS	DUAL PRICES
2)	.000000	.000000
3)	.000000	.000000
4)	.000000	.000000
5)	.000000	.000000
6)	.000000	.000000
7)	.000000	.000000
8)	.000000	.000000
9)	.000000	.000000
10)	.000000	.000000
11)	.000000	.000000
12)	.000000	.000000
13)	.000000	.000000
14)	.000000	.000000
15)	.000000	.000000
16)	.000000	.000000
17)	.000000	.000000
18)	.000000	.000000
19)	.000000	.000000
20)	.000000	.000000
21)	.000000	.000000
22)	.000000	.000000
23)	.000000	.000000
24)	.000000	.000000
25)	.000000	.000000
26)	.000000	.000000
27)	.000000	.000000
28)	.000000	.000000
29)	.000000	.000000
30)	.000000	.000000
31)	1.000000	.000000
32)	.000000	.000000
33)	.000000	.000000
34)	.000000	.000000
35)	.000000	.000000
36)	.000000	.000000

37)	.000000	.000000
38)	1.000000	.000000
39)	.000000	.000000
40)	.000000	.000000
41)	.000000	.000000
42)	.000000	.000000
43)	.000000	.000000
44)	.000000	.000000
45)	.000000	.000000
46)	.000000	.000000
47)	.000000	.000000
48)	.000000	.000000
49)	.000000	.000000
50)	.000000	.000000
51)	.000000	.000000
52)	.000000	.000000
53)	.000000	.000000
54)	1.000000	.000000
55)	.000000	.000000

NO. ITERATIONS = 423

BRANCHES = 20 DETERM. =
1.000E O

A natural question is, How is the ability to reach customers related to the budget? We can answer this question by resolving the model while varying the budget value (the right-hand side value of row 55 in the LINDO model). Figure 8.18 shows how percentage reach (the number of customers reached divided by the total of 53) increases as a function of budget. To get the values shown in the graph, the model was solved for budget values from $0 to $11,000 in increments of $1,000. Note that customers 24, 43, 50, and 52 cannot be reached (see Table 8.2), so that the maximum achievable coverage is 49 (92%). Also, from Figure 8.18, it appears that the effectiveness of increasing the budget diminishes significantly after $6,000.

This prototype model and analysis indicate that this type of analysis would be appropriate for the entire data set of responses when they arrive.

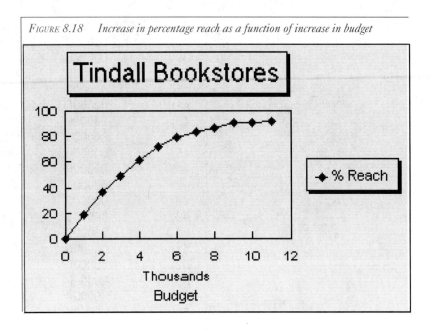

FIGURE 8.18   *Increase in percentage reach as a function of increase in budget*

MORE EXAMPLES AND SOLVED PROBLEMS

In this section we discuss various other applications of integer programming.

EXAMPLE 11. MACRO ALUMINUM CUTTING STOCK PROBLEM

Macro Aluminum provides aluminum rolls of various widths to small companies. Macro buys aluminum rolls of 35 yards in width directly from a nearby steel mill. It then takes orders (in widths from 10 to 35 yards) and fills these orders by cutting the bulk roll into the needed widths. The current orders are shown in Table 8.3. There is currently no inventory of any of these widths. The production manager has developed numerous cutting patterns (ways of cutting up the 35-yard-wide bulk roll) for different combinations of widths. These patterns are shown in Table 8.4 on page 398. Most patterns have some trim loss (scrap). How many rolls should be cut from each pattern in order to to satisfy demand and minimize trim loss? No more than two rolls of each width should be held in inventory.

What is it that Macro needs to decide? Macro needs to decide how many rolls to cut from each of the six patterns and what inventories to maintain. We can define the decision variables:

$$x_i = \text{the number of rolls using cutting pattern } i$$
$$i = 1, 2, 3, 4, 5, 6$$
$$I_j = \text{the number of rolls of width type } j \text{ left over for inventory}$$
$$j = 1, 2, 3, 4$$

TABLE 8.3
*Demand for various
widths*

Width	10 yards	12 yards	15 yards	18 yards
Demand (rolls)	5	3	5	8

What is the objective to be maximized or minimized? The objective is to minimize total trim loss. This is computed by multiplying the number of times we use each pattern by the trim loss per pattern.

$$\text{Min}\quad 5x_1 + 7x_2 + 2x_3 + x_4 + 5x_5$$

How is the problem restricted? Demand for each of the four widths must be satisfied, but no more than two rolls of each width can be kept in inventory. We can model these restrictions using an inventory balance equation for each width. Note that the number of rolls produced in a particular width depends on the type and number of patterns used. For example, 10-yard rolls are produced in the following ways: three every time pattern 1 is used, one every time pattern 2 or 4 is used, and two every time pattern 6 is used. Therefore, the balance equation for 10-yard rolls is

$$3x_1 + x_2 + x_4 + 2x_6 - 5 = I_1$$

— demand

Similarly for the other 3 widths, we have

$$2x_4 + x_5 - 3 = I_2$$
$$x_3 + x_6 - 5 = I_3$$
$$x_2 + x_3 + x_5 - 8 = I_4$$

Finally, the inventory of each width is restricted to two rolls. Note that the x_i's must be integer, but that the I_j's will automatically be integer when the x_i's are integer. Therefore, we need only explicitly restrict the x_i's to be integer. The complete model appears below.

$$\text{Min}\quad 5x_1 + 7x_2 + 2x_3 + x_4 + 5x_5$$
$$\text{subject to}$$
$$3x_1 + x_2 + x_4 + 2x_6 - 5 = I_1$$
$$2x_4 + x_5 - 3 = I_2$$
$$x_3 + x_6 - 5 = I_3$$
$$x_2 + x_3 + x_5 - 8 = I_4$$
$$I_j \leq 2 \quad j = 1, 2, 3, 4$$
$$I_j \geq 0 \quad j = 1, 2, 3, 4$$
$$x_i \geq 0 \quad \text{and integer} \quad i = 1, 2, 3, 4$$

An EXCEL spreadsheet model for this scenario along with selected cell formulas are shown in Figure 8.19. Figure 8.20 shows the model in the *Solver Parameters* dialog

TABLE 8.4
*Cutting patterns for
Macro*

Pattern	10 yard rolls	12 yard rolls	15 yard rolls	18 yard rolls	Trim loss
1	3				5 yards
2	1			1	7 yards
3			1	1	2 yards
4	1	2			1 yard
5		1		1	5 yards
6	2		1		0 yards

box, and the solution is shown in Figure 8.21. The solution to this model is to cut one roll using pattern 2, six rolls using pattern 3, two rolls using pattern 4, and one roll each using patterns 5 and 6. This leaves 26 yards of trim loss and a two-roll inventory for 12- and 15-yard widths.

EXAMPLE 12. THE SEGREGATED STORAGE PROBLEM

The segregated storage problem concerns the optimal assignment of products to storage compartments with the restriction that no more than one product can be stored in any compartment. This segregation of products is important for commodities such as food items, chemicals, and fuels. We illustrate this problem with the following example.[4]

A company has three grain products which must be stored separately, and three storage compartments with different capacities. The storage capacity of each compartment (in tons), the amount of each grain that needs to be stored this month (in tons), and the variable storage cost (per ton per month) are given in Table 8.5. A public facility can be used to store any and all of the commodities at a cost of $240, $220, and $220 per ton per month for grains 1, 2, and 3 respectively. What is the cost-minimizing storage plan?

What is it that needs to be decided? We need to decide which grain to store in each compartment (or in the public facility) in order to minimize the storage cost. Let x_{ij} = the number of tons of grain i to store in compartment j; $i = 1, 2, 3$ and $j = 1, 2, 3$. Because only one grain can be stored in any given compartment, we must know which grain is assigned to which compartment. We define a binary variable $y_{ij} = 1$ if grain i is stored in compartment j, 0 if it is not, $i = 1, 2, 3$ and $j = 1, 2, 3$. Finally, we must decide how much of each grain to store in the public facility. Let z_i = the amount of grain i (in tons) to store in the public facility.

What is the objective to be maximized or minimized? We wish to minimize the storage cost. Using the costs per ton per month given in Table 8.5 we have

$$\text{Min} \quad 200x_{11} + 140x_{12} + 190x_{13} + 240z_1 + 150x_{21} + 130x_{22}$$
$$+ 200x_{23} + 220z_2 + 180x_{31} + 180x_{31} + 180x_{32} + 150x_{33} + 220z_3$$

How is the problem restricted? First, all the grain must be stored. If a_i is the amount (in tons) of grain i available, we have

---

[4]This example is from the reference by Neebe.

FIGURE 8.19   An EXCEL spreadsheet model and selected cell formulas for the Macro cutting stock problem

	A	B	C	D	E	F	G	H	I
1	Macro Aluminum Cutting Stock Problem								
2									
3	Parameters and uncontrollable inputs:								
4									
5				Patterns					
6	Width	1	2	3	4	5	6	Demand	Inventory Bound
7	10	3	1	0	1	0	2	5	2
8	12	0	0	0	2	1	0	3	2
9	15	0	0	1	0	0	1	5	2
10	18	0	1	1	0	1	0	8	2
11	Trim	5	7	2	1	5	0		
12									
13									
14	Decision variables:								
15				Patterns					
16		1	2	3	4	5	6		
17	# Rolls:	0	0	0	0	0	0		
18									
19									
20	Width	10	12	15	18				
21	Inventory	0	2	2	0				
22									
23									
24	Model outputs:								
25									
26	Width	Total	Inventory		Pattern	# Rolls	Trim		
27	10	0	0		1	0	0		
28	12	0	2		2	0	0		
29	15	0	2		3	0	0		
30	18	0	0		4	0	0		
31					5	0	0		
32					6	0	0		
33						Total	0		

Selected cell formulas

	A	B	C	D	E	F
24	Model outputs:					
25						
26	Width	Total	Inventory		Pattern	# Rolls
27	10	=SUMPRODUCT(B17:G17,B7:G7)	=B21		1	=B17
28	12	=SUMPRODUCT(B17:G17,B8:G8)	=C21		2	=C17
29	15	=SUMPRODUCT(B17:G17,B9:G9)	=D21		3	=D17
30	18	=SUMPRODUCT(B17:G17,B10:G10)	=E21		4	=E17
31					5	=F17
32					6	=G17
33						Total

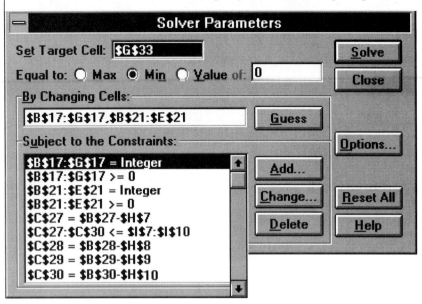

FIGURE 8.20   The Solver Parameters *dialog box for the Macro Cutting stock problem*

FIGURE 8.21   The solution to the Macro Cutting stock problem

	A	B	C	D	E	F	G	H	I
1	Macro Aluminum Cutting Stock Problem								
2									
3	*Parameters and uncontrollable inputs:*								
4									
5				Patterns					
6	Width	1	2	3	4	5	6	Demand	Inventory Bound
7	10	3	1	0	1	0	2	5	2
8	12	0	0	0	2	1	0	3	2
9	15	0	0	1	0	0	1	5	2
10	18	0	1	1	0	1	0	8	2
11	Trim	5	7	2	1	5	0		
12									
13									
14	*Decision variables:*								
15				Patterns					
16		1	2	3	4	5	6		
17	# Rolls:	0	1	6	2	1	1		
18									
19									
20	Width	10	12	15	18				
21	Inventory	0	2	2	0				
22									
23									
24	*Model outputs:*								
25									
26	Width	Total	Inventory		Pattern	# Rolls	Trim		
27	10	5	0		1	0	0		
28	12	5	2		2	1	7		
29	15	7	2		3	6	12		
30	18	8	0		4	2	2		
31					5	1	5		
32					6	1	0		
33						Total	26		

TABLE 8.5
Segregated storage
problem data

	Compartment Storage Cost ($ per ton per month)			
	1	2	3	Amount (Tons)
Grain 1	200	140	190	1
Grain 2	150	130	200	8
Grain 3	180	180	150	7
Capacity (Tons)	3	7	4	

$$\sum_{j=1}^{3} x_{ij} + z_i = a_i \quad i = 1, 2, 3$$

Second, only one type of grain can be stored in any compartment.

$$\sum_{i=1}^{3} y_{ij} \leq 1 \quad j = 1, 2, 3$$

Finally, we must relate the x_{ij} variables to the y_{ij} variables. That is, we must guarantee that grain i cannot be stored in compartment j unless grain i has been assigned to compartment j. If so, we can store only an amount up to the capacity of compartment j (c_j). This is handled using a fixed charge constraint.

$$x_{ij} \leq c_j y_{ij} \quad i = 1, 2, 3 \quad j = 1, 2, 3$$

The complete model is

$$\text{Min} \quad 200x_{11} + 140x_{12} + 190x_{13} + 240z_1 + 150x_{21} + 130x_{22}$$
$$+ 200x_{23} + 220z_2 + 180x_{31} + 180x_{32} + 150x_{33} + 220z_3$$

subject to

$$x_{11} + x_{12} + x_{13} + z_1 = 1$$
$$x_{21} + x_{22} + x_{23} + z_2 = 8$$
$$x_{31} + x_{32} + x_{33} + z_3 = 7$$
$$\sum_{i=1}^{3} y_{ij} \leq 1 \quad j = 1, 2, 3$$
$$x_{ij} \leq c_j y_{ij} \quad i = 1, 2, 3 \quad j = 1, 2, 3$$
$$x_{ij} \geq 0 \quad i = 1, 2, 3 \quad j = 1, 2, 3$$
$$z_i \geq 0 \quad i = 1, 2, 3$$
$$0 \leq y_{ij} \leq 1 \quad \text{and integer} \quad i = 1, 2, 3 \quad j = 1, 2, 3$$

The solution is to store 7 tons of grain 2 in compartment 2 and 1 ton in the public facility, 3 tons of grain 3 in compartment 1, 4 tons in compartment 3, and 1 ton of grain 1 in the public facility. This plan costs $2,510.

EXAMPLE 13. GREENVILLE MILLS EXPANSION

Greenville Mills plans to build a spinning mill.[5] Two mutually exclusive possibilities, Sm1 and Sm2, exist for the spinning mill. At most one of these two will be undertaken. Greenville is also considering building a new cloth mill. Three cloth mill proposals are under consideration, Cm1, Cm2, and Cm3. At most one of these will be selected. The construction of a cloth mill is dependent on the construction of a spinning mill. In particular, Cm1 can be undertaken only if Sm1 is chosen. The other two cloth mill proposals can be chosen only if a new spinning mill is constructed (Sm1 or Sm2). The estimates of net present values (NPV) and initial outlays are given in Table 8.6. The board of Greenville Mills has decided that at least 25 percent of the total initial outlay must be covered by the mill's equity capital, which is currently $8,600,000. What projects should the mill choose in order to maximize net present value?

What is it that Greenville Mills needs to decide? Management needs to decide which of these investments, if any, to undertake. Let x_i = 1 if Smi is chosen, 0 if not, i = 1, 2; y_j = 1 if Cmj is chosen, 0 if not, j = 1, 2, 3.

What is the objective to be maximized or minimized? The objective is to maximize net present value (NPV) of the projects selected. This is shown below in millions of dollars:

$$\text{Max} \quad 6x_1 + 4x_2 + 3.5y_1 + 5.4y_2 + 6y_3$$

How is the problem restricted? First, no more than one spinning mill project and no more than one cloth mill project can be chosen.

$$x_1 + x_2 \le 1$$
$$y_1 + y_2 + y_3 \le 1$$

Second, the company's current capital equity must be at least 25 percent of the initial outlay for the projects.

$$.25(16x_1 + 12.5x_2 + 8.3y_1 + 12y_2 + 15y_3) \le 8.6$$

This can be written as

$$16x_1 + 12.5x_2 + 8.3y_1 + 12y_2 + 15y_3 \le 34.4$$

TABLE 8.6
Project information for
Greenville Mills

	Sm1	Sm2	Cm1	Cm2	Cm3
NPV	$6M	$4M	$3.5M	$5.4M	$6M
Initial Outlay	$16M	$12.5M	$8.3M	$12M	$15M

---

[5]This problem is based on the textile mill problem in the reference by Dano (p. 74).

Third, Cm1 can be chosen only if Sm1 is chosen.

$$y_1 \leq x_1$$

This logical constraint enforces the contingency, because if $x_1 = 0$, then $y_1 = 0$. If $x_1 = 1$, then y_1 can be 0 or 1.

Fourth, Cm2 or Cm3 can only be undertaken if a spinning mill is constructed. This is similar to the previous constraint.

$$y_2 + y_3 \leq x_1 + x_2$$

The complete model for the Greenville Mills investment problem is

$$\text{Max} \quad 6x_1 + 4x_2 + 3.5y_1 + 5.4y_2 + 6y_3$$

subject to

$$x_1 + x_2 \leq 1$$
$$y_1 + y_2 + y_3 \leq 1$$
$$16x_1 + 12.5x_2 + 8.3y_1 + 12y_2 + 15y_3 \leq 34.4$$
$$y_1 \leq x_1 \qquad \text{— important}$$
$$y_2 + y_3 \leq x_1 + x_2$$
$$0 \leq x_i \leq 1 \text{ and integer} \quad i = 1, 2$$
$$0 \leq y_j \leq 1 \text{ and integer} \quad j = 1, 2, 3$$

The solution to this problem is to select Sm1 and Cm3 for a net present value of $12 million.

EXAMPLE 14. LOCK BOX LOCATION

National and international companies face the problem of reducing the amount of time it takes to deposit payments from their customers after the customers have mailed them. Payments in transit or in the process of being cleared through the Federal Reserve Bank (if the check is written from a different bank than the company's) represent delayed capital. For large companies, lost capital and interest can be significant. An approach often used to speed up the payment process is to place "lock boxes" at various locations throughout the country. Lock boxes are post office boxes where payments can be sent. The lock box is checked twice a day by an employee of a nearby bank associated with the Federal Reserve Bank. The bank processes the bills for the company, drastically cutting down the time it takes for the company to gain use of the funds.

Usually, a fixed cost is associated with renting the lock box and hiring the bank to check the box and process the checks. The bank also charges for each check processed. The planning problem, known as the *lock box problem*, is to select the best locations for lock boxes and assignments of customers to them.

For simplicity, assume that we have three potential locations and five customers. The variable monthly costs for assigning a customer to a particular lock box location and the fixed cost of a lock box at that location are given in Table 8.7.

TABLE 8.7
Lock box data

	Location 1	Location 2	Location 3
Customer 1	$ 23	$ 19	$25
Customer 2	$ 22	$ 34	$35
Customer 3	$ 19	$ 19	$37
Customer 4	$ 25	$ 22	$17
Customer 5	$ 22	$ 34	$26
Fixed Cost	$100	$150	$95

What is it that needs to be decided? We would like to determine the least-cost lock box locations and the assignment of customers to those locations. Let $x_{ij} = 1$ if customer i is assigned to the lock box in location j, 0 if not; $i = 1, 2, 3, 4, 5$ and $j = 1, 2, 3$. Let $y_j = 1$ if location j is selected, 0 if not, $j = 1, 2, 3$.

What is the objective to be maximized or minimized? Our objective is to minimize the monthly fixed and variable cost of the lock box operation. In terms of the decision variables we defined

$$\text{Min} \quad 100y_1 + 150y_2 + 95y_3$$
$$+ 23x_{11} + 22x_{21} + 19x_{31} + 25x_{41} + 22x_{51}$$
$$+ 19x_{12} + 34x_{22} + 19x_{32} + 22x_{42} + 34x_{52}$$
$$+ 25x_{13} + 35x_{23} + 37x_{33} + 17x_{43} + 26x_{53}$$

How is the problem restricted? First, every customer must be assigned to exactly one lock box.

$$\sum_{j=1}^{3} x_{ij} = 1 \quad i = 1, 2, 3, 4, 5$$

Second, a customer cannot be assigned to a lock box unless that lock box has been selected. In terms of our decision variables, x_{ij} must be zero if y_j is zero:

$$x_{ij} \le y_j \quad i = 1, 2, 3, 4, 5 \quad j = 1, 2, 3$$

The complete model for determining the cheapest lock box configuration is

$$\text{Min} \quad 100y_1 + 150y_2 + 95y_3$$
$$+ 23x_{11} + 22x_{21} + 19x_{31} + 25x_{41} + 22x_{51}$$
$$+ 19x_{12} + 34x_{22} + 19x_{32} + 22x_{42} + 34x_{52}$$
$$+ 25x_{13} + 35x_{23} + 37x_{33} + 17x_{43} + 26x_{53}$$

subject to

$$\sum_{j=1}^{3} x_{ij} = 1 \quad i = 1, 2, 3, 4, 5$$

$$x_{ij} \le y_j \quad i = 1, 2, 3, 4, 5 \quad j = 1, 2, 3$$
$$0 \le x_{ij} \le 1 \text{ and integer} \quad i = 1, 2, 3, 4, 5 \quad j = 1, 2, 3$$
$$0 \le y_j \le 1 \text{ and integer} \quad j = 1, 2, 3$$

The solution to this small lock box problem is to open a box only at location 1. This results in a monthly total cost of $211.

EXAMPLE 15. CAPITAL BUDGETING AT THE NATIONAL CANCER INSTITUTE[6]

The National Cancer Institute (NCI) in Bethesda, Maryland uses integer programming to help make project funding decisions. The American Stop Smoking Intervention Study (ASSIST) is a multiple-year, multiple-site demonstration project designed to reduce smoking prevalence. The project data are shown in Table 8.8.

Each project has been assigned a value based on the review of the proposals. The objective is to maximize the total rank function value of the projects selected for funding. Each proposal also has a preference coefficient, obtained from the review process, which is designed to take into account other important criteria besides ranking. The total of the preference coefficients for the selected projects must be at least 17. Although many different budgets were considered, suppose that total project funding is $37 million. Table 8.8 gives the cost of each project.

The last three rows in Table 8.8 indicate the region (1, 2, 3, or 4), the region's quartile (1 means the upper 25%, 2 means the next 25%, 3 the third 25%, and 4 the bottom 25%) in terms of percentage of smokers, and the quartile for the decline in smoking rate for each of the proposals. At least one proposal from each of the four regions, at least one proposal from each of the four quartiles of percentage of smokers, and at least one proposal from each quartile for the decline in smoking rate must be selected.

What is it that needs to be decided? NCI needs to decide which projects to fund. Let $x_i = 1$ if project i is funded, 0 if not; $i = 1, 2, 3, 4, 5, 6, 7, 8$.

TABLE 8.8
Example IP for NCI
project selection.

Proposal	1	2	3	4	5	6	7	8
Rank Function	1.9	1.8	1.6	1.5	1.3	1.2	1.1	1.0
Preference	6.3	4.5	8.0	5.2	4.7	7.0	9.1	7.7
Budget ($M)	9.8	7.4	4.9	3.9	8.1	6.1	7.3	5.6
Region	1	3	1	2	4	4	3	2
Smoking Qrt.	3	1	1	2	3	3	4	2
Decline Qrt.	1	3	4	4	2	1	4	3

---

[6] This example is from the reference by Hall et al.

What is the objective to be maximized or minimized? The objective is to maximize the total rank function value of the projects selected. This can be expressed as a function of the x_i's as

$$\text{Max} \quad 1.9x_1 + 1.8x_2 + 1.6x_3 + 1.5x_4 + 1.3x_5 + 1.2x_6 + 1.1x_7 + 1.0x_8$$

How is the problem restricted? First, the total preference score must be at least 17.

$$6.3x_1 + 4.5x_2 + 8x_3 + 5.2x_4 + 4.7x_5 + 7x_6 + 9.1x_7 + 7.7x_8 \geq 17$$

Second, the amount required to fund the selected proposals cannot exceed the budget of $37 million.

$$9.8x_1 + 7.4x_2 + 4.9x_3 + 3.9x_4 + 8.1x_5 + 6.1x_6 + 7.3x_7 + 5.6x_8 \leq 37$$

Third, each of the four regions and each of the four quartiles must have at least one proposal selected.

$$x_1 + x_3 \geq 1$$
$$x_4 + x_8 \geq 1$$
$$x_2 + x_7 \geq 1$$
$$x_5 + x_6 \geq 1$$

$$x_2 + x_3 \geq 1$$
$$x_4 + x_8 \geq 1$$
$$x_1 + x_5 + x_6 \geq 1$$
$$x_7 \geq 1$$

$$x_1 + x_6 \geq 1$$
$$x_5 \geq 1$$
$$x_2 + x_8 \geq 1$$
$$x_3 + x_4 + x_7 \geq 1$$

The complete capital budgeting model is:

$$\text{Max} \quad 1.9x_1 + 1.8x_2 + 1.6x_3 + 1.5x_4 + 1.3x_5 + 1.2x_6 + 1.1x_7 + 1.0x_8$$

subject to

$$6.3x_1 + 4.5x_2 + 8x_3 + 5.2x_4 + 4.7x_5 + 7x_6 + 9.1x_7 + 7.7x_8 \geq 17$$

$$9.8x_1 + 7.4x_2 + 4.9x_3 + 3.9x_4 + 8.1x_5 + 6.1x_6 + 7.3x_7 + 5.6x_8 \leq 37$$

$$x_1 + x_3 \geq 1$$
$$x_4 + x_8 \geq 1$$
$$x_2 + x_7 \geq 1$$
$$x_5 + x_6 \geq 1$$

$$x_2 + x_3 \geq 1$$
$$x_4 + x_8 \geq 1$$
$$x_1 + x_5 + x_6 \geq 1$$
$$x_7 \geq 1$$
$$x_1 + x_6 \geq 1$$
$$x_5 \geq 1$$
$$x_2 + x_8 \geq 1$$
$$x_3 + x_4 + x_7 \geq 1$$
$$0 \leq x_i \leq 1 \quad \text{and integer} \quad i = 1, 2, 3, 4, 5, 6, 7, 8$$

The solution is to select projects 3, 4, 5, 6, 7, 8 for a total ranking function value of 7.7. The cost of funding these proposals is \$35.9 million.

SUMMARY

In this chapter we developed a variety of applications of integer programming models. Many practical applications preclude the use of fractional-valued decision variables, but they can be handled by integer programming. We have also seen that binary variables permit the inclusion of logical yes-no decisions in optimization models, which greatly broadens the types of scenarios that can be modeled using linear mathematical programming models.

We briefly discussed two major approaches to solving integer programming models, the branch and bound and cutting planes methods. Solving IP models is computationally more difficult than solving LP models, and because of this, more care needs to be taken in the development of IP models. Models with integer variables need to be as tight as possible; that is, their LP relaxations should be as close to integer as possible without changing the integer feasible region. Also, any variables whose optimal values can be predetermined should be set prior to solving the model. Integer programming modelling and solution techniques continue to be an important area of academic and commercial research.

CHAPTER REVIEW EXERCISES

I. Terms to Understand

a. Integer program (p. 361)
b. General integer variable (p. 361)
c. Binary integer variable (p. 363)
d. Mixed integer program (p. 364)
e. Linear programming relaxation (p. 367)
f. Branch and bound technique (p. 370)
g. Cutting plane (p. 370)
h. Variable pegging (p. 381)
i. *Titan* (p. 382)

II. Discussion Questions

1. Discuss a planning scenario that would require the use of binary integer variables.
2. Most computer programs solve integer linear programs by solving the linear programming relaxation of the problem coupled with branch and bound. Discuss the relationship between the linear programming relaxation and the corresponding integer program.
3. The model developed for the Tindall Bookstore problem is known as the *maximal set covering* problem. The model finds the solution which maximizes coverage (in the Tindall case, the model seeks to maximize reach) when total coverage is not possible (for example, because of a budget limitation). Discuss how the maximal set covering model might be applied in locating fire or police stations. What does it mean to be "covered" in this situation?
4. Consider the constraint

$$30x_1 + 10x_2 + 12.3x_3 \leq 35$$

   Suppose that the variables are all binary. What valid inequalities (constraints) can you logically derive from this existing constraint?
5. Suppose that $x_i = 1$ if investment project i is selected, 0 if not selected, $i = 1, 2, 3, 4$. How would you model each of the following restrictions (consider each part independently)?
   a. No more than two projects can be selected.
   b. Projects 1 and 4 must be selected.
   c. If project 4 is selected, 3 cannot be selected.
   d. If project 1 is selected, 2 must be selected.

III. Problems

1. Consider the following integer program.
   a. Graph the feasible region to the LP relaxation of this problem.
   b. How many feasible integer points are there to this problem?
   c. Solve the LP relaxation using your graph and the approach discussed in the linear programming chapter.
   d. Solve the integer program using your graph.
   e. Change the objective function to a minimization. What relationship exists between the LP relaxation and the IP in this revised model?

$$\text{Max} \quad 2x_1 + 5x_2$$
$$\text{subject to}$$
$$3x_1 + x_2 \geq 6$$
$$9x_1 + 7x_2 \leq 63$$
$$x_2 \leq 7$$
$$x_1 \leq 5$$
$$x_1, x_2 \geq 0 \quad \text{and integer}$$

2. Consider again the original integer program shown in Problem 1. Suppose that only x_1 is required to be integer; that is, suppose the model is a mixed integer program. How does this change the graph you constructed in Problem 1? Do you think this problem will be easier or more difficult to solve by branch and bound? Why?

3.   Consider the original model in Problem 1. Change the upper bound on x_1 from 5 to 1. Now x_1 is a binary integer variable and x_2 is still a general integer variable. What does the graph of this feasible region look like? Solve this problem using your graph.

4.   The manager for a local bakery must decide on a daily basis how to most effectively deliver to his customers. The bakery has a stable base of regular customers, but also takes special orders which vary from day to day. Possible routes have been determined, based primarily on the regular customers. The table below shows which of today's customers (there are 10 customers, given by customer number) can be served on each of the eight predetermined routes.

Route #	Customers Served
1	1, 4, 5, 6, 9, 10
2	1, 3, 6, 8
3	1, 2, 3, 5, 7
4	1, 2, 4, 6, 7, 9
5	2, 3, 6, 8, 9, 10
6	1, 2, 5, 7, 8, 10
7	1, 2, 3, 6, 8
8	2, 3, 5, 6, 8, 10

Because route drivers reduce the labor available at the bakery, the manager would like to minimize the number of routes required to make all of the deliveries. Formulate a model that will yield the minimum number of routes needed to make all deliveries.

5.   A company is planning the purchase of one of its component parts needed for its finished product. The anticipated demands for the component for the next 12 periods are shown in the following table. The cost to order the component (labor, shipping, and paperwork) is $150. The cost to hold these items in inventory is $1 per component per period. The price of the component is expected to remain stable at $12 per unit, and no quantity discounts are available. Develop a model to minimize the cost of satisfying the company demand for this component.

Period:	1	2	3	4	5	6	7	8	9	10	11	12
Demand:	20	20	30	40	140	360	500	540	460	80	0	20

6.   STAR Co. provides paper to smaller companies whose volumes are not large enough to warrant dealing directly with the paper mill. STAR receives 100-feet-wide paper rolls from the mill and cuts the rolls into smaller rolls of widths 12, 15, and 30 feet. The demands for these widths vary from week to week. The following cutting patterns have been established:

Pattern	Number of: 12'	15'	30'
1	0	6	0
2	0	0	3
3	8	0	0
4	2	1	2
5	7	1	0

Demands this week are 10,000 12' rolls, 1,680 15' rolls, and 3,350 30' rolls. Develop a model that will determine how many 100' rolls to cut into each of the five patterns in order to meet demand and minimize trim loss (leftover paper from a pattern).

7. Change the objective in your model from Problem 6 to one in which the total number of 100' rolls used is minimized. Solve the model from Problem 6 as well as this updated model by using an IP solver. How do the solutions to these two models compare? Under what scenarios would the model which minimizes trim loss be preferred over that which minimizes the number of rolls used (and vice versa)?

8. An investment firm is considering six options for the investment of $2 million that will become available at the beginning of next month. The expected return over the next year, along with the cost of each investment, is shown in the following table, along with conditions placed on each investment due to company policy (considerations of risk, company goals, politics, etc.). Any cash not invested will earn a no-risk fixed rate and be rolled into the funds that will become available next month. Formulate a model to determine which investments to select in order to maximize expected return.

Investment	Cost	Expected Return	Condition
I	$ 200,000	$ 25,000	Only if III
II	$1,000,000	$100,000	Not if I
III	$ 750,000	$150,000	None
IV	$1,000,000	$270,000	Only if I and III
V	$1,000,000	$300,000	Not if III
VI	$ 500,000	$100,000	None

9. Consider the Tindall Bookstore example presented in this chapter. Develop a minimization model for this scenario whose objective is to minimize the number of customers not reached. Solve your model using an IP solver. How does your solution compare to the one presented in the chapter? Can you explain why these models are or are not equivalent?

10. A college intramural four-man basketball team is trying to choose its starting lineup from the eight-man roster given below. The starting lineup is restricted by the conditions that
   a. At most one guard can start.
   b. At most one center can start.
   c. If Tim starts, Tony should be held in reserve.
   d. If Tony starts, then Bill should start.
   e. Tubby must start.

The Roster

Player	Height above 5'8"	Position
Andy	8"	Forward
Bill	0"	Guard
Jeff	0"	Guard
Phil	4"	Forward
Roger	10"	Center
Tim	8"	Center
Tony	8"	Center
Tubby	6"	Forward

The team wants to find the starting roster that maximizes the average height of the starting players and meets the above restrictions.

11. The producers of cassette tapes are faced with the problem of placing songs on either side of the tape so that the total time on each side is as close as possible to being equal in length (they sometimes fail in this endeavor, as evidenced by those blank portions we must endure on certain tapes).

Formulate this problem for the following example:

Song	Run Time (minutes:seconds)
1	2:56
2	3:37
3	3:44
4	3:50
5	4:00
6	4:05
7	4:06
8	4:08
9	4:16
10	4:20

12. Hospital administrators must schedule nurses so that the hospital's patients are provided with adequate care. At the same time, in the face of tighter competition in the health care industry, careful attention must be paid to keeping costs down. From historical records, administrators can project the *minimum* number of nurses to have on hand for the various times of day and days of the week. The nurse scheduling problem seeks to find the minimum total number of nurses required to provide adequate care. Nurses start work at the beginning of one of the four hour shifts given below and work for 8 hours. Formulate and solve the nurse scheduling problem as an integer program for one day for the data given below.

Shift	Time	Minimum Number of Nurses Needed
1	midnight to 4:00 a.m.	5
2	4:00 a.m. to 8:00 a.m.	12
3	8:00 a.m. to 12:00 p.m.	14
4	12:00 p.m. to 4:00 p.m.	8
5	4:00 p.m. to 8:00 p.m.	14
6	8:00 p.m. to 12 midnight	10

13. A company produces four products and has forecasted demand for those four products for the next eight time periods. The holding cost for each product is $10.00 per unit per time period. The processing time per unit is 1 hour, regardless of the product (each product requires processing on the same machine). The cost to set up the machine depends on the product that is about to be produced. Assume that a setup is incurred for a particular product in any period that product is produced. The setup costs are $500 for product

1, $400 for product 2, $300 for product 3, and $300 for product 4. There are 200 hours of machine time available per time period. The demand data are given below. Formulate a model that minimizes the cost of meeting demand and the capacity restrictions.

Product	Time Period							
	1	2	3	4	5	6	7	8
1	0	20	50	10	20	60	40	40
2	50	0	20	40	10	10	20	10
3	0	100	100	150	160	90	100	100
4	10	20	0	0	10	10	20	30

14. Solve the model you developed in problem 13 using LINDO. Resolve the problem using the *Titan* command (if you are using another software package, inspect your model and perform a tightening of the model manually). Discuss why the tighter model is valid (i.e., why is the tighter model equivalent to the first model?).

15. Consider the problem faced by the schedulers of meetings. Suppose that the people who will attend each session are known in advance. If two sessions are scheduled in the same time slot, then the intersection of the two groups will be the number of conflicts in the schedule for that time slot. Let x_{it} be a binary variable which is 1 if session i is assigned to time slot t and 0 if not. Likewise, define x_{jt} for session j. Let y_{ij} be a binary variable which is a 1 if sessions i and j are scheduled for the same time slot. Develop a constraint that will force y_{ij} to be 1 whenever x_{it} and x_{jt} are both 1. Describe a model which could be used to schedule k sessions into l time slots (assume l is less than k) where the number of common people in sessions i and j is C_{ij}.

16. A marketing manager has been charged with assigning sales people to sales territories for a new product about to be introduced over a ten-region area. The manager would like to assign regions that are equitable in terms of potential sales for the four salespeople. Because this is a new product no sales data are available, and the manager has decided to use population as a surrogate for sales potential. The regions and their populations are shown in the following figure.

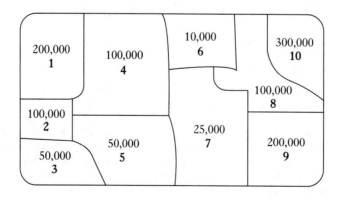

Any one region can be a territory. In addition the following sets should be considered:

Possible Territory
1, 2, 3
1, 2, 4
2, 3, 5
4, 5
1, 4, 5
1, 2
3, 4, 5
4, 5, 6
6, 7, 8
7, 8, 9, 10
4, 5, 6, 7
6, 8, 10
8, 9, 10

Develop a model that will break the ten regions into four sales territories that are as equal as possible in terms of total population.

17.   A problem very similar to the one described in Problem 16 concerns the partitioning of areas into political voting districts. Could the model you developed in Problem 16 be used for this purpose? What additional constraints (if any) might need to be included in the political districting model?

18.   Consider an investor who has $100,000 to invest in 10 mutual fund alternatives with the following restrictions. For diversification, no more than $25,000 can be invested in any one fund. If a fund is chosen for investment, then at least $10,000 will be invested in it. No more than two of the funds can be pure growth funds, and at least one pure bond fund must be selected. The total amount invested in pure bond funds must be at least as much as the amount invested in pure growth funds. Using the following expected returns, formulate and solve a model that will determine the investment strategy which will maximize expected return.

Fund	Type	Expected return
1	growth	13.4%
2	growth	15.3%
3	growth	15.1%
4	growth	14.9%
5	growth & income	15.0%
6	growth & income	12.9%
7	growth & income	14.1%
8	stock and bond	13.8%
9	bond	10.4%
10	bond	11.8%

19. A student has eight computer programs she must submit at the end of the semester. The eight programs are currently saved on her hard drive, but they must be put on diskettes in order to be turned in to the professor. The space requirements for the programs are shown below. Formulate a model that will yield the fewest number of 1.4MB diskettes needed to store all of the programs. Assume that no program can be split over more than one diskette.

Program Assignment #	Space Required
1	.1 MB
2	.9 MB
3	.74MB
4	1.2 MB
5	.3 MB
6	1.1 MB
7	.3 MB
8	1.2 MB

20. Consider the MaBops transportation model in the linear programming chapter (Chapter 4, Example 7). Management is considering the expansion of some of the plants and the possibility of closing others. The current weekly fixed cost associated with each plant is given below, along with the incremental cost associated with expansion (expansion cost is given for the cost of expanding capacity in increments of 5,000 additional units of production). Management is not interested in changing any of the warehousing facilities. Formulate a model that will prescribe the cost-minimizing production/distribution system using the data from Chapter 4.

Plant	Current Fixed Cost	Expansion Cost
Los Angeles	$80,000	$40,000
Denver	$65,000	$18,000
Pensacola	$50,000	$15,000
Cincinnati	$40,000	$14,000

IV. Projects and Cases

1. Camp Sunshine[7] provides a one-day wilderness experience for inner-city children. The camp director at Camp Sunshine must plan a three-meal diet for the campers. The food for the entire day is purchased from McDonald's. The camp must order a breakfast, lunch, and dinner for each child (each child will get the standard meal). The nutritional and cost information of some of the items offered by McDonald's are given in the following table. The diet is subject to the following restrictions:

- At least 100% of the US recommended daily allotment (RDA) is required for vitamins A, C, B1, B2, niacin, calcium, and iron.

- At least 55 grams of protein are required.

---

[7] Thanks to Mr. Jeff Rieder for providing the cost data for this problem. The problem is based on Bosch, R. A. "Big Mac Attack: The Diet Problem Revisited: Eating at McDonald's." *OR/MS Today*, August 1993, pp. 30–31.

| | | | | | | % RDA | | | | | | |
Item	Price	Calories	Protein (g)	Fat (g)	Sodium (mg)	A	C	B1	B2	Niacin	Calcium	Iron
Egg McMuffin	1.36	290	18.2	11.2	740	10	0	30	20	20	25	15
Hot Cakes and Sausage	1.56	590	16.6	25.5	990	4	0	40	26	25	10	14
Scrambled Egs	1.10	140	12.4	9.8	290	10	0	4	15	0	6	10
Hashbrown Potatoes	0.59	130	1.4	7.3	330	0	2	4	0	4	0	0
Biscuit w/Biscuit Spread	0.89	260	4.6	12.7	730	0	0	15	6	8	8	8
Biscuit w/Sausage	0.79	440	13.0	29.0	1080	0	0	35	10	20	8	10
Biscuit w/Sausage and Egg	1.26	520	19.9	34.5	1250	6	0	35	20	20	10	20
Biscuit w/Bacon, Egg and Cheese	1.36	440	17.5	26.4	1230	10	0	25	20	10	20	15
Sausage McMuffin w/Egg	1.36	440	22.6	26.8	980	10	0	45	25	25	25	20
Cheerios w/Milk	0.79	80	3.0	1.1	210	15	15	15	15	15	2	30
Wheaties w/Milk	0.79	90	2.0	0.3	220	20	20	20	20	20	2	20
Apple Bran Muffin	0.76	190	5.0	0.0	230	0	0	0	4	0	2	4
Hamburger	0.59	260	12.3	9.5	500	4	4	20	10	20	10	15
Cheeseburger	0.69	310	15.0	13.8	750	8	4	20	15	20	20	15
Quarter Pounder	1.59	410	23.1	20.7	660	4	6	25	15	35	15	20
Quarter Pounder w/Cheese	1.69	520	28.5	29.2	1150	15	6	25	20	35	30	20
Big Mac	1.65	560	25.2	32.4	950	8	2	30	25	35	25	20
Filet-O-Fish	1.30	440	13.8	26.1	1030	2	0	20	8	15	15	10
McChicken	1.89	490	19.2	28.6	780	2	4	60	15	45	15	15
Chicken McNuggets (6 Piece)	1.59	270	20.0	15.44	580	0	0	8	8	40	0	6
Chicken McNuggets (9 Piece)	2.25	405	30	23.16	870	0	0	12	12	60	0	9
Chicken McNuggets (20 Piece)	4.34	900	67	51	1933	0	0	27	27	133	0	20
Hot Mustard Sauce	0.00	70	0.5	3.6	250	0	0	0	0	0	2	0
Barbeque Sauce	0.00	50	0.3	0.5	340	4	4	0	0	0	0	2
Sweet & Sour Sauce	0.00	60	0.2	0.2	190	6	0	0	0	0	0	0
Honey	0.00	45	0.0	0.0	0	0	0	0	0	0	0	0
Chef Salad	2.69	230	20.5	13.3	490	80	20	20	20	20	25	8
Garden Salad	1.99	110	7.1	6.6	160	80	20	6	10	2	15	6
Chunky Chicken Salad	2.79	140	23.1	3.4	230	70	30	15	10	45	4	6
Side Salad	1.32	60	3.7	3.3	85	45	10	4	4	0	8	4
Croutons	0.00	50	1.39	2.17	140	0	0	4	0	2	0	0
Bacon Bits	0.00	16	1.3	1.19	95	0	0	0	0	0	0	0
Blue Cheese Dressing (0.5 oz.)	0.00	70	0.5	6.9	150	0	0	0	0	0	0	0
Ranch Dressing (0.5 oz.)	0.00	83	0.17	8.6	130	0	0	0	0	0	0	0
1000 Island Dressing (0.5 oz.)	0.00	78	0.2	7.5	100	0	0	0	0	0	0	0

Item	Price	Calories	Protein (g)	Fat (g)	Sodium (mg)	% RDA						
						A	C	B1	B2	Niacin	Calcium	Iron
Lite Vinaigrette Dressing (0.5 oz.)	0.00	15	0.23	0.5	75	0	0	0	0	0	0	0
Red French Dressing (0.5 oz.)	0.00	40	0.07	1.9	110	0	0	0	0	0	0	0
Peppercorn Dressing (0.5 oz.)	0.00	80	0.17	8.7	85	0	0	0	0	0	0	0
Small French Fries	0.70	220	3.13	12.0	110	0	15	10	0	10	0	2
Medium French Fries	0.89	320	4.44	17.1	150	0	20	15	0	15	0	4
Large French Fries	1.10	400	5.61	21.6	200	0	25	15	0	15	0	6
Vanilla Cone	0.39	100	4.0	0.75	80	2	0	2	10	2	10	0
Strawberry Sundae	0.89	210	5.7	1.1	95	4	2	4	20	0	20	0
Hot Fudge Sundae	0.89	240	7.3	3.2	170	4	0	6	20	0	25	2
Hot Caramel Sundae	0.89	270	6.6	2.8	180	6	0	6	20	0	20	0
Apple Pie	0.74	260	2.2	14.8	240	0	20	4	0	0	0	4
Vanilla Lowfat Milk Shake	0.99	290	10.8	1.3	170	6	0	8	30	0	35	0
Chocolate Lowfat Milk Shake	0.99	320	11.6	1.7	240	6	0	8	30	2	35	0
Strawberry Lowfat Milk Shake	0.99	320	10.7	1.3	170	6	0	8	30	2	35	0
McDonaldland Cookies	0.47	290	4.2	9.2	300	0	0	15	10	10	0	10
Chocolaty Chip Cookies	0.55	330	4.2	15.6	280	0	0	10	10	10	2	10
Milk (8 oz.)	0.49	110	9.0	2.0	130	10	4	8	30	0	30	0
Orange Juice (6 oz.)	0.89	80	1.3	0.0	0	0	120	10	0	0	0	0
Orange Drink (12 oz.)	0.65	130	0.0	0.0	10	0	0	0	0	0	0	0
Orange Drink (16 oz.)	0.74	180	0.0	0.0	15	0	0	0	0	0	0	0
Orange Drink (22 oz.)	0.84	240	0.0	0.0	20	0	0	0	0	0	0	0
Orange Drink (32 oz.)	0.99	360	0.0	0.0	25	0	0	0	0	0	0	0
Big Breakfast	1.99	650	21.3	41.8	1580	6	2	39	20	24	10	20
Country Breakfast	2.58	530	18.4	29.8	1350	10	2	23	21	12	14	18
Egg McMuffin Meal	2.29	580	22.2	18.5	1070	10	242	54	20	24	25	15
Bacon Egg and Cheese Meal	2.29	730	21.5	33.7	1560	10	242	49	20	14	20	15
Sausage McMuffin w/Egg Meal	2.29	730	26.6	34.1	1310	10	242	69	25	29	25	20
Sausage Biscuit w/Egg Meal	2.29	810	23.9	41.8	1580	6	242	59	20	24	10	20
Hamburger Happy Meal	1.99	610	15.43	21.5	620	4	19	30	10	30	10	17
Cheeseburger Happy Meal	2.09	660	18.13	25.8	870	8	19	30	15	30	20	17
Chicken McNugget Happy Meal	2.19	530	16.46	22.29	507	0	15	15	5	37	0	6
Big Mac Meal	2.99	1140	30.81	54	1165	8	27	45	25	50	25	26
2 Cheeseburger Meal	2.99	1200	35.61	49.2	1715	16	33	55	30	55	40	36
Quarter Pounder w/Cheese Meal	2.99	1100	34.11	50.8	1365	15	31	40	20	50	30	26
McChicken Sandwich Meal	2.99	1070	24.81	50.2	995	2	29	75	15	60	15	21

- No more than 3 grams of sodium are allowed.
- A maximum of 30% of the calories can come from fat.

a. Develop an integer programming model that will yield the cost minimizing diet subject to the above nutritional requirements.

b. Solve the IP developed in part a. Report the meals and the total cost. Is the diet reasonable in terms of variety? Add any additional constraints you would place on the diet and solve your updated model. Report the new diet and any increase in cost associated with your new constraints.

2. In January, 1979, the banking laws in the state of Ohio were changed to allow greater freedom in the placement of branches throughout the state.[8] The previous law only allowed banks to establish branches in the counties of the bank's principal places of business (ppb). The new law allows a bank to establish branches (upon approval of the superintendent of banks) in any county *contiguous* (sharing a border) to one in which it has a ppb. Milt Drysdale is Vice President in charge of strategic planning for Sun Bank of Cincinnati, which has so far operated primarily in the southern and middle sections of Ohio. Sun currently has ppb's located in Shelby, Butler, Brown, Jackson, Madison, Marion, Licking, Athens, and Belmont counties. Drysdale would like some guidance from you concerning the strategic placement of ppb's as Sun moves into the northern part of Ohio. Specifically, those counties that are not currently open to Sun branches would be judicious choices for ppb's (some counties are more populated than others and population can be thought of as a surrogate for potential business). Opening a ppb is expensive, so Drysdale would like to know how many ppbs should be opened and where they should be located. The population count for the counties of Ohio, as well as a map of Ohio by county are detailed in the following figures. The shaded counties are the current ppb locations, and the territory under consideration is those counties north of the dark border (counties untouched by current ppb's).

County	Population	County	Population	County	Population
1. Williams	36,369	23. Hardin	32,719	45. Franklin	869,132
2. Defiance	39,987	24. Logan	39,155	46. Pickaway	43,662
3. Paulding	21,302	25. Champaign	33,649	47. Ross	65,004
4. Van Wert	30,458	26. Clark	150,236	48. Pike	22,802
5. Mercer	38,334	27. Greene	129,769	49. Scioto	84,545
6. Darke	55,096	28. Clinton	34,606	50. Lawrence	63,849
7. Preble	38,223	29. Brown	31,920	51. Jackson	30,592
8. Butler	258,787	30. Adams	24,328	52. Vinton	11,584
9. Hamilton	873,224	31. Highland	33,477	53. Hocking	24,304
10. Clermont	128,483	32. Fayette	27,467	54. Fairfield	93,678
11. Warren	99,276	33. Madison	33,004	55. Licking	120,981
12. Montgomery	571,697	34. Union	29,536	56. Knox	46,304
13. Miami	90,381	35. Marion	67,974	57. Richland	131,205
14. Shelby	43,089	36. Wyandot	22,651	58. Lorain	274,909
15. Auglaize	42,554	37. Seneca	61,901	59. Ashland	46,178
16. Allen	112,241	38. Sandusky	63,267	60. Cuyahoga	1,498,400
17. Putnam	32,991	39. Ottawa	40,076	61. Medina	113,150
18. Henry	28,383	40. Erie	79,655	62. Wayne	97,408
19. Fulton	37,751	41. Huron	54,608	63. Holmes	29,416
20. Lucus	471,741	42. Crawford	50,075	64. Coshocton	36,024
21. Wood	107,372	43. Morrow	26,480	65. Muskingum	83,340
22. Hancock	64,581	44. Delaware	53,840	66. Perry	31,032

[8]This problem is based on Sweeney, D.J., Mairose, R.L, and R.K. Martin. "Strategic Planning in Bank Location." *American Institute for Decision Sciences Proceedings*, November 1979.

County	Population	County	Population	County	Population
67. Morgan	14,241	75. Stark	378,823	83. Columbiana	113,572
68. Athens	56,399	76. Summit	524,472	84. Carroll	25,598
69. Meigs	23,641	77. Portage	135,856	85. Harrison	18,152
70. Gallia	30,098	78. Geauga	74,474	86. Jefferson	91,564
71. Washington	64,266	79. Lake	212,801	87. Belmont	82,569
72. Noble	11,310	80. Ashtabula	104,215	88. Monroe	17,382
73. Guernsey	42,024	81. Trumbull	241,863		
74. Tuscarawas	84,614	82. Mahoning	289,487		

3. Many large companies are forced to redesign their distribution systems as the demographics of the country change. As the distribution of the population shifts geographically, distribution systems designed years earlier become inefficient, necessitating a distribution system redesign.

    Consider the following map. The company has 14 demand centers, which are denoted by squares. These demand centers are supplied by regional distribution centers (RDC's). Six *potential* sites for RDC's have been identified: Atlanta, Cincinnati, Chicago, Fresno, Lubbock, and Salt Lake City (denoted by circles on the map). The following table shows the mileage from each potential RDC to each demand center. Also shown in the table are the demand (in thousands of truck loads per year) for each of the demand centers. The company would like to operate only three RDC's.

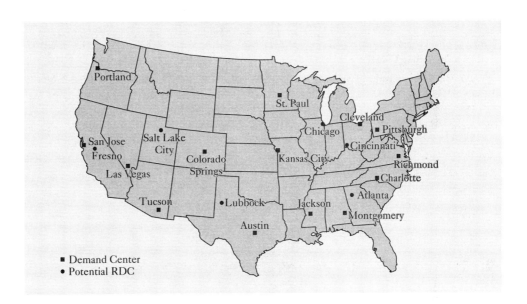

■ Demand Center
● Potential RDC

	Portland	San Jose	Las Vegas	Tucson	Colo. Sprngs	Kansas City	St. Paul	Austin	Jackson	Montgomery	Cleveland	Pitts.	Richmond	Charlotte
Atlanta	2170	2100	1750	1500	1200	680	920	810	350	140	560	530	470	230
Cincinnati	1970	2020	1680	1530	1100	550	610	970	570	490	220	270	400	340
Chicago	1760	1830	1530	1410	940	420	370	980	670	670	340	410	620	590
Fresno	620	110	250	620	820	1380	1490	1350	1710	1940	2050	2160	2320	2170
Lubbock	1390	1160	800	510	430	560	920	310	680	910	1230	1300	1390	1200
Salt Lake Cit	630	570	350	580	390	930	990	1080	1340	1550	1570	1690	1860	1740
Demand (000)	5	15.6	4.25	3.75	4.57	7.5	3	8.7	3.25	12.3	9.6	16.7	8.5	3.2

    The objective is to minimize the *demand-weighted distances* of assignments of demand centers to RDC's. That is, the cost associated with assigning Atlanta to Portland for example, is $(2,170 \times 5 = 10,850)$. In this way, the heavy demand centers are weighted more heavily in the analysis. Finally, assume that each RDC will have as much capacity as needed (an RDC can supply as many demand centers as needed), and that each demand center will be assigned to exactly one RDC. Develop and solve an IP model that will give the optimal RDC locations.

REFERENCES

Anbil, R., Gelman, E., Patty, B., and R. Tanga. "Recent Advances in Crew-Pairing Optimization at American Airlines." *Interfaces*, Vol. 21, No. 1, January–February 1991, pp. 62–74.

Bosch, R.A. "Big Mac Attack: The Diet Problem Revisited: Eating at McDonald's." *OR/MS Today*, August 1993, pp. 30–31.

Camm, J., Raturi, R., and S. Tsubakitani. "Cutting Big M Down to Size." *Interfaces*, Vol. 20, No. 5, September–October 1990, pp. 61–66.

Carraway, R., Cummins, J., and J. Freeland. "Solving Spreadsheet-based Integer Programming Models: An Example from International Telecommunications." *Decision Sciences*, Vol. 21, No. 4, 1990, pp. 808–824.

Dano, S. *Linear Programming in Industry*, 4th Edition. Wien: Springer-Verlag, 1974.

Erkut, E. "Big Mac Attack Revisited." *OR/MS Today*, June 1994, pp. 50–52.

Farley, A. "Planning the Cutting of Photographic Color Paper Rolls for Kodak (Australasia) Pty. Ltd." *Interfaces*, Vol. 21, No. 1, January–February 1991, pp. 92–106.

Gaballa, A. and W. Pearce. "Telephone Sales Manpower Planning at Qantas." *Interfaces*, Vol. 9, No. 3, May 1979, pp. 1–9.

Hall, N., Hershey, J., Kessler, L., and R. Stotts. "A Model for Making Project Funding Decisions at the National Cancer Institute." *Operations Research*, Vol. 40, No. 6, November–December 1992, pp. 1040–1052.

Neebe, A. "An Improved Multiplier Adjustment Procedure for the Segregated Storage Problem." *Journal of the Operational Research Society*, Vol. 38, No. 9, 1987, pp. 815–825.

Nemhauser, G.L. and L.A. Wolsey. *Integer and Combinatorial Optimization*. New York: John Wiley & Sons, 1988.

Salkin, H.M. and K. Mathur. *Foundations of Integer Programming*. New York: Elsevier Science Publishing, North-Holland, 1989.

Sweeney, D., Mairose, R., and K. Martin. "Strategic Planning in Bank Location." *American Institute for Decision Sciences Proceedings*, November 1979.

APPENDIX: SOLVING INTEGER PROGRAMMING PROBLEMS

Because the LP relaxation ignores integer requirements, the objective function value of the IP can never be better than the objective function value of the LP relaxation. In other words, the objective function value of the LP relaxation provides a *bound* on the objective function value of the IP. This bound tells us how good the objective function value of the IP can possibly be—but no better.

> The optimal objective function value of the LP relaxation of a *maximization* integer program provides an *upper bound* on the optimal objective function value of the associated integer program. Likewise, the optimal objective function value of the LP relaxation of a *minimization* integer program provides a *lower bound* on the optimal objective function value of the integer program. These relationships also hold for binary and mixed integer programming models.

Clearly, we can do no worse than any *feasible* solution we may have. Consequently, we know that the optimal IP objective function value must lie between the optimal objective function value of the LP relaxation and the objective function value of the best feasible solution we may have.

Let Z_R^* be the optimal objective function value to the LP relaxation and Z_I the best known feasible integer solution. Let Z_I^* be the optimal objective function value of the IP. For a minimization problem, $Z_R^* \leq Z_I^* \leq Z_I$. For a maximization problem, $Z_I \leq Z_I^* \leq Z_R^*$. These results also hold for binary and mixed integer programs.

We will refer to the difference between Z_I and Z_R^* as the *integrality gap*. Recall that the transportation LP model and the assignment LP model introduced in Chapter 4 have the property that if the right-hand sides of the constraints are integers, the LP solution will be integer (the integrality gap is zero). As we have seen in Example 1, the solution to the LP relaxation will be fractional for many IP models; in these cases the LP relaxation provides us with an objective function value that is the best we can ever hope to achieve with an integer solution to the problem. In what follows we discuss the branch and bound approach in more detail.

The Branch & Bound Approach

Branch and bound is the most common approach to solving IP models. The strategy can be described as "divide and conquer." We start with the LP relaxation. Usually, the solution will be non-integer. In such cases, we add constraints that divide all feasible integer solutions into subsets while rendering the solution to the LP relaxation infeasible. We then solve new LP relaxations over these subsets. As these subsets become smaller, we will eventually find either an integer corner point solution or that we have an infeasible problem. As we have seen, feasible integer solutions establish bounds on the optimal integer solution. If the solution is infeasible, we no longer have to consider that subset. In addition, we often can discard certain subsets from consideration if we can prove that any solution in those subsets can never be better than the best integer solution we have found thus far. We illustrate the approach with the following simple example.

EXAMPLE A1. BRANCH AND BOUND

Consider the integer program

$$\text{Max} \quad 8x_1 + 7x_2$$
$$\text{subject to}$$
$$12x_1 + 10x_2 \leq 45$$
$$x_2 \leq 2.5$$
$$x_1, x_2 \geq 0 \text{ and integer}$$

The feasible region for the LP relaxation of this model is shown in Figure A.1. The dots indicate the points which are feasible to the integer program. The optimal solution to the LP relaxation is corner point b, which is $x_1^* = 1.66667$, $x_2^* = 2.5$ and $z^* = 30.83333$. We know that this solution is not feasible to the IP, because x_1 and x_2 are fractional.

The branch and bound technique selects a fractional-valued variable that is supposed to be integer. In this example, we could select either variable. We will select the variable whose decimal fraction is farthest from the nearest integer (this method is usually used by computer codes). In this example, we select x_2 because it is the "most fractional." In order for x_2 to be integer, it must be either greater than or equal to 3 or less than or equal to 2. Thus, we create two new problems: one being the original LP relaxation with the

FIGURE A.1   *The feasible set for Example A1.*

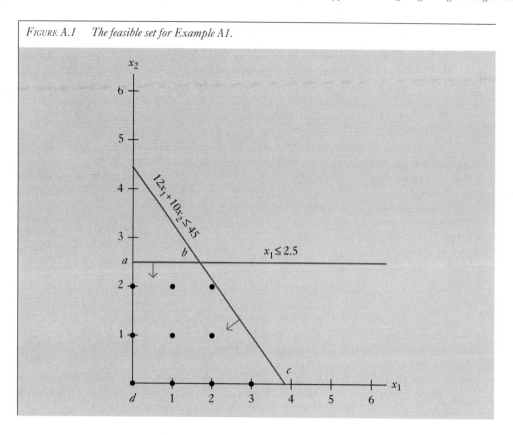

additional constraint $x_2 \leq 2$ (call this subproblem 1), and the other being the original LP relaxation with the additional constraint $x_2 \geq 3$ (subproblem 2). The feasible regions for these two new problems are shown in Figure A.2. Notice that we have excluded from consideration all solutions in which x_2 takes on fractional values between 2 and 3, but have not excluded any feasible integer solutions. This process is known as *branching* and the variable forming the new constraints is referred to as the *branching variable*.

We next solve the LP relaxations for each subproblem. We find that the solution to subproblem 1 is $z = 30.66667$, $x_1 = 2.08333$, $x_2 = 2$. This represents an upper bound on the value of any feasible integer solution that might be found within subproblem 1. Subproblem 2 is infeasible because $x_2 \leq 2.5$ and $x_2 \geq 3$ cannot both hold. Therefore, if any optimal integer solutions exist, they must be found within subproblem 1. The new feasible region is shown in Figure A.3.

The optimal solution in Figure A.3 (labeled b_1) still has a fractional value for x_1. Therefore we must branch on x_1 and create two new subproblems. These are formed by adding branching constraints to the subproblem from which the solution was derived, not the original problem. Thus, we create subproblem 3 by adding the constraint $x_1 \leq 2$ to subproblem 1. We add the restriction $x_1 \geq 3$ to subproblem 1 to create subproblem 4. This is illustrated in Figure A.4.

Solving the linear program corresponding to subproblem 3, we obtain $z = 30$, $x_1 = 2$, $x_2 = 2$. This solution, labeled b_3 in Figure A.4, is integer valued! Thus, it provides a lower bound on the optimal objective function value of the IP. Because the optimal objective function value of subproblem 1 is $z = 30.6666$, we know that the objective function value of the optimal integer solution must be between 30 and 30.6666.

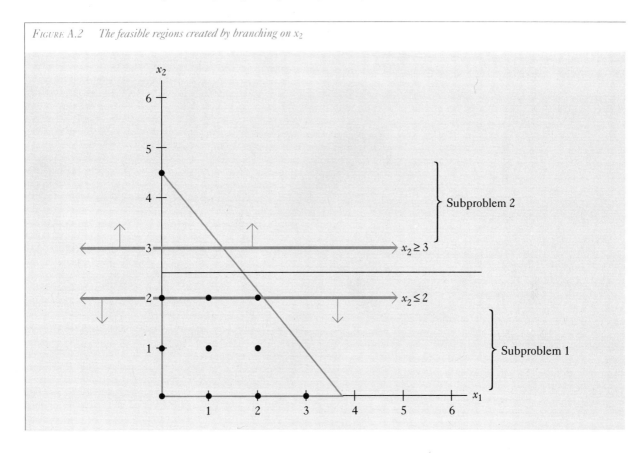

We next solve subproblem 4, obtaining $z = 30.3$, $x_1 = 3$, and $x_2 = .9$. This point is labeled $c4$ in Figure A.4. This solution is not feasible to the IP because x_2 is fractional. However, we also know that $z = 30.3$ is an upper bound on *any* integer solution that might be found within this subproblem. In this problem, the objective function coefficients are integer, so any integer solution must have an integer objective function value. Therefore, the best objective function value that can possibly be achieved by any integer solution in subproblem 4 is at most 30. Because we already have a solution with $z = 30$ in hand (from subproblem 3), we need not consider branching on subproblem 4. Because no other subproblems exist in which the optimal integer solution might lie, our search is complete. The optimal solution to the integer program is therefore $z^* = 30$, $x_1^* = 2$, and $x_2^* = 2$. Obviously, integer programs are generally much more difficult to solve than linear programs, because a series of LP's must be solved in order to find the optimal integer solution.

The branch and bound process can be represented by a *branch and bound tree* as shown in Figure A.5 for this example. The nodes represent the various subproblems, and the constraints that have been added to form a subproblem are shown on the branches leading to that subproblem. The solution to each subproblem is shown next to its node. The objective function value at each node, because it is an LP relaxation over a subregion, indicates the best we can ever hope to achieve down that branch.

As we have seen, we can discontinue our search down a particular branch if a subproblem has an integer solution (as in subproblem 3), if the subproblem is infeasible (as in subproblem 2), or if we can prove that no

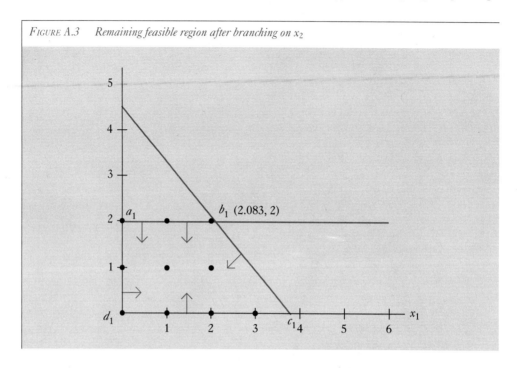

FIGURE A.3   *Remaining feasible region after branching on x_2*

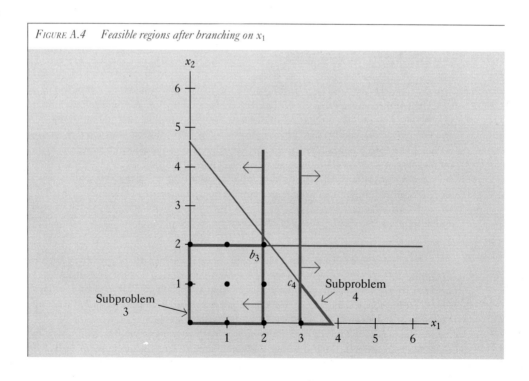

FIGURE A.4   *Feasible regions after branching on x_1*

FIGURE A.5   *The branch and bound tree for Example A1.*

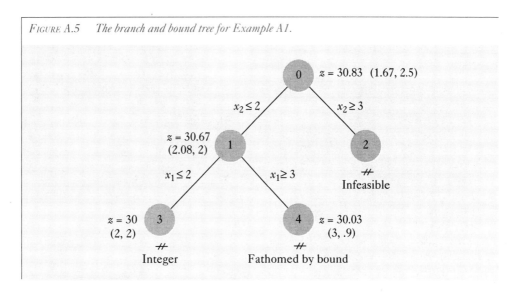

better integer solution can exist in the subregion associated with that subproblem by comparing bounds (as in subproblem 4). When we can discontinue our search down a branch for one of these three reasons, we say that branch has been *fathomed*.

Example A1 illustrated the branch and bound approach for general integer variables. In a similar fashion, branch and bound can also be applied to binary integer variables (where fractional binary variables are forced to zero or one in the branching process) and to mixed integer programs. In MIP's, branching is only done on the set of variables that are restricted to be integer.

CHAPTER 9

NETWORK

MODELING AND

OPTIMIZATION

INTRODUCTION

- A road map is a familiar example of a network. A major problem that cities, counties, and states face is clearing snow from the network of streets in their jurisdictions. In many northern areas of the U.S., as much as 20 percent of the highway maintenance budget is devoted to salting and plowing. Customers demand good service. Thus, routing snow-removal vehicles over the highway network is an important decision. Several Midwestern counties and state Department of Transportation districts use a software package called SnowMaster© to help route snow removal vehicles and to perform strategic planning for fleet mix and depot site selection. SnowMaster© uses various network optimization algorithms to generate efficient routes for snow removal vehicles in an attempt to minimize the distance traveled and improve the level of service to the community. Butler County, Ohio, was able to save $250,000 by reducing its fleet of vehicles, to clear the roads faster than before, and to reduce annual labor and operating costs [Evans and Weant, 1990].

- The Office of Tax Analysis of the Department of the Treasury is charged with evaluating the effects of proposed tax code revisions. These evaluations are based on models that predict the effects of the proposed revisions by using a statistical profile of the nation's population. These statistical profiles generally are derived from existing databases, and the required data must be obtained by merging data from several sources.

  Existing databases do not include the entire population, but consist of samples of tax returns, interviews, and so on. It is not likely that all the databases would contain records on the same individuals, so it is not possible to match records from different databases in order to obtain complete records for the analyses. To resolve this problem, files are merged statistically; that is, files are matched on the basis of their similarity with respect to the attributes common to the two files. This problem can be modeled as a transportation network problem. A real example that was solved in 1978 as a result of President Carter's Tax Reform Initiative consisted of over 100,000 constraints and 25 million variables! If linear programming was used to solve this problem, it would have taken over seven months (of course, computers are much faster today!). Special network-based algorithms solved the problem in about seven hours of computer time [Barr and Turner, 1981].

- St. Vincent's Hospital and Medical Center moved from a 373-bed hillside facility in Portland, Oregon, to a new 403-bed facility 5 miles away in a suburban area. Moving all the patients, equipment, and materials in the hospital was a huge undertaking. Many different activities needed to be planned and scheduled, such as coordinating efforts with the local police, developing moving policies, tagging equipment, preparing patients, and so on. In order to coordinate these activities, a project network was developed that depicted the sequence in which all activities had to be performed. This network became the basic framework on which all plans were based and developed. The network allowed managers to schedule all activities, monitor progress, and determine any needs for reallocation of resources. One manager said that the time spent in developing the network "proved to be a wise investment" [Hanson, 1972].

> A *network* is a collection of points, called *nodes*, which are connected by (undirected) lines that we call *branches*, or by arrows that we call *arcs*.

Examples of networks are shown in Figure 9.1. Branches indicate a connection between two nodes (such as two-way streets between intersections), and the resulting network is called an *undirected network*. Arcs indicate a specific direction (such as a one-way street), and the resulting network is called a *directed network*. Branches and arcs are often defined by the numbers of the pair of nodes they connect. Thus, in Figure 9.1(a), branch *a* connects nodes 1 and 2, and thus can be represented by (1,2) or (2,1), because the direction is irrelevant. In Figure 9.1(b), however, arc *a* is directed from node 1 to node 2, and can only be represented as (1,2), and not by (2,1).

Many different optimization problems can be formulated on networks. For instance, we might be interested in finding the shortest path from one node to another, finding the cheapest way to connect all the nodes, or finding the best way to move objects through a network. The movement of objects through a network is called a *flow*. Flows may represent the distribution of goods from factories to warehouses, the movement of oil through a pipeline, the transfer of cash from one month to another, and countless other examples, both physical and abstract.

Network optimization represents one of the most important areas of management science for several reasons. First, networks can be used to model many diverse applications such as transportation systems, communication systems, vehicle routing problems, production planning, and cash flow analysis. Second, networks are accepted more readily by

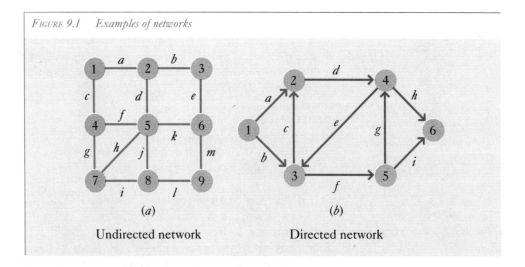

FIGURE 9.1   *Examples of networks*

(a)

Undirected network

(b)

Directed network

managers because they provide a visual picture of the problem under study. Finally, networks have certain mathematical properties that allow management scientists to develop special algorithms able to solve much larger problems than other optimization methods. In this chapter we will discuss modeling and mathematical programming solutions for several important classes of network problems.

BASIC CONCEPTS AND DEFINITIONS

One of the advantages of working with networks is that most of the concepts are highly intuitive and can be easily visualized. In this section, we discuss some basic concepts of networks that are important in understanding various models and algorithms that we will describe later. We will use the networks in Figure 9.1 to illustrate these concepts.

Paths, Cycles, and Trees

A *path* in a network is a sequence of nodes, connected to one another by branches or arcs. You can visualize a path as a means of "walking" from one node to the next along a branch or arc (in either direction). For example, in Figure 9.1(a), two paths are

Path 1: 7-*i*-8-*l*-9-*m*-6

Path 2: 1-*a*-2-*d*-5-*h*-7-*g*-4-*f*-5-*k*-6

A path must start at one node and end at another, and may include a node more than once (as in Path 2). If we can find a path between every pair of nodes in a network, then the network is *connected*.

In a directed network, a path need not follow the directions of the arcs (people sometimes drive the wrong way on one-way streets!). If all arcs are pointed in the same direction, we call the path a *directed path*. Two examples from Figure 9.1(b) are

Path 1: 1-*a*-2-*c*-3-*f*-5

Path 2: 1-*a*-2-*d*-4-*h*-6   *directed path*

Note that only Path 2 is a directed path.

A *cycle* is a path whose first and last nodes are the same. An example of a cycle in Figure 9.1(a) is

1-*c*-4-*g*-7-*h*-5-*d*-2-*a*-1

A cycle in Figure 9.1(b) is

2-*c*-3-*f*-5-*g*-4-*d*-2

As with paths, a cycle in a directed graph need not have all arcs pointing in the same direction. If it does, however, we call it a *directed cycle*.

A *tree* is a connected network that has no cycles. Figure 9.2 shows two examples of trees taken from the networks in Figure 9.1. If a tree contains all nodes of the original network (as is the case in Figure 9.2(a)), then we call it a *spanning tree*.

Figure 9.2   *Examples of trees*

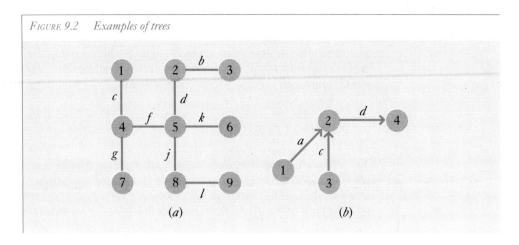

Figure 9.2   *Examples of trees*

Flows in Networks

We stated that a flow is a way of moving objects through a network. When dealing with flows in networks we will assume that the networks are directed. Nodes from which flows originate are called *source nodes*, while nodes at which flows terminate are called *sink nodes*. For example, oil drilling platforms in the Gulf of Mexico would be source nodes for the oil distribution network; the refineries to which the oil is pumped would be sink nodes. Source nodes usually have some supply—the amount of flow available during some time period; sink nodes have a demand—the amount of flow required during the same time period. As objects flow through a network, they are simply routed across branches or arcs to their destinations. At each node we have a fundamental equation that governs this process, which we call *conservation of flow*.

The *conservation of flow* principle in a network states that at any node, the total flow into the node must equal the total flow out, or

$$\text{FLOW OUT} - \text{FLOW IN} = 0$$

Let us write the conservation of flow equations for the network in Figure 9.1(b). We will assume that node 1 is a source having a supply of 30 units and that nodes 4 and 6 are sinks having demands of 10 and 20 units, respectively. Notice that a supply may be viewed as flows into the source node, and a demand may be viewed as a flow out of a sink node. Define x_j to be the flow on arc j. Then at node 1, the conservation of flow equation is

node 1: $(x_a + x_b) - 30 = 0$

                                                 flow out   flow in

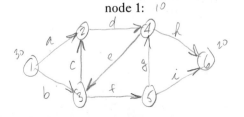

At the remaining nodes, we have   *Flow out– flow in = 0*

node 2: $(x_d) - (x_a + x_c) = 0$

node 3: $(x_c + x_f) - (x_b + x_e) = 0$

node 4: $(x_h + x_e + 10) - (x_d + x_g) = 0$

node 5: $(x_g + x_i) - (x_f) = 0$

node 6: $(20) - (x_h + x_i) = 0$

Now, let us rewrite these equations so that all constant terms are moved to the right-hand side:

node 1: $x_a + x_b$ $= 30$ *Supply*

node 2: $- x_a \quad\quad - x_c + x_d$ $= 0$

node 3: $\quad - x_b + x_c \quad\quad - x_e + x_f$ $= 0$

node 4: $\quad\quad\quad - x_d + x_e \quad\quad - x_g + x_h$ $= -10$ *Demand*

node 5: $\quad\quad\quad\quad\quad\quad - x_f + x_g \quad\quad + x_i = 0$

node 6: $\quad\quad\quad\quad\quad\quad\quad\quad - x_h - x_i = -20$

If you examine these equations closely, you can observe that

1. Each flow variable appears in exactly two equations with opposite signs. The variable has a $+1$ in the row corresponding to the beginning node and a -1 in the row corresponding to the ending node.
2. A positive right-hand side corresponds to a supply; a negative right-hand side corresponds to a demand.

These observations provide an important link between linear programs and the network itself, because they mean that any linear program having these properties can be modeled as a network. For example, suppose we have the following set of constraints (numbered arbitrarily):

1: $x_a - x_b = -50$
2: $x_d - x_a - x_c = 35$
3: $x_b + x_c - x_e = 15$
4: $x_e - x_d = 0$

Each variable satisfies property (1). We can construct a network by drawing an arc for each variable from the node for which its coefficient is -1 to the node for which its coefficient is $+1$. Node 1 has a demand of 50; nodes 2 and 3 have supplies of 35 and 15, respectively. The network is shown in Figure 9.3.

Flows along arcs are often constrained (for instance, by the diameter of a pipe, speed of computer communications, or the capacity of a railcar). We express this limitation by an *arc capacity*, the total amount of flow that is allowed on an arc. Arc capacities are simply upper bounds on the variables corresponding to the flow. For instance, if the flow on arc *a* in Figure 9.1(b) cannot exceed 17, we would define the limit

$$x_a \leq 17.$$

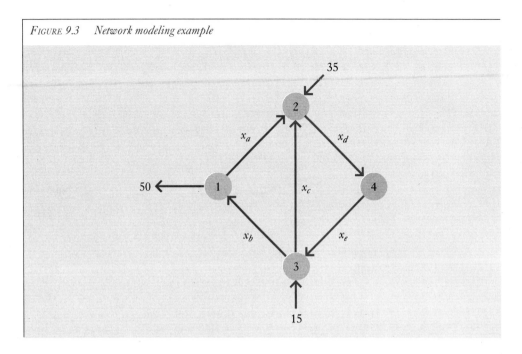

FIGURE 9.3   *Network modeling example*

Most flow problems involve finding an optimal distribution of flow through a network that meets conservation of flow and capacity constraints.

APPLICATIONS OF NETWORK MODELS

Network models arise in many practical settings. In this section, we describe a variety of typical problems involving networks and network flows.

The Transportation Problem

p.150

In Chapter 4, we introduced a special type of linear programming model called the *transportation problem*. The MaBops Inc., example involved distributing a product from four plants to five warehouses at minimum cost (see Table 4.5). This problem can easily be represented as a network flow problem, as shown in Figure 9.4. The four plants are source nodes with supplies of the product as shown. The five warehouses are sink nodes with demands as given. The arcs run from each source to each sink and represent the flow from a plant to a warehouse along with the unit shipping cost. The network flow problem involves shipping the product from the plants in order to meet the demand at the warehouses.

Notice, however, that conservation of flow at all source nodes cannot be guaranteed because the total supply (62,500) exceeds the total demand (59,000). Fortunately, this is

FIGURE 9.4   *MaBops, Inc. distribution network*

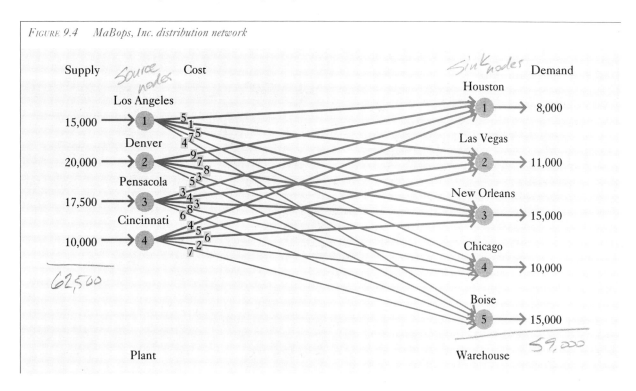

easy to resolve by observing that the excess supply must flow *somewhere*. Therefore, we will create a fictitious demand node (a "dummy destination") to which the excess supply will flow (at zero cost, or at an appropriate holding cost). This is shown in Figure 9.5. The problem now satisfies the conditions for a minimum-cost network flow problem. This problem was solved using linear programming in Chapter 4.

The Transshipment Problem

A problem closely related to the transportation problem is called the *transshipment problem*. Instead of all flows going directly from sources to sinks, the transshipment problem allows flow to be routed through intermediate nodes that are neither sources nor sinks. At intermediate nodes, we have conservation of flow: all flow entering the node must leave it on its journey to the sinks.

Transshipment problems are important generalizations of transportation problems. Many large corporations have distribution networks that can be modeled as transshipment problems. For example, large consumer goods companies such as Procter & Gamble operate dozens of factories along with a set of regional distribution centers. Some products are shipped directly from the factories to major outlets, while others are shipped to the distribution centers for consolidation with other products before being shipped to

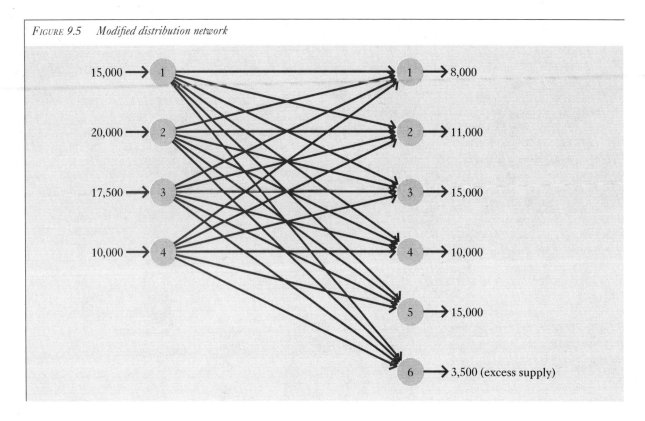

FIGURE 9.5 *Modified distribution network*

outlets. A distribution network of this type is shown in Figure 9.6. As with the transportation problem, the objective is to minimize cost.

Transportation Planning

Trucks that enter a state must file a route plan with the state government. They are not allowed to travel on roads with prohibitive weight restrictions. On the other hand, the trucker wants to reach his or her destination in the shortest possible time. This problem can be approached by constructing a network corresponding to the state highway system and deleting any arcs on which the truck is prohibited from traveling. By knowing the mileage associated with each arc and the legal speed limits, the travel time on each arc can be computed. Using these times as the "length" of the arc, the trucker would want to find the *shortest path* from the point of entry to the final destination.

Equipment Replacement

The operating and maintenance costs of a piece of equipment increase with age. We therefore want to replace the equipment before the costs become excessive. Suppose that

FIGURE 9.6   *Transshipment network example*

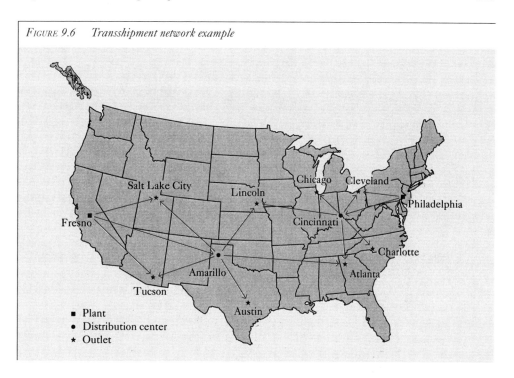

we know the costs over the life of the equipment and can determine the salvage value at the end of each year. Therefore, the total cost of purchasing a new piece of equipment at the beginning of one period and selling it at the beginning of a later period would consist of the purchase cost, plus all operating and maintenance costs during ownership, less the salvage value. The objective is to determine a replacement policy that minimizes the total cost of ownership.

We can model this as a network optimization problem by letting each time period correspond to a node of a network. An arc from node i to node j represents purchasing the equipment at the beginning of period i and keeping it through period $j - 1$. The total cost would be associated with the length of each arc. A small example is given in Figure 9.7. Here, c_{12} represents the cost of purchasing the equipment at the beginning of period 1 and keeping it only for one year; c_{14} represents the cost of purchasing the equipment at the beginning of year 1 and holding it through year 3, and so forth. Any directed path from the first to the last node represents a sequence of purchasing and selling decisions. In Figure 9.7, the path consisting of arcs (1,2) and (2,4) represents purchasing equipment at the beginning of year 1, holding it for one year, replacing it at the beginning of year 2, and holding it for another two years. The minimum-cost policy would be the shortest path through the network.

FIGURE 9.7   *Equipment replacement network example*

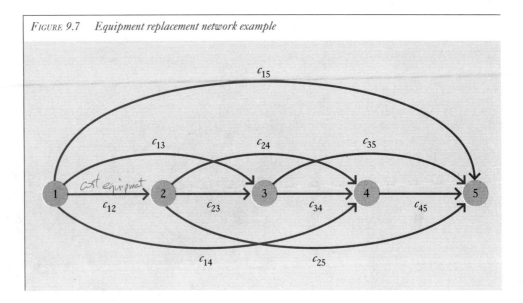

Maximum Flow Problem

In many situations we seek to determine the maximum amount that can be transported from a source to a sink when the arcs of the network have capacity limitations. A typical example is the transportation of oil from a refinery (the source) to a storage facility (the sink) along a network of pipelines. Each pipeline (arc) has a capacity which limits the amount of flow. Another example is the assignment of trains along a railroad network. The flow volume in the rail network is limited by the number of tracks along each link, and by speed limitations that depend on the track condition and grade, or steepness, of the rail line. In either case, the objective is to maximize the total flow from the source to the sink.

Network Design[1]

The production and distribution of natural gas is an important factor in our economy. A problem that the gas industry faces is designing underwater pipeline networks to link gas reserves to processing plants. Several issues are involved, including the configuration of the pipeline system as well as the selection of the best pipe diameters. Figure 9.8 shows one example of an offshore pipeline network in a tree configuration. Trees represent economical ways of linking a set of gas fields to a processing plant using the smallest linear length of pipe. A fundamental problem is to select a tree that connects all the nodes at minimum total cost. This is called the *minimal spanning tree problem* and will be studied later in this chapter.

---

[1]See reference by Rothfarb *et al.*

FIGURE 9.8   Offshore pipeline network

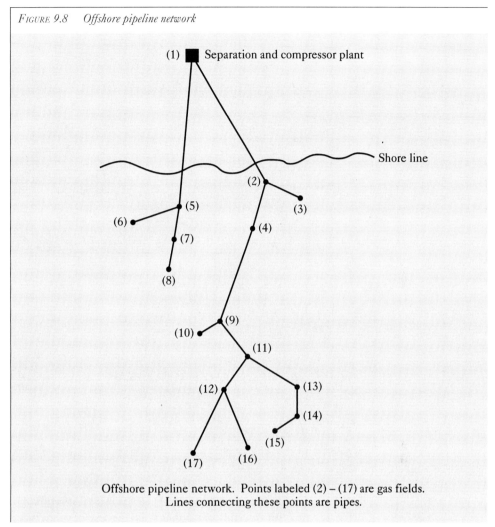

Offshore pipeline network. Points labeled (2) – (17) are gas fields.
Lines connecting these points are pipes.

Project Scheduling   *Gantt chart*

Large projects such as the construction of a building, development of an information system, or completion of a market research study, involve a large number of different activities. Some of the activities can be performed simultaneously; others can be performed only after certain other activities have been completed. The sequence in which activities must be performed can be described by a network. Figure 9.9 shows an example for a product planning and development project. Each arc represents an activity; each node represents the start or finish of an activity. Project managers are interested in knowing

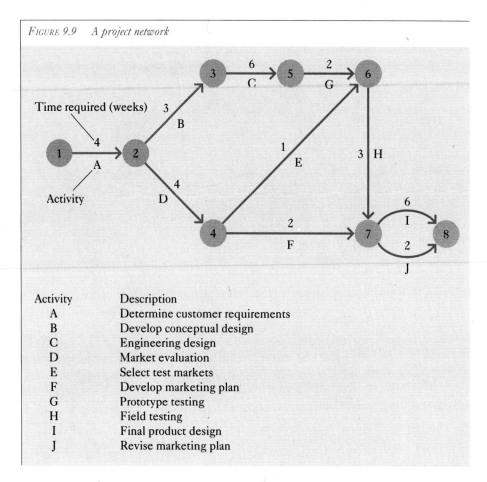

FIGURE 9.9   *A project network*

Activity	Description
A	Determine customer requirements
B	Develop conceptual design
C	Engineering design
D	Market evaluation
E	Select test markets
F	Develop marketing plan
G	Prototype testing
H	Field testing
I	Final product design
J	Revise marketing plan

how long the entire project will take, when each activity should be scheduled, and which activities are critical in the sense that delaying any of them would delay the completion of the project. Later in this chapter, we will discuss how to construct a detailed schedule of activities that minimizes project completion time.

Investment Planning

In Chapter 4 we formulated a linear program for time-based financial planning (Example 11 in Chapter 4). In this example, an investor seeks to determine an optimal sequence of investments that will maximize the amount of cash on hand after five years, with an initial investment of $30,000. Several different investments are available, each earning different returns and having different maturities. The network model for this situation is shown in Figure 9.10. Each node represents the start of a year, and the numbers on the arcs represent the return (principal and interest) for each dollar invested at the start of the

---

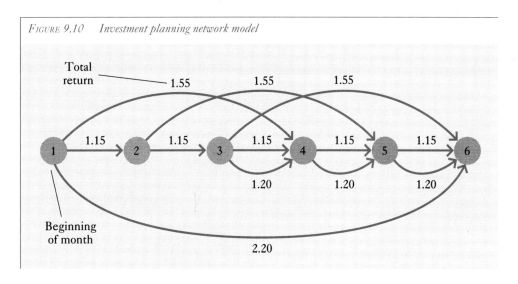

FIGURE 9.10   *Investment planning network model*

year. In this case, conservation of flow applies (that is exactly how the linear programming constraints were developed in Chapter 4), but with one important twist. In this case, the flow that leaves an arc is not the same as the flow that enters. Because of the interest earned, the flow entering an arc is multiplied by a constant greater than 1 when leaving the arc. Such a network is called a *network with gains and losses*. In addition to cash flow management, there are many other examples involving gains and losses. Some examples are modeling scrap and waste in production processes, water evaporation in environmental systems management, and losses due to chemical reactions. Although we will not study special techniques for solving such problems, they represent an important class of practical problems. Usually, it is very easy to conceptualize the network model, and you can then write the conservation of flow equations and solve it as a linear program.

NETWORKS AND MATHEMATICAL PROGRAMMING

Many network problems can be formulated easily as linear or integer programs. In the remainder of this chapter we will discuss mathematical programming models for some important types of network problems and their solution using LINDO and EXCEL SOLVER. Special algorithms exist for solving these models that are faster and more efficient than mathematical programming, especially for large problems. A complete discussion of these, however, is beyond the scope of this book.

EXAMPLE 1. A TRANSSHIPMENT MODEL

Great Northern Industries ships goods from its factory in Minneapolis by rail to two major customer centers in New York and Atlanta. The factory produces 10,000 units each month, 6,000 of which must be shipped to Atlanta, and the remainder to New York. As shown in Figure 9.11(*a*), goods may be shipped directly to Atlanta and on to New York, or through a regional distribution center in Chicago. Figure 9.11(*b*) shows the corresponding network flow model. The numbers beside each arc represent the arc capacities and unit costs.

We can model this problem as a linear program. We follow the same approach discussed in Chapter 4.

What is it that Great Northern needs to decide? Great Northern needs to decide how much to ship from the factory to each location. Let x_{ij} be the flow on the arc from node i to node j (in thousands of units).

FIGURE 9.11   *Distribution system and network flow model*

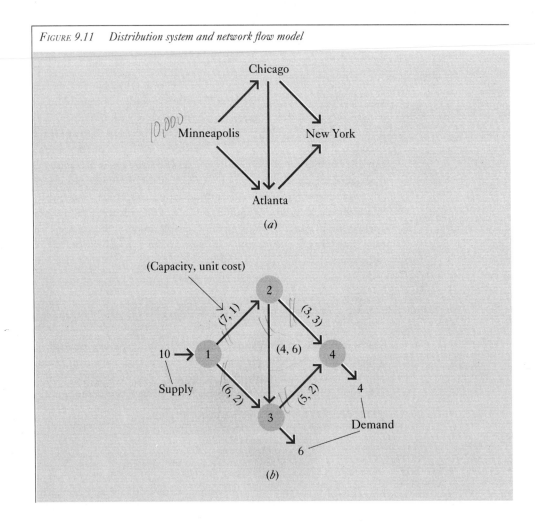

(*a*)

(*b*)

What is the objective to be maximized or minimized? The objective function would be to minimize cost, obtained by multiplying the flow on each arc by the unit cost along the arc.

$$\text{minimize } z = 1x_{12} + 2x_{13} + 6x_{23} + 3x_{24} + 2x_{34}$$

How is the problem restricted? The only restrictions are conservation of flow and arc capacities. Using the conservation of flow principle, we have the equations

$$
\begin{array}{lll}
\text{FLOW OUT} & -\ \text{FLOW IN} & = 0 \\
(x_{12} + x_{13}) & -\ (10) & = 0 \text{ (node 1)} \\
(x_{23} + x_{24}) & -\ (x_{12}) & = 0 \text{ (node 2)} \\
(6 + x_{34}) & -\ (x_{13} + x_{23}) & = 0 \text{ (node 3)} \\
(4) & -\ (x_{24} + x_{34}) & = 0 \text{ (node 4)}
\end{array}
$$

If we rewrite these equations so that all constant terms are on the right-hand side, we have

$$x_{12} + x_{13} = 10$$
$$x_{23} + x_{24} - x_{12} = 0$$
$$x_{34} - x_{13} - x_{23} = -6$$
$$-x_{24} - x_{34} = -4$$

The arc capacity restrictions can be written as

$$x_{12} \le 7$$
$$x_{13} \le 6$$
$$x_{23} \le 4$$
$$x_{24} \le 3$$
$$x_{34} \le 5$$

These, along with the conservation of flow equations, represent a set of constraints for the linear program.

Figure 9.12 shows the solution of this model with LINDO. The solution calls for shipping 4,000 units from Minneapolis to Chicago, 6,000 units from Minneapolis to Atlanta, 1,000 units from Chicago to Atlanta, 3,000 units from Chicago to New York, and 1,000 units from Atlanta to New York, at a total cost of $33,000. Notice that the solution uses all the capacity of the Minneapolis-Atlanta route (x_{13}) and the Chicago-New York route (x_{24}). The dual price for row 7 indicates that the company would realize significant savings if the capacity could be increased, perhaps by negotiating with the rail carrier.

If the capacity on this route is increased to 7, we can reduce the total cost to $28,000 by shipping 2,000 units from Minneapolis to Chicago, 8,000 units from Minneapolis to Atlanta, 2,000 units from Chicago to New York, and 2,000 units from

Atlanta to New York. This is shown in Figure 9.13. From this solution, Great Northern Industries might question the need for the Chicago distribution center, as all product is shipped through Chicago to New York. Perhaps it would be cheaper to ship directly to New York, and considerable savings might result from closing this distribution center.

FIGURE 9.12   *Solution of the Great Northern transshipment problem*

```
MIN       X12 + 2 X13 + 6 X23 + 3 X24 + 2 X34
SUBJECT TO
         2)   X12 + X13 = 10
         3) − X12 + X23 + X24 = 0
         4) − X13 − X23 + X34 = −6
         5) − X24 − X34 = −4
         6)   X12 <= 7
         7)   X13 <= 6
         8)   X23 <= 4
         9)   X24 <= 3
        10)   X34 <= 5
```

OBJECTIVE FUNCTION VALUE

1)	33.000000	

VARIABLE	VALUE	REDUCED COST
X12	4.000000	.000000
X13	6.000000	.000000
X23	1.000000	.000000
X24	3.000000	.000000
X34	1.000000	.000000

ROW	SLACK OR SURPLUS	DUAL PRICES
2)	.000000	−9.000000
3)	.000000	−8.000000
4)	.000000	−2.000000
5)	.000000	.000000
6)	3.000000	.000000
7)	.000000	5.000000
8)	3.000000	.000000
9)	.000000	5.000000
10)	4.000000	.000000

RANGES IN WHICH THE BASIS IS UNCHANGED:

OBJ COEFFICIENT RANGES

VARIABLE	CURRENT COEF	ALLOWABLE INCREASE	ALLOWABLE DECREASE
X12	1.000000	INFINITY	5.000000
X13	2.000000	5.000000	INFINITY
X23	6.000000	INFINITY	5.000000
X24	3.000000	5.000000	INFINITY
X34	2.000000	INFINITY	5.000000

RIGHTHAND SIDE RANGES

ROW	CURRENT RHS	ALLOWABLE INCREASE	ALLOWABLE DECREASE
2	10.000000	.000000	.000000
3	.000000	.000000	.000000
4	−6.000000	.000000	.000000
5	−4.000000	.000000	.000000
6	7.000000	INFINITY	3.000000
7	6.000000	1.000000	3.000000
8	4.000000	INFINITY	3.000000
9	3.000000	1.000000	3.000000
10	5.000000	INFINITY	4.000000

FIGURE 9.13   New solution of the Great Northern transshipment problem

```
MIN      X12 + 2 X13 + 6 X23 + 3 X24 + 2 X34
SUBJECT TO
  2)   X12 + X13 = 10
  3) − X12 + X23 + X24 = 0
  4) − X13 − X23 + X34 = −6
  5) − X24 − X34 = −4
  6)   X12 <= 7
  7)   X13 <= 8          ◄──────── capacity increase
  8)   X23 <= 4
  9)   X24 <= 5
 10)   X34 <= 3
```

OBJECTIVE FUNCTION VALUE

```
  1)     28.000000
```

VARIABLE	VALUE	REDUCED COST
X12	2.000000	.000000
X13	8.000000	.000000
X23	.000000	5.000000
X24	2.000000	.000000
X34	2.000000	.000000

ROW	SLACK OR SURPLUS	DUAL PRICES
2)	.000000	−1.000000
3)	.000000	.000000
4)	.000000	1.000000
5)	.000000	3.000000
6)	5.000000	.000000
7)	.000000	5.000000
8)	4.000000	.000000
9)	1.000000	.000000
10)	3.000000	.000000

ROW   RANGES IN WHICH THE BASIS IS UNCHANGED:

OBJ COEFFICIENT RANGES

VARIABLE	CURRENT COEF	ALLOWABLE INCREASE	ALLOWABLE DECREASE
X12	1.000000	INFINITY	.000000
X13	2.000000	.000000	INFINITY
X23	6.000000	INFINITY	5.000000
X24	3.000000	5.000000	.000000
X34	2.000000	.000000	5.000000

RIGHTHAND SIDE RANGES

ROW	CURRENT RHS	ALLOWABLE INCREASE	ALLOWABLE DECREASE
2	10.000000	.000000	.000000
3	.000000	.000000	.000000
4	−6.000000	.000000	.000000
5	−4.000000	.000000	.000000
6	7.000000	INFINITY	5.000000
7	8.000000	2.000000	1.000000
8	4.000000	INFINITY	4.000000
9	3.000000	INFINITY	1.000000
10	5.000000	INFINITY	3.000000

You might have noticed that all variables in the optimal solution are integers. This is no coincidence—in any network flow problem with integer data, the optimal solution will be integer! This is one of the reasons that network flow models are so appealing, and one of the reasons that special solution procedures can be developed to solve them quickly and easily.

EXAMPLE 2. A MAXIMUM FLOW PROBLEM

Mesov Oil, Inc. owns a pumping station in the Gulf of Mexico and distributes oil through a network of pipelines to a refinery in Louisiana. Pipeline capacities vary, and the company wishes to determine how to route the oil over the network in order to maximize the amount of oil that can be received at the refinery.

Figure 9.14 shows the network. Node s represents the pumping station and node t represents the refinery.

What is it that Mesov Oil needs to decide? The company would like to know how much oil should flow along each arc in the network and the total flow from s to t. The variable v represents the total flow that can be shipped through the network. Let us define x_{ij} as the flow on arc (i,j).

What is the objective function to be maximized or minimized? The objective function is to maximize v, the total flow from s to t, or

$$\text{Maximize } v \quad \text{flow}$$

How is the problem restricted? The only restrictions are conservation flow and arc capacities. The conservation of flow equations at each node are

$$x_{s1} + x_{s2} - v = 0 \qquad \text{(node s)}$$
$$x_{12} + x_{13} - x_{s1} = 0 \qquad \text{(node 1)}$$

FIGURE 9.14   An oil distribution network

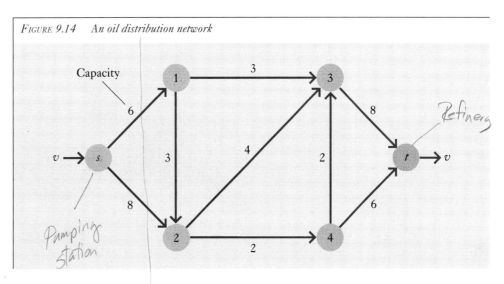

$$x_{23} + x_{24} - x_{s2} - x_{12} = 0 \qquad \text{(node 2)}$$
$$x_{3t} - x_{13} - x_{23} - x_{43} = 0 \qquad \text{(node 3)}$$
$$x_{4t} + x_{43} - x_{24} = 0 \qquad \text{(node 4)}$$
$$v - x_{3t} - x_{4t} = 0 \qquad \text{(node t)}$$

Arc capacity constraints are given by

$$x_{s1} \leq 6$$
$$x_{s2} \leq 8$$
$$x_{12} \leq 3$$
$$x_{13} \leq 3$$
$$x_{23} \leq 4$$
$$x_{24} \leq 2$$
$$x_{43} \leq 2$$
$$x_{3t} \leq 8$$
$$x_{4t} \leq 6$$

Figure 9.15 shows the LINDO output for this maximum flow problem. The maximum flow in the network is 9. Notice that the flows on arcs (1,3), (2,3), and (2,4) are at their capacity (the slack variables are zero). These arcs limit the total amount of flow through the network. What happens if you remove these arcs from the network? It is easy to see that these arcs separate, or cut, the network into two components. Because all flow must pass over arcs that separate the source from the sink, it is always true that the maximum flow is equal to the smallest of these "cuts."

FIGURE 9.15   *LINDO solution to the maximum flow problem*

```
MAX      V
SUBJECT TO
 2) − V + XS1 + XS2 = 0
 3) − XS1 + X12 + X13 = 0
 4) − XS2 − X12 + X23 + X24 = 0
 5) − X13 − X23 + X3T − X43 = 0
 6) − X24 + X43 + X4T = 0
 7)   V − X3T − X4T = 0
 8)   XS1 <= 6
 9)   XS2 <= 8
10)   X12 <= 3
```

11)   X13 <= 3
12)   X23 <= 4
13)   X24 <= 2
14)   X43 <= 2
15)   X3T <= 8
16)   X4T <= 6

OBJECTIVE FUNCTION VALUE

1)   9.000000

VARIABLE	VALUE	REDUCED COST
V	9.000000	.000000
XS1	3.000000	.000000
XS2	6.000000	.000000
X12	.000000	.000000
X13	3.000000	.000000
X23	4.000000	.000000
X24	2.000000	.000000
X3T	7.000000	.000000
X43	.000000	.000000
X4T	2.000000	.000000

ROW	SLACK OR SURPLUS	DUAL PRICES
2)	.000000	.000000
3)	.000000	.000000
4)	.000000	.000000
5)	.000000	1.000000
6)	.000000	1.000000
7)	.000000	1.000000
8)	3.000000	.000000
9)	2.000000	.000000
10)	3.000000	.000000
11)	.000000	1.000000
12)	.000000	1.000000
13)	.000000	1.000000
14)	2.000000	.000000
15)	1.000000	.000000
16)	4.000000	.000000

RANGES IN WHICH THE BASIS IS UNCHANGED:

OBJ COEFFICIENT RANGES

VARIABLE	CURRENT COEF	ALLOWABLE INCREASE	ALLOWABLE DECREASE
V	1.000000	INFINITY	1.000000
XS1	.000000	.000000	1.000000
XS2	.000000	INFINITY	.000000
X12	.000000	.000000	INFINITY
X13	.000000	INFINITY	1.000000
X23	.000000	INFINITY	1.000000
X24	.000000	INFINITY	1.000000
X3T	.000000	.000000	1.000000
X43	.000000	.000000	INFINITY
X4T	.000000	INFINITY	.000000

RIGHTHAND SIDE RANGES

ROW	CURRENT RHS	ALLOWABLE INCREASE	ALLOWABLE DECREASE
2	.000000	.000000	.000000
3	.000000	.000000	.000000
4	.000000	.000000	.000000
5	.000000	.000000	.000000
6	.000000	.000000	.000000
7	.000000	.000000	.000000
8	6.000000	INFINITY	3.000000
9	8.000000	INFINITY	2.000000
10	3.000000	INFINITY	3.000000
11	3.000000	1.000000	3.000000
12	4.000000	1.000000	4.000000
13	2.000000	2.000000	2.000000
14	2.000000	INFINITY	2.000000
15	8.000000	INFINITY	1.000000
16	6.000000	INFINITY	4.000000

EXAMPLE 3. THE SHORTEST ROUTE PROBLEM

As shown in Figure 9.16, Nantucket Airlines operates short commuter flights from the island of Nantucket to a variety of New England cities. A traveler has the choice of a variety of connections to reach her destination (node t), and the time in hours of each flight segment is shown along each branch of the network. What set of flights should she choose in order to reach her destination in the shortest possible time?

FIGURE 9.16   Nantucket Airlines route map

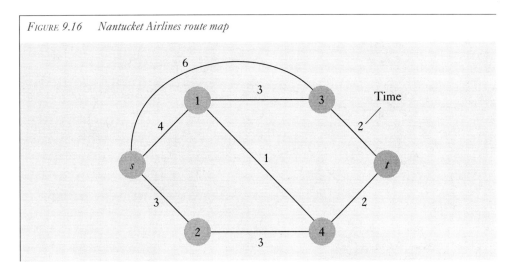

Similar to example 1

This problem is known as the *shortest route problem*. We can model this as a network flow problem and then solve it as a linear program. To model this as a network flow problem, we convert each undirected branch to a pair of oppositely directed arcs. We assign a supply of one unit to node s and a demand of one unit to node t. This new formulation, shown in Figure 9.17, is now a transshipment problem without arc capacities. Because the flight times are treated as unit costs of flow on arcs, the minimum-cost flow of the one unit from s to t must occur over the shortest route. This problem is now exactly analogous to Example 1, but without capacity restrictions.

The corresponding linear program and LINDO solution are shown in Figure 9.18. From the solution we see that the shortest route is along the path s-1-4-t. How would you interpret the sensitivity analysis information for the objective function coefficients? Does it make sense when examining alternate paths in the network?

EXAMPLE 4. THE MINIMUM SPANNING TREE PROBLEM

We defined a spanning tree in a network as a connected network that contains no cycles and includes all nodes of the network. If the branches of a network are assigned some costs, the *minimum spanning tree problem* involves finding a spanning tree whose total cost is the smallest among all possible spanning trees.

One example of such a problem is designing electrical connections on a printed circuit board. Figure 9.19 shows a layout of possible connections that do not interfere with other elements of the circuit board. The numbers by each branch represent the length of the connection—our measure of cost. We seek to connect all nodes of the network at minimum total cost.

FIGURE 9.17   *Network flow model for the shortest route problem*

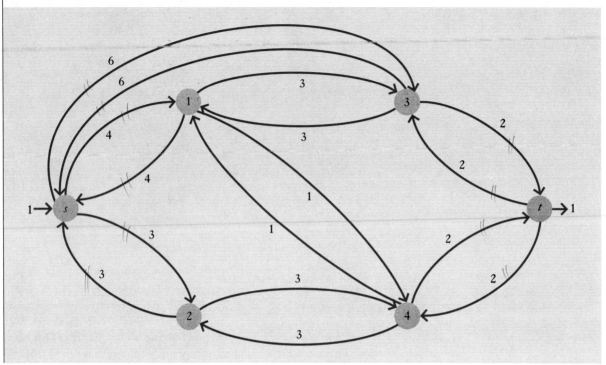

FIGURE 9.18   *LINDO solution to the shortest route problem*

MIN   4 XS1 + 4 X1S + 3 XS2 + 3 X2S + 6 XS3 + 6 X3S + 3 X13 +
           3 X31 + X14 + X41 + 3 X24 + 3 X42 + 2 X3T + 2 XT3 + 2 X4T +
           2 XT4

SUBJECT TO

2)   XS1 − X1S + XS2 − X2S + XS3 − X3S = 1   Node S
3) − XS1 + X1S + X13 − X31 + X14 − X41 = 0   Node 1
4) − XS2 + X2S + X24 − X42 = 0
5) − XS3 + X3S − X13 + X31 + X3T − XT3 = 0
6) − X14 + X41 − X24 + X42 + X4T − XT4 = 0
7) − X3T + XT3 − X4T + XT4 = −1   Node t

OBJECTIVE FUNCTION VALUE

1)   7.000000

VARIABLE	VALUE	REDUCED COST
XS1	1.000000	.000000
X1S	.000000	8.000000
XS2	.000000	.000000
X2S	.000000	6.000000
XS3	.000000	.000000
X3S	.000000	12.000000
X13	.000000	1.000000
X31	.000000	5.000000
X14	1.000000	.000000
X41	.000000	2.000000
X24	.000000	1.000000
X42	.000000	5.000000
X3T	.000000	1.000000
XT3	.000000	3.000000
X4T	1.000000	.000000
XT4	.000000	4.000000

ROW	SLACK OR SURPLUS	DUAL PRICES
2)	.000000	.000000
3)	.000000	4.000000
4)	.000000	3.000000
5)	.000000	6.000000
6)	.000000	5.000000
7)	.000000	7.000000

RANGES IN WHICH THE BASIS IS UNCHANGED:

	OBJ COEFFICIENT RANGES		
VARIABLE	CURRENT COEF	ALLOWABLE INCREASE	ALLOWABLE DECREASE
XS1	4.000000	1.000000	1.000000
X1S	4.000000	INFINITY	8.000000
XS2	3.000000	5.000000	1.000000
X2S	3.000000	INFINITY	6.000000
XS3	6.000000	1.000000	1.000000
X3S	6.000000	INFINITY	12.000000
X13	3.000000	INFINITY	1.000000
X31	3.000000	INFINITY	5.000000
X14	1.000000	1.000000	2.000000
X41	1.000000	INFINITY	2.000000

X24	3.000000	INFINITY	1.000000
X42	3.000000	INFINITY	5.000000
X3T	2.000000	INFINITY	1.000000
XT3	2.000000	INFINITY	3.000000
X4T	2.000000	1.000000	3.000000
XT4	2.000000	INFINITY	4.000000

RIGHTHAND SIDE RANGES

ROW	CURRENT RHS	ALLOWABLE INCREASE	ALLOWABLE DECREASE
2	1.000000	.000000	.000000
3	.000000	.000000	.000000
4	.000000	.000000	.000000
5	.000000	.000000	.000000
6	.000000	.000000	.000000
7	−1.000000	.000000	.000000

What is it we are trying to decide? We would like to find the least-cost spanning tree for the network in Figure 9.19. We must decide whether or not each arc is in the spanning tree. This problem is therefore different from the previous examples because we cannot model it as a flow problem, but must think of it in terms of logical,

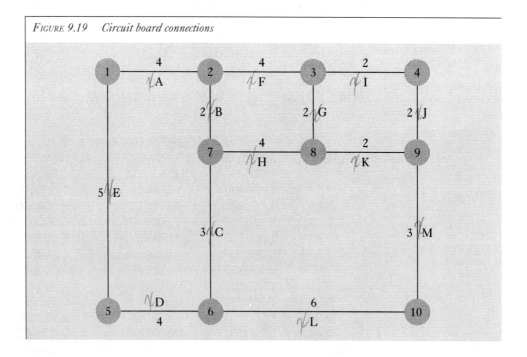

FIGURE 9.19   *Circuit board connections*

zero-one variables. Either a branch is in the spanning tree or it is not. It therefore makes sense to define $x_i = 1$ if branch i is in the tree, and 0 if not.

What is the objective to be maximized or minimized? We would like to minimize the total cost of the spanning tree. This can be expressed as a linear function of our decision variables.

$$\text{Min } 4x_A + 2x_B + 3x_C + \ldots + 3x_M$$

How can we write a set of constraints that would characterize a spanning tree? First, notice that for any tree, there must be at least one branch connected to each node. This tells us that any solution must at least satisfy $\sum x_i \geq 1$, where the summation includes all branches connected to a particular node. For example, at node 1 we must have

$$x_A + x_E \geq 1$$

At node 7 we need

$$x_B + x_C + x_H \geq 1$$

and so forth. Also, because a spanning tree contains exactly one less branch than the number of nodes, we must have exactly 9 branches in the tree, or

10 nodes - 1
= 9

$$x_A + x_B + x_C + x_D + x_E + x_F + x_G + x_H + x_I + x_J + x_K + x_L + x_M = 9$$

The entire IP model can be written as

$$\text{Min } 4x_A + 2x_B + 3x_C + 4s_D + 5x_E + 4x_F + 2x_G + 4x_H + 2x_I$$
$$+ 2x_J + 2x_K + 6x_L + 3x_M$$

node 1 $\quad x_A + x_E \geq 1$

node 2 $\quad x_A + x_B + x_F \geq 1$

$3 \quad x_F + x_G + x_I \geq 1$

$4 \quad x_I + x_J \geq 1$

$5 \quad x_D + x_E \geq 1$

$6 \quad x_C + x_D + x_L \geq 1$

$7 \quad x_B + x_C + x_H \geq 1$

$8 \quad x_G + x_H + x_K \geq 1$

$9 \quad x_J + x_K + x_M \geq 1$

$10 \quad x_L + x_M \geq 1$

$$x_A + x_B + x_C + x_D + x_E + x_F + x_G + x_H + x_I + x_J + x_K + x_L + x_M = 9$$

We may relax the integer requirements by including constraints $x_j \leq 1$, for all j. The LINDO solution is shown in Figure 9.20.

On close examination, you can see that this solution does not provide a spanning tree. Although all variables are 0 or 1, the variables corresponding to branches $I, J, K,$

FIGURE 9.20   *Linear programming solution to the spanning tree model*

OBJECTIVE FUNCTION VALUE

1)   24.000000

VARIABLE	VALUE	REDUCED COST
A	1.000000	4.000000
B	1.000000	2.000000
C	1.000000	3.000000
D	1.000000	4.000000
E	.000000	5.000000
F	.000000	4.000000
G	1.000000	2.000000
H	.000000	4.000000
I	1.000000	2.000000
J	1.000000	2.000000
K	1.000000	2.000000
L	.000000	6.000000
M	1.000000	3.000000

ROW	SLACK OR SURPLUS	DUAL PRICES
2)	.000000	.000000
3)	1.000000	.000000
4)	1.000000	.000000
5)	1.000000	.000000
6)	.000000	.000000
7)	1.000000	.000000
8)	1.000000	.000000
9)	1.000000	.000000
10)	2.000000	.000000
11)	.000000	.000000
12)	.000000	.000000

and G form a cycle that is disconnected from the rest of the tree. If we add a constraint that eliminates this cycle,

$$x_I + x_J + x_K + x_G \leq 3$$

then we get the solution shown in Figure 9.21. This solution is indeed a spanning tree and is the optimal solution.

Unfortunately, there was no guarantee that adding the extra constraint would result in a feasible solution, and we might have ended up with a cycle in some other place. To ensure that no cycles would be formed, we would have to write out a large number of these constraints. There actually is a way of modeling this problem as a linear program, but the

FIGURE 9.21   *Optimal solution to the spanning tree model*

OBJECTIVE FUNCTION VALUE

1)   26.000000

VARIABLE	VALUE	REDUCED COST
A	1.000000	4.000000
B	1.000000	2.000000
C	1.000000	3.000000
D	1.000000	4.000000
E	.000000	5.000000
F	.000000	4.000000
G	.000000	2.000000
H	1.000000	4.000000
I	1.000000	2.000000
J	1.000000	2.000000
K	1.000000	2.000000
L	.000000	6.000000
M	1.000000	3.000000

ROW	SLACK OR SURPLUS	DUAL PRICES
2)	.000000	.000000
3)	1.000000	.000000
4)	.000000	.000000
5)	1.000000	.000000
6)	.000000	.000000
7)	1.000000	.000000
8)	2.000000	.000000
9)	1.000000	.000000
10)	2.000000	.000000
11)	.000000	.000000
12)	.000000	.000000
13)	.000000	.000000

theory is too complicated for this book. Despite the difficulty in modeling the minimum spanning tree problem as a mathematical program, in the Appendix to this chapter we present an incredibly simple algorithm to solve it.

PROJECT SCHEDULING

Figure 9.9 showed a network describing a product planning and development project. As you can see, the network describes the sequence in which activities must be performed.

For example, activity B must follow activity A; however, activities C and D can be performed concurrently. A project manager would like to schedule the activities so that they are performed in the correct sequence and the project is completed as quickly as possible.

Any path in the project network from start to finish represents a sequence of activities that must be performed in sequential order. The time it takes to complete these activities is the length of the path. Thus, the project can be completed *no earlier* than the length of the *longest path* in the network.

> The longest path in a project network is called the *critical path*. Activities on the critical path are the critical activities whose delay would delay the project completion time.

Just knowing the critical path provides no information to a project manager that will be useful in scheduling the individual activities. Instead, we will present an approach that not only finds the critical path, but provides a detailed schedule and sensitivity analysis information. Our goal is to develop a schedule that completes the project in the shortest possible time.

For each activity, we will compute

1. The earliest start time (ES).
2. The earliest finish time (EF).
3. The latest start time (LS).
4. The latest finish time (LF).

For all activities at the starting node, the earliest start time is set to zero. If we know the earliest start time for any activity, then the earliest finish time for that activity must be the earliest start time plus the time it takes to complete the activity. Letting t represent the time for an activity, we have

$$\text{Earliest finish} \quad EF = ES + t \tag{9.1}$$

Because activity A begins the project, its early start time is zero. Thus, the early finish time for activity A is $EF = 0 + 4 = 4$. Now consider the activities B and D that begin at node 2. These activities can start no earlier than the earliest time at which all activities *ending* at node 2 finish. Thus, the early start times for activities B and D are 4. Using equation (9.1), the early finish time for activity B is $4 + 3 = 7$; the early finish time for activity D is $4 + 4 = 8$. We can apply this same approach and find ES and EF for activities C, G, E, and F, as shown in Figure 9.22.

What do we do next? First notice that we cannot assign early start times to activities I and J because we do not yet know when activity H will be completed. We must be careful to select activities in the appropriate order. When can activity H begin? Both activities G and E must be completed before H can begin. Because G can be completed by week 15 and E can be completed by week 9, *both* activities cannot be completed until week 15 (the larger of the early finish times). ES for activity H is therefore 15, and $EF = 15 + 3 = 18$. In a similar fashion, the early start times for activities I and J must be equal to the larger of the early finish times for activities F and H.

FIGURE 9.22   *Partial computation of early start and finish times*

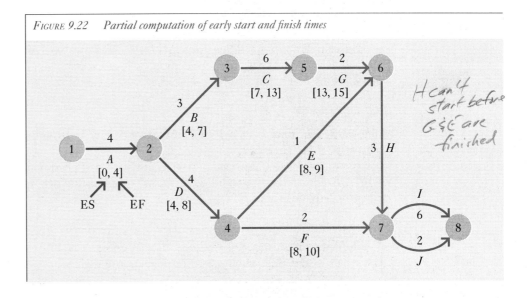

The early start time for any activity leaving a node is equal to the largest early finish time for all activities entering the node.

The complete early start/early finish schedule is shown in Figure 9.23. The largest early finish time at the ending node of the project represents the minimum project completion time. In this example, we see that the project can be completed in no earlier than 24 weeks.

FIGURE 9.23   *Early start/early finish schedule*

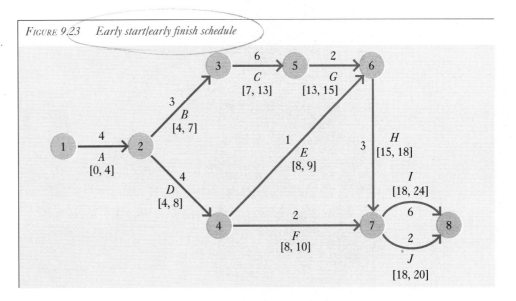

Next, we compute the latest start and latest finish times. We begin at the final node of the project and set the latest finish times for all ending activities equal to the minimum project completion time. Thus, for activities I and J, we set LF = 24. If we know the latest finish time for an activity, we compute the latest start time by "backing up" by the activity time t.

$$\text{Latest start} \qquad \boxed{\text{LS} = \text{LF} - t} \qquad \text{Latest finish} \tag{9.2}$$

The latest start time for activity I is therefore $24 - 6 = 18$, and the latest start time for activity J is $24 - 2 = \cancel{20}\ 22$.

In order for activities I and J to start at their latest possible times, when should activities F and H be completed, *at the latest?* This must be the smaller of the latest start times of activities I and J.

> The latest finish time for all activities that end at a node is equal to the smallest latest start time for all activities leaving the node.

Thus, the latest finish time for activities F and H is the smaller of 18 and 22, or 18. Now we can use equation 9.2 to find the latest start times. We may continue applying these rules and working backwards through the network, resulting in the latest start/latest finish schedule shown in Figure 9.24.

Table 9.1 summarizes these results. In the last column we compute the *slack*—the difference between the early start and latest start (or, the early finish and latest finish).

FIGURE 9.24   *Latest start/latest finish schedule*

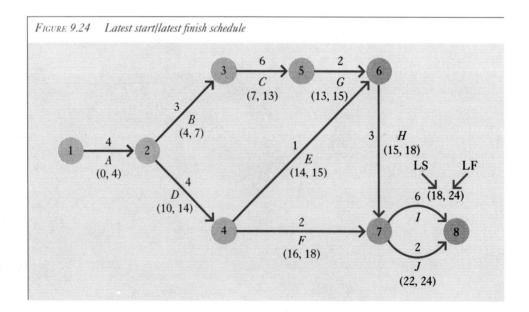

Activity	ES	EF	LS	LF	Slack
A	0	4	0	4	0 ✓
B	4	7	4	7	0 ✓
C	7	13	7	13	0 ✓
D	4	8	10	14	6
E	8	9	14	15	6
F	8	10	16	18	8
G	13	15	13	15	0 ✓
H	15	18	15	18	0 ✓
I	18	24	18	24	0 ✓
J	18	20	22	24	4

√ = critical path

The slack values provide sensitivity analysis information; slack is the amount of time that an *individual* activity can be delayed without delaying the minimum project completion date.

The critical path consists of all activities with zero slack.

The slack on activity *D* is 6. This means that activity *D* can be delayed 6 weeks without delaying the project. Note, however, that if activity *D* is delayed 6 weeks, then activities *E* and *F* cannot start until week 14. In effect, this makes the path *A-D-E -H -I* critical also, because any further delay of activities on this path will increase the project length.

entire path becomes critical if late

As shown in Figure 9.25, it is easy to set up these calculations on a spreadsheet. We need only use the @MAX and @MIN functions to determine the early start and latest finish times as appropriate. If only one activity ends at a node, the early start time for all

FIGURE 9.25   *Spreadsheet model for the product planning and development project*

	A	B	C	D	E	F	G
1	Project Scheduling						
2							
3							
4	Activity	Duration	Early Start	Early Finish	Latest Start	Latest Finish	Slack
5	A	4	0	4	0	4	0
6	B	3	4	7	4	7	0
7	C	6	7	13	7	13	0
8	D	4	4	8	10	14	6
9	E	1	8	9	14	15	6
10	F	2	8	10	16	18	8
11	G	2	13	15	13	15	0
12	H	3	15	18	15	18	0
13	I	6	18	24	18	24	0
14	J	2	18	20	22	24	4

Selected cell formulas

	A	B	C	D	E	F	G
1	Project Scheduling						
2							
3							
4	Activity	Duration	Early Start	Early Finish	Latest Start	Latest Finish	Slack
5	A	4	0	+C5+B5	+F5-B5	@MIN(E6,E8)	+E5-C5
6	B	3	+D5	+C6+B6	+F6-B6	+E7	+E6-C6
7	C	6	+D6	+C7+B7	+F7-B7	+E11	+E7-C7
8	D	4	+D5	+C8+B8	+F8-B8	@MIN(E9,E10)	+E8-C8
9	E	1	+D8	+C9+B9	+F9-B9	+E12	+E9-C9
10	F	2	+D8	+C10+B10	+F10-B10	@MIN(E13,E14)	+E10-C10
11	G	2	+D7	+C11+B11	+F11-B11	+E12	+E11-C11
12	H	3	@MAX(D9,D11)	+C12+B12	+F12-B12	@MIN(E13,E14)	+E12-C12
13	I	6	@MAX(D10,D12)	+C13+B13	+F13-B13	@MAX(D13,D14)	+E13-C13
14	J	2	@MAX(D10,D12)	+C14+B14	+F14-B14	@MAX(D13,D14)	+E14-C14

Decisions in path

activities leaving that node is equal to the early finish time of the preceding activity (e.g., activities *B* through *G*). If more than one activity ends at a node, the early start time for all succeeding activities is the maximum of the early finish times of the preceding activities (e.g., *H* , *I* , and *J*). Because both activities *I* and *J* end at the terminal node, the latest finish time is the maximum of their early finish times. Working backwards, we use the @MIN function to find the latest finish times for the activities ending at a node that has multiple successors (e.g., activity *H*).

With the spreadsheet it is easy to determine the effect of changing an activity time. For instance, we see that activity *D* has a slack of 6. This means that it can be delayed by at most 6 weeks without delaying the entire project. If, for example, the time to complete activity *D* is extended to 11 weeks, the new critical path becomes *A-D-E-H-I* , as shown in Figure 9.26.

FIGURE 9.26   *New schedule with activity* D *duration* = 11

	A	B	C	D	E	F	G
1	Project Scheduling						
2							
3							
4	Activity	Duration	Early Start	Early Finish	Latest Start	Latest Finish	Slack
5	A	4	0	4	0	4	0
6	B	3	4	7	5	8	1
7	C	6	7	13	8	14	1
8	D	11	4	15	4	15	0
9	E	1	15	16	15	16	0
10	F	2	15	17	17	19	2
11	G	2	13	15	14	16	1
12	H	3	16	19	16	19	0
13	I	6	19	25	19	25	0
14	J	2	19	21	23	25	4

Linear Programming Solution

We can formulate the project scheduling problem as a linear program by defining S_{ij} to be the (early) start time for activity (i,j) and F_{ij} to be the (early) finish time for activity (i,j). We assume that node 1 is the beginning of the project and that the project will start at time zero. Therefore, for all activities $(1,j)$, we have

$$\text{Early start} \quad S_{1j} = 0$$

If we know the starting time of activity (i,j), then its completion time will equal the starting time plus the time to perform the activity.

$$\text{Early finish} \quad F_{ij} = S_{ij} + t_{ij} \quad \text{time for activity}$$

However, several activities may end at the same node. The time at which all these activities will be completed (the variable associated with the node) must be at least as large as the completion time of each individual activity. Therefore, the start time of any subsequent activities can be no smaller than the completion time of each activity ending at the node. This is illustrated in Figure 9.27. In this example, S_{67} must be at least as large as F_{56} and F_{46}; that is,

$$S_{67} \geq F_{56}$$

and

$$S_{67} \geq F_{46}$$

If only one activity ends at the node, we may use an equality rather than an inequality because the starting time will be equal to the preceding activity finish time.

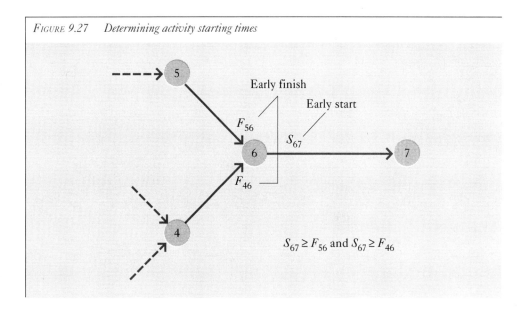

FIGURE 9.27   *Determining activity starting times*

Finally, let T represent the completion time of the entire project. For each terminating activity (i,j), we must have

completion time $T \geq F_{ij}$

The objective is to minimize T.

EXAMPLE 5. A LINEAR PROGRAMMING MODEL FOR PROJECT SCHEDULING

For the product planning and development project shown in Figure 9.23, the following constraints define the linear program:

Minimize T subject to

Early Start Time Constraints

$$S_A = 0$$
$$S_B = F_A$$
$$S_C = F_B$$
$$S_D = F_A$$
$$S_E = F_D$$
$$S_F = F_D$$
$$S_G = F_C$$
$$S_H \geq F_G$$
$$S_H \geq F_E$$
$$S_I \geq F_H$$
$$S_I \geq F_F$$
$$S_J \geq F_H$$
$$S_J \geq F_F$$

Early Finish Time Constraints

$$F_A = S_A + 4$$
$$F_B = S_B + 3$$
$$F_C = S_C + 6$$
$$F_D = S_D + 4$$
$$F_E = S_E + 1$$
$$F_F = S_F + 2$$
$$F_G = S_G + 2$$
$$F_H = S_G + 3$$
$$F_I \geq S_I + 6$$
$$F_J \geq S_J + 2$$

Completion Time Constraints

$$T \geq F_I$$

$$T \geq F_J$$

Figure 9.28 shows the solution of this problem with LINDO. The project can be completed in 24 weeks. If an early finish time constraint has zero slack and a dual price $= -1$, the corresponding activity is on the critical path. We see that activities A, B, C, G, H, and I comprise the critical path. Note that the length of the critical path is the minimum project time.

FIGURE 9.28   *LINDO model and solution to project scheduling example*

```
MIN        T
SUBJECT TO
  2)    SA = 0
  3) − SA + FA = 4
  4) − FA + SB = 0
  5) − FA + SD = 0
  6) − SB + FB = 3
  7) − SD + FD = 4
  8) − FB + SC = 0
  9)    SG − FC = 0
 10) − SC + FC = 6
 11) − FD + SE = 0
 12) − FD + SF = 0
 13) − SE + FE = 1
 14) − SF + FF = 2
 15)    SH − FG >= 0
 16) − FE + SH >= 0
 17) − SH + FH = 3
 18) − FH − SI >= 0
 19) − FF + SI >= 0
 20) − FH + SJ >= 0
 21) − FF + SJ >= 0
 22) − SI + FI >= 6
 23) − SJ + FJ >= 2
 24)    T − FI >= 0
 25)    T − FJ >= 0
 26) − SG + FG = 2
```

OPTIMUM FOUND AT STEP   2

OBJECTIVE FUNCTION VALUE

1)   24.000000

VARIABLE	VALUE	REDUCED COST
T	24.000000	.000000
SA	.000000	1.000000
FA	4.000000	.000000
SB	4.000000	.000000
SD	4.000000	.000000
FB	7.000000	.000000
FD	8.000000	.000000
SC	7.000000	.000000
SG	13.000000	.000000
FC	13.000000	.000000
SE	8.000000	.000000
SF	8.000000	.000000
FE	9.000000	.000000
FF	10.000000	.000000
SH	15.000000	.000000
FG	15.000000	.000000
FH	18.000000	.000000
SI	18.000000	.000000
SJ	22.000000	.000000
FI	24.000000	.000000
FJ	24.000000	.000000

ROW	SLACK OR SURPLUS	DUAL PRICES
2)	.000000	.000000
3)	.000000	−1.000000
4)	.000000	−1.000000
5)	.000000	.000000
6)	.000000	−1.000000
7)	.000000	.000000
8)	.000000	−1.000000
9)	.000000	−1.000000
10)	.000000	−1.000000
11)	.000000	.000000
12)	.000000	.000000
13)	.000000	.000000
14)	.000000	.000000
15)	.000000	−1.000000

16)	6.000000	.000000
17)	.000000	−1.000000
18)	.000000	−1.000000
19)	8.000000	.000000
20)	4.000000	.000000
21)	12.000000	.000000
22)	.000000	−1.000000
23)	.000000	.000000
24)	.000000	−1.000000
25)	.000000	.000000
26)	.000000	−1.000000

No. INTERATIONS = 2

RANGES IN WHICH THE BASIS IS UNCHANGED:

	OBJ COEFFICIENT RANGES		
VARIABLE	CURRENT COEF	ALLOWABLE INCREASE	ALLOWABLE DECREASE
T	1.000000	INFINITY	1.000000
SA	.000000	INFINITY	1.000000
FA	.000000	INFINITY	1.000000
SB	.000000	INFINITY	1.000000
SD	.000000	INFINITY	1.000000
FB	.000000	INFINITY	1.000000
FD	.000000	INFINITY	1.000000
SC	.000000	INFINITY	1.000000
SG	.000000	INFINITY	1.000000
FC	.000000	INFINITY	1.000000
SE	.000000	INFINITY	1.000000
SF	.000000	INFINITY	1.000000
FE	.000000	INFINITY	1.000000
FF	.000000	INFINITY	1.000000
SH	.000000	INFINITY	1.000000
FG	.000000	INFINITY	1.000000
FH	.000000	INFINITY	1.000000
SI	.000000	INFINITY	1.000000
SJ	.000000	.000000	1.000000
FI	.000000	INFINITY	1.000000
FJ	.000000	.000000	1.000000

| | | RIGHTHAND SIDE RANGES | |
ROW	CURRENT RHS	ALLOWABLE INCREASE	ALLOWABLE DECREASE
2	.000000	.000000	.000000
3	4.000000	INFINITY	4.000000
4	.000000	INFINITY	4.000000
5	.000000	6.000000	4.000000
6	3.000000	INFINITY	6.000000
7	4.000000	6.000000	8.000000
8	.000000	INFINITY	6.000000
9	.000000	INFINITY	6.000000
10	6.000000	INFINITY	6.000000
11	.000000	6.000000	8.000000
12	.000000	8.000000	8.000000
13	1.000000	6.000000	9.000000
14	2.000000	8.000000	10.000000
15	.000000	INFINITY	6.000000
16	.000000	6.000000	INFINITY
17	3.000000	INFINITY	8.000000
18	.000000	INFINITY	4.000000
19	.000000	8.000000	INFINITY
20	.000000	4.000000	INFINITY
21	.000000	12.000000	INFINITY
22	6.000000	INFINITY	4.000000
23	2.000000	4.000000	INFINITY
24	.000000	INFINITY	4.000000
25	.000000	4.000000	INFINITY
26	2.000000	INFINITY	6.000000

Clearly, it is easier to find the schedule using the rules presented earlier than by formulating and solving a linear program. However, the LP formulation provides a basis for finding optimal allocations of additional resources in order to reduce project completion times. We can often shorten individual activity times by allocating additional resources, such as additional labor or overtime. In practice, this is called *crashing the activity*. Such reductions in times are not without cost, however. Suppose that C_{ij} represents the cost of reducing the time for activity (i,j) by one unit of time, and m_{ij} the maximum number of time units by which the activity can be reduced. (Obviously, you cannot reduce the activity time to zero!) Let x_{ij} be the actual amount of time that we reduce activity (i,j). The time to complete activity (i,j) becomes

$$\text{Activity time} = t_{ij} - x_{ij}$$

To find the least expensive allocation of resources to reduce the total project completion time to a target value v, we modify the linear programming formulation presented earlier as follows.

1. For each activity whose time can be reduced, modify the early finish time constraint to

$$F_j = S_i + t_{ij} - x_{ij}$$

2. Add constraints limiting the maximum number of time units for which an activity may be crashed.

$$x_{ij} \leq m_{ij}$$

m = maximum reduction

3. Add a constraint representing the target project completion time.

$$T = v$$

v = target value

4. Replace the objective function by

$$\text{Min} \sum C_{ij} x_{ij}$$

EXAMPLE 6. FINDING AN OPTIMAL CRASHING SCHEDULE

For the product planning and development project, suppose that the manager wishes to reduce the project completion time to 20 weeks. The following activities have been identified as ones that can be crashed, along with their unit costs ($1,000/week) and maximum reductions:

Activity	Unit cost, C	Maximum reduction, m
A	2	1
C	1	3
D	2	1
I	5	2

We modify the linear program in Example 5 in the following manner.

1. Include crashing times in early finish constraints.

$$F_A = S_A + 4 - x_A$$
$$F_C = S_C + 6 - x_C$$
$$F_D = S_D + 4 - x_D$$
$$F_F \geq S_I + 6 - x_I$$

2. Add upper limits on crashing.

$$x_A \leq 1$$
$$x_C \leq 3$$
$$x_D \leq 1$$
$$x_I \leq 2$$

3. Add a target constraint.

$$T = 20$$

4. Replace the objective function with

$$\text{Min } 2x_A + 1x_C + 2x_D + 5x_I$$

Figure 9.29 shows the LP solution to this problem. Activity A should be crashed by one week and activity C by three weeks. The total additional cost is $5,000.

FIGURE 9.29   *Linear programming model and solution for project crashing*

```
MIN        2 XA + 2 XD + XC + 5 XI
SUBJECT TO
  2)    SA = 0
  3) − SA + FA + XA = 4
  4) − FA + SB = 0
  5) − FA + SD = 0
  6) − SB + FB = 3
  7) − SD + FD + XD = 4
  8) − FB + SC = 0
  9)    SG − FC = 0
 10) − SC + FC + XC = 6
 11) − FD + SE = 0
 12) − FD + SF = 0
 13) − SE + FE = 1
 14) − SF + FF = 2
 15)    SH − FG >= 0
 16) − FE + SH >= 0
 17) − SH + FH = 3
 18) − FH + SI >= 0
 19) − FF + SI >= 0
 20) − FH + SJ >= 0
 21) − FF + SJ >= 0
 22) − SI + FI + XI >= 6
 23) − SJ + FJ >= 2
 24)    T − FI >= 0
 25)    T − FJ >= 0
 26) − SG + FG = 2
 27)    T = 20
 28)    XA <= 1
 29)    XC <= 3
 30)    XD <= 1
 31)    XI <= 2
```

OPTIMUM FOUND AT STEP 6

OBJECTIVE FUNCTION VALUE

1)   5.000000

VARIABLE	VALUE	REDUCED COST
T	20.000000	.000000
SA	.000000	2.000000
FA	3.000000	.000000
SB	3.000000	.000000
SD	3.000000	.000000
FB	6.000000	.000000
BD	7.000000	.000000
SC	6.000000	.000000
SG	9.000000	.000000
FC	9.000000	.000000
SE	7.000000	.000000
SF	7.000000	.000000
FE	8.000000	.000000
FF	9.000000	.000000
SH	11.000000	.000000
FG	11.000000	.000000
FH	14.000000	.000000
SI	14.000000	.000000
SJ	14.000000	.000000
FI	20.000000	.000000
FJ	16.000000	.000000
XA	1.000000	.000000
XD	.000000	2.000000
XC	3.000000	.000000
XI	.000000	3.000000

ROW	SLACK OR SURPLUS	DUAL PRICES
2)	.000000	.000000
3)	.000000	−2.000000
4)	.000000	−2.000000
5)	.000000	.000000
6)	.000000	−2.000000
7)	.000000	.000000
8)	.000000	−2.000000
9)	.000000	−2.000000
10)	.000000	−2.000000
11)	.000000	.000000
12)	.000000	.000000

13)	.000000	.000000
14)	.000000	.000000
15)	.000000	−2.000000
16)	3.000000	.000000
17)	.000000	−2.000000
18)	.000000	−2.000000
19)	5.000000	.000000
20)	.000000	.000000
21)	5.000000	.000000
22)	.000000	−2.000000
23)	.000000	.000000
24)	.000000	−2.000000
25)	4.000000	.000000
26)	.000000	−2.000000
27)	.000000	2.000000
28)	.000000	.000000
29)	.000000	1.000000
30)	1.000000	.000000
31)	2.000000	.000000

NO. ITERATIONS = 6

RANGES IN WHICH THE BASIS IS UNCHANGED:

	OBJ COEFFICIENT RANGES		
VARIABLE	CURRENT COEF	ALLOWABLE INCREASE	ALLOWABLE DECREASE
T	.000000	INFINITY	INFINITY
SA	.000000	INFINITY	2.000000
FA	.000000	1.000000	3.000000
SB	.000000	1.000000	3.000000
SD	.000000	1.000000	3.000000
FB	.000000	1.000000	3.000000
FD	.000000	1.000000	3.000000
SC	.000000	1.000000	3.000000
SG	.000000	2.000000	3.000000
FC	.000000	2.000000	3.000000
SE	.000000	1.000000	3.000000
SF	.000000	1.000000	3.000000
FE	.000000	1.000000	3.000000
FF	.000000	1.000000	3.000000

SH	.000000	2.000000	3.000000
FG	.000000	2.000000	3.000000
FH	.000000	2.000000	3.000000
SI	.000000	2.000000	3.000000
SJ	.000000	2.000000	.000000
FI	.000000	2.000000	INFINITY
FJ	.000000	2.000000	.000000
XA	2.000000	3.000000	1.000000
XD	2.000000	INFINITY	2.000000
XC	1.000000	1.000000	INFINITY
XI	5.000000	INFINITY	3.000000

RIGHTHAND SIDE RANGES

ROW	CURRENT RHS	ALLOWABLE INCREASE	ALLOWABLE DECREASE
2	.000000	.000000	.000000
3	4.000000	.000000	1.000000
4	.000000	.000000	1.000000
5	.000000	3.000000	3.000000
6	3.000000	.000000	1.000000
7	4.000000	3.000000	7.000000
8	.000000	.000000	1.000000
9	.000000	.000000	1.000000
10	6.000000	.000000	1.000000
11	.000000	3.000000	7.000000
12	.000000	5.000000	7.000000
13	1.000000	3.000000	8.000000
14	2.000000	3.000000	9.000000
15	.000000	.000000	1.000000
16	.000000	3.000000	INFINITY
17	3.000000	.000000	1.000000
18	.000000	.000000	1.000000
19	.000000	5.000000	INFINITY
20	.000000	4.000000	5.000000
21	.000000	5.000000	INFINITY
22	6.000000	.000000	1.000000
23	2.000000	4.000000	16.000000
24	.000000	.000000	1.000000
25	.000000	4.000000	INFINITY
26	2.000000	.000000	1.000000
27	20.000000	1.000000	.000000
28	1.000000	INFINITY	.000000
29	3.000000	1.000000	.000000
30	1.000000	INFINITY	1.000000
31	2.000000	INFINITY	2.000000

MANAGEMENT SCIENCE PRACTICE

In this section we describe how network modeling and solution approaches are used in the SnowMaster© software for routing snow and ice control vehicles.

Routing Snow Removal Vehicles

Snow and ice control efforts represent one of the most important challenges that counties and municipalities face, and in many northern areas of the U.S., as much as 20 percent of the highway maintenance budget is devoted to salting and plowing. Although the cost of an equipped truck approaches six figures, taxpayers are pushing for improved responsiveness. Decisions that managers must make include

- Can I afford more equipment?
- What size trucks should I buy?
- How can I best design my routes?

There are virtually an infinite number of routes and truck fleet configurations to consider. It would take days or weeks to manually lay out a new set of routes, with no assurance that the result will be any better than the original scheme. Computer-based routing and decision support systems help make these decisions easier. SnowMaster© is one such system. SnowMaster© is able to generate multiple sets of routes for any mix of vehicles of varying capacities, assist the manager in finding the minimum number and proper mix of vehicles, determine routes that will service a network within a specified time constraint, and analyze different scenarios of travel speeds and salt spreading rates.

SnowMaster© starts with a network representation of the roads and highways that require service or can be used for travel. (Not all roads in the network may be within the jurisdiction of the county or state agency.) Spreadsheets are typically used to create and edit the data files that represent the network. Figure 9.30 shows a portion of a data file; each row corresponds to a road segment (arc) on a map. Each arc is described by a unique

FIGURE 9.30   *Portion of SnowMaster data file*

A	A	B	C	D	E	F	G	H
1	Arc	Description	Start node	End node	Distance	Speed	Salt Rate	Passes
2	1	City road A	1	3	4.2	25	600	0
3	2	City road B	1	2	1.8	25	600	0
4	3	City road C	1	6	5.8	25	600	0
5	4	Hamilton Rd.	2	4	0.8	25	600	1
6	5	City road B	2	5	2.2	25	600	0
7	6	Milikin Rd.	3	8	1.5	25	600	1
8	7	State Rte 4	3	4	2.1	25	600	0
9	8	Hamilton Rd.	4	7	1.5	25	600	1
10	9	Tylersville Rd.	5	14	2.6	25	600	1
11	10	Mason Rd.	6	14	3.1	25	600	1
12	11	Montgomery Rd.	6	8	0.7	25	600	1
13	12	County line Rd.	7	14	0.6	25	600	1

identifier, the name of the road, beginning and ending node numbers, distance, average travel speed, salt spreading rate (pounds per lane-mile), and the number of *passes*, or times that the vehicle must cross the road segment. A value of zero indicates that it is not under the jurisdiction of the agency, but may be used for travel; a value of one means that it can be serviced in one pass. Some roads may require more than one pass. For example, salt may be spread on both lanes of a two-lane highway in one pass, but a four-lane highway may require two passes.

Given the vehicle fleet configuration or a time constraint to complete service, several heuristics embedded within the software can generate routes. The heuristics essentially determine what arc to service next when the vehicle arrives at an intersection. An important procedure in the software is a shortest path algorithm, and shortest path problems are solved many times during the course of route generation. The first time is when a vehicle is dispatched from the depot. SnowMaster© finds the arc that has an end node that is closest to the depot and that has not yet been serviced. The truck is sent along the shortest route to this node. During the course of generating a route, a truck may find itself at an intersection where there are no other roads requiring service. A shortest path problem is then solved in order to determine the closest unused arc from that point that will send the vehicle to continue its work. Finally, when the truck runs out of salt, it is sent back to the depot along the shortest route.

Figure 9.31 shows one of the typical outputs created by SnowMaster©. Arcs preceded by an asterisk are *deadhead* arcs on which the truck travels while not engaged in salting.

FIGURE 9.31   Example SnowMaster routing output

Begin	End	Description	Travel Time	Salt Used	Cumulative Time
* 1	3	City Road A	0.168		0.168
* 3	8	Millikin Rd.	0.060		0.228
8	9	Liberty Fairfield Rd.	0.040	600.0	0.268
9	10	Kyles Station	0.036	540.0	0.304
* 10	50	Kyles Station	0.032		0.336
* 50	36	So. St. Clair Rd.	0.096		0.432
* 36	37	Princeton Rd.	0.040		0.472
* 37	39	Princeton Rd.	0.050		0.522
39	40	Princeton Rd.	0.031	468.0	0.553
40	38	Dayton Rd.	0.084	1260.0	0.637
38	40	Dayton Rd.	0.084	1260.0	0.721
* 40	38	Dayton Rd.	0.084		0.805
38	34	Dayton Rd.	0.040	606.0	0.846
34	38	Dayton Rd.	0.040	606.0	0.886
* 38	34	Dayton Rd.	0.040		0.926
34	33	Dayton Rd.	0.014	216.0	0.941

	33	34	Dayton Rd.	0.014	216.0	0.955
*	34	33	Dayton Rd.	0.014		0.970
	33	28	Dayton Rd.	0.094	1410.0	1.064
	28	33	Dayton Rd.	0.094	1410.0	1.158
*	33	28	Dayton Rd.	0.094		1.252
	28	22	Dayton Rd.	0.036	546.0	1.288
	22	21	Dayton Rd.	0.041	618.0	1.329
	21	20	Crescentville Rd.	0.054	810.0	1.383
	20	23	Windisch	0.039	588.0	1.422
	23	24	Allen Rd.	0.046	696.0	1.469
	24	28	Rialto Rd.	0.067	1008.0	1.536
*	28	22	Dayton Rd.	0.036		1.572
	22	23	Allen Rd.	0.037	558.0	1.610
*	23	22	Allen Rd.	0.037		1.647
	22	28	Dayton Rd.	0.036	546.0	1.683
*	28	22	Dayton Rd.	0.036		1.720
*	22	21	Dayton Rd.	0.041		1.761
	21	22	Dayton Rd.	0.041	618.0	1.802
*	22	23	Allen Rd.	0.037		1.839
*	23	20	Windisch	0.039		1.878
	20	18	Crescentville Rd.	0.072	1080.0	1.950
	18	19	Crescentville Rd.	0.039	582.0	1.989
*	19	18	Crescentville Rd.	0.039		2.028
*	18	17	Yale Rd.	0.081		2.109
	17	6	Port Union Rd.	0.080	1200.0	2.189
*	6	17	Port Union Rd.	0.080		2.269
	17	26	Port Union Rd.	0.029	432.0	2.298
	26	25	Port Union Rd.	0.025	378.0	2.323
*	25	27	Mills Rd.	0.020		2.344
*	27	15	Beckett Rd.	0.041		2.384
*	15	14	Beckett Rd.	0.026		2.411
*	14	13	Glendale Ave.	0.024		2.435
*	13	7	Hamilton Rd.	0.046		2.481
*	7	4	Hamilton Rd.	0.061		2.542
*	4	2	Hamilton Rd.	0.030		2.572
*	2	1	City Road B	0.072		2.644

Total salt used on route = 9.13 tons
Total travel time on route = 2.64 hours
Time to complete salting on route = 2.32 hours
Total lane miles on route = 66.10
Percent productive time salting = 86.94

İnitially, node 8 is the closest to the depot (node 1), being an end node of an arc requiring service, arc (8,9). After servicing arcs (8,9) and (9,10), there is no arc connected to node 10 requiring service. A shortest path calculation sends the truck to node 39 to service arc (39,40), and so on. After servicing arc (26,25), the truck has effectively run out of salt and is sent back to node 1 along the shortest path from node 5.

In its initial application, Butler County, Ohio was able to retire three trucks (rather than purchasing more as originally intended) at a net capital savings of $251,000 in addition to savings in labor and operating costs. By 1994, SnowMaster© had been deployed extensively in the states of Ohio, Illinois, and Pennsylvania.

Discussion Questions

1. Draw the network corresponding to Figure 9.30. If you have studied the shortest route algorithm in the Appendix to this chapter, find the shortest path from node 1 to node 14.
2. Suppose that a county has four 10-ton trucks but will consider selling any of these and replacing them with either 7- or 14-ton trucks. Explain how SnowMaster© might be used to help the fleet manager in making the best decision.

More Examples and Solved Problems

EXAMPLE 7. MODELING HIGHWAY NETWORKS

In many transportation applications, such as the snow and ice control scenario described in the Management Science Practice section of this chapter, it is necessary to construct detailed networks of highway road systems. Two common types of highway exit configurations are shown in Figure 9.32. How can we construct networks to model these situations?

To model these as networks, we must define a node for each intersection and ensure that all traffic flows in the proper directions. Figure 9.33 shows the network model for the first type of configuration (the second is left as an exercise). You can see that the number of nodes and arcs required to model such configurations can greatly increase the sizes of networks in practical applications. As you can imagine, developing networks for practical applications involving many of these types of highway components is tedious work.

EXAMPLE 8. MODELING TURNS AT INTERSECTIONS

Shortest-path models are designed to find the path in a network that minimizes the total distance. This assumes that the length of the path is a linear function of only the arc distances. Suppose that such a model were applied to a typical city street network by a rapid package delivery service. For example, from your own experience you know that making left-hand turns usually incurs an added delay, while going straight

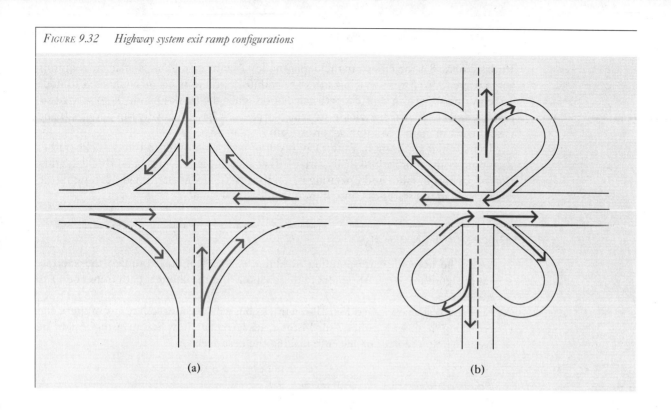

FIGURE 9.32   Highway system exit ramp configurations

(a)   (b)

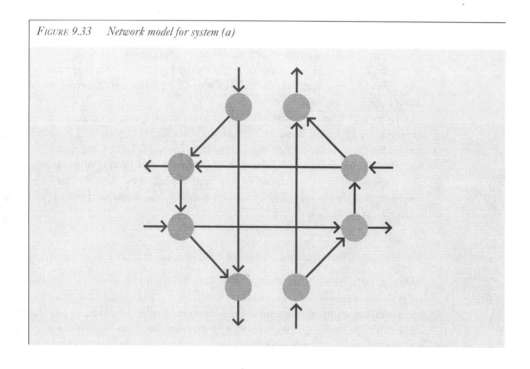

FIGURE 9.33   Network model for system (a)

476

through the intersection or making a right-hand turn do not. Suppose that the network in Figure 9.34 represents a portion of a city street network in which the edge lengths are defined in minutes of travel time. Also, suppose that an additional delay of 1.5 minutes is incurred for a left-hand turn. How can you incorporate this into a shortest path model?

We can create a new network in which the arc lengths represent both the travel time and, if applicable, the turn penalty. In this new network, we overlay a node on each arc of the original network. We draw an arc from one node to another if it is possible to go from that node (an original arc) to the other through a node in the original network. Because each arc in the new network corresponds to traveling through an intersection, we can simply add the turn delay whenever a left-hand turn is made.

Figure 9.35 shows the new network for the example. Arc (a, b) in this new network corresponds to traveling along arc a and passing through node 2 in the original network. Arc (a, e) corresponds to making a right-hand turn through node 2 onto arc e in the original network. Because this is a right-hand turn, no penalty is added. However, to go from arc e to arc i through node 6, we must make a left-hand turn. Thus, the cost on this arc is equal to the cost of arc e (2) plus the penalty of 1.5.

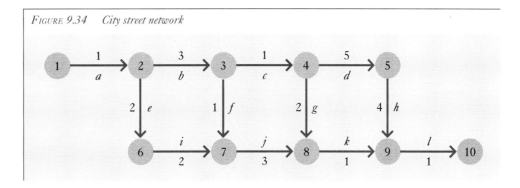

FIGURE 9.34   City street network

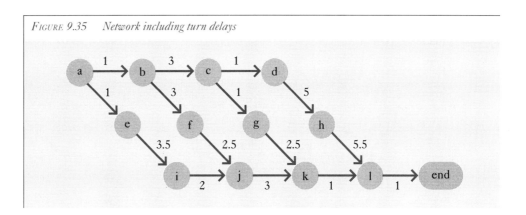

FIGURE 9.35   Network including turn delays

EXAMPLE 9. CONSUMER GOODS TRANSSHIPMENT PROBLEM

A consumer goods company has plants in Fresno, California and Philadelphia, Pennsylvania, and regional distribution centers in Cincinnati, Ohio and Amarillo, Texas. There are eight major outlets for its goods. The distribution system is shown in Figure 9.6 earlier in this chapter.

Plants ship goods to the two distribution centers where different orders for a given outlet are consolidated and then shipped to the outlet. Several of the outlets need full truckloads of a given commodity and therefore occasionally accept product directly from the plants. The company is interested in minimizing the cost of shipping goods. The relevant data are shown in Table 9.2.

For the purpose of this analysis, the data are aggregated to generic truckloads rather than by product. The demand figures are in truckloads and the costs are the roundtrip cost per truck. Bounds are provided on the number of direct full truckloads sent on the possible direct routes shown in Figure 9.6.

This problem can be modeled as a transshipment problem as discussed in Example 1. The decision variables are the amount shipped over each arc in the network

TABLE 9.2
Transshipment data

Plants	Capacity (truckloads)
Fresno	1000
Philadelphia	1500

Outlets	Demand (truckloads)
Salt Lake City	150
Tucson	150
Austin	120
Lincoln	130
Chicago	510
Atlanta	350
Cleveland	400
Charlotte	200

				Shipping cost/truckload ($)						
From/To	SLC	Tuc.	Aus.	Lin.	Chi.	Atl.	Cle.	Char.	Amar.	Cin.
Fresno	490	550							990	
Phil.							350			500
Amar.	680	570	410	470		860				
Cin.				650	240	410	220	350		

Factory direct	Bound
Fresno/Salt Lake	50
Fresno/Tucson	60
Phil./Cleveland	100

and the constraint set consists of conservation of flow equations and bounds on the arc flows. Notice that supply exceeds demand by 485(2,500 − 2,015 = 485), so we have created a dummy outlet with demand of 485. Direct shipments from each plant to the dummy outlet are allowed, with zero cost.

FIGURE 9.36   EXCEL model

	A	B	C	D	E	F	G	H	I	J	K	L	M
1	Transshipment Problem												
2													
3	Parameters and uncontrollable inputs:												
4													
5													
6					Shipping Costs Per Unit ($)								
7		Salt Lake	Tucson	Austin	Lincoln	Chicago	Atlanta	Cleveland	Charlotte	Dummy	Amarillo	Cincinnat	Supply
8	Fresno	$490.00	$550.00								$990.00		1000
9	Philadelphia							$350.00				$500.00	1500
10	Amarillo	$680.00	$570.00	$410.00	$470.00		$860.00						
11	Cincinnati				$650.00	$240.00	$410.00	$220.00	$350.00				
12													
13	Demand	150	150	125	130	510	350	400	200	485			
14													
15													
16	Direct Ship	Bound											
17	Fresno/Salt Lake	50											
18	Fresno/Tucson	60											
19	Philadelphia/Clevela	100											
20													
21													
22	Decision variables:												
23													
24		Salt Lake	Tucson	Amarillo	Dummy			Cleveland	Cincinnati	Dummy			
25	Fresno	0	0	0	0		Philadelphi	0	0	0			
26													
27		Salt Lake	Tucson	Austin	Lincoln	Atlanta							
28	Amarillo	0	0	0	0	0							
29													
30		Lincoln	Chicago	Atlanta	Cleveland	Charlotte							
31	Cincinnati	0	0	0	0	0							
32													
33													
34													
35													
36													
37	Model outputs:												
38													
39		In	Out										
40	Fresno	1000	0		Ship From	Cost				MINIMIZE COST			
41	Philadelphia	1500	0		Fresno	$0							
42	Amarillo	0	0		Philadelp	$0							
43	Cincinnati	0	0		Amarillo	$0							
44	Salt Lake	0	150		Cincinnat	$0			Target cell				
45	Tucson	0	150						=SUM(F41:F47)/1000				
46	Austin	0	125		Total	$0	(000)						
47	Lincoln	0	130										
48	Chicago	0	510										
49	Atlanta	0	350										
50	Cleveland	0	400										
51	Charlotte	0	200										
52	Dummy	0	485										

Selected cell formulas

	A	B	C	D	E	F
36						
37	**Model outputs:**					
38						
39		In	Out			
40	Fresno	=M8	=SUM(B25:E25)		Ship From	Cost
41	Philadelphia	=M9	=SUM(H25:J25)		Fresno	=B25*B8+C25*C8+D25*K8
42	Amarillo	=D25	=SUM(B28:F28)		Philadelphia	=H25*H9+I25*L9
43	Cincinnati	=I25	=SUM(B31:F31)		Amarillo	=B28*B10+C28*C10+D28*D10+E28*E10+F28*G10
44	Salt Lake	=B25+B28	=B13		Cincinnati	=B31*E11+C31*F11+D31*G11+E31*H11+F31*I11
45	Tucson	=C25+C28	=C13			
46	Austin	=D28	=D13		Total	=SUM(F41:F44)/1000
47	Lincoln	=E28+B31	=E13			
48	Chicago	=C31	=F13			
49	Atlanta	=F28+D31	=G13			
60	Cleveland	–H25+E31	=H13			
51	Charlotte	=F31	=I13			
52	Dummy	=E25+J25	=J13			

FIGURE 9.36   *(continued)*

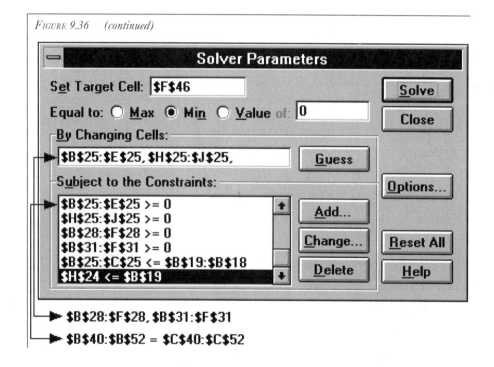

An EXCEL spreadsheet model is shown in Figure 9.36. The solution is shown in Figure 9.37. The total cost is $1,834,000, and the model prescribes as many direct shipments as possible. For the two outlets reached by both distribution centers (Lincoln and Atlanta), Atlanta is supplied solely by the Cincinnati distribution center, whereas Lincoln's demand is supplied by both Amarillo (90) and Cincinnati (40). The solution is shown graphically in Figure 9.38.

FIGURE 9.37   Solution to the network model

	A	B	C	D	E	F	G	H	I	J	K	L	M
1	Transshipment Problem												
2													
3	Parameters and uncontrollable inputs:												
4													
5													
6					Shipping Costs Per Unit ($)								
7		Salt Lake	Tucson	Austin	Lincoln	Chicago	Atlanta	Cleveland	Charlotte	Dummy	Amarillo	Cincinnat	Supply
8	Fresno	$490.00	$550.00								$990.00		1000
9	Philadelphia							$350.00				$500.00	1500
10	Amarillo	$680.00	$570.00	$410.00	$470.00		$860.00						
11	Cincinnati				$650.00	$240.00	$410.00	$220.00	$350.00				
12													
13	Demand	150	150	125	130	510	350	400	200	485			
14													
15													
16	Direct Ship	Bound											
17	Fresno/Salt Lake	50											
18	Fresno/Tucson	60											
19	Philadelphia/Clevela	100											
20													
21													
22	Decision variables:												
23													
24		Salt Lake	Tucson	Amarillo	Dummy				Cleveland	Cincinnat	Dummy		
25	Fresno	50	60	405	485		Philadelphi	100	1400	0			
26													
27		Salt Lake	Tucson	Austin	Lincoln	Atlanta							
28	Amarillo	100	90	125	90	0							
29													
30		Lincoln	Chicago	Atlanta	Cleveland	Charlotte							
31	Cincinnati	40	510	350	300	200							
32													
33													
34													
35													
36													
37	Model outputs:												
38													
39		In	Out										
40	Fresno	1000	1000		Ship From	Cost							
41	Philadelphia	1500	1500		Fresno	$458,450							
42	Amarillo	405	405		Philadelph	$735,000							
43	Cincinnati	1400	1400		Amarillo	$212,850							
44	Salt Lake	150	150		Cincinnati	$427,900							
45	Tucson	150	150										
46	Austin	125	125		Total	$1,834	(000)						
47	Lincoln	130	130										
48	Chicago	510	510										
49	Atlanta	350	350										
50	Cleveland	400	400										
51	Charlotte	200	200										
52	Dummy	485	485										

FIGURE 9.38   *Graphical solution*

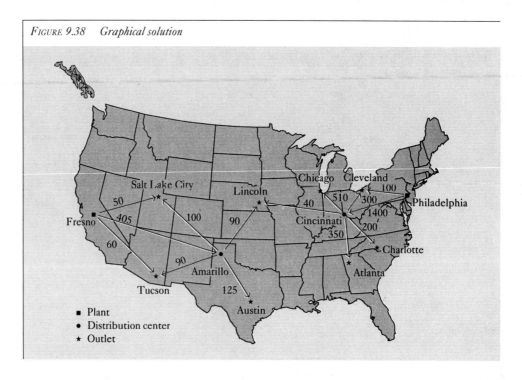

EXAMPLE 10. CONSTRUCTING PROJECT NETWORKS

Constructing a project network correctly often depends on some trial and error. We are usually given a list of activities and their *immediate predecessors*—those activities that must immediately precede a given activity. For example, consider the following table.

Activity	Immediate predecessors
A	None
B	A
C	A
D	A
E	B,C
F	B,C,D
G	E,F

We begin drawing the network with a starting node and connect all activities with no immediate predecessors to this node.

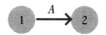

Next, we see that activities B, C, and D all follow activity A. This results in the partial network

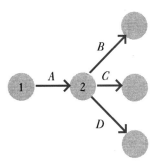

Next, activity E must follow both activities B and C. To model this, we could combine the ending nodes for activities B and C as follows:

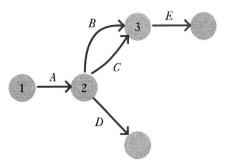

Activity F must follow B, C, and D. We *cannot* combine nodes 2 and 3 because this would force activity D to be an immediate predecessor of activity E, which is not correct. We must use a new device, called a *dummy activity*.

A *dummy activity* is a fictitious arc in a project network that is used to show precedence and has no meaning in the actual set of project activities.

In the figure below, the dummy activity indicates that node 4 (and consequently, activities B and C) is an immediate predecessor of node 5. Thus, at node 5, we see that activity F has as its immediate predecessors activities B, C, and D.

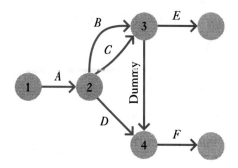

We finally include activity G, resulting in the complete project network shown in Figure 9.39.

FIGURE 9.39   *Complete project network*

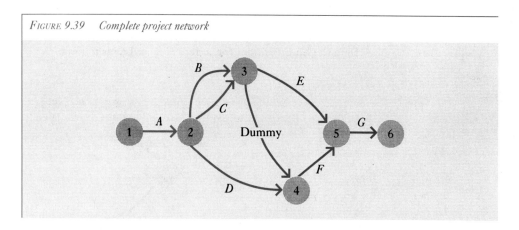

SUMMARY

Because they are visual in nature, network models are very intuitive, and they provide a useful means of communication between management scientists and nontechnical managers. Network flow models represent one of the most versatile and important application areas of management science. Many problems involving the distribution of physical goods, commodities such as oil and natural gas, and information on computer networks can be modeled and solved using network flows. Because many network flow problems are linear programs, we can solve them using LP solvers such as LINDO or spreadsheet optimizers.

Other applications of networks involve finding routes, paths, or trees. For many special types of network problems, such as shortest paths and spanning trees, very efficient algorithms exist to find optimal solutions (see the chapter Appendix).

CHAPTER REVIEW EXERCISES

I. Terms to Understand

You should be able to define the following terms:

a. Network (p. 428)
b. Node (p. 428)
c. Branch (p. 428)
d. Arc (p. 428)
e. Undirected network (p. 428)
f. Directed network (p. 428)
g. Flow (p. 428)
h. Path (p. 429)
i. Connected network (p. 429)
j. Directed path (p. 429)
k. Cycle (p. 429)

l. Directed cycle (p. 429)
m. Tree (p. 429)
n. Spanning tree (p. 429)
o. Source (p. 430)
p. Sink (p. 430)
q. Conservation of flow (p. 430)
r. Transshipment problem (p. 433)
s. Maximum flow problem (p. 436)
t. Shortest route problem (p. 449)
u. Minimum spanning tree problem (p. 449)
v. Critical path (p. 456)

II. Discussion Questions

1. Describe several examples of networks in your daily life.
2. Why are networks an important area of management science?
3. Describe some examples of network problems in which flows do not represent physical items.
4. What is the relationship between the transportation problem and the transshipment problem?
5. Why can most network flow problems be solved as linear programs?
6. Explain the differences between the following types of network flow models in terms of the objective function and constraints:
   a. Transshipment problem
   b. Maximum flow problem
   c. Shortest route problem
7. Why is it difficult to solve minimum spanning tree problems with linear programming?

III. Problems

1. Refer to the network in Figure 9.40. Which of the following are paths, directed paths, cycles, or directed cycles?
   a. 1-*a*-2-*b*-4-*h*-6-*g*-5-*e*-1
   b. 1-*c*-3-*d*-4-*b*-2
   c. 3-*c*-5-*e*-1-*a*-2
   d. 1-*c*-3-*f*-5-*e*-1
2. In Figure 9.40, find a spanning tree for which all paths from node 1 to all other nodes are directed paths.
3. Write the conservation of flow equations for the network in Figure 9.40. How would these change if node 1 is a source having a supply of 25, node 3 a source having a supply of 15, and node 6 a sink having a demand of 40?

FIGURE 9.40   *A directed network*

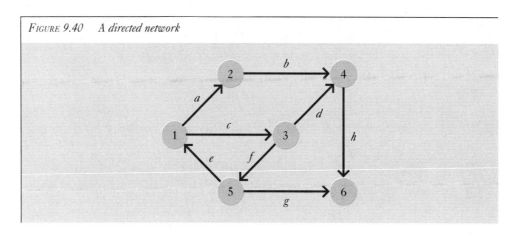

4.   Draw the network flow model corresponding to the linear program

$$\text{Min } 4x_a + 3x_b + 8x_c + 5x_d + 2x_e + 3x_f$$

subject to

$$-x_a + x_b = 6$$
$$x_a + x_c + x_d = 0$$
$$x_e - x_c - x_f = -2$$
$$x_f - x_b = 0$$
$$-x_d - x_e = -4$$
$$\text{all } x \geq 0$$

5.   Draw the network flow model corresponding to the following linear program. (Hint: consider multiplying some equations by -1).

$$\text{Min } 3x_a + 5x_b + 8x_c + 2x_d + 4x_e$$

subject to

$$x_a + x_b = 10$$
$$x_c + x_d - x_a = 5$$
$$x_c + x_e = 15$$
$$x_b + x_d - x_e = 0$$
$$\text{all } x \geq 0$$

6.   Construct a network for which each node is a course required for your degree. Draw an arc from node x to node y if course x is a prerequisite for course y. Interpret each of the following:
     a.   Path
     b.   Directed Path
     c.   Cycle
     d.   Directed Cycle
     e.   Connected Component of the Network

7. The *Knight's Tour* is a classic problem. Starting from any square on an $n \times n$ chessboard, move the knight so that it lands on every space exactly once. Show how a network can be used to solve this problem, and illustrate it on a 4×4 chessboard.

8. Networks are often used to model sources and uses of funds for economic and financial analysis. At a macro level, for example, funds sources arise from household and business savings. These funds ultimately end up in cash, household loans, business loans, and real estate loans. Financial intermediaries—commercial banks, savings and loan associations, and household financing institutions—provide a means of channeling these funds. Funds sources go directly to cash, commercial banks, or savings and loans. S&Ls provide real estate loans, or channel assets to commercial banks. Commercial banks provide funds to household financing institutions, cash, or business loans. Household financing institutions channel assets to cash or household loans. Draw a network that describes these relationships.

9. Suppose that a cable television company wants to connect a subdivision of homes using a minimum amount of cable. The table below shows the lengths of the possible connections that can be made, taking account of natural barriers in the neighborhood. Draw a network that models this situation and discuss the form of the solution.

Node	1	2	3	4	5	6	7	8	9	10	11	12	13	14
1	—	4	—	—	—	—	—	—	—	—	—	—	9	—
2	—	—	4	—	—	—	—	—	—	—	—	—	—	—
3	—	—	—	4	—	—	—	—	—	—	—	—	—	—
4	—	—	—	—	5	3	—	—	—	—	—	—	—	—
5	—	—	—	—	—	—	2	—	—	—	—	—	—	—
6	—	—	—	—	—	—	4	3	7	5	—	—	—	—
7	—	—	—	—	—	—	—	2	—	—	—	—	—	—
8	—	—	—	—	—	—	—	—	6	—	—	—	—	—
9	—	—	—	—	—	—	—	—	—	3	7	—	—	—
10	—	—	—	—	—	—	—	—	—	—	5	6	—	—
11	—	—	—	—	—	—	—	—	—	—	—	9	8	7
12	—	—	—	—	—	—	—	—	—	—	—	—	6	—
13	—	—	—	—	—	—	—	—	—	—	—	—	—	5

10. Find the solution to Problem 8 using an LP solver.

11. Formulate the following shortest route problem as a linear program and solve it using an LP solver.

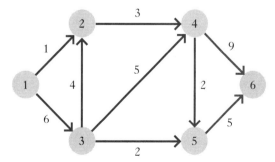

12. In the following network, every turn incurs a delay penalty of 3 in addition to the travel times shown on the arcs. Transform this network into a shortest path problem.

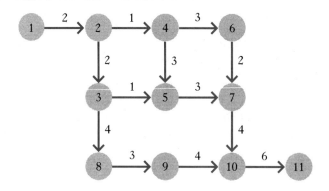

13. Solve the shortest path problem in Problem 12 using an LP solver.
14. Formulate the following transshipment problem as a linear program and solve it using an LP solver.

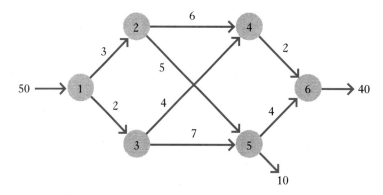

15. Planes R Us has determined that it has the capacity to produce 25, 35, 30, and 10 jets over the next four months. Outstanding orders require that 10, 15, 25, and 20 jets be delivered over these same four months. The unit cost (in millions of dollars) for each of the next four months is estimated to be 1.08, 1.11, 1.10, and 1.13. The jets may be produced earlier than needed, but storage and insurance costs are $16,000 per month for each. Show how to model the problem of determining how many jets to produce each month as a network flow problem. (Hint: Let arcs represent production in each month or inventory holding from one month to the next.)

16. Solve the model developed in Problem 15 using an LP solver.
17. A project for the development of a new product consists of five major activities prior to release to manufacturing. The immediate predecessors and times required for each activity are given in the following table.

Activity		Immediate predecessor	Time (weeks)
A	Design	-	4
B	Development	-	7
C	Engineering specifications	A	6
D	Procurement	A	12
E	Manufacturing planning	C	4

a. Draw the project network.
b. Formulate the linear program to determine a project schedule.
c. Solve the LP using an LP solver.

18. The road network leading from a major interstate highway to the main gate of a major amusement park is shown in Figure 9.41. Because of differences in speed limits and number of lanes, the capacity of each road varies in terms of the flow of vehicles/minute. Construct and solve a linear program to determine the maximum flow rate to the amusement park.

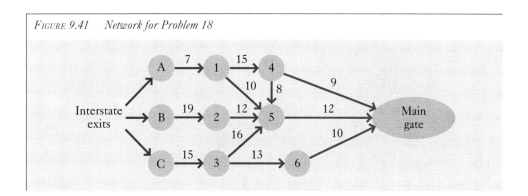

Figure 9.41   Network for Problem 18

19. A corporate fleet manager wants to develop an equipment replacement policy for the next four years. The current price of a car is $14,000. Prices are expected to increase 5 percent each year. The cars depreciate 25 percent for the first 2 years and 15% for the next 2 years. Operating and maintenance costs for the next four years are anticipated to be $2,400, $3,000, $3,600, and $4,800. A car may be replaced every 1, 2, 3, or 4 years. Construct a network model for this problem and explain how to find the best replacement policy.
20. Formulate the network model developed in Problem 19 as a linear program and solve using an LP solver.
21. As shown in the table below, a research and development project consists of four tasks that can be performed at different paces according to the budget allocated to each task. Explain how a network model can be used to find the best strategy to complete the project within 18 months without spending more than $35,000.

	Task 1		Task 2		Task 3		Task 4	
Pace	Time	Cost	Time	Cost	Time	Cost	Time	Cost
Slow	6	6,000	5	8,000	6	2,000	7	10,000
Normal	4	8,000	3	9,000	3	3,000	5	12,000
Fast	3	9,000	2	10,000	1	5,000	3	18,000

22. Formulate Problem 21 as a linear program and solve it using an LP solver.

23. A marketing project consists of the following activities and estimated times in weeks:

Activity		Predecessors	Time
A	Initial planning	none	4
B	Develop training plan	A	6
C	Select trainees	B	4
D	Design brochure	A	3
E	Field test material	J,K,F,I	1
F	Deliver sample products	N	4
G	Print brochure	D	6
H	Prepare advertising	D	4
I	Release advertising	H	1
J	Distribute brochure	G	2
K	Train salespeople	C,G	5
L	Review market survey	E	4
M	Develop prototype	A	7
N	Manufacture sample products	M	3

a. Construct the network for this project.
b. Formulate the scheduling problem as a linear program.
c. Solve the scheduling problem using an LP solver.

24. Consider the project network in Figure 9.42. Write down the immediate predecessors for each activity and formulate the scheduling problem as a linear program.

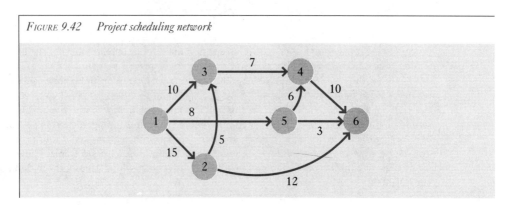

FIGURE 9.42   *Project scheduling network*

IV. Projects and Cases

1.   Figure 9.43 represents the data for an application of the SnowMaster snow and ice control software for a small county road network.

   a.   Draw the network corresponding to this data.

   b.   Use a spreadsheet to determine the total mileage of roads that require service, total amount of salt needed, and the minimum time required to salt all necessary road segments. Why do you think the actual time will be longer? Can you estimate how long a truck might need to accomplish this task (assuming that it has enough capacity)? How did you arrive at this estimate?

FIGURE 9.43   *Road network definition data base*

Arc	Description	Start	End	Distance	Speed	Salt Rate	Passes
1	City Road A	1	3	4.200	25.00	600	0
2	City Road B	1	2	1.800	25.00	600	0
3	City Road C	1	6	5.800	25.00	600	0
4	Hamilton Rd.	2	4	0.750	25.00	600	1
5	City Road B	2	5	2.200	25.00	600	0
6	Millikin Rd.	3	8	1.500	25.00	600	1
7	State Route 4	3	4	2.000	25.00	600	0
8	State Route 4	4	5	1.250	25.00	600	0
9	Hamilton Rd.	4	7	1.530	25.00	600	1
10	Tylersville Rd.	5	14	2.600	25.00	600	1
11	Port Union Rd.	6	17	2.000	25.00	600	1
12	Liberty Fairfield Rd.	7	8	2.200	25.00	600	1
13	Hamilton Rd.	7	13	1.150	25.00	600	1
14	Millikin Rd.	8	11	1.300	25.00	600	1
15	Liberty Fairfield Rd.	8	9	1.000	25.00	600	1
16	Kyles Station	9	10	0.900	25.00	600	1
17	Glendale Ave.	10	11	1.070	25.00	600	0
18	Kyles Station	10	50	0.800	25.00	600	1
19	Glendale Ave.	11	12	1.100	25.00	600	0
20	Glendale Ave.	12	13	1.000	25.00	600	0
21	Princeton Rd.	12	36	1.520	25.00	600	1
22	Glendale Ave.	13	14	0.600	25.00	600	0
23	Beckett Rd.	14	15	0.650	25.00	600	1
24	Tylersville Rd.	14	35	1.960	25.00	600	1
25	Smith Rd.	15	16	0.430	25.00	600	1
26	Beckett Rd.	15	27	1.030	25.00	600	1
27	Yale Rd.	16	17	1.650	25.00	600	0
28	Yale Rd.	17	18	2.030	25.00	600	0
29	Port Union Rd.	17	26	0.720	25.00	600	1
30	Crescentville Rd.	18	19	0.970	25.00	600	1

Arc	Description	Start	End	Distance	Speed	Salt Rate	Passes
31	Crescentville Rd.	18	20	1.800	25.00	600	1
32	Crescentville Rd.	20	21	1.350	25.00	600	1
33	Windisch	20	23	0.980	25.00	600	1
34	Dayton Rd.	21	22	1.030	25.00	600	1
35	Allen Rd.	22	23	0.930	25.00	600	1
36	Dayton Rd.	22	28	0.910	25.00	600	1
37	Allen Rd.	23	24	1.160	25.00	600	1
38	Rialto Rd.	24	25	0.400	25.00	600	1
39	Rialto Rd.	24	28	1.680	25.00	600	1
40	Mills Rd.	25	27	0.510	25.00	600	1
41	Port Union Rd.	25	26	0.630	25.00	600	1
42	Beckett Rd.	27	28	2.020	25.00	600	1
43	West Chester Rd.	28	29	2.310	25.00	600	1
44	Losantiville Rd.	28	35	2.260	25.00	600	0
45	Dayton Rd.	28	33	2.350	25.00	600	1
46	West Chester Rd.	29	30	1.020	25.00	600	1
47	Cox Rd.	29	32	2.650	25.00	600	1

2. This case is an extension of Case 2 in Chapter 2. Please review the information presented there at this time.

    Figure 9.44 shows a portion of the 1994 American League Baseball schedule. Seven umpire crews must be assigned to each series, meeting the constraints described in Case 2, Chapter 2. Assume that crews 1 through 7 are assigned to the first set of series (from left to right in the schedule).

    a. Construct network models for assigning the crews to the next successive series. How do you incorporate the constraints discussed in the case in Chapter 2?

    b. Suppose that the objective is to minimize the total mileage traveled. Table 9.3 on page 494 provides intercity mileage for American League cities. Solve your models using an LP solver. Does your schedule seem reasonable? Do any other issues need to be resolved?

3. Michael Heintzman is an executive in a major corporation and recently accepted a transfer from Boston to Denver. In planning the move, he developed a list of activities that need to be performed:

    1. Find a real estate agent in Denver
    2. Sell his house in Boston
    3. Obtain moving estimates
    4. Sign a moving contract
    5. Cancel utilities at Boston house
    6. Pack
    7. Load moving van
    8. Arrange for car to be driven to Denver
    9. Purchase airline tickets for family
    10. Move belongings to Denver
    11. Have car picked up for delivery to Denver
    12. Fly with family to Denver

FIGURE 9.44 Portion of 1994 American Baseball League schedule

Schedule grid — home team columns grouped by WESTERN DIVISION (SEA, OAK, CAL, TEX, KC, MIN), central teams (CWS, MIL, DET, CLE), and EASTERN DIVISION (TOR, BAL, NYY, BOS). Each cell lists opponent and game time.

1994	SEA	OAK	CAL	TEX	KC	MIN	CWS	MIL	DET	CLE	TOR	BAL	NYY	BOS
04/04	MIN 7:35	TOR 1:05				CAL 7:05				SEA 1:05	CWS 1:35	KC 3:05	TEX 1:05	DET 1:05
04/05	MIN 7:05	TOR 7:05	CLE 11:05	MIL 3:05		CAL 7:05		OAK 1:05		SEA 7:05	CWS 7:35	KC 7:35	TEX 1:05	
04/06	MIN 12:35	TOR 7:35	CLE 7:05	MIL 7:35		CAL 12:15		OAK 6:05		SEA 7:05	CWS 7:35			DET 1:05
04/07		MIN 1:05	CLE 7:35	MIL 7:35										DET 1:05
04/08	MIL 7:35	MIN 7:05	TOR 7:35	BAL 7:35	CLE 1:35	OAK 7:05	BOS 1:35	CAL 6:05			SEA 7:35	TEX 7:35	DET 7:05	
04/09	MIL 7:05	MIN 7:05	TOR 7:05	BAL 7:35	CLE 1:35	OAK 7:05	BOS 1:35	CAL 1:05			SEA 1:35	TEX 1:35	DET 1:35	
04/10	MIL 1:35	MIN 1:05	TOR 1:05	BAL 7:05	CLE 1:35	OAK 1:05	BOS 1:35	CAL 1:05			SEA 1:35	TEX 1:35	DET 1:35	
04/11					BOS 7:05				BAL 1:15					
04/12					BOS 7:05		NYY 7:05		BAL 1:15					
04/13					BOS 7:05		NYY 7:05		BAL 1:15					
04/14							NYY 12:35							
04/15									NYY 7:05					
04/16									NYY 1:15					
04/17									NYY 1:15					
04/18						CLE 7:05			KC 7:05			CAL 7:35	SEA 7:05	
04/19						CLE 7:05		CWS 6:05	KC 3:35		TEX 7:35	CAL 7:35	SEA 7:05	
04/20						CLE 7:05		CWS 6:05	KC 1:15		TEX 7:35	CAL 7:35	SEA 1:05	
04/21						CLE 12:15		CWS 1:05						
04/22				CLE 7:35			DET 7:05	KC 6:05		KC 7:05	MIN 7:35	SEA 1:35	OAK 7:05	CWS 7:05
04/23				CLE 7:35			DET 6:05	KC 1:05		KC 1:05	MIN 1:35	SEA 1:35	OAK 1:35	CWS 1:05
04/24				CLE 2:05			DET 1:35	KC 1:05		KC 1:05	MIN 1:35	SEA 1:35	OAK 1:35	CWS 1:05
04/25	BOS 7:05	BOS 7:35		DET 7:35	TOR 7:05		MIL 7:05			MIN 7:05		OAK 7:35	CAL 7:05	CWS 11:05
04/26	BOS 7:05	BOS 12:15		DET 7:35	TOR 7:05		MIL 7:05			MIN 7:05		OAK 12:35	CAL 1:05	OAK 1:05
04/27	NYY 7:05	NYY 7:05	BAL 7:35	TOR 7:35	DET 7:05	MIL 7:05				CWS 7:05				OAK 7:05
04/28	NYY 7:05	NYY 7:05	BAL 7:05	TOR 7:35	DET 7:05	MIL 7:05				CWS 7:05				OAK 1:05
04/29	BAL 7:35	NYY 1:05	BOS 7:05		MIL 7:05	TOR 7:05			CWS 7:05	TEX 7:05				CAL 7:05
04/30	BAL 7:05	NYY 1:05	BOS 7:05		MIL 7:05	TOR 7:05			CWS 1:15	TEX 1:05				CAL 1:05
05/01	BAL 1:35		BOS 5:05		MIL 1:35	TOR 1:05			CWS 1:15	TEX 1:05				CAL 1:05

493

TABLE 9.3
American League
intercity mileage

	SEA	OAK	CAL	TEX	KC	MIN	CHI	MIL	DET	CLE	TOR	BAL	NY	BOS
SEA		678	954	1670	1489	1399	1720	1694	1932	2023	2124	2334	2421	2469
OAK			337	1467	1498	1589	1846	1845	2079	2161	2286	2457	2586	2704
CAL				1246	1363	1536	1745	1756	1979	2053	2175	2329	2475	2611
TEX					460	853	798	843	982	1015	1186	1209	1383	1555
KC						394	403	483	630	694	822	961	1113	1254
MIN							334	297	528	622	780	936	1028	1124
CHI								74	235	307	430	621	740	867
MIL									237	328	434	641	746	860
DET										95	206	409	509	632
CLE											193	314	425	563
TOR												384	366	463
BAL													184	370
NY														187

13. Find temporary lodging in Denver
14. Locate real estate agent in Denver
15. Find house in Denver
16. Find lawyer in Denver
17. Close on new house
18. Have movers deliver belongings to new house
19. Register children in school system
20. Settle moving claims
21. Insure new house
22. Cancel insurance on Boston house
23. Send change of address to Boston post office to forward mail

Develop a network to represent this project and estimate times for each activity. Solve your problem with LINDO and determine the critical path.

REFERENCES

Barr, R.S. and J.S. Turner. "Microdata File Merging Through Large Scale Network Technology," in *Network Models and Associated Applications* (eds. D. Klingman and J.M. Mulvey). Amsterdam: North-Holland, 1981, pp. 1–22.

Bennington, G.E. "Applying Network Analysis." *Industrial Engineering* Vol. 6, No. 1, Jan 1974, pp. 17–25.

Chachra, V., P.M. Ghare, and J.M. Moore. *Applications of Graph Theory Algorithms.* New York: Elsevier North-Holland, 1979.

Evans, James R. and Edward Minieka. *Optimization Algorithms for Networks and Graphs*, 2nd ed. New York: Marcel Dekker, 1992.

Evans, James R. and Michael Weant. "Strategic Planning for Snow and Ice Control Using Computer-Based Routing Software." *Public Works* Vol. 121, No. 4, April 1990, pp. 60–64.

Hanson, R.S. "Moving the Hospital to a New Location." *Industrial Engineering,* November 1972.

Phillips, Don T. and Alberto Garcia-Diaz. *Fundamentals of Network Analysis.* Englewood Cliffs, NJ: Prentice-Hall, 1981.

Rothfarb, B., H. Frank, D.M. Rosenbaum, K. Steiglitz, and D.J. Kleitman. "Optimal Design of Offshore Natural Gas Pipeline Systems." *Operations Research* Vol. 18, No. 6, 1970, pp. 992–1020.

APPENDIX: NETWORK OPTIMIZATION ALGORITHMS

The Shortest Path Problem

The *shortest path problem* involves finding a path with the smallest possible length between one node and another. Shortest path problems are solved routinely in the SnowMaster©software described in one of the opening scenarios. For instance, when a snow removal vehicle runs out of salt, it would like to return to the salt depot along the shortest path. There are dozens of different algorithms for finding shortest paths in networks, but we will describe only one, called *Dijkstra's algorithm.* We will assume that all arc lengths are non-negative numbers, and define $c(i,j)$ to be the length of the arc (i,j). Our objective is to find the shortest path from node s to node t. However, as we will show, Dijkstra's algorithm will find the shortest path from node s to all other nodes in the network.

Dijkstra's algorithm is implemented by *labeling* nodes in the network. We will state the basic steps of the algorithm, and then illustrate it with an example. First, we assign a temporary label to each node i indicating the length of the current shortest path from s to i, $d(i)$, and the node *immediately preceding i* on the shortest path, n. Thus, each label is written as $[d(i),n]$. Initially, the label on node s is $[0,-]$, indicating that the length of the shortest path from s to itself is zero and that there is no predecessor node. For each node i that is directly connected to s by an arc, we label it $[c(s,i),s]$, indicating that the distance from s to i is $c(s,i)$ and we get there from node 5. We label all other nodes i with $[\infty,-]$. Node s is regarded as *permanently labeled*. We denote permanent labels by marking them with asterisks.

At each step of the algorithm we select the permanently labeled node with the shortest distance; suppose this is node i. For all nodes j that do not have permanent labels and can be reached from node i, determine if $d(i)+c(i,j)$ is *smaller* than $d(j)$ (see Figure 9A.1). In other words, we check to see if the distance of the path to node j that goes through node i is smaller than the length of the currently best-known distance to j. If so, we replace the label on node j by $[d(i)+c(i,j),i]$; otherwise, leave it alone. We repeat this procedure until node j becomes permanently labeled. Notice that if we continue until all nodes have permanent labels, then we will have found the shortest paths from node s to all other nodes. We can trace the paths by using the predecessor nodes in the labels.

EXAMPLE A1.

To illustrate Dijkstra's algorithm, we will find the shortest path from node s to all other nodes in Figure 9.14. The initial labels are shown in Figure 9A.2. Labels on nodes that are permanently labeled are preceded by an asterisk. The node with the smallest temporary label is node 2, so we make this label permanent. Node 4 is the only node reachable from 2 that does not have a permanent label. We see that $d(2)+c(2,4)=3+3=6<d(4)=\infty$. Thus, we replace the label on node 4 with temporary label [6,2], indicating that the shortest known path from s has length 6 and that node 2 is the immediately preceding node on the path. Figure 9A.3 shows the current set of labels.

FIGURE 9A.1   *Revising a distance label d (j)*

$$d(i)\quad i \xrightarrow{\quad c(i,j)\quad} j \quad d(j)$$

$$\text{Is } d(i)+c(i,j)<d(j)?$$

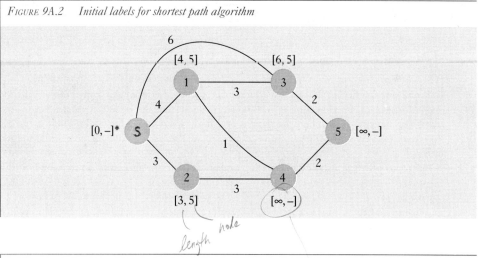

Figure 9A.2   Initial labels for shortest path algorithm

Figure 9A.3   Revised distance labels (first iteration)

Because it now has the smallest temporary label, we next select node 1 and make its label permanent. Nodes 3 and 4 are directly reachable from node 1, so we check to see if we can shorten the lengths to these nodes by going through node 1. For node 3, we have

$$d(1) + c(1, 3) = 4 + 3 = 7 > d(3) = 6$$

Therefore, we do not change the label on node 3. For node 4, we have

$$d(1) + c(1, 4) = 4 + 1 = 5 < d(4) = 6,$$

so we replace the label on node 4 with temporary label [5,1]. This is shown in Figure 9A.4.

Node 4 has the smallest temporary label, so we make it permanent. Node 5 is the only node reachable from 4 that has a temporary label. We check node 4, and

$$d(4) + c(4, 5) = 5 + 2 = 7 < d(5) = \infty.$$

We replace the label on node 5 with [7,4]. The current labels are shown in Figure 9A.5.

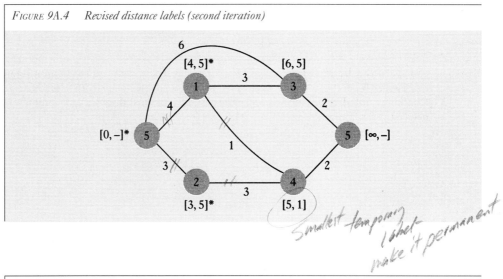

FIGURE 9A.4   *Revised distance labels (second iteration)*

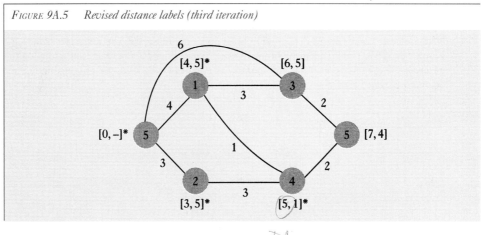

FIGURE 9A.5   *Revised distance labels (third iteration)*

Next, we make the label on node 3 permanent and check to see if we can improve the distance to node 5.

$$d(3) + c(3, 5) = 6 + 2 = 8 > d(5) = 7$$

so we do not change the label on node 5. Because node 5 is the only remaining node, we make its label permanent and we are finished.

The final labels give the lengths of the shortest paths from node s to each node. For example, the shortest distance from s to 5 is $d(5)$, or 7. To find the path, we examine the predecessor node labels beginning at node 5. The label on node 5, [7,4], tells us that we came to node 5 from node 4. Checking the label on node 4, we see that we came from node 1. We came to node 1 from node s. Thus, the shortest path to node 5 is s-1-4-5.

Summary of Dijkstra's Algorithm

1. Label node s with the permanent label $[0, -]$. Label every node i connected to s with a temporary label $[c(s,i),s]$. Assign the label $[\infty, -]$ to all other nodes.
2. Select the node with the smallest temporary label, say node i, and make it permanent. For all nodes j connected to i by arcs that do not have permanent labels, compare the current temporary distance label $d(j)$ with $d(i) + c(i,j)$. If $d(i) + c(i,j) < d(j)$, then label node j with $[d(i) + c(i,j), i]$.
3. Continue until all nodes are labeled permanently. The final distance labels represent the lengths of the shortest paths from s.

Minimum Spanning Tree Algorithm

In Example 4, we presented a minimum spanning tree problem involving the design of circuit board connections. We discussed the difficulty of modeling this problem as a linear or integer program. In this section, we will present algorithms for finding minimum spanning trees. Among all the network algorithms presented in this chapter, minimum spanning tree algorithms are the simplest and most elegant.

Recall that a spanning tree is a connected network without cycles. Therefore, in building a spanning tree, we must ensure that no cycles occur. Suppose that we arbitrarily select the branches according to their alphabetic label. Selecting branches A, B, C and D builds up a tree. However, when we add branch E, we form a cycle (see Figure 9A.6). We clearly need to eliminate one of these branches in order to maintain a tree structure. Because we are striving to minimize the total length of branches in the tree, the obvious branch to eliminate is the one having the largest cost, namely branch E.

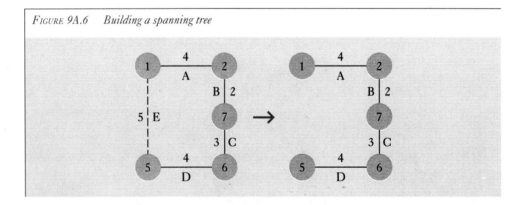

FIGURE 9A.6   Building a spanning tree

Because we have not yet found a spanning tree, we may continue adding other branches. If a cycle is formed, we then delete the branch in the cycle having the largest cost. To guarantee that we find a minimum-cost spanning tree, we must consider every branch in the network. If we continue adding branches in alphabetical order and checking for cycles, we can add branches F and G to build the tree. Adding branch H creates a cycle F-G-H-B. We could eliminate either branch F or H because both have the largest cost in the cycle. Ties can be broken arbitrarily; we will eliminate branch H. The tree now looks like this:

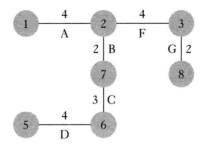

Continuing in this fashion, we

> Add branch I.
>
> Add branch J.
>
> Add branch K and then eliminate branch K from cycle I-J-K-G.
>
> Add branch L.
>
> Add branch M and then eliminate branch L from cycle C-B-F-I-J-M-L.

The final spanning tree is shown in Figure 9A.7.

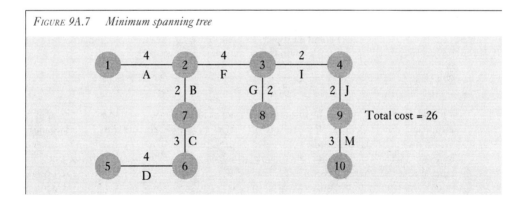

FIGURE 9A.7   *Minimum spanning tree*

This method will always find a minimum cost spanning tree, but requires that you check every branch. A more efficient method called *Kruskal's algorithm* chooses the smallest-cost branch first, then the next smallest, and so on, until a spanning tree is formed. Whenever a cycle is formed, we eliminate the last branch chosen (because it must be the largest one chosen so far). In the example, if we order the branches by smallest cost first, we have (ties ordered arbitrarily):

Branch	Cost	Decision
B	2	in
G	2	in
I	2	in
J	2	in
K	2	out
C	3	in
M	3	in
A	4	in
D	4	in
F	4	in and stop, because we now have
H	4	a spanning tree
E	5	
L	6	

There is no need to examine branches H, E, and L, because we already have a spanning tree and the cost of these branches is at least as large as any branch already in the tree.

Kruskal's algorithm is sometimes called a *greedy* algorithm because it selects branches in a greedy fashion—smallest first.

An Application of Minimum Spanning Trees: Designing Manufacturing Cells

Group technology is an approach to designing manufacturing systems that groups parts into *part families* and machines into *manufacturing cells* for the production of those part families. The machine grouping problem can be solved using spanning trees. We are typically given a machine-part matrix A for which $a_{ij} = 1$ if part j must be processed by machine i, and 0 if otherwise. Denote by M_i the set of parts that require processing by machine i. For any two machines, i and k, define a distance measure $d(i,k)$ as follows:

$$d(i,k) = \frac{|M_i \cup M_k| - |M_i \cap M_k|}{|M_i \cup M_k|}$$

where the symbol $|S|$ means the number of elements in the set S, $\cup$ denotes the union of two sets (all elements in either set), and $\cap$ denotes the intersection of two sets (the elements they have in common).

The numerator is the number of parts requiring processing *only* on machine i or machine k, but not both. The denominator is the number of parts requiring processing on either machine or both. The distance function is a measure of the relative dissimilarity of two different machines with respect to their processing requirements. A value of zero indicates that the two machines have the same set of parts to process, while a value of one means that they process no parts in common.

We construct a network in which each node represents a machine. Each branch (i,k) is assigned the cost $d(i,k)$. The minimum-cost spanning tree in this network minimizes the total dissimilarity that includes all machines. After finding the minimum spanning tree, we can group the machines into K cells by deleting the $K - 1$ largest edges of the spanning tree. This will leave K disconnected trees. The machines corresponding to the vertices in each tree provide the machine groupings.

To illustrate this approach, the matrix A is shown in Figure 9A.8. To illustrate the calculation of $d(i,k)$, consider $i = 1$ and $k = 2$. $M_1 = \{2,3,7,8,9,12,13\}$ and $M_2 = \{2,7,8,11,12\}$. Thus $|M_1 \cup M_2| = 8$ and $|M_1 \cap M_2| = 4$. Therefore $d(1,2) = 4/8 = 0.5$.

FIGURE 9A.8   *Machine-part matrix*

	1	2	3	4	5	6	7	8	9	10	11	12	13
1		1	1				1	1	1			1	1
2		1					1	1			1	1	
3	1					1							
4			1		1					1			
5			1				1	1	1			1	1
6						1							
7				1						1			
8				1						1			
9						1							

The complete matrix of $d(i, k)$ values is shown in the following table.

	1	2	3	4	5	6	7	8	9
1	-	0.50	1.00	0.89	0.14	1.00	1.00	1.00	1.00
2	-	-	1.00	1.00	0.62	1.00	1.00	1.00	1.00
3	-	-	-	1.00	1.00	1.00	1.00	1.00	0.50
4	-	-	-	-	0.87	0.67	0.75	0.75	1.00
5	-	-	-	-	-	1.00	1.00	1.00	1.00
6	-	-	-	-	-	-	1.00	1.00	1.00
7	-	-	-	-	-	-	-	0.00	1.00
8	-	-	-	-	-	-	-	-	1.00

The minimum spanning tree on the network using these distances is shown in Figure 9A.9. Thus, if we wish to form three machine cells, we remove the three largest edges from the tree. The resulting connected components would consist of the vertices {1, 2, 5}, {3, 9}, and {4, 6, 7, 8}. Parts 2, 3, 7, 8, 9, 11, 12, and 13 would be assigned to the first cell, parts 1 and 6 to the second cell, and parts 4, 5, and 10 to the third cell.

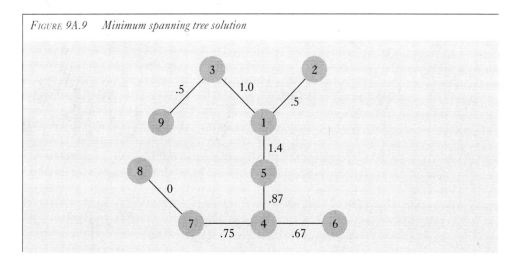

FIGURE 9A.9   *Minimum spanning tree solution*

CHAPTER 10

HEURISTICS

AND

APPROXIMATION

INTRODUCTION

- The College of Law at the University of Cincinnati was experiencing a dramatic increase in the number of examination deferrals granted to students. A deferral is granted if a student has an exam conflict in a given time period or two exams scheduled on a given day. There are two examinations per day, seven days of exams, and two days for deferred exams. In one semester, 66 deferrals were granted out of about 200 second- and third-year students. A heuristic was designed to schedule the exams in such a way as to minimize the conflicts. The technique considers class intersections, time, and room availability. As a result of the heuristic, the number of deferrals decreased by 45 percent. Furthermore, the heuristic typically runs in less than 30 seconds on a PC, saving hours of manual labor that had been required to schedule the exams using a large scheduling board.

- No universal model exists for selecting stocks in an optimal fashion, so financial managers must rely on certain rules and principles to guide their strategies. One strategy that has been proposed is called *disciplined stock selection*. Heuristics that guide this strategy are able to

  1. Keep the portfolio beta (a measure of market risk) between 0.95 and 1.05.
  2. Spread investments over various sectors in line with the S&P 500.
  3. Diversify the portfolio with 60–90 companies.
  4. Avoid establishing an excessive position in any one investment.

  In both simulations and actual practice, this strategy has been shown to exceed the S&P 500 by 2 percent or more [Farrell, 1982].

- Because of the geographic dispersion of special-education schools and students, bus routes servicing these schools tend to be significantly longer than neighborhood routes for non–special-education students. A special-education student is usually picked up at home and delivered to a school specializing in the student's particular disability. One bus may therefore have to deliver students to several different schools. In Tulsa, Oklahoma, approximately 850 students are served by 66 different schools. This problem can be modeled as a very large integer program, whose size and complexity make it too difficult to solve. Instead, a procedure was developed to improve the current routes. This procedure was easy to implement and explain to the school personnel, reduced mileage by about 11 percent (a savings of over $30,000 per year), and reduced the driving time by almost 16 percent [Russell and Morrel, 1986].

In Chapter 1 we introduced you to an important topic in management science: heuristics.

A *heuristic* is a "rule of thumb" to guide decision-making or to find approximate solutions to optimization problems.

The word *heuristic* derives from a Greek word meaning "to discover." In this sense, a heuristic aims at studying the methods and rules of discovery or assisting in problem solving. People use heuristics every day when they

- Take an umbrella when the weather forecast calls for rain.
- Book Thanksgiving airline flights early.
- Use an old golf ball when hitting over water.

Managers also use heuristics routinely in business decisions when they

- Schedule the shortest job first.
- Order more inventory if the stock level is less than half.
- Keep the current ratio (the ratio of current assets to current liabilities) greater than 2 to 1.

The examples at the beginning of this chapter illustrate how heuristics can be applied in order to improve decision-making. In this chapter we provide some basic guidelines for developing heuristics in order to solve practical problems in management science and illustrate these principles for a variety of situations. Also, we discuss how to approximate nonlinear relationships with linear functions so that we can solve certain nonlinear optimization problems with linear programming.

HEURISTICS IN MANAGEMENT SCIENCE

Management scientists use heuristics in many ways. First, they can provide good starting solutions for exact optimization algorithms, as we will illustrate in the following example.

EXAMPLE 1. THE NORTHWEST CORNER RULE FOR THE TRANSPORTATION PROBLEM

P.149

Let us revisit the MaBops Inc. transportation problem (Example 7) in Chapter 4. This problem involved finding a minimum-cost distribution plan for shipping from four plants to five warehouses. Table 10.1 shows the relevant data. In Chapter 4 we developed a linear programming model for this problem.

TABLE 10.1
Data for MaBops, Inc.
(values in the matrix
correspond to unit
transportation costs)

	Houston	Las Vegas	New Orleans	Chicago	Boise	Capacity
Los Angeles	5	1	5	7	4	150
Denver	9	7	8	3	5	200
Pensacola	3	4	3	8	6	175
Cincinnati	4	5	6	2	7	100
Demand	80	110	150	100	150	

Special algorithms based on the simplex method are used to solve transportation problems efficiently. These algorithms start with a feasible solution to the problem, so we need a method that will find a feasible solution quickly. Heuristics are usually used to provide such a feasible solution. A simple heuristic that provides an initial solution to the transportation problem is called the *northwest corner rule*. The northwest corner rule works as follows:

1. Begin in the upper-left (northwest) corner of the cost matrix. This corresponds to the first plant and first warehouse. Ship as much as possible from that plant to that warehouse. How much we can ship is determined by the smaller of the available supply at that plant and the remaining demand at the warehouse. In the Mabops example, the available capacity at Los Angeles is 150 and the demand at Houston is 80, so we can ship a maximum of 80 units. We then subtract the amount shipped from both the capacity at the plant and the demand at the warehouse (one of these will become zero). This is shown in Figure 10.1.

2. If the available capacity at the plant is positive, then move across to the next warehouse. If the available capacity is zero, move down to the next plant. If the demand at the warehouse is zero, move across to the next warehouse. Repeat the allocation procedure described in Step 1. Continue to move across or down, allocating shipments until all demand has been satisfied. Continuing with the MaBops example, we arrive at the solution shown in Figure 10.2. A problem at the end of this chapter will ask you to develop other heuristics for this problem.

The northwest corner rule can be easily implemented on a spreadsheet, as illustrated in Figure 10.3. You need only to subtract the shipments in each row and column from the capacities and demands in order to show the amounts remaining. Thus, as entries are placed in each cell, the remaining capacity and demand at each city are automatically

---

FIGURE 10.1   *Results after the first step in the northwest corner rule*

WAREHOUSE

	Houston	Las Vegas	New Orleans	Chicago	Boise	Available Capacity
Los Angeles	80	~~70~~				~~150~~ ~~70~~
Denver		40	150	10		200 ~~160~~ ~~85~~ 0
Pensacola				90	85	175 ~~85~~ 0
Cincinnati					65	100 35
Remaining Demand	~~80~~ 0	~~40~~ 110	0 ~~150~~	~~90~~ 100	~~65~~ 150	

PLANT

FIGURE 10.2   *Solution obtained by the northwest corner rule*

	Houston	Las Vegas	New Orleans	Chicago	Boise	Available capacity
Los Angeles	80	70				0
Denver		40	150	10		0
Pensacola				90	85	0
Cincinnati					65	0
Remaining demand	0	0	0	0	0	

updated. Because of the iterative nature of heuristics, however, it is generally difficult to use spreadsheets to implement the actual computational processes. Spreadsheets are quite useful in working with the data used in heuristic procedures, however, and we encourage you to use them whenever possible.

Second, heuristics often form the basis for rules that intelligently direct the operation of an optimizing algorithm. For example, in solving large linear programming problems with the simplex method, the decision of which neighboring corner point to visit next is usually based on heuristic principles. This process, however, does not guarantee that the minimum number of steps will be taken to reach the optimal solution.

FIGURE 10.3   *Spreadsheet implementation for the transportation problem*

A	A	B	C	D	E	F	G
1		HOUSTON	LAS VEGAS	NEW ORLEANS	CHICAGO	BOISE	CAPACITY
2	LOS ANGELES						150
3	DENVER						200
4	PENSACOLA						175
5	CINCINNATI						100
6	DEMAND	80	110	150	100	150	

Selected cell formulas

A	A	B	C	D	E	F	G
1		HOUSTON	LAS VEGAS	NEW ORLEANS	CHICAGO	BOISE	CAPACITY
2	LOS ANGELES						150-@SUM(B2..F2)
3	DENVER						200-@SUM(B3..F3)
4	PENSACOLA						175-@SUM(B4..F4)
5	CINCINNATI						100-@SUM(B5..F5)
6	DEMAND	80-@SUM(B2..B5)	110-@SUM(C2..C5)	150-@SUM(D2..D5)	100-@SUM(E2..E5)	150-@SUM(F2..F5)	

Third, heuristics can reduce computational requirements. This is particularly important when we need to solve optimization problems on a real-time basis or when we need a solution quickly.

Heuristic procedures are used extensively to solve large *combinatorial optimization* problems, a group of problems that involves the selection or arrangement of discrete objects. Examples of combinatorial optimization problems include vehicle routing, machine scheduling, job sequencing, and facility location and layout. Integer programming and many network problems that we discussed in previous chapters also fall into this class. Combinatorial optimization problems typically have extremely large numbers of possible solutions that make exhaustive enumeration impossible. Perhaps the most celebrated combinatorial optimization problem is the *traveling salesman problem*, or *TSP*, which is described in the following example.

EXAMPLE 2. THE TRAVELING SALESMAN PROBLEM

A salesman needs to visit a fixed list of cities. He must determine an itinerary that allows him to visit each city *exactly once* and return to his home city in minimum total time. A feasible sequence of cities is called a *tour*. Because of airline schedules, the time to travel from city A to city B may not be the same as the time to travel from city B to city A. In this case, an *n*-city problem has $n! = n(n-1)(n-2)\cdots(2)(1)$ possible solutions. Suppose that there are $n = 21$ cities. If each one could be evaluated in one billionth of a second, it would take over 1,600 years to examine them all!

A simple example of a traveling salesman problem that we will use later in this chapter is shown in Figure 10.4. The cities are represented by nodes of a network, and the branches represent the direct routes between each pair of cities. The distance between each pair of cities is given on the branches. The optimal traveling salesman tour has a cost of 11. Can you find one? (There are alternate optimal solutions.)

FIGURE 10.4   *An example of a traveling salesman problem*

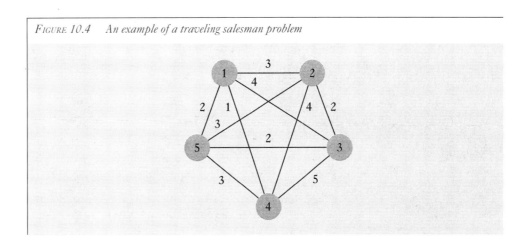

Exact optimization algorithms that solve large traveling salesman problems do not exist. Practical problems may involve hundreds or thousands of "cities" and may preclude the use of an exact solution procedure in a reasonable amount of time. One example involving a large number of locations was discussed in Chapter 1—circuit board drilling. In this example the "cities" are the holes to be drilled, and the problem is to route the drill in minimum time. A heuristic procedure is the only practical alternative for such situations.

There are several reasons why we use heuristics instead of exact optimization algorithms.

1. Exact optimization algorithms may be too costly in terms of time or money to develop and run.
2. Software for exact optimization algorithms (or the expertise to develop them) may not be available. For example, we may be faced with a nonlinear optimization problem and only have a linear programming solver available.
3. In cases where the inputs to the optimization model are only rough estimates, it may be pointless to spend the time and money solving the problem with exact optimization. The exact solution to a fuzzy model is at best a fuzzy solution. A fast near-optimal solution often makes more sense than a time-consuming exact solution to a fuzzy problem. In one case, a heuristic procedure to produce a solution to a large capital budgeting problem was developed and implemented in one day, and the heuristic solution was 99.7 percent of the optimal solution. The algorithm to find the optimal solution had taken six months to develop and took ten times longer to run on a computer.
4. Managers often accept heuristics more easily than other approaches because they are simple and can be readily understood and implemented on a computer. This increases the likelihood that managers will use the recommended solutions. It is often claimed that "a manager would rather live with a problem that cannot be solved than accept a solution that cannot be understood." While they are not optimal, heuristic solutions are usually better than the status quo and provide managers with a sense of improvement.

    The major disadvantage of heuristic algorithms is their inability to produce guaranteed optimal solutions. In many cases you will not know how far away from the optimum a heuristic solution might be, so when decisions are very risky or involve considerable amounts of capital, the use of heuristic algorithms should be weighed carefully.

APPLICATIONS OF HEURISTICS

Decision-makers use heuristics to solve problems in every field. In this section we present several examples of heuristic algorithms and applications.

*   *Delivering "Meals on Wheels"* [Bartholdi, et al., 1983]. Senior Citizen Services, Inc. in Atlanta, Georgia needed to develop a routing system for the "Meals on Wheels" program.

Drivers deliver meals to more than 200 delivery points, whose locations change daily. All meals have to be delivered within four hours, the length of time that the insulated containers will keep the meals properly warm. The objective is to balance the routes so that each driver has a route of similar length. The manager of the program has little time and virtually no resources to devote to this problem. A sophisticated computer system was therefore out of the question.

Instead, a routing heuristic was developed based on the traveling salesman problem. This heuristic requires only the coordinates of the delivery locations (which can be found easily using a map mounted under a plastic grid). From the location, the user needs only to look up its relative position along a "master route" and to sort the locations according to these relative positions. This is easily done using a Rolodex™ file, and also allows the service to add and remove clients on a daily basis. By partitioning the cards into equal sets according to the number of drivers, the routes were easy to determine.

- *Locating Bank Accounts* [Cornuejols, et al., 1977]. The number of days required to clear a check drawn on a bank in one city depends on the city where the check is cashed. A company that pays bills to numerous clients in various locations may find it advantageous to maintain accounts in several strategically located banks. It would then pay bills to clients in one city from a bank in another city that has the largest clearing time. This time, called the *float*, allows the company to continue to earn interest on its funds until the check clears. In a similar fashion, a company that collects funds from clients in different cities may site several different collection points, called *lock boxes*, in order to reduce the float and therefore to maximize its available funds.

  This problem can be modeled as an integer programming problem, but it is so large that it is difficult to solve optimally. For example, one real problem had 737 account locations and 25 client locations. The integer programming model had over 18,000 zero-one variables. Heuristics have been developed that obtain good solutions that are within a small percentage of the optimum.

- *Personnel Scheduling* [Henderson and Berry, 1976]. The demand for telephone operators, fast food restaurant employees, and other service workers usually varies considerably over the course of a day or week. For example, over a one-day period the number of telephone operators needed at General Telephone and Electronics Company in California varied from 2 to 9. Managers of such services face the difficult problem of scheduling starting times, shift lengths, and lunch and relief breaks in a manner that will meet the demand while keeping personnel costs down. Like the lock box problem, these problems can be modeled as large integer programs, but heuristics are needed in order to solve these models in reasonable times.

- *Military Airlift Planning* [Rappoport, et al., 1992]. The Military Airlift Command (MAC) is responsible for planning the allocation of airlift resources for moving cargo and passengers during peacetime and in crisis situations. In 1987 MAC undertook the development of the Airlift Deployment Analysis System, an interactive database that provides MAC with planning, scheduling, and analysis tools for airlift operations. As opposed to commercial air freight operations, there are no scheduled flights on which cargo is assigned. As the military confronts different situations, MAC must schedule flights in a manner that will meet the payload and time demands of the area commander-in-chief. The planning problem has both time and capacity constraints. The schedule depends on the times at which facilities are available at each base, and aircraft have different capacities. Because of all these complexities, a heuristic approach was developed that is extremely fast and provides a good solution as a basis for obtaining improved schedules.

A CLASSIFICATION OF HEURISTIC ALGORITHMS

Heuristic algorithms take many forms, but many of them have similar characteristics. Understanding these similarities often helps in designing a heuristic for a unique problem situation. In this section we will describe some common types of heuristic algorithms and illustrate them using the traveling salesman problem (Example 1).

Construction Heuristics   OR   GREEDY HEURISTICS

Construction heuristics build a feasible solution by adding individual components (for example, nodes or branches in a network or variables in a mathematical program) one at a time and stopping when a feasible solution is obtained. Many construction heuristics are often called *greedy heuristics* because they seek to maximize the improvement at each step. A feasible solution is not usually found until the last step of the heuristic algorithm. One example of a greedy heuristic is the nearest-neighbor heuristic for the TSP.

EXAMPLE 3. THE NEAREST-NEIGHBOR HEURISTIC FOR THE TSP

The nearest-neighbor heuristic for the TSP works as follows. Begin with any city, say x. Define city y as the city not in the current tour that is closest to x. Include the route (x, y) in the tour. Next, define the city closest to y as city z, and add (y, z) to the tour. The current tour is x–y–z. Continue in this fashion until all cities are included. Complete the tour by returning from the last city selected to the starting city x. We illustrate this using the example shown in Figure 10.4.

Step 1. If we select node 1, the closest node not in the tour is node 4. Thus, branch (1,4) is added to the tour.

Step 2. The closest node to node 4 that is not in the tour is node 5. When this node is selected and added, the current tour becomes 1–4–5.

Step 3. Select the closest node to node 5 that is not in the tour. This is node 3, so the current tour is now 1–4–5–3.

Step 4. Only node 2 remains, so we add it to the tour and return to node 1. The final tour is 1–4–5–3–2–1.

The total cost of this tour is $1 + 3 + 2 + 2 + 3 = 11$. Although this is an optimal solution, it is only by coincidence. The nearest-neighbor heuristic does not guarantee an optimal solution.

Improvement Heuristics

Improvement heuristics begin with a feasible solution and successively improve it by a sequence of exchanges or mergers while generally maintaining a feasible solution throughout the process. What we exchange depends on the particular problem. In the following example we illustrate a popular improvement heuristic for the TSP.

EXAMPLE 4. A TOUR IMPROVEMENT HEURISTIC FOR THE TSP *on 2-change*

An improvement heuristic for the traveling salesman problem is called the *2-change heuristic*. Starting with any tour, we consider the effect of removing any two branches in the tour and replacing them with the unique set of two branches that form a different tour. If we find a tour with a lower cost than the current tour, then we use it as the new tour. When no possible exchange can produce a tour that is better than the current tour, we stop. As with the nearest-neighbor heuristic, we have no guarantee that the final solution will be optimal.

To illustrate this for the example in Figure 10.4, suppose that we start with the tour 1-2-3-4-5-1, which has a cost of 15. All 2-changes are shown in Figure 10.5. The costs of the resulting tours are summarized below.

Tour	Cost
1-3-2-4-5-1	15
1-4-3-2-5-1	13
1-2-4-3-5-1	16
1-2-5-4-3-1	18
1-2-3-5-4-1	11

Because the best tour obtained from the 2-change process is 1-2-3-5-4-1, we use it as the new solution. If we find all 2-changes of this tour, we get:

Tour	Cost
1-2-3-5-4-1	11
1-5-3-2-4-1	11
1-2-5-3-4-1	14
1-2-4-5-3-1	16
1-2-3-4-5-1	15

Because no tour has a smaller cost than the current solution, we stop with 1-2-3-5-4-1 as the best solution. We might also choose 1-5-3-2-4-1, which has the same cost.

Many types of heuristic algorithms combine construction with improvement approaches. Usually a construction heuristic is used to obtain an initial feasible solution, and then an improvement heuristic is used to find better solutions.

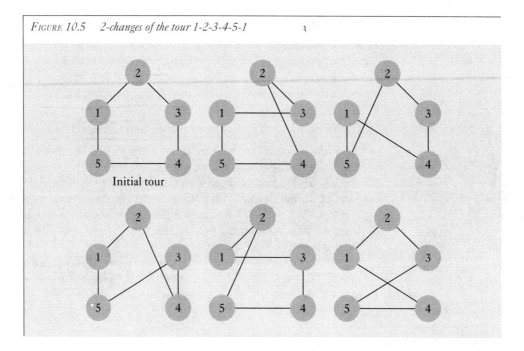

FIGURE 10.5   *2-changes of the tour 1-2-3-4-5-1*

Other Approaches

There are also other generic types of heuristic approaches to optimization problems. These include:

- *Mathematical programming.* We can sometimes solve the linear program relaxation to an integer program form and then modify the solution by rounding the variables in order to obtain a feasible solution.

- *Decomposition.* This refers to solving a problem in stages. In designing a distribution system, for example, we must make simultaneous decisions on where to locate warehouses and how to distribute the products from factories to these warehouses. We can model this problem using mixed integer programming, but suppose that we only have a linear programming software package at our disposal. In this case we might first pick the locations of warehouses and then solve a linear program in order to optimize the transportation flows. We could repeatedly modify the warehouse locations until we found an acceptable solution.

- *Partitioning.* Partitioning heuristics break or *partition* a problem into smaller subproblems, each of which is solved independently. These subproblem solutions are then merged into the overall problem. For example, in a large traveling salesman problem we might partition a map into smaller regions and then solve a TSP within each region. Then we merge them together in order to obtain one tour. This type of approach is often needed for large problems when computational time or computer storage becomes a problem.

HEURISTICS FOR INTEGER PROGRAMMING

One of the most common applications of heuristics involves integer programming. Heuristics for integer programs are important for several reasons. First, it is difficult to solve very large problems optimally in a reasonable amount of computer time. Second, good feasible solutions can speed up the performance of optimizing algorithms. Third, as we discussed in Chapter 8, a good feasible solution provides a bound on the optimal solution. With a bound on the objective function value, it is easy to assess the potential improvement that can be obtained by continuing to search for a better solution. We will restrict our discussion to the 0-1 knapsack problem. Recall that the knapsack problem is formulated as

$$\text{Max} \quad \sum_{j=1}^{n} c_j x_j$$

$$\text{subject to}$$

$$\sum_{j=1}^{n} a_j x_j \leq b$$

$$0 \leq x_j \leq 1 \text{ and integer}$$

We will discuss two heuristic methods for this problem in the following examples.

EXAMPLE 5. A GREEDY HEURISTIC FOR THE 0-1 KNAPSACK PROBLEM

A simple construction heuristic for the knapsack problem is to order the variables in decreasing order of the largest ratio c_j/a_j, and to select the variables to include in the solution one at a time until the inclusion of an additional variable is no longer feasible. To illustrate this we will use the following problem:

$$\text{Max} \quad z = 6x_1 + 8x_2 + 4x_3 + 3x_4 + 6x_5$$

$$\text{subject to}$$

$$3x_1 + 5x_2 + x_3 + 3x_4 + 2x_5 \leq 6$$

$$x_j = 0, 1$$

We first compute the ratios of the objective function coefficients to the constraint coefficients:

Variable	c_j/a_j
x_1	$6/3 = 2.0$
x_2	$8/5 = 1.6$
x_3	$4/1 = 4.0$
x_4	$3/3 = 1.0$
x_5	$6/2 = 3.0$

Therefore, we consider the variables in the order x_3, x_5, x_1, x_2, x_4. We first set $x_3 = 1$. This uses 1 unit of resource from the right-hand side of the constraint and contributes 4 to the objective function. The current solution is therefore $\{x_1 = 0, x_2 = 0, x_3 = 1, x_4 = 0, x_5 = 0\}$, $z = 4$. By setting $x_3 = 1$, we are left with the problem

[handwritten: x_3 is solved. so it's dropped from equation]

$$\text{Max} \quad 6x_1 + 8x_2 + 3x_4 + 6x_5$$
$$\text{subject to}$$
$$3x_1 + 5x_2 + 3x_4 + 2x_5 \leq 5$$
$$x_j = 0, 1$$

We next set $x_5 = 1$ and check for feasibility. (If setting $x_5 = 1$ would be infeasible, we would move on to the next variable on the list.) Because this is feasible, the current solution is $\{x_1 = 0, x_2 = 0, x_3 = 1, x_4 = 0, x_5 = 1\}$, $z = 10$. The problem that remains is

$$\text{Max} \quad 6x_1 + 8x_2 + 3x_4$$
$$\text{subject to}$$
$$3x_1 + 5x_2 + 3x_4 \leq 3$$
$$x_j = 0, 1$$

Next, we set $x_1 = 1$. This uses up all of the remaining resource and therefore we must stop. The final solution is $\{x_1 = 1, x_2 = 0, x_3 = 1, x_4 = 0, x_5 = 1\}$, $z = 16$.

[handwritten below: 6   0   4   0   6]

A second approach is called *neighborhood search*. We encountered the concept of neighborhood search when discussing the 2-change heuristic for the TSP. All tours that can be formed by 2-changes (Figure 10.5) can be thought of as the *neighborhood* of (close to) the given tour. In a similar fashion we can define neighborhoods for integer programming problems. One such neighborhood would be the set of all solutions that differ from a given solution by *exactly* one variable. We would examine all solutions in the neighborhood, and if we find a better feasible solution we let that become the current solution. We continue until no solution in the neighborhood of the current solution improves the objective function. The following example illustrates this process.

[handwritten: Same problem, different approach]

[handwritten left margin: Neighborhood search]

EXAMPLE 6. NEIGHBORHOOD SEARCH FOR THE 0-1 KNAPSACK PROBLEM

We will illustrate a neighborhood search for the knapsack example by using a neighborhood that is defined by all solutions differing from a given solution by exactly one variable. We will start with the solution $\{x_1 = 0, x_2 = 0, x_3 = 0, x_4 = 0, x_5 = 0\}$, $z = 0$. For simplicity we will drop the "$x_j =$" and represent this solution by (0 0 0 0 0). All solutions that differ by exactly one variable are listed below. We determine whether each solution is feasible, and if so, we determine the value of the objective function.

[handwritten: Compare to subject to equation]

$3x_1 + 5x_2 + x_3 + 3x_4 + 2x_5 \leq 6$

st $\geq$

$\text{Max } 6x_1 + 8x_2 + 4x_3 + 3x_4 + 6x_5$

Neighboring solutions	Feasible?		Objective function value
(1 0 0 0 0)	3	yes	6
(0 1 0 0 0)	5	yes	8
(0 0 1 0 0)	1	yes	4
(0 0 0 1 0)	3	yes	3
(0 0 0 0 1)	2	yes	6

The best solution in this neighborhood is (0 1 0 0 0), $z = 8$, and this becomes the current solution. Next, we examine all neighbors of (0 1 0 0 0) by changing the value of each variable, one at a time.

(to subject to equation)

Neighboring solutions	Feasible?		Objective function value
(0 0 0 0 0)	0	yes	0
(1 1 0 0 0)	8	no	
(0 1 1 0 0)	6	yes	12
(0 1 0 1 0)	8	no	
(0 1 0 0 1)	7	no	

Because we have found an improved solution, we continue. The current solution is (0 1 1 0 0), $z = 12$. We now examine all neighbors of this solution.

Neighboring solutions	Feasible?		Objective function value
(1 1 1 0 0)	9	no	
(0 0 1 0 0)	1	yes	4
(0 1 0 0 0)	5	yes	8
(0 1 1 1 0)	9	no	
(0 1 1 0 1)	8	no	

No neighboring solutions are better, so we stop. The final solution is (0 1 1 0 0), $z = 12$. Note that this solution is not as good as the one found with the greedy heuristic. Different starting solutions would yield different results.

We might find better solutions by using a larger neighborhood. Another neighborhood for this problem would be the set of all solutions that differ from a given solution by *at most* two variables. However, increasing the size of the neighborhood results in more computational effort. The decision-maker must therefore make a trade-off between the amount of computation that will be required and the quality of the solution.

DESIGNING HEURISTICS

Designing heuristics is very much an art, and finding the best approaches to use depends on the creativity of the user and her familiarity with the nature of the problem. Designing heuristics requires knowledge, experience, and a lot of experimentation. You must be familiar with the basic heuristic approaches, such as construction and improvement, and it also helps to have seen heuristics applied to many different problems. Finally, you must try many different approaches and experiment with them to find the best. It is good to start with a comprehensive mathematical model of the problem, *even if it cannot be solved using available software*. Developing a model often provides insights into the most effective type of heuristic to use. You might also see relationships with other problems that might stimulate some ideas for heuristics.

Designing a heuristic algorithm requires much the same process that we discussed in Chapter 3 with regard to modeling. We need to understand the environment in which the problem arises, determine the purpose of the heuristic, understand relevant assumptions, know what data are available, and address issues involving software, complexity, and accuracy.

What characteristics do we wish the heuristic to possess? A good heuristic should have the following features:

- *Simplicity*. The effort and data required to implement the algorithm on a computer should be minimal.
- *Computational efficiency*. The heuristic should have low running time and computer storage requirements.
- *Accuracy*. The heuristic should be able to find solutions that are close to optimal solutions.
- *Robustness*. The heuristic should find solutions that are not overly sensitive to changes in model data. Computer running times also should not be highly sensitive to the data. This cannot be said about many optimizing algorithms such as integer programming, whose computational times can double or triple when just one piece of data is changed.

Evaluating Heuristics

For decision making purposes, it is useful to know something about the efficiency and effectiveness of heuristics. Some questions to consider include:

1. Does the heuristic provide a guarantee on the quality of the solution? Solutions using some heuristics are guaranteed not to deviate more than a fixed percentage of the optimal value. However, proving this is rather difficult.
2. What is the average solution quality? This can be assessed by running extensive computational experiments.
3. Does the solution quality depend on problem characteristics such as problem size or problem structure? For example, heuristics that work well for small "toy" problems

may not work as well for larger, real problems. Some heuristics may depend on structural properties of the problem, such as the ratio of zero to nonzero coefficients in the constraints of an integer program or the ratio of the nodes to branches in a network.

4. How does computation time increase as problem size increases? Heuristics that are fast for small problems may be unbearably slow for large problems.

These issues are best left for management science researchers to decide, but practitioners need to be aware of these issues and to be able to find the answers to these questions in order to use heuristics intelligently. Answers can usually be found in the published research literature.

Because it is usually not possible to find the optimal solutions to large problems, we often evaluate heuristics with extensive computational experiments, usually comparing several different heuristics for their computational speed and solution quality. For the traveling salesman problem, for instance, the nearest-neighbor heuristic is very fast. However, experiments have shown that solutions obtained by the nearest-neighbor heuristic are roughly 15 percent above the optimal value. The 2-change heuristic is somewhat slower because more computations are involved, but solutions can be found that are usually within 5 to 7 percent of the optimal value. By using a "3-change" heuristic and cleverly combining construction and improvement heuristics, solutions within 2 or 3 percent of the optimal value can be found. In general, better solutions require higher computational times—another example of the principle that there is no such thing as a free lunch!

Intelligent Approaches to Heuristic Search

Most heuristics in optimization problems are search methods. Neighborhood search, which we discussed earlier, has the disadvantage that it stops once it finds a solution whose neighbors cannot improve the value of the objective function. We call this terminal solution a *local optimum* because it is the best solution only with respect to its particular neighborhood. The best solution to the problem, called the *global optimum* solution, may be quite far away. Frederick Hillier, a renowned Stanford University professor, used the parlance of gambling to suggest some guiding principles for designing heuristics (finding the global optimum does involve an element of luck):

- *Keep your stakes high.* Focus the search on regions where any feasible solutions found should be particularly good ones instead of trying to locate a mediocre solution quickly and then trying to improve it. Good (and poor) solutions tend to be grouped closely together. In integer programming, for example, integer solutions that are close to the optimum LP solution will typically be quite good. Searching around the LP solution has been found to be better than simply rounding in order to find an initial feasible solution quickly.
- *Stick with a winning streak, but don't push your luck.* When a good feasible solution is found, there often is an even better one nearby. You should continue to search for a reasonable period of time until no further improvements can be obtained. Changing one or two variables at a time frequently leads to success, but don't search forever, as the benefits will only be marginal.

- *Shuffle the deck occasionally.* When the search has gotten locked into one well-explored neighborhood, allow it to drift a while to see if it finds better solutions in an entirely different part of the feasible region or search space.
- *Play the field.* The search should move into different regions of good solutions, thereby increasing the chances of "hitting the jackpot" and finding an optimal solution.

Many of these ideas have been incorporated into modern approaches to heuristic search. Three popular approaches are called *tabu search, simulated annealing,* and *genetic algorithms. Tabu search* differs from ordinary local search in that it allows moves to inferior solutions in a effort to avoid being trapped at a local optimum. Both *simulated annealing* and *genetic algorithms* incorporate randomization in order to allow the search to explore different areas of the search space ("shuffling the deck" and "playing the field," as Hillier calls it). Both of these approaches have analogies with physical phenomena. Simulated annealing is derived from statistical mechanics and the physical process of annealing metals, and genetic algorithms draw from the biological principles of evolution and natural selection. Although these approaches are beyond the scope of this book, they are based on many of the elementary principles that we have studied. If you become a serious user of heuristics, you should learn more about them.

APPROXIMATING NONLINEAR RELATIONSHIPS

In the same spirit as heuristics, we often use approximations in management science in order to simplify complex problems. This is particularly true when we have to deal with nonlinear relationships. Problems involving nonlinearities are much more difficult to solve than problems with linear relationships, but by approximating nonlinear relationships with linear relationships we can use linear programming solvers and usually obtain good solutions far more easily.

A common example is a problem where the effectiveness of an additional unit of some resource is not constant but decreases as we increase the amount of that resource. We often call this phenomenon *decreasing or diminishing returns.* The following example shows how to do this.

EXAMPLE 7.[1] OPTIMAL ALLOCATION OF MARKETING EFFORT AMONG NONINTERACTING PRODUCTS

Phillips Inc. sells two products (product 1 and product 2) and uses two marketing instruments (advertising and direct sales calls) to stimulate demand for these products. There is no interaction between the two products in the sense that the price, cost, or demand of one product will not impact the demand of the other product. The company must decide the amount of direct sales and advertising resources to devote to each of the products in the coming quarter.

---

[1]This problem is adapted from Kotler, Philip. *Marketing Decision Making: A Model Building Approach.* Holt Reinhart and Winston Inc., 1971, pp. 171–173.

Phillips has budgeted $25,000 for advertising and has allotted a total of 5,000 hours of labor for direct sales for the quarter. Based on past data and managerial judgement, Phillips has estimated that a dollar of advertising will yield $8 profit when spent on product 1 and $15 when spent on product 2. These estimates hold over the entire range of the advertising budget. Phillips company policy dictates that at least $6,000 but no more than $18,000 be spent on advertising for each product. Likewise, at least 2,000 but no more than 3,500 hours of direct sales labor can be used on each product.

The company has studied the productivity of direct sales, but has found that the effect is not constant. The profit decreases as more time is spent on direct sales. These relationships are shown in Figures 10.6(*a*) and 10.6(*b*).

Although the relationships shown in Figure 10.6 are not linear, we can approximate them with straight line segments. Let us first examine product 1. Figure 10.7 shows an approximation of the nonlinear function with two linear segments, which we have chosen to have equal length (5,000 hours available divided by 2 equals 2,500). The slope of line segment A is $(62,500 - 0)/(2,500 - 0) = 25$. We will therefore use $25 as the profit realized per unit of labor hours expended, up to 2,500 hours. For any additional hours, we will use the slope of line segment B as an estimate of the profit generated per hour of selling. This slope is $(100,000 - 62,500)/(5,000 - 2,500) = 15$.

The relationship between selling hours and profit for product 2 is similar. We can use straight line segments to approximate this relationship as well, but because the relationship is more nonlinear than for product 1, we will use three line segments rather than two. This provides a better approximation (in general, the more line segments are used, the closer the approximation will be to the nonlinear function. However, as we shall see, more line segments increase the size of the model).

The lengths of the intervals of the line segments do not have to be equal. Because product 2's curve is nearly linear for small numbers of labor hours, we will make the first line segment longer than the other two. The linear approximation we use is shown in Figure 10.8. Line segment A has the slope $(90,000 - 0)/(2,000 - 0) = 45$. Line segment B's slope is $(142,500 - 90,000)/(3,500 - 2,000) = 35$, and the slope for line segment C is $(157,500 - 142,500)/(5,000 - 3,500) = 10$. For product 2, therefore, the profits per hour are estimated to be $45 for the first 2,000 hours, $35 for the next 1,500 hours, and $10 for the last 1,500 hours.

Linear Programming Formulation

We will use these *linear approximations* in developing a linear programming model. We will follow the procedure described in Chapter 4.

What Does Phillips Need to Decide? Phillips needs to decide how many labor hours for selling and how much money for advertising to allocate to each of its two products.

Let x_1 = the amount of advertising dollars to spend on product 1
       x_2 = the amount of advertising dollars to spend on product 2

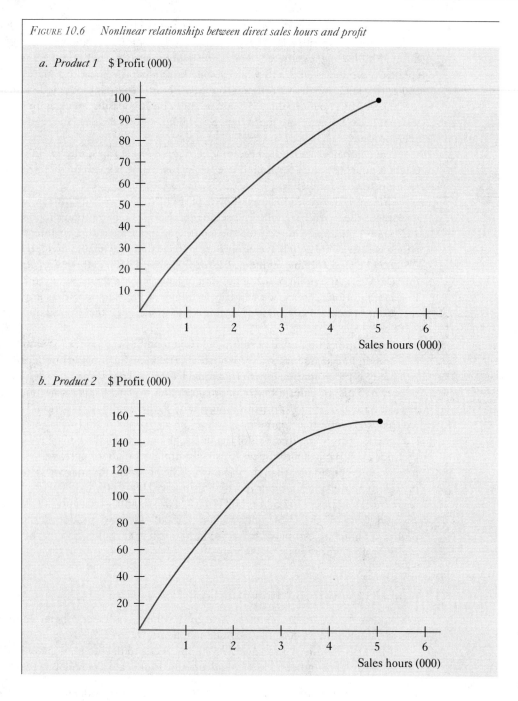

FIGURE 10.6   *Nonlinear relationships between direct sales hours and profit*

a. Product 1 $ Profit (000)

Sales hours (000)

b. Product 2 $ Profit (000)

Sales hours (000)

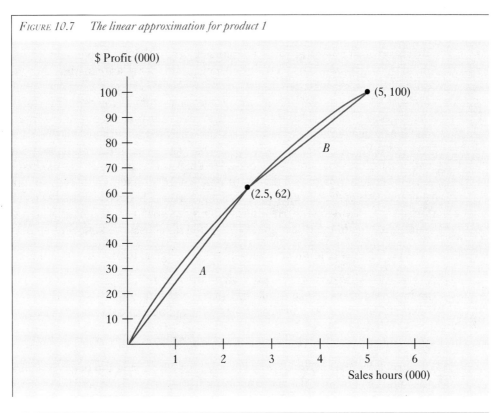

FIGURE 10.7   The linear approximation for product 1

$ Profit (000)

(5, 100)

B

(2.5, 62)

A

1   2   3   4   5   6
Sales hours (000)

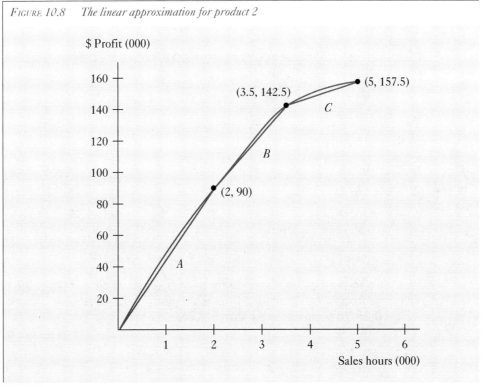

FIGURE 10.8   The linear approximation for product 2

$ Profit (000)

(3.5, 142.5)   (5, 157.5)

C

B

(2, 90)

A

1   2   3   4   5   6
Sales hours (000)

We also need decision variables that represent the number of labor hours to allocate to the selling of each product, but the diminishing returns complicate matters. Because there is a different profit per hour depending on the level of allocation, we need to define a separate decision variable for each range whose marginal profit is constant. This means that we must define a separate decision variable for each linear segment used to approximate the nonlinear function. Consider, for example, the productivity of labor hours allocated to product 1. We can define a decision variable that is the number of labor hours allocated with a marginal profit of $25 per hour. We know that these hours are the first 2,500 hours we allocate to product 1. We then define a second decision variable as the number of hours allocated to product 1 in excess of 3,500 hours (these hours have a marginal profit of $15). We will likewise define three different decision variables for hours allocated to product 2 (corresponding to the three ranges with different constant marginal profits).

Let y_{ij} = the number of sales hours of marginal profit i to allocate to product j

What Is the Objective to Be Maximized or Minimized? Phillips would like to maximize the profit contribution realized from the allocation of its advertising budget and its selling hours allotment for the coming quarter. This can be expressed mathematically as

$$\text{Max}\quad 8x_1 + 15x_2 + 25y_{11} + 15y_{21} + 45y_{12} + 35y_{22} + 10y_{32}$$

How Is the Problem Restricted? First, both the advertising and personal selling have limited budgets. For advertising the budget is in dollars and for selling it is in labor hours. We must ensure that the total dollars expended on advertising does not exceed the budget. This can be expressed in terms of our decision variables as

$$x_1 + x_2 \leq 25,000$$

Likewise, the total number of hours allocated to selling for the two products cannot exceed 5,000 hours.

$$y_{11} + y_{21} + y_{12} + y_{22} + y_{32} \leq 5,000$$

The variables associated with the different levels of hours for selling have upper bounds by their definition.

$$y_{11} \leq 2,500$$
$$y_{21} \leq 2,500$$
$$y_{12} \leq 2,000$$
$$y_{22} \leq 1,500$$
$$y_{32} \leq 1,500$$

Furthermore, we have upper and lower bounds on the amount of advertising dollars and selling hours that can be allocated to each product. The advertising allocations must be no less than $6,000 and no more than $18,000.

$$x_1 \geq 6,000$$
$$x_1 \leq 18,000$$
$$x_2 \geq 6,000$$
$$x_2 \leq 18,000$$

The number of hours allocated to selling of each of the products must be at least 2,000 hours but no more than 3,500 hours. For product 1 this can be written mathematically as

$$y_{11} + y_{21} \geq 2,000$$
$$y_{11} + y_{21} \leq 3,500$$

Similarly for product 2:

$$y_{12} + y_{22} + y_{32} \geq 2,000$$
$$y_{12} + y_{22} + y_{32} \leq 3,500$$

The entire model can be stated as

$$\text{Max} \quad 8x_1 + 15x_2 + 25y_{11} + 15y_{21} + 45y_{12} + 35y_{22} + 10y_{32}$$

subject to

$$x_1 + x_2 \leq 25,000$$
$$y_{11} + y_{21} + y_{12} + y_{22} + y_{32} \leq 5,000$$

$$y_{11} \leq 2,500$$
$$y_{21} \leq 2,500$$

$$y_{12} \leq 2,000$$
$$y_{22} \leq 1,500$$
$$y_{32} \leq 1,500$$

$$x_1 \geq 6,000$$
$$x_1 \leq 18,000$$

$$x_2 \geq 6,000$$
$$x_2 \leq 18,000$$
$$y_{11} + y_{21} \geq 2,000$$
$$y_{11} + y_{21} \leq 3,500$$
$$y_{12} + y_{22} + y_{32} \geq 2,000$$
$$y_{12} + y_{22} + y_{32} \leq 3,500$$
$$x_i, y_{ij} \geq 0 \qquad \text{for all } i \text{ and } j$$

An EXCEL spreadsheet model and the *Solver Parameter* dialog box for this problem are shown in Figure 10.9. The solution to the model shown in the spreadsheet in Figure 10.10 is to invest $7,000 in advertising for product 1 and $18,000 in advertising for product 2, and to allocate 2,000 hours to selling product 1 and 3,000 hours to selling product 2. This plan will yield a profit of $501,000.

FIGURE 10.9   *EXCEL spreadsheet model*

	A	B	C	D	E	F	G
1	Phillips Inc						
2							
3	*Parameters and uncontrollable inputs:*						
4							
5			Bounds:				
6	Product	Profit/Advertising $	Lower	Upper		Advertising Budget:	$25,000
7	1	$8	$6,000	$18,000		Direct Sales Hours:	5000
8	2	$15	$6,000	$18,000			
9							
10	Product	Profit/ Hour	Range:				
11	1	$25	1	2500			
12	1	$15	2501	5000			
13		Total Hour Range:	2000	3500			
14							
15		Profit/ Hour	Range:				
16	2	$45	1	2000			
17	2	$35	2001	3500			
18	2	$10	3501	5000			
19		Total Hour Range:	2000	3500			
20							
21							
22	*Decision variables:*		Selling Hours				
23		Advertising $	$25	$15			
24	Product 1	$0	$0	$0			
25							
26			Selling Hours				
27		Advertising $	$45	$35	$10		
28	Product 2	$0	$0	$0	$0		
29							
30							
31	*Model outputs:*						
32							
33		Advertising $	Selling Hours	Profit			
34	Product 1	$0	0	$0			
35	Product 2	$0	0	$0			
36	Total	$0	0	$0			

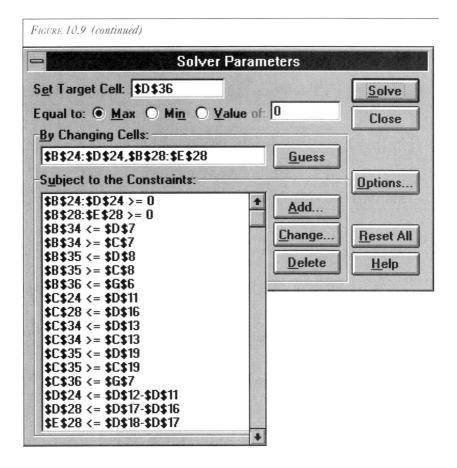

FIGURE 10.9 *(continued)*

Some Practical Considerations

A few words of caution with respect to linear approximations of nonlinear functions are in order. First, we note that the approximations used in Figures 10.7 and 10.8 work in the Phillips example because the slopes of the line segments are smaller as we increase the usage of the resource. Looking at our objective function, because the contribution of the first segment for product 1 is $25 and that of the second segment is only $15, the first segment will always be chosen before the second. This means that any profit-maximizing solution will use up the first segment before using the second (y_{21} will never be positive unless $y_{11} = 2,500$). We are really using the optimization to ensure that the approximation holds correctly. For example, $y_{11} = 0$ and $y_{21} = 2,000$ (with the other variables at their optimal values) is feasible to the constraint set, but it will never be optimal because y_{11} has a higher contribution. Consequently, the type of approximation we have used will work as long as we are maximizing our objective.

FIGURE 10.10   *Optimal solution*

	A	B	C	D	E	F	G
1	Phillips Inc						
2							
3	*Parameters and uncontrollable inputs:*						
4							
5			Bounds:				
6	Product	Profit/Advertising $	Lower	Upper		Advertising Budget:	$25,000
7	1	$8	$6,000	$18,000		Direct Sales Hours:	5000
8	2	$15	$6,000	$18,000			
9							
10	Product	Profit/ Hour	Range:				
11	1	$25	1	2500			
12	1	$15	2501	5000			
13		Total Hour Range:	2000	3500			
14							
15		Profit/ Hour	Range:				
16	2	$45	1	2000			
17	2	$35	2001	3500			
18	2	$10	3501	5000			
19		Total Hour Range:	2000	3500			
20							
21							
22	*Decision variables:*		Selling Hours				
23		Advertising $	$25	$15			
24	Product 1	$7,000	2000	0			
25							
26				Selling Hours			
27		Advertising $	$45	$35	$10		
28	Product 2	$18,000	2000	1000	$0		
29							
30							
31	*Model outputs:*						
32							
33		Advertising $	Selling Hours	Profit			
34	Product 1	$7,000	2000	$106,000			
35	Product 2	$18,000	3000	$395,000			
36	Total	$25,000	5000	$501,000			

Indeed, if we tried to use the approximations in Figures 10.7 and 10.8 with a cost function to be minimized, this approximation would not work! The segments to the right would be chosen (because they have smaller slopes) without the segments to the left being used, essentially yielding a solution that says to use cheaper later hours without using earlier hours. To illustrate this, if we use the same Phillips model that we developed, but with an objective function of minimizing cost, the solution would be

$$x_1 = x_2 = 6,000, \ y_{11} = 0, \ y_{21} = 2,000, \ y_{12} = 0, \ y_{22} = 500, \ y_{32} = 1,500$$

Clearly, this solution does not make operational sense.

We can make the following general statements:

1. When approximating a nonlinear profit function with linear segments in a maximization LP model, the slopes of the line segments must not increase as you move from left to right (increase the value of the decision variable).
2. When approximating a nonlinear cost function with linear segments in a minimization LP model, the slopes of the line segments must not decrease as you move from left to right (increase the value of the decision variable).
3. When approximating a nonlinear function, more segments results in a better approximation, but the number of variables included in the LP model increases (one decision variable is needed for each segment).

MANAGEMENT SCIENCE PRACTICE

In this section we discuss how heuristics helped to improve examination scheduling at the University of Cincinnati College of Law.

College Examination Scheduling[2]

In law school, a student's course grade is typically made up almost entirely by the final exam grade. This increases the pressure on students to perform well on these exams. Being sensitive to this pressure, the University of Cincinnati College of Law instituted a rule that grants an exam deferral upon request to any student who has more than one exam scheduled on a given day. Exams were given over seven days, with two days at the end for taking deferred exams. Two exam periods (morning and afternoon) were used every day.

In the spring of 1992, Law Professor Christo Lassiter noticed that the number of deferrals granted seemed to be increasing at an alarming rate. His conjecture was that students were actually choosing classes based on the tentative exam schedule (which was released before final registration) in order to induce conflicts. A student might schedule two classes that would have exams on the same day so that one of them could be deferred, with a corresponding increase in the amount of time available to prepare for the deferred exam. (This in itself is a rather clever heuristic!) Of the roughly 250 second- and third-year students (first-year students have required schedules), 66 deferrals were granted in the fall semester of 1992 (approximately 25 percent of the students). Professor Lassiter and Associate Dean Barbara Watts, who was responsible for scheduling the exams, contacted Professor Camm of the Department of Quantitative Analysis and Operations

[2]We gratefully acknowledge the members of the student group "Cha-Ching Consulting" who worked on this project: Felicia Collins, Devin Gamboa, Brock Morrison, Ted Russell, and Monica Terhar.

Management, and asked him to explore the possibility of remedying the situation through a better scheduling system. Professor Camm was teaching a project-oriented course to management science majors at that time, so he assigned the project to his students.

The students developed a heuristic approach to scheduling the exams so as to minimize conflicts. The heuristic considers class enrollments and required classroom size as inputs and was coded in PASCAL on a microcomputer. The class enrollment data are needed to find the intersection of the classes in order to calculate conflicts. The heuristic approach is basically a greedy procedure and works as follows:

1. Input the class lists, number of exam days, number of exam periods per day, and classroom capacities. For each pair of classes, calculate the intersection from the class lists.
2. Sort the classes by enrollment size from largest to smallest.
3. Begin with the largest class.
4. Find the feasible time slot for this class that will result in fewest conflicts. If no feasible slot exists, mark that this exam has not been scheduled and go to step 5. Otherwise, assign this exam to that time slot and record it (in the case of ties, take the earliest time slot first).
5. If all exams have been scheduled, go to step 6. Otherwise, choose the next class from the list and go to step 4.
6. Print the schedule and report the total number of deferrals.

Fall semester 1992 was used as a baseline in order to evaluate the quality of this approach. Recall that the Law School had used a seven-day exam schedule, with two extra days for deferrals, and that 66 deferrals had been granted. Using the heuristic procedure with the seven-day time horizon, a schedule with only 36 deferrals was generated (a decrease of 45 percent). Furthermore, the students found that if one of the deferral days was changed to an exam day, the number of deferrals granted dropped to 18 (a 72 percent decrease). The approach was tested over three years of data with similar results. The students concluded that while the approach does not guarantee an optimal solution, it seemed to perform well.

Associate Dean Watts had previously developed the schedule by using a manual approach with a large white board. This often required a day or more of her time. The heuristic requires several input files which can be created by clerical workers, but it runs in less than 30 seconds on the PC available at the Law School. Because of its speed and flexibility, the program can be run for a variety of scenarios, allowing Dean Watts to change the number of days and time periods. The system is currently used to generate a preliminary (based on historical enrollments) and final (based on final enrollment lists) exam schedule.

Discussion Questions

1. Explain why the exam scheduling heuristic is referred to as a greedy heuristic.
2. Some professors, like some students, wish to be finished with the semester as soon as possible. How might professor preference be incorporated into this approach? Likewise, how might student preferences be incorporated (for example, there might

be two exams which are notoriously difficult, so students will want those exams as far apart as possible)?

3. The exam scheduling problem can be modeled as an integer program. Develop the generic integer programming model for this problem. (Hint: Let $x_{it} = 1$ if exam for class i is scheduled for time period t, and 0 if not; let $y_{ij} = 1$ if exams i and j are scheduled in the same time slot, 0 if not.)

MORE EXAMPLES AND SOLVED PROBLEMS

The scope and variety of heuristics in management science is endless. The best way to learn about heuristics is to study a wide variety of different examples. In the following sections we will illustrate heuristics in a variety of decision situations.

EXAMPLE 8. VEHICLE ROUTING

A common problem in distribution involves determining routes from a central depot or warehouse to many customers. Generally, time or capacity restrictions associated with the problem preclude the use of only one route from the depot to all customers and back. We are given the travel times t_{ij} between customer i and customer j (the depot is designated as customer "0"). The Clarke-Wright heuristic begins with an initial solution in which each customer is serviced individually from the depot. This is shown in Figure 10.11. This initial solution is very inefficient, because the vehicle must return to the depot after servicing each customer. An alternative is to combine routes in order to reduce unnecessary travel.

Suppose that we combine the routes for customers i and j as shown in Figure 10.12. The total time required to travel on each route individually is $2t_{0i} + 2t_{0j}$. The

---

FIGURE 10.11   Initial solution for the Clarke-Wright heuristic

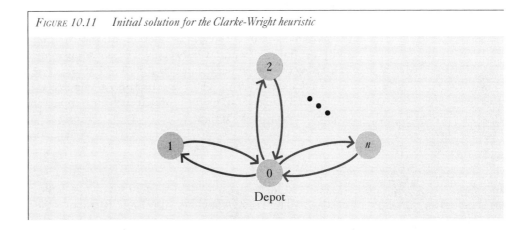

Depot

FIGURE 10.12   *Combining customers i and j in the Clarke-Wright heuristic*

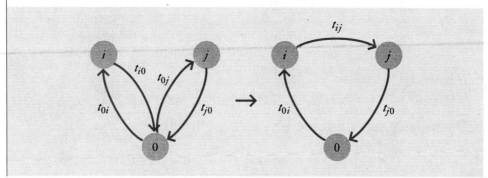

time on the combined route is $t_{0i} + t_{ij} + t_{0j}$. This combined route is better than the individual routes if

$$t_{0i} + t_{ij} + t_{0j} < 2t_{0i} + 2t_{0j}$$

or

$$s_{ij} = t_{0i} + t_{0j} - t_{ij} > 0$$

The term s_{ij} is called the *savings* associated with combining customers i and j on the same route. If the savings is positive, then it is beneficial to link the customers. The Clarke-Wright heuristic can be summarized as follows:

1. Compute the savings s_{ij} for all pairs of customers.
2. Find the pair of customers with the largest savings, and determine if it is feasible to link them. If so, then construct a new route by combining them. If not, try the next-largest savings, and so on.
3. Continue applying step 2 as long as the savings is positive. When all positive savings have been considered, stop.

To illustrate the Clarke-Wright algorithm, suppose that a chain of convenience stores has seven locations in one city. Each week goods must be delivered from a central warehouse to the stores. Items are packaged in standard-size containers. Table 10.2 gives the number of containers that must be delivered for one week and the one-way travel times in minutes between each pair of customers (including the depot). Each delivery vehicle has a capacity for 80 containers. The company would like to make all deliveries within an 8-hour shift on a single day of the week.

Using an initial set of routes in which each customer is serviced individually from the depot requires a total time of

$$2\left(\sum_{j=1}^{7} t_{0j}\right) = 2(20 + 57 + 51 + 50 + 10 + 15 + 90) = 586 \text{ minutes.}$$

This solution takes about 9.8 hours, so all deliveries could not be made during one workday, and fuel costs would be high. Table 10.3 shows the savings s_{ij} for all pairs of customers. The largest savings is 130, corresponding to customers 4 and 7. Because

TABLE 10.2
Travel times t_{ij} and customer requirements

i/j	0	1	2	3	4	5	6	7	Requirements
0	—	20	57	51	50	10	15	90	
1	20	—	51	10	55	25	30	53	46
2	57	51	—	50	20	30	10	47	55
3	51	10	50	—	50	11	60	38	33
4	50	55	20	50	—	50	60	10	30
5	10	25	30	11	50	—	20	90	24
6	15	30	10	60	60	20	—	12	75
7	90	53	47	38	10	90	12	—	30

TABLE 10.3
Savings, s_{ij}

i/j	1	2	3	4	5	6	7
1	—						
2	26	—					
3	61	58	—				
4	15	87	51	—			
5	5	37	50	10	—		
6	5	62	6	5	5	—	
7	57	100	103	130	10	93	—

the total demand is 60, we may combine these routes. The next-largest savings is $s_{37} = 103$. If we try to combine customer 3 with customer 7 (who is already combined with customer 4), the total demand on the new route would be 93, which exceeds the vehicle's capacity. We therefore move on to the next-largest savings, $s_{27} = 100$. Again, this violates the capacity constraint, as does the next-largest savings, $x_{67} = 93$. If we continue with the heuristic, we will obtain the following routes (you should verify this):

Route	Time
0–4–7–0	150
0–3–1–0	81
0–2–5–0	97
0–6–0	30

The total delivery time is reduced to 358 minutes.

EXAMPLE 9. JOB SHOP SCHEDULING

In a job shop, managers must make decisions involving the scheduling and sequencing of jobs. Scheduling refers to the process of assigning start and completion times;

sequencing refers to the process of determining the order in which jobs should be processed. Four major criteria are used to evaluate schedules:

1. *Makespan*, the time needed to process an entire set of jobs.
2. *Flowtime*, the time an individual job spends in the shop.
3. *Lateness*, the difference between the actual completion time and the date a job is scheduled to be finished (the due date).
4. *Tardiness*, the amount by which the actual completion time exceeds the due date. (Tardiness is the maximum of the lateness and zero.)

For a fixed set of jobs on a single machine, we can show that some simple rules will optimize certain criteria. For example, in order to minimize the average flowtime of all jobs in the set, we need only to sequence them according to processing time, beginning with the shortest. If we want to minimize the maximum tardiness or the maximum lateness, we should sequence the jobs according to the earliest due date.

In most real situations, we never deal with a fixed set of jobs or with only a single machine. Jobs continually arrive, and managers must make decisions on which job to process next on each machine. Simulation experiments have shown that the shortest processing time heuristic is very effective if we wish to keep the number of jobs waiting at machines to a minimum. However, jobs that do wait (those with long processing times) usually wait a long time. This can be avoided by modifying the heuristic so that it places higher priorities on jobs that have been waiting for a long time.

If meeting due dates is important, then a heuristic called the *critical ratio rule* is effective. The *critical ratio* is the time remaining until the due date divided by the remaining processing time. For example, if a job requires 8 more days to complete and it is due in 10 days, the critical ratio is $10/8 = 1.25$. Critical ratios greater than 1 mean that the job is ahead of schedule; ratios less than one mean that the job is behind. The critical ratio heuristic chooses jobs according to the smallest critical ratio, as we will illustrate in the following example.

A small manufacturing facility has a lathe, drill press, milling machine, and grinder. Customer orders arrive intermittently over time. The first four orders arrive at times 0, 0, 20, and 30 with due dates 150, 75, 50, and 100 respectively. Machine routing and processing time information is shown in the following table.

Job	Machine routing	Processing time
1	Lathe	10
	Drill press	20
	Grinder	35
2	Drill press	25
	Lathe	20
	Grinder	30
	Milling machine	15

Job	Machine routing	Processing time
3	Drill press	10
	Milling machine	10
4	Lathe	15
	Grinder	10
	Milling machine	20

We will illustrate the critical ratio scheduling rule by deterministically simulating the system. At time 0, job 1 is assigned to the lathe and job 2 to the drill press. Job 1 completes processing on the lathe at time 10. Because its next operation is drilling, it must wait because job 2 is still in progress there. At time 20, job 3 arrives and waits for the drill press. Job 2 completes processing on the drill press at time 25 and moves on to the lathe. At this point, the production manager must choose between sending either job 1 or job 3 to the drill press. The critical ratio for job 1 is

$$(150 - 25)/65 = 1.92$$

The critical ratio for job 3 is

$$(75 - 25)/20 = 2.5$$

Because job 1 has a smaller critical ratio (it is more constrained by time), the manager would assign job 1 to the drill press next. We ask you to complete this example as an exercise.

EXAMPLE 10. ASSEMBLY LINE BALANCING

In a conveyor-paced assembly line, we are given a set of operations to perform and precedence relations among the operations. The precedence relations prescribe the sequence in which the operations must be performed. Figure 10.13 shows an example in which the precedence relations are structured in a network. In this figure, operation A must precede operation D; operations D and E must precede operation G, and so on. The time it takes to perform each operation is listed next to each node. One objective of assembly line balancing is to assign operations to work stations (for example, assemblers) so that the assembly can be performed in the proper sequence defined by the network.

In addition, operations managers usually have some volume requirements that they must meet within a certain time period. To produce n assemblies in t minutes, we must be able to assemble one item in at most t/n minutes. Thus, the maximum time allocated to any work station cannot exceed t/n. This time is called the *cycle time*. If the cycle time is known, we have the problem of assigning operations to workstations so that

1. The total time assigned to any work station does not exceed the cycle time.
2. No precedence relations are violated.

FIGURE 10.13   *Assembly line balancing network*

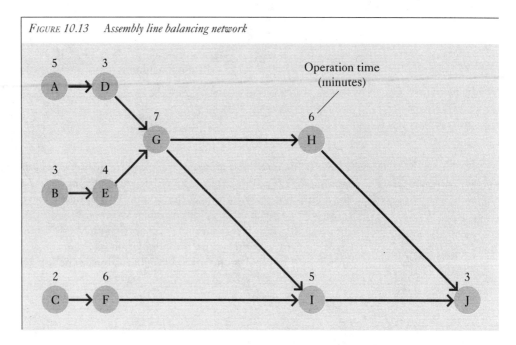

In addition, we would like the line to be as efficient as possible, so we would like to minimize the total idle time. Idle time arises if the amount of work assigned to a workstation is strictly less than the cycle time.

A simple heuristic determines which operations can be performed without violating any precedence restrictions and assigns the operation that has the largest time to a workstation. This process is repeated until all operations have been assigned to work stations. Let us illustrate this using the example in Figure 10.13. The results of applying the heuristic are summarized in Table 10.4.

Suppose that we wish to produce 60 units in an 8-hour (480 minute) shift. This requires us to produce one unit at least every 8 minutes; 8 minutes is therefore the cycle time. We may assign any operation to the next available work station as long as all preceding operations have already been assigned. The initial set of candidates to assign are the operations with no immediate predecessors, A, B, and C. We choose the operation with the largest time (operation A) and assign it to the first work station (see row 1 in Table 10.4). Because operation A is assigned, operation D becomes a candidate. The last column in Table 10.4 shows the set of candidates that we can choose from next. If the cumulative time is less than the cycle time, we continue to try to assign operations to the current work station. If none exist, then we move on to the next work station. In this case, we would choose operation B to assign next. Because the total time assigned to work station 1 is equal to the cycle time, we move to the next work station. You should work through the remainder of this example to verify the results given in Table 10.4. This solution requires 6 work stations. The total

TABLE 10.4
*Heuristic solution to
the assembly line
balancing problem*

Work Station	Operations	Time	Cum. Time	Assignable candidates
1	A	5	5	B, C, D
	B	3	8	C, D, E
2	E	4	4	C, D
	D	3	7	C, G
3	G	7	7	C, H
4	H	6	6	C
	C	2	8	F
5	F	6	6	I
6	I	5	5	J
	J	3	8	

idle time is found by subtracting the cumulative time assigned to each work station from the cycle time and then summing. The total idle time is therefore $0 + 1 + 1 + 0 + 2 + 0 = 4$. A problem at the end of this chapter will ask you to apply the heuristic "choose the shortest available operation next."

EXAMPLE 11. OPTIMIZING MUNICIPAL SERVICES

In the Management Science Practice case in Chapter 9 we described the use of Snow-Master© for snow and ice control applications. The software uses simple heuristics to make decisions about routing service vehicles over the network. Suppose that node 1 represents the depot from which the vehicles are dispatched. The first step is to get to a road segment that requires service. This can be done by finding the shortest path from the depot to any node that is incident with a branch that has not yet been serviced. The shortest-path procedure discussed in the Appendix to Chapter 9 may be used. The next road to service is determined using a heuristic rule that we will discuss shortly. When the vehicle runs out of salt, it returns to the depot along the shortest route. A new route is then created for the next vehicle, and the process continues until all road segments are serviced.

The core of the heuristic lies in deciding which road to take when several choices exist. Several rules have been used in practical applications of this approach, including the following:

1. Select the branch whose end node is closest to the depot.
2. Select the branch whose end node is farthest from the depot.
3. Use rule 2 if the vehicle is more than half full of salt; otherwise, use rule 1.

Each rule will result in different routes, but each has a rationale. For example, rule 1 develops routes that tend to stay close to the depot and then "fan out." Rule 2 creates "spider"-type routes, seeking to move farther away from the depot. Rule 3 takes into consideration the constraint on the vehicle capacity. By moving farther away and then closer, it seeks to reduce the amount of deadheading (non-productive traveling) that will be required when the vehicle runs out of salt. The routes will be "flower-petal" shaped. A case at the end of this chapter will ask you to apply this heuristic approach to the network in Figure 9.43 in Chapter 9.

EXAMPLE 12. PROJECT SCHEDULING WITH LIMITED RESOURCES

In Chapter 9 we showed how to formulate the optimal crashing schedule for a project network as a linear program. Here we show how a heuristic approach might be used to find a good solution. Consider the project network shown in Figure 10.14. By inspection, we see that the critical path is A-D, having a total time of 10. Suppose that we wish to crash activities to reduce the project completion time to 8. The following table shows the unit cost and maximum reduction for each activity:

Activity	Unit cost	Maximum reduction
A	2	1
B	0.5	1
C	3	2
D	1	3
E	2	2

A logical approach is to begin crashing activities on the critical path that have the lowest unit cost. However, note that this network has three paths: A-B-E, A-D, and

FIGURE 10.14   Project network

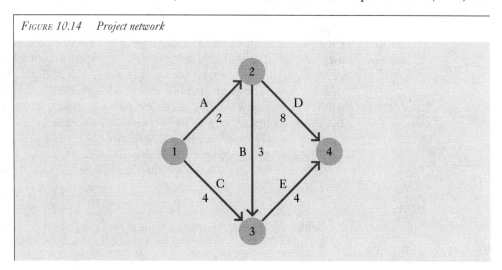

C-E. Path A-B-E has a length of 9, and path C-E has a length of 8. We must be careful to ensure that we do not reduce the length of the critical path below that of some other path, because any further reductions will not reduce the overall project completion time. The heuristic approach can be summarized as follows:

1. Find the critical path(s).
2. Crash activities on the critical path(s) having the lowest unit cost without reducing the length(s) below any other path in the network.
3. Identify the new set of critical paths and continue with Step 2 until the target project time is reached.

Let us illustrate this approach with the example. On the current critical path, A-D, activity D has the lowest unit crashing cost. Although we may crash activity D by 3 units, a reduction of only 1 will make the length of A-D equal to that of A-B-E. At this point, both paths are critical. Because activity A is common to both, crashing activity A will reduce the time on both critical paths simultaneously. We must also consider crashing activities B and D together, or activities E and D together, in order to ensure that the lengths of both paths are reduced. The unit cost for crashing A is 2. Crashing B and D will cost .5 + 1 = 1.5, and crashing E and D will cost 2 + 1 = 3. The lowest cost decision is therefore to crash both B and D by 1 unit, reducing the lengths of the critical paths to our target of 8.

Using this heuristic approach will not guarantee that the lowest-cost solution will be found, because the approach is sequential. What appears to be a good decision at an early stage might force a bad decision later. The linear programming approach described in Chapter 9 takes into account all decisions simultaneously and will always provide the optimum solution. Another drawback of the heuristic approach is that we need to check the lengths of all possible paths; for large problems, this may be difficult to do.

Example 13. Direct-Mail Advertising

In Chapter 8 we described the development of an integer programming model for the Tindall Bookstores problem. A real problem might have responses from thousands of customers and up to 100 magazines from which to choose. This makes the integer programming model very large and quite difficult to solve. An alternative approach is to use a heuristic to select a set of magazines within the budget constraint.

A simple, intuitive heuristic might proceed as follows:

1. Determine the incremental coverage of each magazine list for the sample data. That is, count the number of *additional* customers that would be reached as each list is selected. Initially, this is the total number of subscribers.
2. Select the list with the largest incremental coverage that does not exceed the budget constraint.
3. Compute the incremental coverage of the remaining magazines by deleting all customers that are reached by the list chosen in step 2. Return to step 2.

We will illustrate this approach using the sample data shown in Table 8.2. Initially, the incremental coverage for each list is given in the following table.

List	Incremental coverage
1	9
2	9
3	10
4	9
5	16
6	12
7	7
8	9
9	3
10	11

We would select magazine 5 because it has the highest incremental coverage. Next, we delete each customer who subscribes to magazine 5 and then recompute the incremental coverage.

List	Incremental coverage
1	6
2	8
3	8
4	5
5	0
6	8
7	7
8	5
9	2
10	6

We have a tie among magazines 2, 3, and 6. Because magazines 2 and 3 cost $1,000 while magazine 6 costs $1,500, we will arbitrarily select magazine 2 next. At this point we only have $500 remaining in the budget, so we would add magazine 9, with an incremental coverage of 1, to the solution. This selection reaches 25 of the 53 subscribers, or 47 percent. As you can see, this is a greedy construction heuristic that would be simple to explain to a marketing manager. (The manager might question the wisdom of spending the additional $500 for magazine 9 with such a low incremental coverage. This is why the mathematical solution must be studied in light of the real problem!) A problem at the end of the chapter will ask you to try to devise other heuristics for this problem.

EXAMPLE 14. THE SEGREGATED STORAGE PROBLEM

Another integer programming problem that we introduced in Chapter 8 was the segregated storage problem (Example 12). The problem was formulated to determine the allocation of commodities to storage facilities in such a way as to minimize the cost of storage, while ensuring that no more than one commodity is stored in any private facility.

Figure 10.15 shows the example from Chapter 8 structured as a network. The numbers on the branches represent the *savings* associated with storing a commodity in a facility. Savings are calculated by subtracting the compartment storage cost from the cost of storing in the public facility. In essence, this eliminates the variable corresponding to the public facility from the model. Supplies and capacities are written next to the nodes. We develop a heuristic by noting that, for any commodity-facility combination, the maximum amount that can be stored is the minimum of the commodity supply and the facility capacity. The total cost savings associated with the decision to use the commodity-facility combination is computed by multiplying the maximum amount that can be stored by the unit savings. If we did this for each commodity-facility combination, we could choose the allocation in a greedy fashion. We then delete the facility that was used, update any remaining supply, and repeat until all facilities have been used. Any remaining supply must be allocated to the public facility.

We can illustrate this approach to the example in Figure 10.15 by writing the total cost savings for each commodity-facility combination on the network branches. This is shown in Figure 10.16.

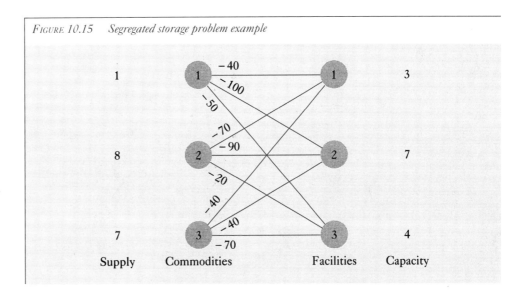

FIGURE 10.15   Segregated storage problem example

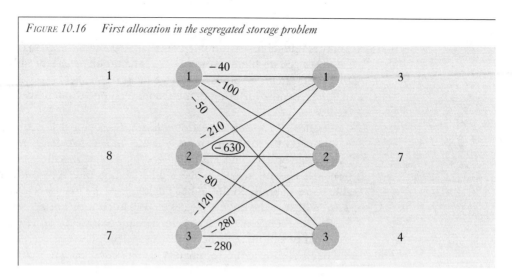

FIGURE 10.16   *First allocation in the segregated storage problem*

For example, the savings achieved by storing commodity 1 in facility 1 is (-40) times the minimum of 1 ton of supply and 3 tons of capacity, or $(-4)(1) = -40$. The largest savings occurs from assigning commodity 2 to facility 2. Because only 7 tons can be stored, 1 ton remains. Deleting facility 2 from further consideration results in the network shown in Figure 10.17. The next largest savings is associated with assigning 4 tons of commodity 3 to facility 3. The final allocation, shown in Figure 10.18, is to assign 3 tons of commodity 3 to facility 1. This happens, only by coincidence, to be the optimal solution!

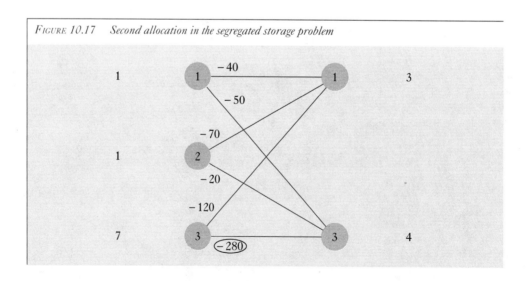

FIGURE 10.17   *Second allocation in the segregated storage problem*

FIGURE 10.18   *Third and final allocation in the segregated storage problem*

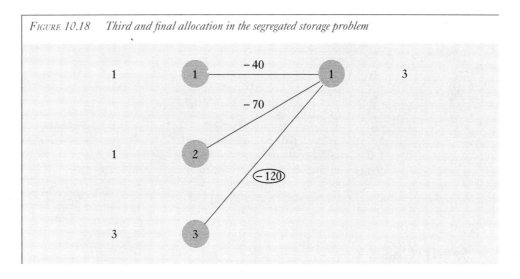

SUMMARY

Heuristics play an important role in management science by providing approaches to solving problems for which exact algorithms either do not exist or are difficult or time-consuming to implement. Heuristics are used

1. To provide good starting solutions to exact optimization algorithms.
2. As a fast solution method used to solve problems frequently or on a real-time basis.
3. To find good approximate solutions to difficult combinatorial optimization problems.

Although heuristics cannot guarantee an optimal solution, they are easy to understand and use and therefore are more readily accepted by managers. Two common heuristic approaches are the greedy method and the neighborhood search. These concepts can be applied to many diverse problems such as the traveling salesman problem, integer programming problems, and many other optimization problems.

Another heuristic-like approach to more complex management science problems is approximation. This is particularly useful when we must deal with nonlinearities in the objective function of a mathematical program. By approximating a nonlinear objective function with a linear function, we can take advantage of linear programming solvers and obtain good solutions.

Designing good heuristics remains a highly creative art. You can learn a lot by studying approaches to different problems and trying to apply the principles to other problems.

CHAPTER REVIEW EXERCISES

I. Terms to Understand

a. Heuristic (p. 503)
b. Northwest corner rule (p. 505)
c. Combinatorial optimization (p. 507)
d. Traveling salesman problem (p. 507)
e. Construction heuristic (p. 510)
f. Greedy heuristic (p. 510)
g. Improvement heuristic (p. 511)

h. 2-Change heuristic (p. 511)
i. Neighborhood search (p. 514)
j. Local optimum (p. 517)
k. Global optimum (p. 517)
l. Linear approximation (p. 519)
m. Critical ratio (p. 532)
n. Cycle time (p. 533)

II. Questions

1. List some heuristics that you use to guide your decision making every day.
2. How does a heuristic algorithm differ from an exact algorithm for an optimization problem? Explain as many features as you can.
3. Make a list of other practical combinatorial optimization problems from your experience at work or school.
4. How would you choose between using an exact algorithm or a heuristic algorithm?
5. State some other examples where the concepts of decomposition and partitioning might be used in developing a heuristic algorithm.
6. Can you think of a physical analogy to the neighborhood search? Can you think of examples when you have used this principle before?
7. List some specific applications of vehicle routing for which the Clarke-Wright heuristic might be used. What factors might complicate the straightforward use of this method?
8. How might you objectively evaluate a heuristic for simplicity, computational efficiency, accuracy, and robustness? Try to develop a "market research" evaluation scale for these criteria. How might this be used?
9. How might you use Hillier's guiding principles in improving the 2-change search heuristic for the TSP? Outline your ideas and apply them to an example (try the case at the end of this chapter).

III. Problems

1. Apply the northwest corner rule heuristic to the Coger Company problem (Problem 10) in Chapter 4.
2. A heuristic for finding an initial solution to a transportation problem is called the *minimum cost rule*. We start by locating the minimum unit cost in the transportation cost matrix, and then we ship as many units as possible between that origin and destination. Next, we move to the next-minimum cost and ship as much as possible. Continue until a feasible solution has been found.
   a. Apply the minimum cost rule to the MaBops, Inc. example.
   b. Apply the minimum cost rule to the Coger Company problem (Problem 10) in Chapter 4.
   c. Compare the results of this rule with the northwest corner rule. Using a standard programming language, which method would probably be faster to run on a computer?

3. Another heuristic for finding an initial solution to the transportation problem is called *Vogel's approximation method*. For each origin and each destination, we identify the least-cost route. Then we compute a penalty corresponding to the unit increase in cost if the *second-best* route must be used instead. We do this for each row and column. Once these penalties are computed, we make an allocation so that the largest penalty is avoided by allocating the shipment to the least-cost cell in the row or column with the largest penalty. After we do this, we must recompute the penalties, because supply or demand for some row or column will be exhausted. We continue until all the supply has been allocated.

    a. Apply this method to the MaBops example (Example 7, Chapter 4).

    b. Compare this heuristic to both the northwest corner rule and minimum-cost rule (Problem 2) using the criteria discussed in this chapter. In general, do you think that Vogel's method would give better solutions than the other methods? Why or why not?

4. The distances between six cities are given in the following matrix:

	1	2	3	4	5	6
1	—	2	1	3	6	3
2		—	3	4	8	5
3			—	4	6	2
4				—	4	5
5					—	8

Find solutions to the traveling salesman problem using the nearest-neighbor heuristic and the 2-change heuristic.

5. With tight budgets at Steger College, all memos and announcements are now routed among the faculty instead of being copied and distributed. The distances between faculty offices are given in the following table. What is the best way to route the memos and return them to the originator?

From To	1	2	3	4	5	6
1	0	9	8	7	6	10
2		0	10	9	15	20
3			0	5	15	25
4				0	20	5
5					0	20

6. Nancy Dennis, a college textbook sales representative, must find the most efficient way to travel from campus to campus. Her territory is Southern Ohio, which includes Miami University, Wright State, Central State, University of Cincinnati, Wilmington College, Ohio University, Dayton, Mt. St. Joseph, Otterbein, Ohio State, Rio Grande, Xavier, Shawnee State, and Wilberforce. Nancy determined the shortest distances between each pair of campuses, as shown in Table 10.5. How should she route her trip in order to visit all schools in the shortest distance?

TABLE 10.5
Distance
matrix for
Problem 6

	Miami	Wright St.	Central St.	UC	Wilmington	Ohio U.	Dayton	Mt. St. Joe	Otterbein	Ohio St.	Rio Grande	Xavier	Shawnee St.	Wilberforce
Miami	—	45	62	36	58	163	61	46	131	121	202	33	169	62
Wright St.		—	18	51	39	128	9	61	87	77	133	53	133	18
Central St.			—	56	21	125	12	66	62	52	115	58	123	1
UC				—	42	138	53	10	130	112	150	3	119	57
Wilmington					—	112	24	52	77	67	127	44	82	25
Ohio U.						—	134	148	84	74	40	140	71	127
Dayton							—	63	82	72	123	55	130	15
Mt. St. Joe								—	132	122	160	13	119	67
Otterbein									—	10	105	132	109	63
Ohio St.										—	95	114	99	53
Rio Grande											—	148	34	113
Xavier												—	122	59
Shawnee St.													—	124
Wilberforce														—

7. Solve the following 0-1 knapsack problem using the greedy and local search heuristics.

$$\text{Max} \quad z = 12x_1 + 8x_2 + 2x_3 + 7x_4 + 16x_5 + 5x_6$$

subject to

$$5x_1 + 2x_2 + 1x_3 + 7x_4 + 4_5 + 8x_6 \leq 13$$

$$x_j = 0, 1$$

8. Solve the following problem using the Clarke-Wright heuristic.

Customer	Demand
1	486
2	541
3	326
4	293
5	24
6	815
7	296

The vehicle capacity is 820, and the distance matrix is given in the following table.

	0	1	2	3	4	5	6
0	—						
1	19	—					
2	57	51					
3	51	10	49	—			
4	49	53	18	50	—		
5	4	25	30	11	68	—	
6	12	80	6	91	62	48	—
7	92	53	47	38	9	94	9

9. Using the direct-mail advertising problem in Chapter 8, develop an alternative heuristic that incorporates the cost of the mailing lists in your decisions.

10. Design a neighborhood search procedure for the direct-mail advertising problem and then apply it to the starting solution found in the chapter. (Example 13)

11. Design a neighborhood search procedure for the segregated storage problem and show that the solution found for the example is at least a local optimum.

12. Design a heuristic method for finding a minimum spanning tree when the number of branches connected to a particular node is restricted. This problem has applications in computer and communication networks. For example, one node might represent a central computing site, and the others might represent terminals that are linked to the central site. Restricting the number of branches connected to the central site guarantees that the computer's load is spread throughout the network.

13. A cellular telephone is subjected to a series of tests. Each test has a fixed cost and a probability that a phone will fail the test. We wish to sequence the tests in such a way that the expected cost of the test sequence is minimized.
    a. Using the following example, compute the costs for each possible sequence and find the optimum.
    b. Devise simple heuristics for finding a solution. Do you think that any of your methods might guarantee an optimum?

Test	Probability of failure	Cost/Item
Drop	.3	$.10
Heat	.05	.14
Vibration	.10	.20
Short	.40	.04
Visual defect	.15	.066

14. Suppose that you have M facilities with existing workloads. You have a group of N incoming jobs of a given size. You want to distribute the workload across the facilities in such a way as to balance the total workload as evenly as possible. Devise a heuristic method for solving this problem and apply it to the following scenario. We have four facilities with current workloads of 150, 170, 220, and 240, respectively. Eight jobs of size 100, 80, 70, 70, 40, 30, 20, and 10 have arrived.

15. There are five possible locations for no more than three new warehouses that will supply five customers. Up to three locations must be chosen on which to build warehouses, and each customer can be supplied

from only one warehouse. The objective is to minimize the total shipping costs from all warehouses to all customers, and no fixed costs are involved. Devise a heuristic method to solve this problem and apply it to the following cost data.

| | Warehouse Sites | | | | |
Customers	A	B	C	D	E
1	80	700	1300	1800	1700
2	1700	350	1300	2500	1800
3	2500	1200	300	1700	1950
4	2750	1650	550	700	850
5	19000	13000	8000	800	900

16. Solve the assembly line balancing problem in this chapter (Example 10), using the rule "choose the assignable operation with the least time first."

17. Consider the following assembly line balancing problem:

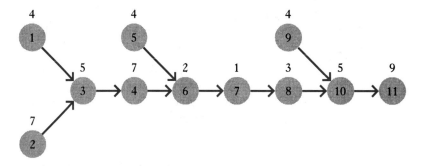

Solve this using both the "largest time first" and "smallest time first" heuristics. Use a cycle time of 10.

18. A building is to be designed in the following rectangular shape:

Assume that diagonal distances are 2 units and that horizontal/vertical distances between adjacent departments are 1 unit. Architects have estimated the frequency of movement between each pair of departments:

From/To	A	B	C	D	E	F
A	0	10	0	5	5	10
B	5	0	0	5	10	5
C	2	10	0	5	5	1
D	5	10	2	0	5	5
E	10	5	0	0	0	5
F	0	10	5	0	5	0

a. Devise a construction heuristic that will obtain a good solution.
b. Show how to use the concept of local search to improve any feasible solution. Apply it to your solution to part (a).

19. The *mean tardiness sequencing problem* is defined as follows. A set of jobs with due dates must be sequenced on a single processor so as to minimize the average tardiness. Tardiness is defined as the difference between the completion time of each job and its due date if the job is late, and is zero if the job is completed by the due date. A small example is given in the following table.

Job	Processing Time	Due Date
1	4	6
2	5	7
3	6	9
4	7	8

Develop at least two different heuristics for this problem and apply them to the example.

20. Use a heuristic approach to determine a good crashing schedule that will meet an 18-day deadline for the following project network:

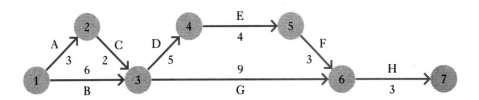

Activity	Unit cost	Maximum reduction
A	150	2
B	50	3
C	200	1
D	150	2
E	100	1
G	100	4

21. Many companies now use electronic data interchange to receive customer payments electronically from banks. A computer system can also automatically apply the payments to customers' accounts. When payment data are transmitted, the system must have a way of allocating the payment to various billing categories and "aging buckets" (such as 30–60 days, etc.). For example, suppose that a customer's account can be described as follows:

	Rent	Sales tax	Late charges	Maintenance	Property tax
Current	$4375.00	262.50	0.00	300.00	0.00
30–60 days	0.00	0.00	0.00	0.00	0.00
60–90 days	0.00	0.00	0.00	0.00	0.00
90–120 days	0.00	0.00	0.00	0.00	0.00
over 120 days	0.00	0.00	0.00	0.00	0.00

Total due: $4937.50

If the full amount of $4,937.50 is received, it can be allocated to all the accounts in the current time bucket in order to clear the account.

However, suppose that the account has the following profile:

	Rent	Sales tax	Late charges	Maintenance	Property tax
Current	$4375.00	262.50	0.00	300.00	0.00
30–60 days	4375.00	262.00	218.75	0.00	630.00
60–90 days	0.00	0.00	150.00	0.00	0.00
90–120 days	0.00	0.00	0.00	0.00	0.00
over 120 days	0.00	0.00	0.00	0.00	0.00

Total due: $10873.75

Suppose that the customer sends in a check for $7,000. How should this payment be allocated to the accounts? Design a heuristic that would allow the system to automatically allocate the payment among the accounts. Be sure that the heuristic is general enough to apply to any situation.

22. Consider the following exam scheduling problem. We would like to schedule the final exams for eight classes over four days. The fifth day is used for deferrals, which are granted to a students if they have more than one exam scheduled on a given day. Using the heuristic approach described in the Management Science Practice section, find a schedule that minimizes the number of deferrals. Assume that room capacity is not an issue and that there is only one exam period each day. The number of students that each pair of classes has in common is shown in Table 10.6.

TABLE 10.6
Data for
Problem 22

	Class							
	1	2	3	4	5	6	7	8
1	0	11	0	11	0	0	2	1
2		0	6	12	34	0	3	9
3			0	9	8	3	4	4
4				0	13	3	5	6
5					0	6	13	21
6						0	1	10
7							0	3
8								0

SA

23. The manager for a two-product line needs to decide how to allocate her print media advertising budget for the next quarter. The profit generated per dollar of advertising for each of the products has been estimated from past data, and these relationships are shown in Figure 10.19. The advertising budget

FIGURE 10.19   Data for Problem 23

Advertising $ (000)	Total Profit (000)
$0	$8.00
$1	$18.40
$2	$24.48
$3	$28.79
$4	$32.14
$5	$34.88
$6	$37.19
$7	$39.19
$8	$40.96

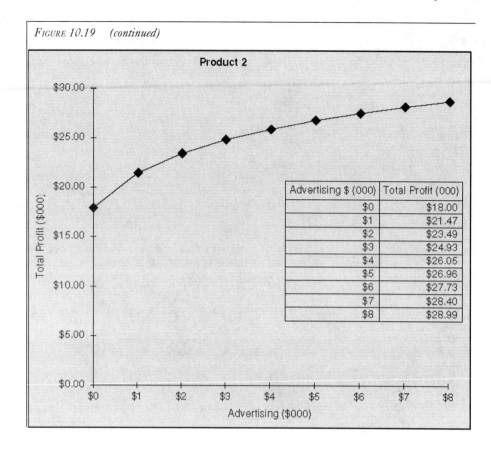

FIGURE 10.19   (continued)

Product 2

Advertising $ (000)	Total Profit (000)
$0	$18.00
$1	$21.47
$2	$23.49
$3	$24.93
$4	$26.05
$5	$26.96
$6	$27.73
$7	$28.40
$8	$28.99

for the coming quarter is $10,000, and at least $2,000 must be allocated to each product. Formulate and solve this allocation problem as a linear program using linear approximations of the functions. Use linear segments over intervals of $1,000.

IV. Projects and Cases

1. In 1962, the Procter & Gamble Company held a contest based on a popular television series *Car 54, Where Are You?* (Check your local cable listings!). The problem was a 33-city traveling salesman problem shown in Figure 10.20. The rules stated that "only completed sections of numbered 'National Interstate', 'U.S.', and 'State' highways are to be considered... Refer to Rand McNally Road Atlas, 1962 edition, which is the sole authority." Fifty-four $1,000 prizes and one $10,000 grand prize were awarded. Using the data given in Table 10.7, apply one or more heuristics and attempt to find a good solution.

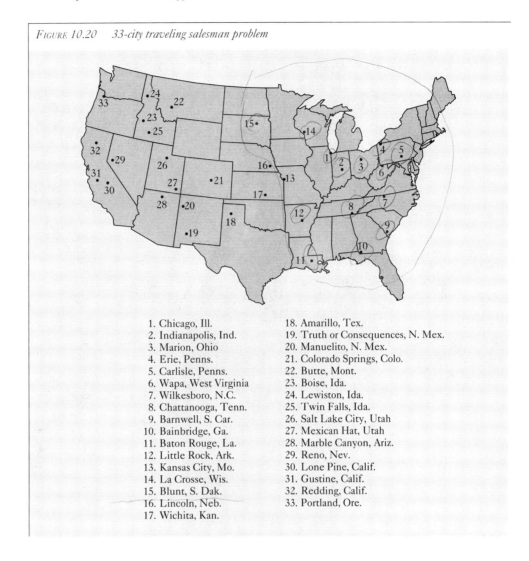

FIGURE 10.20   *33-city traveling salesman problem*

1. Chicago, Ill.	18. Amarillo, Tex.
2. Indianapolis, Ind.	19. Truth or Consequences, N. Mex.
3. Marion, Ohio	20. Manuelito, N. Mex.
4. Erie, Penns.	21. Colorado Springs, Colo.
5. Carlisle, Penns.	22. Butte, Mont.
6. Wapa, West Virginia	23. Boise, Ida.
7. Wilkesboro, N.C.	24. Lewiston, Ida.
8. Chattanooga, Tenn.	25. Twin Falls, Ida.
9. Barnwell, S. Car.	26. Salt Lake City, Utah
10. Bainbridge, Ga.	27. Mexican Hat, Utah
11. Baton Rouge, La.	28. Marble Canyon, Ariz.
12. Little Rock, Ark.	29. Reno, Nev.
13. Kansas City, Mo.	30. Lone Pine, Calif.
14. La Crosse, Wis.	31. Gustine, Calif.
15. Blunt, S. Dak.	32. Redding, Calif.
16. Lincoln, Neb.	33. Portland, Ore.
17. Wichita, Kan.	

2. Jim Wilson works for a company that advertises on benches at bus stops and other locations within cities. He must periodically change the advertising and this requires that he visit all locations in a particular city. One of Jim's responsibilities is Columbus, Ohio, which has 18 ad benches. Jim developed a map showing the locations, major streets, and travel times in minutes along each street. This is shown in Figure 10.21. Use the traveling salesman problem to help Jim find a good route, starting from node 0 (representing his initial entrance into the city).

3. (Finish Case 1 in Chapter 9 before beginning this problem.) Consider the county road network data given in Figure 9-43 in Chapter 9. The depot is at node 1, and the start and end fields denote the node numbers in the network. The last column tells whether or not the road requires salting. The county currently has four 10-ton trucks with which to salt the roads.

TABLE 10.7
Data for 33-city
problem

	1	2	3	4	5	6	7	8	9	10	11	12	13	14	15	16	17	18	19	20	21	22	23	24	25	26	27	28	29	30	31	32	33
1	0																																
2	184	0																															
3	292	195	0																														
4	449	310	215	0																													
5	670	540	380	288	0																												
6	516	357	232	200	211	0																											
7	598	514	434	566	436	381	0																										
8	618	434	493	787	814	642	295	0																									
9	881	697	719	790	632	697	224	320	0																								
10	909	964	955	1020	974	952	541	341	318	0																							
11	978	892	1031	1246	1352	1180	843	538	747	441	0																						
12	654	597	803	1018	1154	1104	766	461	749	634	380	0																					
13	504	503	722	937	1043	806	986	722	1042	954	784	404	0																				
14	276	460	568	725	946	817	874	894	1214	1185	1218	660	452	0																			
15	780	964	1072	1229	1450	1321	1378	1326	1646	1672	1410	1030	626	476	0																		
16	529	644	789	1004	1184	1001	1214	950	1270	1213	1043	632	219	436	419	0																	
17	805	698	917	1132	1238	1055	1113	842	1162	1027	473	195	634	1138	783	256	0																
18	1181	1007	1226	1441	1547	1364	1375	1080	1375	1239	783	473	1046	624	759	563	368	0															
19	1548	1444	1630	1845	1984	1801	1726	1431	1685	1477	1134	1033	1389	967	1094	906	711	404	0														
20	1547	1454	1668	1883	1994	1811	1879	1584	1776	1632	1267	1053	1427	1005	1196	944	749	442	251	0													
21	1239	1167	1353	1568	1707	1524	1584	1313	1633	1498	1151	979	988	525	600	614	471	368	512	507	0												
22	1538	1733	1830	2045	2208	2090	2136	2078	2398	2332	1782	1378	1300	760	1229	1382	1319	1163	930	910	910	0											
23	1999	2158	2291	2448	2669	2515	2597	2500	2820	2675	2336	2164	1707	1860	1375	1582	1658	1545	1389	1156	1237	436	0										
24	1716	1875	2008	2165	2386	2232	2488	2217	2537	2392	2053	1881	1422	1577	1106	1244	1375	1262	1106	873	954	483	283	0									
25	1580	1738	1872	2029	2250	2095	2081	2352	2401	2256	1917	1745	1286	1473	988	1147	1239	1126	970	737	818	379	419	136	0								
26	1425	1569	1717	1874	2109	1926	2115	2115	2164	2019	1680	1508	1118	1335	862	913	1002	889	733	500	581	430	656	373	237	0							
27	1560	1549	1852	2009	2089	1906	1906	2063	1967	1456	1274	1032	1540	1068	1007	944	665	521	282	491	768	994	711	575	603	358	0						
28	1918	1744	1963	2178	2284	2101	2174	1879	2071	1892	1562	1348	1239	1722	1258	1300	1044	737	526	295	802	816	715	432	533	386	545	0					
29	2065	2102	2357	2514	2642	2459	2355	2626	2530	2191	2019	1673	1905	1432	1570	1507	1320	1109	878	842	1124	1022	739	465	849	603	739	739	0				
30	2284	2131	2326	2441	2488	2488	2418	2123	2259	1929	1715	1606	1451	1589	1411	1104	893	662	1143	1004	981	715	599	768	589	768	523	266	0				
31	2340	2348	2543	2658	2888	2705	2869	2598	2773	2434	2262	1916	2148	1675	1813	1750	1468	1102	871	1367	1085	958	675	1033	778	1092	982	243	349	0			
32	2247	2327	2539	2696	2867	2684	2851	2580	2755	2416	2244	1898	2130	1657	1795	1732	1545	1334	1103	1349	1014	814	531	1015	760	1047	964	225	497	266	0		
33	2163	2322	2455	2612	2833	2679	2761	2664	2984	2839	2500	2328	1871	1539	1746	1822	1709	1553	1320	1391	693	346	447	583	820	1158	1355	581	847	710	444	0	
	1	2	3	4	5	6	7	8	9	10	11	12	13	14	15	16	17	18	19	20	21	22	23	24	25	26	27	28	29	30	31	32	33

Source: Rand-McNally Road Atlas, 38th Edition, Rand McNally Company: 1962

FIGURE 10.21   *Jim Wilson's map of Columbus, Ohio*

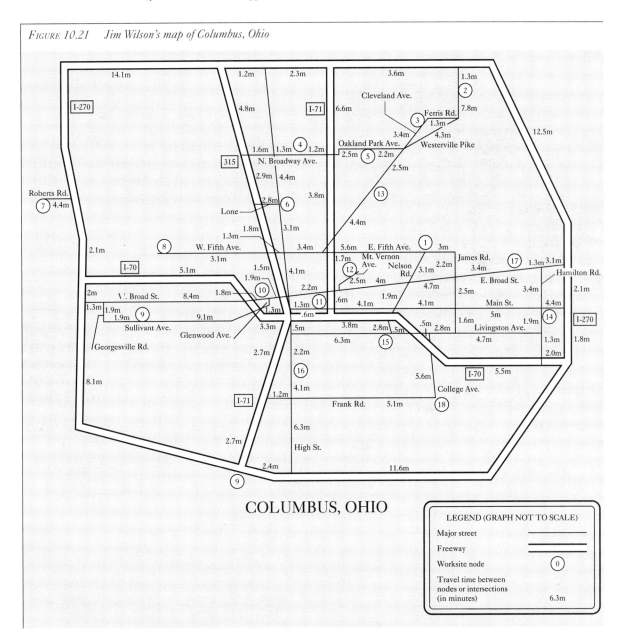

COLUMBUS, OHIO

LEGEND (GRAPH NOT TO SCALE)	
Major street	
Freeway	
Worksite node	⓪
Travel time between nodes or intersections (in minutes)	6.3m

a.   Develop routes that efficiently make use of the trucks. Can any trucks be retired or sold?

b.   The county has the option of replacing any of their fleet with 7- or 12-ton trucks. Should they do so?

c.   A loudmouth local politician is demanding that all the roads be serviced within 1.5 hours. What is the best fleet configuration? You might wish to put the data on a spreadsheet in order to facilitate your calculations.

REFERENCES

Ball, Michael and Michael Magazine. "The Design and Analysis of Heuristics." *Networks*, Vol. 11, 1981, pp. 215–219.

Bartholdi, John J. III, Loren K. Platzman, R. Lee Collins, and William H. Warden III. "A Minimal Technology Routing System for Meals on Wheels." *Interfaces*, Vol. 13, No. 3, June 1983, pp. 1–8.

Cornuejols, Gerard, Marshall L. Fisher, and George L. Nemhauser. "Location of Bank Accounts to Optimize Float: An Analytic Study of Exact and Approximate Algorithms." *Management Science*, Vol. 23, No. 8, April 1977, pp. 789–810.

Evans, James R. *Applied Production and Operations Management*, 4th ed. St. Paul: West Publishing Co., 1993.

Evans, James R. and Frank H. Cullen. "The Segregated Storage Problem: Some Properties and an Effective Heuristic." *AIIE Transactions*, Vol. 9, No. 4, December 1977, pp. 409–413.

Evans, James R. and Edward Minieka. *Optimization Algorithms for Networks and Graphs*, 2nd ed. Revised and Expanded. New York: Marcel Dekker, 1992.

Farrell, James L., Jr. "A Disciplined Stock Selection Strategy." *Interfaces*, Vol. 12, No. 5, October 1982, pp. 19–30.

Foulds, L. R. "The Heuristic Problem-Solving Approach." *Journal of the Operational Research Society*, Vol. 34, No. 10, 1983, pp. 927–934.

Garfinkel, Robert S. and George L. Nemhauser. *Integer Programming*. New York: Wiley, 1972.

Henderson, Willie B. and William L. Berry. "Heuristic Methods for Telephone Operator Shift Scheduling: An Experimental Analysis." *Management Science*, Vol. 22, No. 12, August 1976, pp. 1372–1380.

Hillier, Frederick S. "Heuristics: A Gambler's Roll." *Interfaces*, Vol. 13, No. 3, June 1983, pp. 9–12.

Michael, George C. "A Review of Heuristic Programming." *Decision Sciences*, Vol. 3, 1972, pp. 74–100.

Muller-Merbach, Heiner. "Heuristics and Their Design: A Survey." *European Journal of Operational Research*, Vol. 8, 1981, pp. 1–23.

Russell, Robert A. and Reece B. Morrel. "Routing Special-Education School Buses." *Interfaces*, Vol. 16, No. 5, September–October 1986, pp. 56–64.

Silver, Edward A., R. Victor, V. Vidal, and Dominique de Werra. "A Tutorial on Heuristic Methods." *European Journal of Operational Research*, Vol. 5, 1980, pp. 153–162.

Zanakis, Stelios H. and James R. Evans. "Heuristic 'Optimization': Why, When, and How to Use It." *Interfaces*, Vol. 11, No. 5, October 1981, pp. 84–91.

Zanakis, Stelios H., James R. Evans, and Alkis A. Vazacopoulos. "Heuristic Methods and Applications: A Categorized Survey." *European Journal of Operational Research*, Vol. 43, 1989, pp. 88–110.

PART 3

PROBABILISTIC MODELS IN MANAGEMENT SCIENCE

CHAPTER 11

PROBABILISTIC AND STATISTICAL MODELING

INTRODUCTION

- The tiles of the space shuttle orbiter are critical to its safety at reentry, and their maintenance between flights is time-consuming. NASA consultants developed a probabilistic model to identify the most risk-critical tiles and set priorities in the management of the heat shield. The model included data on the probability of debonding due either to debris hits or to a poor bond, the probability of losing adjacent tiles once the first one is lost, the probability of burn-through given tile loss, and the probability of failure of a critical subsystem under the skin of the orbiter if a burn-through occurs. The model found that 15 percent of the tiles account for about 85 percent of the risk, and that some of the most critical tiles are not in the hottest areas of the orbiter's surface. This helps to set priorities for maintenance, which are estimated to reduce the probability of a shuttle accident attributable to tile failure by about 70 percent [Pate-Cornell and Fischbeck, 1994].

- Managers at Hallmark Cards face critical decision problems in determining the run size or purchase quantity for its merchandise in the face of uncertain demand. For many products, such as calendars, historical sales figures for prior years provide an objective basis for assessing demand uncertainty. On the other hand, for new theme promotions, no historical precedents are available, and demand must be assessed subjectively. Hallmark managers were trained to express their uncertainty in terms of subjective probability judgments and use simple probabilistic decision models that incorporate this information. Using these models, product managers are better able to balance product economics and demand uncertainty, and the entire product management team can better understand, estimate, communicate, and evaluate the impact of uncertainty. In many applications, the contribution to profitability has been substantial [Barron, 1985].

- The Manitoba Telephone System (MTS) wanted to forecast demand for telephones in order to control the inventory in their phone centers. The company's goal was to ensure that 95 percent of demand should be met from inventory. A number of standard forecasting models that were applied to predict customer demand simply did not work because the assumptions required by the models were not satisfied by the data. Instead, a simple intuitive approach was developed using historical data. The model was tested using actual data from a prior year. This analysis showed that service levels could be met consistently using the model and also revealed problems that required human intervention. Nevertheless, the model enabled the company to reduce its stock level by 45 percent and realize significant savings in capital investment [Cohen and Dunford, 1986].

In each of these scenarios, probabilistic and statistical modeling played an important role. An article in the *Harvard Business Review* began with the statement, "Risk, complexity, and uncertainty define the business environment of the 1990s."[1] To better appreciate

---

[1] Nancy A. Nichols, "Scientific Management at Merck: An Interview with CFO Judy Lewent," *Harvard Business Review*, January–February 1994, pp. 89–99.

the truth of this statement, consider the influence diagram developed by an internal consulting group at Du Pont shown in Figure 11.1. This diagram shows the critical decisions and uncertainties that would affect the net present value (NPV), the criterion on which strategic planning decision would be made for one of Du Pont's business units. The actual situation was even more complex, as the uncertainty assessments had to be performed for several different product types in each of three regions.

Probabilistic models and statistical methods are an important part of analysis and problem solving in management science. This is true because, in most practical situations, *the future is uncertain*. Nearly every business decision is subject to *risk*—the chance of an

FIGURE 11.1   *Influence diagram for NPV analysis at Du Pont*

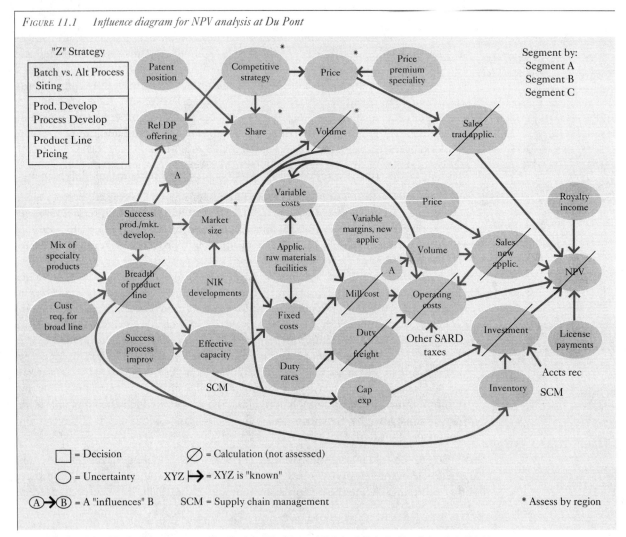

Figure from Krumm and Rolle, "Management and Application of Decision and Risk Analysis in Du Pont," *Interfaces*, Vol. 22, No. 6, Nov–Dec 1992, pp. 84–93.

undesirable consequence such as financial loss. Decision-makers must be able to determine whether a risk is acceptable and what actions should be taken. Like deterministic models, probabilistic models may be descriptive or prescriptive. Descriptive probabilistic models provide an evaluation of decision alternatives to assess the effects of uncertainty and our ability to predict future outcomes. Prescriptive probabilistic models seek the best solution, usually in an expected value sense.

In this chapter we focus on four fundamental issues of probabilistic and statistical modeling:

1. Approaches to modeling uncertainty and analyzing risk
2. Solving probabilistic optimization models
3. The role of statistics in applied management science
4. Forecasting models

The remaining chapters in this book extend these concepts and discuss specific types of models and techniques for dealing with risk and uncertainty in decision making. We assume that the reader has had an introductory course in business statistics. Thus, our focus will be on applications rather than theory development.

Yeah, right,

APPLICATIONS OF PROBABILISTIC AND STATISTICAL MODELS

In this section we describe several examples of probabilistic and statistical models in management science.

- Location is one of the most important decisions for a lodging firm. All hotel chains search for ideal locations and in many cases compete against each other for the same sites. La Quinta Motor Inns, a mid-sized hotel chain that is headquartered in San Antonio, Texas, developed a statistical model that predicted profitability for sites under construction. Input variables were grouped into five categories: competitive factors, demand generators, demographic factors, market awareness, and physical factors. The dependent variable, occupancy, proved to be a very unstable indicator of success; La Quinta settled on forecasting operating margin, which consisted of adding depreciation and interest expenses to profit and dividing by the total revenue. The model was incorporated into a spreadsheet decision model that management uses for selecting sites to minimize the risk of picking an unprofitable site [Kimes and Fitzsimmons, 1990].

- Prudential Securities, Inc., (PSI) uses probabilistic models to quickly and accurately value and trade complex mortgage-backed securities, to properly hedge these securities in inventory, and to structure clients' portfolios to achieve given objectives. One critical model estimates the likely rates of prepayments under different interest-rate and economic environments. The prepayment model is partitioned into four components: housing turnover, refinancing activity, defaults, and all other factors. Modeling of housing turnover, for example, requires the projection of existing home sales for a specified interest rate and economic environment. This projection is adjusted for seasonal variations. By projecting the other three components, PSI can estimate the prepayment rate for the security for a particular month. The model generates a month-by-month schedule of prepayment projections for the remaining term of the security [Ben-Dov et al., 1992].

- In support of the National Materiel Distribution System study, the Operational Research and Analysis Establishment within the Canadian Department of National Defence was asked to examine the operating aspects of the materiel traffic activity in the Canadian Forces. The purpose of the study was to determine whether the system met the approved system objectives: to deliver materiel safely, on time, and at least cost to its destination. Using a random sample of the traffic activity in the western region of Canada, data were collected and analyzed to establish the effectiveness and efficiency of the traffic movement. Statistical inference was used to analyze the performance of the entire materiel traffic system. For example, the analysis established predictions of the percentage of shipments that are delivered before their due dates using low-cost efficiency transport. The findings led to recommendations to improve transportation policies and reduce costs [Ng et al., 1987].

- One of the more difficult jobs confronting hospital administrators is estimating the levels of nurse staffing to meet patient requirements. The further in advance these estimates can be made, the easier it is to plan levels of staffing, vacation time, and training programs. In one short-term acute-care hospital, data from daily reports by shift, ward, and intensity-of-care levels were used to develop statistical models to predict the number of patients in each level of care and, hence, labor requirements. The model supported intuition with more precise information that allowed, for example, hospital management to include part-time nursing schedules in the decision process [Helmer et al., 1980].

- Coaches of sports teams face uncertain decisions all the time. In professional football, for instance, an important decision is whether to attempt a field goal with short yardage required for first down, or to try for the first down. Such decisions are usually made by gut feelings rather than quantitative analysis. Virgil Carter, a former NFL quarterback, and Robert Machol applied statistical analysis to evaluate football strategies. For example, they showed that the expected value of having the ball with first down and 10 yards to go varies from about -1.64 points at one's own goal line and improves at the rate of about $\frac{1}{14}$ point per yard up to about 10 yards from the opponent's goal line, with a larger increase per yard over the last 10 yards. A further analysis of field goal attempts showed that inside the 30-yard line, the run is preferred to the field goal attempt if there are one or two yards to go, and possibly with three. Inside the 10-yard line, the run is preferred to the field goal attempt with up to 5 yards to go. These results are contrary to practice, but many coaches continue to employ the field goal far more than the analysis indicates [Carter and Machol, 1971, 1978].

PROBABILISTIC MODELING AND RISK ANALYSIS

In a deterministic model, such as a linear or integer program, any choice of decision variables leads to a certain outcome. For example, in the knapsack problem (Example 1 in Chapter 4), once the amount of each commodity to haul is decided, we know the total weight of the haul and the total profit. Solution procedures like the simplex method can search efficiently over the range of potential solutions to find the optimal solution. In a real situation, the weight of each commodity and the unit profit can be measured or estimated quite accurately; there should be no uncertainty in any of these model parameters. Thus, we would expect that model predictions will match closely with actual outcomes.

Many decision problems in management science involve the future. As we all know, in the real world, the future is far from certain. Even so, we often assume certainty to develop models that are easy to manipulate or solve. For example, in the Grad & Sons portfolio selection model (Example 8 in Chapter 4), one of the constraints states that the expected return should be at least $40,000. In this model, we *assumed* that the expected rates of return for the four investment options (the constraint coefficients) are fixed. This assumption allows us to formulate and solve the problem as a linear program. However, from any finance courses that you may have taken and from your own experience, you know that future rates of return on stocks and bonds are by no means certain. In addition, the objective function is a subjective estimate of risk per dollar invested. Such judgments are often "best guesses" and are fraught with uncertainty. After the investments are made, we have no assurances that the expected return will actually satisfy the constraint or that the minimum predicted risk will be the same as the actual risk incurred.

We see that we must often make a choice between using a deterministic or a probabilistic model. If we can reasonably assume that uncertain values can be estimated or predicted accurately, then a deterministic model is appropriate. However, if uncertainty is a critical factor, and *if it is important to capture its effect*, then it should be included in the modeling process.

We introduced *risk analysis*—the study of the effects of uncertainty in decision making—briefly in Chapter 2 as an important application of spreadsheets in management science. Many financial models incorporate risk and provide valuable input in decision making. For instance, in preparing a budget, there is usually some uncertainty about future costs. "Fixed" costs such as payroll may vary as employees are hired, leave, or receive promotions during the budget cycle. Variable costs, such as operating supplies and maintenance, are also uncertain. By making assumptions about the nature of this uncertainty, planners can assess the risk of failing to meet a budget or use the information to determine a budget level that meets a prescribed level of risk.

In modeling uncertainty, we may assume either a continuous distribution or a discrete set of values. In the following sections we describe approaches for dealing with each of these situations.

Probabilistic Modeling with Continuous Distributions

When model parameters assume continuous values, we must use continuous probability distributions in our analyses. Table 11.1 summarizes formulas for combining probabilistic variables. When the variables are independent, the correlation coefficient, r, is zero, resulting in considerable simplification.

TABLE 11.1
Formulas for combining probabilistic variables

Function	Mean	Variance[a]
Sum $(x + y)$	$\mu_x + \mu_y$	$\sigma_x^2 + \sigma_y^2 + 2r\sigma_x\sigma_y$
Difference $(x - y)$	$\mu_x - \mu_y$	$\sigma_x^2 + \sigma_y^2 - 2r\sigma_x\sigma_y$
Product $(x \cdot y)$	$\mu_x\mu_y + r_{xy}\sigma_x\sigma_y$	$\mu_x^2\sigma_x^2 + \mu_x^2\sigma_y^2 + 2\mu_x\mu_y r\sigma_x\sigma_y^b$
Quotient (x/y)	μ_x/μ_y^b	$\left(\frac{1}{\mu_y}\right)^2\sigma_x^2 + \left(-\frac{\mu_x^2}{\mu_y^3}\right)^2\sigma_y^2 + 2\left(\frac{1}{\mu_2}\right)\left(\frac{-\mu_x}{\mu_y^3}\right)r\sigma_x\sigma_y^b$

[a] r is the correlation coefficient between x and y.
[b] Approximate for both independent and dependent x and y.

EXAMPLE 1. FINANCIAL RISK ANALYSIS

Suppose that a division determines that its fixed costs are normally distributed with a mean of \$50,000 and a standard deviation of \$4,000, and that variable costs are also normal with a mean of \$100,000 and a standard deviation of \$10,000. Assuming independence, the distribution of total cost is found as follows.

The mean total cost is the sum of the means of the fixed costs and variable costs:

$$\mu_{TC} = \mu_F + \mu_V$$
$$= \$50,000 + \$100,000$$
$$= \$150,000$$

The variance of the total cost is

$$\sigma_{TC}^2 = \sigma_F^2 + \sigma_V^2$$
$$= (4,000)^2 + (10,000)^2$$
$$= 116,000,000$$

Thus, the standard deviation of total cost is $\sqrt{116,000,000} = 10,770$. Figure 11.2 summarizes the distributions of the individual variables and their sum.

Suppose that we wish to set a budget so that there is only a 5 percent chance of exceeding either the allocation to fixed costs or to variable costs. From the distribution of fixed costs, we see that the fixed cost budget, B_F, must satisfy

$$\frac{B_F - 50,000}{4,000} = 1.645$$

The value 1.645 is found from Appendix A and represents the value of a standard normal distribution with an upper-tail probability of 0.05. Solving this equation, we find that $B_F = \$56,580$. Similarly, the variable cost budget, B_V, must satisfy

$$\frac{B_V - 100,000}{10,000} = 1.645$$

Thus, $B_V = \$116,450$.

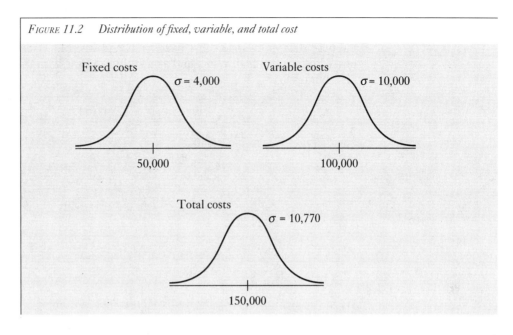

FIGURE 11.2   *Distribution of fixed, variable, and total cost*

The total budget is $B = B_F + B_V = \$56,580 + \$116,450 = \$173,030$. The risk that this budget will be exceeded is found by computing the probability that the total cost will exceed $173,030. The standard normal value corresponding to this level is

$$\frac{173,030 - 150,000}{10,770} = 2.138$$

Rounding 2.138 to 2.14, from Appendix A, we find the upper-tail probability to be .0162. Thus, there is less than a 2 percent chance that the budget will not be met. What overall budget level will provide a 5 percent risk of falling short?

Continuous distributions are often difficult to work with mathematically because analytical solutions may require techniques of calculus with which many readers may not be familiar. (In Chapter 13 we will see how to use computer simulation to get around this problem.) To simplify the calculations, we often use a discrete distribution to represent the range of possible values. Remember, models are *approximations* of reality, and even with such assumptions the results may be entirely adequate for making a decision.

Probabilistic Modeling with Discrete Distributions

Discrete probability distributions have a finite range of values. This can greatly simplify calculations but may result in a loss of accuracy and realism.

EXAMPLE 2. FINANCIAL RISK ANALYSIS-PART 2

Suppose that we estimate that fixed costs and variable costs can assume three values, a low value, a high value, and a most likely value, with the following probability distributions:

Fixed costs	Probability
$40,000	.20
$50,000	.60
$60,000	.20

Variable costs	Probability
$ 80,000	.25
$100,000	.50
$120,000	.25

We have nine possible combinations of outcomes. Assuming independence, the probability of each outcome is the product of the individual probabilities. We may summarize these outcomes and their associated probabilities in the following table.

Fixed costs	Variable costs	Total costs	Probability
40,000	80,000	120,000	(.2)(.25) = .05
40,000	100,000	140,000	(.2)(.50) = .10
40,000	120,000	160,000	(.2)(.25) = .05
50,000	80,000	130,000	(.6)(.25) = .15
50,000	100,000	150,000	(.6)(.50) = .30
50,000	120,000	170,000	(.6)(.25) = .15
60,000	80,000	140,000	(.2)(.25) = .05
60,000	100,000	160,000	(.2)(.50) = .10
60,000	120,000	180,000	(.2)(.25) = .05

We may summarize this information with the following probability distribution:

Total costs	Probability
$120,000	.05
$130,000	.15
$140,000	.15
$150,000	.30
$160,000	.15
$170,000	.15 ←
$180,000	.05

85% ?

Under these assumptions, a budget of $170,000, for example, will be met 95 percent of the time.

Selecting an Appropriate Distribution

One of the difficult tasks of probabilistic modeling is selecting an appropriate probability distribution for the probabilistic components of a model.[2] There are two principal ways to do this: (1) collect and analyze data and (2) estimate probabilities judgmentally. We first consider data analysis.

Data Analysis. When sufficient historical data are available, long-run probabilities may be estimated from the relative proportion of occurrences. The first thing to do is to develop a frequency distribution and histogram and compute estimates of key parameters such as the mean and standard deviation. We may develop an empirical probability distribution from the histogram and use this in our analyses.

EXAMPLE 3. SELECTING A DISTRIBUTION THROUGH DATA ANALYSIS

Figure 11.3 shows a spreadsheet for five years of monthly demand for a product. Using basic statistical calculations, we find that the average demand is 49.25 and the standard deviation is approximately 6.49. The frequency distribution and histogram show that the demand is roughly symmetric, varying from 32 to 65. The probability distribution is obtained by dividing the frequency of each cell by the total number of observations (60). This distribution might be used to assess the risk of running out of stock if a certain inventory level is maintained. For instance, to avoid a high carrying cost, the company might not wish to carry more than 55 units in stock each month. The probability that demand will exceed 55 is estimated to be $.133 + .050 = .183$, or about 18 percent.

In some situations, historical data will show some strange observations, or "outliers," that do not seem to coincide with the rest of the distribution. These might be due to some special cause such as measurement error or chance. Many people have a tendency to exclude them as nonrepresentative of the true pattern of variation. If there is reason to believe that outliers are due to chance, they should not be excluded from the data.

The purpose of data analysis is to make generalizations about the nature of the random variable we are modeling. One of the drawbacks of using an empirical probability distribution is that it may have certain irregularities, especially if we only have a small number of observations. Assuming that the data represent some underlying population, we would like to be able to capture the essence of the entire population. We may do this by fitting one of the well-studied theoretical distributions to our data.

---

[2]An excellent (though more advanced) treatment of this topic can be found in Averill M. Law and W. David Kelton, *Simulation Modeling and Analysis*, New York: McGraw-Hill, 1992.

FIGURE 11.3   *Spreadsheet analysis of demand data*

	A	B	C	D	E	F
1	Monthly Demand					
2						
3	56	52	52	32	50	50
4	46	47	55	40	49	56
5	48	48	52	52	40	50
6	50	56	44	51	54	52
7	42	41	50	52	46	37
8	43	37	45	59	51	61
9	49	47	44	63	48	41
10	48	47	65	59	54	56
11	56	45	48	47	49	58
12	50	44	48	38	50	55
13						
14	Average		49.25			
15	Standard deviation		6.492624			
16	Minimum		32			
17	Maximum		65			
18						
19	Cell	Frequency	Probability			
20	30-35	1	0.017			
21	36-40	5	0.083			
22	41-45	9	0.150			
23	46-50	22	0.367			
24	51-55	12	0.200			
25	56-60	8	0.133			
26	61-65	3	0.050			
27						
28						

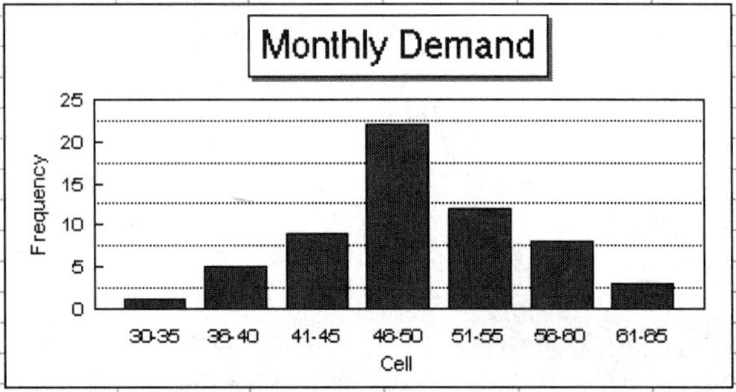

We may wish to fit a theoretical distribution to our available empirical data for the following reasons:

1. A theoretical distribution allows for extreme events that may not be present in the empirical data. Often the assessment of risk depends upon the probability of these extreme values.
2. Using a theoretical distribution "smooths out" any irregularities that may exist in the empirical data.

Many standard types of probability distributions are used to model probabilistic phenomena. The most common continuous distributions are the *uniform, exponential, triangular, and normal* distributions. Characteristics of these distributions are summarized in Figure 11.4. The uniform distribution is often used when a quantity is known to vary between two extremes but little else is known about it. The exponential distribution is used extensively in modeling arrivals of customers to service systems and times to perform tasks. The normal distribution applies when the quantity of interest is a sum of a large number of other quantities (you might recall the central limit theorem from statistics). Finally, the triangular distribution is used often as a rough model in the absence of data when we estimate variation judgmentally. Other distributions, such as the gamma, lognormal, Weibull, and beta, are used in practice but are beyond the introductory scope of this text.

Useful discrete distributions include the discrete uniform and Poisson distributions. These are summarized in Figure 11.5. The discrete uniform distribution, like its continuous counterpart, is often used when few empirical data are available. The Poisson distribution models the number of events that occur in an interval of time or space, when the rate of occurrence is constant. It is often used in inventory situations to model demand.

The first step in selecting a particular distribution is to decide what general type of distribution may be appropriate. This can be done by examining the histogram of data and comparing its shape with various theoretical distributions. A normal distribution is symmetric about the mean; this might be an appropriate model for the data in Figure 11.3. Sometimes knowledge of the variable's role in the model will suggest an appropriate distribution. For example, the interarrival times of customers to service systems often follow an exponential distribution. Another way of hypothesizing a distribution is to compute the parameters of the distribution. For example, in Figure 11.4 we see that the variance of an exponential distribution is equal to the square of its mean. If the computed mean and variance have this relationship and the shape appears to be exponential, then this provides more evidence that an exponential distribution is appropriate.

Once we have determined a possible distribution that might fit the observed data, we need to decide the quality of the fit. This might be done heuristically by simply comparing the frequencies of the empirical data with the expected frequencies of the theoretical distribution. A more formal approach is to use a goodness of fit test. This is a statistical test of hypothesis to assess formally whether the observed data are a sample from a particular distribution.

A popular technique is the *Chi-square goodness of fit test.* To apply the Chi-square test, we group the data into k cells having at least five observations each and compute the expected number of observations in each of these cells for the hypothesized distribution. The Chi-square test examines the differences in the observed and expected frequencies. Large differences suggest that the distributional assumption should be rejected, whereas small differences do not provide sufficient evidence to reject this hypothesis.

Let f_i be the observed frequency in cell i and e_i the expected frequency. The Chi-square statistic is

$$\chi^2 = \sum_{i=1}^{k} \frac{(f_i - e_i)^2}{e_i}$$

FIGURE 11.4   *Common continuous probability distributions in management science*

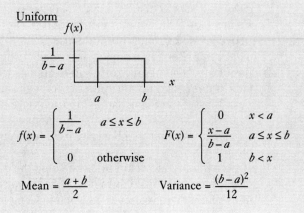

Uniform

$$f(x) = \begin{cases} \dfrac{1}{b-a} & a \leq x \leq b \\ 0 & \text{otherwise} \end{cases} \qquad F(x) = \begin{cases} 0 & x < a \\ \dfrac{x-a}{b-a} & a \leq x \leq b \\ 1 & b < x \end{cases}$$

$$\text{Mean} = \frac{a+b}{2} \qquad\qquad \text{Variance} = \frac{(b-a)^2}{12}$$

FIGURE 11.4   *(continued)*

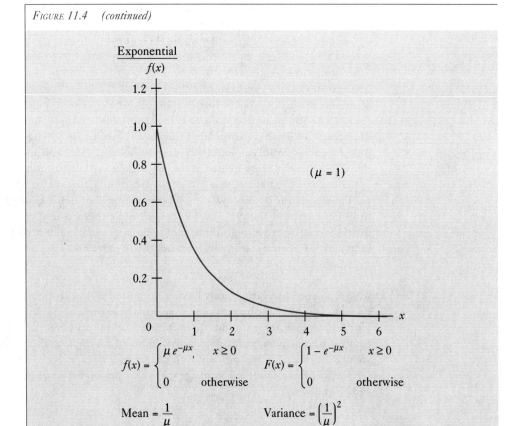

Exponential

$(\mu = 1)$

$$f(x) = \begin{cases} \mu\, e^{-\mu x}, & x \geq 0 \\ 0 & \text{otherwise} \end{cases} \qquad F(x) = \begin{cases} 1 - e^{-\mu x} & x \geq 0 \\ 0 & \text{otherwise} \end{cases}$$

$$\text{Mean} = \frac{1}{\mu} \qquad\qquad \text{Variance} = \left(\frac{1}{\mu}\right)^2$$

FIGURE 11.4   (continued)

Normal

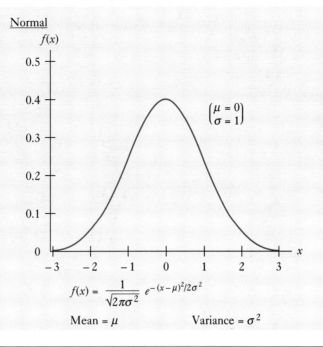

$$f(x) = \frac{1}{\sqrt{2\pi\sigma^2}} \, e^{-(x-\mu)^2/2\sigma^2}$$

Mean $= \mu$ Variance $= \sigma^2$

FIGURE 11.4   (continued)

Triangular

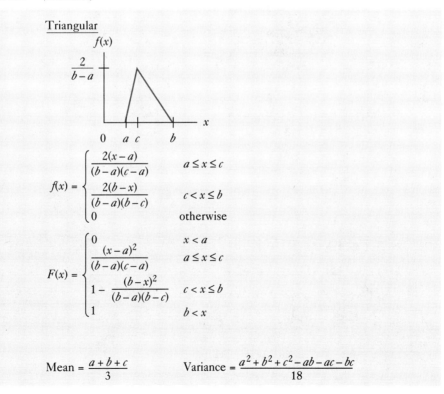

$$f(x) = \begin{cases} \dfrac{2(x-a)}{(b-a)(c-a)} & a \le x \le c \\[2mm] \dfrac{2(b-x)}{(b-a)(b-c)} & c < x \le b \\[2mm] 0 & \text{otherwise} \end{cases}$$

$$F(x) = \begin{cases} 0 & x < a \\[2mm] \dfrac{(x-a)^2}{(b-a)(c-a)} & a \le x \le c \\[2mm] 1 - \dfrac{(b-x)^2}{(b-a)(b-c)} & c < x \le b \\[2mm] 1 & b < x \end{cases}$$

Mean $= \dfrac{a+b+c}{3}$ Variance $= \dfrac{a^2 + b^2 + c^2 - ab - ac - bc}{18}$

569

FIGURE 11.5   *Common discrete probability distributions in management science*

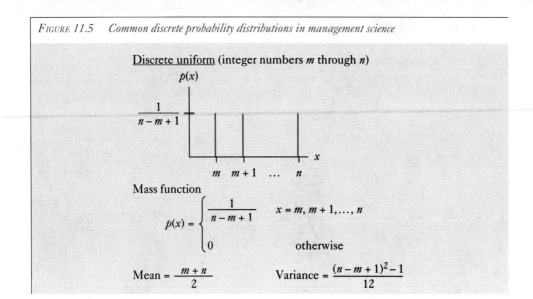

FIGURE 11.5   *(continued)*

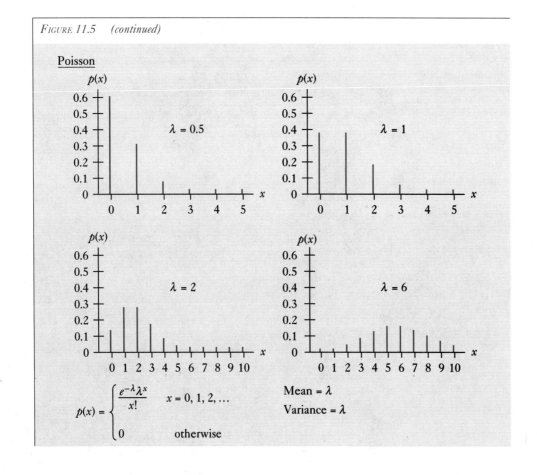

This statistic has a Chi-square distribution with $k - 1 - t$ degrees of freedom, where k is the total number of cells and t is the number of parameters that were estimated from the data. We accept the distributional assumption if $\chi^2 \leq \chi^2_\alpha$ and reject it if $\chi^2 > \chi^2_\alpha$, where α is the significance level of the test. Critical values of Chi-square can be found in Appendix B.

EXAMPLE 4. APPLYING THE CHI-SQUARE TEST

As we noted, it would be reasonable to suspect that the data in Figure 11.3 follow a normal distribution. To apply the Chi-square test, we first need to group the cells to ensure that each group has at least five observations. Thus, we will combine the first two and the last two cells. Figure 11.6 shows the probabilities corresponding to each cell from a normal distribution with the observed mean and standard deviation. We compute these by finding the standard normal value corresponding to the endpoints of the cells and use Appendix A. For example, the standard normal value corresponding to $x = 40$ is

$$\frac{40 - 49.25}{6.492624} = -1.42$$

average

60 observations

standard deviation

From Appendix A, the area to the left of -1.42 (or equivalents, the area to the right of 1.42) under the standard normal distribution is .0778. Multiplying this by 60 gives the expected number of observations in this group. Thus, under the normality assumption, we would expect $.0778(60) = 4.668$ observations. The remaining calculations are summarized as follows

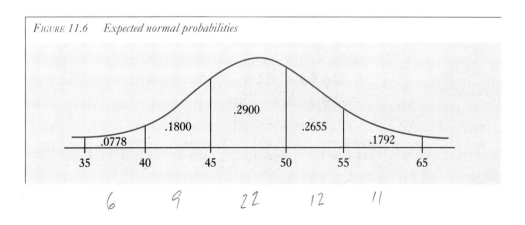

FIGURE 11.6   *Expected normal probabilities*

Group	Observed, f_i	Expected, e_i	$(f_i - e_i)^2 / e_i$
30–40	6	4.668	.380082
41–45	9	10.800	.300000
46–50	22	17.400	1.216092
51–55	12	15.930	.969548
56–65	11	10.752	.005720
			2.871442

For a 5 percent level of significance and two degrees of freedom (we estimated both the mean and standard deviation so we have $5 - 1 - 2 = 2$), the critical value of Chi-square is 5.99146 (see Appendix B). Since the computed value of the Chi-square statistic is only 2.87, we cannot reject the hypothesis of normality. Thus, we could use the normal distribution in any subsequent calculations.

Estimating Probabilities Judgmentally

Most decision makers consider themselves lucky to have historical information from which to base probability estimates. In many cases, both the range of uncertain values and their probability estimates must be estimated judgmentally. A simple approach to estimating a probability distribution is to ask questions carefully.[3]

The first step is to obtain estimates of the most likely, pessimistic (low), and optimistic (high) outcomes. An interview session regarding sales demand might proceed as follows:

Q: What is your best estimate of the most likely value of sales?

A: I think that sales would most likely be around 50,000 units.

Q: Based on your judgment, what are the chances that sales would be less than 50,000?

A: I believe that there is a 50-50 chance that it may be lower or higher than 50,000.

Q: What sales level do you believe that there is less than a 10 percent chance of achieving?

A: There is little chance that sales will drop below 20,000.

Q: Now let's consider the high end. What sales level do you believe sales will not exceed at least 10 percent of the time?

A: I'd say that's about 80,000 units.

At this point, we might stop and use these three estimates. To determine a complete continuous distribution, we continue by considering equidistant points between the low and most likely estimates and between the most likely and high estimates.

---

[3]This procedure is suggested by Wroe Alderson and Paul E. Green, *Planning and Problem Solving in Marketing*, Homewood, IL: Irwin, 1964, pp. 217–223.

Q: Suppose demand is 35,000 units. What do you feel the chances are that it will not exceed this level?

A: Probably 40 percent.

Q: Now suppose sales is 65,000 units. What do you believe are the chances that sales will not exceed 65,000?

A: I suspect it's around .6.

We may plot the information from this interview on a graph and sketch a smooth curve through the points to determine a cumulative probability distribution, shown in Figure 11.7. Often, the interviewer might ask additional questions to test for consistency. For example, the question "Do you believe there is one chance in four that sales will exceed 75,000 units?" seeks to verify that the curve passes through the point (75,000, 0.75) in Figure 11.7. This provides more confidence in the results.

We might want to apply various statistical tests to determine the actual type of distribution, for example, normal or exponential. We will see how to make use of this information using simulation in Chapter 13.

Researchers have conducted many experiments to determine how well decision makers can assess probabilities judgmentally. Some of this research suggests that accurate judgments cannot be obtained by simply asking individuals to provide probabilities. Also, many people underestimate the probability of rare events. When such events are catastrophic, it is especially important to obtain good probability estimates. More sophisticated techniques exist, but they are beyond the scope of this book.

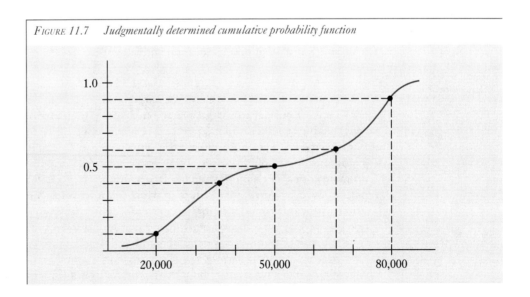

FIGURE 11.7   *Judgmentally determined cumulative probability function*

SOME PROBABILISTIC MODELS IN MANAGEMENT SCIENCE

In this section we illustrate some applications of probabilistic modeling in management science.

p.94

The Economic Order Quantity with Probabilistic Demand

In Chapter 3 we developed the economic order quantity (EOQ) model for minimizing the total cost of placing orders and holding inventory. We assumed that demand was deterministic. Under this assumption, the demand rate follows a smooth curve, and we could place the order at such time to ensure that no shortages would occur before the order was received (you might wish to refer back to Figure 3.4). In many practical situations it is unreasonable to assume that demand is deterministic. In this case, the inventory pattern would resemble that shown in Figure 3.2. Demand is erratic, and inventory managers face the risk of either not being able to satisfy a customer's demand or carrying excess inventory. Thus, the probabilistic nature of demand needs to be incorporated into our modeling efforts. In this section we develop models for inventory decisions in which the demand is probabilistic.

In the EOQ model developed in Chapter 3, we saw that the total annual cost is composed of the cost of placing orders and the cost of holding inventory:

$$\text{Total annual cost} = \frac{DC_0}{Q} + \frac{iCQ}{2}$$

where Q = order quantity
D = annual demand
C = unit cost of the item
C_0 = ordering cost
i = inventory carrying charge

The order quantity that minimizes total annual cost is

$$Q^* = \sqrt{2DC_0/iC}$$

Suppose that the annual demand is a random variable with some probability distribution. We might consider using the average demand, μ_D, in computing Q^*. In Chapter 3 we saw that the economic order quantity is relatively insensitive to changes in the parameters of the model. Therefore, even if the actual value of D would vary from the average, this order quantity should provide a reasonable solution.

A more critical decision is when to place an order. In the EOQ situation, we assumed a continuous review inventory system in which an order is triggered when the inventory position reaches the reorder point, r. In the deterministic case, we computed $r = Dt$, where t is the lead time (time from which the order is placed until it is received). Again, we might consider using the average demand, μ_D, to compute r. Then $\mu_D t$ represents the *average demand during the lead time*. This presents a problem. If the distribution of the lead time demand is symmetric about the mean (for example, normally distributed), then about half the time the actual lead time demand will be less than $\mu_D t$ and half the time it will be greater than $\mu_D t$. This means that 50 percent of the time we will not be able to satisfy customers' demands. This may be unacceptable to the inventory manager.

One way to resolve this is to define a *service level*. A service level is a constraint that represents the probability that a routine demand can be satisfied. For example, we might wish to ensure that demand can be satisfied 95 percent of the time. If we know the probability distribution of the lead time demand, then we can select r to meet the service level constraint.

EXAMPLE 5. SETTING A SERVICE LEVEL

Data Management Supplies (DMS) is a small company that sells various computer peripheral and photocopier supplies to small businesses. One popular item is a toner cartridge for laser printers. Historical data suggest that demand is normally distributed with a mean of 150 every four weeks and a standard deviation of 25. Each cartridge costs $40 from the manufacturer. An order costs $10, and DMS estimates its carrying cost rate to be 20 percent. Lead time is one week.

The expected annual demand, D, is 150(13) = 1950. Applying the EOQ formula, we find that the economic order quantity is

$$Q^* = \sqrt{2D C_0 / i C} \quad \text{—} \quad \text{annual demand}$$
$$\qquad \text{order cost}$$

$$= \sqrt{2(1950)(10)/(.2)(40)} \quad \text{—} \quad \text{cost rate}$$

$$= 69.82, \text{ or about 70 units}$$

Using $Q^* = 70$, DMS will place about $D/Q^* = 1950/70 = 27.86$, or about 28, orders each year.

If X represents the demand over a four-week period, then $.25X$ represents the demand during the lead time. Since X is normally distributed with mean $\mu = 150$ and $\sigma = 25$, then $.25X$ is also normally distributed with

$$\text{Mean} = .25\mu = .25(150) = 37.5$$

and

$$\text{Variance} = (.25)^2\sigma^2 = (.25)^2(25)^2 = 39.0625 \quad \text{Std dev} = \sqrt{39.0625}$$
$$= 6.25$$

Therefore, the standard deviation during the lead time is 6.25.

Suppose that the owner of DMS is willing to allow the lead time demand to exceed the reorder point at most 5 percent of the time. (With 27 orders each year, this will happen only once or twice each year.) This is shown in Figure 11.8. Therefore, the reorder point must satisfy

Reorder point $$\boxed{r = \mu + z\sigma}$$

where z is the number of standard deviations associated with the service level. From Appendix A, we see that the probability of exceeding $z = 1.645$ in a standard normal

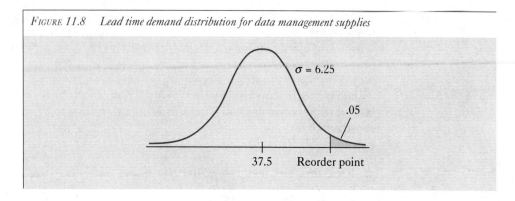

FIGURE 11.8   *Lead time demand distribution for data management supplies*

probability distribution is 0.05. Therefore, the reorder point that meets the required service level is

$$r = 37.5 + 1.645(6.25)$$
$$= 47.78, \text{ or about 48 units}$$

Thus, DMS should place an order for 70 units whenever the inventory position drops to 48 units. Since the average demand during the lead time is only 37.5 units, DMS will carry an average of $48 - 37.5 = 10.5$ units as safety stock. This increases the annual cost for operating this inventory system. The expected annual cost is as follows:

$$\text{Order cost: } (D/Q)C_0 = (1950/70)(10) = \$278.57$$

$$\text{Normal inventory holding: } i\,C\,(Q/2) = .2(40)(70/2) = \$280$$

$$\text{Safety stock holding: } i\,C\,(10.5) = .2(40)(10.5) = \$84$$

$$\text{Total annual cost } = \$642.57$$

DMS is paying about a 13 percent premium to better meet customer demands. (Note that order cost and normal inventory holding costs are not exactly equal—as would be expected—since we rounded the economic order quantity up to 70 units.)

Modeling Uncertainty in Project Management

In Chapter 9 we discussed project management. In particular, we discussed how to calculate the critical path of a project represented by a network (recall that the critical path is the longest path in the network). Figure 11.9 shows the product planning and development network whose critical path we calculated to be A-B-C-G-H-I. The project has expected completion time of 24 weeks (the length of the critical path).

In reality the completion time for each activity is an estimate. Inclement weather, for example, might delay certain activities in a construction project, whereas good weather

FIGURE 11.9   *A project network for product planning and development*

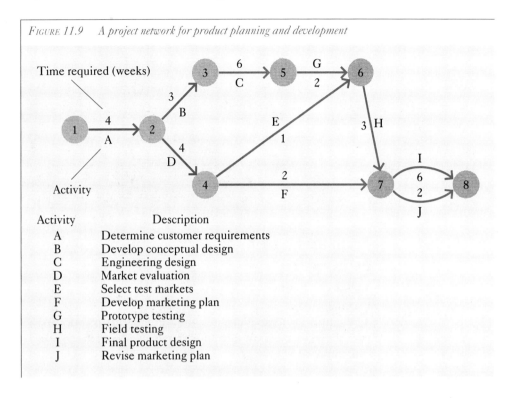

Activity	Description
A	Determine customer requirements
B	Develop conceptual design
C	Engineering design
D	Market evaluation
E	Select test markets
F	Develop marketing plan
G	Prototype testing
H	Field testing
I	Final product design
J	Revise marketing plan

might allow faster-than-planned progress. If the uncertainty of each activity can be quantified, we may capture the variation possible in the overall project completion time. This allows us to make probability statements concerning total project completion. For example, we might wish to know the probability of completing the project in a certain amount of time.

It is often possible to obtain three estimates of an activity's completion time from a person (or persons) closely familiar with the activity: a *pessimistic* time estimate, a *most likely* time estimate, and an *optimistic* time estimate. From these three estimates the expected activity completion time may be calculated using the following formula:

$$t = \frac{o + 4m + p}{6}$$

where t = expected activity time
   o = optimistic time
   m = most likely time
   p = pessimistic time

It is these values that were used in the calculation of the critical path in Chapter 9. To capture the variability, we must also have a measure of the *variance* of each activity time. The variance of each activity time may be calculated using the following formula:

$$\sigma^2 = \left(\frac{p - o}{6}\right)^2$$

where σ^2 is the variance of the activity time and p and o are as defined above.

To distinguish between activities in the project, we may denote t_i to be the expected completion time for activity i and σ_i^2 the variance of the completion time for activity i. We may use these measures of expected activity times and variances to calculate the expected project completion time and variance.

> The expected project completion time, denoted $E(T)$, is the sum of the expected activity times for those activities on the critical path. Under the assumption that the activity times are independent, the variance of the project completion time is the sum of the variances of the activity completion times for those activities on the critical path.

Finally, the fact that the project completion time is the sum of independent activity times allows us to assume that the project completion time is *normally distributed*. As the next example illustrates, knowing the project's mean completion time and variance allows us to make probability statements using the standard normal probability table (Appendix A).

EXAMPLE 6. MODELING THE DISTRIBUTION OF PROJECT COMPLETION TIME

The estimates used in Figure 11.9 might have come from the data shown in the spreadsheet in Figure 11.10. The critical path, as we have seen, is A-B-C-G-H-I. The expected project completion time is therefore as follows: $E(T) = t_A + t_B + t_C + t_G +$

FIGURE 11.10   *Product planning and development data*

	A	B	C	D	E	F
1	**Product Planning & Development Project**					
2						
3			**Time Estimates (Weeks)**			
4	**Activity**	Optimistic	Most Likely	Pessimistic	**Expected**	**Variance**
5	A	1	3	11	4	2.78
6	B	2	3	4	3	0.11
7	C	4	6	8	6	0.44
8	D	2	3	10	4	1.78
9	E	1	1	1	1	0.00
10	F	1	2	3	2	0.11
11	G	1	2	3	2	0.11
12	H	2	3	4	3	0.11
13	I	3	6	9	6	1.00
14	J	1	2	3	2	0.11

Selected cell formulas

	E	F
4	**Expected**	**Variance**
5	=(B5+4*C5+D5)/6	=((D5-B5)/6)^2
6	=(B6+4*C6+D6)/6	=((D6-B6)/6)^2
7	=(B7+4*C7+D7)/6	=((D7-B7)/6)^2
8	=(B8+4*C8+D8)/6	=((D8-B8)/6)^2
9	=(B9+4*C9+D9)/6	=((D9-B9)/6)^2
10	=(B10+4*C10+D10)/6	=((D10-B10)/6)^2
11	=(B11+4*C11+D11)/6	=((D11-B11)/6)^2
12	=(B12+4*C12+D12)/6	=((D12-B12)/6)^2
13	=(B13+4*C13+D13)/6	=((D13-B13)/6)^2
14	=(B14+4*C14+D14)/6	=((D14-B14)/6)^2

$t_H + t_I = 4 + 3 + 6 + 2 + 3 + 6 = 24$ weeks. The variance of the project completion is $\sigma^2 = \sigma_A^2 + \sigma_B^2 + \sigma_C^2 + \sigma_G^2 + \sigma_H^2 + \sigma_I^2 = 2.78 + .11 + .44 + .11 + .11 + 1.00 = 4.55$.

We would like to know, for example, the probability that the project will be completed in four months (28 weeks) or less. That is, we seek $P(T \leq 28)$. Using the standard normal, we have

$$z = \frac{T - E(T)}{\sigma} = \frac{28 - 24}{\sqrt{4.55}} = 1.88$$

From the standard normal table in Appendix A, $P(z \leq 1.88) = 1 - .0301 = .9699$, or roughly a 97 percent chance of being finished in four months or less.

PROBABILISTIC OPTIMIZATION MODELS

Uncertainty makes optimization problems considerably more difficult to solve. First, since there is not a single outcome for any choice of decision variables, we must consider a *range* of outcomes. Second, the concept of an optimal solution becomes fuzzy. We run the risk that any solution we choose may be far from "optimal" once we see what the future holds in store. (Just think of making a spring break vacation decision before you know what the weather will be!) Thus, although we may solve for an "optimal" solution according to some criteria, it is more valuable to evaluate the risk associated with that solution.

> A *probabilistic optimization model* is one in which some of the model input information is not known (or is not assumed to be known) with certainty and is described probabilistically; these model components are *random variables*.

In developing probabilistic optimization models, we often start by constructing a simpler deterministic model and then change deterministic variables into probabilistic variables. As we saw in the Du Pont example in Figure 11.1, influence diagrams provide a convenient means of communicating the role of uncertainty in decision problems. Sometimes different graphical symbols are used to distinguish uncertain variables from others. To illustrate this, we introduce a classic problem in inventory management.

The Single Period Inventory Model with Probabilistic Demand

This problem applies to a variety of practical situations in which a one-time purchase decision must be made in the face of uncertain demand. For example, department store buyers must purchase seasonal clothing well in advance of the buying season; sellers of Christmas trees must decide on how many trees to purchase prior to December; and bookstores must decide on the number of newspapers and magazines to purchase without knowing the actual demand. In all these situations, purchasing too few results in lost opportunity to increase profits, but purchasing too many will usually result in a loss since the excess must be sold at a discount or discarded entirely.

Figure 11.11 shows an influence diagram for this model. The probabilistic element, demand, is enclosed in a diamond to signify that it is a probabilistic quantity. The decision variable (quantity purchased) is enclosed in a rectangle. A graphical scheme like this helps us to communicate the important differences in the model. This approach is by no means standard, but it serves to clarify the key elements in the model to enhance understanding.

Clearly, the decision maker wants to choose a purchase quantity to maximize net profit. We will develop a general model for this problem and then illustrate it with an example. Let us assume that each item costs $\$c$ to purchase and is sold for $\$r$. At the end of the period, any unsold items can be disposed of at $\$s$ each (the salvage value). Clearly, it makes sense to assume that $r > c > s$. We will assume that demand is discrete, that is, it follows a discrete probability distribution. Let d be the number of units demanded during the period with probability $p(d)$ and x be the number purchased.

Notice that we cannot sell more than the minimum of the actual demand and the amount produced. If demand is known, then the optimal decision is obvious: Choose $x = d$. However, if d is not known in advance, we run the risk of overproducing or underproducing. If $x < d$, then we lose the opportunity of realizing additional profit (since we assume that $r > c$), and if $x > d$, we incur a loss (since $c > s$). Because d is uncertain, the value of profit may assume a *range* of values for a fixed production quantity Q. We consider two cases:

Case 1: Quantity purchased (x) greater than or equal to quantity demanded (d). If x is greater than or equal to d, then $(x - d)$ units will be left over and disposed of at a loss. Specifically, the revenue received is $rd + s(x - d)$. Since the purchase cost is cx, the net profit will be

$$\text{Net profit} = rd + s(x - d) - cx$$

Case 2: Quantity purchased (x) less than quantity demanded (d). If x is less than d, then x units will be sold and we will have lost the opportunity to sell an additional $(d - x)$ units at a profit. The net profit would be

$$\text{Net profit} = rx - cx = (r - c)x$$

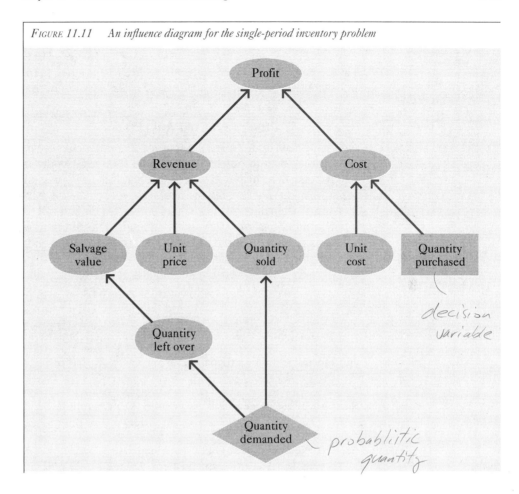

FIGURE 11.11   An influence diagram for the single-period inventory problem

The optimization problem is to choose the best value of x. What does *best* mean under these conditions? With probabilistic models, we may use *expected value* as the criterion for making a decision.

> The expected value of a decision is found by summing the product of the pay-off associated with an outcome and the probability that the outcome will occur.

We develop an expression for the expected profit if x units are purchased. The expected profit is computed by multiplying the net profit obtained for a specific demand d by the probability that the demand is d and summing over all possible values of d. Using the formulas for the two cases described above, we have

$$\text{Expected profit} = \sum_{d=0}^{x} [rd + s(x-d) - cx]p(d) + \sum_{d=x+1}^{\infty} [(r-c)x]p(d)$$

With a discrete set of possible demands, we may enumerate potential combinations of x and d in a table to facilitate our analysis. This is illustrated in the next example.

EXAMPLE 7. THE NEWSBOY PROBLEM

A newsboy has to determine the appropriate number of newspapers to purchase. Each paper costs $0.20 to purchase and is sold for $0.35. At the end of the day, any unsold papers can be disposed of at $0.05 each. If the newsboy purchases at least enough papers to meet the demand, the net profit will be $0.35d + 0.05(x-d) - 0.20x$. If x is less than d, then the newsboy will sell only x papers and will have lost the opportunity to sell an additional $(d-x)$ papers at a profit. The net profit would be $0.35x - 0.20x$.

Let us assume that the demand will vary between 40 and 49, and that the probability of any number of papers within this range is equal to 0.1. Suppose that 43 papers are purchased. If $d = 40$, the net profit is

$$0.35d + 0.05(x-d) - .20x = 0.35(40) + 0.05(43-40) - 0.20(43) = \$5.55$$

Likewise, the net profit for a demand of 41 is

$$0.35d + 0.05(x-d) - 0.20x = 0.35(41) + 0.05(43-41) - 0.20(43) = \$5.85$$

and the net profit for a demand of 42 is

$$0.35d + 0.05(x-d) - .20x = 0.35(42) + 0.05(43-42) - 0.20(43) = \$6.15$$

Similarly, if the demand is 43 or greater, the net profit is

$$0.35x - 0.20x = 0.35(43) - 0.2(43) = \$6.45$$

because the newsboy can only sell 43 papers.

Figure 11.12 shows a spreadsheet designed to calculate the expected profit for any given purchase quantity (input in cell E5). If we vary the purchase quantity, we get the following results:

Purchase quantity	Expected profit
40	$ 6.00
41	6.12
42	6.21
43	6.27
44	6.30
45	6.30
46	6.27
47	6.21
48	6.12
49	6.00

FIGURE 11.12   *Spreadsheet for the newsboy problem*

	A	B	C	D	E
1	**Newsboy problem**				
2					
3	Input Data				
4					
5	*Unit cost*	0.2		*Purchase quantity*	43
6	*Selling price*	0.35			
7	*Salvage value*	0.05			
8					
9	Computations				
10					
11	*Demand*	*Probability*	*Profit*	*Profit x Prob.*	
12	40	0.1	5.55	0.555	
13	41	0.1	5.85	0.585	
14	42	0.1	6.15	0.615	
15	43	0.1	6.45	0.645	
16	44	0.1	6.45	0.645	
17	45	0.1	6.45	0.645	
18	46	0.1	6.45	0.645	
19	47	0.1	6.45	0.645	
20	48	0.1	6.45	0.645	
21	49	0.1	6.45	0.645	
22					
23				*Expected profit*	$6.27

Selected cell formulas

	C	D
11	*Profit*	*Profit x Prob.*
12	@IF($E$5>=A12,$B$6*A12+$B$7*($E$5-A12)-$B$5*$E$5,$B$6*$E$5-$B$5*$E$5)	+B12*C12
13	@IF($E$5>=A13,$B$6*A13+$B$7*($E$5-A13)-$B$5*$E$5,$B$6*$E$5-$B$5*$E$5)	+B13*C13

We see that the optimal purchase quantity is either 44 or 45. It would be easy to investigate changes in the probability distribution or other input data.

Appropriateness of Expected Value Decision Making

The expected value approach is based on the fact that the average outcome for a large number of independent decisions will converge to the expected value of the decision that was selected. The important issue here is a "large number of independent decisions." If an individual or business faces the same decision problem repeatedly, then over the long run the average value of the decision will be close to the expected value. For example, let us consider the airline discounting policy decision that was described in Chapter 1. In this situation, the airline must decide on whether or not to reject a discount fare request in hopes that a customer will purchase the full fare. If p is the probability that the customer will purchase the full fare, then the expected value of rejecting the discount seat request is p times the full fare value. Thus, if a full fare ticket is $560 and $p = .75$, the expected value of .75($560) = $420 means that the discount request should be rejected if the discount fare is less than $420. Since an airline makes many such decisions each day, the expected value criterion is appropriate, because if the full fare is accepted 75 percent of the time, the average sale will be about $420 per customer.

However, suppose only a single decision is to be made. The decision depends on additional factors such as the amount of risk and the decision maker's attitude toward risk. For example, suppose that you could purchase a lottery ticket that would give you a one-in-a-thousand chance of winning a $50,000 automobile. Many people would be willing to pay the expected value of $50 to take this chance. However, few individuals would be willing to pay $5,000 to take a chance at winning $5 million, even though the odds are the same, because few can afford to lose this amount of money. In a one-time decision, we cannot rely on the averages which will hold over the long run. Even if one can afford to lose, such a decision clearly depends on the relative amount at risk. As one Fortune 500 company executive noted, "Most of the decisions we analyze are for a few million dollars. It is adequate to use expected value for these."[4]

Attitudes toward risk also influence decisions. Many investors, for example, are conservative by nature and stick to income or conservative growth mutual funds. Others are aggressive by nature and pursue aggressive growth funds and junk bonds. People who play state lotteries certainly do not apply the expected value criterion, as the expected value of lottery ticket purchases is negative.

Stochastic optimization models are generally based on expected values. Thus, they may not always be the most appropriate choice for a given scenario. In Chapter 12, we will discuss how attitudes toward risk may be explicitly incorporated into the decision-making process.

STATISTICAL MODELING

Statistics plays an important role in every business. Businesses use statistical procedures such as experimental design and sampling for quality control, auditing, and inventory control. Numerous forecasting procedures are used to project important unknowns to aid decision making. Statistics also plays an important role in management science model development. We have seen many models in this book, and it is important to realize that the inputs to these models do not magically appear. Costs, revenues, times, production rates, and other significant model inputs need to be quantified. Often the only way to do this is to collect data from the system being studied and then estimate population parameters or develop prediction equations using statistical analysis techniques. In this section we discuss these issues. We also note that statistics plays an equally important role in the analysis of the *output* of many management science models. For example, in Chapter 13, we will use statistical methods to analyze the results of simulation models.

---

[4]Kirkwood, Craig, "An Overview of Methods for Applied Decision Analysis," *Interfaces*, Vol. 22, No. 6, November–December, 1992, p. 29.

Statistical Techniques in Model Development

Variable cost per unit of product, expected resource usage per unit of product, expected return per dollar invested, the dollar return per minute of advertising, and the expected quantity of demand by product over time are all quantities we have used as inputs to models in earlier chapters. In this section we discuss how statistical techniques may be used to estimate these types of model inputs. We discuss two basic estimation techniques: regression analysis and forecasting techniques.

Linear Regression Analysis

Linear regression analysis allows us to estimate the expected value of some unknown quantity as a function of other variables based on empirical data. The variable we are trying to estimate is called the *dependent variable*. The variables whose values are used to predict the value of the dependent variable are known as the *independent variables*. In linear regression, we assume that the relationship between the dependent variable and independent variables is linear in the model parameters. We may use plots of the data to determine the appropriateness of this technique.

> If *plots* of the dependent variable versus the independent variable indicate a relatively linear relationship, then using linear regression is appropriate.

A regression model with a single independent variable is called a *simple linear regression model*. A regression model with more than one independent variable is called a *multiple linear* regression model. We begin with simple linear regression.

A simple linear regression model has the following form:

$$\hat{y} = b_0 + b_1 x$$

where b_0 = the estimated y-intercept
        b_1 = the estimated slope of the regression line
        $\hat{y}$ = the estimated value of the dependent variable

The values of b_0 and b_1 are calculated to provide the "best-fitting line" to the data points using the least squares measure of fit. That is, the values of b_0 and b_1 minimize the sum of squared error, where error is defined as the observed value of the dependent variable minus the fitted value of the dependent variable, for each of the data points. Suppose we have n data points; that is, we have observed pairs of independent and dependent variable values (x_i, y_i), $i = 1, 2, \ldots, n$. The simple linear regression model is $\hat{y}_i = b_0 + b_1 x_i$, so that the least squares problem with n observations is defined as

$$\text{Min} \sum_{i=1}^{n} (y_i - \hat{y}_i)^2$$

or

$$\text{Min} \sum_{i=1}^{n} (y_i - b_0 - b_1 x_i)^2$$

It turns out that the solution to this problem (the optimal values of b_0 and b_1) can be obtained very easily using calculus. We will not go into the details of that solution here, but the values of b_0 and b_1 giving the best linear fit are easily calculated by the computer.

The interpretation of b_0 and b_1 depends on the data set under consideration, as the following example shows.

EXAMPLE 8. ESTIMATING THE EFFECTS OF ADVERTISING

A company is trying to determine how sales are related to advertising for one of its products. Data are available for the last nine quarters. The amount spent on advertising and the resulting sales figures (both in discounted dollars) are shown in Figure 11.13. As the figure shows, at least over the range of advertising from $1,000 to $5,000, the relationship appears somewhat linear. This suggests that fitting a line to estimate the relationship is a good idea.

Using a computer package with regression options (for example, EXCEL or LOTUS 1-2-3), we may estimate a simple linear regression model:

$$\hat{y} = b_0 + b_1 x$$

FIGURE 11.13   *Advertising and sales data*

	A	B
1	Advertising ($000)	Sales ($000)
2	0.2	52.20
3	0.5	51.07
4	0.8	54.58
5	1	55.89
6	1.1	52.86
7	1.3	56.12
8	1.7	58.10
9	1.7	56.40
10	2	58.08
11	2.2	58.38
12	2.3	57.49
13	2.5	62.40
14	2.7	60.47
15	2.9	63.85
16	3.1	63.75
17	3.3	64.72
18	3.4	65.60
19	3.8	69.10
20	3.9	67.71
21	4	69.50

where b_0 = the estimated y-intercept (expected sales with no advertising)
   b_1 = the change in sales per dollar spent on advertising
   x = dollar amount (in thousands) spent on advertising
   $\hat{y}$ = the estimated sales (in thousands) for x dollars (in thousands) of advertising

The values of b_0 and b_1 that provide the best fit are b_0 = 49.49 and b_1 = 4.69. This regression line is shown in Figure 11.14. The regression line allows us to estimate the sales for a given amount of advertising. For example, suppose we allocate $1,900 for advertising. The estimated sales will be

$$\hat{y} = 49.49 + 4.69(1.9) = 58.4$$

Hence, for an advertising budget of $1,900, expected sales will be $58,400.

Once the linear regression has been applied, a statistic known as the *coefficient of determination*, or r^2 statistic, provides a measure of how well the regression line fits the data. We define the following quantities:

Let $\bar{y}$ = the mean of the dependent variable values. We define

$$\text{SST} = \text{Total sum of squares} = \sum_{i=1}^{n}(y_i - \bar{y})^2$$

$$\text{SSE} = \text{Sum of squared error} = \sum_{i=1}^{n}(y_i - \hat{y}_i)^2$$

$$\text{SSR} = \text{Sum of squares due to regression} = \sum_{i=1}^{n}(\hat{y}_i - \bar{y})^2$$

FIGURE 11.14   *The estimated regression line for sales vs. advertising budget*

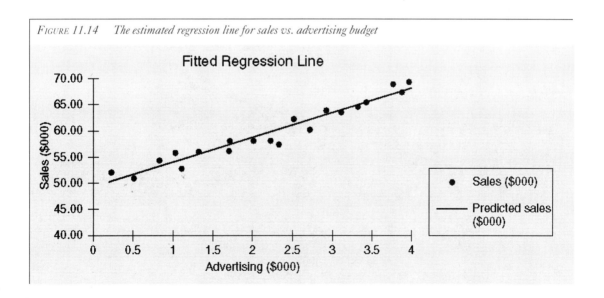

A single component (that of data point 18) for each of these sums from Example 8 is in Figure 11.15. It can be shown that SST = SSE + SSR; that is, the total variation of the data about the mean is equal to the sum of the variation due to error and variation due to the regression.

Then the coefficient of determination is given by

$$r^2 = \frac{SSR}{SST} = \frac{SSR}{SSE + SSR}$$

The *coefficient of determination*, or r^2 statistic, indicates what fraction of the total variation in the dependent variable about its mean is explained by the regression line.

Clearly, by definition, $0 \le r^2 \le 1$. An $r^2 = 1$ implies that all of the variation in the data is explained by the regression equation; that is, all of the data are on the regression line. An $r^2 = 0$ means that none of the variation is explained by the regression line. In this case, the mean of the dependent variable is its best estimate regardless of the value of the independent variable. In Example 8, $r^2 = .94$, which indicates that 94 percent of the variation is explained by the regression line.

The coefficient of determination is a direct measure of how well the regression line fits the data. The higher the value of the r^2, the better the line fits the data.

Figure 11.15   Graphical display of error from Example 8

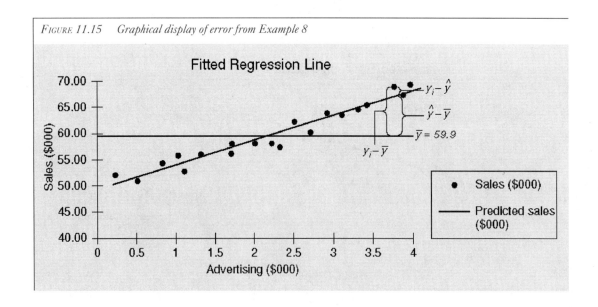

How high the r^2 has to be before a regression is deemed a "good fit" is subjective.

We are sometimes interested in more than just a good fit of the data. We might want to know, for example, if the slope of a regression line is statistically significantly different from zero. To test such a hypothesis, we must view the regression line in a probabilistic manner and make certain assumptions concerning the distribution of the errors. More details in this regard can be found in any standard statistics book (see for example, Anderson, Sweeney, and Williams, 1990, Chapters 13, 14, and 15).

A *multiple* regression model is of the form

$$\hat{y} = b_0 + b_1 x + b_2 x_2 + \cdots + b_k x_k$$

where b_0 = the estimated y-intercept
b_j = the regression coefficient of x_j, $j = 1, 2, \ldots, k$
x_j = the jth independent variable, $j = 1, 2, \ldots, k$
$\hat{y}$ = the estimated value of the dependent variable

Everything previously discussed for simple linear regression is applicable to the multiple regression case. The interpretation of the coefficients of the independent variables is, however, slightly different. In the multiple regression case, b_j is the rate of change of the dependent variable with respect to the independent variable x_j *with all other independent variables held at fixed values*. In terms of its use as a predictive tool, the multiple linear regression is a natural extension of the simple linear regression case: For given values of $x_1, x_2, \ldots, x_k$, we may estimate the value of y using $\hat{y}$ from the estimated regression equation.

EXAMPLE 9. A MULTIPLE REGRESSION MODEL

An inexpensive motel chain[5] that concentrates its efforts in and around college campuses would like to construct a model to help assess new locations under consideration. Data of interest, collected from its current locations, are shown in Table 11.2. The company would like to develop a predictive model based on these data. The model will then be used to estimate the profitability of new sites under consideration.

TABLE 11.2
Motel location data

Location	Average annual profit (thousands)	College students within five miles (thousands)	State population per inn (thousands)
1	$50	16	6
2	$54	15	3.3
3	$55	20	4.3
4	$53	23	3.5
5	$38	6	9
6	$60	25	1.1
7	$52	24	7.2
8	$52	15	2
9	$45	11	3.6
10	$40	11	8

[5]Based on Kimes, Sheryl E., and James A. Fitzsimmons, "Selecting Profitable Hotel Sites at La Quinta Motor Inns," *Interfaces*, Vol. 20, No. 2, March–April, 1990, pp. 12–20.

Figure 11.16 shows plots of average profit versus the number of students within five miles and state population per inn in the given motel's state. Both relationships appear relatively linear, indicating that a multiple linear regression is appropriate. We will therefore estimate the following model:

$$\hat{y} = b_0 + b_1x + b_2x_2$$

where b_0 = the estimated y-intercept
        b_1 = the change in profits per additional 1,000 students within five miles (population held fixed)
        b_2 = the change in profits per additional 1,000 in population per inn (students held fixed)
        x_1 = number of students (in thousands) within five miles
        x_2 = state population (in thousands) per inn
        $\hat{y}$ = the estimated profitability (in thousands of dollars)

Using the linear regression option in EXCEL (to be discussed later in this chapter), the estimated regression equation for the data in Table 11.2, is

$$\hat{y} = 44.335 + .6897x_1 - 1.226x_2$$

FIGURE 11.16   *Plots of profitability vs. independent variables for Example 9*

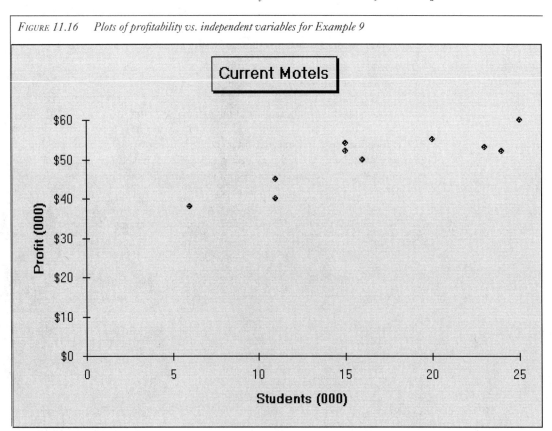

FIGURE 11.16   (continued)

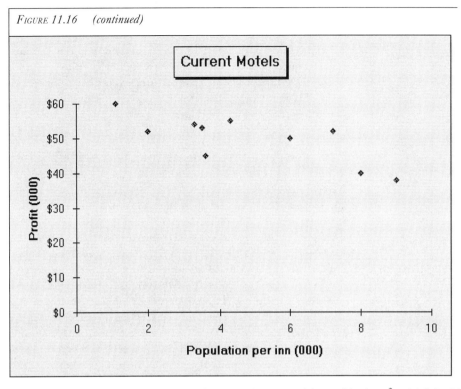

This model provides an excellent fit to the data, as evidenced by its r^2, which is .907. This means that 90.7 percent of the variation in the data is explained by the regression equation. Note that the model has an intuitive appeal in that a greater number of students leads to higher profits. Higher population per inn leads to less profitability (see the relationship shown in the plot in Figure 11.16). As a lower-cost motel, it pays to go to lesser-populated states or more populated states with a high number of inns as an alternative for consumers.

FORECASTING

Businesses of every type need to estimate the future demand for their goods and services. *Forecasting* is the general term used to denote estimation of quantities for some future time based on historical data. The stream of historical data, measured at different points in time, is called a *time series*. For example, 12 data points measuring sales of a product over the last 12 quarters is a time series. The time series would be used to forecast future sales.

Time series can be thought of as having four basic components: trend, cyclical, seasonal, and irregular. *Trend* is the gradual shifting of the time series over a longer period of time. For example, a trend in sales data may be caused by changing demographics. *Trend may be estimated using regression analysis with time as the independent variable.* A regular sequence above or below the trend line is called the *cyclical component* of the time series. Cyclical components are usually due to the business cycle or the state of the economy.

EXAMPLE 10. TREND AND CYCLICAL COMPONENTS

A time series exhibiting trend and cyclical components is shown in Figure 11.17. The trend line was estimated fitting a regression line with sales as the dependent variable and quarter as the independent variable. The estimated trend line is $\hat{y} = 81.758 + 3.799x$. The time series shows three cyclical components (marked by arrows); the first and last are "up cycles," that is, above the trend line, and the middle cycle is a "down cycle" (below the trend line).

A repeating pattern from one year to the next is known as the *seasonal component* of a time series. For example, goods such as hot dogs, cold medicine, and beer typically have demand patterns that repeat year after year. Such a time series is shown in Figure 11.18. Each year there is a drop in sales from the first to the second quarter and then sales increase over the last two quarters.

Finally, the *irregular component* of a time series is the remaining variation in the series that cannot be described as trend, cyclical, or seasonal components. These fluctuations are due to random variability and are short term and nonrepetitive.

In this section we discuss two simple forecasting methods, moving average and exponential smoothing. These two techniques are appropriate for relatively stable time series, those *not* exhibiting significant trend, cyclical, or season components. More advanced techniques may be used to forecast series with seasonal and cyclical components (see Anderson, Sweeney, and Williams, Chapter 16). For a series with trend but neither cyclical nor seasonal components, simple linear regression may be used with time as the independent variable, in the manner discussed in Example 9, to illustrate trend and cyclical components.

FIGURE 11.17   *Trend and cyclical components*

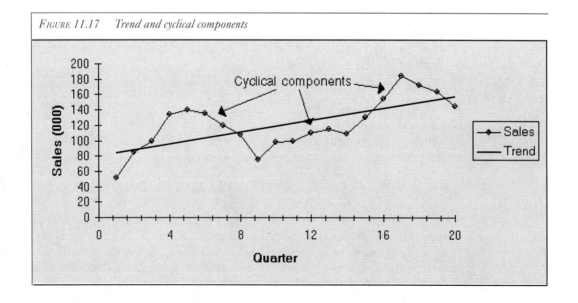

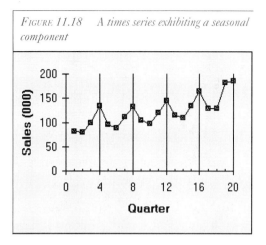

FIGURE 11.18   *A times series exhibiting a seasonal component*

Moving Average

Moving average is a forecasting technique that simply uses the average of the last k (some prespecified number) data points as the forecast for the next period. Let y_t be the known value of the quantity under consideration in time period t. Suppose we have data for $t = 1, 2, 3, \ldots, T$. The moving average forecasts y_{T+1} as

$$y_{T+1} = \frac{\displaystyle\sum_{t=T-k+1}^{T} y_t}{k}$$

That is, the moving average forecast simply averages the last k data points to forecast for the next period. The larger the value of k selected, the more data are included in the forecast. There is no absolute best approach to determining the value of k to use. A common approach is to use trial and error (several different values of k) and check how well the forecasted values fit the data over the time series. One way to measure fit is to use the mean absolute deviation (MAD).

Mean absolute deviation (MAD) is the average of the absolute values of all fore-cast errors over all data points.

MAD can be used to determine a good choice for k or, as we shall see later, to decide among different forecasting techniques.

EXAMPLE 11. COMPUTING A MOVING AVERAGE FORECAST

Atlas Dry Cleaning is a full-service dry cleaning business. Atlas has been in business for over 40 years and has a relatively stable base of satisfied customers. A major portion of Atlas's business is cleaning and starching mens' shirts. Data on the number of shirts cleaned in each of the last 10 weeks is shown in Table 11.3.

Table 11.3
The number of shirts cleaned by Atlas over the last 10 weeks

	Week									
	1	2	3	4	5	6	7	8	9	10
# Shirts	1,061	1,070	1,054	1,075	1,055	1,065	1,054	1,074	1,049	1,062

The data are plotted in Figure 11.19. There do not seem to be trend, cyclical, or seasonal components to these data. A moving average may be used to forecast the number of shirts needing cleaning next week. Suppose we choose the number of periods to be used in the average to be three ($k = 3$). The forecast for week 11 will be the average of the demand in weeks 8, 9, and 10: $(1,074 + 1,049 + 1,062)/3 = 1,061.67$ or 1,062 shirts.

Also, with $k = 3$, to get a better feel for this technique, we may compare the forecasted values with observed data from weeks 4 through 10:

Week	Actual # of shirts	Forecasted # shirts	|Error|
4	1,075	$(1,071 + 1,070 + 1,054)/3 = 1,065$	10.00
5	1,055	$(1,070 + 1,054 + 1,075)/3 = 1,066.33$	11.33
6	1,065	$(1,054 + 1,075 + 1,055)/3 = 1,061.33$	3.67
7	1,054	$(1,075 + 1,055 + 1,065)/3 = 1,065$	11.00
8	1,074	$(1,055 + 1,065 + 1,054)/3 = 1,058$	16.00
9	1,049	$(1,065 + 1,054 + 1,074)/3 = 1,064.33$	15.33
10	1,062	$(1,054 + 1,074 + 1,049)/3 = 1,059$	3.00
			Total: 70.33

The mean absolute deviation is $70.33/7 = 10.05$. The forecasts are plotted along with the observed values in Figure 11.20.

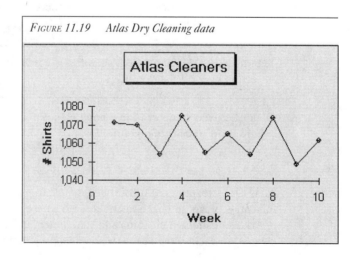

Figure 11.19   Atlas Dry Cleaning data

FIGURE 11.20   Forecasted and observed values for Atlas Dry Cleaning

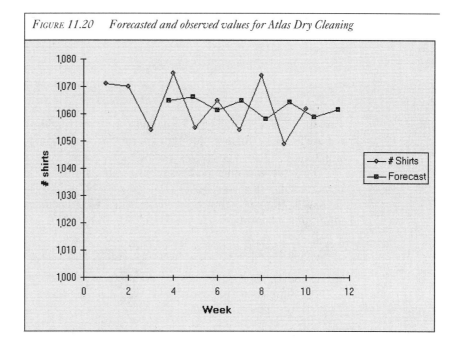

Exponential Smoothing

Exponential smoothing is another simple forecasting technique. Let y_t be the data value in the time series for time period t, and $\hat{y}_t$ be the forecasted value for time period t. Exponential smoothing forecasts using the following model:

$$\hat{y}_2 = y_1$$
$$\hat{y}_{t+1} = \hat{y}_t + \alpha(y_t - \hat{y}_t)$$
$$= \alpha y_t + (1 - \alpha)\hat{y}_t \qquad t = 2, 3, 4, \ldots$$

where α is called the *smoothing constant* $(0 \leq \alpha \leq 1)$. The amount $(1 - \alpha)$ is sometimes referred to as the *damping factor*. As the second equation shows, the forecast for period $t + 1$ is the forecast for period t adjusted by the error for period t. If we overestimated in period t, then $(y_t - \hat{y}_t)$ is negative and the forecast for period $t + 1$ is lower than for period t. If we underestimated for period t, $(y_t - \hat{y}_t)$ is positive and the forecast for period $t + 1$ is higher than for period t.

Exponential smoothing uses a *weighted average* of the data values in the time series to forecast the value in the next period. To see this, consider that $\hat{y}_t = \alpha y_{t-1} + (1 - \alpha)\hat{y}_{t-1}$. By substituting this into the forecast model for period $t + 1$ we have

$$\hat{y}_{t+1} = \alpha y_t + (1 - \alpha)\hat{y}_t$$
$$= \alpha y_t + (1 - \alpha)[\alpha y_{t-1} + (1 - \alpha)\hat{y}_{t-1}]$$
$$= \alpha y_t + \alpha(1 - \alpha)y_{t-1} + (1 - \alpha)^2\hat{y}_{t-1}$$

If we now substitute for $\hat{y}_{t-1}$ and continue in this fashion for the other earlier periods we have

$$\begin{aligned}
\hat{y}_{t+1} &= \alpha y_t + \alpha(1-\alpha)y_{t-1} + \alpha(1-\alpha)^2 y_{t-2} \\
&+ \alpha(1-\alpha)^3 y_{t-3} + \alpha(1-\alpha)^4 y_{t-4} \\
&+ \cdots + \alpha(1-\alpha)^n y_{t-n}
\end{aligned}$$

This shows that the forecast for period $t + 1$ is a weighting of the previous data values. For α close to 0, the more distant data are weighted more heavily. For α close to 1, more importance is placed on the last period's data value.

The value of α must be chosen, just as the value of k must be chosen in the moving average technique. The MAD criterion may be used as a measure of fit as previously discussed. Trial-and-error choices for α with MAD as a measure of fit quality is a common approach to choosing α.

EXAMPLE 12. FORECASTING WITH EXPONENTIAL SMOOTHING

We may apply exponential smoothing to the Atlas Dry Cleaning data given in Table 11.3. Suppose we choose $\alpha = .7$. We have the following forecasts:

Week	Observed # of shirts	Forecasted # of shirts	Error
1	1,071		
2	1,070	1071	-1
3	1,054	$1{,}071 + .7(-1) = 1{,}070.3$	-16.3
4	1,075	$1{,}070.3 + .7(-16.3) = 1{,}058.9$	16.1
5	1,055	$1{,}058.9 + .7(16.1) = 1{,}070.2$	-15.2
6	1,065	$1{,}070.2 + .7(-15.2) = 1{,}059.6$	5.4
7	1,054	$1{,}059.6 + .7(5.4) = 1{,}063.4$	-9.4
8	1,074	$1{,}063.4 + .7(-9.4) = 1{,}056.8$	17.2
9	1,049	$1{,}056.8 + .7(17.2) = 1{,}068.8$	-19.8
10	1,062	$1{,}068.8 + .7(-19.8) = 1{,}054.9$	7.1
11	—	$1{,}054.9 + .7(7.1) = 1{,}059.9$	

A plot of the observed data and the forecasted time series is shown in Figure 11.21. The mean absolute deviation is

$$\text{MAD} = \frac{1 + 16.3 + 16.1 + 15.2 + 5.4 + 9.4 + 17.2 + 19.8 + 7}{9} = 11.93$$

Note that this MAD is higher than that of the moving average forecasted series (MAD for the moving average was 10.05). For a direct comparison between moving average and exponential smoothing, we may compare the MAD for both over weeks 4 through 10, since the moving average provided forecasts only over these weeks. The MAD for exponential smoothing over weeks 4 through 10 is $(16.1 + 15.2 + 5.4 + 9.4 + 17.2 + 19.8 + 7)/7 = 12.87$, compared with the 10.05 for moving average.

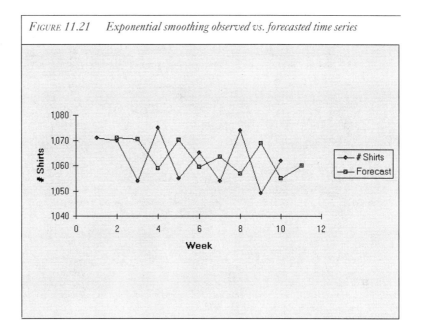

FIGURE 11.21   *Exponential smoothing observed vs. forecasted time series*

STATISTICAL MODELING AND FORECASTING IN A SPREADSHEET

In addition to dedicated statistical packages such as SAS, SPSS, and Minitab, a variety of statistical tools are now available in spreadsheets such as EXCEL and LOTUS 1-2-3. In this section we briefly discuss the use of EXCEL 5.0 and LOTUS 1-2-3 for Windows for forecasting and regression analysis.

Statistical Analysis in EXCEL. EXCEL has the capability of performing simple and multiple linear regression as well as moving average and exponential smoothing. The statistical techniques may be found by selecting the *Tools* option from the main menu, and then the *Data Analysis* option from the submenu. *Moving Average, Exponential Smoothing*, and *Regression* (in addition to other statistical options) are listed. Each of these works in approximately the same format. A dialog box is presented requesting the input data range, a range to place the output, some output options, and the setting of any relevant parameters.

The Exponential Smoothing dialog box is shown in Figure 11.22*a*. The input and output ranges must be specified. The damping factor $= 1 - \alpha$. Its default value is .3; that is, $1 - \alpha = .3$ or $\alpha = .7$. Finally, optional outputs consisting of a chart and standard errors (deviation from the mean error divided by the standard deviation) may be selected.

The Moving Average dialog box is shown in Figure 11.22*b*. Input and output ranges must be specified. If *Labels in First Row* is checked, then the first row of the input range is

FIGURE 11.22a   EXCEL dialog box for exponential smoothing

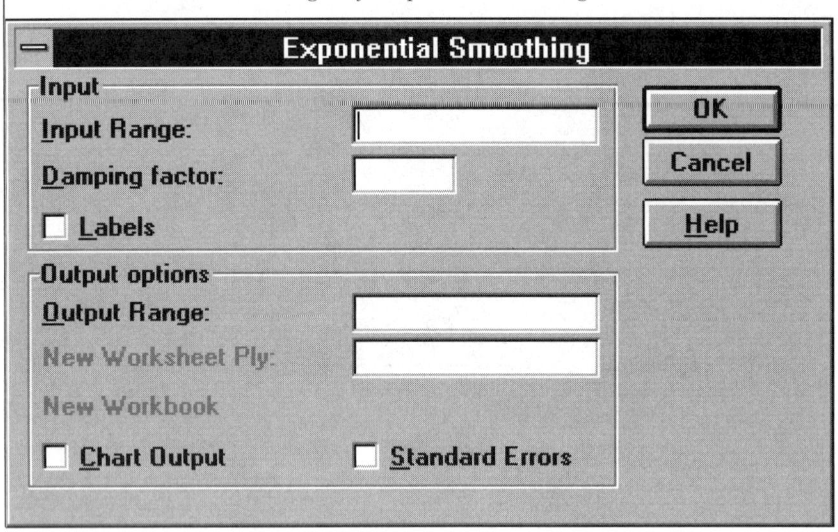

FIGURE 11.22b   EXCEL dialog box for moving average

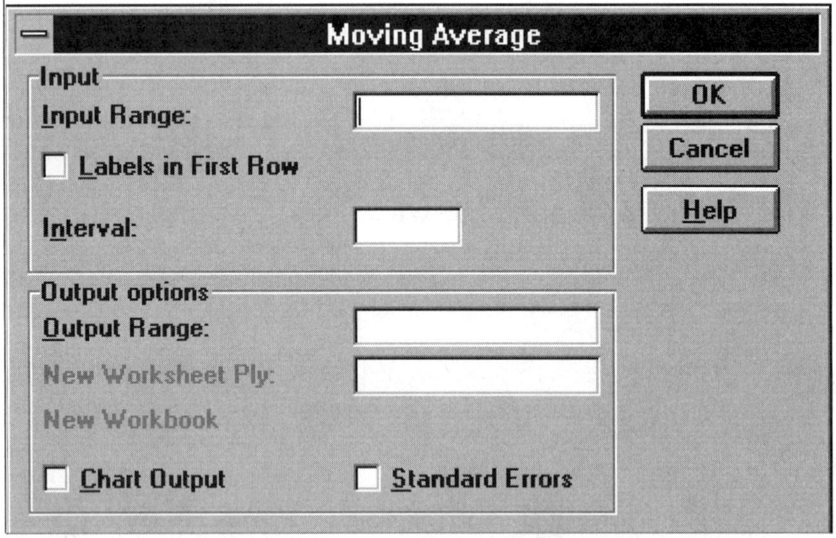

assumed to have labels for the data. *Interval* is the number of data points to be used in the moving average (we referred to this as the parameter k). As in the exponential smoothing option, chart output and standard errors output may be selected.

The Regression dialog box is shown in Figure 11.22c. The *Input Y Range* is the range containing values for the dependent variable and the *Input X Range* is the range of the independent variable data values (a single column or multiple columns). *Output Range* specifies where the output from the regression should be placed in the spreadsheet. The other options deal with validating the assumptions needed to make statistical significance statements about the estimated regression coefficients, so we will forgo discussion of them here.

EXAMPLE 13. EXPONENTIAL SMOOTHING WITH EXCEL

We illustrate in this example the use of EXCEL for exponential smoothing using the Atlas Dry Cleaning data. The 10 weeks of data and Exponential Smoothing dialog box are shown in Figure 11.23. The input data stream is in cells B2 through B12 and includes a blank cell for the week we wish to forecast (week 11). The Output Range has been specified as C2 through C12. The Damping Factor has been set to .3. The

FIGURE 11.22c   EXCEL dialog box for regression

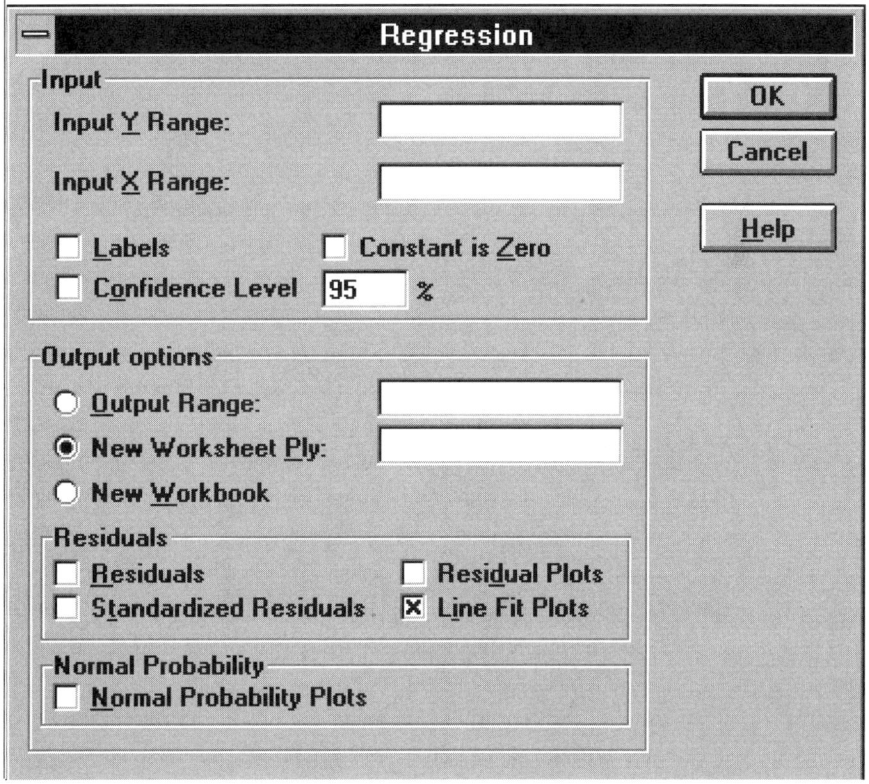

output is also shown in Figure 11.23. Notice that cell C2 has "#N/A" in it. This is because there are no data from which to forecast the first week. The forecasts for the other weeks match those we calculated in Example 12 when rounded to one decimal place.

In addition to the data analysis tools, EXCEL also has *statistical functions* that perform some of these analyses and allow you to report the outcomes to a cell without having to invoke a dialog box. Table 11.4 has a listing of these functions.

These statistical functions are useful when forecasted values or parameter estimates such as intercepts or slopes are part of a larger model in a spreadsheet.

FIGURE 11.23　　EXCEL exponential smoothing of the Atlas Dry Cleaning data

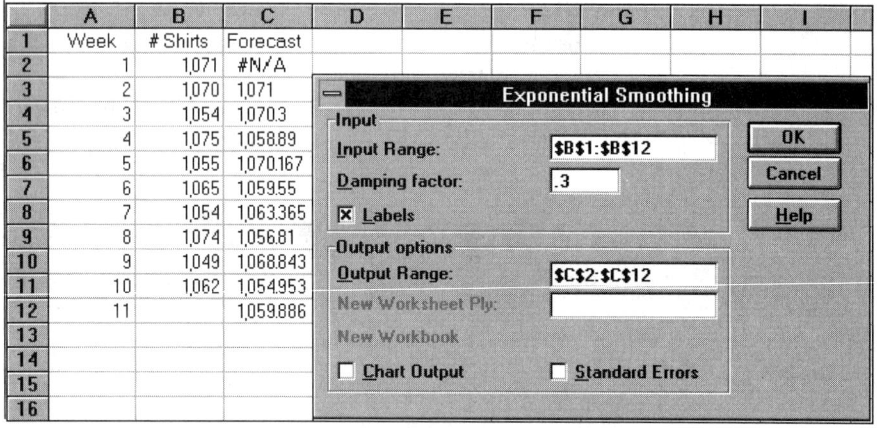

TABLE 11.4
*Statistical functions
available in EXCEL*

FORECAST(*x*, *known_y's*, *known_x's*)—returns a predicted value of *x* based on a simple linear regression of *known_x* and *known_y* arrays.

INTERCEPT(*known_y's*, *known_x's*)—returns the intercept of a simple linear regression line through data points in *known_x's* and *known_y's*.

SLOPE(*known_y's*, *known_x's*)—returns the slope of a simple linear regression through data points in *known_y's* and *known_x's*.

TREND(*known_y's*, *known_x's*, *new_x's*, *const*)—returns values along a linear trend. Fits a straight line using linear regression to the arrays *known_y's* and *known_x's*. Returns the *y* values along that line for the array of *new_x*'s. *Const* is a logical variable (true or false). If *const* = false, then the line is forced to have *intercept* = 0. If *const* = true or is omitted, then the intercept is calculated as is normally with linear regression.

EXAMPLE 14. USING A STATISTICAL MODEL IN A LINEAR PROGRAM

Optcontrol Inc. produces scanning devices used in courtrooms and airports to detect metal weapons. The manager is currently developing a production schedule for next year. He would like to determine the optimal production quantities and inventory levels for each quarter. Production in the current quarter will be 205 units, with 10 units of inventory. The cost to hold inventory for one quarter is $45 per unit. The production cost per unit will vary over the year and is projected to be $590, $525, $505, and $575 over the four quarters. There are also costs associated with changing production levels from one quarter to the next: $85 per unit of increase and $20 per unit of decrease. Finally, sales for the next four quarters must be estimated from the last two years' data. These are shown in Figure 11.24.

Since the data appear linear, linear regression may be used to predict the sales volumes for the next four quarters. We may obtain the optimal production plan by using the following integer programming model:

Let P_t = number of units to produce in quarter t
      I_t = number of units to hold in inventory, end of quarter t
      U_t = increase in production from quarter $t - 1$ to quarter t
      D_t = decrease in production from quarter $t - 1$ to quarter t

$$\text{Min} \sum_{t=1}^{4} [45I_t + 85U_t + 20D_t + c_t P_t]$$

subject to

$$I_{t-1} + P_t - I_t = s_t \qquad t = 1, 2, 3, 4$$

$$P_{t-1} + U_t - D_t = P_t \qquad t = 1, 2, 3, 4$$

$$I_0 = 10$$

$$P_0 = 205$$

$$I_t, P_t, U_t, D_t, \geq 0 \qquad \text{and integer } t = 1, 2, 3, 4$$

where c_t is the production cost per unit in quarter t and s_t is the *forecasted* sales for quarter t.

An EXCEL spreadsheet model of this scenario is given in Figure 11.25. As shown in cells C14 through C17, the TREND function was used to forecast sales for the next four quarters based on the previous eight quarters (the INT function was used to make the forecast integer). The Solver Parameters box and the solution to this model are shown in Figures 11.26a and 11.26b. The minimum total cost for the year is $568,995. The production plan calls for very little inventory and increasing production rates.

Statistical Analysis in LOTUS 1-2-3. LOTUS 1-2-3 4.0 for Windows currently has the capability to perform linear regression analysis (simple or multiple) but does not

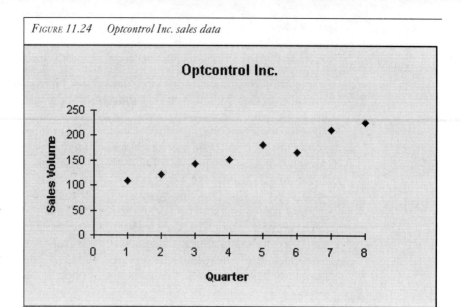

FIGURE 11.24   Optcontrol Inc. sales data

FIGURE 11.25   EXCEL spreadsheet model for Optcontrol Inc.

	A	B	C	D	E	F	G	H	I
1	Optcontrol Inc.								
2									
3	*Parameters and uncontrollable inputs:*								
4									
5	Qtr.:	1	2	3	4	5	6	7	8
6	Sales:	110	122	143	151	182	166	211	226
7									
8	Current Inventory:	10							
9	Current Production Rate:	205							
10	Production Rate Increase Cost/Unit	$85							
11	Production Rate Decrease Cost/Unit	$20							
12	Iventory Holding Cost/Unit/Qtr.	$45							
13	Qtr.	Production Cost/ Unit:	Sales Forecast						
14	1	$590	236						
15	2	$525	252						
16	3	$505	268						
17	4	$575	285						
18									
19	*Decision variables:*								
20									
21		Production Volume	Inventory	Rate Increase	Rate Decrease				
22	Qtr. 1	0.00	0.00	0.00	0.00				
23	Qtr. 2	0.00	0.00	0.00	0.00				
24	Qtr. 3	0.00	0.00	0.00	0.00				
25	Qtr. 4	0.00	0.00	0.00	0.00				
26									
27	*Model outputs:*								
28		Production Cost	Inventory Cost	Rate Increase Cost	Rate Decrease Cost				
29	Qtr. 1	$0	$0	$0	$0				
30	Qtr. 2	$0	$0	$0	$0				
31	Qtr. 3	$0	$0	$0	$0				
32	Qtr. 4	$0	$0	$0	$0				
33									
34	Totals	$0	$0	$0	$0				
35									
36	Total Cost:	$0							

Selected cell formulas

	B	C	D	E
13	Production Cost/ Unit:	Sales Forecast		
14	590	=INT(TREND(B6:I6,B5:I5,9))		
15	525	=INT(TREND(B6:I6,B5:I5,10))		
16	505	=INT(TREND(B6:I6,B5:I5,11))		
17	575	=INT(TREND(B6:I6,B5:I5,12))		
18				
19				
20				
21	Production Volume	Inventory	Rate Increase	Rate Decrease
22	0	0	0	0.00
23	0	0	0	0.00
24	0	0	0	0.00
25	0	0	0	0.00
26				
27				
28	Production Cost	Inventory Cost	Rate Increase Cost	Rate Decrease Cost
29	=B14*B22	=$B$12*C22	=$B$10*D22	=$B$11*E22
30	=B15*B23	=$B$12*C23	=$B$10*D23	=$B$11*E23
31	=B16*B24	=$B$12*C24	=$B$10*D24	=$B$11*E24
32	=B17*B25	=$B$12*C25	=$B$10*D25	=$B$11*E25
33				
34	=SUM(B29:B32)	=SUM(C29:C32)	=SUM(D29:D32)	=SUM(E29:E32)
35				
36	=SUM(B34:E34)			

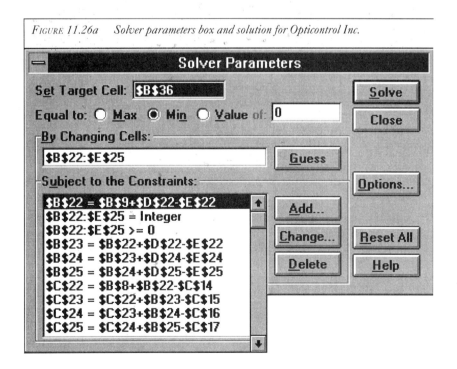

FIGURE 11.26a   *Solver parameters box and solution for Opticontrol Inc.*

FIGURE 11.26b   (continued)

	A	B	C	D	E	F	G	H	I
1	Optcontrol Inc.								
2									
3	*Parameters and uncontrollable inputs:*								
4									
5	Qtr.:	1	2	3	4	5	6	7	8
6	Sales:	110	122	143	151	182	166	211	226
7									
8	Current Inventory:	10							
9	Current Production Rate:	205							
10	Production Rate Increase Cost/Unit	$85							
11	Production Rate Decrease Cost/Unit	$20							
12	Inventory Holding Cost/Unit/Qtr.	$45							
13	Qtr.	Production Cost/ Unit:	Sales Forecast						
14	1	$590	236						
15	2	$525	252						
16	3	$505	268						
17	4	$575	285						
18									
19	*Decision variables:*								
20									
21		Production Volume	Inventory	Rate Increase	Rate Decrease				
22	Qtr. 1	228.00	2.00	23.00	0.00				
23	Qtr. 2	251.00	1.00	0.00	0.00				
24	Qtr. 3	276.00	9.00	25.00	0.00				
25	Qtr. 4	276.00	0.00	0.00	0.00				
26									
27	*Model outputs:*								
28		Production Cost	Inventory Cost	Rate Increase Cost	Rate Decrease Cost				
29	Qtr. 1	$134,520	$90	$1,955	$0				
30	Qtr. 2	$131,775	$45	$0	$0				
31	Qtr. 3	$139,380	$405	$2,125	$0				
32	Qtr. 4	$158,700	$0	$0	$0				
33									
34	Totals	$564,375	$540	$4,080	$0				
35									
36	Total Cost:	$568,995							

have options for moving average or exponential smoothing (although the basic techniques given in this chapter may be performed easily enough in a spreadsheet). The use of linear regression is essentially the same as described for EXCEL 5.0. From the main menu select *Range, Analyze,* and *Regression.* This will invoke the regression dialog box as shown in Figure 11.27. This allows you to specify the ranges of the independent variable(s) (*X-range*) and the dependent variable (*Y-range*) and output range for the results (*Output range*). The *Y-intercept* option allows you to force the line through the origin by selecting *Set to zero.*

MANAGEMENT SCIENCE PRACTICE

In this section we describe how risk assessment was used to evaluate critical safety considerations for the space shuttle.

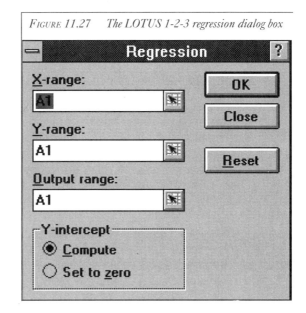

FIGURE 11.27   *The LOTUS 1-2-3 regression dialog box*

Risk Assessment for Space Shuttle Tile Damage[6]

At reentry, the space shuttle orbiter is subjected to high heat loads. Its heat shield is composed of reinforced carbon-carbon in the hottest areas of the nose and edges of wings, protective blankets in the coolest areas on the top, and black tiles (about 25,000) bonded to the bottom surface. After every flight, some tiles are repaired; others have to be replaced.

The potential loss of tiles has been a concern to NASA. Once a tile is lost, adjacent tiles are more vulnerable to heat loads and aerodynamic forces that might cause a burn-through, leading to loss of vehicle and crew. Working with Stanford University, NASA performed a probabilistic risk analysis for the black tiles based on the first 30 flights of the shuttle. The analysis was divided into two parts: the susceptibility of the tiles to damage and the effect of this tile damage on the performance of the shuttle.

A tile fails when the loads on it exceed its capacity to withstand them. The main failure mode is tile debonding because of an external load (a debris hit) that exceeds its design capacity, or because it is unable to withstand a normal load such as vibration due to weakening of one of its components. The severity of increased heating or burn-through due to lost tiles depends on the location, that is, whether critical components such as computers, hydraulic lines, or fuel tanks could be affected.

---

[6]Adaptation and figures from Pate-Cornell *et al.* "Risk Management for the Tiles of the Space Shuttle," *Interfaces*, Vol. 24, No. 1, Jan–Feb, 1994.

Certain tiles have higher probabilities of being damaged by debris, some receive greater heat loading during reentry, and some protect critical flight controls. The orbiter's undersurface was divided into minimal zones ("min-zones") having similar characteristics to facilitate the analysis.

Figure 11.28 shows an influence diagram for the structure of the probabilistic model. The model includes the following for each min-zone:

1. *Initiating events*—probability distributions for the number of tiles initially lost either because of debonding under debris impacts or because of other factors that weakened the bond
2. *Final patch size*—probability distribution of the number of adjacent tiles lost conditional on the loss of the first tile
3. *Burn-through*—probability of burn-through conditional on a failure patch of a given size
4. *System loss*—probability of failure of systems under the skin conditional on a burn-through
5. *Loss of vehicle and crew*—probability conditional on failure of subsystems due to burn-through

The probabilities were estimated using historical frequencies and expert opinion when necessary. Little statistical data were available. Only two tiles had been lost in shuttle flights. The researchers also knew the number and severity of debris hits and the number of tiles that had been found during maintenance to have been poorly bonded. But expert opinion was needed to assess the probability of losing the orbiter if a particular subsystem was exposed to high temperatures and the probability of tile debonding if the bond was weak.

The main results of the analysis are shown in Figure 11.29. This figure shows the min-zones and the risk criticality of each tile (the darker areas being more critical). The analysis

FIGURE 11.28   *Risk analysis influence diagram*

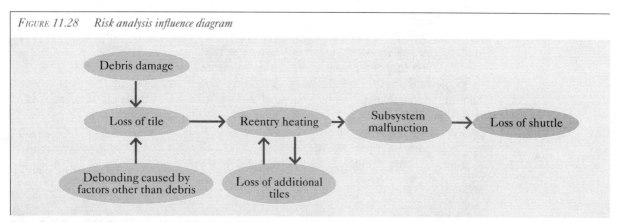

Source: Paté-Cornell, M.-Elisabeth, and Paul S. Fischbeck, "Risk Management for the Tiles of the Space Shuttle," *Interfaces*, Vol. 24, No. 1, January–February, 1994, p. 71.

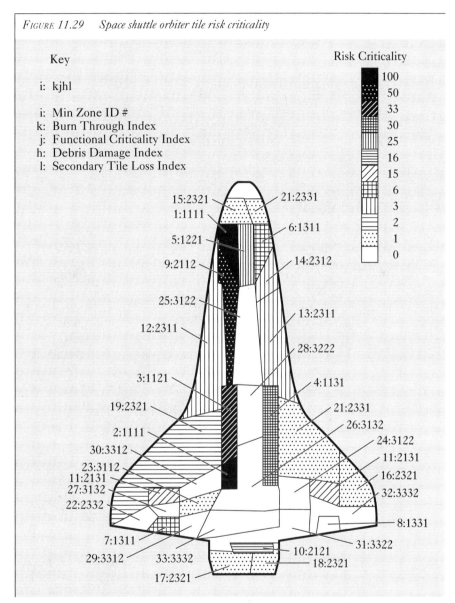

FIGURE 11.29   *Space shuttle orbiter tile risk criticality*

Key

i: kjhl

i: Min Zone ID #
k: Burn Through Index
j: Functional Criticality Index
h: Debris Damage Index
l: Secondary Tile Loss Index

Risk Criticality

100
50
33
30
25
16
15
6
3
2
1
0

15:2321
1:1111
5:1221
9:2112
25:3122
12:2311
3:1121
19:2321
2:1111
30:3312
23:3112
11:2131
27:3132
22:2332
7:1311
29:3312   33:3332
17:2321

21:2331
6:1311
14:2312
13:2311
28:3222
4:1131
21:2331
26:3132
24:3122
11:2131
16:2321
32:3332
8:1331
31:3322
10:2121
18:2321

Source: Paté-Cornell, M.-Elisabeth, and Paul S. Fischbeck, "Risk Management for the Tiles of the Space Shuttle," *Interfaces*, Vol. 24, No. 1, January–February, 1994, p. 74.

demonstrated that the total probability of losing the orbiter on any given mission due to failure of the thermal protection system is on the order of 10^{-3}, with approximately 40 percent of this probability attributable to debris-related problems and 60 percent to problems of debonding caused by other factors. For the total risk, 85 percent of the risk can be attributed to about 15 percent of the tiles. Eight of the 33 min-zones are determined to be the most risk-critical.

Questions for Discussion

1. What factors in shuttle preparation and operation might influence the basic events that could cause loss of the shuttle?
2. How important might this study be in changing organizational attitudes and policies?

MORE EXAMPLES AND SOLVED PROBLEMS

EXAMPLE 15. ELECTRIC UTILITY PLANNING[7]

An electric utility is planning a high-voltage transmission line across its service area. The general characteristics of the transmission line have been selected, but the specific conductor size is still to be determined. The possible conductors differ in both construction and operating costs, and these costs are uncertain. The primary component of the operating cost is the cost of power lost due to heating of the conductor. For a small conductor, this loss is relatively large, whereas for a large conductor it is smaller. Conversely, the construction cost of a small conductor is lower than that of a large conductor. The cost of the lost power is uncertain because the utility company's power generation plants use oil, and its price can vary over time.

   We assume that the construction cost, CC, is given by the product of the construction cost estimate made for a particular conductor size, CCE, and a construction cost variance multiplier, CCVM. The loss cost, LC, for a particular conductor size is given by the product of the loss multiplier associated with that conductor, LM, and the uncertain oil price, PRICE. These data are provided in Table 11.5, and an influence diagram that describes the relationships among these model components is shown in Figure 11.30.

   Figure 11.31 shows a spreadsheet that computes the expected value for each alternative. We see that the medium-size conductor has the lowest expected cost and represents the best decision. A problem at the end of this chapter will ask you to study the sensitivity of this decision with respect to the probability estimates.

---

[7]This is a simplified version of an actual application adapted from Craig W. Kirkwood, "An Overview of Methods for Applied Decision Analysis," *Interfaces*, Vol. 22, No. 6, November–December 1992, pp. 28–39. The actual application is described in Dale M. Crawford, Bruce C. Huntzinger, and Craig W. Kirkwood, "Multiobjective Decision Analysis for Transmission Conductor Selection," *Management Science*, Vol. 24, No. 16, December 1978, pp. 1700–1709.

TABLE 11.5
Cost estimates

Known data	Conductor size		
	Small	Medium	Large
Construction cost estimate	100	200	300
Loss multiplier	11	5	1

Uncertain data		
CCVM:		Probability
Low estimate 1.40		.2
No error 1.00		.6
High estimate .90		.2
Oil price:		
Low price 15		.185
Medium price 20		.630
High price 40		.185

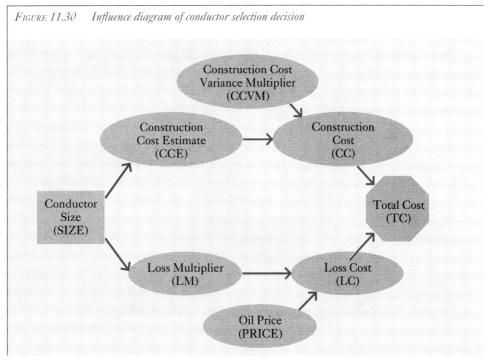

FIGURE 11.30   Influence diagram of conductor selection decision

Figure from Kirkwood, "An Overview of Methods for Applied Decision Analysis," *Interfaces*, Vol. 22, No. 6, Nov–Dec 1992, p. 32.

FIGURE 11.31   Conductor selection spreadsheet

	A	B	C	D	E	F	G	H	I	J	K
1	**Electric Utility Planning Model**										
2											
3	*Model Inputs*										
4											
5	Conductor size	CCE	LM		*Formulas and assumptions*						
6	Small	$100	11								
7	Medium	$200	5		*Construction cost = CCE x CCVM*						
8	Large	$300	1		*Loss cost = LM x PRICE*						
9					*Total cost = construction cost + loss cost*						
10											
11	CCVM		Probability								
12	Low estimate	1.4	0.2								
13	No error	1	0.6								
14	High estimate	0.9	0.2								
15											
16	Oil Price										
17	Low	$15	0.185								
18	Medium	$20	0.63								
19	High	$40	0.185								
20											
21											
22	**Model Output**										
23											
24	CCVM:	Low	Low	Low	No error	No error	No error	High	High	High	
25	PRICE:	Low	Medium	High	Low	Medium	High	Low	Medium	High	Expected
26	Probability:	0.037	0.126	0.037	0.111	0.378	0.111	0.037	0.126	0.037	Value
27	DECISION										
28	Small	$305	$360	$580	$265	$320	$540	$255	$310	$530	$356.53
29	Medium	$355	$380	$480	$275	$300	$400	$255	$280	$380	$325.88
30	Large	$435	$440	$460	$315	$320	$340	$285	$290	$310	$340.78

Selected cell formulas

A	A	B	C	D	E
26	Probability:	+C12*C17	+C12*C18	+C12*C19	+C13*C17
27	DECISION				
28	Small	+B6*B12+C6*B17	+B6*B12+C6*B18	+B6*B12+C6*B19	+B6*B13+C6*B17
29	Medium	+B7*B12+C7*B17	+B7*B12+C7*B18	+B7*B12+C7*B19	+B7*B13+C7*B17
30	Large	+B8*B12+C8*B17	+B8*B12+C8*B18	+B8*B12+C8*B19	+B8*B13+C8*B17

EXAMPLE 16. A PROBABILISTIC MODEL FOR PREVENTIVE MAINTENANCE

A packaging machine in a consumer goods factory shows the following pattern of failure.

Time between failures	Probability of failure (cumulative)
0–100 hours	0
100–150	0.05
150–200	0.10
200–250	0.20
250–300	0.35
300–350	0.55
350–400	0.80
400–450	0.95
450–500	1.0

The cost of repair after breakdown is $600; however, it costs only $120 to perform preventive maintenance on a scheduled basis. What is the best preventive maintenance policy?

We make some simplifying assumptions. First, we assume that maintenance will take place in 50-hour increments. Second, we assume that even if the machine fails and is repaired before the next scheduled maintenance, we will still perform the maintenance on schedule. Third, we assume that once scheduled maintenance is performed, the time to failure follows the distribution given above.

We will compute the expected cost per hour for preventive maintenance at each 50-hour interval. Suppose that we perform preventive maintenance every 100 hours. Then we incur the cost of maintenance, $125, but no cost of breakdowns since the probability of a failure is zero before 100 hours. Thus, the total cost per hour is $125/100 = $1.25. Now suppose that we perform preventive maintenance every 150 hours. There is a 5 percent chance that the machine will fail before the scheduled maintenance and require repair at a cost of $600. Thus the expected cost over the 150 hours is $125 + .05(600) = $155. The expected cost per hour is therefore $155/150 = $1.03. These and other calculations are shown in a spreadsheet in Figure 11.32. It appears that the best maintenance interval is 200 hours.

FIGURE 11.32   Spreadsheet model for preventive maintenance

	A	B	C	D	E	F
1	Preventitive Maintenance					
2						
3	Model Inputs					
4						
5	Repair Cost	$600.00				
6	Maintenance Cost	$125.00				
7						
8	Model Output					
9						
10	Maintenance Interval	Probability	Maintenance	Failure	Total	Cost per
11		of Failure	Cost	Cost	Cost	Hour
12	100	0.00	$125.00	$0.00	$125.00	$1.25
13	150	0.05	$125.00	$30.00	$155.00	$1.03
14	200	0.10	$125.00	$60.00	$185.00	$0.93
15	250	0.20	$125.00	$120.00	$245.00	$0.98
16	300	0.35	$125.00	$210.00	$335.00	$1.12
17	350	0.55	$125.00	$330.00	$455.00	$1.30
18	400	0.80	$125.00	$480.00	$605.00	$1.51
19	450	0.95	$125.00	$570.00	$695.00	$1.54
20	500	1.00	$125.00	$600.00	$725.00	$1.45

Selected cell formulas

	A	B	C	D	E	F
10	Maintenance Interval	Probability	Maintenance	Failure	Total	Cost per
11		of Failure	Cost	Cost	Cost	Hour
12	100	0.00	+$B$6	+$B$5*B12	@SUM(C12..D12)	+E12/A12
13	150	0.05	+$B$6	+$B$5*B13	@SUM(C13..D13)	+E13/A13
14	200	0.10	+$B$6	+$B$5*B14	@SUM(C14..D14)	+E14/A14
15	250	0.20	+$B$6	+$B$5*B15	@SUM(C15..D15)	+E15/A15
16	300	0.35	+$B$6	+$B$5*B16	@SUM(C16..D16)	+E16/A16

EXAMPLE 17. SINGLE PERIOD PROBABILISTIC INVENTORY MODEL WITH CONTINUOUS DEMAND

In Example 7 we developed a model for the newsboy problem when there are a small, discrete number of possible levels of demand. In many cases, the demand follows a continuous probability distribution, such as a uniform or normal distribution, and a decision of how much to purchase must be made. Such a decision is critical for firms such as supermarkets, which operate on low profit margins.

The director of seafood for a major supermarket chain must make a decision of how much shrimp to order for the Christmas season. For a particular market, historical records suggest that the demand is uniform between 200 and 500 lbs. The shrimp is purchased for $5.00/lb. and sells for $5.50/lb. Near the end of its shelf life, it must be discounted, and any surplus can be sold for $4.00/lb. Thus, the company loses $1.00/lb. for purchasing more than the estimated demand. Underestimating the demand results in the lost opportunity of realizing a $.50/lb. profit. What is the best amount of shrimp to purchase?

Figure 11.33 shows the distribution of demand. There is only one decision variable: the amount to order. This problem can be solved easily using an *incremental* or

---

FIGURE 11.33   *Distribution demand for shrimp*

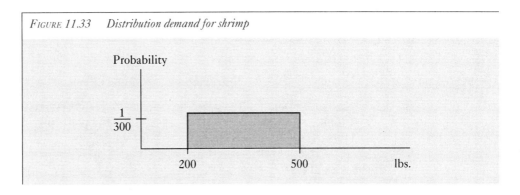

marginal analysis. Rather than computing the total profit that might be expected for each order quantity as we did in the newsboy problem, we may calculate the *change* in the expected profits caused by purchasing one more pound. If we purchase one more pound, only two possibilities exist: (1) It will be sold or (2) it will not be sold. If we purchase the additional pound and it is sold, then no loss is incurred since we made the correct decision. However, if we purchase it and it is not sold, then we incur a loss due to overstocking. In a similar fashion, if we do not purchase the extra pound and it would not have been sold, no loss is incurred. But if it could have been sold, we incur a loss due to understocking.

To illustrate this, note that the expected demand is 350 lbs. Consider the decision to order an additional pound. If we order 351 lbs. and the demand is not greater than 350, then we incur a loss of $1.00. This will occur with a probability $P(\text{Demand} \le 350 \text{ lbs.}) = .50$. The *expected loss* is .5($1.00) = $0.50. On the other hand, if we order 350 lbs. and the actual demand exceeds 350 lbs., then we incur a loss of $0.50. This will occur with a probability $P(\text{Demand} > 350 \text{ lbs.}) = .50$. The *expected loss* is .5($0.50) = $0.25. Clearly, the best decision is to order 350 lbs. We could repeat this for smaller order quantities until the expected loss of not ordering an additional pound exceeds the expected loss of ordering the additional pound. However, we can generalize this approach quite easily.

Let x be the optimal order quantity, L_o the loss due to overstocking, and L_u the loss due to understocking. The expected loss due to overstocking is

$$\text{Expected loss due to overstocking} = L_o P(\text{Demand} \le x)$$

Similarly, the expected loss due to understocking is

$$\text{Expected loss due to understocking} = L_u P(\text{Demand} > x)$$

If one of these expected losses is greater than the other, then we should consider a better order quantity. However, if they are equal, then we are indifferent between ordering x or $x + 1$ pounds. Thus, the breakeven point is the value of x for which

$$L_o P(\text{Demand} \le x) = L_u P(\text{Demand} > x)$$

Since $P(\text{Demand} > x) = 1 - P(\text{Demand} \le x)$, we have

$$L_o P(\text{Demand} \le x) = L_u[1 - P(\text{Demand} \le x)]$$

or

$$P(\text{Demand} \le x) = L_u / (L_o + L_u)$$

For this example, we have

$$P(\text{Demand} \le x) = .50 / (1.00 + .50) = .33$$

Figure 11.34 shows that the optimal purchase quantity can be determined by finding the point at which $P(\text{Demand} \le x) = .33$ on the probability distribution of demand. Thus, 300 pounds should be ordered.

EXAMPLE 18. SEPARATING FIXED AND VARIABLE COSTS

Many optimization models require costs as input data (either directly or as part of a contribution calculation). In Chapter 4, for example, we discussed the difference between fixed and variable costs and their roles in linear programming models. Fixed costs are in general not relevant in a linear program (although they may indeed be relevant in an integer program). Consequently, there is a need to separate cost into fixed and variable portions. One approach to this problem is to use linear regression.

Consider the 10 years of data shown in an EXCEL spreadsheet in Figure 11.35. The graph shows that selling and administrative expenses appear to be linearly related. We would like to determine which portion of these costs is fixed and which portion varies with quantity. We may derive estimates of fixed and variable portions by estimating a simple linear regression model of the form $\hat{y} = b_0 + b_1 x$, where the dependent variable y is selling and administrative expenses and the independent variable x is sales volume. Then the intercept b_0 may be interpreted as the fixed portion of these costs, and the slope b_1 is the variable portion (an estimate of the increase in selling and administrative expenses as sales increases by one unit).

The output from this regression run in EXCEL is shown in Figure 11.36. The fit is very good ($r^2 = 94.3$ percent). The estimates are $b_0 = 107.75$ and $b_1 = 12.33$. Hence our estimate of the fixed portion of selling and administrative expenses is \$107,750 and the variable portion is \$12,331 per 1,000 units, or \$12.33 per unit. The fitted line is shown in Figure 11.37.

FIGURE 11.34   *Optimal purchase quantity for Example 17*

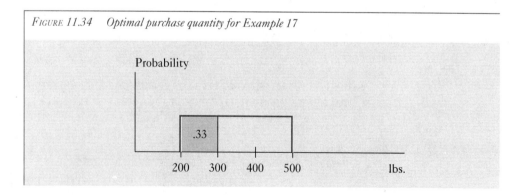

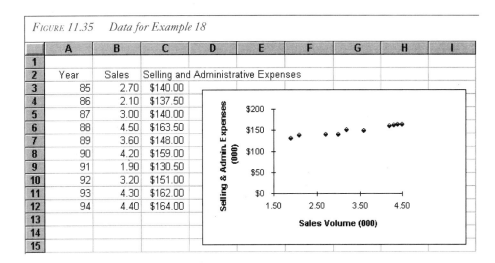

FIGURE 11.35   Data for Example 18

	A	B	C	D	E	F	G	H	I
1									
2	Year	Sales	Selling and Administrative Expenses						
3	85	2.70	$140.00						
4	86	2.10	$137.50						
5	87	3.00	$140.00						
6	88	4.50	$163.50						
7	89	3.60	$148.00						
8	90	4.20	$159.00						
9	91	1.90	$130.50						
10	92	3.20	$151.00						
11	93	4.30	$162.00						
12	94	4.40	$164.00						
13									
14									
15									

FIGURE 11.36   EXCEL regression output for Example 18

	A	B	C	D	E	F	G	H	I
25	SUMMARY OUTPUT								
26									
27	Regression Statistics								
28	Multiple R	0.971184							
29	R Square	0.943199							
30	Adjusted R	0.936099							
31	Standard E	3.087645							
32	Observatio	10							
33									
34	ANOVA								
35		df	SS	MS	F	ignificance F			
36	Regression	1	1266.457	1266.457	132.8421	2.91E-06			
37	Residual	8	76.2684	9.53355					
38	Total	9	1342.725						
39									
40		Coefficient	andard Err	t Stat	P-value	Lower 95%	Upper 95%	wer 95.000	per 95.000%
41	Intercept	107.7479	3.755989	28.68695	2.36E-09	99.08654	116.4092	99.08654	116.4092
42	Sales	12.3311	1.06987	11.52571	2.91E-06	9.863887	14.79814	9.863887	14.79814
43									
44									
45									
46	RESIDUAL OUTPUT								
47					Regression Coefficients				
48	Observation	and Admini	Residuals						
49	1	141.0416	-1.0416						
50	2	133.643	3.857006						
51	3	144.7409	-4.74091						
52	4	163.2374	0.262577						
53	5	152.1395	-4.13951						
54	6	159.5381	-0.53812						
55	7	131.1768	-0.67679						
56	8	147.2071	3.792892						
57	9	160.7712	1.228779						
58	10	162.0043	1.995678						

615

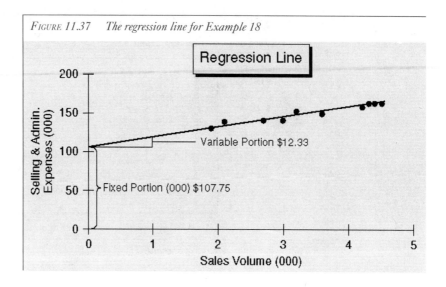

FIGURE 11.37   *The regression line for Example 18*

The remaining portions of the regression output from EXCEL concern the statistical significance of these estimates and allow for the testing of hypotheses concerning them. For example, the *t* Stat in the sales row may be used to test whether or not the slope is significantly different from zero (and likewise for the intercept). However, as previously mentioned, for these tests to be valid, certain assumptions must hold and an analysis of the errors (observed data–fitted estimates) must be conducted. Refer to Anderson, Sweeney, and Williams for a detailed discussion of these issues.

SUMMARY

Probabilistic models and statistical methods are an important part of analysis and problem solving in management science. It is through the use of probability distributions and statistical estimation that we are able to quantify uncertainty and risk, the underlying difficulties in many planning problems.

Statistical methods are extremely important for forecasting and estimating. These techniques are almost always needed to measure or estimate the input parameters for optimization models used in management science. Statistical methods are also often used to verify model assumptions (for example, that the input data come from certain probability distributions). As we shall see in Chapters 13 and 14 on computer simulation, statistical methods are also important for quantifying the reliability of model outputs.

We have seen several examples of probabilistic models in this chapter. The remaining chapters in this text focus on probabilistic management science models.

CHAPTER REVIEW EXERCISES

I. Terms to Understand

a. Risk analysis (p. 561)
b. Discrete probability distribution (p. 563)
c. Continuous probability distribution (p. 561)
d. Chi-square test (p. 568)
e. Stochastic optimization model (p. 579)
f. Independent variable (p. 585)
g. Dependent variable (p. 585)
h. Simple linear regression (p. 585)
i. Multiple linear regression (p. 585)
j. Coefficient of determination (p. 587)
k. r^2 statistic (p. 587)

l. Forecasting (p. 591)
m. Time series (p. 591)
n. Trend component (p. 591)
o. Cyclical component (p. 591)
p. Seasonal component (p. 592)
q. Irregular component (p. 592)
r. Moving average (p. 593)
s. Exponential smoothing (p. 595)
t. Smoothing constant (p. 595)
u. MAD statistic (p. 596)

II. Questions

1. Explain the difference between deterministic and stochastic optimization models. Which type of model is usually more difficult to solve and why?
2. Explain the difference between discrete and continuous probability distributions. Give two examples of phenomena that would follow a discrete distribution and two examples that would follow a continuous distribution.
3. Historical data can be used to construct an empirical frequency-based probability distribution. This empirical distribution may be used directly in modeling. An alternative approach is to fit the data to a known theoretical probability distribution and use the theoretical distribution in modeling. Discuss the advantages and disadvantages of the second approach.
4. Discuss the pros and cons of using an expected value decision criterion. In your opinion, when is this criterion appropriate and when is would it be inappropriate?
5. Discuss a scenario where it is appropriate to estimate probabilities judgmentally.
6. Explain the difference between the least squares measure of fit and the MAD measure of fit in forecasting.
7. List and compare the four components of a time series.
8. Refer to the section on exponential smoothing and Figure 11.21, the exponential smoothing forecast for the Atlas Dry Cleaners time series. Why do you think this technique is called exponential smoothing?

III. Problems[8]

1. Alpha Inc. is considering two projects. Analysis has determined that the return for Project A has an expected value of 15 percent and a standard deviation of 7.5 percent. Project B has an expected return of 23 percent and a standard deviation of 12 percent. Assume that the return for each project is normally distributed.
   a. Which project would you choose based on expected return?
   b. Calculate the probability of achieving a return between 10 percent and 20 percent. Which project would you select based on this?
   c. Calculate the probability of a profit for each project. Which project would you choose based on this?
   d. Which criterion (part a, part b, or part c) would you use for selecting a project? Why?

---

[8]We recommend that all of these problems be done on a spreadsheet.

2. Bill, a manager of a defense department contract, has been charged with developing a budget for next year. Based on past data, he believes that following probabilities are good estimates:

Fixed costs	Probability	Variable costs	Probability
$200,000	.2	$1,000,000	.1
$400,000	.6	$1,200,000	.4
$600,000	.2	$1,600,000	.3
		$1,900,000	.2

Assume that fixed and variable costs are independent.
a. List all possible combinations of fixed and variable costs.
b. Develop the probability distribution for total cost.
c. Approximately what budget is needed so that the probability of running over budget is 5 percent or less?

3. Consider the following sales data (in thousands of dollars):

Month	Sales	Month	Sales
1	5,271	13	4,647
2	4,343	14	5,100
3	5,355	15	5,801
4	4,448	16	3,361
5	4,441	17	4,784
6	4,212	18	3,975
7	5,711	19	6,021
8	4,337	20	4,623
9	5,638	21	5,637
10	4,808	22	4,956
11	5,240	23	4,722
12	5,893	24	6,062

Use the Chi-square goodness of fit test (using a .05 level of significance) to test whether or not sales may be accurately modeled with a normal distribution.

4. Many waiting line models (Chapter 15 concerns the study of queuing, or waiting line models) assume that service times are exponentially distributed. Consider the following grouped data from a post office branch (time is measured in minutes):

Service time	Frequency
$0 \le t \le 0.5$	171
$0.5 \le t \le 1$	189
$1 \le t \le 2$	248
$2 \le t \le 4$	260
$4 \le t \le 10$	132

Use the Chi-square goodness of fit test (.05 level of significance) to determine if these data come from an exponential distribution. (*Hint:* The parameter μ of the exponential distribution must be estimated from the data. μ is interpreted as the average number of services per minute.)

5. Computer simulation (the focus of Chapters 13 and 14) is used extensively in business. Modeling probabilistic components via simulation requires the generation of random numbers. Many computer languages and software packages have the capability of generating "random" numbers uniformly distributed between 0 and 1, which in turn may be used to generate other known probability distributions like those discussed in this chapter.

In the following table are 100 numbers randomly generated from the interval 0 to 5 using EXCEL. Use the Chi-square goodness of fit test (with significance level .05) to test whether or not these numbers correspond to a *uniform distribution* from 0 to 5.

	A	B	C	D	E	F	G	H	I	J
1	0.01	0.60	0.84	1.33	2.86	1.71	3.94	3.63	3.41	1.01
2	2.50	4.38	0.57	2.02	4.64	1.00	0.14	3.03	4.27	0.18
3	3.68	4.09	3.09	2.76	0.46	2.31	4.71	2.95	1.13	4.52
4	3.10	2.86	2.87	3.85	2.42	0.25	1.64	2.76	1.54	1.27
5	1.81	2.16	1.78	2.75	2.20	0.09	0.93	0.40	1.77	3.41
6	4.59	1.82	2.14	0.61	1.56	4.18	4.33	1.26	0.82	2.16
7	2.45	4.56	1.68	2.68	2.67	4.73	3.37	4.74	4.72	0.83
8	4.12	0.56	3.02	4.06	3.33	1.18	1.73	1.57	1.65	1.19
9	4.35	4.09	1.31	0.98	2.17	0.34	2.96	0.52	2.10	0.00
10	2.48	3.90	0.36	3.04	2.38	1.27	4.57	4.07	3.26	4.32

6. Statewise Auto Parts sells a variety of automobile parts. Its highest-volume item is a headlight replacement bulb. Historical data suggest that monthly demand is normally distributed with mean 120 and standard deviation 30. Each bulb costs $9.50 from the manufacturer. An order costs $12 and Statewise estimates that its inventory carrying cost is 22 percent. Lead time is 7 days (assume a 28-day month).

   a. Calculate the economic order quantity (EOQ).

   b. The manager of Statewise is willing to allow the lead time demand to exceed the reorder point at most 5 percent of the time. Calculate the reorder point.

   c. Calculate the expected annual cost based on the lot size and reorder points found in parts a and b.

7. Suppose the manager at Statewise Auto Parts (see Problem 6) decides to use his clout with his current supplier. He intends to threaten to go to a new supplier unless the lead time for headlight bulbs is reduced to one day. How much would such a lead time reduction save Statewise?

8. Lovely Lawns (LL) is a fast-growing lawn care service. Because LL's current supplier of fertilizer has not been reliable, the owner of LL has decided to take bids from three other suppliers and will choose one of them as the replacement.

Past data indicates that LL's weekly customer demand for fertilizer is normally distributed with mean 2,700 pounds and standard deviation 420 pounds. Order costs are $15 and the inventory carrying cost is 25 percent. Evaluate the following bids based on expected annual cost. Which supplier gives the smallest expected annual cost?

	Supplier A	Supplier B	Supplier C
Cost per pound	$2.35	$2.39	$2.40
Promised lead time	7 days	4 days	3 days

9. Bev's Bakery specializes in sourdough bread. Early each morning, Bev must decide how many loaves to bake for the day. Each loaf costs $0.35 to make and sells for $1.15. Bread left over at the end of the day can be sold to a day-old baked goods store for $0.25. Past data indicate that demand is distributed as follows:

Number of loaves	Probability
15	.05
16	.05
17	.1
18	.1
19	.2
20	.4
21	.05
22	.05

a. What is the optimal quantity for Bev to bake each morning?
b. What is the optimal quantity for Bev to bake if the unsold loaves cannot be sold to the day-old store at the end of the day (so that unsold loaves are a total loss)?

10. Midwestern Hardware must decide how many snow shovels to order for the coming snow season. Each shovel costs $6.00 and is sold for $8.50. No inventory is carried from one snow season to the next. Shovels unsold after February are sold at a discount price of $5.00. Past data indicate that sales are highly dependent on the severity of the winter season. Past seasons have been classified as mild or harsh and the following distribution of regular price demand have been tabulated:

Mild winter		Harsh winter	
# of Shovels	Probability	# of Shovels	Probability
250	.5	1,500	.2
300	.4	2,500	.4
350	.1	3,000	.4

Shovels must be ordered from the manufacturer in lots of 200. Develop a spreadsheet to find the optimal quantity for Midwestern to order if the forecast calls for a 70 percent chance of a harsh winter.

11. Perform a sensitivity analysis of the Midwestern Hardware scenario (Problem 10). Find the optimal order quantity and optimal expected profit for probabilities of a harsh winter ranging from .2 to .8 in increments of .2. Plot optimal expected profit as a function of the probability of a harsh winter.

12. The number of tabloids sold per week at Friar's supermarket is normally distributed with mean 85 and standard deviation 12. The market buys the tabloids for $0.45 apiece and sells them for $1.00. At the end of the week, unsold copies are retrieved by the vendor and the market is credited $0.10 for each copy. What quantity should Friar's order to maximize expected profit?

13. A project network, its critical path, the expected activity times (in months) and standard deviations are shown in the following table and in Figure 11.38. Assume that work takes place seven days a week.
a. Calculate the probability of completing the project in 18 months or less.
b. Calculate the probability of completing the project in one year or less.
c. Suppose you are bidding on this project. Your bid must give a project completion date (and there are penalties associated with missing the target completion date). You have decided to use a completion date (time from the start of the project), which you are 90 percent sure of meeting. Calculate this project completion time.

FIGURE 11.38   *Project network with critical path A-E-F-I (time = 15)*

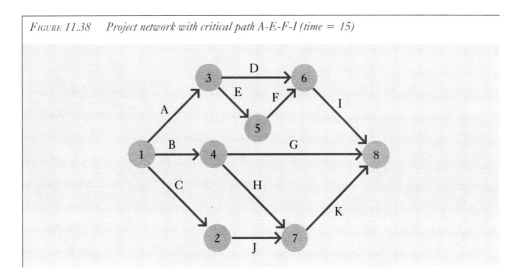

Activity	Expected time	Standard deviation
A	3	.33
B	1	.33
C	3	.20
D	2	.30
E	4	1.00
F	3	1.10
G	7	2.00
H	6	1.50
I	5	.50
J	6	.50
K	3	.10

14.   Consider the project network[9] in Figure 11.39. The following data are believed to hold for this project (all times are in days):

Activity	Optimistic time	Most probable time	Pessimistic time
A	8	9	10
B	10	12	24
C	8	9	10
D	10	14	20
F	7	8	9
G	4	5	6

[9]This problem assumes knowledge of topics from Chapter 9, Network Modeling and Optimization.

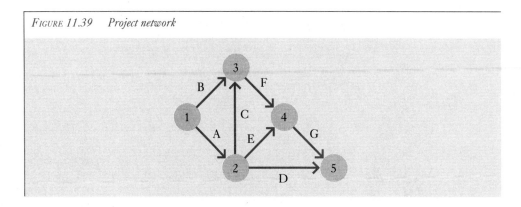

FIGURE 11.39   *Project network*

a.   Calculate the expected time and standard deviation for each activity in this project.
b.   Calculate the critical path for this network.
c.   Calculate the probability that this project will be completed in one month or less (a month is 24 working days).

SA   (15.)   Sales data for the last 12 quarters are shown in Figure 11.40. Forecast sales for the next quarter using the moving average technique with $k = 3$ quarters of data.

SA   (16.)   Consider the sales data presented in Problem 15. Forecast next quarter's sales using exponential smoothing with the following:
a. $\alpha = .2$
b. $\alpha = .3$
c.   Compare the fit of a and b using MAD. Which appears to fit the data better?

SA   (17.)   Alan is a marketing manager. He is about to make a presentation to top management concerning the need for corrective action in production planning because of the increase in the number of stockouts. Data over the last 12 months appear in Figure 11.41. Forecast the number of stockouts for the next three months using linear regression.

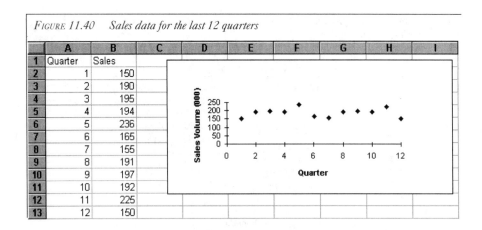

FIGURE 11.40   *Sales data for the last 12 quarters*

	A	B
1	Quarter	Sales
2	1	150
3	2	190
4	3	195
5	4	194
6	5	236
7	6	165
8	7	155
9	8	191
10	9	197
11	10	192
12	11	225
13	12	150

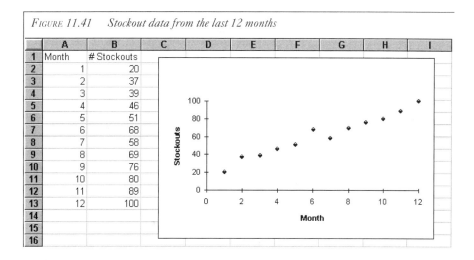

FIGURE 11.41   Stockout data from the last 12 months

18. Consider the stock price behavior shown in Figure 11.42. The stock price given is the price of the stock at the end of each month.

a. Forecast the future stock price using one of the methods discussed in this chapter. Justify using the method you choose.

b. Assuming you've bought the stock at the last price in the data set, how long will you have to hold the stock to realize a return of 10 percent?

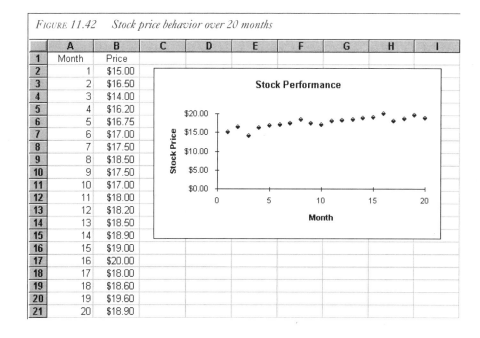

FIGURE 11.42   Stock price behavior over 20 months

19. Lovely Lawns (LL) (see Problem 8) is considering expanding into the landscaping business.[10] LL will focus on upscale homes and has obtained the following data from a landscaping company in a nearby state: LL would like develop a model that will help estimate landscape expenditures as a function of household income and mortgage amount. Develop this model using the data below and multiple linear regression. Estimate the landscape expenditures for a household income of $420,000 and a mortgage amount of $510,000.

Customer #	Landscape expenditures	Household income	Mortgage amount
1	$8,100	$186,000	$242,000
2	$10,800	$204,000	$321,000
3	$5,400	$194,000	$282,000
4	$16,200	$242,000	$340,000
5	$15,600	$238,000	$300,000
6	$18,900	$284,000	$400,000
7	$3,900	$374,000	$480,000
8	$25,200	$460,000	$800,000
9	$13,900	$264,000	$200,000
10	$17,500	$236,000	$310,000
11	$22,000	$421,000	$547,000
12	$12,100	$246,000	$437,000

20. As an alternative to linear regression, linear goal programming[11] may be used to fit a linear model to data. If we take as our goal the estimated line going exactly through every data point (a perfect fit), we may solve for the parameter values that come as close as possible to achieving this goal. Consider the data shown in Figure 11.43.

   We may use linear programming to fit a model of the form $\hat{y} = b_0 + b_1 x$. The objective is to *minimize the sum of the absolute values of the errors* between the observed and fitted values. Let u_i and v_i be the

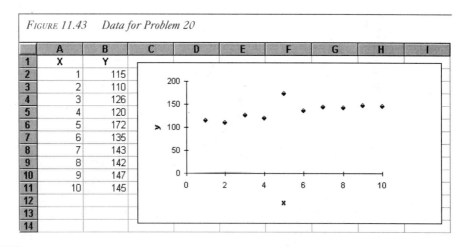

FIGURE 11.43   Data for Problem 20

	A	B
1	X	Y
2	1	115
3	2	110
4	3	126
5	4	120
6	5	172
7	6	135
8	7	143
9	8	142
10	9	147
11	10	145
12		
13		
14		

---

[10]This problem is based on problem 16.24 in Freund, J. E., F. J. Williams, and B. M. Perles, *Elementary Business Statistics* 6th ed. Englewood Cliffs, NJ: Prentice-Hall, 1993.

[11]This problem assumes knowledge of the topics in Chapter 7.

positive and negative difference, respectively, of the observed and fitted values for the i th data point. The following LP will find the optimal values of b_0 and b_1 (and u_i and v_i):

$$\text{Min} \sum_{i=1}^{10} [u_i + v_i]$$

subject to

$$115 - b_0 - 1b_1 = u_1 - v_1$$
$$110 - b_0 - 2b_1 = u_2 - v_2$$
$$126 - b_0 - 3b_1 = u_3 - v_2$$

$$\vdots$$

$$145 - b_0 - 10b_1 = u_{10} - v_{10}$$
$$u_i, v_i \geq 0 \qquad i = 1, 2, 3, \ldots, 10$$

b_0 and b_1 unrestricted

The objective function minimizes the sum of the absolute value of the errors. The constraint set defines the error terms for each data point: observed y − fitted y = error. The error may be positive (positive u_i) or negative (positive v_i). Note that the variables b_0 and b_1 are unrestricted in sign.

a. Solve the above LP problem using an LP solver. What are the optimal values of b_0 and b_1? Plot the fitted line with the observed data.

b. Fit a line to the data using linear regression. What are the estimates of b_0 and b_1? Plot the fitted line with the line from part a.

c. Explain the differences in the two lines. (*Hint:* Consider the objective of linear regression versus the objective of the LP approach.)

IV. Projects and Cases

1. *Fairway Consulting.*[12] Jeff Blain is employed as a systems consultant by Business Systems Solutions (BSS), a large computer consulting firm. Jeff came to BSS from Family Life Mutual, a small insurance company, where he was employed as a systems analyst. Since then, he has maintained a relationship with Family Life by consulting for them on occasion. Jeff likes consulting and has always dreamed of starting his own business.

    Before he quits his job and puts his future on the line, Jeff wants to be reasonably certain that he will be able to make a decent living. In assessing the market for his services, Jeff has categorized potential consulting projects as follows:

    1. *Minor*—simple, basic activities such as software installation and PC setup
    2. *Small*—small programming projects such as designing spreadsheets or databases
    3. *Medium*—more involved projects, such as program maintenance or systems modification
    4. *Large*—in-depth projects, involving systems analysis, design, and implementation
    5. *Major*—large projects that include purchasing hardware, cable installation, and training

    The table below shows a typical distribution of projects in these categories. The table also includes the estimated weekly times required for each category. These are not total completion times but the time that would normally be spent on the project over the course of a week.

---

[12]Our thanks go to Barry Fridley for developing this case.

Category	Number of projects	Weekly time commitment
Minor	18	0.5–3 hours
Small	21	2–10
Medium	12	9–25
Large	6	20–35
Major	3	30–50

From the local chapter of the Data Processing Management Association, Jeff has acquired information about similar, small consulting firms to get a better idea of the number of projects that he could expect in any given week. By analyzing these data, Jeff developed the distribution shown in the table below.

Projects per week	Probability
0	.05
1	.07
2	.10
3	.15
4	.20
5	.15
6	.10
7	.07
8	.05
9	.04
10	.02

Jeff believes that his monthly expenses will be about $2,300, including health insurance, advertising, travel, office supplies, and so on. Being an avid golfer, Jeff decided to name his business Fairway Consulting. To be viable, the business would have to generate enough profit to meet or exceed his current annual income of $45,000.

Determine the potential profitability of the business if the hourly rates are $30, $40, or $50. How many hours per week would Jeff have to work to make the business profitable?

2. *Palmer Company.*[13] It is January, and the mangers of Palmer Company are reviewing their profit plans for the coming year. Last year Palmer had enjoyed a good year and was working close to capacity. Management has ordered a profit analysis of its three products and has available the following information:

	Product A	Product B	Product C
Selling price	$60.00	$30.00	$90.00
Material	$21.00	$11.25	$49.80
Direct labor	6.00	3.00	10.50
Variable overhead	3.70	1.85	6.47
Variable selling & admin.	4.14	3.27	8.28
Contribution margin	$25.16	$10.63	$14.95

Each product requires time in two departments:

	Product A	Product B	Product C
Department 1	0.5 hours	0.25 hours	0.3 hours
Department 2	0.25 hours	0.125 hours	0.75 hours

Yearly capacity in Department 1 is 3,100 hours and in Department 2 is 2,500 hours. Sales volume by product for the last 10 years is shown below.

Year	A	B	C
1	2,028	2,486	1,442
2	1,389	3,000	1,308
3	812	2,654	1,510
4	987	4,195	1,356
5	1,248	4,089	1,423
6	750	4,439	1,515
7	1,069	4,972	1,263
8	1,484	4,956	1,461
9	2,469	5,102	1,342
10	2,400	5,445	1,597

The production manager expressed concern that Palmer seemed to be quickly running out of capacity. These solutions to the limited production problem had already been rejected: (1) Subcontracting the production out to other firms is considered undesirable because of problems with maintaining quality; (2) operating a second shift is impossible because of a shortage of labor; (3) operating overtime would create problems because a large number of Palmer employees are "moonlighting" and would therefore refuse to work more than a regular 40-hour week; and (4) any increase in physical capacity would take a year and would therefore be of no help in the current situation. Price increases have also been rejected; although they would result in higher profits this year, the long-run competitive position of the firm would be weakened.

As a new analyst, you suggest that this year's total sales by product be forecasted from past data. Then if capacity allows, Palmer can produce these quantities. However, if capacity does not allow for the production of forecasted sales, an optimal production plan based on contribution margins, production times, and capacity and forecasted sales may be developed. You are applauded and immediately charged with full responsibility for this project.

Before the meeting breaks the sales manager expresses concern that such an "optimal plan" might not include all products. He informs you that certain customer needs must be met in the coming year. He estimates these requirements to be 1,000 units of A, 2,000 units of B, and 750 units of C.

3. Plan a project you will have to complete in the near future. Break the project down into well-defined tasks.
    a. Draw a network of the project that shows the precedent relationships among tasks.
    b. Give optimistic, most likely, and pessimistic times for each task. Calculate the mean and variance for each activity time.
    c. Calculate the critical path as discussed in Chapter 9. Give the mean and variance of the *project* completion time.
    d. What is the probability you will finish in 80 percent of the expected time?
    e. For what time can you be 90 percent sure of completion in that time or less?

REFERENCES

Anderson, David R., Dennis J. Sweeney, and Thomas A. Williams. *Statistics for Business and Economics*, 4th ed. St. Paul, MN: West Publishing Company, 1990.

Barron, F. Hutton. "Payoff Matrices Pay Off at Hallmark." *Interfaces*, Vol. 15, No. 4, July–August 1985, pp. 20–25.

Ben-Dov, Yosi, Lakhbir Hayre, and Vincent Pica. "Mortgage Valuation Models at Prudential Securities." *Interfaces*, Vol. 22, No. 1, January–February 1992, pp. 55–71.

Carter, Virgil, and Robert E. Machol. "Operations Research on Football." *Operations Research*, Vol. 19, No. 2, 1971, pp. 541–544.

Carter, Virgil, and Robert E. Machol. "Optimal Strategies on Fourth Down." *Management Science*, Vol. 24, No. 16, December 1978, pp. 1758–1762.

Cohen, Rochelle, and Fraser Dunford. "Forecasting for Inventory Control: An Example When 'Simple' Means 'Better'" *Interfaces*, Vol. 16, No. 6, November–December 1986, pp. 95–99.

Freund, John E., Frank J. Williams, and B. M. Peters. *Elementary Business Statistics, the Modern Approach*, 6th ed. Englewood Cliffs, NJ: Prentice Hall, 1993.

Helmer, F. Theodore, Edward B. Oppermann, and J. D. Suver. "Forecasting Nursing Staffing Requirements by Intensity-of-Care Level." *Interfaces*, Vol. 10, No. 3, June 1980, pp. 50–55.

Kimes, Sheryl, and James A. Fitzsimmons. "Selecting Profitable Hotel Sites at La Quinta Motor Inns." *Interfaces*, Vol. 20, No. 2, March–April 1990, pp. 12–20.

Ng, Kevin Y. K., M. Natalie Lam, and John R. Hudson. "Operating Aspects of Materiel Distribution Activity within the Canadian Forces." *Interfaces*, Vol. 17, No. 4, July–August, 1987, pp. 61–70.

Pate-Cornell, M.-Elisabeth, and Paul S. Fischbeck. "Risk Management for the Tiles of the Space Shuttle." *Interfaces*, Vol. 24, No. 1, January–February 1994.

Peterson, Rein, and Edward A. Silver. *Decision Systems for Inventory Management and Production Planning*. New York: John Wiley & Sons, 1979.

Smith, Barry C., John F. Leimkuhler, and Ross M. Darrow. "Yield Management at American Airlines." *Interfaces*, Vol. 22, No. 1, January–February 1992, pp. 8–31.

Springer, Clifford H., Robert E. Herlihy, Robert T. Mall, and Robert I. Beggs. *Probabilistic Models*. Homewood, IL: Irwin, 1968.

CHAPTER 12

DECISION

ANALYSIS

INTRODUCTION

- The athletic board of Santa Clara University had to decide whether to recommend implementing a drug testing program for intercollegiate athletes. One of the board members, who was a management science professor, developed a simple decision model to address the question of whether or not to test a single individual for the presence of drugs. The model focused on the key issue of the reliability of the testing procedures, consequences of testing errors, and the benefits of identifying a drug user compared with the costs of false accusations and nonidentification of users. The model's results surprised many board members. For instance, the model showed that if a test that is 95 percent reliable is applied to a population of 5 percent drug users, only 50 percent of all those that tested positively will actually be drug users. Most board members had read about the reliability of drug tests in various publications and agreed that a 95 percent reliability was a representative value. As a result, the board concluded that a false accusation was more serious than not identifying drug users and rejected the proposal. The university administration later accepted this recommendation [Feinstein, 1990].

- Electric utilities face decisions that can have important impacts on the environment. The impacts stem from the by-products of combustion and other chemicals, equipment, and processes that utilities use to produce electricity. Electric utilities have used decision analysis to make better environmental decisions. For example, utilities use large boilers to boil water and make steam to generate electricity. The cleaning process results in a waste solution that may be hazardous. Whether or not the waste stream will be hazardous is uncertain, as are the costs and effects of the various management strategies. Several courses of action—choice of cleaning agent, whether or not to include a prerinse stage, treatment and disposal method, and cleaning frequency—are available. Using techniques of decision analysis, the consulting firm Decision Focus Incorporated developed a strategy that would save a utility $119,000 for one boiler over a 20-year horizon [Balson et al., 1992].

- The executive vice president of a major bank asked its management science group to develop an approach to identify potentially catastrophic events and select the best alternatives to deal with the risks. In a pilot study, the group studied threats of fire and power failure to several critical services at a data-processing facility at operation's headquarters. The group determined that the potential loss resulting from these threats could exceed $100 million. A lengthy disruption would also have an unfavorable impact on customer relations and future profits. Using techniques of decision analysis, the group evaluated the benefits of alternatives such as fire control modifications and an emergency generator as well as their costs, which ranged upward to $20 million. The study indicated that a small generator for the funds-transfer division was cost justified, but that a large generator for all operations was not [Engemann and Miller, 1992].

Each of these examples involves a choice among alternatives. For example, the Santa Clara University athletic board needed to decide whether or not to implement a drug testing program; electric utilities must choose cleaning agents, treatment and disposal methods, and so on; and the bank had to decide on the size of an emergency generator. Making such choices is called *decision making*. Decision making is difficult because the consequences associated with decision alternatives are different, the consequences are not all equally valued, and there is uncertainty about the consequences of each alternative. Making decisions involves structuring the decision problem, assessing the possible impacts of each alternative, determining the preferences or values of the decision makers, and evaluating the alternatives.

Decision analysis is the study of how people make decisions, particularly when faced with imperfect or uncertain information, as well as a collection of techniques to support the analysis of decision problems.

Why do we have a separate chapter on decision analysis? All of the optimization models and approaches we have studied so far support decision making. The key word, however, is *support*. Models alone provide information with which to make decisions, but people actually make the decisions. For instance, a linear programming model might identify the best solution, but the decision maker is free to choose other solutions, perhaps based upon various qualitative issues. Decision analysis differs from other modeling approaches by explicitly considering preferences and attitudes and modeling the decision process itself. Its purpose is to produce insight and promote creativity to help people make better decisions.

Another distinguishing characteristic of decision analysis versus optimization models is the *number* of decision alternatives. In optimization models such as linear programming, we have an infinite number of possible solutions. In decision analysis problems we typically deal with a small set of alternatives that do not fall along a continuum.

In this chapter we study the techniques known formally as decision analysis. We will discuss both deterministic and probabilistic approaches that explicitly address the uncertainty inherent in many decision-making problems.

THE SCOPE AND IMPORTANCE OF DECISION ANALYSIS

Everybody makes decisions, both personal and professional. Managers are continually faced with decisions involving new products, plant locations, choice of suppliers, new equipment, make versus buy, downsizing, and many others. The ability to make good decisions is the mark of a successful (and promotable) manager. In today's complex business world, intuition and gut feel alone are not sufficient. Successful decision makers critically identify potential alternatives, quantify the expected results of decisions, carefully assess probabilities and preferences, and perform sensitivity analyses on the decision inputs.

The types of decision situations for which the techniques in this chapter apply have the following characteristics:[1]

1. *They must be important.* Decision analysis techniques would not be appropriate for minor decisions where the consequences of a mistake are so small that it is not worth our time to study the situation carefully. Many decision problems involve risks to life and limb, such as foods and drugs and toxic or hazardous materials. In addition, the consequences of many decisions are not felt immediately but may cover a long time period. For example, the lifetime of major facilities is 25 to 100 years, and research and development projects routinely require 5 to 20 years.

2. *They are probably unique.* Decisions that recur can be programmed and then delegated. But the ones that are unusual and perhaps occur only one time cannot be handled this way. Because of the many factors that affect a decision, generating good alternatives requires substantial creativity.

3. *They allow some time for study.* For example, decision analysis techniques would not be useful in making a decision when a small child runs out in front of your automobile or your jet fighter flames out during takeoff.

4. *They are complex.* Practical decision problems involve multiple objectives. For example, in evaluating routes for proposed pipelines, a decision maker would want to minimize environmental impact, minimize health and safety hazards, maximize economic benefit, and maximize social impact. This requires critical value trade-offs among such objectives. Decisions involve many intangibles, such as the goodwill of a client, employee morale, and governmental regulations. Many decisions involve several decision makers. For instance, to build a plant in a new area, corporate management may require approval from stockholders, regulatory agencies, community zoning boards, and perhaps even the courts. Finally, most decisions are closely allied to other decisions. Choices today affect both the alternatives available in the future and the desirability of those alternatives. Thus, there is often a sequence of decisions that must be made.

5. *They involve uncertainty.* If a particular action is taken, the decision maker is not absolutely certain about what outcome will occur. An advertising campaign may fail, a reservoir may break, or a new product may be a complete bomb. Uncertainty is further complicated when little or no data are available, or some data are very expensive or time-consuming to obtain. Natural phenomena such as weather or actions of other influential parties, such as governments or competitors, may cause uncertainty. Faced with such uncertainties, different people view the same set of information in different ways. An important aspect of decision analysis involves understanding decision makers' attitudes toward risk.

Decision problems are by no means trivial. For example, consider the decision of whether an electric utility should replace a transformer in a generating station. This decision depends on the likelihood of an incident, such as a fire, the cost of such an incident,

---

[1] Bruce F. Baird, *Managerial Decisions Under Uncertainty*, New York: John Wiley & Sons, 1989, p. 6; and Ralph L. Keeney, "Decision Analysis: An Overview," *Operations Research*, Vol. 30, No. 5, September–October 1982, pp. 803–838.

and the cost of replacing the unit. It also depends on the risk of a new transformer, the impact of increased efficiency and reliability, and the utility's risk attitude toward a very costly incident that has a very low chance of occurrence. The uncertainties in the occurrence, severity, and cost of incidents make such a decision difficult. By understanding these factors and learning how to analyze decisions in a rational manner, you will be better equipped to make better decisions in the future.

APPLICATIONS OF DECISION ANALYSIS[2]

Decision analysis techniques have been used in many diverse areas of application. In this section we review some of these.

Energy

Many energy-related companies use decision analysis in areas of competitive bidding, product selection, regulation, site selection, and technology choice. For example, one coal company used decision analysis to select a method to haul coal. Alternatives included making a bid to salvage a grounded ship, purchasing a new ship, and subcontracting for delivery. A power company had to choose from among several tower/conductor alternatives for a new electrical transmission line. An electric utility used decision analysis to evaluate and select particulate emission control equipment for a power plant. Decision analysis techniques have also been used to address policy issues related to regulatory actions, such as regulating nuclear material safeguards and nuclear waste management.

Many applications involve site selection, such as selecting nuclear power plant sites, oil wells, and nuclear waste dumps. For example, in choosing among site locations for drilling an oil well, the decision maker must consider geological and engineering factors in addition to attitudes toward risk and money. Both energy producers and energy regulators have applied decision analysis to determine energy-related technology development, for example, the choice between coal and nuclear generating technologies, or selecting the current coal generating technology versus waiting for development of advanced technology.

Manufacturing and Services

Applications in this area include budget allocation, product planning, and strategy. Decision analysis has been used to screen a set of 92 potential geographic information systems for a professional consulting firm and to rank the final candidates. A system reliability decision in the Israeli microelectronics industry involved whether or not to include redundancy in a diode array circuit as well as the choice of a specific packaging technology. In the strategy area, applications include analyzing strategies to regain market share in

---

[2]A comprehensive review of decision analysis applications from which these are adapted is found in James L. Corner and Craig W. Kirkwood, "Decision Analysis Applications in the Operations Research Literature, 1970–1988," Technical Report DIS 89/90-4, Department of Decision and Information Systems, Arizona State University, Tempe, AZ.

the airline industry following settlement of a strike, and analyzing new strategies for merchandising gasoline and other products through full-facility service stations. In the second case, the analysis led to a significant change in marketing strategy that had a large impact on sales. Another application involved the selection of a company with which to place a contract for the development of a computerized financial management system.

Medical Applications

The medical literature has many examples of using decision analysis. These include the decision to operate, equipment selection, treatment strategies, diagnosis of disease, choice of an appropriate cardiac pacemaker, and whether to undertake a national evaluation study on nosocomial infection control. For example, suppose that a patient that comes to the emergency room complaining of abdominal pain. Symptoms and tests might be consistent with appendicitis but might not be totally typical of the problem. The surgeon has to make a decision to perform an immediate operation or keep the patient for observation. If the operation is performed, there is a chance that a normal appendix would be removed if the problem was caused by something else. On the other hand, if it is not performed, delaying the operation might have serious effects if the patient does indeed have appendicitis. Many medical decisions have been successfully modeled with decision analysis with anticipated improvements in patient care.

Public Policy

Applications in the public policy area include acid rain regulation, choice among building development requests for the California Coastal Commission, an evaluation of research recommendations for the Office of Child Development, deciding on prescribed forest burns in the Southwest United States, and an evaluation of the possibility of having two different water quality standards instead of one.

Miscellaneous

In addition to the above categories, decision analysis has been used in some unique ways. For example, decision analysis has been used to consider trajectory decisions for the two 1977 Mariner Jupiter/Saturn space missions, to determine the effectiveness of run/pass or kick options for conversion in the closing moments of a close football game, and selecting among available mortgage instruments.

STRUCTURING DECISION PROBLEMS

Structuring decision problems involves defining alternative decisions that can be made, uncertain outcomes that may result, and criteria by which to evaluate the value of the various combinations of decisions and outcomes.

Generating Alternatives

Decision alternatives represent the choices that a decision maker can make. They might be a simple set of decisions, such as locating a factory from five potential sites or choosing one of three corporate health plan options. Other situations require a more complex sequence of decisions. For example, in new product introduction, a marketing manager might have to decide on whether to test market a new product and then, based on the test market results, decide to conduct further tests, begin a full scale marketing effort, or drop the product from further consideration. In either case, the manager must list the options that are available. Generating viable alternatives might involve some prescreening (perhaps using optimization models). For instance, a company might develop, solve, and perform sensitivity analysis on a mathematical programming model to generate potential plant location sites based on total distribution costs. However, making the final decision would involve many qualitative factors such as labor supply, tax incentives, environmental regulations, future uncertainties, and so on.

Managers must ensure that they have considered all possible options so that the "best" one will be included in the list. This often requires a good deal of creativity to define unusual options that might not normally be considered. Managers must put aside the tendency to jump right into the process of finding a solution to consider creative alternatives.

Defining Outcomes

The second task in structuring decision problems is defining the outcomes that may occur once a decision is made. These outcomes provide the basis for evaluating risks associated with decisions. Outcomes may be quantitative or qualitative. For instance, in selecting the size of a new factory, a company needs to consider the future demand for the product. The demand might be expressed quantitatively in sales units or dollars. If you are planning a spring break vacation to Florida in January, you might define uncertain weather-related outcomes qualitatively: sunny and warm, sunny and cold, rainy and warm, or rainy and cold. We often call the outcomes associated with decisions *states of nature* to reflect the fact that the decision maker does not have control over them.

Decision Criteria

Decision makers must have well-defined criteria on which to evaluate potential options. Decision criteria might be to maximize net profits or social benefits, or to minimize costs or some measure of loss. For example, in a factory sizing decision, sizing the facility too low will result in lost opportunities for market growth and profits, and sizing it too high will result in overcapacity and financial risk. The company might express these outcomes as cash flows and discount them to net present value. A different criterion might involve environmental impact.

To completely structure a decision problem, we must be able to express the value of every combination of decisions and states of nature.

> The value of making a decision D and having state of nature S occur is called the *payoff* and is expressed as $V(D,S)$.

Thus, if we are considering two sizes for a factory (small and large) and define three states of nature (low demand, medium demand, and high demand), we have $2 \times 3 = 6$ combinations. We must determine the payoff for each combination.

Payoffs are summarized in a *payoff table*, a matrix whose rows correspond to decisions and whose columns correspond to states of nature. A payoff table for the two-factory, three-demand example would appear as follows:

	States of Nature		
Decisions	S_1	S_2	S_3
D_1	$V(D_1, S_1)$	$V(D_1, S_2)$	$V(D_1, S_3)$
D_2	$V(D_2, S_1)$	$V(D_2, S_2)$	$V(D_2, S_3)$

Decision Trees

A *decision tree* is a graphical representation of a decision problem. A decision tree consists of the following:

- Decision nodes, represented by squares
- Decision branches, which stem from decision nodes
- State of nature nodes, represented by circles
- State of nature branches, which stem from state of nature nodes

Figure 12.1 shows a decision tree for two decisions and three states of nature. We "read" the tree from left to right. At node 1, a decision node, we have a choice of two decisions. Once this decision is made, we wait to observe what state of nature occurs.

FIGURE 12.1   *Example of a decision tree*

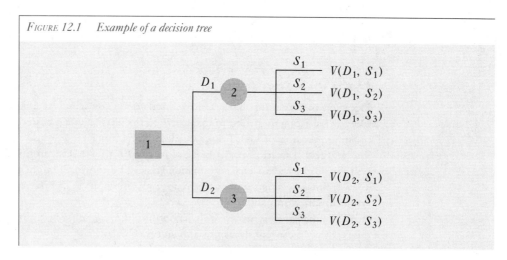

Nodes 2 and 3 are state of nature nodes. For each decision, any of the three states of nature may occur. Thus, each path from node 1 to the end of the tree represents a possible outcome—a sequence of decisions and states of nature. At the end of each path we list the payoff associated with each state of nature. Later in this chapter, we will see how decision trees are extremely useful for modeling multistage decisions.

DECISION MAKING UNDER UNCERTAINTY

In most decision problems in management science, we can either use historical data to determine probabilities of states of nature or estimate them judgmentally. We call such decision problems *decisions under risk*, and we will address them shortly. However, whenever we are faced with a decision problem in which we cannot quantify probabilities associated with states of nature, we have a *decision under uncertainty*. Understanding decision making under uncertainty helps us to understand our own attitudes and preferences toward risk.

EXAMPLE 1. A PERSONAL INVESTMENT DECISION

Rick Martin has $10,000 to invest. As he is expecting to buy a new car in a year, he can tie the money up for only 12 months. Rick is considering three options: a bank CD paying 4.5 percent, a bond mutual fund, and a stock fund. Both the bond and stock funds are sensitive to changing interest rates. If rates remain the same over the coming year, the share price of the bond fund is expected to remain the same, and Rick expects to earn $840. He expects the stock fund to return about $600 in dividends and capital gains. However, if interest rates rise, he anticipates losing about $500 from the bond fund after taking into account the drop in share price and likewise expects to lose $1,000 from the stock fund. If interest rates fall, however, his yield from the bond fund would be $925 and the stock fund would net $1,500. As economic forecasters and investment advisers are giving conflicting advice, Rick is unsure as to the best decision. Table 12.1 summarizes the payoff table for his decision problem.

Before continuing, determine which decision *you* would make. Why? Keep your answer in mind as you read further.

The best decision for Rick's problem clearly depends on which state of nature occurs. If rates remain stable, then obviously the bond fund would be the right decision. However, if you select the bond fund and rates rise, you face a loss of $500; if rates fall, you will make a bit more, but you could have done much better with the stock fund. Clearly, there is no "optimal" solution because the future is uncertain. However, there exist several different strategies for making decisions under uncertainty.

TABLE 12.1
Payoff table for Rick's investment decision

	Rates rise	Rates stable	Rates fall
Bank CD	$450	$450	$450
Bond fund	−$500	$840	$925
Stock fund	−$1,000	$600	$1,500

Laplace Approach

Since the states of nature are completely unpredictable, we might assign an equal probability to each. This approach was proposed by the French mathematician Laplace, who stated the *principle of insufficient reason:* if there is no reason for one state of nature to be more likely than another, treat them as equally likely. Under this assumption, we may evaluate each decision by simply averaging the payoffs. We then select the decision with the best average payoff. For Rick's investment problem we have the following:

$$D_1 \text{ (Bank CD):} \quad \frac{450 + 450 + 450}{3} = \$450$$

$$D_2 \text{ (Bonds):} \quad \frac{-500 + 840 + 925}{3} = \$421.67$$

$$D_3 \text{ (Stocks):} \quad \frac{-1{,}000 + 600 + 1{,}500}{3} = \$366.67$$

Under the Laplace criterion, the best decision would be to invest in the CD. This approach neglects to consider the decision maker's emotions and attitudes toward risk. Some people are naturally aggressive when it comes to investments; others are more cautious. Decision theorists have studied these issues and have proposed various decision criteria that reflect these different attitudes.

Maximax or Optimistic Approach

The aggressive decision maker might seek the option that holds the promise of maximizing his or her gain. This type of decision maker would ask the question, "What is the best I could do from each decision?" For Rick's investment problem, this is summarized below:

Decision	Maximum gain
CD	$450
Bonds	$925
Stocks	$1,500

The aggressive decision maker would attempt to *maximize* the *maximum* gain, or select the stock fund (since $1,500 \geq \$925 \geq \$450$). This criterion is often called the *maximax criterion*. Since the approach of using the maximax criterion focuses on the best payoff of each decision alternative, it is sometimes known as the *optimistic approach*.

Maximin or Pessimistic Approach

A conservative decision maker, on the other hand, might take a more pessimistic attitude and ask, "What is the worst thing that might result from my decision?" This individual focuses on the worst payoff for each decision alternative and would choose the *maximum* of the *minimum* returns. For Rick's investment problem, the minimum returns for each option are as follows:

Decision	Minimum gain
CD	$ 450
Bonds	−$ 500
Stocks	−$1,000

Hence, under this criterion, Rick would choose the CD alternative (since $450 ≥ −$500 ≥ −$1,000). This criterion is called the *maximin criterion*, since it will select the decision that provides the "best of the worst." This approach is sometimes referred to as the *pessimistic approach*.

Minimax Regret

A third approach that considers the decision maker's attitudes is to quantify the *opportunity loss*, or *regret*, associated with making a decision and finding out what state of nature actually occurs. In Rick's investment decision, suppose we choose the bond fund. If rates remain stable, then you could not have done any better by selecting a different decision; in this case, the opportunity loss is zero. However, if rates rise, your best decision would have been to choose the CD. In this case you would have gained an additional $950 (the difference between $450 and −$500). If rates fall, you should have chosen the stock fund. In this case, you forgo the opportunity to earn an additional $1,500 − $925 = $575.

> The *opportunity loss*, or *regret*, for any decision and state of nature is the difference between the *best* decision for that particular state of nature and the payoff for that decision and state of nature.

Opportunity losses can only be nonnegative values! You need to be careful when computing these, especially if some payoffs are negative. For Rick's investment problem, the opportunity losses associated with each decision and state of nature are shown in Table 12.2.

Individuals who use opportunity loss are, in a sense, poor losers ("I should have done *that!*"). Such an individual would be quite upset if he or she missed a large opportunity, so a natural criterion would be to *minimize the maximum opportunity loss* that might occur. This criterion is called *minimax regret*. The approach is to find the maximum regret for each decision alternative and select the decision with the minimum maximum regret. This is summarized below for Rick's investment problem:

Decision	Maximum opportunity loss (regret)
CD	$1,050
Bonds	$950
Stocks	$1,450

TABLE 12.2
Opportunity loss table for Rick's investment

	Rates rise	Rates stable	Rates fall
Bank CD	$450 − $450 = $0	$840 − $450 = $390	$1,500 − $450 = $1,050
Bond fund	$450 − (−$500) = $950	$840 − $840 = $0	$1,500 − $925 = $575
Stock fund	$450 − (−$1,000) = $1,450	$840 − $600 = $240	$1,500 − $1,500 = $0

This investor would choose the bond fund (since $950 ≤ $1,050 ≤ $1,450). This ensures that, no matter what state of nature will occur, Rick will never be further than $950 away from what might have been.

Different criteria, different decisions: what type of decision maker are you?

DECISION MAKING UNDER RISK

In decisions under uncertainty, we assumed complete ignorance about the states of nature. *Decisions under risk* involve probabilistic information about the likelihood of the states of nature. The classical notion of probability is the long-run relative frequency of occurrence of an event. If historical data on past occurrences of states of nature are available, then we can estimate probabilities objectively. For example, an oil company that drills dozens of wells each year would have good information about the likelihood that a drilling site will yield a profitable strike. In most business decisions, however, such historical data are usually not available. Most decision makers will have some personal belief about the likelihood of states of nature. Thus, they may assign probabilities subjectively to states of nature, using techniques discussed in the previous chapter. With probabilities assigned to the states of nature, we may use the expected value criterion to make a decision. The expected value approach is to select the decision alternative with the highest expected payoff. Let $P(S_j)$ = the probability that state of nature S_j occurs and n be the number of states of nature.

The expected value approach is to calculate the expected payoff for each decision alternative:

$$E(D_i) = \sum_{j=1}^{n} P(S_j)V(D_i, S_j)$$

The decision alternative with the highest expected payoff is selected as the optimal decision.

EXAMPLE 2. RICK'S INVESTMENT DECISION UNDER RISK

For Rick's investment problem (Example 1), a careful analysis of the economy leads Rick to believe that the most likely scenario is that interest rates will remain stable over the coming year. He also believes that it is half as likely that rates will rise, and that there is only a small chance that rates will fall. As a result, Rick assigns the following probabilities to the three states of nature:

$$P(S_1) = P(\text{rates rise}) = .3$$

$$P(S_2) = P(\text{rates remain stable}) = .6$$

$$P(S_3) = P(\text{rates fall}) = .1$$

The expected payoff for each decision is as follows:

$$E(D_1) = V(D_1, S_1)P(S_1) + V(D_1, S_2)P(S_2) + V(D_1, S_3)P(S_3)$$
$$= (450)(.3) + (450)(.6) + (450)(.1) = \$450$$

$$E(D_2) = V(D_2, S_1)P(S_1) + V(D_2, S_2)P(S_2) + V(D_2, S_3)P(S_3)$$
$$= (-500)(.3) + (840)(.6) + (925)(.1) = \$446.50$$

$$E(D_3) = V(D_3, S_1)P(S_1) + V(D_3, S_2)P(S_2) + V(D_3, S_3)P(S_3)$$
$$= (-1,000)(.3) + (600)(.6) + (1,500)(.1) = \$210$$

D_1, the bank CD, has the highest expected payoff and would be the recommended decision.

We may perform these calculations directly on the decision tree. This is shown in Figure 12.2. First, we label each state of nature branch with its associated probability. We always work *from right to left*. At each state of nature node, we compute the expected payoff by multiplying the values at the end of the state of nature branches by their associated probabilities and summing. Moving to the left to the decision node, we select the best decision. This operation is sometimes referred to as "folding back" the tree.

Expected Value of Perfect Information

By *perfect information*, we mean knowing in advance what state of nature will occur. Although we never have perfect information in practice, it is worth knowing how much we could improve the value of our decision if we had such information. This is called the *expected value of perfect information*, or *EVPI*. We compute EVPI by asking the following question: If each state of nature occurs, what would be the best decision and payoff? Then we weight these payoffs by the probabilities associated with the states of nature to obtain the expected payoff under perfect information.

> EVPI is the difference between the expected payoff under perfect information and the expected payoff of the optimal decision without perfect information.

We illustrate this with Rick's investment problem.

FIGURE 12.2   *Calculation of expected payoffs and best decision*

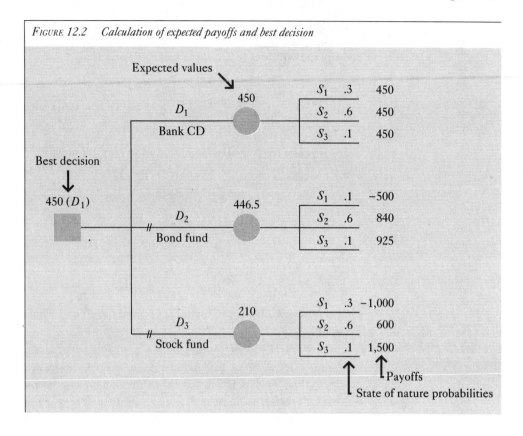

EXAMPLE 3. FINDING EVPI FOR RICK'S INVESTMENT PROBLEM

Refer to Table 12.1. If rates rise (S_1), then the best decision is D_1, the bank CD, yielding $450. If rates remain stable (S_2), then Rick should have chosen the bond fund (D_2), yielding $840. Finally, if rates fall (S_3), then Rick should have picked the stock fund (D_3), yielding $1,500. This is summarized below:

State of nature	Best decision	Payoff	Probability
S_1	D_1	$450	.3
S_2	D_2	$840	.6
S_3	D_3	$1,500	.1

The expected payoff under perfect information is

$$(450)(.3) + (840)(.6) + (1,500)(.1) = \$789$$

In Example 2 we saw that without perfect information, the best decision is to choose D_1 with an expected value of $450. We see that by having perfect information, we can increase our expected payoff by $789 - $450 = $339. This is the expected value of perfect information.

Another way of computing EVPI is to compute the *expected opportunity loss* or *expected regret* for the best decision using the expected value criterion. Let $R(D_i, S_j)$ be the regret for decision alternative D_i under state of nature S_j, and let n be the number of states of nature. The expected opportunity loss for D_i, denoted $\text{EOL}(D_i)$, is

$$\text{EOL}(D_i) = \sum_{j=1}^{n} P(S_j) R(D_i, S_j)$$

Let D^* be the optimal decision using the expected value criterion. Then $\text{EVPI} = \text{EOL}(D^*)$.

For Rick's investment problem, the opportunity loss matrix is shown in Table 12.2. Recall that D_1 is the best decision using the expected value criterion. The expected opportunity loss associated with D_1 is

$$\text{EVPI} = \text{EOL}(D_1) = (0)(.3) + (390)(.6) + (1,050)(.1) = \$339$$

The opportunity loss tells us how much we gain if we could switch our decision based on perfect information. Given a decision from the expected value criterion, the regret for that decision is the potential gain from perfect information. For example, in Rick's investment problem, if we choose D_1, and a person with perfect information tells us that the state of nature is going to be S_1, then we would keep the decision D_1. If a person with perfect information tells us that the state of nature is going to be S_2, then we would switch from D_1 to D_2 for a net gain of $840 - $450 = $390 due to the perfect information. Finally, if the person with perfect information tells us that the state of nature will be S_3, we would switch from D_1 to D_3 for a net gain of $1,500 - $450 = $1,050. We weight these gains by their probabilities to get an expected value (because, if the probabilities are accurate, we will be told that the state of nature will be S_1 30 percent of the time, S_2 60 percent of the time, and S_3 10 percent of the time).

EVPI is the maximum amount that we could improve our outcome by having better information about the future. Therefore, we would never want to pay any more than this amount for better information. For Rick's case, he would never want to pay more than $339 for financial advice that might improve his knowledge of the future interest rates. How much he should actually pay depends on how good the information really is. We will address this later in this chapter.

Sensitivity Analysis and Risk

In Chapter 11 we cautioned you about the dangers of expected value decisions, particularly if the decision is infrequent. Sensitivity analysis provides information about the robustness of decisions to changes or errors in the parameters, especially the probabilities. Sensitivity analysis addresses the question, "How much error in probability estimation can I have without its affecting my decision?" This is particularly important when probabilities are subjective. Spreadsheets are useful tools for performing sensitivity analyses of decision problems.

EXAMPLE 4. SENSITIVITY ANALYSIS FOR RICK'S INVESTMENT PROBLEM

Figure 12.3*a* shows a spreadsheet and graph for performing a sensitivity analysis of probability assumptions for Rick's investment problem. The payoff table and expected value analysis are shown in the upper portion of the spreadsheet. The bottom portion evaluates the expected payoffs for each decision for a range of probability assumptions. The graph in Figure 12.3*b* summarizes the best decisions for each assumption. We see that the stock fund is best only for assumption 1, the bond fund for assumptions 2 through 21, and the CD for the remainder. The graph shows that the stock fund is also more sensitive to the interest-rate assumptions than the bond fund.

Rick's current probability estimates (assumption 22) are at the borderline between the bank CD and bond fund. If rates are more likely to fall or the probability of stability decreases, the bond fund will be more attractive. Therefore, Rick might want to get better information about the future before making a decision.

MULTISTAGE DECISIONS

Thus far, we have considered only single-stage decision problems, that is, problems in which a decision maker makes a decision, awaits the outcome of the state of nature, and receives the payoff. Many business and personal decisions are more complex. Often, you make an initial decision, observe an outcome, and then make additional decisions depending on the outcome. Multistage decision trees are a useful way of modeling complex sequences of decisions.

EXAMPLE 5. NEW PRODUCT INTRODUCTION

A national chain of quick-service restaurants has developed a new specialty sandwich. Initially, it faces two possible decisions: introduce the sandwich nationally, or evaluate it in a regional test market. If it introduces the sandwich nationally, the chain might find either a high or low response to the idea. If it starts with a regional marketing strategy, it might find a low response or a high response at the regional level. This may or may not reflect the national market potential. In any case, the chain needs to decide whether to remain regional, market nationally, or drop the product.

Figure 12.4 shows a decision tree for this example. You can see that it structures the sequence of decisions and outcomes in a convenient graphical fashion. This facilitates communication among managers and provides a basis for further analytical analysis.

FIGURE 12.3a   *Sensitivity analysis for Rick's investment problem*

	A	B	C	D	E	F	G
1	Rick's Investment Decision						
2							
3							
4	Probability	0.3	0.6	0.1			
5		Rates rise	Rates stable	Rates fall	Expected payoff		
6	Bank CD	$450	$450	$450	$450.00		
7	Bond fund	($500)	$840	$925	$446.50		
8	Stock fund	($1,000)	$600	$1,500	$210.00		
9							
10							
11		P(S1)	P(S2)	P(S3)	E(D1)	E(D2)	E(D3)
12	1	0.2	0.4	0.4	$450.00	$606.00	$640.00
13	2	0.2	0.45	0.35	$450.00	$601.75	$595.00
14	3	0.2	0.5	0.3	$450.00	$597.50	$550.00
15	4	0.2	0.55	0.25	$450.00	$593.25	$505.00
16	5	0.2	0.6	0.2	$450.00	$589.00	$460.00
17	6	0.2	0.65	0.15	$450.00	$584.75	$415.00
18	7	0.2	0.7	0.1	$450.00	$580.50	$370.00
19	8	0.2	0.75	0.05	$450.00	$576.25	$325.00
20	9	0.2	0.8	0	$450.00	$572.00	$280.00
21	10	0.25	0.4	0.35	$450.00	$534.75	$515.00
22	11	0.25	0.45	0.3	$450.00	$530.50	$470.00
23	12	0.25	0.5	0.25	$450.00	$526.25	$425.00
24	13	0.25	0.55	0.2	$450.00	$522.00	$380.00
25	14	0.25	0.6	0.15	$450.00	$517.75	$335.00
26	15	0.25	0.65	0.1	$450.00	$513.50	$290.00
27	16	0.25	0.7	0.05	$450.00	$509.25	$245.00
28	17	0.25	0.75	0	$450.00	$505.00	$200.00
29	18	0.3	0.4	0.3	$450.00	$463.50	$390.00
30	19	0.3	0.45	0.25	$450.00	$459.25	$345.00
31	20	0.3	0.5	0.2	$450.00	$455.00	$300.00
32	21	0.3	0.55	0.15	$450.00	$450.75	$255.00
33	22	0.3	0.6	0.1	$450.00	$446.50	$210.00
34	23	0.3	0.65	0.05	$450.00	$442.25	$165.00
35	24	0.3	0.7	0	$450.00	$438.00	$120.00
36	25	0.35	0.4	0.25	$450.00	$392.25	$265.00
37	26	0.35	0.45	0.2	$450.00	$388.00	$220.00
38	27	0.35	0.5	0.15	$450.00	$383.75	$175.00
39	28	0.35	0.55	0.1	$450.00	$379.50	$130.00
40	29	0.35	0.6	0.05	$450.00	$375.25	$85.00
41	30	0.35	0.65	0	$450.00	$371.00	$40.00
42	31	0.4	0.4	0.2	$450.00	$321.00	$140.00
43	32	0.4	0.45	0.15	$450.00	$316.75	$95.00
44	33	0.4	0.5	0.1	$450.00	$312.50	$50.00
45	34	0.4	0.55	0.05	$450.00	$308.25	$5.00
46	35	0.4	0.6	0	$450.00	$304.00	($40.00)

Multistage decision trees are often used in situations in which a decision maker considers acquiring additional information on which to base a key decision. The decision maker must first decide whether it is worth the cost and effort to obtain the information, and if so, how to use the information to improve the decision. Usually this involves *revising* the probabilities assigned initially to the states of nature.

FIGURE 12.3b

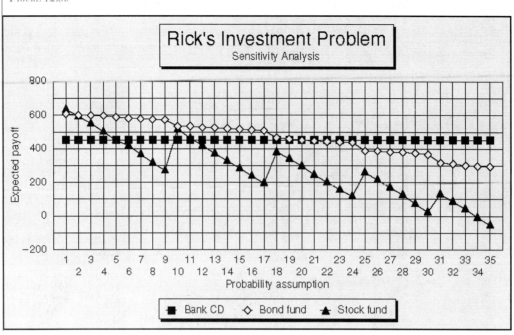

Rick's Investment Problem
Sensitivity Analysis

■ Bank CD ◇ Bond fund ▲ Stock fund

FIGURE 12.4   New product introduction decision tree

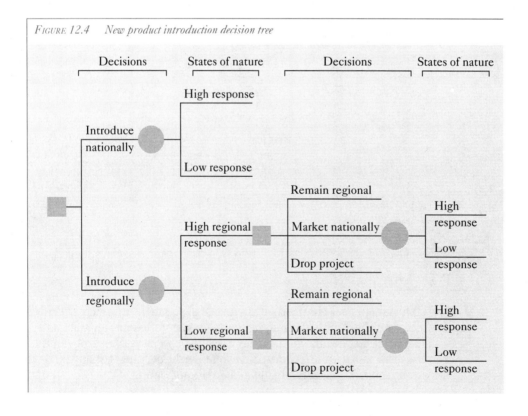

> Initial probabilities assigned to states of nature are called *prior probabilities*, because they are determined before collecting any additional information. Revised probabilities that reflect additional information about the states of nature are called *posterior probabilities*.

Prior probabilities are denoted as $P(S_j)$. In Example 5, assignment of initial estimates for the probabilities of low national demand and high national demand would be prior probabilities. In Rick's investment problem, his initial estimates of the probabilities of interest-rate movements $P(S_1) = .3$, $P(S_2) = .6$, and $P(S_3) = .1$ are prior probabilities also.

Additional information provides an *indicator* of the state of nature that might occur. Such information might be acquired by collecting additional data, performing a market research study, soliciting expert opinion, and so on. We denote the indicators by I_1, I_2, and so on. Thus, in Example 5, the regional introduction of the sandwich provides one of two indicators:

I_1: Low regional demand

I_2: High regional demand

In Rick's investment problem, Rick might hire an economic consultant to provide an indicator of the direction of interest rates.

Posterior probabilities reflect indicator information; in statistical terminology, the states of nature are *conditional* upon the indicators. We denote the probability of a state of nature S_j given an indicator I_k as $P(S_j \mid I_k)$. This is the probability that S_j will occur *after* the indicator I_k has been observed. For instance, if we find a high regional demand in the test market, what is the revised estimate of a high national demand? You might be wondering why we cannot just say that this probability is 1.0; that is, if we observe a high regional demand, why can't we predict a high national demand with certainty? The answer lies in the fact that test marketing and expert opinions are never 100 percent accurate. Test marketing is prone to sampling error, and experts are not always right.

We may quantify the inability of indicators to predict the correct states of nature using the conditional probabilities $P(I_k \mid S_j)$. If S_j is the true state of nature, $P(I_k \mid S_j)$ is the probability that the acquisition of new information results in indicator I_k. These probabilities, which we call *indicator reliabilities*, can be found by evaluating past results. For example, suppose that a market research firm has conducted 100 similar tests. When the final results are known, it finds that in 40 instances the national demand turned out to be high. However, the test market indicators predicted a high national demand only 36 times. The probability of a high national demand indicator given a high national demand would be $\frac{36}{40}$, or 0.90. In other words, the test has a 90 percent reliability of predicting a high national demand when the demand is indeed high.

Once the indicator reliabilities are determined, we may compute the posterior probabilities using Bayes's formula:

$$P(A \mid B) = \frac{P(A \cap B)}{P(B)}$$

Note that Bayes's formula implies

$$P(A \cap B) = P(A \mid B)P(B)$$

These two formulas may be used to generate posterior probabilities using prior probabilities and indicator reliabilities.

Since we need to compute probabilities $P(S_j \mid I_k)$, we substitute S_j for A and I_k for B in Bayes's formula:

$$P(S_j \mid I_k) = \frac{P(S_j \cap I_k)}{P(I_k)}$$

Also, note that if we substitute S_j for B and I_k for A, we have

$$P(I_k \cap S_j) = P(I_k \mid S_j)P(S_j)$$

Since $P(I_k \cap S_j) = P(S_j \cap I_k)$, we now have all the information we need to compute the numerator in the formula above. Furthermore, we may calculate $P(I_k)$ from the prior probabilities and indicator reliabilities as well. To obtain the $P(I_k)$ we may sum all of the possible ways that I_k can occur:

$$P(I_k) = \sum_{j=1}^{n} P(S_j \cap I_k) = \sum_{j=1}^{n} P(I_k \mid S_j)P(S_j)$$

Hence the posterior probabilities we seek may be calculated as follows:

$$P(S_j \mid I_k) = \frac{P(I_k \cap S_j)}{P(I_k)} = \frac{P(I_k \mid S_j)P(S_j)}{\sum_{j=1}^{n} P(I_k \mid S_j)P(S_j)}$$

$P(S_j \mid I_k)$ is the proportion of the total probability $P(I_k)$ that is contributed by S_j. This may seem complicated, but as long as you do the calculations in a step-by-step fashion and carefully keep track of your results, it is not that difficult. The next example illustrates these calculations.

EXAMPLE 6. RICK'S INVESTMENT PROBLEM REVISITED

Rick is thinking about seeing an economic consultant to obtain better information about the future interest-rate trends in order to improve his decision. Rick contacted a highly recommended consultant, C. T. Innes. C. T. agreed to meet with him, give him some general financial advice, and provide his forecasts for a $50 fee.

During the phone conversation, C. T. said, "Of course, you know I can't guarantee my forecasts. Over the years, I've kept some statistics about my predictions and what really happened. When interest rates actually rose, I made the correct forecast 60 percent of the time. Thirty percent of the time, I thought they would remain stable, and in 1 of 10 cases, I forecasted a decline. I predicted that rates would stay the same 80 percent of the time when they actually did. I predicted a rise 10 percent of the time and a decline 10 percent of the time. I've had more trouble predicting the correct movement when rates actually fell. I was correct only half the time. Thirty percent of the time that rates rose, I predicted them to remain stable, and 20 percent of the time I forecast a decline. Do you still want to see me?"

Rick knew that he had all the information he needed to decide whether C. T.'s $50 fee would be worth the information he can provide. The first thing to do is to construct the appropriate decision tree. This is shown in Figure 12.5.

FIGURE 12.5   *Rick's expanded decision tree*

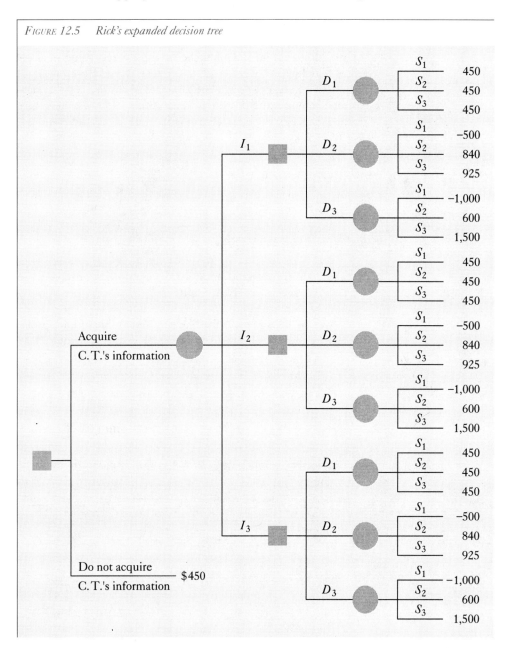

If Rick hires C. T., he will provide one of three indicators:

I_1: Rates are expected to rise

I_2: Rates are expected to remain stable

I_3: Rates are expected to fall

After C. T. provides this advice, Rick must still make a decision and await the outcome for the state of nature. From Example 2 we already know that if he does not seek any additional information, the best expected value decision is to select D_1 for an expected payoff of $450. This is reflected in the bottom branch of the tree.

Rick needs to assign probabilities to all the state of nature branches. Thus, he must compute the posterior probabilities $P(S_j \mid I_k)$ and the probabilities of each indicator $P(I_k)$. From the conversation with C. T., Rick knows the indicator reliabilities $P(I_k \mid S_j)$:

$P(I_k \mid S_j)$	S_1	S_2	S_3
I_1	.6	.1	.2
I_2	.3	.8	.3
I_3	.1	.1	.5

In this table, each column represents a state of nature. Thus, when S_1 actually occurred, C. T. predicted this (I_1) 60 percent of the time; he predicted I_2 30 percent of the time, and so on. By multiplying $P(I_k \mid S_j)$ by the prior probability $P(S_j)$, we obtain the joint probability $P(I_k \cap S_j)$. Thus, $P(I_1 \cap S_1) = (.6)(.3) = .18$, $P(I_2 \cap S_1) = (.3)(.3) = .09$, and so forth. The complete table of joint probabilities is shown below. Adding across each row of this table gives the probabilities $P(I_k)$.

$P(I_k \cap S_j)$	S_1	S_2	S_3	$P(I_k)$
I_1	.18	.06	.02	.26
I_2	.09	.48	.03	.60
I_3	.03	.06	.05	.14

The posterior probabilities $P(S_j \mid I_k)$ are found by dividing the probability $P(I_k \cap S_j)$ by the $P(I_k)$. As you can see, this is simply the ratio of each entry in the above joint probability table to the probability in the right-hand column. For example, $P(S_3 \mid I_1) = .02/.26 = .076923$ (rounding gives .08). These posterior probabilities are shown below.

$P(S_j \mid I_k)$	S_1	S_2	S_3
I_1	.69	.23	.08
I_2	.15	.80	.05
I_3	.21	.43	.36

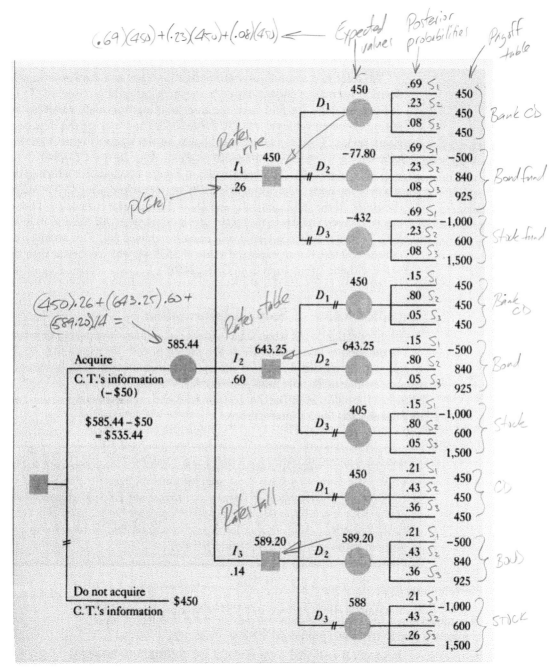

$(.69)(450) + (.23)(450) + (.08)(450) \longleftarrow$ Expected values

Posterior probabilities

Payoff table

				450	.69 S_1	450	} Bank CD
		D_1			.23 S_2	450	
					.08 S_3	450	

Rates rise

I_1 450 .26

$p(I_k)$

D_2	−77.80	.69 S_1	−500	} Bond fund
		.23 S_2	840	
		.08 S_3	925	

D_3	−432	.69 S_1	−1,000	} Stock fund
		.23 S_2	600	
		.08 S_3	1,500	

Rates stable

D_1	450	.15 S_1	450	} Bank CD
		.80 S_2	450	
		.05 S_3	450	

$(450).26 + (643.25).60 + (589.20)/4 =$

585.44

Acquire C. T.'s information (−$50)

$585.44 − $50 = $535.44

I_2 643.25 .60

D_2	643.25	.15 S_1	−500	} Bond
		.80 S_2	840	
		.05 S_3	925	

D_3	405	.15 S_1	−1,000	} Stock
		.80 S_2	600	
		.05 S_3	1,500	

Rates fall

D_1	450	.21 S_1	450	} CD
		.43 S_2	450	
		.36 S_3	450	

I_3 589.20 .14

D_2	589.20	.21 S_1	−500	} Bond
		.43 S_2	840	
		.36 S_3	925	

Do not acquire C. T.'s information — $450

D_3	588	.21 S_1	−1,000	} Stock
		.43 S_2	600	
		.26 S_3	1,500	

Figure 12.6 shows the decision tree with the addition of probabilities on all state of nature branches.

We refer to a solution of a multistage problem as a *decision strategy* because the decision alternative chosen depends on which indicator is observed. To find the best decision strategy, we fold back the tree, working from right to left as before, computing expected values at state of nature nodes and picking the best decision at decision nodes. The calculations are shown on the tree in Figure 12.6. For example, $(.69)(450) + (.23)(450) + (.08)(450) = 450$, $(.69)(-500) + (.23)(840) + (.08)(925) = -77.80$, and so forth. The hash marks in Figure 12.6 indicate which path *not* to take at a decision node. The optimal decision strategy when using C. T.'s information is to choose D_1 if the indicator is I_1, and D_2 if the indicator is I_2 or I_3. That is, the strategy is to invest in CDs if C. T. says that interest rates will rise and to invest in bonds if C. T. says that interest rates will remain stable or fall. This strategy, after netting out the $50 fee, has an expected value of $535.44, which is better than the expected value without information from C. T. ($450).

Expected Value of Sample Information

A natural question to ask when faced with the possibility of acquiring sample information is, "Is the sample information worth the asking price?" We can answer this question by comparing the expected value of the optimal decision with sample information to the expected value using only prior probabilities. The expected value of sample information indicates the value added to the decision by having the extra information (not including any fee charged for the information).

> The expected value of sample information (EVSI) is the expected value of the optimal decision strategy *with* sample information minus the expected value of the optimal decision *without* sample information. If EVSI is greater than the fee charged for the information, then the strategy with the sample information is optimal. Otherwise, the information is not worth the fee, and the optimal decision without sample information should be used.

We note that since sample information is at best perfect, EVSI $\leq$ EVPI. Of course, sample information is rarely perfect, so EVSI is typically less than EVPI.

EXAMPLE 7. EVSI FOR RICK'S INVESTMENT PROBLEM

In Rick's investment problem, given the analysis in Example 6, we may easily calculate the expected value of sample information. The value of the optimal strategy with sample information (before the subtraction of any fees) is $585.44. The expected value of the optimal decision without sample information is $450. Therefore, EVSI = $585.44 − $450 = $135.44. Since EVSI = $135.44 is greater than the $50 fee,

FIGURE 12.6   Decision tree calculations

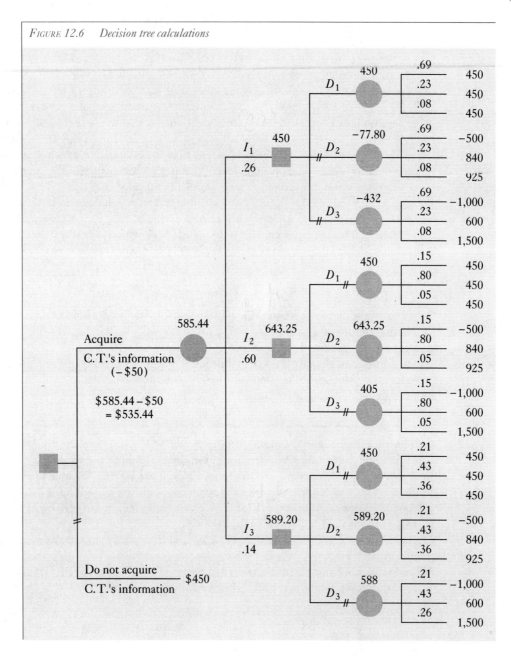

we found that it is optimal to use the sample information. It is also valuable to calculate EVSI, because it gives us *the most* we should ever pay C. T. for information. Finally, from Example 3, we know that the EVPI for Rick is $339. Hence, EVSI = $135.44 < EVPI = $339.

UTILITY AND DECISION MAKING

As we have seen, individual decision makers have different attitudes toward risk. As a result, you may not necessarily choose the best expected value decision. This is easy to illustrate. Several years ago, one of the authors had the opportunity to purchase one of 500 raffle tickets for $100 to win a new Porsche valued at $25,000 as a fundraiser for his old high school alma mater. A decision tree is shown in Figure 12.7. As you can see, the expected value of winning the car was only −$50. Nevertheless, he took the chance (unfortunately not winning). Now suppose he were offered the "opportunity" of purchasing a ticket for $5,000 against a 50 percent chance of winning the car. Although the expected value of taking this chance is much higher, we can state with certainty that he would *not* accept this gamble.

These two situations differ in the amount of money at risk. In the first case, although there was a large chance of losing, the decision maker felt that he could afford $100 at a chance for his dream car. In the second case, although the chance of losing was considerably smaller, the amount at risk was much larger. Neither decision is right or wrong; the decision maker values the consequences differently. An approach for assessing risk attitudes quantitatively is called *utility theory*.

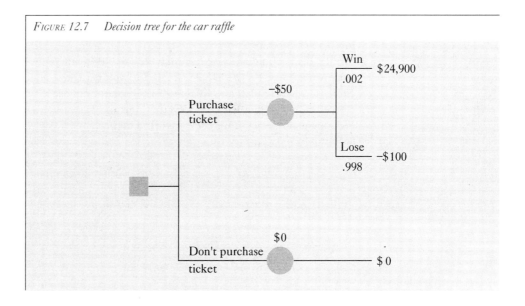

FIGURE 12.7   Decision tree for the car raffle

> *Utility theory* provides an approach for quantifying a decision maker's relative preferences for particular outcomes.

We can determine an individual's utility function by posing a series of decision scenarios. This is best illustrated with an example; we will use Rick's investment problem to do this.

EXAMPLE 8. DETERMINING A UTILITY FUNCTION FOR RICK'S INVESTMENT OUTCOMES

In Example 2, Rick Martin is faced with selecting a decision that could result in a variety of payoffs, from a profit of $1,500 to a loss of $1,000. The first step in determining Rick's utility function is to rank-order the payoffs from highest to lowest. We arbitrarily assign a utility of 1.0 to the highest payoff and a utility of zero to the lowest:

Payoff	Utility
$1,500	1.0
925	
840	
600	
450	
−500	
−1,000	0

Next, for each payoff between the highest and lowest, we present Rick with the following situation: Suppose you have the opportunity of achieving a guaranteed return of P or taking a chance of receiving $1,500 with probability p or losing $1,000 with probability $1 - p$. What value of p would make you indifferent to these two choices? This is illustrated in Figure 12.8. Let us choose $P = \$925$. Because this is a relatively high value, Rick decides that p would have to be at least .9 to take this risk. We repeat this process for each payoff. The probabilities p that Rick selects for each scenario form his utility function:

Payoff	Utility
$1,500	1.0
925	.9
840	.85
600	.80
450	.75
−500	.35
−1,000	0

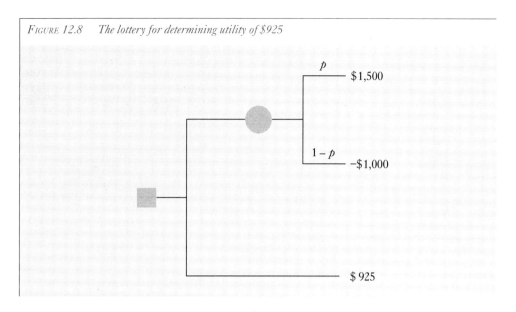

FIGURE 12.8   *The lottery for determining utility of $925*

If we compute the expected value of each of the gambles for the chosen values of p, we see that they are higher than the corresponding payoffs. For example, if $p = .9$, the expected value of taking the gamble is

$$.9(\$1,500) + .1(-\$1,000) = \$1,250$$

This is larger than accepting $925 outright. We can interpret this to mean that Rick requires a premium of $1,250 − $925 = $325 to feel comfortable enough to risk losing $1,000 if he takes the gamble. This indicates that Rick is a *risk-averse individual;* that is, he is relatively conservative. If we graph the utility versus the payoffs, we can sketch Rick's utility function as shown in Figure 12.9.

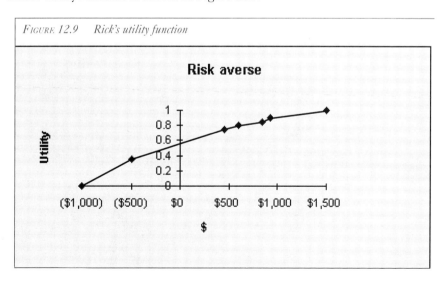

FIGURE 12.9   *Rick's utility function*

Rick's utility function is generally concave downward. This type of curve is characteristic of risk-averse individuals. Such decision makers avoid risk, and a gamble must have a higher expected value than a given payoff to be preferable. Other individuals might be risk taking. What would their utility functions look like? As you might suspect, they are concave upward, as shown in Figure 12.10. These individuals would take a gamble that offers higher rewards even if the expected value is less than a certain payoff. An example of a utility function for a risk-taking individual in Rick's situation would be as follows:

Payoff	Utility
$1,500	1.0
925	.6
840	.55
600	.45
450	.40
−500	.1
−1,000	0

Consider the payoff of $450. This individual would be indifferent between receiving $450 and taking a chance at $1,500 with probability .4 and losing $1,000 with probability .6. The expected value of this gamble is

$$.4(1,500) + .6(-1,000) = \$0$$

Nevertheless, the chance of receiving a higher payoff, even at the risk of a relatively large loss, creates satisfaction.

Finally, some individuals are risk neutral; they prefer neither taking risks nor avoiding them. Their utility function would be linear, as shown in Figure 12.11. For any payoff,

FIGURE 12.10   A risk-taking utility function

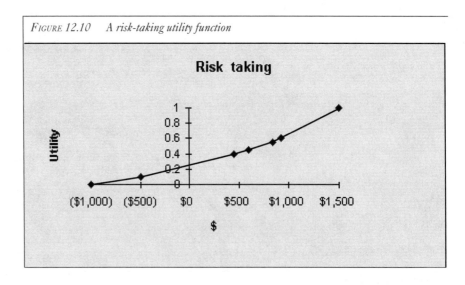

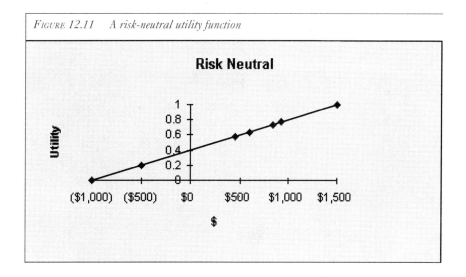

FIGURE 12.11   *A risk-neutral utility function*

the probability of winning the gamble is such that the expected value is the same as the expected payoff. For example, a payoff of 600 would be equivalent to the gamble if

$$600 = p(1,500) + (1 - p)(-1,000)$$

Solving for p we obtain $p = \frac{16}{25}$, or .64. The decision of accepting $600 outright or taking the gamble could be made by flipping a coin.

Expected Utility

A decision maker's utility function can be used in place of payoffs to compute expected values that reflect the decision maker's preferences toward risk. All we need to do is replace the payoffs in the payoff table by their equivalent utilities and compute the expected utility for each decision. We illustrate this approach using Rick's decision problem.

EXAMPLE 9. EXPECTED UTILITY DECISION MAKING

Table 12.3 shows Rick's payoff table after all payoffs are replaced with their utilities. We use the probabilities of states of nature given in Example 1:

$$P \text{ (rates rise)} = P(S_1) = .3$$

$$P \text{ (rates remain stable)} = P(S_2) = .6$$

$$P \text{ (rates fall)} = P(S_3) = .1$$

Let $U(D_i, S_j)$ equal the utility for the payoff of decision alternative D_i under state of nature S_j. We compute the expected utility for each decision as follows:

TABLE 12.3
*Payoff table for Rick's
investment decision*

	Rates rise	Rates stable	Rates fall
Bank CD	.75	.75	.75
Bond fund	.35	.85	.9
Stock fund	0	.8	1

$$EU(D_1) = U(D_1, S_1)P(S_1) + U(D_1, S_2)P(S_2) + U(D_1, S_3)P(S_3)$$
$$= (.75)(.3) + (.75)(.6) + (.75)(.1) = .75$$
$$EU(D_2) = U(D_2, S_1)P(S_1) + U(D_2, S_2)P(S_2) + U(D_2, S_3)P(S_3)$$
$$= (.35)(.3) + (.85)(.6) + (.9)(.1) = .705$$
$$EU(D_3) = U(D_3, S_1)P(S_1) + U(D_3, S_2)P(S_2) + U(D_3, S_3)P(S_3)$$
$$= (0)(.3) + (.8)(.6) + (1)(.1) = .58$$

D_1, the bank CD, has the highest expected utility and would be the recommended decision. This could probably be expected, given the risk-averse nature of Rick's utility function.

Utility theory is based on some key assumptions. If a probability is specified for a gamble, the decision maker must be able to select between receiving the certain payoff or taking the gamble, or be indifferent. Some people find this difficult to do. Second, if a decision maker chooses a probability for the gamble, he or she must truly be indifferent between it and the certain payoff. Some decision makers might not accept a coin flip, despite what they say. Finally, to be consider rational, the utility function must be non-decreasing (since, for example, more money is always at least as valuable as less money).

THE ANALYTIC HIERARCHY PROCESS

The *analytic hierarchy process* (AHP) is a technique developed by Thomas L. Saaty for incorporating multiple criteria into decision making. AHP consists of four major steps:

1. Modeling the decision problem by breaking it down into a hierarchy of interrelated decision elements: decision criteria and decision alternatives.
2. Developing judgmental preferences of the decision alternatives for each criterion and judgmental importance of the decision criteria by pairwise comparisons.
3. Computing relative priorities for each of the decision elements through a set of numerical calculations.
4. Aggregating the relative priorities to arrive at a priority ranking of the decision alternatives.

We will discuss each of these steps and illustrate them using an example.

Modeling the Decision Problem

AHP requires breaking down a complex multicriteria decision problem into a hierarchy of levels. The top level corresponds to the overall objective of the decision process. The second level represents the major criteria (which may be further broken down into subcriteria at the next level). The last level corresponds to the decision alternatives. This is illustrated in Figure 12.12. To better illustrate this process and the subsequent calculations, we introduce a simple example involving the selection of a supplier.

EXAMPLE 10. A SUPPLIER SELECTION DECISION

SpyroTech is a high-technology electronics manufacturer in southern California. Only three companies make a critical film used in the manufacture of microprocessors. Because of the competitive world market and the quality and rapid response demanded by its customers, SpyroTech wants to make its supplier selection decision on three key criteria: quality, price, and service. Thus, the overall objective of the decision is to "select a supplier." This becomes the top level in the decision hierarchy. At the next level, we list the three criteria: quality, price, and service. In this example, there are no subcriteria. Finally, at the third level, we list the decision alternatives, namely, the suppliers. Because each criterion will affect the overall objective, and each supplier is evaluated on each criterion, we connect the elements between successive levels to indicate this. The hierarchical model of this decision problem is shown in Figure 12.13.

FIGURE 12.12   *Hierarchical representation of a decision problem*

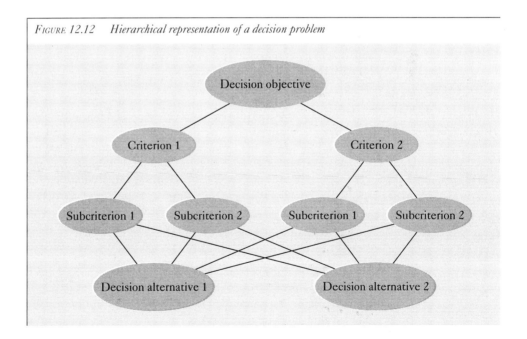

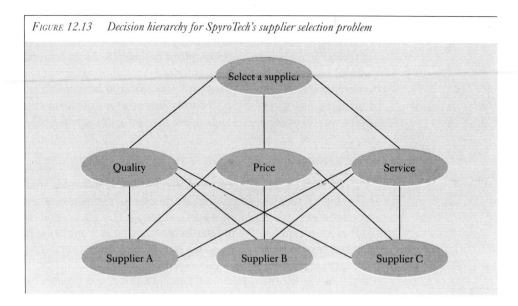

FIGURE 12.13   *Decision hierarchy for SpyroTech's supplier selection problem*

Preference and Importance Comparison

After the decision problem is modeled in this hierarchical fashion, the decision maker must develop a set of comparison matrices that numerically define the relative preference of each decision alternative with respect to each criterion, and also the relative importance of each criterion. This is done by comparing the elements in a pairwise fashion and assigning a numerical score that expresses preference between every two elements. Usually, the following scale is used:

Preference score	Definition
1	Equally important or preferred
3	Moderately important or preferred
5	Strongly important or preferred
7	Very strongly important or preferred
9	Extremely important or preferred

Intermediate values between each category may be used when the decision maker feels that a comparison falls between two categories. For example, if a decision maker feels that one element is more than strongly preferred but not quite very strongly preferred, then a value of 6 would be used.

EXAMPLE 11. DEVELOPING COMPARISON MATRICES

In SpyroTech's decision problem, we first compare each supplier on each of the three criteria. Consider the criterion of quality. Since there are three suppliers, we must compare A with B, B with C, and A with C. When queried as to relative preferences of supplier A and supplier B with respect to quality, SpyroTech's purchasing manager states that supplier B is somewhere between equally and moderately preferred to A, corresponding to a numerical value of 2. Comparing supplier C to A results in a score of 6, with C being between strongly and very strongly preferred to A. In comparing B with C, the manager indicates that supplier C is strongly preferred to supplier B (a score of 5).

We express these data in a matrix called a comparison matrix, in which the value in row i and column j is the preference score of the element of row i when compared with the element in column j. Since each element should be equally preferred to itself, we assign a 1 along the diagonal, as shown below.

Quality	Supplier A	Supplier B	Supplier C
Supplier A	1		
Supplier B	2	1	
Supplier C	6	5	1

We may complete this matrix by making the following assumption:

> If decision element i is n times preferred to or as important as j, then j is $1/n$ times preferred to or as important as i.

Thus, if the preference value of B is 2 when compared to A, the preference value of A is $\frac{1}{2}$ when compared to B. The complete preference matrix is shown below.

Quality	Supplier A	Supplier B	Supplier C
Supplier A	1	$\frac{1}{2}$	$\frac{1}{6}$
Supplier B	2	1	$\frac{1}{5}$
Supplier C	6	5	1

Therefore, it is only necessary to complete either the lower triangular or upper triangular portion of the matrix.

Using the same principles, the purchasing manager would develop preference matrices for price and service, as follows:

Price	Supplier A	Supplier B	Supplier C
Supplier A	1	4	5
Supplier B	$\frac{1}{2}$	1	3
Supplier C	$\frac{1}{5}$	$\frac{1}{3}$	1

Service	Supplier A	Supplier B	Supplier C
Supplier A	1	2	4
Supplier B	$\frac{1}{2}$	1	5
Supplier C	$\frac{1}{4}$	$\frac{1}{5}$	1

Finally, the manager must rate the importance of each criterion with respect to the others. The matrix is shown below; it shows that quality is moderately more important than price; quality is strongly more important than service; and price is moderately more important than service.

Criteria	Quality	Price	Service
Quality	1	3	5
Price	$\frac{1}{3}$	1	3
Service	$\frac{1}{5}$	$\frac{1}{3}$	1

Computing Relative Priorities

The next step in the AHP analysis is to perform various calculations to determine the priority of each of the decision elements using the pairwise comparison information. The exact mathematical basis for this approach is beyond the scope of this book; however, a simplified approximation yields very good results. This procedure is explained as follows:

1. Sum each column of the pairwise comparison matrix. Then divide each element of that column by the column sum. The result is the *normalized comparison matrix*.
2. Compute the average of each row of the normalized comparison matrix. These averages provide the relative priority of the decision elements corresponding to the rows of the matrix.

EXAMPLE 12. COMPUTING RELATIVE PRIORITIES

The pairwise comparison matrix for quality (converted to decimal representation) and column sums are shown below:

Quality	Supplier A	Supplier B	Supplier C
Supplier A	1	.5	.167
Supplier B	2	1	.2
Supplier C	6	5	1
Sum	9	6.5	1.367

If we divide each element in the matrix by the column sum, we obtain the normalized comparison matrix:

Quality	Supplier A	Supplier B	Supplier C
Supplier A	.111	.077	.122
Supplier B	.222	.154	.146
Supplier C	.667	.769	.732

Averaging the rows yields the priorities for each supplier:

Supplier	Row average
A	.103
B	.174
C	.723

We see that the most preferred supplier on the basis of quality is supplier C; supplier B is second; and supplier A is third. This is not surprising as you examine the original quality comparison matrix. We may record these numbers on the links of the hierarchy network as shown in Figure 12.14. This will be useful in developing the final ranking of the decision alternatives. We will compute the priorities for price, service, and the criteria comparison matrices using a spreadsheet shortly.

FIGURE 12.14   *Recording priorities on the decision hierarchy*

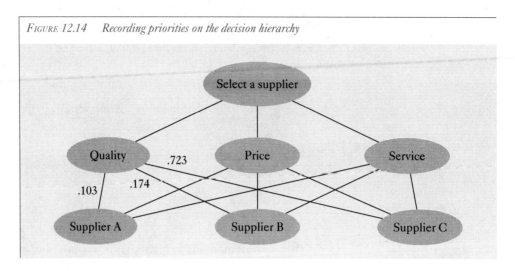

Consistency of Judgments

A critical issue with AHP is the consistency of judgments specified in the pairwise comparison matrices. For example, if you know that A is strongly preferred to B (5), and B is moderately preferred to C (3), then you would expect that A would be at least strongly preferred to C (7 or higher). By considering only one pair at a time, it is easy for the decision maker to specify preference scores that are not consistent with such a chain of relationships, particularly as the number of decision elements increases. Fortunately, AHP provides a measure of the consistency of pairwise comparative judgments. This measure, called the *consistency ratio*, indicates when it might be desirable to reconsider and revise the original judgments in the comparison matrices.

The consistency ratio is computed in the following manner:

1. Multiply each column of the original pairwise comparison matrix by the relative priority of the decision element corresponding to that column, and sum these "weighted columns."
2. Divide each element of the weighted column by the corresponding priority value of that decision element.
3. Average the values computed in step 2; this is denoted as λ_{max}.
4. The consistency index (CI) is defined as

$$CI = \frac{\lambda_{max} - n}{n - 1}$$

   where n is the number of decision elements in the comparison.

5. Compute the consistency ratio (CR) by dividing CI by a random index, RI, found in Table 12.4:

$$CR = \frac{CI}{RI}$$

TABLE 12.4
Random index
values, RI

n	RI
3	.58
4	.90
5	1.12
6	1.24
7	1.32
8	1.41

A consistency ratio of .10 or less is considered acceptable and indicates good consistency of the pairwise comparative judgments. If the consistency ratio is greater than .10, then the decision maker should reexamine the pairwise comparisons.

EXAMPLE 13. COMPUTING A CONSISTENCY RATIO

We will compute the consistency ratio for the quality comparison matrix. We first multiply each column by the relative priority of the decision element corresponding to that column and sum the results:

$$\begin{bmatrix} 1 \\ 2 \\ 6 \end{bmatrix}.103 + \begin{bmatrix} 0.5 \\ 1 \\ 5 \end{bmatrix}.174 + \begin{bmatrix} .167 \\ .2 \\ 1 \end{bmatrix}.723 = \begin{bmatrix} .311 \\ .525 \\ 2.213 \end{bmatrix}$$

Since .311 corresponds to supplier A, .525 to supplier B, and 2.213 to supplier C, we divide these numbers by the priority values corresponding to these suppliers:

$$\text{Supplier A: } \frac{.311}{.103} = 3.008$$

$$\text{Supplier B: } \frac{.525}{.174} = 3.017$$

$$\text{Supplier C: } \frac{2.213}{.7317} = 3.063$$

The average of these values is λ_{max}:

$$\lambda_{max} = \frac{3.008 + 3.017 + 3.063}{3} = 3.029$$

Then

$$\text{CI} = \frac{3.029 - 3}{3 - 1} = .015$$

With $n = 3$, RI $= .58$. Thus

$$\text{CR} = \frac{.0146}{.58} = .025$$

Since CR is less than .10, this indicates a very good consistency among the pairwise comparisons.

Ranking Decision Alternatives

The final step in the AHP is ranking the decision alternatives, taking into account all the decision elements of the hierarchy. This is computed by multiplying the importance of each decision criterion with the priority of each alternative with respect to that criterion and summing across all criteria. This is best illustrated with an example.

EXAMPLE 14.

Figure 12.15 shows a spreadsheet designed to perform all the AHP computations for the supplier selection problem. The relative priorities and importance values are

FIGURE 12.15   AHP in a spreadsheet

	A	B	C	D	E	F	G	H	I	J	K	L	M	N	O
1	Analytic Hierarchy Process														
2	Supplier Selection Example														
3															
4															
5	Quality Comparison Matrix					Normalized Matrices				Priorities		Consistency Ratio Calculations			
6		A	B	C			A	B	C			Weighted sum			
7	A	1	0.5	0.167		A	0.111	0.077	0.122	0.103		0.311	3.008		
8	B	2	1	0.2		B	0.222	0.154	0.146	0.174		0.525	3.017		
9	C	6	5	1		C	0.667	0.769	0.732	0.723		2.213	3.063		
10	Sum	9	6.5	1.367								Lambda max	3.029	CI	0.015
11														CR	0.025
12	Price Comparison Matrix														
13		A	B	C			A	B	C						
14	A	1	4	5		A	0.690	0.750	0.556	0.665		2.109	3.171		
15	B	0.25	1	3		B	0.172	0.188	0.333	0.231		0.709	3.068		
16	C	0.2	0.333	1		C	0.138	0.063	0.111	0.104		0.314	3.023		
17	Sum	1.45	5.333	9								Lambda max	3.087	CI	0.043
18														CR	0.075
19	Service Comparison Matrix														
20		A	B	C			A	B	C						
21	A	1	2	4		A	0.571	0.625	0.400	0.532		1.671	3.141		
22	B	0.5	1	5		B	0.286	0.313	0.500	0.366		1.141	3.117		
23	C	0.25	0.2	1		C	0.143	0.063	0.100	0.102		0.308	3.026		
24	Sum	1.75	3.2	10								Lambda max	3.095	CI	0.047
25														CR	0.082
26	Criteria Comparison Matrix														
27		Quality	Price	Service			Quality	Price	Service						
28	Quality	1	3	5		Quality	0.652	0.692	0.556	0.633		1.946	3.072		
29	Price	0.333	1	3		Price	0.217	0.231	0.333	0.260		0.790	3.033		
30	Service	0.2	0.333	1		Service	0.130	0.077	0.111	0.106		0.320	3.011		
31	Sum	1.533	4.333	9								Lambda max	3.039	CI	0.019
32														CR	0.033
33									Priority Ranking						
34								A	0.295						
35								B	0.209						
36								C	0.495						

Selected cell formulas

A	F	G	H	I	J	K	L	M	N	O
5	Normalized Matrices				Priorities		Consistency Ratio Calculations			
6		A	B	C			Weighted sum			
7	A	+B7/B$10	+C7/C$	+D7/D$10	@AVG(G7..I7)		+B7*$J7+C7*$J8+D7*$J9	+L7/J7		
8	B	+B8/B$10	+C8/C$	+D8/D$10	@AVG(G8..I8)		+B8*$J7+C8*$J8+D8*$J9	+L8/J8		
9	C	+B9/B$10	+C9/C$	+D9/D$10	@AVG(G9..I9)		+B9*$J7+C9*$J8+D9*$J9	+L9/J9		
10							Lambda max	@AVG(M7..M9)	CI	(+M10-3)/2
11									CR	+O10/0.58

Selected cell formulas

A	I	J
33	Priority Ranking	
34	A	+J7*$J$28+J14*$J$29+J21*$J$30
35	B	+J8*$J$28+J15*$J$29+J22*$J$30
36	C	+J9*$J$28+J16*$J$29+J23*$J$30

found in column J of the spreadsheet. We see that for price, supplier A is preferred (.665), followed by suppliers B (.231) and C (.104), respectively. For service, supplier A is preferred (.532), followed by suppliers B (.366) and C (.101). When comparing the criteria with each other, we see that quality is the most important (.633) followed by price (.260) and service (.106). To compute the priorities of the decision alternatives, we multiply the criterion importance value by the relative priority for that criterion and add:

Supplier	Quality weighting		Price weighting		Service weighting	
A	(.633)(.103)	+	(.260)(.665)	+	(.106)(.532)	= .295
B	(.633)(.174)	+	(.260)(.231)	+	(.106)(.366)	= .209
C	(.633)(.713)	+	(.260)(.104)	+	(.106)(.102)	= .495

We see that supplier C is the preferred supplier. Figure 12.16 shows how these calculations follow from the decision hierarchy diagram.

Applications of AHP

The Analytic Hierarchy Process has been used in many different situations; a comprehensive survey is given by Zahedi.[3] Among the various applications of AHP are economics and planning, energy policy and allocation of resources, health, political conflict resolution, material handling and purchasing, flexible manufacturing systems, worker selection and performance measurement, project selection, marketing, database management system selection, office automation, budget allocation, portfolio selection, accounting and auditing education, sociology, and architecture.

---

[3]Fatemeh Zahedi, "The Analytic Hierarchy Process—A Survey of the Method and Its Applications," *Interfaces*, Vol. 16, No. 4, July–August 1986, pp. 96–108.

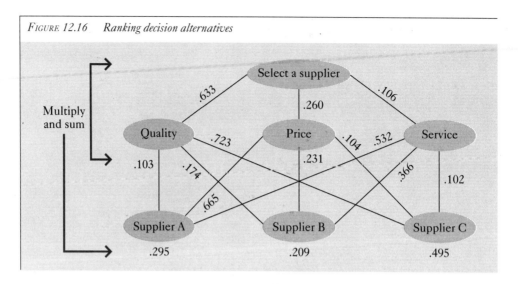

FIGURE 12.16   *Ranking decision alternatives*

In all applications surveyed, some qualitative, as opposed to quantitative, elements play an essential role in the decision problem. This explains why the authors found AHP to be useful. In many cases, no quantification of alternatives was available before, and most cases involved a complex set of interrelated elements that affected the decision.

MANAGEMENT SCIENCE PRACTICE

In this section we show how decision analysis assisted the Santa Clara University athletic board in deciding on a recommendation for implementing a drug testing program for intercollegiate athletes. Unlike the examples we have discussed thus far, the "payoffs" in this decision problem are costs rather than gains. Therefore, the optimal decision based on the expected value criterion is the decision with *lowest expected cost*. More details concerning cost-based payoff tables are given in Example 17 later in this chapter.

Deciding on Intercollegiate Athletic Drug Tests[4]

Figure 12.17 shows the decision tree for testing an individual for drug use. The two main alternatives are "test" or "don't test." The model evaluates the expected cost of testing for drug use compared with that of not testing. If testing is chosen, the test is given and the result, positive or negative, is observed. If the result is positive, action is taken. Since not all those who test positively are actually users, there is some chance of a false accusation, which costs an amount C_1. If the result is negative, then some drug users are not identified, which costs C_2. Nonusers who test negatively might be expected to experi-

---

[4]Adapted from Charles D. Feinstein, "Deciding Whether to Test Student Athletes for Drug Use," *Interfaces*, Vol. 20, No. 3, May–June 1990, pp. 80–87.

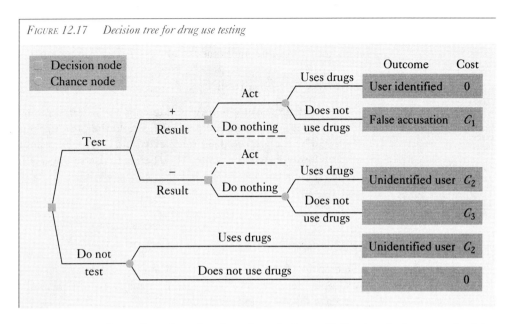

FIGURE 12.17   *Decision tree for drug use testing*

ence some cost C_3, perhaps based on invasion of privacy. Following the lower path of the tree, if the alternative "don't test" were selected, the expected cost is just the cost of an unidentified user, C_2, multiplied by the prior probability that an individual is a drug user. The optimal decision has the lowest expected cost.

The key argument against drug testing revolved around the posterior probabilities. Since the prior probability is the fraction of drug users in the population, the posterior probability is the fraction of drug users among those who tested positively. These posterior probabilities depend on the reliabilities of the test by using Bayes's formula. Table 12.5 shows a table of posterior probabilities for various test reliabilities and prior probabilities. Thus, a test that is 95 percent reliable applied to a population that has 5 percent drug users will yield only a 50 percent posterior probability of drug use; that is, only half of all those that tested positively will actually be drug users!

The athletic board was receptive to this argument and agreed that the incidence of drug abuse was probably no more than 5 percent. Most people had read about the reliability of drug tests in various publications and agreed that the table seemed to capture

TABLE 12.5
Posterior probabilities

		Prior probability that individual is a drug user				
		.05	.083	.100	.125	.166
	.99	.84	.90	.92	.93	.99
Reliability	.95	.50	.63	.68	.73	.80
of the test	.90	.32	.45	.50	.56	.64
	.85	.23	.34	.39	.45	.53
	.75	.14	.21	.25	.30	.38

the range of possible values. They were quite surprised at the posterior probability results and believed that false accusations were more serious than not identifying a drug user. As a result, they recommended that the university not implement a drug testing program.

Questions for Discussion

1. Under what cost assumptions would testing be preferred to not testing?
2. If the costs C_1 and C_2 were equal, what would the posterior probability have to be for testing to be the preferred alternative? Would this assumption be reasonable?
3. The philosopher Voltaire wrote, "It is better to risk saving a guilty person than to condemn an innocent one." Do you agree?

MORE EXAMPLES AND SOLVED PROBLEMS

EXAMPLE 15. THE CARNIVAL GAME[5]

One of the classic examples in decision analysis is known as the carnival game. The example illustrates well all of the approaches to problems under uncertainty and risk we have discussed in this chapter.

A booth at a traveling carnival has the following game. Ten identical boxes sit on the shelf at the back of the booth. There are two "types" of boxes defined by the number of red and black checkers in the box. Each box has 10 checkers in it. A type I box has 4 red checkers and 6 black checkers. A type II box has 9 red checkers and 1 black checker. There are 8 type I boxes and 2 type II boxes. To play the game, you pick a box and guess its type. The payoff table is shown below:

	Type of box	
Guess	Type I	Type II
Type I	$40	−$20
Type II	−$5	$100

Hence, the state of nature is the chosen box's type, and the decision is the type of box to guess. After a play, all of the boxes are randomly shuffled and placed back on the shelf.

What decisions are prescribed by the different criteria we have discussed? First, a player may choose to avoid using probabilities at all and opt for one of the rules under uncertainty. A maximax person (the optimist) would always guess type II:

Guess	Maximum
Type I	$40
Type II	$100 ⟵ Maximax

---

[5]Examples 15 and 16 are based on the example from Howard Raiffa, *Decision Analysis, Introductory Lectures on Choices Under Uncertainty*, New York: Random House, 1968.

A maximin person (the pessimist) would always guess type II:

Guess	Minimum
Type I	−$20
Type II	−$5 ← Maximin

A person using minimax regret (the sore loser) must construct the regret matrix:

	Type of Box	
Guess	Type I	Type II
Type I	$0	$120
Type II	$45	$0

Guess	Maximum regret
Type I	$120
Type II	$45 ← Minimum

Therefore, under minimax regret the optimal decision is always to guess type II.

A player who chooses to use the probabilities may calculate an expected value for each guess:

$$E \text{ (type I guess)} = (40)(.8) + (-20)(.2) = \$28$$

$$E \text{ (type II guess)} = (-5)(.8) + (100)(.2) = \$16$$

The decision tree for this scenario is shown in Figure 12.18. Under the expected value criterion, the optimal decision is to always guess type I.

FIGURE 12.18   *Decision tree for the carnival game*

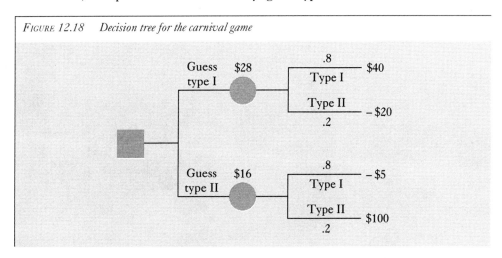

Notice that the expected values of guessing type I and guessing type II are *both* positive! These indicate the expected or average gain *per play* of the game. How long do you think this booth is going to continue to operate before declaring bankruptcy?

Finally, the expected value of perfect information (EVPI) is the expected opportunity loss (regret) for the optimal decision under expected value:

$$\text{EVPI} = \text{EOL (type I guess)} = .8(0) + .2(120) = \$24$$

EXAMPLE 16. THE CARNIVAL GAME WITH SAMPLE INFORMATION

We continue the carnival game of Example 15. Suppose that after the player chooses a box, a checker may be drawn from the box for a $5 fee. After the checker has been drawn, a guess must be made. What is the optimal decision strategy? Is the $5 fee worth it?

A decision tree for this scenario appears in Figure 12.19. The drawn checker is the indicator. The checker will be either red or black, and we may use that information to update the probability that the box is type I or type II.

We have the following probabilities:

Prior: P(Type I) = .8   P(Type II) = .2
Indicator:

P (Checker | Type)	Type I	Type II
Black Checker	.6	.1
Red Checker	.4	.9

FIGURE 12.19   *Decision tree for the carnival game with sampling*

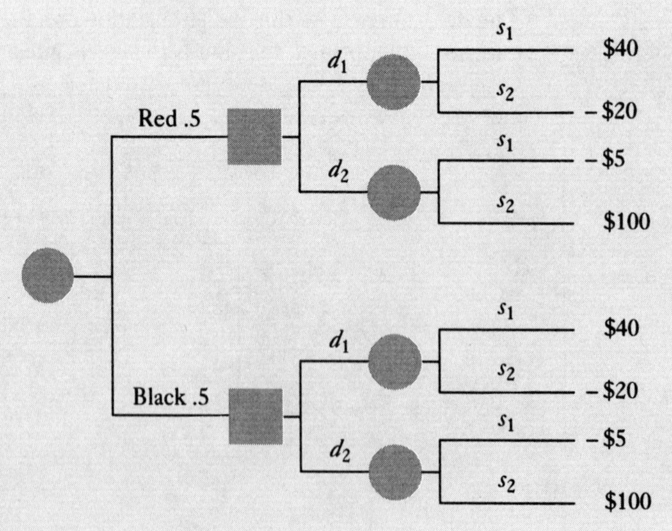

For example, P(black checker | type I) = .6. The joint probabilities are calculated by multiplying each column by its probability:

P (Checker ∩ Type)	Type I	Type II	P (Checker)
Black checker	.48	.02	.5
Red checker	.32	.18	.5

The probability of each indicator is the sum of the row of the joint probability matrix. Hence, P(Black) = .48 + .02 = .5 and P (Red) = .32 + .18 = .5. Now the posterior probabilities may be obtained by simply dividing each row by its indicator probability:

P (Type | Checker)	Type I	Type II
Black checker	.96	.04
Red checker	.64	.36

The decision tree with these posterior and indicator probabilities is shown in Figure 12.20. The tree has been folded back. The optimal strategy when drawing a checker is to guess type I if the checker is black and guess type II if the checker is red. (Does this seem reasonable?) The expected payoff is $35.20. Hence, the gain from using sample information is EVSI = $35.20 − $28 = $7.20. Since the fee is only $5, there is still a net gain of $2.20 over not using sample information. Therefore, the overall optimal decision is to pay the $5 fee and use the optimal strategy with sample information.

EXAMPLE 17. FOREST FIRE MANAGEMENT[6]

Fire is an important tool in contemporary forest management. Prescribed fires are often ignited by forest management personnel under controlled conditions to achieve certain objectives, such as reducing fire hazards, enhancing wildlife habitat, facilitating site preparation for planting seedlings, and controlling diseases and insects. Although it is a highly effective management technique, uncertainties inherent in its use make planning and execution of successful burns challenging.

A simple example is the decision to commit resources to a burn. Two decision alternatives are considered:

D_1: Commit resources to the burn, with an unavoidable cost if the burn is subsequently cancelled.

D_2: Postpone the burn, with a smaller cost associated with the delay in meeting the resource management objectives.

---

[6]Adapted from David Cohan, Stephen M. Haas, David L. Radloff, and Richard F. Yancik, "Using Fire in Forest Management: Decision Making Under Uncertainty," *Interfaces*, Vol. 14, No. 5, September–October 1984, pp. 8–19.

FIGURE 12.20   *Decision tree showing the optimal strategy using sample information for the carnival game*

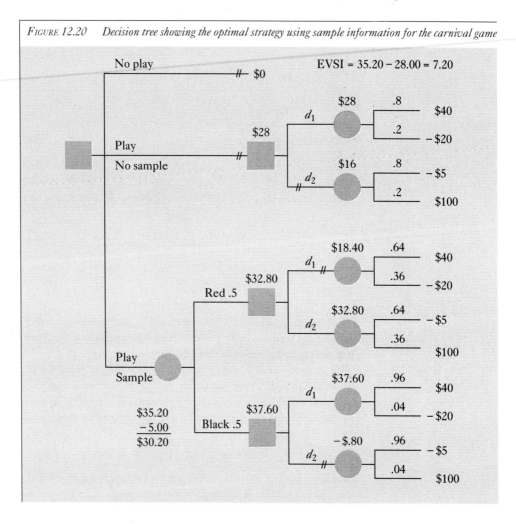

Two uncertainties affect this decision. First is the actual weather conditions on the day of the burn. If the weather is good, the burn can be carried out; if not, it must be canceled. The second uncertainty is the results—will all objectives be met at no additional costs, or will it be only partially successful?

These uncertainties lead to three potential states of nature:

S_1: Good weather and successful outcome

S_2: Good weather and marginal outcome

S_3: Poor weather (the outcome is irrelevant since the burn would be canceled)

Two economic issues are considered: the management costs of preparing and executing the burn and the value of the resources saved from the burn. The cost of preparing for a burn is $1,200, and the cost of executing it is $2,000. If the burn is successful, the value of the resources saved is $6,000; if the burn is only marginal, the value of resources saved is $3,000. If the burn is postponed, costs are estimated to be $300. The forest management would like to minimize the net cost, defined as the management costs less the value of resources saved. The associated *cost* table is as follows:

	S_1	S_2	S_3
D_1	−2,800	200	1,200
D_2	300	300	300

Note that the cost associated with D_1 and S_1 is negative since the value of the resources saved exceeds the cost of the burn (a net gain).

In Rick's investment example, all payoffs are expressed as gains, or profits. The decision criteria change if payoffs are expressed in costs or losses. In this case the aggressive decision maker would choose the decision that would yield the most optimistic outcome. Since our objective is one of cost minimization, the decision maker seeks the minimum payoff for each decision and then chooses the decision that yields the minimum payoff. We call this a *minimin criterion:*

Decision	Minimum cost
D_1	−2,800 ⟵ Best decision
D_2	300

The conservative decision maker is pessimistic and believes the worst will occur. Therefore, this individual would seek to minimize the maximum cost, the *minimax criterion:*

Decision	Minimum cost
D_1	1,200
D_2	300 ⟵ Best decision

If the opportunity loss strategy is used, the minimax regret criterion still applies, since opportunity loss is always a cost, regardless of whether the decision maker's goal is maximization or minimization. However, the way in which opportunity loss is computed differs. The concept is still the same: opportunity loss is the difference in payoffs between any decision and the best decision for a given state of nature. In a cost minimization situation, the best decision has the smallest cost. Thus, for any state of nature, you need to subtract the smallest payoff *from* each decision to compute the opportunity loss. For the fire management problem, we have the opportunity loss matrix given in Table 12.6.

Using the minimax regret criterion, we have

Decision	Maximum opportunity loss
D_1	900 $\leftarrow$ Best decision
D_2	3,100

Using the expected value criterion requires probabilities of the states of nature. From past experience, foresters know that a burn has a .6 probability of being successful. As the decision time approaches, the best estimate they can make about the weather is as good as a coin toss. What is the optimal decision using the expected value criterion?

Recall that the states of nature are defined as follows:

S_1: Good weather and successful outcome

S_2: Good weather and marginal outcome

S_3: Poor weather

From the information provided, we have P(successful outcome) = .6, P(marginal outcome) = .4, P(good weather) = .5, and P(poor weather) = .5. Assuming that the outcome of the burn and the weather are independent (since the burn is attempted only in good weather), then

$$P(S_1) = (.5)(.6) = .3$$

$$P(S_2) = (.5)(.4) = .2$$

$$P(S_3) = .5$$

The expected *cost* for each decision is

$$E(D_1) = .3(-2,800) + .2(200) + .5(1,200) = -\$200$$

$$E(D_2) = .3(300) + .2(300) + .5(300) = \$300$$

The calculations are shown on the decision tree in Figure 12.21. The minimum expected cost is given by D_1 (−$200 cost). This means that the expected value of resources saved will exceed the costs of the burn by $200. This is the best decision since postponing the burn would cost $300.

TABLE 12.6
Opportunity loss matrix

	S_1	S_2	S_3
D_1	0	0	900
D_2	3,100	100	0

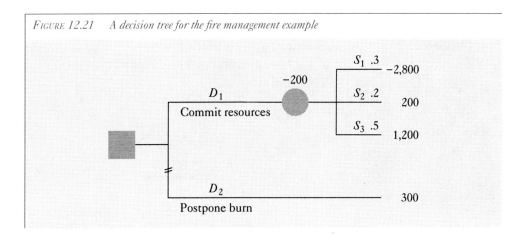

FIGURE 12.21   A decision tree for the fire management example

EXAMPLE 18. AN EQUIPMENT REPLACEMENT DECISION PROBLEM [7]

Electric utilities face decisions that have important impacts on the environment. They must balance the cost of management actions with the risks associated from environmental impacts, particularly the cleanup and liability costs that might result. An important decision that a utility must face is deciding whether to replace a PCB transformer in a generating station. Thus, the utility faces two decision options:

D_1: Replace the transformer at a cost of $75,000.

D_2: Keep the current transformer.

In evaluating this decision, the utility must determine the potential consequences associated with each decision. If it replaces the transformer, the utility can reasonably expect that no serious incidents will occur during the useful life of the equipment. However, if it keeps the current transformer, it runs the risk of an incident such as a fire. In considering this, managers defined the following outcomes:

S_1: Severe incident; cost = $80 million

S_2: Minor incident; cost = $5 million

S_3: No incident; cost = $0

An analysis of the types of incidents and expert judgment of their potential to occur led to assigning probabilities $P(S_1) = .0005$, $P(S_2) = .0040$, and $P(S_3) = .9955$. For what range of utilities would D_1 be preferable to D_2?

First note that the expected value of not replacing the transformer is

($80 million)(.0005) + ($5 million)(.0040) + 0(.9955) = $60,000

[7] Adapted from William E. Balson, Justin L. Welsh, and Donald S. Wilson, "Using Decision Analysis and Risk Analysis to Manage Utility Environmental Risk," *Interfaces*, Vol. 22, No. 6, November–December 1992, pp. 126–139.

On this basis, the recommended decision would be not to replace the transformer. Because of the potential catastrophic loss that can result, utility might be a better approach. Since the highest payoff is $0 and the lowest is −$80 million, we assign a utility of 1 to $0 and a utility of 0 to −$80 million:

Payoff	Utility
0	1
−$75,000	u_1
−$5 million	u_2
−$80 million	0

We can find the risk indifference utilities by finding p so that the expected value of the gamble between $0 and −$80 million is equivalent to the certain payoff, either −$75,000 or −$5 million. For −$75,000, we have

$$-\$75{,}000 = \$0(p) + (-\$80{,}000{,}000)(1 - p)$$

or $p = u_1 = .9990625$. For −$5 million, we have

$$-\$5{,}000{,}000 = \$0(p) + (-\$80{,}000{,}000)(1 - p)$$

or $p = u_2 = .9375$. Thus, the risk indifference utility function is as follows:

Payoff	Utility
0	1
−$75,000	.9990625
−$5 million	.9375
−$80 million	0

We can view this problem more generally by examining the utility payoff matrix:

	S_1	S_2	S_3
D_1	u_1	u_1	u_1
D_2	0	u_2	1

Therefore, expected utilities, EU, for each decision are

$$\text{EU}(D_1) = u_1$$

$$\text{EU}(D_2) = 0(.0005) + u_2(.0040) + 1(.9955) = .004u_2 + .9955$$

D_1 will be preferred to D_2 when $\text{EU}(D_1) > \text{EU}(D_2)$, or

$$u_1 > .004u_2 + .9955$$

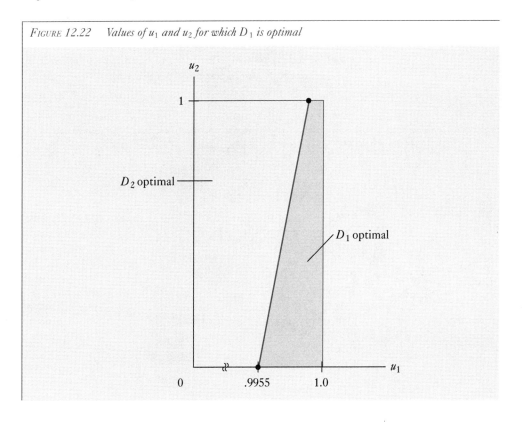

FIGURE 12.22   *Values of u_1 and u_2 for which D_1 is optimal*

This range is shown in the graph in Figure 12.22. We see that for the indifference utilities, $.9990625 < .004(.9375) + .9955 = .99925$. The risk-indifferent decision maker would choose not to replace the generator. A risk-averse individual would probably replace it. However, you might consider whether this approach is really practical, given the precision at which these utilities must be estimated. Would a manager be able to determine utilities to four decimal places? If not, would the utility analysis accurately reflect the decision maker's true preferences?

SUMMARY

In this chapter we have discussed different approaches to making decisions under uncertainty. In the decision analysis framework, the decision maker(s) must choose from a list of decision alternatives in the face of uncertain states of nature, where the resultant payoff or cost depends on both the decision and the state of nature. When the decision maker can estimate the likelihood of the various states of nature, we refer to this process as decision making under risk. Utility functions may be used to incorporate an individual's (or firm's) feelings concerning risk into the decision analysis under risk. The Analytic Hierarchy Process may be used for making multicriteria decisions.

Decision analysis is most applicable to important, unique decisions involving uncertainty. Highly complex decisions with many interconnected parts involving uncertainty are best analyzed by risk analysis using computer simulation. Computer simulation and risk analysis are the topics of the next chapter.

CHAPTER REVIEW EXERCISES

I. Terms to Understand

a.   Decision analysis (p. 631)
b.   Decision alternatives (p. 631)
c.   States of nature (p. 635)
d.   Payoff (p. 636)
e.   Payoff table (p. 636)
f.   Decision tree (p. 636)
g.   Risk (p. 637)
h.   Uncertainty (p. 637)
i.   Principle of insufficient reason (p. 638)
j.   Opportunity loss (regret) (p. 639)

k.   Minimax regret (p. 639)
l.   Expected value of perfect information (p. 641)
m.   Prior probability (p. 647)
n.   Posterior probability (p. 647)
o.   Indicator (p. 647)
p.   Indicator reliability (p. 647)
q.   Utility (p. 653)
r.   Analytic hierarchy process (AHP) (p. 658)

II. Discussion Questions

1.   Why is decision analysis a useful topic to study?
2.   Explain the differences between decision analysis and other techniques of management science, especially optimization models.
3.   What are the key characteristics of situations for which decision analysis techniques apply?
4.   Define several personal decisions that you face. What techniques of decision analysis might be useful to you in structuring and analyzing these decisions?
5.   Discuss the difficulties that managers might face in practice in defining the following:
     a.   Decision alternatives
     b.   States of nature
     c.   Decision criteria
     d.   Payoffs
6.   Explain the fundamental rationale underlying the maximax (minimin), maximin (minimax), and minimax regret criteria. How can you determine which approach a decision maker might prefer?
7.   Of what value is the expected value of perfect information?
8.   Provide a nontechnical summary of the process of evaluating indicator information for decision making.
9.   What are the limitations of expected value decision making? How does utility theory help to overcome these limitations?
10. Explain the purpose of the Analytic Hierarchy Process. What advantages does it have over other techniques of decision analysis?

III. Problems

SA

1. Slaggert Systems is considering becoming certified to the ISO 9000 series of quality standards. Becoming certified is expensive, but the company could lose a substantial amount of business if its major customers suddenly demand ISO certification and the company does not have it. At a management retreat, the senior executives of the firm developed the following payoff table, indicating the net present value of profits over the next five years. What decision should they make under each of the criteria for uncertainty?

	Customer response	
	Standards required	**Standards not required**
Become certified	$550,000	$480,000
Stay uncertified	$300,000	$520,000

HWS

2. Big Bob of Bob's Bagels is trying to decide if he should expand his business. He can choose not to expand, expand by buying an existing business, or expand by opening another (new) location. The net present values (NPV) in thousands of dollars for each alternative under various states of nature are shown in the table below:

	s_1	s_2	s_3	s_4
Do not expand	$290	$290	$290	$290
Buy existing	$510	$130	$580	$150
Open new	$580	$100	$520	$160

a. What is the optimal decision for Bob under the following approaches?
   i. Laplace
   ii. Maximax
   iii. Maximin
   iv. Minimax Regret
b. Bob has accessed the following probabilities: $P(s_1) = .4, P(s_2) = .2, P(s_3) = .3, P(s_4) = .1$. Draw a decision tree of his problem. Find the optimal decision using the expected value criterion. Show your calculations on the decision tree.
c. Calculate the expected value of perfect information (EVPI).

3. The Doorco Corporation is a leading manufacturer of garage doors. All doors are manufactured in their plant in Carmel, Indiana, and shipped to distribution centers or major customers. Doorco recently acquired another manufacturer of garage doors, Wisconsin Door, and is considering moving its wood door operations to the Wisconsin plant. A key consideration in this decision is the transportation and production costs at the two plants and the new construction and relocation costs. Complicating matters is the fact that marketing is predicting a decline in the demand for wood doors. The company developed three scenarios:

1. Demand falls slightly, with no noticeable effect on production.
2. Demand and production decline 20 percent.
3. Demand and production decline 45 percent.

The table below shows the total costs under each decision and scenario.

	Slight decline	20% decline	40% decline
Stay in Carmel	$982,000	$830,000	$635,000
Move to Wisconsin	$993,000	$832,000	$629,000

   a.   What decision should Doorco make under the principle of insufficient reason (Laplace), minimin, minimax, and minimax regret criteria?

   b.   Suppose the probabilities of the three scenarios are estimated to be .15, .45, and .40, respectively. What is the optimal expected cost decision?

4.   Mountain Ski Sports, a chain of ski equipment shops in Colorado, purchases skis from a manufacturer each summer for the coming winter season. The most popular intermediate model costs $150 and sells for $260. Any skis left over at the end of the winter are sold at the store's half-price sale (for $130). Sales over the years are quite stable. Gathering data from all its stores, Mountain Ski Sports developed the following probability distribution for demand:

Demand	Probability
150	.1
175	.3
200	.4
225	.15
250	.05

The manufacturer will take orders only for multiples of 20, so Mountain Ski is considering the following order sizes: 160, 180, 200, 220, and 240.

   a.   Construct a payoff table for Mountain Ski's decision problem of how many pairs of skis to order. What is the best decision from an expected value basis?

   b.   Find the expected value of perfect information.

   c.   What is the expected demand? Is the optimal order quantity equal to the expected demand? Why?

5.   Mad Marty runs a shirt concession at Riverview Music Center. He buys commemorative T-shirts for $15 each and sells them for $25. As people are leaving the music center after the concert, he reduces his price to $10 to sell any remaining shirts. Historically, shirt sales follow the distribution shown below.

Demand	Probability
350	.1
400	.2
450	.3
500	.2
550	.1
600	.1

Marty must purchase lots of 50, so he is considering orders of 350, 400, 450, 500, 550, or 600. Construct a payoff table and determine Mad Marty's optimal ordering decision using the expected value criterion.

6. For the forest fire management problem, find the expected value of perfect information by considering the best strategy for each possible state of nature. Show that this is equal to the expected opportunity loss for the optimal expected value decision. How practical would it be to obtain better information about the states of nature for this decision situation?

7. Perform a sensitivity analysis about the probability of good weather for the forest fire management problem (Example 17). For what range of probabilities would it be better to postpone the burn, all else being equal?

8. Figure 12.23 shows a real-time fire execution decision on a Gifford Pinchot National Forest site in the state of Washington. Determine the optimal decision strategy. Also, perform a sensitivity analysis to determine weather conditions under which it would not be preferable to mobilize resources for the burn.

9. A car rental agency offers you the option of purchasing insurance. Insurance for a week would cost $70. A relatively minor accident might cost you $1,500.
    a. Construct a payoff table for this decision problem. Show the decisions under minimin, minimax, and minimax regret.
    b. What decision would you choose and why? Sketch your utility function for this decision.
    c. Statistics show that the chance of a car renter being involved in an accident during one week is only 0.3 percent. What is the best expected value decision? Would this change your decision from part b?

FIGURE 12.23   *Real-time fire execution decision*

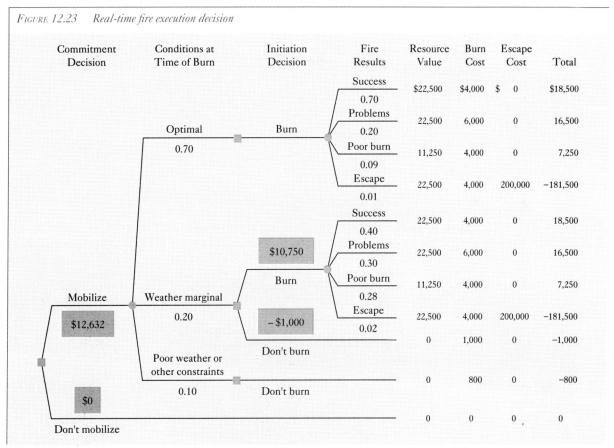

Figure from Cohan et al., "Using Fire in Forest Management: Decision Making under Uncertainty," *Interfaces*, Vol. 14, No. 5, Sept–Oct 1984, p. 17.

10. Dean Kuroff started a business of rehabbing old homes. He recently purchased a circa-1800 Victorian mansion and converted it into a three-family residence. Recently, one of his tenants complained that the refrigerator was not working properly. As Dean's cash flow was not extensive, he was not excited about purchasing a new refrigerator. He is considering two other options: purchase a used refrigerator or repair the current unit. He can purchase a new one for $400, and it will easily last three years. If he repairs the current one, he estimates a repair cost of $150, but he also believes that there is only a 30 percent chance that it will last a full three years and he will end up purchasing a new one anyway. If he buys a used refrigerator for $200, he estimates that there is a .6 probability that it will last at least three years. If it breaks down, he will still have the option of repairing it for $150 or buying a new one. Develop a decision tree for this situation and determine Dean's optimal strategy.

11. In the Tahoe National Forest, prescribed burning is often used to prepare sites for new plantings. An additional objective is to reduce the hazard of wildfire by eliminating heavy concentrations of logging slash. Two treatment techniques are proposed: D_1, broadcast burning, and D_2, yarding of unmerchantable material (YUM) followed by broadcast burning. Foresters have defined three states of nature:

   S_1:   Successful burn

   S_2:   Problems

   S_3:   Escaped fire

   The table below shows the probabilities of each state of nature, which depend on the type of burn.

	S_1	S_2	S_3
D_1	.8485	.150	.0015
D_2	.899	.100	.001

   The value of the resources saved in a burn is $6,620. The first treatment costs $4,550; the second, $4,858. If there is an escaped fire, an additional $40,000 cost is incurred. If problems arise during either type of burn (state of nature S_2) there is also an additional cost. For broadcast burning, the cost is $3,360 with probability .25, $1,750 with probability .5, and $1,050 with probability .25. For YUM and burn, this cost is $3,010 with probability .25, $1,400 with probability .5, and $700 with probability .25. Construct a decision tree for this situation and determine the best decision.

12. *The New York Times* reported (May 21, 1987) that an AIDS test of 100,000 people from the low-risk general public that currently has an incidence of 0.03 percent would identify 28 true positives, 2 false negatives, and 11 false positives.
   a. What is the probability of having AIDS given a positive test?
   b. What is the probability of not having AIDS given a positive test?
   c. What are the probabilities of testing positive and of testing negative if a person in this population has AIDS?
   d. What are the probabilities of testing positive and of testing negative if a person in this population does not have AIDS?
   e. Construct the joint probability table for the test results and whether or not a person has AIDS. What is the probability of a positive test for any individual in the population?

13. Drilling decisions by oil and gas operators involve intensive capital expenditures made in an environment characterized by limited information and high risk. A well site is dry, wet, or gushing. Historically, 50

percent of all wells have been dry, 30 percent wet, and 20 percent gushing. The value (net of drilling costs) for each type of well is as follows:

Dry	−$80,000
Wet	$100,000
Gushing	$200,000

Wildcat operators often investigate oil prospects in areas where deposits are thought to exist by making geological and geophysical examinations of the area before obtaining a lease and drilling permit. This often includes recording shock waves from detonations by a seismograph and using a magnetometer to measure the intensity of the earth's magnetic effect to detect rock formations below the surface. The cost of doing such studies is approximately $15,000. Of course, one may choose to drill in a location based on "gut feel" and avoid the cost of the study.

The geological and geophysical examination classify an area into one of three categories: no structure (NS), which is a bad sign; open structure (OS), which is an "OK" sign; and closed structure (CS), which is hopeful. The following table gives the reliability indicators for these examinations:

	Dry	Wet	Gushing
NS	.6	.3	.1
OS	.3	.4	.4
CS	.1	.3	.5

This table indicates, for example, that $P(\text{OS} \mid \text{Gushing}) = .4$.

a. Draw a decision tree of this problem including the decision of whether or not to perform the geological tests. Calculate any needed probabilities and place them on the decision tree.

b. What is the optimal decision under expected value when no experimentation is conducted?

c. Find the overall optimal strategy by folding back the tree.

14. A patient arrives at an emergency room complaining of abdominal pain. The ER physician must decide on whether to operate or to place the patient under observation for a non–appendix-related condition. If an appendectomy is performed immediately, the doctor runs the risk that the patient does not have appendicitis. If it is delayed and the patient does indeed have appendicitis, the appendix might perforate, leading to a more severe case and possible complications. However, the patient might recover without the operation. Construct a decision tree for the doctor's dilemma. Would utility be a better measure of payoff than actual costs? If so, how might utilities be derived for each path in the tree?

15. A college football team is trailing 14–0 late in the game. The team is getting close to making a touchdown. If they can score now, hold the opponent, and score one more time, they can tie or win the game. The coach is wondering whether to go for an extra-point kick or a two-point conversion now, and what to do if they can score again.

a. Develop a decision tree for the coach's decision. Develop a utility function to represent the final score for each path in the tree.

b. Estimate probabilities for successful kick or two-point conversions. (You might want to do this by some group brainstorming or by calling on experts, such as your school's coach, or a sports journalist.) Using these probabilities and utilities from part a, determine the optimal strategy.

c. Perform a sensitivity analysis on the probabilities to evaluate alternative strategies (such as when the starting kicker is injured).

16. Cathy Crawford is a college student who needs a new car, but she wants to spend only $2,000. Over The Hill Motors sells many used cars to local students, and Cathy found one she is interested in. However, in talking with 10 of her sorority sisters who have bought cars from OTH Motors, three of them said they got a real lemon, whereas the others thought they got the best deal in the world. If it's a lemon, it will cost her an additional $1,000 in repairs. Her other alternative is to buy a car from Jeff Tyler Motors for $2,500 with a warranty that will cover any problems. One of Cathy's classmates is a pretty good mechanic who offers to check out the car's basic systems for $100. He cautions her that he may miss some things because he doesn't have any sophisticated electronic diagnostic equipment. He is confident that if the car is in great shape, he can determine this 90 percent of the time, and if the car has serious problems, he will miss it 20 percent of the time. What should Cathy do?

17. Dean Electronics produces disk drives for personal computers. It will repair any failing drive within one year at no cost. This usually costs the company $50. Records indicate that 5 percent of all drives are returned under warranty. The company is considering a new testing procedure that would cost about $2 per unit and would indicate a potential failure within a year's use. Any drive that fails the test may be repaired at a cost of $10 with virtually no chance of failure within one year. A pilot demonstration with the test equipment and accelerated performance testing (running the drives continuously to simulate a year's use) had the following results:

Actual result	Failure within 1 year	No failure within 1 year
Failure within 1 year	.12	.04
No failure within 1 year	.20	.64

Construct a decision tree for the company's decision problem, determine posterior probabilities and indicator probabilities, and find the optimal decision strategy.

18. Suppose that a decision maker has the following payoff table:

	State of nature	
Decision	S_1	S_2
D_1	90	40
D_2	65	55
D_3	30	80

Determine ranges of $p = P(S_1)$ and $1 - p = P(S_2)$ for which each decision would be optimal using the expected value criterion.

19. Refer to Problem 2. Big Bob's utility function $(U(x) = [x - .00075x^2]/[332.5])$, is shown in Figure 12.24.

a. Is he risk prone, risk averse, or risk neutral?

b. What is Bob's optimal decision using expected utility? Is the solution different from the expected value criterion found in Problem 2? Why or why not?

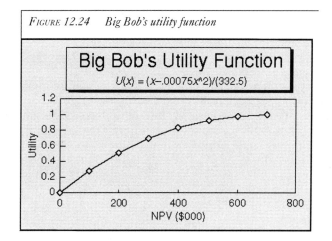

FIGURE 12.24   *Big Bob's utility function*

20.   Rob and Diane are looking for a new house. They have three principal decision criteria: size, neighborhood, and style. They have narrowed down their search to two houses: a turn-of-the-century colonial (C) and a much newer transitional style (T) in a better neighborhood. Using pairwise comparisons, Rob and Diane developed the following preference and importance matrices:

Size	C	T
C	1	3
T	$\frac{1}{3}$	1

Neighborhood	C	T
C	1	$\frac{1}{5}$
T	5	1

Style	C	T
C	1	2
T	$\frac{1}{2}$	1

Criteria	Size	Neighborhood	Style
Size	1	3	$\frac{1}{4}$
Neighborhood	$\frac{1}{3}$	1	$\frac{1}{5}$
Style	4	5	1

a. Develop a decision hierarchy diagram for Rob and Diane's problem.
b. Determine the relative priorities for each criterion and the relative importance of the criteria, and compute the priorities for the two houses.
c. Compute the consistency ratio for each matrix. How might these results influence the answer in part b?

21. StatKeyes, a major marketing research and analysis firm, is seeking to hire a new statistical analyst. Among many applicants, they have selected three finalists: Tim, Scott, and Janet. StatKeyes evaluates their analysts on three criteria: technical ability, writing skills, and maturity. Based on interviews and other application materials, the recruiting team constructed the following preference matrices. Conduct an analysis using the Analytic Hierarchy Process to recommend a selection for the position.

Technical Ability	Tim	Scott	Janet
Tim	1	7	5
Scott	$\frac{1}{7}$	1	3
Janet	$\frac{1}{5}$	$\frac{1}{3}$	1

Writing Skills	Tim	Scott	Janet
Tim	1	2	$\frac{1}{4}$
Scott	$\frac{1}{2}$	1	$\frac{1}{6}$
Janet	4	6	1

Maturity	Tim	Scott	Janet
Tim	1	$\frac{1}{3}$	1
Scott	3	1	2
Janet	1	$\frac{1}{2}$	1

IV. Projects and Cases

1. One of the major decisions that most individuals eventually face is buying a house or condominium and securing a mortgage. A mortgage contract obligates the borrower to make a series of payments over time that will fully amortize the loan. Lenders have available several different types of mortgage instruments, such as fixed-rate (15, 20, or 30 years) and adjustable-rate mortgages (ARMs). The key decisions that borrowers face are the type of mortgage and length of time. ARMs typically have a lower interest rate than fixed-rate mortgages, but many borrowers are reluctant to accept ARMs because of the uncertainty associated with the actual payments they will have to make in the future, particularly if interest rates rise. From the data in Table 12.7 (you may wish to use current data available from a bank or other lender), develop a decision

TABLE *12.7*
Alternative home mortgage contracts

30-year fixed rate: 8.875%

15-year fixed rate: 8.25%

1-year ARM:
   Current rate: 5.5%
   Maximum yearly increase: 2%
   Lifetime increase: 6%

1-year ARM:
   Current rate: 6.75%
   Maximum yearly increase: 1%
   Lifetime increase: 4%

3-year ARM:
   Current rate: 7.5%
   Maximum yearly increase: 2%
   Lifetime increase: 6%
   After 3 years, this becomes a 1-year ARM.

5-year ARM:
   Current rate: 8.125%
   Maximum yearly increase: 2%
   Lifetime increase: 5%
   After 5 years, this becomes a 1-year ARM.

tree to help a would-be borrower make a decision. Use the current Treasury bill index for the margin, and make whatever assumptions you deem appropriate. You might want to use a spreadsheet to compute present values of your cash flows to support your analysis.

2. Many automobile dealers are advertising lease options for new cars. Suppose that you are considering three alternatives:

    1. Purchase the car outright (assuming that you have the cash on hand).
    2. Purchase the car with 20 percent down and a 48-month loan.
    3. Lease the car.

    Select an automobile whose leasing contract is advertised in your newspaper. Using current interest rates and advertised leasing arrangements, perform a decision analysis of these options. Make, but clearly define, any assumptions that may be required.

3. Construct a decision hierarchy for purchasing an automobile. Limit yourself to five criteria. Select three models of automobiles that you would consider buying, visit the showrooms, and pick up some literature about the cars. Using this information, develop your personal preference and importance matrices and conduct an AHP decision analysis. How consistent are you in making pairwise comparisons? Would this analysis help you to actually choose your next car?

REFERENCES

Balson, William E., Justin L. Welsh, and Donald S. Wilson. "Using Decision Analysis and Risk Analysis to Manage Utility Environmental Risk." *Interfaces*, Vol. 22, No. 6, November–December 1992, pp. 126–139.

Bunn, Derek W. *Applied Decision Analysis*. New York: McGraw-Hill, 1984.

Byrd, Jack, Jr., and L. Ted Moore. *Decision Models for Management*. New York: McGraw-Hill, 1982.

Clarke, John R. "The Application of Decision Analysis to Clinical Medicine." *Interfaces*, Vol. 17, No. 2, March–April 1987, pp. 27–34.

Cohan, David, Stephen M. Haas, David L. Radloff, and Richard F. Yancik. "Using Fire in Forest Management: Decision Making Under Uncertainty." *Interfaces*, Vol. 14, No. 5, September–October 1984, pp. 8–19.

Engemann, Kurt J., and Holmes E. Miller. "Operations Risk Management at a Major Bank." *Interfaces*, Vol. 22, No. 6, November–December 1992, pp. 140–149.

Feinstein, Charles D. "Deciding Whether to Test Student Athletes for Drug Use." *Interfaces*, Vol. 20, No. 3, May–June 1990, pp. 80–87.

Heian, Betty C., and James R. Gale, "Mortgage Selection Using a Decision Tree Approach: An Extension." *Interfaces*, Vol. 18, No. 4, July–August, 1988, pp. 72–83.

Janssen, C. T. L., and T. E. Daniel. "A Decision Theory Example in Football." *Decision Sciences*, Vol. 15, No. 2, Spring 1984, pp. 253–259.

Hosseini, Jinoos. "Decision Analysis and Its Application in the Choice Between Two Wildcat Oil Ventures." *Interfaces*, Vol. 16, No. 2, March–April 1986, pp. 75–85.

Moore, Peter G. *Risk in Business Decision*. London: Longman Group Ltd., 1972.

Newman, Joseph W. *Management Applications of Decision Theory*. New York: Harper & Row, 1971.

Raiffa, Howard *Decision Analysis: Introductory Lectures on Choices Under Uncertainty*. New York: Random House, 1968.

CHAPTER 13

COMPUTER

SIMULATION

AND RISK

ANALYSIS

INTRODUCTION

- Certificates of deposit are important to banks as a source of funds. Banks need to effectively manage the spread between the interest they pay out on CDs and the interest earned on loans. Managing CD portfolios is difficult because of uncertainty and fluctuations in interest rates. A model that can assess the impact of various interest-rate scenarios on a bank's CD portfolio is useful for planning purposes. The First National Bank and Trust Company of Tulsa developed and used a simulation model to assess the impact of future interest-rate scenarios in managing its corporate CD portfolio. The model gave an accurate assessment of the effect of changing interest rates on funding costs and profit margins and was expected to be used in the bank's internal systems to project an overall balance sheet [Russell and Hickle, 1986].

- Burger King has used simulation models for many years in designing its facilities and evaluating the impact of new menu items. The models help the company to understand the dynamic aspects of its restaurant operations and the interactions among the customer, delivery, and production subsystems. The models have helped Burger King to design the best configuration of drive-through windows and to predict the financial impact of introducing new specialty sandwiches. Burger King also has several kitchens that can be reconfigured so that they can try out some of the better computer simulation results in an actual physical test setting. The models have helped the corporation gain market share and increase profits by over $30 million annually. Many other major quick-service restaurants such as Pizza Hut, Kentucky Fried Chicken, and Taco Bell use simulation to improve operations and customer service and to reduce costs [Swart and Donno, 1981].

- The Golden West Airport Shuttle, Inc., is a transportation service between suburban Denver and Stapleton International Airport and Central City. The number of passengers requiring transport cannot be predicted with certainty and changes from time to time and from one service point to the other. Trip times vary with the number of service points that a van goes through before reaching its final destination; trip times also depend on weather conditions. The only way to study and experiment with such a system without requiring many simplifying assumptions is computer simulation. A simulation model was built to study the effects of increasing passenger volume on the current fleet size and to estimate the optimal fleet size that will handle increasing volumes with minimal passenger delay [Maurer and Munkonze, undated].

As we have seen in the last two chapters, many problems in management science involve probabilistic variables. In each of the scenarios above, probabilistic variables dominate the systems. In the first case, changes in interest rates are highly uncertain. The pattern of customer arrivals and purchases at Burger King is probabilistic. Finally, in the Golden West situation, passenger volumes, trip times, and weather conditions are probabilistic.

For some problems, probabilistic models and decision analysis techniques are useful analytical approaches for dealing with such decision problems. These techniques usually require some highly simplifying assumptions. Many important problems either do not lend themselves to analytical approaches or involve many interacting probabilistic elements that make analytical approaches difficult to apply. For instance, the distribution of CD maturities does not appear to follow any standard probability distribution. It is virtually impossible to model accurately the flow of transportation vans and passenger waiting because of the randomness in volume and travel. In other problems, formulas may involve sums of random variables from different probability distributions and it is not possible to describe the resulting distribution analytically.

A powerful technique to assist managers in analyzing such problems is called *computer simulation*.

> *Computer simulation* is the process of designing a logical computer model of a system or decision problem and conducting computer-based experiments with the model to describe, explain, and predict the behavior of the system or problem outcomes.

Simulation models are nothing more than logical descriptions of the interrelationships among elements in a decision problem or the sequence of events that occur over time in a system. Spreadsheet models form the basis for many computer simulation experiments. Others require special-purpose programs or "simulation languages" to capture time-dependent behavior of systems. We generate simulation outputs by *sampling* from the distributions of the probabilistic variables. By repeated sampling from these distributions, a simulation generates outputs that show the variation in a system's performance or the uncertainty in decision problems in the same fashion as we might observe them in real life.

Because they are descriptive, simulation models cannot by themselves provide optimal solutions to problems. The decision maker must manipulate the controllable variables, using the simulation model as a tool to evaluate the effects of these variables on the system performance or outcomes from the decision. Simulation models are usually implemented on a computer because of the large number of calculations that are involved. Conceptually, however, the calculations in any simulation can be done with a calculator and pencil and paper.

Simulation has many benefits. Through simulation experiments, we can evaluate proposed systems without building them; experiment with existing systems without disturbing them; and test the limits of systems without destroying them. In this way, simulation can be used for design, analysis, and performance assessment.

As in any modeling approach, there are some drawbacks to using simulation. It requires you to understand fully how a system operates and be able to translate this knowledge into a detailed logical model and computer implementation. A large amount of effort in simulation modeling involves the collection of high-quality data. Therefore, you need a good information system that will capture the required data. You must be able to test the simulation model to see if it works properly and accurately models the actual system in sufficient detail to provide useful answers. These activities all require time and good communication among many individuals. Thus, simulation is often addressed from a project focus. Good management skills are required to coordinate the various activities and people involved in the project.

In this chapter we introduce you to the basic concepts of simulation modeling and analysis. We focus on *Monte Carlo simulation* techniques based on repeated sampling from probability distributions. This approach is extremely useful in evaluating risk in decisions that analytical decision analysis cannot capture. In the next chapter we discuss simulation of more complex systems.

APPLICATIONS OF SIMULATION

Simulation models can be used for a wide variety of problems; thus they are among the most often-used models in management science. They are most useful in situations involving dynamic interactions between elements of the system and for systems that have many probabilistic elements. Simulation has been used extensively in manufacturing systems to evaluate plant designs, technology improvements, different scheduling rules, and material handling systems; in transportation planning to analyze air traffic control systems, air and truck terminal operations, and railroad system performance; in financial planning to study capital investment decisions, cash flow analysis, and corporate budgeting; in health care systems to help schedule operating rooms, plan staffing schedules, and manage inventories; and in many other applications. In this section we present some unique and interesting examples of simulation for complex decision problems.

Planning a New Manufacturing Facility

At AT&T, factories are constantly being modernized. Many proposed changes can be evaluated by experienced manufacturing engineers without the expense of building simulation models. However, one modernization plan was extremely comprehensive and involved new technology and operations policies. The cost of a planning mistake would be very high, so management decided to invest effort in simulation to improve the quality of the planning process.

The most important part of the modernization plan was the consolidation of several older production lines into a single flexible production line called the high-velocity shop (HVS). In the HVS, AT&T builds a variety of data communications products that consist of one or more subassemblies called circuit packs—assemblies of printed wiring boards and electrical components. Figure 13.1 illustrates the product flow and material handling equipment used in the HVS.

The first mission of the project team was to specify the concerns and questions to be addressed with the simulation. These included the following:

1. How large should production lot sizes be?
2. What rules of thumb should be used for scheduling production to achieve even loading and maximize throughput?

3. How large should work-in-process buffers be?
4. How many automated guided vehicles (AGVs) are required?
5. Will the conveyors keep up with the production requirements?
6. What test and repair rules should be used?
7. What trade-offs between capital equipment and inventory can be made?
8. What reductions in setup time should be sought?

FIGURE 13.1   *AT&T high-velocity shop product flow*

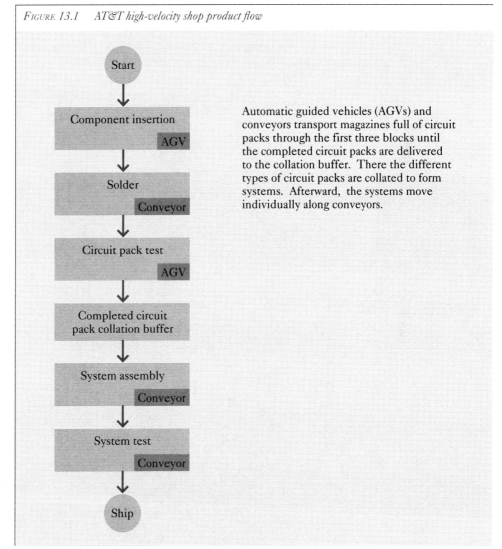

Automatic guided vehicles (AGVs) and conveyors transport magazines full of circuit packs through the first three blocks until the completed circuit packs are delivered to the collation buffer. There the different types of circuit packs are collated to form systems. Afterward, the systems move individually along conveyors.

Figure from Cadley et al., "Insights from Simulating JIT Manufacturing," *Interfaces*, Vol. 19, No. 2, March–April, 1989, pp. 88–97.

The simulation model allowed the managers to answer all these questions. The model also provided some unexpected results. For example, managers found that to meet capacity requirements, they had to schedule preventive maintenance so as not to interfere with production, and that balanced production scheduling was absolutely critical to the shop. The simulation model will continue to be used after the plant is operational to evaluate different scheduling policies and further proposed changes [Cadley et al., 1989].

Running Race Management

The Bolder Boulder is a 10-kilometer running race held each Memorial Day in Boulder, Colorado. From its start with 2,200 participants in 1979, it has grown to 20,000 participants. All runners are individually tagged as they finish, entering a limited number of chutes (see Figure 13.2). As the race grew in size, large numbers of runners began to queue up at the finish line at certain times, causing overcrowding in the chutes and backups into the race course. Possible solutions were identified as follows:

FIGURE 13.2   *Finish line configuration for the Bolder Boulder Race*

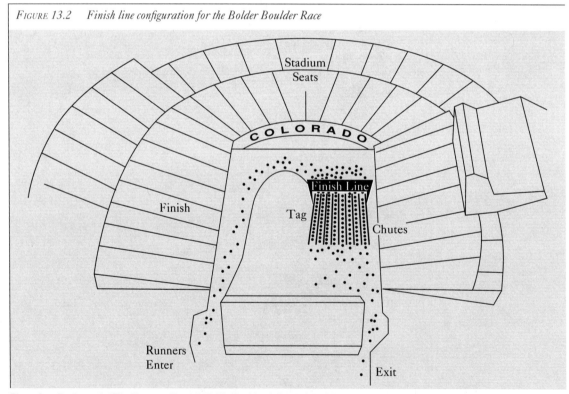

Figure from Farrina et al., "The Computer Runs the Bolder Boulder: A Simulation of a Major Running Race," *Interfaces*, Vol. 19, No. 2, March–April, 1989, pp. 48–55.

- Increasing the number of chutes
- Increasing the length of the chutes
- Modifying the tag procedure to reduce time
- Modifying starting intervals to spread out the runners
- Some combination of these alternatives

Since the race was only run once each year, it was impossible to experiment with these alternatives. A simulation model was constructed to enable the race manager to try proposed solutions and identify a good one. After studying the results of many computer simulations, the race organization decided that the number of chutes should be increased. The 1985 race was conducted using the recommendations derived from the simulation model, and the actual results were very close to those suggested by the model. Overcrowding at the finish line was eliminated and the race was called "the best mass participation race in the United States." The model has been used to study the effects of increased participation and to fine-tune the management decisions [Farina et al., 1989].

Forest Fire Management

The forest industry is an important sector of the economy of Ontario, Canada. As the value of forest resources increases, so does the need for fire managers to improve their operations. One of the most important components of a forest fire management system is the initial attack subsystem, which is designed to start fire-fighting action quickly on newly reported fires. The initial attack dispatch might be a three- to five-person crew that travels to the fire by truck, fixed-wing aircraft, or helicopter. It may also include one or more water-based or amphibious air tankers. The initial attack force constructs a fire line around the fire's perimeter, using digging tools, a flow of high-pressure water from a nearby water source, water dropped from air tankers, and natural barriers such as lakes and rivers.

To help forest fire managers of the Ontario Ministry of Natural Resources evaluate initial attack resources, a simple simulation model of the kinds of fires that occur in Ontario and the resources used to fight them was developed. Specifically, the model indicated that well-trained firefighters equipped with adequate transport would perform well on most fires without air tanker support. However, for a small but important class of fires, air tanker support is critical. The model was useful in planning the acquisition of air tankers and future use of air tankers, transport aircraft, and fire fighters [Martel et al., 1984].

HIV Transmission through Needle Sharing

This application was mentioned in the Management Science Practice section in Chapter 3. Intravenous drug users are a key target group for behavioral change efforts to prevent the spread of HIV, the virus that causes AIDS. This group is the primary source of both heterosexual transmission and parent-to-child transmission of the virus. Researchers have developed a mathematical model that allows the simulation of the spread of HIV infection and HIV-related death through the population of intravenous drug users.

The simulation model has been used to analyze the potential effects of public policy interventions. For example, the model has been used to investigate the potential benefits of a campaign to increase the effectiveness of cleaning shared needles that was promoted in San Francisco in 1986. Questions such as the following were examined:

- How important is the magnitude of the campaign?
- How important is the timeliness of the campaign?
- How might the openness of needle sharing affect the impacts of the campaign's magnitude and timeliness?
- If the campaign results in a greater attraction to needle sharing, to what extent might its benefits be undermined?

For certain assumptions, the model suggested that to be effective, such a campaign should be sufficiently large in its direct impact and must be implemented before the spread of HIV is already well under way. By changing the assumptions underlying the model, the questions raised above could be evaluated.

These examples illustrate the wide variety of practical problems for which simulation can be used, and the types of managerial decisions and policies that can be addressed. We now address the details of building and implementing simulation models [Homer and St. Clair, 1991].

BUILDING SIMULATION MODELS

Building a simulation model involves the following:

1. *Formulating the problem* to determine the objectives of the simulation study, the system performance measures to be computed, and the scenarios to be evaluated
2. *Developing a conceptual model* of the system under study that describes key events and actions that take place
3. *Collecting the data* needed to "drive" the simulation, such as probability distributions of input variables
4. *Developing a logical model* suitable for computer implementation that performs the necessary calculations

As we noted in Chapter 1, the decision to use any management science technique is driven by the need to solve some problem. Decision makers have to deal with various factors beyond their control and must make decisions about the factors they can control. After a decision is made, they can observe the performance of the system. For example, in the Bolder Boulder running race, the race director can decide on the number of chutes, tagging procedure, and so on but cannot control how fast runners finish the race. The purpose of a simulation model is to predict the system performance for any set of management decisions.

> A simulation model translates a set of controllable and uncontrollable inputs into system performance measures.

Any specification of the controllable inputs defines a *scenario*, that is, a particular variation of the system that we wish to study. By comparing the performance of different scenarios, we expect to be able to draw conclusions as to which scenario is the best, if indeed there is a significant difference. Unlike a predictive model, however, scenarios are produced external to the model—by the decision maker—and it is usually feasible to investigate only a limited number of options.

The next step in building a simulation model is to develop a logical flowchart of the system or process under consideration. You must be able to describe in detail the steps that are performed in a decision problem, or how objects flow through a system as they are processed. This flowchart, called a *conceptual model*, can best be characterized as a managerial description of the process. A conceptual model provides the basis for building the actual simulation model that can be implemented on a computer. An example of a conceptual model for AT&T's high-velocity manufacturing facility was shown in Figure 13.1. Another example that was used in Ontario's fire-fighting illustration is shown in Figure 13.3. Constructing conceptual models requires a solid understanding of the system and is best performed by the people who work in the system.

FIGURE 13.3   *Conceptual flowchart of fire attack system*

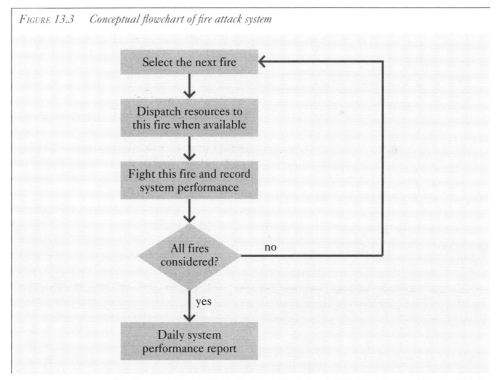

Figure from Farrina et al., "The Computer Runs the Bolder Boulder: A Simulation of a Major Running Race," *Interfaces*, Vol. 19, No. 2, March–April, 1989, pp. 48–55.

The third step in the simulation process is collecting relevant data. For example, in the fire-fighting illustration, data on the incidence of fires (including both the frequency and intensity), number of available firefighters, and number and type of aircraft available are needed. The data should describe the population reasonably. Thus, in the fire-fighting example, simply using one year's historical data would probably not be sufficient. Good data are often not immediately available. Data might have to be collected using time studies or historical records. For proposed systems, one might have to rely on the client's or modeler's best guess.

To actually perform a simulation, we must translate the conceptual model into a logical simulation model (suitable for computer implementation) that computes the performance measures for each scenario. We can implement simulation models on computers in several ways. We might use a spreadsheet, a general-purpose computer programming language, or a special-purpose simulation modeling language. Spreadsheets can handle many simulation problems, particularly those involving risk analysis. Simulating complex systems usually requires special computer programming languages. We discuss this in the next chapter.

To illustrate each of these steps—from problem formulation through a logical simulation model—we present a simple example involving the purchase of new equipment for a distribution facility. Note that this problem can be addressed analytically without simulation. Certainly you would not want to use simulation to solve a real problem that can be solved analytically. However, by comparing the simulation results with the analytical results (which we will do later in this chapter), you will gain a better understanding of the nature and limitations of simulation analysis.

EXAMPLE 1. A SIMULATION MODEL FOR A CAPITAL EQUIPMENT PURCHASE DECISION

A manager of a distribution facility is considering the purchase of a new truck to be used for local deliveries. He presently has one truck, but on days when the dock is very busy, he must rent one or two additional trucks at a higher cost. The loading dock supervisor has been asking that the manager purchase another truck, claiming that the second truck will easily pay for itself. He claims that the daily rental cost is higher than the daily expense of purchasing the new truck. The manager must evaluate this proposal to decide if the supervisor is correct.

In this problem, we have one controllable input—the number of trucks to own. Uncontrollable variables are the actual number of trucks required each day and the costs of ownership and rental. In this example, two scenarios are to be evaluated: (1) owning one truck and renting additional trucks as needed, and (2) owning two trucks and renting an additional truck if necessary. The performance measure of each system is the average daily cost. A conceptual model of this system might look like the one in Figure 13.4. This flowchart describes the sequence of key events and actions in the system and forms the basis for the logical simulation model.

The manager has collected information about the rental and purchase costs of the trucks. From an economic analysis, he determines that the current truck costs $100 per day whether it is used or not. Trucks can be rented for $150 per day, and the purchase of a new truck will cost $120 per day.

FIGURE 13.4   *A conceptual model of the truck decision problem*

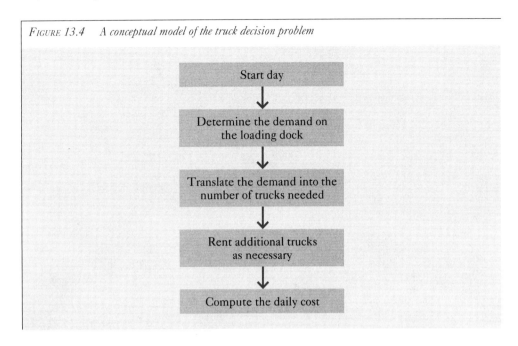

Although the supervisor is correct in that the daily rental cost is higher than the amortized purchase costs, the manager knows that additional trucks are not rented every day. On inspecting records from the past year, it was found that one truck was used 55 percent of the time, two trucks were used 30 percent of the time, and three trucks were used 15 percent of the time. Because of the variability in the need for additional trucks, the best decision is not obvious.

The logical simulation model is shown in Figure 13.5 for the one-truck scenario. This model provides the details necessary to implement the simulation on a spreadsheet or other computer programming language. We begin by initializing the total cost, TC, to zero and setting a variable D, representing the number of days simulated, to one. As we begin a new day, we determine the number of trucks required, N. How this is actually done will be described in the next section. The daily cost is computed as the cost of the one truck that is owned ($100) plus the rental costs for the additional $N - 1$ trucks, $120(N - 1)$. Next, we add the daily cost to TC to keep a running total. Finally, we need to determine whether or not to stop the simulation. If we decide to simulate another day, we increment the day counter, D, by one and repeat the simulation process. If we decide to stop, we compute the average daily cost as TC/D. Determining the number of days to simulate the system is a statistical issue that we address later.

In the next section we discuss the computational details of performing the simulation, specifically, the process of how we determine the number of trucks required and compute the outputs for the simulation.

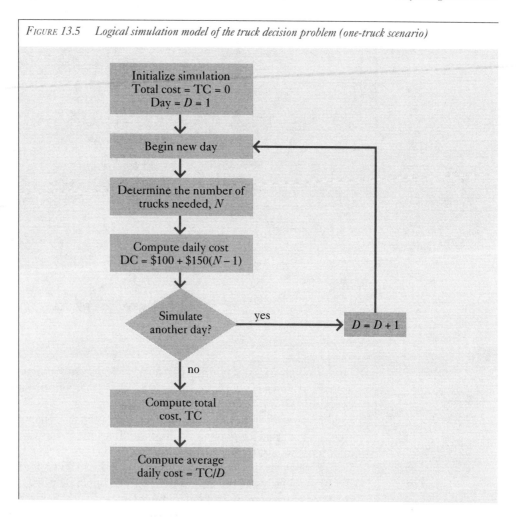

FIGURE 13.5   *Logical simulation model of the truck decision problem (one-truck scenario)*

PERFORMING A SIMULATION

Performing a simulation involves two activities:

1. Developing mechanisms for generating probabilistic outcomes in the simulation
2. Recording and summarizing information from which to compute performance measures from the simulation

The model in Figure 13.5 has one probabilistic element, namely, the number of trucks required each day. From the data collected by the distribution manager, we see that the number of trucks required each day is a random variable with the probability distribution:

Number of trucks required	Probability
1	.55
2	.30
3	.15
	1.00

We assume that the number of trucks required on any given day is independent of the number required on any other day.

Generating Probabilistic Outcomes

We need a mechanism for generating the number of trucks required each day having this probability distribution. That is, if we study the system for a long time, say, 1,000 days, we should expect to see about 55 percent, or 550 days, in which one truck is required; about 30 percent, or 300 days, in which two trucks are required; and about 15 percent, or 150 days, in which three trucks are required. However, we will not be able to predict the specific number of trucks required on a particular day. Thus, in performing the simulation, we wish to pick, on each day, the outcome "one truck required" with a .55 probability, "two trucks required" with a .30 probability, and "three trucks required" with a .15 probability. Can you think of a way to do this?

You might mix 100 poker chips—55 white, 30 blue, and 15 red— in a bowl and draw one at random. You would expect to draw a white chip with a probability of .55; this would correspond to the outcome "one truck required." Similarly, you would expect to draw a blue chip ("two trucks required") with a probability .30 and a red chip ("three trucks required") with a probability .15. If you performed this experiment a large number of times, each time replacing the previously drawn chip and remixing the bowl, what would you expect to see?

Another way would be to take 100 business cards numbered 1 through 100 and sort the cards into three groups. Cards numbered 1 through 55 would correspond to "one truck required"; cards numbered 56 through 85 would correspond to "two trucks required"; and cards numbered 86 through 100 would correspond to "three trucks required." We then shuffle the cards and draw one. All cards have an equal chance of being drawn, but 55 percent of the time we expect to draw a number between 1 and 55, 30 percent of the time a number between 56 and 85, and 15 percent of the time a number between 86 and 100. To repeat the process, we replace the drawn card, reshuffle, and draw again.

The second experiment is more appealing from a quantitative perspective since we are dealing with numbers rather than colors. (Ultimately we wish to implement this procedure on a computer.) We may sample from *any* discrete probability distribution in this fashion by simply grouping the numbers in proportion to the probabilities. In fact, this is the way probabilistic events are simulated on a computer. The only thing we must be able to ensure is that we can draw a number *uniformly*, that is, with equal probability from the entire population of possible numbers (analogous to drawing a card from a deck).

In simulation, probabilistic outcomes are generated using *random numbers*.

> A random number is a number drawn from a uniform probability distribution between 0 and 1.

Sometimes the term *pseudorandom number* is used to denote a computer-generated random number. We make this distinction because "truly random" phenomena occur only in nature; the results of a computer algorithm can be predicted. Many people simply use the term *random number*, and that is what we shall do. Nearly every computer language and spreadsheet package has the ability to generate random numbers quite easily. Appendix C at the end of this book provides a table of random numbers generated on a computer. A portion of this table is reproduced in Table 13.1.

To use random numbers to simulate outcomes from a probability distribution of the number of required trucks, we first find the *cumulative probability distribution* and then assign random number intervals according to this distribution.

EXAMPLE 2. USING RANDOM NUMBERS TO GENERATE PROBABILISTIC OUTCOMES

For the truck data, we have the following:

Number of trucks required	Probability	Cumulative probability
1	.55	.55
2	.30	.85
3	.15	1.00
	1.00	

The cumulative probabilities provide a division of the interval 0 to 1 into smaller intervals proportional to the probabilities of the outcomes we wish to generate. For example, any random number less than .55 will correspond to the outcome "one truck required"; any random number between .55 and .85 will correspond to the outcome "two trucks required"; and any random number between .85 and 1.00 will correspond

TABLE 13.1
Random number
table

Row/column	1	2	3	4	5	6	7	8	9	10
1	0.426	0.332	0.634	0.742	0.826	0.406	0.514	0.924	0.698	0.502
2	0.062	0.491	0.717	0.766	0.574	0.792	0.553	0.788	0.632	0.411
3	0.509	0.965	0.002	0.545	0.254	0.934	0.061	0.687	0.740	0.521
4	0.953	0.563	0.953	0.115	0.160	0.904	0.058	0.052	0.885	0.525
5	0.736	0.219	0.383	0.525	0.007	0.249	0.681	0.818	0.572	0.763

to the outcome "three trucks required." This is summarized below. Let RN = the random number.

Random number interval	Outcome
.000 ≤ RN < .550	1 truck required
.550 ≤ RN < .850	2 trucks required
.850 ≤ RN < 1.000	3 trucks required

To use the random number table to simulate outcomes, let us choose random numbers in succession beginning in row 1, column 1, and move across the row. The first random number is 0.426. This falls in the first interval and corresponds to the outcome "one truck required." The second random number is .332; this also generates the outcome "one truck required." The third random number is .634. Since this lies between .550 and .850, two trucks are required. The results of simulating truck demand for the first 10 days are as follows:

Random number	Outcome (number of trucks required)
.426	1
.332	1
.634	2
.742	2
.826	2
.406	1
.514	1
.924	3
.698	2
.502	1

Observe that in these 10 samples, one truck is needed 50 percent of the time, two trucks are needed 40 percent of the time, and three trucks are needed 10 percent of the time. This corresponds closely to the actual distribution of requirements, considering the small sample size. If we were to continue to simulate the outcomes, this distribution should approach the true distribution.

Conducting the Simulation

Now that we have a mechanism for generating stochastic outcomes in a simulation model, we need only perform the detailed steps in the simulation model in Figure 13.5. We can do this manually or on a computer. We first demonstrate the manual process to illustrate the basic concepts.

EXAMPLE 3. SIMULATING THE TRUCK DECISION PROBLEM

As we step through the flowchart in Figure 13.5 for the first day, we have the following:

Initialize: $TC = 0; D = 1$

Begin new day

Determine number of trucks: Generate a random number (.426). Since this number falls in the interval from 0 to .550, it corresponds to one truck, or $N = 1$.

Compute daily cost: $DC = 100 + 150(0) = 100$

Compute total cost: $TC = 0 + 100 = 100$

We then return to *Begin new day* to simulate another day. The results for 10 days using the random numbers and outcomes generated in the previous section are summarized in Table 13.2. These results show an average daily cost of $190.

To determine whether it is better to purchase two trucks, we would perform a similar simulation for the two-truck scenario and compare the average daily costs. The only changes that need to be made in the simulation model involve the computation of the daily costs. Specifically, if one or two trucks are needed, the daily cost is $220 ($100 for the current truck plus $120 for the new truck). If three trucks are required, the daily cost is $370 ($220 plus the $150 rental cost).

Table 13.3 shows the results for this case. The same sequence of random numbers is used to ensure a valid comparison between the two policies (we will discuss this later). The average daily cost for this scenario is $235. Thus, it appears that the proposal to purchase a second truck is not economical.

Would you expect the same numerical results if a different sequence of random numbers was used? Probably not. (Try it, using a different sequence of random numbers from

TABLE 13.2
Simulation results
for one-truck
scenario

Day	Random number	Outcome	Daily cost	Cumulative total cost
1	.426	1	$100	$ 100
2	.332	1	100	200
3	.634	2	250	450
4	.742	2	250	700
5	.826	2	250	950
6	.406	1	100	1,050
7	.514	1	100	1,150
8	.924	3	400	1,550
9	.698	2	250	1,800
10	.502	1	100	1,900

Average daily cost = $1,900/10 = $190

Day	Random number	Outcome	Daily cost	Total cost
1	.426	1	$220	$ 220
2	.332	1	220	440
3	.634	2	220	660
4	.742	2	220	880
5	.826	2	220	1,100
6	.406	1	220	1,320
7	.514	1	220	1,540
8	.924	3	370	1,910
9	.698	2	220	2,130
10	.502	1	220	2,350

Average daily cost = $2,350/10 = $235

Table 13.1.) One simulation experiment is only a *sample* from an infinite population of possible experiments. This is one of the major limitations of simulation. We need to run a simulation multiple times to be able to capture the variation in the results. At best, we can draw only statistical inferences about the results, and our conclusions are subject to sampling errors.

The process of simulation by sampling from probability distributions using random numbers is often called *Monte Carlo simulation*. This term was coined by scientists who worked on the development of the atom bomb and is taken from the random behavior of casino games at Monte Carlo.

SPREADSHEET SIMULATION

A spreadsheet is a natural tool for performing Monte Carlo simulation. Simulations on spreadsheets can be implemented in the following way:

1. Develop the spreadsheet model in the usual way.
2. For each probabilistic variable, assign the appropriate probability distribution.
3. Generate random observations of each probabilistic variable and "solve" the entire spreadsheet to give one trial of the simulation.
4. Collect output data for important variables in a frequency distribution and analyze the data.

To do this, we need to be able to generate probabilistic outcomes within the spreadsheet environment.

Generating Probabilistic Outcomes in Lotus 1-2-3

The Lotus 1-2-3 function @RAND provides uniformly distributed random numbers between 0 and 1 and can be used in the same manner as random number tables. Placing @RAND in a cell creates a random number in that cell. The random numbers in

Table 13.1 were created in this fashion. (Note that if the automatic recalculation feature is on, the random number function will produce a new value whenever a formula is put in a new cell. The automatic recalculation feature can be suppressed by the command /Worksheet Global Recalculation Manual. The F9 key recalculates the spreadsheet. Therefore, if the manual mode is on, pressing F9 will change all random numbers.)

To generate outcomes from a discrete probability distribution, the Lotus 1-2-3 function @VLOOKUP (vertical lookup) is useful. The function @VLOOKUP uses three arguments:

1. The value to look up
2. The table range
3. The number of the column whose value we want (the leftmost column is zero)

The general form of the function is @VLOOKUP(CELL, TABLE RANGE, COLUMN OFFSET). The @VLOOKUP function compares the value found in CELL to each row in the first column of the TABLE RANGE. When it locates a row containing a value *larger* than the value in CELL, it returns to the next-lower row and picks up the number found in the corresponding column designated by COLUMN OFFSET (the first column is 0).

To illustrate this, recall the probability distribution of the number of trucks required:

Random number range	Number of trucks
0–.55	1
.55–.85	2
.85–1.00	3

We first put the data in a table, say, in cells A4 through C6:

	A	B	C
4	0	.55	1
5	.55	.85	2
6	.85	1.00	3

Now consider the formula @VLOOKUP(B9,$A$4..$C$6,2). Cell B9 is the one in which the random number used to generate the number of trucks is found. The range $A$4..$C$6 represents the range of the table in which the data are located. Suppose the random number in cell B9 is .624. The function would search column A until it finds the first number larger than .624, which is .85 in cell A6. Then it returns to the next-lower row (row 5) and picks the number in column 2 (that is, column C; remember that the first column is labeled zero) as the value of the function. Thus, the outcome is two trucks.

EXAMPLE 4. A SPREADSHEET SIMULATION

Figure 13.6 shows a spreadsheet that was developed for the capital equipment purchase decision problem. The data lookup table is given in cells A4 through C6 as described above. In cells B9 through B18, random numbers are generated using the @RAND function and formatted to three decimal places. Cells C9 through C18 use

FIGURE 13.6   *Spreadsheet for equipment purchase decision*

A	A	B	C	D	E
1	Capital Equipment Decision Simulation				
2					
3	*Random Number Range*		*No. Trucks*		
4	0	0.55	1		
5	0.55	0.85	2		
6	0.85	1	3		
7				*One Truck*	*Two trucks*
8	*Trial*	*Random No.*	*No. Trucks*	*Daily Cost*	*Daily cost*
9	1	0.812	2	$250	$220
10	2	0.638	2	$250	$220
11	3	0.666	2	$250	$220
12	4	0.982	3	$400	$370
13	5	0.138	1	$100	$220
14	6	0.603	2	$250	$220
15	7	0.548	1	$100	$220
16	8	0.320	1	$100	$220
17	9	0.023	1	$100	$220
18	10	0.832	2	$250	$220
19					
20	AVERAGE DAILY COST			$205	$235

Selected cell formulas

A	A	B	C	D	E
7				*One Truck*	*Two trucks*
8	*Trial*	*Random No.*		*Daily Cost*	*Daily cost*
9	1	@RAND	@VLOOKUP(B9,$A$4..$C$6,2)	100+150*(C9-1)	220+150*@MAX(C9-2,0)
10	2	@RAND	@VLOOKUP(B10,$A$4..$C$6,2)	100+150*(C10-1)	220+150*@MAX(C10-2,0)
11	3	@RAND	@VLOOKUP(B11,$A$4..$C$6,2)	100+150*(C11-1)	220+150*@MAX(C11-2,0)

the @VLOOKUP function to generate the simulated outcomes. Daily costs are computed in cells D9 through D18 for the one-truck case and E9 through E18 for the two-truck case and are averaged in cells D20 and E20.

Each time the F9 (recalculation) key is pressed, Lotus 1-2-3 recalculates all cell formulas. This includes generating new values for the @RAND function. Therefore, it is easy to repeat the simulation using new sets of random numbers by simply pressing the F9 key.

A more sophisticated method for simulating a system a large number of times is to create a large table to capture the data. This may be rather awkward to do manually. An experienced spreadsheet user could write a macro to repeat the simulation as many times as needed and put the results in a table from which a histogram can be constructed. Several "add-on" software packages are available to do this automatically and provide custom reports. Two of these are "@Risk" and "Crystal Ball."[1] We will demonstrate Crystal Ball later in this chapter.

---

[1] @Risk, Palisade Corp., Newfield, NY; Crystal Ball, version 3.0, Decisioneering, Denver, Colorado.

Generating Probabilistic Outcomes in EXCEL 5.0

Generating probabilistic outcomes in EXCEL is considerably easier than in Lotus 1-2-3. There is no need to use the table lookup function in EXCEL. Once the data are specified (the values and their probabilities), EXCEL performs the table lookup internally. To generate probabilistic outcomes from a discrete distribution, select the *Tools* option in the main menu, and then *Data Analysis* and *Random Number Generation*. The Random Number Generation dialog box, as shown in Figure 13.7, will appear.

EXCEL allows you to generate from known discrete data, as well as from many of the well-known theoretical distributions we discussed in Chapter 11 (this will be discussed in more detail later). The default distribution is discrete data, as shown in Figure 13.7. Using the dialog box, the number of variables must be specified (the number of different outputs that follow this distribution) as well as the number of random numbers to draw from this distribution. The range that contains the discrete values and their probabilities must be specified. You may specify a *seed*, which is simply a number that EXCEL uses to start the simulation. If you do not specify a seed, EXCEL will choose one for you. However, specifying your own seed allows you to repeat the same simulation (for example, for debugging purposes). To get back the same simulation as a previous run, you specify

FIGURE 13.7　　*The EXCEL random number generation dialog box*

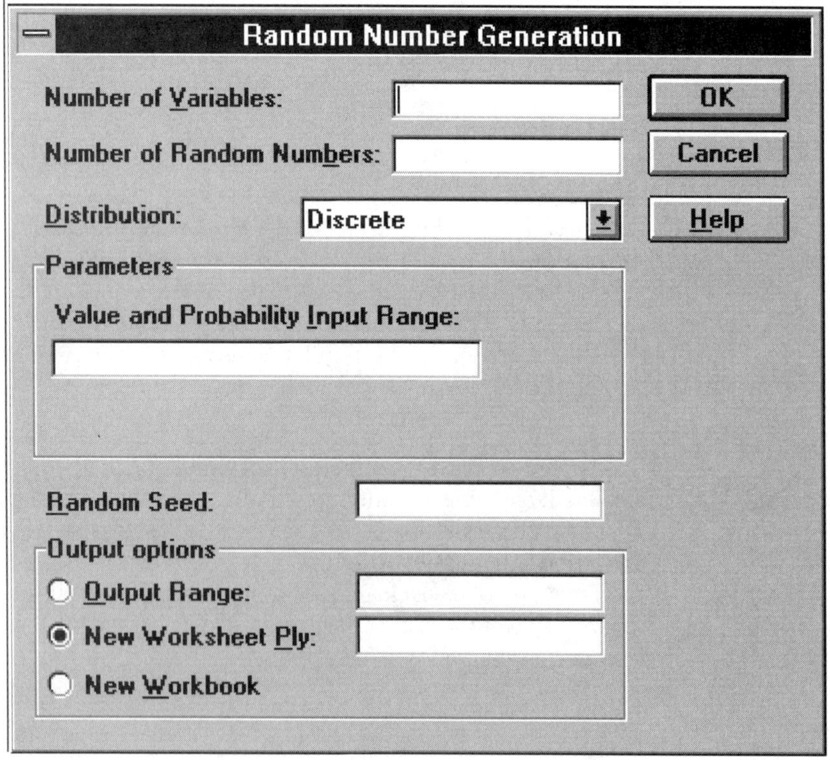

the seed used for that run. Finally, the output range is where the simulated data will appear in the spreadsheet. We illustrate the use of EXCEL using the capital equipment decision problem from Example 1.

EXAMPLE 5. USING EXCEL FOR SIMULATION

We illustrate the use of EXCEL for simulation with discrete data using Example 1, the capital equipment decision. A basic spreadsheet with selected cell formulas and the random number generation dialog box are shown in Figure 13.8. We wish to simulate 10 days and compare the average cost for the one-truck and two-truck scenarios. The data and their probabilities are in cells A4 through B6, and we choose (arbitrarily) a random number seed of 43. The probabilistic outputs will be placed in cells B10 through B19, which will then allow the daily costs and their average to be calculated. The average costs appear in cells C21 and D21. The simulation results are shown in Figure 13.9.

FIGURE 13.8   EXCEL simulation spreadsheet and dialog box

	A	B	C	D
1	**Capital Equipment Decision Simulation**			
2				
3	*No. Trucks*	*Probability*		
4	1	0.55		
5	2	0.3		
6	3	0.15		
7				
8			1 Truck	2 Trucks
9	Trial	No. Trucks	Daily Cost	Daily Cost
10	1	0	($50)	$220
11	2	0	($50)	$220
12	3	0	($50)	$220
13	4	0	($50)	$220
14	5	0	($50)	$220
15	6	0	($50)	$220
16	7	0	($50)	$220
17	8	0	($50)	$220
18	9	0	($50)	$220
19	10	0	($50)	$220
20				
21		Average	($50)	$220

Selected cell formulas

	A	B	C	D
8			1 Truck	2 Trucks
9	Trial	No. Trucks	Daily Cost	Daily Cost
10	1	0	=100+150*(B10-1)	=220 + 150*MAX(B10-2,0)
11	2	0	=100+150*(B11-1)	=220 + 150*MAX(B11-2,0)
12	3	0	=100+150*(B12-1)	=220 + 150*MAX(B12-2,0)

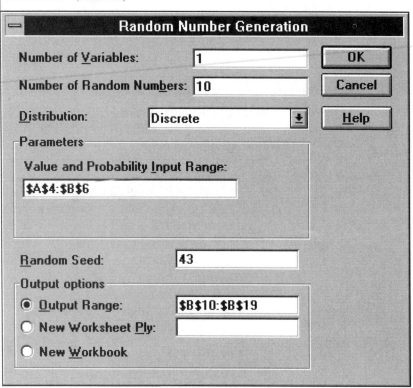

FIGURE 13.8 (continued)

Random Number Generation

Number of Variables: `1`

Number of Random Numbers: `10`

Distribution: `Discrete`

OK

Cancel

Help

Parameters

Value and Probability Input Range:

`$A$4:$B$6`

Random Seed: `43`

Output options

◉ Output Range: `$B$10:$B$19`

○ New Worksheet Ply:

○ New Workbook

FIGURE 13.9   EXCEL capital equipment simulation results

	A	B	C	D
1	Capital Equipment Decision Simulation			
2				
3	No. Trucks	Probability		
4	1	0.55		
5	2	0.3		
6	3	0.15		
7				
8			1 Truck	2 Trucks
9	Trial	No. Trucks	Daily Cost	Daily Cost
10	1	1	$100	$220
11	2	1	$100	$220
12	3	1	$100	$220
13	4	2	$250	$220
14	5	2	$250	$220
15	6	1	$100	$220
16	7	1	$100	$220
17	8	1	$100	$220
18	9	3	$400	$370
19	10	3	$400	$370
20				
21		Average	$190	$250

ANALYZING SIMULATION OUTPUT

Real systems exhibit variability; they behave in ways that are not completely predictable. Therefore, we should expect a simulation model to capture this variability. This is done through the use of random numbers to drive the simulation. The random numbers used in a simulation are a *sample* from an infinite population of possible random number sequences. Therefore, the output of a simulation model is *also* a sample from some infinite population of outcomes. Each time we run the simulation with a different sequence of random numbers, we would expect different results. In this sense, a simulation is an *experiment*. We would like to be able to characterize the population of outcomes and make statistical statements about the performance measures in which we are interested.

Similarly, if we run the simulation longer, say, 100 days instead of 10 days, we would also expect different results. Therefore, how we interpret the results of a simulation experiment should depend on (1) how many times we run the simulation model and (2) the length of each run. Because of variability, the interpretation of simulation results requires statistical analysis. In this section we show how to use some elementary statistical concepts to analyze simulation results and illustrate them using the capital equipment decision problem. We will use this model because of its simplicity and the fact that we can compute expected values analytically. This will allow us to compare the simulation results in order to understand these issues of variability better. In practical applications of simulation, we cannot solve the problem analytically, so we must rely on the statistical conclusions we make.

Replication

A single simulation experiment is called a *run*. The performance measures from a single simulation run, such as daily cost, number of customers waiting, or waiting time, are observations drawn from the population of possible simulation experiments. We would like to characterize this population.

Let us consider the scenario of owning one truck. We first note that if only one truck is required, then the daily cost is $100. If two trucks are required, the daily cost is $250; and if three are required, the daily cost is $400. Thus, the daily cost has the following discrete probability distribution:

i	Cost, x_i	Probability, $f(x_i)$
1	100	.55
2	250	.30
3	400	.15

By multiplying the cost associated with each level of requirements by the probability that it will occur, we arrive at the expected cost per day:

$$\text{Expected cost} = E(x) = \sum_{i=1}^{3} x_i f(x_i)$$

$$= \$100(.55) + \$250(.30) + \$400(.15) = \$190$$

Observe that the average daily cost determined by the one simulation run (Table 13.2) was $190—simply a coincidence! In general, how close would the simulated results be to the expected value? To answer this question, we need to know something about the variation in the sample mean.

The variance of the cost per day is

$$\text{Variance} = \sum_{i=1}^{3} [x_i - E(x)]^2 f(x_i) = \sum_{i=1}^{3} x_i^2 f(x_i) - [E(x)]^2$$

$$= 100^2(.55) + 250^2(.30) + 400^2(.15) - 190^2 = 12{,}150$$

Therefore, the standard deviation is $\sigma = \sqrt{12{,}150} = 110.23$. This holds *for any one day* of the simulation. In other words, the cost for a simulation of a single day has a mean of $190 and a standard deviation of 110.23. We can see that simulating only a single day can produce a result over a rather wide range.

The variation in the *sample mean* is characterized by the standard error. The standard error of the mean for an n-day simulation is $\sigma/\sqrt{n}$. For a 10-day simulation, the standard error of the mean is $110.23/\sqrt{10} = 34.86$. Therefore, the average daily cost from a 10-day simulation run has a mean of $190 and a standard deviation of 34.86. This means that a single 10-day simulation experiment would still provide a rather wide range of outcomes for the mean cost, although you can see that the variation is much smaller than for a single simulated trial.

Because any simulation exhibits variability, we should be cautious when interpreting the results of only one simulation run. In fact, we should *never* draw conclusions on the basis of only a single run.

To make valid statistical statements about the performance measures, we need to *replicate* the simulation experiment, that is, repeat the experiment several times. Using the spreadsheet model, we ran the one-truck scenario four times. The results are summarized below:

Run	Average daily cost
1	190
2	235
3	175
4	145

We may compute the mean and standard deviation of these four observations. Let x_i be the outcome from the ith replication and N the number of replications. The mean, $\bar{x}$, and sample standard deviation, s, are given below:[2]

---

[2] If you are using a spreadsheet, be sure to use the correct function for the (unbiased) standard deviation.

$$\bar{x} = \frac{\sum_{i=1}^{N} x_i}{N}$$

$$= \frac{190 + 235 + 175 + 145}{4} = 186.25$$

$$s = \sqrt{\frac{\sum_{i=1}^{N}(x_i - \bar{x})^2}{N - 1}}$$

$$= 37.5$$

Note that these values are fairly close to the exact values we calculated analytically.

Since we now have a measure of the variability of the simulated results, we may construct a confidence interval for the average daily cost. A $100(1 - \alpha)$ percent confidence interval for x is

$$\bar{x} \pm t_{N-1, \alpha/2} \frac{s}{\sqrt{N}}$$

For example, a 95 percent confidence interval for x is

$$186.25 \pm 3.18 \frac{37.5}{\sqrt{4}}$$

or $[126.625, 245.875]$, where $t_{3,.025} = 3.18$ is found in Appendix D. Of course, we can obtain a smaller confidence interval for the mean by increasing the number of replications, N.

Comparing Two Systems

In the capital equipment decision problem, our real goal was to determine whether or not the two-truck ownership policy would be more economical than the one-truck policy. We may answer this question by comparing simulated results for both policies. One way would be to make independent simulation runs of the two-truck scenario and compare the results. The best way to do this, however, is to make paired comparisons of the results *using the same random numbers to generate the uncontrollable factors in the simulation model.* The advantage of this approach is that the observed differences between the systems are more likely to be due to the controllable factors (that is, number of trucks owned) than to just random noise. In simulation terminology, we call this approach *common random numbers.* This approach actually results in tighter confidence intervals than if we had made independent simulation runs.

To illustrate this approach, we use the same random numbers to generate the demand for trucks. For example, we have the following for the first run:

			1 Truck		2 Truck	
Day	RN	N	DC	TC	DC	TC
1	.106	1	100	100	220	220
2	.863	3	400	500	370	590
3	.996	3	400	900	370	960
4	.822	2	250	1150	220	1,180
5	.361	1	100	1250	220	1,400
6	.629	2	250	1500	220	1,620
7	.359	1	100	1600	220	1,840
8	.008	1	100	1700	220	2,060
9	.228	1	100	1800	220	2,280
10	.001	1	100	1900	220	2,500
Average daily cost =			190		250	

If we do this for each of the remaining three runs, we obtain the results in Table 13.4.

> To compare two policies, we construct a confidence interval for the average difference.

The average difference is

$$\bar{x} = \frac{60 + 35 + 60 + 90}{4} = 61.25$$

The standard deviation of the differences is

$$s = 22.5$$

Thus, a 95 percent confidence interval for the average difference is

$$61.25 \pm 3.18\frac{22.5}{\sqrt{4}}$$

or [25.475, 97.025].

If this confidence interval contains zero, then we would conclude that there is no significant difference between the systems. Because in this case the confidence interval does not contain zero, we may conclude that there is a significant difference and that the one-truck system is less costly.

TABLE 13.4
Comparison of scenarios for capital equipment decision problem

Run	One-truck scenario	Two-truck scenario	Difference*
1	190	250	60
2	235	265	35
3	175	235	60
4	145	235	90

*Two-truck scenario average minus one-truck scenario average.

Increasing Run Length

Suppose we increase the length of a single simulation run, say, to 30 days. Then the standard error of the mean is $\sigma/\sqrt{n}$ or $110.23/\sqrt{30} = 20.125$. Similarly, if we increase the length to 100 days, the standard error decreases to $110.23/\sqrt{100} = 11.023$. Observe that as n increases, the standard error gets smaller and we obtain a more precise estimate of the true average value.

> The longer we run a simulation (that is, by increasing the number of samples), the more accurate will be the estimate of the average value.

Using the one-truck scenario, four runs were made for 100 and 1,000 days each. The results are shown in Table 13.5. Not only does the standard deviation get smaller, thus providing tighter confidence intervals, but the average value gets closer to the true expected value.

In the capital equipment simulation model, each day of a simulation run is an independent experiment. In this case, there is little difference in running the simulation four times for 10 days each or one time for 40 days. In either case, we have 40 independent observations from which to estimate the statistical error in estimating the mean. However, in simulating dynamic systems that we will discuss in the next chapter, and for problems in which we are interested in the performance over a fixed time horizon, we must replicate rather than just increase the number of trials in a single simulation run to obtain useful statistical conclusions.

SIMULATION AND RISK ANALYSIS

The process of characterizing a probability distribution of outcomes for a decision problem allows managers to evaluate risk. Some industries, such as the insurance and nuclear power industries, define risk as the probability of catastrophic loss. In this book, we define *risk* as the inability to predict the outcomes or consequences of a decision. For example, Merck & Co., a major pharmaceutical manufacturer, invests approximately $1 billion per

TABLE 13.5
Results for increasing run length (average daily cost)

Run	100 Days	1,000 Days
1	200.5	189.25
2	199.0	190.3
3	193.0	192.85
4	187.0	189.85
Mean	194.875	190.5625
Std. dev.	6.17	1.58

year in drug research, a highly risky venture.[3] At the beginning of a project, the company may know whether there is a market for a specific treatment that includes many thousands of people, and after some research and development they may know that a certain compound may be effective. But they may not know whether it will prove safe and effective enough to be turned into a marketable drug. They must decide whether or not to continue to invest in the research, which may not yield a profit for another 10 or 15 years.

Risk analysis is an approach that is aimed at developing a probability profile of key decision variables, such as revenue, cash flow, or some other economic measure, particularly when they are affected by numerous uncontrollable, probabilistic variables. Such profiles provide a much better source of information on which to base a decision than simply using expected values from traditional decision analysis. Monte Carlo simulation is an effective approach to performing a risk analysis. Figure 13.10 shows the general approach.

We illustrated the basic ideas of risk analysis in Examples 1 and 2 in Chapter 11. Recall that in these examples, both the fixed costs and variable costs were assumed to be random variables. Because of the simplifying assumptions, it was possible to develop the distribution of total costs analytically. As the number of interacting variables increases and the assumptions no longer allow neat analytical results, Monte Carlo simulation becomes

FIGURE 13.10   *Risk analysis using Monte Carlo simulation*

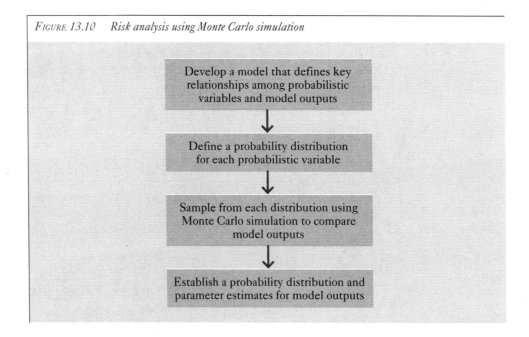

---

[3]Nancy A. Nichols, "Scientific Management at Merck: An Interview with CFO Judy Lewent," *Harvard Business Review*, January–February, 1994, pp. 89–99.

necessary. We will use these examples to illustrate simulation risk analysis and show how simulated results compare with the analytical results.

EXAMPLE 6. FINANCIAL RISK ANALYSIS WITH DISCRETE DISTRIBUTIONS

Figure 13.11 shows a spreadsheet model for Example 2 in Chapter 11. Although only 10 simulated trials are shown, Table 13.6 shows the results of 100 trials compared with the theoretical distribution derived in Chapter 11. We see that the simulated results agree quite closely with the expected analytical results. Of course, with a larger sample size, we would expect to find even closer agreement.

In many simulations we must generate outcomes from continuous probability distributions such as the uniform, normal, exponential, and triangular. Simulated outcomes from arbitrary probability distributions are called *random variates*. In the next section we show how to use random numbers to generate outcomes from these distributions.

Generating Outcomes from Common Probability Distributions

In this section we present some formulas for generating random variates from some of the more common probability distributions used in applications. The derivations of these formulas are beyond the scope of this book, but they can be found in many books devoted exclusively to simulation and statistics. All of these formulas transform random numbers to random variates. In each of the following, R represents a random number.

FIGURE 13.11   Spreadsheet model for financial risk analysis (discrete case)

	A	B	C	D	E	F
1	Financial Risk Analysis					
2						
3	*Random Number Range*		*Fixed Costs*			
4	0	0.2	$40,000			
5	0.2	0.8	$50,000			
6	0.8	1	$60,000			
7						
8	*Random Number Range*		*Variable Costs*			
9	0	0.25	$80,000			
10	0.25	0.75	$100,000			
11	0.75	1	$120,000			
12						
13	Monte Carlo Simulation					
14						
15	Trial	Random Number	Fixed Costs	Random Number	Variable Costs	Total Cost
16	1	0.243	$50,000.00	0.613	$100,000.00	$150,000.00
17	2	0.486	$50,000.00	0.222	$80,000.00	$130,000.00
18	3	0.903	$60,000.00	0.508	$100,000.00	$160,000.00
19	4	0.559	$50,000.00	0.365	$100,000.00	$150,000.00
20	5	0.663	$50,000.00	0.050	$80,000.00	$130,000.00
21	6	0.730	$50,000.00	0.447	$100,000.00	$150,000.00
22	7	0.546	$50,000.00	0.051	$80,000.00	$130,000.00
23	8	0.878	$60,000.00	0.163	$80,000.00	$140,000.00
24	9	0.800	$50,000.00	0.855	$120,000.00	$170,000.00
25	10	0.151	$40,000.00	0.124	$80,000.00	$120,000.00

Selected cell formulas

A	A	B	C	D	E	F
15	Trial	Random number	Fixed Costs	Random number	Variable Costs	Total Cost
16	1	@RAND	@VLOOKUP(B16,$A$4..$C$6,2)	@RAND	@VLOOKUP(D16,$A$9..$C$11,2)	+C16+E16
17	2	@RAND	@VLOOKUP(B17,$A$4..$C$6,2)	@RAND	@VLOOKUP(D17,$A$9..$C$11,2)	+C17+E17
18	3	@RAND	@VLOOKUP(B18,$A$4..$C$6,2)	@RAND	@VLOOKUP(D18,$A$9..$C$11,2)	+C18+E18

Uniform Distribution. To generate uniform random variates over the interval $[a, b]$, use the formula

$$U = a + (b - a)R$$

This makes sense if you observe that if $R = 0, U = a$, and if $R = 1, U = b$. For any random number between 0 and 1, we generate a uniform random variate between a and b.

Normal Distribution. Several methods exist to generate normally distributed random variates with mean 0 and variance 1. One approach is to add six independent random numbers and subtract six independent random numbers:

$$z = R + R + R + R + R + R - R - R - R - R - R - R$$

It may seem strange, but it works (and is actually based on the Central Limit Theorem of statistics). Another formula involves the natural logarithm and cosine functions but is easy to use in spreadsheets since these functions are built into the software:

$$z = \sqrt{(-2 \ln R_1)} \cos(2\pi R_2)$$

In this formula, we need two random numbers, R_1 and R_2. We multiply the square root of -2 by the natural logarithm of R_1, and multiply this by the cosine of 2π times R_2.

To generate a normal random variate x with mean μ and standard deviation σ, we generate a normal random variate with mean 0 and variance 1 as above, multiply it by σ, and add μ:

$$x = \sigma z + \mu$$

TABLE 13.6
Comparison of simulated results with analytical results

Total cost	Frequencies	
	Simulated distribution	Expected distribution
$120,000	.09	.05
$130,000	.14	.15
$140,000	.15	.15
$150,000	.29	.30
$160,000	.17	.15
$170,000	.12	.15
$180,000	.04	.05

Exponential Distribution. To generate a random variate from an exponential distribution having a mean m, we multiply the negative of the mean by the natural logarithm of a random number:

$$E = -m \ln(R)$$

Triangular Distribution. For a triangular random variate T with a lower limit a, mode m, and upper limit b, first generate a random number R. Then,

$$\text{if } R \le \frac{m-a}{b-a}, \text{ then } T = a + (b-a)\sqrt{R(m-a)/(b-a)}$$

$$\text{if } R > \frac{m-a}{b-a}, \text{ then } T = a + (b-a)\left[1 - \sqrt{(1-R)\left(1 - \frac{m-a}{b-a}\right)}\right]$$

Using Lotus 1-2-3

@RAND in Lotus 1-2-3 can be used to generate probabilistic outcomes from many other distributions within a spreadsheet. You can use the formulas given above to do this. Simply substitute @RAND whenever a random number R is used.

EXAMPLE 7. FINANCIAL RISK ANALYSIS WITH NORMAL DISTRIBUTIONS

Figure 13.12 shows a spreadsheet for performing a Monte Carlo risk analysis simulation for Example 1 in Chapter 11. In that example, we assumed that the fixed and variable costs were normally distributed and showed that the distribution of total cost was normal with mean $150,000 and standard deviation 10,770. In this spreadsheet, we used the first approach to generate normal random variates. Fifty simulated observations have a mean of $149,395.75 and a standard deviation of $10,143.09. We could use a Chi-square test (see Chapter 11) to check for normality of the distribution.

Using EXCEL 5.0

The formulas previously described for generating some of the known probability functions using uniform random numbers between 0 and 1 are not all explicitly needed in EXCEL. For some of the distributions, EXCEL uses those formulas implicitly to generate from the distributions you select. To generate probabilistic outcomes from a known distribution, select the *Tools* option in the main menu, and then *Data Analysis* and *Random Number Generation*. From the Random Number Generation dialog box (discussed previously with regard to discrete data), select from the distribution list the distribution desired for each outcome. Any parameters of the distribution will be requested in the dialog box.

The following distributions are available (in addition to the Discrete data distribution): Bernoulli, Binomial, Normal, Poisson, Normal, and Uniform. We illustrate the use of this option in EXCEL in the following example.

FIGURE 13.12   Spreadsheet for financial risk analysis (continuous case)

	A	B	C	D	E
1	**Financial Risk Analysis**				
2					
3	*Assumptions*				
4					
5	Fixed costs are normal, mean $50,000, standard deviation $4,000				
6					
7	Variable costs are normal, mean $100,000, standard deviation $10,000				
8					
9					
10	Monte Carlo Simulation				
11					
12	Trial	Fixed Costs	Variable Costs	Total Cost	
13	1	$43,957.12	$102,957.88	$146,915.00	
14	2	$55,277.55	$89,221.77	$144,499.32	
15	3	$51,420.18	$125,292.22	$176,712.40	
16	4	$48,707.58	$104,225.11	$152,932.70	
17	5	$50,349.05	$93,473.47	$143,822.52	
18	6	$42,564.39	$86,149.68	$128,714.07	
19	7	$42,307.30	$96,635.83	$138,943.13	
20	8	$54,089.75	$102,035.49	$156,125.24	
21	9	$47,633.68	$104,010.30	$151,643.98	
22	10	$52,996.90	$100,666.11	$153,663.01	
23	11	$50,197.23	$105,628.75	$155,825.99	
24	12	$49,505.76	$118,419.81	$167,925.56	
25	13	$47,113.76	$98,452.72	$145,566.47	
26	14	$55,013.75	$85,163.70	$140,177.45	
27	15	$46,356.87	$110,771.09	$157,127.96	
28	16	$42,924.33	$103,894.39	$146,818.72	
29	17	$49,805.97	$98,767.29	$148,573.26	
30	18	$51,087.28	$104,261.66	$155,348.94	
31	19	$50,556.23	$95,891.01	$146,447.23	
32	20	$46,374.33	$103,206.76	$149,581.09	
33	21	$51,656.71	$108,964.89	$160,621.60	
34	22	$48,196.87	$100,258.42	$148,455.29	
35	23	$57,069.02	$101,362.66	$158,431.68	
36	24	$43,770.73	$101,090.92	$144,861.65	
37	25	$48,412.42	$101,994.69	$150,407.11	
38	26	$49,707.26	$102,598.47	$152,305.73	
39	27	$48,024.69	$97,357.89	$145,382.58	
40	28	$55,601.59	$103,657.16	$159,258.75	
41	29	$49,555.05	$121,611.00	$171,166.05	
42	30	$51,797.61	$96,628.93	$148,426.54	
43	31	$47,976.14	$102,990.50	$150,966.64	
44	32	$42,262.37	$93,352.32	$135,614.69	
45	33	$47,326.32	$89,928.28	$137,254.61	
46	34	$46,351.60	$90,515.45	$136,867.05	
47	35	$48,058.05	$91,871.26	$139,929.31	
48	36	$50,355.96	$94,757.90	$145,113.86	
49	37	$54,757.61	$91,873.40	$146,631.02	
50	38	$47,593.06	$86,655.07	$134,248.13	
51	39	$48,592.54	$92,991.81	$141,584.35	
52	40	$54,027.08	$98,832.44	$152,859.53	
53	41	$46,353.89	$114,060.48	$160,414.37	
54	42	$46,656.53	$108,668.64	$155,325.17	
55	43	$45,682.60	$97,879.48	$143,562.08	
56	44	$52,674.28	$114,654.37	$167,328.64	
57	45	$53,679.69	$89,743.82	$143,423.51	
58	46	$48,935.21	$109,797.92	$158,733.13	
59	47	$51,112.13	$100,254.83	$151,366.96	
60	48	$53,392.66	$94,139.58	$147,532.24	
61	49	$47,855.38	$104,157.79	$152,013.17	
62	50	$52,066.14	$70,271.92	$122,338.06	
63					
64			Average	$149,395.75	
65			Standard deviation	$10,143.09	

EXAMPLE 8. FINANCIAL RISK ANALYSIS IN EXCEL

An EXCEL spreadsheet for performing the financial analysis described in Example 7 is shown in Figure 13.13, along with the two Random Number Generation dialog boxes (one for fixed cost and one for variable cost). Each of the costs is chosen to be normally distributed (fixed cost has mean $50,000 and standard deviation $4,000; variable costs have mean $100,000 and standard deviation $10,000). The probabilistic outcomes are sent to their respective columns. The results of the simulation are shown in Figure 13.14 (page 727).

Using Crystal Ball for Risk Analysis

Crystal Ball (available from Decisioneering, Denver, CO) is a user-friendly, graphically oriented risk analysis program that works in conjunction with Lotus 1-2-3 or Microsoft EXCEL. Its advantages lie in allowing a user to select from a wide variety of standard probability distributions for input variables, automatically constructing probability distributions of outcomes from Monte Carlo simulations, and providing a complete report to assist you in interpreting the results of a simulation.

Once Crystal Ball has been added to your spreadsheet package you will have additional options: *Cell* and *Run*. The *Cell* option allows you to define selected cells as either probabilistic cells or as forecast cells (an output cell). A cell is defined as a probabilistic cell by selecting the cell and choosing *Define Assumption* from the *Cell* submenu. The Distribution Gallery shown in Figure 13.15 (page 728) will appear. From this gallery, you may choose the distribution you would like for the selected cell. To define an output cell, select the cell you desire and then select *Define Forecast* from the *Cell* submenu. A probability distribution of this cell will be constructed from the simulation.

From the *Run* option you may define run settings by selecting *Run Preferences*. The Run Preferences dialog box will appear with a variety of options. This box allows you to set the number of trials. The *Run Preferences* dialog box is shown in Figure 13.16 (page 729). The first box, Maximum Number of Trials, has been set to 1,000 in this example.

From the *Run* option, selecting *Run* will begin the simulation. The distribution of the output cell(s) will appear on the screen as the simulation is running, and the simulation will stop when the maximum number of trials is reached. Selecting *Create Report* from the *Run* option will create a report of the simulation. A variety of options are available in the report, including a listing of the input assumptions and additional statistics such as the percentiles of the output distribution(s). We illustrate the use of Crystal Ball in the following example.

EXAMPLE 9. FINANCIAL RISK ANALYSIS WITH CRYSTAL BALL

Figure 13.17 (page 729) shows a spreadsheet set up to simulate the financial analysis situation discussed in Examples 7 and 8. The spreadsheet is very simple. We put the means of fixed and variable cost into cells B12 and C12, and cell D12 is the sum of these costs. Cells B12 and C12 are defined as being normally distributed by selecting *Define Assumption* from the *Cell* option. The distribution settings are shown in Figure 13.18 (page 730). Cell D12 is defined as an output cell by selecting D12 and then *Cell* and *Define Forecast*.

FIGURE 13.13   EXCEL spreadsheet and dialog boxes
for the financial analysis problem

	A	B	C	D	E	F
1	**Financial Risk Analysis**					
2						
3	Assumptions					
4						
5	Fixed costs are normal, mean $50,000, standard deviation $4,000					
6						
7	Variable costs are normal, mean $100,000, standard deviation $10,000					
8						
9						
10	Monte Carlo Simulation					
11	Trial	Fixed Costs	Variable Costs	Total Costs		
12	1	$0	$0	$0		
13	2	$0	$0	$0		
14	3	$0	$0	$0		
15	4	$0	$0	$0		
16	5	$0	$0	$0		
17	6	$0	$0	$0		
18	7	$0	$0	$0		
19	8	$0	$0	$0		
20	9	$0	$0	$0		
21	10	$0	$0	$0		
22	11	$0	$0	$0		
23	12	$0	$0	$0		
24	13	$0	$0	$0		
25	14	$0	$0	$0		
26	15	$0	$0	$0		
27	16	$0	$0	$0		
28	17	$0	$0	$0		
29	18	$0	$0	$0		
30	19	$0	$0	$0		
31	20	$0	$0	$0		
32	21	$0	$0	$0		
33	22	$0	$0	$0		
34	23	$0	$0	$0		
35	24	$0	$0	$0		
36	25	$0	$0	$0		
37	26	$0	$0	$0		
38	27	$0	$0	$0		
39	28	$0	$0	$0		
40	29	$0	$0	$0		
41	30	$0	$0	$0		
42	31	$0	$0	$0		
43	32	$0	$0	$0		
44	33	$0	$0	$0		
45	34	$0	$0	$0		
46	35	$0	$0	$0		
47	36	$0	$0	$0		
48	37	$0	$0	$0		
49	38	$0	$0	$0		
50	39	$0	$0	$0		
51	40	$0	$0	$0		
52	41	$0	$0	$0		
53	42	$0	$0	$0		
54	43	$0	$0	$0		
55	44	$0	$0	$0		
56	45	$0	$0	$0		
57	46	$0	$0	$0		
58	47	$0	$0	$0		
59	48	$0	$0	$0		
60	49	$0	$0	$0		
61	50	$0	$0	$0		
62						
63			Average	$0		
64			Standard deviation	$0		

FIGURE 13.13   (continued)

Random Number Generation

Number of Variables:	`1`
Number of Random Numbers:	`50`
Distribution:	`Normal` ⬥

Parameters

Mean =	`50000`
Standard Deviation =	`4000`

Random Seed: `8`

Output options

- ⊙ **Output Range:** `$B$12:$B$61`
- ○ **New Worksheet Ply:**
- ○ **New Workbook**

Buttons: **OK**, **Cancel**, **Help**

The maximum number of trials was set to 1,000. The basic report output is shown in Figure 13.19 (page 731). After 1,000 trials, the total cost has a mean of $149,808 and a standard deviation of $10,934 (recall from Example 7 that the theoretical distribution of total cost should be normal with mean $150,000 and standard deviation of $10,770). After 1,000 trials, the empirical data are fairly close to what the theory indicates should occur.

MANAGEMENT SCIENCE PRACTICE

In this section we discuss further details of the opening scenario about simulating a certificate of deposit (CD) portfolio at the First National Bank and Trust Company of Tulsa, Oklahoma.

Simulating a CD Portfolio[4]

At the First National Bank and Trust Company, managers wanted to assess the impact of various interest-rate scenarios on portfolio yield. The mean portfolio yield reflects the

---

[4]Adapted from Robert A. Russell and Regina Hickle, "Simulation of a CD Portfolio," *Interfaces*, Vol. 16, No. 3, May–June, 1986, pp. 49–54.

FIGURE 13.13   *(continued)*

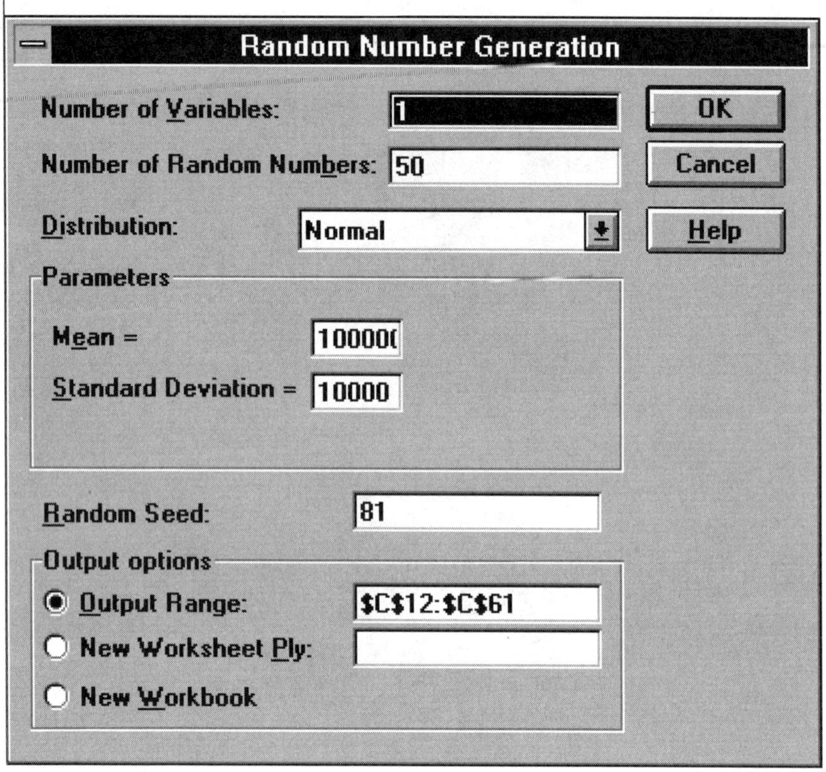

bank's cost of offering the CDs. By calculating the mean portfolio yield under a variety of future interest-rate scenarios, the bank can more effectively estimate risk and plan for profitability. The specific statistic calculated in the simulation analysis is mean dollar weighted yield, where the interest rates of larger CDs are weighted more heavily in calculating the overall portfolio yield.

The "jumbo" CD portfolio of the bank was composed primarily of corporate CDs with a minimum investment of $100,000. The total portfolio consisted of approximately $270 million. Typically 10 to 30 CDs mature on any given day and are "rolled over" for a specified length of time. This maturity period depends on two factors: the cash flow requirements of the corporation (who buys the CD) and anticipated return on investment. The bank has no way of knowing what maturity periods will be chosen for rollovers.

To determine the probability distribution of maturity periods, data were collected on CD renewals for three months. The data consisted of the dollar amount, rate, and time to maturity of all CDs renewing on a given day. Table 13.7 (page 732) shows a distribution of 908 observations. This distribution, which follows no common probability distribution (notice the spikes at 14, 30, 60, 90, and 120 days), was used to generate maturity periods in the simulation analysis.

*FIGURE 13.14   Simulation results for the financial analysis
problem using EXCEL*

	A	B	C	D	E	F
1	**Financial Risk Analysis**					
2						
3	Assumptions					
4						
5	Fixed costs are normal, mean $50,000, standard deviation $4,000					
6						
7	Variable costs are normal, mean $100,000, standard deviation $10,000					
8						
9						
10	Monte Carlo Simulation					
11	Trial	Fixed Costs	Variable Costs	Total Costs		
12	1	$52,890	$93,004	$145,894		
13	2	$51,912	$108,821	$160,733		
14	3	$48,540	$99,026	$147,566		
15	4	$46,515	$103,875	$150,390		
16	5	$52,962	$106,032	$158,994		
17	6	$50,944	$89,667	$140,611		
18	7	$44,417	$101,135	$145,552		
19	8	$49,823	$100,701	$150,524		
20	9	$52,073	$75,849	$127,921		
21	10	$51,270	$98,739	$150,009		
22	11	$40,954	$117,281	$158,235		
23	12	$52,195	$110,871	$163,067		
24	13	$52,552	$89,355	$141,907		
25	14	$51,902	$82,594	$134,496		
26	15	$49,815	$103,913	$153,728		
27	16	$50,386	$130,304	$180,690		
28	17	$47,277	$83,641	$130,918		
29	18	$56,214	$96,366	$152,580		
30	19	$50,418	$101,269	$151,687		
31	20	$44,510	$103,219	$147,730		
32	21	$52,492	$101,588	$154,080		
33	22	$53,698	$88,522	$142,220		
34	23	$44,821	$110,957	$157,778		
35	24	$52,205	$95,413	$147,619		
36	25	$46,236	$107,108	$153,344		
37	26	$52,862	$110,304	$163,166		
38	27	$50,196	$88,398	$138,594		
39	28	$47,869	$86,413	$134,281		
40	29	$53,597	$107,246	$160,843		
41	30	$49,009	$104,823	$153,831		
42	31	$49,742	$100,599	$150,341		
43	32	$49,423	$94,454	$143,877		
44	33	$46,840	$92,240	$139,080		
45	34	$49,169	$109,924	$159,093		
46	35	$52,054	$111,701	$163,754		
47	36	$47,211	$124,965	$172,177		
48	37	$46,882	$103,263	$150,144		
49	38	$49,050	$106,060	$155,110		
50	39	$53,851	$98,849	$152,700		
51	40	$36,810	$109,828	$146,638		
52	41	$39,542	$110,731	$150,273		
53	42	$44,668	$98,045	$142,713		
54	43	$50,748	$99,483	$150,232		
55	44	$49,481	$96,188	$145,670		
56	45	$41,869	$106,347	$148,216		
57	46	$54,811	$89,350	$144,161		
58	47	$50,409	$110,412	$160,820		
59	48	$48,301	$110,056	$158,357		
60	49	$48,617	$96,649	$145,266		
61	50	$49,785	$80,069	$129,854		
62						
63			Average	$149,609		
64			Standard Deviation	$9,351		

FIGURE 13.15   Distribution gallery of Crystal Ball

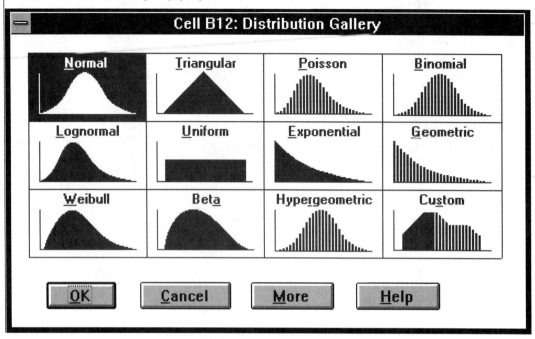

In constructing the simulation model, several assumptions were made. Since 95 percent of the CDs are renewed, a 100 percent renewal rate was assumed to simplify the analysis. Also, all CDs were assumed to roll over at their original dollar value. Finally, interest rates were assumed to be a function of maturity period and are input to the model.

The final input is the CD portfolio itself. Aggregated data were used instead of updated data on each individual CD, because the portfolio manager did not have easy access to complete data for individual CDs but received aggregate daily reports.

In using the model, the bank simulated various interest-rate scenarios, summarized in Table 13.8 (page 732). Table 13.9 (page 733) shows the results of simulating the portfolio for 60 days using the scenarios in Table 13.8 and running 20 replications. The simulation can help predict the impact on the spread between prime earning rates and CD funding costs. Also, if the portfolio manager can estimate how much CD costs are going to change, he can plan a more effective strategy for hedging against these costs in the CD futures market. From Table 13.8, the manager concluded that a half-point rise in interest rates after 30 days would cause the portfolio to increase by 33 basis points. Similarly, a half-point decline after 30 days would cause the cost of the portfolio to decrease 32.6 basis points. The cost of offering more competitive rates (Scenario A) for longer-term CDs appears to cost 13 basis points relative to the level approach of Scenario B.

FIGURE 13.16   *The run preferences dialog box of Crystal Ball*

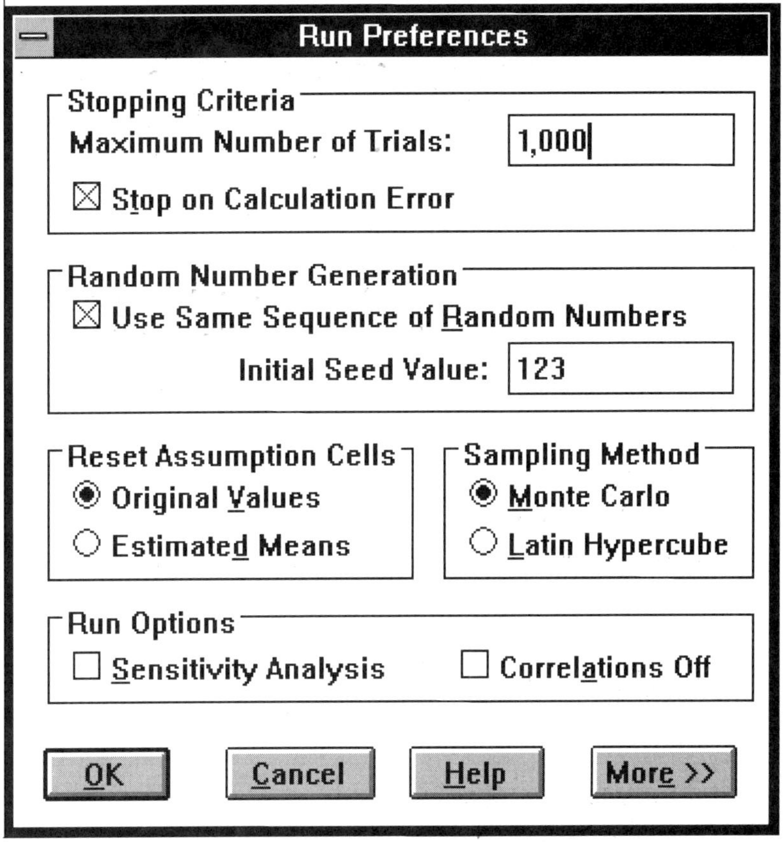

FIGURE 13.17   *Spreadsheet for financial risk analysis to be used with Crystal Ball*

	A	B	C	D	E
1	**Financial Risk Analysis**				
2					
3	*Assumptions*				
4					
5	Fixed costs are normal, mean $50,000, standard deviation $4,000				
6					
7	Variable costs are normal, mean $100,000, standard deviation $10,000				
8					
9					
10	Monte Carlo Simulation				
11		Fixed Costs	Variable Costs	Total Cost	
12		$50,000.00	$100,000.00	$150,000.00	

FIGURE 13.18   *Distribution settings for fixed and variable costs*

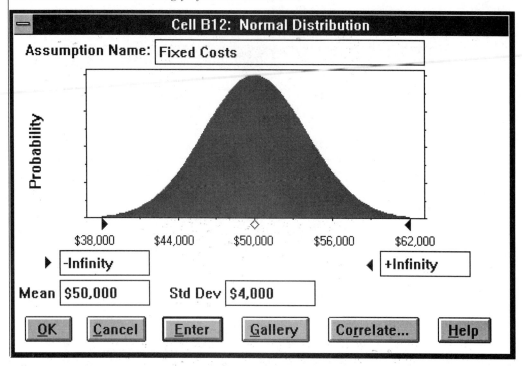

FIGURE 13.18   *(continued)*

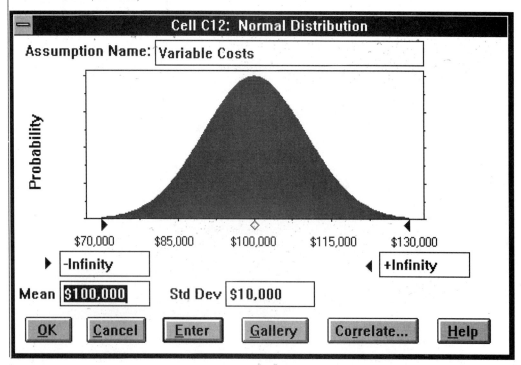

*F*IGURE *13.19   Report from Crystal Ball simulation*

Crystal Ball Report
Simulation started on 1/6/95 at 10:37:28
Simulation stopped on 1/6/95 at 10:38:24

Forecast: Total Costs   **Cell: D12**

Summary:
Display Range is from $120,000 to $180,000
Entire Range is from $111,845 to $185,350
After 1,000 Trials, the Std. Error of the Mean is $346

Statistics:	Value
Trials	1000
Mean	$149,808
Median (approx.)	$149,431
Mode (approx.)	$151,170
Standard Deviation	$10,934
Variance	$119,550,888
Skewness	0.05
Kurtosis	3.14
Coeff. of Variability	0.07
Range Minimum	$111,845
Range Maximum	$185,350
Range Width	$73,505
Mean Std. Error	$345.76

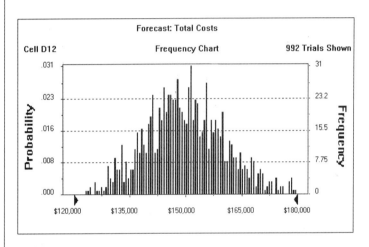

Assumption: Fixed Costs   **Cell: B12**

Normal distribution with parameters:
Mean $50,000
Standard Dev. $4,000

Selected range is from -Infinity to +Infinity

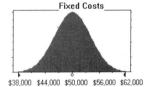

Assumption: Variable Costs   **Cell: C12**

731

TABLE 13.7
Distribution of three months' data on maturity periods

Maturity period (days)	Probability	Maturity period (days)	Probability	Maturity period (days)	Probability
7	0.119	33	0.013	69	0.001
8	0.035	34	0.002	70	0.001
9	0.004	35	0.005	77	0.001
10	0.010	36	0.001	79	0.001
11	0.015	38	0.001	87	0.001
12	0.022	40	0.002	89	0.001
13	0.011	41	0.001	90	0.032
14	0.206	42	0.001	91	0.012
15	0.032	43	0.002	92	0.004
16	0.003	44	0.001	98	0.001
17	0.014	45	0.004	99	0.001
18	0.020	46	0.001	112	0.001
19	0.003	47	0.001	116	0.001
20	0.007	49	0.001	119	0.003
21	0.009	50	0.001	120	0.009
22	0.002	52	0.001	122	0.001
23	0.002	53	0.001	123	0.002
24	0.004	55	0.002	133	0.001
25	0.001	57	0.001	147	0.001
27	0.005	60	0.044	180	0.003
28	0.032	61	0.012	181	0.003
29	0.007	62	0.005	182	0.003
30	0.152	63	0.004	184	0.001
31	0.055	64	0.001	272	0.001
32	0.024	65	0.002		

Questions for Discussion

1. What effect do you think the simplifying assumptions might have had on the simulation results?
2. Explain how to use the distribution in Table 13.7 to generate maturity periods.
3. What effect did the issuance of a $42 million block of fixed-rate CDs have on Scenario C?

TABLE 13.8
Interest-rate scenarios

Scenario	Days to maturity							
	7	14	30	60	90	120	150	180 (or more)
A (1 to 60 days)	9.85	10.00	10.15	10.30	10.45	10.60	10.75	10.75
B (1 to 60 days)	9.85	10.00	10.15	10.15	10.15	10.15	10.15	10.15
C (1 to 30 days)	9.85	10.00	10.15	10.30	10.45	10.60	10.75	10.75
(31 to 60 days)	10.35	10.50	10.65	10.80	10.95	11.10	11.25	11.25
D (1 to 30 days)	9.85	10.00	10.15	10.30	10.45	10.60	10.75	10.75
(31 to 60 days)	9.35	9.50	9.65	9.80	9.95	10.10	10.25	10.25
E	Same as C except issue $42,000,000 of new 60-day CDs at 10.30 percent. This block is in addition to existing portfolio.							

TABLE 13.9
Simulation results
for CD portfolio

Scenario	Mean yield	Standard deviation	Minimum yield	Maximum yield
A	10.25	0.0407	10.16	10.32
B	10.12	0.0124	10.08	10.13
C	10.58	0.0399	10.53	10.65
D	9.92	0.0729	9.78	10.11
E	10.54	0.0346	10.50	10.60

MORE EXAMPLES AND SOLVED PROBLEMS

In this section we present some additional examples to help you gain a better understanding of simulation modeling. There are no simple formulas or algorithms for building simulation models; successful simulation modeling depends on the ability to think logically.

EXAMPLE 10. SIMULATING THE NEWSBOY PROBLEM

In Chapter 11 we developed a model for the single-period inventory model with probabilistic demand. The analytical approach computes the expected profit for a particular purchasing decision. In this example we show how to simulate this problem. Simulation has the advantage of providing a distribution of profit so that we may assess the risk associated with an ordering decision. This is not available with the analytical approach.

We will use the situation described in Example 7 of Chapter 11 as an illustration. In that example, we assumed that demand is uniformly distributed between 40 and 49. Each paper costs $0.20 and is sold for $0.35. Any unsold papers can be disposed of at $0.05 each.

Figure 13.20 describes the process of simulating the profit for a fixed order quantity Q. We generate the demand, S, by assigning the following random number intervals:

Random number intervals	Demand
0–.1	40
.1–.2	41
.2–.3	42
.3–.4	43
.4–.5	44
.5–.6	45
.6–.7	46
.7–.8	47
.8–.9	48
.9–1.0	49

FIGURE 13.20   *Simulation model for the newsboy problem*

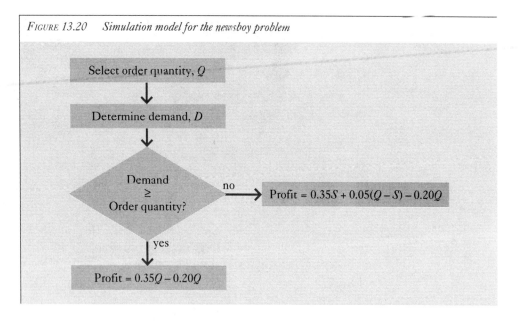

If $D \geq Q$, then we have sold all that we purchased and realized a profit of $0.35Q - 0.20Q$. If $D < Q$, then we have $Q - D$ papers left over. D papers are sold for \$0.35 each, and the remainder is disposed of for \$0.05 each. Thus, the net profit is $0.35D + 0.05(Q - D) - 0.20Q$. We may repeat this simulation a large number of times and then compute the average profit and the profit distribution. Then we may evaluate other order quantities and select the best. Figure 13.21 shows a spreadsheet designed to evaluate each order quantity between 40 and 49. The simulation shows that purchasing 43 papers yields the highest expected profit. However, as the graph in Figure 13.21 shows, the expected profit is relatively insensitive to the number of papers purchased. As this increases, we see that the spread between the highest and lowest possible profits increases. Thus, although the newsboy might earn a higher profit by purchasing more newspapers, he also runs a greater risk of a low profit.

Notice that we could not have made these observations using the analytical expected value analysis as we did in Chapter 11. The newsboy might now wish to incorporate some concepts of utility and decision analysis that we discussed in the last chapter to make a final decision.

EXAMPLE 11. A SIMULATION MODEL FOR PROCESSING CRIMINAL COURT CASES[5]

Figure 13.22 (page 736) illustrates a simplified process for processing felony cases through the District of Columbia court system. Following an arrest, the first steps are

---

[5]Adapted from Jean G. Taylor and Joseph A. Navarro, "Simulation of a Court System for the Processing of Criminal Cases," *Simulation*, May 1968, pp. 235–240.

FIGURE 13.21   *Spreadsheet model for the newsboy problem*

	A	B	C	D	E	F	G	H	I	J	K	L
1	Newsboy Problem											
2												
3	Parameters and Uncontrollable Variables			Assumptions								
4												
5	Unit cost	0.2		Demand is uniform between 40 and 49								
6	Selling price	0.35										
7	Salvage value	0.05										
8												
9			Order Quantity									
10	Trial	Demand	40	41	42	43	44	45	46	47	48	49
11	1	49	$6.00	$6.15	$6.30	$6.45	$6.60	$6.75	$6.90	$7.05	$7.20	$7.35
12	2	43	$6.00	$6.15	$6.30	$6.45	$6.30	$6.15	$6.00	$5.85	$5.70	$5.55
13	3	42	$6.00	$6.15	$6.30	$6.15	$6.00	$5.85	$5.70	$5.55	$5.40	$5.25
14	4	42	$6.00	$6.15	$6.30	$6.15	$6.00	$5.85	$5.70	$5.55	$5.40	$5.25
15	5	46	$6.00	$6.15	$6.30	$6.45	$6.60	$6.75	$6.90	$6.75	$6.60	$6.45
16	6	44	$6.00	$6.15	$6.30	$6.45	$6.60	$6.45	$6.30	$6.15	$6.00	$5.85
17	7	43	$6.00	$6.15	$6.30	$6.45	$6.30	$6.15	$6.00	$5.85	$5.70	$5.55
18	8	42	$6.00	$6.15	$6.30	$6.15	$6.00	$5.85	$5.70	$5.55	$5.40	$5.25
19	9	43	$6.00	$6.15	$6.30	$6.45	$6.30	$6.15	$6.00	$5.85	$5.70	$5.55
20	10	45	$6.00	$6.15	$6.30	$6.45	$6.60	$6.75	$6.60	$6.45	$6.30	$6.15
21	11	43	$6.00	$6.15	$6.30	$6.45	$6.30	$6.15	$6.00	$5.85	$5.70	$5.55
22	12	48	$6.00	$6.15	$6.30	$6.45	$6.60	$6.75	$6.90	$7.05	$7.20	$7.05
23	13	49	$6.00	$6.15	$6.30	$6.45	$6.60	$6.75	$6.90	$7.05	$7.20	$7.35
24	14	41	$6.00	$6.15	$6.00	$5.85	$5.70	$5.55	$5.40	$5.25	$5.10	$4.95
25	15	41	$6.00	$6.15	$6.00	$5.85	$5.70	$5.55	$5.40	$5.25	$5.10	$4.95
26	16	40	$6.00	$5.85	$5.70	$5.55	$5.40	$5.25	$5.10	$4.95	$4.80	$4.65
27	17	43	$6.00	$6.15	$6.30	$6.45	$6.30	$6.15	$6.00	$5.85	$5.70	$5.55
28	18	47	$6.00	$6.15	$6.30	$6.45	$6.60	$6.75	$6.90	$7.05	$6.90	$6.75
29	19	49	$6.00	$6.15	$6.30	$6.45	$6.60	$6.75	$6.90	$7.05	$7.20	$7.35
30	20	45	$6.00	$6.15	$6.30	$6.45	$6.60	$6.75	$6.60	$6.45	$6.30	$6.15
31		Avg. profit	$6.00	$6.14	$6.24	$6.30	$6.29	$6.26	$6.20	$6.12	$6.03	$5.93
32		Standard dev.	$0.00	$0.07	$0.15	$0.26	$0.36	$0.48	$0.58	$0.68	$0.76	$0.84
33		Minimum	6	5.85	5.7	5.55	5.4	5.25	5.1	4.95	4.8	4.65
34		Maximum	6	6.15	6.3	6.45	6.6	6.75	6.9	7.05	7.2	7.35

FIGURE 13.21   *(continued)*

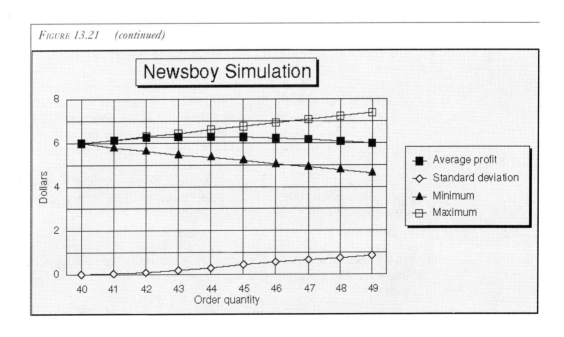

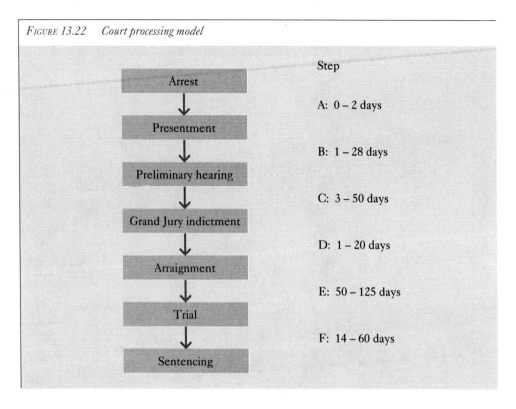

FIGURE 13.22   *Court processing model*

Step

A: 0 – 2 days

B: 1 – 28 days

C: 3 – 50 days

D: 1 – 20 days

E: 50 – 125 days

F: 14 – 60 days

presentment and a preliminary hearing, which occurs before a judge of the Court of General Sessions. The case is then processed in the office of the U.S. Attorney, Grand Jury Unit, which votes on an indictment. Arraignment is a proceeding in which the accused appears, is advised of the formal charge, and enters a plea. Following arraignment, trial preparation proceeds, the case is placed on a calendar, and finally progresses to trial. If the defendant is convicted, the final step is sentencing.

Figure 13.22 also shows the delays incurred at each step of the process. We will assume that these times are uniformly distributed. Thus, the time between arrest and presentment is anywhere between zero and two days. The objective of the simulation is to determine the distribution of time to proceed through the entire process, from arrest to sentencing.

To simulate this system, we need to be able to generate probabilistic outcomes from a uniform distribution between a and b. As discussed earlier in this chapter, we do this using random numbers as follows:

$$U = a + (b - a)R \tag{13.15}$$

Thus, to simulate the time from presentment to the preliminary hearing (see Figure 13.22), we use the formula

$$1 + (28 - 1)R = 1 + 27R \tag{13.16}$$

To illustrate one trial of the simulation, we will use the first six random numbers in row 1 of Table 13.1. (For simplification, we will round the randomly generated times to integers.)

Step	Random number	Simulated time
A	.426	$0 + 2(.426) = .852$, or 1 day
B	.332	$1 + 27(.332) = 9.964$, or 10 days
C	.634	$3 + 47(.634) = 32.798$, or 33 days
D	.742	$1 + 19(.742) = 15.098$, or 15 days
E	.826	$50 + 75(.826) = 111.95$, or 112 days
F	.406	$14 + 46(.406) = 32.676$, or 33 days

Thus, the total processing time for one simulated trial is 204 days. To find a reasonable statistical distribution of processing times, this system would have to be simulated many times. A problem at the end of this chapter asks you to develop a spreadsheet for simulating this problem.

EXAMPLE 12. SIMULATING A PROJECT NETWORK

In Chapter 11 we showed how to incorporate uncertainty in activity times in a project network. The analytical calculations provide the expected project completion time and an estimate of the variance. We assumed that the critical path is defined by the *expected* activity times. We were also able to assess the risk that the project time will exceed a certain amount by assuming that the distribution of project times is normally distributed. These assumptions are rather severe. Depending on the actual realization of activity times, different paths might be critical, and the distribution of project times may be far from normal. Simulation provides a means of obtaining a more accurate assessment of the distribution of project completion times.

To illustrate this, consider the small project network shown in Figure 13.23. All times are assumed to be triangular; thus, $T(a, m, b)$ represents a triangular distribution with lower limit a, mode m, and upper limit b. Figure 13.24 shows a spreadsheet for simulating activity times and finding the critical path. We see that path BD is critical only in 5 of the 50 trials. The expected project time is 7.652, but there is considerable variation; the completion time varies from 5.681 to 9.736. You may construct a histogram of the project time and use it to make probability statements. We ask you to do this in a problem at the end of this chapter.

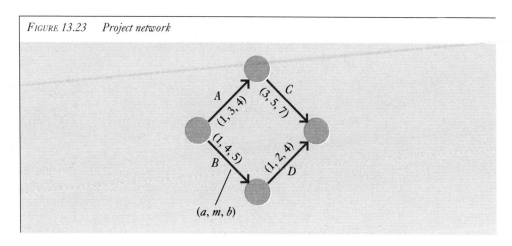

FIGURE 13.23   Project network

EXAMPLE 13. RISK ANALYSIS FOR A NEW PRODUCT PROPOSAL

Rattel Toys is considering introducing a new action toy based on an anticipated blockbuster movie to be released next summer. The toy is expected to have a marketable lifetime of only one year. The price is proposed to be $7.95, and marketing expects to sell 900,000 units. Fixed production costs are estimated to be $675,000 and per unit variable cost $3.00. Selling costs are expected to be $875,000 and general and administrative costs $300,000. Figure 13.25 shows a simple spreadsheet for computing the net profit under these conditions. The net profit is expected to be $2,605,000.

All these estimates, however, are uncertain. Many movies have been surprise hits, and others have been enormous flops. Upon further analysis, the management team estimates that sales will be normal with mean 900,000 and standard deviation 300,000; fixed costs will be uniform between $625,000 and $725,000; variable costs triangular with $a = \$2.75$, $m = \$3.00$, and $b = \$3.25$; and selling costs normal with mean $875,000 and standard deviation $50,000. How risky is this project?

Because the costs are characterized by several different types of distributions, a Monte Carlo simulation will provide a profile of the profit distribution. Figure 13.26 shows a report generated by Crystal Ball. In simulating 1,000 trials, we see that the mean is close to the expected value. We also see that the distribution of net profit has a standard deviation of $1,486,187 and varies from −$2.6 million to almost $8 million. The percentile summary shows that there is about a 15 percent chance of making less than $1 million, and almost a 20 percent chance of exceeding $4 million. What would you recommend?

FIGURE 13.24   Spreadsheet for project network simulation

	A	B	C	D	E	F	G	H	I	J	K	L	M	N
1	**Project Network Simulation**													
2														
3	*Triangular distribution parameters*													
4														
5	Activity	a	m	b	(b-a)	(m-a)/(b-a)								
6	A	1	3	4	3	0.666667								
7	B	1	4	5	4	0.75								
8	C	3	5	7	4	0.5								
9	D	1	2	4	3	0.333333								
10														
11	Trial	RN	A	RN	B	RN	C	RN	D	Path AC	Path BD	Project time	Critical Path	
12	1	0.337	2.422	0.360	3.078	0.008	3.258	0.216	1.804	5.681	4.882	5.681	1	
13	2	0.230	2.176	0.156	2.370	0.894	6.079	0.170	1.713	8.255	4.083	8.255	1	
14	3	0.778	3.184	0.919	4.431	0.568	5.141	0.793	2.885	8.325	7.316	8.325	1	
15	4	0.682	3.024	0.021	1.504	0.235	4.372	0.023	1.264	7.396	2.768	7.396	1	
16	5	0.049	1.543	0.049	1.771	0.268	4.465	0.446	2.177	6.008	3.948	6.008	1	
17	6	0.088	1.728	0.704	3.907	0.598	5.208	0.437	2.162	6.936	6.068	6.936	1	
18	7	0.275	2.284	0.373	3.116	0.970	6.512	0.561	2.377	8.796	5.494	8.796	1	
19	8	0.320	2.386	0.341	3.022	0.081	3.803	0.026	1.279	6.189	4.301	6.189	1	
20	9	0.161	1.982	0.142	2.304	0.858	5.933	0.415	2.126	7.915	4.430	7.915	1	
21	10	0.617	2.924	0.289	2.863	0.844	5.822	0.060	1.425	8.806	4.288	8.806	1	
22	11	0.489	2.713	0.588	3.656	0.144	4.074	0.691	2.639	6.787	6.296	6.787	1	
23	12	0.991	3.831	0.196	2.535	0.107	3.924	0.724	2.714	7.756	5.248	7.756	1	
24	13	0.395	2.540	0.269	2.797	0.006	3.217	0.912	3.274	5.758	6.071	6.071	2	
25	14	0.999	3.941	0.625	3.738	0.326	4.615	0.322	1.982	8.555	5.720	8.555	1	
26	15	0.189	2.065	0.991	4.810	0.535	5.072	0.794	2.888	7.137	7.698	7.698	2	
27	16	0.055	1.572	0.601	3.686	0.687	5.417	0.688	2.631	6.989	6.317	6.989	1	
28	17	0.026	1.395	0.972	4.665	0.133	4.032	0.564	2.382	5.427	7.047	7.047	2	
29	18	0.214	2.134	0.765	4.030	0.105	3.915	0.843	3.029	6.049	7.060	7.060	2	
30	19	0.956	3.636	0.690	3.877	0.760	5.615	0.676	2.605	9.250	6.482	9.250	1	
31	20	0.706	3.062	0.354	3.062	0.975	6.550	0.851	3.054	9.611	6.116	9.611	1	
32	21	0.198	2.091	0.156	2.369	0.391	4.768	0.600	2.451	6.858	4.820	6.858	1	
33	22	0.137	1.905	0.981	4.724	0.036	3.534	0.897	3.213	5.439	7.937	7.937	2	
34	23	0.404	2.558	0.130	2.250	0.395	4.778	0.131	1.626	7.336	3.876	7.336	1	
35	24	0.546	2.810	0.078	1.970	0.197	4.255	0.146	1.662	7.065	3.631	7.065	1	
36	25	0.109	1.808	0.821	4.153	0.789	5.702	0.660	2.572	7.510	6.725	7.510	1	
37	26	0.934	3.557	0.151	2.344	0.767	5.635	0.898	3.219	9.192	5.564	9.192	1	
38	27	0.574	2.856	0.719	3.938	0.085	3.825	0.341	2.011	6.681	5.949	6.681	1	
39	28	0.789	3.205	0.734	3.968	0.554	5.112	0.396	2.097	8.317	6.065	8.317	1	
40	29	0.831	3.287	0.511	3.477	0.678	5.395	0.559	2.373	8.682	5.850	8.682	1	
41	30	0.549	2.815	0.755	4.010	0.667	5.368	0.989	3.741	8.183	7.751	8.183	1	
42	31	0.920	3.510	0.287	2.856	0.113	3.951	0.444	2.174	7.461	5.030	7.461	1	
43	32	0.620	2.928	0.740	3.979	0.339	4.647	0.045	1.368	7.575	5.348	7.575	1	
44	33	0.880	3.401	0.277	2.823	0.269	4.467	0.380	2.072	7.868	4.895	7.868	1	
45	34	0.578	2.863	0.093	2.056	0.154	4.111	0.231	1.832	6.974	3.888	6.974	1	
46	35	0.840	3.308	0.335	3.004	0.232	4.363	0.872	3.122	7.761	6.126	7.761	1	
47	36	0.667	3.001	0.634	3.759	0.124	3.997	0.451	2.185	6.997	5.944	6.997	1	
48	37	0.369	2.488	0.901	4.372	0.616	5.247	0.665	2.582	7.734	6.954	7.734	1	
49	38	0.753	3.139	0.224	2.641	0.394	4.776	0.126	1.615	7.916	4.256	7.916	1	
50	39	0.981	3.761	0.478	3.395	0.125	4.000	0.706	2.673	7.761	6.068	7.761	1	
51	40	0.820	3.265	0.071	1.924	0.534	5.069	0.351	2.027	8.334	3.951	8.334	1	
52	41	0.732	3.103	0.606	3.696	0.179	4.198	0.616	2.483	7.301	6.178	7.301	1	
53	42	0.200	2.096	0.148	2.332	0.214	4.307	0.153	1.677	6.404	4.009	6.404	1	
54	43	0.908	3.475	0.662	3.819	0.256	4.430	0.143	1.655	7.904	5.475	7.904	1	
55	44	0.754	3.141	0.756	4.011	0.979	6.594	0.161	1.695	9.736	5.706	9.736	1	
56	45	0.433	2.613	0.082	1.991	0.090	3.851	0.332	1.997	6.463	3.988	6.463	1	
57	46	0.913	3.490	0.207	2.576	0.759	5.611	0.300	1.948	9.101	4.524	9.101	1	
58	47	0.049	1.544	0.252	2.737	0.972	6.526	0.948	3.443	8.070	6.180	8.070	1	
59	48	0.314	2.372	0.167	2.416	0.109	3.932	0.280	1.917	6.304	4.333	6.304	1	
60	49	0.606	2.907	0.538	3.542	0.615	5.246	0.843	3.030	8.153	6.571	8.153	1	
61	50	0.345	2.438	0.377	3.126	0.736	5.546	0.612	2.473	7.984	5.599	7.984	1	
62														
63											Average	7.652		
64											Stand. dev	0.940		
65											Minimum	5.681		
66											Maximum	9.736		

739

FIGURE 13.25   *Rattel Toys Spreadsheet*

A	A	B
1	New Product Risk Analysis	
2		
3	Price	$7.95
4	Sales	900000
5	Fixed costs	$675,000.00
6	Variable cost	$3.00
7	Selling costs	$875,000.00
8	Adm. costs	$300,000.00
9		
10	Revenue	$7,155,000.00
11	Fixed costs	$675,000.00
12	Variable costs	$2,700,000.00
13	Selling costs	$875,000.00
14	Adm. costs	$300,000.00
15		
16	Net profit	$2,605,000.00

SUMMARY

Computer simulation is the process of designing a logical model of a system or decision problem and then conducting computer-based experiments with the model to describe, explain, and predict the behavior of the system or problem outcomes. Because simulation is not limited by restrictive assumptions, it can be used to model and analyze a much wider variety of practical problems than analytical approaches. Simulation is used for design, analysis, and performance assessment.

Simulation modeling begins with a conceptual model—a flowchart—that describes the logic of the system or process being analyzed. Once a conceptual model is developed, the analyst can collect the necessary data to drive the model. The conceptual model must then be translated into a logical model that can be implemented on a computer. Probabilistic outcomes in a simulation model are generated using random numbers. A random number is a number drawn from a uniform probability distribution between 0 and 1. Random variates are outcomes drawn from arbitrary probability distributions.

Monte Carlo simulation is basically repeated sampling from probability distributions. For problems consisting of many different types of distributions, Monte Carlo simulation provides a distribution of outcomes from which a manager can assess risk. Computer software such as Crystal Ball provides automatic Monte Carlo simulations of spreadsheet models and comprehensive reports.

Because simulation is a sampling experiment, statistical analysis is necessary to draw conclusions from the simulation outputs. Variability is decreased by replicating simulation experiments and by lengthening individual simulation runs. Through statistical analysis, we may construct confidence intervals for key performance measures obtained from simulations.

In the next chapter we discuss dynamic simulation models in which time is a crucial factor, and special computer languages for simulation modeling.

FIGURE 13.26   *Crystal ball report for Rattel Toys new product proposal*

Crystal Ball Report
Simulation started on 5/17/94 at 11:12:39
Simulation stopped on 5/17/94 at 11:13:27

Forecast: Net profit   Cell: B16

    Summary:
        Display Range is from ($2,000,000.00) to $7,000,000.00
        Entire Range is from ($2,607,765.40) to $7,917,099.09
        After 1,000 Trials, the Std. Error of the Mean is $46,997.38

Statistics:	Value
Trials	1000
Mean	$2,634,433.89
Median (approx.)	$2,566,959.64
Mode (approx.)	$1,654,804.72
Standard Deviation	$1,486,187.64
Variance	2.21E+12
Skewness	0.08
Kurtosis	2.98
Coeff. of Variability	0.56
Range Minimum	($2,607,765.40)
Range Maximum	$7,917,099.09
Range Width	$10,524,864.49
Mean Std. Error	$46,997.38

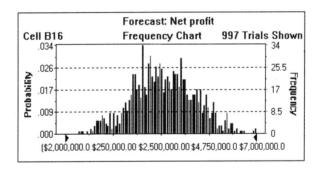

Forecast: Net profit (cont'd)   Cell: B16

    Percentiles:

Percentile	Value (approx.)
0%	($2,607,765.40)
10%	$816,323.85
20%	$1,378,527.03
30%	$1,830,219.13
40%	$2,206,385.58
50%	$2,566,959.64
60%	$3,027,422.46
70%	$3,423,984.32
80%	$3,917,650.59
90%	$4,588,610.70
100%	$7,917,099.09

End of Forecast

Figure 13.26   (continued)

Assumption: Sales   Cell: B4

    Normal distribution with parameters:
      Mean $900,000.00
      Standard Dev. $300,000.00

    Selected range is from -Infinity to +Infinity
    Mean value in simulation was $905,511.06

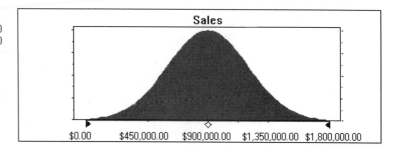

Assumption: Fixed costs   Cell: B5

    Uniform distribution with parameters:
      Minimum $625,000.00
      Maximum $725,000.00

    Mean value in simulation was $673,686.41

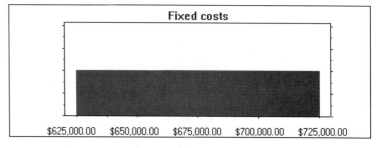

Assumption: Variable cost   Cell: B6

    Triangular distribution with parameters:
      Minimum $2.75
      Likeliest $3.00
      Maximum $3.25

    Selected range is from $2.75 to $3.25
    Mean value in simulation was $3.00

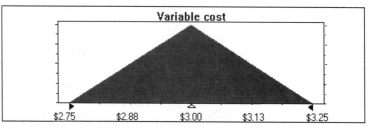

Assumption: Selling costs   Cell: B7

    Normal distribution with parameters:
      Mean $875,000.00
      Standard Dev. $50,000.00

    Selected range is from -Infinity to +Infinity
    Mean value in simulation was $873,354.60

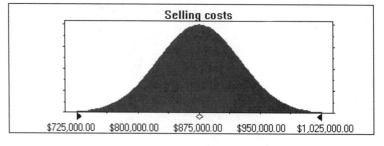

CHAPTER REVIEW EXERCISES

I. Terms to Understand

a.   Computer simulation (p. 692)

b.   Scenario (p. 698)

c.   Conceptual simulation model (p. 698)

d.   Logical simulation model (p. 700)

e.   Random number (p. 703)

f.   Pseudorandom number (p. 703)

g.   Monte Carlo simulation (p. 706)

h.   Random variate (p. 719)

i.   Simulation run (p. 713)

j.   Replication (p. 712)

k.   Common random numbers (p. 714)

l.   Crystal Ball (p. 722)

II. Discussion Questions

1.   Explain why simulation models are descriptive and usually probabilistic.

2.   What are the benefits of using simulation models? The disadvantages?

3.   Describe some potential applications of simulation to problems of your own experience. How difficult would it be to build simulation models for these situations?

4.   Explain the steps involved in building simulation models. Which would you say are the most difficult? Why?

5.   What are the two major activities involved in performing a simulation?

6.   Explain different ways of generating outcomes from probability distributions.

7.   Why are random numbers so appealing for simulation experiments?

8.   Explain why it is not good practice to draw conclusions on the basis of only one simulation experiment.

9.   Discuss the advantages and limitations of using spreadsheets for simulation.

10.   Discuss the effects of varying the length of simulation runs.

11.   Why do we replicate simulation experiments? What would be the impact of *not* replicating?

12.   Describe the best way to use random numbers when comparing two or more different systems using simulation experiments.

13.   What is the effect of increasing the run length on simulation output?

III. Problems

1.   For the capital equipment decision problem described in this chapter, generate 10 observations for the number of trucks required per day using row 3 of the random number table (Table 13.1).

2.   Using the results from Problem 1, simulate both the one- and two-truck scenarios and determine the average daily cost for each strategy. How did your results differ from Tables 13.2 and 13.3? Why?

3.   Using a spreadsheet, generate 50, 100, and 500 outcomes from each of the following distributions. Construct histograms for each data set and use a Chi-square goodness of fit test to test the hypotheses that the data are drawn from the distribution from which they were generated.

a.   Uniform between 0 and 1

b.   Normal with mean 50 and standard deviation 10

c.   Exponential with mean 1

4.   Simulate 25 outcomes for the CD maturity periods in Table 13.7. Compute the mean and standard deviation and construct a 95 percent confidence interval for the average. How do your results compare with the expected value of 30.59? Simulate 100 outcomes. What differences do you observe?

5.   Four runs of the two-truck scenario for the capital equipment decision problem were performed with the following results:

Run	Average daily cost
1	280
2	220
3	250
4	235

Find a 99 percent confidence interval for the average daily cost.

6.   The table below shows the results of five runs of a simulation model. Construct 95 percent confidence intervals for the average waiting time and average idle time.

Run	Waiting time	Idle time
1	15.2	6.4
2	15.6	7.2
3	23.6	8.0
4	10.6	9.6
5	21.4	7.0

7.   Using the computer program or spreadsheet template for the capital equipment decision problem (Example 1), run five simulations and construct a 90 percent confidence interval for the average daily cost.

8.   Compute analytically the expected value and standard error of the mean for the two-truck scenario in the capital equipment decision problem. What conclusions do you reach regarding the best scenario on the basis of the analytical results?

9.   Using row 2 of Table 13.1, generate 10 outcomes from a uniform distribution between 3 and 7.

10.   Construct a spreadsheet for the court processing model (Figure 13.22). Simulate 100 outcomes and construct a distribution of total processing times.

11.   Using row 1 of Table 13.1, generate 10 outcomes from an exponential probability distribution having a mean of 5.

12.   A sample of 445 patients of a St. Louis hospital revealed the following data for length of time in surgery:

Length of stay (hours)	Frequency
.01—.50	181
.51—1.00	103
1.01—1.50	64
1.51—2.00	42
2.01—2.50	22
2.51—3.00	13
3.01—3.50	8
3.51—4.00	5
4.01—6.00	7

Design a procedure for generating the number of hours in surgery as input to a simulation model. Assume that the times within an interval are uniformly distributed.

13.   A local pharmacy orders 75 copies of a weekly newsmagazine. Depending on the cover story, demand for the magazine varies. Historical records suggest that the probability distribution of demand is as follows:

Number of magazines	Probability
60	.15
70	.20
75	.25
80	.20
85	.20

The pharmacy purchases the magazines for $1.25 and sells them for $2.00. Any magazines left over at the end of the month are donated to hospitals and other health care facilities. Is the 75-copy order quantity the most profitable? Conduct simulation analyses to answer this question.

14.   Using the table of random numbers in Appendix C, simulate 30 trials of the felony criminal processing example in this chapter and construct a histogram of the simulated times. What does the distribution look like?

15.   An electrical system is composed of two components, A and B, as shown below.

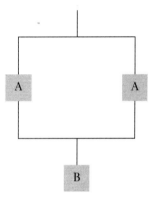

The reliability—the probability that the component will work properly during a given length of time—is .7 for component A and .9 for component B. The system fails if both A components fail or if the B component fails. Simulate this system to estimate the reliability of the entire system.

16.   Consider the capital equipment purchase example. Is it better to simulate, say, four replications of 10 days each, or to make one simulation run of 40 days, or does it not make a difference? Try to answer this question statistically and verify your results using simulation experiments. Under what circumstances might one approach be preferable?

17.   A buyer for a large department store must make a decision on the purchase of fall merchandise in May. Clearly, there is an element of risk. If enough merchandise is not purchased, the store will forgo

TABLE 13.10
Probability distribu-
tion of coat sales
demand

Sales	Probability
50	.1
60	.2
70	.3
80	.2
90	.1
100	.1

the opportunity to gain additional profit. If too much is purchased, the store will have to sell the surplus at a loss at the end of the season to make room for the spring line. For a particular style of winter coat, marketing researchers have estimated a probability distribution for the sales of the merchandise, shown in Table 13.10. The coats are purchased for $55 and sold for $135. However, any that are left over at the end of the season are sold for $40. What is the best quantity to order to maximize expected profit?

18. In the seasonal ordering decision problem (Problem 17), we ran five replications of the model. For order quantities of 80 and 90, we obtained the following results:

Run	$Q = 80$	$Q = 90$	Difference
1	5,165	5,157.5	7.50
2	5,355	5,252	103.00
3	5,545	5,584	–40.00
4	5,782.5	5,775	7.50
5	5,117.5	5,062.5	55.00

Is there a significant difference between these order quantities?

19. Consider the simple profit model in Chapter 1:

$$P = (p - c)Q - F$$

Develop a financial simulation model for a new product proposal and construct a distribution of profits under the following assumptions. Price is fixed at $1,000. Variable costs are unknown and follow the distribution:

Costs, c	Probability
$500	.20
$600	.40
$700	.20
$800	.20

Quantity sold is also variable and follows the following distribution:

Quantity sold, Q	Probability
120	.25
140	.50
160	.25

Fixed costs are estimated to follow the following distribution:

Fixed costs, F	Probability
$45,000	.20
$50,000	.50
$55,000	.30

Would you conclude that this product is a good investment?

20. A company is considering two investments. Both cost $10 million and have a 10-year life. Investment A expects to generate an annual net cash flow of $1.3 million, and investment B expects to generate a net annual cash flow of $1.4 million. However, the distribution of annual net cash flow is triangular with a = $900,000 and b = $1.7 million for investment A, and a = −$600,000 and b = $3.4 million for investment B. Make a recommendation of which investment to choose.

IV. Projects and Cases

1. A plant manager is considering investing in a new $30,000 machine. Use of the new machine is expected to generate a cash flow of about $8,000 per year for each of the next five years. However, the cash flow is uncertain, and the manager estimates that the actual cash flow will be normally distributed with a mean of $8,000 and a standard deviation of $500. The interest rate is estimated to be 9 percent and assumed to remain constant over the next five years. The company evaluates capital investments using net present value and internal rate of return. How risky is this investment? Develop an appropriate simulation model and conduct experiments and statistical output analysis to answer this question. (*Hint:* in Lotus 1-2-3 you will need to use the functions @NPV and @IRR.)

2. TakeAim is a new software company that develops and markets productivity software for municipal government applications. In developing their income statement, the following formulas are used:
    1. Gross profit = Net sales − Cost of sales
    2. Net operating profit = Gross profit − Administrative expenses
    3. Net income before taxes = Net operating profit − Interest expense
    4. Net income = Net income before taxes − Taxes

    Net sales in the first year (in hundreds of thousands of dollars) is uniformly distributed between 6 and 12. The net sales is expected to increase each year by 5 percent plus or minus 1 percent. Cost of sales (in hundreds of thousands of dollars) is normally distributed, with mean of 5.6 and standard deviation 0.2, and is expected to increase an average of 5 percent per year. Selling expenses has a fixed component that is uniform between $75,000 and $110,000. The variable component is estimated to be 7 percent of net sales. Administrative expenses is normal, with a mean of $50,000 and standard deviation of $4,000, and will increase 3 percent per year on average. Interest expenses are $10,000 in year 1 and will decline by $1,000 each year. The company is taxed at a 50 percent rate.

Develop a profile of net income over a five-year period and write a report to management.

3. You are considering investing in (purchasing) an apartment complex. Before deciding to invest, you would like to do a risk analysis of the situation to assess whether or not the investment is a good idea for you.

    The complex has 40 units. Historical data indicate that the number of units rented in a given month are distributed uniformly between 30 and 40 units. The rent per unit, which you are not likely to change since demand is very price sensitive, is $600 per month. Monthly expenses for the entire complex seem to be distributed normally with mean $11,000 and standard deviation $1,500.

    a. Simulate at least 100 months. What is the maximum amount made in any of these months? What is the worst month?

    b. According to the simulation results, what is the probability of making a profit in any given month?

    c. Suppose your debt payments on this complex will be $2,400 per month. Would you take this investment? Defend your decision using the simulation output data.

REFERENCES

Cadley, John A., Helen E. Heintz, and Lisa Vogrich Allocco. "Insights from Simulating JIT Manufacturing." *Interfaces*, Vol. 19, No. 2, March–April 1989, pp. 88–97.

Carson, John S. "Convincing Users of Model's Validity Is Challenging Aspect of Modeler's Job." *Industrial Engineering*, June 1986, pp. 74–85.

Cebry, Michael E., Anura H. deSilva, and Fred J. DeLisio. "Management Science in Automating Postal Operations: Facility and Equipment Planning in the United States Postal Service." *Interfaces*, Vol. 22, No. 1, January–February 1992, pp. 110–130.

Evans, James R. "A Little Knowledge Can Be Dangerous: Handle Simulation with Care." *Production and Inventory Management*, Vol. 33, No. 2, pp. 51–54, 1992.

Farina, Ron, Gary A. Kochenberger, and Tom Obremski. "The Computer Runs the Bolder Boulder: A Simulation of a Major Running Race." *Interfaces*, Vol. 19, No. 2, March–April 1989, pp. 48–55.

Hertz, David B. *Risk Analysis and Its Applications*. New York: John Wiley & Sons, 1983.

Homer, Jack B., and Christian L. St. Clair. "A Model of HIV Transmission Through Needle Sharing." *Interfaces*, Vol. 21, No. 3, May–June 1991, pp. 26–49.

Kelton, W. David. "Statistical Analysis Methods Enhance Usefulness, Reliability, of Simulation Models." *Industrial Engineering*, Vol. 28, No. 9, September 1986, pp. 74–84.

Law, Averill M. and W. David Kelton. *Simulation Modeling and Analysis*. New York: McGraw-Hill, 1991.

Martel, D. L., R. J. Drysdale, G. E. Doan, and D. Boychuk. "An Evaluation of Forest Fire Initial Attack Resources." *Interfaces*, Vol. 14, No. 5, September–October 1984, pp. 30–32.

Maurer, Ruth A. and Fines H. Munkonze. "A Simulation Model of an Airport Shuttle Service." Department of Mathematical and Computer Sciences, Colorado School of Mines, Golden CO 80401-1887.

Ravindran, A., B. L. Foote, A. B. Badiru, L. M. Leemis, and Larry Williams. "An Application of Simulation and Network Analysis to Capacity Planning and Material Handling Systems at Tinker Air Force Base." *Interfaces*, Vol. 19, No. 1, January–February 1991, pp. 102–115.

Russell, Robert and Regina Hickle. "Simulation of a CD Portfolio." *Interfaces*, Vol. 16, No. 3, May–June 1986, pp. 49–59.

Schmitz, Homer H. and N. K. Kwak. "Monte Carlo Simulation of Operating-Room and Recovery-Room Usage." *Operations Research*, Vol. 20, No. 6, 1972, pp. 1171–1180.

Swart, William and Luca Donno. "Simulation Modeling Improves Operations, Planning, and Productivity of Fast Food Restaurants." *Interfaces*, Vol. 11, No. 6, December 1981, pp. 35–47.

Thesen, Arne and Laurel E. Travis. *Simulation for Decision Making.* St. Paul, MN: West Publishing Co., 1992.

Watson, Hugh J. and John H. Blackstone, Jr. *Computer Simulation* (2nd ed.). New York: John Wiley & Sons, 1989.

CHAPTER 14

SIMULATING

DYNAMIC

SYSTEMS

INTRODUCTION

- A project team developed a simulation model to aid reconstruction efforts after a disastrous fire at Tinker Air Force Base, one of five jet engine overhaul bases in the Air Force materiel system. The model has been used extensively to determine the appropriate number of machines to use, and the optimal design and routing scheme for the material handling system. The new design has decreased material handling by over 50 percent, saved $4.3 million by eliminating excess machine capacity, and saved $1.8 million from improved labor efficiency [Ravindran et al., 1989].

- The United States Postal Service delivers over 500 million pieces of mail each day to over 100 million delivery locations. The Postal Service uses a comprehensive simulation model for capacity planning and the evaluation of technology investment. The model has three major components: a mail operations component that models the flow of each stream of mail through sorting operations; a work force component that assigns staff to each sorting method; and a financial model to calculate yearly costs. The system can identify bottlenecks and cost impacts of various automation alternatives. The annual labor savings from their automation program is over $4 billion per year [Cebry et al., 1992].

- A small Canadian sporting wear company, Chlorphylle Haute Technologie, Inc., was investigating the use of Japanese just-in-time production scheduling methods. A simulation model, written in FORTRAN and taking six months to construct and test, showed that these methods can reduce the work-in-progress by over 60 percent and reduce the time to complete an order by 20 percent. Yet management was skeptical of the model. A "visual interactive" simulation model was built with animation capabilities and graphical output to help management better understand the numerical results of the previous simulations. The visual simulation model convinced the production manager to try the new methods [Gravel and Price, 1991].

Each of these applications involves complex systems with many interacting elements. For example, the engine overhaul facility at Tinker AFB consists of 900,000 square feet of floor space in which engines are periodically overhauled, completely modified, or upgraded. Over 10 million component parts are produced each year. Postal sorting involves cancellation, sorting to primary destinations, sorting to secondary destinations, sorting to zip codes, sorting to carrier routes, and preparation for delivery. Also, the events that take place in these systems occur over time. Simulating such systems is considerably different from Monte Carlo simulation discussed in the previous chapter. The complexity of these systems and dynamic relationships makes formal mathematical modeling virtually impossible.

Thus there is much more to simulation than simply generating random numbers and replicating numerical outcomes on spreadsheets. In this chapter we focus on *dynamic simulation models*—those that involve the passage of time. Although simple dynamic simulations can be implemented on spreadsheets, sophisticated simulation languages are usually necessary to implement complex problems. We will provide a brief overview of such special programming languages, and recent innovations such as visual modeling and animation. We also address the issues of *verification* and *validation*—ensuring that the simulation model works correctly and represents the real system adequately.

DYNAMIC SIMULATION MODELS

The truck purchase decision example in Chapter 13 shows how a simple simulation model is designed and implemented. This type of simulation model is called a *static* model. A second type of simulation model is called a *dynamic* model. The nature of a simulation model can be determined by asking a simple question: Is the operation of the system independent of or dependent on time? In other words, do you have to record the *time* at which various events in the system take place in order to find the information you seek? If the operation of the system is independent of time, then we have a static situation. The truck example is a static simulation model. As the simulation progresses, we need only know the number of trucks that are required each day; we do not need to know when trucks arrived or are dispatched for delivery, for example.

If time is an important factor, then we have a dynamic situation. For example, suppose we wish to simulate the process of loading and dispatching the trucks during the day. We would have to know when the trucks arrive, whether all the merchandise is ready to be loaded, how much time it takes to load the trucks, and so on. Trucks may be delayed because of the lack of availability of the merchandise or because of limited resources such as labor or forklift trucks. To obtain useful information about the process, we would have to record the times at which important events took place.

> Static simulation models are independent of time; dynamic simulation models depend on time and must incorporate a simulation "clock" to maintain a log of events.

To better illustrate the concept of a dynamic simulation model, we present the following example.

EXAMPLE 1. A DYNAMIC INVENTORY SIMULATION

Murthy Manufacturing Inc. (MMI) produces a variety of automobile aftermarket components. The demand for a certain type of rebuilt alternator fluctuates each month between 120 and 170, with any demand in this range being equally likely. MMI likes to keep its production level at 145 units per week, but this may also fluctuate because of variations in labor availability, defect rates, material delays, and so on. In approximately 4 of every 10 weeks, production falls to 130, and 10 percent of the time MMI can produce 150 units each week. MMI likes to maintain an inventory level of at least

200 units. If inventory falls below 200 units, MMI authorizes overtime to produce an extra run of 100 units. MMI management would like to know how often overtime is necessary or, equivalently, how long the inventory requirement can be maintained.

In this situation, we see that both demand and production are random variables. We cannot simply sample from these distributions in a Monte Carlo fashion and compute average results since the inventory level depends on previous events. In addition, we must keep track of time to examine how long the inventory remains above 200 units.

The fundamental equation that governs this system each week is

$$\text{Ending inventory} = \text{Beginning inventory} + \text{Production} - \text{Demand}$$

Let us assume that we begin with an initial inventory of 250 units in the first week. We randomly generate a value for production and demand using the techniques described in the last chapter. This provides a value for the ending inventory that week, which also becomes the beginning inventory for the next week. If at any time the inventory falls below 200, we add an extra 100 units to the production for that week.

Figure 14.1 shows a spreadsheet designed to simulate this system. Notice that we use the @IF function to determine if an overtime production run is necessary. Figure 14.2 shows a graph of the ending inventory and production levels each week. The spikes clearly show when additional production is used. In this simulation, we see that the inventory level fell below the required 200 units three times, or about every 30 to 35 weeks.

As we emphasized in the last chapter, we should never base a conclusion on a single simulation run. This is particularly true for dynamic simulations since the data within a simulation run are correlated; that is, they are not independent trials as in Monte Carlo simulations. If you repeat this simulation several times, you will find that the number of extra production runs generally varies from three to six times during the 100-week simulation. Thus, MMI can expect to require overtime approximately every 15 to 35 weeks.

This example illustrated the essence of dynamic simulation: the necessity of keeping track of events as they occur over time. Most practical dynamic simulation models are more complex than the one in this example. In the next section, we discuss some of the key issues in modeling and simulating more complex dynamic systems.

Building Dynamic Simulation Models

Many important dynamic simulation models involve the processing of customers at service facilities. "Customers" might represent people, messages, manufacturing jobs, and so on. In a typical manufacturing facility, for instance, jobs are processed at machine centers and routed to other machine centers for further processing. Because of variations in processing times, jobs usually end up waiting at machine centers to be processed. The production manager would be interested in how long jobs have to wait, the average time to complete processing, machine utilization, and so on. For a large facility, this would

FIGURE 14.1   Spreadsheet model for Murthy Manufacturing, Inc.

	A	B	C	D	E	F
1	Dynamic Inventory Simulation					
2						
3	Formulas and Assumptions					
4						
5	Ending Inventory=beginning inventory + production - demand					
6	Demand is uniform between 120 and 170 units/week					
7	Production has the distribution					
8	Production Probability					
9	130	0.4				
10	145	0.5				
11	150	0.1				
12	If inventory < 200, production increases by 100 for one week					
13						
14	Lookup Table					
15	Random Number range	Production				
16	0	0.4	130			
17	0.4	0.9	145			
18	0.9	1	150			
19						
20	Week	Beg. Inv.	Demand	Rand. no.	Production	End. Inv.
21	1	250	133	0.955656	150	267
22	2	267	155	0.201925	130	242
23	3	242	157	0.344106	130	215
24	4	215	139	0.296207	130	206
25	5	206	137	0.129616	130	199
26	6	199	142	0.276315	230	287
27	7	287	121	0.326991	130	296
28	8	296	157	0.273301	130	269
29	9	269	144	0.41847	145	270
30	10	270	131	0.733934	145	284
31	11	284	131	0.754592	145	298
32	12	298	141	0.243737	130	287
33	13	287	144	0.854775	145	288
34	14	288	130	0.497621	145	303
35	15	303	145	0.746198	145	303
36	16	303	137	0.930618	150	316
37	17	316	164	0.547713	145	297
38	18	297	140	0.549504	145	302
39	19	302	145	0.055939	130	287
40	20	287	128	0.000336	130	289
41	21	289	152	0.407977	145	282
42	22	282	163	0.160486	130	249
43	23	249	134	0.870038	145	260
44	24	260	156	0.828244	145	249
45	25	249	135	0.487665	145	259
46	26	259	129	0.339607	130	260
47	27	260	158	0.538332	145	247
48	28	247	157	0.342896	130	220
49	29	220	122	0.410711	145	243
50	30	243	161	0.144899	130	212
51	31	212	135	0.620968	145	222
52	32	222	150	0.400549	145	217
53	33	217	121	0.705462	145	241
54	34	241	154	0.917516	150	237
55	35	237	154	0.440085	145	228
56	36	228	145	0.65399	145	228
57	37	228	150	0.690859	145	223
58	38	223	133	0.215306	130	220
59	39	220	152	0.806645	145	213
60	40	213	133	0.888379	145	225
61	41	225	169	0.64761	145	201
62	42	201	138	0.808769	145	200
63	43	208	169	0.483637	145	184
64	44	184	137	0.656824	245	292
65	45	292	132	0.430228	145	305
66	46	305	162	0.97855	150	293
67	47	293	144	0.333229	130	279
68	48	279	149	0.608258	145	275
69	49	275	169	0.759187	145	251
70	50	251	152	0.494741	145	244
71	51	244	125	0.368062	130	249
72	52	249	120	0.285773	130	259
73	53	259	169	0.045702	130	220
74	54	220	125	0.77978	145	240
75	55	240	157	0.580245	145	228
76	56	228	129	0.010025	130	229
77	57	229	150	0.388374	130	209
78	58	209	139	0.88051	145	215
79	59	215	156	0.696096	145	204
80	60	204	134	0.524983	145	215
81	61	215	139	0.876533	145	221
82	62	221	164	0.645827	145	202
83	63	202	140	0.425964	145	207
84	64	207	129	0.715943	145	223
85	65	223	162	0.40074	145	206
86	66	206	131	0.940217	150	225
87	67	225	131	0.268189	130	224
88	68	224	142	0.307214	130	212
89	69	212	137	0.439599	145	220
90	70	220	136	0.353819	130	214
91	71	214	151	0.675555	145	208
92	72	208	122	0.361596	130	216
93	73	216	137	0.522424	145	224
94	74	224	139	0.010967	130	215
95	75	215	135	0.372452	130	210
96	76	210	160	0.61007	145	195
97	77	195	142	0.689029	245	298
98	78	298	145	0.1053	130	283
99	79	283	159	0.898493	145	269
100	80	269	168	0.138843	130	231
101	81	231	146	0.389557	130	215
102	82	215	133	0.703923	145	227
103	83	227	161	0.452284	145	211
104	84	211	146	0.923685	150	215
105	85	215	138	0.761485	145	222
106	86	222	133	0.687217	145	234
107	87	234	122	0.282846	130	242
108	88	242	159	0.360692	130	213
109	89	213	127	0.307614	130	216
110	90	216	123	0.440968	145	238
111	91	238	137	0.487278	145	246
112	92	246	153	0.611427	145	238
113	93	238	133	0.162318	130	235
114	94	235	124	0.825891	145	256
115	95	256	157	0.994659	150	249
116	96	249	131	0.288154	130	248
117	97	248	169	0.213998	130	209
118	98	209	153	0.540287	145	201
119	99	201	150	0.902102	150	201
120	100	201	151	0.834133	145	195
121						
122		Average	143.55		143	240.54

involve keeping track of a lot of information over time. This is exactly what a dynamic simulation model does. We illustrate the process of building and simulating a dynamic model for a much simpler situation: processing customers at a supermarket service desk.

EXAMPLE 2. A DYNAMIC SIMULATION MODEL FOR CUSTOMER SERVICE IMPROVEMENT AT A SUPERMARKET

The front desk manager in a large supermarket provides services, such as one-day picture developing, that are not handled by the cashiers. Customers arrive at

FIGURE 14.2   *Graph of production and ending inventory levels*

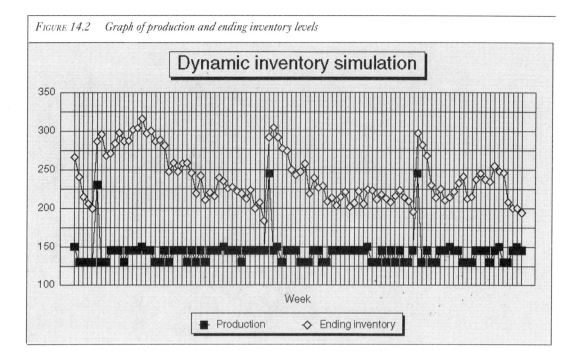

random intervals and may have to wait if another customer is being serviced. Because of problems involving check approvals by the cashiers, the store manager is considering requiring that all checks be approved at the front desk. However, with the addition of this new activity, the store manager is concerned about the length of time that customers must wait and the additional burden put on the front desk manager. Thus, performance measures that we expect from a simulation of this process are the average waiting time per customer and the percentage of time that the front desk manager would spend approving checks.

A conceptual model of this system is shown in Figure 14.3. The system is simple. Customers arrive for service. They wait if the manager is busy. They receive the service and finally leave the system.

The next step in the modeling process is to collect relevant data. From Figure 14.3 we note that we need to know the arrival pattern of customers and the time required for service. Clearly these are probabilistic activities since they will vary from one customer to the next. For arrivals, we could specify either the actual *times* that customers arrive for service or the *times between successive arrivals*. The second approach works better for simulation purposes because we need only know the time that the last customer arrived to generate the arrival time of the next customer.

From an analysis of current service demands at the front desk and check-cashing activities at the cashiers, the manager estimated the following arrival distribution.

FIGURE 14.3   *A conceptual model of a front desk supermarket operation*

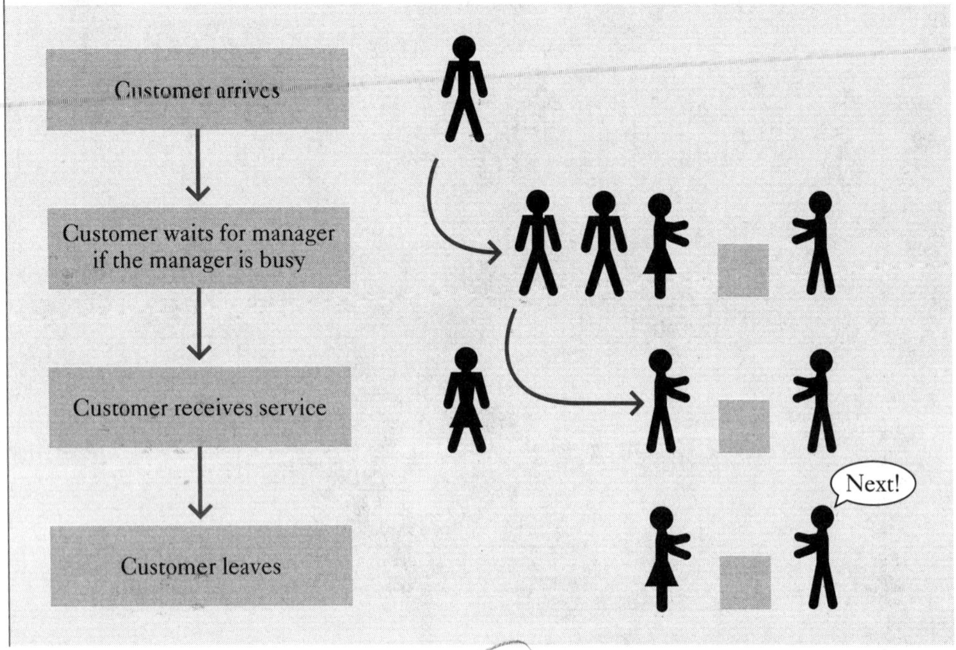

Time between arrivals (seconds)	Probability
20	.4
40	.3
60	.2
80	.1

In addition, the distribution of service times was determined to be the following:

Service time (seconds)	Probability
15	.2
25	.4
35	.3
45	.1

Developing a detailed simulation model requires a bit of logical thought.

A key question to ask in developing any model is this: What do we need to know to compute the performance measures we want?

In this example, we are interested in the *waiting time* of customers and the *idle time* of the front desk manager. We note the following:

1. The waiting time of any customer is equal to the time at which the customer begins service minus the time the customer arrived.
2. The front desk manager is idle if the time at which a customer arrives is *greater* than the time at which the previous customer completed service. The idle time is the difference between these two times.

Thus, to compute the waiting time of a customer we need to know the *time that service begins* and the *arrival time* of the customer. To find the idle time of the manager, we need to know the time that the customer arrives and the *time that the previous customer completed service*. The front desk manager remains busy when a customer arrives if the arrival time is less than the time that the previous customer will complete service.

We now make the following observations:

1. If a customer arrives at time t and the manager is not busy, then that customer can begin service immediately upon arrival.
2. If a customer arrives at time t and the manager is busy, then that customer will begin service at the time that the *previous* customer completes service (which will be greater than t).
3. In either case, the time at which a customer completes service is computed as the time that the customer begins service plus the time it takes to perform the service.

Notice that in this case, unlike Example 1 in which we incremented time by a fixed amount (a week) during the course of the simulation, we move the simulation clock forward to the time at which the next logical event occurs. This type of simulation is called *event-driven*.

EXAMPLE 3. SIMULATING THE SUPERMARKET OPERATION

Figure 14.4 translates these observations into a detailed logical model (simulation flowchart). We may use this flowchart to step through a simulation manually, or as a basis for constructing a spreadsheet or other computer model. We use the following variables:

$$\text{ARRIVAL.TIME}(I) = \text{Arrival time of customer } I$$

$$\text{START.TIME}(I) = \text{Time service for customer } I \text{ is started}$$

$$\text{COMPLETION.TIME}(I) = \text{Time service for customer } I \text{ is completed}$$

$$\text{WAIT.TIME}(I) = \text{Waiting time for customer } I$$

$$\text{IDLETIME} = \text{Idle time incurred by the manager}$$

$$\text{TBA} = \text{Time between arrivals (from previous customer to current customer)}$$

$$\text{ST} = \text{Service time}$$

The two probabilistic elements in this problem are the time between customer arrivals, TBA, and the service time, ST. Using the probability distributions for the arrival and service times, we have the following random number assignments:

FIGURE 14.4   *Simulation flowchart for a supermarket operation*

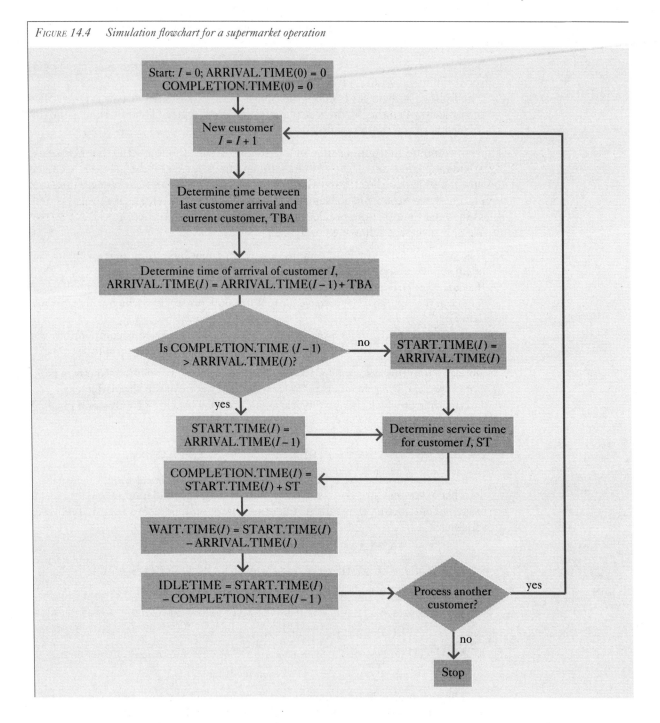

Arrival Distribution Random number interval	Time between arrivals	Service Time Distribution Random number interval	Service time
0–.4	20 seconds	0–.2	15 seconds
.4–.7	40	.2–.6	25
.7–.9	60	.6–.9	35
.9–1.0	80	.9–1.0	45

.953 ⟹ 80 seconds
.563 ⟹ 25 seconds

p. 704

Table 14.1 shows the results for a simulation of 10 customers. The random numbers were chosen from Table 13.1 beginning with row 4 and moving across the rows. Let us walk through the flowchart for the first customer, $I = 1$. The first random number in row 4 is .953; thus TBA = 80, indicating that the first customer arrives to the system at time 80. Since the completion time of customer 0 is defined to be zero to initialize the simulation, the manager is not busy and customer 1 will begin service at its arrival time, 80. The next random number is .563; thus, the service time, ST, is 25. Customer 1 will complete service at time 105 (start time + ST). Since customer 1 did not wait, the waiting time is zero. However, the manager was idle from time 0 until the arrival of the customer, or 80 seconds.

For the ten customers, the total waiting time is 35 seconds. Thus, the average waiting time per customer is $35/10 = 3.5$ seconds. The total idle time for the manager is 215 seconds. Since the length of the simulation is 475 seconds, the percent idle time is $215/475 = 45.2$ percent. The manager can attend to other duties about 45 percent of the time.

Building Dynamic Simulation Models on Spreadsheets

In general, building dynamic simulation models on spreadsheets is difficult to do, particularly for systems that have many interacting elements. For such situations, special-purpose simulation languages, discussed in the next section, are much better. However, for most models that we discuss in this book, spreadsheets can be easily constructed. The following example shows the development of a spreadsheet for the supermarket operation example.

EXAMPLE 4. A SPREADSHEET FOR THE SUPERMARKET SIMULATION

Table 14.1 showed an organization of the input and output data in a spreadsheet format using the logic and equations given in Figure 14.4. We can easily implement this on a spreadsheet as shown in Figure 14.5. The @VLOOKUP function is used to generate the time between arrivals and service times from the arrival distribution and service time distribution tables. The start time for any customer is the maximum of the arrival time and the time of service of the previous customer. This is implemented using the @MAX function. Waiting time is simply the difference between the start time and arrival time; idle time for the server is computed from the arrival time of the current customer and the completion time of the last customer.

TABLE 14.1
Simulation of the
supermarket front
desk operation

Customer	Random number	TBA	Arrival time	Start time	Random number	ST	Completion time	Waiting time	Idle time
1	.953	80	80	80	.563	25	105	0	80
2	.953	80	160	160	.115	15	175	0	55
3	.160	20	180	180	.904	45	225	0	5
4	.058	20	200	225	.052	15	240	25	0
5	.885	60	260	260	.525	25	285	0	20
6	.736	60	320	320	.219	25	345	0	35
7	.383	20	340	340	.525	25	365	5	0
8	.007	20	360	360	.249	25	385	5	0
9	.681	40	400	400	.818	35	435	0	15
10	.572	40	440	440	.763	35	475	0	5

FIGURE 14.5   Spreadsheet implementation of the supermarket operation simulation model

	A	B	C	D	E	F	G	H	I	J
1	SUPERMARKET OPERATION SIMULATION									
2										
3	ARRIVAL DISTRIBUTION				SERVICE TIME DISTRIBUTION					
4	RANDOM NO.	RANGE		TBA	RANDOM NO.	RANGE	ST			
5	0	0.4		20	0	0.2	15			
6	0.4	0.7		40	0.2	0.4	25			
7	0.7	0.9		60	0.4	0.7	35			
8	0.9	1		80	0.7	1	45			
9										
10		RANDOM	TIME BET.	ARRIVAL	START	RANDOM	SERVICE	COMPL.	WAIT	IDLE
11	CUSTOMER	NUMBER	ARRIVALS	TIME	TIME	NUMBER	TIME	TIME	TIME	TIME
12	1	0.085	20	20	20	0.047	15	35	0	20
13	2	0.847	60	80	80	0.693	35	115	0	45
14	3	0.538	40	120	120	0.994	45	165	0	5
15	4	0.172	20	140	165	0.141	15	180	25	0
16	5	0.681	40	180	180	0.780	45	225	0	0
17	6	0.636	40	220	225	0.613	35	260	5	0
18	7	0.342	20	240	260	0.125	15	275	20	0
19	8	0.087	20	260	275	0.633	35	310	15	0
20	9	0.610	40	300	310	0.169	15	325	10	0
21	10	0.269	20	320	325	0.530	35	360	5	0
22										
23								AVERAGE	8	7

Selected cell formulas

	A	B	C	D	E	F	G	H	I	J
3	ARRIVAL DISTRIBUTION				SERVICE TIME DISTRIBUTION					
4	RANDOM NO. RANGE			TBA	RANDOM NO. RANGE		ST			
5	0	0.4		20	0	0.2	15			
6	0.4	0.7		40	0.2	0.4	25			
7	0.7	0.9		60	0.4	0.7	35			
8	0.9	1		80	0.7	1	45			
9										
10		RANDOM		TIME BET.	ARRIVAL	START	RANDOM		SERVICE	COMPL.	WAIT	IDLE
11	CUSTOMER	NUMBER		ARRIVALS	TIME	TIME	NUMBER		TIME	TIME	TIME	TIME
12	1	@RAND	@VLOOKUP(B12,$A$5..$C$8,2)	+C12			@RAND	@VLOOKUP(F12,$E$5..$G$8,2)	+E12+G12	+E12-D12	+E12
13	2	@RAND	@VLOOKUP(B13,$A$5..$C$8,2)	+D12+C13	@MAX(D13,H12)	@RAND	@VLOOKUP(F13,$E$5..$G$8,2)	+E13+G13	+E13-D13	+E13-H12
14	3	@RAND	@VLOOKUP(B14,$A$5..$C$8,2)	+D13+C14	@MAX(D14,H13)	@RAND	@VLOOKUP(F14,$E$5..$G$8,2)	+E14+G14	+E14-D14	+E14-H13
15	4	@RAND	@VLOOKUP(B15,$A$5..$C$8,2)	+D14+C15	@MAX(D15,H14)	@RAND	@VLOOKUP(F15,$E$5..$G$8,2)	+E15+G15	+E15-D15	+E15-H14
16	5	@RAND	@VLOOKUP(B16,$A$5..$C$8,2)	+D15+C16	@MAX(D16,H15)	@RAND	@VLOOKUP(F16,$E$5..$G$8,2)	+E16+G16	+E16-D16	+E16-H15
17	6	@RAND	@VLOOKUP(B17,$A$5..$C$8,2)	+D16+C17	@MAX(D17,H16)	@RAND	@VLOOKUP(F17,$E$5..$G$8,2)	+E17+G17	+E17-D17	+E17-H16
18	7	@RAND	@VLOOKUP(B18,$A$5..$C$8,2)	+D17+C18	@MAX(D18,H17)	@RAND	@VLOOKUP(F18,$E$5..$G$8,2)	+E18+G18	+E18-D18	+E18-H17
19	8	@RAND	@VLOOKUP(B19,$A$5..$C$8,2)	+D18+C19	@MAX(D19,H18)	@RAND	@VLOOKUP(F19,$E$5..$G$8,2)	+E19+G19	+E19-D19	+E19-H18
20	9	@RAND	@VLOOKUP(B20,$A$5..$C$8,2)	+D19+C20	@MAX(D20,H19)	@RAND	@VLOOKUP(F20,$E$5..$G$8,2)	+E20+G20	+E20-D20	+E20-H19
21	10	@RAND	@VLOOKUP(B21,$A$5..$C$8,2)	+D20+C21	@MAX(D21,H20)	@RAND	@VLOOKUP(F21,$E$5..$G$8,2)	+E21+G21	+E21-D21	+E21-H20
22											
23									AVERAGE	@AVG(I12..I21)	@AVG(J12..J21)

COMPUTER IMPLEMENTATION OF SIMULATION MODELS

We may implement simulation models on a computer in one of three basic ways:

1. With a spreadsheet (if appropriate)
2. With a general-purpose programming language
3. With a special-purpose simulation language

The choice depends on the complexity of the model and the user's familiarity with these options. We have used spreadsheets in several examples thus far. In this section, we will discuss the other alternatives.

General-Purpose Programming Languages

If the logical flowchart for a simulation model is written correctly, then it should be rather easy to translate it into a computer programming language. Many simulation models have been written in general-purpose programming languages such as FORTRAN, C, BASIC, and PASCAL. Of course, the developer must be familiar with the particular language and must write a variety of specialized routines for generating stochastic outcomes, computing statistical measures, monitoring simulated time, and so forth. This is one of the drawbacks of using a general-purpose language. Figure 14.6 shows a computer program written in Microsoft QuickBASIC™ for the capital equipment decision problem example in Chapter 13. If you are familiar with any general-purpose computer programming language, the code should be very easy to follow and corresponds to the flowchart in Figure 14.4 quite closely. The only difference is that the code was written to accommodate both scenarios and any number of simulated days. These are specified in the initialization section of the program. The variable SCENARIO is set to 1 for a one-truck scenario, or 2 for a two-truck scenario. DAYS corresponds to the number of days to be simulated.

In a similar fashion, the code for the supermarket operation example developed in Chapter 5 is shown in Figure 14.7. An example of the output generated by this program is given in Figure 14.8.

Special-Purpose Simulation Languages

One of the drawbacks of using a general-purpose programming language for simulation is that the programmer must include all the details for file management, advancing time, computing statistics, and so on. Most computer simulation programs have many elements in common. These include generating random numbers, collecting statistical information, producing summary reports, and advancing the simulation clock in dynamic situations. It would be foolish to attempt to write a computer program from scratch for each new simulation problem. Special-purpose *simulation languages* have been developed that automatically take care of many details of simulation calculations and reporting, thus allowing the user to concentrate on the modeling process itself. Programs written in a simulation language are much more compact than those in a general-purpose language. Modern

---

FIGURE 14.6   Microsoft QuickBasic program for the capital equipment decision example

```
'SIMULATION PROGRAM FOR TRUCK DECISION PROBLEM

'initialize variables
CLS
TC = 0
D = 1
SCENARIO = 1 'set SCENARIO = 2 for 2 trucks
DAYS = 10 'DAYS = number of simulated days
PRINT "DAY R.N. N DC TC"
RANDOMIZE TIMER
FOR D = 1 TO DAYS
'Begin new day

'Generate random number and determine number of trucks
R = RND(1)
IF R < .55 THEN N = 1
IF R >= .55 AND R < .85 THEN N = 2
IF R >= .85 THEN N = 3

'Compute daily cost, total cost, and print summary
IF SCENARIO = 1 THEN
DC = 100 + 150 * (N − 1)
END IF

IF SCENARIO = 2 THEN
IF N <= 2 THEN DC = 220
IF N = 3 THEN DC = 370
END IF
```

```
            TC = TC + DC
            PRINT USING ' ### .### ## ### ####'; D; R; N; DC; TC

            NEXT D

            'Compute average cost and print results
            AC = TC / DAYS
            PRINT "NUMBER OF DAYS SIMULATED = "; DAYS
            PRINT "AVERAGE DAILY COST = "; AC
            END
```

FIGURE 14.7   Microsoft QuickBasic program for the supermarket operation example

```
'SIMULATION PROGRAM FOR SUPERMARKET OPERATION
DIM ARRIVAL.TIME(1000), COMPLETION.TIME(1000), START.TIME(1000), WAIT.TIME(1000)
'Initialize variables
CLS
NCUSTOMERS = 20 'NCUSTOMERS = number of simulated customers
ARRIVAL.TIME(0) = 0
COMPLETION.TIME(0) = 0
TOTAL.IDLE.TIME = 0
TOTAL.WAITING.TIME = 0
RANDOMIZE TIMER
PRINT "CUST. R.N. TBA ARR START R.N. ST COMP WAIT IDLE"
'Simulate the arrival of a new customer
FOR I = 1 TO NCUSTOMERS
'Generate random number and determine time between arrivals
R1 = RND(1)
IF R1 < .4 THEN TBA = 20
IF R1 >= .4 AND R1 < .3 THEN TBA = 40
IF R1 >= .7 AND R1 < .9 THEN TBA = 60
IF R1 >= .9 THEN TBA = 80
'Compute arrival time, completion time, and start time
ARRIVAL.TIME(I) = ARRIVAL.TIME(I − 1) + TBA
IF COMPLETION.TIME(I − 1) > ARRIVAL.TIME(I) THEN
    START.TIME(I) = COMPLETION.TIME(I − 1)
ELSE
    START.TIME(I) = ARRIVAL.TIME(I)
END IF
'Generate random number and determine service time
R2 = RND(1)
IF R2 < .2 THEN ST = .15
IF R2 >= .2 AND R2 < .6 THEN ST = 25
```

```
IF R2 >= .6 AND R2 < .9 THEN ST = 35
IF R2 >= .9 THEN ST = 45
'Compute completion time, waiting time, and idle time, and print summary
COMPLETION.TIME(I) = START.TIME(I) + ST
WAIT.TIME(I) = START.TIME(I) - COMPLETION.TIME(I - 1)
PRINT USING "### .### ## #### #### .### ## #####";
    I; R1; TBA; ARRIVAL.TIME(I); START.TIME(I); R2; ST; COMPLETION.TIME(I);
PRINT USING "### ###"; WAIT.TIME(I); IDLETIME
'Accumulate total idle time and total waiting time
TOTAL.IDLE.TIME = TOTAL.IDLE.TIME + IDLETIME
TOTAL.WAITING.TIME = TOTAL.WAITING.TIME + WAIT.TIME(I)
NEXT I
'Compute and print summary statistics
PERCENT.IDLETIME = 100 * TOTAL.IDLE.TIME / COMPLETION.TIME(NCUSTOMERS)
AVERAGE.WAITING.TIME = TOTAL.WAITING.TIME / NCUSTOMERS
PRINT "AVERAGE WAITING TIME PER CUSTOMER = "; AVERAGE.WAITING.TIME
PRINT "PERCENT IDLE TIME = "; PERCENT.IDLETIME
END
```

FIGURE 14.8   Example output for the supermarket operation example

CUST.	R.N.	TBA	ARR	START	R.N.	ST	COMP	WAIT	IDLE
1	.634	0	0	0	.983	45	45	0	0
2	.527	0	0	45	.556	25	70	45	0
3	.174	20	20	70	.142	15	85	50	0
4	.958	80	100	100	.787	35	135	0	15
5	.158	20	120	135	.412	25	160	15	0
6	.733	60	180	180	.961	45	225	0	20
7	.393	20	200	225	.685	35	260	25	0
8	.237	20	220	260	.730	35	295	40	0
9	.490	20	240	295	.435	25	320	55	0
10	.111	20	260	320	.989	45	365	60	0
11	.322	20	280	365	.360	25	390	85	0
12	.321	20	300	390	.649	35	425	90	0
13	.722	60	360	425	.274	25	450	65	0
14	.493	60	420	450	.647	35	485	30	0
15	.437	60	480	485	.243	25	510	5	0
16	.486	60	540	540	.216	25	565	0	30
17	.336	20	560	565	.981	45	610	5	0
18	.224	20	580	610	.398	25	635	30	0
19	.855	60	640	640	.486	25	665	0	5
20	.772	60	700	700	.808	35	735	0	35

AVERAGE WAITING TIME PER CUSTOMER = 30
PERCENT IDLE TIME = 14.28571

languages have database capabilities that provide sophisticated data analysis and reporting, graphical report displays (bar charts, pie charts, and histograms), and even animation to allow users to observe the dynamics of a simulation in progress. Among the most popular languages are SLAM (Simulation Language for Alternative Modeling), SIMAN, GPSS (General Purpose Systems Simulator), and SIMSCRIPT. These languages provide the basic building blocks to simulate nearly any type of situation. We will briefly describe some of the features of the SLAM language.

SLAM models are built by combining *network symbols* that perform certain logic operations to model the system being studied. An example of a SLAM network model and associated computer code for the supermarket operation example are shown in Figure 14.9. The network consists of four basic elements: a CREATE node that generates customer arrivals to the system according to the probability distribution specified for the time between arrivals (a variable called DPROBN—Discrete PROBability distributioN). Customers go to a QUEUE node, where they wait for service. The QUEUE node is followed by a SERVICE ACTIVITY, with service time given by another discrete probability distribution. The numbers below the service activity indicate that there is one server and provide a number to the activity that is used in the output report.

All the logic required to keep track of waiting customers, their times of arrival, start and completion of service, and status of the server are built into the QUEUE node and SERVICE ACTIVITY symbols. You can see how a simulation language takes much of the programming burden away from the user. Finally, the TERMINATE node "destroys" the customer; that is, customers leave the system. The value of 100 in this node means that the simulation will stop after 100 customers have been processed. You can see that the network corresponds to the conceptual model shown in Figure 14.3.

The graphical network modeling approach is one of the advantages to using SLAM; in most cases, the logical flow of customers or other objects through the network is similar

---

Figure 14.9   SLAM network model and computer statements for the supermarket example

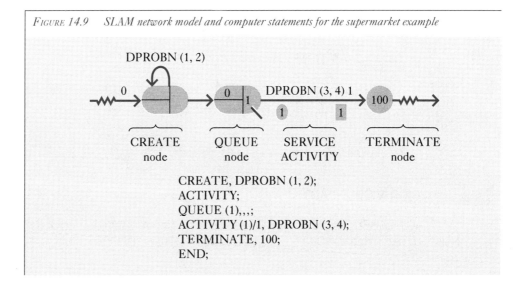

```
CREATE, DPROBN (1, 2);
ACTIVITY;
QUEUE (1),,,;
ACTIVITY (1)/1, DPROBN (3, 4);
TERMINATE, 100;
END;
```

to the flow in the actual system. This makes the network a good communication vehicle between the end user and the simulation analyst. Using the SLAMSYSTEM software package, which runs in a Microsoft Windows environment on a PC, the user can build the network graphically on the computer with a mouse, and the software actually creates the computer code automatically from the network model. No programming is necessary!

Figure 14.10 shows the output generated from running the SLAM model. We will discuss a few key parts of the output. CURRENT TIME tells us that the simulation ended after 4,085 seconds (the time at which the 100th customer completed service). Under "File Statistics," line 1 for QUEUE tells us that on the average, .181 customers waited in line; the maximum number waiting was 2; and the average waiting time was 7.4 seconds. Under "Service Activity Statistics," we see that the average utilization of the front desk manager was .681. This represents the fraction of time spent servicing customers. The longest time the server was idle was 65 seconds, and the longest time the server was busy was 225 seconds.

SLAM, GPSS, SIMSCRIPT, and other simulation languages are widely used in business and industry. Although they require some startup time to learn, they make it easy to model and analyze very complex systems that would be difficult or impossible to simulate with general-purpose languages or spreadsheets.

FIGURE 14.10   *SLAM simulation output for the model in Figure 14.8*

SLAM II SUMMARY REPORT

SIMULATION PROJECT SUPERMARKET   BY EVANS J.

DATE 1/ 1/1995   RUN   NUMBER   1   OF   1

CURRENT TIME   .4085E+04
STATISTICAL ARRAYS CLEARED AT TIME   .0000E+00

FILE STATISTICS

FILE NUMBER	AVERAGE LABEL/TYPE	STANDARD LENGTH	MAXIMUM DEVIATION	CURRENT LENGTH	AVERAGE LENGTH	WAIT TIME
1	QUEUE	.181	.427	2	0	7.400
2	CALENDAR	1.681	.466	3	1	19.956

SERVICE   ACTIVITY   STATISTICS

ACT NUM	ACT LABEL OR START NODE	SER CAP	AVERAGE UTIL	STD DEV	CUR UTIL	AVERAGE BLOCK	MAX IDL TME/SER	MAX BSY TIME/SER	ENT CNT
1	QUEUE	1	.681	.47	0	.00	65.00	225.00	100

Simulators[1]

A *simulator* is a parameter-driven simulation that requires no programming. The user need only input a set of data that describes the system; the programs prompt users for the required information. Most simulators have been developed for specific applications, such as manufacturing, network communications, nuclear power plant analysis, and cardiovascular physiology. Among the popular manufacturing simulators are SIMFACTORY II.5, XCELL+, WITNESS, and ProModelPC. Because of their narrow scope, some simulators require the analyst to make some crucial approximations in modeling the real system.

To create a simulation model using a simulator, one must select several basic features of the system being modeled. For example, in manufacturing, one must consider the following:

- The types of parts moving through the system
- The types of stations (machines, palletizers, inspection sites) in the system
- The capacity of the stations
- The processing time of the parts in each station
- The routing of parts through the system
- The scheduling of part arrivals

Other characteristics that may be included are machine downtime, labor requirements, and material handling equipment.

Simulators provide graphical, animated models of the system. Figure 14.11 shows a typical simulator's animation capability. In this situation, parts are produced in a continuous

---

FIGURE 14.11   Simulator animation

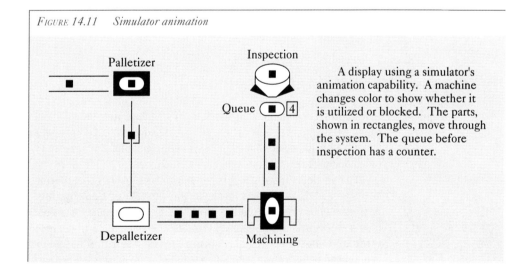

A display using a simulator's animation capability. A machine changes color to show whether it is utilized or blocked. The parts, shown in rectangles, move through the system. The queue before inspection has a counter.

---

[1] Adapted from Banks, J. *et al.*, "The Simulator: New Member of the Simulation Family." *Interfaces*, Vol. 21, No. 2, March–April, 1992, pp. 76–86.

fashion and flow by conveyor to a palletizer. The palletizer station loads parts onto a pallet to be moved by a transporter. The parts are then depalletized at the next station. They then go to an automated machining center. From the machining center, parts are transported by conveyor to an inspection station. In the animation of the simulation, a machine changes color to show whether it is running or idle. The parts, shown as rectangles, move through the system on the computer screen. The queue before the inspection station has a counter displaying the number of parts waiting. The user can control the speed of animation and zoom in on a particular segment of the animation.

Table 14.2 summarizes the various features among four different manufacturing simulators. Basic features are needed to model any realistic manufacturing system that requires material handling. The *routes* feature allows the modeler to enter the path that parts will follow; the *schedules* feature to enter the processing time of parts on different machines, the interarrival distribution of parts, and other time-related characteristics; and the *capacities* feature to enter the number of parts that can be processed at any time. Using the *downtimes* feature, the modeler can incorporate the possibility of machine breakdowns; the *transporters* feature includes a wide variety of material handling equipment such as automated guided vehicles or forklifts; and the *conveyors* feature allows for different types of equipment such as belt conveyors, roller conveyors, and towlines.

In the *robust features* section, *programming* refers to the ability to incorporate special characteristics into the model, and *conditional routing* refers to the ability to send parts to different locations depending on conditions such as whether a machine is up or down. *Global variables* are information such as the number of parts completed that are available to all parts of the simulation and can be used, for example, as criteria in conditional routing. With an interface to other software, the modeler can incorporate logic written in another language. The last section, *Qualitative Considerations*, compares important features relevant to the user. As you can see, simulators can provide a powerful tool for simulating a wide variety of problems.

VERIFICATION AND VALIDATION

In Chapter 1 we stated that models are only approximations to reality. Users of management science models have the right to be skeptical of a model's predictions. A challenging task is to build an accurate model and convince the end user that the model is a valid representation of the real system under study.

Two important considerations when dealing with simulation models are verification and validation. *Verification* refers to the process of determining if a simulation program performs as intended. In other words, have we correctly translated the conceptual model into a working simulation program? Is the computer implementation free from logical errors and bugs? *Validation* is concerned with determining whether the conceptual model is an accurate representation of the real system under investigation.

Several verification techniques exist; many of these are the same used by programmers in writing and debugging computer code. For example, care in developing the logical flowchart will help to minimize logical errors. It is often easier to conceptualize the

TABLE 14.2
Manufacturing simulator
feature summary
(Source: Banks et al. 1992)

Basic Features	SIMFACTORY	XCELL+	WITNESS	ProModelPC
Routes	Yes	Yes	Yes	Yes
Schedules	Yes	Yes	Yes	Yes
Capacities	Yes	Yes	Yes	Yes
Downtimes	Yes	No	Yes	Yes
Transporters	Yes	Build*	Yes	Yes
Conveyors	Yes	Build*	Yes	Yes
Robust Features	**SIMFACTORY**	**XCELL+**	**WITNESS**	**ProModelPC**
Programming	No	No	Possible	Some**
Conditional Routing	No	No	Yes	Yes
Part Attributes	No	No	Yes	Yes
Global Variables	No	No	Yes	Yes
Interface to Other Software	No	No	Yes	No
Qualitative Considerations	**SIMFACTORY**	**XCELL+**	**WITNESS**	**ProModelPC**
Easy to Use	Yes	Yes	Yes	Yes
Easy to Learn	Yes	No	No	No
High Quality Interface	Yes	No	Yes	Yes
Quality Documentation	Yes	No	Yes	No
High Quality Animation	Yes	No	Yes	Yes
Standard Output Reports	Yes	Yes	Yes	Yes
On-Line Help	Yes	Yes	Yes	Yes
Compilation/Run Time Warnings	Yes	Yes	Yes	Yes
System Trace	Yes	***	Yes	Yes
Special Constructs	**SIMFACTORY**	**XCELL+**	**WITNESS**	**ProModelPC**
Robots	No	No	No	Yes
Cranes	No	No	No	Yes
	SIMFACTORY	**XCELL+**	**WITNESS**	**ProModelPC**
Cost	$15,000	$8,000	$25,000	$1,500– $7,000#

*Must be constructed from available elements.

**To attain maximum utilization of the simulator beyond basic concepts.

***By stepping through the animation.

Price dependent on the number of operations purchased.

problem in smaller pieces, or modules, and write the computer code in modules that can be linked together. The code can be checked by someone other than the programmer. The outputs from the model should also be studied for reasonableness. Sometimes some simple analytical results can be used for comparison. We did this with the capital equipment decision problem. Had the results been far from the expected results, we might have suspected a programming error. Modern simulation languages have built-in tools to assist in verifying the correctness of a program.

The purpose of simulation modeling is to be able to make decisions about the system that are similar to those that would be made if you were experimenting with the real system. Validation typically consists of three steps:

1. Develop a model with high face validity.
2. Validate model assumptions.
3. Validate model output.

The model should seem reasonable to those who understand the real system. This is called *face validity* and is important in gaining acceptance from the users of the model. Face validity can be strengthened by maintaining good communication with the user during the model development stages. Successful simulation models are usually the result of team efforts involving managers, engineers, and workers involved in the system.

The more complex a system is, the harder it is to validate. Many assumptions are made in simulation models, particularly in regard to the probability distributions used to drive the simulation and behavior of system entities. Thus the probability distributions used to describe probabilistic elements of a simulation should be validated by comparing them with actual data from the system. Similarly, assumptions made regarding the behavior of customers, service personnel, and so on must have a rational basis.

The most objective and scientific means of validation is to compare the output of the model with data from the real system for the same inputs. The idea is to match as closely as possible the inputs used in the real system and the inputs used in the model. The system outputs should closely approximate the model outputs.

One should always remember that a real system constantly changes; thus, validation is never really finished. Data need to be periodically updated and the model needs to be retested.

MANAGEMENT SCIENCE PRACTICE

In this section we describe some of the issues involved in developing the simulation model for Tinker Air Force Base that we introduced in the opening scenario. This is an excellent example because it involves everything from collecting data to validation.

Designing an Air Force Repair Center Using Simulation[2]

Tinker Air Force Base is one of five overhaul bases in the Air Force Logistics Command. It overhauls and repairs six types of jet engines and various aircraft and engine

---

[2]Adaptation from Ravindran *et al.*, "An Application of Simulation and Network Analysis to Capacity Planning and Material Handling Systems at Tinker Air Force Base, *Interfaces*, Vol. 19, No. 1, Jan–Feb, 1989, pp. 102–115.

accessories, and it manages selected Air Force assets worldwide. Engines are received for periodic overhaul or modification. The engine is disassembled, and each part is inspected for wear and possible repair. Individual parts are repaired or replaced with new parts. The majority of parts are overhauled and returned to service for a fraction of the cost of a new part.

In 1984 a fire devastated one building at the base. The Air Force requested assistance to develop a simulation of the engine overhaul process to assist in redesign and layout of approximately 900,000 square feet of production floor space. A team from the University of Oklahoma received the contract.

Objectives of the study included a means to predict and forecast varying resource requirements as workload mixes changed. The baseline database consisted of 117 fields with over 2,500 records and provided information on each engine part, the annual requirement of each end item, the sequential routes of the part and machine/process time requirements, size and weight of the part (for storage estimation), and number of units per assembly required of each part.

The simulation model, called TIPS—Tinker Integrated Planning Simulation—was written in the SLAM language. The model included a three-shift operation; transfers to other operations such as painting, plating, and heat treatment; and storage facilities. The model included sick leave, training leave, and vacations for machine operators. Several assumptions had to be made because no data on arrival times of engines were available. Arrivals were assumed to be deterministic, based on the annual volume of demand.

The model was so large that it exceeded the computer storage limitations of the SLAM language. The team needed the assistance of Pritsker & Associates, developers of SLAM, to extend the software's storage capabilities. The model integrated both machine and labor resources to support bottleneck analysis, space analysis, and conveyor-routing analysis. They designed the model for *managers* and held two training sessions at the base to allow managers to use TIPS for decision making.

To ensure that the model worked correctly, the team developed it incrementally, which made debugging the programs easier. They also analyzed the outputs of each model component for reasonableness and consistency. To validate the model, they made a diagnostic check of how closely the simulation matched the actual system by cross-checking model assumptions and comparing results statistically to actual historical data.

The simulation output consisted of the standard SLAM summary report (similar to Figure 14.10) and a custom report at a level of detail suitable for prompt managerial decision making. The statistics in the output included the following:

- Machine availability by shift for each process
- Maximum number of waiting jobs in front of each process
- Average processing time
- Average waiting time for each process
- Number of units of each type entering and leaving the system
- Time spent in storage waiting for a specific process
- Utilization level of each process per shift
- Total time in the system including waiting, handling, and processing

The TIPS program proved valuable in aiding the transition to the new layout by estimating performance measures that helped determine the number of machines of each type to have in the facility. In one particular instance, the Production and Engineering Department called for 24 workstations of a certain type. The simulation model indicated that between 11 and 13 workstations were needed. As a result, only 12 workstations were installed, and this has proved to be sufficient.

Discussion Questions

1. Under what conditions would it be reasonable at assume that engines arrived at the facility in a deterministic fashion?
2. How might the managers use the output information to make decisions on the facility design?
3. The data for the simulation consisted of over 250,000 elements. How might the team verify the accuracy of the input data?

MORE EXAMPLES AND SOLVED PROBLEMS

EXAMPLE 5. A SIMULATION MODEL OF A CONTINUOUS REVIEW INVENTORY SYSTEM

In Chapter 3 we developed a total cost model of a continuous review inventory system and discussed the economic order quantity. That model assumed a constant demand rate, a constant lead time, and no back orders. In realistic situations, neither the demand nor the lead time will be constant and back orders may accumulate. Simulation provides a convenient way of evaluating the impact of different ordering policies. The decision maker can choose specific combinations of the order quantity Q and reorder point r and compare the costs of operating the inventory system under these different policies. We would like to develop a simulation model for such a situation.

The flowchart in Figure 3.2 provides a conceptual model of the process. We need to translate this into a more detailed, logical model. This is shown in Figure 14.12. We begin each day by determining if any orders will arrive, assuming that all orders arrive at the beginning of the day. If the current level of back orders is zero, then the stock level is increased by the amount of the order, Q. If back orders have accumulated, we subtract Q from the current level of back orders. If the result is still positive, this means that we still have no inventory in stock and are carrying back orders until the next order arrives. If the result is negative, it means that we have filled all back orders and have some stock remaining. (Notice that in the box with "Stock = Stock − Back order," a negative value for back order will yield a positive level of stock.)

Next we generate the demand D for that day and decrease the inventory position by D. If the position is at or below the reorder point r, we place an order by increasing the position by Q and generating the lead time. If we have sufficient stock to meet the demand, we decrease the stock level by D. If not, the stock level drops to zero and the number of back orders increases by the difference. This completes the operation of the system for one day.

FIGURE 14.12   Simulation model of a continuous review inventory system

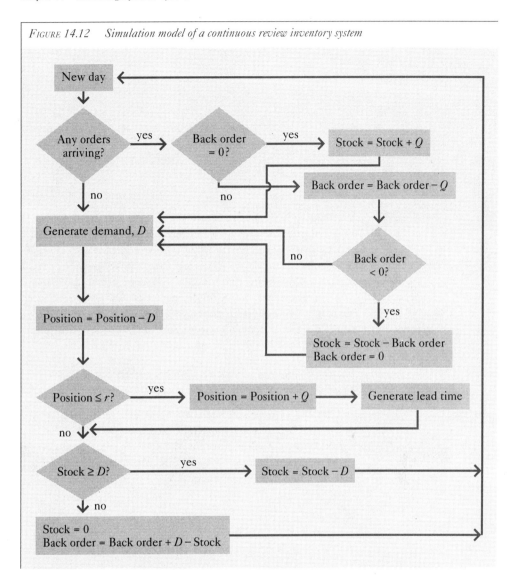

Figure 14.13 shows the results of simulating this system for 10 days using the following initial values and probability distributions:

Stock = 10
Position = 10
Back order = 0
Q = 7
r = 5

Demand	Probability	Random number range
1	.4	0–.4
2	.3	.4–.7
3	.2	.7–.9
4	.1	.9–1.0

Lead time	Probability	Random number range
1	.3	0–.3
2	.5	.3–.8
3	.2	.8–1.0

We used Table 13.1 to generate the random numbers. At the end of the simulation, we may compute the average stock level, average number of back orders, and number of orders. In this case, we find that the average stock level was 6.0, no back orders were accumulated, and three orders were placed. We could use this information to compute the cost of operating the inventory system. If we feel, for instance, that the average stock level is too high, we might reduce Q. Or if we feel that the order cost is too high, we might decrease r (of course, we would run the risk of incurring back orders). We could run the simulation with new values to determine the effects of these changes and move toward the best solution.

EXAMPLE 6. ANALYZING MULTIPLE RUNS OF THE SUPERMARKET OPERATION EXAMPLE

In Chapter 13 we discussed the importance of making replications of simulation experiments. We may use the same statistical approaches for analyzing the results of dynamic models. To illustrate this, the supermarket operation simulation was replicated six times with 20 customers. The results are given in Table 14.3. What conclusions can you draw from these data?

FIGURE 14.13   *Simulation of 10 days for a continuous review inventory system*

Day	Arrival?	R.N.	D	Stock	Back order	Position	Order?	R.N.	Lead time	Arrival time
Start				10	0	10				
1	N	.426	2	8	0	8	N			
2	N	.332	1	7	0	7	N			
3	N	.634	2	5	0	5	Y	.742	2	5
4	N	.826	3	2	0	9	N			
5	Y	.406	2	7	0	7	N			
6	N	.514	2	5	0	5	Y	.924	3	9
7	N	.698	2	3	0	10	N			
8	N	.502	2	1	0	8	N			
9	Y	.062	1	7	0	7	N			
10	N	.491	2	5	0	5	Y	.717	2	12

TABLE 14.3
Results of six replica-
tions of the supermar-
ket simulation

Run	Average waiting time per customer	Percent idle time
1	10.50	38.99
2	3.76	54.87
3	89.33	0.00
4	5.52	57.99
5	3.00	51.42
6	12.25	25.49

The average and standard deviation for the waiting time and percent idle time are as follows:

	Waiting time	Percent idle time
Average	20.73	38.13
Std. dev.	33.81	22.21

We see that there is considerable variability in these output measures. A 95 percent confidence interval is given by

$$x \pm t_{5,.025} \frac{s}{\sqrt{6}}$$

For the waiting time we have

$$20.73 \pm 2.57 \left(\frac{33.81}{\sqrt{6}}\right) \quad \text{or} \quad (-14.74, 56.20)$$

(Note that the physical lower limit is zero.) For percent idle time we have

$$38.13 \pm 2.57 \left(\frac{22.21}{\sqrt{6}}\right) \quad \text{or} \quad (14.83, 61.43)$$

From these computations, we might conclude that the risks of long waiting times for customers might be too high. Modifications of the system might be considered to reduce this risk.

EXAMPLE 7. A SIMULATION MODEL FOR TOOL REPLACEMENT POLICIES [3]

A manager is considering changing the replacement policy for three drill bits in a single drill press on the shop floor. The present policy is to replace a drill bit when it breaks or becomes inoperable. One of the supervisors recommended that a new policy be used in which all three drill bits are replaced when any one bit breaks or

---

[3] Adapted from Larry W. Cornwell and Doan T. Modianos, "Management Tool: Using Spreadsheets for Simulation Models," *Production and Inventory Management Journal*, Vol. 31, No. 3, Third Quarter 1990, 7–17.

needs replacement. It costs $100 each time the drill press must be shut down. A drill bit costs $50, and the variable cost of replacing a drill bit is $10 per bit.

The company that supplies the drill bits has historical evidence that the reliability of a single drill bit is described by an exponential probability distribution with the mean number of failures per hour equal to 0.01. The company would like to compare the cost of the two replacement policies.

We shall develop a simulation model for the current policy in which each bit is replaced as it fails. Analysis of the proposed policy will be left as an exercise. Because each bit is replaced as it fails, we can simulate each drill bit independently. We need to simulate the time at which each drill bit will fail and compute the replacement cost ($160 per replacement). This can be done easily on a spreadsheet. We need to be able to generate outcomes from an exponential probability distribution. As discussed earlier in Chapter 13, to generate a random outcome from an exponential probability distribution with mean μ, we use the formula

$$E = -\mu \ln(R)$$

Therefore, if the mean time between failures is 100 hours, we may generate outcomes from an exponential distribution using the formula $-100 \ln(R)$, where R is a random number. We must use a new random number each time we apply this formula.

Figure 14.14 shows a spreadsheet model for this example. We simulated 20 failures for each drill bit. In row 26 we compute the average cost per unit time. For example, for drill bit 1 the average cost per unit time is

$$\frac{\$3,200}{1,674.18 \text{ hours}} = \$1.91$$

For all three drill bits, the total running time was 5,679.32 hours and the total replacement cost was $9,600. Therefore, the average cost per unit time for the system is $9,600/5,679.32 = \$1.69$. We can compare this with the alternative policy of replacing all three bits when any one of them fails.

SUMMARY

Dynamic simulation models involve the passage of time. To develop and implement a dynamic model, we need to have a simulation "clock" to trace the occurrence of events over time and record relevant information to compute performance measures.

Implementing simulation models requires basic logical ability to develop the appropriate computer code. Spreadsheets and special-purpose simulation languages have a variety of features that simplify the process of implementing simulation models. Although our orientation is biased toward spreadsheet implementation, we advise you to investigate alternatives should you begin to use simulation frequently in practice.

Any simulation model requires verification of input data and validation of results. Without them, there is no assurance that the model will provide any useful information for decision making.

FIGURE 14.14   Spreadsheet model for individual drill bit replacement

	A	B	C	D	E	F	G	H	I	J	K	L	M	N	O
1	Drill Bit Replacement Simulation Model														
2															
3	Drill Bit 1					Drill Bit 2					Drill Bit 3				
4	Time	R.N.	Running Time	Time of Failure	Total Cost	Time	R.N.	Running Time	Time of Failure	Total Cost	Time	R.N.	Running tim	Time of Failure	Total Cost
5	0.00	0.44	81.92	81.92	$160.00	0.00	0.64	44.98	44.98	$160.00	0.00	0.31	117.83	117.83	$160.00
6	81.92	0.62	48.19	130.11	$320.00	44.98	0.64	43.97	88.96	$320.00	117.83	0.36	103.23	221.05	$320.00
7	130.11	0.69	37.50	167.61	$480.00	88.96	0.12	208.37	297.32	$480.00	221.05	0.90	10.11	231.16	$480.00
8	167.61	0.64	44.79	212.40	$640.00	297.32	0.02	403.36	700.68	$640.00	231.16	0.35	103.85	335.01	$640.00
9	212.40	0.99	0.60	212.99	$800.00	700.68	0.67	40.09	740.77	$800.00	335.01	0.54	60.89	395.90	$800.00
10	212.99	0.28	126.42	339.41	$960.00	740.77	0.54	61.29	802.06	$960.00	395.90	0.03	349.90	745.79	$960.00
11	339.41	0.31	115.92	455.34	$1,120.00	802.06	0.95	5.61	807.67	$1,120.00	745.79	0.05	300.13	1045.92	$1,120.00
12	455.34	0.82	19.47	474.80	$1,280.00	807.67	0.85	16.53	824.21	$1,280.00	1045.92	0.70	36.17	1082.10	$1,280.00
13	474.80	0.01	425.22	900.02	$1,440.00	824.21	0.66	41.37	865.58	$1,440.00	1082.10	0.43	84.46	1166.55	$1,440.00
14	900.02	0.22	150.18	1050.20	$1,600.00	865.58	0.48	72.43	938.01	$1,600.00	1166.55	0.73	31.78	1198.33	$1,600.00
15	1050.20	0.52	64.97	1115.16	$1,760.00	938.01	0.34	107.29	1045.30	$1,760.00	1198.33	0.75	29.17	1227.50	$1,760.00
16	1115.16	0.91	9.13	1124.30	$1,920.00	1045.30	0.41	88.11	1133.41	$1,920.00	1227.50	0.51	66.85	1294.35	$1,920.00
17	1124.30	0.22	151.89	1276.18	$2,080.00	1133.41	0.36	102.48	1235.89	$2,080.00	1294.35	0.05	303.55	1597.90	$2,080.00
18	1276.18	0.97	2.81	1279.00	$2,240.00	1235.89	0.54	61.10	1297.00	$2,240.00	1597.90	0.60	51.77	1649.68	$2,240.00
19	1279.00	0.57	55.82	1334.82	$2,400.00	1297.00	0.72	33.45	1330.45	$2,400.00	1649.68	0.74	30.33	1680.01	$2,400.00
20	1334.82	0.36	102.38	1437.20	$2,560.00	1330.45	0.18	172.31	1502.76	$2,560.00	1680.01	0.31	118.02	1798.03	$2,560.00
21	1437.20	0.62	48.55	1485.75	$2,720.00	1502.76	0.17	178.91	1681.67	$2,720.00	1798.03	0.53	63.30	1861.33	$2,720.00
22	1485.75	0.73	31.88	1517.63	$2,880.00	1681.67	0.57	56.88	1738.55	$2,880.00	1861.33	0.68	38.42	1899.75	$2,880.00
23	1517.63	0.93	7.64	1525.27	$3,040.00	1738.55	0.52	65.47	1804.02	$3,040.00	1899.74	0.65	42.83	1942.57	$3,040.00
24	1525.27	0.23	148.91	1674.18	$3,200.00	1804.02	0.09	237.14	2041.16	$3,200.00	1942.57	0.81	21.41	1963.98	$3,200.00
25															
26				Average	$1.91				Average	$1.57				Average	$1.63

Selected cell formulas

	A	B	C	D	E	F	G	H	I	J	K	L	M	N	O
3	Drill Bit 1					Drill Bit 2					Drill Bit 3				
4	Time	R.N.	Running Time	Time of Failure	Total Cost	Time	R.N.	Running Time	Time of Failure	Total Cost	Time	R.N.	Running time	Time of Failure	Total Cost
5	0.00	@RAND	-100*@LN(B5)	+A5+C5	160	0	@RAND	-100*@LN(G5)	+F5+H5	160	0	@RAND	-100*@LN(L5)	+K5+M5	160
6	+D5	@RAND	-100*@LN(B6)	+A6+C6	+E5+160	+I5	@RAND	-100*@LN(G6)	+F6+H6	+J5+160	+N5	@RAND	-100*@LN(L6)	+K6+M6	+O5+160
7	+D6	@RAND	-100*@LN(B7)	+A7+C7	+E6+160	+I6	@RAND	-100*@LN(G7)	+F7+H7	+J6+160	+N6	@RAND	-100*@LN(L7)	+K7+M7	+O6+160
8	+D7	@RAND	-100*@LN(B8)	+A8+C8	+E7+160	+I7	@RAND	-100*@LN(G8)	+F8+H8	+J7+160	+N7	@RAND	-100*@LN(L8)	+K8+M8	+O7+160
9	+D8	@RAND	-100*@LN(B9)	+A9+C9	+E8+160	+I8	@RAND	-100*@LN(G9)	+F9+H9	+J8+160	+N8	@RAND	-100*@LN(L9)	+K9+M9	+O8+160
10	+D9	@RAND	-100*@LN(B10)	+A10+C10	+E9+160	+I9	@RAND	-100*@LN(G10)	+F10+H10	+J9+160	+N9	@RAND	-100*@LN(L10)	+K10+M10	+O9+160
11	+D10	@RAND	-100*@LN(B11)	+A11+C11	+E10+160	+I10	@RAND	-100*@LN(G11)	+F11+H11	+J10+160	+N10	@RAND	-100*@LN(L11)	+K11+M11	+O10+160

CHAPTER REVIEW EXERCISE

I. Terms to Understand

a.   Dynamic simulation model (p. 752)

b.   Event-driven (p. 757)

c.   Simulation language (p. 762)

d.   Simulator (p. 767)

e.   Verification (p. 768)

f.   Validation (p. 768)

g.   Face validity (p. 770)

II. Discussion Questions

1. Explain the differences between static and dynamic simulation models.
2. Describe a general approach for developing a conceptual model for a dynamic simulation model.
3. Explain the three principal ways of implementing simulation models on a computer.
4. What are the advantages and drawbacks with using (a) general-purpose computer programming languages, (b) spreadsheets, and (c) special-purpose simulation languages to implement computer simulation models?
5. Describe some of the features of a simulation language such as SLAM.

6. Why are simulators used? What advantages do they offer over other means of simulation modeling and analysis?
7. Explain the difference between verification and validation. Can these concepts apply to other approaches in management science besides simulation?
8. Discuss some ways in which simulation models can be validated.

III. Problems

1. Complete the following table:

Customer	Arrival time	Processing time	Start	End	Time waiting
1	3.2	3.7			
2	10.5	3.5			
3	12.8	4.3			
4	14.5	3.0			
5	17.2	2.8			
6	19.7	4.2			
7	21.1	2.8			
8	26.9	2.3			
9	32.7	2.1			
10	36.9	4.8			

2. Using row 2 of Table 13.1, simulate 20 days of the supermarket operation example (Example 3). Express your results in a table similar to Table 14.1.
3. Using row 2 of Table 13.1, simulate 20 days of the continuous review inventory system (Example 5). Express your results in a table similar to Figure 14.13.
4. Compare the results of Problem 2 with the scenario in which the lead time distribution is changed to the following:

Lead time	Probability
1	.1
2	.4
3	.5

How do the average inventory, number of orders, and average back order level change?

5. Unstructural Dynamo Research (UDR) is a company that produces software designed to enhance company creativity. UDR itself has lately become less than creative and has had trouble getting new products to the market. The current stock price for the company is $9.75 per share. The daily changes in stock price over the last 500 trading days have been analyzed, resulting in the following frequency counts:

Price change	Frequency
-5	1
-1	20
$-\frac{1}{2}$	55
$-\frac{3}{8}$	95
0	212
$+\frac{3}{8}$	100
$+\frac{1}{2}$	10
$+1$	5
$+2$	2
	Total: 500

Simulate the stock performance over the next 20 trading days using the following random numbers: .14, .78, .67, .58, .97, .04, .95, .71, .32, .62, .84, .84, .19, .57, .56, .94, .30, .07, .88, .23.

What is the high and low stock price and on which days did they occur (that is, what were the best days to sell and buy this stock)?

6. A drive-through-only restaurant is considering adding more workers to its crew during the lunchtime rush (11:00 A.M.–1:00 P.M.). The following data have been collected for this period of the day (all times are in minutes):

Time between arrivals	Frequency
3	21
3.5	32
4	39
4.5	6
5	2
	Total: 100

Service time	Frequency
1	2
1.5	5
2	10
2.5	24
3	36
3.5	23
	Total: 100

The owner would like to perform a simulation to see if an increase in crew size would be beneficial.

a.   Draw a conceptual model for this scenario similar to that shown in Figure 14.3.

b.   Simulate the arrival and service of 15 customers using the random numbers given below. Use average wait per customer, percentage of time server is idle, and longest waiting line length as the output measure.

Time between arrivals: .92, .83, .85, .58, .05, .09, .61, .77, .43, .35, .05, .87, .13, .22, .63

Service times: .12, .75, .14, .72, .20, .82, .74, .08, .01, .69, .36, .35, .52, .99, .41

c.   Assume that adding to the crew will cut all service times in half. Use the simulation from part a to calculate new output measures and compare these with those from part b. Does an increase in crew size seem warranted? Why?

7.   The hot dog vendors at Bench Field face the problem of how many hot dogs to order from a catering service for sale at its games. The catering service requires that a fixed amount be ordered for every game in a given month. At the end of a month, the order size may be changed.

Past observation at Bench Field indicates that the sales of hot dogs is dependent primarily on the team's performance. If the team is playing well, sales are high, but if the team is mediocre or a loser, sales are low. The following probabilities have been obtained from past data:

Current record (% wins)	Sales
.55 to 1.00	300 dogs
.35 to .54	125
.00 to .34	35

Hot dogs cost $0.35 apiece, regardless of the quantity ordered, and are sold for $1.00 apiece. Hot dogs left over at the end of the day are donated to a nearby zoo for animal feed (at a total loss). The manager of the vendors would like to evaluate orders of size 100, 150, and 250.

Simulate the first 20 games of the season using the random numbers given below. This year's team is virtually the same team as last year (their record was 34 wins and 26 losses). Keep track of total profit or loss over the 20 days for the three different order sizes. Which appears best?

Random numbers: .27, .76, .17, .25, .17, .67, .62, .32, .61, .47, .81, 70, .77, .55, .57, .07, .32, .02, .12, .24.

8.   Retailers often observe that daily demand for a product is related to the number of units on the shelf (even beyond the fact that the number of units on the shelf is an upper limit on sales). Customers seem to buy more if the shelf is full. The following table shows the probabilities for different sales levels, given the number of units on the shelf for one product:

Units on the shelf (start of day)	Demand			
	0	10	20	30
0–20	.1	.7	.20	0
20–50	0	.1	.6	.3
50–100	0	0	.3	.7

Assume that 100 units is the maximum amount that can be stored on the shelf and that no storage space is available beyond that for this product. The profit per unit sold is $4.75, ordering cost to replenish the shelf is $17 (regardless of the order quantity and whether goods arrive overnight in time to be placed on the shelf for the next day), and demand over available units is simply lost (a stockout), which is estimated to cost $6 per unit. Evaluate the following two stocking policies with a 20-day simulation.

Policy 1:   Restock with 80 more units whenever the number of units on the shelf drops below 21.

Policy 2:   Restock every two days with whatever amount is needed to bring the number of units on the shelf up to 100.

Assume that there are currently 63 units on the shelf. Use the following random numbers: .10, .62, .86, .34, .45, .57, .06, .32, .89, .93, .37, .21, .45, .34, .66, .31, .26, .18, .43, .56.

9. Consider the following distributions for time between arrival of jobs and service times:

HW

Time between arrivals	Probability
$\frac{1}{2}$ hour	.2
1 hour	.4
$1\frac{1}{2}$ hours	.3
2 hours	.1

Service times	Probability
$\frac{1}{4}$ hour	.2 .21
$\frac{1}{2}$ hour	.2 .20
1 hour	.3
$1\frac{1}{2}$ hours	.2 .19
2 hours	.1

discrete distribution in ARENA (NU-BASED) PROGRAM

Simulate the system performance for 10 jobs under two different service rules:

First In First Out (FIFO)—jobs are served in the order in which they arrive.

Last In First Out (LIFO)—the last job to arrive is the next one served.

Compare these two rules on average amount of time a job must wait to be served and the longest wait of any job. Which rule appears to be better and why? Use the following random numbers:

Job number	Random number for time between arrivals	Random number for service
1	—	.11
2	.54	.63
3	.10	.24
4	.87	.42
5	.53	.47
6	.70	.33
7	.54	.73
8	.39	.43
9	.42	.55
10	.18	.26

use this data for Excel

10. A university computer center services students and faculty researchers. During the mornings, demand for student services occurs uniformly every 1.9 to 2.6 minutes. Demand for research support occurs every 10 to 15 minutes. The average service time in minutes for student services is 0.75 minutes (distributed exponentially); for faculty research, 3.5 minutes (distributed exponentially).
   a. Develop a logical simulation model for this system.
   b. Show how to generate the probabilistic inputs for this model.
   c. Simulate 60 minutes of operation to determine the waiting time for each class of user and mean idle time for the system.

11. The children's board game Hi-Ho Cherry-O!® works as follows. Each child has a tree with 10 cherries. The object of the game is to pick all the cherries into a bucket. A spinner is divided into seven equal sections:
   1. Pick 1 cherry
   2. Pick 2 cherries
   3. Pick 3 cherries
   4. Pick 4 cherries
   5. Dog eats 2 cherries (place 2 back on the tree)
   6. Bird eats 2 cherries (place 2 back on the tree)
   7. Spill the bucket (place all cherries back on the tree)
      a. Develop conceptual and logical flowcharts for this game.
      b. Simulate this game five times (until all cherries have been picked) to estimate the mean number of moves required to finish the game.

12. Passengers wait for an airport shuttle service that arrives every 15 minutes. Passengers arrive within each 5-minute period according to the following distribution:

Number of passengers	Probability
0	.2
1	.1
2	.2
3	.3
4	.15
5	.05

The shuttle holds 10 passengers. Develop a simulation model to find the probability that some passengers will not be able to board the shuttle and must wait for the next one. Is this a static or dynamic simulation model?

13. A refuse collection company in a small city currently uses trash collection vehicles with a 15-ton capacity. Trucks are dispatched from the landfill at 6:00 A.M., travel to their collection routes, pick up refuse until the truck is full, return to the landfill, and continue until 2:00 P.M., at which point they return to the landfill, dump the refuse, and wait until the next morning. The tables below provide data on the operation.

Tons collected/hour	Probability
1	.05
2	.25
3	.30
4	.25
5	.15

Travel time to or from landfill	Probability
30 minutes	.15
40	.30
50	.45
60	.10

The time to dump the refuse is constant at 15 minutes.

    a.   Develop conceptual and logical simulation models for this system. Management is interested in determining the productivity of the trucks.

    b.   Show how to generate the probabilistic inputs for your model.

    c.   Simulate 5 days' operation for one truck. What percent of time is the truck performing useful work?

    d.   If a 25-ton truck is used, how much will productivity be expected to increase?

    e.   How might the simulation results be used to make a decision on whether to purchase the larger trucks? What other information is needed?

14. Run the spreadsheet model for the drill bit replacement simulation and find a 90 percent confidence interval for the average cost per time using 3 replications. Repeat this exercise using 10 replications. How much tighter is the new confidence interval?

15. Develop and implement a computer simulation model for the computer center problem (Problem 10). Analyze the output using methods discussed in Chapter 13.

16. Develop and implement a computer simulation model to solve the Hi-Ho Cherry-O!® board game problem (Problem 11). Analyze the output using methods discussed in Chapter 13.

17. Develop and implement a computer simulation model to solve the airport shuttle problem (Problem 12). Analyze the output using methods discussed in Chapter 13.

18. Develop and implement a computer simulation model to solve the refuse collection problem (Problem 13). Analyze the output using methods discussed in Chapter 13.

19. Water flows into a regional water reservoir in the mountains.[4] The amount of water flowing into the reservoir is a function of rainfall and snow melts. Water leaving the reservoir is a function of evaporation and the controlled flow of stream water through a gate. Too much water flowing through the gate at any one time will result in downstream flooding, but too little water through the gate may cause the reservoir itself to overflow. The decision maker's problem is to determine a constant gate flow rate that maintains a balance between the two extremes. Probability distributions for the input and output processes are given below. The initial water level is 100,000 gallons. Develop a spreadsheet model for this system, assuming that the controlled flow rate is 2,000 gallons/day. Conduct appropriate simulation experiments and analyze the results using the methods discussed in this chapter. What output information would be important to the manager of this system?

Water input (thousands of gallons/day)	
Amount	Probability
10	.2
20	.2
30	.3
40	.2
50	.1

[4]Adapted from Mark G. Simkin and Manalur Sandilya, "Simulation on Spreadsheets," undated paper, College of Business, University of Nevada, Reno.

Water output (thousands of gallons/day)

Amount	Probability
5	.15
10	.10
20	.25
30	.25
40	.25

20. Expensive tools are kept in a tool crib at many manufacturing facilities. Workers needing tools receive formal authorization and are issued the tools at the tool crib and return them when they are finished. Suppose that workers arrive every 4 ± 2 minutes and the time it takes to issue a tool is 3 ± 1 minutes. Design and implement a simulation model to determine the average waiting time of workers and idle time of the tool crib clerk.

IV. Projects and Cases

1. Study the elevator system in a building with which you are familiar. Draw a conceptual model for simulating the elevator operation. What data would be needed for your model? How would you collect these data?

2. The Southern California Gas Company serves over 13 million people and receives over 40,000 calls daily.[5] Over 400 customer service representatives (CSRs) handle the calls. The objectives of the Service Bureau Operations are to provide good service to customers without excessive staffing of customer service representatives. Performance measures of the system include the following:

   - Total number of calls received
   - Total number of calls answered
   - Average number of calls waiting
   - Average available CSRs
   - Average CSR utilization
   - Average customer waiting time
   - Percentage of customers who hang up before getting service

   The system operates as follows. Incoming calls arrive at the switchboard. If all lines are busy, the caller receives a busy signal and hangs up. Otherwise, the system checks to see if a CSR is available. If there is, the call is automatically routed to a CSR. If not, the caller is asked to wait for the next available CSR. Some callers decide not to wait and abandon the call. Those who do wait are routed to the next available CSR.
   a. Draw a conceptual flowchart of this system.
   b. What data must be collected for a useful simulation model?
   c. What controllable variables would be important? What system alternatives should be studied?

3. The Anderson Fitness Club[6]

   The Anderson Fitness Club is a full-service exercise facility that features a full-circuit Nautilus system, Lifecycles, Stairmasters, and free weights. Although the main attraction is the Nautilus machines, many people join to use more than one type of exercise system during their workout. These people generally do not like to wait between exercises because it allows them to cool down.

---

[5] Adapted from Mehdi Danesh, "Simulation in Optimal Staffing of Customer Service Representatives," Southern California Gas Company Operations Research & Planning Models, May 9, 1989.

[6] The authors acknowledge the contribution of Mr. David Minning in preparing this case.

The clientele of the club consists of professionals of all ages; therefore, the busiest times are weeknights from 5 to 9 P. M.. Seventy-five percent of all members exercise at this time. Therefore, it is extremely important that there be a sufficient number of machines available. Currently, a first-come, first- served basis is used. If an exercise machine is being used, a chalkboard is provided for a waiting list. The club has three Stairmasters, three Lifecycles, one rack of free weights, and a 15-station Nautilus. Everyone who wishes to use the Nautilus machines must start at the beginning of the circuit.

Because of the popularity of the Stairmasters, they tend to be used the most and have a line of people waiting during the busiest times. One of the reasons that this occurs may be that when people are waiting for the Nautilus, they sometimes want to use the Stairmaster. Only a small number of members ride the Lifecycles because of the age of the machines and the declining popularity of stationary bicycles.

Lately the manager of the club has been receiving complaints about the lines at the Stairmasters during the busy times. The owners of the club are not very receptive to purchasing another machine because of cash flow problems. In addition, they do not believe that an additional machine is needed because of its low utilization during the day. However, the manager is convinced that members will not renew their membership if waiting times continue to be long.

The manager conducted a phone survey of 200 members and found out that 80 percent of them used the Stairmaster equipment. Of these people, 70 percent wished to use both the Nautilus and the Stairmaster. Using a sign-in sheet over several weeks, she also determined that the customers arrived to use the Stairmaster machines on average every 6.85 minutes. An exponential distribution was reasoned to be a good model of this arrival pattern. The maximum time that a person could use the Stairmaster is 15 minutes. About 85 percent use it for the maximum time. The remaining 15 percent stop after 10 minutes.

Build a conceptual model and logical simulation flowchart for this problem. Conduct a simulation of this system to determine the effect that an additional Stairmaster would have on the waiting times and lines. Discuss how the simulation results might be used to justify an additional Stairmaster. What additional data are necessary to make an informed decision?

4.   A small wholesale distributor sells an electronic cruise control unit for automobiles. The distribution of daily demand is given below:

Daily demand	Probability
0	.1770
1	.0770
2	.3850
3	.2731
4	.0879

The lead time distribution is as follows:

Lead time (days)	Frequency
14	.10
15	.75
16	.10
17	.05

Unit cost is $54.90 for order sizes less than 117 units, and $49.40 for order sizes of 117 units or more. The item sells for $61.73. Other information obtained from company records includes the following:

1. Annual usage is 525 units.
2. Order cost is $5.00 per order.
3. Back order cost is $5.00 per stockout.
4. Unit storage cost is $1.48 per year.
5. Starting inventory is 117 units.
6. The company operates 260 days per year.

Determine the best reorder point and reorder level for this situation using simulation analysis.

REFERENCES

Banks, Jerry, et al. "The Simulator: New Member of the Simulation Family." *Interfaces*, Vol. 21, No. 2, March–April 1992, pp. 76-86.

Bodily, Samuel E. "Spreadsheet Modeling as a Stepping Stone." *Interfaces*, Vol. 16, No. 5, September–October, 1986, pp. 34–52.

Cebry, Michael E., Anura H. deSilva, and Fred J. DeLisio. "Management Science in Automating Postal Operations: Facility and Equipment Planning in the United States Postal Service." *Interfaces,* Vol. 22, No. 1, January–February, 1992, pp. 110–130.

Cornwell, Larry W., and Doan T. Modianos. "Management Tool: Using Spreadsheets for Simulation Models." *Production and Inventory Management*, Vol. 31, No. 3, Third Quarter 1990, pp. 8–17.

Gravel, Marc, and Wilson L. Price. "Visual Interactive Simulation Shows How to Use the Kanban Method in Small Business." *Interfaces*, Vol. 21, No. 5, September–October, 1991, pp. 22–33.

Maurer, Ruth A., and Fines H. Munkonze. "A Simulation Model of an Airport Shuttle Service." Department of Mathematical and Computer Sciences, Colorado School of Mines, Golden, CO.

Ravindran, A., B. L. Foote, A. B. Badiru, L. M. Leemis, and Larry Williams. "An Application of Simulation and Network Analysis to Capacity Planning and Material Handling Systems at Tinker Air Force Base." *Interfaces*, Vol. 19, No. 1, January–February, 1989, pp. 102–115.

Russell, Robert, and Regina Hickle. "Simulation of a CD Portfolio." *Interfaces*, Vol. 16, No. 3, May–June 1986, pp. 49–59.

Saunders, Gary. "How to Use a Microcomputer Simulation to Determine Order Quantity." *Production and Inventory Management Journal*, Vol. 28, No. 4, Fourth Quarter, 1987.

Thesen, Arne, and Laurel E. Travis. *Simulation for Decision Making.* St. Paul, MN: West Publishing Co., 1992.

CHAPTER 15

MODELING

AND ANALYSIS

OF QUEUEING

SYSTEMS

INTRODUCTION

- L.L. Bean is widely known for retailing high-quality outdoor goods and apparel, primarily through mail and telephone orders. In 1989 about 65 percent of the total annual sales volume was generated through orders taken at two telemarketing centers. In managing telemarketing call centers, decisions must be made on the number of telephone lines (trunks) to install, the number of sales agent positions to establish, and other capacity considerations such as facilities, equipment, automatic call distributors, and other support equipment. L.L. Bean conservatively estimated that it lost $10 million of profit in 1988 because it allocated telemarketing resources suboptimally. In some half-hour periods, 80 percent of calls dialed received busy signals because the system was full; those who got through might have waited 10 minutes for an available agent. The cost of keeping those customers waiting was as much as $25,000 in one day.

  A management science team was charged with defining and implementing models for better resource management. Using waiting-line models, L.L. Bean was able to optimize its resources, improve profits by up to $10 million per year, and realize intangible benefits in customer satisfaction. The project cost only $40,000 [Quinn, Andrews, and Parsons, 1991].

- The rise of aircraft hijacking in the 1970s led to security screening as an essential feature of modern air travel. Passenger screening is costly to implement and operate and can delay passengers and aircraft departures during congested periods. In designing a major international airport during the early days of security screening, Lockheed Aircraft Service Company studied different types of screening concepts. The "sterile concourse" system screens passengers at each concourse entrance. This system is commonly used throughout the world today. When the concept was new, questions were raised as to whether the system would delay scheduled aircraft operations and cause unacceptable congestion and waiting times in the ticket lobbies where the waiting lines would form. A major issue was determining the number of screening systems needed to service passengers at a reasonable rate. Using passenger demand forecasts, Lockheed calculated expected waiting-line lengths. At the time the study was performed, Lockheed's model indicated that a single-unit system would handle demand with high reliability for the next 10 years, but after that time, a two-unit system would be needed unless the airport itself was expanded [Gilliam, 1979].

- The American Red Cross collects over six million units of blood each year in the United States. Blood is collected at over 400 fixed and mobile sites operated daily by the 52 blood services regions throughout the country. The Red Cross was concerned that excessive waiting lines and the time required to donate blood were affecting donors' willingness to make future blood donations. A management science team developed a simulation model of the service process to analyze new processing strategies in an effort to reduce waiting times. In implementing the recommendations, donor processing times improved markedly, and customer satisfaction surveys indicated that repeat donors noticed improvements [Brennen, Golden, and Rappoport, 1992].

Each of these applications deals with the management of waiting lines. A waiting line is also called a *queue* (the French word for "line"). The analysis of waiting lines, called *queueing theory,* applies to any situation in which customers arrive to a system, wait, and receive service. The objectives of queueing theory are to improve customer service and reduce operating costs.

Queueing theory had its origins in 1908 with a Danish telephone engineer, A. K. Erlang, who began to study congestion in the telephone service of the Copenhagen Telephone Company. Erlang developed mathematical formulas to predict waiting times and line lengths. Over the years, queueing theory has found numerous applications in telecommunications and computer systems and has expanded to many other service systems. As consumers began to differentiate firms by their quality of service, reducing waiting times has become an obsession with many firms. Quick-service restaurants take waiting seriously—some have dedicated staffs that study ways to speed up service.

In this chapter we study how queueing theory is applied to management science problems. Both analytical modeling and simulation modeling approaches will be discussed and illustrated.

QUEUEING SYSTEMS

A large part of our lives involves waiting—waiting for traffic lights, in banks, on the telephone, in quick-service restaurants, at ticket counters, in grocery stores, and in many other places. Experts have estimated that Americans wait an average of 30 minutes per day. This translates to 37 billion hours each year! In both manufacturing and service organizations, there is a growing need to manage waiting lines effectively. Every minute spent waiting is wasted and costs money.

All queueing systems have three elements in common:

1. *Customers* that wait for service. Customers need not be people but can be machines awaiting repair, airplanes waiting to take off, subassemblies waiting for a machine, computer programs waiting for processing, or telephone calls awaiting a customer service representative.
2. *Servers* that provide the service. Again, servers need not be only people, such as clerks, customer service representatives, or repairpersons; servers may be airport runways, machine tools, repair bays, ATMs, or computers.
3. A *waiting line* or *queue.* The queue is the set of customers waiting for service. In many cases, a queue is a physical line, as you experience in a bank or grocery store. In other situations, a queue may not even be visible or even in one location, as with computer jobs waiting for processing or telephone calls waiting for an open line.

To understand the operation of a queueing system, we need to describe the characteristics of the customer, server, and queue, and how the system is configured.

Customer Characteristics

Customers arrive to the system according to some *arrival process*. The arrival process can be deterministic or probabilistic. Examples of deterministic arrivals would be parts feeding from an automated machine to an assembly line or patients arriving at appointed times to a medical facility. Most arrival processes, such as people arriving at a supermarket, are probabilistic. We can describe a probabilistic arrival process by a probability distribution representing the number of arrivals during a specific time interval, or by a distribution that represents the time between successive arrivals.

The *arrival rate* may be constant or may vary with time. For instance, the demand for service at a quick-service restaurant is low in the mid-morning and mid-afternoon but peaks during the breakfast, lunch, and dinner hours. Individual customers may arrive singly and independently (telephone calls to a mail order company) or in groups (a pallet-load of parts arriving at a machine center, or patrons at a movie theater).

The *calling population* is the set of potential customers. In many applications, the calling population is assumed to be infinite; that is, an unlimited number of possible customers can arrive to the system. This would be the case with telephone calls to a mail order company or shoppers at a supermarket. In other situations, the calling population is finite. One example would be a factory in which failed machines await repair.

Once in line, customers may not always stay in the same order as they arrived. It is common for customers to *renege*, or leave a queue, before being served if they get tired of waiting. In queueing systems with multiple queues, customers may *jockey*, or switch lines if they perceive another to be moving faster. Some customers may arrive at the system, determine that the line is too long, and decide not to join the queue. This behavior is called *balking*.

Service Characteristics

Service occurs according to some *service process*. The time it takes to serve a customer may be deterministic or probabilistic. In the probabilistic case, the service time is described by some probability distribution. The average service time might vary during the day (taking orders and serving dinner might be longer than for breakfast). Service times might depend on the type of customer. The service process may include one or several servers. The service characteristics of multiple servers may be identical or different. In some systems, certain servers may only service specific types of customers. In many systems, such as restaurants and department stores, managers vary the number of servers to adjust to busy or slack periods.

Queue Characteristics

The order in which customers are served is defined by the *queue discipline*. The most common queue discipline is first-come, first-served (FCFS). In some situations, a queue may be structured as last-come, first-served (LCFS); just think of the in-box on a clerk's desk. In computer processing systems, jobs are usually serviced according to some priority; for example, small student jobs have higher priority than larger research jobs, no matter when they were submitted.

System Configuration

The customers, servers, and queues in a queueing system can be arranged in various ways. Three common queueing configurations are as follows:

1. One or more parallel servers fed by a single queue (see Figure 15.1). This is the typical configuration used by many banks and airline ticket counters.
2. Several parallel servers fed by their own queues (see Figure 15.2). McDonald's uses this type of system, as do most supermarkets and discount retailers.
3. A combination of several queues in series. This structure is common when multiple processing operations exist, such as in manufacturing facilities and many service systems. The example of a typical voting facility is shown in Figure 15.3.

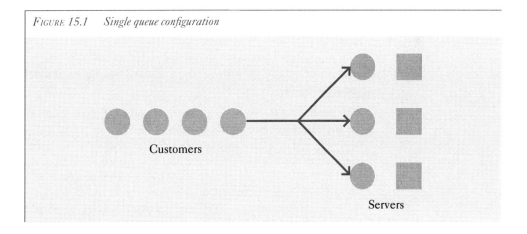

FIGURE 15.1   Single queue configuration

Customers

Servers

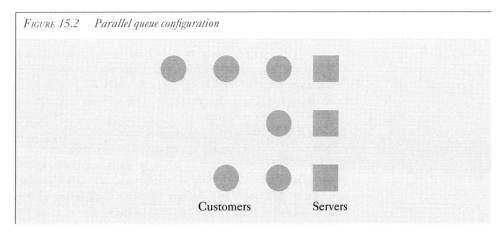

FIGURE 15.2   Parallel queue configuration

Customers   Servers

FIGURE 15.3   *Queues in series in a typical voting facility*

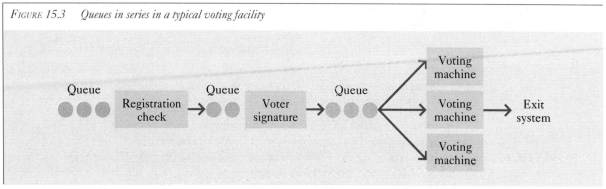

Figure from Grant, III, "Reducing Voter Waiting Time," *Interfaces*, Vol. 10, No. 5, October 1980, pp. 19–25.

APPLICATIONS OF QUEUEING MODELS

Queueing models have wide applicability. In addition to the applications cited in the chapter introduction, we provide the following examples to illustrate the value of using queueing analysis.

- *Toll booths.* At Port Authority tunnels and bridges in New York, toll-plaza activities involve hundreds of traffic officers, with millions of dollars of payroll expenses. In a classic application of queueing analysis, the Port Authority undertook a study to balance expenses and employee and customer satisfaction. Specifically, the purposes of the study were to evaluate the grade of service given to customers as a function of traffic volume, to establish optimum standards of service, and to develop a more precise method of controlling expenses and service while providing for toll-collector rest periods [Edie, 1954].

  Data collected included the traffic arrivals at the toll plaza, the number of cars in each toll-lane queue, and the toll-transaction count and times. The pattern of arrivals was found to depend on the volume. At low volumes, the number of arrivals followed a Poisson probability distribution; at high volumes, a normal distribution; and at peak volumes, a uniform distribution. The scheduling procedure developed through queueing theory saved a yearly equivalent of 10 times the cost of the study. In addition, the scheduling procedure offered better service to the public and benefits to toll-collection personnel.

- *Tool cribs.* The Boeing Company used queueing models to determine the optimum number of clerks to station at tool cribs. Boeing maintained about 60 tool cribs scattered among several plants to provide tools required by their mechanics. The supervisor wanted to reduce the mechanics' idle time by increasing the number of crib clerks. Management did not like this idea, since adding crib clerks would increase overhead. The best economic solution was obtained from a queueing model, which balanced the cost between the two conflicting objectives. The model justified a personnel reduction, which resulted in a savings of about $10,000 per month [Brigham, 1955].

- *Teller staffing.* The Bankers Trust Company of New York used a queueing model for teller staffing. The study was motivated by management's concern with rising labor costs and the need to maintain high levels of customer service. Data collection and analysis determined that a standard queueing model could be used. The output of the model provided management with the appropriate staffing requirements based on the expected customer arrival rate, the average service time, and the service level desired. Bankers Trust used the model to establish teller staffing policies at more than 100 branches. They reduced the number of tellers by an average of one per branch while maintaining comparable levels of service, and the total benefit of the project was over $1 million per year [Deutsch and Mabert, 1980].

- *Health care.* A queueing model assisted in a cost/benefit analysis of a telemetry system at Long Community Hospital in Greensboro, North Carolina. The telemetric unit is used to monitor ambulatory cardiac patients. The purpose of the study was to determine the number of units needed to provide a satisfactory level of patient service while simultaneously maximizing revenue. Records of patient arrival and service times were used to obtain the data for the model. The analysis revealed that the current number of units was resulting in a loss of approximately $20,000 per year. Adding four additional units would not only eliminate this loss but would also reduce patient waiting time by almost 100 percent [Scott and Hailey, 1981].

- *Security checkpoints.* Vehicles entering a secured work facility at the Westinghouse Hanford Company each morning pass through a security gate. Normally two security guards checked vehicles, drivers, and passengers. Upon approaching the gate, vehicles formed one line that extended past the available queue space onto the adjacent highway, resulting in a major traffic safety problem. A study was conducted to minimize the queue length while also minimizing the number of security guards at the gate. Using a simulation model, the study showed that a significant improvement could be achieved using the same number of guards in two parallel traffic lines rather than the obvious solution of increasing the number of guards. The study was so successful that several other queueing studies were initiated shortly thereafter [Landauer and Becker, 1989].

MODELING QUEUEING SYSTEMS

The inputs to a queueing model were described earlier in this chapter.

- Arrival process
- Service process
- Queue discipline
- System configuration

A queueing model translates these inputs into measures of system performance. Thus, queueing models are *descriptive* in nature. The two basic measures by which we evaluate the performance of a queueing system are as follows:

1. The quality of the service provided to the customer.
2. The efficiency of the service operation and the cost of providing the service.

Various numerical measures of performance can be used to evaluate the quality of the service provided to the customer. These include the following:

- Waiting time in the queue
- Time in the system (waiting time plus service time)
- Completion by a deadline

The efficiency of the service operation can be evaluated by computing such measures as the following:

- Average queue length
- Average number of customers in the system (queue plus in service)
- Throughput—the rate at which customers are served
- Server utilization—percentage of time servers are busy
- Percentage of customers who balk or renege

Usually we can use these measures to compute an operating cost in order to compare alternative system configurations.

The most common measures of queueing system performance and the symbols used to denote them are given in Table 15.1. These measures are called the *operating characteristics* of the queueing system.

We may summarize the relationships among the customer, service, and queueing characteristics using the influence diagram in Figure 15.4.

Modeling the Arrival Process

In many queueing systems, customers arrive in a random fashion and independently of each other. For example, calls to a mail order company may arrive at any time during the work day, and each call is initiated independently of the others. We need to specify the

TABLE 15.1
Measures of queueing system performance

Measure	Symbol
Average number in the system (queue plus service)	L
Average number in the queue	L_q
Average waiting time in the system (queue plus service)	W
Average time in the queue	W_q
Probability that the system is empty (servers are idle)	P_0

FIGURE 15.4   *Influence diagram of queueing systems*

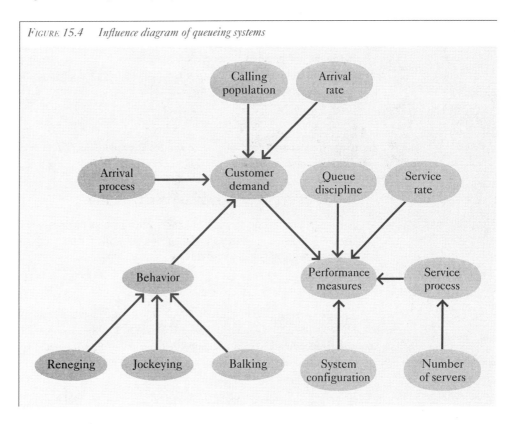

probability distribution that governs the arrival process. We have a *Poisson process* if we can assume that

1. Customers arrive one at a time, independently of each other and at random.
2. Past arrivals do not influence future arrivals; that is, the probability that a customer arrives at any point in time does not depend on when other customers arrived (sometimes we say that the system has *no memory*).
3. The probability of an arrival does not vary over time.

The key assumption is number 3. In many real systems, the rate at which customers arrive may be relatively constant over short intervals of time but most likely will vary over the day or week (just think of any fast-food restaurant). If we use the mathematical formulas in the next section in real applications, we must ensure that these assumptions are met.

One way to validate these assumptions is simply to collect empirical data about the pattern of arrivals. Not only can we observe and record the actual times of individual arrivals in order to determine the probability distribution and check if the arrival rate is constant over time, but we can also observe if customers arrive individually or in groups, and whether they balk, jockey, or renege. This information is vital in using the correct models for queueing analysis and obtaining useful results.

If the arrival pattern is described by a Poisson process, then the Poisson probability distribution can be used to describe the probability that a particular number of customers arrives during a specified time interval. The Poisson distribution with mean λ is

$$f(x) = \lambda^x \frac{e^{-\lambda}}{x!} \qquad \text{for } x = 0, 1, 2, \ldots$$

In using the Poisson distribution to model arrivals to a queueing system, the parameter λ is called the *mean arrival rate* and is expressed in dimensions of customers per unit time.

EXAMPLE 1. A POISSON ARRIVAL PROCESS

Arrivals at an airline ticket counter follow a Poisson process with a mean of two customers per minute. Thus, $\lambda = 2$. The probability that x customers will arrive during any one-minute period is given by

$$f(x) = (2)^x \frac{e^{-2}}{x!}$$

We may compute this function for any nonnegative integer value of x. Figure 15.5 shows the results for x from 0 to 10, computed on a LOTUS 1-2-3 spreadsheet using the function @POISSON. Figure 15.6 is a histogram of this distribution. The Poisson distribution is typically skewed to the right.

The Poisson Process and the Exponential Distribution

In the previous example, an arrival rate of two customers per minute means that on the average, customers arrive every half-minute, or every 30 seconds. Thus, an equivalent way

FIGURE 15.5   *Spreadsheet calculation of Poisson distribution*

A	A	B	C
1	Poisson Distribution		
2			
3	Mean	2	
4			
5	x	f(x)	Cumulative
6	0	0.135335	0.135335
7	1	0.270671	0.406006
8	2	0.270671	0.676676
9	3	0.180447	0.857123
10	4	0.090224	0.947347
11	5	0.036089	0.983436
12	6	0.01203	0.995466
13	7	0.003437	0.998903
14	8	0.000859	0.999763
15	9	0.000191	0.999954
16	10	0.000038	0.999992

FIGURE 15.6   Histogram of Poisson arrivals

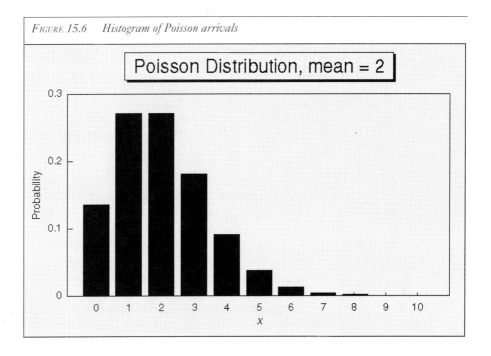

of expressing arrivals is to state the *mean interarrival time* between successive customers. If λ is the mean arrival rate, the mean interarrival time, $\bar{t}$, is simply the reciprocal of λ:

$$\bar{t} = \frac{1}{\lambda}$$

If the arrival process is Poisson, then the distribution of the interarrival times has an exponential probability distribution. This is summed up in the following statement:

> If the number of arrivals follows a Poisson process with mean λ, then the time between arrivals has an exponential distribution with a mean service rate λ.

Recall that the exponential probability distribution is

$$f(t) = \lambda e^{-\lambda t} \quad \text{for } t \geq 0$$

It has mean $1/\lambda$ and has a cumulative distribution function

$$F(t) = 1 - e^{-\lambda t} \quad \text{for } t \geq 0$$

Thus, $F(t)$ is the probability that the time between successive arrivals will be less than or equal to t. This result also implies that if the time between arrivals is exponentially distributed with a mean $1/\lambda$, then the *number of arrivals* in a length of time T is Poisson with mean λT.

EXAMPLE 2. COMPUTING INTERARRIVAL TIME PROBABILITIES

For the situation in Example 1 with an arrival rate of two customers per minute, the mean interarrival time is 0.5 minutes per customer. Thus, the distribution of interarrival times is exponential with the cumulative distribution function

$$F(t) = 1 - e^{-2t}$$

This specifies the probability that the next customer will arrive within t minutes of the current time. Figure 15.7 shows a spreadsheet tabulation of this function for values of t up to 2 minutes using the LOTUS 1-2-3 function @EXP. A graph of the cumulative probability distribution is shown in Figure 15.8.

The Poisson process applies to many real-world arrival processes. If this assumption is made in a queueing study, some attempt should be made to validate it. Goodness of fit tests discussed in Chapter 11 can be used to determine how well observed data follow the Poisson or exponential distribution. Failure to validate this assumption might suggest that different queueing models or approaches such as simulation be used.

FIGURE 15.7 Spreadsheet tabulation of interarrival time probabilities

A	A	B	C
1	Exponential Distribution		
2			
3	Mean	2	
4			
5	x	F(x)	
6	0	0	
7	0.1	0.181269	
8	0.2	0.32968	
9	0.3	0.451188	
10	0.4	0.550671	
11	0.5	0.632121	
12	0.6	0.698806	
13	0.7	0.753403	
14	0.8	0.798103	
15	0.9	0.834701	
16	1	0.864665	
17	1.1	0.889197	
18	1.2	0.909282	
19	1.3	0.925726	
20	1.4	0.93919	
21	1.5	0.950213	
22	1.6	0.959238	
23	1.7	0.966627	
24	1.8	0.972676	
25	1.9	0.977629	
26	2	0.981684	

Selected cell formulas

A	A	B
1	Exponential Distribution	
2		
3	Mean	2
4		
5	x	F(x)
6	0	1-@EXP(-A6*$B$3)
7	0.1	1-@EXP(-A7*$B$3)
8	0.2	1-@EXP(-A8*$B$3)
9	0.3	1-@EXP(-A9*$B$3)
10	0.4	1-@EXP(-A10*$B$3)

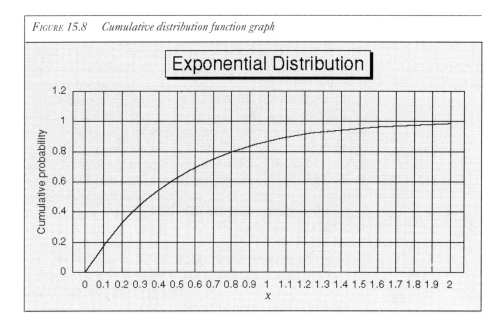

FIGURE 15.8   *Cumulative distribution function graph*

Modeling the Service Process

In many queueing models, we make the assumption that service times follow an exponential distribution:

$$f(t) = \mu e^{-\mu t}, \quad t \geq 0$$
$$F(t) = 1 - e^{-\mu t}, \quad t \geq 0$$

The parameter μ is called the *mean service rate* and represents the average number of customers served per unit time. The average service *time* is $1/\mu$.

EXAMPLE 3. EXPONENTIAL SERVICE TIMES

The mean service rate in processing customers at an airline ticket counter is three customers per minute. Thus, the mean service time is one-third of a minute. If the distribution of service times is exponential, then the probability that a customer is served in t minutes or less is

$$F(t) = 1 - e^{-3t}, \quad t \geq 0$$

Assuming exponential services is often reasonable and simplifies the mathematics involved in calculating performance measures. One reason that the exponential distribution describes many service phenomena is that it has a useful property—the probability of small service times is large. For example, the probability that t exceeds the mean is only 0.368. This means that we see a large number of short service times and a few long ones. Think of your own experience in grocery stores. Most customers' service times are relatively short; however, every once in a while you see a shopper with a large number of groceries (who gets out the checkbook only *after* all of the groceries are scanned!). Many real-world applications have been found to have exponentially distributed service times.

The exponential distribution, however, does not seem to be as common in modeling service processes as the Poisson is in modeling arrival processes. Management scientists have found that many queueing systems have service time distributions other than the exponential. In many applications, service times are constant or follow a normal distribution or some other probability distribution. As we shall see, we can develop queueing models for which the service time distribution does not even have to be known. We will need to know only the average service rate and the standard deviation of the service time. As with the arrival process, you should attempt to validate the service time distribution by collecting data from the system and analyzing the data using the goodness of fit test that we reviewed in Chapter 11.

Note that the unit of time that we use in modeling both arrival and service processes can be arbitrary. For example, a mean arrival rate of 2 customers per minute is equivalent to 120 customers per hour. We must be careful, however, to express the arrival rate and service rate in the same time units.

ANALYTICAL APPROACHES

Because of the variety of assumptions that can be made, D. G. Kendall developed a taxonomy for queueing models that simplifies discussion and communication. We characterize a queueing model using the notation A/B/s, where

A = Arrival distribution
B = Service time distribution
s = Number of servers

Symbols used to specify the arrival and service time distributions include

M = Exponential distribution (Poisson process)
G = General (arbitrary) distribution of service times
GI = General (arbitrary) distribution of arrivals
D = Deterministic (constant) value

Thus, a queueing model with Poisson arrivals, exponential service times, and a single server is denoted as $M/M/1$; a model with Poisson arrivals, general service times, and two servers is denoted as $M/G/2$. Where does the M come from? Recall that a Poisson process has the *m*emoryless property.

We will describe analytical approaches to some of the basic queueing models. Much research on queueing models has been conducted, but the mathematics becomes rather complex. Except for special cases, queueing models in general are rather difficult to formulate and solve even when the distribution of arrivals and departures is known. We will not be concerned with the mathematical derivation of queueing formulas. Rather, we will present them and show how they can be used.

The M/M/1 Queueing Model

The M/M/1 queueing model is the simplest. It assumes that arrivals follow a Poisson process with mean arrival rate λ, that service times are exponentially distributed with mean service rate μ, and that the queue discipline is FCFS. For this model, the operating characteristics are as follows:

$$\text{Average number in the queue} = L_q = \frac{\lambda^2}{\mu(\mu - \lambda)}$$

$$\text{Average number in the system} = L = \frac{\lambda}{\mu - \lambda}$$

$$\text{Average waiting time in the queue} = W_q = \frac{\lambda}{\mu(\mu - \lambda)}$$

$$\text{Average time in the system} = W = \frac{1}{\mu - \lambda}$$

$$\text{Probability that the system is empty} = P_0 = 1 - \frac{\lambda}{\mu}$$

We note that these formulas are valid only if $\lambda < \mu$. If $\lambda \geq \mu$ (that is, the rate of arrivals is at least as great as the service rate), the numerical results become nonsensical. In practice, this means that the queue will never "average out" but will grow indefinitely (we will discuss this further in the section on simulation). It should be obvious that when $\lambda > \mu$, the server will not be able to keep up with the demand. However, it may seem a little strange that this will occur even when $\lambda = \mu$. You would think that an equal arrival rate and service rate should result in a "balanced" system. This *would* be true in the deterministic case when both arrival and service rates are constant. However, when any variation exists in the arrival or service pattern, the queue will eventually build up indefinitely. The reason is that individual arrival times and service times vary in an unpredictable fashion even though their averages may be constant. As a result, there will be periods of time in which demand is low and the server is idle. This time is lost forever, and the server will not be able to make up for periods of heavy demand at other times. This also explains why queues form when $\lambda < \mu$.

EXAMPLE 4. COMPUTING M/M/1 OPERATING CHARACTERISTICS

For the airline ticket counter example used in the previous examples, we have $\lambda = 2$ customers/minute and $\mu = 3$ customers per minute. Using the formulas given above, we have

$$L_q = \frac{\lambda^2}{\mu(\mu - \lambda)} = \frac{2^2}{3(3 - 2)} = \frac{4}{3} = 1.33 \text{ customers}$$

$$L = \frac{\lambda}{\mu - \lambda} = \frac{2}{3 - 2} = 2.00 \text{ customers}$$

$$W_q = \frac{\lambda}{\mu(\mu - \lambda)} = \frac{2}{3(3 - 2)} = .67 \text{ minutes}$$

$$W = \frac{1}{\mu - \lambda} = \frac{1}{3 - 2} = 1.00 \text{ minutes}$$

$$P_0 = 1 - \frac{\lambda}{\mu} = 1 - \frac{2}{3} = .33$$

These results indicate that on the average, 1.33 customers will be waiting in the queue. In other words, if we took photographs of the waiting line at random times, we would find an average of 1.33 customers waiting. If we include any customers in service, the average number of customers in the system is 2. Each customer can expect to wait an average of .67 minutes in the queue, and spend an average of 1 minute in the system. About one-third of the time, we would expect to see the system empty and the server idle.

The $M/M/1$ queueing model (and all analytical queueing models) provides *steady-state* values of operating characteristics. By steady state we mean that the probability distribution of the operating characteristics does not vary with time. This means that no matter when we observe the system, we would expect to see the same average values of queue lengths, waiting times, and so on. This usually does not happen in practice, even if the average arrival rate and average service rate are constant over time.

To understand this, think of an amusement park that opens at 10:00 A.M. When it opens, there are no customers in the system and hence no queues at any of the rides. As customers arrive, it will take some time for queues to build up. For the first hour or so, the lines and waiting times for popular rides grow longer but then eventually decrease. This is called the *transient period*. Eventually (if the arrival and service rates remain constant), the lines will stabilize and reach steady state. Mathematical queueing models provide only steady-state results. Thus, if we are interested in how long it takes to reach steady state, for example, we must resort to other methods of analysis, such as simulation.

Sensitivity Analysis

Spreadsheets can be useful in dealing with queueing models since they allow managers to study the effects of variations in assumptions. For example, we might be uncertain of our estimate of the arrival rate and want to know how the performance measures would change if our estimate varied by as much as 20 percent. The spreadsheet in Figure 15.9 and its accompanying graph shown in Figure 15.10 are designed to answer this question. Each column B through J of the spreadsheet provides the operating characteristics for a constant service rate of 3 customers per minute, with the arrival rate varying from 1.6 to 2.4 customers per minute (a 20 percent variation from the original figure of 2 customers per minute). We see that the average numbers in the queue and system are the most sensitive

FIGURE 15.9 *Spreadsheet for M/M/1 queueing model analysis*

	A	B	C	D	E	F	G	H	I	J
1	M/M/1 Queueing Model									
2										
3	Lambda	1.6	1.7	1.8	1.9	2	2.1	2.2	2.3	2.4
4	Mu	3.00	3.00	3.00	3.00	3.00	3.00	3.00	3.00	3.00
5										
6	Average number in queue	0.61	0.74	0.90	1.09	1.33	1.63	2.02	2.52	3.20
7	Average number in system	1.14	1.31	1.50	1.73	2.00	2.33	2.75	3.29	4.00
8	Average time in queue	0.38	0.44	0.50	0.58	0.67	0.78	0.92	1.10	1.33
9	Average waiting time in system	0.71	0.77	0.83	0.91	1.00	1.11	1.25	1.43	1.67
10	Probability system is empty	0.47	0.43	0.40	0.37	0.33	0.30	0.27	0.23	0.20

Selected cell formulas

	A	B	C
1	M/M/1 Queueing Model		
2			
3	Lambda	1.6	1.7
4	Mu	3.00	3.00
5			
6	Average number in queue	+B3^2/(B4*(B4-B3))	+C3^2/(C4*(C4-C3))
7	Average number in system	+B3/(B4-B3)	+C3/(C4-C3)
8	Average time in queue	+B3/(B4*(B4-B3))	+C3/(C4*(C4-C3))
9	Average waiting time in system	1/(B4-B3)	1/(C4-C3)
10	Probability system is empty	1-B3/B4	1-C3/C4

FIGURE 15.10 *Graph of performance measures as arrival rate varies*

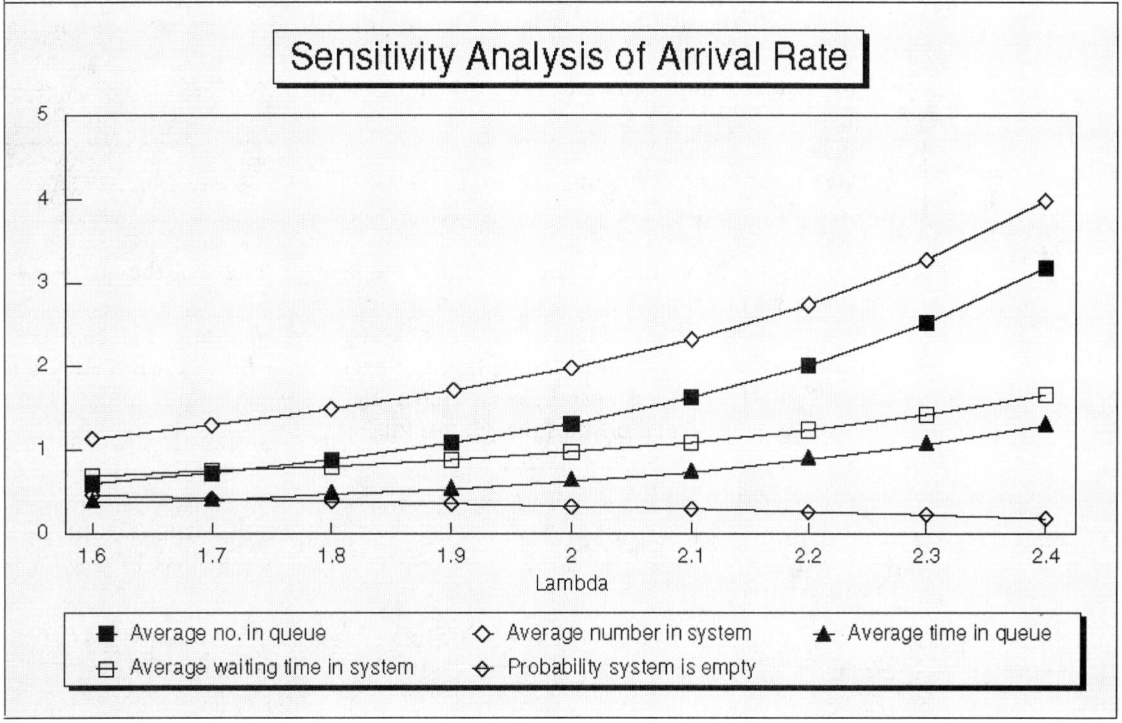

Sensitivity Analysis of Arrival Rate

- ■ Average no. in queue
- ◇ Average number in system
- ▲ Average time in queue
- ⊟ Average waiting time in system
- ⬦ Probability system is empty

to a 20 percent error in our estimate of λ. Waiting times are less sensitive. We also see that as the arrival rate increases, the average number in the queue and system increases at a growing rate while the probability that the system is empty gradually declines. This makes sense because the demand on the system is growing (more customers will have to wait), and the increased demand requires that the server is busy more often. What do you think happens as λ approaches the mean service rate of 3?

Little's Law

MIT Professor John D. C. Little has made many contributions to the field of management science. He is most famous for recognizing a simple yet powerful relationship among operating characteristics in queueing systems. *Little's Law*, as it has become known, is stated as follows:

> For *any* steady-state queueing system, $L = \lambda W$.

This states that the average number of customers in a system is equal to the mean arrival rate times the average time in the system. An intuitive explanation of this result can be seen in the following way. Suppose that you arrive at a queue and spend W minutes in the system (waiting plus service). During this time, more customers will arrive at a rate λ. Thus, when you complete service, a total of λW customers will have arrived after you. This is precisely the number of customers that remain in the system when you leave, or L.

Using similar arguments, we can show the following:

> For *any* steady-state queueing system, $L_q = \lambda W_q$.

This is similar to the first result and states that the average length of the queue equals the mean arrival rate times the average waiting time.

These results provide an alternative way of computing operating characteristics instead of using the formulas provided earlier. For example, if L is known, then we may compute W by L/λ. Also, W_q can be computed as L_q/λ.

Two other general relationships that are useful are

$$L = L_q + \frac{\lambda}{\mu}$$

and

$$W = W_q + \frac{1}{\mu}$$

The first relationship states that the average number in the system is equal to the average queue length plus λ/μ. This makes sense if you recall that the probability that the system is empty is $P_0 = 1 - \lambda/\mu$. Thus, λ/μ is the probability that at least one customer is in the system. If there is at least one customer in the system, then the server must be busy. The term λ/μ simply represents the expected number of customers in service.

The second relationship states that the average time in the system is equal to the average waiting time plus the average service time. This makes sense because the time spent in the system for any customer consists of the waiting time plus the time in service. An exercise at the end of this chapter will ask you to show that these relationships are the same mathematically as the formulas presented earlier for the M/M/1 queueing system.

The M/G/1 Queueing Model

This model applies to situations in which we have Poisson arrivals and arbitrary service times. As we noted earlier, we may not be able to make the assumption that service times follow an exponential distribution. Through empirical analysis of service time data, we may not even find a fit with any known distribution. With the M/G/1 model, all we need to know is the mean service time $1/\mu$ and the variance of the service time, σ^2. These statistics can be calculated easily from data that we can collect. The operating characteristics for the M/G/1 model are given below.

$$L_q = \frac{\lambda^2\sigma^2 + (\lambda/\mu)^2}{2(1 - \lambda/\mu)}$$

$$L = L_q + \frac{\lambda}{\mu}$$

$$W_q = \frac{L_q}{\lambda}$$

$$W = W_q + \frac{1}{\mu}$$

$$P_0 = 1 - \frac{\lambda}{\mu}$$

Notice that σ^2 appears explicitly in L_q and implicitly in L, W_q, and W. Thus, as the variance of the service time increases, the line lengths and waiting times increase. Conversely, as σ^2 decreases, the operating characteristics improve. When $\sigma^2 = 0$, we have a constant service time. In this case,

$$L_q = \frac{(\lambda/\mu)^2}{2(1 - \lambda/\mu)}$$

EXAMPLE 5. AN M/G/1 QUEUEING MODEL

Customers arrive at the airline ticket counter at an average rate of two per minute. Two employees rotate shifts at the counter. Ken is relatively new and can service an average of three customers each minute. Sharon is an experienced employee and can service customers at a faster rate, five per minute. However, Sharon likes to engage in spirited conversation; the standard deviation of her service times is 1.0, whereas Ken's is 0.5. How will the performance of their queues compare?

Since Sharon is nearly twice as fast, you might think that her operating characteristics would be superior. Intuition fails us here because it is difficult to take into account the difference in the variance of service times. Figure 15.11 shows a spreadsheet for the $M/G/1$ model comparing three scenarios. Ken's parameters and operating characteristics are found in column B; Sharon's are found in column D. Even though Sharon is faster, the higher variance causes higher waiting times and queue lengths. In column C, we see that if Sharon reduced her variance to 0.5, her operating characteristics would improve greatly.

FIGURE 15.11   *Spreadsheet for $M/G/1$ queueing example*

A	A	B	C	D
1	M/G/1 Queueing Model			
2				
3	Lambda	2	2	2
4	Mu	3	5	5
5	Sigma	0.5	0.5	1
6				
7	Average number in queue	2.166667	0.966667	3.466667
8	Average number in system	2.833333	1.366667	3.866667
9	Average time in queue	1.083333	0.483333	1.733333
10	Average waiting time in system	1.416667	0.683333	1.933333
11	Probability system is empty	0.333333	0.6	0.6

Selected cell formulas

A	A	B	C	D
1	M/G/1 Queueing Model			
2				
3	Lambda	2	2	2
4	Mu	3	5	5
5	Sigma	0.5	0.5	1
6				
7	Average number in queue	(B3^2*B5^2+(B3/B4)^2)/(2*(1-B3/B4))	(C3^2*C5^2+(C3/C4)^2)/(2*(1-C3/C4))	(D3^2*D5^2+(D3/D4)^2)/(2*(1-D3/D4))
8	Average number in system	+B7+B3/B4	+C7+C3/C4	+D7+D3/D4
9	Average time in queue	+B7/B3	+C7/C3	+D7/D3
10	Average waiting time in system	+B9+1/B4	+C9+1/C4	+D9+1/D4
11	Probability system is empty	1-B3/B4	1-C3/C4	1-D3/D4

Models for Multiple Servers

The queueing models we have discussed thus far assume that we have a single server. You have probably experienced many situations, such as in banks or your college advising or cashier's office, where several servers are available. Customers form a single queue (behind the ubiquitous "Wait Here for Next Available Server" sign) and are served by the next available server (as shown in Figure 15.1). Many telephone-based customer service operations operate in this manner. We may compute the same operating characteristics for such a system; the mathematical formulas are only more complicated.

If we let s be the number of servers, then the operating characteristics for an $M/M/s$ queueing system are as follows:

$$P_0 = \frac{1}{\sum_{n=0}^{s-1} \frac{(\lambda/\mu)^n}{n!} \frac{(\lambda/\mu)^s}{s!} \left(\frac{1}{1-\lambda/s\mu}\right)}$$

$$L_q = P_0 \frac{(\lambda/\mu)^{s+1}}{(s-1)!(s-\lambda/\mu)^2}$$

$$W_q = \frac{L_q}{\lambda}$$

$$W = W_q + \frac{1}{\mu}$$

$$L = \lambda W$$

As with the $M/M/1$ model, steady state will only occur if the arrival rate is less than the service rate. However, since we have multiple servers, the combined service rate is $s\mu$. Therefore, steady state will occur when $\lambda < s\mu$; otherwise, the queue will grow indefinitely.

EXAMPLE 6. AN M/M/*s* QUEUEING MODEL

Figure 15.12 shows a spreadsheet that provides the operating characteristics for an $M/M/s$ queueing system for two to eight servers using the arrival and service rates for the airline ticket counter example that we used in previous examples. (This spreadsheet uses the LOTUS 1-2-3 table lookup function @HLOOKUP to compute the summation and the term $(\lambda/\mu)^s/s!$ in the denominator of P_0. You may wish to consult a LOTUS 1-2-3 manual if you are not familiar with this function. Also, @FACT performs the factorial function.) Comparing these results with Example 4, you can see that for two servers, the queue length and average time in the queue become negligible—a significant decrease. The probability that the system is empty increases to .5, meaning that half of the time both servers will be idle.

FIGURE 15.12   Multiple server model spreadsheet

	A	B	C	D	E	F	G	H	I	J
1	Multiple Server Queue									
2										
3	Lambda	2								
4	Mu	3								
5	Number of servers	2	3	4	5	6	7	8		
6										
7										
8	Average number in queue	0.083	0.009	0.001	0.000	0.000	0.000	0.000		
9	Average number in system	0.750	0.676	0.668	0.667	0.667	0.667	0.667		
10	Average time in queue	0.042	0.005	0.001	0.000	0.000	0.000	0.000		
11	Average waiting time in system	0.375	0.338	0.334	0.333	0.333	0.333	0.333		
12	Probability system is empty	0.500	0.512	0.513	0.513	0.513	0.513	0.513		
13										
14										
15										
16	Lookup table	0	1	2	3	4	5	6	7	8
17		1.0000	0.6667	0.2222	0.0494	0.0082	0.0011	0.0001	0.0000	0.0000
18				1.6667	1.8889	1.9383	1.9465	1.9476	1.9477	1.9477
19				0.2222	0.0494	0.0082	0.0011	0.0001	0.0000	0.0000

Selected cell formulas

	A	B
1	Multiple Server Queue	
2		
3	Lambda	2
4	Mu	3
5	Number of servers	2
6		
7		
8	Average number in queue	(($B$3/$B$4)^(B5+1)/(@FACT(B5-1)*(B5-$B$3/$B$4)^2))*B12
9	Average number in system	+B11*$B$3
10	Average time in queue	+B8/$B$3
11	Average waiting time in system	+B10+1/$B$4
12	Probability system is empty	1/(@HLOOKUP(B5,$D$16..$H$18,2)+@HLOOKUP(B5,$D$16..$H$19,3)*(1/(1-($B$3/(B5*$B$4)))))
13		
14		
15		
16	Lookup table	0
17		1.0000
18		
19		

Selected cell formulas

	C	D
1		
2		
3		
4		
5	3	4
6		
7		
8	(($B$3/$B$4)^(C5+1)/(@FACT(C5-1)*(C5-$B$3/$B$4)^2))*C12	(($B$3/$B$4)^(D5+1)/(@FACT(D5-1)*(D5-$B$3/$B$4)^2))*D12
9	+C11*$B$3	+D11*$B$3
10	+C8/$B$3	+D8/$B$3
11	+C10+1/$B$4	+D10+1/$B$4
12	1/(@HLOOKUP(C5,$D$16..$H$18,2)+@HLOOKUP(C5,$D$16..$H$19,3)*(1/(1-($B$3/(C5*$B$4)))))	1/(@HLOOKUP(D5,$D$16..$H$18,2)+@HLOOKUP(D5,$D$16..$H$19,3)*(1/(1-($B$3/(D5*$B$4)))))
13		
14		
15		
16	1	2
17	($B$3/$B$4)^C16/@FACT(C16)	($B$3/$B$4)^D16/@FACT(D16)
18		+B17+C17
19		(($B$3/$B$4)^D16)/@FACT(D16)

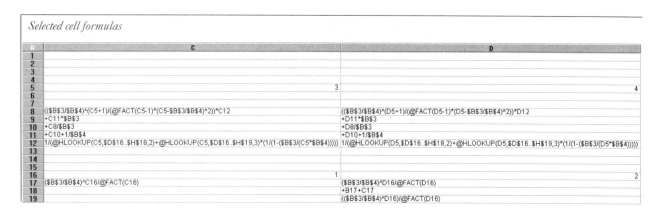

A Model for Finite Calling Populations

All the models we have considered so far assume that the calling population is infinite; that is, an unlimited number of customers may seek service. With this assumption, the mean arrival rate remains constant regardless of how many customers are in the system. In many applications, though, the calling population is finite. One example would be a factory in which the "customers" are machines that have failed and are waiting for repair. Clearly if all machines are down, then no further arrivals can take place. Thus, the mean arrival rate depends on the number of customers in the system. Another example is an office copy machine; the calling population consists only of the workers in the office.

To model this situation, we assume that the arrival rate of each customer follows a Poisson process with mean λ. (In the previous models, λ represented the mean arrival rate for the system, not an individual customer. We define N to be the number of customers in the population. The operating characteristics for this model are

$$P_0 = \frac{1}{\displaystyle\sum_{n=0}^{N} \frac{N!}{(N-n)!}(\lambda/\mu)^n}$$

$$L_q = N - \frac{\lambda + \mu}{\lambda}(1 - P_0)$$

$$L = L_q + (1 - P_0)$$

$$W_q = \frac{L_q}{(N-L)\lambda}$$

$$W = W_q + 1/\mu$$

EXAMPLE 7. A FINITE CALLING POPULATION MODEL

A large business school has eight photocopiers. Each copier averages 60 hours between breakdowns in a random fashion. Thus, the mean arrival rate for each copier is $\lambda = \frac{1}{60}$ copiers per hour and follows a Poisson process. Service times, which extend from the time service is called until the repairperson arrives, are exponentially distributed with a mean of 30 hours. Thus, the mean service rate is $\mu = \frac{1}{30}$ machines per hour.

Figure 15.13 shows a spreadsheet that computes the operating characteristics for the finite calling population model. We see that, on average, about five copiers are inoperable and waiting for repair for an average of 150 hours. There is virtually no chance that all eight copiers are functioning normally since $P_0 = .001$. What can the school do to provide better service to its faculty and staff? One alternative is to purchase more reliable machines that do not fail as often. Another alternative is to add more machines. How would you make this decision?

FIGURE 15.13   *Spreadsheet queueing model for finite calling populations*

	A	B	C	D	E	F	G	H	I	J	K	L
1	Finite Calling Population Model											
2												
3	Lambda	0.016667										
4	Mu	0.033333										
5	Number in population	8										
6												
7	Average number in queue	5.003										
8	Average number in system	6.002										
9	Average time in queue	150.206										
10	Average waiting time in system	180.206										
11	Probability system is empty	0.001										
12												
13												
14												
15												
16	Lookup table	0	1	2	3	4	5	6	7	8	9	10
17		1	4	14	42	105	210	315	315	157.5	ERR	ERR
18		1	5	19	61	166	376	691	1006	1163.5	ERR	ERR

Selected cell formulas

	A	B	C
1	Finite Calling Population Model		
2			
3	Lambda	0.05	
4	Mu	0.5	
5	Number in population	6	
6			
7	Average number in queue	+$B$5-($B$3+$B$4)*(1-$B$11)/$B$3	
8	Average number in system	+B7+1-B11	
9	Average time in queue	+B7/(($B$5-$B$8)*$B$3)	
10	Average waiting time in system	+B9+1/$B$4	
11	Probability system is empty	1/(@HLOOKUP($B$5,C16..L18,2))	
12			
13			
14			
15			
16	Lookup table	0	1
17		((@FACT($B$5)/@FACT($B$5-B16))*($B$3/$B$4)^B16)	((@FACT($B$5)/@FACT($B$5-C16))*($B$3/$B$4)^C16)
18		1	+B18+C17

Distribution of Customers in a Queueing System

For the $M/M/1$, $M/M/s$, and finite calling population queueing models, we computed P_0, the probability that the system is empty. We can develop similar formulas for P_n, the probability that exactly n customers will be in the system. This allows us to construct a distribution of the number of customers that might be found in such a system. These formulas are given below.

    $M/M/1$ Model:

$$P_n = \left(\frac{\lambda}{\mu}\right)^n P_0$$

$M/M/s$ Model:

If $n \leq s$:

$$P_n = \frac{(\lambda/\mu)^n}{n!} P_0$$

If $n > s$:

$$P_n = \frac{(\lambda/\mu)^n}{s! s^{(n-s)}} P_0$$

Finite Calling Population Model:

$$P_n = \frac{N!}{(N-n)!} \left(\frac{\lambda}{\mu}\right)^n P_0$$

for $n = 0, 1, \ldots, N$. We may easily incorporate these into the spreadsheets we have presented for these queueing systems; we leave that to you as an exercise at the end of the chapter.

OPTIMIZING QUEUEING SYSTEMS

In Example 6 we saw that an increase in the number of servers caused dramatic changes in the operating characteristics of the queueing system. Managers would be interested if the added cost of more servers were beneficial. Therefore, managers face a fundamental economic problem of balancing the cost of providing higher levels of service with the benefits to customers of smaller lines and waiting times. Queueing theory helps managers to determine the best values for service rates, number of service facilities, and size of service facilities.

In many situations, attaching a dollar cost to waiting is not relevant until customers begin to leave. Making a decision on the number of servers would require some behavioral consumer research to determine how much waiting customers are willing to tolerate before they leave the system (or how long the lines can be before customers balk). Spreadsheets can certainly provide the "what if?" capability to assess these trade-offs.

In other situations, the cost of waiting is related to resources that are tied up. For example, in factories, you can use a worker's salary or the value of an idle machine as a measure of the cost of waiting. If it is possible to attach a cost to waiting, then we can develop economic models for this decision problem. Figure 15.14 shows an influence diagram that describes the relationships among these factors. We see that the key managerial decision is the number of servers to have. However, managers might also be able to affect the service rate by changing the technology of the service process, or changing the arrival rate through demand management strategies. We will consider only the number of servers as a decision variable in the following model.

To develop a mathematical model, let

C_w = Cost of waiting per customer per time period
C_s = Cost per server per time period

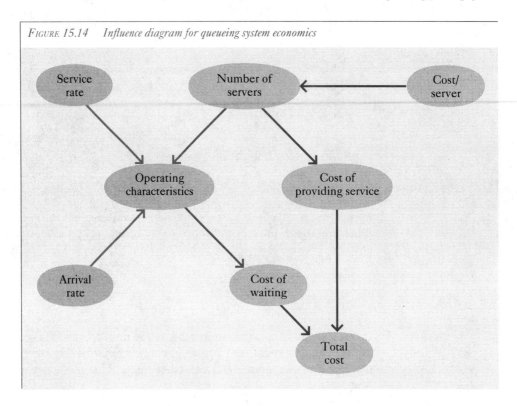

FIGURE 15.14   *Influence diagram for queueing system economics*

The total cost of providing s servers is

$$\text{Total cost} = C_w L + C_s s$$

It might seem strange that the waiting cost is multiplied by L rather than W. However, recall that L is the average number of customers in the system *at any instant in time*. Hence, L is independent of time. Note that C_w is expressed as the cost per customer per time and L has dimensions of number of customers. Then $C_w L$ would have dimensions of cost per time.

EXAMPLE 8. FINDING AN OPTIMAL NUMBER OF SERVERS

Prescriptions at a hospital pharmacy arrive at an average rate of 22 per hour. One pharmacist can fill a prescription in about five minutes, or at a rate of 12 per hour. Pharmacists are paid $30.00 per hour, and hospital administrators have attached a cost of $100 per hour to waiting on prescriptions. What is the optimal number of pharmacists to have?

Figure 15.15 shows a spreadsheet designed to answer this question. First, notice that since $\lambda = 22$ and $\mu = 12$, the ratio of λ/μ is greater than one, indicating that a single server cannot handle the volume of demand without the queue growing indef-

Figure 15.15   Queue optimization spreadsheet

	A	B	C	D	E	F	G	H	I	J
1	Queue Optimization Spreadsheet									
2										
3	Lambda	22								
4	Mu	12								
5	Waiting cost/customer/time, C	$100.00								
6	Cost/server/time, Cs	$30.00								
7										.
8	Number of servers	1	2	3	4	5	6	7	8	
9	Average number in queue	-4.033	9.645	0.580	0.115	0.025	0.005	0.001	0.000	
10	Average number in system	-2.200	11.478	2.413	1.948	1.858	1.839	1.834	1.834	
11	Average time in queue	-0.183	0.438	0.026	0.005	0.001	0.000	0.000	0.000	
12	Average waiting time in system	-0.100	0.522	0.110	0.089	0.084	0.084	0.083	0.083	
13	Probability system is empty	-0.833	0.043	0.140	0.156	0.159	0.160	0.160	0.160	
14										
15	Customer cost	($403.33)	$964.49	$58.00	$11.47	$2.51	$0.53	$0.11	$0.02	
16	Server cost	$30.00	$60.00	$90.00	$120.00	$150.00	$180.00	$210.00	$240.00	
17	Total cost	($373.33)	$1,024.49	$148.00	$131.47	$152.51	$180.53	$210.11	$240.02	
18										
19	Lookup table	0	1	2	3	4	5	6	7	8
20			1.0000	1.8333	1.6806	1.0270	0.4707	0.1726	0.0527	0.0138	0.0032
21				2.8333	4.5139	5.5409	6.0116	6.1842	6.2369	6.2507
22				1.6806	1.0270	0.4707	0.1726	0.0527	0.0138	0.0032

Selected cell formulas

	B	C	D
8	1	(($B$3/$B$4)^(C8+1)/(@FACT(C8-1)*(C8-$B$3/$B$4)^2))*C13	3
9	+B3^2/(B4*(B4-B3))	+C12*$B$3	(($B$3/$B$4)^(D8+1)/(@FACT(D8-1)*(D8-$B$3/$B$4)^2))*D13
10	+B9+B3/B4	+C9/$B$3	+D12*$B$3
11	+B3/(B4*(B4-B3))	+C11+1/$B$4	+D9/$B$3
12	+B11+1/B4	1/(@HLOOKUP(C8,$D$19..$H$21,2)+@HLOOKUP(C8,$D$19..$H$22,3)*(1/(1-($B$3/(C8*$B$4)))))	+D11+1/$B$4
13	1-B3/B4		1/(@HLOOKUP(D8,$D$19..$H$21,2)+@HLOOKUP(D8,$D$19..$H$22,3)*(1/(1-($B$3/(D8*$B$4)))))
14		+$B$5*C9	
15	+$B$5*B9	+$B$6*C8	+$B$5*D9
16	+$B$6*B8	+$B$5*C9+C8*$B$6	+$B$6*D8
17	+$B$5*B9+B8*$B$6		+$B$5*D9+D8*$B$6
18			1
19		0	($B$3/$B$4)^C19/@FACT(C19)	2
20		1	($B$3/$B$4)^D19/@FACT(D19)
21			+B20+C20
22			(($B$3/$B$4)^D19)/@FACT(D19)

initely. This is reflected in column B of the spreadsheet with negative values for the operating characteristics. The *minimum* number of servers, s, must satisfy $\lambda < s\mu$. In this case, we see that we need at least two servers. As the number of servers increases, the operating characteristics improve. Also note that eventually the average number in the queue falls to zero and all the waiting time in the system is taken up in service. At this point we are paying for more pharmacists with nothing to do!

The optimal number of servers balances the waiting and service cost. Row 17 in the spreadsheet gives the total cost for a given number of servers. We see that the minimum total cost occurs for four servers (see Figure 15.16). We might wish to experiment with different estimates of the waiting cost to examine the sensitivity of this solution to our economic estimates. What would happen if the waiting cost estimate were doubled?

FIGURE 15.16   *Cost curves for finding the optimum number of servers*

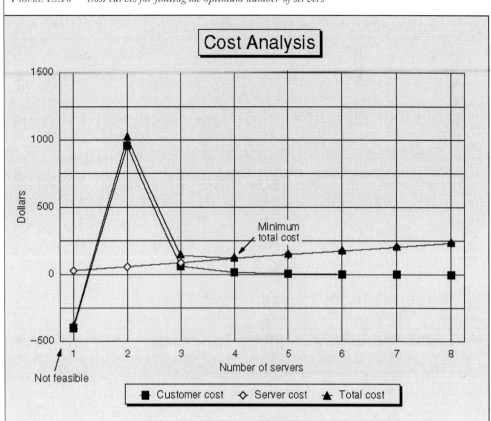

Meeting Service Level Constraints

When costs are difficult to quantify, an alternative way of determining the optimal number of servers is to set a *service level*, that is, specify a value for P_0, the probability that a customer does not have to wait. To understand this better, let us consider the $M/M/1$ queueing model. For this model,

$$P_0 = 1 - \lambda/\mu$$

Suppose a manager desires a service level of 0.80. That is, the probability that a customer will wait for service is $1 - .80 = 0.20$. This means that λ/μ must be no greater than 0.20. Since the manager probably would not be able to control the arrival rate, meeting this constraint means that the service rate must satisfy

$$\mu > \frac{\lambda}{0.2}$$

or

$$\mu > 5\lambda$$

Thus, the service rate must be at least five times the arrival rate. This might be accomplished through the use of technology such as scanners or other automated equipment that can provide fast service, or it may require additional servers.

Because the formula for P_0 is rather complicated for the multiple server model, management scientists have developed tables to make this analysis easier. One example is given in Table 15.2. The body of the table gives the upper limit on λ/μ for which the service level is met. For example, to achieve a service level of 0.8 with four servers, λ/μ cannot exceed 2.1024. The table may be used as follows:

Step 1. Calculate $\mu = 1/$mean service time.

Step 2. Choose the column corresponding to the required service level.

Step 3. Multiply each entry in the column by μ. These entries provide upper limits on the arrival rate that meet the service level constraint.

Step 4. Use s servers whenever the arrival rate is between the values computed for rows $s - 1$ and s.

EXAMPLE 9. CHOOSING SERVERS TO MEET SERVICE LEVEL CONSTRAINTS

The number of customers arriving at a quick service restaurant varies considerably over the course of a day and week. One of the important decisions that the franchise manager must make is the scheduling of part-time employees during the week. The manager has set a service level of .6; thus, 40 percent of the time, customers should not have to wait to place their orders. The mean service time has been estimated to be two minutes. Therefore, $\mu = 0.5$ customers/minute.

From Table 15.2, we multiply the numbers in the column corresponding to $P_0 = $ .6 by $\frac{1}{2}$. The first few are shown below.

Number of servers	Upper limit on arrival rate (customers/minute)
1	.2000
2	.5583
3	.9518
4	1.3624

Thus, if the arrival rate is between .5583 and .9518 customers per minute (33.5 and 57.1 customers per hour), three servers should be used. This information will help the manager to plan staffing levels and ensure consistent service at any time of the week.

TABLE 15.2
Service level table for M/m/s queue

Number of Servers, c	Required Service Level										
	0.9500	0.9000	0.8500	0.8000	0.7500	0.7000	0.6500	0.6000	0.5500	0.5000	0.2500
1	0.0500	0.1000	0.1500	0.2000	0.2500	0.3000	0.3500	0.4000	0.4500	0.5000	0.7500
2	0.3422	0.5000	0.6278	0.7403	0.8431	0.9390	1.0298	1.1165	1.2000	1.2808	1.6559
3	0.7879	1.0395	1.2313	1.3930	1.5364	1.6675	1.7888	1.9036	2.0121	2.1155	2.5844
4	1.3184	1.6527	1.8985	2.1024	2.2802	2.4402	2.5872	2.7247	2.8543	2.9773	3.5242
5	1.9051	2.3129	2.6071	2.8470	3.0552	3.2409	3.4106	3.5685	3.7160	3.8562	4.4719
6	2.5317	3.0066	3.3438	3.6173	3.8521	4.0613	4.2520	4.4278	4.5918	4.7468	5.4242
7	3.1879	3.7254	4.1024	4.4063	4.6661	4.8964	5.1059	5.2982	5.4777	5.6468	6.3805
8	3.8684	4.4637	4.8782	5.2102	5.4935	5.7441	5.9700	6.1778	6.3715	6.5530	7.3399
9	4.5684	5.2176	5.6681	6.0266	6.3317	6.6003	6.8427	7.0653	7.2723	7.4655	8.3024
10	5.2848	5.9855	6.4688	6.8524	7.1778	7.4644	7.7223	7.9583	8.1777	8.3827	9.2664
11	6.0153	6.7652	7.2798	7.6876	8.0325	8.3355	8.6083	8.8575	9.0887	9.3046	10.2320
12	6.7574	7.5543	8.0993	8.5298	8.8935	9.2120	9.4989	9.7607	10.0027	10.2296	11.1992
13	7.5106	8.3520	8.9259	9.3790	9.7606	10.0941	10.3942	10.6677	10.9207	11.1577	12.1680
14	8.2731	9.1574	9.7595	10.2337	10.6325	10.9808	11.2934	11.5786	11.8418	12.0882	13.1375
15	9.0434	9.9707	10.5993	11.0930	11.5083	11.8714	12.1966	12.4927	12.7660	13.0218	14.1086
16	9.8223	10.7895	11.4438	11.9579	12.3888	12.7652	13.1028	13.4091	13.6926	13.9569	15.0805
17	10.6074	11.6137	12.2931	12.8266	13.2731	13.6628	14.0114	14.3286	14.6215	14.8944	16.0531
18	11.3989	12.4434	13.1478	13.6985	14.1606	14.5636	14.9231	15.2505	15.5527	15.8335	17.0266
19	12.1957	13.2770	14.0056	14.5751	15.0513	15.4667	15.8372	16.1747	16.4855	16.7741	18.0008
20	12.9981	14.1160	14.8673	15.4540	15.9450	16.3722	16.7536	17.1005	17.4199	17.7171	18.9758
21	13.8059	14.9582	15.7321	16.3360	16.8411	17.2808	17.6723	18.0286	18.3559	18.6609	19.9516
22	14.6176	15.8051	16.6009	17.2212	17.7403	18.1909	18.5927	18.9575	19.2934	19.6062	20.9274
23	15.4340	16.6543	17.4720	18.1095	18.6411	19.1027	19.5145	19.8888	20.2332	20.5530	21.9039
24	16.2535	17.5074	18.3462	18.9993	19.5442	20.0175	20.4388	20.8216	21.1730	21.5007	22.8813
25	17.0778	18.3637	19.2228	19.8915	20.4489	20.9931	21.3645	21.7552	22.1152	22.4491	23.8594

Table from Agnihothri and Taylor, "Staffing a Centralized Appointment Scheduling Department at Lourdes Hospital," *Interfaces*, Vol. 21, No. 5, September–October 1991, pp. 1–11.

SIMULATION OF QUEUEING SYSTEMS

Queueing systems lend themselves well to simulation analysis for several reasons. First, mathematical models of queueing systems require restrictive assumptions, such as Poisson arrivals and exponential service times; most practical situations are messier.[1] The typical real-life situation has multiple servers and nonexponential service times. Many service systems such as restaurants and retail stores vary the number of servers, the service time, and even the queue discipline to adjust to busy or slack periods. In many situations, customers arrive in batches, not individually. Average service times may vary from one server to another. When we cannot validate the assumptions required by analytical models, they cannot provide useful results. Even for simple cases such as the $M/M/s$ queue, the mathematical formulas can get quite complicated, and for many realistic problems it is not even possible to derive a mathematical formula. Simulation, on the other hand, can be used to model nearly any situation, regardless of the assumptions made.

A second drawback of analytical queueing models is that they provide only *steady-state* values for operating characteristics. For systems that do not run continuously (as is the case with most service operations) steady state may not even be reached before the system closes. Operating managers may be more interested in transient behavior than in steady-state results.

We simulated a queueing system in Chapter 14. The spreadsheet developed for the supermarket operation simulation example can be modified easily to simulate $M/M/1$ queueing systems. Figure 15.17 shows a portion of a spreadsheet for simulating an $M/M/1$ system (the actual spreadsheet simulates the service of 1,000 customers). The key modifications are the calculations of the average waiting and idle times. The average waiting times (column L) are found by dividing the cumulative waiting time (column K) by the number of customers served (column C). The average idle time (column N) is found by dividing the cumulative idle time (column M) by the time when service is completed (column H). Note that we are not computing the idle time *per customer*, but the *fraction* of time the server is idle, or equivalently, the fraction of time that no customers are in the system. This corresponds to P_0. In the range A14. .B18, we compute the expected waiting time and idle time as determined by analytical formulas and the actual simulation results.

We see that even for the simulation of 1,000 customers, the simulated values are not that close to the expected values. This can be explained by examining a graph of the average waiting time (see Figure 15.18). We see that during the first half of the simulation, the average waiting time starts very low and varies dramatically. This is the transient period during which the queueing system is "warming up." Eventually, however, you can see that the average waiting time levels off and approaches steady state. Notice, however, that the statistical averages include all the data during the transient period; this biases the overall average and shows why the simulated value is less than the expected, steady-state value.

---

[1] Jack Byrd, "The Value of Queueing Theory," *Interfaces*, Vol. 8, No. 3, May 1978, pp. 22–26.

FIGURE 15.17   M/M/1 queueing system spreadsheet

	A	B	C	D	E	F	G	H	I	J	K	L	M	N
1	Single Server Queueing		CUSTOMER	TIME BETWEEN ARRIVALS	ARRIVAL TIME	START TIME	SERVICE TIME	COMPLETION TIME	WAIT TIME	IDLE TIME	CUMULATIVE WAIT TIME	AVERAGE WAIT TIME	CUMULATIVE IDLE TIME	AVERAGE IDLE TIME
2	Simulation Spreadsheet													
3														
4			1	0.3893	0.3893	0.3893	0.0498	0.4391	0.0000	0.3893	0.0000	0.0000	0.3893	0.8866
5	Mean arrival rate (customers/time)	2	2	0.2173	0.6066	0.6066	0.0563	0.6629	0.0000	0.1675	0.0000	0.0000	0.5569	0.8400
6	Mean service rate (customers/time	3	3	1.4476	2.0542	2.0542	0.4503	2.5045	0.0000	1.3913	0.0000	0.0000	1.9402	0.7778
7			4	0.2413	2.2955	2.5045	0.3352	2.8397	0.2090	0.0000	0.2090	0.0523	1.9482	0.6860
8			5	0.1695	2.4651	2.8397	0.7875	3.6273	0.3747	0.0000	0.5837	0.1167	1.9482	0.5371
9			6	0.1569	2.6220	3.6273	0.1782	3.8055	1.0053	0.0000	1.5890	0.2648	1.9482	0.5119
10			7	0.4589	3.0809	3.8055	0.1121	3.9176	0.7246	0.0000	2.3136	0.3305	1.9482	0.4973
11			8	0.3129	3.3938	3.9176	0.4446	4.3622	0.5238	0.0000	2.8374	0.3547	1.9482	0.4466
12			9	0.2649	3.6587	4.3622	0.0439	4.4061	0.7035	0.0000	3.5409	0.3934	1.9482	0.4422
13			10	0.2938	3.9525	4.4061	0.4821	4.8882	0.4535	0.0000	3.9945	0.3994	1.9482	0.3985
14	Expected waiting time	0.6667	11	0.2843	4.2368	4.8882	0.4397	5.3729	0.6514	0.0000	4.6458	0.4223	1.9482	0.3657
15	Expected idle time	0.3333	12	0.7058	4.9427	5.3729	0.2736	5.6015	0.3852	0.0000	5.0311	0.4193	1.9482	0.3478
16			13	0.2898	5.2325	5.6015	0.1404	5.7420	0.3690	0.0000	5.4001	0.4154	1.9482	0.3393
17	Average waiting time	0.5945	14	0.0324	5.2649	5.7420	0.0902	5.8321	0.4771	0.0000	5.8772	0.4198	1.9482	0.3340
18	Average idle time	0.3703	15	0.1219	5.3868	5.8321	0.1862	6.0183	0.4453	0.0000	6.3225	0.4215	1.9482	0.3237
19			16	0.8029	6.1897	6.1897	0.2726	6.4623	0.0000	0.1714	6.3225	0.3952	2.1195	0.3280
20			17	0.7426	6.9323	6.9323	0.4775	7.4098	0.0000	0.4699	6.3225	0.3719	2.5894	0.3495
21			18	0.4272	7.3595	7.4098	2.8515	10.2613	0.0504	0.0000	6.3729	0.3540	2.5894	0.2524
22			19	0.9018	8.2612	10.2613	0.1329	10.3942	2.0001	0.0000	8.3729	0.4407	2.5894	0.2491
23			20	1.3775	9.6387	10.3942	0.0334	10.4277	0.7555	0.0000	9.1285	0.4564	2.5894	0.2483

Selected cell formulas

	C	D	E	F	G	H	I	J	K	L	M	N
4	1	-(1/$B$5)*@LN(@RAND)	+D4	@MAX(E4,H3)	-(1/$B$6)*@LN(@RAND)	+F4+G4	+F4-E4	+F4-H3	+I4	+K4/C4	+J4	+M4/H4
5	2	-(1/$B$5)*@LN(@RAND)	+E4+D5	@MAX(E5,H4)	-(1/$B$6)*@LN(@RAND)	+F5+G5	+F5-E5	+F5-H4	+K4+I5	+K5/C5	+M4+J5	+M5/H5
6	3	-(1/$B$5)*@LN(@RAND)	+E5+D6	@MAX(E6,H5)	-(1/$B$6)*@LN(@RAND)	+F6+G6	+F6-E6	+F6-H5	+K5+I6	+K6/C6	+M5+J6	+M6/H6
7	4	-(1/$B$5)*@LN(@RAND)	+E6+D7	@MAX(E7,H6)	-(1/$B$6)*@LN(@RAND)	+F7+G7	+F7-E7	+F7-H6	+K6+I7	+K7/C7	+M6+J7	+M7/H7

FIGURE 15.18   Graph of average waiting time

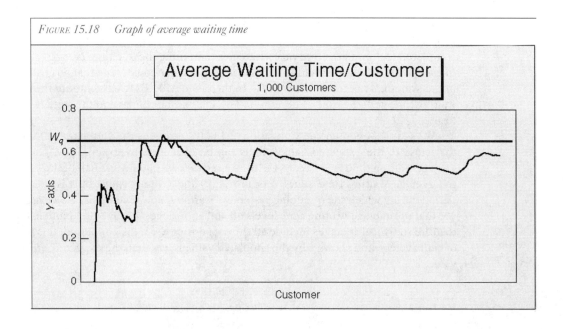

Since steady-state averages do not tell us anything about the behavior of queueing systems during transient periods or the variation of the performance measures, making decisions based only on averages can be dangerous. For example, although the average waiting time in a queueing system in steady state might be 34 seconds, the waiting times of individual customers might be as long as several minutes. Thus, it is useful to know other statistical information, such as the distribution of the average waiting time, confidence intervals about the mean, and the minimum and maximum values. Simulation can be used to obtain such information and provide a manager with better decision making capabilities.

MANAGING QUEUEING SYSTEMS

Understanding the characteristics of the customers, servers, queue discipline, and system configuration is the first step toward analyzing queueing systems to improve their performance. Companies need to conduct research to understand customers' attitudes. They must ask questions such as these: How long do customers expect to wait? At what point does the wait time result in a significant decrease in customer satisfaction? What is the relationship between wait time and customer satisfaction? Are waiting time expectations correlated with the time that customers actually are willing to wait? Once these questions are addressed, companies can consider a variety of improvements to their queueing systems. Improvements to queueing systems can involve technical as well as psychological solutions.

Technical Solutions

The most straightforward type of technical solution is simply to add more servers. For example, Zayre department stores developed a policy that if more than three people are in line at a checkout register, they will open another register. One major supermarket firm developed a forecasting model to predict customer demand for checkout services one-half hour into the future based on counts of arriving and departing customers obtained through sensors at the entrance and exit doors. The model was designed to assist the store manager in opening and closing checkout counters in the short term.

Most banks have installed automatic teller machines (ATMs) to shift demand away from the human tellers. In many cases, this strategy has backfired because customers want the human interaction as part of the service. Restaurants have shifted some of the work to the customer by introducing self-service beverage bars in efforts to speed service. Drive-through windows and menu packages (for example, burger, fries, and a drink ordered together) are other innovations designed to reduce service times. Although the differences may only be a few seconds, the cumulative effects can be significant.

Some key questions to consider include the following:[2]

---

[2]Randolph W. Hall, "From Trade-Offs to Trade-Ups: The New Face of 'Queueing Theory,'" *APICS—The Performance Advantage*, July 1992, pp. 32–33.

1. Are servers idle when customers are waiting? If so, retrain employees and consider improving the maintenance of the equipment that servers may use.
2. Are resources used inflexibly? If so, alternate employees or equipment between direct customer service and "back room" activities.
3. Are employees operating below peak efficiency? If so, automate the process, improve communication, or redesign the job.

Another approach is to make simple changes in staffing schedules. This often eliminates queueing problems at little or no cost. We can use Table 15.2 to determine the best staffing policies as customer demand varies over time.

Psychological Solutions

Customers become frustrated when a person enters a line next to them and receives service first. Of course, *that* customer feels a certain sense of satisfaction. People expect to be treated fairly; in queueing situations that means "first-come, first-served." In the mid-1960s, Chemical Bank was one of the first to switch to a serpentine line (one line feeding into several servers) from multiple parallel lines. American Airlines copied this at their airport counters and most others followed suit. Studies have shown that customers are happier when they wait in a serpentine line, rather than in parallel lines, even if that type of line increases their wait.

Understanding the psychological perception of waiting is as important in addressing queueing problems as are mathematical and simulation approaches. We discussed some of these issues in earlier chapters. Creative solutions that do not rely on technical approaches can be quite effective. One example involved complaints of tenants waiting for elevators in a high-rise building. Rather than pursuing an expensive technical solution of installing a faster elevator, the building manager installed mirrors in the elevator lobbies to help the tenants pass the time. This is commonly found in many hotels today. Another example occurred at the Houston airport. Passengers complained about long waits when picking up their baggage. The airline solved the problem by moving the baggage to the farthest carousel from the planes. While the total time to deliver the baggage was not changed, the fact that passengers had to walk farther and wait less eliminated the complaints.

Nothing is worse than not knowing when the next bus will arrive. Not knowing how long a wait will be creates anxiety. To alleviate this kind of uncertainty, the Disney theme parks inform people how long of a wait to expect by placing signs at various points along the queue. Chemical Bank pays customers who wait in line more than seven minutes $5. This was chosen because research indicated that waits up to 10 minutes were tolerable. Customers have provided good feedback; they do not seem to mind waiting longer if they receive something for it.

Florida Power and Light, the first overseas winner of Japan's Deming Prize for quality, developed a system that informed customers of the estimated waiting time for telephone calls, allowing customers to call back later if the wait would be too long.[3] Consumer re-

---

[3] Bob Graessel and Pete Zeidler, "Using Quality Function Deployment to Improve Customer Service," *Quality Progress,* November 1993, pp. 59–63.

search revealed that customers would wait 94 seconds without knowing the length of wait. It also showed that customers began to be dissatisfied after waiting about 2 minutes. But when customers knew the length of wait, they were willing to wait 105 seconds longer—a total of 199 seconds! Thus, Florida Power and Light knew that it could buy more time, without sacrificing customer satisfaction, by giving customers a choice of holding for a predicted period of time or deferring the call to a later time. The system, called Smartqueue, was implemented, and virtually all customers considered it helpful in subsequent satisfaction surveys. From the company's perspective, Smartqueue increased the time customers were willing to wait without being dissatisfied by an appreciable amount.

Other methods of changing customers' perceptions involve distractions. Time spent without anything to do seems longer than occupied time. Large amusement parks such as Disney and Busch Gardens have roving entertainers to distract the crowds that are waiting. Since 1959, the Manhattan Savings Bank has offered live entertainment and even dog and boat shows during the busy lunchtime hours. Supermarkets place "impulse" items such as candy, batteries, and other small items as well as magazines near checkouts to grab customers' attention. The Postal Service has been experimenting with video displays that not only distract customers but also inform them of postal procedures so that they can speed up their transactions.

The Importance of Culture.[4] Sociologists have discovered that queueing is an acquired social trait that began in Great Britain during the world wars and was passed on to North America and other European countries. In some parts of the world, particularly in southern Europe and Latin America, waiting is virtually nonexistent. Disney found this out after opening Euro-Disney and expecting ticket buyers to line up in the same fashion as those at their U.S. parks—they don't. In some Arab countries, where women hold a subordinate position, it is common for men to cut in front of women. Try to model that mathematically!

These issues tell us that solving management science problems must address a variety of behavioral and social factors in addition to technical solutions. It is important for managers and management scientists alike to look beyond technical approaches when addressing important problems.

MANAGEMENT SCIENCE PRACTICE

In this section we describe some details of the telemarketing queueing study conducted at L.L. Bean.

Queueing Models for Telemarketing at L.L. Bean[5]

L.L. Bean is widely known for retailing high-quality outdoor goods and apparel, with more than 85 percent of sales generated through mail orders and telephone orders via

---

[4]Malcolm Gladwell, "Queue & A: The Long and Short of Standing in Line," *The Washington Post National Weekly Edition*, December 21–27, 1992, p. 38.

[5]Adaptation and figure from Quinn, *et al.*, "Allocating Telecommunications Resources at L.L. Bean, Inc." *Interfaces*, Vol. 21, No. 1, January–February, 1991, pp. 75–91.

800-number service, which was introduced in 1986. About 65 percent of total annual sales volume is generated through orders taken at two telemarketing centers located in Maine. The telephone system at L.L. Bean is shown in Figure 15.19. An arriving call (point 1 in Figure 15.19) seizes one of the trunk lines if one is available; otherwise it is routed to a busy signal. The call arrives at an L.L. Bean switch (point 2); the switch checks the queue length; if the queue is full, the call is routed to a busy signal, freeing the trunk. Otherwise, the call enters the queue. Callers may abandon the call (hang up) while waiting for an agent, freeing the trunk and queue position (point 3). When one of the agents is available, the call is serviced, freeing a queue position (point 4). When the call is completed, a trunk and an agent are freed (point 5). From a strategic planning perspective, L.L. Bean can control the number of trunks, number of agent positions, and queue capacity. In the short term, decisions must be made to staff on a half-hourly basis, 24 hours a day, seven days a week to meet expected demand. In the intermediate term, the most critical decision is the number of agents to hire and train. These decisions affect the longer-term capacity issues as well as the short-term staffing issues.

The critical nature of these decisions can be understood by considering that during the three-week period before Christmas in 1989, the number of telephone agents increased from 500 to 1,275, telephone trunks expanded from 150 to 576, and the overall operational capacity was 18 percent of the annual call volume.

L.L. Bean estimated that in 1988 it lost at least $10 million of profit by allocating telemarketing resources suboptimally. Customer service had become unacceptable; in some half-hours, 80 percent of the calls dialed received a busy signal because the trunks were full. Those customers who got through might have waited 10 minutes for an available agent. As a consequence, the company launched a project to better allocate resources and manage its queues.

A mathematical model was developed for the key decision variables:

1. Number of trunks
2. Number of agents scheduled
3. Queue capacity (maximum number of wait positions)

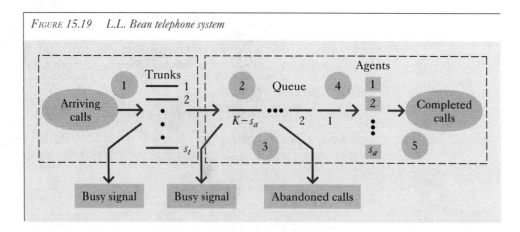

FIGURE 15.19   *L.L. Bean telephone system*

The model searches for the combination of resources that minimizes the expected costs of trunking, labor, connect time, and lost-order profits. The cost calculations are derived as follows:

1. The expected trunking costs are calculated to include average charges for both installation and monthly maintenance.
2. The expected labor costs are calculated as the number of agents times the fully loaded pay rate.
3. The expected connect costs are calculated by using the expected connect time per call multiplied by the number of calls times the 800-number service rate.
4. The expected cost of permanently lost orders is calculated in two steps. First, the percentage of calls generating orders is multiplied by the expected number of permanently lost calls to get expected lost orders. This result is then multiplied by the average value of an order. The expected number of permanently lost calls is the sum of the expected lost calls due to busy signals from the trunks, the expected lost calls due to busy signals from the agent queue, and the expected lost calls due to call abandonment.

A finite capacity queueing model ($M/M/s/K$, where K is the system capacity) was used to determine the rate of busy signals at the trunks. Caller abandonment was estimated by a simple linear regression model with the average queue time per caller as the independent variable. The most questionable assumption was the agent time distribution. A sample of 1,240 observations was tested using a Chi-square goodness of fit test to corroborate the validity of the exponential distribution assumption.

Table 15.3 shows the results of three-week peak periods before and after the optimization effort. In addition to the gains in profit, managers also report operational benefits, indicating that L.L. Bean's reputation in the eyes of calling customers has improved and that the number of problems that agents experience has been drastically reduced; customers used to vent their frustrations at long waits on the agents. In addition, the project's findings have had a major influence on strategic thinking at the company, raising management's service-level perspective on resource allocation.

TABLE 15.3
Performance improvements at L.L. Bean

Criterion measured	1988 (before)	1989 (after)	% change
Calls answered	1,260,530	1,562,457	+24.0
Orders taken	1,038,557	1,211,759	+16.7
Revenues generated	$85,367,372	$99,273,655	+16.3
Percent abandoned callers	11.2	2.1	−81.3
Percent calls spending <20 seconds in queue	25.0	77.0	+208.0
Average speed of answer	93 seconds	15 seconds	−83.9

Discussion Questions

1. Construct influence diagrams for the expected cost components.
2. Propose a procedure for finding the optimal number of trunks, number of agents, and queue capacity that minimizes expected costs.
3. Explain why linear regression produced a good fit for caller abandonment.

MORE EXAMPLES AND SOLVED PROBLEMS

EXAMPLE 10. ANALYSIS OF A DRIVE-THROUGH SERVICE

Don McHardy, owner of McHardy's Burger Palace, is considering adding a drive-through window to his restaurant. Studies of similar operations have shown that arrivals generally follow a Poisson process, but it is not clear that service times are always exponentially distributed. The data indicate that service times appear to be exponential on some days but not on others. During the busy lunch period, Don found that an average of 15 customers per hour would use the drive-through. Service times average 2.5 minutes with a standard deviation of 1.5 minutes. What queue lengths and waiting lines can Don expect? How long would the lines get?

Since it is not clear whether an $M/M/1$ or $M/G/1$ model is appropriate, we will analyze both of them. First, note that $\lambda = 15/60 = .25$ customers per minute, and $\mu = 1/2.5 = .4$ customers per minute. The operating characteristics for the $M/M/1$ model are as follows:

$$L_q = \frac{\lambda^2}{\mu(\mu - \lambda)} = 1.04 \text{ customers}$$

$$L = \frac{\lambda}{\mu - \lambda} = 1.67 \text{ customers}$$

$$W_q = \frac{\lambda}{\mu(\mu - \lambda)} = 4.17 \text{ minutes}$$

$$W = \frac{1}{\mu - \lambda} = 6.67 \text{ minutes}$$

$$P_0 = 1 - \frac{\lambda}{\mu} = .375$$

The operating characteristics for an $M/G/1$ model with a variance of $(1.5)^2 = 2.25$ are as follows:

$$L_q = \frac{\lambda^2 \sigma^2 + (\lambda/\mu)^2}{2(1 - \lambda/\mu)} = .71 \text{ customers}$$

$$L = L_q + \frac{\lambda}{\mu} = 1.33 \text{ customers}$$

$$W_q = \frac{L_q}{\lambda} = 2.83 \text{ minutes}$$

$$W = W_q + \frac{1}{\mu} = 5.33 \text{ minutes}$$

$$P_0 = 1 - \frac{\lambda}{\mu} = .375$$

Comparing these performance measures for the two systems, we have the following:

Measure	M/M/1	M/G/1
L_q	1.04	.71
L	1.67	1.33
W_q	4.17	2.83
W	6.67	5.33
P_0	.375	.375

The largest differences are in the waiting times; with exponential service times, waiting times are somewhat larger. In either case, the differences are insignificant to the decision of opening up the drive-through. Thus, no matter how the service times are distributed, Don can be reasonably assured that line lengths and waiting times are reasonable.

EXAMPLE 11. AIRLINE SECURITY SCREENING

Security measures at airport terminals, such as walk-through metal detectors and X rays of carry-on baggage, arose in the 1970s because of the rise of airline hijackings (see the relevant chapter opening scenario). Typically, screening can be accomplished at a rate of 11 passengers per minute, although this may vary slightly depending on the particular equipment.

In designing new airport terminals, planners need to know how many security units to install to minimize congestion and to plan space for future expansion. A growing airport in a southern U.S. city is planning a new international terminal. Airport planners have estimated that during peak travel times, passengers will arrive at a rate of 20 per minute, but this is forecasted to grow to 40 over the next 10 years. What security screening plans should they take?

Since the arrival rate exceeds the service rate, we see that a single service facility is not feasible. We will assume that arrivals follow a Poisson distribution and that service times are exponential. We may use the multiple server model spreadsheet to analyze this situation. Figure 15.20 shows the results when the arrival rate is varied from 20 to 40 passengers per minute. With the current demand, a two-server system is not unreasonable. Although about eight or nine passengers are expected in the queue, the average waiting time in the queue is less than a half-minute. As the arrival rate increases to 30, however, a two-server system is not sufficient. When demand hits 40, the terminal will require four servers. Because of the fixed costs of installation, it might be a wise decision to install three screening systems initially, and plan to expand to four at a later time.

FIGURE 15.20   *Analysis of airport security screening* $\lambda = 20$

	A	B	C	D	E	F	G	H
1	Multiple Server Queue							
2								
3	Lambda	20						
4	Mu	11						
5	Number of servers	2	3	4	5	6	7	8
6								
7								
8	Average number in queue	8.658	0.558	0.110	0.024	0.005	0.001	0.000
9	Average number in system	10.476	2.376	1.928	1.842	1.823	1.819	1.818
10	Average time in queue	0.433	0.028	0.006	0.001	0.000	0.000	0.000
11	Average waiting time in system	0.524	0.119	0.096	0.092	0.091	0.091	0.091
12	Probability system is empty	0.048	0.143	0.159	0.162	0.162	0.162	0.162

$\lambda = 30$

	A	B	C	D	E	F	G	H
1	Multiple Server Queue							
2								
3	Lambda	30						
4	Mu	11						
5	Number of servers	2	3	4	5	6	7	8
6								
7								
8	Average number in queue	-5.900	8.332	0.859	0.209	0.057	0.015	0.004
9	Average number in system	-3.173	11.059	3.586	2.936	2.784	2.742	2.731
10	Average time in queue	-0.197	0.278	0.029	0.007	0.002	0.001	0.000
11	Average waiting time in system	-0.106	0.369	0.120	0.098	0.093	0.091	0.091
12	Probability system is empty	-0.154	0.022	0.055	0.063	0.065	0.065	0.066

$\lambda = 40$

	A	B	C	D	E	F	G	H
1	Multiple Server Queue							
2								
3	Lambda	40						
4	Mu	11						
5	Number of servers	2	3	4	5	6	7	8
6								
7								
8	Average number in queue	-5.213	-8.137	8.062	1.127	0.314	0.097	0.031
9	Average number in system	-1.577	-4.500	11.699	4.763	3.950	3.734	3.667
10	Average time in queue	-0.130	-0.203	0.202	0.028	0.008	0.002	0.001
11	Average waiting time in system	-0.039	-0.113	0.292	0.119	0.099	0.093	0.092
12	Probability system is empty	-0.290	-0.038	0.010	0.022	0.025	0.026	0.027

EXAMPLE 12. A TRUCK FLEET EXPANSION PROBLEM

The internal transport system in an electronics manufacturing company consisted of three trucks. Many complaints were being made about the lack of truck availability, but management had resisted adding a fourth truck because of the expense. In a meeting to discuss the problem, supervisors and managers decided to conduct a study to determine the value of adding a fourth truck to the fleet.

The daily cost of an extra truck was computed by adding the daily pay for two drivers (one for each shift), other operating expenses, and depreciation. This amounted to $120 per day, or $7.50 per hour. In studying the effects of delays on production, the accounting department estimated the average waiting cost per hour to be $28. Each hour an average of 4.6 truck requests are made. The average time that each truck is used is 20 minutes. Should the fourth truck be purchased?

To analyze this problem, we may use the spreadsheet developed in Figure 15.15. Figure 15.21 shows the results. This analysis indicates that the fourth truck is not justified, although the difference is marginal. In fact, simple sensitivity analysis of the parameters in the spreadsheet shows that the fourth truck would be justified if one of the following were true:

1. The waiting cost C_w increases to $36 (as it might due to inflation or other productivity demands).
2. The rate of truck requests increases to 4.9.
3. The time each truck is used increases to 21.5 minutes.

Clearly, errors in the estimation of these parameters might suggest that the fourth truck is justifiable. In addition, adding the fourth truck would reduce frustration to

FIGURE 15.21   *Economic analysis of the truck queueing problem*

	A	B	C	D	E
1	Queue Optimization Spreadsheet				
2					
3	Lambda	4.6			
4	Mu	3			
5	Waiting cost/customer/time, C	$28.00			
6	Cost/server/time, Cs	$7.50			
7					
8	Number of servers	1	2	3	4
9	Average number in queue	-4.408	2.186	0.260	0.050
10	Average number in system	-2.875	3.720	1.794	1.583
11	Average time in queue	-0.958	0.475	0.057	0.011
12	Average waiting time in syste	-0.625	0.809	0.390	0.344
13	Probability system is empty	-0.533	0.132	0.203	0.214
14					
15	Customer cost	($123.43)	$61.22	$7.29	$1.39
16	Server cost	$7.50	$15.00	$22.50	$30.00
17	Total cost	($115.93)	$76.22	$29.79	$31.39

the employees and improve the morale in the plant. Because the economics of adding the fourth truck is not overwhelmingly negative, the improvement in employee morale may be the most important factor in making the decision.

SUMMARY

The understanding and optimization of waiting lines is important to most managers, particularly as many organizations have turned their attention toward improving customer service and quality. The key elements of queueing systems are the customer characteristics and arrival pattern, service process characteristics, queue discipline, and system configuration. Simple analytical models require that arrivals follow a Poisson process and that service times be exponential or that at least the variance be known. Figure 15.22 provides a summary of the model selection process for those that we have introduced in this chapter.

One of the drawbacks of analytical queueing models is that they provide only steady-state results. To understand the dynamics of waiting lines, particularly over short time periods, simulation should be used. Finally, queueing is a cultural and psychological phenomenon. Managers need to understand the social and behavioral implications in designing systems that involve waiting.

FIGURE 15.22   *Summary of queueing approaches in this chapter*

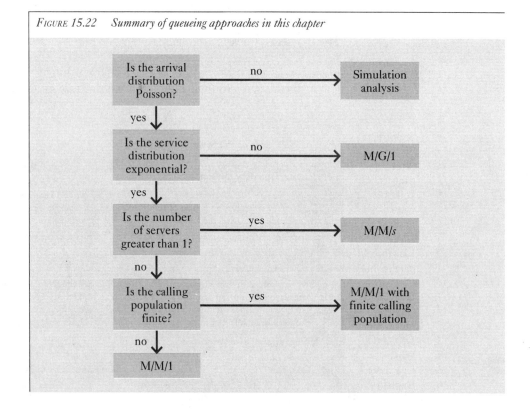

CHAPTER REVIEW EXERCISES

I. Terms to Understand

You should be able to define the following terms:

a.	Queue (p. 789)		k.	Operating characteristics (p. 794)
b.	Queueing theory (p. 789)		l.	Poisson process (p. 795)
c.	Arrival process (p. 790)		m.	Mean arrival rate (p. 796)
d.	Arrival rate (p. 790)		n.	Mean interarrival time (p. 797)
e.	Calling population (p. 790)		o.	Mean service rate (p. 799)
f.	Reneging (p. 790)		p.	Kendall taxonomy (p. 800)
g.	Jockeying (p. 790)		q.	Little's law (p. 804)
h.	Balking (p. 790)		r.	Steady state (p. 802)
i.	Service process (p. 790)		s.	Transient period (p. 802)
j.	Queue discipline (p. 790)			

II. Questions

1. Describe several situations in which you were part of a waiting line system. How did the system operate?
2. Describe the customers, servers, and queueing system associated with the following:
    a. A self-service gasoline station
    b. A full-service gasoline station
    c. Your school's registration office
    d. Your school's central computer center
    e. Your local automobile license agency
    f. An airport runway
3. Can you think of any queueing systems in which the arrival rate remains constant all the time?
4. Suppose that you observed the time between touchdown of successive airplanes on a runway. Would this be a Poisson process? Why or why not?
5. A university career development center schedules job interviews every hour of the day. If you record the time that each candidate arrives, would you observe a Poisson process? Why or why not?
6. You observe the time of arrival to an automatic teller machine between 11:00 A.M. and 1:00 P.M. during a weekday. Would you expect this to be a Poisson process? Why or why not?
7. List the informal rules that you use to decide to renege, jockey, or balk at a queue.
8. List three examples (different from the book) that have FCFS, LCFS, and priority queue disciplines.
9. List three examples (different from the book) that have servers fed by a single queue, several separate parallel queues, and a series of queues.
10. Discuss the ways in which managers would typically evaluate the performance of queueing systems.
11. Explain the assumptions behind a Poisson process. How might these be validated in a real application?
12. Could an analytical queueing model be of any use to a manager of a typical service facility such as a quick-service restaurant or a mini food mart? Why or why not?
13. Explain the intuition behind Little's Law.
14. Why is the $M/G/1$ queueing model useful in many practical situations?
15. List three queueing examples (different from the book) that have finite calling populations.
16. Explain the basic approach to optimizing queueing systems.

17. How can you tell when a queue has reached steady state?

18. Explain different technical and psychological approaches for solving queueing problems in practice.

19. A study in Northern California surveyed 95 grocery store shoppers to better understand their attitudes about the types of queueing systems used in grocery stores.[6] The survey asked the following questions:

- *Are you familiar with the waiting-line system used inside banks and post offices?* All 95 respondents answered yes.
- *Do you shop at only one grocery store?* Forty-nine of the 95 respondents answered yes.
- *Would you continue to shop at a grocery store that implemented the same type of waiting-line system that is used inside of banks?* Seventy-five of the 95 respondents answered yes.

    a. Why do you think that grocery stores have not adopted the single service line concept that is prevalent in many other service systems?

    b. Of the 21 percent of customers answering no to question 3, 60 percent shop at only one store. Twenty-four percent of the customers who are loyal to a single store would shop elsewhere. Why do you think this is so?

    c. Of the respondents who indicated that they would not shop at a store that implemented a single-service line system, 40 percent were not store-loyal customers. What might explain this result?

20. Suppose that you interviewed people waiting in line and asked them how long they thought they had waited and compared their responses to actual waiting times. What would you expect? What implications does this have for a manager?

21. Do you believe the following statements are true or false? Explain your reasoning.
    a. Unoccupied time feels longer than occupied time.
    b. Anxiety makes waits seem shorter.
    c. Uncertain waits are longer than known waits (as with appointments).
    d. The more valuable the service, the longer the customer will wait.
    e. Waiting in a group feels longer than waiting alone.

III. Problems

1. The manager of Servani's Bakery believes that arrivals follow a Poisson process with an average arrival rate of eight customers per hour. What is the probability that only three customers will arrive in a one-hour period? More than 10 customers? Exactly eight?

2. For Servani's Bakery in Problem 1, what is the mean interarrival time? What is the probability that the next customer will arrive within five minutes of the current customer? More than 15 minutes later?

3. The mean service time at Servani's Bakery is six minutes. What is the probability that a customer is served within one minute? Within three minutes? In greater than six minutes?

4. For the arrival and service rates given in Problems 1 and 3, compute the operating characteristics for Servani's Bakery if only one employee is available to service the customers.

5. A group of students studied the arrivals of customers to a bank in Oklahoma. They observed the following frequency distribution:

---

[6]Michael T. Jones, Arlene M. O'Berski, and Gail Tom, "Quickening the Queue in Grocery Stores," *Interfaces*, Vol. 10, No. 3, June 1980, pp. 90–92.

Interarrival time (sec)	Frequency
0–19	208
20–39	108
40–59	64
60–79	33
80–99	19
100–119	13
> 119	10

Can you conclude that the arrival process is Poisson?

6. Student jobs arrive to a computer processing operation at a rate of 12 per minute. The average processing time is four seconds. Find
   a. The average number of jobs waiting
   b. The average waiting time per job
   c. The average utilization of the computer processor

7. Michael's Tire Company performs free tire balance and rotation for the life of any tires purchased there on a first-come, first-served basis. One mechanic handles this and can usually complete the job in an average of 20 minutes. Customers arrive at an average rate of two per hour for this service.
   a. How long will a customer expect to wait before being served?
   b. How long will a customer expect to spend at the shop?
   c. How many customers will be waiting, on the average?
   d. What is the probability that the mechanic will be idle?

8. Suppose that the arrival rate to a queueing system is 10 customers per hour. Using manual calculations or a spreadsheet, sketch a graph of the average number in the system and average time in the system as the service rate varies from 1 to 10. What implications does this information have for managers who design service systems?

9. Modify the spreadsheet in Figure 15.8 to perform sensitivity analysis on the service rate if the arrival rate is fixed. For the situation in Example 4 (the airline ticket counter), determine the sensitivity of the operating characteristics if the service rate varies by 20 percent. Which parameter—the arrival rate or the service rate—is more sensitive?

10. For the $M/M/1$ queue, show that the operating characteristics satisfy the following equations:
   a. $L = \lambda W$
   b. $L = L_q + \lambda/\mu$
   c. $L_q = \lambda W_q$
   d. $W = W_q + 1/\mu$

11. For the $M/G/1$ queueing model, suppose that $\lambda = 6$ and $\mu = 9$. Develop a spreadsheet and graphs for examining the sensitivity of the operating characteristics for the variance σ^2 as it varies from 0 to 3. What conclusions can you reach?

12. Show that the $M/G/1$ model is equivalent to the $M/M/1$ model if the service time distribution is exponential. (*Hint:* What is the variance of the exponential distribution?)

13. A college office has one photocopier. Faculty and staff arrive according to a Poisson process at a rate of five per hour. Copying times average eight minutes but do not follow an exponential distribution. The standard deviation of copying times is estimated to be two minutes. What are the operating characteristics for this system?

14. Guests purchasing season passes at an amusement park must have their pictures taken for the pass. During the peak sales period, guests arrive at a rate of eight per hour to purchase a pass. The times to take and develop their pictures are nearly constant at five minutes. What is the average number of people waiting for their pictures to be taken?

15. Servani's Bakery (Problem 4) is considering adding an additional employee. How would the operating characteristics change if the additional employee is hired? How much would customer demand have to increase before the waiting times and queue lengths are approximately the same as the current situation?

16. Star Savings and Loan is opening up a new branch in Union Township. Market research shows that they can expect an average of 35 customers per hour on Saturdays. Transaction times typically average four minutes.
    a. What is the minimum number of tellers that will be needed?
    b. Compute the operating characteristics for your answer to part a and up to three additional tellers.
    c. How many tellers would you hire if you were the bank manager?

17. Star Savings and Loan is planning to install a drive-through window. Transaction times at the drive-through are expected to average three minutes because customers would use it for simpler transactions. The arrival rate is expected to be 10 customers per hour.
    a. Compute the operating characteristics for the drive-through window queueing system.
    b. The demand for drive-through services is expected to increase over the next several years. If you were the bank manager, how high would you let the average arrival rate increase before considering adding a second drive-through window?

18. Seven college secretaries share one laser printer connected to a local area network. Each secretary submits documents to be printed at an average rate of two per hour. The printer prints an average of 10 documents each hour.
    a. What is the average number of documents waiting to be printed?
    b. How long will a secretary expect to wait for the document?
    c. What percentage of the time will the printer be busy?

19. For Servani's Bakery (Problem 4), find the probability that n customers are in the bakery, for n from 0 to 10.

20. For Michael's Tire Company (Problem 7), find the probability that n customers will be waiting in the customer lounge, for $n = 0$ through 8.

21. Using your answer to part c in Problem 6, compute the probability that n customers will be in the bank, for $n = 0$ to 2 times the number of tellers. Would this information change your decision?

22. Modify the spreadsheets for the $M/M/1$ and $M/M/s$ queueing models to include a probability distribution for P_n, the number of customers in the system.

23. An automated call distributor handles incoming calls for L.L. Jean, a mail order clothes company. Customer service representatives (CSRs) are paid $7 per hour. Because excessive waiting can affect sales and profitability significantly, waiting is valued at $10 per minute. During the October–November sales season, an average of 150 calls per hour arrive. The average duration of each call is six minutes. How many CSRs should be hired during this season?

24. A new manager has arrived at L.L. Jean (Problem 23). She recognizes that waiting cost cannot be estimated. Instead, she wants no more than 10 percent of all callers to wait for an available customer service representative. How many CSRs should be hired? What if no more than 25 percent are allowed to wait?

25. An upscale downtown department store offers personalized shopping service for busy businesspeople. Customer representatives are salaried, earning $15 per hour. When not attending to clients, they work elsewhere in the store. During the midday period from 11:00 to 1:00, clients arrive at a rate of eight per hour. Each client takes an average of 45 minutes to service. The store manager wants no more than one client to wait on the average. How many representatives should be assigned to this shopping service to meet this goal? What value is the manager implicitly placing on customer waiting?

26. Modify the spreadsheet in Figure 15.17 to use normally-distributed service times. Simulate 1,000 customers with an arrival rate of two customers per hour and a service time having a mean of 0.33 hours per customer and a standard deviation of 0.57. How do your results compare with the exponential assumption in Figure 15.17? (Note that the mean and standard deviation are the same.)

27. Simulate Servani's Bakery (Problem 4) to determine how long it takes to reach a reasonable steady state. Would the analytical results of the $M/M/1$ model be applicable to the real decision problem?

28. Simulate an $M/M/1$ queueing system with $\lambda = 5$ and $\mu = 7$ for 100, 200, 500, and 1,000 customers (using five replications each). Compute confidence intervals for the average waiting times. How do your results compare with the expected waiting time? What does this say about the use of analytical models in real situations?

IV. Projects and Cases

1. *The South-Side Fitness Club.*[7] The South-Side Fitness Club is a full-service exercise facility that features a full-circuit Nautilus system, Lifecycles, Stairmasters, and free weights. Although the main attraction is the Nautilus, many people who join use more than one type of exercise system during their workout. They generally do not wish to wait between exercises because it allows them to cool down.

     The clientele of the club are professionals of all ages, so the busiest times of the week are evenings from 5 to 9 P.M. Seventy-five percent of all members exercise at this time. Therefore, it is extremely important that exercise machines be available with minimal waiting. Currently, three Stairmasters, three Lifecycles, one rack of free weights, and the Nautilus system are available. Anyone wishing to use the Nautilus machines must start at the beginning of the circuit.

     The Stairmasters have increased in popularity, and the club manager has been receiving many complaints about waiting. The club owners are resisting purchasing another machine; every time they visit the club during the day, the machines are idle. The manager conducted a random phone survey of 20 percent of the members and learned that 80 percent of those surveyed like to use the Stairmaster. The average length of a workout on the machine is 15 minutes. With the help of her fitness staff, she found that members arrive at the club during the evenings at an average rate of 8.75 people per hour. The cost of leasing and servicing the Stairmaster machines amounts to $130 per month.

     a. What assumptions would you make about the distribution of arrivals and service times? Specifically, should service times be modeled as an exponential distribution or are they constant?

     b. Compute the operating characteristics with and without the extra machine assuming that service times are exponentially distributed.

     c. Repeat part b, assuming that service times are constant at 15 minutes.

     d. What cost would you attach to waiting time? Study the optimal number of machines to have under various waiting time cost scenarios. What would your recommendation be?

2. *Calahan Research Products.*[8] Calahan Research Products is a growing biological research products company. Since the company was started 10 years ago, it has specialized in plastic products designed for use in the laboratory. Recently, Calahan expanded its product line to include cutting-edge equipment used in microbiological and biochemical research. This decision quadrupled revenues and almost doubled its customer base last quarter. Management expects continued growth in the company as it expands and improves existing product lines.

     Most customers place orders over the telephone. Customer service representatives record all necessary information by hand and begin processing the order. In anticipation of increased business from the introduction of new products, Michael Carter, the Customer Service Supervisor, hired a third customer

---

[7]Our appreciation goes to David Minning for developing this case.
[8]We wish to thank Robin Heltzel for providing this case.

service representative to handle telephone orders. However, he has received complaints from customers of waiting up to three minutes to talk with a representative. He fears that this may jeopardize current business and future growth. Mr. Carter wants to improve the system so that customers will not wait more than 15 seconds on average.

Two options are possible. He could hire an additional CSR at a cost of $20,000 per year. Alternatively, the company could purchase a computer system at a cost of $125,000 that would reduce order processing time by providing faster access to information in a customer's history file. Mr. Carter and a co-worker collected data on current operations. On the average, calls arrive randomly at a rate of 1 per minute. The average service time for a call is 2.2 minutes. Mr. Carter estimates that the new computer system would reduce the service time to an average of 1.4 minutes per call.

    a.   How many additional CSRs would Mr. Carter have to hire to meet his goal?

    b.   What effect would the computer system have over the current operation?

    c.   What recommendations would you make?

3.   *The Midwestin Hotel.* Customer satisfaction is the most important objective at the Midwestin Hotel. Consumer research has shown that a critical factor in customer satisfaction is check-in time. The hotel currently has five clerks on duty. During peak times, 90 guests arrive each hour and spend three minutes checking in. A quality improvement team is considering two ideas to improve service. One is to have a dedicated clerk serve corporate customers exclusively. Corporate customers account for 30 percent of their business. Because of prearranged billing information, this will allow the hotel to reduce the registration time for these customers to two minutes on average. A second suggestion is to use a new automated kiosk to allow guests to check themselves in. Approximately 20 percent of the guests might be willing to do this. How would you analyze this information, and what recommendations would you make?

REFERENCES

Agnihothri, S. R. and P. F. Taylor. "Staffing a Centralized Appointment Scheduling Department at Lourdes Hospital." *Interfaces,* Vol. 21, No. 5, September–October, 1991, pp. 1–11.

Bennett, G. Kimble, and Brian J. Melloy. "Applying Queueing Theory Helps Minimize Waiting Time and Costs of Available Resources." *Industrial Engineering,* Vol. 16, No. 7, July 1984, pp. 86–91.

Brennen, John E., Bruce L. Golden, and Harold K. Rappoport. "Go with the Flow: Improving Red Cross Bloodmobiles Using Simulation Analysis." *Interfaces,* Vol. 22, No. 5, September–October, 1992, pp. 1–13.

Brigham, Georges. "On a Congestion Problem in an Aircraft Factory." *Operations Research,* Vol. 3, 1955, pp. 412–428.

Deutsch, Howard and Vincent A. Mabert. "Queueing Theory and Teller Staffing: A Successful Application." *Interfaces,* Vol. 10, No. 5, October 1980, pp. 63–69.

Edie, Leslie C. "Traffic Delays at Toll Booths." *Journal of the Operations Research Society of America,* Vol. 2, No. 2, 1954, pp. 107–138.

Gilliam, Ronald R. "An Application of Queueing Theory to Airport Passenger Security Screening." *Interfaces,* Vol. 9, No. 4, August 1979, pp. 117–122.

Grant, Floyd H., III. "Reducing Voter Waiting Time." *Interfaces,* Vol. 10, No. 5, October 1980, pp. 19–25.

Landauer, Edwin G. and Linda C. Becker. "Reducing Waiting Time at Security Checkpoints." *Interfaces,* Vol. 19, No. 5, September–October, 1989, pp. 57–65.

Quinn, Phil, Bruce Andrews, and Henry Parsons. "Allocating Telecommunications Resources at L.L. Bean, Inc." *Interfaces,* Vol. 21, No. 1, January–February, 1991, pp. 75–91.

Scott, Tom and William Hailey. "Queue Modelling Aids Economic Analysis at Health Center." *Industrial Engineering,* Vol. 13, No. 2, February 1981, pp. 56–61.

APPENDIX A

Normal Curve Areas

The following table gives the standard normal probability in right-hand tail. For negative values of z, areas are found by symmetry. For the probability area to the left of the specified value of z, subtract the area given in the table from 1.

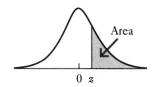

Area

0 z

Second decimal place of z

z	.00	.01	.02	.03	.04	.05	.06	.07	.08	.09
0.0	.5000	.4960	.4920	.4880	.4840	.4801	.4761	.4721	.4681	.4641
0.1	.4602	.4562	.4522	.4483	.4443	.4404	.4364	.4325	.4286	.4247
0.2	.4207	.4168	.4129	.4090	.4052	.4013	.3974	.3936	.3897	.3859
0.3	.3821	.3783	.3745	.3707	.3669	.3632	.3594	.3557	.3520	.3483
0.4	.3446	.3409	.3372	.3336	.3300	.3264	.3228	.3192	.3156	.3121
0.5	.3085	.3050	.3015	.2981	.2946	.2912	.2877	.2843	.2810	.2776
0.6	.2743	.2709	.2676	.2643	.2611	.2578	.2546	.2514	.2483	.2451
0.7	.2420	.2389	.2358	.2327	.2296	.2266	.2236	.2206	.2177	.2148
0.8	.2119	.2090	.2061	.2033	.2005	.1977	.1949	.1922	.1894	.1867
0.9	.1841	.1814	.1788	.1762	.1736	.1711	.1685	.1660	.1635	.1611
1.0	.1587	.1562	.1539	.1515	.1492	.1469	.1446	.1423	.1401	.1379
1.1	.1357	.1335	.1314	.1292	.1271	.1251	.1230	.1210	.1190	.1170
1.2	.1151	.1131	.1112	.1093	.1075	.1056	.1038	.1020	.1003	.0985
1.3	.0968	.0951	.0934	.0918	.0901	.0885	.0869	.0853	.0838	.0823
1.4	.0808	.0793	.0778	.0764	.0749	.0735	.0722	.0708	.0694	.0681
1.5	.0668	.0655	.0643	.0630	.0618	.0606	.0594	.0582	.0571	.0559
1.6	.0548	.0537	.0526	.0516	.0505	.0495	.0485	.0475	.0465	.0455
1.7	.0446	.0436	.0427	.0418	.0409	.0401	.0392	.0384	.0375	.0367
1.8	.0359	.0352	.0344	.0336	.0329	.0322	.0314	.0307	.0301	.0294
1.9	.0287	.0281	.0274	.0268	.0262	.0256	.0250	.0244	.0239	.0233
2.0	.0228	.0222	.0217	.0212	.0207	.0202	.0197	.0192	.0188	.0183
2.1	.0179	.0174	.0170	.0166	.0162	.0158	.0154	.0150	.0146	.0143
2.2	.0139	.0136	.0132	.0129	.0125	.0122	.0119	.0116	.0113	.0110
2.3	.0107	.0104	.0102	.0099	.0096	.0094	.0091	.0089	.0087	.0084
2.4	.0082	.0080	.0078	.0075	.0073	.0071	.0069	.0068	.0066	.0064
2.5	.0062	.0060	.0059	.0057	.0055	.0054	.0052	.0051	.0049	.0048
2.6	.0047	.0045	.0044	.0043	.0041	.0040	.0039	.0038	.0037	.0036
2.7	.0035	.0034	.0033	.0032	.0031	.0030	.0029	.0028	.0027	.0026
2.8	.0026	.0025	.0024	.0023	.0023	.0022	.0021	.0021	.0020	.0019
2.9	.0019	.0018	.0017	.0017	.0016	.0016	.0015	.0015	.0014	.0014
3.0	.00135									
3.5	.000 233									
4.0	.000 031 7									
4.5	.000 003 40									
5.0	.000 000 287									

Reprinted with the permission of Simon & Schuster from the Macmillan college text *Introduction to Statistics*, 3rd ed., by Ronald E. Walpole. Copyright © 1982 by Ronald E. Walpole.

APPENDIX B

Percentage Points of the χ^2 Distributions

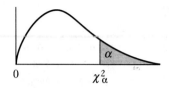

d.f.	$\chi^2_{0.995}$	$\chi^2_{0.990}$	$\chi^2_{0.975}$	$\chi^2_{0.950}$	$\chi^2_{0.900}$
1	0.0000393	0.0001571	0.0009821	0.0039321	0.0157908
2	0.0100251	0.0201007	0.0506356	0.102587	0.210720
3	0.0717212	0.114832	0.215795	0.351846	0.584375
4	0.206990	0.297110	0.484419	0.710721	1.063623
5	0.411740	0.554300	0.831211	1.145476	1.61031
6	0.675727	0.872085	1.237347	1.63539	2.20413
7	0.989265	1.239043	1.68987	2.16735	2.83311
8	1.344419	1.646482	2.17973	2.73264	3.48954
9	1.734926	2.087912	2.70039	3.32511	4.16816
10	2.15585	2.55821	3.24697	3.94030	4.86518
11	2.60321	3.05347	3.81575	4.57481	5.57779
12	3.07382	3.57056	4.40379	5.22603	6.30380
13	3.56503	4.10691	5.00874	5.89186	7.04150
14	4.07468	4.66043	5.62872	6.57063	7.78953
15	4.60094	5.22935	6.26214	7.26094	8.54675
16	5.14224	5.81221	6.90766	7.96164	9.31223
17	5.69724	6.40776	7.56418	8.67176	10.0852
18	6.26481	7.01491	8.23075	9.39046	10.8649
19	6.84398	7.63273	8.90655	10.1170	11.6509
20	7.43386	8.26040	9.59083	10.8508	12.4426
21	8.03366	8.89720	10.28293	11.5913	13.2396
22	8.64272	9.54249	10.9823	12.3380	14.0415
23	9.26042	10.19567	11.6885	13.0905	14.8479
24	9.88623	10.8564	12.4011	13.8484	15.6587
25	10.5197	11.5240	13.1197	14.6114	16.4734
26	11.1603	12.1981	13.8439	15.3791	17.2919
27	11.8076	12.8786	14.5733	16.1513	18.1138
28	12.4613	13.5648	15.3079	16.9279	18.9392
29	13.1211	14.2565	16.0471	17.7083	19.7677
30	13.7867	14.9535	16.7908	18.4926	20.5992
40	20.7065	22.1643	24.4331	26.5093	29.0505
50	27.9907	29.7067	32.3574	34.7642	37.6886
60	35.5346	37.4848	40.4817	43.1879	46.4589
70	43.2752	45.4418	48.7576	51.7393	55.3290
80	51.1720	53.5400	57.1532	60.3915	64.2778
90	59.1963	61.7541	65.6466	69.1260	73.2912
100	67.3276	70.0648	74.2219	77.9295	82.3581

5% ↙ degrees of freedom

$\chi^2_{0.100}$	$\chi^2_{0.050}$	$\chi^2_{0.025}$	$\chi^2_{0.010}$	$\chi^2_{0.005}$	d.f.
2.70554	3.84146	5.02389	6.63490	7.87944	1
4.60517	5.99147	7.37776	9.21034	10.5966	2
6.25139	7.81473	9.34840	11.3449	12.8381	3
7.77944	9.48773	11.1433	13.2767	14.8602	4
9.23635	11.0705	12.8325	15.0863	16.7496	5
10.6446	12.5916	14.4494	16.8119	18.5476	6
12.0170	14.0671	16.0128	18.4753	20.2777	7
13.3616	15.5073	17.5346	20.0902	21.9550	8
14.6837	16.9190	19.0228	21.6660	23.5893	9
15.9871	18.3070	20.4831	23.2093	25.1882	10
17.2750	19.6751	21.9200	24.7250	26.7569	11
18.5494	21.0261	23.3367	26.2170	28.2995	12
19.8119	22.3621	24.7356	27.6883	29.8194	13
21.0642	23.6848	26.1190	29.1413	31.3193	14
22.3072	24.9958	27.4884	30.5779	32.8013	15
23.5418	26.2962	28.8454	31.9999	34.2672	16
24.7690	27.5871	30.1910	33.4087	35.7185	17
25.9894	28.8693	31.5264	34.8053	37.1564	18
27.2036	30.1435	32.8523	36.1908	38.5822	19
28.4120	31.4104	34.1696	37.5662	39.9968	20
29.6151	32.6705	35.4789	38.9321	41.4010	21
30.8133	33.9244	36.7807	40.2894	42.7956	22
32.0069	35.1725	38.0757	41.6384	44.1813	23
33.1963	36.4151	39.3641	42.9798	45.5585	24
34.3816	37.6525	40.6465	44.3141	46.9278	25
35.5631	38.8852	41.9232	45.6417	48.2899	26
36.7412	40.1133	43.1944	46.9630	49.6449	27
37.9159	41.3372	44.4607	48.2782	50.9933	28
39.0875	42.5569	45.7222	49.5879	52.3356	29
40.2560	43.7729	46.9792	50.8922	53.6720	30
51.8050	55.7585	59.3417	63.6907	66.7659	40
63.1671	67.5048	71.4202	76.1539	79.4900	50
74.3970	79.0819	83.2976	88.3794	91.9517	60
85.5271	90.5312	95.0231	100.425	104.215	70
96.5782	101.879	106.629	112.329	116.321	80
107.565	113.145	118.136	124.116	128.299	90
118.498	124.342	129.561	135.807	140.169	100

From Thompson, Catherine M. "Tables of the Percentage Points of the χ^2-Distribution." *Biometrika*, Vol. 32, 1941, pp. 188–189.

Random Number Table (generated by Excel)

Row/Column	1	2	3	4	5	6	7	8	9	10	11	12
1	0.426	0.332	0.634	0.742	0.826	0.406	0.514	0.924	0.698	0.502	0.911	0.060
2	0.062	0.491	0.717	0.766	0.574	0.792	0.553	0.788	0.632	0.411	0.880	0.038
3	0.509	0.965	0.002	0.545	0.254	0.934	0.061	0.687	0.740	0.521	0.732	0.623
4	0.953	0.563	0.953	0.115	0.160	0.904	0.058	0.052	0.885	0.525	0.663	0.093
5	0.736	0.219	0.383	0.525	0.007	0.249	0.681	0.818	0.572	0.763	0.708	0.886
6	0.804	0.148	0.576	0.918	0.488	0.071	0.691	0.474	0.446	0.331	0.483	0.473
7	0.619	0.401	0.978	0.461	0.902	0.820	0.123	0.215	0.925	0.358	0.293	0.510
8	0.964	0.581	0.771	0.147	0.488	0.632	0.466	0.346	0.519	0.196	0.186	0.828
9	0.377	0.811	0.693	0.476	0.397	0.662	0.777	0.236	0.334	0.447	0.899	0.637
10	0.662	0.314	0.984	0.594	0.918	0.921	0.159	0.693	0.893	0.760	0.646	0.378
11	0.850	0.373	0.976	0.999	0.892	0.469	0.040	0.694	0.300	0.291	0.859	0.113
12	0.538	0.544	0.772	0.648	0.942	0.981	0.546	0.968	0.354	0.733	0.018	0.298
13	0.426	0.948	0.661	0.776	0.892	0.981	0.434	0.312	0.281	0.123	0.159	0.441
14	0.098	0.718	0.386	0.279	0.973	0.075	0.813	0.191	0.616	0.146	0.198	0.455
15	0.993	0.062	0.090	0.511	0.609	0.109	0.092	0.580	0.641	0.875	0.447	0.855
16	0.520	0.254	0.236	0.769	0.132	0.455	0.872	0.115	0.456	0.069	0.274	0.171
17	0.210	0.221	0.806	0.902	0.458	0.563	0.513	0.620	0.658	0.267	0.377	0.423
18	0.084	0.355	0.073	0.295	0.109	0.884	0.426	0.155	0.542	0.247	0.262	0.152
19	0.867	0.953	0.039	0.315	0.679	0.117	0.383	0.845	0.187	0.961	0.800	0.603
20	0.781	0.324	0.658	0.032	0.484	0.813	0.061	0.246	0.496	0.042	0.891	0.257
21	0.110	0.249	0.014	0.982	0.359	0.678	0.002	0.800	0.749	0.403	0.841	0.126
22	0.108	0.296	0.220	0.929	0.018	0.621	0.142	0.276	0.210	0.606	0.727	0.242
23	0.825	0.550	0.613	0.142	0.626	0.804	0.344	0.108	0.340	0.534	0.393	0.651
24	0.598	0.769	0.452	0.820	0.958	0.833	0.797	0.258	0.960	0.664	0.420	0.156
25	0.947	0.942	0.417	0.030	0.321	0.838	0.289	0.906	0.725	0.024	0.059	0.062
26	0.112	0.870	0.364	0.012	0.883	0.710	0.768	0.895	0.337	0.853	0.347	0.532
27	0.981	0.707	0.676	0.115	0.903	0.309	0.043	0.698	0.515	0.165	0.065	0.838
28	0.412	0.741	0.739	0.025	0.116	0.118	0.421	0.691	0.534	0.979	0.436	0.029
29	0.524	0.899	0.210	0.498	0.881	0.753	0.296	0.018	0.800	0.112	0.198	0.389
30	0.066	0.959	0.500	0.626	0.254	0.096	0.677	0.269	0.014	0.133	0.461	0.694
31	0.054	0.084	0.801	0.872	0.557	0.620	0.132	0.819	0.613	0.595	0.267	0.778
32	0.202	0.398	0.755	0.818	0.812	0.014	0.160	0.056	0.101	0.054	0.569	0.486
33	0.782	0.923	0.090	0.955	0.355	0.412	0.234	0.982	0.022	0.783	0.152	0.712
34	0.149	0.430	0.803	0.940	0.555	0.731	0.345	0.970	0.515	0.651	0.343	0.223
35	0.840	0.730	0.515	0.798	0.514	0.717	0.410	0.861	0.116	0.442	0.944	0.235
36	0.493	0.887	0.888	0.540	0.509	0.667	0.971	0.300	0.378	0.092	0.166	0.613
37	0.586	0.674	0.324	0.882	0.441	0.291	0.976	0.271	0.677	0.053	0.231	0.008
38	0.576	0.678	0.975	0.162	0.212	0.186	0.516	0.400	0.746	0.355	0.175	0.518
39	0.313	0.788	0.185	0.392	0.486	0.841	0.016	0.816	0.812	0.034	0.040	0.599
40	0.984	0.463	0.336	0.724	0.221	0.198	0.014	0.381	0.163	0.669	0.579	0.112
41	0.137	0.427	0.441	0.603	0.438	0.682	0.067	0.974	0.329	0.738	0.482	0.676
42	0.031	0.310	0.219	0.623	0.406	0.391	0.981	0.439	0.306	0.729	0.640	0.089
43	0.347	0.333	0.519	0.753	0.508	0.891	0.244	0.836	0.141	0.365	0.625	0.510
44	0.799	0.720	0.394	0.240	0.077	0.999	0.751	0.980	0.216	0.102	0.070	0.573
45	0.005	0.978	0.548	0.333	0.095	0.155	0.349	0.912	0.476	0.467	0.624	0.714
46	0.738	0.939	0.838	0.986	0.452	0.499	0.990	0.212	0.181	0.728	0.153	0.891
47	0.061	0.322	0.695	0.192	0.099	0.939	0.987	0.905	0.171	0.176	0.648	0.590
48	0.372	0.960	0.363	0.562	0.517	0.166	0.669	0.330	0.766	0.929	0.351	0.865
49	0.789	0.656	0.271	0.356	0.083	0.138	0.219	0.870	0.841	0.833	0.621	0.022
50	0.149	0.116	0.452	0.574	0.802	0.872	0.290	0.986	0.059	0.819	0.699	0.777

Row/Column	13	14	15	16	17	18	19	20	21	22	23	24	25	26
1	0.207	0.717	0.651	0.010	0.294	0.326	0.165	0.575	0.871	0.990	0.353	0.389	0.540	0.893
2	0.937	0.582	0.748	0.070	0.762	0.853	0.163	0.725	0.332	0.823	0.334	0.587	0.764	0.049
3	0.299	0.512	0.803	0.682	0.659	0.782	0.053	0.423	0.965	0.275	0.362	0.081	0.394	0.301
4	0.185	0.710	0.381	0.186	0.151	0.123	0.094	0.562	0.371	0.745	0.414	0.950	0.467	0.781
5	0.454	0.657	0.193	0.065	0.770	0.902	0.652	0.803	0.123	0.417	0.555	0.223	0.038	0.450
6	0.056	0.469	0.797	0.468	0.903	0.504	0.741	0.136	0.452	0.050	0.964	0.567	0.818	0.115
7	0.119	0.030	0.035	0.461	0.404	0.792	0.821	0.114	0.715	0.098	0.012	0.721	0.829	0.543
8	0.546	0.519	0.541	0.195	0.947	0.408	0.782	0.171	0.622	0.459	0.748	0.885	0.761	0.873
9	0.243	0.161	0.107	0.942	0.601	0.069	0.016	0.570	0.870	0.144	0.131	0.247	0.650	0.735
10	0.947	0.620	0.930	0.109	0.462	0.597	0.539	0.381	0.209	0.077	0.685	0.925	0.398	0.740
11	0.227	0.515	0.501	0.254	0.578	0.222	0.837	0.676	0.651	0.106	0.518	0.703	0.138	0.592
12	0.327	0.306	0.664	0.730	0.540	0.313	0.209	0.890	0.195	0.392	0.502	0.449	0.121	0.028
13	0.701	0.285	0.899	0.089	0.528	0.361	0.396	0.247	0.645	0.638	0.475	0.879	0.334	0.251
14	0.928	0.808	0.663	0.949	0.052	0.821	0.877	0.318	0.578	0.324	0.193	0.708	0.983	0.648
15	0.928	0.304	0.433	0.653	0.553	0.522	0.046	0.361	0.719	0.336	0.124	0.205	0.053	0.443
16	0.518	0.141	0.442	0.036	0.239	0.753	0.088	0.205	0.738	0.255	0.564	0.924	0.880	0.721
17	0.102	0.274	0.636	0.909	0.547	0.167	0.487	0.155	0.254	0.173	0.697	0.009	0.746	0.033
18	0.208	0.753	0.789	0.732	0.059	0.187	0.248	0.912	0.339	0.430	0.652	0.170	0.541	0.714
19	0.333	0.945	0.542	0.432	0.272	0.055	0.788	0.882	0.610	0.219	0.025	0.174	0.133	0.238
20	0.798	0.644	0.032	0.578	0.832	0.845	0.652	0.675	0.815	0.643	0.292	0.795	0.881	0.521
21	0.588	0.396	0.441	0.250	0.446	0.125	0.361	0.117	0.126	0.778	0.753	0.619	0.400	0.166
22	0.142	0.363	0.671	0.132	0.201	0.323	0.412	0.945	0.950	0.615	0.612	0.050	0.728	0.387
23	0.388	0.100	0.336	0.604	0.096	0.554	0.413	0.528	0.420	0.598	0.313	0.496	0.232	0.853
24	0.605	0.788	0.663	0.242	0.955	0.770	0.061	0.698	0.595	0.961	0.744	0.085	0.479	0.084
25	0.516	0.896	0.628	0.018	0.967	0.646	0.904	0.130	0.283	0.329	0.197	0.516	0.456	0.432
26	0.109	0.094	0.143	0.020	0.724	0.899	0.125	0.843	0.055	0.168	0.535	0.958	0.695	0.244
27	0.541	0.557	0.061	0.591	0.277	0.703	0.548	0.397	0.935	0.866	0.539	0.305	0.600	0.605
28	0.825	0.823	0.849	0.673	0.104	0.765	0.438	0.407	0.168	0.474	0.519	0.813	0.173	0.262
29	0.430	0.081	0.456	0.914	0.585	0.550	0.887	0.172	0.939	0.747	0.563	0.200	0.123	0.075
30	0.020	0.443	0.051	0.863	0.218	0.183	0.482	0.638	0.614	0.062	0.962	0.901	0.537	0.663
31	0.022	0.380	0.269	0.526	0.057	0.844	0.967	0.762	0.542	0.245	0.907	0.399	0.606	0.080
32	0.110	0.330	0.244	0.727	0.261	0.232	0.531	0.689	0.486	0.482	0.233	0.572	0.858	0.347
33	0.661	0.523	0.502	0.299	0.924	0.847	0.652	0.123	0.725	0.336	0.366	0.849	0.700	0.702
34	0.440	0.555	0.411	0.240	0.057	0.711	0.890	0.045	0.652	0.689	0.297	0.924	0.355	0.623
35	0.755	0.174	0.003	0.682	0.390	0.809	0.099	0.560	0.761	0.173	0.087	0.800	0.084	0.095
36	0.818	0.394	0.112	0.054	0.148	0.982	0.996	0.329	0.933	0.624	0.615	0.239	0.701	0.427
37	0.550	0.398	0.672	0.182	0.792	0.619	0.433	0.818	0.531	0.238	0.732	0.430	0.237	0.297
38	0.349	0.968	0.197	0.489	0.467	0.092	0.671	0.673	0.643	0.727	0.214	0.882	0.951	0.635
39	0.895	0.482	0.623	0.020	0.286	0.877	0.155	0.004	0.411	0.827	0.661	0.424	0.304	0.775
40	0.581	0.908	0.422	0.810	0.104	0.590	0.308	0.281	0.510	0.301	0.232	0.807	0.651	0.882
41	0.290	0.934	0.824	0.333	0.836	0.050	0.296	0.219	0.985	0.015	0.651	0.945	0.816	0.367
42	0.516	0.471	0.745	0.475	0.215	0.932	0.275	0.358	0.512	0.125	0.696	0.333	0.138	0.786
43	0.983	0.305	0.240	0.864	0.791	0.859	0.883	0.322	0.389	0.768	0.187	0.883	0.574	0.766
44	0.494	0.992	0.577	0.481	0.592	0.892	0.297	0.060	0.659	0.228	0.834	0.341	0.565	0.990
45	0.406	0.003	0.027	0.519	0.833	0.564	0.704	0.724	0.545	0.355	0.858	0.788	0.461	0.215
46	0.504	0.095	0.794	0.485	0.930	0.883	0.136	0.613	0.262	0.221	0.691	0.556	0.691	0.919
47	0.736	0.746	0.786	0.706	0.578	0.299	0.947	0.621	0.083	0.709	0.889	0.410	0.460	0.561
48	0.934	0.553	0.756	0.846	0.327	0.591	0.306	0.264	0.698	0.108	0.329	0.060	0.960	0.671
49	0.849	0.818	0.436	0.872	0.598	0.100	0.709	0.582	0.226	0.906	0.336	0.233	0.678	0.328
50	0.302	0.226	0.146	0.248	0.039	0.825	0.142	0.219	0.231	0.972	0.402	0.700	0.903	0.934

Random Number Table (continued)

Row/Column	27	28	29	30	31	32	33	34	35	36	37	38	39	40
1	0.180	0.495	0.869	0.738	0.820	0.031	0.963	0.159	0.031	0.230	0.086	0.970	0.046	0.889
2	0.383	0.415	0.903	0.117	0.658	0.333	0.383	0.610	0.471	0.725	0.564	0.407	0.813	0.245
3	0.766	0.143	0.194	0.501	0.698	0.766	0.043	0.887	0.474	0.422	0.748	0.876	0.837	0.414
4	0.022	0.906	0.465	0.571	0.148	0.504	0.348	0.061	0.765	0.887	0.017	0.041	0.516	0.591
5	0.200	0.822	0.365	0.939	0.812	0.284	0.457	0.095	0.443	0.923	0.478	0.614	0.933	0.906
6	0.872	0.747	0.928	0.755	0.300	0.664	0.840	0.224	0.682	0.923	0.521	0.787	0.245	0.287
7	0.561	0.718	0.031	0.978	0.275	0.092	0.653	0.035	0.884	0.275	0.009	0.436	0.729	0.231
8	0.020	0.518	0.525	0.535	0.331	0.222	0.931	0.494	0.738	0.703	0.708	0.509	0.615	0.392
9	0.456	0.298	0.449	0.381	0.685	0.211	0.604	0.174	0.738	0.142	0.384	0.574	0.935	0.527
10	0.905	0.913	0.669	0.709	0.222	0.595	0.803	0.521	0.865	0.268	0.460	0.063	0.079	0.974
11	0.269	0.667	0.030	0.244	0.287	0.835	0.458	0.372	0.022	0.186	0.991	0.266	0.131	0.684
12	0.665	0.806	0.350	0.949	0.541	0.846	0.459	0.233	0.995	0.192	0.440	0.795	0.066	0.848
13	0.304	0.274	0.844	0.591	0.786	0.996	0.179	0.078	0.866	0.078	0.123	0.203	0.041	0.631
14	0.827	0.321	0.577	0.600	0.645	0.216	0.743	0.872	0.550	0.240	0.748	0.732	0.036	0.520
15	0.338	0.372	0.876	0.748	0.870	0.127	0.464	0.702	0.025	0.093	0.840	0.060	0.573	0.345
16	0.116	0.535	0.882	0.281	0.522	0.709	0.228	0.485	0.617	0.982	0.696	0.360	0.755	0.490
17	0.627	0.132	0.299	0.635	0.960	0.948	0.721	0.817	0.903	0.161	0.425	0.259	0.149	0.991
18	0.659	0.977	0.441	0.660	0.078	0.377	0.972	0.754	0.073	0.524	0.252	0.419	0.566	0.577
19	0.886	0.821	0.563	0.634	0.210	0.570	0.378	0.344	0.613	0.807	0.203	0.630	0.357	0.090
20	0.373	0.593	0.819	0.338	0.121	0.467	0.706	0.576	0.466	0.996	0.192	0.588	0.925	0.410
21	0.282	0.960	0.564	0.205	0.310	0.229	0.317	0.381	0.119	0.862	0.020	0.113	0.453	0.130
22	0.820	0.312	0.890	0.222	0.854	0.086	0.456	0.305	0.920	0.974	0.463	0.498	0.009	0.757
23	0.963	0.843	0.685	0.881	0.107	0.544	0.708	0.837	0.970	0.377	0.141	0.174	0.753	0.524
24	0.301	0.884	0.942	0.319	0.134	0.546	0.156	0.058	0.838	0.475	0.822	0.961	0.647	0.836
25	0.165	0.357	0.988	0.823	0.575	0.727	0.017	0.506	0.674	0.619	0.869	0.077	0.438	0.313
26	0.478	0.142	0.524	0.334	0.289	0.026	0.258	0.992	0.705	0.691	0.253	0.825	0.379	0.270
27	0.420	0.475	0.339	0.573	0.174	0.627	0.488	0.773	0.243	0.578	0.660	0.673	0.807	0.537
28	0.299	0.345	0.047	0.993	0.778	0.733	0.895	0.954	0.750	0.119	0.219	0.363	0.916	0.842
29	0.901	0.358	0.740	0.172	0.129	0.037	0.862	0.567	0.927	0.883	0.005	0.866	0.512	0.661
30	0.517	0.753	0.669	0.495	0.464	0.199	0.607	0.418	0.765	0.231	0.254	0.602	0.775	0.699
31	0.424	0.448	0.664	0.293	0.645	0.149	0.622	0.754	0.679	0.524	0.877	0.407	0.792	0.978
32	0.576	0.096	0.517	0.994	0.792	0.879	0.173	0.115	0.852	0.360	0.951	0.500	0.381	0.180
33	0.162	0.480	0.657	0.554	0.614	0.581	0.550	0.600	0.384	0.302	0.011	0.176	0.263	0.387
34	0.141	0.100	0.751	0.520	0.643	0.701	0.584	0.246	0.383	0.938	0.861	0.368	0.415	0.894
35	0.576	0.799	0.003	0.647	0.821	0.868	0.861	0.475	0.372	0.405	0.802	0.603	0.266	0.453
36	0.071	0.704	0.514	0.251	0.158	0.732	0.672	0.714	0.959	0.757	0.336	0.457	0.684	0.238
37	0.609	0.904	0.720	0.473	0.195	0.838	0.718	0.447	0.259	0.015	0.112	0.393	0.333	0.159
38	0.093	0.149	0.305	0.528	0.300	0.609	0.444	0.248	0.635	0.401	0.860	0.108	0.298	0.987
39	0.672	0.614	0.683	0.902	0.135	0.766	0.394	0.927	0.642	0.353	0.747	0.202	0.770	0.252
40	0.981	0.580	0.790	0.539	0.447	0.893	0.640	0.855	0.213	0.510	0.880	0.369	0.438	0.120
41	0.455	0.773	0.145	0.343	0.435	0.716	0.856	0.022	0.670	0.079	0.905	0.425	0.925	0.591
42	0.502	0.325	0.601	0.056	0.785	0.005	0.554	0.483	0.862	0.032	0.685	0.495	0.487	0.542
43	0.082	0.887	0.432	0.761	0.846	0.983	0.078	0.736	0.044	0.429	0.363	0.754	0.139	0.403
44	0.924	0.500	0.135	0.152	0.795	0.898	0.643	0.315	0.868	0.110	0.351	0.225	0.821	0.853
45	0.661	0.616	0.113	0.315	0.802	0.034	0.835	0.709	0.453	0.023	0.697	0.657	0.932	0.855
46	0.358	0.102	0.900	0.294	0.605	0.119	0.960	0.598	0.772	0.779	0.295	0.253	0.021	0.823
47	0.747	0.508	0.406	0.253	0.350	0.860	0.280	0.613	0.994	0.734	0.300	0.439	0.447	0.844
48	0.723	0.246	0.437	0.708	0.497	0.426	0.943	0.405	0.702	0.108	0.462	0.792	0.804	0.723
49	0.749	0.901	0.112	0.240	0.797	0.138	0.075	0.883	0.603	0.522	0.489	0.037	0.688	0.417
50	0.608	0.701	0.332	0.452	0.337	0.601	0.580	0.251	0.157	0.956	0.676	0.642	0.448	0.185

Row/Column	41	42	43	44	45	46	47	48	49	50
1	0.880	0.645	0.740	0.968	0.194	0.949	0.385	0.469	0.072	0.005
2	0.137	0.995	0.046	0.835	0.675	0.933	0.133	0.177	0.921	0.106
3	0.311	0.211	0.807	0.435	0.900	0.181	0.647	0.799	0.743	0.136
4	0.960	0.277	0.929	0.038	0.384	0.219	0.935	0.112	0.121	0.049
5	0.352	0.953	0.738	0.917	0.398	0.547	0.875	0.415	0.175	0.420
6	0.842	0.839	0.262	0.052	0.090	0.508	0.888	0.649	0.771	0.396
7	0.763	0.016	0.320	0.887	0.263	0.853	0.567	0.567	0.862	0.371
8	0.421	0.819	0.968	0.602	0.625	0.783	0.136	0.571	0.351	0.417
9	0.803	0.088	0.588	0.427	0.186	0.718	0.286	0.797	0.997	0.560
10	0.692	0.142	0.049	0.844	0.539	0.831	0.479	0.495	0.472	0.578
11	0.428	0.933	0.871	0.220	0.620	0.766	0.725	0.855	0.345	0.260
12	0.413	0.414	0.537	0.632	0.921	0.937	0.922	0.331	0.126	0.041
13	0.046	0.240	0.839	0.518	0.514	0.539	0.568	0.242	0.237	0.838
14	0.905	0.659	0.907	0.403	0.372	0.073	0.726	0.262	0.369	0.807
15	0.115	0.973	0.104	0.477	0.922	0.817	0.174	0.287	0.968	0.809
16	0.762	0.306	0.739	0.324	0.179	0.500	0.232	0.393	0.995	0.657
17	0.350	0.855	0.386	0.784	0.749	0.478	0.614	0.162	0.368	0.957
18	0.511	0.336	0.896	0.868	0.222	0.181	0.243	0.737	0.214	0.547
19	0.843	0.150	0.781	0.969	0.442	0.567	0.090	0.747	0.845	0.418
20	0.749	0.997	0.019	0.469	0.634	0.920	0.240	0.679	0.870	0.616
21	0.850	0.407	0.169	0.315	0.888	0.727	0.271	0.741	0.668	0.151
22	0.793	0.983	0.605	0.408	0.759	0.619	0.224	0.591	0.236	0.463
23	0.559	0.310	0.286	0.766	0.306	0.643	0.584	0.935	0.773	0.683
24	0.365	0.492	0.451	0.601	0.423	0.577	0.451	0.737	0.908	0.843
25	0.582	0.294	0.489	0.748	0.413	0.663	0.966	0.049	0.883	0.549
26	0.355	0.073	0.756	0.427	0.069	0.226	0.855	0.144	0.833	0.447
27	0.489	0.092	0.757	0.305	0.654	0.251	0.147	0.039	0.207	0.324
28	0.187	0.655	0.646	0.267	0.770	0.207	0.427	0.574	0.012	0.918
29	0.142	0.853	0.944	0.446	0.759	0.423	0.957	0.281	0.513	0.661
30	0.812	0.673	0.421	0.900	0.658	0.209	0.347	0.267	0.887	0.755
31	0.111	0.006	0.834	0.134	0.427	0.826	0.715	0.538	0.854	0.233
32	0.883	0.702	0.287	0.420	0.806	0.453	0.133	0.613	0.965	0.278
33	0.974	0.508	0.001	0.795	0.410	0.617	0.217	0.118	0.720	0.992
34	0.107	0.490	0.873	0.825	0.079	0.254	0.599	0.394	0.702	0.281
35	0.750	0.644	0.043	0.773	0.774	0.798	0.360	0.126	0.902	0.650
36	0.343	0.814	0.292	0.937	0.008	0.542	0.908	0.775	0.176	0.560
37	0.277	0.038	0.184	0.631	0.626	0.158	0.933	0.218	0.862	0.781
38	0.451	0.049	0.056	0.808	0.189	0.767	0.480	0.673	0.579	0.951
39	0.800	0.011	0.800	0.700	0.088	0.489	0.605	0.765	0.861	0.465
40	0.431	0.872	0.595	0.268	0.268	0.085	0.065	0.688	0.067	0.046
41	0.544	0.974	0.892	0.792	0.789	0.219	0.640	0.828	0.658	0.864
42	0.891	0.993	0.686	0.771	0.024	0.232	0.739	0.230	0.998	0.239
43	0.577	0.979	0.036	0.469	0.670	0.130	0.371	0.858	0.039	0.645
44	0.362	0.326	0.560	0.201	0.583	0.000	0.114	0.015	0.072	0.254
45	0.717	0.114	0.841	0.793	0.374	0.313	0.970	0.521	0.968	0.660
46	0.501	0.509	0.971	0.782	0.307	0.705	0.545	0.568	0.440	0.818
47	0.786	0.873	0.453	0.944	0.008	0.008	0.536	0.553	0.639	0.780
48	0.711	0.175	0.013	0.761	0.371	0.570	0.608	0.914	0.267	0.639
49	0.976	0.173	0.128	0.626	0.550	0.503	0.036	0.061	0.206	0.290
50	0.201	0.879	0.959	0.012	0.576	0.422	0.641	0.085	0.828	0.325

APPENDIX D

Percentage Points of the *t* Distributions

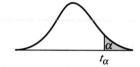

t.100	t.050	t.025	t.010	t.005	d.f.
3.078	6.314	12.706	31.821	63.657	1
1.886	2.920	4.303	6.965	9.925	2
1.638	2.353	3.182	4.541	5.841	3
1.533	2.132	2.776	3.747	4.604	4
1.476	2.015	2.571	3.365	4.032	5
1.440	1.943	2.447	3.143	3.707	6
1.415	1.895	2.365	2.998	3.499	7
1.397	1.860	2.306	2.896	3.355	8
1.383	1.833	2.262	2.821	3.250	9
1.372	1.812	2.228	2.764	3.169	10
1.363	1.796	2.201	2.718	3.106	11
1.356	1.782	2.179	2.681	3.055	12
1.350	1.771	2.160	2.650	3.012	13
1.345	1.761	2.145	2.624	2.977	14
1.341	1.753	2.131	2.602	2.947	15
1.337	1.746	2.120	2.583	2.921	16
1.333	1.740	2.110	2.567	2.898	17
1.330	1.734	2.101	2.552	2.878	18
1.328	1.729	2.093	2.539	2.861	19
1.325	1.725	2.086	2.528	2.845	20
1.323	1.721	2.080	2.518	2.831	21
1.321	1.717	2.074	2.508	2.819	22
1.319	1.714	2.069	2.500	2.807	23
1.318	1.711	2.064	2.492	2.797	24
1.316	1.708	2.060	2.485	2.787	25
1.315	1.706	2.056	2.479	2.779	26
1.314	1.703	2.052	2.473	2.771	27
1.313	1.701	2.048	2.467	2.763	28
1.311	1.699	2.045	2.462	2.756	29
1.282	1.645	1.960	2.326	2.576	inf.

From Merrington, Maxine. "Table of Percentage Points of the *t*-Distribution." *Biometrika*, Vol. 32, 1941, p. 300.

ANSWERS TO SELECTED EXERCISES

CHAPTER 1

2. NI = $C + I$ + GS

C = j(TI) + kT

T = r(TI)

I = s(TI)

Combining terms, we have NI = j(TI) + kr(TI) + s(TI) + GS. Thus, NI is essentially a function of total income and government spending.

8. Let N = Profit

p = Price

D = Demand

C = Cost

N = $pD - C$

= $p(2,000 - 3p) - 5,000 - 40D$

= $2,000p - 3p^2 - 5,000 - 40(2,000 - 3p)$

= $2,000p - 3p^2 - 5,000 - 80,000 + 120p$

= $-3p^2 + 2,120p - 85,000$

Profit is maximized at $289,533, at a price of $353.

6. A predictive model is appropriate here since the decision maker is interested in predicting what demand will be for a given price. A graph of the data shows:

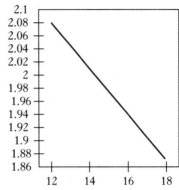

This is best represented mathematically as a linear model: $D = a - bP$.

13.

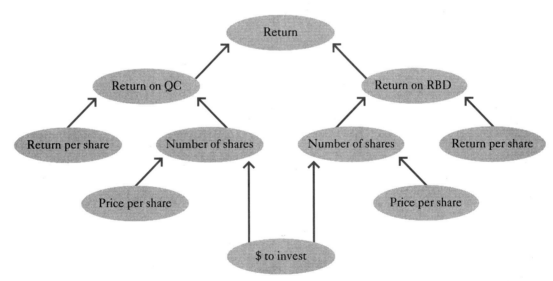

Let QC be the number of shares of QC purchased and let RBD be the number of shares of RBD purchased. Then a model can be written:

Max   5 QC + 3 RBD

subject to   20QC + 15RBD ≤ 2,000

QC ,   RBD ≥ 0

The optimal solution is to purchase 100 shares of QC, giving a return of $500.

CHAPTER 2

2.

	A	B	C	D	E	F	G
1	Profit Calculation	Spreadsheet					
2							
3	Parameters and uncontrollable variables			Formulas and assumptions			
4							
5	Unit Price	$40					
6	Unit Cost	$24		<- Formula for this cell is @VLOOKUP(B12,A24..B26,I)			
7	Fixed Cost	$400,000					
8	Sales	0		Assume sales = quantity produced			
9							
10	Decision Variable						
11							
12	Quantity produced						
13							
14	Model outputs						
15							
16	Revenue	$0		Revenue = unit price * sales			
17	Cost	$400,000		Cost = fixed cost + unit cost * quantity produced			
18	Profits	($400,000)					
19							
20							
21							
22	Look-up Table for Unit Cost Discounts						
23							
24	0	$24.00					
25	20,001	$22.50					
26	25,001	$21.00					
27							
28							
29							
30	What-If Table						
31		Quantity	Revenue	Cost	Profit		
32			$0	$400,000	($400,000)		
33		15,000	$600,000	$760,000	($160,000)		
34		16,000	$640,000	$784,000	($144,000)		
35		17,000	$680,000	$808,000	($128,000)		
36		18,000	$720,000	$832,000	($112,000)		
37		19,000	$760,000	$856,000	($96,000)		
38		20,000	$800,000	$880,000	($80,000)		
39		21,000	$840,000	$872,500	($32,500)		
40		22,000	$880,000	$895,000	($15,000)		
41		23,000	$920,000	$917,500	$2,500		
42		24,000	$960,000	$940,000	$20,000		
43		25,000	$1,000,000	$962,500	$37,500		
44		26,000	$1,040,000	$946,000	$94,000		
45		27,000	$1,080,000	$967,000	$113,000		
46		28,000	$1,120,000	$988,000	$132,000		
47		29,000	$1,160,000	$1,009,000	$151,000		
48		30,000	$1,200,000	$1,030,000	$170,000		

5.

	A	B	C	D	E	F	G	H
1			Product 1	Cost per		Product 2		
2		Cost per	Input Units	Unit		Input Units	Cost per	
3	Cost Components	Input Unit	Req'd			Req'd	Unit	
4								
5	Material Cost	$3	3.0	$9.00		2.0	$6.00	
6	Machine Cost	$70	0.1	$7.00		0.2	$14.00	
7	Labor Cost	$9	0.2	$1.80		0.3	$2.70	
8	Selling Cost	$30	0.5	$15.00		0.2	$6.00	
9	Advertising Cost	$2	2.5	$5.00		1.5	$3.00	
10								
11	Total Cost per Unit			$37.80			$31.70	

CHAPTER 3

3. Total annual cost $= DC_0/Q + iCQ/2$

$$\text{EOQ} = \sqrt{(2DC_0/iC)}$$
$$- \sqrt{(2(6,000)(75)/(.08)(3.50))}$$
$$= \sqrt{(3,214,285.6)}$$
$$= 1,792.84$$

Total cost $= (6,000)(75)/1,793 + (.08)(3.50)(1,793)/2$
$$= 250.98 + 251.02 = 502$$

$D = 4,000$:	$\text{EOQ} = 1,464$	Total cost $= 409.88$
$D = 5,000$:	$\text{EOQ} = 1,637$	Total cost $= 458.26$
$D = 7,000$:	$\text{EOQ} = 1,937$	Total cost $= 542.22$
$D = 8,000$:	$\text{EOQ} = 2,071$	Total cost $= 579.66$

6. Total cost $= (1/2)(1 - D/P)(QiC) + (D/Q)C_0$
$$= (.5)(1 - (10,000/50,000))(Q(.2)(1.35))$$
$$+ (10,000/Q)(400)$$
$$= .108Q + 4,000,000/Q$$
$$\text{EOQ} = 6,100$$

9.

	A	B
1	Variable	Value
2	D =	3000
3	i =	0.2
4	C =	$70
5	C0 =	$50
6	CB =	$25
7	CH =	$14
8	Optimal policies:	
9	Q* =	183
10	B* =	66

12. Optimal Solution:

	A	B	C	D	E
1	x1 =	3.5			
2	x2 =	0			
3	x3 =	0			
4	Objective =	15.75			
5	Constr. 1:	10.5	>=	10	Feasible
6	Constr. 2:	7	>=	7	Feasible
7	Constr. 3:	17.5	>=	5	Feasible

17. Let $F =$ the number of firefighters hired

Hours to build break $= (.5 \text{ min}/\text{ft})(5,280 \text{ ft}/\text{mi})(1 \text{ hr}/60 \text{ min}) (3 \text{ mi})/F = 132/F$

Firefighter cost $= 30F + (12)(F)(132/F)$
$$= 30F + 1,584$$

Time until fire reaches break $=$ Hours to build break $= 132/F$

Timber cost $= (\$4,000/mi^2)(3mi)(40ft/min)(1mi/5,280ft)(60min/hr)(132/F)$

$\qquad = 720,000/F$

Total cost $= 30F + 1,584 + 720,000/F$

Firebreak location (ft from start) $= (40\ ft/min)(60\ min/hr)(132/F) = 316,800/F$

CHAPTER 4

1. Let   RT = number of regular tables to produce

    DT = number of deluxe tables to produce

    Max   200RT + 425DT

    subject to   .5RT + DT ≤ 45

    $\qquad\qquad$ 4RT + 4DT ≤ 240

    $\qquad\qquad$ RT , DT ≥   0

[Handwritten note:] 2 types of tables RT & DT each table needs 4 legs – 240 in shop ½ hour to sand RT 1 hour to sand DT 45 hours available to sand

	A	B	C	D
1	Tommy's Tables Model			
2				
3	Parameters and Uncontrollable Variables			
4				
5		Regular	Deluxe	
6		Tables	Tables	
7	Profit ($/Table)	200	425	Maximum
8	Finishing (Hrs/Table)	0.5	1	45
9	Table Legs (Legs/Table)	4	4	240
10				
11	Decision Variables:			
12				
13		Regular	Deluxe	
14		Tables	Tables	
15	Qty. Produced	0	45	
16				
17				
18	Model Outputs:			
19				
20		Amount	Available	
21	Finishing	45	0	
22	Table Legs	180	60	
23				
24	Total Profit	$19,125.00		

	A	B	C
20		Amount	Available
21	Finishing	=B8*B15+C8*C15	=D6-B21 *D8-B21*
22	Table Legs	=B9*B15+C9*C15	=D9-B22
23			
24	Total Profit	=B7*B15+C7*C15	

3. Let X_i = number of dollars invested in option i:

Max $.05X_1 + .047X_2 + .04X_3 + .0575X_4$

subject to $X_1 + X_2 + X_3 + X_4 \leq 400,000$

$$X_1 \qquad\qquad\qquad \leq 200,000$$
$$X_2 \qquad\qquad \leq 200,000$$
$$X_3 \qquad \leq 200,000$$
$$X_4 \leq 200,000$$
$$X_1\ , X_2\ , X_3\ , X_4 \geq \qquad 0$$

This model can be solved by inspection as well. Since each dollar invested contributes one dollar to the investment limit, we would invest $200,000 in the option with the highest return (option 4) and $200,000 in the option with the next highest return (option 1).

This problem is similar to the knapsack problem except that there are limits on the amount of each item that can go into the knapsack.

7. Let P = number of cans of Party Mix to produce

M = number of cans of Mixed to produce

D = number of cans of Delightful Mix to produce

Max $2.25P + 3.37M + 6.49D$

subject to

$$.5P + (.55)(.5)M \qquad\qquad \leq 500 \quad \text{(Peanuts)}$$
$$(.25)(.5)M + (.4)(.5)D \leq 175 \quad \text{(Cashews)}$$
$$(.1)(.5)M + (.2)(.5)D \leq 100 \quad \text{(Brazil nuts)}$$
$$(.1)(.5)M + (.4)(.5)D \leq 80 \quad \text{(Hazelnuts)}$$
$$P\ , \qquad M\ , \qquad D \geq 0$$

13. Let GI_1 = amount invested in Growth & Income 1

GI_2 = amount invested in Growth & Income 2

GI_3 = amount invested in Growth & Income 3

I_1 = amount invested in Index 1

I_2 = amount invested in Index 2

MM = amount invested in Money Market

Max $.15\,GI_1 + .1\,GI_2 + .16\,GI_3 + .1I_1 + .13I_2 + .08\,MM$

subject to $GI_1 + GI_2 + GI_3 + I_1 + I_2 + MM \leq 75,000$

$$GI_1 \qquad\qquad\qquad\qquad \leq 37,500$$
$$GI_2 \qquad\qquad\qquad \leq 37,500$$
$$GI_3 \qquad\qquad \leq 37,500$$
$$I_1 \qquad \leq 37,500$$
$$I_2 \leq 37,500$$
$$MM \leq 37,500$$
$$GI_1 + GI_2 + GI_3 \geq 2MM$$
$$GI_1, GI_2, GI_3, I_1, I_2, MM \geq 0$$

17. Let x_i = number of reservationists starting on day i.

Min $x_1 + x_2 + x_3 + x_4 + x_5 + x_6 + x_7$

subject to

$$x_4 + x_5 + x_6 + x_7 + x_1 \geq 75 \quad \text{(Monday)}$$
$$x_5 + x_6 + x_7 + x_1 + x_2 \geq 50 \quad \text{(Tuesday)}$$
$$x_6 + x_7 + x_1 + x_2 + x_3 \geq 45 \quad \text{(Wednesday)}$$
$$x_7 + x_1 + x_2 + x_3 + x_4 \geq 60 \quad \text{(Thursday)}$$
$$x_1 + x_2 + x_3 + x_4 + x_5 \geq 90 \quad \text{(Friday)}$$
$$x_2 + x_3 + x_4 + x_5 + x_6 \geq 75 \quad \text{(Saturday)}$$
$$x_3 + x_4 + x_5 + x_6 + x_7 \geq 45 \quad \text{(Sunday)}$$
$$x_i \geq 0$$

CHAPTER 5

6. a. The optimal objective function value is 150.000.

b. $X_1^* = 0.00$, $X_2^* = 25.000$

c. Constraint 5 is binding because it has zero slack or surplus.

9. Revise the selling hour constraint to have a limit of 6,000 hours to get the following solution: $S_1^* = 7,000$, $S_2^* = 18,000$, $A_1^* = 2,500$, $A_2^* = 3,500$, Profit = \$546,000, where S_i = selling hours for product i and A_i is advertising dollars for product i.

11. a. Let x_i = the number of nurses to start work on day i,

$$i = 1, 2, \ldots, 7$$

```
MIN    700 X1 + 700 X2 + 700 X3 + 700 X4
       + 700 X5 + 700 X6 + 700 X7
SUBJECT TO
  2)    X1 + X4 + X5 + X6 + X7 >=    16   (Sunday)
  3)    X1 + X2 + X5 + X6 + X7 >=    15   (Monday)
  4)    X1 + X2 + X3 + X6 + X7 >=    12   (Tuesday)
  5)    X1 + X2 + X3 + X4 + X7 >=    14   (Wednesday)
  6)    X1 + X2 + X3 + X4 + X5 >=    15   (Thursday)
  7)    X2 + X3 + X4 + X5 + X6 >=    18   (Friday)
  8)    X3 + X4 + X5 + X6 + X7 >=    19   (Saturday)
END
```

b. Solution is $x_1 = 0, x_2 = 3, x_3 = 3, x_4 = 4, x_5 = 6, x_6 = 2$, and $x_7 = 4$ for a total cost of \$15,400.

c. Only Thursday is *not* a bottleneck (positive surplus in row 6).

13. Solution to the Very Good Juice problem (4.6):
   a. Maximum profit is $112,000.
   b. 10,000 gallons of apple juice A
      15,000 gallons of cherry juice C
      30,000 gallons of lemon juice L
      40,000 gallons of orange juice O
      10,000 gallons of pineapple juice P
   c. Product A is at the minimum
      Product C is at the minimum
      Product L is in between
      Product O is at the minimum
      Product P is at the minimum
   d. The straining department is a candidate for expansion because it has zero slack.

18. Solution to Corry's grade problem: Midterm 20%, final 60%, assignments 10%, and participation 10%. This will give him an overall score of 91.4%.

CHAPTER 6

3. a. X1 = 0.25, X2 = 12.50, objective function value = 9.625.
   b. Constraints 2 and 4 are binding because they have zero slack or surplus.

5. a. The minimum-cost plan costs $107,850 with production of 90, 270, 0, and 180 units. This requires inventory of 0, 120, 0, and 0 units.
   b. All of the constraints are binding (they are = type).
   c. The dual prices indicate how much cost will increase for an increase in demand of 1 in a given quarter.
   d. The current solution will remain optimal since the allowable increase on the objective function coefficient of Q_1 is infinity.

CHAPTER 7

5. a. Let X_i = amount to produce in week $i, i = 1, 2, \ldots 6$
   I_i = amount of inventory at the end of week $i, i = 1, 2, \ldots 6$
   S_i = amount of lost sales, week $i, i = 1, 2, \ldots 6$

   Min $I_1 + I_2 + I_3 + I_4 + I_5 + I_6 + S_1 + S_2 + S_3 + S_4 + S_5 + S_6$

   subject to
   $$X_1 - I_1 + S_1 = 2{,}000$$
   $$I_1 + X_2 - I_2 + S_2 = 2{,}900$$
   $$I_2 + X_3 - I_3 + S_3 = 1{,}500$$
   $$I_3 + X_4 - I_4 + S_4 = 1{,}700$$
   $$I_4 + X_5 - I_5 + S_5 = 3{,}000$$
   $$I_5 + X_6 - I_6 + S_6 = 2{,}300$$
   $$X_i \leq 2{,}500 \quad i = 1, 2, \ldots 6$$
   $$X_i, S_i, I_i \geq 0 \quad i = 1, 2, \ldots 6$$

   Solution is $X_1 = 2{,}000, X_2 = 2{,}500, X_3 = 1{,}500, X_4 = 1{,}700, X_5 = 2{,}500, X_6 = 2{,}300$, all $I_i = 0, S_2 = 400$, and $S_5 = 500$, all other $S_i = 0$. Objective function value = 900.
   b. Keep same model as in part a, but weight I_i by .33 and S_i by .67 in the objective function. Solution is $X_1 = 2{,}400, X_2 = 2{,}500, X_3 = 1{,}500, X_4 = 2{,}200, X_5 = 2{,}500, X_6 = 2{,}300, I_1 = 400$, and $I_4 = 500$, all other $I_i = 0, S_i = 0$ for all i. Objective function value = 299.7.

7. a. Constraints 2, 3, 4, and 7 are binding.
   b. Risk will increase by .875 per unit increase in required return (up to an increase of 1,000).
   c. These dual prices indicate the per unit improvement in the objective function value for increases in the amount allowed in options 1 and 2.
   d. This dual price indicates the improvement in the objective function for an increase in the amount of money to invest. For an increase of $1, the risk will drop by .02125 (for an increase of up to $42,857.13).
   e. The allowable increase in the coefficient of A_3 is .035. Since $.04 + .035 = .075 > .06$ the current solution will remain optimal.

9. a. These dual prices indicate the increase in profit for an increase in the amount of inputs 1, 2, and 3, respectively.
   b. The dual price of row 8 is $1.50. The allowable increase is 105,000. Therefore we know that an increase of 12,000 will result in an increase in profit of $12{,}000 \times 1.5 = \$18{,}000$.
   c. The current coefficient of SB is 20. The allowable decrease, from the objective function coefficient ranges section, is 1.5. Since the drop in price is 1 (i.e., $20 - 19$), the current solution remains optimal.

13. a. $239.25, 142.5 quarts of Southern Tang and 22.5 quarts of Yankee Sweet.
   b. Each additional quart of A will increase profit by $1, and each additional quart of B, by $3.
   c. Current coefficient is $-\$1$, can decrease to $-\$2$ and have the current solution remain optimal. Therefore, for a cost of $1.50, the current solution will remain optimal.
   d. An increase of 50 quarts is less than the allowable increase of 285, therefore the shadow price of $1 will hold. This assumes a cost of $1. The net benefit from the purchase will be $(\$1 - .5) \times 50 = \$25$.

8. Goal Achievement: Priority 1: 0, Priority 2: 220,000, and Priority 3: 65,000.

11. a. Let X_i = pounds of ingredient i to use in making a 75 pound batch, $i = 1, 2, 3, 4$. All other variables are deviational variables.

$$\text{Min} \qquad P_u \qquad\qquad + F_0 + (B_u + B_0) \qquad + C_0$$

$$
\begin{array}{lllll}
\text{subject to} & .20X_1 + .25X_2 + .08X_3 + \ .0X_4 + P_u - P_o & & = .18(75) & \text{(Protein)} \\
& .05X_1 + .25X_2 + .10X_3 + .00X_4 & + F_u - F_o & = 1.0(75) & \text{(Fat)} \\
& X_1 - \ \ X_2 & + B_u - B_o & = \quad 0 & \text{(Balance)} \\
& .15X_1 + .10X_2 + .08X_3 + .00X_4 & + C_u - C_o = .10(75) & \text{(Cost)} \\
& X_1 + \ \ X_2 + \ \ X_3 + \ \ X_4 & = \quad 75 & \text{(Total Batch)}
\end{array}
$$

All variables are nonnegative.

b. Solution: Priority 1: $P_u = 0$, Priority 2: $B_o = 0$, Priority 3: $B_u + B_o = 18$, Priority 4: $C_o = .7$ (total batch is over by \$.70). $X_1 = 40$, $X_2 = 22$, $X_3 = 0$, $X_4 = 13$.

13. Same result as in 11(b).

16. Solution is (3,3).

CHAPTER 8

5. Let $\ \ x_t$ = number of units to order during period t

$\qquad I_t$ = number of units left over as inventory at the end of period t

$\qquad d_t$ = number of units demanded during period t

$\qquad h$ = cost to hold one unit for one period

$\qquad A$ = cost to place an order

$$y_t = \begin{cases} 1 & \text{if an order is placed during period } t \\ 0 & \text{otherwise} \end{cases}$$

$$\text{Min} \ \sum_{t=1}^{12} (Ay_t + hI_t)$$

$$
\begin{array}{lll}
\text{subject to} & I_{t-1} + x_t - I_t = d_t & t = 1, 2, \ldots, 12 \\[2mm]
& x_t \qquad\qquad \leq \left(\displaystyle\sum_{j=t}^{12} d_j \right) y_t & t = 1, 2, \ldots, 12 \\[4mm]
& x_t, I_t \qquad\quad \geq 0 \\[1mm]
& y_t \qquad\qquad \geq 0 \text{ and binary}
\end{array}
$$

9. Tindall Bookstore: Minimize the number of customers *not* reached. Let the variable definitions be $Z_i = 1$ if customer i is *not* reached, 0 if reached; x_j as before.

$$\text{Min} \sum_{i=1}^{53} Z_i$$

$$
\begin{array}{ll}
\text{subject to} & \displaystyle\sum_{j=1}^{10} C_j X_j \leq 3{,}000 \\[4mm]
& \displaystyle\sum_{j=1}^{10} a_{ij} X_j + Z_i \geq 1 \quad i = 1, 2, \ldots, 53
\end{array}
$$

Models can be shown to be equivalent by using that $Z_i = 1 - y_i$ from example in chapter.

11. Total time on each side of tape is close

Let $x_i = \begin{cases} 1 & \text{if song } i \text{ is on side 1} \\ 0 & \text{if not} \end{cases}$

$y_i = \begin{cases} 1 & \text{if song } i \text{ is on side 2} \\ 0 & \text{if not} \end{cases}$

$$\text{Min} \quad \sum_{i=1}^{10} t_i x_i - \sum_{i=1}^{10} t_i y_i$$

subject to $\quad x_i \quad + y_i = 1 \quad i = 1, 2, \ldots, 10$

$$\sum_{i=1}^{10} t_i x_i - \sum_{i=1}^{10} t_i y_i \geq 0$$

where t_i = running time of song in minutes (converted to decimal fraction).

13. Production scheduling:

Let x_{ij} = number of units of product i to produce in time period j

$\quad I_{ij}$ = number of units of product i in inventory at the end of period j

$\quad d_{ij}$ = demand for product i in period j

$\quad H$ = holding cost for each unit of product per time period (= \$10.00)

$\quad S_i$ = set-up cost for product i

$\quad P$ = processing time per unit regardless of product (= 1 hour)

$\quad y_{ij} = \begin{cases} 1 & \text{if product } i \text{ incurs a setup charge in period } j \\ 0 & \text{otherwise} \end{cases}$

$$\text{Min} \qquad \sum_{j=1}^{8} \sum_{i=1}^{4} (H I_{ij} + S_i y_{ij})$$

subject to $\quad \sum_{i=1}^{4} P x_{ij} \quad \leq 200 \qquad j = 1, 2, \ldots, 8$

$\qquad\qquad I_{i(j-1)} + x_{ij} - I_{ij} = d_{ij} \qquad i = 1, 2, 3, 4$

$\qquad\qquad\qquad\qquad\qquad\qquad\qquad\qquad j = 1, 2, \ldots, 8$

$\qquad\qquad x_{ij} \quad \leq \left(\sum_{t=j}^{8} d_{it} \right) y_{ij}$

$\qquad\qquad x_{ij}, I_{ij} \quad \geq 0$

$\qquad\qquad y_{ij} \qquad \geq 0 \text{ and binary} \quad \text{for all } i, j$

19. Note that we will not need more than 8 disks.

Let X_{ij} = 1 if program i is on disk j, 0 if not.

$\quad Y_j$ = 1 if disk j is used, 0 if not.

$$\text{Min} \qquad \sum_{j=1}^{8} Y_j$$

subject to $\qquad X_{ij} \leq Y_j \quad \text{for all } i, j$

$\qquad\qquad \sum_{j=1}^{8} X_{ij} = 1 \quad i = 1, 2, \ldots, 8$

$\qquad\qquad \sum_{i=1}^{8} S_i X_{ij} \leq 1.4 \quad j = 1, 2, \ldots, 8$

where S_i = the space required for program i.

CHAPTER 9

10. Let x_{ij} = 1 if arc (i,j) is in the spanning tree, 0 otherwise.

```
MIN   4 X12 + 9 X113 + 3 X23 + 4 X34 + 5 X45 + 3 X46 + 2 X57 + 4 X67
+2 X68 + 7 X69 + 5 X610 + 2 X78 + 6 X89 + 3 X910 + 7 X911 + 5 X1011
+ 6 X1012 + 9 X1112 + 8 X1113 + 7 X1114 + 6 X1213 + 5 X1314
              SUBJECT TO
        2)    X12 + X113 > = 1
        3)    X12 + X23 > = 1
        4)    X23 + X34 > = 1
        5)    X34 + X45 + X46 > = 1
        6)    X45 + X57 > = 1
        7)    X46 + X67 + X68 + X69 > = 1
        8)    X57 + X67 + X78 > = 1
        9)    X68 + X78 + X89 > = 1
       10)    X69 + X89 + X910 + X911 > = 1
       11)    X610 + X910 + X1011 + X1012 > = 1
       12)    X911 + X1011 + X1112 + X1113 + X1114 > = 1
       13)    X1012 + X1112 + X1213 > = 1
       14)    X113 + X1113 + X1213 + X1314 > = 1
       15)    X1114 + X1314 > = 1
      END

LP OPTIMUM FOUND AT STEP      14

              OBJECTIVE FUNCTION VALUE
        1)    28.00000

VARIABLE    VALUE        REDUCED COST
     X12    1.000000         .000000
    X113     .000000        5.500000
     X23     .000000         .000000
     X34    1.000000         .000000
     X45     .000000         .000000
     X46     .000000         .000000
     X57    1.000000         .000000
     X67     .000000        4.000000
     X68    1.000000         .000000
     X69     .000000        5.500000
    X610     .000000        3.500000
     X78     .000000         .000000
     X89     .000000        2.500000
    X910    1.000000         .000000
    X911     .000000        2.000000
   X1011     .000000         .000000
   X1012     .000000         .000000
   X1112     .000000        1.000000
   X1113     .000000        3.000000
   X1114    1.000000         .000000
   X1213    1.000000         .000000
   X1314     .000000         .000000
```

13. Let $x_{ij} = 1$ if arc (i,j) is in the shortest path, 0 otherwise.

```
MIN 2 X12 + X24 + 3 X46 + 28 X411 + 5 X23 + 5 X67 + 4 X35 + 3 X57
   + 4 X38 + 13 X711 + 6 X89 + 4 X910 + 6 X1011
                     SUBJECT TO
        2)      X12 = 1
        3)    - X12 + X24 + X23 = 0
        4)    - X23 + X35 + X38 = 0
        5)    - X24 + X46 + X411 = 0
        6)    - X35 + X57 = 0
        7)    - X46 + X67 = 0
        8)    - X67 - X57 + X711 = 0
        9)    - X38 + X89 = 0
       10)    - X89 + X910 = 0
       11)    - X910 + X1011 = 0
       12)     X711 + X1011 = 1
END

LP OPTIMUM FOUND AT STEP      2

             OBJECTIVE FUNCTION VALUE

        1)      24.00000

    VARIABLE        VALUE      REDUCED COST
        X12       1.000000          .000000
        X24       1.000000          .000000
        X46       1.000000          .000000
        X411       .000000        24.000000
        X23        .000000          .000000
        X67       1.000000          .000000
        X35        .000000         3.000000
        X57        .000000          .000000
        X38        .000000         3.000000
        X711      1.000000          .000000
        X89        .000000          .000000
        X910       .000000          .000000
        X1011      .000000          .000000
```

16.

```
        MIN     1.08 P1 + 1.11 P2 + 1.1 P3 + 1.13 P4 + 0.016 I1 + 16 I2 + 0.016 I3
                SUBJECT TO
        2)      P1 <= 25
        3)      P2 <= 35
        4)      P3 <= 30
        5)      P4 <= 10
        6)      P1 −   I1 =      10
        7)      P2 +   I1 − I2 = 15
        8)      P3 +   I2 − I3 = 25
        9)      P4 +   I3 =      20
END

LP OPTIMUM FOUND AT STEP      5

        OBJECTIVE FUNCTION VALUE

        1)      157.2500

VARIABLE         VALUE     REDUCED COST
        P1     25.000000        .000000
        P2      5.000000        .000000
        P3     30.000000        .000000
        P4     10.000000        .000000
        I1     15.000000        .000000
        I2      5.000000        .000000
        I3     10.000000        .000000
```

20. Let $x_{ij} = 1$ if arc (i, j) is in the shortest path, 0 otherwise.

```
MIN 25000 X15 + 18100 X14 + 12400 X13 + 5900 X12 + 20955 X25
+ 13950 X24 + 6675 X23 + 16118 X35 + 7456 X34 + 8852 X45

            SUBJECT TO
    2)      X15  + X14 + X13 + X12 = 1
    3)      − X12 + X25 + X24 + X23 = 0
    4)      − X13 − X23 + X35 + X34 = 0
    5)      − X14 − X24 − X34 + X45 = 0
    6)      X15  + X25 + X35 + X45 = 1
LP OPTIMUM FOUND AT STEP     2
    OBJECTIVE FUNCTION VALUE
    1)      25000.00
VARIABLE     VALUE    REDUCED COST
    X15     1.000000       .000000
    X14      .000000   1952.000000
    X13      .000000       .000000
    X12      .000000       .000000
    X25      .000000   1855.000000
    X24      .000000   3702.000000
    X23      .000000    175.000000
    X35      .000000   3518.000000
    X34      .000000   3708.000000
    X45      .000000       .000000
```

23. a.

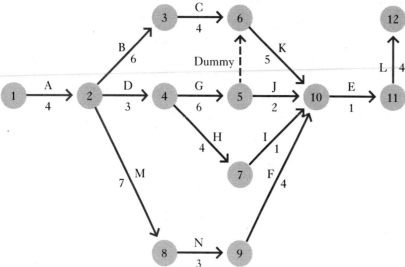

b. Let S_i = Start time of activity i

F_i = Finish time of activity i

T = Project completion time

Min T

subject to $S_A = 0$ $S_M = S_A$

$S_B = F_A$ $S_N = S_M$

$S_C = F_B$ $F_A = S_A + 4$

$S_D = F_A$ $F_B = S_B + 6$

$S_E \geq F_F$ $F_C = S_C + 4$

$S_E \geq F_I$ $F_D = S_D + 3$

$S_E \geq F_J$ $F_E = S_E + 1$

$S_E \geq F_K$ $F_F = S_F + 4$

$S_F = F_N$ $F_G = S_G + 6$

$S_G = F_D$ $F_H = S_H + 4$

$S_H = F_D$ $F_I = S_I + 1$

$S_I = F_H$ $F_J = S_J + 2$

$S_J = F_G$ $F_K = S_K + 5$

$S_K \geq F_C$ $F_L = S_L + 4$

$S_K \geq F_G$ $F_M = S_M + 7$

$S_L = F_E$ $F_N = S_N + 3$

$T \geq F_L$

$S_i, F_i, T \geq 0$

c.

```
MIN T
SUBJECT TO
    2)      SA  = 0
    3)      SB − FA  =    0
    4)      SC − FB  =    0
    5)    − FA + SD  =    0
    6)      SE − FF >= 0
    7)      SE − FI >= 0
    8)      SE − FJ >= 0
    9)      SE − FK >= 0
   10)      SF − FN  =    0
   11)      SG − FD  =    0
   12)    − FD + SH  =    0
   13)      SI − FH  =    0
   14)      SJ − FG  =    0
   15)      SK − FC >= 0
   16)    − FG + SK >= 0
   17)      SL − FE  =    0
   18)    − SA + SM  =    0
   19)    − SM + SN  =    0
   20)    − SA + FA  =    4
   21)    − SB + FB  =    6
   22)    − SC + FC  =    4
   23)    − SD + FD  =    3
   24)    − SE + FE  =    1
   25)      FF − SF  =    4
   26)    − SG + FG  =    6
   27)    − SH + FH  =    4
   28)      FI − SI  =    1
   29)      FJ − SJ  =    2
   30)      FK − SK  =    5
   31)    − SL + FL  =    4
   32)    − SM + FM  =    7
   33)      FN − SN  =    3
   34)      T  − FL >= 0
END
```

```
LP OPTIMUM FOUND AT STEP      9

        OBJECTIVE FUNCTION VALUE

   1)     24.00000

VARIABLE     VALUE       REDUCED COST
   T       24.000000       .000000
   SA        .000000      1.000000
   SB       4.000000       .000000
   FA       4.000000       .000000
   SC      10.000000       .000000
   FB      10.000000       .000000
   SD       4.000000       .000000
   SE      19.000000       .000000
   FF       7.000000       .000000
   FI      12.000000       .000000
   FJ      15.000000       .000000
   FK      19.000000       .000000
   SF       3.000000       .000000
   FN       3.000000       .000000
   SG       7.000000       .000000
   FD       7.000000       .000000
   SH       7.000000       .000000
   SI      11.000000       .000000
   FH      11.000000       .000000
   SJ      13.000000       .000000
   FG      13.000000       .000000
   SK      14.000000       .000000
   FC      14.000000       .000000
   SL      20.000000       .000000
   FE      20.000000       .000000
   SM        .000000       .000000
   SN        .000000       .000000
   FL      24.000000       .000000
   FM       7.000000       .000000
```

CHAPTER 10

1. Columbus-Toledo: 1,200
   Columbus-Dayton: 1,800
   Indianapolis-Bowling Green: 900
   Indianapolis-St. Louis: 700

4. **a.** One solution starting at node 1 is
      1-3-6-2-4-5-1—Cost = 22
   b. Starting with the tour 1-2-3-4-5-6-1

7. **a.** Greedy solution: $x_1 = x_2 = x_3 = x_5 = 1$
   b. Local search (starting from $x_i = 0$) yields
      same solution as part a.

8. Routes:
   0 - 4 - 7 - 0
   0 - 1 - 3 - 0
   0 - 2 - 5 - 0
   0 - 6 - 0

13. a. Expected cost for sequence given:

Test	P(failure)	Cost	P(fail after test)	Cumulative Cost	Expected Cost
Drop	.3	.10	$.3 = .30$	.10	.03
Heat	.05	.14	$(.7)(.05) = .35$	.24	.0084
Vib.	.1	.20	$(.7)(.95)(.1) = .0665$	.44	.02926
Short.	.4	.04	$(.7)(.95)(.9)(.4) = .2394$	.48	.114912
Visual	.15	.066	—	—	.066
					$\overline{\$.248572}$

16.

Station	Operations
1	C,B
2	E
3	A,D
4	F
5	G
6	I
7	H
8	J Total idle time = 20

23. Product 1:   8,000

Product 2:   2,000

Profit: $38,450

CHAPTER 11

1. a. Project B, since 23% > 15%.
b. Project A: $P(10\% \le x \le 20\%) = .494$
Project B: $P(10\% \le x \le 20\%) = .2618$
Therefore, select Project A.
c. Project A: $P(x \ge 0) = .9772$
Project B: $P(x \ge 0) = .9724$
Therefore, select Project A.

3. Accept normality of the data.

8.

Supplier	Expected Annual Cost
A	$ 1,978.94
B	1,822.27
C	1,767.36

Therefore, select Supplier C.

13. a. .9693
b. .0307
c. 17.056 months

15. Forecast for next quarter's demand is 189.

16. a. $\alpha = .2$ MAD = 29.59
b. $\alpha = .3$ MAD = 30.20
c. $\alpha = .2$ fits better(29.59 < 30.20)

17. Forecast for next three months: 103, 109, 115.
Regression equation: $y = 19.51 + 6.395X$.

CHAPTER 12

1. Laplace, maximax, maximin, and minimax regret all give "become certified" as the best decision.

5. Optimal order quantity, based on expected value, is to order 500 shirts. Expected profit = $4,250.

9. a. *Minimin*—do not buy insurance.
Minimax—buy insurance.
Minimax regret—buy insurance.
c. Expected cost (buy insurance) = $70.
Expected cost (not buy insurance) = $4.5.

13. a.

$P(S_j / I_k)$	S_1	S_2	S_3
I_1	.7317	.2195	.0488
I_2	.4286	.3429	.2285
I_3	.2083	.3750	.4167

b. Drill; Expected profit = $30,000.
c. Conduct study:

If NS—don't drill

If OS or CS—drill

Expected profit = $44,942.44.

19. a. Risk averse
b. Optimal decision for expected utility is to buy an existing business (d_2).
Optimal decision for expected value using dollars (NPV) is open a new business (d_3).
c. Solutions are different because of Bob's risk aversion (there is a wide spread in the payoffs for d_3).

21. In order of preference: Tim, Scott, Janet.

CHAPTER 13

4. (Answers will vary) Approximate confidence intervals: $N = 25$: $\{20, 37\}$; $N = 100$: $\{25, 35\}$. Larger sample sizes should result in tighter confidence intervals.

6. Waiting time $\{10.81, 23.75\}$
Idle time $\{6.11, 9.17\}$

13. Profit is maximized at 70 magazines.

17. Profit is maximized at 90 coats.

20. Simulation analysis suggests investment A.

CHAPTER 14

1.

Customer	Arrival time	Start time	Service time	Completion time	Wait time	Idle time
1	3.2	3.2	3.7	6.9	0.0	3.2
2	10.5	10.5	3.5	14.0	0.0	3.6
3	12.8	14.0	4.3	18.3	1.2	0.0
4	14.5	18.3	3.0	21.3	3.8	0.0
5	17.2	21.3	2.8	24.1	4.1	0.0
6	19.7	24.1	4.2	28.3	4.4	0.0
7	21.1	28.3	2.8	31.1	7.2	0.0
8	26.9	31.1	2.3	33.4	4.2	0.0
9	32.7	33.4	2.1	35.5	0.7	0.0
10	36.9	36.9	4.8	41.7	0.0	1.4
Averages					2.56	0.82

6. b. Arrival distribution:

Random number range		Time between arrivals
0.00	0.21	3.0
0.21	0.53	3.5
0.53	0.92	4.0
0.92	0.98	4.5
0.98	1.00	5.0

Service Distribution:

Random number range		Time between arrivals
0.00	0.02	1.0
0.02	0.07	1.5
0.07	0.17	2.0
0.17	0.41	2.5
0.41	0.77	3.0
0.77	1.00	3.5

Customer	Arrival random number	Time between arrivals	Arrival time	Start time	Service random number	Service time	Completion time	Customer wait time	Server idle time
1	0.92	4.5	4.5	4.5	0.12	2.0	6.5	0.0	4.5
2	0.83	4.0	8.5	8.5	0.75	3.0	11.5	0.0	2.0
3	0.85	4.0	12.5	12.5	0.14	2.0	14.5	0.0	1.0
4	0.58	4.0	16.5	16.5	0.72	3.0	19.5	0.0	2.0
5	0.05	3.0	19.5	19.5	0.20	2.5	22.0	0.0	0.0
6	0.09	3.0	22.5	22.5	0.82	3.5	26.0	0.0	0.5
7	0.61	4.0	26.5	26.5	0.74	3.0	29.5	0.0	0.5
8	0.77	4.0	30.5	30.5	0.08	2.0	32.5	0.0	1.0
9	0.43	3.5	34.0	34.0	0.01	1.0	35.0	0.0	1.5
10	0.35	3.5	37.5	37.5	0.69	3.0	40.5	0.0	2.5
11	0.05	3.0	40.5	40.5	0.36	2.5	43.0	0.0	0.0
12	0.87	4.0	44.5	44.5	0.35	2.5	47.0	0.0	1.5
13	0.13	3.0	47.5	47.5	0.52	3.0	50.5	0.0	0.5
14	0.22	3.5	51.0	51.0	0.99	3.5	54.5	0.0	0.5
15	0.63	4.0	55.0	55.0	0.41	3.0	58.0	0.0	0.5

Avg. wait per customer:	0.00
Longest waiting line length:	0.0
Percent of time server is idle:	31.9%

10. b. Student demand: $x = 1.9 + .7R$
Faculty demand: $x = 10 + 5R$
Student service time: $x = .65 + .2R$
Faculty service time: $x = 3.25 + .5R$
where R is a random number.

12. Simulation analysis should find a very low probability of waiting (approximately, less than .1).

CHAPTER 15

1. $P(x = 3) = .0286$
$P(x \geq 10) = .2834$
$P(x = 8) = .1396$

3. $P(x \leq 1) = .1535$
$P(x \leq 3) = .3935$
$P(x > 6) = .4346$

6. $L_q = 3.2$
$W_q = 16$ sec.
$\lambda/\mu = .80$

13. $L_q = .7083$
$L = 1.375$
$W_q = 8.5$
$W = 16.5$
$P_0 = .333$

18. $L_q = 1.723$
$W = .2959$
$1 - P_0 = .8795$

20.

n	P_n	n	P_0
0	.3333	4	.0658
1	.2222	5	.0439
2	.1481	6	.0293
3	.0988	7	.0195
		8	.0130

24. Using Table 15-2, use 22 servers for a 90% service level; 19 for a 75% service level.